# INSTRUCTOR'S RESOURCE MANUAL
## FOR KOZIER AND ERB'S
# FUNDAMENTALS OF NURSING
## CONCEPTS, PROCESS, AND PRACTICE

### EIGHTH EDITION

**LINDA ROBERTSON, PhD, CRNP**
Associate Professor
La Roche College Pittsburgh
Pittsburgh, Pennsylvania
(Instructor's Resource Manual)

**TAMMY OWEN, MSN, RN**
Assistant Professor
West Kentucky Community and Technical College
Paducah, Kentucky
(Test Bank)

**PAMELA FOWLER, MS, RN, C**
Assistant Professor
Rogers State University
Claremore, Oklahoma
(Test Bank)

**KATHRYN G. MAGORIAN, MSN, RN**
Mount Marty College
Yankton, South Dakota
(Test Bank)

**PATRICIA B. LISK, BSN**
Instructor
Augusta Technical College
Augusta, Georgia
(Test Bank)

**JANE J. BENEDICT RN, BSN, MSN**
Associate Professor of Nursing
Pennsylvania College of Technology
Williamsport, Pennsylvania
(Classroom Response
System Questions)

**PEARSON**
Prentice
Hall

Upper Saddle River, New Jersey 07458

**Cover Photo:** Kaleidoscopic XXII: September 11, 2002 © Paula Nadelstern

**Pearson Prentice Hall**™ is a trademark of Pearson Education, Inc.
**Pearson**® is a registered trademark of Pearson plc
**Prentice Hall**® a registered trademark of Pearson Education, Inc.

Pearson Education Ltd.
Pearson Education Singapore, Pte. Ltd.
Pearson Education Canada, Ltd.
Pearson Education—Japan

Pearson Education Australia PTY, Limited
Pearson Education North Asia Ltd.
Pearson Education de Mexico, S.A. de C.V.
Pearson Education Malaysia. Pte. Ltd.
Pearson Education, Upper Saddle River, New Jersey

10 9 8 7 6 5 4 3 2 1
ISBN 13 978-0-13-188936-1
ISBN 10    0-13-188936-2

# CONTENTS

# PREFACE

Nurses today must be able to grow and evolve to meet the demands of a dramatically changing health care system. The eighth edition of *Kozier and Erb's Fundamentals of Nursing* addresses the many concepts of contemporary professional nursing that students will need to learn and embrace to be effective members of the collaborative health care team. This accompanying Instructor's Resource Manual is designed to support your teaching in this stepped-up environment and to reduce your preparation time for class. It will help you provide an optimal learning experience for your students and their many learning needs.

Each chapter in the Instructor's Resource Manual is thoroughly integrated with the corresponding chapter in *Kozier and Erb's Fundamentals of Nursing,* eighth edition. Chapters are organized by learning outcomes, and the teaching unit flows from these outcomes. You will find the following features to support the objectives:

- The **Concepts for Lecture** in this manual may be used in their entirety for class presentation or they may be merged with the classroom activities for a mixture of teaching styles that will meet the needs of students with various learning styles.

- The **Lecture Outlines** can be found on your Instructor's Resource DVD-ROM in PowerPoint. The number in the slide icon ▤ refers to the Concept for Lecture to which the slide correlates. Some lecture concepts have more than one slide, in which case the slide icon may contain a letter after the Concept for Lecture number.

- Suggestions for Classroom and Clinical Activities attempt to go beyond the traditional activities that have been the mainstay of nursing education for many years.

- The Resource Library identifies for you—the instructor—all the specific media resources and activities available for that chapter on the *Prentice Hall Nursing MediaLink DVD-ROM*, Companion Website, and Instructor's Resource DVD-ROM. Chapter by chapter, the Resource Library helps you decide what resources from the DVD-ROM, Companion Website, and Instructor's Resource DVD-ROM to use to enhance your course and your students' ability to apply concepts from the book into practice.

This Instructor's Resource Manual also contains a new *Strategies for Success* module that includes discussion on learning theories, planning for instruction, how to use effective pedagogies, assessing learning, and more. There is also a guide on *Teaching Nursing to Students Who Speak English as a Nonnative Language.* This tool is intended to guide you in reaching across cultural barriers to train nurses.

The following additional resources are also available to accompany this textbook. For more information or sample copies, please contact your Prentice Hall sales representative:

- **Study Guide (ISBN 0-13-188938-9)**—This workbook incorporates strategies for students to focus their study and increase comprehension of concepts of nursing care. It contains a variety of activities such as multiple-choice, fill-in-the-blank, case studies, and more.

- **Clinical Handbook (ISBN 0-13-188933-8)**—This clinical handbook serves as a portable, quick reference to fundamentals of nursing. Topics include lab values, diagnostic tests, standard precautions documentation, NANDA diagnoses, and much more. This handbook will allow students to bring the information they learn from class into any clinical setting.

- **Prentice Hall Nursing MediaLink DVD-ROM**—This DVD-ROM is packaged with the textbook. It provides an interactive study program that allows students to practice answering NCLEX®-style questions with rationales for right and wrong answers. It also contains an audio glossary, animations and video tutorials, and a link to the Companion Website (an Internet connection is required).
*Note: Prentice Hall Nursing MediaLink CD-ROM version is available for purchase on www. MyPearsonStore.com.*

- **Companion Website (*www.prenhall.com/ berman*)**—This online study guide is designed to help students apply the concepts presented in the book. Each chapter-specific module features learning outcomes, NCLEX® review questions with rationales, chapter outlines for lecture notes, case studies, critical-thinking web links, an audio glossary, and more.

- **Instructor's Resource DVD-ROM (ISBN 0-13-188940-0)**—This cross-platform DVD-ROM provides text slides and illustrations in PowerPoint for use in classroom lectures. It also contains an electronic test bank, animations, and video clips from the Student DVD-ROM. This supplement is available to faculty upon adoption of the textbook.
*Note: Instructor's Resource CD-ROM also available upon request.*

- **Online Course Management Systems**—Also available are online companions for schools using course management systems. The OneKey Course Management Solutions feature interactive assessment modules, electronic test bank, PowerPoint images, animations and video clips, and more. For more information about adopting an online course management system to accompany *Kozier and Erb's Fundamentals of Nursing*, eighth edition, please contact your Prentice Hall sales representative.

It is our hope that the information provided in this manual will decrease the time it takes you to prepare for class and will optimize the learning experience for your students.

# Teaching Nursing to Students Who Speak English as a Nonnative Language

We are fortunate to have so many multinational and multilingual nursing students in the United States in the 21st century. As our classrooms become more diverse, there are additional challenges to communication, but we in the nursing education community are ready. Our goal is to educate competent and caring nurses to serve the health needs of our diverse communities.

We know that English as a nonnative language (ENNL) students experience higher attrition rates than their native English-speaking counterparts. This is a complex problem. However, there are teaching strategies that have helped many students be successful.

The first step toward developing success strategies is understanding language proficiency. Language proficiency has four interdependent components. Each component is pertinent to nursing education. *Reading* is the first aspect of language. Any nursing student will tell you that there are volumes to read in nursing education. Even native speakers of English find the reading load heavy. People tend to read more slowly in their nonnative language. They also tend to recall less. Nonnative speakers often spend inordinate amounts of time on reading assignments. These students also tend to take longer to process exam questions.

*Listening* is the second component of language. Learning from lectures can be challenging. Some students are more proficient at reading English than at listening to it. It is not uncommon for ENNL students to understand medical terminology, but to become confused by social references, slang, or idiomatic expressions used in class. The spoken language of the teacher may be different in accent or even vocabulary from that experienced by immigrant students in their language education. ENNL students may not even hear certain sounds that are not present in their native languages. Words such as *amoxicillin* and *ampicillin* may sound the same. Asian languages do not have gender-specific personal pronouns (he, she, him, her, etc.). Asian students may become confused when the teacher is describing a case study involving people of different genders.

*Speaking* is the third component of language proficiency. People who speak with an accent are often self-conscious about it. They may hesitate to voice their questions or to engage in discussion. Vicious cycles of self-defeating behavior can occur in which a student hesitates to speak, resulting in decreased speaking skills, which results in more hesitation to speak. Students may develop sufficient anxiety about speaking that their academic outcomes are affected. Students tend to form study groups with others who have common first languages. Opportunities to practice English are therefore reduced, and communication errors are perpetuated. When the teacher divides students into small groups for projects, ENNL students often do not participate as much as others. If these students are anxious about speaking, they may withdraw from classroom participation. ENNL students may feel rejected by other students in a small-group situation when their input is not sought or understood.

The fourth aspect of language is *writing*. Spelling and syntax errors are common when writing in a nonnative language. Teachers often respond to student writing assignments with feedback that is too vague to provide a basis for correction or improvement by ENNL students. When it comes to writing lecture notes, these students are at risk of missing important details because they may not pick up the teacher's cues about what is important. They might miss information when they spend extra time translating a word or concept to understand it, or they might just take more time to write what is being said.

Another major issue faced by ENNL nursing students is the culture of the learning environment. International students were often educated in settings where students took a passive role in the classroom. They may have learned that faculty are to be respected, not questioned. Memorization of facts may have been emphasized. It may be a shock to them when the nursing faculty expect assertive students who ask questions and think critically. These expectations cannot be achieved unless students understand them.

Finally, the European American culture, which forms the context for nursing practice, creates challenges. Because they are immersed in European American culture and the culture of nursing, faculty may not see the potential sources of misunderstanding. For example, if a teacher writes a test question about what foods are allowed on a soft diet, a student who understands therapeutic diets may miss the question if he or she does not recognize the names of the food choices. Nursing issues with especially high culture connection include food, behavior, law, ethics, parenting, games, or choosing the right thing to say. These topics are well represented in psychiatric nursing, which makes it a difficult subject for ENNL students.

## MINIMIZING CULTURE BIAS ON NURSING EXAMS

Our goal is not to eliminate culture from nursing or from nursing education. Nursing exists in a culture-dependent context. Our goal is to practice transcultural nursing and to teach nursing without undue culture bias.

Sometimes our nursing exam questions will relate to culture-based expectations for nursing action. The way to make these questions fair is to teach transcultural nursing and to clarify the cultural expectations of a nursing student in the European-American-dominated health care system. Students must learn the cultural aspects of the profession before they can practice appropriately within it. Like other cultures, the professional culture of nursing has its own language (for example, medical terminology and nursing diagnoses). We have our own accepted way of dress and our own implements, skills, taboos, celebrations, and behavior. The values accepted by our culture are delineated in the American Nurses Association Code of Ethics, and are passed down to our students during nursing education.

It is usually clear to nursing educators that students are not initially aware of all the aspects of the professional culture, and that these must be taught. The social context of nursing seems more obvious to educators, and is often overlooked in nursing education. Some aspects of the social context of nursing were mentioned above (food, games, social activities, relationships, behavior, what to say in certain situations). Students must also learn these social behaviors and attitudes if they are to function fully in nursing. If they do not already know about American hospital foods, what to say when someone dies, how to communicate with an authority figure, or what game to play with a 5-year-old child, they must learn these things in nursing school.

Try for yourself the following test. It was written without teaching you the cultural expectations first.

## CULTURE-BIASED TEST

1. Following radiation therapy, an African American client has been told to avoid using her usual hair care product due to its petroleum content. Which product should the nurse recommend that she use instead?
   A. Royal Crown hair treatment
   B. Dax Wave and Curl
   C. Long Aid Curl Activator Gel
   D. Wave Pomade

2. A Jewish client is hospitalized for pregnancy-induced hypertension during Yom Kippur. How should the nurse help this client meet her religious needs based on the tradition of this holy day?
   A. Order meals without meat-milk combinations.
   B. Ask a family member to bring a serving of *Marror* for the client.
   C. Encourage her to fast from sunrise to sunset.
   D. Remind her that she is exempt from fasting.

3. Based on the Puerto Rican concept of *compadrazco*, who is considered part of the immediate family and responsible for care of children?
   A. Parents, grandparents, aunts, uncles, cousins, and godparents
   B. Mother, father, and older siblings
   C. Mother, father, and any blood relative
   D. Parents and chosen friends (*compadres*) who are given the honor of child care responsibility

4. A 60-year-old Vietnamese immigrant client on a general diet is awake at 11 PM on a summer night. What is the best choice of food for the nurse to offer to this client?
   A. Warm milk
   B. Hot tea
   C. Ice cream
   D. Iced tea

5. Which of the following positions is contraindicated for a client recovering from a total hip replacement?
   A. Side-lying using an abductor pillow
   B. Standing
   C. Walking to the restroom using a walker
   D. Sitting in a low recliner

When you took this test, did it seem unfair? It was intended to test nursing behaviors that were based on culture-specific situations. Your immigrant and ENNL students are likely to face questions like these on every exam.

Question 1 is about hair care products for black hair. Option C is the only one that does not contain petroleum. Students could know this, if they were given the information before the exam. Otherwise the question is culture-biased.

Question 2 is about the Jewish holiday Yom Kippur. To celebrate this holiday, it is customary to fast from sunrise to sunset, but people who are sick, such as the client in the question, are exempted from fasting. This question is only unfair if students did not have access to the information.

Question 3 expects you to know about *compadrazco*, in which parents, grandparents, aunts, uncles, cousins, and godparents are all considered immediate family. This can be an important point if you are responsible for visiting policies in a pediatrics unit.

Question 4 tests knowledge about the preferred drink for an immigrant Vietnamese client. Many people in Asia feel comforted by hot drinks and find cold drinks to be unsettling.

Question 5 does not seem so biased. If you understand total hip precautions, it is a pretty simple question, unless you have never heard of a "low recliner." An ENNL student who missed this question said, "I saw the chairs in clinical called 'geri chairs' and I know that the client cannot bend more than 90 degrees, but 'low recliner' was confusing to me. I imagined someone lying down (reclining) and I think this would not dislocate the prosthesis."

The best way to avoid culture bias on exams is to know what you are testing. It is acceptable to test about hip precautions, but not really fair to test about the names of furniture. The same is true of foods. Test about therapeutic diets, but not about the recipes (an African immigrant student advised us to say "egg-based food" instead of "custard").

Behavior in social and professional situations is especially culture-bound. Behavior-based questions are common on nursing exams. Make behavior expectations explicit. Especially when a student is expected to act in a way that would be inappropriate in his or her social culture, these are very difficult questions. For example, we expect nurses to act assertively with physicians and clients. It is inappropriate for many Asian students to question their elders. When a client is their elder, these students will choose the option that preserves respect for the client over one that provides teaching. We must make our expectations very clear.

Finally, talk with your ENNL and immigrant students after your exams. They can provide a wealth of information about what confused them or what was ambiguous. Discuss your findings with your colleagues and improve your exams. Ultimately your exams will be clearer and more valid.

The following strategies were developed originally to help ENNL students. An interesting revelation is that they also help native English speakers who have learning styles that are not conducive to learning by lecture, who read slowly, or who have learning disabilities or other academic challenges.

## STRATEGIES FOR PROMOTING ENNL STUDENT SUCCESS

1. You cannot decrease the reading assignment because some students read slowly, but you can help students prioritize the most important areas.
2. Allow adequate time for testing. The NCLEX® is not a 1-minute-per-question test anymore. Usually 1.5 hours is adequate for a 50-item multiple-choice exam.
3. Allow students to tape lectures if they want to. You might have lectures audiotaped and put in the library for student access.
4. Speak clearly. Mumbling and rapid anxious speech are difficult to understand. If you have a problem with clarity, provide handouts containing the critical points. You want to teach and test nursing knowledge, not note-taking skills.
5. Avoid slang and idiomatic expressions. This is hard to do, but you can do it with practice. When you do use slang, explain it. This is especially important on exams. When in doubt about whether a word is confusing, think about what the dictionary definition would be. If there are two meanings, use another word.
6. Allow the use of translation dictionaries on exams. You can stipulate that students must tell you what they are looking up, so they cannot find medical terminology that is part of the test.
7. Be aware of cultural issues when you are writing exams. Of course you will test on culture-specific issues, but be sure you are testing what you want to test (e.g., the student's knowledge of diets, not of recipes).
8. Feel free to use medical terminology. After all, this is nursing school. However, when you use an important new term, write it on the board so students can spell it correctly in their notes.
9. In clinical, make the implied explicit. It seems obvious that safety is the priority. However, if a student thinks the priority is respecting her elders, there could be a disaster when a client with a new hip replacement demands to get out of bed.
10. Hire a student who takes clear and accurate lecture notes to post his or her notes for use by ENNL and other students. The students will still attend class and take their own notes, but will have this resource to fill in the details that they miss.
11. SOA (spell out abbreviations).
12. Many international students learned to speak English in the British style. If something would be confusing to a British person, they will find it confusing.

13. Provide opportunities for students to discuss what they are learning with other students and faculty. A faculty member might hold a weekly discussion group where students bring questions. It can be interesting to find a student having no trouble tracing the path of a red cell from the heart to the portal vein, but having difficulty understanding what cream of wheat is ("I thought it was a stalk of grain in a bowl with cream poured on it").
14. Make it clear that questions are encouraged. If you think a student who is not asking questions may not understand, ask the student after class if he or she has questions. Make it easier for students to approach you by being approachable. Learn their names, and learn to pronounce them correctly. Hearing you try to pronounce their names might be humorous for them, and it will validate how difficult it is to speak other languages.
15. Take another look at basing grades on class participation. You may be putting inordinate demands on the ENNL students. Of course nurses must learn to work with others, but the nurse who talks most is not necessarily the best.
16. Be a role model for communication skills. You might even say in class when you talk about communication that if you respect a person who is trying to communicate with you, you will persist until you understand the message. Say, "Please repeat that," or "I think you said to put a chicken on my head, is that correct?" or "You want me to do what with the textbook?" It may be considered socially rude to ask people to repeat themselves. Make it clear that this is not a social situation. In the professional role, we are responsible for effective communication. We cannot get away with smiling and nodding our heads.
17. In clinical, if a student has an accent that is difficult for the staff to understand, discuss clarification techniques (#16 above) with the student and staff member. Make it explicit that it is acceptable for the student to ask questions and for the staff to ask for clarification.
18. If your college has a writing center where students can receive feedback on grammar and style before submitting papers, have students use it. If you are not so fortunate, view papers as a rough draft instead of a final product. Give specific feedback about what to correct and allow students to resubmit.
19. Make any services that are available to ENNL students available to all students (such as group discussions and notes). These services may meet the learning needs of many students while preventing the attitude that "they are different and they get something I don't."
20. Faculty attitudes are the most important determinant of a successful program to promote the success of ENNL nursing students. Talk with other faculty about the controversial issues. Create an organized program with a consistent approach among the faculty. The rewards will be well worth the work.

# STRATEGIES FOR SUCCESS

**Sandra DeYoung, EdD, RN**
William Paterson University Wayne, New Jersey

## IMPROVING OUR TEACHING

Every faculty member wants to be a good teacher, and every teacher wants the students to learn. In particular, we want to achieve the student learning outcomes that our educational institutions say we must achieve. How can we best meet both goals? We cannot just teach as we were taught. We have to learn a variety of teaching methods and investigate best practices in pedagogy. We also have to learn how to measure student learning outcomes in practical and efficient ways. The next few pages will introduce you to principles of good teaching and ways to evaluate learning. Keep in mind that this is only an introduction. For a more extensive study of these principles and pedagogies, you might consult the resources listed at the end of this introduction.

## LEARNING THEORY

In order to improve our teaching, we must have some familiarity with learning theory. Nurses who come into educational roles without psychology of learning courses in their background should read at least an introductory-level book on learning theories. You should, for example, know something about stages and types of learning, how information is stored in memory and how it is retrieved, and how knowledge is transferred from one situation to another.

## BEHAVIORIST THEORIES

Behaviorist theories are not in as much favor today as they were 25 years ago, but they still help to explain simple learning. Conditioning and reinforcement are concepts with which most educators are familiar. Conditioning explains how we learn some simple movements and behaviors that result in desired outcomes, such as a nurse responding when an alarm sounds on a ventilator. Reinforcement refers to the fact that behavior which is rewarded or reinforced tends to reoccur. Therefore, reinforcement is a powerful tool in the hands of an educator.

## COGNITIVE LEARNING THEORIES

Cognitive learning theories are much more sophisticated. They deal with how we process information by perceiving, remembering, and storing information. All of these processes are a part of learning. One of the most useful concepts in cognitive theory is that of mental schemata.

*Schemata* (plural) are units of knowledge that are stored in memory. For example, nurses must develop a schema related to aseptic technique. Once a schema is stored in memory, related information can be built on it. For instance, changing a dressing is easier to learn if the learner already has a schema for asepsis.

*Metacognition* is another concept identified in cognitive theories. This concept refers to thinking about one's thinking. To help learners who are having difficulty mastering certain material, you might ask them to think about how they learn best and help them evaluate whether they really understand the material.

*Transfer of learning* occurs when a learner takes information from the situation in which it is learned and applies it to a new situation. Transfer is most likely to occur if the information was learned well in the first place, if it can be retrieved from memory, and if the new situation is similar to the original learning situation. Educators can teach for transfer by pointing out to students how a concept is applied in several situations so that learners know the concept is not an isolated one, and the students begin to look for similar patterns in new situations.

## ADULT LEARNING THEORIES

Adult learning theories help to explain how learning takes place differently for adults than for children. Adults usually need to know the practical applications for the information they are given. They also want to see how it fits with their life experiences. When teaching adults, nurse educators need to keep in mind adult motivation for learning.

## LEARNING STYLE THEORIES

Learning style theories abound. Research has shown that some learners are visually oriented, some are more auditory or tactile learners, some are individualistic and learn best alone, others learn best by collaboration, some deal well with abstract concepts, and others learn better with concrete information. Measurement instruments that can determine preferred learning styles are readily available. Although not many educators actually measure their students' learning styles, they should keep learning styles in mind when they plan their instruction.

## PLANNING FOR INSTRUCTION

With some background knowledge of how students learn, the nurse educator can begin to plan the learning experiences. Planning includes developing objectives, selecting content, choosing pedagogies, selecting assignments, and planning for assessment of learning. All nurse educators come to the teaching process already knowing how to write objectives. Objectives can be written in the cognitive, psychomotor, and affective domains of learning. In the cognitive domain, they can be written at the knowledge, comprehension, application, analysis, and synthesis levels of complexity. The critical aspect of objectives is to keep referring to them as you plan your lesson or course. They will help you focus on the "need to know" versus the "nice to know" material. They will help you decide which assignments will be most suitable, and they will guide your development of evaluation tools.

## SELECTING ASSIGNMENTS

Selecting and developing out-of-class assignments calls for creativity. You may use instructor's manuals such as this for ideas for assignments or you may also develop your own. To encourage learning through writing, you can assign short analysis papers, position papers, or clinical journals, all of which promote critical thinking. Nursing care plans of various lengths and complexity may be assigned. You may create reading guides with questions to help students read their textbooks analytically. You might also ask students to interview or observe people to achieve various objectives.

## USING EFFECTIVE PEDAGOGIES

Selecting teaching methods or pedagogies takes considerable time. You must consider what you are trying to achieve. To teach facts, you may choose to lecture or assign a computer tutorial. To change attitudes or motivate learners, you may use discussion, role-playing, or gaming. Developing critical thinking may be done effectively using critical-thinking exercises, concept maps, group projects, or problem-based learning. There are traditional pedagogies, activity-based pedagogies, and technology-based pedagogies.

## TRADITIONAL PEDAGOGIES

Traditional pedagogies include lecture, discussion, and questioning. Lecturing is an efficient way to convey a great deal of information to large groups of people. However, the lecture creates passive learning. Learners just sit and listen (or not) and do not interact with the information or the lecturer. Research has shown that students learn more from active learning techniques (i.e., from being able to talk about, manipulate, deduce, or synthesize information). If you are going to lecture, it would be wise to intersperse lecture with discussion and questioning.

Discussion gives students an opportunity to analyze and think critically about information that they have read or were given in a lecture. By discussing key concepts and issues, they can learn the applicability of the concepts and see how they can transfer to varied situations. Discussions can be formal or informal, but they generally work best if they are planned. For a formal discussion, students must be held accountable for preparing for it. The teacher becomes a facilitator by giving an opening statement or question, guiding the discussion to keep it focused, giving everyone a chance to participate, and summarizing at the end.

Questioning is a skill that develops over time. The first principle to learn is that you have to give students time to answer. Most teachers wait only 1 second before either repeating the question or answering it themselves. You should wait at least 3 to 5 seconds before doing anything, to allow students time to think and prepare a thoughtful answer. Research has revealed that most instructor-posed questions are at a very low level (lower-order), eliciting recall of facts. But questioning can be used to develop critical thinking if it is planned. Higher-order questions are those that require students to interpret information, to apply it to different situations, to think about relationships between concepts, or to assess a situation. If you ask higher-order questions during your classes or clinical experiences, students will rise to the occasion and will be challenged to provide thoughtful answers.

## ACTIVITY-BASED PEDAGOGIES

Activity-based teaching strategies include cooperative learning, simulations, games, problem-based learning, and self-learning modules, among others. Cooperative learning is an old pedagogy that has received more research support than any other method. This approach involves learners working together and being responsible for the learning of group members as well as their own learning. Cooperative learning groups can be informal, such as out-of-class study groups, or they can be formally structured in-class groups. The groups may serve to solve problems, develop projects, or discuss previously taught content.

Simulations are exercises that can help students to learn in an environment that is low risk or risk-free. Students can learn decision making, for example, in a setting where no one is hurt if the decision is the wrong one. Simulations in skill laboratories are frequently used to teach psychomotor skills. Simulations can be written (case studies), acted out (role-playing), computer-based (clinical decision-making scenarios), or complex technology-based (active simulation manikins).

Games can help motivate people to learn. Factual content that requires memorization (such as medical terminology) can be turned into word games such as crossword puzzles or word searches. More complex games can teach problem solving or can apply previously learned information. Board games or simulation games can be used for these purposes.

Problem-based learning (PBL) provides students with real-life problems that they must research and analyze and then develop possible solutions. PBL is a group activity. The instructor presents the students with a brief problem statement. The student group makes lists of what they know and don't know about the problem. They decide what information they must collect in order to further understand the problem. As they collect the information and analyze it, they further refine the problem and begin to investigate possible solutions. The educator serves as a facilitator and resource during the learning process and helps keep the group focused.

Self-learning modules are a means of self-paced learning. They can be used to teach segments of a course or an entire course or curriculum. Modules should be built around a single concept. For example, you might design a module for a skill lab based on aseptic technique, or you could develop a module for a classroom course around the concept of airway impairment. Each module contains components such as an introduction, instructions on how to use the module, objectives, a pretest, learning activities, and a post-test. Learning activities within a module should address various learning styles. For example, you should try to include activities that appeal to visual learners and tactile learners, conceptual learners and abstract learners, and individual learners and collaborative learners. Those activities could be readings, audiovisuals, computer programs, group discussion, or skills practice. The educator develops and tests the module and then acts as facilitator and evaluator as learners work through the module.

## TECHNOLOGY-BASED PEDAGOGIES

Technology-based pedagogies include computer simulations and tutorials, Internet use, and distance learning applications. Computer simulations include decision-making software in which a clinical situation is enacted and students are asked to work through the nursing process to solve problems and achieve positive outcomes. They also include simulation games such as SimCity, which can be a useful tool in teaching community health principles. Computer tutorials are useful for individual remedial work such as medication calculations or practice in answering multiple-choice test questions.

The Internet is a rich resource for classroom use and for out-of-class assignments. There are hundreds of websites that can be accessed for health-related information. Students need to be taught how to evaluate the worth of these websites. The criteria they should apply to this evaluation include identifying the intended audience, the currency of the information, the author's credentials or the affiliated organization, and content accuracy. Students may not know how to identify online journal sources compared to other websites. It is worth spending time, therefore, teaching students how to use the Internet before giving them such assignments. If your classroom is Internet access enabled, you can visually demonstrate how to identify and use appropriate websites. For example, if you want students to find relevant information for diabetic teaching, you can show them the differing value of information from official diabetes associations versus pharmaceutical sites versus chat rooms or public forums.

You may be using this instructor's manual in a distance learning course. Distance learning takes the forms of interactive television classes, webcasting, or online courses. In any form of distance learning, students are learning via the technology, but they are also learning about technology and becoming familiar with several computer applications. Those applications may include synchronous and asynchronous applications, streaming video, and multimedia functions.

## ASSESSING LEARNING

You can assess or evaluate learning in a number of ways. Your first decision is whether you are just trying to get informal, ungraded feedback on how well students are learning in your class, or whether you are evaluating the students for the purpose of assigning a grade. Following are a number of techniques that can be used for one or both purposes.

## CLASSROOM ASSESSMENT TECHNIQUES

Classroom assessment techniques (CATs) are short, quick, ungraded, in-class assessments used to gauge students' learning during or at the end of class. Getting frequent feedback on students' understanding helps educators to know if they are on the right track and if students are benefiting from the planned instruction. If you wait until you give a formal quiz or examination, you may have waited too long to help some students who are struggling with the material. The most popular CAT is probably the *minute paper*. This technique involves asking students to write down, in 1 or 2 minutes, usually at the end of class, what was the most important thing they learned that day or what points remain unclear. A related technique is the *muddiest point*, in which you ask the class to write down what the "muddiest" part of the class was for them. In nursing, *application cards* can be especially useful. After teaching about a particular concept or body of knowledge, and before you talk about the applications of the information, ask the students to fill out an index card with one possible clinical application of the information. This technique fosters application and critical thinking. Always leave class time during the following session to give feedback on the CAT results.

Another means of doing a quick assessment of learning in the classroom is the use of a *classroom (or student) response system,* sometimes called *clicker* technology. By the use of radio frequency technology, a laptop computer, a projector, and student remote controls (the clickers), an instructor can pose a written question on the screen and ask students to use their clickers to select the correct answer. The answers are then tallied and can be projected as a graph of results on the screen. This technology permits quick assessment of student understanding of critical information and keeps students active during a lecture. Classroom response systems are often made available by publishers in conjunction with their textbooks.

## TESTS AND EXAMINATIONS

Tests and examinations are also used to assess or evaluate learning. Tests should be planned carefully to measure whether learning objectives have been met. You should form a test plan in which you decide the number of test items to include for each objective as well as the complexity of the items. Just as objectives can be written at the knowledge through synthesis levels of knowing, test items can be written at each level, too. Some types of items lend themselves to the lower levels of knowing, such as true-false and matching items, while multiple-choice and essay questions can be used to test higher levels.

## TRUE-FALSE QUESTIONS

True-false questions are used simply to determine if the student can identify the correctness of a fact or principle. This type of question should be used sparingly, because the student has a 50% chance of guessing the correct answer. Well-written true-false questions are clear and unambiguous.

The entire statement should be totally true or totally false. An example of a question that is ambiguous is:

(T F) A routine urinalysis specimen must be collected with clean technique and contain at least 100 mL.

The answer to this question is false because the specimen does not require 100 mL of volume. However, the clean technique part of the question is true. Because part of the statement is true and part is false, the question is misleading. A better question is:

(T F) A routine urinalysis specimen must be collected with clean technique.

True-false questions can be made more difficult by requiring the student to explain why the statement is true or false.

## MATCHING QUESTIONS

Matching questions also test a low level of learning—that of knowledge. They are most useful for determining if students have learned definitions or equivalents of some type. They should be formatted in two columns, with the premise words or statements on the left and the definitions or responses on the right. You should have more responses than premises so that matching cannot be done simply by process of elimination. Instructions should be given that indicate if responses can be used more than once or even not used at all. An example of a matching question is:

Match the definition on the right with the suffix on the left. Definitions can be used only once or not at all.

| _____ 1. –itis | a. presence of |
| _____ 2. –stalsis | b. abnormal flow |
| _____ 3. –rrhage | c. inflammation |
| _____ 4. –iasis | d. discharge or flow |
| _____ 5. –ectomy | e. contraction |
| | f. surgical removal of |

## MULTIPLE-CHOICE QUESTIONS

Multiple-choice questions can be written at the higher levels of knowing, from application through evaluation. At these higher levels they can test critical thinking. A multiple-choice question has two parts. The first part, the question, is also called the *stem*. The possible answers are called *options*. Among the options, the correct one is called the *answer*, while the incorrect options are termed *distractors*. You can word stems as questions or as incomplete statements that are completed by the options. For example, an item written as a question is:

What is a quick way to assess the approximate literacy level of a patient?

a. Pay attention to her vocabulary as she speaks.
b. Give her an instruction sheet to read.
c. Administer a literacy test.
d. Ask her whether she graduated from high school.

The same knowledge can be tested by a stem written as an incomplete statement:

A quick way to assess the approximate literacy level of a patient is to

a. pay attention to her vocabulary as she speaks.
b. give her an instruction sheet to read.
c. administer a literacy test.
d. ask her whether she graduated from high school.

Notice the differing formats of each item. When the stem is a question it is also a complete sentence, so each option should be capitalized because each is also a complete sentence and each ends with a period. When the stem is an incomplete statement, it does not end with a period, so the options that complete the statement do not begin with a capital letter but do end with a period. Stems should be kept as brief as possible to minimize reading time. Avoid negatively stated stems. For example, a poor stem would be:

Which of the following is not a good way to assess a patient's literacy level? It is too easy for readers to miss the word *not* and therefore answer incorrectly. If you feel compelled to write negative stems occasionally, be sure to capitalize or underline the word *not*, or use the word *except* as in the following example:

All of the following are good ways to assess a patient's literacy level EXCEPT In this case, the reader is less likely to miss the negative word because of the sentence structure and also because the word *except* is capitalized.

Options usually vary from three to five in number. The more options you have, the more difficult the item. However, it is often difficult to write good distractors. Be sure that your options are grammatically consistent with the stem. Next is a test item in which all of the options do not fit grammatically with the stem:

The lecture method of teaching is best suited to

a. when the audience already knows a lot about the topic.
b. large audiences.
c. times when you are in a hurry to cover your material and don't want to be interrupted.
d. young children.

Not only are the options grammatically inconsistent, they are also of varied lengths. Attempt to keep the options about the same length. The following restatement of the item corrects the problems with grammar and with length:

The lecture method of teaching is best suited to

a. an audience that already knows the topic.
b. an audience that is very large.
c. times when you must cover your material quickly.
d. an audience of young children.

Distractors that make no sense should never be used. Instead, try to develop distractors that reflect incorrect ideas that some students might hold about a topic.

## ESSAY QUESTIONS

Essay-type questions include short answer (restricted-response questions) and full essays (extended-response questions). These types of items can be used to test higher-order thinking. Extended-response essays are especially suited to testing analysis, synthesis, and evaluation levels of thinking. An example of an essay that might test these higher-order levels of thinking is:

Explain how exogenous cortisone products mimic a person's normal cortisol functions and why long-term cortisone administration leads to complications. Also explain how nursing assessment and intervention can help to reduce those complications.

The educator must plan how the essay is going to be graded before the test is given. An outline of required facts and concepts can be developed and points given to each. Then a decision must be made as to whether it is appropriate to give points for writing style, grammar, spelling, and so on.

## TEST ITEM ANALYSIS

After a test is given, an analysis of objective items can be conducted. Two common analyses are *item difficulty* and *item discrimination*. Most instructors want to develop questions that are of moderate difficulty, with around half of the students selecting the correct answer. A mixture of fairly easy, moderate, and difficult questions can be used. The difficulty index can be calculated by dividing the number of students who answered the question correctly by the total number of students answering the question.

The resulting fraction, converted to a percentage, gives an estimate of the difficulty, with lower percentages reflecting more difficult questions.

Item discrimination is an estimate of how well a particular item differentiates between students who generally know the material and those that don't. In other words, a discriminating item is one that most of the students who got high scores on the rest of the examination got right and most of the students who got low scores got wrong. The discrimination index can be calculated by computer software or by hand using a formula that can be found in tests and measurement textbooks.

## HELPFUL RESOURCES

These few pages are but an introduction to teaching techniques. To be fully prepared for the educator role, you will need to enroll in formal courses on curriculum and teaching or do more self-learning on educational topics. For more information, you might consult the following print and Web-based resources:

DeYoung, S. (2003). *Teaching Strategies for Nurse Educators*. Upper Saddle River, NJ: Prentice Hall.

Websites:
*www.crlt.umich.edu/tstrategies/teachings.html*
*www.gmu.edu/facstaff/part-time/strategy.html*
*www.ic.arizona.edu/ic/edtech/strategy.html*

# UTILIZING FUNCTIONAL HEALTH PATTERNS FRAMEWORK

To assist faculty who utilize the Functional Health Patterns Framework in using this text, the following chart has been developed to facilitate locating content related to specific patterns. The chart is a matrix between the book chapters and specific patterns. For some patterns, content can be found in several chapters and for other patterns, concentrated primarily within one. Faculty may want to use this chart in conjunction with the Concept Maps to organize content to be examined within the Functional Health Patterns structure.

## FUNCTIONAL HEALTH PATTERNS

| BOOK CHAPTER | HEALTH PERCEPTION- HEALTH MANAGEMENT | NUTRITIONAL- METABOLIC | ELIMINATION | ACTIVITY- EXERCISE | REST- SLEEP | COGNITIVE- PERCEPTUAL | SELF-PERCEPTION- SELF-CONCEPT | ROLE- RELATIONSHIP | SEXUALITY- REPRODUCTIVE | COPING- STRESS- TOLERANCE | VALUE- BELIEF |
|---|---|---|---|---|---|---|---|---|---|---|---|
| **UNIT ONE:** The Nature of Nursing | | | | | | | | | | | |
| 1 | | | | | | | | | | | |
| 2 | | | | | | | | | | | |
| 3 | | | | | | | | | | | |
| 4 | | | | | | | | | | | |
| 5 | | | | | | | | | | | X |
| **UNIT TWO:** Contemporary Health Care | | | | | | | | | | | |
| 6 | X | | | | | | | | | | |
| 7 | X | | | | | | | | | | |
| 8 | | | | | | | | | | | |
| 9 | | | | | | | | | | | |
| **UNIT THREE:** The Nursing Process | | | | | | | | | | | |
| 10 | | | | | | | | | | | |
| 11 | | | | | | | | | | | |
| 12 | | | | | | | | | | | |
| 13 | | | | | | | | | | | |
| 14 | | | | | | | | | | | |
| 15 | | | | | | | | | | | |

| | Health Perception-Health Management | Nutritional-Metabolic | Elimination | Activity-Exercise | Rest-Sleep | Cognitive-Perceptual | Self-Perception-Self-Concept | Role-Relationship | Sexuality-Reproductive | Coping-Stress-Tolerance | Value-Belief |
|---|---|---|---|---|---|---|---|---|---|---|---|
| **UNIT FOUR:** Health Beliefs and Practice | | | | | | | | | | | |
| 16 | X | | | | | | | | | | |
| 17 | X | | | | | | | | | | X |
| 18 | X | X | | | | X | X | X | | | X |
| 19 | X | X | | X | X | X | X | | | X | X |
| **UNIT FIVE:** Life Span Development | | | | | | | | | | | |
| 20 | X | | | | | X | X | X | X | X | X |
| 21 | X | | | | | X | X | X | X | X | X |
| 22 | X | | | | | X | X | X | X | X | X |
| 23 | X | | | | | X | X | X | X | X | X |
| 24 | | | | | | | | X | | | |
| **UNIT SIX:** Integral Aspects of Nursing | | | | | | | | | | | |
| 25 | | | | | | | | | | | |
| 26 | | | | | | | | | | | |
| 27 | | | | | | X | | | | | |
| 28 | | | | | | | | | | | |
| **UNIT SEVEN:** Assessing Health | | | | | | | | | | | |
| 29 | | X | | | | | | | | | |
| 30 | | X | | X | | X | X | | X | X | |

xvii

# Chapter 1
# Historical and Contemporary Nursing Practice

## Resource Library

 **PRENTICE HALL NURSING MEDIALINK DVD-ROM**

Audio Glossary
NCLEX® Review
Video: *The History of Nursing*

 **COMPANION WEBSITE**

Additional NCLEX® Review
Case Study: Evolution of Nursing
MediaLink Activities:
    *Florence Nightingale*
    *American Association of Colleges of Nursing*
    *Sigma Theta Tau*
Links to Resources

### IMAGE LIBRARY

**Figure 1.1** The Knights of Saint Lazarus (established circa 1200) dedicated themselves to the care of people with leprosy, syphilis, and chronic skin conditions.

**Figure 1.2** Harriet Tubman (1820–1913) was known as "The Moses of Her People" for her work with the Underground Railroad.

**Figure 1.3** Sojourner Truth (1797–1883), abolitionist, Underground Railroad agent, preacher, and women's rights advocate, was a nurse for over 4 years during the Civil War and worked as a nurse and counselor for the Freedmen's Relief Association after the war.

**Figure 1.4** Dorothea Dix (1802–1887) was the Union's Superintendent of Female Nurses during the Civil War.

**Figure 1.5** A, Section 21 in Arlington National Cemetery honors the nurses who served in the Armed Services in World War I. B, The "Spirit of Nursing" monument that stands in Section 21. C, Monument plaque.

**Figure 1.6** Recruiting poster for the Cadet Nurse Corps during World War II.

**Figure 1.7** Vietnam Women's Memorial.

**Figure 1.8** Sairy Gamp, a character in Dickens' book Martin Chuzzlewit, represented the negative image of nurses in the early 1800s.

**Figure 1.9** Considered the founder of modern nursing, Florence Nightingale (1820–1910) was influential in developing nursing education, practice, and administration.

**Figure 1.10** Clara Barton (1812–1912) organized the American Red Cross, which linked with the International Red Cross when the U.S. Congress ratified the Geneva Convention in 1882.

**Figure 1.11** Linda Richards (1841–1930) was America's first trained nurse.

**Figure 1.12** Mary Mahoney (1845–1926) was the first African American trained nurse.

**Figure 1.13** Lillian Wald (1867–1940) founded the Henry Street Settlement and Visiting Nurse Service (circa 1893), which provided nursing and social services and organized educational and cultural activities.

**Figure 1.14** Nursing leader and suffragist Lavinia L. Dock (1858–1956) was active in the protest movement for women's rights that resulted in the U.S. Constitution amendment allowing women to vote in 1920.

**Figure 1.15** Nurse activist Margaret Sanger, considered the founder of Planned Parenthood, was imprisoned for opening the first birth control information clinic in Baltimore in 1916.

**Figure 1.16** Mary Breckinridge, a nurse who practiced midwifery in England, Australia, and New Zealand, founded the Frontier Nursing Service in Kentucky in 1925 to provide family-centered primary health care to rural populations.

**Figure 1.17** Nurses practice in a variety of settings.

# LEARNING OUTCOME 1

Discuss historical and contemporary factors influencing the development of nursing.

## CONCEPTS FOR LECTURE

1. Recurring themes of women's roles and status, religious (Christian) values, war, societal attitudes, and visionary nursing leadership have influenced practice.

Traditional female roles of wife, mother, daughter, and sister have always included caring, nurturing, comforting, and supporting. In addition, women generally occupied subservient and dependent roles.

Christian values, self-denial, spiritual calling, and devotion to duty and work had a significant impact on nursing. Examples include the establishment of houses of care and healing in early Rome, orders of knights that provided care to the sick and injured during the Crusades, and the Order of Deaconesses who established a small hospital and training school where Florence Nightingale received her training in nursing.

War created a need for nurses, and a number of early nursing leaders emerged during wartime. Florence Nightingale is well known for her service during the Crimean War. Harriet Tubman, Sojourner Truth, Mother Biekerdyke, Clara Barton, and Dorothea Dix provided care during the American Civil War. During World War II the Cadet Nurse Corps was established, and nurses continue to volunteer to provide care in time of war.

Throughout nursing's history, societal attitudes about nurses have evolved, with images such as the poorly educated woman, guardian angel or angel of mercy, doctor's handmaiden, heroine, sex object, tyrannical mother, and body expert.

In the early 1990s, the Tri-Council for Nursing initiated an effort to improve the image of nursing, and the Johnson & Johnson corporation launched a "Campaign for Nursing's Future."

Many nursing leaders have made contributions to nursing's history and to women's history. Florence Nightingale (1820–1910) was the founder of modern nursing. Clara Barton (1812–1912) helped establish the American Red Cross. Linda Richards (1841–1930) was the United States' first trained nurse and is credited with pioneer work in psychiatric and industrial nursing. Mary Mahoney (1845–1926) was the United States' first black professional nurse, and she worked for acceptance of blacks into nursing and the promotion of equal rights. Lillian Wald (1867–1940) was the founder of public health nursing and with Mary Brewster founded the Henry Street Settlement and Visiting Nurse Service. Lavinia L. Dock (1858–1956) worked for passage of the 19th Amendment, campaigned for legislation to allow nurses to control their profession, and, with the assistance of Mary Adelaide Nutting and Isabel Hampton Robb, founded the American Society of Superintendents of Training Schools for Nurses of the United States and Canada, the precursor to the National League for Nursing. Margaret Higgins Sanger

## POWERPOINT LECTURE SLIDES

*(NOTE: The number on each PPT Lecture Slide directly corresponds with the Concepts for Lecture.)*

 Evolution of Nursing Practice
- Women's roles and status
- Religious (Christian) values
- War
- Societal attitudes
- Visionary nursing leadership

 Influences on Contemporary Nursing Practice
- Economics
- Changing demands for nurses
- Consumer demand
- Family structure
- Science and technology
- Information and telecommunications
- Legislation
- Demographics
- Nursing shortage
- Collective bargaining
- Work of nursing associations

## CONCEPTS FOR LECTURE *continued*

(1879–1966) is considered the founder of Planned Parenthood. Mary Breckinridge (1881–1965) established the Frontier Nursing Service and started one of the first midwifery training schools.

2. Contemporary nursing practice is influenced by economics, changing demands for nurses, consumer demand, family structure, science and technology, information and telecommunications, legislation, demographics, the nursing shortage, collective bargaining, and the work of nursing associations.

---

### SUGGESTIONS FOR CLASSROOM ACTIVITIES

- Have the students write a paper on one of the historical or contemporary factors influencing nursing.
- Have the students write a paper about one of the historical nursing leaders.

### SUGGESTIONS FOR CLINICAL ACTIVITIES

- Arrange a tour of hospital units employing advanced technologies.

---

## LEARNING OUTCOME 2

Identify the essential aspects of nursing.

### CONCEPTS FOR LECTURE

1. Definitions of nursing include nursing as caring, an art, a science, client centered, holistic, adaptive, a helping profession, and concerned with health promotion, maintenance, and restoration.

    Nursing theorists describe what nursing is as well as the interrelationships among nurses, nursing, the client, the environment, and intended outcomes. There is current interest by nurse researchers in the concept of caring.

    The definition of nursing developed by the American Nurses Association has evolved over the years. The current definition states that "nursing is the protection, promotion, and optimization of health and abilities, prevention of illness and injury, alleviation of suffering through the diagnosis and treatment of human response, and advocacy in the care of individuals, families, communities, and population."

2. *Consumer*, *patient*, and *client* are terms used to identify the recipients of nursing; however, many nurses use the term *client* since it emphasizes the responsibility of people for their own health.

### POWERPOINT LECTURE SLIDES

*(NOTE: The number on each PPT Lecture Slide directly corresponds with the Concepts for Lecture.)*

1. Definitions of Nursing

2. Recipients of Nursing
   - Consumer
   - Patient
   - Client

---

## SUGGESTIONS FOR CLASSROOM ACTIVITIES

- Have each student develop a definition of nursing. Then compile a class definition. Repeat this activity prior to graduation, comparing the two definitions.
- Have the students compare the ANA definition of nursing and the definition of nursing in the state nurse practice act.
- Have the students debate which term—consumer, patient, or client—should be used to designate the recipient of nursing care.

## SUGGESTIONS FOR CLINICAL ACTIVITIES

- Have the students ask nurses about their definitions of nursing.

## LEARNING OUTCOME 3

Identify four major areas within the scope of nursing practice.

### CONCEPTS FOR LECTURE

1. Four major areas within the scope of nursing practice are promoting health and wellness, preventing illness, restoring health, and caring for the dying.

    Promoting health and wellness involves behaviors that enhance quality of life and maximize personal potential by enhancing healthy lifestyles.

    The goal of illness prevention is to maintain optimal health by preventing disease.

    Restoring health includes providing direct care, performing diagnostic and assessment procedures, consulting with other health care professionals, and teaching and rehabilitating clients.

    Care of the dying involves comforting and caring for dying clients, assisting clients to live as comfortably as possible until death, and helping support persons cope with death.

### POWERPOINT LECTURE SLIDES

*(NOTE: The number on each PPT Lecture Slide directly corresponds with the Concepts for Lecture.)*

 The Scope of Nursing Practice
- Promotion of health and wellness
- Prevention of illness
- Restoration of health
- Care for the dying

## SUGGESTIONS FOR CLASSROOM ACTIVITIES

- Invite a panel of nurses whose positions represent the four major areas within the scope of practice to discuss their responsibilities.

## SUGGESTIONS FOR CLINICAL ACTIVITIES

- Arrange for groups of students to visit an outpatient clinic, an inpatient unit, a rehabilitation unit, and a hospice unit. Have the students report on the types of nursing activities observed on the various units.

## LEARNING OUTCOME 4

Identify the purposes of nurse practice acts and standards for nursing practice.

### CONCEPTS FOR LECTURE

1. The common purpose of nurse practice acts is to protect the public.

    Nurse practice acts regulate the practice of nursing in the United States and Canada and are unique in each jurisdiction.

### POWERPOINT LECTURE SLIDES

*(NOTE: The number on each PPT Lecture Slide directly corresponds with the Concepts for Lecture.)*

 Nurse Practice Acts
- Common purpose
- Legal acts

Establishing and implementing standards of practice are major functions of a professional organization.

2. The purpose of the American Nurses Association Standards of Practice is to describe the responsibilities for which nurses are accountable. These standards are generic in nature, by using the nursing process as a foundation, and provide for the practice of nursing regardless of area of specialization.

Nursing specialty organizations further develop standards for nurses practicing in specialty roles.

- Regulate practice
- Jurisdiction specific

 Standards of Nursing Practice
- ANA: Standards of Professional Performance
- Specialty nursing organizations

## SUGGESTIONS FOR CLASSROOM ACTIVITIES

- Obtain copies of the state's nurse practice act for the students. Have the students compare the nurse practice act with the ANA's scope and standards of practice.
- Have the students compare the state nurse practice act with the nurse practice act from another state.
- Have the students obtain standards of practice from a nursing specialty organization and compare these with the ANA standards and the nurse practice act.

## SUGGESTIONS FOR CLINICAL ACTIVITIES

- Ask the students to give examples of how the ANA standards of care are operationalized on the clinical unit.

## LEARNING OUTCOME 5

Describe the roles of nurses.

### CONCEPTS FOR LECTURE

1. Nurses assume a number of roles, often concurrently, while providing care to clients. These roles include caregiver, communicator, teacher, client advocate, counselor, change agent, leader, manager, case manager, and research consumer.

As caregivers, nurses perform activities that assist the client physically and psychologically.

As communicators, nurses communicate with clients, support persons, other health care professionals, and people in the community.

As educators, nurses educate clients about their health and health care procedures, teach unlicensed assistive personnel, and share expertise with other nurses and health care personnel.

As client advocates, nurses act to protect clients. They represent clients' needs and wishes to other health professionals and assist clients to exercise rights and speak up for themselves.

As counselors, nurses provide emotional, intellectual, and psychological support to help clients recognize and cope with stressful psychological or social problems, develop improved interpersonal relationships, and promote personal growth.

### POWERPOINT LECTURE SLIDES

*(NOTE: The number on each PPT Lecture Slide directly corresponds with the Concepts for Lecture.)*

 Roles and Functions of Nurses
- Caregiver
- Communicator
- Teacher
- Client advocate
- Counselor
- Change agent
- Leader
- Manager
- Case manager
- Research consumer

As change agents, nurses not only assist clients to make modifications in behavior but also act to make changes in the health care system.

As leaders, nurses influence others to work together to accomplish specific goals whether working with individual clients, other health professionals, or community groups.

As managers, nurses manage care for individuals, families, and communities. They delegate nursing activities to ancillary personnel and other nurses, supervising and evaluating their performance.

As case managers, nurses work with multidisciplinary health care teams to measure effectiveness of case management plans and to monitor outcomes.

As research consumers, nurses are aware of the process of research, are sensitive to protection of the rights of human subjects, participate in the identification of researchable problems, and discriminately use research findings to improve client care.

| SUGGESTIONS FOR CLASSROOM ACTIVITIES | SUGGESTIONS FOR CLINICAL ACTIVITIES |
|---|---|
| • Ask the students to give examples of how nurses enact these roles. <br> • Invite a group of nurses to discuss how they enact these roles. | • Have students "shadow" a nurse, observing how the nurse enacts the various roles. |

## LEARNING OUTCOME 6

Describe the expanded career roles and their functions.

### CONCEPTS FOR LECTURE

1. Expanded career roles such as nurse practitioner, clinical nurse specialist, nurse midwife, nurse educator, nurse researcher, and nurse anesthetist require advanced education in these roles and allow greater independence and autonomy.

Nurse practitioners specialize in areas such as care of adults, pediatrics, family practice, school nursing, or gerontology. They provide care for clients with non-emergent acute or chronic illness, provide ambulatory care, and practice in health care agencies or community-based settings.

Clinical specialists are experts in a specialized area of practice and provide direct care, educate clients and other health care professionals, provide consulting services, conduct research, and manage care.

Nurse midwives give prenatal and postnatal care and manage deliveries in normal pregnancies.

### POWERPOINT LECTURE SLIDES

*(NOTE: The number on each PPT Lecture Slide directly corresponds with the Concepts for Lecture.)*

 Expanded Career Roles
- Nurse practitioner
- Nurse administrator
- Clinical nurse specialist
- Nurse educator
- Nurse anesthetist
- Nurse midwife
- Nurse researcher

Nurse educators are responsible for classroom and clinical education, frequently have expertise in a particular area of practice, and are employed in nursing programs at educational institutions and in hospital staff education.

Nurse researchers investigate nursing problems to improve nursing care and to refine and expand nursing knowledge. They are employed in academic institutions, teaching hospitals, and research centers.

Nurse anesthetists carry out preoperative visits and assessments, and administer anesthesia for surgery under the supervision of a physician prepared in anesthesiology.

---

## SUGGESTIONS FOR CLASSROOM ACTIVITIES

- Invite a panel of nurses in expanded roles to discuss their education, roles, and responsibilities.
- Have each student write a short paper on an expanded role of interest to the student.
- Have the students explore the scope and standards of practice for one of the expanded roles.
- Ask the students to investigate the educational and licensing requirements for one of the expanded nursing roles.

## SUGGESTIONS FOR CLINICAL ACTIVITIES

- Assign the students to observe a nurse functioning in an expanded role. Have the students share their observations with the clinical group.

---

## LEARNING OUTCOME 7

Discuss the criteria of a profession and the professionalization of nursing.

### CONCEPTS FOR LECTURE

1. Criteria of a profession include requirements for prolonged and specialized education to acquire a body of knowledge pertinent to the role to be performed, an orientation toward service, ongoing research, a code of ethics, autonomy, and a professional organization.

Nursing is gaining recognition as a profession and as such is striving to meet the characteristics of a profession.

Nursing is establishing a well-defined body of knowledge and expertise through the use of nursing conceptual frameworks, which give direction to nursing practice, education, and ongoing research.

Nursing has a tradition of service to others guided by rules, policies, and a code of ethics.

Research in nursing is evolving with federal funding and professional support establishing centers for nursing research with an increased focus on research pertaining to practice-related issues.

The nursing profession places a high value on the worth and dignity of others, requiring integrity of its members regardless of personal cost. Nursing

### POWERPOINT LECTURE SLIDES

*(NOTE: The number on each PPT Lecture Slide directly corresponds with the Concepts for Lecture.)*

 Criteria of a Profession
- Prolonged, specialized education
- Orientation toward service
- Ongoing research
- Code of ethics
- Autonomy
- Professional organization

has established its own code of ethics and has set up means to monitor professional behavior.

To be autonomous, a profession must regulate itself and set standards for its members. It must have legal authority to define the scope, function, and roles of the profession and to determine its goals and responsibilities. The nursing profession is striving to achieve autonomy in the formation of policy and in control of its activity through professional organizations and nursing regulatory bodies.

---

## SUGGESTIONS FOR CLASSROOM ACTIVITIES

- Have the students debate whether nursing is a profession.
- Have the students compare nursing with another profession, using the criteria of a profession.

---

# LEARNING OUTCOME 8

Discuss Benner's levels of nursing proficiency.

## CONCEPTS FOR LECTURE

1. Benner (2001) describes five stages of proficiency: novice, advanced beginner, competent, proficient, and expert.

   A novice has no experience. Performance is limited, inflexible, and governed by rules and regulations rather than by experience.

   An advanced beginner demonstrates marginally acceptable performance, recognizes meaningful aspects of a real situation, and has experienced enough real situations to make judgments about them.

   A competent nurse has 2 to 3 years of experience, demonstrates organizational and planning abilities, and is able to differentiate important factors from less important aspects of care, coordinating multiple complex care demands.

   A proficient nurse has 3 to 5 years of experience perceiving situations as a whole, uses maxims as guides for what to consider in a situation, has a holistic understanding of the client, and focuses on long-term goals.

   An expert nurse's performance is fluid, flexible, and highly proficient, no longer requiring rules, guidelines, or maxims to understand a situation. The expert nurse demonstrates a highly skilled, intuitive, analytic ability in new situations, often taking action because "it felt right."

## POWERPOINT LECTURE SLIDES

*(NOTE: The number on each PPT Lecture Slide directly corresponds with the Concepts for Lecture.)*

 Benner's Stages of Nursing Expertise
- Stage I: Novice
- Stage II: Advanced Beginner
- Stage III: Competent
- Stage IV: Proficient
- Stage V: Expert

## LEARNING OUTCOME 9

Relate essential nursing values to attitudes, personal qualities, and professional behaviors.

### CONCEPTS FOR LECTURE

1. Through nursing education programs, nurses develop, clarify, and internalize professional values.

   These values are stated in a code of ethics, standards of nursing practice, and nurse practice acts.

   The National Student Nurses' Association has developed a Code of Academic and Clinical Conduct to provide guidance for the student in personal development of an ethical foundation for the profession of nursing and to assist in the holistic development of the student.

### POWERPOINT LECTURE SLIDES

*(NOTE: The number on each PPT Lecture Slide directly corresponds with the Concepts for Lecture.)*

 Critical Values of Nursing
- Code of ethics
- Standards
- Nurse practice acts
- NSNA's *Code of Academic and Clinical Conduct*

## LEARNING OUTCOME 10

Explain the functions of national and international nurses' associations.

### CONCEPTS FOR LECTURE

1. The American Nurses Association (ANA) is the national professional organization for nursing in the United States. Purposes of the organization are to foster high standards of nursing practice and to promote the educational and professional advancement of nurses so that all people may have better nursing care.

   The Canadian Nurses Association (CNA) is the national nursing association in Canada. It develops

### POWERPOINT LECTURE SLIDES

*(NOTE: The number on each PPT Lecture Slide directly corresponds with the Concepts for Lecture.)*

 National and International Nursing Organizations
- American Nurses Association (ANA)
- Canadian Nurses Association (CNA)
- National League for Nursing (NLN)
- National League for Nursing Accrediting Commission (NLNAC)

standards and a code of ethics, prepares licensure examinations, and offers research grants, fellowships, and scholarships to Canadian nurses.

The National League for Nursing (NLN) is an organization of individuals and agencies. Its purpose is to foster the development and improvement of all nursing services and nursing education. Non-nurses may become members of the NLN. The National League for Nursing Accrediting Commission (NLNAC), an independent body within the NLN, provides voluntary accreditation for educational programs in nursing.

The International Council of Nurses (ICN) is a federation of national nurses' associations working together for the mission of representing nursing worldwide, advancing the profession, and influencing health policy.

The National Student Nurses' Association (NSNA) is the official professional organization for nursing students.

The Canadian University Student Nurses Association is similar to the NSNA.

Sigma Theta Tau, International is the international honor society in nursing. Its purpose is professional rather than social, with membership attained through academic achievement.

- International Council of Nurses (ICN)
- The National Student Nurses' Association (NSNA)
- Sigma Theta Tau, International

---

## SUGGESTIONS FOR CLASSROOM ACTIVITIES

- Have the students debate the following topic: All nurses should join and participate in the ANA or CNA, and all nursing students should join and participate in the NSNA or the Canadian University Student Nurses Association.
- Have the students write a short paper on one of the professional nursing organizations, describing membership requirements, cost of membership, benefits of membership, the organizational chart, and purposes of the organization.
- Invite members of several nursing organizations to discuss their organizations.

# CHAPTER 2
## NURSING EDUCATION, RESEARCH, AND EVIDENCE-BASED PRACTICE

## RESOURCE LIBRARY

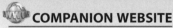 **PRENTICE HALL NURSING MEDIALINK DVD-ROM**

Audio Glossary
NCLEX® Review
Videos: *LPW/LVN*
*Nursing Assistants*
*The Health Care Team*

 **IMAGE LIBRARY**

**COMPANION WEBSITE**

Additional NCLEX® Review
Case Study: *Nursing Profession*
Application Activity: *Entry into Practice*
Links to Resources

**Figure 2.1** Nursing students learn to care for clients in community settings.
**Figure 2.2** A nurse practitioner holds a master's degree and assumes an advanced practice role.

**Figure 2.3** It is important for clients to be fully informed before they participate in a research study.

---

## LEARNING OUTCOME 1

Describe the different types of educational nursing programs.

### CONCEPTS FOR LECTURE

1. Types of educational programs include practical or vocational nursing, registered nursing, graduate nursing, continuing education, and in-service education.

    There are two types of entry-level generalist nurses: the registered nurse (RN), and the licensed practical or vocational nurse (LPN, LVN). Practical or vocational nursing programs are provided by community colleges, vocational schools, hospitals, or independent health agencies. These programs are 5 to 12 months in duration with classroom and clinical experiences, and graduates take the NCLEX-PN examination for licensure.

    There are three major types of RN nursing programs: diploma, associate degree (ADN), and baccalaureate degree (BSN). Although these programs vary considerably, all RN program graduates take the NCLEX-RN® examination for licensure.

    Diploma programs are hospital-based educational programs that provide a rich clinical experience for nursing students. These programs are often associated with colleges or universities. Associate degree programs are usually 2-year programs offered primarily in community colleges, although some 4-year colleges also have ADN programs. Baccalaureate degree programs are generally 4 years in duration and offer liberal arts, sciences, humanities, and nursing courses.

    Graduate nursing programs include master's degree and doctoral programs. Master's programs generally take from 1.5 to 2 years to complete and provide specialized knowledge and skills that enable nurses to assume advanced roles in practice, education,

### POWERPOINT LECTURE SLIDES

*(NOTE: The number on each PPT Lecture Slide directly corresponds with the Concepts for Lecture.)*

 Types of Nursing Education
- Practical or vocational nursing
- Registered nursing
    - Diploma
    - Associate degree
    - Baccalaureate
- Graduate nursing
    - Master's
    - Doctoral
- Continuing education and in-service education

---

administration, and research. Doctoral programs further prepare the nurse for advanced clinical practice, administration, education, and research.

Continuing education (CE) refers to formalized experiences designed to enlarge the knowledge or skills of practitioners. CE courses tend to be more specific and shorter.

An in-service education program is administered by an employer and is designed to upgrade the knowledge or skills of employees.

## SUGGESTIONS FOR CLASSROOM ACTIVITIES

- Invite nurses who have obtained master's and doctoral degrees to discuss the programs, why they decided to obtain advanced education, and their current positions.
- To provide a historical perspective, invite nurses who graduated from diploma schools in the 1960s or the Cadet Nurse Corps to discuss their education programs.
- Review the state nursing law to determine the difference between the functions of the LPN/LVN and the RN.
- Review the state nursing law to determine the qualifications necessary for licensure and license renewal.

## SUGGESTIONS FOR CLINICAL ACTIVITIES

- Assign students to interview nurses who graduated from various types of education programs to determine why these nurses selected the type of nursing program attended.

# LEARNING OUTCOME 2

Discuss aspects of entry to professional nursing practice.

## CONCEPTS FOR LECTURE

1. The American Nurses Association (ANA) has endorsed the bachelor of science in nursing (BSN) as entry level for professional nursing practice. The graduate with an associate degree in nursing would be considered a technical nurse and be licensed under the legal title associate nurse (AN). The proposal sparked sharp debate among graduates, students, and educators. Some believe the proposal undervalues associate degree graduates.

The ANA cannot legislate these changes as each state has the responsibility to define the legal boundaries of nursing practice and to designate the criteria for licensure. Therefore, each state needs to adopt the ANA proposal, if desired. If the proposal is implemented, a grandfather clause would need to be considered for AD or diploma graduates who were educated in these programs before the date of the licensure regulation change. The ANA proposal for licensure changes does not mention diploma or LPN/LVN programs.

The proposal entails that new standardized examinations be developed to test the two levels of competence.

Perspectives about entry into practice are changing. The American Association of Colleges of Nursing

## POWERPOINT LECTURE SLIDES

*(NOTE: The number on each PPT Lecture Slide directly corresponds with the Concepts for Lecture.)*

 1   Entry to Professional Practice
- ANA's resolution
- Debate
- Implications
- AACN's support for articulation

(AACN) provides a fact sheet supporting articulation from associate degree programs to baccalaureate and higher degree programs and desires to strengthen collaboration between ADN and BSN programs.

| SUGGESTIONS FOR CLASSROOM ACTIVITIES | SUGGESTIONS FOR CLINICAL ACTIVITIES |
|---|---|
| • Have the students debate the pros and cons of establishing the BSN degree as entry level for professional nursing practice. | • Have the students ask several staff nurses to react to the ANA 1985 proposal and report findings in a clinical conference.<br>• Have the students determine the institution's educational requirements for various nursing positions.<br>• Obtain the job descriptions of aides, LPNs/LVNs, and RNs. Compare and contrast roles and responsibilities. |

## LEARNING OUTCOME 3

Explain the importance of continuing nursing education.

### CONCEPTS FOR LECTURE

1. Continuing education (CE) refers to formalized experiences designed to enlarge the knowledge or skills of practitioners.

   The purposes of CE programs include keeping nurses abreast of new techniques and knowledge, attaining expertise in a specialized area of practice, and providing nurses with information essential to nursing practice.

   Some states require nurses to obtain a certain number of CE credits to renew their licenses.

### POWERPOINT LECTURE SLIDES

*(NOTE: The number on each PPT Lecture Slide directly corresponds with the Concepts for Lecture.)*

 Continuing Education
- Definition
- Purpose
- Licensure requirements

| SUGGESTIONS FOR CLASSROOM ACTIVITIES | SUGGESTIONS FOR CLINICAL ACTIVITIES |
|---|---|
| • Have the students investigate the continuing education requirements as established by the state's nurse practice act. | • Have the students review the in-service schedule for the month.<br>• Have the students attend one in-service education program at the institution.<br>• Review the mandatory in-service education programs at the institution.<br>• Have each student locate one CE article in a nursing journal and review the journal's requirements to obtain these CE credits. |

## LEARNING OUTCOME 4

Identify ways the nurse can participate in research activities in practice.

### CONCEPTS FOR LECTURE

1. Nurses generate, publish, and apply research in practice to improve client care and enhance nursing's scientific knowledge base.

### POWERPOINT LECTURE SLIDES

*(NOTE: The number on each PPT Lecture Slide directly corresponds with the Concepts for Lecture.)*

According to the ANA standards, the RN integrates research findings into practice, utilizes the best evidence available to guide practice, and actively participates in research activities according to the level of education and position of the RN. According to the ANA standards, examples of research activities in which the RN may participate include identifying clinical problems specific to research, participating in data collection, participating in a formal committee or program, sharing research activities and/or findings with peers and others, conducting research, critically analyzing and interpreting research for application to practice, and incorporating research as a basis for learning.

There has been an increased emphasis on the importance of evidence-based practice (EBP), that is, the use of some form of substantiation in making clinical decisions. This substantiation or evidence can arise from tradition, authority, experience, trial and error, logic or reason, or research.

Although the focus for all nurses is use of research findings in practice, the degree of participation in research depends on the nurse's educational level, position, experience, and practice environment.

1 Participation in Research
- Purpose
  - ANA standards
  - Evidence-based practice (EBP)
- Degree of participation

## SUGGESTIONS FOR CLASSROOM ACTIVITIES

- Invite a nurse researcher to discuss the use of research findings in clinical practice.
- Have the students explore the National Institute for Nursing Research on the Internet and report on the mission, scientific goals and objectives, and examples of research contributions of NINR-supported researchers.

## SUGGESTIONS FOR CLINICAL ACTIVITIES

- Invite a member of the nursing research committee of the institution to discuss the role of research in the institution.

# LEARNING OUTCOME 5

Differentiate the quantitative approach from the qualitative approach in nursing research.

## CONCEPTS FOR LECTURE

1. The two major approaches in nursing research to investigate diverse phenomena are quantitative and qualitative research.
2. Quantitative research progresses through systematic, logical steps according to a specific plan under conditions of control with data analyzed using statistical procedures. Quantitative research is most frequently associated with a philosophical doctrine that emphasizes the rational and the scientific. It is often viewed as "hard" science and uses deductive reasoning and the measurable attributes of human experience.
3. Qualitative research is often associated with naturalistic inquiry, which explores the subjective and complex experiences of human beings. Qualitative research seeks to understand the human experience as it is lived through careful collection and analysis of materials that

## POWERPOINT LECTURE SLIDES

*(NOTE: The number on each PPT Lecture Slide directly corresponds with the Concepts for Lecture.)*

1 Types of Nursing Research
- Quantitative
- Qualitative

2 Quantitative
- Logical steps
- Specific plan
- Controlled conditions
- Statistical analysis

3 Qualitative
- Naturalistic inquiry
- Explores human experiences
- Identifies themes and patterns

are narrative and subjective. Using the inductive method, data are analyzed by identifying themes and patterns to develop a theory or framework that helps explain the processes under observation.

Each type of research is appropriate for specific types of research questions.

---

## SUGGESTIONS FOR CLASSROOM ACTIVITIES

• Have the students find one example of a quantitative and a qualitative nursing research study and write a paper comparing and contrasting the type of research question, methods, and analysis used.

## SUGGESTIONS FOR CLINICAL ACTIVITIES

• Have the students make a list of appropriate research questions that could be addressed by quantitative and qualitative research methods from their current clinical practice.

---

# LEARNING OUTCOME 6

Describe the nurse's role in protecting the rights of human subjects in research.

## CONCEPTS FOR LECTURE

1. All clients must be informed and understand the consequences of consenting to participate in a research study. They must be able to assess the risks and potential benefits to either themselves or to the development of knowledge.

For years adults have been the focus of medical research; however, the American Academy of Pediatrics has identified the need to conduct pediatric research so that children can benefit from advances in medical science. Because of their vulnerability, extra precaution must be taken to ensure that children's rights are upheld and that they are not harmed; therefore, pediatric expertise is needed on review panels.

All nurses who practice in settings where research is conducted or participate in research share a role in safeguarding the following rights: the right not to be harmed, the right to full disclosure, the right of self-determination, and the right of privacy and confidentiality.

The risk of harm is exposure to the possibility of injury going beyond everyday situations. These risks may be physical, emotional, legal, financial, or social. The right to full disclosure is the act of making clear the client's role in a research situation; deception either by withholding information or by giving false or misleading information must not occur. The right of self-determination means that participants should feel free from constraints, coercion, or any undue influence to participate in a study. Hidden inducements must be strictly avoided. The right of privacy means that anonymity of the study participant is ensured, and confidentiality means that any information a participant relates will not be made public or available to others without the participant's consent. This may require the use of pseudonyms, code numbers, and reporting only aggregate or group data in published research.

## POWERPOINT LECTURE SLIDES

*(NOTE: The number on each PPT Lecture Slide directly corresponds with the Concepts for Lecture.)*

 Protection of Rights of Human Research Subjects
• Safeguard the following rights:
  ○ Right not to be harmed
  ○ Right to full disclosure
  ○ Right of self-determination
  ○ Right of privacy and confidentiality

---

## SUGGESTIONS FOR CLASSROOM ACTIVITIES

- Invite a nurse researcher to discuss protection of the rights of human subjects in the studies the researcher has completed.
- Obtain copies of several consent forms used in nursing research studies, and have the students review these for inclusion of all of the rights of research subjects.

## SUGGESTIONS FOR CLINICAL ACTIVITIES

- Ask a member of the institutional review board to discuss the board's roles and obligations and how rights of human subjects are protected.

## LEARNING OUTCOME 7

Identify the steps of the research process.

### CONCEPTS FOR LECTURE

1. The steps in quantitative research include stating a research question or problem; defining the purpose or rationale; reviewing the literature; formulating the hypothesis and defining variables; selecting a research design to test the hypothesis; selecting the population, sample, and setting; conducting a pilot study; collecting the data; analyzing the data; and communicating conclusions or implications.

2. Steps in qualitative research differ in many ways. For example, dependent and independent variables are not used and variables are not manipulated to test a hypothesis. Because the intent of qualitative research is to thoroughly describe and explain a phenomenon, the researcher collects narrative data through interviews or observations, transcribes the data, organizes data around some type of categorization scheme, and integrates themes to present a description or theory. Some common qualitative research traditions include ethnography, phenomenology, and grounded theory.

### POWERPOINT LECTURE SLIDES

*(NOTE: The number on each PPT Lecture Slide directly corresponds with the Concepts for Lecture.)*

 Quantitative Research Process
- State a research question or problem
- Define the purpose or rationale
- Review the literature
- Formulate a hypothesis and defining variables
- Select a research design
- Select population, sample, and setting
- Conduct pilot study
- Collect the data
- Analyze the data
- Communicate conclusions or implications

 Qualitative Research Steps
- Collect narrative data through interviews or observations
- Transcribe the data
- Organize data around some type of categorization scheme to present a description or theory
- Integrate themes to present a description or theory
- Common qualitative research traditions include:
  ○ Ethnography
  ○ Phenomenology
  ○ Grounded theory
- Grounded theory

## SUGGESTIONS FOR CLASSROOM ACTIVITIES

- Have the students find one quantitative and one qualitative study in a nursing research journal and identify the steps in the research process.

## SUGGESTIONS FOR CLINICAL ACTIVITIES

- Arrange for the students to attend a research conference.

# CHAPTER 3
## NURSING THEORIES AND CONCEPTUAL FRAMEWORKS

## RESOURCE LIBRARY

 **PRENTICE HALL NURSING MEDIALINK DVD-ROM**

Audio Glossary
NCLEX® Review

**COMPANION WEBSITE**

Additional NCLEX® Review
Case Study: Theories
Application Activities:
  *The Growth of Nursing Theory*
  *Shaping Watson's Theory*
Links to Resources

**IMAGE LIBRARY**

**Figure 3.1** The living tree of nursing theories.
**Figure 3.2** The major components of Orem's self-care deficit theory. R indicates a relationship between components; < indicates a current or potential deficit where nursing would be required.

**Figure 3.3** King's conceptual framework for nursing: dynamic interacting systems.
**Figure 3.4** King's model of transactions.
**Figure 3.5** Neuman's client system.

---

## LEARNING OUTCOME 1

Differentiate the terms *concept, conceptual framework, theory, paradigm,* and *metaparadigm for nursing.*

### CONCEPTS FOR LECTURE

1. Concepts are often called the building blocks of theories. They may be abstract ideas or mental images of phenomena or reality. Examples include mass, energy, ego, and id.
2. A conceptual framework is a group of related ideas, statements, or concepts. The term *conceptual framework* is often used interchangeably with the terms *conceptual model* and *grand theories.* One example is Freud's structure of the mind (id, ego, and superego).
3. Broadly speaking, a paradigm refers to a pattern of shared understanding and assumptions about reality and the world. A paradigm includes notions of reality that are largely unconscious, taken for granted, and culturally related. Examples are time and space.
4. Metaparadigms are concepts that can be superimposed on other concepts. In nursing, these are person, environment, health, and nursing.
5. A theory is defined as a supposition or system of ideas that is proposed to explain a given phenomenon. A theory articulates significant relationships between concepts. Theories offer ways of looking at or conceptualizing the central interests of a discipline. They are used to describe, predict, and control phenomena. An example is Freud's theory of the unconscious.

### POWERPOINT LECTURE SLIDES

*(NOTE: The number on each PPT Lecture Slide directly corresponds with the Concepts for Lecture.)*

**1** Concepts
- Abstract ideas or mental images of phenomena or reality
- Often called the "building blocks" of theories
- Examples:
  ○ Mass
  ○ Energy
  ○ Ego
  ○ Id

**2** Conceptual Framework
- Group of related ideas, statements, or concepts
- Often used interchangeably with the terms "conceptual model" and "grand theories"
- Examples:
  ○ Freud's structure of the mind (id, ego, and superego)

**3** Paradigm
- A pattern of shared understanding and assumptions about reality and the world
- Include notions of reality that are largely unconscious or taken for granted
- Are derived from cultural beliefs

---

- Examples:
  - time
  - space

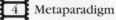 Metaparadigm
- Concepts that can be superimposed on other concepts
- Four major metaparadigms in nursing:
  - Person
  - Environment
  - Health
  - Nursing

5. Theory
- Supposition or system of ideas proposed to explain a given phenomenon
- Attempt to explain relationships between concepts
- Offer ways to conceptualize central interests of a discipline
- Example:
  - Freud's theory of the unconscious

## SUGGESTIONS FOR CLASSROOM ACTIVITIES

- Have the students identify concepts, conceptual frameworks, theories, and paradigms used in the curriculum of the program.

## LEARNING OUTCOME 2

Identify the purposes of nursing theory in nursing education, research, and clinical practice.

### CONCEPTS FOR LECTURE

1. In many cases, nursing theory guides knowledge development and directs education, research, and practice although each influences the other.

    Nursing theory helped to establish nursing's place in academia and became more firmly established in these settings than in clinical practice. In the past, many nursing programs organized curriculum around a conceptual framework. Although all nursing programs are organized around concepts, today many programs have abandoned theory-driven conceptual frameworks.

    Nurse scholars have repeatedly insisted that nursing research identifies the philosophical assumptions or conceptual frameworks from which it proceeds because new theoretical perspectives are based upon previous assumptions about people and the world. Perspectives can help generate new ideas, research questions, and interpretations.

    Where nursing theory has been employed in a clinical setting, the primary contribution has been the facilitation of reflecting, questioning, and thinking about what nurses do.

    In addition, practice theories that describe relationships among variables as applied to specific clinical situations are important contributors to effective evidence-based practice (EBP).

### POWERPOINT LECTURE SLIDES

*(NOTE: The number on each PPT Lecture Slide directly corresponds with the Concepts for Lecture.)*

1. Purposes of Nursing Theory
- Link among nursing theory, education, research, and clinical practice
- Contributes to knowledge development
- May direct education, research, and practice

<table>
<tr><td>

**SUGGESTIONS FOR CLASSROOM ACTIVITIES**

- Discuss the conceptual framework or concepts used in the educational program.
- Have the students identify the theoretical or conceptual framework for a nursing research study.

</td><td>

**SUGGESTIONS FOR CLINICAL ACTIVITIES**

- Have the students determine whether the nursing department has identified a theoretical or conceptual framework for the institution and how this framework is implemented.
- Invite a nurse from the agency to discuss the conceptual framework used within the institution.

</td></tr>
</table>

# LEARNING OUTCOME 3

Identify the components of the metaparadigm for nursing.

## CONCEPTS FOR LECTURE

1. Collectively, the concepts of person or client, environment, health, and nursing are the metaparadigm for nursing.

   Person or client is the recipient of nursing care and includes individuals, families, groups, and communities.

   Environment is the internal and external surroundings that affect the client. It includes people in the physical environment, such as families, friends, and significant others.

   Health is the degree of wellness or well-being that the client experiences.

   Nursing is the attributes, characteristics, and actions of the nurse providing care on behalf of, or in conjunction with, the client.

## POWERPOINT LECTURE SLIDES

*(NOTE: The number on each PPT Lecture Slide directly corresponds with the Concepts for Lecture.)*

 1 Metaparadigms of Nursing
- Person or client
- Environment
- Health
- Nursing

<table>
<tr><td>

**SUGGESTIONS FOR CLASSROOM ACTIVITIES**

- Have the students investigate how the metaparadigm is used in the curriculum of the school.
- Have the students compare and contrast the definitions of the concepts of patient or client, environment, health, and nursing in the textbook and in the school's curriculum.
- Divide the students into groups and assign one of the theories/models of nursing presented in the text to each group. Ask the students to identify the metaparadigm definitions for the assigned model and then compare and contrast among these models.

</td><td>

**SUGGESTIONS FOR CLINICAL ACTIVITIES**

- Have the students ask RNs in various positions to define the metaparadigm concepts and compare and contrast the definitions obtained from these nurses.

</td></tr>
</table>

# LEARNING OUTCOME 4

Describe the major purpose of theory in the sciences and practice disciplines.

## CONCEPTS FOR LECTURE

1. Theories in the natural sciences provide a foundation and direction for research, which often produces tangible results such as knowledge that can be used to control nature, disease, and foreign threats.

## POWERPOINT LECTURE SLIDES

*(NOTE: The number on each PPT Lecture Slide directly corresponds with the Concepts for Lecture.)*

 1 Natural Sciences
- Theories provide a foundation and direction for research

2. In the practice disciplines, theories work like lenses through which the practitioners are invited to interpret the world of interest such as the market workforce, the human mind, pain, and suffering. The usefulness comes from helping to interpret phenomena from unique perspectives and building new understandings, relationships, and possibilities.

- Often produced tangible results
  - Examples: knowledge that can be used to control nature, disease, and foreign threats

 Practice Disciplines
- Theories work like lenses to interpret the world of interest
- Usefulness comes from helping to interpret phenomenon from unique perspectives
- Building new understandings, relationships, and possibilities

## SUGGESTIONS FOR CLASSROOM ACTIVITIES

- Invite a colleague who teaches in the natural sciences to discuss the role of theory and research in that discipline.
- Invite a colleague from another practice discipline to discuss the role of theory and research in that discipline. Compare how theory and research are used in that practice discipline to how these are used in nursing.

# LEARNING OUTCOME 5

Identify one positive and one negative effect of using theory to understand clinical practice.

## CONCEPTS FOR LECTURE

1. Debates about the role of theory in nursing practice provide evidence that nursing is maturing, both as an academic discipline and as a clinical profession.

   Theory can be used to broaden perspectives in nursing and facilitate altruistic and humanistic values of the profession.

   At the same time, rational and predictive theory can produce language and social practices that are superimposed onto the lives of vulnerable clients and do violence to the fragility of human dignity.

   Theory can either liberate or enslave.

## POWERPOINT LECTURE SLIDES

*(NOTE: The number on each PPT Lecture Slide directly corresponds with the Concepts for Lecture.)*

 Use of Theory to Understand Clinical Practice
- Debates provide evidence that nursing is maturing
- Positive effects
  - Broadening perspectives in nursing
  - Facilitating the altruistic and humanistic values
- Negative effects
  - Produce language and social practices that are superimposed onto lives of clients
  - Do violence to the fragility of human dignity

## SUGGESTIONS FOR CLASSROOM ACTIVITIES

- Divide the students into groups and assign one of the theories/models of nursing presented in the text to each group. Ask the students to develop a list of positive and negative effects of using the assigned theory/model to understand practice. Share the findings.

## SUGGESTIONS FOR CLINICAL ACTIVITIES

- Invite a nurse from administration, a nurse from in-service education, and a staff nurse to discuss the positive and negative effects of using theory to understand clinical practice.

# CHAPTER 4
## LEGAL ASPECTS OF NURSING

## RESOURCE LIBRARY

 **PRENTICE HALL NURSING MEDIALINK DVD-ROM**

Audio Glossary
NCLEX® Review
Video:
   *Collective Bargaining*
   *Understanding Legal and Ethical Issues*

 **COMPANION WEBSITE**

Additional NCLEX® Review
Case Study: Legal Aspects of Obstetrics
Application Activities:
   *Nurse Practice Act*
   *Collective Bargaining*
   *Good Samaritan Act*
Links to Resources

 **IMAGE LIBRARY**

**Figure 4.1** Overview of sources of law.
**Figure 4.2** Anatomy of a lawsuit.
**Figure 4.3** Obtaining informed consent is the responsibility of the person performing the procedure.

**Figure 4.4** Sample advance health care directive.
**Figure 4.5** An overview of the types of law in nursing practice.
**Figure 4.6** Clear and accurate documentation is the nurse's best defense against potential liability.

---

## LEARNING OUTCOME 1

List sources of law and types of laws.

### CONCEPTS FOR LECTURE

1. The primary sources of law include constitutions, statutes, administrative agencies, and decisions of courts.
2. Laws can be divided into different types of laws. The two main types are public law and private or civil law.

   Public law refers to the body of law that deals with relationships between individuals and the government and government agencies. Criminal laws, which deal with actions against the safety and welfare of the public, are an important segment of public law.

   Private or civil law is the body of law that deals with relationships among private individuals. Categories of civil law include contract law and tort law.

### POWERPOINT LECTURE SLIDES

*(NOTE: The number on each PPT Lecture Slide directly corresponds with the Concepts for Lecture.)*

**1** Sources of Law
   • Constitutions
   • Statutes
   • Administrative agencies
   • Decisions of courts

**2** Types of Law
   • Public
      ○ Criminal
   • Private or civil
      ○ Contract law
      ○ Tort law

---

### SUGGESTIONS FOR CLASSROOM ACTIVITIES

• Provide the students with a list of situations that might occur in nursing practice and have them classify the problems under the type of law involved (for example, a nurse witnesses a health care provider strike a client).

---

# LEARNING OUTCOME 2

Describe ways nurse practice acts, standards of care, and agency policies and procedures affect the scope of nursing practice.

## CONCEPTS FOR LECTURE

1. Each state has a nurse practice act, which protects the public, by legally defining and describing the scope of nursing practice and legally controlling practice through licensing requirements. While similar, they do differ from state to state. Standards of care are the skills and learning commonly possessed by members of a profession. They are used to evaluate the quality of care nurses provide. Therefore, standards of care become legal guidelines for nursing practice. There are two categories of standards of care: internal and external. Internal standards include job descriptions, education, expertise, and institutional polices and procedures. External standards consist of nurse practice acts; standards developed by professional organizations, nursing specialty practice organizations, and federal organizations; and federal guidelines.

## POWERPOINT LECTURE SLIDES

*(NOTE: The number on each PPT Lecture Slide directly corresponds with the Concepts for Lecture.)*

1 Legal Aspects Related to Scope of Nursing Practice
- Nurse Practice Acts (NPA)
  ○ Define and describe scope of nursing practice
  ○ Control practice through licensing
- Standards of care
  ○ Internal
  ○ External

## SUGGESTIONS FOR CLASSROOM ACTIVITIES

- Obtain copies of the nurse practice act, standards for the American Nurses Association, and the standards of several specialty nursing organizations. Have the students identify how these affect the scope of practice and protect the public.
- Have the students review the licensing requirements for the state and relate these to public safety.

## SUGGESTIONS FOR CLINICAL ACTIVITIES

- Obtain the policy and procedures books for the institution. Have the students review several policies and procedures, relating these to the nurse practice act, standards, and client safety.

# LEARNING OUTCOME 3

Compare and contrast the state-based licensure model and the mutual recognition model for multistate licensure.

## CONCEPTS FOR LECTURE

1. A license is a legal permit that a government agency grants to engage in the practice of a profession and to use a particular title. A nursing license is mandatory in all states.

   Historically, licensure for nurses was state based. The state board of nursing licensed all nurses practicing in the state, and a nurse who wished to practice in multiple states was required to obtain a separate license in each state.

   Changes in health care delivery and telecommunications raised questions about state-based models. Telehealth, the delivery of health services over distances, made it possible for the nurse to electronically interact with a client in another state to provide health information or intervention. If the nurse was not licensed to practice in both states, the nurse would be practicing across state lines without a license.

## POWERPOINT LECTURE SLIDES

*(NOTE: The number on each PPT Lecture Slide directly corresponds with the Concepts for Lecture.)*

 1 Licensure Models
- State-Based
  ○ Separate license required for each state
  ○ Challenged by changes in health care delivery
- Mutual recognition
  ○ A new regulatory model developed by NCSBN
  ○ Allows for multistate licensure
  ○ State legislatures initiate and establish a compact (NLC)

In response, the National Council of State Boards of Nursing (NCSBN) developed a new regulatory model, the mutual state recognition model, which allows for multistate licensure (see Box 4–1).

The state legislatures initiate and decide on the establishment of an interstate compact called the Nurse Licensure Compact (NLC), an agreement between two or more states to create a mutual recognition model. Then, a nurse who is not under discipline can practice across state lines with one license. However, the nurse must still contact the other state's board of nursing and provide proof of licensure. The nurse is held accountable for knowing and practicing the nursing practice laws and regulations in the state where the client is located at the time of care.

Only states that have adopted the RN and LPN/LVN NLC may implement a compact for advanced practice registered nurses.

## SUGGESTIONS FOR CLASSROOM ACTIVITIES

- Have the students access the NCSBN website to determine whether the state participates in the mutual recognition model.
- Have the students review the state licensure requirements and compare them to another state.
- Give the students examples of telehealth situations, and have the students determine whether multiple licensure would be required for a nurse involved in these situations.

# LEARNING OUTCOME 4

Describe the purpose and essential elements of informed consent.

## CONCEPTS FOR LECTURE

1. Informed consent is an agreement by a client to accept a course of treatment or a procedure after being provided complete information, including the benefits and risks of treatment, alternatives to the treatment, and prognosis if not treated by a health care provider. Informed consent is based upon the principle of autonomy; each person has the right to decide what can or cannot be done to his or her person.

There are three major elements of informed consent: The consent must be given voluntarily, the consent must be given by a client or individual with the capacity and competence to understand, and the client or individual must be given enough information to be the ultimate decision maker.

For consent to be voluntarily given, the client must not feel coerced or give consent to avoid disapproval of the health care provider. Therefore, it is important for the person obtaining the consent to invite and answer client questions.

## POWERPOINT LECTURE SLIDES

*(NOTE: The number on each PPT Lecture Slide directly corresponds with the Concepts for Lecture.)*

 Informed Consent
- Purpose
  - Provides client with complete information prior to obtaining agreement by client to accept a course of treatment
  - Based upon principle of autonomy
- Essential elements
  - Consent must be voluntary
  - Consent must be given by client or individual with capacity to understand

In order to be certain that the client understands, it is important to consider the problem of illiteracy and other language barriers. The consent form must be read to the client or an interpreter must be used when appropriate.

The client also has the right of refusal even after a consent has been signed. It is important to verify that the pros and cons of refusal are understood by the client and that the client is making an informed decision.

## SUGGESTIONS FOR CLASSROOM ACTIVITIES

- Discuss the difference between obtaining informed consent and witnessing the client's signature on a consent form.
- Obtain informed consent forms from clinical agencies, and compare the information on the forms with the general guidelines given in the textbook for information to be included on a consent form.

## SUGGESTIONS FOR CLINICAL ACTIVITIES

- Review procedures for which written informed consent is necessary in the clinical agency.
- Review policies for obtaining informed consent forms in the institution.

# LEARNING OUTCOME 5

Describe the purpose of the following legislative acts: Good Samaritan Acts and Americans with Disabilities Act.

## CONCEPTS FOR LECTURE

1. The Americans with Disabilities Act (ADA) prohibits discrimination on the basis of disability in employment, public services, and public accommodation. It is about productivity, economic independence, and the ability to move about freely in society.

    The purposes of ADA are to provide a clear and comprehensive national mandate for eliminating discrimination against individuals with disabilities; to provide clear, strong, consistent, enforceable standards addressing the discrimination against individuals with disabilities; and to ensure that the federal government plays a central role in enforcing standards established under the act.

2. Good Samaritan acts are laws designed to protect health care providers who provide assistance at the scene of an emergency against claims of malpractice unless it can be shown that there was a gross departure from the normal standard of care or willful wrongdoing on their part.

## POWERPOINT LECTURE SLIDES

*(NOTE: The number on each PPT Lecture Slide directly corresponds with the Concepts for Lecture.)*

1 The Americans with Disabilities Act (ADA)
- Prohibits discrimination on the basis of disability
- Purpose
  - Provide national mandate
  - Provide enforceable standards
  - Ensure government role in enforcing

2 Good Samaritan Acts
- Protect health care providers providing assistance at an emergency scene against claims of malpractice

## SUGGESTIONS FOR CLASSROOM ACTIVITIES

- Have the students compare the state's Good Samaritan act with the general description supplied in the textbook. Most Good Samaritan acts can be located online.
- Develop questions regarding the ADA, and assign students to go to the ADA website Q & A section to obtain answers and report findings to the class.

## SUGGESTIONS FOR CLINICAL ACTIVITIES

- Invite a hospital representative to discuss accommodations made for clients with disabilities to comply with ADA requirements, for example, clients who have hearing and vision disabilities.

# LEARNING OUTCOME 6

Discuss the impaired nurse and available diversion or peer assistance programs.

## CONCEPTS FOR LECTURE

1. The impaired nurse refers to a nurse whose ability to perform the functions of a nurse is diminished by chemical dependency on drugs, alcoholism, or mental illness.
2. Professional nursing organizations such as the American Nurses Association (ANA), the American Association of Nurse Anesthetists (AANA), the International Nurses Society on Addictions (IntNSA), and the National Student Nurses' Association (NSNA) have passed resolutions to ensure that student nurses and nurses with chemical dependencies receive treatment and support, not discipline and derision.

    Employers must have policies and procedures for identifying and intervening in situations involving a possibly impaired nurse in order to protect the clients and to recognize the problem early so that appropriate treatment may be instituted.

    In many states, impaired nurses who voluntarily enter a diversion program (sometimes called a peer assistance program) do not have their nursing license revoked if they follow treatment requirements. However, their practice is closely supervised within specific guidelines.

    These programs require counseling and participation in support groups with periodic progress reports, and the nurse may petition for reinstatement of a full license after a specified period of time and evidence of recovery as determined by the state board.

    The ADA protects a nurse who is either in a treatment program or who has completed a program.

## POWERPOINT LECTURE SLIDES

*(NOTE: The number on each PPT Lecture Slide directly corresponds with the Concepts for Lecture.)*

1. The Impaired Nurse
   - Functions diminished due to:
     ○ Chemical dependency on drugs
     ○ Alcoholism
     ○ Mental illness

2. Diversion or Peer Assistance Programs
   - State boards of nursing
   - Institutional policies
   - Diversion programs require
     ○ Counseling
     ○ Participation in support groups
     ○ Periodic progress reports

## SUGGESTIONS FOR CLASSROOM ACTIVITIES

- Discuss the impaired nurse program for the state.
- Have the students discuss what they would do if they recognized that a peer had come to the clinical setting while intoxicated.

## SUGGESTIONS FOR CLINICAL ACTIVITIES

- Review the institution's policy and procedures for the impaired health professional.

# LEARNING OUTCOME 7

Recognize the nurse's legal responsibilities with selected aspects of nursing practice.

## CONCEPTS FOR LECTURE

1. Nurses need to know the legal aspects related to their many different roles. These include legal aspects related to informed consent, delegation, violence, abuse and neglect, the ADA (see Outcome 5), controlled substances, the impaired nurse (see Outcome 6), sexual harassment, abortions, death and related issues (advanced health care directives, autopsy, certification of death, do-not-resuscitate orders, euthanasia, inquests, and organ donations).

## POWERPOINT LECTURE SLIDES

*(NOTE: The number on each PPT Lecture Slide directly corresponds with the Concepts for Lecture.)*

1. Selected Nursing Legal Responsibilities
   - Informed consent
   - Delegation
   - Violence, abuse, and neglect
   - ADA
   - Controlled substances
   - Impaired nurse

- Sexual harassment
- Abortions
- Death and related issues

The nurse's role in informed consent is not to explain the procedure but to witness the client's signature on the form. The nurse's signature confirms three things: the consent was voluntarily given, the signature is authentic, and the client appears competent to give consent.

From a legal perspective, the nurse's authority to delegate is based on laws and regulations. Therefore, the nurse must be familiar with the state's nurse practice act (NPA). The nurse needs to know whether the NPA permits delegation, whether the NPA provides a list of what can be delegated, and whether the NPA has issued any guidelines explaining nurses' responsibility when delegating.

Because of the many roles and settings in which nurses practice, nurses are often in positions to identify and assess cases of violence, abuse, or neglect. As a result, nurses are often included as mandatory reporters and must report situations to the proper authorities.

Nurses must be familiar with the sexual harassment policy and procedures in the institutions in which they work. The policy and procedures will include information regarding the reporting procedure, to whom incidents should be reported, the investigative process, and how confidentiality will be protected.

Abortion laws provide specific guidelines about what is legally permissible; however, the Supreme Court and state legislatures continue to struggle with this issue. Many statutes include conscience clauses that give hospitals the right to deny admission to abortion clients and give health care personnel the right to refuse to participate in abortions.

The Patient Self-Determination Act (1991) requires all health care facilities receiving Medicare and Medicaid reimbursement to recognize advance directives, ask clients whether they have advance directives, and provide educational materials advising clients of their rights to declare their personal wishes regarding treatment decisions. Nurses should learn the law regarding patient self-determination for the state in which they practice as well as the policies and procedures for implementation in the institutions in which they work.

The law describes under what circumstances an autopsy or postmortem examination, the examination of the body after death, must be performed. It is the responsibility of the physician or, in some instances, of a designated person to obtain consent for an autopsy.

The formal determination of death, or pronouncement, must be performed by a physician, a coroner, or a nurse. The granting of authority to nurses to pronounce death is regulated by the state or province; however, by law a death certificate must be completed when a person dies.

The ANA (2003) makes the following recommendations related to DNR orders: the competent client's wishes should take priority; when the client is incompetent, advance health directives or the proxy decision maker should make the health care decisions; the DNR decision should always be the subject of explicit discussion; the DNR order should be clearly documented, reviewed, and updated periodically; and a DNR order is separate from other aspects of the client's care and does not imply that other types of care should be withdrawn. Nurses should be familiar with the federal and state or provincial laws and the policies of the agency concerning withholding life-sustaining measures.

Euthanasia is the act of painlessly putting to death persons with incurable or distressing disease. Euthanasia is illegal in both Canada and the United States, leading to criminal charges of homicide or to a civil lawsuit for withholding treatment or providing an unacceptable standard of care. Voluntary euthanasia refers to situations in which the dying individual desires some control over the time and manner of death. In some states where right-to-die statutes exist, physicians are permitted to prescribe lethal doses of medication.

An inquest is a legal inquiry into the cause or manner of death. It is conducted under the jurisdiction of a coroner or medical examiner. Agency policy dictates who is responsible for reporting deaths to the coroner or medical examiner.

Under the Uniform Anatomical Gift Act and the National Organ Transplant Act in the United States and the Human Tissue Act in Canada, people 18 years or older and of sound mind may donate all or any part of their own bodies for medical or dental education, research, advancement of medical or dental science, therapy, or transplantation. Nurses may serve as witnesses for people consenting to donate organs. If there is no valid donor card, health care workers are required to discuss with survivors of a potential organ donor the option to make an anatomical gift.

## SUGGESTIONS FOR CLASSROOM ACTIVITIES

- Ask the students to bring in magazine and newspaper articles about health-related legal issues. Use these as a basis for discussion.
- Distribute procedures that a nurse might consider delegating to an unlicensed assistive person. Have the students discuss in small groups whether the procedure fits the criteria for delegation.
- Review the state's requirements for reporting child and adult abuse.
- Review the school's policy and procedures related to sexual harassment.
- Review the state's advance health care directive and health care proxy requirements. Ask the students to investigate the requirements for emergency personnel who come to the client's home to comply with advance health care directives.
- Have the students investigate who has the authority to declare a person deceased in the state.
- Review the ANA's Code of Ethics for Nurses to determine what the code states about the nurse who has moral concerns about an aspect of medical care such as abortion.

# LEARNING OUTCOME 8

Differentiate crimes from torts and give examples in nursing.

## CONCEPTS FOR LECTURE

1. A crime is an act committed in violation of public (criminal) law and punishable by a fine or imprisonment. It does not have to be intended in order to be a crime (for example, a nurse may accidentally administer an additional and lethal dose of a narcotic to relieve discomfort).

   Crimes can be classified as either a felony or a misdemeanor. A felony is a crime of a serious nature, such as murder, punishable by a term in prison. A misdemeanor is an offense of a less serious nature and is usually punishable by a fine, a short-term jail sentence, or both.

   A nurse who administers an additional and lethal dose of a narcotic may be charged with second-degree murder or manslaughter (a felony). A nurse who slaps a client's face could be charged with a misdemeanor.

2. A tort is a civil wrong committed against a person or a person's property. Tort liability almost always is based on fault, which is something done incorrectly (an unreasonable act of commission) or something that should have been done but was not (act of omission). (See Outcomes # 9, 10, and 11.)

## POWERPOINT LECTURE SLIDES

*(NOTE: The number on each PPT Lecture Slide directly corresponds with the Concepts for Lecture.)*

**1** Crimes
  • Felony
    ○ Serious nature, e.g., murder
    ○ Punishable by term in prison
  • Misdemeanor
    ○ Less serious
    ○ Punishable by fine or short-term sentence

**2** Torts
  • Civil wrong against a person or property
  • Based on fault
    ○ Something done incorrectly
    ○ Something omitted

---

SUGGESTIONS FOR CLASSROOM ACTIVITIES

• Invite a guest speaker who is both a nurse and an attorney, or an attorney familiar with health-related legal issues, to discuss legal aspects related to nursing.

---

# LEARNING OUTCOME 9

Discriminate between negligence and malpractice.

## CONCEPTS FOR LECTURE

1. Negligence and malpractice are examples of unintentional torts.

   Negligence is misconduct or practice that is below the standard expected of an ordinary, reasonable, and prudent person. Such conduct places another person at risk for harm.

## POWERPOINT LECTURE SLIDES

*(NOTE: The number on each PPT Lecture Slide directly corresponds with the Concepts for Lecture.)*

**1** Negligence
  • Misconduct or practice below expected standard
  • Places another person at risk for harm

Gross negligence involves extreme lack of knowledge, skill, or decision making that the person clearly should have known would put another person at risk for harm.

2. Malpractice is negligence that occurred while the person was performing as a professional. It applies to physicians, dentists, and lawyers, and generally includes nurses (Box 4–4).

- Applies to anyone

 Malpractice
- Negligence that occured while the person was performing as a professional
  - Applies to physicians, dentists, lawyers, and generally includes nurses

### SUGGESTIONS FOR CLASSROOM ACTIVITIES

- Invite a guest speaker who is both a nurse and an attorney, or an attorney familiar with health-related legal issues, to discuss legal aspects related to nursing. Provide students with several case studies illustrating negligence or malpractice and have students identify these.

## LEARNING OUTCOME 10

Delineate the elements of malpractice.

### CONCEPTS FOR LECTURE

1. Six elements must be present for a case of nursing malpractice to be proven: duty, breach of duty, foreseeability, causation, harm or injury, and damages.

    Duty means the nurse must have (or should have had) a relationship with the client that involves providing care and following an acceptable standard of care and also has a general duty of care, even if not specifically assigned to a client, and the client needs help.

    Breach of duty means that there is a standard of care that is expected in the specific situation but that the nurse did not observe. Standards can come from documents published by national or professional organizations, boards of nursing, institutional policies and procedures, or textbooks or journals, or they may be stated by expert witnesses.

    Foreseeability means that a link must exist between the nurse's act and the injury.

    Causation means that it must be proved that the harm occurred as a direct result of the nurse's failure to follow the standard of care and the nurse could have (or should have) known that failure to follow the standard could result in such harm.

    The client or plaintiff must demonstrate some type of harm or injury (physical, financial, or emotional) as a result of the breach of duty owed the client.

    If malpractice caused the injury, the nurse is held liable for damages that may be compensated. The goal of awarding damages is to assist the injured party to his or her original position so far as financially possible (Guido, 2006).

### POWERPOINT LECTURE SLIDES

*(NOTE: The number on each PPT Lecture Slide directly corresponds with the Concepts for Lecture.)*

 Elements of Malpractice
- Duty
- Breach of duty
- Forseeability
- Causation
- Harm or injury
- Damages

### SUGGESTIONS FOR CLASSROOM ACTIVITIES

- Invite a guest speaker who is both a nurse and an attorney, or an attorney familiar with malpractice, to discuss legal ramifications for nurses.

# LEARNING OUTCOME 11

Compare and contrast intentional torts (assault/battery, false imprisonment, invasion of privacy, defamation) and unintentional torts (negligence, malpractice).

## CONCEPTS FOR LECTURE

1. Unintentional torts (negligence and malpractice) do not require intent but do require the element of harm.
2. With intentional torts the defendant executed the act on purpose or with intent. No harm need be caused by intentional torts for liability to exist. Also, since no standard is involved, no expert witnesses are needed.

   Four intentional torts relate to nursing: assault/battery, false imprisonment, invasion of privacy, and defamation (libel/slander).

   Assault is an attempt or threat to touch another person unjustifiably. It is the act that causes the person to believe a battery is about to occur (for example, verbally threatening a client).

   Battery is the willful touching of a person (or the person's clothes or even something the person is carrying) that may or may not cause harm. To be actionable at law, the touching must be wrong in some way (for example, performing a procedure without consent).

   False imprisonment is the unjustifiable detention of a person without legal warrant to confine the person. If it is accompanied by forceful restraint or threat of restraint, it is battery (for example, the application of restraints in violation of institutional policy).

   Invasion of privacy is a direct wrong of a personal nature. Individuals have the right to withhold themselves and their lives from public scrutiny. An example of invasion of privacy would be sharing client information with those not directly involved in the client's care. There are four types of invasion: use of a client's name or likeness for profit without consent, unreasonable intrusion, public disclosure of private facts, and putting a person in a false light.

   Defamation is communication that is false, or made with a careless disregard for the truth, and results in injury to the reputation of a person.

   Two types of defamation include libel and slander. Libel is defamation by means of print, writing, or pictures. Slander is defamation by the spoken word, stating unprivileged (not legally protected) or false words by which a reputation is damaged. Examples of defamation include writing negative comments about another health care professional in nursing notes and verbally telling a client that another health care professional is incompetent.

## POWERPOINT LECTURE SLIDES

*(NOTE: The number on each PPT Lecture Slide directly corresponds with the Concepts for Lecture.)*

1. Unintentional Torts
   - Negligence
   - Malpractice

2. Intentional Torts
   - Assault and battery
     - Assault is attempt or threat to touch unjustifiably
     - Battery is willful touching that may or may not cause harm
   - False imprisonment
     - Unjustifiable detention without legal warrant
   - Invasion of privacy
     - Direct wrong of a personal nature
   - Defamation (slander and libel)
     - Communications that are false
     - Slander-defamation by the spoken word
     - Libel-defamation by means of print, writing, or pictures

## SUGGESTIONS FOR CLASSROOM ACTIVITIES

- Discuss informed consent and its relationship to battery.
- Give the students a list of situations and ask them to determine whether the incidents are acceptable or represent examples of unintentional or intentional torts.
- Review the type of client information that is reportable in the state.

## SUGGESTIONS FOR CLINICAL ACTIVITIES

- Review the institution's policies and procedures regarding the use of restraints and discharge against medical advice.

# LEARNING OUTCOME 12

Describe the four specific areas of the Health Insurance Portability and Accountability Act (HIPAA) and their impact on nursing practice.

## CONCEPTS FOR LECTURE

1. HIPAA includes four specific areas: electronic transfer of information among organizations; standardized numbers for identifying providers, employers, and health plans; a security rule that provides for a uniform level of protection of all health information; and a privacy rule that sets standards defining appropriate disclosure of protected health information and gives clients new rights to understand and control how their health information is used.

2. Examples of how HIPAA compliance affects nursing practice include the following: a client's name cannot be posted near or on a room door; charts must be kept in a secure, nonpublic location; printed copies of protected health information should not be left unattended in a printer or fax machine; access to protected health information is limited to those authorized to obtain the information; a password is needed to access a client's electronic information; a notice informing clients of their rights about privacy and their health information should be posted or provided; voice levels should be lowered to minimize disclosure of information; and health care providers need to stay current with HIPAA regulations (see Box 4–5).

## POWERPOINT LECTURE SLIDES

*(NOTE: The number on each PPT Lecture Slide directly corresponds with the Concepts for Lecture.)*

**1** Four Specific Areas of HIPAA
- Electronic transfer of information among organizations
- Standardized numbers for identifying providers, employers, and health plans
- Security rule
- Privacy rule

**2** Impact of HIPAA
- Client's name cannot be posted near or on a room door
- Charts must be kept in a secure, nonpublic location
- Printed copies of protected health information should not be left unattended in a printer or fax machine
- Access to protected health information is limited to those authorized to obtain the information
- Password is needed to access a client's electronic information
- A notice informing clients of their rights about privacy and their health information should be posted or provided
- Voice levels should be lowered to minimize disclosure of information
- Need to stay current with HIPAA regulations

## SUGGESTIONS FOR CLASSROOM ACTIVITIES

- Review how HIPAA regulations impact nursing education.

## SUGGESTIONS FOR CLINICAL ACTIVITIES

- Review the information the institution distributes to clients regarding HIPAA regulations.
- Review the institution's regulations for students regarding HIPAA.
- Invite a nurse in-service educator to discuss actions the institution has taken to comply with HIPAA regulations.

# LEARNING OUTCOME 13

Describe the purpose of professional liability insurance.

## CONCEPTS FOR LECTURE

1. Because of the increase in numbers of malpractice lawsuits against health professionals, nurses are advised to carry their own liability insurance.

   Liability insurance coverage usually defrays all costs of defending a nurse, including the cost of retaining an attorney. It also covers all costs incurred by the nurse up

## POWERPOINT LECTURE SLIDES

*(NOTE: The number on each PPT Lecture Slide directly corresponds with the Concepts for Lecture.)*

**1** Professional Liability Insurance
- Necessary due to increasing numbers of malpractice lawsuits

**CONCEPTS FOR LECTURE** *continued*

to the face value of the policy, including a settlement made out of court. In return, the insurance company may have the right to make the decision about the claim and settlement.

**POWERPOINT LECTURE SLIDES** *continued*

- Nurses advised to carry own insurance
- Insurance covers costs up to face value of policy

---

### SUGGESTIONS FOR CLASSROOM ACTIVITIES

- Have the students review several applications for professional liability insurance, focusing on coverage and cost.
- Have the students debate the necessity of obtaining professional liability coverage.
- Review the school's liability coverage for students.

### SUGGESTIONS FOR CLINICAL ACTIVITIES

- Ask a representative of the human resources department to discuss the institution's liability coverage for employees.
- Have the students interview staff nurses to determine whether the nurses carry their own liability insurance and what influenced their decisions.

---

# LEARNING OUTCOME 14

List information that needs to be included in an incident report.

### CONCEPTS FOR LECTURE

1. The following information is included on an incident report: identification of the client by name, initials, and hospital or identification number; date, time, and place of the incident; description of the facts of the incident (no conclusions or blame); incorporation of the client's account of the incident in quotes; identification of all witnesses; and identification of any equipment by number and any medication by name and dosage.

### POWERPOINT LECTURE SLIDES

*(NOTE: The number on each PPT Lecture Slide directly corresponds with the Concepts for Lecture.)*

 Information Included on an Incident Report:
- Identification of the client by name, initials, and hospital or identification number
- Date, time, and place of the incident
- Description of the facts of the incident (no conclusions or blame)
- Incorporation of the client's account of the incident in quotes
- Identification of all witnesses
- Identification of any equipment by number and any medication by name and dosage

---

### SUGGESTIONS FOR CLASSROOM ACTIVITIES

- Obtain several incident report forms and have the students compare information included with the guidelines presented in class.

### SUGGESTIONS FOR CLINICAL ACTIVITIES

- Review the institution's policy and procedure for completing an incident report.

---

# LEARNING OUTCOME 15

Identify ways nurses and nursing students can minimize their chances of liability.

### CONCEPTS FOR LECTURE

1. Nurses and nursing students can minimize their chances of liability by following these recommendations (see Practice Guidelines: Legal Protection for Nurses in the text): function within the scope of education, job description, and nurse practice act; follow procedures and policies of the employing agency;

### POWERPOINT LECTURE SLIDES

*(NOTE: The number on each PPT Lecture Slide directly corresponds with the Concepts for Lecture.)*

 Minimizing Chance of Liability
- Function within the scope of education, job description, and nurse practice act
- Follow procedures and policies

## CONCEPTS FOR LECTURE *continued*

build and maintain good rapport with clients; always check the identity of the client to make sure it is the right client; observe and monitor the client, accurately communicating and recording significant changes in the client's condition; promptly and accurately document all assessments and care given; be alert when implementing nursing interventions, giving each task full attention and skill; perform procedures correctly and appropriately; make sure the correct medications are given in the correct dose, by the right route, at the scheduled time, and to the right client; when delegating nursing responsibilities, make sure the person who is delegated a task understands what to do and that the person has the required knowledge and skill; protect clients from injury; report all incidents involving clients; always check any order that a client questions; know own strengths and weaknesses and ask for assistance and supervision in situations for which the nurse feels inadequately prepared; and maintain clinical competence.

## POWERPOINT LECTURE SLIDES *continued*

- Build and maintain good rapport
- Always check identity
- Observe and monitor
- Accurately communicate and record significant changes
- Promptly and accurately document all assessments and care
- Be alert when implementing nursing interventions
- Perform procedures correctly and appropriately
- Administer the right medication, in the right dose, via the right route, at the right time, to the right client
- Delegate appropriately
- Protect clients from injury
- Report all incidents
- Always check any order that is questioned
- Know own strengths and weaknesses
- Maintain clinical competence

## SUGGESTIONS FOR CLASSROOM ACTIVITIES

- Have the students select five of the recommendations for minimizing liability and write a short paper on how they will operationalize these recommendations.

## SUGGESTIONS FOR CLINICAL ACTIVITIES

- Ask the students to identify ways in which nurses follow the recommendations for minimizing liability in the clinical facility.

# CHAPTER 5
## VALUES, ETHICS, AND ADVOCACY

### RESOURCE LIBRARY

 **PRENTICE HALL NURSING MEDIALINK DVD-ROM**

Audio Glossary
NCLEX® Review
End of Unit Concept Map Activity

 **COMPANION WEBSITE**

Additional NCLEX® Review
Case Study: Ethics Committee
Application Activities:
  *AIDS Resources*
  *Privacy*
Links to Resources

 **IMAGE LIBRARY**

**Figure 5.1** An ethics committee contemplates all aspects of the case being considered.

**Figure 5.2** When there is a need for ethical decisions or client advocacy, many different persons contribute to the final outcome.

---

### LEARNING OUTCOME 1

Explain how cognitive development, values, moral frameworks, and codes of ethics affect moral decisions.

#### CONCEPTS FOR LECTURE

1. Ethical and moral decisions require persons to think and reason. Reasoning is a cognitive function; therefore, it develops over the life span.
2. Values are enduring beliefs or attitudes about the worth of a person, object, idea, or action that may be unspoken or even unconscious. Values underlie all moral dilemmas and influence decisions and actions, including nurses' ethical decision making.
3. Moral development is the process of learning to tell the difference between right and wrong and of learning what ought and ought not to be done. This process begins in childhood and continues throughout life. Moral development theories address this development.

   Moral theories provide different frameworks through which nurses can view and clarify moral and ethical dilemmas. Nurses can use moral theories in developing explanations for their ethical decisions and actions.
4. A code of ethics is a formal statement of a group's ideals and values. It serves as a standard for professional actions. One of the purposes of nursing codes of ethics is to provide ethical standards for professional behavior.

#### POWERPOINT LECTURE SLIDES

*(NOTE: The number on each PPT Lecture Slide directly corresponds with the Concepts for Lecture.)*

**1** Cognitive Development
  • Moral decisions require persons to think and reason
  • Reasoning is a cognitive function
  • Ability to make decisions develops over the life span

**2** Values
  • Enduring beliefs or attitudes about the worth of a person, object, idea, or action
  • May be unspoken or even unconscious
  • Underlie all moral dilemmas
  • Influence decisions and actions including nurses' ethical decision making

**3** Moral Development
  • Process of learning difference between right and wrong
  • Begins in childhood and continues throughout life
  • Moral development theories provide frameworks to view and clarify moral and ethical dilemmas

**4** A Code of Ethics
  • Formal statement of a group's ideals and values
  • Serves as a standard for professional actions
  • Provides ethical standards for professional behavior

## SUGGESTIONS FOR CLASSROOM ACTIVITIES

- Ask the students to complete the Questionnaire for Values Clarification in Table 5–2 and identify their top five essential values. Have the students write a short paper on how these values would affect moral decision making.
- Divide the students into three groups. Provide the students with an ethical dilemma. Ask one group to respond to the situation using the teleological model, another using the deontological model, and the third using the caring model. Report results to the class.

## SUGGESTIONS FOR CLINICAL ACTIVITIES

- Have the students discuss how beliefs and attitudes about client characteristics—age, gender, socioeconomic status, citizenship, previous and expected future contributions to society, health behaviors, and compliance—affect providers' actions.

---

## LEARNING OUTCOME 2

Explain how nurses use knowledge of values to make ethical decisions and facilitate ethical decision making by clients.

### CONCEPTS FOR LECTURE

1. Nurses need to identify clients' values as they influence and relate to a particular health problem.

   When clients hold unclear or conflicting values that are detrimental to their health, the nurse should use values clarification as an intervention.

   Values clarification assists individuals to identify values, permitting them to change values and act based on freely chosen values. This is an important step in understanding ethical problems and making ethical decisions.

   The following steps can help clarify values: list alternatives, examine possible consequences of choices, choose freely, feel good about the choice, affirm the choice, act on the choice, and act with a pattern.

   When implementing these seven steps to clarify values, the nurse does not impose personal values since what the nurse would choose in his or her own life may not be relevant to the client's circumstances.

### POWERPOINT LECTURE SLIDES

*(NOTE: The number on each PPT Lecture Slide directly corresponds with the Concepts for Lecture.)*

[1] To Help Clarify Values
- List alternatives
- Examine possible consequences of choices
- Choose freely
- Feel good about the choice
- Affirm the choice
- Act on the choice
- Act with a pattern

---

## SUGGESTIONS FOR CLASSROOM ACTIVITIES

- Develop several moral or ethical dilemmas related to clients. Have the students use the steps in values clarification to assist the clients to make an ethical decision.

## SUGGESTIONS FOR CLINICAL ACTIVITIES

- Have the students describe situations where the clients' unclear or conflicting values were detrimental to their health.

---

## LEARNING OUTCOME 3

When presented with an ethical situation, identify the moral issues and principles involved.

### CONCEPTS FOR LECTURE

1. Moral issues are those that arouse conscience, are concerned with important values and norms, and evoke words such as *good, bad, wrong, should,* and *ought.*
2. Moral principles are statements about broad, general, philosophic concepts that provide the foundation for moral rules, which are specific prescriptions for actions.

### POWERPOINT LECTURE SLIDES

*(NOTE: The number on each PPT Lecture Slide directly corresponds with the Concepts for Lecture.)*

[1] Moral Issues
- Arouse conscience
- Concerned with important values and norms
- Evoke words such as *good, bad, wrong, should,* and *ought*

---

Principles are useful in ethical discussions. Even if a disagreement is about which action is right in a situation, individuals may be able to agree on the principles that apply and this agreement may serve as a basis for the solution to the problem.

3. The six major moral principles are autonomy, nonmaleficence, beneficence, justice, fidelity, and veracity. Autonomy refers to the right to make one's own decisions. Inward autonomy exists if individuals have the ability to make choices, and outward autonomy exists if their choices are not limited or imposed by others. Nonmaleficence is the duty to do no harm; harm may be intentional or nonintentional. Beneficence means doing good. Justice is often referred to as fairness. Fidelity means to be faithful to agreements and promises, and veracity refers to telling the truth.

 Moral Principles
- Statements about broad, general, philosophic concepts
- Provide the foundation for moral rules which are specific prescriptions for actions
- Useful in ethical discussions
- May be able to agree on principles that apply
- May serve as a basis for the solution to the problem

 Six Major Moral Principles
- Autonomy
- Nonmaleficence
- Beneficence
- Justice
- Fidelity
- Veracity

---

### SUGGESTIONS FOR CLASSROOM ACTIVITIES

- Have the students bring a newspaper or magazine article about ethical and moral dilemmas to class. Divide the students into groups and ask each group to determine which moral principle would best apply as a basis for a solution.

### SUGGESTIONS FOR CLINICAL ACTIVITIES

- Assign several students to interview an RN about ethical and moral dilemmas encountered in clinical practice. Discuss these dilemmas in a clinical conference.

---

## LEARNING OUTCOME 4

Explain the uses and limitations of professional codes of ethics.

### CONCEPTS FOR LECTURE

1. A code of ethics is a formal statement of a group's ideals and values. It is a set of ethical principles that is shared by members of the group, reflects their moral judgments over time, and serves as a standard for their professional actions.

    Nursing codes of ethics have the following purposes: to inform the public about the minimum standards of the profession and to help them understand professional nursing conduct; to provide a sign of the profession's commitment to the public it serves; to outline the major ethical considerations of the profession; to provide ethical standards for professional behavior; to guide the profession in self-regulation; and to remind nurses of the special responsibility they assume when caring for the sick.

    Since recent ethical problems have occurred largely because of social and technological changes and nurses' conflicting loyalties and obligations, codes of ethics must include standards that reflect moral judgments over time.

### POWERPOINT LECTURE SLIDES

*(NOTE: The number on each PPT Lecture Slide directly corresponds with the Concepts for Lecture.)*

 Professional Codes of Ethics
- Purposes
    - To inform the public about the minimum standards of the profession
    - Help them understand professional nursing conduct
    - Provide a sign of the profession's commitment to the public
    - Outline major ethical considerations of the profession
    - Provide ethical standards for professional behavior
    - Guide the profession in self-regulation
    - Remind nurses of the special responsibility assumed when caring for the sick

## LEARNING OUTCOME 5

Discuss common ethical issues currently facing health care professionals.

### CONCEPTS FOR LECTURE

1. Common ethical problems nurses encounter are issues in the care of HIV/AIDS clients, abortions, organ transplantation, end-of-life decisions, cost-containment issues (resource allocation), and management of personal health information.

   The ANA (1994) states that the moral obligation to care for an HIV-infected client cannot be set aside unless the risk exceeds the responsibility. Other ethical issues center on HIV testing of all providers and patients, and releasing test results to insurance companies, sexual partners, or caregivers.

   The debate over abortion pits the principle of sanctity of life against the principle of autonomy and the woman's right to control her own body. Conscience clauses in some state laws permit individuals and agencies to refuse to assist with abortions; however, nurses have no right to impose their values on others although nursing codes of ethics support clients' rights to information and counseling in making decisions.

   Ethical issues related to organ transplantation include allocation of organs, selling of body parts, involvement of children as potential donors, consent, clear definition of death, conflicts of interest between potential donors and recipients, and conflict with some religious beliefs.

   Many moral problems surrounding end-of-life decisions can be resolved if clients complete advance directives. Advance directives guide caregivers as to the client's wishes about treatment and provide a voice for clients when they have lost the capacity to make or communicate decisions.

   Active euthanasia is forbidden by law, but assisted suicide is legal in some states. However, the ANA (1995) states that active and assisted suicide are in violation of the *Code for Nurses*. Passive euthanasia, commonly referred to as withdrawing or withholding life-sustaining therapy (WWLST), involves the withdrawal of extraordinary means of life support. WWLST is legally and ethically more acceptable to many people.

   Some treatments help to prolong life but do not necessarily restore health. Individuals often have misunderstandings about which treatments are life sustaining.

### POWERPOINT LECTURE SLIDES

*(NOTE: The number on each PPT Lecture Slide directly corresponds with the Concepts for Lecture.)*

 1 Common Ethical Issues
- Issues in the care of HIV/AIDS clients
- Abortions
- Organ transplantation
- End-of-life decisions
- Cost-containment issues (resource allocation)
- Management of personal health information

They need help to fully understand treatments and need to know that decisions can be changed, if desired. A nurse is morally obligated to withhold food and fluids if administering is more harmful than withholding and must honor the wishes of a competent and informed client's refusal of food and fluids. The ANA Code of Ethics for Nurses (2001) supports this position through the nurse's role as advocate and the moral principle of autonomy.

Allocation of scarce health resources is an urgent issue as medical costs continue to rise and more stringent cost-containment measures are implemented. The moral principle of autonomy cannot be applied if it is not possible to give each client what he or she chooses. Therefore, the principle of justice, attempting to choose what is most fair to all, may be applied by health care providers.

Nursing care is also a health resource. Some nurses are concerned that staff is not adequate to give the level of care they value. Some states have enacted a nurse-to-client ratio. With a shortage of nursing, an ethical dilemma arises when, in order to provide adequate staffing, facilities may turn away needy clients.

Privacy is both a legal and ethical mandate. Clients must be able to trust that nurses will reveal details of their situation only as appropriate and will communicate only the information necessary to provide health care.

## SUGGESTIONS FOR CLASSROOM ACTIVITIES

- Have the students bring newspaper or magazine articles about controversial bioethical and moral dilemmas to class for discussion.
- Have each student select an ethical problem and write a paper about the controversy and issues surrounding the problem.

## SUGGESTIONS FOR CLINICAL ACTIVITIES

- Discuss a clinical situation in which one of the ethical issues was related to end-of-life decisions. Discuss how the issue was resolved.
- Ask a member of the institution's ethics committee, preferably a nurse representative, to discuss the types of issues brought to the committee and the process used by the committee to assist with these issues.

# LEARNING OUTCOME 6

Describe ways in which nurses can enhance their ethical decision making and practice.

## CONCEPTS FOR LECTURE

1. Several strategies help nurses enhance their ethical decision making and practice. These strategies include becoming aware of personal values and ethical aspects of nursing; becoming familiar with nursing codes of ethics; seeking continuing education to remain knowledgeable about ethical issues in nursing; respecting the values, opinions, and responsibilities of other health care professionals; participating in or establishing ethics rounds; serving on institutional ethics committees; and striving for collaborative practice.

## POWERPOINT LECTURE SLIDES

*(NOTE: The number on each PPT Lecture Slide directly corresponds with the Concepts for Lecture.)*

1 Strategies to Enhance Ethical Decision Making
- Becoming aware of personal values and ethical aspects of nursing
- Becoming familiar with nursing code of ethics
- Seeking continuing education to remain knowledgeable about ethical issues in nursing
- Respecting the values, opinions, and responsibilities of other health care professionals
- Participating in or establishing ethic rounds
- Serving on institutional ethics committees
- Striving for collaborative practice

## SUGGESTIONS FOR CLASSROOM ACTIVITIES

- Discuss the structure and function of institutional ethics committees.
- Discuss how striving for collaborative practice can assist the nurse to enhance ethical decision making.

## SUGGESTIONS FOR CLINICAL ACTIVITIES

- Review the structure and function of the institution's ethics committee.
- Ask the students to review the Internet for continuing education announcements about ethical issues and bring these to class.

# LEARNING OUTCOME 7

Discuss the advocacy role of the nurse.

## CONCEPTS FOR LECTURE

1. An advocate is one who expresses and defends the cause of another. Nurses function as client advocates as well as advocates for the profession and the public.

2. The overall goal of the client advocate is to protect clients' rights by informing clients about their rights, providing them with information to make informed decisions, supporting clients in their decisions, and mediating directly on the client's behalf.

   When people are ill and enter the complex health care system, they may be unable to assert their rights and may need an advocate to help them assert these rights.

3. Values basic to client advocacy include the belief that the client is a holistic, autonomous being who has the right to make choices and decisions; the client has the right to expect a nurse–client relationship based on shared respect, trust, and collaboration in solving problems; and that it is the nurse's responsibility to ensure that the client has access to health care services. (See Box 5-8.)

4. In other societies, health care decisions may be made by the head of the family or another member of the community. Therefore, the nurse must be aware of the client's and family's views and traditions.

   Advocacy requires accepting and supporting the client's right to decide even if the nurse believes the decision to be wrong.

5. To act as professional and public advocates, nurses need an understanding of ethical issues in nursing and health care as well as knowledge of the laws and regulations that affect nursing and the health of society.

## POWERPOINT LECTURE SLIDES

*(NOTE: The number on each PPT Lecture Slide directly corresponds with the Concepts for Lecture.)*

**1** Advocacy Role
- Express and defend the cause of another

**2** Overall Goal of Advocacy
- Overall goal is to protect clients' right
  - Inform clients of rights
  - Provide clients with information to make informed decisions
  - Support clients in their decisions
  - Mediate directly on the clients' behalf

**3** Values Basic to Client Advocacy
- Client is holistic, autonomous with right to make choices and decisions
- Client has right to expect nurse-client relationship with shared respect, trust, and collaboration
- It is the nurse's responsibility to ensure client has access to health care services

**4** Cultural Differences
- Nurse must be aware of client and family views and traditions

**5** Professional and Public Advocacy
- Understanding of ethical issues in nursing
- Knowledge of laws and regulations affecting nursing and health care

## SUGGESTIONS FOR CLASSROOM ACTIVITIES

- Invite a nurse active in the political arena to discuss the role of professional and public advocate.
- Present the students with a situation in which it appears as if the client had made an unwise decision and ask students to discuss how the nurse should respond to this situation.

## SUGGESTIONS FOR CLINICAL ACTIVITIES

- Have the students describe a situation they have observed in which they thought the nurse acted as a client advocate. Discuss the effects of this nurse's action on the client.
- Have the students describe a situation in which they thought the nurse could or should have acted as the client advocate. What were the effects of the nurse's action on the client? Did the student take any action at this time? What might the student have done?

# CHAPTER 6
## HEALTH CARE DELIVERY SYSTEMS

## RESOURCE LIBRARY

 **PRENTICE HALL NURSING MEDIALINK DVD-ROM**

Audio Glossary
NCLEX® Review
Videos:
   *Long-Term Care Facilities*
   *Using Health Care Technology Systems*

 **COMPANION WEBSITE**

Additional NCLEX® Review
Case Study: Delivery Systems
Application Activities:
   *Where Do Elders Live?*
   *Issues Plaguing Women and Children*
   *Health Care and Indigents*
   *The Competent Case Manager*
Links to Resources

 **IMAGE LIBRARY**

**Figure 6.1** Various health care settings.
**Figure 6.2** Although all members of the health care team individualize care for the client based on the expertise of their own discipline, there are areas of overlap facilitated through teamwork.

**Figure 6.3** Number of nurses per 100,000 population map.
**Figure 6.4** Medicare helps defray the costs of health care.

---

## LEARNING OUTCOME 1

Differentiate health care services based on primary, secondary, and tertiary disease prevention categories.

### CONCEPTS FOR LECTURE

1. Health care services are often described in a way correlated with levels of disease prevention: primary, secondary, and tertiary prevention.
2. Primary prevention consists of health promotion and illness prevention. Health promotion emphasizes client participation in order to maintain the highest level of wellness individually possible. Primary prevention programs address areas such as adequate and proper nutrition, weight control, exercise, and stress reduction. Illness prevention programs may be directed to the client or community and involve practices such as immunization programs, identifying risk factors, and helping people to reduce these risks.
3. Secondary prevention consists of diagnosis and treatment; is offered in hospitals, freestanding diagnostic and treatment facilities, and outpatient surgical units (surgi-centers); and includes early detection of disease through routine screening of the population and focused screening of those at increased risk. Community-based agencies often provide screening services.
4. The goal of tertiary prevention, which consists of rehabilitation, health restoration, and palliative care, is to help people move to their previous level of health or to the highest level they are capable of given their current

### POWERPOINT LECTURE SLIDES

*(NOTE: The number on each PPT Lecture Slide directly corresponds with the Concepts for Lecture.)*

**1** Types of Health Care Services
- Primary prevention
- Secondary prevention
- Tertiary prevention

**2** Primary Prevention
- Health promotion
- Illness prevention

**3** Secondary Prevention
- Diagnosis
- Early detection
- Treatment

**4** Tertiary Prevention
- Rehabilitation
- Health restoration
- Palliative care

health status. Rehabilitation emphasizes assisting clients to function adequately in the physical, mental, social, economic, and vocational areas of their lives. It may begin in the hospital but eventually leads back to the community for further treatment and follow-up. When people cannot be returned to health, palliative care (providing comfort and treatment for symptoms) and end-of-life care become important. These services may be conducted in many settings, including the home.

---

## SUGGESTIONS FOR CLASSROOM ACTIVITIES

- Provide the students with a list of health care services and ask them to classify the services as primary, secondary, or tertiary prevention.

## SUGGESTIONS FOR CLINICAL ACTIVITIES

- Divide the class into three groups. Assign each group an observational experience in a different type of health care agency: primary, secondary, or tertiary. Have the groups share their observations with the class.

---

# LEARNING OUTCOME 2

Describe the functions and purposes of the health care agencies outlined in this chapter.

## CONCEPTS FOR LECTURE

1. Government agencies are established at the federal, state, and local levels to provide public health services.

    Physicians' offices are primary care settings providing routine health screening, illness diagnosis, and treatment.

    Ambulatory care centers have diagnostic and treatment facilities providing medical, nursing, laboratory, and radiological services, as well as minor surgery services. These centers permit clients to live at home while obtaining health care and make costly hospital beds available for more seriously ill clients.

    Occupational health clinics are run by companies that recognize the value of healthy employees and encourage healthy lifestyles by providing exercise facilities and coordinating health promotion activities.

    Hospitals (governmental or nongovernmental) may be for-profit or not-for-profit facilities. They may provide acute inpatient, outpatient or ambulatory care services, emergency room services, and hospice services.

    Subacute care is a variation of inpatient care designed for someone who has an acute illness, injury, or exacerbation of a disease process. Clients may be admitted after, or instead of, acute hospitalization or to administer one or more technically complex treatments.

    Extended care facilities, formerly called nursing homes, often provide independent living quarters for seniors, assisted living, skilled nursing and extended care facilities for those chronically ill or unable to care for themselves. In addition, they may provide care for clients of all ages who require rehabilitation or custodial care.

    Extended care facilities have programs that are oriented to the needs of the elderly because chronic illness occurs most often in this age group.

## POWERPOINT LECTURE SLIDES

*(NOTE: The number on each PPT Lecture Slide directly corresponds with the Concepts for Lecture.)*

 1 Health Care Agencies
- Government agencies
- Physicians' offices
- Ambulatory care centers
- Occupational health clinics
- Hospitals
- Subacute care
- Extended care facilities (formerly called nursing homes)
- Retirement and assisted-living centers
- Rehabilitation centers
- Home health care agencies
- Day-care centers
- Rural Care Hospitals
- Hospice services
- Crisis centers
- Mutual support or self-help groups

---

Retirement and assisted living centers are intended to meet the needs of people who are unable to remain at home but do not require hospital or nursing home care. Many offer meals, laundry services, nursing care, transportation, and social activities.

Rehabilitation centers play a role in assisting clients to restore their health and recuperate. Some centers are specialized for drug and alcohol rehabilitation.

Home health care agencies offer education to clients and families and also provide comprehensive care to acute, chronic, and terminally ill clients.

Day-care centers serve many functions and many age groups. Some centers provide care for infants and children while parents work, and others provide care for adults who cannot be left home alone but do not need to be in an institution. These centers provide care involving socializing, exercise programs, and stimulation.

Rural primary care hospitals, created by several federal acts, receive federal funding to remain open and provide the breadth of services needed for rural residents, including interface with regional tertiary care centers.

Hospice services provide interdisciplinary health care services for the dying in the home or another health care setting. The central concept is not saving a life but improving or maintaining the quality of life until death.

Crisis centers provide emergency services to clients experiencing life crises. Some also provide direct counseling; however, the primary purpose is to help people cope with an immediate crisis and then provide guidance and support for long-term therapy.

Mutual support or self-help groups focus on nearly every major health problem or life crisis people experience. These types of groups arose largely because people felt their needs were not being met by the existing health care system.

## SUGGESTIONS FOR CLASSROOM ACTIVITIES

- Ask each student to write a short paper on a health care agency, further exploring the purpose and function.
- Invite a panel of speakers from retirement or assisted living centers, day-care centers, crisis centers, and self-help groups to discuss the purpose and functions of these groups.

## SUGGESTIONS FOR CLINICAL ACTIVITIES

- Assign the students to an observational experience in a variety of health care agencies. Have students share these observations.

# LEARNING OUTCOME 3

Identify the roles of various health care professionals.

## CONCEPTS FOR LECTURE

1. Providers of health care, also known as the health care team or health care professionals, are nurses and individuals from other disciplines who coordinate skills to assist clients and their support persons to restore health and promote wellness.

## POWERPOINT LECTURE SLIDES

*(NOTE: The number on each PPT Lecture Slide directly corresponds with the Concepts for Lecture.)*

 1 Health Care Professionals
- Nurses
- Alternative (complementary) care providers

The role of the nurse varies with the needs of the client, the nurse's credentials, and the type of employment setting. A registered nurse (RN) assesses a client's health status, identifies health problems, and develops and coordinates care. A licensed vocational nurse (LVN) or licensed practical nurse (LPN), provides direct client care under the direction of an RN, physician, or other licensed practitioner. Advanced practice nurses (APNs) provide direct care as nurse practitioners, nurse midwives, certified registered nurse anesthetists, and clinical nurse specialists.

Alternative (complementary) care providers provide care not commonly considered part of Western medicine. Examples include chiropractors, herbalists, and massage therapists.

A case manager's role is to ensure that clients receive fiscally sound, appropriate care in the best facility.

Dentists diagnose and treat dental problems and are actively involved in preventive measures to maintain healthy oral structures.

Dietitians use specialized knowledge about diets required to maintain health and to treat disease. Nutritionists have special knowledge about nutrition and food. In the community setting, they recommend healthy diets and provide broad advisory services about the purchase and preparation of foods.

Occupational therapists (OTs) assist clients with impaired function to gain skills to perform activities of daily living.

Paramedical technologists include laboratory, radiological, and nuclear medicine technologists, among others. Their roles depend on area of education; for example, laboratory technologists examine specimens to facilitate diagnosis and prescription of a therapeutic regimen.

Pharmacists prepare and dispense pharmaceuticals in hospital and community settings and monitor and evaluate the actions and effects of medications on clients. Clinical pharmacists guide physicians in prescribing medications. Pharmacist assistants administer medication or work in the pharmacy under the direction of the pharmacist.

Physical therapists (PTs) assist clients with musculoskeletal problems treating movement dysfunctions by means of heat, water, exercise, massage, and electric current. Physical therapy aides also work with PTs and clients.

Physicians are responsible for the medical diagnosis and for determining the therapy required by a person who has a disease or injury. Therapy may now include health promotion and disease prevention. Some physicians are general practitioners, while others have a specialty practice.

Physician assistants perform certain tasks under the direction of a physician, including diagnosing and treating diseases, conditions, and injuries.

Podiatrists diagnose and treat foot conditions including performing surgery and prescribing medications for these conditions.

- Case managers
- Dentists
- Dietitians
- Nutritionists
- Occupational therapists
- Paramedical technologists
- Pharmacists
- Physical therapists
- Physicians
- Physician assistants
- Podiatrists
- Respiratory therapists
- Social workers
- Spiritual support personnel
- Unlicensed assistive personnel (UAPs)

Respiratory therapists are skilled in therapeutic measures used in the care of clients with respiratory problems.

Social workers counsel clients and their support persons regarding problems in day-to-day living such as assisting with financial concerns and finding suitable living situations.

Spiritual support personnel are religious or spiritual advisers who attend to the spiritual needs of clients.

Unlicensed assistive personnel (UAPs) are health care staff who assume delegated aspects of basic care. They include certified nurse assistants, hospital attendants, nurse technicians, patient care technicians, and orderlies.

---

## SUGGESTIONS FOR CLASSROOM ACTIVITIES

- Invite a panel of health care professionals, such as physical, occupational, and respiratory therapists, a paramedical technologist, and a social worker, to describe their role and functions.

## SUGGESTIONS FOR CLINICAL ACTIVITIES

- Obtain the job descriptions of LPNs/LVNs and unlicensed assistive personnel. Have the students discuss the roles and functions of these health care personnel.
- Invite the hospital chaplain to discuss this role.

---

# LEARNING OUTCOME 4

Describe the factors that affect health care delivery.

## CONCEPTS FOR LECTURE

1. Factors that affect health care delivery include the increasing number of elderly persons, advances in technology, economics, women's health, uneven distribution of services, access to health insurance, the homeless and the poor, HIPAA, and demographic changes.

The number of elderly people is increasing. Long-term illnesses are prevalent in this age group, requiring special housing, treatment services, financial support, and social networks.

Scientific knowledge and technology related to health care is rapidly increasing, leading to improved diagnosis, early recognition of diseases, and new treatment options; however, technology may come at a high price because of the expense of the equipment and training specialized personnel. In addition, use of computers is commonplace in health care agencies permitting increased storage and retrieval of data. The World Wide Web and Internet have increased client access to medical information.

Paying for health care is becoming a greater problem. Major reasons for increasing costs include existing equipment and facilities becoming obsolete as research uncovers new and better methods in health care, inflation, total population growth, the increased number of people seeking assistance in health agencies as people recognize that health is everyone's right, reductions in

## POWERPOINT LECTURE SLIDES

*(NOTE: The number on each PPT Lecture Slide directly corresponds with the Concepts for Lecture.)*

 Factors that Affect Health Care Delivery
- Increasing number of elderly
- Advances in technology
- Economics
- Women's health issues
- Uneven distribution of services
- Access to health insurance
- Homeless and the poor
- HIPAA
- Demographic changes

the number of people who provide health services, increases in the number of uninsured people, and the cost of prescription drugs.

The women's movement has changed health care practices. Until recently women's health care focused on reproductive aspects of health, disregarding many health care concerns unique to women. Investigators are recognizing the need for research that examines women equally to men in health issues.

Uneven distribution of health services exists in the United States due to uneven distribution of health care professionals, particularly in remote and rural locations, as well as the increasing number of health care personnel providing specialized services. Specialization can lead to fragmentation of care and increased cost of care.

Another problem is access to health insurance which is related to income. Low income has been associated with relatively higher rates of illness; thus, those with the greatest need for health care are often those least able to pay for it.

Because of the conditions in which homeless people live, health problems are often exacerbated and sometimes become chronic. Physical, mental, social, and emotional factors create health challenges for the homeless and the poor. Limited access to health care services significantly contributes to general poor health of the homeless and poor in the United States.

The Health Insurance Portability and Accountability Act (HIPAA) has changed how health care is practiced. These new regulations were instituted to protect the privacy of individuals by safeguarding individually identifiable health care records. Violations of HIPAA by health care providers or agencies can result in heavy fines for this breach of trust.

Demographic changes include an increase in the number of single-parent families, many of whom are headed by women who work and require assistance with child care or when a child is sick at home.

Recognition of cultural and ethnic diversity is also increasing. Health care agencies are employing means to meet the challenges that diversity presents.

## SUGGESTIONS FOR CLASSROOM ACTIVITIES

- Have the students debate whether health care is a right or privilege.
- Invite guest speakers to address health care delivery to the elderly, the poor, and the homeless in your community.

## SUGGESTIONS FOR CLINICAL ACTIVITIES

- Have students collect current articles in the popular media on access to health care and other issues related to health care delivery. Use these as a basis for discussion.

# LEARNING OUTCOME 5

Compare various systems of payment for health care services.

## CONCEPTS FOR LECTURE

1. Medicare is a national and state health insurance program for adults over 65 years. The Medicare plan is divided into two parts. Part A provides insurance toward hospitalization, home care, and hospice care. Part B, which is voluntary, provides partial coverage of outpatient and physician services to people eligible for Part A.

   Part D is the voluntary prescription drug plan. Most clients pay a monthly premium for Parts B and D coverage and all pay a deductible and coinsurance. Medicare does not cover dental care, dentures, eyeglasses, hearing aids or examinations to prescribe and fit hearing aids, or most routine physical examinations and associated diagnostic tests.

2. Medicaid is a federal public assistance program paid out of general taxes to people who require financial assistance. Each state contributes to the program and each state program is distinct.

3. Supplemental Security Income benefits are available for people with disabilities, those who are blind, and also people not eligible for Social Security. Payments are not restricted to health care cost and may be used to purchase medicines or to cover costs of extended health care.

4. The State Children's Health Insurance Program (SCHIP) was established by the U.S. government to provide insurance coverage for poor and working-class children. Coverage includes visits to primary health care providers, prescription medicines, and hospitalization. State eligibility requirements vary.

5. Congress established the prospective payment system to curtail health care costs by limiting the amount paid to hospitals that are reimbursed by Medicare. Reimbursement is made according to a classification system known as diagnostic-related groups (DRGs).

6. There are two types of private insurance plans: not-for-profit and for-profit. Private health insurance pays either the entire bill or more often 80% of the costs of health care services. These plans may be purchased either as an individual plan or as part of a group plan through a person's employer, union, student association, or similar organizations.

7. Health care group plans provide blanket medical service in exchange for a predetermined monthly payment. These plans include Health Maintenance Organizations, Preferred Provider Organizations, Preferred Provider Arrangements, Independent Practice Associations, and Physician/Hospital Organizations.

   A Health Maintenance Organization (HMO) is a group health care agency that provides health maintenance and treatment services to voluntary enrollees. A fee is set without regard to the amount or kind of service, and the plan emphasizes client wellness. HMO clients are limited in their ability to select health care providers

## POWERPOINT LECTURE SLIDES

*(NOTE: The number on each PPT Lecture Slide directly corresponds with the Concepts for Lecture.)*

1 Medicare
- For adults over 65
- Part A provides hospitalization, home care, hospice
- Part B provides partial outpatient and physician services (voluntary)
- Part D prescription plan (voluntary)
- Does not cover dental, eyeglasses, hearing aids, etc.

2 Medicaid
- Financial assistance
- Each state is distinct

3 Supplemental Security Income
- Benefits for people with disabilities
- For those not eligible for Social Security

4 State Children's Health Insurance Program (SCHIP)
- Insurance coverage for poor and working class children
- Includes primary care, prescriptions, hospitalization

5 Prospective Payment System
- Limits amount paid to hospitals that are reimbursed by Medicare

6 Private Insurance Plans
- Not-for-profit and for-profit
- Most often pay 80% of costs

7 Health Care Group Plans
- Provide blanket medical service in exchange for monthly payment
  - Health Maintenance Organization (HMO)
  - Preferred Provider Organization (PPO)
  - Preferred Provider Arrangements (PPA)
  - Independent Practice Associations (IPA)
  - Physician/Hospital Organizations (PHO)

and services, but available services are at a reduced and predetermined cost to the client.

A Preferred Provider Organization (PPO) consists of a group of providers and perhaps a health care agency that provides an insurance company or employer with a health service at a discounted rate. PPOs provide clients with a choice of health care providers and services, but they tend to be slightly more expensive than HMO plans.

A Preferred Provider Arrangement (PPA) is similar to a PPO. The main difference is that PPAs can be contracted with individual health care providers, whereas PPOs involve an organization of health care providers.

An Independent Practice Association (IPA) provides care in offices just as the providers belonging to a PPO. The difference is that clients pay a fixed prospective payment to the IPA, and the IPA pays the provider. At the end of the fiscal year, any surplus money is divided among the providers. Any loss is assumed by the IPA.

A Physician/Hospital Organization (PHO) is a joint venture between a group of private practice physicians and a hospital. PHOs combine both resources and personnel to provide managed care alternatives and medical services. PHOs work with a variety of insurers to provide services.

## SUGGESTIONS FOR CLASSROOM ACTIVITIES

- Invite a guest speaker knowledgeable about Medicare Part D to discuss this addition to Medicare.
- Invite a human resource representative from a local hospital to discuss, compare, and contrast the health care plans offered to hospital employees. Have students discuss how they would select the best plan for themselves.

## SUGGESTIONS FOR CLINICAL ACTIVITIES

- Direct the students to determine the insurance coverage of their clients. Discuss in conference how this coverage might influence the type of care the client receives in the health care setting.
- Invite a representative from the institution's billing office to discuss the process used to bill clients and insurance companies.

# CHAPTER 7
## COMMUNITY NURSING AND CARE CONTINUITY

## RESOURCE LIBRARY

### 🔘 PRENTICE HALL NURSING MEDIALINK DVD-ROM

Audio Glossary
NCLEX® Review

### 🌐 COMPANION WEBSITE

Additional NCLEX® Review
Case Studies:
    *The Amish*
    *Community Health Nursing*
Application Activities:
    *Community Nursing Standards*
    *Government Services*
Links to Resources

### 📖 IMAGE LIBRARY

**Figure 7.1** Communities may consist of several types of neighborhoods.
**Figure 7.2** The community assessment wheel, the assessment segment of the community-as-partner model.

**Figure 7.3** Model of an integrated health care delivery system.
**Figure 7.4** Some parish-based health services provide care to community residents in addition to members of the congregation.

---

## LEARNING OUTCOME 1

Discuss factors influencing health care reform.

### CONCEPTS FOR LECTURE

1. Escalating health care costs, expanding technology, changing patterns of demographics, shorter hospital stays, increasing client acuity and limited access to health care are some of the factors motivating change in health care. In addition, the location of client care is expanding out of traditional settings into the community.

    Both consumers and health care professionals have had major dissatisfaction with the current health care system, which focuses on acute, hospital-based care.

    Plans to reform the health care system have been proposed nationally and internationally, but no single plan has been adopted.

2. Nurses, professional organizations, and consumers influence health care reform.

    In 1991 the ANA published *Nursing's Agenda for Health Care Reform,* which set forth the ANA's recommendations for health care reform (Box 7–1). The majority of these recommendations have still not been implemented.

    Consumers are effecting changes in health care delivery systems by adopting health-related values that support an increased emphasis on health care services and programs that promote wellness and restoration and prevent disease.

### POWERPOINT LECTURE SLIDES

*(NOTE: The number on each PPT Lecture Slide directly corresponds with the Concepts for Lecture.)*

 Factors Influencing Health Care Reform
- Health care costs
- Expanding technology
- Changing patterns of demographics
- Shorter hospital stays
- Increasing client acuity
- Limited access to health care

**2** Influence of Nurses, Professional Organizations, and Consumer Influence:
- ANA
- Move toward wellness
- *Healthy People 2010*
- WHO

Another major influence promoting health care reform has been the work on *Healthy People 2000 and 2010.* These projects present health-related objectives providing a framework for national health promotion, health protection, and disease prevention.

Previous to this, the World Health Organization (1978) produced a report entitled *Primary Health Care.* The term primary health care (PHC) incorporates equitable distribution, appropriate technology, a focus on health promotion and disease prevention, community participation, and a multisectional approach.

---

## SUGGESTIONS FOR CLASSROOM ACTIVITIES

- Discuss *Nursing's Agenda for Health Care Reform* (Box 7–1). Ask the students to identify which items on the agenda have been implemented and which are yet to be addressed.
- Have the students collect newspaper articles related to health care reform for a specific period of time and write a short paper comparing and contrasting issues discussed in the articles to issues presented in the textbook.

---

# LEARNING OUTCOME 2

Describe community-based health care, including the Pew Health Professions Commission recommendations for health competencies for future health practitioners.

## CONCEPTS FOR LECTURE

1. Community-based health care (CBHC) is a primary health care system that provides health-related services in places where people spend their time, for example, in the home, in shelters, at work, at school, and so on.

   The care is directed toward a specific group within the geographical neighborhood. The group may be established by a physical boundary, an employer, a school district, a managed care insurance provider, or a specific medical need or category.

2. To be truly effective, a CBHC system needs to provide easy access to care, be flexible in responding to the care needs that individuals and families identify, promote care between and among health care agencies through improved communication mechanisms, provide appropriate support for family caregivers, and be affordable.

   Nurses working in community-based integrated health care systems need to have specific knowledge and skills. In 1991, the Pew Health Professions Commission report *Healthy America: Practitioners for 2005* identified 17 competencies (skills) that future health professionals would require (see Outcome 6).

## POWERPOINT LECTURE SLIDES

*(NOTE: The number on each PPT Lecture Slide directly corresponds with the Concepts for Lecture.)*

1. Community-based Health Care (CBHC)
   - Primary health care system
   - Services provided within context of peoples' lives
   - Care is directed toward a specific geographical group

2. Effective CBHC Systems
   - Provides easy access to care
   - Is flexible in responding to needs
   - Promotes communication among agencies
   - Supports family caregivers
   - Is affordable

---

## SUGGESTIONS FOR CLASSROOM ACTIVITIES

- Invite nurses working in a variety of community-based health care settings to discuss the goals, purposes, and roles of the nurse in these settings.
- Discuss the characteristics of an ideal health care system as written in 1992 with the reality of the health care system today.

## SUGGESTIONS FOR CLINICAL ACTIVITIES

- Have the students apply the characteristics of an ideal health care system with what they have observed in the institution.

---

# LEARNING OUTCOME 3

Describe various community-based frameworks, including integrated health care systems, community initiatives and coalitions, and case management.

## CONCEPTS FOR LECTURE

1. Various approaches are emerging to address community health, including integrated health care systems, community initiatives and coalitions, managed care, case management, and outreach programs using lay health workers.

   An integrated health care system, sometimes referred to as *seamless care*, is one that makes all levels of care—primary, secondary, and tertiary—available in an integrated form. Its goals are to facilitate care across settings, recovery, positive health outcomes, and the long-term benefits of modifying harmful lifestyles through health promotion and disease prevention.

   Community initiatives are being sponsored by some hospitals or local community agencies. These initiatives, called *healthy cities* and *healthier communities,* involve members of the community to establish health priorities, set measurable goals, and determine actions to reach these goals.

   Community coalitions bring together individuals and groups for the shared purpose of improving the community's health. They may focus on single or multifaceted problems.

   Case management tracks a client's needs and services through a variety of care settings to ensure continuity. The case manager is familiar with clients' health needs and resources available through their insurance coverage so they can receive cost-effective care and assists the client and family to understand and navigate their way through the health care system.

   Outreach programs using lay health workers are a method of linking underserved or high-risk populations with the formal health care system, minimizing or reducing barriers to health care, increasing access to services, and improving the health status of the community. Interested and committed lay health workers are identified who will assist their neighbors through outreach networks. Nurses provide training, consultation, and support to these individuals.

## POWERPOINT LECTURE SLIDES

*(NOTE: The number on each PPT Lecture Slide directly corresponds with the Concepts for Lecture.)*

 Community-Based Frameworks
- Various approaches emerging to address community health including:
  - Integrated health care systems
  - Community initiatives and coalitions
  - Managed care
  - Case management
  - Outreach programs

## SUGGESTIONS FOR CLASSROOM ACTIVITIES

- Have the students explore their community of origin for examples of community initiatives, coalitions, and outreach programs and report findings to the class.

## SUGGESTIONS FOR CLINICAL ACTIVITIES

- Invite a case manager from the institution to discuss the role.

# LEARNING OUTCOME 4

Differentiate community health care settings from traditional settings.

## CONCEPTS FOR LECTURE

1. Traditionally, community services have been provided in county and state health departments (public health nursing), in schools (school nursing), in workplaces (occupational nursing), and in homes (home health care and hospice nursing).

    Over time numerous other settings have been established, including day-care centers, senior centers, storefront clinics, homeless shelters, mental health centers, crisis centers, drug rehabilitation programs, and ambulatory care centers.

2. More recent settings for community nursing practice include nurse-managed community nursing centers, parish nursing, and telehealth centers.

    Nurse-managed community nursing centers provide primary care to specific populations and are staffed by nurse practitioners and community health nurses with physicians' consultation available as needed. There are various categories of these settings: community outreach, institution-based, school-based, and wellness centers.

    Parish nursing is nondenominational and includes nurses from all religious faiths. Roles of parish nurses include: personal health counselor, health educator, referral source, facilitator, and integrator of faith and health.

    Telehealth projects use communication and information technology to provide health information and services to people in rural, remote, or underserved areas using video conferences or "video clinics."

## POWERPOINT LECTURE SLIDES

*(NOTE: The number on each PPT Lecture Slide directly corresponds with the Concepts for Lecture.)*

1. Traditional Settings
   - County and state health departments
   - Schools
   - Work places
   - Homes
   - Numerous additional settings

2. Community Health Care Settings Now
   - Nurse-managed community nursing centers
   - Parish nursing
   - Telehealth centers

## SUGGESTIONS FOR CLASSROOM ACTIVITIES

- Invite nurses who practice in the roles of parish nurse or in a nurse-managed or telehealth center to discuss these roles.

## SUGGESTIONS FOR CLINICAL ACTIVITIES

- Arrange for each student to have an observational experience in a different community health care setting, such as day-care centers, senior centers, homeless shelters, crisis centers, or other community health care settings, and share observations with the group.

# LEARNING OUTCOME 5

Differentiate community-based nursing from traditional institutional-based nursing.

## CONCEPTS FOR LECTURE

1. As in traditional institutional-based nursing, community-based nursing (CBN) is nursing care directed toward specific individuals. However, CBN involves nursing care that is not confined to one practice setting, extending beyond institutional boundaries.

2. CBN involves a network of nursing services: nursing wellness centers, ambulatory centers, acute care, long-term care nursing services, telephone advice, home health, school health, and hospice services.

## POWERPOINT LECTURE SLIDES

*(NOTE: The number on each PPT Lecture Slide directly corresponds with the Concepts for Lecture.)*

1. Community-based Nursing (CBN)
   - Care directed toward specific individuals
   - Extends beyond institutional boundaries

2. CBN Network
   - Nursing wellness centers
   - Ambulatory centers

- Acute care
- Long-term care nursing services
- Telephone advice
- Home health
- School health
- Hospice services

---

## Suggestions for Classroom Activities

- Invite nurses working in a variety of community-based health care settings to discuss the goals, purposes, and roles of the nurse in these settings.

---

## Learning Outcome 6

Discuss competencies community-based nurses need for practice.

### Concepts for Lecture

1. In 1991, the Pew Health Profession Commission identified 17 competencies (skills) that future health care professionals would require: to care for the community's health, expand access to effective care, provide contemporary clinical care, emphasize primary care, participate in coordinated care, ensure cost-effective and appropriate care, practice prevention, involve patients and families in decision-making processes, promote healthy lifestyles, access and use technology appropriately, improve the health care system, manage information, understand the role of the physical environment, practice counseling on ethical issues, accommodate expanded accountability, participate in a racially and culturally diverse society, and continue to learn.

2. To achieve these competencies, nurses need the following knowledge: (a) determinants of a healthy community; (b) primary and secondary preventive strategies for people of all ages; (c) health promotion strategies for individuals, families, and communities; (d) how to participate in collaborative and interdisciplinary teamwork; (e) determinants of an accessible, cost-effective, integrated health care system; (f) decision-making processes that involve active participation by consumers and balance cost and quality of care; and (g) concepts of information management.

   Community-based nurses also require up-to-date clinical skills and knowledge of complex technology, public health policy, and strategies to influence and effect change.

### PowerPoint Lecture Slides

*(NOTE: The number on each PPT Lecture Slide directly corresponds with the Concepts for Lecture.)*

 Pew Commission Competencies for Future Practitioners
- Care for the community's health
- Expand access to effective care
- Provide contemporary clinical care
- Emphasize primary care
- Participate in coordinated care
- Ensure cost-effective and appropriate care
- Practice prevention
- Involve patients and families in decision-making processes
- Promote healthy lifestyles
- Access and use technology appropriately
- Improve the health care system
- Manage information
- Understand the role of the physical environment
- Practice counseling on ethical issues
- Accommodate expanded accountability
- Participate in a racially and culturally diverse society
- Continue to learn

 Achieving Pew Competencies
- Nurses need the following knowledge:
  - Determinants of a healthy community
  - Primary and secondary preventive strategies for people of all ages
  - Health promotion strategies for individuals, families, and communities
  - How to participate in collaborative and interdisciplinary teamwork
  - Determinants of an accessible, cost-effective integrated health care system

- Decision-making processes that involve active participation by consumers
- Balance cost and quality care
- Concepts of information management
- Also require up-to-date clinical skills
- Knowledge of complex technology and public health policy
- Strategies to influence and effect change

## SUGGESTIONS FOR CLASSROOM ACTIVITIES

- Have the students debate the pros and cons of community-based nursing.
- Obtain the curriculum for a community nursing program or course and compare the competencies identified in the text with the competencies developed in the curriculum or course.

# LEARNING OUTCOME 7

Explain essential aspects of collaborative health care: definitions, objectives, benefits, and the nurse's role.

## CONCEPTS FOR LECTURE

1. The ANA's (1992) operational definition of collaboration is a collegial working relationship with another health care provider in the provision of client care.

   In addition, the ANA states that collaborative practice may include discussion of the diagnosis and cooperation in the management and delivery of care. Each collaborator is available for consultation either in person or by communication device, but need not be physically present on the premises at the time the actions are performed. The client-designated health care provider is responsible for the overall direction and management of client care.

   The objective of collaborative health care is to provide optimal health care for the client.
2. The collaborative role of the nurse occurs with peers, with other health care professionals, with nursing professional groups, and with legislators (see Box 7-7).

   To fulfill a collaborative role the nurse needs to assume accountability and increased authority in practice areas.
3. Key elements necessary for collaboration include effective communication, mutual respect, trust, and an effective decision-making process.

## POWERPOINT LECTURE SLIDES

*(NOTE: The number on each PPT Lecture Slide directly corresponds with the Concepts for Lecture.)*

**1** Collaborative Health Care
- ANA's Definition of Collaborative Health Care
- Objective
  - Provide optimal health care for the client

**2** Collaborative Role of the Nurse
- Peers
- Other health care professionals
- Nursing professional groups
- Legislators

**3** Key Elements Necessary for Collaboration
- Effective communication
- Mutual respect
- Trust
- Effective decision-making process
- Accountability and increased authority in practice areas

## SUGGESTIONS FOR CLASSROOM ACTIVITIES

- Have the students discuss how they believe mutual trust and respect can be developed within their class and how this might relate to the development of collegial working relationships in the clinical area.

## SUGGESTIONS FOR CLINICAL ACTIVITIES

- Have the students report on instances in which they have observed collaboration in the clinical setting, and instances they have observed when collaboration should have occurred and did not. Compare and contrast each situation.

# LEARNING OUTCOME 8

Identify various types of communities.

## CONCEPTS FOR LECTURE

1. A community is a collection of people who share some attribute of their lives and interact with each other in some way.

   A community may be made up of people who live in the same locale, attend a particular church, or even share a particular interest such as art.

   Groups that constitute a community because of a particular interest are often referred to as a *community of interest*.

   A community can also be defined as a social system, in which the members interact formally or informally and form networks that operate for the benefit of all people in the community.

   In community health, the community may be viewed as having a common health problem.

## POWERPOINT LECTURE SLIDES

*(NOTE: The number on each PPT Lecture Slide directly corresponds with the Concepts for Lecture.)*

 Types of Communities
- Collection of people who share same attribute
  - Live in same locale
  - Attend particular church
  - Share particular interest (community of interest)
- A social system that interacts to form networks that operate for the benefit of all
- A community health community may have a common health problem

## SUGGESTIONS FOR CLASSROOM ACTIVITIES

- Ask the students to identify communities within the educational institution and clinical institutions.
- Discuss how the educational community operates for the benefit of all within the institution.

## SUGGESTIONS FOR CLINICAL ACTIVITIES

- Discuss the institution as a community of interest.

# LEARNING OUTCOME 9

Describe the role of the nurse in providing continuity of care.

## CONCEPTS FOR LECTURE

1. Continuity of care is the coordination of health care services by health care providers for clients moving from one health care setting to another and between and among health care professionals. It ensures uninterrupted and consistent services for the client from one level to another, maintains client-focused individualized care, and helps optimize the client's health status.

   To provide continuity of care, nurses need to accomplish the following: initiate discharge planning for all clients when admitted to any health care setting; involve the client and the client's family or support persons in the planning process; and collaborate with other health care professionals as needed to ensure that biopsychosocial, cultural, and spiritual needs are met.

2. Discharge planning is the process of preparing a client to leave one level of care for another. Effective discharge planning involves ongoing assessment to obtain comprehensive information about the client's ongoing needs and nursing care plans to ensure the client's and caregiver's needs are met. Discharge planning may include health team conferences and family conferences.

## POWERPOINT LECTURE SLIDES

*(NOTE: The number on each PPT Lecture Slide directly corresponds with the Concepts for Lecture.)*

 Continuity of Care
- Coordination of Services Includes
  - Initiation of discharge planning on admission
  - Involvement of the client and support persons
  - Collaboration with other health care professionals

 Discharge Planning
- May include health team conferences and family conferences
- Assessment
  - Client's personal and health data
  - Abilities to perform activities of daily living
  - Disabilities/limitations
  - Caregiver's responsibilities/abilities
  - Financial resources
  - Community support
  - Home hazard appraisals
  - Need for health care assistance

Areas to assess prior to discharge include the client's personal and health data, abilities to perform activities of daily living, disabilities/limitations, caregiver's responsibilities/abilities, financial resources, community support, home hazard appraisals, and need for health care assistance (see Box 7-8).

3. Health care teaching is often required for clients to understand their situation, to make health care decisions, and to learn new health care behaviors. Prior to discharge, it is essential that the client and caregiver understand information about medications, dietary and activity restrictions, signs of complications that need to be reported to the physician, follow-up appointments and telephone numbers, and where supplies can be obtained. Clients or caregivers also need to demonstrate safe performance of any necessary treatments.

The nurse may need to make a referral to a home health care agency for follow-up teaching, and care may be necessary.

 Health Care Teaching
- Information about medications
  - Dietary and activity restrictions
  - Signs of complications that need to be reported to the physician
  - Follow-up appointments and telephone numbers
  - Where supplies can be obtained
  - Safe performance of any necessary treatments
- Home Care Referrals

---

## SUGGESTIONS FOR CLASSROOM ACTIVITIES

- Using a client case study, have the students review the assessment information necessary to plan for client discharge using parameters listed in Box 7-8.
- Invite a panel of home care coordinators to discuss the services provided and funding requirements for the home care agencies.

## SUGGESTIONS FOR CLINICAL ACTIVITIES

- Have the students discuss the steps taken to ensure continuity of care for their clients (for example, from physician's office or emergency department to inpatient unit, to and from operating suite).
- Have the students discuss the discharge plan for their clients.
- Obtain permission for students to observe a health team or family conference.
- Assign students to assist a nurse to provide discharge teaching for clients.

# CHAPTER 8
## HOME CARE

## RESOURCE LIBRARY

### PRENTICE HALL NURSING MEDIALINK DVD-ROM

Audio Glossary
NCLEX® Review

### COMPANION WEBSITE

Additional NCLEX® Review
Case Study: Home Care Nursing
Application Activities:
*Hospice Nursing*
*Duties of the Home Health Assistant*
*Home Care of a Diabetic Client*
Links to Resources

### IMAGE LIBRARY

**Figure 8.1** Home care nurses perform skilled direct care such as changing dressings.
**Figure 8.2** MedicAlert emblems.
**Figure 8.3** Interviewing the home care client.
**Figure 8.4** The nurse monitors the client's response to treatments and therapy.

**Figure 8.5** Determining the success of the care plan includes comparing assessment findings to previous values. Weighing this tube-fed baby provides critical data about her progress.

## LEARNING OUTCOME 1

Define home health care.

### CONCEPTS FOR LECTURE

1. Historically, home care consisted primarily of nurses providing private duty care in clients' homes and care of the ill by their own family members.

    Home care today involves a wide range of health care professionals providing services in the home setting to people recovering from an acute illness, or who are disabled, or those with a chronic condition.

    In the not-too-distant past, home health care occurred at the end of the client care continuum—that is, after discharge from the acute care setting. Today, the trend is changing to use of home health care services to avoid hospitalization.

### POWERPOINT LECTURE SLIDES

*(NOTE: The number on each PPT Lecture Slide directly corresponds with the Concepts for Lecture.)*

**1** Home Health Care
- Historically
  - Private duty care in client's home
  - Care of the ill by family members
- Today
  - Wide range of health care professionals
  - Services for recovery from acute illness, disabilities or chronic conditions

### SUGGESTIONS FOR CLASSROOM ACTIVITIES

- Give examples of situations in which home care may be used as an alternative to hospitalization.

Compare the characteristics of home health nursing to those of institutional nursing care.

### CONCEPTS FOR LECTURE

1.  Home health care nursing or visiting nursing includes the nursing services and products provided to clients in their homes that are needed to maintain, restore, or promote their physical, psychological, and social well-being.

    Hospice nursing, support and care of the dying person and family, is often considered a subspecialty because services are frequently delivered in the client's home.

    Home health care nursing differs from institutional nursing in a number of ways. The home health care nurse must function independently in a variety of unfamiliar home settings and situations.

    Because the home is the client's and family's territory, power and control issues in delivering care differ from those in the hospital. For example, the nurse enters the home with the permission of the client and family.

    Health care that is provided in the home is often given with other family members present. Families may feel freer to question advice, to ignore directions, to do things differently, and to set their own priorities and schedules than in the institution.

### POWERPOINT LECTURE SLIDES

*(NOTE: The number on each PPT Lecture Slide directly corresponds with the Concepts for Lecture.)*

 Characteristics of Home Health Nursing
- Function independently
- Variety of unfamiliar home settings and situations
- Power and control issues
- Care provided in home
- Presence of family members

### SUGGESTIONS FOR CLASSROOM ACTIVITIES

- Invite a panel of home health care nurses and nurses who work in institutions to compare the characteristics of home health nursing with institutional nursing.
- Have students discuss the advantages and disadvantages they perceive in caring for the client and family in the home.

### SUGGESTIONS FOR CLINICAL ACTIVITIES

- Arrange for all or several students to have an observational experience with a home health care nurse. Ask the students to keep a journal of the differences and similarities in the practice of nursing in the home as compared to the practice of nursing in an institution.

Describe the types of home health agencies, including reimbursement and referral sources.

### CONCEPTS FOR LECTURE

1.  There are several different types of home health agencies: official or public, voluntary or private not-for-profit, private, proprietary, institutional-based, and private duty agencies. All must meet specific standards for licensing, certification, and accreditation.

    Official or public agencies are operated by state or local governments and financed primarily by tax funds.

    Voluntary or private not-for-profit agencies are supported by donations, endowments, charities such as the United Way, and third-party reimbursement.

    Private, proprietary agencies are for-profit organizations and are governed by either individual owners or national corporations. Some of these agencies participate in third-party reimbursement, and others rely on "private-pay" sources.

### POWERPOINT LECTURE SLIDES

*(NOTE: The number on each PPT Lecture Slide directly corresponds with the Concepts for Lecture.)*

 Types of Home Health Agencies
- Official or public
  - Operated by state or local governments
  - Financed primarily by tax funds
- Voluntary or private not-for-profit
  - Supported by donations, endowments, charities
- Private, proprietary
  - For-profit organizations
  - Governed by individual owners or national corporations
  - Some rely on third-party, others rely on private-pay sources

Institutional-based agencies operate under a parent organization, such as a hospital, and are funded by the same sources as the parent organization.

Private duty agencies (also referred to as a registry) contract with individual practitioners to care for clients in the home and may also supply staff to hospitals, clinics, and other settings. Commercial insurance generally provides limited reimbursement or otherwise the client must pay privately.

2. Home care agencies receive reimbursement for services from various sources: Medicare, Medicaid, private insurance companies, and private pay. Medicare and Medicaid programs provide reimbursement for home health care services; however, they have strict guidelines governing reimbursement. Other payers typically negotiate reimbursement rates; not-for-profit agencies like Visiting Nurses Associations are reimbursed by public and private insurance plans plus charitable donations.

Durable medical equipment (DME) companies provide health care equipment for client use in the home. Because of the cost of DME, nurses need to ensure that clients have either Medicare/Medicaid or a DME benefit with commercial insurance companies or are able to pay privately.

3. Clients may be referred to home health care providers by a physician, nurse, social worker, therapist, discharge planner, or family member.

Home care cannot begin, however, without a physician's order and a physician-approved treatment plan. This is a legal and reimbursement requirement.

- Institutional-based
  - Funded by same source as parent organization
- Private Duty Agencies (Registry)
  - Contract with individual practitioners
  - May also supply staff to hospitals
  - Limited reimbursement through commercial insurance
  - Private pay

 Reimbursement Sources
- Medicare and Medicaid
- Private insurance companies
- Private pay
- Durable medical equipment (DME) funding

Referral Process
- Health care providers
- Family
- Actual service requires physician's order

## SUGGESTIONS FOR CLASSROOM ACTIVITIES

- Invite a panel of guest speakers to discuss home health care delivery in your community. Ask each to discuss the types of client services and types of nursing care provided. Ask the panel members to address the process of reimbursement.

## SUGGESTIONS FOR CLINICAL ACTIVITIES

- Arrange for a variety of home care clinical experiences for the students. Assign students to keep a journal of their experiences. Journal notes should include a summary of each home visit, nursing assessment information, plan of care, client and nurse safety issues, infection control, and caregiver support. Have each student share the highlights of the experience during clinical conference.
- Arrange for a discharge planner or case manager to discuss the home care referral process in the institution.

# LEARNING OUTCOME 4

Describe the roles of the home health nurse.

## CONCEPTS FOR LECTURE

1. Major roles of the home health nurse are those of advocate, caregiver (provider of direct care), educator, and case manager or coordinator.

As an advocate, the nurse explores and supports the client's choices in health care and ensures that the client's rights and desires in terms of health care are upheld.

## POWERPOINT LECTURE SLIDES

*(NOTE: The number on each PPT Lecture Slide directly corresponds with the Concepts for Lecture.)*

 Roles of Home Health Nurse
- Advocate
- Caregiver (provider of direct care)
- Educator
- Case manager or coordinator

The home health nurse's major role as caregiver is to assess and diagnose the client's actual and potential health problems, plan care, and evaluate the client's outcomes. The home health nurse may also provide direct care for specific procedures and treatments; however, much of the home health care nurse's time is spent teaching others to provide required care.

The educator's role of the home health nurse focuses on teaching illness care, the prevention of problems, and the promotion of wellness or well-being in the client, the family, and other related persons. It may involve teaching others with whom the client interacts. Education is ongoing and can be considered the crux of home care practice; its goal is to help clients learn to manage as independently as possible.

The home health care nurse coordinates the activities of all other home health team members involved in the treatment plan. The nurse is the main contact to report any changes in the client's condition and to bring about a revision in the plan of care as needed. Documentation of care coordination is a legal and reimbursement requirement.

## SUGGESTIONS FOR CLASSROOM ACTIVITIES

- Invite a panel of home health care nurses to discuss how they enact the roles of client advocate, caregiver, educator, and case manager.

## SUGGESTIONS FOR CLINICAL ACTIVITIES

- Arrange for a variety of home care clinical experiences for students. Assign students to keep a journal of their experiences in which they document how the home health nurse enacted the roles of client advocate, caregiver, educator, and case manager.

# LEARNING OUTCOME 5

Identify the essential aspects of the home visit.

## CONCEPTS FOR LECTURE

1. The goal of the initial visit is to obtain a comprehensive clinical picture of the client's needs and begins with the documents received from the referral agency prior to the initial visit.

    During this initial visit the home health nurse obtains a health history, examines the client, observes the relationship of the client and caregiver, and assesses the home and community environment.

    The nurse also discusses what the client and family can expect from home care, what other health care providers may be needed to help the client achieve independence, and the frequency of home visits.

2. Following this initial assessment, the nurse determines whether further consults and support personnel are needed and develops a plan of care.

3. The data required by Medicare for the nursing plan of care include: all pertinent diagnoses; a notation of the client's mental status; types of services, supplies, and equipment ordered; frequency of visits; client's

## POWERPOINT LECTURE SLIDES

*(NOTE: The number on each PPT Lecture Slide directly corresponds with the Concepts for Lecture.)*

**1** Initial Home Care Visit
- Goal
- Review of referral documents
- Obtain a health history
- Examine the client
- Observe the relationship of the client and caregiver
- Assess the home and community environment
- Discuss what the client and family can expect from home care
- Frequency of home visits

**2** Following Initial Assessment
- Determine whether further consults and support personnel needed
- Develop nursing care plan

prognosis; client's rehabilitation potential; client's functional potential; activities permitted; client's nutritional requirements; client's medications and treatments; safety measures to prevent injury; discharge plans; and any other items the home health agency or primary care provider wishes to include.

4. On subsequent home visits, the nurse observes the same parameters assessed on the initial home visit and relates findings to the expected outcomes of goals.

5. Documentation of care given and the client's progress toward goal achievement at each visit is essential. Notes must also reflect plans for subsequent visits and when the client may be sufficiently prepared for self-care and discharge from the agency.

**3** Medicare's Requirements for Nursing Care Plan
- All pertinent diagnoses
- Mental status
- Types of services, supplies, equipment ordered
- Frequency of visits
- Client's prognosis, rehabilitation potential, functional potential, nutritional requirements, medications and treatments
- Activities permitted
- Safety measures
- Discharge plans
- Any other items agency or primary care provider wishes to add

**4** Subsequent Visits
- Review all previous parameters
- Evaluate progress towards goals

**5** Documentation

## SUGGESTIONS FOR CLASSROOM ACTIVITIES

- Obtain copies of the forms several home health care agencies use to "open a case." Review these with the students.
- Review the Medicare requirements for the nursing plan of care listed in Box 8-1.

## SUGGESTIONS FOR CLINICAL ACTIVITIES

- Arrange for a variety of home care clinical experiences for the students. Assign students to keep a journal of their experiences. Journal notes should include a summary of each home visit, including the components of the nursing process enacted during the visit and the type of documentation the home health care nurse completed. Have the students share their observations.

# LEARNING OUTCOME 6

Discuss the safety and infection control dimensions applicable to the home care setting.

## CONCEPTS FOR LECTURE

1. Hazards in the home are major causes of falls, fire, poisoning, and other injuries. The appraisal of such hazards and suggestions for remedies is an essential nursing function (see the Home Care Assessment box for home hazard appraisal).

2. Areas to assess for potential hazards include: walkways and stairways, floors, furniture, bathrooms, kitchen, bedrooms, electrical equipment, fire protection, toxic substances, communication devices, and medications.

3. Other aspects of client safety relate to emergency situations. The home health care nurse can assist the client and caregivers as follows: list all emergency numbers by each telephone, list all client medications and potential side effects in a central location, help the client and family apply for a medical alert system, enroll in a program to place all the client's vital medical information in one place for emergency personnel to have in the event of a life-threatening situation, and recommend the client enroll in an emergency response system.

## POWERPOINT LECTURE SLIDES

*(NOTE: The number on each PPT Lecture Slide directly corresponds with the Concepts for Lecture.)*

**1** Safety in the Home Care Setting
- Possible emergencies include:
  - Falls
  - Fire
  - Poisoning
  - Injuries

**2** Assessment of Home Hazards
- Walkways and stairways
- Floors and furniture
- Bathroom, kitchen, bedroom
- Electrical equipment
- Fire protection
- Toxic substance and medication safety
- Communication devices

**3** Emergency Preparation Measures
- List all emergency numbers by each telephone
- List all client medications and potential side effects in a central location

4. Some less desirable living locations pose additional personal safety concerns for the nurse. Many home health agencies may have contracts with security firms to escort nurses needing to see clients in unsafe neighborhoods, and the nurse should have preestablished mechanisms to signal for help and avoid taking personal belongings to these visits. Home health agencies provide training in ways to decrease personal risk.

5. The goal of infection control in the home is to protect clients, caregivers, and the general community from the transmission of disease. The nurse's major role in infection control is health teaching. Although some modifications in techniques may be indicated in the home setting, all the basic principles of asepsis still apply.

   An important aspect of infection control involves handling of the nurse's equipment and supplies. The nurse needs to follow agency protocols about aseptic practice in the home.

- Help client and family apply for a medical alert system
- Enroll in a program to place all client's vital medical information in one place for emergency personnel
- Recommend the client enroll in an emergency response system

**4** Nurse Safety
- Contracts with security firms to escort nurses
- Preestablished mechanisms to signal for help
- Training to decrease personal risk

**5** Infection Control in the Home Care Setting
- Goal is to protect from transmission of disease
- Teach principles of asepsis
- Follow agency's protocol for aseptic practice

---

## SUGGESTIONS FOR CLASSROOM ACTIVITIES

- Have the students explore their state health department website to determine the process to be followed to enroll in a program to place all medical information in a location for emergency personnel access.
- Ask the students to investigate how to assist a client to obtain a MedicAlert device or an emergency response system.
- Discuss situations in which aseptic principles are modified in the home (e.g., when clean technique may be used).

## SUGGESTIONS FOR CLINICAL ACTIVITIES

- Have a student contact the local health department or municipal sanitation department to find out the accepted way to dispose of dressings, syringes, and other materials contaminated with blood or body fluids.

---

# LEARNING OUTCOME 7

Identify ways the nurse can recognize and minimize caregiver role strain.

## CONCEPTS FOR LECTURE

1. Signs of caregiver overload (strain) include the following: difficulty performing routine tasks for the client, reports of declining physical energy and insufficient time for caregiving, concern that caregiving responsibilities interfere with other roles, anxiety about the ability to meet future care needs of the client, feelings of anger and depression, and a dramatic change in the home environment's appearance.

2. The nurse needs to encourage caregivers to express their feelings and at the same time convey understanding about the difficulties associated with caregiving and acknowledge the caregivers' competence.

   A realistic appraisal of the situation can be obtained by asking a caregiver to describe a typical day.

   Activities that are commonly done by nurses and aides can be challenging to caregivers. Demonstrating

## POWERPOINT LECTURE SLIDES

*(NOTE: The number on each PPT Lecture Slide directly corresponds with the Concepts for Lecture.)*

**1** Signs of Caregiver Role Strain (Overload)
- Difficulty performing routine tasks for the client
- Reports of declining physical energy
- Insufficient time for caregiving
- Concern that caregiving responsibilities interfere with other roles
- Anxiety about ability to meet future care needs of client
- Feelings of anger and depression
- Dramatic change in the appearance of home environment

**2** Minimizing Caregiver Role Strain (Overload)
- Encourage caregivers to express feelings
- Convey understanding

## CONCEPTS FOR LECTURE *continued*

these activities in the home and allowing caregivers to perform them with the nurse's supervision increases caregiver confidence and increases the likelihood of caregivers asking for assistance in other situations.

When activities for which assistance is required are identified, the nurse and caregiver need to identify possible sources of help such as volunteer and agency sources.

Caregivers may benefit from a weekend respite— a program some hospitals provide in which the client is admitted to a skilled unit for observation and care, enabling the caregiver a break from ongoing health care needs.

Caregivers need to be reminded of the importance of caring for themselves by getting adequate rest, eating nutritious meals, asking for help, delegating household chores, and making time for leisure activities or simply some time alone.

Family members other than the caregiver may require help to learn ways to support the caregiver.

## POWERPOINT LECTURE SLIDES *continued*

- Acknowledge the caregivers' competence
- Demonstrate care activities in the home
- Encourage return demonstration by caregivers
- Identify possible sources of outside help
- Investigate a weekend respite, if desired
- Remind caregivers to care for themselves
- Help other family members to learn ways to support the caregivers

## SUGGESTIONS FOR CLASSROOM ACTIVITIES

- Discuss the multiple roles that many middle-aged caregivers occupy, how the obligations of each role may contribute to caregiver overload, and possible measures to reduce this stress.
- Have students investigate respite programs in the local community and report findings to the class.

## SUGGESTIONS FOR CLINICAL ACTIVITIES

- Determine whether the institution offers a weekend respite program, and ask a representative of the institution to discuss this program.
- Have students interview client caregivers to determine what measures they are taking to ensure their own physical and psychological health.

# CHAPTER 9
## NURSING INFORMATICS

## RESOURCE LIBRARY

 **PRENTICE HALL NURSING MEDIALINK DVD-ROM**

Audio Glossary
NCLEX® Review
End of Unit Concept Map Activity

 **COMPANION WEBSITE**

Additional NCLEX® Review
Case Study: *Computerizing Clinical Documentation*
Application Activities:
    *Confidentiality Laws*
    *Working on the Hospital Informatics Committee*
    *Informatics Certification Exam*
Links to Resources

**IMAGE LIBRARY**

**Figure 9.1** An electronic address book is a type of database.

**Figure 9.2** Client list screen.

**Figure 9.3** This screen shows an MAR (medication administration record) for several regularly scheduled medications.

**Figure 9.4** This screen displays the client's vital signs.

**Figure 9.5** One of the strengths of an electronic medical record is its ability to alert the clinician to potential drug interactions using warnings like the one displayed.

**Figure 9.6** Lab results are displayed in a trend view graph.

**Figure 9.7** This screen displays a summary view of all available results for a particular client.

## LEARNING OUTCOME 1

Define the common components of desktop computers.

### CONCEPTS FOR LECTURE

1. Hardware, the physical parts of the computer, allows the user to enter data, perform actions of the computer's processing, and produce the output. The common components of the computers include: central processing unit (CPU) and one or more types of data input and output devices. In addition, applications or software is required to instruct the hardware to perform certain tasks.

    The CPU is the box that contains the computer hardware necessary to process and store data. Also located with the CPU are the power supply, disk drives, chips, and connections for all the other computer hardware, referred to as peripherals.

    Input devices are used to enter information into the computer. They include the keyboard, mouse, finger, and light pen or wand.

    Other possible input devices include a microphone for voice commands, scanners, and analog-to-digital converters. Scanners allow data to be copied from a paper version or other "hardcopy" text or graphics. Analog signals such as those from biometric devices convert data to digital signals that can be stored on the computer.

### POWERPOINT LECTURE SLIDES

*(NOTE: The number on each PPT Lecture Slide directly corresponds with the Concepts for Lecture.)*

 Components of Desktop Computers
- Central processing unit (CPU)
- Input devices
- Computer memory or storage
- Output devices

In order for data to be kept for later retrieval, the computer must store this data in electronic form. Data and instructions are loaded into random-access memory (RAM), which is lost when the computer is turned off. To save work, the computer stores data on magnetic hard drives or removable storage devices, e.g. portable or compact disks or flash drives.

Output devices permit the results of computer data entry to be displayed. They include the computer screen or monitor, printer, or methods to output data in audio and video displays.

| SUGGESTIONS FOR CLASSROOM ACTIVITIES | SUGGESTIONS FOR CLINICAL ACTIVITIES |
|---|---|
| • Ask the person responsible for the computer labs in the college to discuss the equipment available in the lab. | • Review the types of input and output devices used in the clinical area. |

## LEARNING OUTCOME 2

Recognize the uses of word processing, database, spreadsheet, and communications software in nursing.

### CONCEPTS FOR LECTURE

1. Computer software, also called applications, are programs that instruct the hardware to perform certain tasks. Most commonly used software includes word processing, databases, spreadsheets, utilities such as communications, and presentation graphics.

   Word processing applications save and manipulate words.

   Database programs are used to manage detailed information. They can be used to quickly search an extremely large number of records and fields for commonalities and then help the user generate detailed and complex reports. Examples include hospital client databases and pharmacy databases.

   Electronic spreadsheets are programs that manipulate words and numbers. They are used for managing budgets but are also useful for working with staffing, scheduling, invoicing, research, and other analyses.

   Communication devices require software to guide the computer in connecting to a remote device and knowing what data to send or receive. An important type of communications software is electronic mail (e-mail).

   Presentation graphics programs create charts, graphics, tables, pictures, videos, audio, and other non-text files. Many integrated software packages include graphics programs that can easily exchange materials with word processing and spreadsheet programs. Users can create "slide shows."

### POWERPOINT LECTURE SLIDES

*(NOTE: The number on each PPT Lecture Slide directly corresponds with the Concepts for Lecture.)*

1. Uses of Software in Nursing
   • Word processing
   • Databases
   • Spreadsheets
   • Communications
   • Presentation graphics

# LEARNING OUTCOME 3

Describe the uses of computers in nursing education.

## CONCEPTS FOR LECTURE

1. Computers are used extensively in all aspects of nursing education. They enhance academics for both students and faculty in a number of ways: literature access and retrieval, computer-assisted instruction (CAI), classroom technologies, distance learning, testing, and student and course management.

   Computers have improved literature access and retrieval by presenting catalogs and text of materials in a way that can be searched systematically. In addition, complete publications and materials are available in computerized formats.

   Computer-assisted instruction (CAI) helps nursing students and nurses learn and demonstrate learning. CAI is classified according to format: tutorial, drill and practice, simulation, or testing. CAI may be used by employers for required annual competency testing mandated by accrediting bodies and may also be an acceptable means of demonstrating continuing education activities required for licensure renewal.

   Many educational buildings are wired to accommodate technology including wireless technology. Projectors and liquid crystal display (LCD) panels permit computer screens to be displayed to the classroom, which allows faculty to use capabilities of the computer instead of overhead transparencies, slides, or writing on the board.

   There are several models of distance learning: asynchronous and synchronous. In asynchronous models, persons involved are not interacting at the same "real" time. The student receives course materials, communicates with faculty and other students, and submits assignments completely through mail, phone, fax, e-mail, website, and electronic "dropbox." Synchronous models involve groups of students at distant sites interacting in real time through specially equipped classrooms or through the use of chat and instant messaging.

   Another use of computerized delivery of knowledge is through e-books or a personal digital assistant (PDA). Entire textbooks are available on computers and can be searched and annotated. PDAs can store reference materials for access in various settings.

## POWERPOINT LECTURE SLIDES

*(NOTE: The number on each PPT Lecture Slide directly corresponds with the Concepts for Lecture.)*

 Computers in Nursing Education
- Literature access and retrieval
- Computer-assisted instruction (CAI)
- Classroom technologies
- Strategies for distance learning
- Testing
- Student and course management

The computer is ideal for conducting certain types of learning evaluations. Large databases of test banks can be accessed and the computer can generate different exams for each student. Answers can be scored electronically and the results analyzed quickly.

Computers are also useful for maintaining results of students' grades and attendance using spreadsheets. They may be used for faculty and course evaluation and may be used by the registrar's office to maintain student records. Students may use computers to register for classes, check their tuition bills, and see their transcripts from campus or anywhere that has a computer with Internet access.

## SUGGESTIONS FOR CLASSROOM ACTIVITIES

- Invite the college librarian to demonstrate searching the nursing cumulative indexes held by the college library.
- Demonstrate the various types of CAI used by the school of nursing.
- Describe the type of distance learning used by the college.
- Discuss the NCLEX-RN ® process and procedures.
- Demonstrate use of the college computerized system for registration and obtaining grades and transcripts.

## SUGGESTIONS FOR CLINICAL ACTIVITIES

- Send the students forms used for clinical preparation through the college e-mail system. Discuss the advantages and disadvantages of this process.
- Discuss the use of PDAs in the clinical setting (e.g., as reference for medications, laboratory values, and the nursing process).

## LEARNING OUTCOME 4

Discuss the advantages of and concerns about computerized client documentation systems.

## CONCEPTS FOR LECTURE

1. Computer-based patient records (CPRs) or electronic medical records (EMRs) permit electronic client data retrieval by caregivers, administrators, accreditors, and other persons who require the data.

   Providers can easily retrieve specific data such as trends in vital signs, immunization records, and current problems. The system can be designed to warn providers about conflicting medications or client parameters that indicate dangerous conditions. In addition, all text is legible and can be searched for keywords.

   Maintaining privacy and security of data is a significant issue. One way that computers can protect data is by user authentication via passwords or biometric identifiers (e.g., fingerprints or retinal scans).

   The American Nurses Association (ANA) developed a position statement on privacy, confidentiality of medical records, and the nurse's role (Box 9–3).

   Additional policies and procedures for protecting confidentiality of CPRs are evolving as the use of computer systems becomes more widespread.

## POWERPOINT LECTURE SLIDES

*(NOTE: The number on each PPT Lecture Slide directly corresponds with the Concepts for Lecture.)*

1 Computer-Based Patient Records (CPRs)
- Warning systems
  - Legible
  - Searchable
- Concerns
  - Privacy and security of data
  - No national standards

Currently there are no national standards for CPRs, for the specific data that should be included, nor for how the records should be organized. HIPAA regulations are playing a key role in establishing these.

---

### SUGGESTIONS FOR CLASSROOM ACTIVITIES

- Discuss the ANA position statement on privacy, confidentiality, and the nurse's role.
- Invite a nurse informaticist to discuss this role and the benefits of and concerns about computerized patient record systems.

### SUGGESTIONS FOR CLINICAL ACTIVITIES

- Review the policies and procedures for accessing computerized patient records in the institution.
- Demonstrate how to access the various components of the system.
- Discuss how security is maintained in the institution for the client's computerized patient record and the student's responsibility.

---

## LEARNING OUTCOME 5

Identify computer applications used in client assessment and care.

### CONCEPTS FOR LECTURE

1. Once CPRs are established, nurses can retrieve and display a client's physiologic parameters across time.

   Standardized nursing care plans, care maps, critical pathways, or other prewritten treatment protocols can be stored in the computer and easily placed in the electronic medical record (EMR), permitting the nurse and other health care personnel to examine progress and variance from plans.

   Computers assist nurses and other health care providers to monitor the client (for example, pulse oximetry, ECG/telemetry, and fetal apnea monitors).

   In various specialty areas of health care, clients undergo diagnostic procedures in which computers play a role. Examples include computerized axial tomography (CAT), magnetic resonance imaging (MRI), and positron emission tomography (PET), and these may be linked to directly store data in the CPR (Figure 9-7).

   Telehealth, using technology to transmit electronic data about clients to persons at distant locations and to provide primary health care to clients in remote areas, is another form of computer-assisted health care.

   Computer networks are being used in innovative ways in home care, permitting clients and families to access health care information, to e-mail a health care provider with questions or concerns, and to send data about their health status.

   Nurses who visit clients in the home are using notebook computer systems to record assessments and transmit data to the main office.

   Software programs allow the case manager to enter client data and integrate this with predesigned case-tracking templates.

### POWERPOINT LECTURE SLIDES

*(NOTE: The number on each PPT Lecture Slide directly corresponds with the Concepts for Lecture.)*

 1 Computers in Client Assessment and Care
- Display physiologic parameters
- Store and retrieve standardized plans of care
- Monitor client progress and variance from plans
  - Clinically monitor clients
- Sophisticated diagnostic testing
  - Telehealth
  - Client access to health information
- Use of notebook computer in home care
- Track progress in case management

- If possible, invite an individual involved in telehealth to describe the process, advantages, and disadvantages.
- Ask each student to select a health information website and evaluate this site using the criteria for evaluating Internet health information in Box 9-1.

**SUGGESTIONS FOR CLINICAL ACTIVITIES**

- Demonstrate various computer monitoring devices available in the clinical area (e.g., tympanic thermometer, pulse oximetry, cardiopulmonary telemetry).
- Demonstrate how the institution uses computerized care planning.
- Demonstrate the institution's intravenous or feeding pumps, showing the alarm systems.

## LEARNING OUTCOME 6

List ways computers may be used by nurse administrators in the areas of human resources, facilities management, finance, quality assurance, and accreditation.

### CONCEPTS FOR LECTURE

1. Computers may be used in human resources to maintain a database on each employee, including demographic information, licensure, salary, certification in life support, and health requirements.

    Many aspects of managing buildings and nonnursing services can be facilitated by computers, such as environmental control, security devices, and inventory management.

    Computers may be used to facilitate billing, budget development, and forecasting and planning.

    Computers can facilitate the accumulation of data for individuals and groups of clients and the analysis of data for quality assurance.

    The Joint Commission on Accreditation of Healthcare Organizations (JCAHO) has mandated that hospitals have online mechanisms to monitor quality indicators to reduce the difficulty and time involved in the accreditation process.

    Health care agencies must maintain databases of policies and procedures, standards of care, and employee accomplishment of JCAHO requirements such as continuing education and in-service education.

### POWERPOINT LECTURE SLIDES

*(NOTE: The number on each PPT Lecture Slide directly corresponds with the Concepts for Lecture.)*

1. Computers in Nursing Administration
   - Human Resources
   - Facilities management
   - Finance
   - Quality assurance
   - Accreditation

### SUGGESTIONS FOR CLASSROOM ACTIVITIES

- Invite a panel of nurse administrators to discuss how computers assist in completing tasks in the areas of personnel, facilities management, finance, quality assurance, and accreditation.

### SUGGESTIONS FOR CLINICAL ACTIVITIES

- Invite a representative from nursing administration to discuss the influence of JCAHO on computerization of the institution's records, policies, and procedures and how this has influenced the nursing administrator's role.

## LEARNING OUTCOME 7

Identify the role of computers in each step of the research process.

### CONCEPTS FOR LECTURE

1. Computers are invaluable assistants in the conduct of both qualitative and quantitative research in each step of the research process: problem identification, literature review, research design, data collection and analysis, and research dissemination.

### POWERPOINT LECTURE SLIDES

*(NOTE: The number on each PPT Lecture Slide directly corresponds with the Concepts for Lecture.)*

 Computers in the Research Process
   - Problem identification and literature review
     - Search databases for current research
     - Availability of full text journal articles

The computer can be useful in locating current literature about the problem and related concepts to help identify and describe the problem.

The time-consuming review of literature can be made less time consuming by computer access to on-line or CD-ROM bibliographic databases that facilitate searches. In addition, the increase in availability of full-text journal articles online has made electronic literature searches even more productive.

During research design, computers may be used to search the literature for instruments that have already been established or to design and test instruments that need to be developed for the study.

Forms can be created on the computer for data collection. When data have been collected and coded, other programs can be used to calculate descriptive and analytic statistics, and to display output in tables, charts, lists, and other easily read formats.

Computer word processing programs are used to author the final reports of research and to send the reports to various readerships.

Computers are frequently used to present research at meetings.

In addition, information about grant funding may be found online; applications may be downloaded and then submitted electronically.

- Research design
  - Search the literature for instruments
  - Design and test instruments
- Data collection and analysis
  - Create forms for data collection
  - Calculate descriptive and analytic statistics
  - Display output in tables, charts, lists, and other easily read formats
- Research dissemination
  - Word processing programs used to author the final reports
  - Send the reports to various readerships
  - Frequently used to present research at meetings
- Grants
  - Locate
  - Download and submit funding applications

## SUGGESTIONS FOR CLASSROOM ACTIVITIES

- Invite a nurse researcher or nursing student enrolled in a doctoral program to discuss the use of computers in each step of the research process.

# CHAPTER 10
# CRITICAL THINKING
# AND THE NURSING PROCESS

## RESOURCE LIBRARY

 **PRENTICE HALL NURSING MEDIALINK DVD-ROM**

Audio Glossary
NCLEX® Review
Video: Thinking Critically

 **COMPANION WEBSITE**

Additional NCLEX® Review
Case Study: *Examining an Increase in Pressure Ulcers*
Application Activity: *Practicing Critical Thinking*
Links to Resources

**IMAGE LIBRARY**

**Figure 10.1** Mind Map for Critical Thinking in Nursing.

## LEARNING OUTCOME 1

Discuss the skills and attitudes of critical thinking.

### CONCEPTS FOR LECTURE

1. Critical-thinking skills include the ability to do critical analysis, to perform inductive and deductive reasoning, to make valid inferences, to differentiate facts from opinions, to evaluate the credibility of information sources, to clarify concepts, and to recognize assumptions.

   Critical analysis is the application of a set of questions to a particular situation or idea to determine essential information and ideas and to discard superfluous information and ideas.

   In inductive reasoning, generalizations are formed from a set of facts or observations. Inductive reasoning moves from specific examples (premises) to generalized conclusions—for example, from clinical signs and symptoms to diagnosis. Deductive reasoning is reasoning from the general premise to the specific conclusion. The premise must be valid or the conclusion may not be valid.

   It is important to differentiate statements of fact, inference, judgment, and opinion in critical thinking. A fact can be verified through investigation. Inferences are conclusions drawn from facts, going beyond facts to make a statement about something not currently known. Judgments are evaluation of facts or information that reflect values or other criteria; a type of opinion. Opinions are beliefs formed over time and include judgments that may fit facts or be in error.

   Evaluating the credibility of information sources is an important step in critical thinking because not all sources are accurate or reliable. It may be necessary to check information with other sources or other informants.

### POWERPOINT LECTURE SLIDES

*(NOTE: The number on each PPT Lecture Slide directly corresponds with the Concepts for Lecture.)*

[1] Critical-Thinking Skills
   - Critical analysis
   - Inductive and deductive reasoning
   - Make valid inferences
   - Differentiate facts from opinions
   - Evaluate the credibility of information sources
   - Clarify concepts
   - Recognize assumptions

[2] Critical-Thinking Attitudes
   - Independence
   - Fair-mindedness
   - Insight
   - Intellectual humility
   - Intellectual courage
   - Integrity
   - Perseverance
   - Confidence
   - Curiosity

Clarifying concepts means that agreeing on the meaning of terms is important since individuals may have different interpretations of words or situations.

2. Critical thinkers have certain attitudes, including independence, fair-mindedness, insight, intellectual humility, intellectual courage, integrity, perseverance, confidence, and curiosity.

Critical thinking requires that individuals think for themselves, examine a wide range of ideas, learn from them, and make their own judgments. Critical thinkers are not easily swayed by the opinion of others, but take responsibility for their own views.

Fair-mindedness means assessing all viewpoints with the same standards and not basing judgments on personal or group bias or prejudice. It helps one to consider opposing points of view and to try to understand new ideas fully before rejecting or accepting them.

Critical thinkers are open to the possibility that their personal biases or social pressures and customs could unduly affect their own thinking. They actively examine their own biases and bring them to awareness each time they think or make a decision.

Intellectual humility means having the awareness of the limits of one's own knowledge.

With an attitude of courage, one is willing to consider and examine fairly one's own ideas or views, especially those to which one may have a strong negative reaction. This type of courage comes from recognizing that beliefs are sometimes false or misleading. Courage is needed to be true to new thinking, especially if social penalties for nonconformity are severe.

Intellectual integrity requires that individuals apply the same rigorous standards of proof to their own knowledge and beliefs as they apply to the knowledge and beliefs of others.

Critical thinkers show perseverance in finding effective solutions. This determination enables them to clarify concepts and sort out related issues in spite of frustration resisting the temptation to find a quick and easy answer.

Critical thinkers believe that well-reasoned thinking will lead to trustworthy conclusions. They cultivate an attitude of confidence in the reasoning process and examine emotion-laden arguments using the standards for evaluating thoughts.

The mind of the critical thinker is filled with questions. The critical thinker may value traditions but is not afraid to examine traditions to be sure they are still valid.

## SUGGESTIONS FOR CLASSROOM ACTIVITIES

- Ask the students to describe individuals they know who demonstrate one or more of the critical-thinking attitudes. How do they believe this influences the person's actions?
- Divide the students into groups. Assign each group one of the critical-thinking attitudes. Ask each group to develop a description of a nurse who demonstrates this attitude and share it with the group.

## SUGGESTIONS FOR CLINICAL ACTIVITIES

- Ask the students to share situations in which they have used trial and error in problem solving. Discuss reasons why trial and error may or may not be a good problem-solving method to use in patient care.
- At the completion of a clinical day, have the students write down all the ways they used creativity in their client care. How did this affect the outcomes of their client care?

# LEARNING OUTCOME 2

Describe the significance of developing critical-thinking abilities in order to practice safe, effective, and professional nursing care.

## CONCEPTS FOR LECTURE

1. Critical thinking is essential to safe, competent, skillful nursing practice.

    Decisions about client care and distribution of limited resources force nurses to think and act in areas where there are neither clear answers nor standard procedures and where conflicting forces turn decision making into a complex process.

2. The top ten reasons to improve thinking include: things change and will continue to change; clients are sicker with multiple problems; there is more consumer involvement; nurse must be able to move from one setting to another; rapid change and information explosion require new learning and workplace skills; consumers and payers require evidence of benefits, efficiency, and results; today's progress may create new problems that can't be solved with old ways of thinking; redesigning care delivery and nursing curriculum are useless if nurses don't have the thinking skills needed to deal with today's world; it is possible to improve thinking; and the ability to focus thinking to get results can make the difference between success and failure. (See Box 10–1.)

## POWERPOINT LECTURE SLIDES

*(NOTE: The number on each PPT Lecture Slide directly corresponds with the Concepts for Lecture.)*

 Significance of Critical Thinking
- Essential for safe, competent, skillful nursing practice
- Rapid and continuing growth of knowledge
- Make complex and important decisions
- Draw meaningful information from other subject areas
- Work in rapidly changing, stressful environments
- Recognize important cues, respond quickly, and adapt interventions

 Top 10 Reasons to Improve Thinking
- Things change
- Sicker client
- More consumer involvement
- Move from one setting to another
- Rapid change and information explosion
- Requirement for evidence of benefits, efficiency, and results
- New problems can't be solved with old ways of thinking
- Thinking skills needed to deal with today's world
- Possible to improve thinking
- Difference between success and failure

## SUGGESTIONS FOR CLASSROOM ACTIVITIES

- Using the top 10 reasons to improve thinking (See Box 10-1 in the text book), have the students discuss why each of the reasons creates a need for nurses to improve their thinking.
- Give situations where routine actions may be inadequate to deal with these situations. Ask the students to discuss how critical thinking could assist nurses to deal with these situations.

## SUGGESTIONS FOR CLINICAL ACTIVITIES

- During clinical conference, ask the students to give examples of clinical situations where nurses must apply critical thinking to their nursing practice.
- Ask the students to describe clinical situations in which they applied critical-thinking skills.

# LEARNING OUTCOME 3

Discuss the relationships among the nursing process, critical thinking, the problem-solving process, and the decision-making process.

## CONCEPTS FOR LECTURE

1. There is a relationship between the following: nursing process, critical thinking, problem solving process and decision-making process.
2. The nursing process is a systematic, rational method of planning and providing individualized nursing care.
3. The problem-solving process is obtaining information that clarifies the nature of a problem and suggests possible solutions.
4. Decision making is a critical-thinking process for choosing the best actions to meet a desired goal.
5. Critical thinking underlies each step of the nursing, problem-solving, and decision-making processes. Nurses are expected to use critical thinking to solve client problems and to make better decisions.

    The nursing process is a modified problem-solving process.

    Table 10–5 presents a comparison between the nursing process and the decision-making process.

## POWERPOINT LECTURE SLIDES

*(NOTE: The number on each PPT Lecture Slide directly corresponds with the Concepts for Lecture.)*

1. Relationships Among Processes
   - Critical thinking
   - Nursing process
   - Problem-solving process
   - Decision-making process

2. Nursing Process
   - Method of planning and providing individualized care
   - Modified problem-solving process
   - Assess, diagnose, plan, implement, evaluate

3. Problem-Solving Process
   - Clarifies the nature of a problem and suggests possible solutions

4. Decision-Making Process
   - Choosing the best actions to meet a desired goal
     - Identify purpose
     - Set and weigh criteria
     - Seek and examine alternatives
     - Project, implement, and evaluate outcome

5. Critical Thinking
   - Underlies each step of the nursing, problem-solving, and decision-making processes

## SUGGESTIONS FOR CLASSROOM ACTIVITIES

- In order to assist students to recognize the differences and similarities among critical thinking, problem solving, and decision making, obtain several children's puzzles that do not have borders. Place each puzzle into a bag without the picture to show what the completed puzzle represents. Take one piece from each puzzle. Exchange the pieces for two of the puzzles. Hide another piece in the classroom, keep one piece, and so on, so that there is a problem to be solved. Divide the students into groups and ask each group to complete the puzzles. Have one group member record the process used to complete the puzzles, focusing on critical-thinking skills and attitudes, problem solving, and decision-making steps. Have each group report findings to the class. Use the findings as a basis to discuss these processes and critical thinking.
- Have groups of students draw a diagram of the relationship among critical-thinking, problem-solving, and decision-making processes on butcher block paper. The MIND MAP in the text (Figure 10–1) may provide a starting point. Post diagrams and have the students discuss the drawings. Discuss how the nursing process would fit into these diagrams.

## SUGGESTIONS FOR CLINICAL ACTIVITIES

- Have the students share examples of the use of decision-making and problem-solving processes as they apply the nursing process to care of assigned clients.

Explore ways of demonstrating critical thinking.

## CONCEPTS FOR LECTURE

1. The nurse might benefit from a rigorous personal assessment to determine which attitudes of critical thinking he or she already possesses and which need to be cultivated.

   The nurse first determines which attitudes are held strongly and form a base for thinking and which are minimally held or not at all.

   The nurse can also reflect on situations where he or she made decisions that were later regretted and analyze thinking processes and attitudes or ask a friend or trusted colleague to assess them.

   Reflection, at every step of critical thinking and nursing care, helps examine the ways in which the nurse gathers and analyzes data, makes decisions, and determines the effectiveness of interventions.

   The nurse needs to make deliberate efforts to cultivate critical-thinking abilities. For example, to develop fair-mindedness the nurse could deliberately seek out information that is in opposition to his or her own views in order to practice understanding and learning to be open to other viewpoints.

   Nurses should increase their tolerance for ideas that contradict previously held beliefs and then should practice suspending judgment.

   Nurses may attend conferences in clinical or educational settings that support open examination of all sides of an issue demonstrating respect for opposing viewpoints.

   Nurses need to review the standards for evaluating thinking and apply these to their own thinking. If nurses are aware of their own thinking—while they are thinking—they can detect thinking errors.

   Nurses in leadership positions should be aware of the climate for thinking they establish and actively create a stimulating environment that encourages differences of opinion and fair examination of ideas and options.

   Leaders should encourage colleagues to examine evidence carefully before they come to conclusions and to avoid "group think," the tendency to defer unthinkingly to the will of the group.

## POWERPOINT LECTURE SLIDES

*(NOTE: The number on each PPT Lecture Slide directly corresponds with the Concepts for Lecture.)*

 Demonstrating Critical Thinking
- Rigorous personal assessment
- Reflection
- Analysis of thinking processes and attitudes
- Cultivation of critical-thinking abilities
- Attendance at conferences
- Awareness of own thinking—while thinking
- Create environments that support critical thinking

## SUGGESTIONS FOR CLASSROOM ACTIVITIES

- Administer a critical-thinking inventory to the students. Discuss how knowledge of one's own style can be useful.
- Develop a list of controversial issues in health care (e.g., abortion, euthanasia, withholding fluids and food at the end of life). Ask the students to identify their position on each. Have the students write a short paper taking the viewpoint opposite to their viewpoint. Ask them to include in the paper how this exercise helped them learn about critical-thinking attitudes.

## SUGGESTIONS FOR CLINICAL ACTIVITIES

- Ask the nurse administrator on the unit to discuss how he or she creates an environment that supports critical thinking on the clinical unit.
- Give the students a clinical situation. For example, it is time for the schedule to be developed for the winter holidays. The administrator has listed the following options for making this decision: the administrator will decide, staff can submit requests and the administrator will then decide, the staff will decide as a group, or the selection will be random. Have the students decide which option they would like, using critical-thinking skills and attitudes. Discuss the process and how this exercise contributed to developing critical-thinking skills.

# CHAPTER 11
## ASSESSING

## RESOURCE LIBRARY

**PRENTICE HALL NURSING MEDIALINK DVD-ROM**

Audio Glossary
NCLEX® Review
Animations:
    Anatomical Landmarks
    Introduction to Body Systems
A & P Review:
    Anterior View
    Posterior View
    Body Cavity
    Lymphatic System
    Body Organization

**COMPANION WEBSITE**

Additional NCLEX® Review
Case Study: *Down Syndrome Client*
Application Activity: *Care of a Disorganized Elderly
    Client*
Links to Resources

**IMAGE LIBRARY**

**Figure 11.1** The nursing process in action.
**Figure 11.2** The five overlapping phases of the
nursing process.

**Figure 11.3** Assessing.
**Figure 11.4** Assessment for Amanda Aquilini.

## LEARNING OUTCOME 1

Describe the phases of the nursing process.

### CONCEPTS FOR LECTURE

1. The five phases of the nursing process are assessing, diagnosing, planning, implementing, and evaluating.
2. Assessing includes collecting, organizing, validating, and documenting data in order to establish a database about the client's response to health concerns or illness and the ability to manage health care.
3. Diagnosing includes analyzing and synthesizing data in order to identify client strengths as well as health problems that can be prevented or resolved by collaborative and independent nursing interventions and to develop a list of nursing and collaborative problems.
4. Planning includes determining how to prevent, reduce, or resolve the identified priority client problems; how to support client strengths; and how to implement nursing interventions in an organized, individualized, and goal-directed manner in order to develop an individualized care plan that specifies client goals/desired outcomes, and related nursing interventions.
5. Implementing includes carrying out (or delegating) and documenting the planned nursing interventions in order to assist the client to meet desired goals/outcomes, promote wellness, prevent illness and disease, restore health, and facilitate coping with altered functioning.

### POWERPOINT LECTURE SLIDES

*(NOTE: The number on each PPT Lecture Slide directly corresponds
with the Concepts for Lecture.)*

**1** Phases of the Nursing Process
- Assessing
- Diagnosing
- Planning
- Implementing
- Evaluating

**2** Assessing
- Collecting data
- Organizing data
- Validating data
- Documenting data
    ○ Goals
- Establish a database about the client's response to health concerns or illness

**3** Diagnosing
- Analyzing and synthesizing data
    ○ Goals
- Identify client strengths

6. Evaluating includes measuring the degree to which goals/outcomes have been achieved and identifying factors that positively or negatively influence goal achievement in order to determine whether to continue, modify, or terminate the plan of care. (See Table 11–1.)

- Identify health problems that can be prevented or resolved
- Develop a list of nursing and collaborative problems

**4** Planning
- Determining how to prevent, reduce, or resolve identified priority client problems
- Determining how to support client strengths
- Determining how to implement nursing interventions in an organized, individualized, and goal-directed manner
  ○ Goals
- Develop an individualized care plan that specifies client goals/desired outcomes
- Related nursing interventions

**5** Implementing
- Carrying out (or delegating) and documenting planned nursing interventions
  ○ Goals
- Assist the client to meet desired goals/outcomes
- Promote wellness
- Prevent illness and disease
- Restore health
- Facilitate coping with altered functioning

**6** Evaluating
- Measuring the degree to which goals/outcomes have been achieved
- Identifying factors that positively or negatively influence goal achievement
  ○ Goals
- Determine whether to continue, modify, or terminate the plan of care

---

**SUGGESTIONS FOR CLASSROOM ACTIVITIES**

- Provide the students with a list of activities representative of the various phases of the nursing process and ask them to classify each activity into the appropriate phase.

**SUGGESTIONS FOR CLINICAL ACTIVITIES**

- Have the students identify elements of the nursing process performed throughout their clinical day.

---

## LEARNING OUTCOME 2

Identify major characteristics of the nursing process.

**CONCEPTS FOR LECTURE**

1. The nursing process has distinctive characteristics that enable the nurse to respond to the changing health status of the client. These characteristics include its cyclic and dynamic nature, client centeredness, a focus on problem solving and decision making, interpersonal and collaborative style, universal applicability, and use of critical thinking.

**POWERPOINT LECTURE SLIDES**

*(NOTE: The number on each PPT Lecture Slide directly corresponds with the Concepts for Lecture.)*

**1** Characteristics of the Nursing Process
- Cyclic and dynamic nature
- Client centeredness
- Focus on problem solving and decision making
- Interpersonal and collaborative style
- Universal applicability
- Use of critical thinking

| SUGGESTIONS FOR CLASSROOM ACTIVITIES | SUGGESTIONS FOR CLINICAL ACTIVITIES |
|---|---|
| • Give examples of how inadequate or inaccurate assessment data affect the other phases of the nursing process.<br>• Give examples of goals written as client goals and goals written as nursing goals. Ask the students to identify the patient-centered goals.<br>• Have the students discuss why the nursing process can be used in all types of health care agencies and with clients across the life span. | • Have the students provide examples of problem solving, decision making, and critical thinking that they employed or observed other nurses employ while providing care using the nursing process. |

## LEARNING OUTCOME 3

Identify the purpose of assessing.

### CONCEPTS FOR LECTURE

1. The purpose of assessing is to establish a database about the client's response to health concerns or illness and the ability to manage health care needs and is a continuous process carried out during all phases of the nursing process.
2. There are four types of assessment: initial assessment, problem-focused assessment, emergency assessment, and time-lapsed reassessment. (See Table 11–3.)
3. Initial assessment is performed within a specified time after admission to a health care agency for the purpose of establishing a complete database for problem identification, reference, and future comparison.
4. Problem-focused assessment is an ongoing process integrated with nursing care to determine the status of a specific problem identified in an earlier assessment.
5. Emergency assessment occurs during any physiologic or psychologic crisis of the client to identify the life-threatening problems and to identify new or overlooked problems.
6. Time-lapsed reassessment occurs several months after the initial assessment to compare the client's current status to baseline data previously obtained.

### POWERPOINT LECTURE SLIDES

*(NOTE: The number on each PPT Lecture Slide directly corresponds with the Concepts for Lecture.)*

**1** Assessment
- Establishes a database of information
  ○ Client's responses to health concerns or illness
  ○ Ability to manage health care needs
- A continuous process

**2** Types of Assessment
- Initial
- Problem-focused
- Emergency
- Time-lapsed

**3** Initial Assessment
- Performed within a specified time period
- Establish complete database
- Problem identification
- Reference
- Future comparison

**4** Problem-Focused Assessment
- Ongoing process
- Integrated with nursing care
- Determines status of a specific problem

**5** Emergency Assessment
- Performed during physiologic or psychologic crises
- Identify life-threatening problems
- Identify new or overlooked problems

**6** Time-Lapsed Assessment
- Occurs several months after initial assessment
- Compares current status to baseline

| SUGGESTIONS FOR CLASSROOM ACTIVITIES | SUGGESTIONS FOR CLINICAL ACTIVITIES |
|---|---|
| • Provide examples of the four types of assessment and have the students identify similarities and differences in these. | • Have the students compare and contrast the initial, problem-focused, and emergency assessments of several clients.<br>• Review the assessment forms used in the institution. |

## LEARNING OUTCOME 4

Identify the four major activities associated with the assessing phase.

### CONCEPTS FOR LECTURE

1. The assessment process involves four closely related activities: collecting, organizing, validating, and documenting data. Collecting data is the process of gathering information about a client's health status. Organizing data is categorizing data systematically using a specified format. Validating data is the act of "double-checking" or verifying data to confirm that it is accurate and factual. Documenting is accurately and factually recording data.

### POWERPOINT LECTURE SLIDES

*(NOTE: The number on each PPT Lecture Slide directly corresponds with the Concepts for Lecture.)*

1 Assessment Activities
- Collecting data
- Organizing data
- Validating data
- Documenting data

## LEARNING OUTCOME 5

Differentiate objective and subjective data and primary and secondary data.

### CONCEPTS FOR LECTURE

1. Subjective data, also referred to as symptoms or covert data, are apparent only to the person affected and can be described only by that person. Subjective data include the client's sensations, feelings, values, beliefs, attitudes, and perception of personal health status and life situations.
2. Objective data, also referred to as signs or overt data, are detectable by an observer or can be measured or tested against an accepted standard. Objective data can be seen, heard, felt, or smelled, and are obtained through observation or physical examination. (See Table 11-4.)
3. The primary source of data is the client.
4. All sources of data other than the client are considered secondary sources or indirect sources. These include family and other support people, other health care professionals, records and reports, laboratory and diagnostic analyses and relevant literature. All data from secondary sources should be validated, if possible.

### POWERPOINT LECTURE SLIDES

*(NOTE: The number on each PPT Lecture Slide directly corresponds with the Concepts for Lecture.)*

1 Subjective Data (Symptoms or Covert Data)
- Apparent only to the person affected
- Can be described only by person affected
- Includes sensations, feelings, values, beliefs, attitudes, and perception of personal health status and life situations

2 Objective Data (Signs or Overt Data)
- Detectable by an observer
- Can be measured or tested against an accepted standard
- Can be seen, heard, felt, or smelled
- Obtained through observation or physical examination

3 Primary Data
- The client is the source

4 Secondary Data
- All other sources of data
- Should be validated, if possible

---

### SUGGESTIONS FOR CLASSROOM ACTIVITIES

- Give the students a case study. Ask them to identify subjective and objective data as well as primary and secondary sources.
- Discuss methods of validating secondary sources.

### SUGGESTIONS FOR CLINICAL ACTIVITIES

- Have each student discuss the assessment data for his or her client. Ask the students to identify subjective and objective data as well as primary and secondary sources.

# LEARNING OUTCOME 6

Identify three methods of data collection, and give examples of how each is useful.

## CONCEPTS FOR LECTURE

1. The principal methods used to collect data are observing, interviewing, and examining.
2. To observe means to gather data by using the senses. Although nurses observe mainly through sight, most of the senses are engaged during careful observation.

   Observation is useful for gathering data such as skin color or lesions (vision), body or breath odors (smell), lung or heart sounds (hearing), and skin temperature (touch).
3. Interviewing is a planned communication or a conversation with a purpose. Interviewing is useful to identify problems of mutual concern, evaluate change, teach, provide support, or provide counseling or therapy.
4. Examining, referred to as physical examination or physical assessment, is a systematic data collection method that uses observation (i.e., the senses of sight, hearing, smell, and touch) and techniques of inspection, auscultation, palpation, and percussion to detect health problems. Examining is useful for assessing all body parts and comparing findings on each side of the body.

## POWERPOINT LECTURE SLIDES

*(NOTE: The number on each PPT Lecture Slide directly corresponds with the Concepts for Lecture.)*

**1** Methods of Data Collection
- Observing
- Interviewing
- Examining

**2** Observing
- Gathering data using the senses
- Used to obtain following types of data:
  - Skin color (vision)
  - Body or breath odors (smell)
  - Lung or heart sounds (hearing)
  - Skin temperature (touch)

**3** Interviewing
- Planned communication or a conversation with a purpose
- Used to
  - Identify problems of mutual concern
  - Evaluate change
  - Teach
  - Provide support
  - Provide counseling or therapy

**4** Examining (Physical Examination or Physical Assessment)
- Systematic data-collection method
- Uses observation and inspection, auscultation, palpation, and percussion
- Used to obtain data such as
  - Obtaining blood pressure
  - Pulses
  - Heart and lungs sounds
  - Skin temperature and moisture
  - Muscle strength

## SUGGESTIONS FOR CLASSROOM ACTIVITIES

- Set up a manikin in the nursing laboratory incorporating various types of equipment. Include in the setup several problems, such as a dressing that is partially unattached or the "client's" hand hanging over the bed. Give the students 5 minutes to observe the scenario. Discuss observations made and the process used to make the observations.
- Discuss examples of how the sense of smell is used in client assessment.

## SUGGESTIONS FOR CLINICAL ACTIVITIES

- Have the students develop a systematic assessment to use when assessing their clients on entry into the client's room. The assessment should include observation, interviewing, and examining.
- Have the students employ the assessment process developed and report results. Ask the students to modify the process based on these results.
- Assign several students to interview staff nurses about the systematic assessment process they use in their clinical practice and report the findings to the group.

## LEARNING OUTCOME 7

Compare directive and nondirective approaches to interviewing.

### CONCEPTS FOR LECTURE

1. The interviewing approach can be directive or nondirective.
2. A directive interview is highly structured and elicits specific information. The nurse establishes the purpose of the interview and controls the interview. Nurses frequently use directive interviews to gather and to give information when time is limited (e.g., in an emergency situation).
3. During a nondirective interview, or rapport-building interview, the nurse allows the client to control the purpose, subject matter, and pacing. A combination of directive and nondirective approaches is usually appropriate during the information-gathering interview.

### POWERPOINT LECTURE SLIDES

*(NOTE: The number on each PPT Lecture Slide directly corresponds with the Concepts for Lecture.)*

**1** Approaches to Interviewing
- Directive
- Nondirective

**2** Directive Approach
- Nurse establishes purpose
- Nurse controls the interview
- Used to gather and give information when time is limited, e.g., in an emergency

**3** Nondirective Approach (Rapport-Building)
- Client controls the purpose, subject matter, and pacing
- Combination of directive and nondirective approaches usually appropriate during the information-gathering interview

### SUGGESTIONS FOR CLASSROOM ACTIVITIES

- Role-play an admission interview with one student playing the role of the client, another the client's family member, and another the nurse. Ask the other students to identify directive and nondirective components of the interview.
- Present several clinical situations and ask the students to identify which type of interviewing would best meet the needs of the client and why.

### SUGGESTIONS FOR CLINICAL ACTIVITIES

- Ask the students to describe clinical situations where either a directive or nondirective interview was used. Discuss the outcomes of the interviews and ask students how they would modify the approach, if necessary, for future interviews.

## LEARNING OUTCOME 8

Compare closed and open-ended questions, providing examples and listing advantages and disadvantages of each.

### CONCEPTS FOR LECTURE

1. Questioning techniques for interviewing include both closed and open-ended questions.
2. Closed questions are restrictive and generally require only "yes" or "no" or short factual answers giving specific information. Closed questions often begin with "when," "where," "who," "what," "do," or "is." Examples of closed questions are "What medications did you take?" or "Are you having pain now?" Closed questions are more effectively controlled by interviewer, require less effort from the client, may be less threatening, obtain information more rapidly than if volunteered, are easily documented, and easier for the unskilled interviewer to use; however, closed questions may provide too little information, may not reveal how client feels, may inhibit volunteering of information by the client, may inhibit communication and convey lack of interest. (See Box 11-2).

### POWERPOINT LECTURE SLIDES

*(NOTE: The number on each PPT Lecture Slide directly corresponds with the Concepts for Lecture.)*

**1** Questioning Techniques
- Closed questions
- Open-ended questions

**2** Closed Question
- Restrictive
  - Yes or no
  - Short/factual
- Less effort and information from client
- "What medications did you take?"
- "Are you having pain now?"

**3** Open-Ended Question
- Specify broad topic to be discussed
- Invite longer answers

3. Open-ended questions invite clients to discover and explore, elaborate, clarify, or illustrate their thoughts or feelings. An open-ended question specifies only the broad topic to be discussed, invites answers longer than one or two words, and gives clients the freedom to divulge only the information that they are ready to disclose. The open-ended question is useful at the beginning of an interview or to change topics and to elicit attitudes. Open-ended questions may begin with "what" or "how." Examples of open-ended questions include "How have you been feeling lately?" or "What would you like to talk about today?" Box 11–2 lists selected advantages and disadvantages of open-ended questions.

- Get more information from client
- Useful to change topics and elicit attitudes
- "How have you been feeling lately?"
- "What would you like to talk about today?"

## SUGGESTIONS FOR CLASSROOM ACTIVITIES

- Divide the students into groups. Assign each group a client scenario (e.g., a client with an injured ankle who enters an emergency department, or a client arriving for same-day surgery). Have each group demonstrate the use of open-ended and closed questions to obtain required data from the client.
- Provide examples of the advantages and disadvantages of open-ended and closed questions.

## SUGGESTIONS FOR CLINICAL ACTIVITIES

- Ask the students to present examples of open-ended and closed questions used with their clients during the clinical day. Discuss whether the answers provided to the questions elicited the information needed and how the students would modify the questions if necessary.
- Discuss situations the students have observed in the clinical setting when the type of question asked was inappropriate and how they would rephrase the question to obtain the needed information.
- Have the students list the types of questions asked during shift report. Identify whether the questions were closed or open-ended.

## LEARNING OUTCOME 9

Describe important aspects of the interview setting.

### CONCEPTS FOR LECTURE

1. Each interview is influenced by time, place, seating arrangement, distance, and language.
2. Nurses need to plan interviews for when clients are physically comfortable and interruptions are minimal. Schedule interviews in the home at a time selected by the client.
3. A well-lit, well-ventilated room that is relatively free of noise, movements, and distractions encourages communication. A place where others cannot overhear or see the client is necessary.

    In the hospital, if the nurse stands and looks down on the client, the nurse risks intimidating the client. Sitting at a 45-degree angle to the bed is less formal than sitting behind a table or standing at the foot of the bed. The client may feel less confronted if there is an overbed table between the client and nurse during the initial interview. A seating arrangement with the nurse behind a desk and the

### POWERPOINT LECTURE SLIDES

*(NOTE: The number on each PPT Lecture Slide directly corresponds with the Concepts for Lecture.)*

1. The Interview Setting
   - Time
   - Place
   - Seating arrangements
   - Distance
   - Language

2. Time
   - Client free of pain
   - Limited interruptions

3. Place
   - Private
   - Comfortable environment
   - Limited distractions

client seated across suggests a formal, superior and subordinate setting. If both parties sit on chairs at right angles to a desk or table a few feet apart, a less formal atmosphere is created and the nurse and client feel on equal terms. In groups, a horseshoe or circular chair arrangement can avoid a superior or head-of-the-table position.

5. The distance between the interviewer and interviewee should be neither too small nor too great because people feel uncomfortable when talking to someone who is too close or too far away.

6. Failure to communicate in a language the client can understand is a form of discrimination. The nurse must convert medical terminology into common English usage. Interpreters or translators are needed if the client and the nurse do not speak the same language or dialect.

4 Seating Arrangement
- Hospital
- Office or clinic
  - Group

5 Distance
- Comfortable

6 Language
- Use easily-understood terminology
- Interpreter or translator

---

### SUGGESTIONS FOR CLASSROOM ACTIVITIES

- Demonstrate various seating arrangements and ask the students to identify the advantage or disadvantage of each.
- Demonstrate distance and its influence on the interview setting.

### SUGGESTIONS FOR CLINICAL ACTIVITIES

- Discuss the institution's availability of interpreters.
- Ask the students to discuss methods to arrange the interview setting in the clinical area to best facilitate an admission interview.

---

## LEARNING OUTCOME 10

Contrast various frameworks used for nursing assessment.

### CONCEPTS FOR LECTURE

1. Most schools of nursing and health care agencies have developed their own structured assessment format. Many are based on selected nursing models or frameworks. Examples include Gordon's functional health patterns, Orem's self-care model, and Roy's adaptation model. The assessment formats flow from the model or framework selected (See Boxes 11-4, 11-5, and 11-6). Wellness models are used to assist clients to identify health risks and to explore lifestyle and health behaviors, beliefs, values, and attitudes that influence levels of wellness.

2. Nonnursing models and frameworks from other disciplines may also be helpful for organizing data and are narrower than the model required in nursing; therefore, they usually must be used in combination with other approaches to obtain a complete history. Examples include body systems model, Maslow's hierarchy of needs, and developmental theories.

### POWERPOINT LECTURE SLIDES

*(NOTE: The number on each PPT Lecture Slide directly corresponds with the Concepts for Lecture.)*

1 Frameworks for Nursing Assessment
- Nursing Models Framework
  - Gordon's functional health pattern framework
  - Orem's self-care model
  - Roy's adaptation model
- Wellness Models

2 Nonnursing Models
- Body systems model
- Maslow's hierarchy of needs
- Developmental theories

---

### SUGGESTIONS FOR CLASSROOM ACTIVITIES

- Discuss the nursing model or framework used by the school and how this influences nursing assessment.

### SUGGESTIONS FOR CLINICAL ACTIVITIES

- Review the nursing assessment forms used in the institution. Discuss the model underlying these forms.

---

# CHAPTER 12
## DIAGNOSING

## RESOURCE LIBRARY

 **PRENTICE HALL NURSING MEDIALINK DVD-ROM**

Audio Glossary
NCLEX® Review

 **COMPANION WEBSITE**

Additional NCLEX® Review
Case Study: *Selecting Nursing Diagnoses for Client with Pneumonia*
Application Activity: *Resources for a Chronically Ill Child*
Links to Resources

 **IMAGE LIBRARY**

**Figure 12.1** Diagnosing.
**Figure 12.2** Decision tree for differentiating among nursing diagnoses, collaborative problems, and medical diagnoses.

**Figure 12.3** Taxonomy II.

---

## LEARNING OUTCOME 1

Differentiate various types of nursing diagnoses.

### CONCEPTS FOR LECTURE

1. There are five types of nursing diagnoses: actual, risk, wellness, possible, and syndrome.
2. An actual diagnosis is a client problem that is present at the time of the nursing assessment. An actual nursing diagnosis is based on the presence of associated signs and symptoms.
3. A risk diagnosis is a clinical judgment that a problem does not exist, but the presence of risk factors indicates that a problem is likely to develop unless nurses intervene. There are no current signs or symptoms at present.
4. A wellness diagnosis "describes human responses to levels of wellness in an individual, family, or community that have a readiness enhancement."
5. A possible diagnosis is one in which evidence about a health problem is incomplete or unclear. It requires more data to either support or refute it.
6. A syndrome diagnosis is associated with a cluster of other diagnoses.

### POWERPOINT LECTURE SLIDES

*(NOTE: The number on each PPT Lecture Slide directly corresponds with the Concepts for Lecture.)*

**1** Types of Nursing Diagnosis
- Actual
- Risk
- Wellness
- Possible
- Syndrome

**2** Actual Diagnosis
- Problem present at the time of the assessment
- Presence of associated signs and symptoms

**3** Risk Diagnosis
- Problem does not exist
- Presence of risk factors

**4** Wellness Diagnosis
- Readiness for enhancement

**5** Possible Diagnosis
- Evidence about a health problem incomplete or unclear
- Requires more data to either support or to refute it

**6** Syndrome Diagnosis
- Associated with a cluster of other diagnoses

## Suggestions for Classroom Activities

- Provide the students with a list of nursing diagnoses. Ask the students to classify these according to type of nursing diagnosis.
- Provide the students with one or more case studies. Have the students decide whether there is no problem, a potential problem, a possible problem, or an actual problem. Discuss rationales for the classifications.

## Suggestions for Clinical Activities

- Have the students identify the types of nursing diagnoses established for their clients using the criteria in the textbook.

---

# LEARNING OUTCOME 2

Identify the components of a nursing diagnosis.

## Concepts for Lecture

1. A nursing diagnosis has three components: the problem and its definition, the etiology, and the defining characteristics.
2. The problem statement, or diagnostic label, describes the client's health problem or response for which nursing therapy is given. It describes the health status clearly and concisely in a few words. The purpose of the diagnostic label is to direct the formation of client goals and desired outcomes. It may also suggest some nursing interventions.
3. The etiology (related factors and risk factors) component of a nursing diagnosis identifies one or more probable causes of the health problem, gives direction to the required nursing therapy, and enables the nurse to individualize the client's care. Differentiating possible causes is essential because each may require different nursing interventions.
4. Defining characteristics are the cluster of signs and symptoms that indicate the presence of a particular diagnostic label. For actual nursing diagnoses, the defining characteristics are the client's subjective and objective signs. For risk diagnoses, no signs and symptoms exist; thus the factors that cause the client to be more vulnerable to the problem form the etiology.

## PowerPoint Lecture Slides

*(NOTE: The number on each PPT Lecture Slide directly corresponds with the Concepts for Lecture.)*

1 Components of a Nursing Diagnosis
- Problem
- Etiology
- Defining characteristics

2 Problem Statement (Diagnostic Label)
- Describes the client's health problem or response

3 Etiology (Related Factors and Risk Factors)
- Identifies one or more probable causes of the health problem

4 Defining Characteristics
- Cluster of signs and symptoms indicating the presence of a particular diagnostic label (actual diagnoses)
- Factors that cause the client to be more vulnerable to the problem (risk diagnoses)

---

## Suggestions for Classroom Activities

- Using a nursing diagnosis handbook, develop a list of diagnostic labels, etiologies, and defining characteristics. Divide the students into groups. Have the students classify the items in the list into the appropriate components.

## Suggestions for Clinical Activities

- Have the students identify the components of the nursing diagnoses listed in the care plans for their assigned clients.

# LEARNING OUTCOME 3

Compare nursing diagnoses, medical diagnoses, and collaborative problems.

## CONCEPTS FOR LECTURE

1. Differences among nursing diagnoses, medical diagnoses, and collaborative problems are based on description, orientation, responsibility for diagnosing, treatment orders, nursing focus, nursing actions, duration, and classification system. (See Table 12–3.)

2. Nursing diagnoses describe human responses to disease processes or health problems. They consist of one-, two-, or three-part statements including problem and etiology. Nursing diagnoses are oriented to the client. The nurse is responsible for diagnosing and ordering most interventions to prevent and treat the health problem. Most interventions are independent nursing actions, and the nursing diagnosis may change frequently. There is a classification system in development and being used but it is not universally accepted.

3. Medical diagnoses describe disease and pathology, do not consider human responses, usually consist of a few words, and are oriented to pathology. The primary care provider is responsible for diagnosing and ordering primary interventions. Nurses implement medical orders for treatment and monitor the status of the client's condition; nursing actions are primarily dependent. Diagnosis remains the same while disease is present, and there is a well-developed classification system accepted by the medical profession.

4. Collaborative problems involve human responses, mainly physiologic complications of disease, tests, or treatments. They consist of two-part statements of situation/pathophysiology and the potential complication. Collaborative problems are oriented to pathophysiology, and nurses are responsible for diagnosing. Nurses collaborate with physicians and other health care professionals to prevent and treat. Medical orders are required for definitive treatment. The nursing focus is to prevent and monitor for onset and status of condition. There are some independent nursing actions, but primarily for monitoring and preventing. The duration of the problem is present when the disease or situation is present, and there is no universally accepted classification system.

## POWERPOINT LECTURE SLIDES

*(NOTE: The number on each PPT Lecture Slide directly corresponds with the Concepts for Lecture.)*

**1** Nursing and Medical Diagnosis, and Collaborative Problems
- Differences based on
  - Description
  - Orientation
  - Responsibility for diagnosing
  - Treatment orders
  - Nursing focus
  - Nursing actions
  - Duration
  - Classification system

**2** Nursing Diagnosis
- Describes human responses to disease processes/health problems
- Oriented to the client
- Nurse responsible for diagnosing, treatment orders, actions
- May change frequently
- Classification system in development

**3** Medical Diagnosis
- Describes disease and pathology
- Does not consider human responses
- Oriented to pathology
- Physician responsible for diagnosing and treatment orders
- Nurse implements orders and monitors client status
- Nursing actions dependent
- Diagnosis remains as long as disease present
- Well-developed and accepted classification

**4** Collaborative Problems
- Physiologic complications of disease, tests, treatments
- Oriented to pathophysiology
- Nurse and physician diagnose
- Physician orders definitive treatment
- Independent nursing action for monitoring and preventing
- Dependent nursing actions for treatment
- Present when disease/situation present
- No classification system

## LEARNING OUTCOME 4

Identify basic steps in the diagnostic process.

### CONCEPTS FOR LECTURE

1. The diagnostic process includes analyzing data; identifying health problems, risks, and strengths; and formulating diagnostic statements. To analyze data, the nurse must compare data against standards (identify significant cues), cluster the cues (generate tentative hypotheses), and identify gaps and inconsistencies.

   To analyze data, the nurse compares data with standards or norms, generally accepted measures, rules, models, or patterns, looking for negative or positive changes in the client's health status or pattern, variation from norms of the population, or a developmental delay. (See Table 12–4.) Another step in analyzing is to cluster cues to determine the relationship of facts, determining whether patterns are present or represent isolated incidents, and whether the data are significant. Data clustering involves making inferences about the data, interpreting possible meaning of the cues, and labeling the cues with tentative diagnostic hypotheses. Inconsistencies are conflicting data. Possible sources of conflicting data are measurement errors, expectations, and inconsistent or unreliable reports. All inconsistencies must be clarified before valid patterns can be established. The nurse and the client then identify problems that support tentative actual, risk, and possible diagnoses, and the nurse must determine whether the client's problem is a nursing diagnosis, a medical diagnosis, or a collaborative problem. The nurse and client must establish the client's strengths, resources, and abilities to cope. The last step in the diagnostic process is formulating diagnostic statements (see Outcomes 5, 6, and 7).

### POWERPOINT LECTURE SLIDES

*(NOTE: The number on each PPT Lecture Slide directly corresponds with the Concepts for Lecture.)*

 **1** Steps in Diagnostic Process
- Analyzing data
  - Compare data against standards
  - Cluster cues
  - Identify gaps and inconsistencies
- Identifying health problems, risks, and strengths
- Formulating diagnostic statements

## SUGGESTIONS FOR CLASSROOM ACTIVITIES

- Using a case study, demonstrate how to use the steps in the diagnostic process, pointing out the use of critical-thinking skills and the decision-making process in this phase of the nursing process.
- Using another case study, divide the students into small groups. Have each group use the steps in the diagnostic process to derive nursing diagnoses and collaborative problems. Compare and contrast results.

## SUGGESTIONS FOR CLINICAL ACTIVITIES

- Demonstrate how to use a nursing diagnosis manual or handbook to develop nursing diagnoses from a student's client data. Emphasize how the nursing diagnoses are individualized for the specific client.
- Ask the students to derive nursing diagnoses and collaborative problems from their client's data. Have the students review the process and outcomes.
- Ask the students to develop a list of their own strengths, resources, and abilities to cope with the stress of the clinical area. Relate this to assisting clients to identify strengths and resources and the ability to cope with health problems.

# LEARNING OUTCOME 5

Describe various formats for writing nursing diagnoses.

## CONCEPTS FOR LECTURE

1. Most nursing diagnoses are written as two-part or three-part statements, but there are variations. The basic two-part statement includes *problem (P)*, a statement of the client's response (NANDA label), and *etiology (E)*, factors contributing to or probable causes of the response. The two parts are joined by the words *related to* rather than *due to* since *related to* merely implies a relationship (See Box 12–1).

   The basic three-part nursing diagnosis statement is called the PES format and includes the following: *problem (P)*, a statement of the client's response (NANDA label); *etiology (E)*, factors contributing to or probable causes of the response; and *signs and symptoms (S)*, defining characteristics manifested by the client. (See Box 12–2). Actual nursing diagnoses can be documented in the PES format because the signs and symptoms have been identified. The format cannot be used for risk diagnoses because the client does not have signs and symptoms.

   One-part statements, such as wellness diagnoses and syndrome nursing diagnoses, consist of a NANDA label only. NANDA has specified that any new wellness diagnoses will be developed as one-part statements beginning with the words *readiness for enhanced*.

2. There are five variations of the basic formats:
   - Writing *unknown etiology* when the defining characteristics are present but the nurse does not know the cause or contributing factors
   - Using the phrase *complex factors* when there are too many etiologic factors or when they are too complex to state in a brief phrase
   - Using the word *possible* to describe either the problem or the etiology when the nurse believes more data are needed about the client's problem or the etiology

## POWERPOINT LECTURE SLIDES

*(NOTE: The number on each PPT Lecture Slide directly corresponds with the Concepts for Lecture.)*

 Formats for Writing Nursing Diagnoses
- Basic two-part statement
  - Problem (P)
  - Etiology (E)
- Basic three-part statement
  - Problem (P)
  - Etiology (E)
  - Signs and symptoms (S)
- One-part statement
  - Wellness (readiness for enhanced)
  - Syndrome

 Variations
- Unknown etiology
- Complex factors
- Possible
- Secondary
- Other additions for precisions

- Using *secondary* to divide the etiology into two parts, thereby making the statement more descriptive and useful (the part following *secondary to* is often a pathophysiologic or disease process or a medical diagnosis)
- Adding a second part to the general response or NANDA label to make it more precise

---

## SUGGESTIONS FOR CLASSROOM ACTIVITIES

- Using a client database, demonstrate how to develop two-part and three-part nursing diagnostic statements. Give the students another database and have them develop types of diagnostic statements.
- Provide examples of when the variations of the basic formats are necessary.

## SUGGESTIONS FOR CLINICAL ACTIVITIES

- Review the format used by the institution for stating nursing diagnoses.
- Compare and contrast the format used by the institution with the format required for student care plans.
- Ask the students to write nursing diagnoses for their clients adding the *secondary to* component to the diagnosis to make the statement more descriptive and useful.
- Compare and contrast complete diagnostic statements for clients with the same diagnostic label but different etiologies or defining characteristics.

---

# LEARNING OUTCOME 6

Describe the characteristics of a nursing diagnosis.

## CONCEPTS FOR LECTURE

1. Nursing diagnoses have diagnostic labels, which are the standardized NANDA names for diagnoses. The client's problem, consisting of the diagnostic label plus etiology, is called a nursing diagnosis. Professional nurses are responsible for making nursing diagnoses, even though other nursing personnel may contribute data to the process of diagnosing and may implement specified nursing care. The domain of nursing diagnoses includes only those health states that nurses are educated and licensed to treat. A nursing diagnosis is a judgment made only after thorough, systematic data collection. Nursing diagnoses describe a continuum of health states: deviations from health, presence of risk factors, and areas of enhanced personal growth.

## POWERPOINT LECTURE SLIDES

*(NOTE: The number on each PPT Lecture Slide directly corresponds with the Concepts for Lecture.)*

 Characteristics of a Nursing Diagnosis
- Have diagnostic labels
- Consist of the diagnostic label plus etiology
- Professional nurses responsible for making nursing diagnoses
- A judgment made only after thorough, systematic data collection
- Describes a continuum of health states

---

## SUGGESTIONS FOR CLASSROOM ACTIVITIES

- Have students review the nursing practice act of the state to determine whether the nurse is responsible for making nursing diagnoses. Have students review the definition of nursing diagnoses used in the nursing practice act of the state.

---

# LEARNING OUTCOME 7

List guidelines for writing a nursing diagnosis statement.

## CONCEPTS FOR LECTURE

1. The following are guidelines for writing nursing diagnosis statements:
   - Write statements in terms of a problem instead of a need.
   - Word the statement so that it is legally advisable.
   - Use nonjudgmental statements.
   - Be sure both elements of the statement do not say the say thing.
   - Be sure cause and effect are stated correctly.
   - Word diagnosis specifically and precisely.
   - Use nursing terminology rather than medical terminology to describe the client's response.
   - Using nursing terminology rather than medical terminology to describe the probable cause of the client's response. (See Table 12–6.)

2. To improve diagnostic reasoning and avoid diagnostic reasoning errors, the nurse should do the following: verify diagnoses by talking with the client and family, build a good knowledge base and acquire clinical experience, have a working knowledge of what is normal, consult resources, base diagnoses on patterns (that is, behavior over time) rather than an isolated incident, and improve critical-thinking skills.

## POWERPOINT LECTURE SLIDES

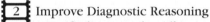 Guidelines for Writing a Diagnostic Statement
- State in terms of a problem, not a need.
- Word the statement so that it is legally advisable.
- Use nonjudgmental statements.
- Make sure that both elements of the statement do not say the same thing.
- Be sure that cause and effect are correctly stated.
- Word the diagnosis specifically and precisely.
- Use nursing terminology rather than medical terminology to describe the client's response and probable cause of client's response.

2 Improve Diagnostic Reasoning
- Verify diagnoses by talking with the client and family.
- Build a good knowledge base and acquire clinical experience.
- Have a working knowledge of what is normal.
- Consult resources.
- Base diagnoses on patterns.
- Improve critical-thinking skills.

## SUGGESTIONS FOR CLASSROOM ACTIVITIES

- Review common problems that past students have had with writing nursing diagnoses.
- Provide the students with a list of properly written and improperly written nursing diagnoses. Have the students identify each type and correct the improperly written diagnoses.

## SUGGESTIONS FOR CLINICAL ACTIVITIES

- Ask the students to critique the nursing diagnoses developed from their client's database using the guidelines listed in Table 12-6 in the textbook.
- Discuss resources available to consult on the clinical area to verify data.

# LEARNING OUTCOME 8

Describe the evolution of the nursing diagnosis movement, including work currently in progress.

## CONCEPTS FOR LECTURE

1. The first taxonomy—a classification system or set of categories arranged based on a single principle or set of principles—was alphabetical. In 1982, NANDA accepted the "nine patterns of unitary man" as an organizing principle. In 1984, NANDA renamed the "patterns of unitary man" as "human response patterns." Having undergone refinements, revisions, and acceptance of new diagnoses, the taxonomy, now called Taxonomy II, has three levels: domains, classes, and nursing diagnoses. The diagnoses are coded according to seven axes: diagnostic concept, time, unit of care, age, health

## POWERPOINT LECTURE SLIDES

 Evolution of Nursing Diagnosis
- First taxonomy alphabetical
- Taxonomy II
  - Domains
  - Classes
  - Nursing diagnoses
  - Seven axes
- Process for acceptance on new diagnosis

status, descriptor, and topology. Review and refinements of diagnostic labels continue. Nurses submit diagnoses to the Diagnostic Review Committee for review and staging. NANDA's board of directors gives final approval for incorporation of a diagnosis into the official list of labels. Diagnoses on the NANDA list are not finished products but are approved for clinical use and further study. This system includes classification of nursing interventions (NIC) and nursing outcomes (NOC), which are being developed by other research groups and are linked to NANDA diagnostic labels.

- NIC
- NOC

## LEARNING OUTCOME 9

List advantages of a taxonomy of nursing diagnoses.

### CONCEPTS FOR LECTURE

1. Research groups are examining what nurses do from these three different perspectives (diagnoses, interventions, and outcomes) to clarify and communicate the role nurses play in the health care system. The development of a standardized nursing language would facilitate clarification and communication. In addition, a standardized language will also enable nurses to implement a Nursing Minimum Data Set needed for computerized records.

### POWERPOINT LECTURE SLIDES

*(NOTE: The number on each PPT Lecture Slide directly corresponds with the Concepts for Lecture.)*

 Advantages of a Taxonomy of Nursing Diagnoses
- Development of a standardized nursing language
- Nursing minimum data set

### SUGGESTIONS FOR CLASSROOM ACTIVITIES

- Have the students debate the pros and cons of developing a standardized nursing language.

### SUGGESTIONS FOR CLINICAL ACTIVITIES

- Invite a staff nurse, nurse administrator, and nurse educator to discuss the use of NANDA, NIC, and NOC in the institution. If the institution does not use NANDA, NIC, and NOC, ask the panel to discuss this decision.

# CHAPTER 13
## PLANNING

## RESOURCE LIBRARY

 **PRENTICE HALL NURSING MEDIALINK DVD-ROM**

Audio Glossary
NCLEX® Review

 **COMPANION WEBSITE**

Additional NCLEX® Review
Case Study: *Client Struck by a Car*
Application Activity: *Client with Peptic Ulcers*

 **IMAGE LIBRARY**

**Figure 13.1** Planning.
**Figure 13.2** Documents that may be included in a complete client care plan.
**Figure 13.3** Standards of care for thrombophlebitis.

**Figure 13.4** A standardized care plan for the nursing diagnosis of Deficient Fluid Volume.
**Figure 13.5** A sample pathophysiology concept map.
**Figure 13.6** Nurse Medina and Amanda collaborate to set goals and outcome criteria and develop a care plan.

## LEARNING OUTCOME 1

Compare and contrast initial planning, ongoing planning, and discharge planning.

### CONCEPTS FOR LECTURE

1. Planning begins with the first client contact and continues until the nurse–client relationship ends, usually when the client is discharged from the health care agency. All planning is multidisciplinary, involves all health care providers interacting with the client, and includes the client and family to the fullest extent possible in every step.
2. Initial planning is usually performed by the nurse who completes the admission assessment. This type of planning results in the initial comprehensive plan of care.
3. Ongoing planning is done by all nurses who work with the client. Individualization of the initial plan occurs as new information is obtained and the client's response to care is evaluated. Ongoing planning also occurs at the beginning of a shift as nurses plan care to be given for the shift.
4. Discharge planning is the process of anticipating and planning for needs after discharge. Effective discharge planning begins at the first client contact and involves comprehensive and ongoing assessment to obtain information about the client's ongoing needs.

### POWERPOINT LECTURE SLIDES

*(NOTE: The number on each PPT Lecture Slide directly corresponds with the Concepts for Lecture.)*

**1** Planning
- Begins with first client contact
- Continues until nurse–client relationship ends (discharge)
- Multidisciplinary

**2** Initial Planning
- Based on admission assessment
- Results in the initial comprehensive plan of care

**3** Ongoing Planning
- Done by all nurses who work with the client
- Individualization of initial plan
- Also occurs at the beginning of a shift

**4** Discharge Planning
- Process of anticipating and planning for needs after discharge
- Begins at first client contact
- Involves comprehensive and ongoing assessment

### SUGGESTIONS FOR CLASSROOM ACTIVITIES

- Discuss the use of multidisciplinary care plans or critical pathways as other types of planning, and relate these to nursing care planning.

### SUGGESTIONS FOR CLINICAL ACTIVITIES

- Review the care plan forms used in the institution, comparing the initial plan, ongoing plan, and discharge plan.
- Ask the students to give examples of how they employ daily planning to provide care for their clients.

# LEARNING OUTCOME 2

Identify activities that occur in the planning process.

## CONCEPTS FOR LECTURE

1. Activities that occur in the planning phase include prioritizing problems/diagnoses, formulating goals/desired outcomes, selecting nursing interventions, and writing nursing interventions.

## POWERPOINT LECTURE SLIDES

*(NOTE: The number on each PPT Lecture Slide directly corresponds with the Concepts for Lecture.)*

**1** Activities in the Planning Process
- Prioritizing problems/diagnoses
- Formulating client goals/desired outcomes
- Selecting nursing interventions
- Writing individualized nursing interventions

## SUGGESTIONS FOR CLASSROOM ACTIVITIES

- Discuss how poor planning in any of the activities of planning can affect client care.
- Provide the students with a list of nursing diagnoses and ask them to prioritize these. Ask students to provide the criteria they used to prioritize these diagnoses.

## SUGGESTIONS FOR CLINICAL ACTIVITIES

- Invite a staff nurse from the clinical unit to discuss the planning process he or she uses to develop nursing care plans.

# LEARNING OUTCOME 3

Explain how standards of care and preprinted care plans can be individualized and used in creating a comprehensive nursing care plan.

## CONCEPTS FOR LECTURE

1. Most health agencies have a variety of preprinted, standardized plans for providing essential nursing care to specified groups of clients who have certain needs in common. Examples include standards of care, standardized care plans, protocols, policies, and procedures.
2. Standards of care describe nursing actions for clients with similar medical conditions rather than individuals, and they describe achievable rather than ideal nursing care. They define interventions for which nurses are held accountable. They are written from the perspective of the nurse's responsibilities, and do not contain medical interventions.
3. Standardized care plans are preprinted guides for nursing care of a client who has a need that arises frequently in the agency (such as a specific nursing diagnosis). They are written from the perspective of what care the client can expect.
4. Protocols are preprinted and indicate the actions commonly required for a particular group of patients. They may include both physician's orders and nursing interventions (for example, a protocol for admitting a client to the intensive care unit).
5. Policies and procedures are developed to govern the handling of frequently occurring situations. A policy covers a situation pertinent to client care (for example, a policy specifying the number of visitors a client may have).

## POWERPOINT LECTURE SLIDES

*(NOTE: The number on each PPT Lecture Slide directly corresponds with the Concepts for Lecture.)*

**1** Standardized Plans
- Standards of care
- Standardized care plans
- Protocols
- Policies and procedures

**2** Standards of Care
- Describe nursing actions for clients with similar medical conditions
- Describe achievable rather than ideal nursing care
- Define interventions for which nurses accountable
- Written from the perspective of the nurse's responsibilities
- Do not contain medical interventions

**3** Standardized Care Plans
- Guides for nursing care of clients with frequently arising needs
- Written from the perspective of what care the client can expect

**4** Protocols
- Indicate the actions commonly required for a particular groups of clients
- May include both physician's orders and nursing interventions
- Example: protocol for admitting a client to the intensive care unit

6. Regardless of whether care plans are handwritten, computerized, or standardized, nursing care must be individualized to fit the unique needs of each client. In practice, a care plan usually consists of both preprinted and nurse-created sections. Nurses use standardized care plans for predictable, commonly occurring problems and create an individual plan for unusual problems or problems needing special attention.

**5** Policies and Procedures
- Developed to govern the handling of frequently occurring situations
- Covers a situation pertinent to client care
- Example: policy specifying the number of visitors a client may have

**6** Individualization of Standardized Care Plans
- Must include unique needs of each client
- Usually consists of both preprinted and nurse-created sections
- Standardized care plans for predictable, commonly occurring problems
- Individual plan for unusual problems or problems needing special attention

## SUGGESTIONS FOR CLASSROOM ACTIVITIES

- Show various types of standardized written care plans used in different clinical settings. Have the students examine the similarities and differences among the various care plans.
- Using the standardized plans in the textbook, ask the students to give examples of how these can be individualized.

## SUGGESTIONS FOR CLINICAL ACTIVITIES

- Review the various types of standardized care plans used in the institution and how individualization of the plans can occur.
- Review several protocols and policies specific for the clinical unit. Have the students identify differences among the standardized care plans, protocols, and policies.
- Bring to conference a variety of standardized care plan references. Examine a medical diagnosis, nursing diagnosis, or collaborative problem in the various texts. Ask the students to discuss how the nurse would individualize these plans for a particular client.

# LEARNING OUTCOME 4

Identify essential guidelines for writing nursing care plans.

## CONCEPTS FOR LECTURE

1. Use the following guidelines when writing nursing care plans. Date and sign the plan. The date is essential for evaluation, review, and future planning. The nurse's signature indicates accountability. Use category headings; for example, "Nursing Diagnosis," "Goals/Desired Outcomes." Use standardized/approved medical or English symbols and key words rather than complete sentences to communicate ideas unless the agency policy dictates otherwise. Be specific. Writing specific times during a 24-hour period will help to clarify interventions. Refer to a procedure book or other sources of information rather than including all the steps on a written plan. Tailor the plan to the unique characteristics of the client by ensuring that the client's choices, such as preferences about the times of care and the methods used, are included. Ensure that the nursing care plan incorporates preventive and health maintenance aspects as well as restorative ones. Ensure that

## POWERPOINT LECTURE SLIDES

*(NOTE: The number on each PPT Lecture Slide directly corresponds with the Concepts for Lecture.)*

 **1** Guidelines for Writing Nursing Care Plans
- Date and sign the plan
- Use category headings
- Use standardized/approved terminology and symbols
- Be specific
- Refer to other sources
- Individualize the plan to the client
- Incorporate prevention and health maintenance
- Include discharge and home care plans

the plan contains interventions for ongoing assessment of the client. Include collaborative and coordination activities in the plan. Include plans for the client's discharge and home care needs.

### SUGGESTIONS FOR CLASSROOM ACTIVITIES

- Give the students a list of standardized/approved medical or English symbols that may be used in care plans. Discuss why it is important to adhere to this list.
- Review the differences between a student care plan or concept map and the client care plan used in an institution.

### SUGGESTIONS FOR CLINICAL ACTIVITIES

- Review the guidelines students are expected to follow when writing student care plans or concept maps for their assigned clients.

---

# LEARNING OUTCOME 5

Identify factors that the nurse must consider when setting priorities.

### CONCEPTS FOR LECTURE

1. Priority setting is the process of establishing a preferential sequence for addressing nursing diagnoses and interventions. Nurses can group nursing diagnoses as having high, medium, or low priority. Life-threatening problems, such as loss of respiratory or cardiac functions, are designated as high priority, health-threatening problems, such as acute illness and decreased coping abilities, are considered to be medium priority, and a problem that arises from normal developmental needs or only requires minimal nursing support is low priority (see Table 13–1).
2. Factors that must be considered when setting priorities are the following:
   - The client's health values and beliefs
   - The client's priorities
   - Resources available to the nurse and client
   - Urgency of the health problem
   - The medical treatment plan

### POWERPOINT LECTURE SLIDES

*(NOTE: The number on each PPT Lecture Slide directly corresponds with the Concepts for Lecture.)*

 Setting Priorities
- Establishing a preferential sequence for addressing nursing diagnoses and interventions
  - High priority (life-threatening)
  - Medium priority (health-threatening)
  - Low priority (developmental needs)

2 Factors to Consider When Setting Priorities
- Client's health values and beliefs
- Client's priorities
- Resources available to the nurse and client
- Urgency of the health problem
- Medical treatment plan

### SUGGESTIONS FOR CLASSROOM ACTIVITIES

- Provide the students with a list of nursing diagnoses. Divide the students into groups. Ask each group to rank the diagnoses as high, medium, or low priority and to provide the rationale for the ranking. Share the ranking with the class.
- Ask the students to identify what additional data would have been useful to consider when ranking the above diagnoses.

### SUGGESTIONS FOR CLINICAL ACTIVITIES

- Have the students share the nursing diagnoses established for their assigned clients. Discuss prioritizing the diagnoses using Maslow's hierarchy of needs or the prioritizing system used by the school.
- Have the students share situations in which they experienced clients whose priorities conflicted with theirs. How did they handle the conflict? In retrospect, what other strategies might have been useful?

# LEARNING OUTCOME 6

State the purposes of establishing client goals/desired outcomes.

## CONCEPTS FOR LECTURE

1. The goals/desired outcomes describe, in terms of observable client responses, what the nurse hopes to achieve by implementing the nursing interventions.
2. Goals/desired outcomes serve the following purposes:
   - Provide direction for planning nursing interventions
   - Serve as criteria for evaluating client progress
   - Enable the client and nurse to determine when the problem has been resolved
   - Help motivate the client and nurse by providing a sense of achievement

## POWERPOINT LECTURE SLIDES

*(NOTE: The number on each PPT Lecture Slide directly corresponds with the Concepts for Lecture.)*

1. Goals/Desired Outcomes
   - Describe what the nurse wants to achieve

2. Purpose of Goals/Desired Outcomes
   - Provides direction for planning nursing interventions
   - Serves as criteria for evaluating client progress
   - Enables determination of problem resolution
   - Helps motivate by providing a sense of achievement

## SUGGESTIONS FOR CLASSROOM ACTIVITIES

- Review the terminology used by the school for goals/desired outcomes.
- Relate the process of setting personal goals/desired outcomes to the process used in establishing client goals/desired outcomes.

## SUGGESTIONS FOR CLINICAL ACTIVITIES

- Discuss why it is important for the nurse to establish specific client goals/desired outcomes.
- Review the terminology used in the institution for goals/desired outcomes.
- Ask the students to give examples of how they have used client goals to assist with care.

# LEARNING OUTCOME 7

Discuss the Nursing Outcomes Classification, including an explanation of how to use the outcomes and indicators in care planning.

## CONCEPTS FOR LECTURE

1. Standardized or common nursing language is required in all phases of the nursing process if nursing data are to be included in computerized databases that are analyzed and used in nursing practice. Since 1991 nurse researchers and leaders have been developing the Nursing Outcomes Classification (NOC), a taxonomy for describing client outcomes that respond to nursing interventions. In the taxonomy, over 330 outcomes belong to one of seven domains and a class within the domains. Each NOC outcome is assigned a four-digit identifier (see Table 13–3). A NOC outcome is similar to a goal in traditional language. It is an individual, family, or community state, behavior, or perception measured along a continuum in response to a nursing intervention(s). The NOC outcomes are broadly stated and conceptual. To be measured, an outcome must be made more specific by identifying the indicators that apply to a particular client. An indicator is a more concrete individual, family, or community state, behavior, or perception that serves as a cue for measuring an outcome and is similar to desired outcomes in traditional language. Indicators are stated in neutral terms, but each outcome includes a five-point scale (a measure) that is used to rate the client's status on each indicator.

## POWERPOINT LECTURE SLIDES

*(NOTE: The number on each PPT Lecture Slide directly corresponds with the Concepts for Lecture.)*

1. Nursing Outcomes Classification (NOC)
   - Taxonomy for describing client outcomes that respond to nursing interventions
   - NOC outcome similar to a goal in traditional language
   - Outcomes broadly stated and conceptual
   - Made more specific by identifying indicators that apply to client
   - Includes a five-point scale (a measure) used to rate the client's status

2. To Write a Desired Outcome Using the NOC Taxonomy Indicate:
   - Label
   - Indicators that apply to the client
   - Location on the measuring scale desired for each indicator
   - Can be stated in traditional language

2.  When using the NOC taxonomy to write a desired outcome on a care plan, the nurse writes the label, the indicators that apply to the particular client, and the location on the measuring scale that is desired for each indicator. NOC outcomes can be stated in traditional language.

## SUGGESTIONS FOR CLASSROOM ACTIVITIES

- Discuss how the use of NOC could benefit the profession of nursing.
- Debate the pros and cons of using the NOC system.

## SUGGESTIONS FOR CLINICAL ACTIVITIES

- Invite a representative from nursing administration to discuss how NOC is used in the institution or why NOC is not used in the institution.

# LEARNING OUTCOME 8

Describe the relationship of goals/desired outcomes to the nursing diagnoses.

## CONCEPTS FOR LECTURE

1.  Goals are derived from the client's nursing diagnosis—primarily from the diagnostic label. The diagnostic label contains the unhealthy response: It states what should change. For every nursing diagnosis, the nurse must write the desired outcome or outcomes that, when achieved, directly demonstrate resolution of the problem. When developing goals/desired outcomes, the nurse should address the following questions:
    - What is the client's problem?
    - What is the opposite, healthy response?
    - How will the client look or behave if the healthy response is achieved (what will the nurse be able to see, hear, measure, palpate, smell, or otherwise observe with the senses)?
    - What must the client do and how well must the client do it to demonstrate problem resolution or to demonstrate the capability of resolving the problem?

## POWERPOINT LECTURE SLIDES

*(NOTE: The number on each PPT Lecture Slide directly corresponds with the Concepts for Lecture.)*

 Goals/Desired Outcomes and Nursing Diagnosis
- Goals derived from diagnostic label
- Diagnostic label contains the unhealthy response (problem)
- Goal/desired outcome demonstrates resolution of the unhealthy response (problem)

## SUGGESTIONS FOR CLASSROOM ACTIVITIES

- Provide the students with a list of various types of nursing diagnoses. Ask the students to use the questions provided in the text to develop related goals/desired outcomes.

## SUGGESTIONS FOR CLINICAL ACTIVITIES

- Review the nursing diagnoses for several of the students' assigned clients. Ask the students to derive goals/desired outcomes for these diagnoses.

# LEARNING OUTCOME 9

Identify guidelines for writing goals/desired outcomes.

## CONCEPTS FOR LECTURE

1.  The goal/desired outcome statement usually has the following components: subject, verb, condition or modifier, and criterion of desired performance (see Table 13–4). The subject is the client, any part of the client, or some attribute of the client such as pulse. The word

## POWERPOINT LECTURE SLIDES

*(NOTE: The number on each PPT Lecture Slide directly corresponds with the Concepts for Lecture.)*

 Components of Goal/Desired Outcome Statements
- Subject
- Verb

"client" is often omitted in goals since it is assumed that the subject is the client unless otherwise indicated. The verb specifies an action that the client is expected to perform. Verbs that denote directly observable behaviors must be used. Examples include: apply, identify, name, or demonstrate. (See Box 13-1) Conditions or modifiers may be added to verbs to explain the circumstances under which the behavior is observed. They explain what, where, when, or how. The criterion of desired performance indicates the standard by which performance is evaluated or the level at which the client will perform the specified behavior. They may specify time or speed, accuracy, distance, and quality.

2. Guidelines for writing goals/desired outcomes include the following:
   • Write goals/desired outcomes in terms of client responses, not nurse activities.
   • Be sure that goals/desired outcomes are realistic for the client's capabilities, limitations, and designated time span, if it is indicated.
   • Ensure that goals/outcomes are compatible with the therapies of other professionals.
   • Make sure that each goal/desired outcome is derived from only one nursing diagnosis.
   • Use observable, measurable terms for goals/desired outcomes.
   • Make sure the client considers the goals/desired outcomes important and values them.
   (See Table 13-4.)

   • Condition or modifier
   • Criterion of desired performance

 Guidelines for Writing Goal/Outcome Statements
   • Write in terms of the client responses
   • Must be realistic
   • Ensure compatibility with the therapies of other professionals
   • Derive from only one nursing diagnosis
   • Use observable, measurable terms

---

## SUGGESTIONS FOR CLASSROOM ACTIVITIES

• Hand out a list of goals/desired outcomes statements. Ask the students to identify the subject, verb, conditions, and criteria for each statement.
• Provide the students with a list of improperly stated goals/desired outcomes. Ask the students to identify and correct the errors.

## SUGGESTIONS FOR CLINICAL ACTIVITIES

• Have each student develop goals/desired outcomes for clients. Ask another student to identify the verb, conditions, and criteria in these goals/desired outcomes.
• Review verbs that are not specific and should not be used in goal setting (e.g., understand, know).

---

# LEARNING OUTCOME 10

Describe the process of selecting and choosing nursing interventions.

## CONCEPTS FOR LECTURE

1. Nursing interventions and activities are the actions a nurse performs to achieve client goals/desired outcomes. They should focus on eliminating or reducing the etiology of the nursing diagnosis, which is the second clause of the diagnostic statement. When it is not possible to change the etiologic factors, the nurse chooses interventions to treat the signs and symptoms or defining characteristics in NANDA terminology. Interventions for risk diagnoses should focus on measures to reduce the client's risk factors, which are also found in the second clause. Correct identification of

## POWERPOINT LECTURE SLIDES

*(NOTE: The number on each PPT Lecture Slide directly corresponds with the Concepts for Lecture.)*

 Nursing Interventions and Activities
   • Actions nurse performs to achieve goals/desired outcomes
   • Focus on eliminating or reducing etiology of nursing diagnosis
   • Treat signs/symptoms and defining characteristics

the etiologies provides the framework for choosing successful nursing intervention.

2. Nursing interventions include both direct and indirect care. Direct care is an intervention performed through interaction with the client. Indirect care is an intervention performed away from but on behalf of the client such as interdisciplinary collaboration or management of the care environment. Other types of nursing interventions include (a) independent interventions, those activities that nurses are licensed to initiate on the basis of their knowledge and skills; (b) dependent interventions, activities carried out under the primary care provider's orders or supervision, or according to specified routines; and (c) collaborative interventions, actions the nurse carries out in collaboration with other health team members. The nurse must choose interventions that are most likely to achieve the goal/desired outcome. In addition, the nurse must consider the risks and benefits of each intervention which requires nursing knowledge and experience.

3. The best nursing interventions will meet the following criteria:
   - Safe and appropriate for the client's age, health, and condition
   - Achievable with the resources available
   - Congruent with the client's values, beliefs, and culture
   - Congruent with other therapies
   - Based on nursing knowledge and experience or knowledge from relevant sciences
   - Within established standards of care as determined by state laws, professional associations (ANA), and the policies of the institution

**2** Types of Nursing Interventions
   - Direct
   - Indirect
   - Independent interventions
   - Dependent interventions
   - Collaborative interventions

**3** Criteria for Choosing Appropriate Intervention
   - Safe and appropriate for the client's age, health, and condition
   - Achievable with the resources available
   - Congruent with the client's values, beliefs, and culture
   - Congruent with other therapies
   - Based on nursing knowledge and experience or knowledge from relevant sciences
   - Within established standards of care

## SUGGESTIONS FOR CLASSROOM ACTIVITIES

- Provide the students with a list of nursing diagnoses. Ask the students to develop several interventions for these diagnoses. Be certain to include risk diagnoses in the list.
- Provide a list of interventions. Ask the students to identify the independent, dependent, and collaborative interventions.
- Although interventions are written in much the same way as goals/desired outcomes, discuss the differences.

## SUGGESTIONS FOR CLINICAL ACTIVITIES

- Demonstrate how nursing interventions are written and recorded on the clinical unit.
- Ask the students to use the questions presented in the text to critique the interventions they have written for their assigned clients.
- Invite the clinical unit nurse manager to discuss the process used to delegate nursing activities on the clinical unit.

## LEARNING OUTCOME 11

Discuss the Nursing Interventions Classification, including an explanation of how to use the interventions and activities in care planning.

### CONCEPTS FOR LECTURE

1. A taxonomy of nursing interventions referred to as the Nursing Interventions Classification System (NIC) was developed by the Iowa Intervention Project and was first published in 1992. It is updated every 4 years.

### POWERPOINT LECTURE SLIDES

*(NOTE: The number on each PPT Lecture Slide directly corresponds with the Concepts for Lecture.)*

**1** Nursing Interventions Classification (NIC)
   - Taxonomy of nursing interventions
   - Developed by the Iowa Intervention Project

2. This taxonomy consists of three levels: level 1 domains, level 2 classes, and level 3 interventions (see Table 13-6).
3. More than 514 interventions have been developed. Each broadly stated intervention includes a label (name), a definition, and a list of activities that outline key actions of nurses in carrying out interventions (see Box 13-2). All NIC interventions have been linked to NANDA nursing diagnostic labels. Each nursing diagnosis contains suggestions for several interventions, so nurses need to select the appropriate interventions based on their judgment and knowledge of the client (see Box 13-3).
4. When writing individualized nursing interventions on a care plan, the nurse should record customized activities rather than the broad intervention labels.

- First published in 1992
- Updated every 4 years

**2** Levels of NIC
- Consists of three levels:
  - Level 1 domains
  - Level 2 classes
  - Level 3 interventions

**3** NIC Interventions
- More than 514 interventions developed
- Each intervention includes:
  - A label (name)
  - A definition
  - A list of activities that outline key actions

**4** NIC Interventions
- Linked to NANDA diagnostic labels
- Select appropriate intervention and customize

---

## SUGGESTIONS FOR CLASSROOM ACTIVITIES

- Discuss how the use of NIC could benefit the profession of nursing.
- Debate the pros and cons of using the NIC system.

## SUGGESTIONS FOR CLINICAL ACTIVITIES

- Invite a representative from nursing administration to discuss how NIC is used in the institution or why NIC is not used in the institution.
- Select several nursing diagnoses and review suggested NIC interventions. Have students suggest ways to individualize the interventions.

# CHAPTER 14
## IMPLEMENTING AND EVALUATING

## RESOURCE LIBRARY

###  PRENTICE HALL NURSING MEDIALINK DVD-ROM

Audio Glossary
NCLEX® Review

### COMPANION WEBSITE

Additional NCLEX® Review
Case Study: *Treating a Client for Pain*
Application Activity: *Analyzing Effective Quality Assurance*
Links to Resources

### IMAGE LIBRARY

**Figure 14.1** Implementing.
**Figure 14.2** Amanda agrees to practice deep-breathing exercises q3h during the day.
**Figure 14.3** Evaluating.

**Figure 14.4** Upon assessment of respiratory excursion, Nurse Medina detects failure of the client to achieve maximum ventilation.

## LEARNING OUTCOME 1

Explain how implementing relates to other phases of the nursing process.

### CONCEPTS FOR LECTURE

1. The first three nursing process phases provide the basis for the nursing actions performed during the implementing phase. In turn, the implementing phase provides the actual nursing activities and client responses that are examined in the final phase, evaluating. Using data acquired during assessment, the nurse can individualize the care given in the implementing phase.

### POWERPOINT LECTURE SLIDES

*(NOTE: The number on each PPT Lecture Slide directly corresponds with the Concepts for Lecture.)*

 The Nursing Process—Implementing, assessment, diagnosis, and planning provide basis for nursing actions (implementing)
  - Nursing activities and client responses examined during evaluating phase
  - Nursing activities individualized based on assessment data

### SUGGESTIONS FOR CLASSROOM ACTIVITIES

- Provide a client case study much like the one in the text. Have the students develop a concept map, using the CMap Tool provided on the Prentice Hall Nursing MediaLink DVD, demonstrating the relationships between the steps in the process.

### SUGGESTIONS FOR CLINICAL ACTIVITIES

- Have students present one nursing diagnosis, goals/desired outcomes, and plan for their clients. Discuss the relationship to the implementation phase.

# LEARNING OUTCOME 2

Describe three categories of skills used to implement nursing interventions.

## CONCEPTS FOR LECTURE

1. To implement the care plan successfully, nurses need cognitive, interpersonal, and technical skills. Although these skills are distinct from one another, nurses use them in various combinations and with different emphasis depending on the activity.
2. Cognitive skills (intellectual) include problem solving, decision making, critical thinking, and creativity.
3. Interpersonal skills are all of the activities, verbal and nonverbal, people use when interacting directly with one another. The effectiveness of a nursing action often depends largely on the nurse's ability to communicate with others. Nurses use therapeutic communication to understand the client and in turn to be understood. Interpersonal skills are necessary for all nursing activities: caring, comforting, advocating, referring, counseling, and supporting, for example. These skills include conveying knowledge, attitudes, feelings, interest, and appreciation of the client's cultural values and lifestyle.
4. Technical skills are purposeful "hands-on" skills such as manipulating equipment or giving injections. These skills are often called tasks, procedures, or psychomotor skills. Psychomotor refers to physical actions that are controlled by the mind; they are not reflexive. Technical skills require knowledge and, frequently, manual dexterity.

## POWERPOINT LECTURE SLIDES

*(NOTE: The number on each PPT Lecture Slide directly corresponds with the Concepts for Lecture.)*

1 Successful Implementation
- Cognitive skills
- Interpersonal skills
- Technical skills

2 Cognitive Skills (Intellectual)
- Problem solving
- Decision making
- Critical thinking
- Creativity

3 Interpersonal Skills
- Verbal and nonverbal
- Effectiveness depends largely on ability to communicate
- Therapeutic communication
- Include conveying knowledge, attitudes, feelings, interest
- Appreciation of the client's cultural values and lifestyle

4 Technical Skills
- Purposeful "hands-on" skills
- Often called tasks, procedures, or psychomotor skills
- Psychomotor refers to physical actions that are controlled by the mind, not reflexive
- Require knowledge and frequently manual dexterity

## SUGGESTIONS FOR CLASSROOM ACTIVITIES

- Provide the students with examples of how nurses use the three types of skills in various combinations and concurrently.
- Discuss the meaning of the term *psychomotor,* stressing the importance of cognition when performing nursing skills. Ask students to provide examples illustrating the association of cognition and motor skills.

## SUGGESTIONS FOR CLINICAL ACTIVITIES

- Ask the students to provide examples from clinical experience of how they or staff nurses employ the three types of skills in various combinations and concurrently in the clinical setting.

# LEARNING OUTCOME 3

Discuss the five activities of the implementing phase.

## CONCEPTS FOR LECTURE

1. The five activities of the implementing phase are reassessing the client, determining the nurse's need for assistance, implementing nursing interventions, supervising delegated care, and documenting nursing

## POWERPOINT LECTURE SLIDES

*(NOTE: The number on each PPT Lecture Slide directly corresponds with the Concepts for Lecture.)*

1 Five Activities of the Implementing Phase

activities. Before implementing an intervention, the nurse must reassess the client to make sure the intervention is still needed. New data may indicate a need to change the priorities of care or the nursing activities. When implementing some nursing interventions, the nurse may require assistance for one or more of the following reasons: the nurse is unable to implement the nursing activity safely or efficiently alone; assistance would reduce stress on the client; or the nurse lacks the knowledge or skills to implement a particular nursing activity. When implementing nursing interventions, it is important to explain to the client what interventions will be done, what sensations to expect, what the client is expected to do, and what the expected outcome is. It is important to ensure privacy. Nurses also coordinate client care. This involves scheduling client contacts with other departments and serving as a liaison among the members of the health care team. If care is delegated, the nurse is responsible for the client's overall care and must ensure that the activities have been implemented according to the care plan. The nurse completes the implementing phase by recording the interventions and client responses in the progress notes. Care must not be recorded in advance because the nurse may determine on reassessment that the intervention should not or cannot be implemented. The nurse may record routine or recurring activities in the client record at the end of the shift, keeping a personal record of these interventions on a worksheet. Nursing activities are communicated verbally as well as in writing.

- Reassessing the client
- Determining the nurse's need for assistance
- Implementing nursing interventions
- Supervising delegated care
- Documenting nursing activities

## SUGGESTIONS FOR CLASSROOM ACTIVITIES

- Discuss situations in which the nurse may need to obtain assistance when implementing nursing interventions and how the nurse may obtain this assistance.

## SUGGESTIONS FOR CLINICAL ACTIVITIES

- During clinical conference, ask the students to discuss and evaluate how registered nurses use delegation. Have the students identify aspects of client care that cannot be delegated to a non-RN staff member.
- Ask the students to describe how they keep a record of routine or recurring activities prior to recording these on the client's record.

# LEARNING OUTCOME 4

Identify guidelines for implementing nursing interventions.

## CONCEPTS FOR LECTURE

1. Base nursing interventions on scientific knowledge, nursing research, and professional standards (evidence-based practice) when these exist. Be aware of the scientific rationale as well as possible side effects or complications of all interventions. Clearly understand the interventions to be implemented and question any that are not understood. This requires knowledge of

## POWERPOINT LECTURE SLIDES

*(NOTE: The number on each PPT Lecture Slide directly corresponds with the Concepts for Lecture.)*

1 Implementing Nursing Interventions
- Evidence-based practice
- Clearly understand interventions
- Adapt activities to client
- Implement safe care

each intervention, its purpose in the client's plan of care, and any considerations and changes in the client's condition that may affect the order. Adapt activities to the individual client. A client's beliefs, values, age, health status, and environment are factors that can affect the success of nursing action. Implement safe care. Provide teaching, support, and comfort. Explain the purpose of interventions, what the client will experience, and how the client can participate. The client must have sufficient knowledge to agree to the plan of care and to assume responsibility for as much self-care as possible. Be holistic. Respect the dignity of the client and enhance the client's self-esteem. Provide privacy and encourage clients to make own decisions. Encourage clients to participate actively in implementing the nursing interventions. This enhances clients' sense of independence and control.

- Provide teaching, support, and comfort
- Be holistic
- Respect the dignity of the client
- Encourage active client participation

## SUGGESTIONS FOR CLASSROOM ACTIVITIES

- Discuss the importance of understanding the scientific rationale for nursing interventions. Give examples of how knowledge from science and the liberal arts can be used to provide these rationales.
- Discuss evidence-based practice and its relationship to nursing interventions.
- Provide examples of how the client's age, beliefs, values, health status, and environment can affect the success of nursing actions. Ask the students to identify ways to incorporate this knowledge to promote the effectiveness of nursing interventions.

## SUGGESTIONS FOR CLINICAL ACTIVITIES

- Require students to include the scientific rationale for nursing interventions in their student care plans. Required documentation for each rationale.
- Have the students describe how they have demonstrated respect for their client and enhanced their client's self-esteem.

## LEARNING OUTCOME 5

Explain how evaluating relates to other phases of the nursing process.

## CONCEPTS FOR LECTURE

1. Evaluating is a planned, ongoing, purposeful activity in which clients and health care professionals determine the client's progress toward achievement of goals/outcomes and the effectiveness of the nursing care plan. Successful evaluation depends on the effectiveness of the steps that precede it. Assessment data must be accurate and complete so the nurse can formulate appropriate nursing diagnoses and goals/desired outcomes. The goals/desired outcomes must be stated concretely in behavioral terms to be useful for evaluating client responses. Without the implementing phase in which the plan is put into action, there would be nothing to evaluate. The evaluating and assessing phases overlap.

   During the assessment phase the nurse collects data for the purpose of making diagnoses. During the evaluation step the nurse collects data for the purpose

## POWERPOINT LECTURE SLIDES

*(NOTE: The number on each PPT Lecture Slide directly corresponds with the Concepts for Lecture.)*

1. Nursing Process—Evaluating
   - Depends on the effectiveness of phases that precede
   - Assessing and nursing diagnosis must be accurate
   - Goals/desired outcomes must be stated behaviorally to be useful for evaluating
   - Without implementing phase, there would be nothing to evaluate
   - Evaluating and assessing phases overlap

of comparing the data to preselected goals and judging the effectiveness of the nursing care. The act of assessing (data collection) is the same. The differences lie in when the data are collected and how the data are used.

---

## SUGGESTIONS FOR CLASSROOM ACTIVITIES

- Provide a client case study much like the one in the text. Have the students develop a concept map demonstrating the relationships between the steps in the process.
- Have the students indicate on the concept map or verbally how assessment is incorporated in the assessing, implementing, and evaluating phases of the nursing process.

## SUGGESTIONS FOR CLINICAL ACTIVITIES

- Have each student share one goal/desired outcome for a client. Ask another student to list the data that must be collected to determine whether the goal/desired outcome has been met.

---

# LEARNING OUTCOME 6

Describe five components of the evaluation process.

## CONCEPTS FOR LECTURE

1. The evaluation process has five components: collecting data related to the desired outcomes (NOC indicators), comparing the data with outcomes, relating nursing activities to outcomes, drawing conclusions about problem status, and continuing, modifying, or terminating the nursing care plan. Using the clearly stated, precise, and measurable goals/desired outcomes as a guide, the nurse collects data so that conclusions can be drawn about whether goals have been met. Data must be recorded concisely and accurately to facilitate the next part of the evaluating process. The nurse and client compare the client's actual responses with the goals/desired outcomes. If NOC indicators are being used with the outcomes, scores on the scales after intervention would be compared with those measured at baseline to determine improvement. The next aspect of the evaluating process is determining whether the nursing activities had any relation to the outcomes. It should never be assumed that a nursing activity was the cause of or the only factor in meeting, partially meeting, or not meeting a goal. The nurse must collect data about what the client actually did to meet the goal/desired outcome to establish the relationship (or lack of) between the nursing actions and the client's responses. Drawing conclusions about the problem status involves using judgments about goal achievement to determine whether the care plan was effective in resolving, reducing, or preventing client problems.

## POWERPOINT LECTURE SLIDES

*(NOTE: The number on each PPT Lecture Slide directly corresponds with the Concepts for Lecture.)*

 1 Components of the Evaluation Process
- Collecting data related to the desired outcomes (NOC indicators)
- Comparing the data with outcomes
- Relating nursing activities to outcomes
- Drawing conclusions about problem status
- Continuing, modifying, or terminating the nursing care plan

---

After drawing conclusions about the status of the client's problems, the nurse modifies the care plan as indicated. This is done according to agency policy.

Before making individual modifications to a care plan if the problem was only partially resolved or not resolved, the nurse must first determine why the plan as a whole was not completely effective. (See Outcome 7.)

## SUGGESTIONS FOR CLASSROOM ACTIVITIES

- Provide examples of goals/desired outcomes and client responses. Have the students decide whether these goals have been met, partially met, or not met. Have the students provide a rationale for their decisions.
- Ask the students to give examples of situations where they achieved personal goals or solved problems without the use of previously developed plans to achieve the goals. Why do the students think this happened? What was wrong with the plans? Relate this to goals/outcomes and nursing interventions.
- Describe various client situations in which goals/outcomes have been met. What conclusions can be drawn regarding the clients' problems: actual problem resolved, potential problem prevented, or incremental progress toward problem resolution accomplished?

## SUGGESTIONS FOR CLINICAL ACTIVITIES

- Using the case of a student's actual client, discuss a desired goal/outcome that was not met. Analyze the case to determine possible reasons for this, and what modifications are needed.
- Discuss how the institution indicates problem resolution on the client's records.

## LEARNING OUTCOME 7

Describe the steps involved in reviewing and modifying the client's care plan.

## CONCEPTS FOR LECTURE

1. Before making modifications to the care plan, the nurse must review the entire care plan and critique each step of the nursing process. During assessing phase were data complete, accurate, validated, and does any new data require changes in the care plan? Are nursing diagnoses relevant, accurate, supported by data, clearly stated in the correct format and has the status of any problem changed or been resolved? Do any new nursing diagnoses require new goal? Are goals realistic and is enough time allowed for achievement? Do the goals address all aspects of the problem and does the client still concur with the goals? Are nursing interventions related to goals, address all aspects of the goals, clear, specific, detailed, supported with rationale, are available resources available to implement the intervention, are any new interventions required, and were the interventions actually carried out? During implementing phase was the client's input obtained, were the goals and nursing interventions acceptable to the client, did caregivers have the knowledge and skills to correctly perform the interventions and was the client given explanation prior to implementing? (See Table 14-1.) Even if all sections of the care plan

## POWERPOINT LECTURE SLIDES

*(NOTE: The number on each PPT Lecture Slide directly corresponds with the Concepts for Lecture.)*

1. Reviewing and Modifying the Care Plan
   - Critique each phase of the nursing process
   - Check whether the interventions were
     - Carried out
     - Were unclear or unreasonable

2. Make Necessary Modifications
   - Implement the modified plan
   - Begin nursing process again

appear to be satisfactory, the manner in which the plan was implemented may have interfered with goal achievement. The nurse should check whether the interventions were carried out, or were unclear or unreasonable in terms of external constraints such as money, staff, time, and equipment.

2. After making necessary modifications to the care plan, the nurse implements the modified plan and begins the nursing process cycle again.

---

### SUGGESTIONS FOR CLASSROOM ACTIVITIES

- Review the checklist in Table 14-1 in the textbook and discuss how this may be used to critique the phases of the nursing process, including the process as used in developing student care plans.

### SUGGESTIONS FOR CLINICAL ACTIVITIES

- Have students use the checklist in Table 14-1 in the textbook to review and modify the care plans for their clients.

---

## LEARNING OUTCOME 8

Differentiate quality improvement from quality assurance.

### CONCEPTS FOR LECTURE

1. A quality-assurance (QA) program is an ongoing, systematic process designed to evaluate and promote excellence in the health care provided to clients. QA frequently refers to evaluation of the level of care provided in a health care agency, but it may be limited to evaluation of the performance of one nurse or more broadly involve evaluation of the quality of care in an agency or even in a country.

2. Quality improvement (QI) follows client care rather than organizational structure, focuses on process rather than individuals, and uses a systematic approach with the intention of *improving* the quality of care rather than *ensuring* the quality of care. QI studies often focus on identifying and correcting a system's problems.

   QI is also known as continuous quality improvement (CQI), total quality management (TQM), performance improvement (PI), or persistent quality improvement (PQI).

### POWERPOINT LECTURE SLIDES

*(NOTE: The number on each PPT Lecture Slide directly corresponds with the Concepts for Lecture.)*

**1** Quality Assurance
- Ongoing, systematic process
- Evaluate and promote excellence provision of health care
- May evaluate the level of care provided
- May be evaluation of performance of one nurse or an agency or country

**2** Quality Improvement
- Focus on process
- Uses a systematic approach to improve the quality of care
- Often focus on identifying and correcting a system's problems
- Also known as:
  - Continuous quality improvement (CQI)
  - Total quality management (TQM)
  - Performance improvement (PI)
  - Persistent quality improvement (PQI)

---

### SUGGESTIONS FOR CLASSROOM ACTIVITIES

- Invite a nurse responsible for quality improvement to discuss the responsibilities of this role and the flow of the nurse's findings throughout the institution.

### SUGGESTIONS FOR CLINICAL ACTIVITIES

- Ask a representative of the quality improvement or quality assurance program to explain the process used in the institution and the types of issues addressed.

---

# LEARNING OUTCOME 9

Name the two components of an evaluation statement.

## CONCEPTS FOR LECTURE

1. The evaluation statement consists of two parts: a conclusion and supporting data.
    The conclusion is a statement that the goal/desired outcome was met, partially met, or not met. The supporting data are the list of client responses that support the conclusion.

## POWERPOINT LECTURE SLIDES

*(NOTE: The number on each PPT Lecture Slide directly corresponds with the Concepts for Lecture.)*

**1** Components of an Evaluation Statement
- Conclusion
- Supporting data

## SUGGESTIONS FOR CLASSROOM ACTIVITIES

- Provide a list of several evaluation statements. Ask the students to identify the two parts of each evaluation statement.

## SUGGESTIONS FOR CLINICAL ACTIVITIES

- Have students include the two part evaluation statement on their student care plans.

# LEARNING OUTCOME 10

Describe three components of quality evaluation: structure, process, and outcomes.

## CONCEPTS FOR LECTURE

1. Quality assurance evaluation involves three components of care: structure, process, and outcome. Each requires different criteria and methods, and each has a different focus.
2. Structure evaluation focuses on the setting in which the care is given. It answers the question "What effect does the setting have on the quality of care?" Structure standards describe desirable environmental and organizational characteristics that influence care.
3. Process evaluation focuses on how the care was given. It answers questions such as "Is the care relevant to the client's needs?" and "Is the care appropriate, complete, and timely?" Process standards focus on the manner in which the nurse uses the nursing process.
4. Outcome evaluation focuses on demonstrable changes in the client's health status as a result of nursing care. Outcome criteria are written in terms of client responses or health status.

## POWERPOINT LECTURE SLIDES

*(NOTE: The number on each PPT Lecture Slide directly corresponds with the Concepts for Lecture.)*

**1** Components of Quality Evaluation
- Structure
- Process
- Outcome

**2** Structure
- Focuses on the setting
- Effect setting has on care
- Describe desirable environmental and organizational characteristics

**3** Process
- Focuses on how the care was given
- Relevance of care to client needs
- How nurse uses the nursing process

**4** Outcome
- Focuses on demonstrable client health changes resulting from nursing care
- Outcome criteria written in terms of client responses or health status

# CHAPTER 15
## DOCUMENTING AND REPORTING

## RESOURCE LIBRARY

 **PRENTICE HALL NURSING MEDIALINK DVD-ROM**

Audio Glossary
NCLEX® Review
End of Unit Concept Map Activity

**COMPANION WEBSITE**

Additional NCLEX® Review
Case Study: Client with Delirium Tremens
Application Activities:
   *Establishing a Documentation System*
   *HIPAA and Client Privacy*
Links to Resources

### IMAGE LIBRARY

**Figure 15.1** An example of narrative notes.
**Figure 15.2** A client's problem list in the POMR.
**Figure 15.3** Examples of nursing progress notes using SOAP, SOAPIER, and APIE formats.
**Figure 15.4** Sample vital signs graphic record.
**Figure 15.5** Sample of a daily nursing assessment form used in CBE.

**Figure 15.6** Sample skin assessment flow sheet.
**Figure 15.7** A bedside computer.
**Figure 15.8** Excerpt from a critical pathway documentation form.
**Figure 15.9** The 24-hour clock.
**Figure 15.10** Correcting a charting error.

---

## LEARNING OUTCOME 1

List the measures used to maintain the confidentiality of client records.

### CONCEPTS FOR LECTURE

1. Access is restricted to health professionals involved in giving care to the client. The institution or agency is the rightful owner of the client's record. However, the client has rights to the same document.

   For purposes of education and research, most agencies allow students and graduate health professionals access to client records for use in client conferences, clinics, rounds, client studies, and written papers.

   The student or graduate is bound by a strict ethical code and legal responsibility to hold all information in confidence by not using a name or any statements in the notations that would identify the client.

   Health care agencies have developed policies and procedures to ensure the privacy and confidentiality of client information stored in computers.

2. The following are some suggestions for ensuring confidentiality and security of computerized records:
   - A personal password is required to enter and sign off computer files.
   - Personal passwords should not be shared.
   - Never leave the computer terminal unattended after logging on.
   - Do not leave client information displayed on the monitor where others may see it.

### POWERPOINT LECTURE SLIDES

*(NOTE: The number on each PPT Lecture Slide directly corresponds with the Concepts for Lecture.)*

**1** Maintaining Confidentiality of Records
   - Restrict access
   - Ethical codes and legal responsibility
   - Policies and procedures to ensure privacy and confidentiality

**2** Security for Computerized Records
   - Passwords required and should not be shared
   - Never leave the computer terminal unattended after logging on
   - Do not leave client information displayed
   - Shred all unneeded computer-generated worksheets
   - Know the facility's policy and procedure for correcting an entry error
   - Follow agency procedures for documenting sensitive material
   - IT personnel must install a firewall

- Shred all unneeded computer-generated worksheets.
- Know the facility's policy and procedure for correcting an entry error.
- Follow agency procedures for documenting sensitive material such as a diagnosis of AIDS.
- Information technology (IT) personnel must install a firewall to protect the server from unauthorized access.

---

### SUGGESTIONS FOR CLASSROOM ACTIVITIES

- Invite a speaker who is an administrator or lawyer to discuss the importance of maintaining confidentiality in client records.
- Invite a speaker from an institution's information technology department to discuss computer security for clients' records.

### SUGGESTIONS FOR CLINICAL ACTIVITIES

- Review the students' responsibility for maintaining privacy and confidentiality of clients' records.

---

## LEARNING OUTCOME 2

Discuss reasons for keeping client records.

### CONCEPTS FOR LECTURE

1. Client records are kept for a number of purposes: communication, planning client care, auditing health agencies, research, education, reimbursement, legal documentation, and health care analysis.

   Client records serve as a vehicle by which health professionals who interact with a client communicate with each other to prevent fragmentation, repetition, and delays in client care.

   Each health professional uses data from the client's record to plan care for that client.

   An audit is a review of client records for quality assurance purposes. Accrediting agencies may review client records to determine if a particular agency is meeting stated standards.

   The information contained in the record can be a valuable source of data for research. Treatment plans for clients with the same diagnosis can yield information helpful in treating other clients.

   The health record can frequently provide a comprehensive view of the client, the illness, effective treatment strategies, and factors that affect the outcomes of illness for education of students in the health disciplines.

   Documentation helps a facility receive reimbursement from the federal government. For Medicare reimbursement the record must contain the correct diagnostic-related group (DRG) codes and reveal that the appropriate care has been given.

   Other insurance companies and other third-party payers also require appropriate documentation for reimbursement. If additional care, treatment, or length of stay becomes necessary for the client's welfare, thorough charting will help justify these needs.

### POWERPOINT LECTURE SLIDES

*(NOTE: The number on each PPT Lecture Slide directly corresponds with the Concepts for Lecture.)*

 Purposes of Client Records
- Communication
- Planning client care
- Auditing health agencies
- Research
- Education
- Reimbursement
- Legal documentation
- Health care analysis

The client's record is a legal document and is usually admissible in court as evidence.

Information from records may assist health care planners to identify agency needs such as overutilized and underutilized services, costs of various services, and those services that cost the agency money and those that generate revenue.

---

## SUGGESTIONS FOR CLASSROOM ACTIVITIES

• Invite staff members from a medical record and billing department to discuss the importance of documentation in reference to their responsibilities.

## SUGGESTIONS FOR CLINICAL ACTIVITIES

• Review the importance of the clinical chart as a means of communication among health care providers and as an educational tool for students.

---

# LEARNING OUTCOME 3

Compare and contrast different documentation methods: source-oriented and problem-oriented medical records, PIE, focus charting, charting by exception, computerized records, and the case management model.

## CONCEPTS FOR LECTURE

1. In the source-oriented record, the traditional client record, each person or department makes notations in separate sections of the client's chart. Information about a particular problem is distributed throughout the record (see Table 15–1). Narrative charting is used which consists of written notes that include routine care, normal findings, and client problems, often in chronological order.

   Source-oriented records are convenient and disciplines can easily locate the forms on which to record data; however, information about a particular problem is scattered throughout the chart, which can lead to decreased communication among health team members, an incomplete picture of the client's care, and a lack of coordination of care.

2. In the problem-oriented medical record (POMR) or problem-oriented record (POR), the data are arranged according to the problem the client has rather than the source of the information. Health team members contribute to the problem list, plan of care for each problem, and progress notes. Progress notes are documented in the SOAP, SOAPIE, or SOAPIER format: *S*ubjective data, *O*bjective data, *A*ssessment (interpretation or conclusions), *P*lan, *I*nterventions, *E*valuation, and *R*evisions. This format encourages collaboration, problem lists alert caregivers to clients' needs, and makes it easier to track the status of the problems; however, caregivers differ in ability to use the format, problem lists must be current, and documentation is somewhat inefficient since assessment and interventions that apply to more than one problem must be repeated.

3. The PIE documentation model groups information into three categories: *P*roblem, *I*nterventions, and *E*valuation of nursing care. It consists of a client

## POWERPOINT LECTURE SLIDES

*(NOTE: The number on each PPT Lecture Slide directly corresponds with the Concepts for Lecture.)*

**1** Source-Oriented
   • Traditional client record
   • Each discipline makes notations in a separate section
   • Information about a particular problem distributed throughout the record
   • Narrative charting used

**2** Problem-Oriented Medical Records (POMR)
   • Data arranged according to client problem
   • Health team contributes to the problem list, plan of care, and progress notes for each problem
   • Uses SOAP, SOAPIE, SOAPIER documentation
   • Encourages collaboration
   • Easier to track status of problems
   • Vigilance required to maintain problem list
   • Less efficient documentation process

**3** PIE
   • Groups information into three categories: **P**roblem, **I**nterventions, **E**valuation
   • Consists of client assessment, flow sheet, and progress notes

**4** Focus Charting
   • Focus on client concerns and strengths
   • Progress notes organized into **DAR** format
   • Holistic perspective of client and client's needs
   • Nursing process framework for the progress notes

**5** Charting by Exception (CBE)
   • Incorporates flow sheets, standards of nursing care, bedside chart forms

assessment flow sheet and progress notes. The PIE system eliminates the traditional care plan and incorporates an ongoing care plan into the progress notes; however, the nurse must review all the nursing notes before giving care to determine which problems are current and which interventions were effective.

4. Focus charting is intended to make the client and the client's concerns and strengths the focus of care. The focus may be a condition, a nursing diagnosis, a medical diagnosis, a behavior, a sign or symptom, an acute change in the client's condition, or a client's strength. Progress notes are organized into the DAR format: data, action, and response. Focus charting provides a holistic perspective of the client and the client's needs and provides a nursing process framework for the progress notes.

5. Charting by exception (CBE) is a documentation system in which any abnormal or significant findings or exceptions to norms are recorded. CBE incorporates three elements: flow sheets, standards of nursing care, and bedside access to chart forms. Agencies using CBE must develop standards of nursing practice that identify minimum criteria for client care regardless of clinical area. Care is documented using only a check mark if these standards are met. If not all standards are met (an exception), an asterisk is made on the flow sheet with reference to the nurses' notes. All exceptions to the standards are fully described in narrative form on the nurses' notes. This type of documentation eliminates lengthy, repetitive charting and makes changes in the client's condition more obvious.

6. Computerized documentation systems are being developed to manage the huge volume of information required in contemporary health care. Computers store the client's database, add new data, create and revise care plans, and document the client's progress. Multiple flow sheets are not necessary because information can be easily retrieved in a variety of formats. The computerization of clinical records has made it possible to transmit information from one care setting to another.

7. The case management model emphasizes quality, cost-effective care delivered within an established length of stay. It uses a multidisciplinary approach to planning and documenting client care, using critical pathways that identify outcomes certain groups of clients are expected to achieve on each day of care along with the interventions necessary for each day. The case management model incorporates graphics and flow sheets. Progress notes use some type of CBE. If the client deviates from what is planned on the critical pathway, a variance occurs. The nurse writes a note documenting the unexpected event, the cause, and actions taken to correct the situation or justify the actions taken (see Table 15–2).

- Agencies develop standards of nursing practice
- Documentation according to standards involves a check mark
- Exceptions to standards described in narrative form on nurses' notes

 **6** Computerized Documentation
- Developed to manage volume of information
- Use of computers to store the client's database, new data, create and revise care plans, and document client's progress
- Information easily retrieved
- Possible to transmit information from one care setting to another

**7** Case Management Model
- Quality, cost-effective care delivered within an established length of stay
- Uses a multidisciplinary approach
- Use of critical pathways
- Use of CBE
- Documentation of variance include:
  ○ Actions taken to correct the situation
  ○ Justify the actions taken

## SUGGESTIONS FOR CLASSROOM ACTIVITIES

- Give students a database about a client in a clinical setting. Have them document information from the database in several different documentation methods.
- Obtain documentation forms from several institutions. Compare and contrast the methods used.

## SUGGESTIONS FOR CLINICAL ACTIVITIES

- Examine a client record and compare documentation by nurses, primary care providers, and other health care providers. What are the similarities and differences in the documentation? What are the advantages and disadvantages of having multiple providers record problems and plans on the same forms?
- If possible, arrange to visit an institution that uses computerized records. Discuss with the staff who uses the system the advantages and disadvantages over handwritten records.
- Review the institution's policy and procedure for documentation.

# LEARNING OUTCOME 4

Explain how various forms in the client record (e.g., flow sheets, progress notes, care plans, critical pathways, Kardexes, discharge/transfer forms) are used to document steps of the nursing process (assessment, diagnosis, planning, implementation, and evaluation).

## CONCEPTS FOR LECTURE

1. The client record should describe the client's ongoing status and reflect the full range of the nursing process.

   Assessment data are located in initial assessment forms, various flow sheets, and progress notes (nurses' notes).

   Nursing diagnoses are found in care plans, critical pathways, progress notes, and problem lists.

   Planning activities are found in nursing care plans, critical pathways, and Kardexes.

   Implementation is found in progress notes and flow sheets.

   Evaluation is located in progress notes.

   All steps in the nursing process are recorded on discharge and referral documents.

## POWERPOINT LECTURE SLIDES

*(NOTE: The number on each PPT Lecture Slide directly corresponds with the Concepts for Lecture.)*

1. Documenting the Nursing Process
   - Assessment data: initial assessment forms, flow sheets, progress notes (nurses' notes)
   - Nursing diagnoses: care plans, critical pathways, progress notes, problem lists
   - Planning: nursing care plans, critical pathways, Kardex
   - Implementation: progress notes, flow sheets
   - Evaluation: progress notes
   - All steps in the process recorded on discharge and referral documents

## SUGGESTIONS FOR CLINICAL ACTIVITIES

- Obtain copies of the documentation forms used in the institution. Ask the students to locate where the various components of the nursing process are documented.

# LEARNING OUTCOME 5

Compare and contrast the documentation needed for clients in acute care, home health care, and long-term care settings.

## CONCEPTS FOR LECTURE

1. Requirements for documentation in long-term care settings are based on professional standards, federal and state regulations, and policies of the health care agency.

   Laws influencing the kind and frequency of documentation required are the Health Care Financing Administration and the Omnibus Budget Reconciliation Act (OBRA) of 1987.

## POWERPOINT LECTURE SLIDES

*(NOTE: The number on each PPT Lecture Slide directly corresponds with the Concepts for Lecture.)*

1. Long-Term Care Documentation
   - Based on professional standards, federal and state regulations and the policies of the health care agency
   - Laws and requirements influencing:
     - Health Care Financing Administration

OBRA law requires that a comprehensive assessment (Minimum Data Set [MDS] for Resident Assessment and Care Screening) be performed within 4 days of admission. A formulated plan of care must be completed within 7 days, and the reassessment and care screening process must be reviewed every 3 months.

Documentation must also comply with requirements set by Medicare and Medicaid. These vary based on level of service provided.

2. General guidelines for long-term care documentation include:
   - complete the assessment/screening forms (MDS) within the time period specified by regulatory bodies
   - keep a record of any visits and of phone calls from family, friends, and others regarding the client
   - write nursing summaries and progress notes that comply with the frequency and standards required by regulatory bodies
   - review and revise plan of care every 3 months or whenever health status changes
   - document and report any changes in client's condition to primary care provider and client's family within 24 hours
   - document all measures implemented in response to changes in client's condition
   - make sure progress notes address progress related to goals and outcomes defined in plan of care
3. In 1985 the Health Care Financing Administration mandated that home health care agencies standardize their documentation methods to meet requirements for Medicare and Medicaid and other third-party disbursements. Two records are required: a home health certification and plan of treatment form, and a medical update and patient information form.
4. Guidelines for home care documentation include:
   - complete the comprehensive nursing assessment and develop plan of care to meet Medicare and other third-party payers
   - write progress notes at each visit noting any change in client's condition, nursing interventions, client responses, and vital signs as indicated
   - provide monthly nursing progress summary to the attending physician and reimbursement to confirm need to continue services
   - keep a copy of the plan of care in client's home and update as client's condition changes
   - report changes in plan of care to primary care provider and document that these were reported
   - encourage client or home caregiver to record data when appropriate
   - write a discharge summary for the primary care provider to approve and to notify reimbursers that services have been discontinued

   - Omnibus Budget Reconciliation Act (OBRA) of 1987
   - Medicare and Medicaid

**2** Documentation Guidelines:
   - Complete assessments, screening forms and plan of care within time period
   - Keep a record of any visits and phone calls
   - Write nursing summaries and progress notes according to specified time periods
   - Review and revise the plan of care every 3 months or when status changes
   - Document and report any change
   - Document all measures implemented in response to a change
   - Make sure progress notes address the client's progress in relation to the goals

**3** Home Care Documentation
   - Laws and requirements influencing
     - Health Care Financing Administration (1985)
     - Medicare and Medicaid
     - Other third-party payers
   - Two records are required:
     - Home health certification and plan of treatment form
     - Medical update and client information form

**4** Home Care Documentation Guidelines
   - Complete a comprehensive nursing assessment and plan of care
   - Write a progress note at each visit
   - Provide a monthly progress nursing summary
   - Keep a copy of the care plan in the client's home
   - Report and document changes in the plan of care
   - Encourage the client or home caregiver to record data
   - Write a discharge summary

| SUGGESTIONS FOR CLASSROOM ACTIVITIES | SUGGESTIONS FOR CLINICAL ACTIVITIES |
|---|---|
| • Invite nurses from a home health care agency and a long-term setting to discuss the documentation process required in this agency.<br>• Obtain forms used by home health care agencies and long-term care settings for documentation. If possible obtain the policies and procedures for documentation in these settings. | • If the institution has a home care department, invite a nurse from the department to review the regulations for documentation. Have students compare and contrast with documentation in acute care settings. |

## LEARNING OUTCOME 6

Identify and discuss guidelines for effective recording that meets legal and ethical standards.

### CONCEPTS FOR LECTURE

1. Because the client's record is a legal document and may be used to provide evidence in court, health care personnel must not only maintain confidentiality but also meet legal standards in the process of recording.
2. Factors to be considered include timing, legibility, permanence, accepted terminology, correct spelling, signature, accuracy, sequence, appropriateness, completeness, conciseness, and legal prudence.
   - Timing: Document the date and time of each recording in the format required by the agency. Follow the agency's policy about the frequency of documenting, adjusting as a client's condition indicates. In addition, documenting should be done as soon as possible after the assessment or intervention. No recording should be done before providing the care.
   - Legibility: All entries must be legible and easy to read. Printing or easily understood handwriting is usually permissible. Follow agency policies.
   - Permanence: All entries are made in dark ink so that the record is permanent and changes can be identified. Dark ink reproduces well in duplication processes. Follow agency policies.
   - Accepted terminology: Use only commonly accepted abbreviations, symbols, and terms that are specified by the agency. When in doubt about whether to use an abbreviation, write the term out in full (see Table 15-4). Follow JCAHO requirements by conforming to the agency's "Do Not Use" list of abbreviations, acronyms, and symbols (see Table 15-5).
   - Correct spelling: Correct spelling is essential for accuracy in recording. If unsure how to spell a word, look it up in a dictionary or other resource book.
   - Signature: Each recording is signed by the nurse making it, including name and title. Some agencies have a signature sheet and after signing this signature sheet, nurses can use their initials. With computerized documenting, each nurse has a code that allows documentation to be identified.

### POWERPOINT LECTURE SLIDES

*(NOTE: The number on each PPT Lecture Slide directly corresponds with the Concepts for Lecture.)*

1. Legal and Ethical Standards for Documentation
   - Client's record is a legal document
   - May be used to provide evidence in court

2. Factors To Be Considered Include:
   - Timing
   - Legibility
   - Permanence
   - Accepted terminology
   - Correct spelling
   - Signature
   - Accuracy
   - Sequence
   - Appropriateness
   - Completeness
   - Conciseness
   - Legal prudence

- Accuracy: The client's name and identifying information should be stamped or written on each page of the record. Before making an entry, check that it is the correct chart. Notations must be accurate and correct; accurate notations consist of facts or observations rather than opinions or interpretations. When describing, avoid general terms such as *large, good,* or *normal,* which can be interpreted differently. When a mistake in recording has been made, draw a line through it and write the words *mistaken entry* above or next to the original entry, with your initials or name (follow agency policy). Do not erase, blot out, or use correction fluid. Follow agency policy for correcting documentation errors in computerized documentation. Write on every line but never between lines. If a blank appears in a notation, draw a line through the blank space so that no additional information can be recorded at any other time or by any other person, and sign the notation.
- Sequence: Document events in the order in which they occur. Update or delete problems as needed.
- Appropriateness: Record only information that pertains to the client's health problems and care. Recording irrelevant information may be considered an invasion of privacy or libelous.
- Completeness: Information that is recorded needs to be complete and helpful to the client and health care professionals. Nurses' notes need to reflect the nursing process. Care that is omitted because of the client's condition or refusal of treatment must also be recorded including what was omitted, why it was omitted, and who was notified.
- Conciseness: Recordings need to be brief as well as complete to save time in communication. The client's name and the word *client* are omitted. End each thought or sentence with a period.
- Legal prudence: Accurate, complete documentation should give legal protection to the nurse, the client's other caregivers, the health care facility, and the client. The record provides proof of the quality of care given. Documentation is usually viewed by juries and attorneys as the best evidence of what really happened to the client.

## SUGGESTIONS FOR CLASSROOM ACTIVITIES

- Provide examples of errors in charting. Divide the students into groups and have each group determine and demonstrate the best way to correct the errors in a clear and legal manner. Share the groups' corrections with the class and critique.
- If possible, show a DVD or videotape of court proceedings where documentation is an important component of the process.

## SUGGESTIONS FOR CLINICAL ACTIVITIES

- Review the policy and procedure for correcting errors in charting and late entries for the institution.
- Have the students write a narrative note for their assigned clients. Ask the students to exchange notes with a classmate. Critique the notes using the guidelines for documentation in the text.

# LEARNING OUTCOME 7

Identify essential guidelines for reporting client data.

## CONCEPTS FOR LECTURE

1. The purpose of reporting is to communicate specific information to a person or group of people. A report, whether oral or written, should be concise, including pertinent information but no extraneous detail. In addition to change-of-shift reports and telephone reports, reporting can also include the sharing of information or ideas with colleagues and other health professionals about some aspect of a client's care (e.g., care plan conference and nursing rounds).

2. Key elements of a change-of-shift report include the following: follow a particular order (e.g., room numbers); provide basic identifying information for each client; for new clients provide the reason for admission or medical diagnoses, surgery, diagnostic tests, and therapies in the past 24 hours; include significant changes in the client's condition and present information in order; provide exact information; report the client's need for emotional support; include current nurse and primary care provider-prescribed orders; provide a summary of newly admitted clients, including diagnosis, age, general condition, plan of therapy, and significant information about the client's support people; report on clients who have been transferred or discharged; clearly state priorities of care and care that is due after the shift begins; and be concise (see Box 15–3).

3. Health professionals frequently report about a client by telephone. Nurses inform primary care provider about a change in a client's condition. A nurse may report to another nurse on another unit about a transferred client. The nurse receiving a telephone report should document the date and time, the name of the person giving the information, and the subject of the information received, and sign the notation. If there is any doubt about the information, the nurse receiving the information should repeat it back to the sender to ensure accuracy. When giving a telephone report to a primary care provider, it is important to be concise and accurate. Begin with your name and relationship to the client, the client's name and medical diagnosis, changes in nursing assessment, vital signs related to baseline, significant laboratory data, and related nursing interventions. The nurse should have the client's chart ready to give the primary care provider any further information. After reporting, the nurse should document the date, time, and content of the call.

4. Primary care provider often order therapy for a client by telephone. Most agencies have specific policies about who may take such an order as may state nursing boards of nursing. Guidelines for taking telephone orders include: know the state nursing board's position on who can give and accept; know the agency's policy; ask prescriber to speak slowly and clearly, to spell our medication name if nurse is unfamiliar with

## POWERPOINT LECTURE SLIDES

*(NOTE: The number on each PPT Lecture Slide directly corresponds with the Concepts for Lecture.)*

**1** Guidelines for Reporting Client Data
- Should be concise, including pertinent information but no extraneous detail
- Types of reporting:
  - Change-of-shift report
  - Telephone reports
  - Care plan conference
  - Nursing rounds

**2** Guidelines for Change-of-Shift Report
- Follow a particular order
- Provide basic identifying information
- For new clients provide the reason for admission or medical diagnosis/es, surgery, diagnostic tests, and therapies in the past 24 hours
- Significant changes in client's condition
- Provide exact information
- Report client's need for emotional support
- Include current nurse and primary care provider-prescribed orders
- Provide a summary of newly admitted clients, including diagnosis, age, general condition, plan of therapy, and significant information about the client's support people
- Report on clients who have been transferred or discharged
- Clearly state priorities of care and care due after the shift begins
- Be concise

**3** Guidelines for Receiving and Giving a Telephone Report
- When receiving a report:
  - Document date and time
  - Record the name of person giving the information
  - Record the subject of the information received
  - Repeat information to ensure accuracy
  - Sign the notation
- When giving a report:
  - Be concise and accurate
  - State name and relationship to client
  - State the client's name, medical diagnosis, changes in nursing assessment, vital signs related to baseline, significant laboratory data, related nursing interventions
  - Have chart ready to give any further information needed
  - Document the date, time, and content of the call

it; question the drug, dosage, or changes if seem inappropriate for the client; write the order down or enter into a computer; read the order back; use words instead of abbreviations; write the order on the physician's order sheet, record date, time, indicate it was a telephone order, sign name with credentials; when writing a dosage always put a number before a decimal, but never after a decimal; write out units; transcribe the order; follow agency protocol about signing telephone orders; and never follow a voice-mail order, call the prescriber for the order.

5. A care plan conference is a meeting of nurses to discuss possible solutions to certain problems. Other health professionals may be invited to attend the conference to offer their expertise. Care plan conferences are most effective when there is a climate of respect—that is, nonjudgmental acceptance of others even though their values, opinions, and beliefs may seem different.

6. Nursing rounds are procedures in which two or more nurses visit selected clients at their bedside to obtain information that helps plan nursing care, to provide clients the opportunity to discuss their care, and to evaluate the nursing care the clients have received. The nurse assigned to the client provides a brief summary of the client's nursing needs and the interventions being implemented. To facilitate the client's participation in nursing rounds, nurses need to use terms that the client can understand.

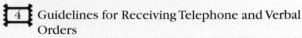

**4** Guidelines for Receiving Telephone and Verbal Orders
- Know the state nursing board's position on who can give and accept
- Know the agency policy
- Ask prescriber to speak slowly and clearly
- Ask prescriber to spell out the medication if unfamiliar
- Question the drug, dosage, or changes if seem inappropriate
- Write the order down or enter into a computer
- Read the order back to the prescriber
- Use words instead of abbreviations
- Write the order on the physician's order sheet, record date, time, indicate it was a telephone order, and sign name with credentials
- When writing a dosage always put a number before a decimal, but never after a decimal
- Write out units
- Transcribe the order
- Follow agency protocol about signing the telephone order
- Never follow a voice-mail order

**5** Care Plan Conference
- Meeting of nurses to discuss possible solutions to certain problems
- Other health care professionals may be invited
- Most effective in climate of respect

**6** Nursing Rounds
- Two or more nurses visit client at bedside
  - Obtain information to help plan nursing care
  - Provide client opportunity to discuss care
  - Evaluate nursing care client has received
- Assigned nurse provides brief summary of client's nursing needs and interventions being implemented

---

**SUGGESTIONS FOR CLASSROOM ACTIVITIES**

- Divide the students into groups. Have each group role-play a change-of-shift report, a telephone report to a physician, and a transfer report to another unit using data that you provide. Ask group members to assist each other by making suggestions for improvement and identifying strengths.

**SUGGESTIONS FOR CLINICAL ACTIVITIES**

- Review the institution's policies and procedures for taking verbal orders and reports.
- Assign the students to attend change-of-shift reports, nursing care conferences, or nursing rounds in the clinical facility. Ask the students to report observations including how the activity was organized, the type of information exchanged, and positive and negative aspects of the activity.
- Have students give an end-of-shift report on their client to the clinical group using the guidelines presented in the text.

# LEARNING OUTCOME 8

Identify prohibited abbreviations, acronyms, and symbols that cannot be used in any form of clinical documentation.

## CONCEPTS FOR LECTURE

1. In 2004, JCAHO developed National Patient Safety Goals (NPSGs) to reduce communication errors. These goals are required to be implemented by all organizations accredited by JCAHO. As a result, the accredited organizations must develop a "Do Not Use" list of abbreviations, acronyms, and symbols. This list must include those banned by JCAHO (see Table 15–5). Many of the banned abbreviations are related to medication administration such as U, IU, MS, and S.C. Other banned abbreviations are derived from Latin such as H.S., A.S., A.D., Q.D., or Q.O.D.

## POWERPOINT LECTURE SLIDES

*(NOTE: The number on each PPT Lecture Slide directly corresponds with the Concepts for Lecture.)*

 Prohibited Abbreviations, Acronyms, and Symbols
- JCAHO National Patient Safety Goals (2004)
- "Do Not Use" list
- Many banned abbreviations refer to medications
- Others derived from Latin

## SUGGESTIONS FOR CLASSROOM ACTIVITIES

- Review the information in Table 15–5 with the students, stressing the rationale for inclusion on the "Do Not Use" list.
- Provide examples of how these terms can be misinterpreted.

## SUGGESTIONS FOR CLINICAL ACTIVITIES

- Review the institution's "Do Not Use" list and give students a copy of this.
- Obtain copies of the approved abbreviation list for the institution and distribute to the students.

# CHAPTER 16
## HEALTH PROMOTION

## RESOURCE LIBRARY

###  PRENTICE HALL NURSING MEDIALINK DVD-ROM

Audio Glossary
NCLEX® Review

### COMPANION WEBSITE

Additional NCLEX® Review
Case Study: Health Promotion Program
Care Plan Activity: Health Promotion, Health Fair, and
  Nursing Students
Application Activity: *Health Belief Model*
Links to Resources

### 📖 IMAGE LIBRARY

**Figure 16.1** An open system with a feedback
mechanism.
**Figure 16.2** The homeostatic regulators of the body:
autonomic nervous system, endocrine system, and
specific organ systems.
**Figure 16.3** Maslow's needs.

**Figure 16.4** The Health Promotion Model (revised).
**Figure 16.5** The stages of change are rarely linear.
**Figure 16.6** Strategies to promote behavioral change
for each stage of change.

---

## LEARNING OUTCOME 1

Explain the relationship of individuality and holism to nursing practice.

### CONCEPTS FOR LECTURE

1. Assessing and planning health care of the client is enhanced when the nurse understands the concepts of individuality, holism, homeostasis, and human needs.
2. To help clients attain, maintain, or regain an optimal level of health, nurses need to understand clients as unique individuals who are different from every other human being. Nurses need to focus on both a total care context and an individualized care context. In the total care context, nurses consider all the principles and areas that apply when taking care of any client of that age and condition. In the individualized context, nurses become acquainted with clients as individuals, using the total care principles that apply to this person at this time.
3. Nurses are concerned with the individual as a whole, complete, or holistic person, not as an assembly of parts.

    When applied in nursing, the concept of holism emphasizes that nurses must keep the whole person in mind and strive to understand how one area of concern relates to the whole person. Nurses must also consider the relationship of the client to the environment and to others.

### POWERPOINT LECTURE SLIDES

*(NOTE: The number on each PPT Lecture Slide directly corresponds with the Concepts for Lecture.)*

**1** Assessing and Planning Health Care
  • Enhanced when nurses understand
    ○ Individuality
    ○ Holism
    ○ Homeostasis
    ○ Human needs

**2** Individuality
  • Each individual is a unique being
  • Focus on total care and individualized care context
  • Total care context considers all the principles that apply when taking care of any client
  • Individualized care context means using the total care principles that apply to the person at this time

**3** Holism
  • Concerned with the individual as a whole, not as an assembly of parts
  • Strive to understand how one area of concern relates to the whole person
  • Consider the relationship of individuals to the environment and to others

## LEARNING OUTCOME 2

Give four main characteristics of homeostatic mechanisms.

### CONCEPTS FOR LECTURE

1. Homeostasis is the tendency of the body to maintain a state of balance or equilibrium while constantly changing. Homeostatic mechanisms have four main characteristics:
   - Self-regulation
   - Compensatory
   - Regulated by negative feedback systems
   - May require several feedback mechanisms to correct only one physiologic imbalance

### POWERPOINT LECTURE SLIDES

*(NOTE: The number on each PPT Lecture Slide directly corresponds with the Concepts for Lecture.)*

 Characteristics of Homeostatic Mechanisms
- Self-regulatory
- Compensatory
- Regulated by negative feedback systems
- Feedback mechanisms

**SUGGESTIONS FOR CLASSROOM ACTIVITIES**

- Have the students give examples of how changes may occur within the internal or external environment of a person and yet a state of balance is maintained.

**SUGGESTIONS FOR CLINICAL ACTIVITIES**

- Have the students give examples of homeostatic mechanisms that they observed in their clients.

## LEARNING OUTCOME 3

Identify theoretical frameworks used in individual health promotion.

### CONCEPTS FOR LECTURE

1. A variety of theoretical frameworks provide the nurse with a holistic overview of health promotion. Two major theoretical frameworks that nurses use in promoting health of an individual are needs theories and developmental stage theories.

   In needs theories, human needs are ranked on an ascending scale according to how essential the needs are for survival.

   Maslow (1970) ranked human needs on five levels in ascending order: physiologic, safety and security, love and belonging, self-esteem, and self-actualization.

   Kalish (1983) adapted Maslow's hierarchy, adding one more level between physiologic and safety and security-stimulation needs.

   Human needs serve as a framework for assessing behaviors, assigning priorities to desired outcomes, and planning nursing interventions.

### POWERPOINT LECTURE SLIDES

*(NOTE: The number on each PPT Lecture Slide directly corresponds with the Concepts for Lecture.)*

 Theoretical Frameworks Used in Individual Health Promotion
- Two major theoretical frameworks
  ○ Needs theories
    – Maslow
    – Kalish
  ○ Developmental stage theories

Developmental stage theories categorize a person's behavior or tasks into approximate age ranges or in terms that describe the features of an age group.

These theories allow nurses to describe typical behaviors of an individual within a certain age group, explain the significance of those behaviors, predict behaviors that might occur in a given situation, and provide a rationale to control behavioral manifestations.

---

### SUGGESTIONS FOR CLASSROOM ACTIVITIES

- Develop a list of nursing diagnoses. Assist the students to use Maslow's hierarchy of needs to prioritize these diagnoses. Discuss the pros and cons of using this method to prioritize diagnoses.
- Provide examples of developmental stage theories and how these may be used to help identify health promotion needs.

### SUGGESTIONS FOR CLINICAL ACTIVITIES

- Have the students prioritize the nursing diagnoses for their assigned clients using Maslow's hierarchy of needs.

---

## LEARNING OUTCOME 4

Identify Maslow's characteristics of the self-actualized person.

### CONCEPTS FOR LECTURE

1. The self-actualized person has the following characteristics (see Figure 16–3):
   - Is realistic, sees life clearly, and is objective about his or her observations
   - Judges people correctly
   - Has superior perception, is more decisive
   - Has a clear notion of right and wrong
   - Is usually accurate in predicting future events
   - Understands art, music, politics, and philosophy
   - Possesses humility, listens to others carefully
   - Is dedicated to some work, task, duty, or vocation
   - Is highly creative, flexible, spontaneous, courageous, and willing to make mistakes
   - Is open to new ideas
   - Is self-confident and has self-respect
   - Has a low degree of self-conflict, personality is integrated
   - Respects self, does not need fame, possesses a feeling of self-control
   - Is highly independent, desires privacy
   - Can appear remote and detached
   - Is friendly, loving, and governed more by inner directives than by society
   - Can make decisions contrary to popular opinion
   - Is problem centered rather than self-centered
   - Accepts the world for what it is

### POWERPOINT LECTURE SLIDES

*(NOTE: The number on each PPT Lecture Slide directly corresponds with the Concepts for Lecture.)*

 Maslow's Characteristics of the Self-Actualized Person
- Realistic, sees life clearly, and is objective
- Judges people correctly
- Has superior perception, is more decisive
- Has clear notion of right and wrong
- Is usually accurate in predicting future events
- Understands art, music, politics, and philosophy
- Possesses humility, listens to others carefully
- Is highly creative, flexible, spontaneous, courageous, and willing to make mistakes
- Is open to new ideas
- Is self-confident and has self respect
- Has low degree of self-conflict; personality is integrated
- Respects self, does not need fame, possesses a feeling of self control
- Is highly independent, desires privacy
- Can appear remote and detached
- Is friendly, loving, and governed more by inner directives than by society
- Can make decisions contrary to popular opinion
- Is problem-centered rather than self-centered
- Accepts the world for what it is

# LEARNING OUTCOME 5

Describe how the *Healthy People 2010* leading health indicators can help improve the health of a community.

## CONCEPTS FOR LECTURE

1. *Healthy People 2010* presents a comprehensive 10-year strategy for promoting health and preventing illness, disability, and premature death.

    Its two major goals are to increase quality and years of healthy life and to eliminate health disparities.

2. To support these goals, *Healthy People 2010* is organized around 28 focus areas to improve health (see Box 16–2). It also establishes a set of leading health indicators that reflect the major public health concerns in the United States at the beginning of the 21st century (see Box 16–3).

    It is expected that these indicators will help develop action plans to improve the health of both individuals and communities.

    The foundation for *Healthy People 2010* is the belief that individual health is closely linked to community health and the reverse; thus the vision for *Healthy People 2010* is "Healthy People in Healthy Communities."

    As a result, partnerships are important to improve individual and community health. Businesses, local government, and civic, professional, and religious organizations can all participate.

## POWERPOINT LECTURE SLIDES

*(NOTE: The number on each PPT Lecture Slide directly corresponds with the Concepts for Lecture.)*

1 *Healthy People 2010*
- Two major goals are:
  - To increase quality and years of healthy life
  - To eliminate health disparities

2 *Healthy People 2010*
- Organized around 28 focus areas to improve health
- Establishes a set of leading health indicators reflecting public health concerns
- Indicators will help develop action plans to improve the health of both individuals and communities
- Individual health closely linked to community health and reverse
- Vision is "healthy people in healthy communities"

**SUGGESTIONS FOR CLASSROOM ACTIVITIES**

- Have the students generate examples that illustrate the meaning of "Healthy People in Healthy Communities."
- Divide the students into groups, and assign a leading health indicator (see Box 16–3). Ask the group to give examples of community programs for the indicator that would improve the health of the community and people in the community.

**SUGGESTIONS FOR CLINICAL ACTIVITIES**

- Ask the students to identify problems their clients demonstrated that may be attributed to one of the leading health indicators (e.g., lack of physical mobility, tobacco use, overweight and obesity).

# LEARNING OUTCOME 6

Differentiate health promotion from health protection or illness prevention.

## CONCEPTS FOR LECTURE

1. Considerable differences appear in the literature regarding the use of the terms *health promotion, health protection,* and *illness prevention*. The individual's motivation for the behavior is the major difference.

## POWERPOINT LECTURE SLIDES

*(NOTE: The number on each PPT Lecture Slide directly corresponds with the Concepts for Lecture.)*

1 Health Promotion, Health Protection, and Illness Prevention

2. Health promotion is not disease oriented. It is motivated by a personal, positive approach to wellness, and seeks to expand positive health potential.
3. Health protection/illness prevention is illness or injury specific, is motivated by avoidance of illness, and seeks to thwart the occurrence of insults to health and well-being (see Box 16–4).

- The difference is the individual's motivation for behavior

 Health Promotion
  - Not disease oriented
  - Motivated by personal, positive approach to wellness
  - Seeks to expand positive potential for health

 Health Protection or Illness Prevention
  - Illness or injury specific
  - Motivated by avoidance of illness
  - Seeks to thwart the occurrence of insults to health and well-being

---

**SUGGESTIONS FOR CLASSROOM ACTIVITIES**

- Provide examples of healthy behaviors. Have the students classify these as health promotion, health protection, or illness prevention. Discuss any difficulties encountered.

**SUGGESTIONS FOR CLINICAL ACTIVITIES**

- Have the students identify health promotion, health protection, or illness prevention activities appropriate for their assigned clients.
- Have the students discuss whether health promotion, health protection, or illness prevention activities are or should be a component of care for the clients on the clinical unit of this institution.

---

## LEARNING OUTCOME 7

Identify various types and sites of health promotion programs.

**CONCEPTS FOR LECTURE**

1. Health promotion programs are found in many settings. They may be offered to individuals and families in the home or in the community setting and at schools, hospitals, or worksites.

   The type of program depends on the current concerns and the expertise of the sponsoring department or group.

   For example, the local health department may offer a town-wide immunization program, the fire department may disseminate fire prevention information, and the police may offer a bicycle safety program for children, or a safe-driving campaign for young adults.

   Programs offered by health care organizations initially began with a specific focus on prevention such as infection control or fire prevention and gradually expanded to include issues related to employee health and lifestyle such as smoking cessation and exercise. Increasingly, hospitals have offered a variety of these programs to the community.

   School health promotion programs may serve as a foundation for children of all ages to gain basic knowledge about personal hygiene and issues in the health science providing a cost-effective and convenient setting for health-focused programs. The school nurse may teach programs about basic nutrition, dental care, activity

**POWERPOINT LECTURE SLIDES**

*(NOTE: The number on each PPT Lecture Slide directly corresponds with the Concepts for Lecture.)*

 Health Promotion Programs
  - Types of programs
    - Health promotion
    - Specific protection
    - Screening for early detection of disease
  - Sites for programs
    - In home
    - Community
    - Schools
    - Health care organizations
    - Worksites

and play, drug and alcohol abuse, for example. Classroom teachers may include health-related topics in their lesson plans.

   Worksite programs for health promotion have developed out of the need for businesses to control the rising cost of health care and employee absenteeism. Worksite programs may include health promotion programs that affect all employees such as air quality standards for the office or plant; programs aimed at specific populations, such as accident prevention for the machine worker; screening programs such as blood pressure screening; or health enhancement programs, such as fitness information and relaxation techniques.

---

### SUGGESTIONS FOR CLASSROOM ACTIVITIES

- Ask the students to brainstorm ways to provide health promotion activities for various age groups on the campus or in the community.
- Invite a panel of guest speakers to discuss health promotion for the elderly, poor, and homeless in your community.

### SUGGESTIONS FOR CLINICAL ACTIVITIES

- Invite a representative from the institution's community outreach program or human resources department to discuss the various types of health promotion programs offered by the institution and how these programs were selected.

---

## LEARNING OUTCOME 8

Discuss the Health Promotion Model.

### CONCEPTS FOR LECTURE

1. The Health Promotion Model (revised) (HPM) is a competence or approach-oriented model in which the motivational source for behavior change is based on the individual's subjective value of the change—that is, how the client perceives the benefits of changing the given health behavior (see Figure 16–4).
2. There are a number of variables in this model: individual characteristics and experiences, behavior-specific cognitions and affect, commitment to a plan of action, immediate competing demands and preferences, and behavioral outcomes.

   Individual characteristics and experiences include personal factors and prior related experiences. Some personal factors, categorized as biological, psychological, and sociocultural, can be changed and others cannot. Nursing intervention usually focuses on factors that can be modified; however, it can be just as important to focus on factors that cannot be changed, such as family history.

   Prior health-related behavior includes previous experience, knowledge, and skill in health-promoting behavior. Individuals who made a habit of previous health-promoting behaviors and received a positive benefit as a result will engage in future health-promoting

### POWERPOINT LECTURE SLIDES

*(NOTE: The number on each PPT Lecture Slide directly corresponds with the Concepts for Lecture.)*

1 Health Promotion Model (HPM)
- Competence or approach-oriented model
- Motivational source for behavior changes based on individual's subjective value of the change

2 Variables of HPM
- Individual characteristics and experiences
  ○ Prior related behaviors
  ○ Personal factors
- Behavior-specific cognitions and affect
  ○ Perceived benefits of action
  ○ Perceived barriers to action
  ○ Perceived self-efficacy
  ○ Activity-related affect
  ○ Interpersonal factors
  ○ Situational influences
- Commitment to a plan of action
- Immediate competing demands and preferences
- Behavioral outcome

behaviors in contrast to those persons with a history of barriers to achieving the behavior.

Behavior-specific cognitions and affect include a set of variables that is of major motivational significance for acquiring and maintaining health-promoting behaviors that can be modified through nursing interventions. These variables include perceived benefits of action, perceived barriers to action, perceived self-efficacy, activity-related affect, interpersonal influences, and situational influences.

Commitment to action includes specifying strategies for carrying out and reinforcing the behavior.

Immediate competing demands and preferences can interfere with carrying out the plan to change behavior. A competing demand is a behavior over which an individual has a low level of control. Not responding to this demand may cause a more negative outcome than not performing the health-promoting behavior.

Competing preferences are behaviors over which an individual has a high level of control; however, this control depends on the individual's ability to be self-regulating or to not "give in."

The health-promoting behavior is the outcome of the HPM and is directed toward obtaining positive health outcomes for the client.

---

## SUGGESTIONS FOR CLASSROOM ACTIVITIES

- Have each student identify one health promotion behavior that he or she has attempted to change or would like to change. Ask the student to write a short paper applying the variables of the HPM to this behavior. For example, has the student attempted to change this behavior before? If so, what happened and how might this prior attempt at behavior change influence this attempt to change the behavior?
- Provide additional examples of how the variables in the model may affect behavioral change.

## SUGGESTIONS FOR CLINICAL ACTIVITIES

- Have the students discuss the pros and cons of fear as a motivating factor for behavior change.

---

# LEARNING OUTCOME 9

Explain the stages of health behavior change.

## CONCEPTS FOR LECTURE

1. Health behavior change is a cyclic phenomenon in which a person goes through several stages (see Figure 16–5).

    In the Transtheoretical Model (TTM) proposed by Prochaska, Redding, and Evers, there are six stages: precontemplation, contemplation, preparation, action, maintenance, and termination. If the person is not successful in changing behaviors, relapse occurs.

## POWERPOINT LECTURE SLIDES

*(NOTE: The number on each PPT Lecture Slide directly corresponds with the Concepts for Lecture.)*

 Stages of Health Behavior Change
- Precontemplation
- Contemplation
- Preparation
- Action
- Maintenance
- Termination

In the precontemplation stage, the person does not think about changing behavior in the next 6 months and may be uninformed or underinformed about the consequences of the risk behaviors. If a person has tried changing previously and was unsuccessful, he or she may now see the behavior as "fate" or believe that change is hopeless.

In the contemplation stage, the person acknowledges having a problem, seriously considers making a specific behavior change, actively gathers information, and verbalizes plans to change in the near future (e.g., next 6 months). Some people stay in this stage for months or years. When contemplators begin to transition to preparation, their thinking is marked by two changes: focusing on the solution and thinking more about the future than the past.

The preparation stage occurs when the person intends to take action in the immediate future, may have started making small behavioral changes, and makes the final specific plans to accomplish the change.

In the action stage, the person actively implements the behavioral and cognitive strategies of the action plan. This stage requires the greatest commitment of time and energy.

In the maintenance stage, the person strives to prevent relapse by integrating newly adopted behaviors into his or her lifestyle. This stage lasts until the person no longer experiences temptation to return to previous unhealthy behaviors. Without a commitment, there will be a relapse.

In the termination stage, the individual has complete confidence that the problem is no longer a temptation or threat. Experts debate whether some behaviors can be terminated versus requiring continual maintenance (see Box 16–6).

## SUGGESTIONS FOR CLASSROOM ACTIVITIES

- Provide the students with examples of statements clients may make about a health-promoting behavior. Ask the students to identify the stage of change that each statement may represent and to supply their rationale. Example: "It is my right to decide whether I smoke, and I have decided that I am going to smoke."
- Have the students debate the following statement: Some health promotion, health protection, or illness prevention behaviors may require continual maintenance.

## SUGGESTIONS FOR CLINICAL ACTIVITIES

- Have the students provide examples from client interactions that demonstrate the TTM stages.

Discuss the nurse's role in health promotion.

## CONCEPTS FOR LECTURE

1. The nurse's role in health promotion includes:
   - Model healthy lifestyle behaviors and attitudes.
   - Facilitate client involvement in the assessment, implementation, and evaluation of health goals.
   - Teach clients self-care strategies to enhance fitness, improve nutrition, manage stress, and enhance relationships.
   - Assist clients, families, and communities to increase their levels of health.
   - Educate clients to be effective health care consumers.
   - Assist clients, families, and communities to develop and choose health-promoting options.
   - Guide clients' development in effective problem solving and decision making.
   - Reinforce clients' personal and family health-promoting behaviors.
   - Advocate in the community for changes that promote a healthy environment.

## POWERPOINT LECTURE SLIDES

*(NOTE: The number on each PPT Lecture Slide directly corresponds with the Concepts for Lecture.)*

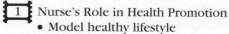 Nurse's Role in Health Promotion
- Model healthy lifestyle
- Facilitate client involvement
- Teach self-care strategies
- Assist clients to increase levels of health
- Educate clients to be effective health care consumers
- Assist clients to develop and choose health-promoting options
- Guide development of effective problem solving and decision making
- Reinforce clients' personal and family health-promoting behaviors
- Advocate in the community for changes that promote a healthy environment

## SUGGESTIONS FOR CLASSROOM ACTIVITIES

- Have students debate the following statement: The nurse's role in health promotion includes modeling healthy lifestyle behaviors and attitudes.
- Invite several community health nurses to discuss the nurse's role in health promotion in their agencies.

# LEARNING OUTCOME 11

Assess the health of individuals.

## CONCEPTS FOR LECTURE

1. Plans for health promotion are based on a thorough assessment of the individual's health status.

   Components of this assessment are the health history and physical examination, physical fitness, lifestyle, spiritual health, social support system, and health risk assessments, health beliefs review, and life-stress review.

## POWERPOINT LECTURE SLIDES

*(NOTE: The number on each PPT Lecture Slide directly corresponds with the Concepts for Lecture.)*

 Assessment of Health
- Health history
- Physical examination
- Physical fitness assessment
- Lifestyle assessment
- Spiritual health assessment
- Social support system review
- Health risk assessment
- Health beliefs review
- Life-stress review

## SUGGESTIONS FOR CLASSROOM ACTIVITIES

- Have the students perform health assessments on a partner, using the information presented in the textbook.
- Have the students perform the Life Change Index assessment in Box 16–8 on themselves and discuss the results.

## SUGGESTIONS FOR CLINICAL ACTIVITIES

- Have the students review the health history and physical examination of their assigned clients to identify health risks. Compare and contrast findings.

# LEARNING OUTCOME 12

Develop, implement, and evaluate plans for health promotion.

## CONCEPTS FOR LECTURE

1. Health promotion plans need to be developed according to the needs, desires, and priorities of the client. The client decides on goals, activities or interventions to achieve these goals, the frequency and duration of the activities, and the method of evaluation. Another essential aspect of planning is identifying support resources available to the client.

2. Implementing is the "doing" part of the behavior change. Self-responsibility is emphasized. Nursing interventions may include supporting, counseling, facilitating, teaching, consulting, enhancing the behavior change, and modeling (see Figure 16–6).

3. Evaluating takes place on an ongoing basis, both during the attainment of short-term goals and after the completion of long-term goals.

   During evaluation, the client may decide to continue with the plan, reorder priorities, change strategies, or revise the health protection/health promotion contract. Evaluation of the plan is a collaborative effort between the nurse and the client.

## POWERPOINT LECTURE SLIDES

*(NOTE: The number on each PPT Lecture Slide directly corresponds with the Concepts for Lecture.)*

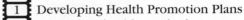 Developing Health Promotion Plans
- Based on health needs, desires, and priorities of the client
- Client decides on:
  - Goals
  - Activities or interventions to achieve these goals
  - Frequency and duration of activities
  - Method of evaluation

2 Implementing Health Promotion Plans
- Emphasis on self responsibility
- Nursing interventions include:
  - Supporting
  - Counseling
  - Facilitating
  - Teaching
  - Consulting
  - Enhancing the behavior change
  - Modeling

3 Evaluating Health Promotion Plans
- Ongoing
- Collaborative effort
- Client actions may include:
  - Continue the plan
  - Reorder priorities
  - Change strategies

---

## SUGGESTIONS FOR CLASSROOM ACTIVITIES

- Assign students to plan, organize, and implement a health promotion day on campus.

---

# CHAPTER 17
## HEALTH, WELLNESS, AND ILLNESS

## RESOURCE LIBRARY

### ⊙ PRENTICE HALL NURSING MEDIALINK DVD-ROM

Audio Glossary
NCLEX® Review

 **COMPANION WEBSITE**

Additional NCLEX® Review
Care Plan: Health Care Promotion in a Senior Citizen
   Residence
Case Study: Nonadherent Diabetic Client
Application Activity: *Multidisciplinary Care and
   Resources*
Links to Resources

### 📖 IMAGE LIBRARY

**Figure 17.1** Satisfaction with work enhances a sense of well-being and contributes to wellness.
**Figure 17.2** The seven components of wellness.
**Figure 17.3** The agent-host-environment triangle.

**Figure 17.4** Dunn's health grid: its axes and quadrants.
**Figure 17.5** Illness-wellness continuum.
**Figure 17.6** The health belief model.

---

## LEARNING OUTCOME 1

Differentiate health, wellness, and well-being.

### CONCEPTS FOR LECTURE

1. Health, wellness, and well-being have many definitions and interpretations.
2. Traditionally health was defined in terms of the presence or absence of disease.

   The World Health Organization (WHO) defines health as "a state of complete physical, mental, and social well-being and not merely the absence of disease or infirmity." This definition reflects concern for the total individual and places health in the context of the environment.

   Health has also been defined in terms of role and performance. Talcott Parson conceptualized health as the ability to maintain normal roles.

   The President's Commission on Health Needs of the Nation (1953) stated: "Health is not a condition, it is an adjustment. It is not a state but a process. The process adapts the individual not only to our physical but also our social environment."

   In 1980 the ANA defined health as "a dynamic state of being in which the developmental and behavioral potential of an individual is realized to the fullest extent possible" (p. 5). In this definition health includes striving toward optimal functioning. In 2004 the ANA also stated that health was "an experience that is often expressed in terms of wellness and illness, and may occur in the presence or absence of disease or injury" (p. 48).

### POWERPOINT LECTURE SLIDES

*(NOTE: The number on each PPT Lecture Slide directly corresponds with the Concepts for Lecture.)*

**1** Health, Wellness, and Well-Being
   • Many definitions and interpretations

**2** Health
   • Presence or absence of disease
   • Complete physical, mental, social well-being
   • Ability to maintain normal roles
   • Process of adaptation to physical and social environment
   • Striving toward optimal wellness
   • Individual definitions

**3** Wellness
   • State of well-being
   • Basic aspects of wellness include:
      ○ Self-responsibility
      ○ An ultimate goal
      ○ A dynamic, growing process
      ○ Daily decision making in areas related to health
      ○ Whole being of the individual

**4** Well-Being
   • Subjective perception of vitality and feeling well
   • Described objectively, experienced, measured
   • Can be plotted on a continuum

Many people define and describe health as being free of disease and pain as much as possible; being able to be active and to do what they want or must; and being in good spirits most of the time.

3. Wellness is a state of well-being. Basic aspects of wellness include self-responsibility; an ultimate goal; a dynamic, growing process; daily decision making in the areas of nutrition, stress management, physical fitness, preventive health care, and emotional health; and, most importantly, the whole being of the individual.

4. "Well-being is a subjective perception of vitality and feeling well . . . can be described objectively, experienced, and measured . . . and can be plotted on a continuum." It is a component of health.

---

### SUGGESTIONS FOR CLASSROOM ACTIVITIES

- Have the students develop their own definitions of health and wellness.
- Have the students interview a school-age child, an adolescent, a middle-aged adult, and an elderly adult, asking each to define health and wellness. Have the students report their findings. Record the results. Have the class analyze the results, looking for patterns across the groups and within the groups. If possible, compare and contrast results given by men and women. Compare to definitions given in the textbook.

### SUGGESTIONS FOR CLINICAL ACTIVITIES

- Have the students ask their clients and several different types of health care professionals to define health and wellness. Compare and contrast definitions of the clients and the health care professionals.

---

# LEARNING OUTCOME 2

Describe five dimensions of wellness.

### CONCEPTS FOR LECTURE

1. The dimensions of wellness are: physical, social, emotional, intellectual, spiritual, occupational, and environmental.

2. The physical dimension of wellness is the ability to carry out daily tasks, to achieve fitness (e.g., pulmonary, cardiovascular, gastrointestinal), to maintain adequate nutrition and proper body fat, to avoid abusing drugs and alcohol or using tobacco products, and generally to practice positive lifestyle habits.

3. The social dimension of wellness includes the ability to interact successfully with people and within the environment of which each person is a part, to develop and maintain intimacy with significant others, and to develop respect and tolerance for those with different opinions and beliefs.

4. The emotional dimension is the ability to manage stress and to express emotions appropriately. Emotional wellness involves the ability to recognize, accept, and express feelings and to accept one's limitations.

### POWERPOINT LECTURE SLIDES

*(NOTE: The number on each PPT Lecture Slide directly corresponds with the Concepts for Lecture.)*

**1** Dimensions of Wellness
- Physical
- Social
- Emotional
- Intellectual
- Spiritual
- Occupational
- Environmental

**2** Physical Dimension
- Ability to carry out daily tasks
- Achieve fitness
- Maintain nutrition
- Avoid abuses

**3** Social Dimension
- Interact successfully
- Develop and maintain intimacy
- Develop respect and tolerance for others

5. The intellectual dimension includes the ability to learn and use information effectively for personal, family, and career development. Intellectual wellness involves striving for continued growth and learning to deal with new challenges effectively.

6. The spiritual dimension of wellness is the belief in some force (nature, science, religion, or a higher power) that serves to unite human beings and provide meaning and purpose to life. It includes a person's own morals, values, and ethics.

7. The occupational dimension of wellness is the ability to achieve a balance between work and leisure time. A person's beliefs about education, employment, and home influence personal satisfaction and relationships with others.

8. The environmental dimension of wellness is the ability to promote health measures that improve the standard of living and quality of life in the community. This includes influences such as food, water, and air.

**4** Emotional Dimension
- Ability to manage stress
- Ability to express emotions

**5** Intellectual Dimension
- Ability to learn and use information effectively

**6** Spiritual Dimension
- Belief in some force that serves to unite

**7** Occupational Dimension
- Ability to achieve balance between work and leisure

**8** Environmental Dimension
- Ability to promote health measures that improve standard of living and quality of life in the community

## SUGGESTIONS FOR CLASSROOM ACTIVITIES

- Divide the students into seven groups and assign each a component of wellness. Ask the students to provide examples of wellness behavior in each component.

# LEARNING OUTCOME 3

Compare various models of health outlined in this chapter.

## CONCEPTS FOR LECTURE

1. Models of health include the clinical model, the role performance model, the adaptive model, the eudemonistic model, the agent-host-environment model, and the health-illness continuum.

2. The clinical model provides the narrowest interpretation of health. People are viewed as physiologic systems with related functions. Health is identified by the absence of signs and symptoms of disease or injury. It is considered the state of not being "sick." In this model the opposite of health is disease or injury.

3. In the role performance model, health is defined in terms of the individual's ability to fulfill societal roles. People who can fulfill their roles are healthy even if they have clinical illness. Sickness is the inability to perform one's role.

4. In the adaptive model, health is a creative process. Disease is a failure in adaptation, or maladaptation. The aim of treatment is to restore the ability of the person to adapt. Extreme good health is flexible adaptation to the environment and interaction with the environment to maximum advantage. The focus of this model is stability, although there is also an element of growth and change.

5. The eudemonistic model incorporates a comprehensive view of health. Health is seen as a condition of

## POWERPOINT LECTURE SLIDES

*(NOTE: The number on each PPT Lecture Slide directly corresponds with the Concepts for Lecture.)*

**1** Models of Health
- Clinical Model
- Role Performance Model
- Adaptive Model
- Eudemonistic Model
- Agent-Host-Environment Model
- Health-Illness Continuum

**2** Clinical Model
- Provides the narrowest interpretation of health
- People viewed as physiologic systems
- Health identified by the absence of signs and symptoms of disease or injury
- State of not being "sick"
- Opposite of health is disease or injury

**3** Role Performance Model
- Ability to fulfill societal roles
- Healthy even if clinically ill if roles fulfilled
- Sickness is the inability to perform one's role

**4** Adaptive Model
- Creative process

actualization or realization of a person's potential. In this model the highest aspiration of people is fulfillment and complete development, which is actualization. Illness in this model is a condition that prevents self-actualization.

6. The agent-host-environment model, also called the ecologic model, has three dynamic, interactive elements: agent (any environmental factor or stressor that by its presence or absence can lead to illness or disease), host (one or more persons who may or may not be at risk of acquiring a disease), and environment (all factors external to the host that may or may not predispose the person to the development of disease). Because each of the agent-host-environment factors constantly interacts with the others, health is an ever-changing state. When the variables are in balance, health is maintained. When variables are not in balance, disease occurs.

7. Health-illness continua (grids or graduated scales) can be used to measure a person's perceived level of wellness. Health and illness or disease can be viewed as the opposite ends of a health continuum. People move back and forth within this continuum day by day. The ranges in which people can be thought of as healthy or ill are considerable. Examples include Dunn's high-level wellness grid, Travis's illness-wellness continuum, and the 4+ model of wellness.

- Disease is a failure in adaptation or maladaptation
- Extreme good health is flexible adaptation to the environment
- Focus is stability
- Element of growth and change

**5** Eudemonistic Model
- Comprehensive view of health
- Condition of actualization or realization of a person's potential
- Illness is a condition that prevents self-actualization

**6** Agent-Host-Environment Model (Ecologic Model)
- Three dynamic, interactive elements:
  ○ Agent
  ○ Host
  ○ Environment
- Each of factors constantly interacts with the others
- When in balance, health is maintained
- When not in balance, disease occurs

**7** Health-Illness Continua (Grids or Graduated Scales)
- Measure person's perceived level of wellness
- Health and illness/disease opposite ends of a health continuum
- Move back and forth within this continuum day by day
- Wide ranges of health or illness

## SUGGESTIONS FOR CLASSROOM ACTIVITIES

- Have the students classify their definitions of health and wellness into the model of health that best fits their definitions. Discuss how their definitions and models of health may affect their nursing practice.
- Have the students discuss this statement: "The highest aspiration of people is fulfillment and complete development, which is self-actualization."

## LEARNING OUTCOME 4

Identify factors affecting health status, beliefs, and practices.

### CONCEPTS FOR LECTURE

1. Many factors influence a person's health status, beliefs, behaviors and practices. These factors may or may not be under conscious control. People can usually control their health behaviors and can choose healthy or unhealthy activities. In contrast, people have little or no choices over their genetic makeup, age, gender, culture, and sometimes their geographical environments.

   Factors affecting health status, beliefs, and practices include internal variables and external variables.

2. Internal variables are biologic, psychologic, and cognitive dimensions.

### POWERPOINT LECTURE SLIDES

*(NOTE: The number on each PPT Lecture Slide directly corresponds with the Concepts for Lecture.)*

**1** Factors Affecting Health Status, Beliefs, and Practices
- Internal variables
- External variables

**2** Internal Variables
- Biologic dimension (genetic makeup, gender, age, and developmental level)
- Psychologic dimension (mind–body interactions and self-concept)
- Cognitive dimension (intellectual factors include lifestyle choices and spiritual and religious beliefs)

Biologic dimension variables include genetic make-up, gender, age, and developmental level. Psychologic dimension variables include mind–body interactions and self-concept. Cognitive dimension variables include lifestyle choices and spiritual and religious beliefs.

3. External variables are physical environment, standards of living, family and cultural beliefs, and social support networks.

**3** External Variables
- Physical environment
- Standards of living
- Family and cultural beliefs
- Social support networks

## SUGGESTIONS FOR CLASSROOM ACTIVITIES

- Provide examples of how various factors influence health status, health beliefs, and health practices.

## SUGGESTIONS FOR CLINICAL ACTIVITIES

- Have the students discuss situations in which their health beliefs and a client's health beliefs were different, or provide an example of this type of situation. How was this demonstrated? How did the students respond in this situation? What would they do differently, if anything?

# LEARNING OUTCOME 5

Describe factors affecting health care adherence.

## CONCEPTS FOR LECTURE

1. Adherence is the extent to which an individual's behavior coincides with medical or health advice. The degree of adherence may range from disregarding every aspect of the recommendations to following the total therapeutic plan.

2. Factors influencing adherence include client motivation to become well; degree of lifestyle change necessary; perceived severity of the health care problem; value placed on reducing the threat of illness; difficulty in understanding and performing specific behaviors; degree of inconvenience of the illness itself or of the regimens; complexity, side effects, and duration of the proposed therapy; specific cultural heritage that may make adherence difficult; degree of satisfaction and quality and type of relationship with the health care providers; and overall cost of prescribed therapy.

## POWERPOINT LECTURE SLIDES

*(NOTE: The number on each PPT Lecture Slide directly corresponds with the Concepts for Lecture.)*

**1** Adherence
- Extent to which individual's behavior coincides with medical/health advice
- Ranges from total disregard to following total plan

**2** Factors Affecting Health Care Adherence
- Client motivation
- Degree of lifestyle change necessary
- Perceived severity of problem
- Value placed on reducing the threat of illness
- Difficulty in understanding and performing specific behaviors
- Degree of inconvenience of the illness itself or of the regimens
- Complexity, side effects, and duration of the proposed therapy
- Specific cultural heritage that may make adherence difficult
- Degree of satisfaction and quality and type of relationship with the health care providers
- Overall cost of prescribed therapy

## SUGGESTIONS FOR CLASSROOM ACTIVITIES

- Provide the students with a case study in which the client did not follow all or some of the health advice (e.g., adherence to an exercise plan or nutrition guidelines). Have students brainstorm possible factors that may have contributed to this outcome and possible nursing interventions to assist the client.

## SUGGESTIONS FOR CLINICAL ACTIVITIES

- Discuss discharge planning for several of the students' clients and how the students can assist the clients to adhere to the discharge plan.

# LEARNING OUTCOME 6

Differentiate illness from disease and acute illness from chronic illness.

## CONCEPTS FOR LECTURE

1. Illness is a highly personal state in which the person's physical, emotional, intellectual, social, developmental, or spiritual functioning is thought to be diminished. It is not synonymous with disease and may or may not be related to disease. Illness is highly subjective. Only the individual person can say he or she is ill.

2. Disease can be described as an alteration in body function resulting in a reduction of capacities or a shortening of the normal life span.

3. Acute illness is typically characterized by severe symptoms of relatively short duration. Symptoms often appear abruptly and subside quickly and, depending upon the cause, may or may not require intervention by health care professionals. Following an acute illness, most people return to their normal level of wellness.

4. A chronic illness lasts for an extended period, usually 6 months or longer and often for the person's life. Chronic illnesses usually have a slow onset and often have periods of remissions, when symptoms disappear, and exacerbations, when the symptoms reappear. Care needs to be focused on promoting the highest level possible of independence, sense of control, and wellness. In addition, many must learn how to live with increasing physical limitations and discomfort.

## POWERPOINT LECTURE SLIDES

*(NOTE: The number on each PPT Lecture Slide directly corresponds with the Concepts for Lecture.)*

**1** Illness
- A highly personal state
- Person's physical, emotional, intellectual, social, developmental, or spiritual functioning is diminished
- Not synonymous with disease
- May or may not be related to disease
- Only person can say he or she is ill

**2** Disease
- Alteration in body function
- A reduction of capacities or a shortening of the normal life span

**3** Acute Illness
- Characterized by severe symptoms of relatively short duration
- Symptoms often appear abruptly, subside quickly
- May or may not require intervention by health care professionals
- Most people return to normal level of wellness

**4** Chronic Illness
- Lasts for an extended period
- Usually has a slow onset
- Often have periods of remissions and exacerbations
- Care includes promoting independence, sense of control, and wellness
- Learn how to live with physical limitations and discomfort

---

## SUGGESTIONS FOR CLASSROOM ACTIVITIES

- Discuss the statement that illness is "not synonymous with disease and may or may not be related to disease." Have the students provide examples to illustrate their statements.
- Provide examples of an acute illness (or disease) and a chronic illness (or disease). Ask the students to compare and contrast the onset, duration, interventions, and recovery.

## SUGGESTIONS FOR CLINICAL ACTIVITIES

- Have the students identify clients who have an acute illness (disease) and those who have a chronic illness (disease). Compare and contrast the client's responses to the different types of illnesses in terms of influence on the client's roles, treatment, and discharge plans.

# LEARNING OUTCOME 7

Identify Parson's four aspects of the sick role.

## CONCEPTS FOR LECTURE

1. Parsons (1979) described four aspects of the sick role.
   - Clients are not held responsible for their condition.
   - Clients are excused from certain social roles and tasks.
   - Clients are obligated to try to get well as quickly as possible.
   - Clients or their families are obligated to seek competent help.

## POWERPOINT LECTURE SLIDES

*(NOTE: The number on each PPT Lecture Slide directly corresponds with the Concepts for Lecture.)*

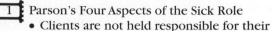 Parson's Four Aspects of the Sick Role
   - Clients are not held responsible for their condition
   - Clients are excused from certain social roles and tasks
   - Clients are obligated to try to get well as quickly as possible
   - Clients or their families are obligated to seek competent help

### SUGGESTIONS FOR CLASSROOM ACTIVITIES

- Discuss how these aspects of the sick role are enacted by clients.

### SUGGESTIONS FOR CLINICAL ACTIVITIES

- Have the students provide examples of clients' behavior that illustrate one of the four aspects of the sick role.

# LEARNING OUTCOME 8

Explain Suchman's stages of illness.

## CONCEPTS FOR LECTURE

1. Suchman (1979) described five stages of illness. Not all clients progress through each stage. Others may progress through only the first two stages and then recover.
   - Stage 1—Symptom experience: The person comes to believe something is wrong.
   - Stage 2—Assumption of the sick role: The person accepts the sick role and seeks confirmation from family and friends.
   - Stage 3—Medical care contact: The person seeks advice of a health professional either on his or her own initiative or at the urging of significant others.
   - Stage 4—Dependent client role: After accepting the illness and seeking treatment, the client becomes dependent on the professional for help.
   - Stage 5—Recovery or rehabilitation: The client is expected to relinquish the dependent role and resume former roles and responsibilities.

## POWERPOINT LECTURE SLIDES

*(NOTE: The number on each PPT Lecture Slide directly corresponds with the Concepts for Lecture.)*

1 Suchman's Stages of Illness
   - Stage 1: Symptom experience
   - Stage 2: Assumption of the sick role
   - Stage 3: Medical care contact
   - Stage 4: Dependent client role
   - Stage 5: Recovery or rehabilitation

### SUGGESTIONS FOR CLASSROOM ACTIVITIES

- Have the students provide examples from their own experiences of the stages of illness.
- Discuss the nurse's role for clients in the various stages of illness.

### SUGGESTIONS FOR CLINICAL ACTIVITIES

- Have the students discuss the stage of illness that their clients are experiencing and how the clients are demonstrating this stage. Have the students discuss their role in assisting the clients in this stage.

# LEARNING OUTCOME 9

Describe effects of illness on individuals' and family members' roles and functions.

## CONCEPTS FOR LECTURE

1. Ill clients may experience behavioral and emotional changes, changes in self-concept and body image, and lifestyle changes.

   Behavioral and emotional changes associated with short-term illness are generally mild and short-lived. More acute responses are likely with severe, life-threatening, chronic, or disabling illness.

   Ill clients are also vulnerable to loss of autonomy. Family interactions may change so that the client may no longer be involved in making family decisions or even decisions about his or her own health care.

   Illness also often necessitates a change in lifestyle such as changing diet, activity, and exercise.

2. A person's illness affects not only the person who is ill but also the family or significant others. The kind of effect and its extent depend chiefly on three factors: the member of the family who is ill, the seriousness and length of the illness, and the cultural and social customs the family follows.

3. The changes that can occur in the family include role changes, task reassignments, increased demands on time, increased stress due to anxiety about the outcome of the illness, conflict about unaccustomed responsibilities, financial problems, loneliness as a result of separation and pending loss, and changes in social customs.

## POWERPOINT LECTURE SLIDES

*(NOTE: The number on each PPT Lecture Slide directly corresponds with the Concepts for Lecture.)*

**1** Impact of Illness on the Client
- Behavioral and emotional changes
- Loss of autonomy
- Self-concept and body image changes
- Lifestyle changes

**2** Impact of Illness on Family
- Depend on three factors:
  - Member of the family who is ill
  - Seriousness and length of the illness
  - Cultural and social customs the family follows

**3** Changes that Can Occur in the Family Include the Following:
- Role changes
- Task reassignments
- Increased demands on time
- Anxiety about outcomes
- Conflict about unaccustomed responsibilities
- Financial problems
- Loneliness as a result of separation and pending loss
- Change in social customs

---

## SUGGESTIONS FOR CLASSROOM ACTIVITIES

- Invite a guest speaker who is related to a client with a chronic condition to discuss the effects of the client's condition on the family.

## SUGGESTIONS FOR CLINICAL ACTIVITIES

- During clinical conference, have students describe how an assigned client's illness has affected the roles and functions of each of the client's family members.

# Chapter 18
## Culture and Heritage

## Resource Library

 **PRENTICE HALL NURSING MEDIALINK DVD-ROM**

Audio Glossary
NCLEX® Review

**COMPANION WEBSITE**

Additional NCLEX® Review
Care Plan Activity: Client in the ICU
Case Study: Conveying Cultural Sensitivity
Application Activity: *Chinese Childbearing Beliefs*
Links to Resources

**IMAGE LIBRARY**

**Figure 18.1** Celebrations of the passage to adulthood are often based on culture or religion: for example, the Jewish bar mitzvah at age 13 and the Mexican quinceañera or "sweet fifteen" party.

**Figure 18.2** Symbols of the HEALTH traditions model and themes.

## Learning Outcome 1

Describe the role of federal agencies, initiatives, and laws on provision of cultural health care.

### Concepts for Lecture

1. The U.S. Department of Health and Human Services (DHHS) houses the Office of Minority Health "to improve and protect the health of racial and ethnic minority populations through the development of health policies and programs that will eliminate health disparities." In collaboration with other organizations, it developed the *National Standards for Culturally and Linguistically Appropriate Services in Health Care* (CLAS).

   The Centers for Disease Control and Prevention (CDC) also has an Office of Minority Health to "promote health and quality of life by preventing and controlling the disproportionate burden of disease, injury, and disability among racial and ethnic minority populations."

   The purpose of the National Center on Minority Health and Health Disparities (NCMHD) in the National Institutes of Health "is to promote minority health and to lead, coordinate, support, and access the NIH effort to reduce and ultimately eliminate health disparities."

   The nursing profession plays a major role in REACH: Racial and Ethnic Approaches to Community Health, which strives to eliminate racial and ethnic disparities in infant mortality, in screening and management of breast and cervical cancer, cardiovascular diseases, diabetes, HIV infections/AIDS, and child and adult immunizations.

### PowerPoint Lecture Slides

*(NOTE: The number on each PPT Lecture Slide directly corresponds with the Concepts for Lecture.)*

 1  Cultural Health Care
   - Office of Minority Health
     - U.S. Department of Health and Human Services (DHHS)
     - Centers for Disease Control and Prevention (CDC)
   - National Center on Minority Health and Health Disparities (NCMHD)
   - Racial and Ethnic Approaches to Community Health (REACH)
   - Health Resources and Services Administration
   - National Healthcare Disparities Report

One of the major goals of *Healthy People 2010* is to eliminate health disparities by gender, race or ethnicity, education, income, disability, geographic location, and sexual orientation. To achieve this goal, the Health Resources and Services Administration (HRSA) aims to increase the number of under-represented racial and ethnic groups entering the nursing profession.

Current nursing practice has been influenced by the *National Healthcare Disparities Report*, which is a comprehensive overview of disparities in health care among racial, ethnic, and socioeconomic groups in the general U.S. population and among priority populations. This report indicates that, although overall the quality of health care has improved, differences in access and quality of care between whites and minorities have deceased overall, and the quality and access disparity for Hispanics has widened.

## SUGGESTIONS FOR CLASSROOM ACTIVITIES

• Discuss the Office of Minority Health standards for culturally and linguistically appropriate health care for health care organizations (*www.omhrc.gov*).

## SUGGESTIONS FOR CLINICAL ACTIVITIES

• Invite a staff nurse to discuss how the institution operationalizes the above standards.

## LEARNING OUTCOME 2

Discuss the components of culturally focused nursing, heritage consistency, and health traditions.

### CONCEPTS FOR LECTURE

1. Cultural nursing care is the provision of nursing care across cultural boundaries and takes into account the context in which the client lives as well as the situations in which the client's health problems arise.

   Professional nursing care is culturally sensitive, culturally appropriate, and culturally competent.

   Culturally sensitive implies that nurses possess some basic knowledge of and constructive attitudes toward the health traditions observed among the diverse cultural groups found in the setting in which they practice. Culturally appropriate implies that nurses apply the underlying background knowledge that must be possessed to provide a client with the best possible care. Culturally competent implies that, within the delivered care, nurses understand and attend to the total context of the client's situation and use a complex combination of knowledge, attitudes, and skills.

2. Heritage consistency relates to the observance of beliefs and practices of a person's traditional cultural system. It has been expanded in an attempt to study the degree to which a person's lifestyle reflects his or her traditional culture. The model of heritage consistency has four overlapping components: culture, ethnicity, religion, and socialization.

### POWERPOINT LECTURE SLIDES

*(NOTE: The number on each PPT Lecture Slide directly corresponds with the Concepts for Lecture.)*

1. Culturally Focused Nursing
   • Culturally sensitive
   • Culturally appropriate
   • Culturally competent

2. Heritage Consistency
   • Observance of beliefs and practices of a person's traditional cultural system
   • Degree to which a person's lifestyle reflects his or her traditional culture

3. HEALTH Traditions Model
   • Predicated on the concept of holistic health
   • Describes what people do to maintain, protect, and restore health
   • Describes health as a balance of person-body, mind, and spirit

3. The HEALTH traditions model is predicated on the concept of holistic health and describes what people do from a traditional perspective to maintain, protect, and restore health. This model describes health as a balance of all aspects of the person—body, mind, and spirit.

   The HEALTH traditions model consists of nine interrelated facets, represented by traditional methods of maintaining health, traditional methods of protecting health, and traditional methods of restoring health (see Table 18–2).

## SUGGESTIONS FOR CLASSROOM ACTIVITIES

- Invite representatives from various religions to discuss the traditions of the religions they represent. In addition, ask the representatives to discuss the variations in adherence to the traditions found among their group members.

## SUGGESTIONS FOR CLINICAL ACTIVITIES

- Have students identify symbolic items used to maintain, protect, or restore physical, mental or spiritual health by clients of different heritage.

# LEARNING OUTCOME 3

Describe examples of the different health views of culturally diverse people.

## CONCEPTS FOR LECTURE

1. Three views of health beliefs include magico-religious, scientific, and holistic. In the magico-religious health belief view, health and illness are controlled by supernatural forces. Individuals may believe that illness is the result of "being bad" or opposing God's will. Getting well is also viewed as dependent on God's will. Some cultures believe that magic can cause illness through spells or hexes. Such illnesses may require magical treatments in addition to scientific treatment.

2. Scientific or biomedical health belief is based on the belief that life and life processes are controlled by physical and biochemical processes that can be manipulated by humans. Illness is caused by germs, bacteria, or a breakdown of the human machine, the body. Clients will expect a pill, a treatment, or surgery to cure the problem.

3. The holistic health belief holds that the forces of nature must be maintained in balance or harmony. Human life is one aspect of nature that must be in harmony with the rest of nature. When the natural balance or harmony is disturbed, illness results.

## POWERPOINT LECTURE SLIDES

*(NOTE: The number on each PPT Lecture Slide directly corresponds with the Concepts for Lecture.)*

1 Magico-Religious Health View
- Health and illness are controlled by supernatural forces
- May believe that illness a result of "being bad" or opposing God's will
- Getting well is also dependent on God's will
- Some cultures believe magic can cause illness

2 Scientific (Biomedical) Health View
- Life and life processes are controlled by physical and biomechanical processes
- Illness is caused by germs, bacteria, or a breakdown of the human machine
- Belief that pills, treatments, or surgery will cure

3 Holistic Health View
- Forces of nature must be maintained in balance or harmony
- Human life is one aspect of nature
- When the natural balance is disturbed then illness results

## SUGGESTIONS FOR CLASSROOM ACTIVITIES

- Invite members of diverse cultures within the community to discuss health beliefs.
- Show videotaped interviews of people discussing various health beliefs.

## SUGGESTIONS FOR CLINICAL ACTIVITIES

- Ask the students to propose ways in which to discover the primary health beliefs of their clients and how these beliefs will influence care, including health teaching.

# LEARNING OUTCOME 4

Differentiate biomedical care from folk healing.

## CONCEPTS FOR LECTURE

1. Folk medicine is defined as those beliefs and practices relating to illness prevention and healing that derive from cultural traditions rather than from modern medicine's scientific base. Folk medicine is thought to be more humanistic than biomedical health care.

   The consultation and treatment takes place in the community of the recipient, frequently in the home of the healer. It may be less expensive than scientific or biomedical care.

   A frequent component of treatment is some ritual practiced on the part of the healer or the client to cause healing to occur.

   Folk healing is more culturally based and it is often more comfortable and less frightening for the client.

## POWERPOINT LECTURE SLIDES

*(NOTE: The number on each PPT Lecture Slide directly corresponds with the Concepts for Lecture.)*

**1** Folk Medicine
- Health and illness beliefs and practices derived from cultural traditions
- Thought to be more humanistic than biomedical health care
- Consultation and treatment takes place in the community
- May be less expensive than biomedical care
- Frequently includes ritual practice on the part of the healer or the client
- Often more comfortable and less frightening for the client

## SUGGESTIONS FOR CLASSROOM ACTIVITIES

- Invite healers from various cultural groups to talk to the class about illness prevention and healing as they practice these.
- Ask students from different cultural groups to share their groups' views of health, nurses, and nursing, and how these views may affect client care.

## SUGGESTIONS FOR CLINICAL ACTIVITIES

- Ask several staff nurses to describe how they have negotiated with clients who employ folk healing that conflicts with the biomedical plan of care.

# LEARNING OUTCOME 5

Identify factors related to communication with culturally diverse clients and colleagues.

## CONCEPTS FOR LECTURE

1. Communicating effectively with clients of various ethnic and cultural backgrounds is critical to providing culturally competent nursing care. There are cultural variations in both verbal and nonverbal communication.
2. The most obvious cultural difference is in verbal communication: vocabulary, grammatical structure, voice qualities, intonation, rhythm, speed, pronunciation, and silence.

   Initiating verbal communication may be influenced by cultural values.

   Verbal communication becomes even more difficult when an interaction involves people who speak different languages. The assistance of a translator or interpreter may be required. Techniques for therapeutic communication are listed in Practice Guidelines: Verbal Communication with Clients Who Have Limited Knowledge of English.

   Nurses must remember that clients for whom English is a second language may lose command of their English when they are in stressful situations. Clients may forget and revert to their primary language when they are ill or distressed.

## POWERPOINT LECTURE SLIDES

*(NOTE: The number on each PPT Lecture Slide directly corresponds with the Concepts for Lecture.)*

**1** Communication with Culturally Diverse Clients
- Cultural variation
  - Verbal communication
  - Nonverbal communication

**2** Verbal Communication
- Vocabulary, grammatical structure, voice qualities, intonation, rhythm, speed, pronunciation
- Initiation of verbal communication
- Interaction between people who speak different languages

**3** Nonverbal Communication Behaviors
- Meaning to the client
- Meaning in the client's culture
- Use of
  - Silence
  - Touch
  - Eye movement

3. Nurses must be aware of two aspects of nonverbal communication behaviors: what nonverbal behaviors mean to the client and what specific nonverbal behaviors mean in the client's culture.

Nonverbal communication can include the use of silence, touch, eye movement, facial expressions, and body posture.

Some cultures are comfortable with silence. Other cultures consider it appropriate to speak before others have finished talking. Others view silence as a sign of respect. For others, silence may indicate agreement.

Touching is a learned behavior that can have both positive and negative meanings. Cultures dictate what forms of touch are appropriate for individuals of the same and opposite gender.

Facial expressions can vary between cultures. Some cultures smile and use facial expressions, and others are less open in response. Facial expressions can also convey a meaning opposite to what is felt or understood.

Eye movement during communication has cultural foundations. In some cultures direct eye contact is regarded as important, conveys self-confidence, openness, interest, and honesty. In these cultures lack of eye contact may be interpreted as secretiveness, shyness, guilt, lack of interest, or even a sign of mental illness. In other cultures direct eye contact is considered rude, but intermittent eye contact may be acceptable.

Body posture and hand gestures are also culturally learned. A gesture can be accepted in one culture and be offensive in another.

- Facial expressions
- Body posture

---

## SUGGESTIONS FOR CLASSROOM ACTIVITIES

- Invite international students from the educational institution to discuss appropriate verbal and nonverbal communication used in their cultures.

## SUGGESTIONS FOR CLINICAL ACTIVITIES

- Invite several interpreters used by the institution to describe their role and how nurses can best utilize their services.
- Review agency policy and procedures for obtaining and using the services of an interpreter.

---

# LEARNING OUTCOME 6

Recognize the core practice competencies of culturally competent nursing care.

## CONCEPTS FOR LECTURE

1. Include cultural assessment of the client and family as part of overall assessment.

Learn the rituals, customs, and practices of the major cultural groups with whom you come into contact. Learn to appreciate the richness of diversity and consider it an asset rather than a hindrance in your practice. Don't make assumptions about beliefs or practices. Ask about the client's use of cultural or alternative approaches to healing.

## POWERPOINT LECTURE SLIDES

*(NOTE: The number on each PPT Lecture Slide directly corresponds with the Concepts for Lecture.)*

 Core Practice Competencies
- Include cultural assessment of the client and family
- Learn the rituals, customs, and practices of the major cultural groups
- Don't make assumptions about beliefs or practices

Identify your personal biases, attitudes, prejudices, and stereotypes. Recognize that it is the client's (or family's) right to make their own health care choices. Explain in detail the client's condition and the treatment plan if the client is willing for you to do this. Convey respect and cooperate with traditional helpers and caregivers. Campinha-Bacote's model of cultural competence (2003) is also of special relevance to understand the core practice competencies of culturally appropriate nursing care. In this model, nurses are encouraged to integrate into their practice the following five constructs: cultural awareness, cultural knowledge, cultural skills, cultural encounters, and cultural desires.

- Ask about the client's use of cultural or alternative approaches to healing
- Identify your personal biases, attitudes, prejudices, and stereotypes
- Recognize that it is the client's (or family's) right to make their own health care choices
- Convey respect and cooperate with traditional helpers and caregivers

## SUGGESTIONS FOR CLASSROOM ACTIVITIES

- Ask the students to use available resources to identify the most common cultural groups served by the health care agencies in the community. Have the students select one group and investigate health beliefs of this group.

## SUGGESTIONS FOR CLINICAL ACTIVITIES

- If possible, arrange for students to observe in a clinic or community agency where clients of diverse cultural heritage are seen. Have the students make observations of interventions that address this diversity. Discuss observations in post-conference.

## LEARNING OUTCOME 7

Identify methods of heritage assessment.

### CONCEPTS FOR LECTURE

1. An assessment interview questionnaire is a tool that can be used to ask the client questions specific to the heritage assessment. This tool facilitates communication with clients and their families and is designed to determine if clients are identifying with their traditional cultural heritage (heritage consistency) or if they have acculturated into the dominant culture (see the Assessment Interview: Heritage Assessment Tool). Several factors are indicative of heritage consistency. These can be explored by the nurse to determine the depth to which a person identifies with his or her traditional heritage.

2. Before a heritage assessment begins, the nurse should determine what language the client speaks and the client's degree of fluency in the English language. The nurse needs to spend some time with clients, introduce some social conversation, and convey a genuine desire to understand the client's values and beliefs. How and when questions are asked requires sensitivity and clinical judgment. Timing is important in introducing questions, and sensitivity is needed in phrasing questions.

### POWERPOINT LECTURE SLIDES

*(NOTE: The number on each PPT Lecture Slide directly corresponds with the Concepts for Lecture.)*

1 Heritage Assessment
- Tool used to assess cultural heritage
- Facilitates communication with clients and their families
- Designed to determine identification with traditional cultural heritage
- Designed to determine degree of heritage consistency

2 Before Beginning the Assessment
- Determine what language the client speaks
- Determine client's degree of fluency in the English language
- Spend some time to develop trust
- Introduce some social conversation
- Convey a genuine desire to understand values and beliefs
- Introduce questions in a timely manner
- Use sensitivity in phrasing questions

## LEARNING OUTCOME 8

Plan culturally sensitive, appropriate, and competent nursing interventions.

### CONCEPTS FOR LECTURE

1. Nursing diagnoses developed by NANDA are based on Western cultural beliefs. Nurses must provide appropriate care to clients of any culture. This is accomplished through developing cultural sensitivity and considering how a client's culture influences his or her responses to health conditions.

   A potential outcome is that the client can "promote, maintain, and/or regain mutually desired and obtainable levels of health within the realities of their life circumstances."

   There are several steps involved:
   - Nurses must become aware of their own cultural heritage.
   - The nurse must become aware of the client's heritage and health traditions as described by the client.
   - The nurse must become aware of adaptations the client made to live in a North American culture.
   - The nurse must form a nursing plan with the client that incorporates his or her cultural beliefs regarding the maintenance, protection, and restoration of health.

### POWERPOINT LECTURE SLIDES

*(NOTE: The number on each PPT Lecture Slide directly corresponds with the Concepts for Lecture.)*

1. Culturally Sensitive Care Planning
   - Provide appropriate care to clients of any culture
     - Become aware of own cultural heritage
     - Become aware of client's heritage and health traditions
     - Become aware of adaptations client made to live in North American culture
     - Form a nursing plan that incorporates cultural beliefs regarding maintenance, protection, and restoration of health

# CHAPTER 19
## COMPLEMENTARY AND ALTERNATIVE HEALING MODALITIES

## RESOURCE LIBRARY

### ⊚ PRENTICE HALL NURSING MEDIALINK DVD-ROM

Audio Glossary
NCLEX® Review
End of Unit Concept Map Activity

### ⊕ COMPANION WEBSITE

Additional NCLEX® Review
Care Plan Activity: Lyme Disease
Case Study: Complementary Alternative Medicine
Application Activity: *Support for Alternative Therapies*
Links to Resources

### 📖 IMAGE LIBRARY

**Figure 19.1** Massage over the shoulders and back.
**Figure 19.2** Acupuncture involves the insertion of thin, sterile needles.

**Figure 19.3** Foot reflex areas.
**Figure 19.4** Listening to music can provide a variety of therapeutic benefits.

## LEARNING OUTCOME 1

Describe concepts basic to alternative practices.

### CONCEPTS FOR LECTURE

1. Several concepts are common to most alternative practices: holism, humanism, balance, spirituality, energy, and healing environments.
2. Holism is a paradigm of the whole systems belief that people are more than physical bodies with fixable and replaceable parts. Combined mental, emotional, spiritual, relationship, and environmental components, referred to as holism, are considered to play crucial and equal roles in a person's state of health. Interventions are individualized within the entire context of the person's life.
3. Humanism is a perspective that includes propositions such as the mind and body are indivisible, people have the power to solve their own problems, people are responsible for the patterns of their lives, and well-being is a combination of personal satisfaction and contributions to the larger community.
4. Balance consists of mental, physical, emotional, spiritual, and environmental components. Not only does each component have to be balanced, equilibrium is needed among the components.
5. Spirituality includes the drive to become all that one can, and is bound to intuition, creativity, and motivation. It is the dimension that involves relationship with oneself, with others, and with a higher power. Spirituality gives people meaning and purpose in their lives. It involves significant meaning in the entirety of life, including illness and death.

### POWERPOINT LECTURE SLIDES

*(NOTE: The number on each PPT Lecture Slide directly corresponds with the Concepts for Lecture.)*

**1** Concepts Basic to Alternative Practices
  • Holism
  • Humanism
  • Balance
  • Spirituality
  • Energy
  • Healing environment

**2** Holism
  • Paradigm of whole systems
  • Belief that people are more than physical bodies
  • Combined mental, emotional, spiritual, relationship, and environmental components
  • Interventions individualized within the entire context of the person's life

**3** Humanism
  • Mind and body are indivisible
  • People have the power to solve own problems
  • People are responsible for the patterns of their lives
  • Well-being is a combination of personal satisfaction and contributions to the larger community

**4** Balance
  • Consists of mental, physical, emotional, spiritual, and environmental components

6. Energy is viewed as the force that integrates the body, mind, and spirit. It is that which connects everything. Grounding relates to one's connection with the ground and to one's whole contact with reality. Being grounded suggests stability, security, independence, having a solid foundation, and living in the present rather than escaping into dreams. Centering refers to the process of bringing oneself to the center or middle; being fully connected to the part of their bodies where all energies meet. It is the process of focusing one's mind on the center of energy allowing one to operate intuitively and with awareness, and to channel energy throughout the body.

    For information on healing environments, see Outcome 2.

- Each component needs to be balanced
- Equilibrium needed among the components

 Spirituality
- Includes the drive to become all that one can
- Bound to intuition, creativity, and motivation
- Relationship with oneself, with others, and with a higher power
- Gives people meaning and purpose in lives
- Involves significant meaning in the entirety of life

 Energy
- Force that integrates the body, mind, and spirit
- Grounding
- Connection with the ground
- Contact with reality
- Centering
- Focusing one's mind on the center of energy allowing one to operate intuitively and with awareness, channeling energy throughout the body

### SUGGESTIONS FOR CLASSROOM ACTIVITIES

- Have the class debate the pros and cons of alternative healing modalities and medical therapies.

### SUGGESTIONS FOR CLINICAL ACTIVITIES

- Assign students to review nursing assessment or nursing history forms for their various clinical sites. In clinical conference, have the students discuss the appropriateness of these forms for inclusion of client information regarding alternative healing modalities and medical therapies.

## LEARNING OUTCOME 2

Give examples of healing environments.

### CONCEPTS FOR LECTURE

1. Healing environments are created when nurses use hands, heart, and mind to provide holistic nursing care.

    Healing environments are created by providing knowledge, skills, and the support that allow clients to tap into their inner wisdom and make healthy decisions.

    Healing environments are a synthesis of the medical-curing approach and the nursing-healing approach.

    Healing environments are created when time is taken to be with clients in deeply caring ways, to become still and enter the other's subjective world, and to be wholly present for that person.

    Nurses must also create healing environments for themselves. They need to learn how to restore energy and replenish themselves.

### POWERPOINT LECTURE SLIDES

*(NOTE: The number on each PPT Lecture Slide directly corresponds with the Concepts for Lecture.)*

 Healing Environments
- Created when nurses provide holistic nursing care
- Created by providing knowledge, skills, and the support
- Synthesis of medical-curing and nursing-healing approach
- Created when time is taken to be with clients in a deeply caring way
- Nurses need to create healing environments for self

# LEARNING OUTCOME 3

Develop a self-care plan using alternative practices.

## CONCEPTS FOR LECTURE

1. Clarify values and beliefs. Identify those things that are important, meaningful, and valuable to you, and assess whether your actions are consistent with your beliefs. For example, do you value time spent with your children and time reading or listening to music?

   Set realistic goals. Identify long-term goals and then short-term goals that will help you meet the long-term goals. For example, a long-term goal might be to experience an increase in emotional and physical comfort, and a short-term goal might be to take a 30-minute walk each evening.

   Challenge the belief that others always come first. Over involvement with clients leads to overwork and overly solicitous helping that neglects the clients' responsibilities, autonomy, and resources. It leaves little time for fulfillment of personal needs. Learn to ask for what you need, acknowledge that you are doing the best you can, and affirm that you can meet your own needs as well as care for others. Learn to manage stress.

2. Managing Stress
   - Acknowledge the mind–body connection—the relationship among thoughts, feelings, behaviors, and the physiologic response to stress.
   - Monitor stress warning signals. Invoke the relaxation response on a regular basis such as once a day for 20 minutes or twice a day for 10 minutes.
   - Develop the skill of personal presence— physically "being there" and psychologically "being with" a client or other person. To be available to others in this way requires practicing the skill of being present to yourself. Focus full attention on the activity you are doing at the moment.
   - Maintain and enhance physical health. Eat healthy, balanced meals; exercise regularly; and obtain adequate rest.
   - Develop a support network. Fellow nurses can often provide perspectives and insights to help cope with commonly shared experiences.

## POWERPOINT LECTURE SLIDES

(NOTE: The number on each PPT Lecture Slide directly corresponds with the Concepts for Lecture.)

1. Self-Care Plan
   - Clarify values and beliefs
   - Set realistic goals
   - Challenge the belief that others always come first
   - Learn to manage stress

2. Managing Stress
   - Acknowledge the mind–body connection
   - Monitor the stress warning signals
   - Invoke the relaxation response on a regular basis
   - Develop the skill of personal presence
   - Maintain and enhance physical health
   - Develop a support system

## LEARNING OUTCOME 4

Explain how herbs are similar to many prescription drugs.

### CONCEPTS FOR LECTURE

1. Conventional primary care providers use plant-derived products regularly. Thirty percent of all prescription drugs in the United States are derived from plants (e.g., aspirin from willow tree bark, morphine from opium poppy, atropine from nightshade).

   The vast majority of herbal medicines present no danger if taken appropriately. Some can cause serious side effects if taken in excess or, for some, if taken over a prolonged period of time.

   Herbs can also interact with drugs, and caution should be used when combining herbs with prescription and over-the-counter (OTC) medications. (See Practice Guidelines: Cautions and Contraindications for Popular Herbal Preparations.)

   Although herbs can be quite effective, like prescription drugs it is important to caution people about becoming dependent on them.

   Pregnant and breast-feeding women should be cautioned not to take herbs internally except for mild herb teas.

   Nurses must be open to exploring and discussing their clients' uses of and questions regarding herbal medicine. This allows for evaluation of herbal intake against known and potential adverse interactions with prescriptions and OTC medications.

### POWERPOINT LECTURE SLIDES

*(NOTE: The number on each PPT Lecture Slide directly corresponds with the Concepts for Lecture.)*

1. Herbs and Prescription Drugs
   • Many prescription drugs derived from plants
   • Most herbal medicines present no danger if taken appropriately
   • Some can cause serious side effects if taken in excess, or over a prolonged period of time
   • Caution when combining with prescription and over-the-counter medications
   • Caution about becoming dependent on herbal remedies
   • Caution pregnant and breast-feeding women not to take herbs

## LEARNING OUTCOME 5

Discuss how naturopathic medicine may be the model health care system of the future.

### CONCEPTS FOR LEARNING

1. Naturopathic medicine is not only a system of medicine but also a way of life with emphasis on client responsibility, client education, health maintenance, and disease prevention.

### POWERPOINT LECTURE SLIDES

*(NOTE: The number on each PPT Lecture Slide directly corresponds with the Concepts for Lecture.)*

1. Naturopathic Medicine
   • A system of medicine

It may be the model health system of the future with the movement toward healthy lifestyles, healthy diets, and preventive health care.

2. Naturopathic physicians do not provide emergency care nor do major surgery. They rarely prescribe drugs, and they treat clients in private practice and outpatient clinics, not in hospitals.

3. The goal of treatment is the restoration of health and normal body functions rather than the application of a particular therapy. Virtually every CAM therapy is utilized. Physicians mix and match different approaches, customizing treatment for each person. The least invasive intervention to support the body's natural healing processes is a primary consideration.

- A way of life
- Emphasis on responsibility, health maintenance, and disease prevention
- Model health system of the future

**2** Naturopathic Physicians
- Do not provide emergency care or do major surgery
- Rarely prescribe drugs
- Treat clients in private practice and outpatient clinics

**3** Goal of Naturopathic Treatment
- Restoration of health and normal body functions
- Customized to client
- Primary consideration is least invasive method

---

## SUGGESTIONS FOR CLASSROOM ACTIVITIES

- Invite a panel of alternative and complementary health care providers to discuss alternative healing modalities and medical therapies.

---

# LEARNING OUTCOME 6

Identify the role of manual healing methods in health and illness.

## CONCEPTS FOR LECTURE

1. Manual healing methods include chiropractic, massage, acupuncture/acupressure/reflexology, and hand-mediated biofield therapies.

2. The goals of chiropractic interventions are to reduce or eliminate pain; to correct spinal dysfunction thereby restoring biomechanical balance to reestablish shock absorption, leverage, and range of motion; to strengthen muscles and ligaments by spinal rehabilitative exercises in order to increase resistance to further injury; and to practice preventive maintenance to ensure the problem does not recur.

3. Massage aids the ability of the body to heal itself and is aimed at achieving or increasing health and well-being.

4. Acupuncture, acupressure, and reflexology are treatments rooted in the traditional Eastern philosophy that *qi*, or life energy, flows through the body along pathways known as meridians, forming tiny whirlpools close to the skin's surface at places called acupuncture points. When the flow of energy becomes blocked or congested, people experience discomfort or pain on a physical level, may feel frustrated or irritable on an emotional level, and may experience a sense of vulnerability or lack of purpose in life on a spiritual level. The goal of care is to recognize and manage disruption before illness or disease occurs. Practitioners bring balance to the body's energies, which promotes optimal health and well-being and facilitates people's own healing capacity.

## POWERPOINT LECTURE SLIDES

*(NOTE: The number on each PPT Lecture Slide directly corresponds with the Concepts for Lecture.)*

**1** Manual Healing Methods
- Chiropractic
- Massage
- Acupuncture/acupressure/reflexology
- Hand-mediatiated biofield therapies

**2** Chiropractic
- Reduce or eliminate pain
- Correct spinal dysfunction
- Muscles and ligaments strengthened by spinal rehabilitative exercises
- Preventive maintenance to ensure the problem does not recur

**3** Massage
- Aids the ability of the body to heal itself
- Aimed at achieving or increasing health and well-being

**4** Acupuncture/Acupressure/Reflexology
- Treatments rooted in the traditional philosophy of *qi*, or life energy
- Blocked or congested energy causes pain, frustration, and irritability
- Goal of care is to recognize and manage disruption before illness or disease occurs by applying pressure or stimulation to specific points on the body

5. Hand-mediated biofield therapies include therapeutic touch (TT), healing touch (HT), and reiki. All three approaches could be simply defined as the use of the hands on or near the body with the intention to heal. The goals are to accelerate the person's own healing process and to facilitate healing at all levels of body, mind, emotions, and spirit. All three are forms of treatment and are not designed to diagnose physical conditions, nor are they meant to replace conventional surgery, medicine, or drugs in treating organic disease. These therapies are helpful for people with a variety of medical and nursing diagnoses.

5 Hand-Mediated Biofield Therapies
- Includes therapeutic touch (TT), healing touch (HT), and reiki
- Use of hands on or near with intention to heal
- Goal of care is to accelerate person's own healing process
- Facilitate healing of body, mind, emotions, and spirit

---

**SUGGESTIONS FOR CLASSROOM ACTIVITIES**

- Invite a nurse who is a practitioner of TT, HT, Reiki, or massage to provide a demonstration to the class.

**SUGGESTIONS FOR CLINICAL ACTIVITIES**

- Arrange clinical experiences for students that allow them to learn about healing modalities available in the community or offered in the clinical setting.

---

## LEARNING OUTCOME 7

Describe the goals that yoga, meditation, hypnotherapy, guided imagery, qigong, and t'ai chi have in common.

**CONCEPTS FOR LECTURE**

1. Mind–body therapies include yoga, meditation, hypnotherapy, guided imagery, qigong, and t'ai chi.
2. In mind–body therapies, clients focus on realigning or creating balance in mental processes to bring about healing. The goal of mind-body therapies is to decrease stress and bring increased relaxation to the body and mind.

**POWERPOINT LECTURE SLIDES**

*(NOTE: The number on each PPT Lecture Slide directly corresponds with the Concepts for Lecture.)*

 1 Mind–Body Therapies
- Yoga
- Meditation
- Hypnotherapy
- Guided imagery
- Qigong
- T'ai chi

 2 Common Goals
- Creating balance
- Reducing stress
- Increasing relaxation of the body

---

**SUGGESTIONS FOR CLASSROOM ACTIVITIES**

- Demonstrate the use of guided imagery.
- Obtain a DVD of a yoga session and t'ai chi for the class to view.

**SUGGESTIONS FOR CLINICAL ACTIVITIES**

- Have the students investigate the community to locate classes in yoga, t'ai chi, and other alternative and complementary healing modalities. Have the students share the resources with the class.

# LEARNING OUTCOME 8

Explain the theory underlying bioelectromagnetics and infrared photoenergy therapy.

## CONCEPTS FOR LECTURE

1. Bioelectromagnetics is the emerging science that studies how living organisms interact with electromagnetic fields. It works on the principle that every animal, plant, and mineral has an electromagnetic field that enables organic and inorganic objects, such as crystals, to communicate and interact as part of a single, unified energy system. Magnetic fields are able to penetrate the body and affect the functioning of cells, tissues, organs, and systems.
2. Infrared photoenergy therapy is believed to work by increasing energy inside cells, as well as by improving circulation.

## POWERPOINT LECTURE SLIDES

*(NOTE: The number on each PPT Lecture Slide directly corresponds with the Concepts for Lecture.)*

**1** Bioelectromagnetics
- Every animal, plant, and mineral has an electromagnetic field
- Enables organic and inorganic objects to communicate and interact
- Penetrate the body affecting the functioning of cells, tissues, organs, and systems

**2** Infrared Photoenergy Therapy
- Increase energy inside cells
- Improve circulation

---

## SUGGESTIONS FOR CLASSROOM ACTIVITIES

- Invite a member of the college science department to discuss the basics of electromagnetic fields and human beings.

---

# LEARNING OUTCOME 9

Compare the various types of detoxification.

## CONCEPTS FOR LECTURE

1. Detoxification is the belief that physical impurities and toxins must be cleared from the body to achieve better health. Hydrotherapy, colonics, and chelation therapy are types of detoxification.
2. Hydrotherapy is the use of water as a healing treatment. The use of hot and cold moisture in the form of solid, liquid, or gas makes use of the body's response to heat and cold. Hydrotherapy is used to decrease pain, decrease fever, reduce swelling, reduce cramps, induce sleep, and improve physical and mental tone.
3. Colonics, or colon therapy, is based on the idea that a high-fat, Western diet leads to an accumulation of a thick, glue-like substance in the colon, which in turn produces toxins that lead to disease. Colonics is the procedure for washing the inner walls of the colon by filling it with water or herbal solutions and then draining it. Colon cleansing is a controversial method of detoxification.
4. Chelation therapy is the introduction of chemicals into the bloodstream that bind with heavy metals in the body.

## POWERPOINT LECTURE SLIDES

*(NOTE: The number on each PPT Lecture Slide directly corresponds with the Concepts for Lecture.)*

**1** Detoxification
- Belief that physical impurities and toxins must be cleared
- Types
  - Hydrotherapy
  - Colonics
  - Chelation therapy

**2** Hydrotherapy
- Use of water as a healing treatment
- Makes use of the body's response to heat and cold
- Used to
  - Decrease pain and fever
  - Reduce swelling and cramps
  - Induce sleep
  - Improve physical and mental tone

**3** Colonics or Colon Therapy
- Colonics is the procedure for washing the inner walls of the colon by filling it with water or herbal solutions and then draining it

**4** Chelation Therapy
- Introduction of chemicals into the bloodstream that bind with heavy metals in the body

## LEARNING OUTCOME 10

Discuss uses of animals, prayer, and humor as treatment modalities.

### CONCEPTS FOR LECTURE

1. Animal-assisted therapy: The use of specifically selected animals as a treatment modality in health and human service settings has been shown to be a successful intervention for people with a variety of physical or psychological conditions. For example, throwing a ball for a dog increases upper extremity range of motion, ambulating with a dog improves mobility, and attending to the animal and the situation increases attention and concentration. Resident animals live in long-term health care facilities. Residents who have regular visits by the animals are more receptive to treatment, have a greater incentive to recover, and have an increased will to live. The contributions companion animals (personal pets) make to the emotional well-being of people include providing unconditional love and opportunities for affection, achievement of trust, responsibility, and empathy toward others. Companion animals provide a reason to get up in the morning and a source of reassurance.

2. Prayer: Prayer is most often defined simply as a form of communication and fellowship with the Deity or Creator. It is also defined as an "active process of appealing to a higher spiritual power, specifically for health reasons" when used with CAM. Prayer is a self-care strategy that provides comfort, increases hope, and promotes healing and psychological well-being.

3. Humor: Humor is the ability to discover, express, or appreciate the comical or bizarre; to be amused by one's own imperfections or the whimsical aspects of life; and to see the funny side of an otherwise serious situation. Humor in nursing is defined as helping the client "to perceive, appreciate, and express what is funny, amusing, or ludicrous in order to establish relationships, relieve tension, release anger, facilitate learning or cope with painful feeling." Humor has physiologic benefits that involve alternating states of stimulation and relaxation. Humor brings out and integrates people's positive emotions—hope, faith, will to live, festivity, purpose, and determination—and therefore has healing properties.

### POWERPOINT LECTURE SLIDES

*(NOTE: The number on each PPT Lecture Slide directly corresponds with the Concepts for Lecture.)*

1. Animal-Assisted Therapy
   • Physical or psychological conditions
   • Resident animals
   • Companion animals

2. Prayer
   • Form of communication and fellowship with the Deity or Creator
   • Self-care strategy
   • Provides comfort, increases hope, and promotes healing and psychological well-being

3. Humor
   • Establish relationships
   • Relieve tension and anxiety
   • Release anger and aggression
   • Facilitate learning
   • Cope with painful feelings

## SUGGESTIONS FOR CLASSROOM ACTIVITIES

- Have the students discuss the pros and cons of the use of humor in emergency situations (e.g., cardiopulmonary resuscitation).
- Have the students investigate the difference between the types of humor men and women enjoy and how this may be applied clinically.

## SUGGESTIONS FOR CLINICAL ACTIVITIES

- Arrange for several students to observe a facility in which there is a resident animal. Ask them to record their observations of the interactions of the animal with clients, clients' families, and staff, and share these with the rest of the students.
- Have the students provide examples of when they have used humor in the clinical setting. What was the result?
- Have the students give examples of the use of prayer that they have observed in the clinical area. Ask them to discuss how they would respond if their clients asked them to pray with them.

# CHAPTER 20
## CONCEPTS OF GROWTH AND DEVELOPMENT

## RESOURCE LIBRARY

### PRENTICE HALL NURSING MEDIALINK DVD-ROM

Audio Glossary
NCLEX® Review

### COMPANION WEBSITE

Additional NCLEX® Review
Case Study: Treating a Six-Year-Old Client
Care Plan Activity: Child with Developmental
   Problems
Application Activity: *Discharging a Young Client*
Links to Resources

### IMAGE LIBRARY

**Figure 20.1** Cephalocaudal and proximodistal growth.

**Figure 20.2** Trust is established when the infant's basic needs are met.

**Figure 20.3** Assistive devices help maintain independence and self-esteem, which also helps the older adult's ego integrity to adapt and cope with the reality of aging.

**Figure 20.4** Young adults develop meaningful relationships and begin considering a home and family for themselves.

**Figure 20.5** School-age (7 to 11 years) children can understand cause-and-effect and concrete relationships or problems.

---

## LEARNING OUTCOME 1

Differentiate between the terms *growth* and *development*.

### CONCEPTS FOR LECTURE

1. *Growth* and *development* both refer to dynamic processes and are often used interchangeably but have different meanings.
2. Growth is physical change and increase in size. It can be measured quantitatively. Indicators of growth include height, weight, and bone size, for example. Patterns of physiological growth are similar for all people. However, growth rates vary during different stages of growth and development. Growth is most rapid during prenatal, neonatal, infancy, and adolescent stages. Growth slows during childhood and is minimal in adulthood.
3. Development is an increase in the complexity of function and skill progression. It is the capacity and skill of a person to adapt to the environment. Examples of development of abilities include learning to walk, talk, and run. Development is the behavioral aspects of growth.
4. Growth and development are independent, interrelated processes. Growth generally takes place during the first 20 years of life. Development takes place during that time and also continues after that point.

### POWERPOINT LECTURE SLIDES

*(NOTE: The number on each PPT Lecture Slide directly corresponds with the Concepts for Lecture.)*

**1** Growth and Development
   • Both refer to dynamic processes
   • Terms often used interchangeably
   • Have different meanings

**2** Growth
   • Physical change and increase in size
   • Measure quantitatively
   • Examples: height, weight, head circumference

**3** Development
   • Increase in the complexity of function and skill progression
   • Capacity and skill of a person to adapt to the environment
   • Examples: learning to walk, run, talk

**4** Growth and Development
   • Independent but interrelated
   • Growth—first 20 years of life
   • Development—during and after growth

**SUGGESTIONS FOR CLASSROOM ACTIVITIES**

• Provide examples of indicators of growth and development. Ask the students to classify the examples.

**SUGGESTIONS FOR CLINICAL ACTIVITIES**

• If appropriate for the setting, demonstrate use of growth charts for each gender.

## LEARNING OUTCOME 2

Describe essential principles related to growth and development.

### CONCEPTS FOR LECTURE

1. Growth and development are continuous, orderly, sequential processes influenced by maturational, environmental, and genetic factors. All humans follow the same pattern of growth and development. The sequence of each stage is predictable although the time of onset, the length of the stage, and the effects of each stage vary with the person. Learning can either help or hinder the maturational process, depending upon what is learned. Each developmental stage has its own characteristics. Growth and development occur in a cephalocaudal direction: starting at the head and moving to the trunk, legs, and feet. Growth and development occur in a proximodistal direction: from the center of the body outward. Development proceeds from simple to complex, or from single acts to integrated acts. Development becomes increasingly differentiated. Certain stages of growth and development are more critical than others. The pace of growth and development is uneven (see Box 20–1).

### POWERPOINT LECTURE SLIDES

*(NOTE: The number on each PPT Lecture Slide directly corresponds with the Concepts for Lecture.)*

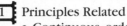 Principles Related to Growth and Development
- Continuous, orderly, sequential processes
- Same pattern of growth and development
- Sequence predictable
- Learning may affect
- Each developmental stage has its own characteristics
- Cephalocaudal growth occurs from the head downward
- Proximodistal growth occurs from the center outward
- Development proceeds from simple to complex
- Development becomes increasingly differentiated
- Certain stages of growth and development more crititcal than others
- Pace can be uneven

### SUGGESTIONS FOR CLASSROOM ACTIVITIES

• Have the students provide examples demonstrating the principles of growth and development.

### SUGGESTIONS FOR CLINICAL ACTIVITIES

• Arrange for students to have an observational experience in a pediatric wellness clinic. Ask them to keep a log of observations of the principles of growth and development. Have the students share their observations in a clinical conference.

## LEARNING OUTCOME 3

List factors that influence growth and development.

### CONCEPTS FOR LECTURE

1. Many factors influence growth and development, including genetics, temperament, family, nutrition, environment, health, and culture.

### POWERPOINT LECTURE SLIDES

*(NOTE: The number on each PPT Lecture Slide directly corresponds with the Concepts for Lecture.)*

1 Factors Influencing Growth and Development
- Genetics
- Temperament
- Family
- Nutrition
- Environmental
- Health
- Culture

# LEARNING OUTCOME 4

Explain the concept of temperament.

## CONCEPTS FOR LECTURE

1. Temperament is the way individuals respond to their external and internal environment. This sets the stage for interactive dynamics of growth and development.

   Temperament may persist throughout the life span, though caution must be taken not to irrevocably "label" or categorize infants and children. The "goodness of fit" between children's temperamental qualities and the demand of their environment contribute to positive growth and development. When parents understand the child's temperament, they are better able to shape environment to meet the child's needs.

2. Chess and Thomas identified nine temperamental qualities seen in children's behavior: activity level, sensitivity, intensity, adaptability, distractibility, approach/withdrawal, mood, persistence, and regularity (see Table 20–5).

## POWERPOINT LECTURE SLIDES

(NOTE: The number on each PPT Lecture Slide directly corresponds with the Concepts for Lecture.)

**1** Temperament
- Response to external and internal environment
- Stage for interactive dynamics of growth and development
- May persist throughout the life span
- Caution not to irrevocably "label" or categorize
- "Goodness of fit"

**2** Nine Temperamental Qualities (Chess & Thomas)
- Activity level
- Sensitivity
- Intensity
- Adaptability
- Distractibility
- Approach/withdrawal
- Mood
- Persistence
- Regularity

# LEARNING OUTCOME 5

Describe the stages of growth and development according to various theorists.

## CONCEPTS FOR LECTURE

1. The rate of a person's growth and development is highly individual; however, the sequence of growth and development is predictable (see Table 20–1).

   The neonatal period is from birth to 28 days. Behavior is largely reflexive but develops to more purposeful behavior.

   During infancy (1 month to 1 year), physical growth is rapid.

   During toddlerhood (1 to 3 years), motor development permits increased physical autonomy, and psychosocial skills increase.

## POWERPOINT LECTURE SLIDES

(NOTE: The number on each PPT Lecture Slide directly corresponds with the Concepts for Lecture.)

**1** Stages of Growth and Development
- Neonatal (birth to 28 days)
  - Behavior largely reflexive
  - Develops to more purposeful behavior
- Infancy (1 month to 1 year)
  - Physical growth rapid
- Toddlerhood (1 to 3 years)
  - Motor development permits increased physical autonomy
  - Psychosocial skills increase

For preschoolers (3 to 6 years), the world is expanding. New experiences and social roles are tried during play. Physical growth slows.

School age (6 to 12 years) includes the preadolescent period (10 to 12 years). Peer groups have an increasing influence on behavior. Physical, cognitive, and social development increase, and communication skills improve.

During adolescence (12 to 20 years), self-concept changes with biologic development. Values are tested, physical growth accelerates, and stress increases, especially in the face of conflicts.

During young adulthood (20 to 40 years), a personal lifestyle develops. The young adult establishes a relationship with a significant other and a commitment to something.

Middle adulthood (40 to 65 years) includes lifestyle changes due to other changes. For example, children leave home and occupational goals change.

During older adulthood, the young-old (65 to 74 years) adapt to retirement and changing physical abilities. Chronic illness may develop.

The middle-old (75 to 84 years) adapt to decline in speed of movement and reaction time. Increasing dependence on others may be necessary.

The old-old (85 and over) may develop increasing physical problems.

- Preschool (3 to 6 years)
  - World is expanding
  - New experiences and social role tried during play
  - Physical growth slows
- School age (6 to 12 years)
  - Includes preadolescent period (10 to 12 years)
  - Peer group increasingly influences behavior
  - Physical, cognitive, social development increase
  - Communication skills improve
- Adolescence (12 to 20 years)
  - Self-concept changes with biologic development
  - Values tested
  - Physical growth accelerates
  - Stress increases, especially in face of conflicts
- Young adulthood (20 to 40 years)
  - A personal lifestyle develops
  - Establishes a relationship with a significant other and a commitment to something
- Middle adulthood (40 to 65 years)
  - Lifestyle changes due to other changes
  - Example: children leave home, occupational goals change
- Older adulthood (Young-old, 65 to 74 years)
  - Adaptation to retirement and changing physical abilities often necessary
  - Chronic illness may develop
- Middle-Old (75 to 84 years)
  - Adapts to decline in speed of movement, reaction time, and increasing dependence on others may be necessary
- Old-Old (85 and over)
  - Increasing physical problems may develop

---

## SUGGESTIONS FOR CLASSROOM ACTIVITIES

- Divide the students into groups. Assign each group one or two developmental stages. Ask the groups to provide examples to illustrate the major characteristics of each assigned developmental stage. Have the groups share with the class.
- Invite a panel of nurses who care for infants, children, adolescents, adults, and the elderly to discuss how they incorporate the stages and various theories of growth and development into their nursing practice.

## SUGGESTIONS FOR CLINICAL ACTIVITIES

- Have the students provide examples of how clients demonstrate characteristics of their developmental stage.

# LEARNING OUTCOME 6

Describe characteristics and implications of Freud's five stages of development.

## CONCEPTS FOR LECTURE

1. According to Freud's theory of psychosexual development, the personality develops in five overlapping stages from birth to adulthood (see Table 20–2).
2. The oral stage is from birth to 1 1/2 years. The mouth is the center of pleasure (gratification and exploration). Security is the primary need. The major conflict is weaning. Feeding produces pleasure and a sense of comfort and safety. Feeding should be pleasurable and provided when required.
3. The anal stage is from 1 1/2 to 3 years. The anus and bladder are the source of pleasure (sensual satisfaction, self-control). The major conflict is toilet training. Controlling and expelling feces provide pleasure and a sense of control. Toilet training should be a pleasurable experience.
4. The phallic stage is from 4 to 6 years. The genitals are the center of pleasure; masturbation offers pleasure. Fantasy, experimentation with peers, and questioning adults about sexual topics become common. The major conflict is the Oedipus or Electra complex, which resolves when the child identifies with the parent of the same gender, identifies with the parent of the opposite sex, and later takes on a love relationship outside the family. This stage encourages identity.
5. The latency stage is from 6 years to puberty. Energy is directed to physical and intellectual activities. Sexual impulses tend to be repressed. Relationships develop between peers of the same gender. The child should be encouraged in physical and intellectual pursuits. Encourage sports and other activities with same-gender peers.
6. The genital stage is puberty and after. Energy is directed toward full sexual maturity and function and development of skills needed to cope with the environment. Encourage separation from parents and achievement of independence and decision making.

## POWERPOINT LECTURE SLIDES

*(NOTE: The number on each PPT Lecture Slide directly corresponds with the Concepts for Lecture.)*

**1** Freud's Stages of Development
- Oral
- Anal
- Phallic
- Latency
- Genital

**2** Oral (Birth to 1 1/2 Years)
- Mouth center of pleasure (gratification and exploration)
- Security primary need
- Major conflict: weaning
- Feeding produces pleasure, sense of comfort, safety
- Feeding should be pleasurable and provided when required

**3** Anal (1 1/2 to 3 Years)
- Anus and bladder source of pleasure (sensual satisfaction, self-control)
- Major conflict: toilet training
- Toilet training should be a pleasurable experience

**4** Phallic (4 to 6 Years)
- Genitals center of pleasure
- Masturbation offers pleasure
- Fantasy, experimentation with peers
- Questioning adults about sexual topics
- Major conflict: Oedipus/Electra complexes
- Resolves when the child identifies with parent of same gender

**5** Latency (6 Years to Puberty)
- Energy directed to physical and intellectual activities
- Sexual impulses tend to be repressed
- Develop relationship between peers of the same gender
- Encourage child with physical and intellectual pursuits
- Encourage sports and other activities with same gender peers

**6** Genital (Puberty and After)
- Energy directed toward full sexual maturity and function
- Development of skills needed to cope with the environment
- Encourage separation from parents
- Achievement of independence and decision making

## LEARNING OUTCOME 7

Identify Erikson's eight stages of development.

### CONCEPTS FOR LECTURE

1. Erikson's stages of development reflect both positive and negative aspects of the critical life periods. The resolution of conflicts at each stage enables the person to function effectively in society (see Table 20-3). Failure to resolves crises damages the ego.

    The infancy stage is from birth to 18 months. The central task at this stage is trust versus mistrust.

    The early childhood stage is from 18 months to 3 years. The central task is autonomy versus shame and doubt.

    The late childhood stage is from 3 to 5 years. The central task is initiative versus guilt.

    The school-age stage is from 6 to 12 years. The central task is industry versus inferiority.

    The stage of adolescence is from 12 to 20 years. The central task is identity versus role confusion.

    The stage of young adulthood is from 18 to 25 years. The central task is intimacy versus isolation.

    Adulthood is from 25 to 65 years. The central task of this stage is generativity versus stagnation.

    The maturity stage is from 65 years to death. The central task is integrity versus despair.

### POWERPOINT LECTURE SLIDES

*(NOTE: The number on each PPT Lecture Slide directly corresponds with the Concepts for Lecture.)*

1 Erikson's Eight Stages of Development
- Infancy (birth to 18 months)—trust versus mistrust
- Early childhood (18 months to 3 year)—autonomy versus shame and doubt
- Late Childhood (3 to 5 years)—Initiative versus guilt
- School-Age (6 to 12 years)—industry versus inferiority
- Adolescence (12 to 20 years)—identity versus role confusion
- Young adult (18 to 25 years)—intimacy versus isolation
- Adulthood (25 to 65 years)—generativity versus stagnation
- Maturity (65 years to death)—integrity versus despair

## LEARNING OUTCOME 8

Identify developmental tasks associated with Havighurst's six age periods.

### CONCEPTS FOR LECTURE

1. Havighurst believed that learning is basic to life and people continue to learn throughout life. Developmental tasks arise at or about a certain period of life. Successful achievement of these tasks leads to happiness and success in later tasks while failure to accomplish these tasks leads to unhappiness, disapproval by society and difficulty achieving later tasks.
2. Infancy and early childhood: The child is learning to walk; learning to eat solid foods; learning to talk; learning to control the elimination of body wastes;

### POWERPOINT LECTURE SLIDES

*(NOTE: The number on each PPT Lecture Slide directly corresponds with the Concepts for Lecture.)*

1 Havighurst's Six Age Periods
- Infancy and early childhood
- Middle childhood
- Adolescence
- Early adulthood
- Middle age
- Later maturity

learning sex differences and sexual modesty; achieving psychologic stability; forming simple concepts of social and physical reality; learning to relate emotionally to parents, siblings, and other people; and learning to distinguish right from wrong and developing a conscience.

3. Middle childhood: The child is learning physical skills necessary for ordinary games; building wholesome attitudes toward oneself as a growing organism; learning to get along with age-mates; learning an appropriate masculine or feminine social role; developing fundamental skills in reading, writing, and calculating; developing concepts necessary for everyday living; developing conscience, morality, and a scale of values; achieving personal independence; and developing attitudes toward social groups and institutions.

4. Adolescence: The adolescent is achieving new and more mature relations with age-mates of both sexes, achieving a masculine or feminine social role, accepting one's physique and using the body effectively, achieving emotional independence from parents and other adults, achieving assurance of economic independence, selecting and preparing for an occupation, preparing for marriage and family life, developing intellectual skills and concepts necessary for civic competence, desiring and achieving socially responsible behaviors, and acquiring a set of values and an ethical system as a guide to behavior.

5. Early adulthood: The young adult is concerned with selecting a mate, learning to live with a partner, starting a family, rearing children, managing a home, getting started in an occupation, taking on civic responsibility, and finding a congenial social group.

6. Middle age: The middle-aged adult is focused on achieving adult civic and social responsibility, establishing and maintaining an economic standard of living, assisting teenage children to become responsible and happy adults, developing adult leisure-time activities, relating oneself to one's spouse as a person, accepting and adjusting to the physiologic changes of middle age, and adjusting to aging parents.

7. Later maturity: The older adult is concerned with adjusting to decreasing physical strength and health, adjusting to retirement and reduced income, adjusting to death of a spouse, establishing an explicit affiliation with one's age group, meeting social and civil obligations, and establishing physical living arrangements (see Table 20–4).

 Infancy and Early Childhood
- Learning to walk and talk
- Eat solid foods
- Control elimination
- Learning sex differences and modesty
- Achieving psychologic stability
- Learning to relate emotionally
- Learning to distinguish right from wrong
- Developing a conscience

 Middle Childhood
- Learning physical skills for ordinary games
- Building wholesome attitudes toward oneself
- Learning to get along with peers
- Learning appropriate gender social role
- Developing fundamental skills in reading, writing, math
- Developing concepts for everyday living
- Developing conscience, morality, scale of values
- Achieving personal independence
- Developing attitudes toward social groups and institutions

 Adolescence
- Achieving more mature relationships with peers
- Achieving gender role
- Accepting one's own body
- Using the body effectively
- Achieving emotional independence from parents
- Achieving economic independence
- Preparing for an occupation
- Preparing for marriage and family life
- Developing intellectual skills and concepts for civic competence
- Achieving socially responsible behaviors
- Acquiring a set of values and an ethical system

 Early Adulthood
- Selecting a mate
- Learning to live with a partner
- Starting a family
- Rearing children
- Managing a home
- Getting started in an occupation
- Taking on civic responsibilities
- Finding a congenial social group

 Middle Age
- Achieving adult civic role and social responsibilities
- Establishing and maintaining an economic standard of living
- Assisting teenage children to become happy adults
- Developing adult leisure-time activities
- Relating oneself to one's spouse as a person
- Accepting and adapting to physiologic changes
- Adjusting to aging parents

7 Later Maturity
- Adjusting to decreasing physical strength and health
- Adjusting to retirement and reduced income
- Adjusting to death of spouse
- Establishing an explicit affiliation with peers
- Meeting social and civic obligations
- Establishing physical living arrangements

# LEARNING OUTCOME 9

Compare Peck's and Gould's stages of adult development.

## CONCEPTS FOR LECTURE

1. Peck believes that although physical capabilities and functions decrease with old age, mental and social capacities tend to increase in the latter part of life. Peck proposes three development tasks during old age in contrast to Erikson's one (integrity versus despair):

2. Ego differentiation versus work-role preoccupation. An adult's identity and feelings of worth are highly dependent on the work role. On retirement, adults may experience feelings of worthlessness unless they derive their sense of identity from a number of roles so that one role can replace the work role as a source of self-esteem.

3. Body transcendence versus body preoccupation. The adult must adjust to decreasing physical capacities and at the same time maintain feelings of well-being.

4. Ego transcendence versus ego preoccupation. This task is the acceptance without fear of one's death as inevitable and being actively involved in one's own future beyond death.

5. Gould believes that transformation is a central theme of adulthood and that adults continue to change over the period of time considered to be adulthood. Gould describes seven stages of adult development:
   - Stage 1 (ages 16–18): Individuals consider themselves part of a family instead of individuals and want to separate from their parents.
   - Stage 2 (ages 18–22): Although individuals have established autonomy, they feel it is in jeopardy; they feel they could be pulled back into the family.
   - Stage 3 (ages 22–28): Individuals feel they are established as adults and autonomous from their families. They see themselves as well defined but still feel the need to prove themselves to their parents. This is the time for growing and building a future.
   - Stage 4 (ages 29–34): Marriage and careers are well established. Individuals question what life is all about, wish to be accepted as they are, and are no longer trying to prove themselves.

## POWERPOINT LECTURE SLIDES

*(NOTE: The number on each PPT Lecture Slide directly corresponds with the Concepts for Lecture.)*

1 Peck's Stages of Adult Development
- Ego differentiation vs. work-role preoccupation
- Body transcendence vs. body preoccupation
- Ego transcendence vs. ego preoccupation

2 Ego Differentiation vs. Work-Role Preoccupation
- If identity and feelings of worth are dependent on work role
- On retirement may experience feelings of worthlessness
- Unless derive sense of identity from a number of roles

3 Body Transcendence vs. Body Preoccupation
- Must adjust to decreasing physical capacities
- At the same time maintain feelings of well-being

4 Ego Transcendence vs. Ego Preoccupation
- Acceptance without fear of one's death as inevitable
- Being actively involved in one's own future beyond death

5 Gould's Stages of Adult Development
- Stage 1 (ages 16–18)
  - Part of family instead of individuals
  - Want to separate from family
- Stage 2 (ages 18–22)
  - Established autonomy but feel its in jeopardy
  - Feel could be pulled back into family
- Stage 3 (ages 22–28)
  - Established as adult and autonomous from family
  - Well-defined but still feels need to prove self to parents
  - Time for growing and building a future
- Stage 4 (ages 29–34)
  - Marriage and career
  - Well established
  - Questions what life is all about

- Stage 5 (ages 35–43): This is a period of self-reflection. Individuals question values and life itself. They see time as finite, with little time left to shape the lives of adolescent children.
- Stage 6 (ages 43–50): The personality is set. Time is accepted as finite. The individual is interested in social activities with friends and spouse and desires both sympathy and affection from spouse.
- Stage 7 (ages 50–60): This is a period of transformation, with a realization of mortality and a concern for health. There is an increase in warmth and a decrease in negativism. The spouse is seen as a valuable companion.

- ○ Wishes to be accepted as are
- ○ No longer trying to prove self
- Stage 5 (ages 35–43)
  - ○ Self-reflection, questions values and life itself
  - ○ See time as finite, with little time left to shape lives of adolescent children
- Stage 6 (ages 43–50)
  - ○ Personality set
  - ○ Time accepted as finite
  - ○ Interested in social activities with friends and spouse
  - ○ Desire both sympathy and affection from spouse
- Stage 7 (age 50–60)
  - ○ Period of transformation
  - ○ Realization of mortality and concern for health
  - ○ Increase in warmth and a decrease in negativism
  - ○ Spouse is seen as valuable companion

## SUGGESTIONS FOR CLASSROOM ACTIVITIES

- Have the students compare Peck's and Gould's developmental tasks of the adult with Erikson's.
- Many adults do not choose to marry or have children, or have become divorced. Have the students discuss the application of Peck's and Gould's theories to these situations.

## SUGGESTIONS FOR CLINICAL ACTIVITIES

- Invite nurses from the institution who work with adults in various stages to discuss how they apply Peck's and Gould's theories in their nursing practice.
- Have students apply Peck's or Gould's stages to one of their clients and share with the group.

## LEARNING OUTCOME 10

Explain Piaget's theory of cognitive development.

### CONCEPTS FOR LECTURE

1. Cognitive development refers to the manner in which people learn to think, reason, and use language. It involves a person's intelligence, perceptual ability, and ability to process information.
2. Cognitive development represents a progression of mental abilities from illogical to logical thinking, from simple to complex problem solving, and from understanding concrete ideas to understanding abstract ideas.
3. Piaget is the most widely known cognitive theorist. According to Piaget, cognitive development is an orderly, sequential process in which a variety of experiences must exist before intellectual abilities can develop. This process is divided into five major phases: sensorimotor, preconceptual, intuitive thought, concrete operations, and formal operations.
4. In each phase, the person uses three primary abilities: assimilation, accommodation, and adaptation.

### POWERPOINT LECTURE SLIDES

*(NOTE: The number on each PPT Lecture Slide directly corresponds with the Concepts for Lecture.)*

1 Cognitive Development
- Manner in which people learn to think, reason and use language
- Involves
  - ○ Intelligence
  - ○ Perceptual ability
  - ○ Ability to process information

2 Cognitive Development
- Progression of mental abilities
  - ○ From illogical to logical
  - ○ From simple to complex problem solving
  - ○ Understanding concrete ideas to understanding abstract ideas

3 Piaget's Cognitive Development Theory
- Sensorimotor

## CONCEPTS FOR LECTURE *continued*

Assimilation is the process through which humans encounter and react to new situations by using the mechanisms already possessed. Accommodation is a process of change whereby cognitive processes mature sufficiently to allow the person to solve problems that were unsolvable before. Adaptation, or coping behavior, is the ability to handle the demands made by the environment (see Table 20-6).

## POWERPOINT LECTURE SLIDES *continued*

- Preconceptual
- Intuitive thought
- Concrete operations
- Formal operation

 Three Primary Abilities of Each Phase
- Assimilation
  - Encounter and react to new situations by using the mechanisms already possessed
- Accommodation
  - Process of change
  - Cognitive processes mature to solve problems that were unsolvable
- Adaptation, or coping behavior
  - The ability to handle the demands made by the environment

---

## SUGGESTIONS FOR CLASSROOM ACTIVITIES

- Provide the students with examples of problem-solving processes and skills that are learned in each of Piaget's five phases. Ask the students to classify these into the appropriate phase.
- Have the students discuss whether all people are able to attain the formal operations phase.

## SUGGESTIONS FOR CLINICAL ACTIVITIES

- Have the students provide examples of assimilation, accommodation, and adaptation processes as these apply to learning in the clinical setting.

---

# LEARNING OUTCOME 11

Compare Kohlberg's and Gilligan's theories of moral development.

## CONCEPTS FOR LECTURE

1. Kohlberg's theory specifically addresses moral development in children and adults. The morality of an individual's decision was not his concern rather he focused on the reasons an individual makes a decision.

   According to Kohlberg, moral development progresses through three levels and six stages. The levels and stages are not always linked to a certain developmental stage, because some people progress to a higher level of moral development than others (see Table 20-7).

2. Gilligan's theory is based on research with women subjects. She reported that women often consider the dilemmas Kohlberg used in his research to be irrelevant. Women scored consistently lower on Kohlberg's scale of moral development in spite of the fact that they approached moral dilemmas with considerable sophistication. Gilligan believes that most frameworks for research in moral development do not include the concepts of caring and responsibility.

   Gilligan found that moral development proceeds through three levels and two transitions, with each level representing a more complex understanding of the relationship of self and others and each transition resulting in a crucial reevaluation of the conflict between selfishness and responsibility.

## POWERPOINT LECTURE SLIDES

*(NOTE: The number on each PPT Lecture Slide directly corresponds with the Concepts for Lecture.)*

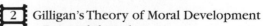 Kohlberg's Theory of Moral Development
- Addresses moral development in children and adults
- Focused on the reasons an individual makes a decision
- Moral development progresses through three levels and six stages
- Levels and stages are not always linked to a certain developmental stage
- Some people progress to a higher level of moral development than others

Gilligan's Theory of Moral Development
- Research based on women
- Includes the concepts of caring and responsibility
- Three levels and two transitions
- Each level representing a more complex understanding of the relationship of self and others
- Each transition resulting in a crucial reevaluation of the conflict between selfishness and responsibility

## LEARNING OUTCOME 12

Compare Fowler's and Westerhoff's stages of spiritual development.

### CONCEPTS FOR LECTURE

1. Fowler describes the development of faith as a force that gives meaning to a person's life. He believes the development of faith is an interactive process between the person and the environment.

   Fowler's stages of spiritual development (see Table 20-8) were influenced by the work of Piaget, Kohlberg, and Erikson. In each of Fowler's stages, new patterns of thought, values, and beliefs are added to those already held by the individual. Therefore, the stages must follow in sequence.

   Faith stages, according to Fowler, are separate from the cognitive stages of Piaget. They evolve from a combination of knowledge and values.

2. Westerhoff describes faith as a way of being and behaving that evolves from an experienced faith guided by parents and others during a person's infancy and childhood to an owned faith that is internalized in adulthood and serves as a directive for personal action (see Table 20-9).

### POWERPOINT LECTURE SLIDES

*(NOTE: The number on each PPT Lecture Slide directly corresponds with the Concepts for Lecture.)*

 Fowler's Theory of Spiritual Development
- Describes faith is a force that gives meaning to a person's life
- An interactive process between the person and environment
- Influenced by the work of Piaget, Kohlberg, and Erikson
- In each stage new patterns of thought, values, and beliefs added
- Stages must follow in sequence
- Faith stages are separate from the cognitive stages of Piaget
- Evolve from a combination of knowledge and values

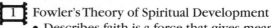 Westerhoff's Theory of Spiritual Development
- Describes faith as a way of being and behaving
- Evolves from an experienced faith guided by parents and others to an owned faith
- Faith serves as a directive for personal action

# Chapter 21
## Promoting Health from Conception through Adolescence

## Resource Library

### PRENTICE HALL NURSING MEDIALINK DVD-ROM

Audio Glossary
NCLEX® Review
Videos & Animations:
   *Adolescent Ear*
   *Cellullar Division of a Zygote*
   *Conception*
   *Drowning*
   *Identifying Child Abuse*
   *Oogenesis*
   *SIDS*
   *Spermatogenisis*

### COMPANION WEBSITE

Additional NCLEX® Review
Case Study: *Motor and Social Development in Infancy*
Care Plan Activity: *Teen with Lymphocytic Leukemia*
Application Activities:
   *Safety Tips for Children*
   *Playground Bullies*
Links to Resources

### IMAGE LIBRARY

**Figure 21.1** Measuring an infant head to heel, from the top of the head to the base of the heels.

**Figure 21.2** An infant's head circumference is measured around the skull, above the cycbrows and around the occiput.

**Figure 21.3** The bones of the skull, showing the fontanels and suture lines.

**Figure 21.4** An infant sits without support at 6 months of age.

**Figure 21.5** Place infant on back for sleeping. Note the infant's tonic neck reflex.

**Figure 21.6** A toddler has enough gross and fine motor ability to jump and kick a ball.

**Figure 21.7** Keep medicines and other poisonous materials locked away.

**Figure 21.8** A preschooler brushing her teeth.

**Figure 21.9** Preschoolers often identify with the parent of the same sex and like to mimic behavior.

**Figure 21.10** Expanding cognitive skills enable school-age children to interact cooperatively in activities of an increasingly complex nature, as shown by the children playing this board game.

**Figure 21.11** Teach children never to touch guns without a parent present.

**Figure 21.12** Adolescent peer group relationships enhance a sense of belonging, self-esteem, and self-identity.

**Figure 21.13** To prevent motor vehicle crashes, insist on driver's education classes and enforce rules about safe driving.

---

## LEARNING OUTCOME 1

Identify tasks characteristic of different stages of development from infancy through adolescence.

### CONCEPTS FOR LECTURE

1. Neonates and infants (birth to 1 year): A neonate's basic task is adjustment to the environment outside the uterus, which requires breathing, sleeping, sucking, eating, swallowing, digesting, and eliminating.

2. Toddlers (1 to 3 years): Toddlers develop from having no voluntary control to being able to walk and speak. They also learn to control their bladder and bowels, and they acquire a wide variety of information about their environment.

### POWERPOINT LECTURE SLIDES

*(NOTE: The number on each PPT Lecture Slide directly corresponds with the Concepts for Lecture.)*

 **1** Neonates and Infants (Birth to 1 Year)
   • Adjustment to environment outside the uterus

**2** Toddlers (1 to 3 Years)
   • Progress from no control to walking and speaking

---

3. Preschoolers (4 to 5 years): During the preschool period, physical growth slows, but control of the body and coordination increase greatly. A preschooler's world enlarges as he or she meets relatives and neighbors, and forms friendships.

4. School-age children (6 to 12 years): The school-age period starts when the deciduous teeth are shed. This period includes the preadolescent (prepuberty) period. It ends with the onset of puberty. In general, this period is one of significant growth. Skills learned in this stage are particularly important in relationship to work in later life and in willingness to try new tasks.

5. Adolescents (12 to 18 years): This is the period in which the person becomes physically and psychologically mature and acquires a personal identity. At the end of this critical period in development, the person should be ready to enter adulthood and assume its responsibilities.

- Control elimination
- Acquire information about environment

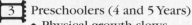 Preschoolers (4 and 5 Years)
- Physical growth slows
- Control of body and coordination greatly increases
- World enlarges with relatives, friends, etc.

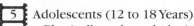 School-age Children (6 to 12 Years)
- Deciduous teeth are shed
- Includes preadolescence (or prepuberty)
- Period ends with onset of puberty
- Skills learned are important for later life

Adolescents (12 to 18 Years)
- Physically and psychologically matures
- Acquires personal identity
- Ready to enter adulthood

---

# LEARNING OUTCOME 2

Describe usual physical development from infancy through adolescence.

## CONCEPTS FOR LECTURE

1. Neonates and infants (0 to 1 year):
   - **Weight:** The infant weighs 2.7 to 3.8 kg (6.0 to 8.5 lb) at birth; loses 5% to 10% after birth but regains it in about 1 week; gains weight at a rate of 150 to 210 g (5 to 7 oz) per week for 6 months; doubles birth weight by 5 months; and triples birth weight by 12 months.
   - **Length:** Average length at birth is 50 cm (20 in.). The infant gains 13.75 cm (5.5 in.) by 6 months and gains another 7.5 cm (3 in.) by 12 months.
   - **Head and chest circumference:** Average head circumference is 35 cm (14 in.); chest circumference is usually about 2.5 cm (1 in.) less than head circumference. By about 9 to 10 months, the head equals chest circumference; after 1 year, chest circumference is larger than head. The anterior fontanel closes between 9 to 18 months and the posterior fontanel closes between 2 and 3 months.
   - **Vision:** The newborn follows large moving objects and blinks in response to bright light and sound. The pupils respond slowly; the newborn cannot focus on close objects. At 1 month, the infant can focus gaze on objects and follow moving objects. At 4 months, the infant recognizes a parent's smile, has almost complete color vision, and follows objects through a 180-degree arc. At 5 months, the infant reaches for objects. By 6 to 10 months, the infant can fix on an object and follow it in all directions. By 12 months, depth perception is fully developed and the child is able to recognize a change in levels (such as the edge of a bed).

## POWERPOINT LECTURE SLIDES

*(NOTE: The number on each PPT Lecture Slide directly corresponds with the Concepts for Lecture.)*

 Neonates and Infants
- Doubles birth weight by 5 mo; triples birth weight by 12 mo
- Gain 13.75 cm (5.5 inches) in length by 6 mo.; another 7.5 cm (3 in.) by 12 months
- At birth, head circumference larger than chest circumference; 9 to 10 mo, head equals chest; after 1 yr chest larger than head
- Anterior fontanel closes between 9 and 18 mo; posterior fontanel between 2 and 3 mo
- 1 mo focus gaze on close objects; 4 mo almost complete color vision, follows objects in 180° arc; 5 mo reaches for objects; follows in all directions; 12 mo depth perception developed
- Intact hearing at birth; 2–3 mo vocalizes to voices; 3–6 mo pauses to listen, responds to angry/happy voices; 6–9 mo words begin to have meaning; 9–12 mo understands some words, uses gestures, one word speech; 12 mo responds to simple commands
- Smell and taste functional shortly after birth
- Well-developed sense of touch at birth
- Infant reflexes disappear as voluntary movements develop
- Motor development improves significantly in a short time

 Neonates and Infants
- Weight
  - Doubles by 5 mo
  - Triples by 12 mo

- **Hearing:** The newborn has intact hearing at birth, responds to loud noises with the Moro reflex, and can distinguish sounds within a few days. At 2 to 3 months the infant can actively coo, smile, or gurgle to sounds and voices. By 3 to 6 months, the infant looks for sounds, pausing an activity to listen, and responds with distress or pleasure to angry or happy voices. By 6 to 9 months, individual words begin to take on meaning, and the baby may look at named objects or people. By 9 to 12 months, the baby understands many words, uses gestures, and may articulate one or two words with a specific reference. By 12 months, the child responds to simple commands.
- **Smell and taste:** These senses are functional shortly after birth. The newborn prefers sweet tastes, is able to recognize the smell of the mother's milk, and responds by turning toward the mother.
- **Touch:** The sense of touch is well developed at birth. The newborn responds positively when touched, held, and cuddled. Because of poor regulation of body temperature, the newborn is sensitive to extreme temperatures. The newborn responds to pain diffusely but cannot isolate discomfort.
- **Reflexes:** The rooting, sucking, Moro, palmar grasp, plantar, tonic neck, stepping, and Babinski reflexes are present at birth (see Box 21-2). They disappear during the first year in an orderly sequence to permit development of voluntary movements. The newborn can also yawn, stretch, sneeze, burp, and hiccup at birth.
- **Motor development:** The newborn is initially uncoordinated. By 1 month, the infant lifts the head momentarily when prone, turns the head when prone, and has head lag when pulled to a sitting position. By 4 months, there is minimal head lag. By 6 months the infant can sit without support; by 9 months, he or she can reach, grasp a rattle, and transfer it from hand to hand; and by 12 months, the child can turn pages in a book, put objects into a container, walk with some assistance, and help to dress self (see Table 21-1).

2. Toddlers (1 to 3 years):
- **Appearance:** The toddler appears chubby, with relatively short legs and a large head. The face appears small when compared to the skull. As the child grows, the face becomes better proportioned. Toddlers have pronounced lumbar lordosis and a protruding abdomen. The abdominal muscles develop with growth, and the abdomen flattens.
- **Weight:** By 2 years, weight is about four times birth weight. Between 1 and 2 years, weight gain is about 2 kg (5 lb); between 2 and 3 years, weight gain is about 1 to 2 kg (2 to 5 lb). A 3-year-old weighs about 13.6 kg (30 lb).

- Length
  - Gains 13.75 cm (5.5 in.) by 6 mo
  - Additional 7.5 cm (3 in.) by 12 mo
- Head and Chest Circumference
  - Head > chest at birth
  - Head = chest 9–10 mo
  - Head < chest after 1 yr
- Vision
  - Birth-blinks in response to bright light
  - 1 mo: focus on objects
  - 4 mo: almost complete color vision, follows object in 180° arc
  - 5 mo: reaches for objects
  - 6–10 mo: focus on object and follow in all directions
  - 12 mo: depth perception developed
- Hearing
  - Intact at birth; Moro reflex to loud noises
  - 2–3 mo: vocalize to sounds and voices
  - 3–6 mo: looks for sounds, pauses to listen, responds to angry/happy voices
  - 6–9 mo: may look at named objects/people
  - 9–12 mo: understands some words, uses gestures, says one or two words
  - 12 mo: responds to simple commands
- Smell and Taste
  - Intact at birth
- Touch
  - Well developed at birth
  - Poor temperature regulation
  - Diffuse response to pain
- Reflexes
  - Reflexes present at birth
  - Disappear to permit voluntary movement
- Motor development
  - Uncoordinated at birth
  - 1 mo: lifts head when prone, head lag present
  - 4 mo: minimal head lag
  - 6 mo: sits without support
  - 9 mo: reach, grasp, transfer object from hand to hand
  - 12 mo: fine motor skills begin to develop

**2** Toddlers
- Lose the "baby look" by age 2
- Gain 3–5 kg (7–10 lb) between ages 1 and 3
- Height spurts between ages 1 and 2, then slows
- By 24 mo, head circumference 80% adult size
- Vision continues to mature; 20/40 at age 2
- Hearing, taste, smell, and touch increasingly developed
- Fine and gross motor skills improve

**3** Preschoolers
- Body appears out of proportion as extremities grow more quickly
- Weight gain generally slow
- Doubles birth length by age 5

- **Height:** Between ages 1 and 2 years, average growth is 10 to 12 cm (4 to 5 in.); between ages 2 and 3 years, growth slows to 6 to 8 cm (2 ½ to 3 ½ in.).
- **Head circumference:** Head circumference increases about 2.5 cm (1 in.) on average each year. By 24 months the head is 80% of average adult size and the brain is 70% of adult size.
- **Vision:** Acuity is fairly well established at 1 year, 20/70 at 18 months, and 20/40 at 2 years. Accommodation is fairly well developed by 18 months. By 3 years the child can look away from a toy prior to reaching out and picking it up.
- **Hearing, taste, smell, and touch:** These senses are increasingly developed and associated with each other. A 3-year-old's hearing is at adult levels. Taste buds are sensitive to natural flavors or food. A 3-year-old will prefer familiar odors and tastes. Touch is very important; the child is often soothed by tactile sensation.
- **Motor abilities:** Fine motor coordination and gross motor skills improve during this period. At 18 months the toddler can pick up raisins or cereal pieces and place them into a receptacle, hold a spoon and cup, walk upstairs with assistance, and probably crawl down. The 2-year-old can hold a spoon and put it into the mouth correctly, run, has a steady gait, can balance on one foot, and ride a tricycle. Most 3-year-olds are toilet trained, with occasional accidents at night or when playing.

3. Preschoolers (4 to 5 years):
- **Appearance:** The child appears taller and thinner; the brain is almost adult size at 5 years. The extremities grow more quickly than the body, making the body appear out of proportion. The child appears slender with an erect posture.
- **Weight:** Gain is generally slow. By 5 years the child has added 3 to 5 kg (7 to 12 lb), weighing around 18 to 20 kg (40 to 45 lb).
- **Height:** The child grows about 5 to 6.25 cm (2 to 2.5 in.) each year, doubling birth length by 4 years and measures about 102 cm (41 in.).
- **Vision:** The child is generally hyperopic (farsighted) and unable to focus on near objects. Normal vision for 5-year-olds is approximately 20/30.
- **Hearing and taste:** Hearing has reached optimal levels, and the ability to listen has matured. The child shows food preferences and may develop food jags.
- **Motor abilities:** Children are able to wash their hands and face, and brush their teeth by 5 years. They are self-conscious about exposing their bodies and go to the bathroom without telling others. They can run with increasing skill each year. By 5 years they can run skillfully, jump three steps, balance on their toes, and dress without assistance.

- 20/30 normal vision at age 5
- Hearing at optimal levels
- Shows taste preferences
- Motor abilities strengthen as child begins to master physical activities

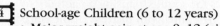 School-age Children (6 to 12 years)
- Major weight gain at age 9–12 (girls) and 10–12 (boys)
- Growth spurt at age 10–12 (girls) and 12–14 (boys)
- 20/20 vision established between ages 9–11
- Well-developed senses of hearing and touch
- Increased perspiration and other prepubertal changes
- Motor abilities well developed during this period

 Adolescents
- Body parts reach adult size, beginning with head, hands, and feet
- Rapid growth in height and weight for boys, slower in girls
- Glandular changes cause increased sweat and acne
- Primary and secondary sexual characteristics develop

4. School-age children (6 to 12 years):
   - **Weight:** Average weight gain is about 3.2 kg (7 lb) per year between 6 and 12 years; major weight gain occurs from age 10 to 12 for boys and from age 9 to 12 for girls.
   - **Height:** At 6 years, boys and girls are about the same height. The growth spurt for girls occurs at age 10 to 12 and for boys at 12 to 14. The extremities grow more quickly than the trunk. By age 6, thoracic curvature develops and lordosis disappears.
   - **Vision:** By 6 to 8 years, depth and distance perception is accurate. By age 6, the child has full binocular vision, eye muscles are well developed and coordinated, and the child can focus on one object at the same time. The child develops 20/20 vision between 9 and 11 years of age.
   - **Hearing and touch:** Auditory perception is fully developed; the child can identify fine differences in voices. The child has a well-developed sense of touch and can locate points of heat and cold on all body surfaces. Stereognosis is developed.
   - **Prepubertal changes:** Endocrine functions slowly increase at ages 9 to 13. Perspiration increases, sebaceous glands become more active, and leukorrhea occurs prior to puberty.
   - **Motor abilities:** Muscular skills and coordination are perfected in the middle years (6 to 10). By 9 years most children are skilled in games of interest. Fine motor control is sufficient for activities such as drawing, building models, or playing musical instruments.

5. Adolescents (12 to 18 years):
   - **Appearance:** Growth is accelerated, with sudden, dramatic physical changes (adolescent growth spurt). The head, hands, and feet are first to grow to adult status, next the extremities. The adolescent looks leggy, awkward, and uncoordinated until the trunk grows to full size. The shoulders, chest, and hips grow. The skull and facial bones change proportion, the forehead becomes more prominent, and jawbones develop.
   - **Weight and height:** Boys reach their maximum height at about 18 to 19 years; between ages 10 and 18 their weight doubles. Girls reach their maximum height at about 15 to 16 years; between 10 and 18 they gain an average of 25 kg (55 lb).
   - **Glandular changes:** Eccrine and apocrine glands increase secretion and become fully functional after puberty. Sebaceous glands also become active, and primary and secondary sex characteristics develop. For males the first noticeable sign of puberty is the appearance of pubic hair and the enlargement of the scrotum and testes. First ejaculation occurs about age 14 years, and fertility follows several months later. Sexual maturity is achieved by age 18. For females

often the first noticeable sign is appearance of the breast bud (thelarche) although appearance of hair along the labia may precede this. Menarche occurs about 1 $\frac{1}{2}$ to 2 years later, and ovulation is usually established 1 to 2 years after that. The female internal reproductive organs reach adult size about age 18 to 20.

| SUGGESTIONS FOR CLASSROOM ACTIVITIES | SUGGESTIONS FOR CLINICAL ACTIVITIES |
|---|---|
| • Show Tanner's sexual maturity rating tables.<br>• If possible, ask students to obtain their physical development records from their parents and compare their developmental milestones to those in the text. | • Arrange for the students to have a clinical experience or observation in a well-child clinic. Have students perform physical screenings and compare to milestones as listed in the text. |

# LEARNING OUTCOME 3

Trace psychosocial development according to Erikson from infancy through adolescence.

## CONCEPTS FOR LECTURE

1. According to Erikson the central crisis at this stage is trust versus mistrust. Resolution determines how the person approaches subsequent developmental stages. Fulfillment of needs is required to develop a basic sense of trust.

Erikson sees the period from 18 months to 3 years as the time when the central developmental task is autonomy versus shame and doubt. Toddlers begin to assert themselves with frequent use of the word "no." They become frustrated by restraints to behavior and between 1 and 3 may have temper tantrums. With guidance from their parents, toddlers slowly gain control over their emotions.

Erikson writes that the major developmental crisis of the preschooler is initiative versus guilt. Erikson views the success of this milestone as determining the individual's self-concept. Preschoolers must learn what they can do; as a result, they imitate behavior, and their imaginations and creativity become lively.

According to Erikson, the central task of school-age children is industry versus inferiority. They begin to create and develop a sense of competence and perseverance and are motivated by activities that provide a sense of worth. They work hard to succeed, but are always faced with the possibility of failure which can lead to inferiority. If they have been successful in previous stages, they are motivated to be industrious and to cooperate with others toward a common goal.

According to Erikson, the psychosocial task of the adolescent is the establishment of identity. The danger of this stage is role confusion. The inability to settle on an occupational identity commonly disturbs the adolescent. Less commonly, doubts about sexual identity arise.

## POWERPOINT LECTURE SLIDES

*(NOTE: The number on each PPT Lecture Slide directly corresponds with the Concepts for Lecture.)*

 Psychosocial Development (Erikson)
- Neonates and infants
  - Trust versus mistrust
- Toddlers
  - Autonomy versus shame and doubt
- Preschoolers
  - Initiative versus guilt
- School-age children
  - Industry versus inferiority
- Adolescents
  - Identity versus role confusion

Because of dramatic body changes, the development of a stable identity is difficult. Adolescents help one another through this identity crisis by forming cliques and a separate youth culture; cliques often exclude those who are "different."

| SUGGESTIONS FOR CLASSROOM ACTIVITIES | SUGGESTIONS FOR CLINICAL ACTIVITIES |
|---|---|
| • Discuss nursing interventions to assist children and parents to meet the central tasks of each age. | • Arrange for an observational experience at a day-care center or school. Have students keep observations of the children's activities and responses. Share in clinical conference relating observations to Erikson's tasks. |

## LEARNING OUTCOME 4

Explain cognitive development according to Piaget from infancy through adolescence.

### CONCEPTS FOR LECTURE

1. Piaget refers to the initial period of cognitive development as the sensorimotor phase. This phase has six stages, three of which take place during the first year. From 4 to 8 months, infants begin to have perceptual recognition. By 6 months, they respond to new stimuli and remember objects and look for them a short time. By 12 months, they have a concept of both space and time, experiment to reach a goal such as a toy on a chair, and proceed from the reflexive ability of the newborn to using one or two actions to attain a goal by the age of 1 year.

2. According to Piaget, the toddler completes the fifth and sixth stages of the sensorimotor phase and starts the preconceptual phase at about 2 years of age. In the fifth stage the toddler solves problems by a trial-and-error process; by stage 6 the toddler can solve problems mentally. During the preconceptual phase, toddlers develop considerable cognitive and intellectual skills, learn about the sequence of time, and have some symbolic thought. Concepts start to develop when words represent classes of objects or thoughts.

3. The preschooler's cognitive development, according to Piaget, is the phase of intuitive thought. Children are still egocentric, but this subsides as they experience their expanding world. They learn through trial and error, think of only one idea at a time, and do not understand relationships. They start to understand that words are associated with objects in late toddlerhood or the early preschool years. Preschoolers become concerned about death as something inevitable, but they do not explain it. They also associate death with others rather than themselves. By the age of 5, children can count pennies. Reading skills develop at this age; they like fairy tales, and books about animals and other children.

### POWERPOINT LECTURE SLIDES

*(NOTE: The number on each PPT Lecture Slide directly corresponds with the Concepts for Lecture.)*

**1** Neonates and Infants
- Sensorimotor phase
  - Perceptual recognition (4–8 mo)
  - Responds to new stimuli, remembers objects, looks for them (6 mo)
  - Concept of both space and time develops (12 mo)

**2** Toddlers
- Completes sensorimotor phase
  - Trial-and-error problem solving
  - Solving problems mentally
- Preconceptual Phase (2 yr)
  - Learn sequence of time
  - Develop some symbolic thought

**3** Preschoolers
- Intuitive thought phase
- Still egocentric, but subsiding
  - Learn through trial and error
  - Think of one idea at a time
  - Do not understand relationships
  - 5 yr-count pennies, reading skills develop

**4** School-Age Children
- Concrete operations phase
  - Cooperative interactions
  - Intuitive reasoning
  - Cause and effect
  - Concepts of money and time learned
  - Reading skills well developed

**5** Adolescents
- Formal operations phase

4. According to Piaget, the ages 7 to 11 years mark the phase of cognitive operations. The child changes from egocentric interactions to cooperative interactions, develops increased understanding of concepts that are associated with specific objects, develops logical reasoning from intuitive thinking, learns to add and subtract, and learns about cause and effect. Money is a concept that gains meaning; most 7- to 8-year-olds know the value of most coins. The concept of time is also learned. Not until age 9 or 10 are children able to understand the long periods of time in the past. They begin to read a clock by age 6. Reading skills are usually well developed in later childhood. By age 9 most are self-motivated, compete with themselves, and like to plan in advance. By 12 they are motivated by inner drive rather than competition with peers. They like to talk and discuss different subjects and to debate.

5. Cognitive abilities mature during adolescence. Between the ages of 11 and 15 begins Piaget's formal operations stage. The main feature of this stage is that children think beyond the present and beyond the world of reality. Adolescents are highly imaginative and idealistic, consider things that do not exist but that might be and consider ways things could be or ought to be, and in social interactions often practice this increasing ability to think abstractly. Parents may misunderstand their child's intent, seeing the teen as being argumentative or contrary. The child becomes more informed about the world and environment. Adolescents use this new information to solve everyday problems, and can communicate with adults on most subjects. The capacity to absorb and use knowledge is great. Adolescents usually select their own areas for learning and explore interests from which they may evolve a career plan. Study habits and learning skills developed in adolescence are used throughout life.

- ○ Thinking beyond the present
- ○ Idealistic thinking
- ○ Abstract thinking

## SUGGESTIONS FOR CLASSROOM ACTIVITIES

- Discuss nursing interventions to assist children and parents to develop the cognitive abilities of each age.

## SUGGESTIONS FOR CLINICAL ACTIVITIES

- Arrange for observational experience at a day-care center or school. Have students keep observations of the children's activities and responses. Share in clinical conference relating observations to Piaget's cognitive stages of development.

# LEARNING OUTCOME 5

Describe moral development according to Kohlberg from childhood through adolescence.

## CONCEPTS FOR LECTURE

1. Infants associate right and wrong with pleasure and pain; what gives them pleasure is right. When they receive abundant positive responses from parents, they learn that certain behaviors are wrong or good and that pain or pleasure is the consequence. In later months and years, children can tell easily and quickly by changes in

## POWERPOINT LECTURE SLIDES

*(NOTE: The number on each PPT Lecture Slide directly corresponds with the Concepts for Lecture.)*

 Neonates and Infants
- No related stage
- Pleasure/pain
- Parent tone of voice, facial expressions

parental facial expressions and voice tones that their behavior is either approved or disapproved.

2. According to Kohlberg, the first level of moral development is the preconventional level when children respond to punishment and reward. During the second year of life, they begin to know that some activities elicit affection and approval. They also recognize that certain rituals such as repeating phrases from prayers also elicit approval and provide a sense of security. By age 2, children are learning what attitudes parents hold about moral matters.

3. Preschoolers are capable of prosocial behavior—that is, any action that a person takes to benefit someone else. They do not have a fully formed conscience; however, they do develop some internal controls. Moral behavior is learned largely through modeling, initially after parents and later significant others. Preschoolers usually behave well in social settings and control their behavior because they want love and approval from their parents. Moral behavior may mean taking turns at play or sharing.

4. Some school-age children are at Kohlberg's stage 1 of the preconventional level, punishment and obedience, and act to avoid being punished; however, some are at stage 2, instrumental-relativist orientation. At this stage, they do things to benefit themselves; fairness becomes important. Later in childhood most progress to the conventional level, which has two stages: Stage 3 is the "good boy–nice girl" stage, and stage 4 is the law and order orientation. Children usually reach the conventional level between 10 and 13. Concrete interests of the individual shift to the interests of the group. Motivation for moral action is to live up to what significant others think of the child.

5. According to Kohlberg, the young adolescent is usually at the conventional level of moral development. Most still accept the Golden Rule; want to abide by social order and existing laws; examine their own values, standards, and morals; and may discard values adopted from parents in favor of values they consider more suitable. When adolescents move into the postconventional or principled level, they start to question the rules and laws of society. Right thinking and right action become a matter of personal values and opinions, which may conflict with societal laws. They consider the possibility of rationally changing the law and emphasize individual rights; not all adolescents or even adults proceed to the postconventional level.

**2** Toddlers
- Preconventional level
  - Stage 1: Punishment and reward

**3** Preschoolers
- Prosocial behavior
- Modeling moral behavior

**4** School-Age Children
- Preconventional level
  - Stage 1: Punishment and reward
  - Stage 2: Instrumental-relativist
- Conventional level
  - Stage 3: "Good boy-nice girl"
  - Stage 4: Law and order

**5** Adolescents
- Conventional level (young adolescent)
- Postconventional or principled level

---

**SUGGESTIONS FOR CLASSROOM ACTIVITIES**

- Discuss nursing interventions to assist children and parents to morally develop (e.g., development of family "rules").

**SUGGESTIONS FOR CLINICAL ACTIVITIES**

- Arrange for an observational experience at a day-care center or school. Have students keep observations of the children's activities and responses. Share in clinical conference relating observations to Kohlberg's stages.

---

# LEARNING OUTCOME 6

Describe spiritual development according to Fowler throughout childhood and adolescence.

## CONCEPTS FOR LECTURE

1. According to Fowler, the toddler's stage of spiritual development is undifferentiated. Toddlers may be aware of some religious practice. They are primarily involved in learning knowledge and emotional reactions rather than establishing spiritual beliefs. The toddler may repeat prayers at bedtime, conforming to a ritual, because praise and affection result. Parental or caregiver response enhances the toddler's sense of security.

Many preschoolers enroll in Sunday school or faith-oriented classes. They usually enjoy the social interaction of these classes. Ages 4 to 6 years are the intuitive-projection stage of spiritual development; faith is primarily a result of the teaching of significant others. Preschoolers learn to imitate religious behavior although they don't understand the meaning of the behavior. They require simple explanations of spiritual matters and use their imagination to envision such ideas as angels or the devil.

According to Fowler, the school-age child is in stage 2 of spiritual development (mythic-literal). The child learns to distinguish fantasy from fact. Spiritual facts are those beliefs that are accepted by a religious group; fantasy is the thoughts and images formed in the child's mind. Parents and religious advisers help the child distinguish fact from fantasy. These people still influence the child more than peers in spiritual matters. When children do not understand events, they use fantasy to explain them. They need to have concepts such as prayer presented in concrete terms, they ask many questions about God and religion, and they generally believe God is good and always present to help. Just before puberty, children become aware that their prayers are not always answered and become disappointed. Some will reject religion, and others will continue to accept it; the decision is largely influenced by the parents. If the child continues religious training, the child is ready to apply reason rather than blind belief in most situations.

According to Fowler, the adolescent or young adult reaches the synthetic-conventional stage of spiritual development. As they encounter different groups in society, adolescents are exposed to a wide variety of opinions, beliefs, and behaviors regarding religious matters. They may reconcile the difference in one of the following ways: by deciding any differences are wrong, compartmentalizing the differences, or obtaining advice from a significant other. They believe that various religious beliefs and practices have more similarities than differences; focus is on interpersonal rather than conceptual matters.

## POWERPOINT LECTURE SLIDES

*(NOTE: The number on each PPT Lecture Slide directly corresponds with the Concepts for Lecture.)*

 1 Spiritual Development (Fowler)
- Toddlers
  - Undifferentiated
- Preschoolers
  - Intuitive-projective
- School-age children
  - Mythic-literal
- Adolescents
  - Synthetic-conventional

## LEARNING OUTCOME 7

Identify assessment activities and expected characteristics from birth through late childhood.

### CONCEPTS FOR LECTURE

1. Neonates and infants:
   - Health assessment occurs immediately at birth and continues for the promotion of wellness; newborns can be assessed immediately by the Apgar scoring system (see Table 21–2).
   - Development can be assessed by observing the infant's behavior and by using standardized tests such as the Denver Developmental Screening Test (DDST-II).
   - Physical development: The infant demonstrates growth in the normal range, manifests appropriately sized fontanels for age, manifests vital signs in the normal range, and displays the ability to habituate to stimuli and to calm self.
   - Motor development: The infant performs gross and fine motor skills in the normal range, exhibits reflexes appropriate for age, displays symmetric movements, and exhibits no hyper- or hypotonia.
   - Sensory development: The infant follows a moving object; responds to sounds, such as talking or clapping; and can coo, babble, laugh, and imitate sounds as expected for age range.
   - Psychosocial development: The infant interacts appropriately with parents through body movements and vocalization.
   - Development in activities of daily living: The baby eats and drinks appropriate amounts of breast milk, formula, or solid foods; exhibits an elimination pattern normal for age; and exhibits a normal rest and sleep pattern.
2. Toddlers:
   - It is essential that nurses do accurate and timely assessments to promote health and detect problems early, thus allowing for early interventions.
   - Assessment activities for toddlers are similar to those for infants in terms of measuring weight, length (height), and vital signs.
   - Physical development: The toddler should demonstrate physical growth (weight, height, head circumference) within normal range, manifest vital signs within normal range for age, and exhibit vision and hearing abilities within normal range.

### POWERPOINT LECTURE SLIDES

*(NOTE: The number on each PPT Lecture Slide directly corresponds with the Concepts for Lecture.)*

 Neonates and Infants
- Apgar scoring
- Denver Developmental Screening Test (DDST-II)
- Physical development
  ◦ Growth in normal range
  ◦ Appropriately size fontanels
  ◦ Vital signs in normal range
  ◦ Ability to habituate to stimuli and calm self
- Motor development
  ◦ Gross and fine skills in normal range
  ◦ Appropriate reflexes
  ◦ Symmetrical movements
  ◦ No hyper- or hypotonia
- Sensory development
  ◦ Follows moving objects
  ◦ Responds to sound
  ◦ Coos, babbles, laughs
  ◦ Imitate sounds
- Psychosocial development
  ◦ Interacts with parents through movement and vocalizations
- Development in activities of daily living (ADL)
  ◦ Eats, drinks appropriate amounts
  ◦ Exhibits elimination patterns normal for age
  ◦ Exhibits normal rest and sleep patterns

2 Toddlers
- Physical development
  ◦ Physical growth in normal range
  ◦ Vital signs in normal range
  ◦ Vision, hearing within normal range
- Motor development
  ◦ Achieves gross and fine motor milestones
- Psychosocial development
  ◦ Achieves milestones
- Development in ADL
  ◦ Feeds self
  ◦ Eats variety of foods
  ◦ Begins to develop bowel and bladder control
  ◦ Rest and sleep patterns appropriate for age

- Motor development: The toddler performs gross and fine motor milestones within normal range for the age (e.g., walks up steps with assistance, balances on one foot, copies a circle).
- Psychosocial development: The toddler performs psychosocial development milestones for the age (e.g., expresses likes and dislikes, displays curiosity and asks questions, begins to play and communicate with children).
- Development in activities of daily living: The toddler feeds self, eats and drinks a variety of foods, begins to develop bowel and bladder control, exhibits a rest and sleep pattern appropriate for age, and dresses self.

3. Preschoolers:
- During assessment the preschooler can often participate in answering questions with assistance from parents or caregivers. Preschoolers can describe the types of activities they enjoy.
- Physical development: Preschoolers demonstrate physical growth (weight, height) within normal range, manifest vital signs within normal range for age, and exhibit vision and hearing abilities within normal range.
- Motor development: The preschooler performs gross and fine motor milestones within normal range for age (e.g., jumps rope, climbs playground equipment, prints letters and numbers).
- Psychosocial development: The preschooler performs psychosocial milestones for age (e.g., separates easily from parents, displays imagination and creativity, exhibits increasing vocabulary).
- Development in activities of daily living: The child demonstrates development of toilet training, performs simple hygiene measures, dresses and undresses self, engages in bedtime rituals, and demonstrates the ability to put self to sleep.

4. School-age children:
- During assessment the nurse responds to questions from the parent or other caregiver, gives appropriate feedback, and lends support. The nurse also demonstrates interest in the child and enthusiasm for the child's strength.
- Physical development: The school-age child demonstrates physical growth (height, weight) within normal range, manifests vital signs within normal range, exhibits vision and hearing abilities within normal range, and demonstrates male or female prepubertal changes within normal range.
- Motor development: The child possesses coordinated motor skills for age (e.g., climbs a tree, throws and catches a ball, plays a musical instrument).
- Psychosocial development: The child performs psychosocial milestones for age (e.g., interacts well with parents, becomes less dependent on family, articulates an understanding of right and wrong, expresses self in a logical manner).

 Preschoolers
- Physical development
  - Physical growth within normal range
  - Vital signs in normal range
  - Vision, hearing within normal range
- Motor development
  - Achieves gross and fine motor milestone
- Psychosocial Development
  - Achieves milestones
- Development in ADL
  - Control of bowel and bladder functions
  - Performs simple hygiene activities
  - Dresses and undresses self
  - Engages in bedtime rituals
  - Demonstrates ability to put self to sleep

 School-Age Children
- Physical development
  - Physical growth within normal range
  - Vision, hearing within normal range
  - Vital signs in normal range
  - Demonstrate male or female prepubertal changes
- Motor development
  - Possesses coordinated motor skills for age
- Psychosocial development
  - Achieves milestones
- Development in ADL
  - Concern for personal cleanliness and appearance
  - Expresses need for privacy

 Adolescents
- Physical development
  - Physical growth within normal range
  - Demonstrates male or female sexual development within standards
  - Vital signs within normal range for gender
  - Hearing, vision within normal range
- Psychosocial development
  - Interacts well with parents and others
  - Likes self
  - Has plans for future
  - Chooses lifestyle and interests that fit own identity
  - Determines own beliefs and values
  - Begins to establish a sense of identity in family
  - Seeks help from appropriate people as needed
- Development in ADL
  - Knowledge of physical development, menstruation, reproduction, and birth control
  - Exhibits healthy lifestyle practice
  - Demonstrates concern for personal cleanliness and appearance

## CONCEPTS FOR LECTURE *continued*

- Development in activities of daily living: The child demonstrates concern for personal cleanliness and appearance, and expresses the need for privacy.
5. Adolescents:
   - Adolescents are usually self-directed in meeting their health needs. Because of maturation changes, however, they need teaching and guidance in a number of health care areas.
   - Physical development: The adolescent should exhibit physical growth within normal range for age and gender, demonstrate male or female sexual development consistent with standards, manifest vital signs within normal range for age and gender, and exhibit vision and hearing abilities within normal range.
   - Psychosocial development: The adolescent interacts well with parents, teachers, peers, siblings, and persons in authority; likes self; thinks and plans for the future; chooses a lifestyle and interests that fit own identity; determines own beliefs and values; begins to establish a sense of identity in the family; and seeks help from appropriate persons about problems.
   - Development in activities of daily living: The adolescent demonstrates knowledge of physical development, menstruation, reproduction, and birth control; exhibits healthy lifestyle practices in nutrition, exercise, recreation, sleep patterns, and personal habits; and demonstrates concern for personal cleanliness and appearance.

---

### SUGGESTIONS FOR CLASSROOM ACTIVITIES

- Demonstrate physical assessment of growth in the nursing laboratory (e.g., height and weight, head circumference).
- Show an audiovisual presentation of the performance of the Denver Developmental Screening Test (DDST).

### SUGGESTIONS FOR CLINICAL ACTIVITIES

- Arrange for the students to perform the DDST on children of various ages.
- Arrange for the students to have a clinical experience in a well-child clinic. Have them perform or observe physical screenings. Ask the students to present observations in clinical conference and compare findings with milestones in the text.

---

## LEARNING OUTCOME 8

Identify essential activities of health promotion and protection to meet the needs of infants, toddlers, preschoolers, school-age children, and adolescents.

---

### CONCEPTS FOR LECTURE

1. Health promotion guidelines for infants:
   - Health examinations are at 2 weeks, 2 months, 4 months, 5 months, and 12 months.
   - Protective measures should include immunizations, fluoride supplementation as necessary, screening for tuberculosis and phenylketonuria, prompt attention for illness, and appropriate skin hygiene and clothing.

### POWERPOINT LECTURE SLIDES

*(NOTE: The number on each PPT Lecture Slide directly corresponds with the Concepts for Lecture.)*

 Neonates and Infants
- Health examinations
  - Birth, 2 weeks, 2, 4, 5, and 12 mo
- Protective measures
  - Immunizations
  - Fluoride supplementation as needed

- Infant safety: Review the importance of supervision; car seat, crib, playpen, bath, and home environment safety measures; feeding measures; and providing toys without small parts or sharp edges.
- Nutrition: Review breast-feeding and bottle-feeding techniques, formula preparation, feeding schedule, introduction of solid foods, and the need for iron supplementation at 4 to 6 months.
- Elimination: Topics include characteristics and frequency of stool and urine elimination, and diarrhea and its effects.
- Rest/sleep: Establish usual sleep and rest patterns.
- Sensory stimulation: Touch stimulation should include holding, cuddling, and rocking. Provide colorful, moving toys to stimulate vision. Screen the newborn for hearing loss with follow-up at 3 months and early intervention by 6 months if appropriate. Soothing voice tones, music, and singing help to stimulate hearing. Provide toys appropriate for development.
- Additional safety and health concerns for infancy include failure to thrive, infant colic, crying, child abuse (including shaken baby syndrome), and sudden infant death.

2. Health promotion guidelines for toddlers:
- Health examinations should occur at 15 and 18 months, then as recommended by the primary care provider. Dental visits should start at age 3, hearing tests by 18 months or earlier.
- Protective measures should include immunizations, screening for tuberculosis and lead poisoning, and fluoride supplementation as needed.
- Toddler safety: Review the importance of supervision and teaching the child to obey commands, home environment safety measures, outdoor safety, and appropriate toys.
- Nutrition: Review the importance of nutritious meals and snacks, teaching simple mealtime manners, dental care, and elimination/toilet training techniques.
- Rest/sleep: Deal with sleep disturbances.
- Play: Provide adequate space, a variety of activities, and toys that allow "acting on" behaviors and provide motor and sensory stimulation.
- Additional safety and health concerns for toddlers include accidents, visual problems, dental caries, and respiratory tract and ear infections.

3. Health promotion guidelines for preschoolers:
- Health examinations should take place every 1 to 2 years.
- Protective measures include immunizations, screening for tuberculosis, vision and hearing screening, regular dental screenings, and fluoride treatment.
- Preschooler safety includes educating the child about simple safety rules, teaching the child to play safely, and educating to prevent poisoning.

- Screening for TB and PKU
- Prompt attention to illness
- Appropriate hygiene
- Infant safety
  - Importance of supervision
  - Home environmental safety
  - Feeding measures
  - Appropriate toys
- Nutrition
  - Breast and formula feeding
  - Solid foods
  - Iron supplementation
- Elimination
  - Characteristics
  - Frequency
  - Diarrhea
- Rest/Sleep
  - Patterns
- Sensory stimulation
  - Touch stimulation
  - Visually stimulating toys
  - Hearing loss screening and intervention
- Additional safety and health concerns for infants
  - Failure to thrive
  - Infant colic
  - Crying
  - Child abuse including shaken baby syndrome
  - Sudden infant death

2 Toddlers
- Health examinations
  - 15, 18 months and then as recommended by primary care provider
- Protective measures
  - Immunizations
  - Screening for TB, lead poisoning
  - Fluoride supplementation as needed
- Toddler safety
  - Supervision
  - Teaching
  - Home environment safety
  - Outdoor safety
  - Appropriate toys
- Nutrition
  - Nutritious meals and snacks
  - Mealtime manners
  - Dental care
- Elimination
  - Toilet training
- Rest/Sleep
  - Sleep disturbances
- Play
  - Adequate space
  - Toys for "acting on" behavior
  - Motor and sensory stimulation

- Nutrition: Review the importance of nutritious meals and snacks.
- Elimination: Teach proper hygiene.
- Rest/sleep: Deal with sleep disturbances.
- Play: Provide time for group play activities, teach the child simple games that require cooperation and interaction, and provide toys and dress-up for role-playing.
- In addition, preschoolers often have health problems similar to those they had as a toddler. Respiratory tract and communicable diseases, accidents, and dental caries continue to be problems. Congenital abnormalities such as cardiac disorders and hernias are often corrected at this age.

4. Health promotion guidelines for school-age children:
   - Health examinations include annual physical examinations or as recommended.
   - Protective measures include immunizations; screening for tuberculosis; periodic vision, speech, and hearing screenings; regular dental screenings and fluoride treatment; and providing accurate information about sexual issues.
   - School-age child safety: Children should use proper equipment when participating in sports and other physical activities. Encourage children to take responsibility for their own safety.
   - Nutrition: It is important that the child does not skip meals, eats a balanced diet, and limits foods that may lead to obesity.
   - Elimination: Use positive approaches for elimination problems.
   - Play and social interactions: Provide opportunities for a variety of organized group activities, accept realistic expectations of the child's ability, act as role models in acceptance of other persons who may be different, and provide a home environment that limits TV viewing and video games and encourages completion of homework and healthy exercise.
   - School-age children continue to have as many communicable diseases, dental caries, and accidents as preschoolers. The increasing number of overweight children is another health risk.

5. Health promotion guidelines for adolescents:
   - Health examinations should occur as recommended by the primary care provider.
   - Protective measures include immunizations, screening for tuberculosis, periodic vision and hearing screenings, regular dental assessments, and providing accurate information about sexual issues.
   - Adolescent safety issues include the adolescent's taking responsibility for using motor vehicles safely, making certain that proper precautions are taken during all athletic activity, and parents keeping lines of communication open and being alert to signs of substance abuse and emotional disturbances in the adolescent.

- Additional safety and health concerns for toddlers
  - Injuries
  - Visual problems
  - Respiratory and ear infections
  - Dental caries

**3** Preschoolers
- Health examinations
  - Every 1–2 years
- Protective measures
  - Immunizations
  - Screening for TB, vision, hearing, dental
  - Fluoride treatment
- Preschooler safety
  - Education
  - Play safety
  - Prevention of poisoning
- Nutrition
  - Nutritious meals and snacks
- Elimination
  - Proper hygiene
- Rest/Sleep
  - Sleep disturbances
- Play
  - Group play activities
  - Teach simple cooperative and interactive games
  - Toys for "dress-up"
- Additional safety and health concerns for preschoolers
  - Injuries
  - Visual problems
  - Dental caries
  - Respiratory tract and ear infections
    - Communicable disease
    - Congenital abnormalities correction

**4** School-Age Children
- Physical Development
  - As recommended
- Protective Measures
  - Immunizations
  - Screening for TB
  - Periodic vision, speech, hearing, dental screening
  - Fluoride treatment
  - Sexual education
- Safety
  - Sports safety
  - Education
- Nutrition
  - No skipped meals
  - Balanced diet
  - Obesity
- Play and social interaction
  - Organized group activities
  - Parental expectations
  - Parental responsibilities

- Nutrition and exercise: Stress the importance of healthy snacks and appropriate patterns of food intake and exercise, factors that may lead to nutritional problems, and balancing sedentary activities with regular exercise.
- Social interactions: The adolescent should be encouraged to succeed in school, establish relationships that promote discussion of feelings, concerns, and fears. Parents need to encourage adolescent peer group activities that promote appropriate moral and spiritual values, act as role models for appropriate social interactions, provide a comfortable home environment for appropriate adolescent peer group activities and expect adolescent to participate in and contribute to family activities.

6. Adolescents face many health risks, including the consequences of risky behavior, such as injury related to accidents, sexually transmitted disease, and teen pregnancy. Psychological and emotional challenges may lead to psychological problems, the developing brain is more susceptible to addiction, and the first manifestations of schizophrenia may appear. In the late adolescence with communal living (college dorms), adolescents are at increased risk for infectious diseases such as measles and pneumococcal meningitis.

- Additional safety and health concerns for school-age children
  - Communicable Diseases
  - Dental Cavities
  - Injuries
  - Obesity

 Adolescents
- Health examinations
  - As recommended
- Protective measures
  - Immunizations
  - Periodic screenings for TB, vision, hearing, dental screening
  - Accurate sexual information
- Safety issues
  - Motor vehicle safety
  - Sports safety
  - Substance abuse
  - Emotional disturbances
- Nutrition and exercise
  - Health snacks
  - Appropriate food intake and exercise
- Social interaction
  - Positive relationships
  - Peer group activities
  - Home environment
  - Family responsibilities and participation

 Additional Safety and Health Concerns for Adolescents
- Consequences of Risky Behavior
  - Injury
  - Sexually transmitted disease
  - Teen pregnancy
- Psychological and emotional challenges
  - Addiction
  - Schizophrenia may appear
  - Suicide
- Infectious diseases

---

### SUGGESTIONS FOR CLASSROOM ACTIVITIES

- Divide the students into five groups. Assign each an age group. Have each group develop safety measures for the assigned age group and share these with the class.

### SUGGESTIONS FOR CLINICAL ACTIVITIES

- Arrange for students to have a clinical experience in a well-child clinic. Have them observe the anticipatory guidance given in this setting. Ask the students to present observations in clinical conference and compare findings with health promotion guidelines given in the text.

# CHAPTER 22
# PROMOTING HEALTH IN YOUNG AND MIDDLE-AGED ADULTS

## RESOURCE LIBRARY

### 💿 PRENTICE HALL NURSING MEDIALINK DVD-ROM

Audio Glossary
NCLEX® Review

### 🌐 COMPANION WEBSITE

Additional NCLEX® Review
Case Study: *Developmental Phases of Adulthood*
Care Plan Activity: *Parenting Responsibilities*
Application Activity: *College Student with Manic Depression*
Links to Resources

### 📖 IMAGE LIBRARY

**Figure 22.1** Many young women combine active careers with motherhood.

**Figure 22.2** Middle-aged adults have time to pursue interests that may have been put aside for child care.

---

## LEARNING OUTCOME 1

Compare and contrast the following generational groups: Baby boomers, Generation X, and Generation Y.

### CONCEPTS FOR LECTURE

1. Baby Boomers (born 1945–1964), Generation X (born 1965–1978), and Generation Y (born 1979–2000) compose cohorts that share specific life events and have their own world views. Baby Boomers are characterized by an individualistic outlook, tend toward a "workaholic" orientation, want to be respected at work, but feel role overload.
2. Gen Xers were frequently raised in two-worker households where long work hours were common. They may now be less impressed with corporate values, be more skeptical, and resist authority, but they enjoy challenges and opportunities to creatively problem solve.
3. Generation Y (or Millennials) have come of age in an increasingly multicultural America. They are technologically sophisticated (and dependent), and they enjoy public affirmations of their efforts.

### POWERPOINT LECTURE SLIDES

*(NOTE: The number on each PPT Lecture Slide directly corresponds with the Concepts for Lecture.)*

 **1** Baby Boomers (Years 1945–1964)
- An individualistic outlook
- "Workaholic" orientation
- Respect at work, but feel role overload

**2** Generation X (Gen Xers) (Born 1965–1978)
- Frequently raised in two-worker households
- Less impressed with corporate values
- More skeptical
- Resist authority
- Enjoy challenges and opportunities to creatively problem solve

**3** Generation Y (or Millennials) (Born 1979–2000)
- Part of an increasingly multi-cultural America
- Technologically sophisticated (and dependent)
- Enjoy public affirmations of efforts

---

### SUGGESTIONS FOR CLASSROOM ACTIVITIES

- Have the students write a short paper on one of the generational groups, including the current research on the group and historical, social, and political context shared by the group.

### SUGGESTIONS FOR CLINICAL ACTIVITIES

- Have the students apply the characteristics of the generational groups to assigned clients.

---

# LEARNING OUTCOME 2

Describe the usual physical development occurring during young and middle adulthood.

## CONCEPTS FOR LECTURE

1. Young adults (ages 20 to 40 years) are in the prime physical years. The musculoskeletal system is well developed and coordinated, athletic endeavors reach their peak, and all other body systems are functioning at peak efficiency. Weight and muscle mass may change as a result of diet and exercise. Extensive physical changes occur in pregnant and lactating women.

2. Physical changes occurring in middle-aged adults (40 to 65 years) include changes in (a) appearance: hair thins, gray hair appears, skin turgor and moisture decreases, subcutaneous fat decreases, wrinkling occurs, and fatty tissue is redistributed resulting in fat deposits in abdominal areas; (b) the musculoskeletal system: skeletal muscle bulk decreases around age 60, thinning intervertebral discs cause a decrease in height of about 1 inch, calcium is lost from bone, and muscle growth continues in proportion to use; (c) the cardiovascular system: blood vessels lose elasticity and become thicker; (d) sensory perception: visual acuity declines, often by 40 years presbyopia develops, auditory acuity especially for high-frequency sounds decreases (presbycusis), and taste sensation also diminishes; (e) metabolism: slows resulting in weight gain; (f) the gastrointestinal system: gradual decrease in tone of large intestines may predispose to constipation; (g) the urinary system: nephron units are lost and glomerular filtration rate decreases; and (h) sexuality: hormonal changes occur in men (climacteric) and women (menopause). (See Table 22–1.)

## POWERPOINT LECTURE SLIDES

*(NOTE: The number on each PPT Lecture Slide directly corresponds with the Concepts for Lecture.)*

**1** Young Adults (20–40)
- Prime physical years
- Musculoskeletal system well developed and coordinated
- Other body systems functioning at peak efficiency
- Choices affect weight and muscle mass
- Physical changes in pregnant and lactating women

**2** Middle-Aged Adults (40–65)
- Appearance changes
- Skeletal muscle bulk decreases
- Thinning of intervertebral discs
- Calcium loss from bone
- Blood vessels lose elasticity and become thicker
- Decline in visual acuity
- Presbyopia
- Presbycusis
- Decreased taste sensation
- Gradual decrease in tone of large intestine may lead to constipation
- Urinary system affected as glomerular filtration rate decreases
- Hormonal changes affect sexuality: menopause, climacteric

## SUGGESTIONS FOR CLASSROOM ACTIVITIES

- Invite a panel of healthy young and middle-aged adults to discuss the positive aspects of aging.
- Have the class debate the pros and cons of the recent trend in cosmetic surgery to reverse some of the physical changes of aging.

## SUGGESTIONS FOR CLINICAL ACTIVITIES

- Have the students discuss the physical changes observed in their young and middle-aged adult clients. Discuss how these changes may alter nursing care for these clients.

# LEARNING OUTCOME 3

Identify characteristic tasks of development during young and middle adulthood.

## CONCEPTS FOR LECTURE

1. According to Freud's theory, young adults are in the genital stage in which energy is directed toward attaining a mature sexual relationship. Young adults are in Erikson's stage of intimacy versus isolation. They have the following tasks according to Havighurst: selecting a mate, learning to live with a partner, starting a family, rearing children, managing a home, getting started in an occupation, taking on civic responsibility, and finding

## POWERPOINT LECTURE SLIDES

*(NOTE: The number on each PPT Lecture Slide directly corresponds with the Concepts for Lecture.)*

**1** Young Adults
- Havighurst development tasks:
  ○ Selecting a mate
  ○ Learning to live with a partner
  ○ Starting a family
  ○ Rearing children

a congenial social group. According to Nelson and Barry (2005) young adults have the following characteristics: separation from parents, exploration of new identities for self, personal discovery and self discovery, and high risk behaviors (see Box 22–1).

2. According to Erikson, middle-aged adults are in the generativity versus stagnation phase of development. According to Havighurst, middle-aged adults have the following developmental tasks: achieving adult civic and social responsibility, establishing and maintaining an economic standard of living, assisting teenage children to become responsible and happy adults, developing adult leisure-time activities, relating oneself to one's spouse as a person, accepting and adjusting to the physiologic changes of middle age, adjusting to aging parents, balancing the needs of multiple constituencies, and maintaining work as a central theme. Slater (2003) added the additional developmental tasks of inclusivity versus exclusivity, pride versus embarrassment (in children, work, or creativity), responsibility versus ambivalence (making choices about commitments), career productivity versus inadequacy, parenthood versus self-absorption, being needed versus alienation, and honesty versus denial (with oneself) (see Box 22–3).

- ○ Managing a home
- ○ Getting started in an occupation
- ○ Taking on civic responsibility
- ○ Finding a congenial social group
- • Nelson and Barry (2005) characteristics
  - ○ Separation from parents
  - ○ Exploration of new identities
  - ○ Personal discovery and self discovery
  - ○ High risk behaviors

**2** Middle-Aged Adults
- • Havighurst developmental tasks:
  - ○ Achieving adult civic and social responsibility
  - ○ Establishing and maintaining an economic standard of living
  - ○ Assisting teenage children to become responsible and happy adults
  - ○ Developing adult leisure-time activities
  - ○ Relating oneself to one's spouse as a person
  - ○ Accepting and adjusting to the physiologic changes of middle age
  - ○ Adjusting to aging parents
  - ○ Balancing the needs of multiple constituencies
  - ○ Maintaining work as a central theme
- • Slater (2003) additional developmental tasks:
  - ○ Inclusivity versus exclusivity
  - ○ Pride versus embarrassment (in children, work, or creativity)
  - ○ Responsibility versus ambivalence (making choices about commitments)
  - ○ Career productivity versus inadequacy
  - ○ Parenthood versus self-absorption
  - ○ Being needed versus alienation
  - ○ Honesty versus denial (with oneself)

---

## SUGGESTIONS FOR CLASSROOM ACTIVITIES

- • Invite a panel of clinical specialists and nurse practitioners who work with adults of various ages to discuss the benefits and challenges of working with clients of these ages.

## SUGGESTIONS FOR CLINICAL ACTIVITIES

- • Discuss how knowing about the client's developmental stage can influence nursing care for these clients.

---

# LEARNING OUTCOME 4

Explain changes in cognitive development throughout adulthood.

## CONCEPTS FOR LECTURE

1. Young adults are able to use formal operations characterized by the ability to think abstractly and employ logic. Recently researchers have proposed a concept of postformal thought as a further stage of cognitive development.

   Postformal thought includes creativity, intuition, and the ability to consider information in relationship to other ideas, to possess an understanding of the

## POWERPOINT LECTURE SLIDES

*(NOTE: The number on each PPT Lecture Slide directly corresponds with the Concepts for Lecture.)*

**1** Young Adults
- • Use formal operations
- • May demonstrate postformal thought

temporary or relative nature of knowledge, and to comprehend and balance arguments created by both logic and emotion. Few adults achieve this cognitive stage, but those who do are marked by greater tolerance and skills of noting and resolving complex problems.

2. The middle-aged adult's cognitive and intellectual abilities change very little. Reaction time may diminish during the later part of the middle years. Memory and problem solving are maintained through middle adulthood. Learning continues and can be enhanced by increased motivation. Genetic, environmental, and personality factors in early and middle adulthood account for the large difference in the ways in which individuals maintain mental abilities.

 Middle-Aged Adults
- Reaction time
- Little change in cognitive and intellectual abilities
- Maintain memory and problem solving
- Continues learning
- Influence of genetic, environmental, and personality factors

---

## SUGGESTIONS FOR CLASSROOM ACTIVITIES

- Discuss the influence of genetic, environmental, and personality factors on how individuals maintain mental abilities. Have students provide additional examples to illustrate this influence.
- Discuss the concept of postformal thought. Have the students discuss whether this cognitive level is as uncommon as researchers maintain. Ask students to support their opinions.

---

# LEARNING OUTCOME 5

Describe moral development according to Kohlberg throughout adulthood.

## CONCEPTS FOR LECTURE

1. Young and middle-aged adults who have mastered the previous stages of Kohlberg's theory of moral development now enter the postconventional level. The individual is able to separate self from the expectations and rules of others and to define morality in terms of personal principles.

   In stage 5, a social contract orientation, the individual believes that rights of others take precedence.

   Recent research demonstrates that moral development continues throughout adulthood and that few individuals attain stage 5, before age 40.

## POWERPOINT LECTURE SLIDES

*(NOTE: The number on each PPT Lecture Slide directly corresponds with the Concepts for Lecture.)*

 Moral Development (Kohlberg)—Adulthood.
- May enter postconventional level
  - Define morality in terms of personal principles
- May progress to stage 5
  - Believes rights of others take precedence
- Recent research demonstrates
  - Moral development continues throughout adulthood
  - Few attain stage 5 before age 40

---

## SUGGESTIONS FOR CLASSROOM ACTIVITIES

- Review Gilligan's theory of moral development. Have the students debate the differences proposed in the development of moral behavior in men and women.

## SUGGESTIONS FOR CLINICAL ACTIVITIES

- Have the students present examples of Kohlberg's stages observed in the clinical setting.

# LEARNING OUTCOME 6

Describe spiritual development according to Fowler throughout adulthood.

## CONCEPTS FOR LECTURE

1. According to Fowler, the individual enters the individuating reflective period sometime after 18 years. The individual focuses on reality, may ask philosophical questions regarding spirituality, and may be self-conscious about spiritual matters. The religious teaching from childhood may now be accepted or redefined. The young adult may depend on spirituality and seek guidance from a Higher Power, but do so privately (Cavendish, Luise, Bauer, et al., 2001).

2. Not all adults progress through Fowler's stages to the fifth, called the paradoxical-consolidative stage. At this stage the individual can view "truth" from a number of viewpoints. Fowler believes that only some individuals after the age of 30 years reach this stage.

3. In middle age, people tend to be less dogmatic about religious beliefs, and religion offers more comfort to middle-aged persons than it did previously. They often rely on spiritual beliefs to help them deal with illness, death, and tragedy.

## POWERPOINT LECTURE SLIDES

*(NOTE: The number on each PPT Lecture Slide directly corresponds with the Concepts for Lecture.)*

**1** Spiritual Development (Fowler)—Adulthood
- Young adults
  - Individuating reflective period (after 18 years)
  - Focuses on reality
  - May ask philosophical questions regarding spirituality
  - May be self-conscious about spiritual matters
  - Religious teaching from childhood accepted or redefined

**2** After 30 Years Some Reach the Paradoxical-Consolidative Stage
- View "truth" from a number of viewpoints

**3** Middle-Aged Adults
- Less dogmatic about religious beliefs
- Religion offers more comfort than previously
- Often rely on spiritual beliefs to deal with illness, death, and tragedy

---

### SUGGESTIONS FOR CLASSROOM ACTIVITIES

- Invite a panel of religious and spiritual practitioners to discuss the development of faith in adults and the influence of faith on daily lives of adults.

### SUGGESTIONS FOR CLINICAL ACTIVITIES

- Have the students provide examples of the influence of faith in health care observed in the clinical setting.

---

# LEARNING OUTCOME 7

Identify selected health problems associated with young and middle-aged adults.

## CONCEPTS FOR LECTURE

1. Health problems that occur in young adulthood include injuries, suicide, hypertension, substance abuse (including smoking), sexually transmitted infections (STIs), eating disorders (including obesity), violence, abuse of women, and certain malignancies (testicular cancer and cervical cancer).

2. Leading causes of death in middle adulthood include injuries (motor vehicle and occupational accidents), chronic disease such as cancer (in men, cancer of the lung and bladder; in women, breast cancer followed by cancer of the colon and rectum, uterus, and lung), and cardiovascular disease (coronary heart disease). Other health problems include obesity, alcoholism, and mental health alterations (anxiety and depression).

## POWERPOINT LECTURE SLIDES

*(NOTE: The number on each PPT Lecture Slide directly corresponds with the Concepts for Lecture.)*

**1** Young Adults
- Injuries
- Suicide
- Hypertension
- Substance abuse (including smoking)
- Sexually transmitted infections (STI)
- Eating disorders (obesity)
- Violence
- Abuse of women
- Certain malignancies (testicular cancer and cervical cancer)

**2** Middle-Aged Adults
- Injuries
- Cancer
  - Cancer of the lung and bladder (men)
  - Breast cancer followed by cancer of the colon and rectum, uterus, and lung (women)

- Cardiovascular disease
- Obesity
- Alcoholism
- Mental health alterations
  - Anxiety
  - Depression

## SUGGESTIONS FOR CLASSROOM ACTIVITIES

- Divide the students into groups. Assign each group a health problem associated with young or middle-aged adults. Ask each group to develop a plan to assist the adult to prevent or obtain early diagnosis and treatment for this problem. Have groups share their work.

## SUGGESTIONS FOR CLINICAL ACTIVITIES

- Have the students relate examples of health problems associated with young and middle-aged adults that they have observed in their assigned clients.

# LEARNING OUTCOME 8

Identify developmental assessment guidelines for young and middle-aged adults.

## CONCEPTS FOR LECTURE

1. Developmental assessment guidelines for the young adult:

   **Physical development:** The young adult should exhibit weight within normal range for age and gender, manifest vital signs within normal range for age and gender, demonstrate visual and hearing abilities within normal range, and exhibit appropriate knowledge and attitudes about sexuality.

   **Psychosocial development:** The young adult should feel independent from parents; have a realistic self-concept; like self and direction life is going; interact well with family; cope with stresses of change and growth; have well-established bonds with a significant other; have a meaningful social life; demonstrate emotional, social, and economic responsibility; and have a set of values that guide behavior.

   **Development in activities of daily living (ADL):** It is important for the young adult to have a healthy lifestyle.

2. Developmental assessment guidelines for the middle-aged adult:

   **Physical development:** The middle-aged adult should exhibit weight, vital signs, and visual and hearing abilities within normal range; exhibit appropriate knowledge and attitudes about sexuality; and verbalize any changes in eating, elimination, or exercise.

   **Psychosocial development:** The middle-aged adult should accept the aging body, feel comfortable and respect self, enjoy the new freedom to be independent, accept changes in family roles, interact effectively and share companionable activities with a life partner, expand and renew previous interests, pursue charitable and altruistic activities, and have a meaningful philosophy of life.

   **Development in ADL:** It is important to follow preventive health practices.

## POWERPOINT LECTURE SLIDES

*(NOTE: The number on each PPT Lecture Slide directly corresponds with the Concepts for Lecture.)*

 Young Adults
- Physical development
  - Weight, vital signs, vision and hearing
  - Knowledge and attitudes about sexuality
- Psychosocial development
  - Independence from parents
  - Self-concept
  - Direction in life
  - Family interactions
  - Coping skills
  - Relationship with significant other
  - Emotional, social, and economic responsibilities
  - Values
- Development in activities of daily living
  - Lifestyle

 Middle-aged Adults
- Physical development
  - Weight, vital signs, vision and hearing
  - Knowledge and attitudes about sexuality
  - Changes in eating, elimination, exercise
- Psychosocial development
  - Response to physical changes
  - Comfort with self
  - Independence
  - Changes in family roles
  - Relationship with life partner
  - Interests
  - Civic involvement
  - Philosophy of life
- Development in activities of daily living
  - Preventive health practices

## LEARNING OUTCOME 9

List examples of health promotion topics for young and middle adulthood.

### CONCEPTS FOR LECTURE

1. Health promotion topics for the young adult:
   - **Health tests and screening:** These include routine physical examinations, immunizations as recommended, regular dental assessments, periodic vision and hearing screenings, professional breast examinations, Papanicolaou smear, testicular examination, screening for cardiovascular disease, tuberculosis skin test, and smoking history and counseling, if needed.
   - **Safety:** These include motor vehicle safety, sun protection, and workplace and water safety measures.
   - **Nutrition and exercise:** Review the importance of adequate iron intake, and nutritional and exercise factors that may lead to cardiovascular disease.
   - **Social interactions:** These include encouraging personal relationships that promote discussion of feelings, concerns, and fears; and setting short- and long-term goals for work and career choices.

2. Health promotion topics for the middle-aged adult:
   - **Health tests and screening:** The middle-aged adult should have routine physical examinations, immunizations as recommended, regular dental assessments, tonometry for signs of glaucoma and other eye diseases, breast self-examination, testicular self-examination, screening for cardiovascular disease, screening for tuberculosis, and screenings for colorectal, breast, cervical, uterine, and prostate cancer, smoking history and counseling as needed.
   - **Safety:** Issues include motor vehicle safety reinforcement, workplace safety measures, and home safety measures.
   - **Nutrition and exercise:** The middle-aged adult needs to understand the importance of adequate protein, calcium, and vitamin D; nutrition and exercise factors that may lead to cardiovascular disease; and the importance of an exercise program that emphasizes skill and coordination.
   - **Social interactions:** Issues include the possibility of a midlife crisis, providing time to expand and to review previous interests, and retirement planning with a partner if appropriate.

### POWERPOINT LECTURE SLIDES

*(NOTE: The number on each PPT Lecture Slide directly corresponds with the Concepts for Lecture.)*

**1** Young Adults
- Health tests and screening
  - Routine physical examinations as recommended
  - Immunizations
  - Dental, vision, hearing screenings
  - Breast and testicular examinations
  - Papanicolaou smear
  - Screening for cardiovascular disease, TB, smoking
- Safety
  - Motor vehicle safety
  - Sun protection
  - Workplace and water safety
- Nutrition and exercise
  - Adequate iron intake
  - Proper nutrition and exercise
- Social Interactions
  - Positive personal relationships
  - Occupational long and short term goals

**2** Middle-Aged Adults
- Health-tests and screening
  - Routine physical examinations as recommended
  - Immunizations
  - Dental, tonometry screening
  - Breast, testicular examinations
  - Screening for cardiovascular disease
  - Screening for colorectal, breast, cervical, uterine, and prostate cance
  - Smoking history and counseling
- Safety
  - Motor vehicle safety
  - Workplace safety
  - Home safety measures
- Nutrition and exercise
  - Adequate protein, calcium, vitamin D
  - Proper nutrition and exercise to prevent cardiovascular disease
  - Exercise program

- Social interactions
  - Midlife crisis
  - Interest
  - Retirement planning

---

**SUGGESTIONS FOR CLASSROOM ACTIVITIES**

- Have the students plan and implement a health fair for young and middle-aged adults in the educational institution. The fair should include posters, presentations, and literature that address major health problems of these age groups.

**SUGGESTIONS FOR CLINICAL ACTIVITIES**

- Have the students participate in health fairs held at regional malls or health institutions.
- Have the students provide examples of health promotion activities incorporated into their client's plan of care.

---

# CHAPTER 23
## PROMOTING HEALTH IN ELDERS

## RESOURCE LIBRARY

### 💿 PRENTICE HALL NURSING MEDIALINK DVD-ROM

Audio Glossary
NCLEX® Review
Videos & Animations:
   *Alzheimer's Disease*
   *Cardiovascular System*
   *Cultural Diversity*
   *Elder Mistreatment and Abuse*
   *Gastrointestinal*
   *Geritourinary and Renal System*
   *Immune System*
   *Nursing Issues and the Elderly*
   *Nutrition and Aging*
   *Respiratory System*
   *Sleep and the Elderly*
   *The Study of Aging*

### 🌐 COMPANION WEBSITE

Additional NCLEX® Review
Case Study: *Home Health and Elderly Siblings*
Care Plan Activity: *Elderly Client with Nose Bleed*
Application Activity: *Gerontology as a Nusing Speciality*
Links to Resources

### 📖 IMAGE LIBRARY

**Figure 23.1** A regular program of exercise is important for maintenance of joint mobility and muscle tone and can promote socialization.

**Figure 23.2** Many elders find creative outlets during retirement.

**Figure 23.3** Retirement provides time for enjoying hobbies.

**Table 23.5** Normal Physical Changes Associated with Aging.

## LEARNING OUTCOME 1

Identify the different categories of elders as they range from 65 to 100 years of age.

### CONCEPTS FOR LECTURE

1. The categories of elders include young-old (65 to 75 years), old (75 to 85 years), old-old (85 to 100 years), and elite old (over 100 years).

### POWERPOINT LECTURE SLIDES

*(NOTE: The number on each PPT Lecture Slide directly corresponds with the Concepts for Lecture.)*

🎞 **1** Categories of Elders
   • Young-old (65 to 75 years)
   • Old (75 to 85 years)
   • Old-old (85 to 100 years)
   • Elite old (over 100 years)

## LEARNING OUTCOME 2

Describe the demographic, socioeconomic, ethnicity, and health characteristics of elders in the United States.

### CONCEPTS FOR LECTURE

1. There are demographic, socioeconomic, ethnic, and health characteristics for elders.
2. Demographic characteristics: People are living longer; adults 85 years and older are the fastest growing of all age groups in the United States.

### POWERPOINT LECTURE SLIDES

*(NOTE: The number on each PPT Lecture Slide directly corresponds with the Concepts for Lecture.)*

🎞 **1** Characteristics of Elders in the United States

## CONCEPTS FOR LECTURE *continued*

3. Socioeconomic characteristics (gender, marital status, education, income, living arrangements): Women have a longer life expectancy and are more likely to be widowed. Men are more likely to remarry. Higher education is associated with higher income. Educational levels for older adults are gradually increasing with an increased percentage of those over age 65 who have completed high school. Usually older adults have lower incomes, and people over 85 years have the lowest median income. Living arrangements are linked to income and health status. Most older adults live in a variety of community settings; only 4.3% live in nursing homes. Older people who live alone are more likely to live in poverty than married people in the same age category. Older women are twice as likely to be living along.

4. Ethnicity characteristics: The number of minority elders is increasing; however, the higher proportion of the elder white population will continue. The nonwhite elder population is expected to increase, with elder Hispanics being the fastest growing subpopulation.

5. Health characteristics: Chronic health problems and disabilities increase as age increases. The vast majority (73%) of older Americans rate their health as good, very good, or excellent even though most have chronic health conditions and 20% report disability. Disease is not a normal outcome of aging.

## POWERPOINT LECTURE SLIDES *continued*

- Demographic
- Socioeconomic
- Ethnicity
- Health

**2** Demographic
- Longer life spans
- Fastest growing age group is 85 yr and over

**3** Socioeconomic
- Women have longer life expectancy
- Men more likely to remarry
- Educational level gradually increasing
- Lower incomes
- Most live in community settings
- Poverty level more likely when live alone

**4** Ethnicity
- Number of minority elders increasing
- Elder Hispanic fastest growing subpopulation

**5** Health
- Chronic health problems and disabilities increase
- 73% rate health as good, very good, or excellent
- 20% report disability and most have chronic disease

## SUGGESTIONS FOR CLASSROOM ACTIVITIES

- Discuss the implications of the characteristics of elders to nursing practice.

## SUGGESTIONS FOR CLINICAL ACTIVITIES

- Have students compare and contrast the characteristics of elders in the United States to their clinical clients.

---

# LEARNING OUTCOME 3

Describe ageism and its contribution to the development of negative stereotypes about elders.

## CONCEPTS FOR LECTURE

1. Ageism describes the deep and profound prejudice in American society against older adults. It is discrimination based solely on age, and it exists among some professionals.

    Ageism contributes to the development of negative stereotypes about older adults. Stereotypes occur when younger people do not understand or identify with elders as unique human beings, and generalizations of undesirable characteristics are made. Many negative attitudes are based on myths and incorrect information (see Table 23-3).

## POWERPOINT LECTURE SLIDES

*(NOTE: The number on each PPT Lecture Slide directly corresponds with the Concepts for Lecture.)*

**1** Ageism
- Discrimination based solely on age
- Exists among some professionals
- Negative stereotypes based on myths and incorrect information

## SUGGESTIONS FOR CLASSROOM ACTIVITIES

- Ask the students to develop a questionnaire derived from Table 23-3 in the text book: Myths and Realities of Aging. Have them administer this questionnaire to students, faculty, and staff of your institution. Review the results.

## SUGGESTIONS FOR CLINICAL ACTIVITIES

- Have the students observe comments and actions of personnel on the clinical unit for indications of beliefs about elders. Compare and contrast to Table 23-3.

## LEARNING OUTCOME 4

Compare and contrast gerontology and geriatrics.

### CONCEPTS FOR LECTURE

1. Gerontology is a term used to define the study of aging and older adults. It is a multidisciplinary and specialized area within various disciplines, including nursing, psychology, and social work.
2. Geriatrics is associated with the medical care, e.g., diseases and disabilities, of the elderly.

### POWERPOINT LECTURE SLIDES

*(NOTE: The number on each PPT Lecture Slide directly corresponds with the Concepts for Lecture.)*

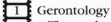 Gerontology
- The study of aging and older adults
- Multidisciplinary
- Specialized area within various disciplines including nursing

2 Geriatrics
- Associated with the medical care (diseases, disabilities) of the elderly

---

### SUGGESTIONS FOR CLASSROOM ACTIVITIES

- Have students explain why the term *gerontological* is used to describe the nursing specialty instead of the term *geriatric*.

---

## LEARNING OUTCOME 5

Describe the development of gerontological nursing and the roles of the gerontological nurse.

### CONCEPTS FOR LECTURE

1. Gerontological nursing involves advocating for the health of older persons at all levels of prevention.

   In the 1960s, gerontological nursing became a subspecialty of nursing. In the 1980s, gerontological nursing leaders stated that most practicing nurses did not have sufficient knowledge about gerontology. This prompted discussion of how to prepare nurses for gerontological nursing.

   Since the 1990s the nursing profession has recognized the importance of preparing all practicing nurses with basic gerontological knowledge. As a result, schools of nursing provide classes or courses about nursing care of the elderly.

   Practicing gerontological nurses can obtain gerontological nursing certification through the American Nurses Association.

   Advanced practice in gerontological nursing requires a master's degree in nursing, of which there are two options: the gerontological clinical nurse specialist and the gerontological nurse practitioner.

   The roles of the gerontological nurse are provider of care, teacher, manager, advocate, and research consumer.

   As a provider of care, the nurse gives direct care to older adults in a variety of settings. As a teacher, the nurse often focuses on modifiable risk factors. The gerontological nurse manager balances the concerns of the elder, family, and nursing and other interdisciplinary team members. As an advocate, the nurse helps elders remain independent and strengthens their autonomy

### POWERPOINT LECTURE SLIDES

*(NOTE: The number on each PPT Lecture Slide directly corresponds with the Concepts for Lecture.)*

 Gerontological Nursing
- Historical development
- Certification through the American Nurses Association
- Advanced practice
- Roles
  - Provider of care
  - Teacher
  - Manager
  - Advocate
  - Research consumer

and decision making. Being a research consumer requires the nurse to read the latest professional literature for evidence-based practice to improve quality of nursing care for the elderly.

---

| **SUGGESTIONS FOR CLASSROOM ACTIVITIES** | **SUGGESTIONS FOR CLINICAL ACTIVITIES** |
|---|---|
| • Invite a panel of gerontological nurses, clinical specialists, and nurse practitioners to discuss their roles and specialty. | • Arrange for several students to have an observational experience with an advanced practice gerontological nurse. Have the students report their observations of the roles enacted by these nurses to the rest of the students. |

---

# LEARNING OUTCOME 6

Describe the different care settings for elders.

## CONCEPTS FOR LECTURE

1. Gerontological nurses practice in many settings, including acute care facilities, long-term care facilities, and the community.

    Elders are the majority of clients cared for in acute care. People who are 65 and older use the emergency department (ED) at a higher rate than any other age group. Nurses in this setting focus on protecting the health of older adults with the goal of returning clients to prior level of independence.

    The objective of long-term care is to provide a place of safety and care to attain optimal wellness and independence for each individual. The clients in this setting are often referred to as residents. Long-term care includes many different levels of care such as assisted living, intermediate care, skilled care, and Alzheimer's units.

    Elders who do not feel safe living alone or who require additional help with ADLs may desire assisted living. When residents require additional assistance, they may enter intermediate care. Skilled care units or skilled nursing facilities (SNFs) are for those who require a higher level of nursing care because the acuity level requires a greater nurse-to-patient ratio. Many long-term care facilities offer specialized units for clients with Alzheimer's disease.

    Gerontological nurses may also work in hospice and care for dying persons and their families. The majority of hospice patients are elders.

    Rehabilitation may be found in several settings: acute care hospitals, subacute or transitional care, and long-term care facilities. The goal is to maintain physical independence.

    Gerontological nurses provide nursing care in many types of community settings, including home health care for those who are homebound due to severity of illness or disability, nurse-run clinics focusing on managing chronic illnesses, and adult day care where the focus is on social activities or health care. The level of nursing care can vary.

## POWERPOINT LECTURE SLIDES

*(NOTE: The number on each PPT Lecture Slide directly corresponds with the Concepts for Lecture.)*

 Care Settings for Older Adults
- Acute care facilities
- Long-term care facilities
  - Assisted living
  - Intermediate care
  - Skilled care or skilled nursing facilities (SNF)
  - Alzheimer's units
  - Hospice
  - Rehabilitation
- Community
  - Hospice
  - Home health care
  - Nurse-run clinics
  - Adult day care

**SUGGESTIONS FOR CLASSROOM ACTIVITIES**

- Invite nurses who practice in various community settings with elders to discuss their roles and the services offered in their settings.

**SUGGESTIONS FOR CLINICAL ACTIVITIES**

- Arrange for the students to observe in an adult day-care center. Have students record observations of the services offered, types of clients in the setting, and interactions among clients and staff and clients with other clients. Ask the students to report their observations in a clinical conference.
- Arrange for students to tour a residential community for individuals who are elderly. Ask the administrator to discuss the various types of services available in this setting.

## LEARNING OUTCOME 7

List the common biologic theories of aging.

### CONCEPTS FOR LECTURE

1. Common biologic theories of aging include the wear-and-tear, endocrine, free-radical, genetic, cross-linking, and immunological theories (see Table 23–4).
2. Wear-and-tear theories propose that humans are like cars that run down over time.
3. Endocrine theories propose that events in the hypothalamus and pituitary are responsible for decline.
4. Free radical theories propose that free radical resulting from oxidation of organic material cause biochemical changes in cells. Cells can no longer regenerate.
5. Genetic theories propose the cells are preprogrammed for predetermined number of cell divisions. After this, cells die.
6. Cross-linking theories propose that irreversible aging of proteins cause ultimate failure of tissues and organs.
7. Immunological theories propose that the immune system becomes less efficient causing decreased resistance to infectious diseases and viruses.

### POWERPOINT LECTURE SLIDES

*(NOTE: The number on each PPT Lecture Slide directly corresponds with the Concepts for Lecture.)*

**1** Biological Theories of Aging
  - Wear-and-tear
  - Endocrine
  - Free-radical
  - Genetic
  - Cross-linking
  - Immunological theories

**2** Wear-and-Tear
  - Vital parts run down with time, leading to aging and death

**3** Endocrine
  - Hormonal changes in hypothalamus and pituitary result in organism's decline

**4** Free-Radical
  - Cells unable to regenerate due to biochemical changes caused by free radicals

**5** Genetic
  - Organism genetically programmed for a predetermined number of cell divisions, after which the organism dies

**6** Cross-linking
  - Irreversible aging of proteins cause ultimate failure of tissues and organs

**7** Immunological Theories
  - Less-effective immune system reduces resistance to infectious disease and viruses

### SUGGESTIONS FOR CLASSROOM ACTIVITIES

- Discuss the hypotheses underlying the various biological theories of aging.

## LEARNING OUTCOME 8

Describe the usual physical changes that occur during older adulthood.

**CONCEPTS FOR LECTURE**

1. There are numerous normal physical changes associated with aging, involving the integumentary, neuromuscular, sensory-perceptual, pulmonary, cardiovascular, gastrointestinal, urinary, genital, immunological, and endocrine systems.

2. Integumentary: Changes include increased skin dryness, pallor, and fragility; progressive wrinkling and sagging of the skin; brown "age spots" on exposed body parts; decreased perspiration; thinning and graying of scalp, pubic, and axillary hair; and slower nail growth and increased thickening with ridges.

3. Neuromuscular: Older adults experience decreased speed and power of skeletal muscle contractions, slowed reaction time, loss of height (stature), loss of bone mass, joint stiffness, impaired balance, and greater difficulty in complex learning and abstraction.

4. Sensory-perceptual: Aging leads to loss of visual acuity, increased sensitivity to glare, decreased ability to adjust to darkness, arcus senilis, progressive loss of hearing, decreased sense of taste (especially the sweet sensation at the tip of the tongue), decreased sense of smell, and an increased threshold for sensations of pain, touch, and temperature.

5. Pulmonary: Changes associated with aging include decreased ability to expel foreign or accumulated matter, decreased lung expansion, less effective exhalation, reduced vital capacity, increased residual volume, and dyspnea following intense exercise.

6. Cardiovascular: Older adults are more likely to experience reduced cardiac output and stroke volume (particularly during increased activity or unusual demands that may result in shortness of breath on exertion and pooling of blood in the extremities), reduced elasticity and increased rigidity of arteries, increases in diastolic and systolic blood pressure, and orthostatic hypotension.

7. Gastrointestinal: Changes include delayed swallowing time, increased tendency for indigestion, and increased tendency for constipation.

8. Urinary: Aging may be accompanied by reduced filtering ability of the kidney and impaired renal function, less effective concentration of urine, urinary urgency and urinary frequency, tendency for nocturnal frequency, and retention of residual urine.

9. Genitals: Typical changes include prostate enlargement (benign) in men, multiple changes in women (shrinking and atrophy of the vulva, cervix, uterus, fallopian tubes, and ovaries; reduction in secretions; and changes in vaginal flora); changes in sexual function include increased time to sexual arousal, decreased firmness of erection, increased refractory period (men), and decreased vaginal lubrication and elasticity (women).

**POWERPOINT LECTURE SLIDES**

*(NOTE: The number on each PPT Lecture Slide directly corresponds with the Concepts for Lecture.)*

**1** Usual Physical Changes During Older Adulthood (see Table 23–5)

**2** Integumentary
- Skin dryness, pallor, fragility
- Wrinkling and sagging
- "Age spots"
- Decreased perspiration
- Thinning, graying of body hair
- Slower growth and thickening of nails

**3** Neuromuscular
- Decreased speed and power of muscles
- Slowed reaction time
- Loss of height
- Loss of bone mass
- Joint stiffness
- Impaired balance
- Greater difficulty with complex learning and abstraction

**4** Sensory-Perceptual
- Loss of visual acuity
- Increased sensitivity to glare
- Decreased ability to adjust to darkness
- Arcus senilis
- Presbycusis
- Decreased sense of taste and smell
- Increased threshold for pain, touch, and temperature

**5** Pulmonary
- Decreased ability to expel accumulated matter
- Decreased lung expansion
- Less effective exhalation
- Reduced vital capacity
- Increased residual volume
- Dyspnea with exertion

**6** Cardiovascular
- Reduce stroke volume and cardiac output
- Reduced elasticity and increased rigidity of arteries
- Increased systolic and diastolic blood pressure
- Orthostatic hypotension

**7** Gastrointestinal
- Delayed swallowing time
- Increased indigestion
- Constipation

**8** Urinary
- Reduced filtering
- Impaired renal function

10. Immunological: The older person is more likely to have decreased immune response, lowered resistance to infections, poor response to immunization, and decreased stress response.
11. Endocrine: Insulin resistance is increased.

- Less effective concentration of urine
- Urgency and frequency
- Nocturia
- Retention

 Genital
- Prostate enlargement
- Atrophy of vulva, cervix, uterus, fallopian tubes and ovaries
- Reduction in vaginal secretions
- Changes in vaginal flora
- Changes in sexual functioning

 Immunological
- Decreased immune system function
- Lowered resistance to infection
- Poor response to immunizations
- Decreased stress response

 Endocrine System
- Increased insulin resistance

## SUGGESTIONS FOR CLASSROOM ACTIVITIES

- Obtain or make items to simulate some of the normal physical changes that occur with aging (e.g., glasses to simulate visual disturbance). Obtain various walkers, quad canes, and wheelchairs. Have students attempt to maneuver around campus using these items with other students assisting as necessary. Ask the students to share their feelings and barriers encountered.

## SUGGESTIONS FOR CLINICAL ACTIVITIES

- Have students assess their clients for the normal physical changes of aging. Compare and contrast findings.

## LEARNING OUTCOME 9

List the common psychosocial theories about aging.

### CONCEPTS FOR LECTURE

1. The disengagement theory was developed in the early 1960s by Cumming and Henry. It proposed that aging involves mutual withdrawal (disengagement) between the older person and others in the elderly person's environment.

   The activity theory, developed by Havighurst, claims the best way to age is to stay active physically and mentally. The continuity theory, developed by Atchley, states that people maintain their values, habits, and behavior in old age. A person who is accustomed to having people around will continue to do so, and the person who prefers not to be involved with others is more likely to disengage.

### POWERPOINT LECTURE SLIDES

*(NOTE: The number on each PPT Lecture Slide directly corresponds with the Concepts for Lecture.)*

 Psychological Theories About Aging
- Disengagement theory (Cumming and Henry)
  - Aging involves mutual withdrawal between elder and the elder's environment
- Activity theory (Havighurst)
  - The best way to age is to stay active physically and mentally
- Continuity theory (Atchley)
  - People maintain their values, habits, and behaviors into old age

## SUGGESTIONS FOR CLASSROOM ACTIVITIES

- Invite a panel of nursing professionals who work with elders to discuss how they use psychological theories of aging in their nursing practice.

# LEARNING OUTCOME 10

Describe developmental tasks of the older adult.

## CONCEPTS FOR LECTURE

1. According to Erikson the developmental task at this time is ego integrity versus despair. People who attain ego integrity view life with a sense of wholeness and derive satisfaction from past accomplishments. They view death as an acceptable completion of life.

   By contrast, people who despair often believe they have made poor choices during life and wish they could live life over.

   Many people have difficulty with Erikson's singular developmental task because the "young-old" and "old-old" differ in both physical characteristics and psychosocial responses.

   Peck (1968) proposed three developmental tasks of the elder: ego differentiation versus work-role preoccupation, body transcendence versus body preoccupation, and ego transcendence versus ego preoccupation.

2. Additional developmental tasks:
   - From 65 to 75 years, older adults adjust to decreasing physical strength and health; to retirement and to lower and fixed income; to death of parents, spouses, and friends; to new relationships with adult children; to leisure time; to slower physical and cognitive responses; to keeping active and involved; and to making satisfying living arrangements as aging progresses.
   - Adults 75 years and older adjust to living alone, to the possibility of moving into a nursing home, and to their own mortality. They focus on safeguarding physical and mental health, remaining in touch with other family members, and finding meaning in life.

## POWERPOINT LECTURE SLIDES

*(NOTE: The number on each PPT Lecture Slide directly corresponds with the Concepts for Lecture.)*

 1 Developmental Tasks of the Older Adult
   - Developmental Tasks according to Erikson and Peck
     - Erikson
       - Ego integrity versus despair
     - Peck
       - Ego differentiation versus work-role preoccupation
       - Body transcendence versus body preoccupation
       - Ego transcendence versus ego preoccupation

2 Additional Developmental Tasks
   - (65–75 years)
     - Adjusting to:
       - Decreasing physical strength and health
       - Retirement
       - Lower and fixed income
       - Death of parents, spouses and friends
       - New relationships with adult children
       - Leisure time
       - Slower physical and cognitive responses
     - Keeping active and involved
     - Making satisfying living arrangements
   - (75 years and older)
     - Adapting to living alone
     - Adjusting to the possibility of moving into a nursing home
     - Adjusting to the idea of one's own death
     - Safeguarding physical and mental health
     - Remaining in touch with other family members
     - Finding meaning in life

## SUGGESTIONS FOR CLASSROOM ACTIVITIES

- Review Peck's three developmental tasks and give examples of behaviors that demonstrate positive and negative resolution of these tasks.

## SUGGESTIONS FOR CLINICAL ACTIVITIES

- Have the students provide examples of statements made or behaviors observed in their clients that demonstrate positive and negative resolution of the developmental tasks appropriate for the client's age group.

# LEARNING OUTCOME 11

Describe psychosocial changes that the older adult adjusts to during the aging process.

## CONCEPTS FOR LECTURE

1. Psychosocial changes that the older adult adjusts to during the aging process include retirement, economic change, grandparenting, relocation, maintaining independence and self-esteem, facing death, and grieving.

## POWERPOINT LECTURE SLIDES

*(NOTE: The number on each PPT Lecture Slide directly corresponds with the Concepts for Lecture.)*

1 Psychosocial Changes in the Older Adult

Retirement: A majority of people in the United States over age 65 are unemployed. However, many who are healthy continue to work, offering these people a better income, a sense of self-worth, and the chance to continue long-established routines. Retirement usually causes income to decrease by 35% or more and requires a process of adaptation. Those who learned early in life to lead well-balanced and fulfilling lives are generally more successful in retirement.

Economic change: The financial needs of elders vary considerably. Adequate financial resources enable the older person to remain independent. Problems with income are often related to low retirement benefits, lack of pension plans for many workers, and the increased length of the retirement years. Older members of minority groups often have greater financial problems than older whites, and older women of all ages usually have lower incomes than men.

Grandparenting: Older adults traditionally provide gifts, money, and other forms of support for younger family members. They also provide a sense of continuity, family heritage, rituals, and folklore. However, the rate of grandparents being the primary caregiver for their grandchildren is increasing for the following reasons: substance abuse, incarceration, teen pregnancy, emotional problems, and parental death. They often experience stress, anxiety, financial hardships, and potential deteriorating health.

Relocation: A variety of factors may lead to relocation. The house or apartment may be too large or too expensive, work involved in maintaining the house may be burdensome or impossible, or the person may need living arrangements all on one floor or more accessible bathroom facilities. Making the decision to move is stressful, but adjustment will be easier for elders making a voluntary move. More living choices and options are available for the older adult today.

Maintaining independence and self-esteem: Most American elders thrive on independence and want to look after themselves even if they have to struggle to do so. They need this sense of accomplishment. Elders appreciate the same thoughtfulness, consideration, and acceptance of their abilities as younger people do. Values and standards held by older people need to be accepted.

Facing death and grieving: When a mate dies, the remaining partner inevitably experiences feelings of loss, emptiness, and loneliness. Some widows and widowers remarry, particularly widowers since they are less inclined to maintain a household. More women than men face bereavement because women usually live longer. Independence established prior to loss of a partner makes this adjustment period easier. A person who has some meaningful friendships, economic security, ongoing interests in the community, private hobbies, and a peaceful philosophy of life copes more easily with bereavement. Successful relationships with children and grandchildren are of inestimable value.

- Retirement
- Economic change
- Grandparenting
- Relocation
- Maintaining independence and self-esteem
- Facing death and grieving

# LEARNING OUTCOME 12

Explain changes in cognitive abilities while aging.

## CONCEPTS FOR LECTURE

1. Piaget's phases of cognitive development end with formal operations; however, research on cognitive ability and aging is currently being conducted.

Intellectual capacity includes perception, cognitive agility, memory, and learning.

Perception is the ability to interpret the environment, which depends on the acuteness of the senses. If senses are impaired the ability to perceive the environment and react appropriately is diminished. Changes in the cognitive structures occur as a person ages; however, the effect of these changes on the cognitive functioning of the adult is not yet known. Lifelong mental activity, particularly verbal activity, helps elders retain a high level of cognitive function and helps maintain long-term memory.

Changes in cognitive abilities are more often a difference in speed than ability. Overall, the older adult maintains intelligence, problem solving, judgment, creativity, and other well-practiced cognitive skills.

Intellectual loss generally reflects a disease process. Cognitive impairment that interferes with social or occupational functions should always be regarded as abnormal.

Memory includes sensory memory (momentary perception of stimuli from the environment), storage in short-term memory (also includes recent memory), and encoding in which the information leaves short-term memory and enters long-term memory. In elders, retrieval from long-term memory can be slower, especially if the information is not frequently used. Most age-related differences, however, occur in short-term memory. Older adults tend to forget the recent past.

Older people need additional time for learning, largely because of the problem of retrieving information. Motivation is important; elders have more difficulty in learning information they do not consider meaningful.

## POWERPOINT LECTURE SLIDES

*(NOTE: The number on each PPT Lecture Slide directly corresponds with the Concepts for Lecture.)*

 Changes to Cognitive Abilities While Aging
- Formal operations (Piaget)
- Intellectual capacity
  - Perception
    - Ability to interpret the environment
    - Depends on acuteness of senses
    - Effect of changes in cognitive structures unknown
    - Importance of lifelong mental activity
  - Cognitive agility
    - Change in speed
    - Abilities remain
  - Memory
    - Retrieval from long-term memory increased
    - Most change in short-term memory
  - Learning
    - Additional time required
    - Motivation important

# LEARNING OUTCOME 13

Compare and contrast Kohlberg's and Gilligan's theories of moral reasoning in elders.

## CONCEPTS FOR LECTURE

1. According to Kohlberg, moral development is completed in the early adult years. He has hypothesized that an older person at the preconventional level obeys rules to avoid pain and displeasure of others. At stage 1 a person defines good and bad in relation to self, whereas older people at stage 2 may act to meet another's needs as well as their own. Elders at the conventional level follow society's rules of conduct in response to the expectations of others. Moral reasoning does not decline with age.

2. Gilligan challenged Kohlberg's stages as not being applicable to women. She believed that women base moral judgment on connectedness to others and the value of relationships while Kohlberg based his stages on concepts of justice, objectivity, and preservation of rights.

3. Older adults begin to make moral decisions that are consistent with both Kohlberg and Gilligan. Older men consider relationships as well as justice in moral decisions and older women add justice to factors considered in moral situations.

4. Values and belief patterns that are important to older adults may be different than those held by younger people because they developed during a time that was very different from today. In addition, a large number of today's elders are either foreign-born or first-generation citizens. Cultural background, life experience, gender, religion, and socioeconomic status all influence one's values.

## POWERPOINT LECTURE SLIDES

*(NOTE: The number on each PPT Lecture Slide directly corresponds with the Concepts for Lecture.)*

**1** Kohlberg's Theory on Moral Reasoning in Elders
- Based stages on concepts of justice, objectivity, and preservation of right
- Believed moral development complete in early adult years
- Does not decline with age

**2** Gilligan's Theory on Moral Reasoning in Elders
- Focused on women
- Based theory on connectedness to others and the value of relationships

**3** Older Adults and Moral Reasoning
- Older men consider relations as well as justice
- Older women add justice

**4** Values and Belief Patterns May Differ from Younger Due To
- Influence of time period
- Foreign-born or first-generation citizens
- Cultural background
- Life experience
- Gender
- Religion
- Socioeconomic status

## SUGGESTIONS FOR CLASSROOM ACTIVITIES

- Have the students debate the concepts underlying Kohlberg's and Gilligan's theories of moral development in terms of differences between genders.
- Discuss the statement that "the values and belief patterns that are important to older adults may be different than those held by younger people" as a potential reason for intergenerational conflict. Have the students suggest possible resolutions.

# LEARNING OUTCOME 14

Describe spirituality and aging.

## CONCEPTS FOR LECTURE

1. Elders can contemplate new religious and philosophical views and try to understand ideas missed previously or interpreted differently. They may derive a sense of worth by sharing experiences or views. In contrast, the older adult who has not matured spiritually may feel impoverished or despair as the drive for economic and professional success lessens.

   Many elders take their faith and religious practice very seriously and display a high level of spirituality. This may be because they grew up in a time when religion was much more important than it is for younger people today.

## POWERPOINT LECTURE SLIDES

*(NOTE: The number on each PPT Lecture Slide directly corresponds with the Concepts for Lecture.)*

**1** Spirituality and Aging.
- Capable of contemplating new religious and philosophical views
- Understanding ideas missed previously or interpreted differently
- May derive sense of worth by sharing experiences or views
- Many take faith and religious practice very seriously

2. Involvement in religion often helps older adults resolve issues related to the meaning of life, to adversity, or to good fortune. It may also be an important coping resource, leading to enhanced well-being.

- Display a high level of spirituality
- Importance of religion in youth
- May be feel impoverished or despair if not matured spiritually

 Benefits to Spirituality
- Helps resolve issues related to
  ○ Meaning of life
  ○ Adversity
  ○ Good fortune
    – May be an important coping resource

---

### SUGGESTIONS FOR CLASSROOM ACTIVITIES

- Invite a group of elders from various religious and spiritual groups to discuss the influence of their beliefs on coping with health as well as psychosocial issues related to aging.

### SUGGESTIONS FOR CLINICAL ACTIVITIES

- Ask students to provide examples of how their clients in various age groups used their religious or spiritual beliefs to cope with health-related problems.

---

# LEARNING OUTCOME 15

Describe selected health problems associated with elders.

## CONCEPTS FOR LECTURE

1. Health problems the older adult may experience include injuries, chronic disabling illnesses, drug use and misuse, alcoholism, dementia, and elder abuse. Leading causes of death in people age 65 and over are heart disease, cancer, cerebrovascular disease (stroke), lower respiratory disease, pneumonia/influenza, and diabetes mellitus.

   *Healthy People 2010* (2000) reported that falls account for 87% of all fractures among adults 65 years and older. Vision is limited, reflexes are slowed, and bones are brittle; therefore, caution is required. Driving, particularly at night, requires caution because accommodation is impaired and peripheral vision is diminished. Driving in fog or other hazardous conditions should be avoided.

   Fires are a hazard for the elder with a failing memory. They can forget to turn off an iron, the stove is left on, or a cigarette is not extinguished. Decreased sensitivity to pain and heat may lead to burns.

   Many elders die from hypothermia due to lowered metabolism and loss of normal insulation from thinning subcutaneous tissue.

   Persons with Alzheimer's disease or other types of dementia experience increasing safety needs as their condition deteriorates.

   Many older adults are afflicted with one or more chronic disabling illnesses that may seriously impair their functioning. Examples include arthritis, osteoporosis, heart disease, stroke, obstructive lung disease, hearing and vision alterations, and cognitive dysfunction. Acute diseases may create chronic health problems. Examples include pneumonia, fractures, and trauma from falls or motor vehicle crashes.

## POWERPOINT LECTURE SLIDES

*(NOTE: The number on each PPT Lecture Slide directly corresponds with the Concepts for Lecture.)*

 Selected Health Problems of Older Adults
- Injuries
- Chronic disabling illnesses
- Drug use and misuse
- Alcoholism
- Dementia
- Elder abuse

Chronic illnesses bring changes to the client and family. They may create the need for increasing help with ADLs, and health care expenses often escalate. Family roles may need to be altered and lifestyles changed.

The average elder in the United States takes four to five prescription drugs and two over-the-counter (OTC) medications and may take herbal remedies, vitamins, and food supplements. The complexities involved in self-administration may lead to a variety of misuse situations including taking too much or too little, combining alcohol and medications, combining prescription drugs with OTC drugs and herbal remedies, taking medication at the wrong time, or taking someone else's medication. Another potential misuse occurs when multiple primary care providers prescribe medication and the client fails to tell each what has been previously prescribed.

Additionally, the pharmacodynamics of drugs are altered in older adults. Variations in absorption, distribution, metabolism, and excretion of drugs are related to physiologic changes associated with aging.

There are two types of older alcoholics: those who began drinking alcohol in their youth and those who began excessive alcohol use later in life to help them cope with the changes and problems of their older years. Chronic drinking has major effects on all body systems, frequently leading to accidents and death. Some medications have an increased effect and others a decreased effect when combined with alcohol.

Dementia is a progressive loss of cognitive functions and must be differentiated from delirium, an acute and reversible syndrome. The most common causes of delirium are infection, medications, and dehydration. The most common type of dementia is Alzheimer's disease (AD). The symptoms of AD may vary somewhat but are progressive and exhibit a steady decline in cognitive and physical abilities, lasting between 7 and 15 years and ending in death. Many people with AD are cared for in the home. AD is devastating for the families and caregivers. Caregivers may experience physical and emotional exhaustion. The burden of care is frequently on women—wives and daughters.

Elder mistreatment may affect either gender; however, the victims are most often women over 75 years of age, physically or mentally impaired, and dependent for care on the abuser. Abuse may involve physical, psychologic, or emotional abuse; sexual abuse; financial abuse; violation of human or civil rights; and active or passive neglect. Elder abuse or neglect may occur in private homes, senior citizens' homes, nursing homes, hospitals, and long-term care facilities. Many abusers are either sons or daughters; others include spouses, other relatives, and health care providers.

Elders at home may fail to report abuse or neglect because they are ashamed to admit that their children have mistreated them or may fear retaliation or fear being sent to an institution. They may lack financial resources or lack the mental capacity to be aware of abuse or neglect. Legally competent adults cannot be forced to leave the abusive situation and in many cases decide to stay.

## SUGGESTIONS FOR CLASSROOM ACTIVITIES

- Have the students investigate the state's law and reporting requirements for elder abuse.
- Have the students investigate the services offered by the state's department on aging.
- Have the students locate respite services in the community.

## SUGGESTIONS FOR CLINICAL ACTIVITIES

- Review the institution's policies and procedures related to elder abuse.
- Ask the students to develop a list of potential safety hazards in the home and measures to help elders and their families reduce these hazards.
- Compare and contrast dementia and delirium in terms of possible causes, signs, and symptoms seen in clients clinically.

# LEARNING OUTCOME 16

List examples of health promotion topics for older adulthood.

## CONCEPTS FOR LECTURE

1. Health promotion topics and guidelines for older adults include safety, nutrition and exercise, elimination, and social interaction.

   Safety: Topics include home safety measures to prevent falls, fire, burns, scalds, and electrocution; working smoke and CO detectors; motor vehicle safety reinforcement, especially driving at night; and precautions to prevent pedestrian accidents, elder driver skills.

   Nutrition and exercise: Review the importance of a well-balanced diet with fewer calories; the importance of sufficient amounts of vitamin D and calcium to prevent osteoporosis; nutritional and exercise factors that may lead to cardiovascular disease; the importance of 30 minutes of moderate physical activity and 20 minutes of vigorous physical activity three times a week.

   Elimination: Review the importance of adequate roughage in the diet, adequate exercise, and at least six 8-ounce glasses of fluid daily to prevent constipation.

   Social interactions: Encourage intellectual and recreational pursuits; encourage personal relationships that promote discussion of feelings, concerns, and fears; assess risk factors for elder abuse, and identify the availability of social community centers and programs for seniors.

## POWERPOINT LECTURE SLIDES

*(NOTE: The number on each PPT Lecture Slide directly corresponds with the Concepts for Lecture.)*

1. Health Promotion Topics for Older Adulthood
   - Safety
   - Nutrition and Exercise
   - Elimination
   - Social interaction

develop sex role orientation and behaviors similar to children in the general population. Legal issues for same-sex couples are significant and constantly changing.

Single adults living alone represent a significant portion of today's society. Singles include young, self-supporting adults who have recently left the nuclear family as well as older adults living alone. Young adults typically move in and out of living situations and may fall into different categories of family types at various times. Older adults may find themselves single through divorce, separation, or the death of a spouse, but they generally live alone for the remainder of their lives.

**PRENT**

Audio Glo
NCLEX® R
End of Uni
Video and
Settings

**IMAG**

Figure 24
Figure 24
are chang
Figure 24

Describe t

**CONCEPTS F**

1. Function
resource
bers; pro
nutrition
ronment
influenc
its meml
    Each
to cultu
methods
coping r

**SUGGESTI**

• Review
• Clarify f

## SUGGESTIONS FOR CLASSROOM ACTIVITIES

• Have the students investigate the laws of the state regarding gay and lesbian couples.
• Have the students write a short paper on one of the types of family, including roles, functions, and common challenges.

## SUGGESTIONS FOR CLINICAL ACTIVITIES

• Have students determine the family type of assigned clients, including members of the family, roles, and responsibilities.

# LEARNING OUTCOME 3

Identify theoretical frameworks used in family health promotion.

## CONCEPTS FOR LECTURE

1. Major theoretical frameworks used in family health promotion include systems theory and structural-functional theory.

    The family unit can also be viewed as a system. Its members are interdependent, working toward specific purposes and goals. Families are open systems, continually interacting with and influenced by other systems in the community. Boundaries regulate the input from other systems that interact with the family system and regulate output from the family to the community or society. Boundaries protect the family from the demands and influences of other systems.

    Families are likely to welcome input from without, encourage members to adapt beliefs and practices to meet changing demands of society, seek out information, and use community resources.

    The structural-functional theory focuses on family structure and function. The structural component of the theory addresses the membership of the family and the relationship among family members. The functional aspect of the theory examines the effects of intrafamily relationships on the family system, as well as their effects on other systems.

    Nurses generally use a combination of theoretical frameworks in promoting the health of individuals and families.

## POWERPOINT LECTURE SLIDES

*(NOTE: The number on each PPT Lecture Slide directly corresponds with the Concepts for Lecture.)*

 Theoretical Frameworks Used in Family Health Promotion
• Systems theory
    ○ Family unit is an open system
    ○ Continually interacting with and influenced by other systems
    ○ Boundaries regulate input and output
• Structural-functional theory
    ○ Structure component addresses membership and relationships
    ○ Functional component examines effects of relationships on family and other systems
• Combination of theoretical frameworks

## LEARNING OUTCOME 4

Identify the components of a family health assessment.

### CONCEPTS FOR LECTURE

1. Components of the family assessment include family structure, family roles and functions, physical health status, interaction patterns, family values, and coping resources.
2. A family's structure is determined by size, type (nuclear, extended, or other type of family), and the age and gender of family members.
3. A family's roles and functions include certain family members working outside the home, their type of work and satisfaction with it, household roles and responsibilities, how tasks are distributed, how child-rearing responsibilities are shared, who is the major decision maker and what methods of decision-making are used, the family members' satisfaction with roles, and the way decisions are made.
4. The family's physical health status is affected by the current physical health status of each member, perceptions of own and other family members' health, preventive health practices, routine health care, and when and why the primary care provider was last seen.
5. Interaction patterns are ways of expressing affection, love, sorrow, anger, and so on. They are determined by the significance of the family members to each other and by the openness of communication among all family members.
6. Family values may include cultural and religious orientations; the degree to which cultural practices are followed; use of leisure time and whether leisure time is shared with the total family unit; the family's view of education, teachers, and the school system; health values; and how much emphasis is put on exercise, diet, and preventive health care.
7. Coping resources are determined by the degree of emotional support offered to one another, availability of support persons and affiliation outside the family, sources of stress, methods of handling stressful situations and conflicting goals of family members, and the financial ability to meet current and future needs.

### POWERPOINT LECTURE SLIDES

*(NOTE: The number on each PPT Lecture Slide directly corresponds with the Concepts for Lecture.)*

**1** Family Health Assessment
- Family structure
- Family functions
- Physical health status
- Interaction patterns
- Family values
- Coping resources

**2** Family Structure
- Size and type
- Age and gender of members

**3** Family Roles and Functions
- Members working outside the home
- Type of work and satisfaction with work
- Household roles and responsibilities
- How tasks are distributed
- How child-rearing responsibilities are shared
- Satisfaction with roles and way decisions are made

**4** Physical Health Status
- Current physical health status of members
- Perceptions of own and other members' health
- Preventive health practices
- Routine health care
- When and why primary care provider was last seen

**5** Interaction Patterns
- Ways of expressing emotions
- Most significant family member in client's life
- Openness of communication

**6** Family Values
- Cultural and religious orientations
- Degree to which practices are followed
- Use of leisure time and whether shared by all members
- View of education and educational system
- Health values
- Emphasis on exercise, diet, and preventive health care

7  Coping Resources
  • Degree of support of members
  • Availability of support systems outside of family
  • Source of stress, methods of coping
  • Financial status

| **SUGGESTIONS FOR CLASSROOM ACTIVITIES** | **SUGGESTIONS FOR CLINICAL ACTIVITIES** |
|---|---|
| • Ask the students to complete a family assessment on their own family.<br>• Demonstrate how to complete a genogram. | • Ask the students to complete a family assessment including a genogram on their assigned client and share with the class. |

## LEARNING OUTCOME 5

Identify common risk factors regarding family health.

### CONCEPTS FOR LECTURE

1. Common risk factors regarding family health include maturity factors, heredity factors, gender or race, sociologic factors, and lifestyle factors.

    Families with members at both ends of the age continuum are at risk of developing health problems. Families entering childbearing and child-rearing phases experience changes in roles, responsibilities, and expectations. Adolescent mothers, due to their developmental level and lack of knowledge about parenting, and single-parent families, due to role overload, are more likely to develop health problems. Many elderly persons feel a lack of purpose and decreased self-esteem which in turn reduce their motivation to engage in health-promoting behaviors.

    Persons born into families with a history of certain diseases are at greater risk of developing these conditions.

    Gender or race may predispose individuals to specific health risks. For example, men are at greater risk of having cardiovascular disease at an earlier age than women. Women are at risk of developing osteoporosis, particularly after menopause. Sickle-cell anemia is a hereditary disease limited to people of African descent, for example.

    Poverty is a major sociologic problem that affects not only the family but also the community and society. When ill, the poor are likely to put off seeking services until the illness reaches an advanced state and requires longer or more complex treatment.

    Many diseases are preventable, the effects can be minimized, or the onset of disease can be delayed through lifestyle modifications. Other important lifestyle considerations are exercise, stress management, and rest.

### POWERPOINT LECTURE SLIDES

*(NOTE: The number on each PPT Lecture Slide directly corresponds with the Concepts for Lecture.)*

 Family Health Risk Factors
  • Maturity
  • Heredity
  • Gender or race
  • Sociologic
  • Lifestyle

# LEARNING OUTCOME 6

Develop nursing diagnoses, outcomes, and interventions pertaining to family functioning.

## CONCEPTS FOR LECTURE

1. Data gathered during a family assessment may lead to the following nursing diagnoses:
   - Interrupted family processes: a change in family relationships
   - Readiness for enhanced family coping: effective management of adaptive tasks by family members involved with the client's health challenge, who exhibit desire and readiness for enhanced health and growth in regard to self and in relation to the client
   - Disabled family coping: behavior of significant person (family member or other primary person) that disables his or her capacities to effectively address tasks essential to either person's adaptation to the health challenge
   - Impaired parenting: inability of the primary caretaker to create, maintain, or regain an environment that promotes the optimum growth and development of the child
   - Impaired home maintenance: inability to independently maintain a safe growth-promoting immediate environment
   - Caregiver role strain: difficulty in performing family caregiving role
2. Nursing needs to focus on assisting the family to plan realistic goals/outcomes and strategies that enhance family functioning, such as improving communication skills, identifying and utilizing support systems, and developing and rehearsing parenting skills.
3. Anticipatory guidance may assist well-functioning families in preparing for predictable developmental transitions that occur in the life of families. (See Identifying Nursing Diagnoses, Outcomes, and Interventions: Clients with Disruption in Family Health in textbook.)

## POWERPOINT LECTURE SLIDES

*(NOTE: The number on each PPT Lecture Slide directly corresponds with the Concepts for Lecture.)*

1. Diagnoses
   - Interrupted family processes coping
   - Readiness for enhanced family
   - Disabled family coping
   - Impaired parenting
   - Impaired home maintenance
   - Caregiver role strain

2. Outcomes
   - Improving communication skills
   - Identifying and utilizing support systems
   - Developing and rehearsing parenting skills
   - Anticipatory guidance

3. Interventions
   - Based on medical diagnoses, nursing diagnoses, and selected goals or outcomes

# LEARNING OUTCOME 7

Develop outcome criteria for specific nursing diagnoses related to family functioning.

## CONCEPTS FOR LECTURE

1. Nursing needs to focus on assisting the family to plan realistic goals/outcomes and strategies that enhance family functioning, such as improving communication skills, identifying and utilizing support systems, and developing and rehearsing parenting skills.

   Specific outcome criteria will depend on the nursing diagnoses derived from the assessment data.

## POWERPOINT LECTURE SLIDES

*(NOTE: The number on each PPT Lecture Slide directly corresponds with the Concepts for Lecture.)*

1. Outcome Criteria for Nursing Diagnoses
   - Dependent upon the following:
     - Assessment data
     - Diagnostic label
     - Etiology of nursing diagnosis

## SUGGESTIONS FOR CLASSROOM ACTIVITIES

- Have students look up suggestion outcome criteria for the nursing diagnoses listed in Outcome # 6 in a nursing diagnoses reference book.

## SUGGESTIONS FOR CLINICAL ACTIVITIES

- Have the students develop a family care plan for an assigned client.

# CHAPTER 25
## CARING

## RESOURCE LIBRARY

 **PRENTICE HALL NURSING MEDIALINK DVD-ROM**

Audio Glossary
NCLEX® Review

**COMPANION WEBSITE**

Additional NCLEX® Review
Case Study: *Six C's of Caring in Nursing*
Care Plan Activity: *Care of Client After Motor Vehicle Crash*
Application Activity: *Watson's Theory of Human Caring*
Links to Resources

**IMAGE LIBRARY**

**Figure 25.1** Theory of bureaucratic caring.
**Figure 25.2** The four ways of knowing.
**Figure 25.3** Regular activity and exercise is an effective self-care practice.

**Figure 25.4** Yoga is a mind–body self-care strategy to help restore peace and balance.

---

## LEARNING OUTCOME 1

Discuss the meaning of caring.

### CONCEPTS FOR LECTURE

1. There are a number of definitions of caring in the text. Caring means that people, relationships, and things matter.
2. Mayeroff (1990) has proposed that to care for another person is to help him grow and actualize himself. Caring is a process that develops over time, resulting in a deepening and transformation of the relationship.

   According to Mayeroff, the caring process has benefits for the one giving care. By caring and being cared for, each person "finds his place" in the world. Major ingredients of caring provide further description of this process: knowing (understanding the other's needs and how to respond to these needs); alternating rhythms (moving back and forth between the immediate and long-term meaning of behavior, considering the past); patience (enabling the other to grow in his or her own way and time); honesty (having an awareness and openness to one's own feelings and a genuineness in caring for others); trust (letting go, allowing the other to grow in his or her own way and own time); humility (acknowledging that there is always more to learn, and that learning may come from any source); hope (believing in the possibilities of the other's growth); and courage (going into the unknown, informed by insight from past experience).

### POWERPOINT LECTURE SLIDES

*(NOTE: The number on each PPT Lecture Slide directly corresponds with the Concepts for Lecture.)*

**1** Meaning of Caring
- Number of definitions
- People, relationships, and things matter

**2** Mayeroff
- Growth and actualization
- A process
- Benefits for the one giving care and one receiving care
- Major ingredients of caring:
  - Knowing
  - Alternating rhythms
  - Patience
  - Honesty
  - Trust
  - Humility
  - Hope
  - Courage

**3** Summary of Definitions
- Multidimensional concept
- Five viewpoints
  - Caring as a moral imperative
  - Caring as an affect
  - Caring as a human trait

3. Caring is a multidimensional concept. In a comprehensive review of this concept, Morse et al. (1990) identified definitions of caring that were summarized as the following five viewpoints: caring as a moral imperative, caring as an affect, caring as a human trait, caring as an interpersonal relationship, and caring as a therapeutic intervention.

- ○ Caring as an interpersonal relationship
- ○ Caring as a therapeutic intervention

## SUGGESTIONS FOR CLASSROOM ACTIVITIES

- Have each student select a definition of caring that most reflects his or her understanding of this concept. Ask the students to write several paragraphs explaining the rationale for their selection.
- Provide examples of the major ingredients of caring as listed in the text.

## SUGGESTIONS FOR CLINICAL ACTIVITIES

- Ask several staff nurses to share what the concept of caring means to their practice.
- Have students interview clients on their perception of caring and non-caring behaviors of nurses. Also, ask students to interview several nurses on the same topic. Compare and contrast findings.

## LEARNING OUTCOME 2

Identify nursing theories focusing on caring.

### CONCEPTS FOR LECTURE

1. Several nursing theorists focus on caring: Leininger, Ray, Roach, Boykin and Schoenhofer, Watson, Swanson, and Benner and Wrubel.
2. Leininger's theory of culture care diversity and universality is based on the assumption that nurses must understand different cultures in order to function effectively. This theory focuses on both differences and similarities among persons in diverse cultures. Nurses must understand these in order to give care that is reasonably congruent with clients' beliefs, lifeways, and values.
3. Ray's theory of bureaucratic caring focuses on caring in organizations as cultures. The theory suggests that caring in nursing is contextual and is influenced by the organizational structure.
4. Roach focuses on caring as a philosophical concept and proposes that caring is the human mode of being. All persons are caring and develop their caring abilities by being true to self, being real, and being who they truly are. Although it is not unique to nursing, caring is the center of all attributes used to describe nursing.

    Roach defines these attributes as the six Cs of caring: compassion, competence, confidence, conscience, commitment, and comportment.
5. Boykin and Schoenhofer propose the theory of nursing as caring. They suggest that the purpose of the discipline and profession of nursing is to know persons and nurture them as persons living in caring and growing in caring. Caring in nursing is "an altruistic, active expression of love, and is intentional and embodied recognition of value and connectedness."

### POWERPOINT LECTURE SLIDES

*(NOTE: The number on each PPT Lecture Slide directly corresponds with the Concepts for Lecture.)*

**1** Theories of Caring
- Leininger
- Ray
- Roach
- Boykin
- Schoenhofer
- Watson
- Swanson
- Benner
- Wrubel

**2** Culture Care Diversity and Universality (Leininger)
- Understanding culture essential for nursing care

**3** Theory of Bureaucratic Caring (Ray)
- Caring is contextual influenced by organizational structure

**4** Caring, the Human Mode of Being (Roach)
- Center of all attributes used to describe nursing
- Six "Cs" of caring

**5** Nursing as Caring (Boykin and Schoenhofer)
- Purpose of the discipline and profession of nursing

**6** Theory of Human Caring (Watson)
- Basis for nursing's role in society
- Essence and moral ideal of nursing

6. Watson's theory of human care views caring as the essence and the moral ideal of nursing. Human care is the basis for nursing's role in society; indeed nursing's contribution to society lies in its moral commitment to human care.

7. Swanson defines caring as "a nurturing way of relating to a valued 'other' toward whom one feels a personal sense of commitment and responsibility." The theory focuses on caring processes as nursing interventions. The five caring processes include knowing, being with, doing for, enabling, and maintaining belief (see Table 25–1).

8. Benner and Wrubel (1989) described nursing as a relationship in which caring is primary because it sets up the possibility of giving and receiving help. Caring practice requires attending to the particular client over time, determining what matters to the person, and using this knowledge in clinical judgments.

7 Theory of Caring (Swanson)
- Caring processes in nursing interventions
- Five caring processes

8 Primacy of Caring (Benner and Wrubel)
- Nursing as a relationship
- Caring is primary
- Possibility of giving and receiving help

---

### SUGGESTIONS FOR CLASSROOM ACTIVITIES

- If a specific theory of caring is used in the school of nursing, explore this theory in greater detail including how to apply concepts from this theory to nursing care.
- Divide students into groups and assign a theory to each group. Ask the students to translate the theory into their own words. Have nursing theory books and resources available for students to use as needed.

### SUGGESTIONS FOR CLINICAL ACTIVITIES

- Discuss Ray's theory of bureaucratic caring. Ask students to supply examples of how they have observed this theory operationalized in the clinical setting.

---

## LEARNING OUTCOME 3

Analyze the importance of different types of knowledge in nursing.

### CONCEPTS FOR LECTURE

1. Nursing involves different types of knowledge that are integrated to guide nursing practice. Nurses require scientific knowledge (empirical knowledge), therapeutic use of self (personal knowledge), moral/ethical knowledge (ethical knowing), and creative action (aesthetic knowing). An understanding of each type of knowledge is important for the student of nursing because only by integrating all ways of knowing can the nurse develop a professional practice.

   Knowledge about the empirical world is systematically organized into laws and theories for the purpose of describing, explaining, and predicting phenomena of special concern to the discipline of nursing. Empirical knowledge ranges from factual, observable phenomenon to theoretical analysis.

   Aesthetic knowing is the art of nursing and is expressed by the individual nurse through his or her creativity and style in meeting the needs of the client. Empathy, compassion, holism, and sensitivity are important modes in aesthetic pattern of knowing.

### POWERPOINT LECTURE SLIDES

*(NOTE: The number on each PPT Lecture Slide directly corresponds with the Concepts for Lecture.)*

1 Types of Knowledge in Nursing
- Empirical knowing
  - The science of nursing
- Aesthetic knowing
  - The art of nursing
- Personal knowing
  - The therapeutic use of self
- Ethical knowing
  - The moral component

---

Personal knowledge is concerned with the knowing, encountering, and actualizing of the concrete, individual self. Personal knowing promotes wellness and integrity in personal encounters, achieves engagement rather than detachment, and denies the manipulative or impersonal approach.

Ethical knowing focuses on matters of obligation or what ought to be done, and goes beyond simply following the ethical codes of the discipline. Nursing care involves a series of deliberate actions or choices that are subject to the judgment of right or wrong.

## SUGGESTIONS FOR CLASSROOM ACTIVITIES

- Provide examples of the types of knowledge and ask students to supply additional examples. Discuss the importance of these various types of knowledge to nursing practice using the examples generated to illustrate.

## SUGGESTIONS FOR CLINICAL ACTIVITIES

- Have the students supply examples of how they have used the various types of knowledge in care of their clients.

# LEARNING OUTCOME 4

Describe how nurses demonstrate caring in practice.

## CONCEPTS FOR LECTURE

1. Nurse theorists and researchers have studied the question of "how does a nurse demonstrate caring?" and have identified caring attributes and behaviors. Because caring is contextual, a nursing approach used with a client in one situation may be ineffective in another. Caring encounters are influenced by the diversity of human responses, the nurse's workload, and the preferences of the nurse and client. When clients perceive the encounter to be caring, their sense of dignity and self-worth are increased, and feelings of connectedness are expressed.

Caring in practice is demonstrated by knowing the client, nursing presence, empowering the client, compassion, and competence.
- **Knowing the client:** Caring attends to the totality of the client's experience. The nurse aims to know who the client is, in his or her uniqueness. The nurse's knowing the client ultimately increases the possibilities for therapeutic interventions to be perceived as relevant.
- **Nursing presence:** By being emotionally present to the client and family, the nurse conveys that they and their experiences matter. Physical presence is combined with the promise of availability, especially in a time of need. Covington (2003) has defined caring presence as an "interpersonal, intersubjective human experience of connection within a nurse-client relationship that makes it safe for sharing oneself with another" (p. 312).

## POWERPOINT LECTURE SLIDES

*(NOTE: The number on each PPT Lecture Slide directly corresponds with the Concepts for Lecture.)*

**1** Caring in Practice
- Caring encounters are demonstrated by
  - Knowing the client
  - Nursing presence
  - Empowering the client
  - Compassion
  - Competence

- **Empowering the client:** Swanson (1993) has identified the caring behavior of enabling, defined as "facilitating the other's passage through life transitions and unfamiliar events" (p. 356). Enabling also includes coaching, informing, explaining, supporting, assisting, guiding, focusing, and validating.
- **Compassion:** The nurse must be able to identify with the client, appreciate the pain and discomfort of illness, or imagine "walking in the client's shoes" in regard to some part of the client's life experience. Attending to spiritual needs and comfort are also part of compassionate care. Comfort is often associated with compassionate care. For example, bathing, positioning, talking, touching, and listening are often performed to increase the client's comfort.
- **Competence:** The nurse employs the necessary knowledge, judgment, skills, and motivation to respond adequately to the client's needs. Compassion without competence is meaningless and dangerous.

---

## SUGGESTIONS FOR CLASSROOM ACTIVITIES

- Share specific examples from your practice of caring in nursing practice.
- Invite a panel of nurses who work with clients of varying ages in various types of settings, including intensive care, emergency department, home care, hospice, and other long-term care settings, to discuss how they demonstrate caring in their practice.

## SUGGESTIONS FOR CLINICAL ACTIVITIES

- Ask the students to share examples of how they have demonstrated caring with assigned clients and examples of instances when they have observed other nurses demonstrating caring attributes and behavior.
- Have students share situations where they failed to show caring in practice (e.g., a situation in which personal needs were prioritized over the client's needs). Help students analyze these situations and develop another possible approach to these situations.

---

# LEARNING OUTCOME 5

Evaluate the importance of self-care for the professional nurse.

---

## CONCEPTS FOR LECTURE

1. As nurses take on multiple commitments to family, work, school, and community, they risk exhaustion, burnout, and stress.

    Mayeroff (1990) describes caring for self as helping oneself grow and actualize one's possibilities.

    Caring for self means taking the time to nurture oneself. This involves initiating and maintaining behaviors that promote healthy living and well-being.

    Self-awareness and self-esteem are intimately connected to self-care. Individuals with high self-esteem can critically problem solve and tackle obstacles more effectively. Self-care activities build self-esteem leading to feelings of comfort and accomplishment.

    Types of self-care activities include creating a healthy lifestyle, proper nutrition, activity and exercise, recreation, avoiding unhealthy patterns, and using mind–body therapies such as guided imagery, meditation, storytelling, music therapy, and yoga.

## POWERPOINT LECTURE SLIDES

*(NOTE: The number on each PPT Lecture Slide directly corresponds with the Concepts for Lecture.)*

 Self Care for the Professional Nurse
- Helping oneself grow and actualize
- Self-care builds self-esteem
- Creating a healthy lifestyle
  ○ Proper nutrition
  ○ Activity and exercise
  ○ Recreation
  ○ Avoiding unhealthy patterns
- Using mind-body therapies
  ○ Guided imagery
  ○ Meditation
  ○ Storytelling
  ○ Music therapy
  ○ Yoga

---

# LEARNING OUTCOME 6

Identify the value of reflective practice in nursing.

## CONCEPTS FOR LECTURE

1. Critical thinking, self-analysis, and reflection are required in order to learn from one's experience. The student matures as a practitioner by thinking about how values and standards guide practical experience. Reflection is thinking from a critical point of view, analyzing why one acted in a certain way, and assessing the results of one's actions. In order to develop oneself as a caring practitioner, reflection on practice must be personal and meaningful. Reflective practice is a method of self-examination that involves thinking back over what happened in a nursing situation. It includes becoming aware of how one feels about oneself and recognizing how one thinks and acts. This exploration leads to new understandings and appreciations. Reflection provides a method to explore alternative forms of nursing knowledge, including empirical, aesthetics, personal, and ethical types.

   Reflective practice requires discipline, actions, openness, and trust. It is a form of self-evaluation. Reflective journaling provides a space for the student to look at and acknowledge the deeper self. Guidance from a mentor or teacher can help the student view a nursing situation from many perspectives. Guidance helps the student find meaning in an event, understand and learn through it, and emerge at a higher level of understanding.

## POWERPOINT LECTURE SLIDES

*(NOTE: The number on each PPT Lecture Slide directly corresponds with the Concepts for Lecture.)*

 The Value of Reflective Practice in Nursing
- Reflective practice
  - Method of self-examination
  - Involves thinking over what happened in a nursing situation
  - Includes becoming aware of how one feels about oneself
  - Recognizing how one thinks and acts
  - Leads to new understandings and appreciations
  - Requires discipline, action, openness, and trust
- Reflective journaling
  - Guidance from a mentor

# CHAPTER 26
## COMMUNICATING

## RESOURCE LIBRARY

###  PRENTICE HALL NURSING MEDIALINK DVD-ROM

Audio Glossary
NCLEX® Review
Videos and Animations:
  *Communicating Effectively*
  *Communications*

### 📖 IMAGE LIBRARY

**Figure 26.1** Improving student nurse self-talk.
**Figure 26.2** The communication process.
**Figure 26.3** Appropriate forms of touch can communicate caring.
**Figure 26.4** Nonverbal communication sometimes conveys meaning more effectively than words.

### COMPANION WEBSITE

Additional NCLEX® Review
Case Study: *Facilitating Communication*
Care Plan Activity: *Treating an Immigrant Family*
Application Activity: *Communication Resources*
Links to Resources

**Figure 26.5** The nurse's facial expression communicates warmth and caring.
**Figure 26.6** Personal space influences communication in social and professional interactions.
**Figure 26.7** The nurse conveys attentive listening through a posture of involvement.

---

## LEARNING OUTCOME 1

Describe factors influencing the communication process.

### CONCEPTS FOR LECTURE

1. Many factors influence the communication process. Some of these are development, gender, values and perceptions, personal space, territoriality, roles and relationships, environment, congruence, and attitudes.

   Language, psychosocial, and intellectual development moves through stages across the life span. Knowledge of a client's developmental stage will allow the nurse to modify the message accordingly.

   From an early age, females and males communicate differently. Girls tend to use language to seek confirmation, minimize differences, and establish intimacy. Boys use language to establish independence and negotiate status within a group. These differences can continue into adulthood, so the same communication may be interpreted differently by a man and a woman.

   Values are standards that influence behavior, and perceptions are the personal view of an event. Because each person has unique personality traits, values, and life experiences, each will perceive and interpret messages and experiences differently. It is important for the nurse to be aware of a client's values and to validate or correct perceptions to avoid creating barriers in the nurse–client relationship.

### POWERPOINT LECTURE SLIDES

*(NOTE: The number on each PPT Lecture Slide directly corresponds with the Concepts for Lecture.)*

 Factors Influencing the Communication Process
- Development
- Gender
- Values and perceptions
- Personal space
  - Intimate (touching to $1\frac{1}{2}$ feet)
  - Personal ($1\frac{1}{2}$ to 4 feet)
  - Social (4 to 12 feet)
  - Public (12 to 15 feet)
- Territoriality
- Roles and relationships
- Environment
- Congruence
- Interpersonal attitudes

---

Personal space is the distance people prefer in interactions with others. Middle-class North Americans use definite distances in various interpersonal relationships. Communication is altered in accordance with four distances: intimate (touching to $1\frac{1}{2}$ feet), personal ($1\frac{1}{2}$ to 4 feet), social (4 to 12 feet), and public (12 to 15 feet).

Intimate distance is characterized by body contact, heightened sensations of body heat and smell, and vocalizations that are low. Vision is intense, restricted to a small body part, and may be distorted. It is a natural protective instinct for people to maintain a certain amount of space immediately around them, and the amount varies with cultures.

Personal distance is less overwhelming. Voice tones are moderate, and body heat and smell are noticed less. More of the person is perceived so that nonverbal behaviors are seen with less distortion. Much communication occurs at this distance. Communication at a close personal distance can convey involvement by facilitating the sharing of thoughts and feelings.

Social distance is characterized by a clear visual perception of the whole person. Body heat and odor are imperceptible, eye contact is increased, and vocalizations are loud enough to be overheard by others. Communication is therefore more formal and is limited to seeing and hearing. The person is protected and out of reach for touch or personal sharing of thoughts or feelings. It is expedient for communicating with several people at the same time or within a short time.

Public distance requires loud, clear vocalizations with careful enunciation. Although the faces and forms of people are seen at public distance, individuality is lost. The perception is of the group or people or the community.

Territoriality is the concept of the space and things that an individual considers as belonging to the self. Territories marked off by people may be visible to others. This human tendency to claim territory must be recognized by health care providers. Clients often feel the need to defend their territory when it is invaded by others.

Choice of words, sentence structure, and tone of voice vary considerably from role to role. In addition, the specific relationship between communicators is significant.

The nurse communicates differently when meeting the client for the first time than the nurse who has previously developed a relationship with the client.

People usually communicate most effectively in a comfortable environment. Temperature extremes, excessive noise, and a poorly ventilated environment can all interfere with communication, as may lack of privacy and environmental distractions.

Congruence means that the verbal and nonverbal aspects of the message match. This is usually readily seen by nurses; however, clients are often just as adept at reading a nurse's expression or body language. If there is an incongruence, the body language or nonverbal communication is usually the one with the true meaning.

Attitudes convey beliefs, thoughts, and feelings about people and events. Attitudes such as caring, warmth, respect, and acceptance facilitate communication; whereas condescension, lack of interest, and coldness inhibit communication.

Caring and warmth convey feelings of emotional closeness; respect is an attitude that emphasizes the other person's worth and individuality; acceptance emphasizes neither approval or disapproval but a willingness to receive the client's honest feelings.

## SUGGESTIONS FOR CLASSROOM ACTIVITIES

- Have each student find a partner. Have one partner stand 12 to 15 feet away from the other; then gradually move from public to social to personal and then intimate space. As this is occurring, ask the other person to monitor the feelings that he or she is experiencing. Reverse the roles. Discuss findings.
- Move the notebook, books, or some personal belonging of several students. Have the students describe the feelings experienced. Relate this to the concept of territoriality.
- Assign several students emotions and ask them to attempt to convey the assigned emotion nonverbally. Have other students attempt to identify this emotion.

## SUGGESTIONS FOR CLINICAL ACTIVITIES

- Have the students identify ways in which they can control the environment in order to facilitate communication with their clients.
- Have the students provide examples of situations in which they observed incongruence between verbal and nonverbal communication of a client. How might the students clarify this situation?

# LEARNING OUTCOME 2

Discuss nurse–client communication as a dynamic process.

## CONCEPTS FOR LECTURE

1. Nurse–client relationships are referred to by some as interpersonal relationships, by others as therapeutic relationships, and by still others as helping relationships.

   Helping is a growth-facilitating process that strives to achieve two basic goals: (a) to help clients manage their problems in living more effectively and develop unused or underused opportunities more fully, and (b) to help clients become better at helping themselves in their everyday lives.

   A helping relationship may develop over weeks of working with a client or within minutes.

   The keys to the helping relationship are the development of trust and acceptance between the nurse and the client and an underlying belief that the nurse cares about and wants to help the client.

## POWERPOINT LECTURE SLIDES

*(NOTE: The number on each PPT Lecture Slide directly corresponds with the Concepts for Lecture.)*

 1 Nurse–Client Relationships
- Therapeutic relationship
- Growth-facilitating process
- Achieve two basic goals:
  ○ Help clients manage problems in living
  ○ Become better at helping themselves in their everyday lives
- Development of trust and acceptance
- Influenced by personal and professional characteristics of nurse and client
- Good communication skills
- Sincere interest in the client's welfare

The helping relationship is influenced by the personal and professional characteristics of the nurse and the client.

Consideration of age, gender, appearance, diagnosis, education, values, ethnicity, cultural background, personality, expectations, and setting combined with good communication skills and sincere interest in the client's welfare will enable the nurse to create a helping relationship.

## SUGGESTIONS FOR CLASSROOM ACTIVITIES

- Have the students provide examples of how to help the client develop trust in the nurse.
- Have the students discuss the possible influence appearance may have on communication between the nurse and client. For example, what effect might a clean, pressed lab coat and uniform versus a wrinkled, soiled lab coat and uniform have on communication between the client and nurse?

## SUGGESTIONS FOR CLINICAL ACTIVITIES

- Have the students discuss how age, gender, diagnosis, education, values, ethnicity, and cultural background of assigned clients have influenced communication.

## LEARNING OUTCOME 3

Describe four phases of the helping relationship.

## CONCEPTS FOR LECTURE

1. The helping relationship process can be described in terms of four sequential phases, each characterized by identifiable tasks and skills: preinteraction phase, introductory phase, working (maintaining) phase, and termination phase (see Table 26–4).
2. In the preinteraction phase, the nurse reviews pertinent assessment data, considers potential areas of concern, and develops plans for interaction.
3. The introductory phase consists of three stages: opening the relationship, clarifying the problem, and structuring and formulating the contract obligations to be met by both the nurse and the client.
   - **Opening the relationship:** The nurse and client identify each other by name. If the nurse initiates, it is important to give the client an idea of what to expect. When the client initiates, the nurse needs to help the client express concerns and reasons for seeking help, often with open-ended questions.
   - **Clarifying the problem:** The client may not initially see the problem clearly; the nurse helps to clarify the problem.
   - **Structuring and formulating the contract:** The nurse and client develop a sense of trust and verbally agree about location, frequency and length of the meetings, overall purpose of the relationship, how confidential material will be handled, tasks to be accomplished and duration, and indications for termination of the relationship.

## POWERPOINT LECTURE SLIDES

*(NOTE: The number on each PPT Lecture Slide directly corresponds with the Concepts for Lecture.)*

**1** Four Phases of the Helping Relationship
- Preinteraction
- Introductory
- Working (maintaining)
- Termination

**2** Preinteraction Phase
- Reviews pertinent assessment data and knowledge
- Considers potential areas of concern
- Develops plans for interaction

**3** Introductory Phase
- Stage 1: Opening the relationship
- Stage 2: Clarifying the problem
- Stage 3: Structuring and formulating the contract

**4** Working Phase
- Stage 1: Exploring and understanding thoughts and feelings
- Stage 2: Facilitating and taking actions

**5** Termination Phase
- Nurse and client accept feelings of loss
- Client accepts the end of the relationship without feelings of anxiety or dependence

4. The working phase has two stages: exploring and understanding thoughts and feelings, and facilitating and taking actions.
   - **Exploring and understanding thoughts and feelings:** The nurse assists the client to explore and understand thoughts and feelings and acquires an understanding of the client. The client explores thoughts and feelings associated with problems, develops the skill of listening, and gains insight into personal behavior.
   - **Facilitating and taking action:** The nurse plans programs within the client's capabilities and considers long- and short-term goals. The client needs to learn to take risks, and the nurse needs to reinforce successes and help the client recognize failures realistically.
5. In the termination phase, the nurse and client accept feelings of loss. The client accepts the end of the relationship without feelings of anxiety or dependence.

---

## SUGGESTIONS FOR CLASSROOM ACTIVITIES

- Divide the students into triads. Have two of the students role-play the nurse and the client. Have the third student observe the interaction and note facilitating and inhibiting communication. Provide a situation (for example, the client wishes to establish an exercise program), and have the "nurse" and "client" work through the stages of the helping relationship. Discuss the observations.

## SUGGESTIONS FOR CLINICAL ACTIVITIES

- Assign students to perform admission interviews, paying attention to the phases of the helping relationship. Discuss outcomes in clinical conference.

---

# LEARNING OUTCOME 4

Identify features of effective groups.

## CONCEPTS FOR LECTURE

1. Three main functions are required for any group to be effective: it must maintain a degree of group unity or cohesion, it needs to develop and modify its structure to improve effectiveness, and it must accomplish its goals.

   Features of effective groups include the following:
   - The atmosphere is comfortable and relaxed, and people are able to demonstrate their interest and involvement.
   - The group's purpose—its goals, tasks, and outcomes—is clarified, understood, and modified so that members can commit to the purpose through cooperation.
   - Leadership and member participation are democratic. There may be a shift in leadership from time to time depending on knowledge and experience.
   - Communication is open. Ideas and feelings are encouraged.

## POWERPOINT LECTURE SLIDES

*(NOTE: The number on each PPT Lecture Slide directly corresponds with the Concepts for Lecture.)*

 Features of Effective Groups
- Comfortable, relaxed atmosphere
- Clearly defined purpose
- Democratic leadership and member participation
- Open communication
- Group decision making
- Cohesion
- Tolerance of conflict
- Shared power
- Problem solving a high priority
- Creativity encouraged

---

- Decisions are made by the group, although various decision-making procedures appropriate to the situation may be instituted.
- Cohesion is facilitated through valuing group members, with open expression of feelings, trust, and support.
- Conflict is tolerated. The reasons for disagreement or conflicts are carefully examined and the group seeks to resolve them.
- Power is determined by the members' abilities and the information they possess; power is shared.
- Problem solving is a high priority. Constructive criticism is frequent, frank, relatively comfortable, and oriented toward problem solving.
- Creativity is encouraged.

## SUGGESTIONS FOR CLASSROOM ACTIVITIES

- Have the students identify a group of which they are members. Have them discuss how this group models or fails to model the features of an effective group.

## SUGGESTIONS FOR CLINICAL ACTIVITIES

- Have the students identify features of effective groups that they have observed in the staff of the clinical facility. Ask them to identify any problem areas noted and provide suggestions for how to overcome these.

# LEARNING OUTCOME 5

Identify types of groups helpful in promoting health and comfort.

## CONCEPTS FOR LECTURE

1. Common types of health care groups include task groups, teaching groups, self-help groups, self-awareness groups, therapy groups, and work-related social support groups. Task groups are work-related with a focus on completion of a specific task. Teaching groups impart information to the participants. Self-help groups are small, voluntary organizations composed of individuals who share a similar health, social, or daily living problem. Self-awareness groups develop or use interpersonal strengths. Therapy groups work toward self-understanding, more satisfactory way of relating or handling stress, and changing patterns of behavior toward health. Work-related social support groups assist member to buffer stress related to vocational stress.

## POWERPOINT LECTURE SLIDES

*(NOTE: The number on each PPT Lecture Slide directly corresponds with the Concepts for Lecture.)*

[1] Groups Helpful in Promoting Health and Comfort
- Task
- Teaching
- Self-help
- Self-awareness/Growth
- Therapy
- Work-related social support

## SUGGESTIONS FOR CLASSROOM ACTIVITIES

- Have each student identify and write a short report on a self-help group, including purpose, group structure, and conduct of the group.

## SUGGESTIONS FOR CLINICAL ACTIVITIES

- Discuss the types of groups that the clinical agency supports.

### CONCEPTS FOR LECTURE

1. Communication is an integral part of the nursing process. Nurses use communication skills in each phase of the nursing process. Communication is also important when caring for clients who have communication problems.

2. Assessing: The nurse must determine communication impairments or barriers and communication style, cultural influence, age, and development.
   - Impairments in communication include language deficits, sensory deficits, cognitive impairments, structural deficits, and paralysis.
   - Style of communication includes both verbal and nonverbal communication. Psychological illness may influence the ability to communicate.
   - Verbal communication includes the content of the message, the themes, and verbalized emotions. In addition, the nurse must consider pattern (e.g., slow, rapid, quiet, spontaneous, hesitant, evasive); vocabulary; presence of hostility, aggression, assertiveness, reticence, hesitance, anxiety, or loquaciousness; difficulties with verbal communication; and refusal or inability to speak.
   - Nonverbal communication must be considered in relationship to the client's culture. It is important to pay attention to facial expression, gestures, body movements, affect, tone of voice, posture, and eye contact.

3. Diagnosing: *Impaired Verbal Communication* may be used as a nursing diagnosis when "an individual experiences a decreased, delayed, or absent ability to receive, process, transmit, and use a system of symbols—anything that has meaning (i.e., transmits meaning)." Communication problems may be receptive or expressive.
   - If the client has a psychiatric illness or a coping problem causing communication problems, another diagnosis may be more useful such as *Fear* or *Anxiety*.
   - Other nursing diagnoses used for clients experiencing communication problems that involve impaired communication as the etiology could include the following: *Anxiety, Powerlessness, Situational Low Self-esteem, Social Isolation, and Impaired Social Interaction*. All of these are related to impaired verbal communication.

4. Planning: The client and nurse determine outcomes and begin planning ways to promote effective communication. The overall outcome is to reduce or resolve the factors impairing the communication. Specific nursing interventions will be planned for the stated etiology.
   - Examples of outcome criteria include the following: communicates that needs are being met;

### POWERPOINT LECTURE SLIDES

*(NOTE: The number on each PPT Lecture Slide directly corresponds with the Concepts for Lecture.)*

**1** Communication Skills and the Nursing Process
   - Communication is integral to the nursing process
   - Used in each phase

**2** Assessing
   - Determine communication impairments or barriers
   - Communication style
   - Cultural influence
   - Age and development

**3** Diagnosing
   - Impaired Verbal Communication (NANDA)
   - Fear or Anxiety
   - Impaired Verbal Communication may be Etiology

**4** Planning
   - Determine outcomes
   - Plan ways to promote effective communication
   - Overall outcome is to reduce or resolve the factors impairing the communication
   - Specific nursing interventions planned for the stated etiology

**5** Implementing
   - Manipulate the environment
   - Providing support
   - Employing measures to enhance communication
   - Educating the client and support person

**6** Evaluating
   - Client communication
     - Listen actively
     - Observe nonverbal cues
     - Use therapeutic communication skills

begins to establish a means of communication; perceives the message accurately as evidenced by appropriate verbal and/or nonverbal responses; communicates effectively; regains maximum communication abilities; expresses minimum fear, anxiety, frustration, and depression; and uses resources appropriately.

5. Implementing: Interventions to facilitate communication with clients who have problems with speech or language include manipulating the environment, providing support, employing measures to enhance communication, and educating the client and support person.

6. Evaluating: To establish whether outcomes have been met, the nurse must listen actively, observe nonverbal cues, and use therapeutic communication skills to determine that communication was effective.

---

### SUGGESTIONS FOR CLASSROOM ACTIVITIES

- Divide the students into two groups. Provide each group with a case study. One client case study should provide evidence that the client has *Impaired Verbal Communication* as a nursing diagnosis, and the other case study should provide evidence that *Impaired Verbal Communication* is the etiology for another nursing diagnosis. Have students develop a care plan for the client in the assigned case study. Share care plans with the class.

### SUGGESTIONS FOR CLINICAL ACTIVITIES

- Have the students provide examples of clients who have had *Impaired Verbal Communication* as either a nursing diagnosis or the etiology of another nursing diagnosis. Discuss care plans developed for these clients.

---

## LEARNING OUTCOME 7

State why effective communication is imperative among health professionals.

### CONCEPTS FOR LECTURE

1. Effective communication among health professionals is imperative to prevent medical errors as a result of communication problems, to promote better client outcomes, to preserve a nurse's professional integrity while ensuring a client's safety, and to maintain a better working environment.

### POWERPOINT LECTURE SLIDES

*(NOTE: The number on each PPT Lecture Slide directly corresponds with the Concepts for Lecture.)*

 Communication Among Health Professionals
- Effective communication is important for:
  - Prevention of medical errors
  - Promotion of better client outcomes
  - Preservation of nurse's professional integrity
  - Maintenance of client's safety
  - Maintenance of a better working environment

---

### SUGGESTIONS FOR CLASSROOM ACTIVITIES

- Have the students provide examples of situations in which effective communication could affect client outcomes and maintain a positive working environment.
- Discuss methods to improve communication to help eliminate medical errors.

### SUGGESTIONS FOR CLINICAL ACTIVITIES

- Have the students observe communication among various members of the health care team. Discuss positive and negative examples of the observed interactions. Have students provide suggestions for improving communication.

---

# LEARNING OUTCOME 8

Differentiate major characteristics between assertive and nonassertive communication.

## CONCEPTS FOR LECTURE

1. Assertive communication promotes client safety by minimizing miscommunication with colleagues. People who are assertive are honest, direct, and appropriate while being open to ideas and respecting the rights of others.

   An important characteristic of assertive communication includes the use of "I" statements versus "you" statements. "I" statements encourage discussion, and "you" statements place blame and put the listener in a defensive position.

2. Nonassertive communication includes two types of interpersonal behaviors: submissive and aggressive.

3. When people use a submissive communication style, they allow their rights to be violated by others. They meet the demands and requests of others without regard to their own feelings and needs because they believe their own feelings are not important. Some experts believe that these individuals are insecure and try to maintain their self-esteem by avoiding conflict.

4. There is a fine line between assertive and aggressive communication. Assertive communication is an open expression of ideas and opinions while respecting the rights and opinions of others. Aggressive communication strongly asserts the person's legitimate rights and opinions with little regard or respect for the rights and opinions of others. Aggressive communication is often perceived as a personal attack because it humiliates, dominates, controls, or embarrasses the other person. By lowering the other person's self-esteem, the person using aggressive communication may feel superior. Aggressive communication can take several forms, including screaming, sarcasm, rudeness, belittling jokes, and even direct personal insults.

## POWERPOINT LECTURE SLIDES

*(NOTE: The number on each PPT Lecture Slide directly corresponds with the Concepts for Lecture.)*

**1** Assertive Communication
- Promotes client safety by minimizing miscommunication with colleagues
- Honest, direct and appropriate
- Open to ideas
- Respecting the rights of others.
- Use of the "I" statements versus the "you" statements
- "I" statements encourage discussion
- "You" statements place blame and put the listener in a defensive position

**2** Nonassertive Communication
- Submissive
- Aggressive

**3** Submissive Communication
- Allow rights to be violated by others
- Meet the demands and requests of others without regard to own feelings and needs
- Believe own feelings not important
- May be insecure and try to maintain self-esteem by avoiding conflict

**4** Aggressive Communication
- Strongly asserts the person's legitimate rights and opinions with little regard or respect for the rights and opinions of others
- Often perceived as a personal attack by the other person
- Humiliates, dominates, controls, or embarrasses the other person
- By lowering other person's self-esteem, may feel superior
- Several forms including:
  - Screaming, sarcasm
  - Rudeness, belittling jokes
  - Direct personal insults

## SUGGESTIONS FOR CLASSROOM ACTIVITIES

- Provide the students with a situation in which there is a conflict. Have them role-play an assertive and nonassertive approach to this conflict. Have the students discuss feelings experienced during this role play.

## SUGGESTIONS FOR CLINICAL ACTIVITIES

- Have the students discuss situations in which they have demonstrated a nonassertive communication style in the clinical setting. Discuss how the students could restructure the nonassertive communication situation.
- Discuss examples of aggressive communication, methods to avoid this style of communication, and how to respond to those who demonstrate this style of communication.

# CHAPTER 27
## TEACHING

## RESOURCE LIBRARY

 **PRENTICE HALL NURSING MEDIALINK DVD-ROM**

Audio Glossary
NCLEX® Review

 **COMPANION WEBSITE**

Additional NCLEX® Review
Case Study: *Planning a Rural Health Education Program*
Care Plan Activity: *Discharge of Client with Cardiomyopathy*
Application Activity: *Overseeing a Health Fair*
Links to Resources

### IMAGE LIBRARY

**Figure 27.1** Learning is facilitated when the client is interested and actively involved.
**Figure 27.2** Teaching materials and strategies should be suited to the client's age and learning abilities.

**Figure 27.3** Teaching activities may need to include hands-on client participation.

## LEARNING OUTCOME 1

Discuss the importance of the teaching role of the nurse.

### CONCEPTS FOR LECTURE

1. Teaching the client is a major aspect of nursing practice and an important independent nursing function.

   The American Hospital Association's *Patient's Bill of Rights* mandates client education as a right of all clients.

   State nurse practice acts include client teaching as a function of nursing, making this a legal and professional responsibility.

   The Joint Commission on Accreditation of Healthcare Organization (JCAHO) expanded its standards of client education by nurses to include evidence that patients and their significant others understand what they have been taught.

   This requirement means that providers must consider the literacy level, educational background, language skills, and culture of every client during the education process.

### POWERPOINT LECTURE SLIDES

*(NOTE: The number on each PPT Lecture Slide directly corresponds with the Concepts for Lecture.)*

**1** Importance of the Teaching Role
   - Major aspect of nursing practice
   - Independent nursing function
   - The American Hospital Association's *Patient's Bill of Rights*
   - State nurse practice acts
     ○ The JCAHO's standards

### SUGGESTIONS FOR CLASSROOM ACTIVITIES

- Have the students review the nurse practice act of the state and the ANA Scope and Standards of Practice to determine the importance of the teaching role of the nurse as represented in these documents.

### SUGGESTIONS FOR CLINICAL ACTIVITIES

- Have students present examples of teaching they incorporated in daily care for their assigned clients.
- Discuss how the institution fulfills the mandated JCAHO standards on patient education.

# LEARNING OUTCOME 2

Describe the attributes of learning.

## CONCEPTS FOR LECTURE

1. The attributes of learning include:
   - An experience that occurs inside the learner.
   - The discovery of the personal meaning and relevance of ideas.
   - A consequence of experience.
   - A collaborative and cooperative process.
   - An evolutionary process.
   - A process that is both intellectual and emotional.

## POWERPOINT LECTURE SLIDES

*(NOTE: The number on each PPT Lecture Slide directly corresponds with the Concepts for Lecture.)*

**1** Attributes of Learning
- Experience that occurs inside the learner
- Discovery of the personal meaning and relevance of ideas
- Consequence of experience
- Collaborative and cooperative process
- Evolutionary process
- Process that is both intellectual and emotional

## SUGGESTIONS FOR CLASSROOM ACTIVITIES

- Have the students write their own definitions of learning and teaching and compare to the attributes listed in the textbook.
- Have students generate examples that illustrate the attributes of learning.

# LEARNING OUTCOME 3

Compare and contrast andragogy, pedagogy, and geragogy.

## CONCEPTS FOR LECTURE

1. Andragogy is the art and science of teaching adults. The following concepts relate to teaching adults: As people mature, they move from dependence to independence. An adult's previous experiences can be used as a resource for learning. An adult's readiness to learn is often related to a developmental task or social role (e.g., perceiving a need in his or her life situation). An adult is more oriented to learning when the material is useful immediately, not sometime in the future.

2. Pedagogy is the discipline concerned with helping children learn. Parents can be taught the teaching loop: (a) alerting—get the child's attention by calling his or her name, touching the child, and making a noise; (b) instructing—give the child a short, specific instruction about what is to be done, or model or demonstrate the behavior; (c) performing—give the child opportunity to practice the task, play with the toy, and explore the materials being used (give "enough time," but with some structure or direction); and (d) reinforcing—give the child feedback; a positive or negative comment that is specific to the task lets children know how they have done and encourages them to continue to learn.

   See Lifespan Considerations: Special Teaching Considerations in the textbook.

3. Geragogy is the term used to describe the process involved in stimulating and helping elders to learn. The following concepts relate to teaching elders: The material

## POWERPOINT LECTURE SLIDES

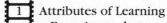

*(NOTE: The number on each PPT Lecture Slide directly corresponds with the Concepts for Lecture.)*

**1** Andragogy
- Teaching adults
- Concepts related to teaching adults:
  ○ More independent in learning situation
  ○ Previous experiences can be used as a resource for learning
  ○ Readiness to learn is often related to a development task or social role
  ○ Immediate application of material is important

**2** Pedagogy
- Teaching children
- Concepts related to teaching children:
  ○ Alerting
  ○ Instructing
  ○ Performing
  ○ Reinforcing

**3** Geragogy
- Teaching elders
- Concepts related to teaching elders:
  ○ Material must be practical and meaningful
  ○ Set achievable goals with client/family
  ○ Increase time for teaching
  ○ Incorporate rest periods

must be practical and have meaning for them individually, especially if the information is new to them. Health promotion is a priority. Set achievable goals with the client and family. If developing new written materials, use large print and buff-colored paper. Written materials should be developed at the fifth- to sixth-grade reading level. Increase time for teaching and allow for rest periods. Verbal presentations should be well organized. Ensure minimal distraction, repeat information if necessary, and use return demonstration with psychomotor skills. Determine where clients obtain most of their health information. Use examples that they can relate to in their daily lives. Be aware of sensory deficits, and use the setting in which the individual is most comfortable (group or individual). If noncompliance is a problem, determine its cause. Respect the lifetime or knowledge and experience accumulated. Use positive reinforcement and ongoing evaluation of material learned.

- ○ Reduce distractions
- ○ Accommodate for sensory alterations
- ○ Use positive reinforcement and ongoing evaluation

## SUGGESTIONS FOR CLASSROOM ACTIVITIES

- Give the students a teaching topic: for example, teaching the food pyramid. Divide the students into groups and assign them an age group. Have the students discuss how to present this topic to this age group. Have the groups share with the class and compare and contrast strategies.

## SUGGESTIONS FOR CLINICAL ACTIVITIES

- Have the students review teaching materials used in the clinical setting. Evaluate for appropriateness for the age groups represented in the clinical agency.

# LEARNING OUTCOME 4

Discuss the learning theories of behaviorism, cognitivism, and humanism and how nurses can use each of these theories.

## CONCEPTS FOR LEARNING

1. Thorndike, Pavlov, Skinner, and Bandura are major behaviorism theorists. Thorndike's contribution is that learning should be based on the learner's behavior. An act is called a response when it can be traced to the effects of a stimulus. Behaviorists closely observe responses and then manipulate the environment to bring about the intended change. To modify a person's attitude and response, a behaviorist would either alter the stimulus condition in the environment or change what happens after a response occurs.

   Skinner's and Pavlov's work focused on conditioning behavioral responses to a stimulus that causes the response or behavior. Skinner also introduced the importance of positive reinforcement. According to Bandura, most learning comes from observational learning and instruction; his research focuses on imitation and modeling.

   Nurses applying behavioristic theory will provide sufficient practice time, immediate and repeat testing and redemonstration, provide opportunity for trial and

## POWERPOINT LECTURE SLIDES

*(NOTE: The number on each PPT Lecture Slide directly corresponds with the Concepts for Lecture.)*

1 Behaviorism, Cognitivism, and Humanism
- Behaviorism (Thorndike, Pavlov, Skinner, Bandura)
  - ○ Learning is based on the learner's behavior
  - ○ Stimulus and response
  - ○ Conditioning
  - ○ Positive reinforcement
  - ○ Observational learning and instruction (imitation and modeling)
  - ○ Nurses using behaviorism will:
    - – Provide sufficient practice time
    - – Provide immediate and repeat testing and redemonstration
    - – Provide opportunity for trial and error problem-solving
    - – Select teaching strategies that avoid distracting information and evoke desired response

error problem-solving, select teaching strategies that avoid distracting information and evoke desired response, praise correct behavior and positive feedback, and provide role models of desired behavior.

2. Cognitivism depicts learning as a complex cognitive activity in which learning is largely a mental or intellectual or thinking process. The learner structures and processes information. Perceptions are selectively chosen by the individual, and *personal characteristics have an impact on how a cue is perceived.*

    Cognitivists also emphasize the importance of social, emotional, and physical contexts in which learning occurs. Major cognitive theorists include Piaget, Lewin, and Bloom.

    Nurses applying cognitive theory will provide social, emotional, physical environment conducive to learning, encourage positive teaching-learning relationships, select multisensory teaching strategies, recognize personal characteristics have impact on how cues are perceived, develop appropriate approaches to target different learning styles, assess developmental and individual readiness to learn and adapt to developmental stage, and select behavioral objectives and teaching strategies that encompass cognitive, affective, and psychomotor learning.

3. Humanistic learning theory focuses on both cognitive and affective qualities of the learner. Learning is believed to be self-motivated, self-initiated, and self-evaluated. Each individual is viewed as a unique composite of biologic, psychologic, social, cultural, and spiritual factors. Learning is best when it is relevant to the learner. Autonomy and self-determination are important. The learner is an active participant who identifies learning needs and takes the initiative to meet these needs. Maslow and Rogers are prominent humanistic theorists.

    Nurses applying humanistic theory will convey empathy, encourage learner to establish goals, promote self learning, serve as facilitator, mentor or resource for learners, use active learning strategies, expose the learner to new, relevant information, ask appropriate questions, and encourage the learner to seek new answers.

    – Praise correct behavior and positive feedback
    – Provide role models of desired behavior.

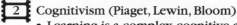 Cognitivism (Piaget, Lewin, Bloom)
- Learning is a complex cognitive activity
- Learner structures and processes information
- Perception chosen by learner
- Personal characteristics impact perceptions
- Social, emotional, and physical contexts
- Nurses using cognitive theory will:
  ○ Provide social, emotional, physical environment conducive to learning
  ○ Encourage positive teaching-learning relationships
  ○ Select multisensory teaching strategies
  ○ Recognize personal characteristics have impact on how cues are perceived
  ○ Develop appropriate approaches to target different learning styles
  ○ Assess developmental and individual readiness to learn
  ○ Adapt teaching to developmental stage
  ○ Select behavioral objectives and teaching strategies that encompass cognitive, affective and psychomotor learning.

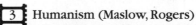 Humanism (Maslow, Rogers)
- Learning is self-motivated, self-initiated, and self-evaluated
- Focus on cognitive and affective qualities of learner
- Learning best when relevant to the learner
- Autonomy and self-determination of learner important
- Learner is an active participant and takes responsibility for meeting learning needs
- Nurses using humanistic theory will:
  ○ Convey empathy
  ○ Encourage learner to establish goals
  ○ Promote self learning
  ○ Serve as facilitator, mentor or resource for learners
  ○ Use active learning strategies
  ○ Expose the learner to new, relevant information
  ○ Ask appropriate questions
  ○ Encourage the learner to seek new answers.

---

## SUGGESTIONS FOR CLASSROOM ACTIVITIES

- Have the students provide additional examples of when each of these theories can be appropriately used in teaching clients or other health care providers.

## SUGGESTIONS FOR CLINICAL ACTIVITIES

- Discuss use of the various theories of learning as applied in the clinical setting.

---

# LEARNING OUTCOME 5

Describe the three domains of learning.

## CONCEPTS FOR LECTURE

1. Domains of learning: cognitive, affective, and psychomotor.
2. The cognitive domain, the "thinking" domain, includes six intellectual abilities and thinking processes: knowledge, comprehension, application, analysis, synthesis, and evaluation.
3. The affective domain, known as the "feeling" domain, is divided into categories that specify the degree of a "person's depth of emotional response to tasks." It includes feelings, emotions, interests, attitudes, and appreciations.
4. The psychomotor domain, the "skill" domain, includes motor skills such as giving an injection.

## POWERPOINT LECTURE SLIDES

*(NOTE: The number on each PPT Lecture Slide directly corresponds with the Concepts for Lecture.)*

**1** Three Domains of Learning
- Cognitive
- Affective
- Psychomotor

**2** Cognitive ("Thinking" Domain)
- Knowledge
- Comprehension
- Application
- Analysis
- Synthesis
- Evaluation

**3** Affective ("Feeling" Domain)
- Feelings
- Emotions
- Interests
- Attitudes
- Appreciations

**4** Psychomotor ("Skill" Domain)
- Motor skills

## SUGGESTIONS FOR CLASSROOM ACTIVITIES

- Provide the students with a list of learning topics. Have them classify these topics according to the domains of learning.
- Discuss the importance of knowing the rationale for performing psychomotor skills in nursing rather simply learning the motor skill component of these skills.

## SUGGESTIONS FOR CLINICAL ACTIVITIES

- Have the students provide examples of teaching they have performed or have observed in the clinical setting, and ask them to categorize each example into the appropriate domain.

# LEARNING OUTCOME 6

Identify factors that affect learning.

## CONCEPTS FOR LECTURE

1. Factors that can facilitate or hinder learning include motivation, readiness, active involvement, relevance, feedback, nonjudgmental support, organizing material from simple to complex, repetition, timing, environment, emotions, physiologic events, culture, and psychomotor ability.

## POWERPOINT LECTURE SLIDES

*(NOTE: The number on each PPT Lecture Slide directly corresponds with the Concepts for Lecture.)*

**1** Factors Affecting Learning
- Motivation
- Readiness
- Active involvement
- Relevance
- Feedback
- Nonjudgmental support
- Organizing material from simple to complex
- Repetition

- Timing
- Environment
- Emotions
- Physiologic events
- Culture
- Psychomotor ability

## SUGGESTIONS FOR CLASSROOM ACTIVITIES

- Have the students provide examples of how the nurse can manipulate the factors that affect learning in order to assist the client to learn.

## SUGGESTIONS FOR CLINICAL ACTIVITIES

- Have the students identify physiologic events as demonstrated by their clients that could affect the clients' readiness to learn and how the nurse may modify these situations to promote learning, if possible.

---

# LEARNING OUTCOME 7

Discuss the implications of using the Internet as a source of health information.

## CONCEPTS FOR LECTURE

1. Using the Internet to locate health information is common. Online usage for health care is growing twice as fast as any other type of online usage.
2. Certain groups of users are more likely to search the Internet for health information: women, adults younger than 65, college graduates, people with online experience, and those with broadband (high speed) access.
3. Twenty-two percent of American adults have never used the Internet. These groups are those with a high school education or less and those who are older than 65 years of age.
4. Nurses need to know and be able to integrate this technology into the teaching plans for those clients who use the Internet. On the other hand, nurses also need to apply effective teaching strategies for those clients who do not use the Internet.

## POWERPOINT LECTURE SLIDES

*(NOTE: The number on each PPT Lecture Slide directly corresponds with the Concepts for Lecture.)*

**1** The Internet and Health Information
- Online health information
  - Healthcare online usage growing twice as fast as any other online type of usage

**2** Groups Most Likely to Use the Internet for Health Information:
- Women
- Adults younger than 65
- College graduates
- People with online experience
- Those with broadband (high-speed) access

**3** Groups Less Likely to Use the Internet
- High school education of less
- 65 years of age or older

**4** Implications for Use of Internet for Client Teaching:
- Integrate into teaching plan for users of Internet
- Apply other strategies for those who do not use

## SUGGESTIONS FOR CLASSROOM ACTIVITIES

- Present the students with a framework for evaluating a health-related Internet site. Have them use this framework to evaluate a health-related Internet site of their choice.

## SUGGESTIONS FOR CLINICAL ACTIVITIES

- Have the students interview clients to determine whether the Internet is used to obtain health information and, if so, which sites are most often used. Have the students critique these sites and present their findings in a clinical conference.

# LEARNING OUTCOME 8

Assess learning needs of learners and the learning environment.

## CONCEPTS FOR LECTURE

1. A comprehensive assessment of learning needs incorporates data from the nursing history and physical assessment and addresses the client's support system. It also considers client characteristics that may influence the learning process, such as readiness to learn, motivation to learn, and reading and comprehension level. Learning needs change as the client's health status changes, so nurses must constantly reassess them.

2. Several elements in the nursing history provide clues to learning needs, including age, the client's understanding and perceptions of the health problem, health beliefs and practices, cultural factors, economic factors, learning style, and the client's support system. In the textbook, Assessment Interview: Learning Needs and Characteristics presents questions that may facilitate the assessment process.

3. The general survey part of the physical examination provides useful clues to the client's learning needs, such as mental status, energy level, and nutritional status. Other parts reveal data about the client's physical capacity to learn and to perform self-care activities. Additional areas to assess include readiness to learn, motivation, and health literacy.

## POWERPOINT LECTURE SLIDES

*(NOTE: The number on each PPT Lecture Slide directly corresponds with the Concepts for Lecture.)*

**1** Assessment of Learning Needs
- Nursing history
- Physical examination

**2** Nursing History
- Age
- Client's understanding of the health problem
- Health beliefs and practices
- Cultural factors
- Economic factors
- Learning style
- Client's support system
- Readiness to learn
- Motivation to learn
- Health literacy

**3** Physical Examination
- General survey provides useful clues, such as:
  - Mental status
  - Energy level
  - Nutritional status
- Remainder of physical exam reveals additional information, such as:
  - Visual ability
  - Hearing ability
  - Muscle coordination

## SUGGESTIONS FOR CLASSROOM ACTIVITIES

- Discuss methods to use to assess an individual's health literacy skills.
- Have the students identify methods to assess an individual's learning style.

## SUGGESTIONS FOR CLINICAL ACTIVITIES

- Have the students use the Assessment Interview presented in the text to assess the learning needs and characteristics of their assigned client.

# LEARNING OUTCOME 9

Identify nursing diagnoses, outcomes, and interventions that reflect the learning needs of clients.

## CONCEPTS FOR LECTURE

1. Nursing diagnoses for clients with learning needs can be designated in two ways: as the client's primary concern or problem, or as the etiology of a nursing diagnosis.

   One diagnostic label that is appropriate when the client's learning needs are the primary concern is *Deficient Knowledge:* the absence or deficiency of cognitive information related to a specific topic. The area of deficiency should always be included in the diagnosis.

## POWERPOINT LECTURE SLIDES

*(NOTE: The number on each PPT Lecture Slide directly corresponds with the Concepts for Lecture.)*

**1** Nursing Diagnoses Related to Learning Needs
- Primary problem or etiology for other nursing diagnoses
- NANDA diagnoses when used as the primary problem:
  - Deficient knowledge (specify)

If this diagnosis is used, one client goal must be "client will acquire knowledge about. . . ." The nurse needs to provide information that has the potential to change the client's behavior.

Another nursing diagnostic label where a learning need may be the primary concern is *Health-Seeking Behavior:* active seeking by a person in stable health of ways to alter personal health habits and/or the environment in order to move toward a higher level of health. The client may or may not have an altered response of dysfunction but may be seeking information to improve health or prevent illness.

A third nursing diagnostic label where a learning need may be the primary concern is *Noncompliance:* behavior of person and/or caregiver that fails to coincide with a health-promoting or therapeutic plan agreed upon by the person (and/or family and/or community) and health care professional. In the presence of an agreed-on, health-promoting or therapeutic plan, the person's or caregiver's behavior is fully or partially nonadherent and may lead to clinically ineffective or partially effective outcomes.

*Noncompliance* should be used with caution. In general, the diagnosis is associated with the intent to comply but situational factors make it difficult. It should not be used for a client who is unable to follow instructions or for a client who makes an informed decision to refuse or not follow the medical treatment.

2. One example of deficient knowledge as the etiology is *Risk for Infection* related to deficient knowledge (sexually transmitted diseases and their prevention). Other diagnostic labels may be *Risk for Impaired Parenting, Anxiety, Risk for Injury, Ineffective Breastfeeding, Impaired Adjustment, Ineffective Coping*, and *Ineffective Health Maintenance*.

3. Learning outcomes can be considered the same as desired outcomes for other nursing diagnoses. State the client's behavior or performance, not the nurse's behavior. Reflect an observable, measurable activity. The nurse may add conditions or modifiers as required to clarify what, where, when, or how the behavior will be performed. Include criteria specifying the time by which learning should have occurred. Learning outcomes can reflect the learner's command of simple to complex concepts. The nurse must be specific about what behaviors and knowledge (cognitive, affective, and psychomotor) clients must have to be able to positively influence their health status.

4. Interventions include choosing the content, which is determined by the learning outcome; selecting teaching strategies, which should be suited to the individual and to the material to be learned (see Table 27–3); and organizing the learning experience.

- Health-seeking behavior
- Noncompliance

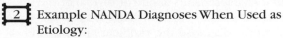 Example NANDA Diagnoses When Used as Etiology:
- Risk for impaired parenting
- Risk for injury
- Ineffective health maintenance

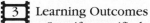 Learning Outcomes
- Specify specific knowledge or skills client must acquire
- State in terms of the client
- State in observable, measurable terms
- Add conditions or modifiers as needed
- Add criteria specifying the time for achievement

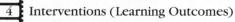 Interventions (Learning Outcomes)
- Selecting content
- Selecting teaching strategies
- Organizing learning experiences

## SUGGESTIONS FOR CLASSROOM ACTIVITIES

- Present the students with a case study in which the defining characteristics of one or several of the nursing diagnoses related to knowledge are present. Have the students diagnose the problem and provide rationale for their diagnoses.

## SUGGESTIONS FOR CLINICAL ACTIVITIES

- Have the students use the information obtained from the assessment interview of their clients' learning needs and characteristics to develop an appropriate care plan.

# LEARNING OUTCOME 10

Describe the essential aspects of a teaching plan.

## CONCEPTS FOR LECTURE

1. Essential aspects of a teaching plan include the nursing diagnosis, long- and short-term goals, learning outcomes (see Outcome # 9), content outline, and teaching and evaluation methods.

2. Content is determined by learning outcomes. Nurses can select among many sources of information. However, the content must be accurate; current; based on learning outcomes; adjusted for the learner's age, culture, and ability; consistent with the information the nurse is teaching; and selected with consideration of how much time and what resources are available.

3. Teaching strategies should be suited to the individual and to the material to be learned. Teaching strategies and methods include explanation or description (lecture), one-to-one discussion, answering questions, demonstration, discovery, group discussion, practice, printed and audiovisual materials, role-playing, and modeling. Special teaching strategies include contracting, group teaching, computer-assisted learning programs, discovery/problem solving, and behavior modification.

   The written teaching plan that the nurse uses as a resource to guide future teaching sessions might also include actual information and skills taught, teaching strategies used, time framework and content for each class, teaching outcomes, and methods of evaluation.

## POWERPOINT LECTURE SLIDES

*(NOTE: The number on each PPT Lecture Slide directly corresponds with the Concepts for Lecture.)*

**1** A Teaching Plan Should Include:
- Nursing diagnosis
- Long and short term goals
- Learning outcomes
- Content outline
- Teaching and evaluation methods

**2** Content Must Be
- Accurate
- Current
- Based on learning outcomes
- Adjusted for the learner's age, culture, and ability
- Consistent with information nurse is teaching
- Carefully selected with time and resources in mind

**3** Teaching Strategies
- Lecture
- One-to-one discussion
- Answering questions
- Demonstration
- Group discussion
- Practice
- Printed and audiovisual materials
- Role-playing
- Modeling
- Contracting
- Group teaching
- Computer-assisted learning programs
- Discovery/problem solving
- Behavior modification

## SUGGESTIONS FOR CLASSROOM ACTIVITIES

- Have each student develop a teaching plan for a health promotion topic for freshmen college students using the components listed in the textbook.

## SUGGESTIONS FOR CLINICAL ACTIVITIES

- Have the students develop and implement a teaching plan for their assigned client.

# LEARNING OUTCOME 11

Discuss guidelines for effective teaching.

## CONCEPTS FOR LECTURE

1. When a client is ready to change a health behavior and when implementing a teaching plan, the nurse may find the following guidelines helpful:
   - Rapport between teacher and learner is essential.
   - The teacher who uses the client's previous learning in the present situation encourages the client and facilitates learning new skills.
   - The optimal time for each session depends largely on the learner.
   - The nurse teacher must be able to communicate clearly and concise.
   - Using a layperson's vocabulary enhances communication.
   - The pace of each teaching session also affects learning.
   - An environment can detract from or assist learning.
   - Teaching aids can foster learning and help focus a learner's attention.
   - Teaching that involves a number of the learner's senses often enhances learning.
   - Learning is more effective when learners discover the content for themselves.
   - Repetition reinforces learning.
   - It is helpful to employ "organizers" to introduce material to be learned.
   - The anticipated behavioral changes that indicate learning has taken place must always be within the context of the client's lifestyle and resources.

## POWERPOINT LECTURE SLIDES

*(NOTE: The number on each PPT Lecture Slide directly corresponds with the Concepts for Lecture.)*

 Guidelines for Effective Teaching
- Establish rapport
- Use client's previous learning to encourage further learning
- Choose the best times for learning
- Communicate clearly and concisely
- Use a layperson's vocabulary
- Be sensitive to teaching pace (too fast or too slow)
- Choose the best environment for learning
- Use teaching aids to foster learning and focus attention
- Involve the senses
- Allow learners to discover content for themselves
- Use repetition to reinforce learning
- Employ "organizers" to introduce material
- Choose appropriate anticipated behavioral changes within the context of client's lifestyle and resources

## SUGGESTIONS FOR CLASSROOM ACTIVITIES

- Invite a panel of nurses from various types of clinical agencies to discuss how they incorporate the guidelines for effective teaching with the clients in their agencies.
- Discuss the importance of providing effective teaching within the context of early discharge from the acute care setting.

## SUGGESTIONS FOR CLINICAL ACTIVITIES

- Have the students observe a nurse providing discharge instructions to a client. Have the students identify examples of effective teaching and ineffective teaching in this situation. Ask them to suggest ways to improve the teaching, if appropriate.

# LEARNING OUTCOME 12

Discuss strategies to use when teaching clients of different cultures.

## CONCEPTS FOR LECTURE

1. Nurses should consider the following guidelines when teaching clients from various ethnic backgrounds:
   - Obtain teaching materials, pamphlets, and instructions in languages used by the client.
   - Use visual aids such as pictures, charts, or diagrams to communicate meaning.
   - Use concrete rather than abstract words.

## POWERPOINT LECTURE SLIDES

*(NOTE: The number on each PPT Lecture Slide directly corresponds with the Concepts for Lecture.)*

 Teaching Clients of Different Cultures
- Obtain teaching materials, pamphlets, and instructions in languages used by client
- Use visual aids, such as pictures, charts, or diagrams to communicate meaning

- Allow time for questions.
- Avoid the use of medical terminology or health care language.
- If understanding another's pronunciation is a problem, validate brief information in writing.
- Use humor very cautiously, and do not use slang words or colloquialisms.
- Do not assume that a client who nods, uses eye contact, or smiles is indicating an understanding of what is being taught.
- Invite and encourage questions during teaching.
- When explaining procedures or functioning related to personal areas of the body, it may be appropriate to have a nurse of the same gender do the teaching.
- Include the family in planning and teaching, consider the client's time orientation.
- Identify cultural health practices and beliefs.

- Use concrete rather than abstract words
- Allow time for questions
- Avoid the use of medical terminology or health care language
- If understanding another's pronunciation is a problem, validate brief information in writing
- Use humor very cautiously
- Do not use slang word or colloquialisms
- Do not assume that a client who nods, uses eye contact, or smiles is indicating an understanding of what is being taught
- Invite and encourage questions during teaching
- When explaining procedures or functioning related to personal areas of the body, may be appropriate to have a nurse of the same gender do the teaching
- Include family in planning and teaching
- Consider the client's time orientation
- Identify cultural health practices and beliefs

## SUGGESTIONS FOR CLASSROOM ACTIVITIES

- Invite nurses with various cultural backgrounds to discuss the implications of their culture for client teaching.

## SUGGESTIONS FOR CLINICAL ACTIVITIES

- Invite several individuals who function as interpreters in the clinical agency to discuss their role and guidelines for use of interpreters in the health care setting.
- Obtain samples of educational material developed for use by clients of different cultures.

## LEARNING OUTCOME 13

Identify methods to evaluate learning.

### CONCEPTS FOR LECTURE

1. The evaluation method is determined by measuring against the predetermined learning outcomes. The best method for evaluating depends on the type of learning. In cognitive learning, the client demonstrates acquisition of the knowledge by direct observation, written measurements, oral questioning, self-reports, or self-monitoring. The acquisition of psychomotor skill is best evaluated by observing how well the client carries out the skill. Affective learning is more difficult to evaluate. Whether attitudes or values have been learned may be inferred by listening to the client's responses to questions, noting how the client speaks about relevant subjects, and observing the client's behavior that expresses feelings and values.

### POWERPOINT LECTURE SLIDES

*(NOTE: The number on each PPT Lecture Slide directly corresponds with the Concepts for Lecture.)*

 Methods to Evaluate Learning
- Cognitive learning
  - Direct observation
  - Written measurements
  - Oral questioning
  - Self-reports or self-monitoring
- Psychomotor skill
  - Observing how well the client carries out the skill
- Affective learning
  - More difficult to evaluate
  - Inferred by the following:
    - Listening to the client's responses to questions
    - Noting how the client speaks about relevant subjects
    - Observing the client's behavior

## SUGGESTIONS FOR CLASSROOM ACTIVITIES

• Provide the students with several examples of learning goals/outcomes and related interventions. Ask them to identify appropriate methods of evaluation.

## SUGGESTIONS FOR CLINICAL ACTIVITIES

• Have the students provide examples of how they have evaluated their clients' learning. Discuss any problems encountered and how these might be overcome.

# LEARNING OUTCOME 14

Demonstrate effective documentation of teaching–learning activities.

## CONCEPTS FOR LECTURE

1. Documentation of the teaching process is essential because it provides a legal record that the teaching took place and communicates the teaching to other health professionals. If teaching is not documented, legally it did not occur.

    It is also important to document the responses of the client and support people to teaching activities.

    The parts of the teaching process that should be documented in the client's chart include diagnosed learning needs, learning outcomes, topics taught, client outcomes, need for additional teaching, and resources provided.

## POWERPOINT LECTURE SLIDES

*(NOTE: The number on each PPT Lecture Slide directly corresponds with the Concepts for Lecture.)*

 Documentation

• Provides a legal record that the teaching took place
• Communicates teaching to other health professionals
• Document responses of the client and support people to teaching activities
• Parts of the teaching process that should be documented included the following:
  ○ Diagnosed learning needs
  ○ Learning outcomes
  ○ Topics taught
  ○ Client outcomes
  ○ Need for additional teaching
  ○ Resources provided

## SUGGESTIONS FOR CLASSROOM ACTIVITIES

• Obtain examples from various institutions of chart forms used to document teaching, and share these with the class.

## SUGGESTIONS FOR CLINICAL ACTIVITIES

• Show the students how teaching is documented in the clinical agency. Compare to the guidelines presented in the textbook.

# CHAPTER 28
## LEADING, MANAGING, AND DELEGATING

## RESOURCE LIBRARY

###  PRENTICE HALL NURSING MEDIALINK DVD-ROM

Audio Glossary
NCLEX® Review
End of Unit Concept Map Activity
Videos and Animations:
 *Building and Managing Teams*
 *Delegating Successfully*
 *Handling Conflict*
 *Initiating and Managing Change*
 *Introduction to Nursing Management*
 *Leading and Managing*
 *Managing Stress and Time*
 *Motivating and Developing Staff*

### 📖 IMAGE LIBRARY

**Figure 28.1** Nurses as leaders and managers.

### COMPANION WEBSITE

Additional NCLEX® Review
Case Study: *Nurse as Manager and Delegator*
Application Activity: *Nursing World*
Links to Resources

**Figure 28.2** Delegation decision-making grid.

---

## LEARNING OUTCOME 1

Compare and contrast leadership and management.

### CONCEPTS FOR LECTURE

1. Leaders may or may not be officially appointed to the position. They have power and authority to enforce decisions only as long as followers are willing to be led. Leaders influence others toward goal setting, either formally or informally. They are interested in risk taking and exploring new ideas. Leaders relate to people personally in an intuitive and empathetic manner, feel rewarded by personal achievements, and may or may not be successful managers. Leaders manage relationships and focus on people.

2. Managers are appointed officially to the position. They have power and authority to enforce decisions and to carry out predetermined policies, rules, and regulations. Managers maintain an orderly, controlled, rational, and equitable work environment. They relate to people according to their roles. Managers feel rewarded when fulfilling organizational missions or goals. They are managers as long as the appointment holds. They manage resources and focus on systems.

### POWERPOINT LECTURE SLIDES

*(NOTE: The number on each PPT Lecture Slide directly corresponds with the Concepts for Lecture.)*

**1** Leaders
- May or may not be officially appointed to the position
- Have power and authority to enforce decisions only as long as followers are willing to be led
- Influence others toward goal setting, either formally or informally
- Are interested in risk taking and exploring new ideas
- Relate to people personally in an intuitive and empathetic manner
- Feel rewarded by personal achievements
- May or may not be successful managers
- Manage relationships
- Focus on people

**2** Managers
- Appointed officially to the position
- Have power and authority to enforce decisions
- Carry out predetermined policies, rules, and regulations
- Maintain an orderly, controlled, rational, and equitable structure

- Relate to people according to their roles
- Feel rewarded when fulfilling organizational mission or goals
- Are managers as long as the appointment holds
- Manage resources
- Focus on system

---

**SUGGESTIONS FOR CLASSROOM ACTIVITIES**

- Have the students provide examples of individuals who are leaders, those who are managers, and those who are both leaders and managers. Have the students provide rationales for their responses.

**SUGGESTIONS FOR CLINICAL ACTIVITIES**

- Have the students identify leaders and managers on the clinical unit.

---

# LEARNING OUTCOME 2

Differentiate formal from informal leaders.

## CONCEPTS FOR LECTURE

1. The formal leader, or appointed leader, is selected by an organization and given official authority to make decisions and act.
2. An informal leader is not officially appointed to direct the activities of others, but because of seniority, age, or special abilities, is recognized by the group as its leader and plays an important role in influencing colleagues, co-workers, or other group members to achieve the group's goals.

## POWERPOINT LECTURE SLIDES

*(NOTE: The number on each PPT Lecture Slide directly corresponds with the Concepts for Lecture.)*

**1** Formal Leader
- Appointed leader
- Selected by an organization
- Given official authority to make decisions and act

**2** Informal Leader
- Not officially appointed
- Recognized by the group as its leader because of seniority, age, or special abilities
- Plays an important role in influencing group members to achieve the group's goals

---

**SUGGESTIONS FOR CLASSROOM ACTIVITIES**

- From their own experience with groups, have students provide examples of abilities of individuals who were the informal group leader and why these abilities were important to the group.

**SUGGESTIONS FOR CLINICAL ACTIVITIES**

- Have the students provide examples from the clinical setting of individuals who they believe are informal leaders. They should provide a rationale for their response.

---

# LEARNING OUTCOME 3

Compare and contrast different leadership styles.

## CONCEPTS FOR LECTURE

1. The classic leadership theories describe the following leadership styles: autocratic (authoritarian), democratic (participative, consultative), laissez-faire (nondirective, permissive), bureaucratic, and situational. Contemporary leadership theories describe the following leadership styles: charismatic, transactional, transformational, and shared.

## POWERPOINT LECTURE SLIDES

*(NOTE: The number on each PPT Lecture Slide directly corresponds with the Concepts for Lecture.)*

**1** Classic Leadership Styles
- Autocratic
  - Authoritarian

---

An autocratic leader makes decisions for the group, believes individuals are externally motivated and are incapable of independent decision making, determines policies, and gives orders and directions to the group. At times, the autocratic style is the most effective. When urgent decisions are necessary, one person must assume responsibility for making decisions without being challenged. When group members are unable to make or do not wish to participate in making a decision, the autocratic style solves the problem and enables the group to move on. It can also be effective when a project must be completed quickly and efficiently.

A democratic (participative, consultative) leader encourages group discussion and decision making; acts as a catalyst or facilitator, actively guiding the group toward achieving the group goals; and assumes individuals are internally motivated, are capable of making decisions, and value independence. The participative leader provides constructive feedback, offers information, makes suggestions, asks questions, and has faith in the group members to accomplish goals. This leadership style has been shown to be less efficient and more cumbersome than autocratic. It allows for more self-motivation and creativity among group members; it also calls for a great deal of cooperation and coordination among group members.

The laissez-faire (nondirective, permissive) leader recognizes the group's need for autonomy and self-regulation, assumes a "hands off" approach, and presupposes the group is internally motivated. However, group members may act independently and at cross purposes because of a lack of cooperation and coordination. Laissez-faire leadership is most effective for groups whose members have both personal and professional maturity so that once a decision is made the members become committed to it and have the required expertise to implement it. Individual members then perform tasks in their area of expertise while the leader acts as a resource person.

The bureaucratic leader does not trust self or others to make decisions and instead relies on the organization's rules, policies, and procedures to direct the group's work efforts. Group members are usually dissatisfied with the leader's inflexibility and impersonal relations with them.

The situational leader flexes the task and relationship behaviors, considers the staff members' abilities, knows the nature of the task to be done, and is sensitive to the context or environment in which the task takes place. The task-orientation focuses the leader on activities that encourage the group to get a task done.

2. A charismatic leader is rare and is characterized by an emotional relationship between the leader and the group members. The followers of a charismatic leader often overcome extreme hardship to achieve the group's goal because of faith in the leader.

- Democratic
  - Participative
  - Consultative
- Laissez-faire
  - Nondirective
  - Permissive
- Bureaucratic
  - Follows organization's rules, policies, procedures
- Situational
  - Task-orientation

 Contemporary Leadership Styles
- Charismatic
  - Emotional relationship
- Transactional
  - Relationship based on exchange of resource valued by followers
- Transformational
  - Empowers the group to share organization's vision
- Shared
  - Emerge in relationship to need of work to be done

The transactional leader has a relationship with followers based on an exchange for some resource valued by the followers. These incentives are used to promote loyalty and performance. The transactional leader represents the traditional manager, focused on the daily tasks or achieving organizational goals, while understanding and meeting the needs of the group.

The transformational leader fosters creativity, risk taking, commitment, and collaboration by empowering the group to share in the organization's vision. This type of leader inspires others with a clear, attractive, and attainable goal and enlists them to participate in attaining the goals. Independence, individual growth, and change are facilitated.

Shared leadership recognizes that a professional workforce is made up of many leaders. No one person is considered to have knowledge or ability beyond that of other members. Appropriate leadership is thought to emerge in relation to the challenges that confront the work group. Shared governance is a method that aims to distribute decision making among a group of people.

---

**SUGGESTIONS FOR CLASSROOM ACTIVITIES**

- Divide the class into small groups, each representing one of the leadership styles described in the text. Give the groups a situation that requires a decision to be made. Have each group role-play how a leader of its assigned style would handle the situation. Discuss the effectiveness of the resulting processes in arriving at a decision.

**SUGGESTIONS FOR CLINICAL ACTIVITIES**

- Invite a group of nurse leaders/managers to discuss their leadership styles.

---

# LEARNING OUTCOME 4

Identify characteristics of an effective leader.

**CONCEPTS FOR LECTURE**

1. Effective leaders
   - use a leadership style that is natural to them.
   - use a leadership style appropriate to the task and the members.
   - assess the effects of their behavior on others and the effects of others' behavior on themselves.
   - are sensitive to forces acting for and against change, express an optimistic view about human nature, and are energetic.
   - are open and encourage openness, so that real issues are confronted.
   - facilitate personal relationships.
   - plan and organize activities of the group.
   - are consistent in behavior toward group members.

**POWERPOINT LECTURE SLIDES**

*(NOTE: The number on each PPT Lecture Slide directly corresponds with the Concepts for Lecture.)*

 Characteristics of an Effective Leader
- Natural and appropriate leadership style
- Able to assess effects of behaviors
- Sensitive to forces acting for and against change
- Optimistic view about human nature
- Energetic
- Open and encourage openness
- Facilitate personal relationships
- Plan and organize activities of the group
- Consistent in behavior
- Delegate tasks and responsibilities, not merely to get tasks performed

## CONCEPTS FOR LECTURE *continued*

- delegate tasks and responsibilities to develop members' abilities (not merely to get tasks performed).
- involve members in all decisions.
- value and use group members' contributions.
- encourage creativity.
- encourage feedback about their leadership style.
- assess for and promote use of current technology.

## POWERPOINT LECTURE SLIDES *continued*

- Involve members in all decisions
- Value and use group members' contributions
- Encourage creativity
- Encourage feedback about their leadership style
- Assess for and promote use of current technology

## SUGGESTIONS FOR CLASSROOM ACTIVITIES

- Have the students provide suggestions for how a leader can demonstrate openness and encourage openness in group members, encourage creativity, and demonstrate an optimistic view about human nature.

## SUGGESTIONS FOR CLINICAL ACTIVITIES

- Have the students identify the characteristics of an effective clinical leader or manager.

## LEARNING OUTCOME 5

Compare and contrast the levels of management.

### CONCEPTS FOR LECTURE

1. Traditional management is divided into three levels of responsibility: first-level, middle-level, and upper-level management.
2. First-level managers are responsible for managing the work of nonmanagerial personnel and the day-to-day activities of specific work groups. Their primary responsibility is to motivate staff to achieve the organization's goals. They communicate staff issues to upper administration and report administrative messages back to staff.
3. Middle-level managers supervise a number of first-level managers and are responsible for the activities in the departments they supervise. They serve as liaisons between first-level and upper-level managers.
4. Upper-level (top-level) managers are organizational executives who are primarily responsible for establishing goals and developing strategic plans. Nurse executives are registered nurses who are responsible for the management of nursing within the organization and the practice of nursing.

### POWERPOINT LECTURE SLIDES

*(NOTE: The number on each PPT Lecture Slide directly corresponds with the Concepts for Lecture.)*

**1** Levels of Management
- First level
- Middle level
- Upper level

**2** First Level
- Manage nonmanagerial personnel
- Motivate staff to achieve organizational goals
- Communicate staff issues to upper administration and administrators messages to staff

**3** Middle Level
- Manage first-level managers
- Responsible for activities of departments supervised

**4** Upper Level
- Establish goals and develop strategic plans
- Responsible for management of nursing and practice of nursing

## SUGGESTIONS FOR CLASSROOM ACTIVITIES

- Invite a panel of nurses who function at different levels of management to discuss their positions and responsibilities with the class.

## SUGGESTIONS FOR CLINICAL ACTIVITIES

- Invite the nurse manager from the clinical setting to discuss his or her functions within the institution as well as the responsibilities of his or her supervisor and those who report to the manager.

# LEARNING OUTCOME 6

Describe the four functions of management.

## CONCEPTS FOR LECTURE

1. The four management functions are planning, organizing, directing, and coordinating. These functions help to achieve the broad goal of quality client care.
2. Planning is an ongoing process that involves assessing a situation; establishing goals and objectives based on assessment of a situation or future trends; and developing a plan of action that identifies priorities, delineates who is responsible, determines deadlines, and describes how the intended outcome is to be achieved and evaluated.
3. Organizing is also an ongoing process. After identifying the work and evaluating human and material resources, the manager arranges the work into smaller units. This involves determining responsibilities, communicating expectations, and establishing the chain of command for authority and communication.
4. Directing is the process of getting the organization's work accomplished. It involves assigning and communicating expectations about the task to be completed, providing instruction and guidance, and making ongoing decisions.
5. Coordinating is the process of ensuring that plans are carried out, evaluating outcomes, measuring results or actions against standards or desired outcomes, and then reinforcing effective actions or changing ineffective ones.

## POWERPOINT LECTURE SLIDES

*(NOTE: The number on each PPT Lecture Slide directly corresponds with the Concepts for Lecture.)*

**1** Four Functions of Management
- Planning
- Organizing
- Directing
- Coordinating

**2** Planning
- Assessing a situation
- Establishing goals and objectives
- Developing a plan of action
- Delineating who is responsible
- Determining deadlines
- Describing how outcomes are achieved and evaluated

**3** Organizing
- Determining responsibilities
- Communicating expectations
- Establishing chain of command

**4** Directing
- Assigning and communicating expectations
- Providing instruction/guidance
- Ongoing decision making

**5** Coordinating
- Ensuring plans are carried out
- Evaluating outcomes
- Measuring results or actions against standards or outcomes
- Reinforcing effective actions or changing ineffective ones

## SUGGESTIONS FOR CLASSROOM ACTIVITIES

- Invite a panel of nurse managers from different settings (community, acute care, long-term care) to discuss the functions of managers in their setting.

## SUGGESTIONS FOR CLINICAL ACTIVITIES

- Assign students to observe the functioning of nurse managers within the institution. Have them keep track of the types of activities the managers perform during the observation period. Have students classify the activities into the functions of managers and share this with the group in a clinical conference.

# LEARNING OUTCOME 7

Discuss the roles and functions of nurse managers.

## CONCEPTS FOR LECTURE

1. The nurse manager reasons with logic, exploring assumptions, alternatives, and the consequences of actions. Managers use both verbal and written communication. Effective managers communicate assertively,

## POWERPOINT LECTURE SLIDES

*(NOTE: The number on each PPT Lecture Slide directly corresponds with the Concepts for Lecture.)*

**1** The Nurse Manager:
- Reasons with logic

expressing their ideas clearly, accurately, and honestly. One of the greatest responsibilities of managers is their accountability for human, fiscal, and material resources. Budgeting and determining variances between the actual and budgeted expenses are crucial skills for any manager. Managers are responsible for ensuring that employees develop through appropriate learning opportunities. In addition to personnel development, the manager is responsible for building and managing the work team. Nurse managers are often in a position to manage conflict among people, groups, or teams. The effective nurse manager uses time effectively and assists others to do the same.

- Communicates assertively
- Assumes accountability for human, fiscal, and material resources
- Develops employees through appropriate learning opportunities
- Is responsible for building and managing the work team
- Manages conflict among people, groups, or teams
- Uses time effectively and assists others to do the same

### SUGGESTIONS FOR CLASSROOM ACTIVITIES

- Discuss the difference between a mentor and a preceptor.

### SUGGESTIONS FOR CLINICAL ACTIVITIES

- Have student interview staff nurses to determine how the nurse manager enacts the roles and functions of manager as described in the text.

## LEARNING OUTCOME 8

Identify the skills and competencies needed by a nurse manager.

### CONCEPTS FOR LECTURE

1. To be effective managers, nurses need to be able to think critically, communicate well, manage resources effectively and efficiently, enhance employee performance, build and manage teams, manage conflict, manage time, and initiate and manage change.

### POWERPOINT LECTURE SLIDES

*(NOTE: The number on each PPT Lecture Slide directly corresponds with the Concepts for Lecture.)*

 Skills and Competencies of a Nurse Manager
- Critical thinking
- Communicating
- Managing resources
- Enhancing employee performance
- Building and managing teams
- Managing conflict
- Managing time

### SUGGESTIONS FOR CLASSROOM ACTIVITIES

- Discuss the importance of resource management in the current health care environment.
- Discuss conflict management.

### SUGGESTIONS FOR CLINICAL ACTIVITIES

- Invite the nurse manager of the clinical setting to discuss management of resources on the unit.

## LEARNING OUTCOME 9

Describe the characteristics of tasks appropriate to delegate to unlicensed and licensed assistive personnel.

### CONCEPTS FOR LECTURE

1. Principles used by the nurse to determine delegation to unlicensed assistive personnel (UAP) include:
   - The nurse must assess the client prior to delegating tasks.

### POWERPOINT LECTURE SLIDES

*(NOTE: The number on each PPT Lecture Slide directly corresponds with the Concepts for Lecture.)*

 Principles of Delegating to Unlicensed Assistive Personnel
- Assess the client

- The client must be medically stable or in a chronic condition and not fragile.
- The task must be considered routine for this client and must not require a substantial amount of scientific knowledge or technical skills.
- The task must be considered safe for this client and must have a predictable outcome.
- The nurse must learn the agency's procedure and policies for delegation.
- The nurse must know the scope of practice and the customary knowledge, skills, and job description for each health care discipline represented on the team.
- The nurse must be aware of individual variations in work abilities and experiences.
- When unsure about an assistant's abilities to perform a task, observe while the person performs it or demonstrate before allowing the person to perform the task independently.
- The nurse must clarify reporting expectations.
- The nurse must create an atmosphere that fosters communication, teaching, and learning (see Box 28–3).

Examples of tasks that may be delegated include: taking vital signs, measuring and recording intake and output, assisting with client transfer and ambulation, bathing, feeding, gastrostomy feeding (if established), attending to safety, weighing, performing simple dressing changes, suctioning chronic tracheostomies, and performing CPR.

Examples of tasks that may not be delegated include assessment, interpretation of data, making nursing diagnoses, creation of the nursing care plan, evaluation of care, care of invasive lines, administration of parenteral medications, insertion of nasogastric tubes, client education, performing triage, and giving telephone advice.

- Client must be medically stable or in a chronic condition and not fragile
- Task routine for this client
- Not require a substantial amount of scientific knowledge or technical skills
- Considered safe for this client
- Have a predictable outcome
- Follow agency's procedure and policies for delegation
- Know UAP's scope of practice
- Know customary knowledge, skills, and job description for UAP
- Know work abilities and experiences of UAP
- Observe performance or demonstrate task when unsure about abilities
- Clarify reporting expectations
- Create an atmosphere that fosters communication, teaching, and learning

## SUGGESTIONS FOR CLASSROOM ACTIVITIES

- Provide the students with a list of clients and relevant information about the clients. Provide a list of unlicensed assistive personnel with relevant characteristics as listed in the delegation decision-making grid (see Figure 28.2 in the textbook) and a list of tasks to be completed for the client in the case study. Have the students decide which task can be delegated to which UAP. Discuss results.

## SUGGESTIONS FOR CLINICAL ACTIVITIES

- Have the students identify tasks that are usually delegated to unlicensed assistive personnel in the clinical setting. Have them discuss client situations in which these tasks should not be assigned to UAP or, if delegated, what additional nursing action should be taken to ensure that the task is safely performed.

# LEARNING OUTCOME 10

List the five rights of delegation.

## CONCEPTS FOR LECTURE

1. The National Council of State Boards of Nursing (NCSBN) published the five "rights" of delegation: right task, under the right circumstances, to the right person, with the right directions and communication, and the right supervision and evaluation.

## POWERPOINT LECTURE SLIDES

*(NOTE: The number on each PPT Lecture Slide directly corresponds with the Concepts for Lecture.)*

 Five Rights of Delegation
- Right task
- Right circumstances
- Right person
- Right directions and communication
- Right supervision and evaluation

## SUGGESTIONS FOR CLASSROOM ACTIVITIES

- Provide students with a list of tasks that are often delegated to unlicensed assistive personnel. Have the students identify the type of directions, communication, supervision, and evaluation that should accompany these tasks.

## SUGGESTIONS FOR CLINICAL ACTIVITIES

- Have the students describe how the five rights of delegation are enacted on the clinical unit.

# LEARNING OUTCOME 11

Describe the role of the leader/manager in planning for and implementing change.

## CONCEPTS FOR LECTURE

1. The leader/manager is often the change agent. The change agent is the person who initiates, motivates, and implements change. An important aspect of planning change is establishing the likelihood of the acceptance for the change and then determining the criteria by which that acceptance can be identified. The leader/manager can make change easier by involving people in the process. To facilitate acceptance of the change, the leader/manager needs to identify common driving and restraining forces.

## POWERPOINT LECTURE SLIDES

*(NOTE: The number on each PPT Lecture Slide directly corresponds with the Concepts for Lecture.)*

 The Leader/Manager and Implementing Change
- Leader/manager often becomes the change agent
- Establish likelihood of acceptance
- Determine criteria
- Involve people in the process
- Facilitate acceptance

## SUGGESTIONS FOR CLASSROOM ACTIVITIES

- Have students identify a change they would like to occur in the academic setting. Ask students to identify common driving and restraining forces related to this change. Using the guidelines for dealing with resistance to change, have the students develop a plan for instituting this change.

## SUGGESTIONS FOR CLINICAL ACTIVITIES

- Identify a recent change made in the clinical setting. Ask key individuals involved in the change to describe the process used in making this change.

# CHAPTER 29
## VITAL SIGNS

## RESOURCE LIBRARY

 **PRENTICE HALL NURSING MEDIALINK DVD-ROM**

Audio Glossary
NCLEX® Review
Skills Checklists:
   *Assessing a Peripheral Pulse*
   *Assessing an Apical-Radial Pulse*
   *Assessing an Apical Pulse*
   *Assessing Blood Pressure*
   *Assessing Body Temperature*
   *Assessing Respirations*
   *Measuring Oxygen Saturation*

**COMPANION WEBSITE**

Additional NCLEX® Review
Case Study: *Assessing Vital Signs*
Care Plan Activity: *Client with Pneumonia*
Application Activity: *Joanna Briggs Institute*
Links to Resources

### 📖 IMAGE LIBRARY

**Figure 29.2** As long as heat production and heat loss are properly balanced, body temperature remains constant.

**Figure 29.3** Range of oral temperatures during 24 hours for a healthy young adult.

**Figure 29.4** Terms used to describe alterations in body temperature (oral measurements) and ranges in Celsius (centigrade) and Fahrenheit scales.

**Figure 29.5** An electronic thermometer. Note the probe and probe cover.

**Figure 29.6** A chemical thermometer showing a reading of 99.2°F.

**Figure 29.7** A temperature-sensitive skin tape.

**Figure 29.8** An infrared (tympanic) thermometer used to measure the tympanic membrane temperature.

**Figure 29.9** A temporal artery thermometer.

**Figure 29.10** Axillary thermometer placement.

**Figure 29.11** Pull the pinna of the ear back and up for placement of a tympanic thermometer in a child over 3 years of age, back and down for children under age 3.

**Figure 29.12** Nine sites for assessing pulse.

**Figure 29.13** Location of the apical pulse for a child under 4 years, a child 4 to 6 years, and an adult.

**Figure 29.14** A Doppler ultrasound stethoscope (DUS).

**Figure 29.15** Respiratory inhalation.

**Figure 29.16** Respiratory exhalation.

**Figure 29.17** A, A blood pressure cuff and bulb; B, the bladder inside the cuff.

**Figure 29.18** An aneroid sphygmomanometer and cuff.

**Figure 29.19** Blood pressure monitors register systolic and diastolic blood pressures and often other vital signs.

**Figure 29.20** Three standard cuff sizes: a small cuff for an infant, small child, or frail adult; a normal adult-size cuff; and a large cuff for measuring the blood pressure on the leg or on the arm of an obese adult.

**Figure 29.21** Determining that the bladder of a blood pressure cuff is 40% of the arm circumference or 20% wider than the diameter of the midpoint of the limb.

**Figure 29.22** Korotkoff's sounds can be differentiated into five phases. In the illustration the blood pressure is 138/90 or 138/102/90.

**Figure 29.23** Pediatric blood pressure cuffs (with manometers).

**Figure 29.24** Fingertip oximeter sensor (adult).

**Figure 29.25** Fingertip oximeter sensor (cordless).

**Figure 29.26** Fingertip oximeter sensor (child).

**Figure 29.27** Vital signs monitor.

**Skill 29.1** Assessing Body Temperature

**Skill 29.2** Assessing a Peripheral Pulse

**Skill 29.3** Assessing an Apical Pulse

**Skill 29.4** Assessing an Apical-Radial Pulse

**Skill 29.5** Assessing Respirations

**Skill 29.6** Assessing Blood Pressure

**Skill 29.7** Measuring Oxygen Saturation

# LEARNING OUTCOME 1

Describe factors that affect the vital signs and accurate measurement of them.

## CONCEPTS FOR LECTURE

1. The vital signs are body temperature, pulse, respirations, and blood pressure.
2. Vital signs monitor functions of the body and reflect changes that might not be observed. Assessing vital signs should not be an automatic or routine procedure; this should be a thoughtful, scientific assessment.
3. Factors affecting body temperature include:
   - Age affects body temperature, pulse, respirations, and blood pressure and is discussed in outcome # 2.
   - Diurnal variations: (circadian rhythms) refer to body temperature changes throughout the day, which can vary as much as 1.0°C (1.8°F) between early morning and late afternoon. The point of highest temperature is usually reached between 4 PM and 6 PM, and the lowest is reached during sleep between 4 PM and 6 PM.
   - Exercise: Hard work or strenuous exercise can increase body temperature.
   - Hormones: Women usually experience more hormone fluctuations than men. Progesterone secretion at the time of ovulation raises body temperature by about 0.3°C to 0.6°C (0.5°F to 1.0°F) above basal temperature.
   - Environment: Extremes in environmental temperature can affect a person's temperature regulatory system. If the temperature is very warm and the body temperature cannot be modified by convection, conduction, or radiation, the person's body temperature will increase. Similarly, if the client has been outside in cold weather without suitable clothing or if there is a medical condition preventing the client from controlling the temperature in the environment, the person's body temperature will be low.
   - Pyrexia: is a body temperature above the usual range. Hyperthermia is a fever, and a very high fever (41°C or 105.8°F) is called hyperpyrexia. During a fever and the resolution of a fever, the person goes through several phases as the core body temperature reaches the new set point (chill, plateau, and flush or crisis phases).
   - Hypothermia: is a core body temperature below the lower limit of normal due to excessive heat loss, inadequate heat production to counteract heat loss, and impaired hypothalamic thermoregulation.
4. Factors affecting the pulse include:
   - Gender: After puberty, the average male's pulse rate is slightly lower than the female's.
   - Exercise: The pulse rate normally increases with exercise. The rate of increase in the professional athlete is often less than the average person because of greater cardiac size, strength, and efficiency.

## POWERPOINT LECTURE SLIDES

*(NOTE: The number on each PPT Lecture Slide directly corresponds with the Concepts for Lecture.)*

**1** Vital Signs
- Monitor functions of the body
- Should be a thoughtful, scientific assessment

**2** Factors Affecting Body Temperature
- Age
- Diurnal variations (circadian rhythms)
- Exercise
- Hormones
- Stress
- Environment

**3** Factors Affecting Pulse
- Age
- Gender
- Exercise
- Fever
- Medications
- Hypovolemia
- Stress
- Position changes
- Pathology

**4** Factors Affecting Respirations
- Exercise
- Stress
- Environmental temperature
- Medications

**5** Factors Affecting Blood Pressure
- Age
- Exercise
- Stress
- Race
- Gender
- Medications
- Obesity
- Diurnal variations
- Disease process

**6** Factors Affecting Depth of Respiration
- Body position
- Medications

**7** Factors Affecting Blood Pressure
- Exercise
- Stress
- Race
- Gender
- Medications
- Obesity
- Diurnal variations
- Disease process

- Fever: affects the pulse because the pulse rate increases in response to the lower blood pressure that results from peripheral vasodilatation associated with elevated body temperature and because of the increased metabolic rate.
- Medications: Some medications decrease the pulse; others increase the pulse.
- Hypovolemia: Loss of blood from the vascular system normally increases the pulse rate.
- Stress: affects pulse because the sympathetic nervous stimulation increases the overall activity of the heart. In addition, the rate and force of the heartbeat increases. Fear, anxiety, and the perception of severe pain stimulate the sympathetic nervous system.
- Position change: When a person is sitting or standing, the blood usually pools in dependent vessels. Pooling results in a transient decrease in the venous blood return to the heart and a subsequent reduction in blood pressure and an increase in heart rate.
- Pathology: Certain diseases such as some heart conditions or those that impair oxygenation can alter the resting pulse rate.

5. Several factors influence respiratory rate:
   - Factors that increase the rate include exercise (increases metabolism), stress (readies the body for "flight or fight"), increased environmental temperature, and lowered oxygen concentration at increased altitudes.
   - Factors that decrease the rate include decreased environmental temperature, certain medications (e.g., narcotics), and increased intracranial pressure.

6. Two of the factors that affect depth of respirations include:
   - Body position: The depth is suppressed due to an increase in the volume of blood inside the thoracic cavity and the compression of the chest.
   - Medications: Certain medications can depress the respiratory center in the brain, thereby depressing the respiratory rate and depth.

7. Factors affecting blood pressure include:
   - Exercise: increases the cardiac output and hence the blood pressure.
   - Stress: affects blood pressure because stimulation of the sympathetic nervous system increases cardiac output and vasoconstriction of the arterioles, thus increasing the blood pressure reading. However, severe pain can decrease blood pressure greatly inhibiting the vasomotor center and producing vasodilatation.
   - Race: African American males over 35 years have higher blood pressures than European males of the same age.
   - Gender: After puberty, females usually have lower blood pressures than males of the same age. After menopause, women generally have higher blood pressures than before.

- Medications: Various medications may either increase or decrease blood pressure.
- Obesity: predisposes to hypertension in both children and adults.
- Diurnal variations: have an effect on blood pressure, which is usually lowest early in the morning when the metabolic rate is lowest. It rises throughout the day and peaks in the late afternoon or early evening.
- Disease process: Any disease process affecting the cardiac output, blood volume, blood viscosity, and/or compliance of the arteries has a direct effect on the blood pressure.

## SUGGESTIONS FOR CLASSROOM ACTIVITIES

- Have the students monitor their own body temperatures in the morning on arising, in the late afternoon, and between 2 AM and 4 AM and report findings.
- Have several students run up and down a flight of stairs after obtaining baseline radial, apical, temperature, and blood pressures on these students. Have other students obtain radial, apical, body temperature, and blood pressures on these students and compare to baseline values.

## SUGGESTIONS FOR CLINICAL ACTIVITIES

- Have the students obtain vital signs on their assigned clients and compare and contrast findings based on the factors that may affect vital signs.

## LEARNING OUTCOME 2

Identify the variations in normal body temperature, pulse, respirations, and blood pressure that occur from infancy to old age.

### CONCEPTS FOR LECTURE

1. The body temperature of an infant is greatly influenced by the temperature of the environment. Children's temperatures continue to be more variable than those of adults until puberty. Many older people, particularly those over 75 years, are at risk of hypothermia for a variety of reasons such as inadequate diet, loss of subcutaneous fat, lack of activity, and decreased thermoregulatory efficiency.

2. As age increases, the pulse gradually decreases overall. Table 29-2 lists variations in pulse and respiration by age.

3. The respiratory rhythm of an infant may be less regular than an adult's. Some newborns display "periodic breathing" pausing for a few seconds between respirations.

4. Newborns have a mean systolic pressure of about 75 mm Hg. The pressure rises with age, reaching a peak at the onset of puberty, and then tends to decline somewhat. In elders, elasticity of the arteries is decreased, which produces an elevated systolic pressure, and the diastolic pressure may also be high.

### POWERPOINT LECTURE SLIDES

*(NOTE: The number on each PPT Lecture Slide directly corresponds with the Concepts for Lecture.)*

**1** Temperature
- Infants—unstable; newborns must be kept warm to prevent hypothermia
- Children—tympanic or temporal artery sites preferred
- Elders—tends to be lower than that of middle-aged adults

**2** Pulse
- Infants—newborns may have heart murmurs that are not pathological
- Children—the apex of the heart is normally located in the fourth intercostal space in young children; fifth intercostal space in children 7 years old and older
- Elders—often have decreased peripheral circulation

**3** Respirations
- Infants—some newborns display "periodic breathing"

- Children—diaphragmatic breathers
- Elders—anatomic and physiologic changes cause respiratory system to be less efficient

 Blood Pressure
- Infants—arm and thigh pressures are equivalent under 1 year of age
- Children—thigh pressure is 10 mm Hg higher than arm
- Elders—client's medication may affect how pressure is taken

## SUGGESTIONS FOR CLASSROOM ACTIVITIES

- Discuss the standards for blood pressure in infants and children.
- Provide students with clinical situations, e.g. a crying infant and have students decide the order in which to obtain the vital signs providing rationales for the order.

## SUGGESTIONS FOR CLINICAL ACTIVITIES

- Have students obtain vital signs on assigned clients comparing findings based upon age. Have students compare findings to standards for the age group.

# LEARNING OUTCOME 3

Compare methods of measuring body temperature.

## CONCEPTS FOR LECTURE

1. Body temperature may be measured using the oral, rectal, axillary, tympanic membrane, and skin/temporal artery sites.

    The oral site is accessible and convenient; however, the thermometer can break if bitten, can be inaccurate if the client has just ingested hot or cold food and fluid or smoked, and could injure the mouth following oral surgery.

    The rectal site is reliable; however, it is inconvenient and more unpleasant for clients, difficult for clients who cannot turn to the side, and could injure the rectum following rectal surgery. The presence of stool may interfere with thermometer placement. If the stool is soft, the thermometer may be embedded in stool rather than against the wall of the rectum. The site is contraindicated for clients who have diarrhea, diseases or surgery of the rectum, hemorrhoids, and clotting disorders. Some authorities recommend avoiding this route for the client who has had a myocardial infarction believing that inserting the rectal thermometer may cause vagal stimulation leading to arrhythmias.

    The axillary site is safe and noninvasive; however, the thermometer must be left in place a long time to obtain an accurate reading. This is the preferred site for assessing temperature in newborns; however, it may be inaccurate when assessing fevers.

    The tympanic membrane measurement is readily accessible, reflects the core temperature, and is very fast. However, it can be uncomfortable and involves risk of injuring the membrane if the probe is inserted too far. Repeated measurements may vary, right and left measurements can differ, and presence of cerumen can affect the reading.

## POWERPOINT LECTURE SLIDES

*(NOTE: The number on each PPT Lecture Slide directly corresponds with the Concepts for Lecture.)*

1 Sites for Measuring Body Temperature
- Oral
- Rectal
- Axillary
- Tympanic membrane
- Skin/temporal artery

2 Types of Thermometers
- Electronic
- Chemical disposable
- Infrared (tympanic)
- Scanning infrared (temporal artery)
- Temperature-sensitive tape
- Glass mercury

Temporal artery measurement is safe, noninvasive, and very fast; however, it requires electronic equipment that may be expensive or unavailable. Variation in technique is needed if the client has perspiration on the forehead. Body temperature may also be measured on the forehead with chemical thermometers.

2. Body temperature may be measured using electronic, chemical disposable, infrared (tympanic), scanning infrared (temporal artery) thermometers or temperature-sensitive tape. The traditional glass mercury thermometer is rarely encountered in health care facilities since mercury is toxic to humans.

## SUGGESTIONS FOR CLASSROOM ACTIVITIES

- Have several students drink ice water and others drink a hot beverage after obtaining baseline oral temperature readings. Compare the results.
- Have students locate research studies comparing various methods of obtaining body temperature. Discuss findings.

## SUGGESTIONS FOR CLINICAL ACTIVITIES

- Investigate the equipment available to obtain temperature readings on the clinical unit. Have the students read the procedures for accurately using this equipment.

## LEARNING OUTCOME 4

Describe appropriate nursing care for alterations in body temperature.

### CONCEPTS FOR LECTURE

1. Nursing interventions for clients with fever include the following: monitor vital signs; assess skin color and temperature; monitor white blood cell count, hematocrit values, and other pertinent laboratory reports for indication of infection or dehydration; remove excess blankets when the client feels warm, but provide extra warmth when the client feels chilled; provide adequate nutrition and fluids; measure intake and output; reduce physical activity to limit heat production; administer antipyretic as ordered; provide oral hygiene to keep mucous membranes moist; provide a tepid sponge bath to increase heat loss through conduction; and provide dry clothing and bed linens.
2. Nursing care for clients with hypothermia includes providing a warm environment, providing dry clothing, applying warm blankets, keeping limbs close to the body, covering the client's scalp with a cap or turban, supplying warm oral or intravenous fluids, and applying warming pads.

### POWERPOINT LECTURE SLIDES

*(NOTE: The number on each PPT Lecture Slide directly corresponds with the Concepts for Lecture.)*

 Fever
- Monitor vital signs
- Assess skin color and temperature
- Monitor laboratory results for signs of dehydration or infection
- Remove excess blankets when the client feels warm
- Provide adequate nutrition and fluid
- Measure intake and output
- Reduce physical activity
- Administer antipyretic as ordered
- Provide oral hygiene
- Provide a tepid sponge bath
- Provide dry clothing and bed linens

 Hypothermia
- Provide warm environment
- Provide dry clothing
- Apply warm blankets
- Keep limbs close to body
- Cover the client's scalp
- Supply warm oral or intravenous fluids
- Apply warming pads

## SUGGESTIONS FOR CLASSROOM ACTIVITIES

- Have the students investigate the care for temperature alterations in different cultures.
- Have students review antipyretic medications.
- Discuss the role of fever in the body's immunologic response to infection.

## SUGGESTIONS FOR CLINICAL ACTIVITIES

- Have the students provide examples of clients whose temperature readings were elevated or decreased. Discuss factors contributing to the temperature alterations and the nursing care provided for the clients.

# LEARNING OUTCOME 5

Identify nine sites used to assess the pulse and state the reasons for their use.

## CONCEPTS FOR LECTURE

1. The nine sites used to assess the pulse are radial, temporal, carotid, apical, brachial, femoral, popliteal, posterior tibial, and pedal (dorsalis pedis). The radial site is readily accessible. The temporal site is used when the radial pulse is not accessible. The carotid site is used during cardiac arrest/shock in adults and is used to determine circulation to the brain. The apical site is routinely used for infants and children up to 3 years of age. It is used to determine discrepancies with radial pulse, and it is used in conjunction with some medications. The brachial site is used to measure blood pressure and is used during cardiac arrest in infants. The femoral site is used in cases of cardiac arrest/shock and is used to determine circulation to a leg. The popliteal site is used to determine circulation to the lower leg. The posterior tibial is used to determine circulation to the foot. The dorsalis pedis (pedal, dorsal pedal) is used to determine circulation to the foot.

## POWERPOINT LECTURE SLIDES

*(NOTE: The number on each PPT Lecture Slide directly corresponds with the Concepts for Lecture.)*

 Pulse Sites
- Radial site
  - Readily accessible
- Temporal
  - When radial pulse is not accessible
- Carotid
  - During cardiac arrest/shock in adults
  - Determine circulation to the brain
- Apical
  - Infants and children up to 3 years of age
  - Discrepancies with radial pulse
  - Monitor some medications
- Brachial
  - Blood pressure
  - Cardiac arrest in infants
- Femoral
  - Cardiac arrest/shock
  - Circulation to a leg
- Popliteal
  - Circulation to lower leg;
- Posterior tibial
  - Circulation to the foot
- Dorsalis pedis (pedal, dorsal pedal)
  - Circulation to the foot

## SUGGESTIONS FOR CLASSROOM ACTIVITIES

- Provide the students with a drawing of the vascular system and have them identify the pulse sites.
- Have the students locate the pulse sites on a partner.

## SUGGESTIONS FOR CLINICAL ACTIVITIES

- Have the students identify the pulse sites on their assigned clients, with the clients' permission. Discuss any difficulties in locating these.

# LEARNING OUTCOME 6

List the characteristics that should be included when assessing pulses.

## CONCEPTS FOR LECTURE

1. When assessing the pulse, the nurse collects the following data: the rate, rhythm, volume, arterial wall elasticity, and presence or absence of bilateral equality.
2. Rate is the number of beats per minute (BPM). An excessively fast heart rate (>100BPM in an adult) is referred to as tachycardia and an excessively slow heart rate (< 60 BPM in an adult) is called bradycardia.
3. Rhythm is the pattern of beats and intervals between beats. Equal time elapses between beats of a normal pulse. A pulse with an irregular rhythm is referred to as a dysrhythmia or arrhythmia.
4. Volume (also called pulse strength or amplitude) refers to the force of blood with each beat. Normally this is equal with each beat. This can range from absent to bounding.
5. Elasticity of the arterial wall refers to its expansibility or its deformity. A healthy, normal artery feels straight, smooth, soft, and pliable.
6. The nurse should assess the corresponding pulse on the other side of the body as a comparison when assessing the adequacy of the blood flow to areas of the body.

## POWERPOINT LECTURE SLIDES

*(NOTE: The number on each PPT Lecture Slide directly corresponds with the Concepts for Lecture.)*

**1** Characteristics of the Pulse
  - Rate
  - Rhythm
  - Volume
  - Arterial wall elasticity
  - Bilateral equality

**2** Rate
  - Beats per minute
  - Tachycardia
  - Bradycardia

**3** Rhythm
  - Equality of beats and intervals between beats
  - Dysrhythmias
  - Arrhythmia

**4** Volume
  - Strength or amplitude
  - Absent to bounding

**5** Arterial Wall Elasticity
  - Expansibility or deformity

**6** Presence or Absence of Bilateral Equality
  - Compare corresponding artery

## SUGGESTIONS FOR CLASSROOM ACTIVITIES

- Discuss the scientific basis for the characteristics that should be included when assessing pulses.
- Divide the students into pairs and have one student obtain the radial pulse of his or her partner, noting the characteristics of the pulse. Have the student go up and down a flight of steps several times and have the partner reassess the pulse characteristics. Discuss findings.

## SUGGESTIONS FOR CLINICAL ACTIVITIES

- Have the students obtain the radial pulse on their assigned clients, comparing right and left pulses and noting the characteristics of the pulse. Discuss findings based on each client's physical and psychological condition.

# LEARNING OUTCOME 7

Explain how to measure the apical pulse and the apical-radial pulse.

## CONCEPTS FOR LECTURE

1. Apical pulse: See Skill 29.3.
2. Apical-radial pulse: See Skill 29.4.

## POWERPOINT LECTURE SLIDES

*(NOTE: The number on each PPT Lecture Slide directly corresponds with the Concepts for Lecture.)*

**1** Measuring Apical Pulse
  - Skill 29.3

**2** Apical-Radial Pulse
  - Skill 29.4

## LEARNING OUTCOME 8

Describe the mechanics of breathing and the mechanisms that control respirations.

### CONCEPTS FOR LECTURE

1. During inhalation the following processes normally occur:
   - diaphragm contracts (flattens).
   - ribs move upward and outward.
   - sternum moves outward, thus enlarging the thorax and permitting the lungs to expand.
2. During exhalation the following processes normally occur:
   - diaphragm relaxes.
   - ribs move downward and inward.
   - sternum moves inward, thus decreasing the size of the thorax as the lungs are compressed.
3. Normally, breathing is carried out automatically and effortlessly. Respiration is controlled by respiratory centers in the medulla oblongata and the pons of the brain and by chemoreceptors located centrally in the medulla and peripherally in the carotid and aortic bodies. These centers and receptors respond to changes in the concentration of oxygen ($O_2$), carbon dioxide ($CO_2$), and hydrogen ($H^+$) in the arterial blood.

### POWERPOINT LECTURE SLIDES

*(NOTE: The number on each PPT Lecture Slide directly corresponds with the Concepts for Lecture.)*

**1** Inhalation
   - Diaphragm contracts (flattens)
   - Ribs move upward and outward
   - Sternum moves outward
   - Enlarging the size of the thorax

**2** Exhalation
   - Diaphragm relaxes
   - Ribs move downward and inward
   - Sternum moves inward
   - Decreasing the size of the thorax

**3** Respiratory Control Mechanisms
   - Respiratory centers
     ○ Medulla oblongata
     ○ Pons
   - Chemoreceptors
     ○ Medulla
     ○ Carotid and aortic bodies
     ○ Both respond to $O_2$, $CO_2$, $H^+$ in arterial blood

### SUGGESTIONS FOR CLASSROOM ACTIVITIES

- Discuss how body positioning can assist a person with the mechanics of respiration.

## LEARNING OUTCOME 9

Identify the components of a respiratory assessment.

### CONCEPTS FOR LECTURE

1. The rate, depth, rhythm, quality, and effectiveness of respirations should be assessed.
2. Rate is described as breaths per minute. Breathing that is normal in rate is called eupnea; abnormally slow respirations are called bradypnea; and abnormally rapid respirations are called tachypnea or polypnea. Apnea is absence of breathing. Table 29–2 lists normal respiratory rates across the lifespan.

### POWERPOINT LECTURE SLIDES

*(NOTE: The number on each PPT Lecture Slide directly corresponds with the Concepts for Lecture.)*

**1** Components of Respiratory Assessment
   - Rate
   - Depth
   - Rhythm
   - Quality
   - Effectiveness

3. Depth can be established by watching the movement of the chest. Depth is generally described as normal, deep, or shallow.
4. Rhythm refers to regularity of inhalation and expiration. Normally respirations are equally spaced. Rhythm can be described as regular or irregular.
5. Quality (character) refers to aspects of breathing that are different from normal, effortless breathing. Two such aspects are the amount of effort the client must exert to breathe and sound of breathing. A client who can breathe only with substantial effort has labored respirations. Normal breaths are silent, but a number of abnormal sounds such as wheezes can be produced that are audible.
6. Effectiveness is measured in part by the uptake of oxygen from air into the blood and release of carbon dioxide from blood into expired air. The amount of hemoglobin in arterial blood that is saturated with oxygen can be measured indirectly through pulse oximetry.

**2** Rate
- Breaths per minute
- Eupnea
- Bradypnea
- Tachypnea

**3** Depth
- Normal
- Deep
- Shallow

**4** Rhythm
- Regular
- Irregular

**5** Quality
- Effort
- Sounds

**6** Effectiveness
- Uptake and transport of $O_2$
- Transport and elimination of $CO_2$

## SUGGESTIONS FOR CLASSROOM ACTIVITIES

- Discuss how the nurse assesses each of the components of respiration.
- Play audiotapes of clients experiencing difficulty breathing, e.g. wheezes, crackles.
- Discuss characteristics of sputum and of coughing.

## SUGGESTIONS FOR CLINICAL ACTIVITIES

- Have the students assess the respirations of their assigned clients, paying attention to the components of the respiratory assessment. Compare and contrast findings based upon clients' physical and psychological conditions.

## LEARNING OUTCOME 10

Differentiate systolic from diastolic blood pressure.

### CONCEPTS FOR LECTURE

1. Arterial blood pressure is a measure of the pressure exerted by the blood as it flows through the arteries.

   The systolic blood pressure is the pressure of the blood as a result of the contraction of the ventricles—that is, the pressure of the height of the blood wave.

   The diastolic blood pressure is the pressure when the ventricles are at rest. The diastolic pressure is the lower pressure present at all times within the arteries.

   Blood pressure is measured in millimeters of mercury and recorded as a fraction, example is 120/80. The systolic blood pressure in this example is 120 and the diastolic blood pressure is 80. The mathematical difference between the systolic and diastole pressures is called the pulse pressure. A normal pulse pressure is about 40 mm Hg but can be as high as 100 mm Hg during exercise. A consistently high pulse pressure is associated with arteriosclerosis and a consistently low pulse pressure with severe heart failure, for example. The pulse pressure in the example above is 40 mm Hg.

### POWERPOINT LECTURE SLIDES

*(NOTE: The number on each PPT Lecture Slide directly corresponds with the Concepts for Lecture.)*

**1** Systolic and Diastolic Blood Pressure
- Systolic
  - Contraction of the ventricles
- Diastolic
  - Ventricles are at rest
  - Lower pressure present at all times
- Measured in mm Hg
- Recorded as a fraction, e.g., 120/80
- Systolic = 120 and Diastolic = 80
- Pulse Pressure—difference between systolic and diastolic pressures

## LEARNING OUTCOME 11

Describe five phases of Korotkoff's sounds.

### CONCEPTS FOR LECTURE

1. Phase 1 is the pressure level at which the first faint, clear tapping or thumping sounds are heard. These sounds gradually become more intense. The first tapping sound heard during deflation of the cuff is the systolic blood pressure.

    Phase 2 is the period during deflation when the sounds have a muffled, whooshing, or swishing sound.

    Phase 3 is the period during which the blood flows freely through an increasingly open artery and the sounds become crisper and more intense and again assume a thumping quality but softer than in phase 1.

    Phase 4 is the time when the sounds become muffled and have a soft, blowing quality.

    Phase 5 is the pressure level when the last sound is heard. This is followed by a period of silence. The pressure at which the last sound is heard is the diastolic blood pressure in adults.

### POWERPOINT LECTURE SLIDES

*(NOTE: The number on each PPT Lecture Slide directly corresponds with the Concepts for Lecture.)*

1. Korotkoff's Sounds
   - Phase 1
     - First faint, clear tapping or thumping sounds
     - Systolic pressure
   - Phase 2
     - Muffled, whooshing, or swishing sound
   - Phase 3
     - Blood flows freely
     - Crisper and more intense sound
     - Thumping quality but softer than in phase 1
   - Phase 4
     - Muffled and have a soft, blowing sound
   - Phase 5
     - Pressure level when the last sound is heard
     - Period of silence
     - Diastolic pressure

## LEARNING OUTCOME 12

Describe methods and sites used to measure blood pressure.

### CONCEPTS FOR LECTURE

1. The blood pressure is assessed directly or indirectly. Direct (invasive monitoring) measurement involves the insertion of a catheter into the brachial, radial, or femoral artery. Arterial pressure is represented as wavelike forms displayed on a monitor. Two noninvasive, indirect methods of measuring blood pressure are the auscultatory and palpatory methods.

### POWERPOINT LECTURE SLIDES

*(NOTE: The number on each PPT Lecture Slide directly corresponds with the Concepts for Lecture.)*

1. Measuring Blood Pressure
   - Direct (Invasive Monitoring)
   - Indirect
     - Auscultatory
     - Palpatory

The auscultatory method is most commonly used. The equipment required is a sphygmomanometer, a cuff, and a stethoscope. When taking a blood pressure using a stethoscope, the nurse identifies phases of sounds called Korotkoff's sounds. First the nurse pumps the cuff up to about 30 mm Hg above the point where the pulse is no longer felt; then the pressure is slowly released (2 to 3 mm Hg/second) while the nurse observes the readings on the manometer and relates them to the sounds heard through the stethoscope.

The palpatory method is sometimes used when Korotkoff's sounds cannot be heard and electronic equipment to amplify the sounds is not available, or to prevent misdirection from the presence of an auscultatory gap. In the palpatory method, instead of listening for the blood flow sounds, the nurse uses light to moderate pressure to palpate the pulsations of the artery as the pressure in the cuff is released. The pressure is read from the sphygmomanometer when the first pulsation is felt.

Blood pressure is usually assessed in the client's upper arm using the brachial artery. Assessing the blood pressure on a client's thigh is indicated if the blood pressure cannot be measured on either arm and when the blood pressure in one thigh is to be compared with the blood pressure in the other thigh.

- Sites
  - Upper arms (brachial artery)
  - Thighs (popliteal artery)

## SUGGESTIONS FOR CLASSROOM ACTIVITIES

- Have the students practice obtaining blood pressure recordings on various classmates, listening for the various Korotkoff's phases, or on an electronic blood pressure arm.
- Have the students obtain thigh blood pressure recordings on each other.
- Have the students obtain blood pressure recordings on their partners using the palpatory method.

## SUGGESTIONS FOR CLINICAL ACTIVITIES

- Have the students obtain blood pressure readings on their assigned clients using both electronic and manual blood pressure equipment. Discuss any difficulties. Compare and contrast readings based upon the clients' physical and psychological conditions.

## LEARNING OUTCOME 13

Discuss measurement of blood oxygenation using pulse oximetry.

### CONCEPTS FOR LECTURE

1. A pulse oximeter is a noninvasive device that estimates a client's arterial blood oxygen saturation ($SaO_2$) by means of a sensor attached to the client's finger (see Figure 29.24), toe, nose, earlobe, or forehead (or around the hand or foot of a neonate).

   The pulse oximeter can detect hypoxemia before clinical signs and symptoms, such as the development of dusky skin color and dusky nail bed color.

   Normal $SpO_2$ is 95% to 100%, and an $SpO_2$ below 70% is life threatening.

### POWERPOINT LECTURE SLIDES

*(NOTE: The number on each PPT Lecture Slide directly corresponds with the Concepts for Lecture.)*

 1 Pulse Oximetry
- Noninvasive devise
- Estimates arterial blood oxygen saturation ($SpO_2$)
- Normal $SpO_2$ 85-100%; < 70% life threatening
- Detects hypoxemia before clinical signs and symptoms
- Sensor, photodetector, pulse oximeter unit

The pulse oximeter sensor has two parts: two light-emitting diodes (LEDs) that transmit red and infrared lights through nails, tissue, and venous and arterial blood, and a photodetector placed directly opposite the LEDs. The photodetector measures the amount of red and infrared light absorbed by oxygenated and de-oxygenated hemoglobin in peripheral arterial blood and reports it as $SpO_2$.

The oximeter unit consists of an inlet connection for the sensor cable, a faceplate that indicates the oxygen saturation measurement (expressed as a percentage), and the pulse rate. Cordless units are available. Preset alarms signal high and low readings.

2. Factors affecting $SpO_2$ include hemoglobin, circulation, activity, and carbon monoxide poisoning. In the hemoglobin is fully saturated, the $SpO_2$ will appear normal even if the total hemoglobin level is reduced; the reading will not be accurate in the area under the sensor has impaired circulation; shivering and excessive movement of the sensor site may interfere with accurate readings; and the pulse oximeter cannot discriminate between hemoglobin saturated with oxygen and carbon monoxide.

3. Skill 29.7 presents the procedure for measurement of oxygen saturation:

**2** Factors that Affect Accuracy
- Hemoglobin level
- Circulation
- Activity
- Carbon monoxide poisoning

**3** Measuring Oxygenation
- Skill 29.7

---

**SUGGESTIONS FOR CLASSROOM ACTIVITIES**

- Have the students practice obtaining pulse oximetry readings on each other. Have several students place their hands in cold water or apply dark nail polish or move fingers and then obtain readings. Compare and contrast.

**SUGGESTIONS FOR CLINICAL ACTIVITIES**

- If possible, obtain pulse oximetry equipment used in the institution. Have the students read the procedure for the proper use of this equipment.

---

# LEARNING OUTCOME 14

Identify when it is appropriate to delegate measurement of vital signs to unlicensed assistive personnel.

**CONCEPTS FOR LECTURE**

1. Prior to delegating measurement of vital signs to unlicensed assistive personnel (UAP), the nurse must have assessed the individual client and determined that the client is medically stable or in a chronic condition and not fragile and that the vital sign measurement is considered routine for this client. Under those circumstances the UAP may measure, record, and report vital signs, but the interpretation rests with the nurse.

2. Routine measurement of the client's temperature can be delegated to the UAP or to family members/caregivers in nonhospital settings. The nurse must explain the appropriate type of thermometer and site to be used and ensure that the person knows when to report an abnormal temperature and how to record the findings. The nurse is responsible for interpreting an abnormal temperature and determining the appropriate response.

**POWERPOINT LECTURE SLIDES**

*(NOTE: The number on each PPT Lecture Slide directly corresponds with the Concepts for Lecture.)*

**1** General Considerations Prior to Delegation
- Nurse assesses to determine stability of client
- Measurement is considered to be routine
- Interpretation rests with the nurse

**2** Body Temperature
- Routine measurement may be delegated to UAP
- UAP reports abnormal temperatures
- Nurse interprets abnormal temperature and determines response

**3** Pulse
- Radial or brachial pulse may be delegated to UAP
- Nurse interprets abnormal rates or rhythms and determines response

## Concepts for Lecture *continued*

3. Measurement of the client's radial or brachial pulse can be delegated to the UAP or family members/caregivers in nonhospital settings. Reports of abnormal pulse rates or rhythms require reassessment by the nurse, who also determines appropriate action if the abnormality is confirmed. Unlicensed personnel are generally not delegated obtaining other peripheral pulses due to the skill required in locating and interpreting, and they are generally not delegated the task of obtaining pulses by Doppler ultrasound devices.

   Due to the degree of skill and knowledge required, unlicensed personnel are generally not responsible for assessing the apical pulse. Unlicensed assistive personnel are generally not responsible for assessing apical-radial pulses using the one-nurse technique. The UAP may perform the radial pulse count for the two-nurse technique.

4. Counting and observing respirations may be delegated to the UAP. The follow-up assessment, interpretation of abnormal respirations, and determination of appropriate responses are done by the nurse.

5. Blood pressure measurement may be delegated to the UAP. The interpretation of abnormal blood pressure readings and determination of appropriate responses are done by the nurse.

6. Application of the pulse oximeter sensor and recording of the $SpO_2$ value may be delegated to the UAP. Interpretation of the $SpO_2$ value and determination of appropriate responses are done by the nurse.

## PowerPoint Lecture Slides *continued*

- UAP are generally not responsible for assessing apical or one person apical-radial pulses

**[4]** Respirations
- Counting and observing respirations may be delegated to UAP
- Nurse interprets abnormal respirations and determines response

**[5]** Blood Pressure
- May be delegated to UAP
- Nurse interprets abnormal readings and determines response

**[6]** Oxygen Saturation
- Application of the pulse oximeter sensor and recording the $SpO_2$ may be delegated to UAP
- Nurse interprets oxygen saturation value and determines response

---

### Suggestions for Classroom Activities

- Provide the students with client situations and ask whether it would appropriate to delegate vital sign measurement to unlicensed assistive personnel for these clients.

### Suggestions for Clinical Activities

- Discuss the policy for delegation of vital signs to unlicensed assistive personnel in this institution.

---

# CHAPTER 30
## HEALTH ASSESSMENT

## RESOURCE LIBRARY

**PRENTICE HALL NURSING MEDIALINK DVD-ROM**

Audio Glossary
NCLEX® Review
End of Unit Concept Map Activity
Videos and Animations:
*Barking Cough (14 month old with upper respiratory infection)*
*Crackles (age: 8 months, recovering from cardiac surgery*
*Continuous Murmur (caused by patent Ductus Arteriosus)*
*Fast Breathing (3 month old with Bronchiolitis, Fixed S2 Split*
*Inspiratory and Expiratory Crackles (age: 3 months with Bronchiolitis)*
*Normal Heart Sound (12 year-old, heart rate is approximately 65 beats per minute)*
*Normal Heart Sound (recorded from a child, heart rate is approximately 100 beats per minute)*
*Normal Lung Sounds (4 month old)*
*Normal Lung Sounds (4 year-old)*
*Physiological S2 Split (12 year-old)*
*Rhonchi (recorded from a midnight back of a 5 year-old with pneumonia)*
*Squawks (5 year-old with pneumonia)*
*Stridor (16 year-old female)*
Skills Checklists:
*Assessing Appearance and Mental Status*
*Assessing the Abdomen*
*Assessing the Breasts and Axillae*
*Assessing the Ears and Hearing*
*Assessing the Eye Structures and Visual Acuity*
*Assessing the Female Genitals and Inguinal Area*
*Assessing the Hair*
*Assessing the Heart and Central Vessels*
*Assessing the Male Genitals and Inguinal Area*
*Assessing the Mouth and Oropharynx*
*Assessing the Musculoskeletal System*
*Assessing the Nails*
*Assessing the Neck*
*Assessing the Neurological System*
*Assessing the Nose and Sinuses*
*Assessing the Peripheral Vascular System*
*Assessing the Rectum and Anus*
*Assessing the Skin*
*Assessing the Skull and Face*
*Assessing the Thorax and Lungs*

**COMPANION WEBSITE**

Additional NCLEX® Review
Case Study: *Performing Physical Assessments*
Care Plan Activity: *Client Care After Motor Vehicle Crash*
Application Activity: *Physical Exam Study Guide*
Links to Resources

# LEARNING OUTCOME 1

Identify the purposes of the physical examination.

## CONCEPTS FOR LECTURE

1. The purposes of the physical examination include the following:
   - obtain baseline data about the client's functional abilities
   - supplement, confirm, or refute data obtained in the nursing history
   - obtain data that will help establish nursing diagnoses and plans of care
   - evaluate the physiologic outcomes of health care and thus the progress of a client's health problem
   - make clinical judgments about a client's health status
   - identify areas for health promotion and disease prevention

## POWERPOINT LECTURE SLIDES

*(NOTE: The number on each PPT Lecture Slide directly corresponds with the Concepts for Lecture.)*

**1** Purposes of the Physical Examination
- Obtain baseline data
- Supplement, confirm, or refute data from the history
- Help establish nursing diagnoses and plans of care
- Evaluate physiologic outcomes and progress
- Make clinical judgments
- Identify areas for health promotion and disease prevention

## SUGGESTIONS FOR CLASSROOM ACTIVITIES

- Provide examples to illustrate the various purposes of the physical examination.

## SUGGESTIONS FOR CLINICAL ACTIVITIES

- Have the students review the nursing physical examinations performed on their assigned clients and identify the purposes of these examinations.
- Compare and contrast the nursing physical examinations to the physical examinations performed by the physicians

# LEARNING OUTCOME 2

Explain the four methods used in physical examination.

## CONCEPTS FOR LECTURE

1. The four primary techniques used in the physical examination are inspection, palpation, percussion, and auscultation.
2. Inspection is visual examination using the sense of sight. It should be deliberate, purposeful, and systematic. The nurse inspects with the naked eye and with lighted instruments. Inspection is frequently used to assess moisture, color, and texture of body surfaces, as well as shape, position, size, color, and symmetry of the body. In addition to visual observations, olfactory (smell) and auditory (hearing) cues are also noted.
3. Palpation is examination of the body using the sense of touch. The pads of the fingers are used to determine texture, temperature, vibration, position, size, consistency and mobility of organs or masses, distention, pulsations, and the presence of pain upon pressure. Palpation can be light or deep. For light palpation the nurse presses gently over area while moving the hand in a circle. Deep palpation requires nurse practitioner skill and should be used with caution.

## POWERPOINT LECTURE SLIDES

*(NOTE: The number on each PPT Lecture Slide directly corresponds with the Concepts for Lecture.)*

**1** Methods used in Physical Examination
- Inspection
- Palpation
- Percussion
- Auscultation

**2** Inspection
- Deliberate, purposeful, and systematic visual examination
  - Moisture, color, texture of body surfaces
  - Shape, position, size, symmetry of the body

**3** Palpation
- Examination using sense of touch
  - Texture
  - Temperature
  - Vibration

4. Percussion is the act of striking the body surface to elicit sounds that can be heard or vibration that can be felt. There are two types of percussion: direct and indirect. Direct percussion refers to striking the area directly and indirect percussion involves striking an object (finger) held against the area to be assessed. Percussion is used to determine the size and shape of internal organs by establishing borders. Percussion elicits five types of sounds: flatness, dullness, resonance, hyperresonance, and tympany indicating whether the tissues are fluid filled, air filled or solid.

5. Auscultation is the process of listening to sounds produced within the body. Auscultation can be direct, using the unaided ear, or indirect, using the stethoscope. A stethoscope is used primarily to listen to sounds from within the body. Sounds are described according to pitch (high or low), intensity (loud or soft), duration (long or short), and quality (subjective description).

- ○ Position, size, consistency, mobility of organs or masses
- ○ Distention
- ○ Pulsation
- ○ Presence of pain upon pressure
- • Light and deep
- • Flatness, dullness, resonance, hyperresonance, tympany

 Percussion
- • Striking body surface to elicit sounds or vibrations
  - ○ Direct—striking body directly
  - ○ Indirect—striking of an object held against the body
- • Determine size, shape, borders of internal organs

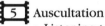 Auscultation
- • Listening to sounds produced within the body
  - ○ Direct—use of unaided ear
  - ○ Indirect—use of stethoscope
- • Pitch, intensity, duration, quality

## SUGGESTIONS FOR CLASSROOM ACTIVITIES

- • Set up an inspection unit in the nursing laboratory. Position a manikin in an orthopneic position. Apply wounds, dressings, and so on. Divide the students into groups and give each group a specific amount of time to inspect the client. Compare and contrast findings from each group.
- • Demonstrate use of the otoscope and ophthalmoscope. Have the students practice using these instruments.
- • Have the students practice palpation and percussion on each other.
- • Identify the parts of a stethoscope. Have the students practice listening to heart, lung, and abdominal sounds on each other.

## SUGGESTIONS FOR CLINICAL ACTIVITIES

- • Have the students practice listening to heart, lung, and abdominal sounds on assigned clients. Compare and contrast findings as related to the clients' medical and nursing diagnoses.
- • Have the students enter the room of an assigned client. Give them a 3-minute time limit to visually inspect the client and the client's environment. Have them report on their findings.
- • If possible, assign students to assist with an admission physical examination performed by a nurse practitioner and identify the techniques used during this assessment.

# LEARNING OUTCOME 3

Explain the significance of selected physical findings.

## CONCEPTS FOR LECTURE

1. Physical findings may either be normal or represent deviations from normal.

   The initial assessment of physical findings provides baseline data about the client's functional abilities against which subsequent assessment findings are compared.

   Knowledge of the normal structure and function of body parts and systems is an essential requisite to conducting a physical assessment.

## POWERPOINT LECTURE SLIDES

*(NOTE: The number on each PPT Lecture Slide directly corresponds with the Concepts for Lecture.)*

[1] Normal Findings on Physical Examination
- • Assessment helps the nurse:
  - ○ Establish nursing diagnoses
  - ○ Plan the client's care
  - ○ Evaluate the outcomes of nursing care

Significant deviations from normal should be reported to the client's primary care provider.

Normal findings and deviations from normal are indicated in each skill in this chapter.

- Appearance and mental status (Skill 30.1)
- Skin (Skill 30.2):
- Hair (Skill 30.3)
- Skull and Face (Skill 30.5)
- Eye Structures and Visual Acuity (Skill 30.6)
- Ears and Hearing (Skill 30.7)
- Nose and Sinuses (Skill 30.8)
- Mouth and Oropharynx (Skill 30.9)
- Neck (Skill 30.10)
- Thorax and Lungs (Skill 30.11)
- Heart, Central Vessels, and Peripheral Vascular System (Skill 30.12, 30.13)
- Breast and Axilla (Skill 30.14)
- Abdomen (Skill 30.15)
- Musculoskeletal System (Skill 30.16)
- Neurologic System (Skill 30.17)
- Female Genitals and Inguinal Area (Skill 30.18)
- Male Genitals and Inguinal Area (Skill 30.19)
- Rectum and Anus (Skill 30.20)

## SUGGESTIONS FOR CLASSROOM ACTIVITIES

- Provide the students with several physical examination documentations. Have the students identify normal and deviations from normal in these examinations.

## SUGGESTIONS FOR CLINICAL ACTIVITIES

- Have the students perform appropriate physical examinations on their assigned clients and discuss normal findings and deviations from normal as these relate to the clients' medical and nursing diagnoses and plans of care.

# LEARNING OUTCOME 4

Identify expected outcomes of health assessment.

## CONCEPTS FOR LECTURE

1. Data obtained in the physical health assessment help the nurse establish nursing diagnoses, plan the client's care, and evaluate the outcomes of nursing care.

## POWERPOINT LECTURE SLIDES

*(NOTE: The number on each PPT Lecture Slide directly corresponds with the Concepts for Lecture.)*

 Outcomes of Physical Health Assessment
- Nursing diagnoses
- Plan the client's care
- Evaluate the outcomes of nursing care

## SUGGESTIONS FOR CLASSROOM ACTIVITIES

- Divide the students into groups. Give each group a client case study. Have the students identify normal findings and deviations from normal in the client's data. Then ask them to identify one appropriate nursing diagnosis and plan of care for the client. Share with the class.

## SUGGESTIONS FOR CLINICAL ACTIVITIES

- Have the students develop a plan of care derived from the health assessment for their assigned clients.

# LEARNING OUTCOME 5

Identify the steps in selected examination procedures.

## CONCEPTS FOR LECTURE

1. Each procedure includes planning, obtaining appropriate equipment, preparing the client, implementing the procedures, and evaluating the findings. Steps in assessment of each body system are listed in the skills in the text.

## POWERPOINT LECTURE SLIDES

*(NOTE: The number on each PPT Lecture Slide directly corresponds with the Concepts for Lecture.)*

1 Steps in Examination Procedures
- Planning
- Obtaining appropriate equipment
- Preparing the client
- Implementation of the procedures
- Evaluation of findings

## SUGGESTIONS FOR CLASSROOM ACTIVITIES

- Show the students a videotape or DVD demonstrating physical examination of the various body systems.
- Demonstrate the examination techniques and have the students return demonstrate the techniques.
- Use breast and testicular models to demonstrate these examinations. Have students do return demonstrations.

## SUGGESTIONS FOR CLINICAL ACTIVITIES

- Assign the students to perform appropriate physical assessment examinations on their clients. Discuss the findings and any difficulties encountered.

# LEARNING OUTCOME 6

Describe suggested sequencing to conduct a physical health examination in an orderly fashion.

## CONCEPTS FOR LECTURE

1. The health assessment is conducted in a systematic and efficient manner that results in the fewest position changes for the client.
2. The head-to-toe framework proceeds from the general survey and vital signs to the head (hair, scalp, cranium, face, eyes and vision, ears and hearing, nose and sinuses, mouth and oropharynx, and cranial nerves).
3. The neck (muscles, lymph nodes, trachea, thyroid gland, carotid artery, and neck veins) is examined next.
4. The examination of the upper extremities (skin and nails, muscle strength and tone, range of motion, brachial and radial pulses, biceps and triceps reflexes, and sensation) follows.
5. The examination of the chest and back proceeds by inspecting the skin, chest shape and size, lungs, heart, spinal column, breasts and axillae.
6. The assessment continues to the abdomen where the skin, abdominal sounds, specific organs, and femoral pulses are checked.
7. The genitals, the testicles, the vagina and the urethra are observed.
8. The anus and rectum are observed.
9. Lastly, the lower extremities are inspected. These consist of the skin and toenails, gait and balance, range of motion, popliteal, posterior tibial, and pedal pulses, and tendon and plantar reflexes.

## POWERPOINT LECTURE SLIDES

*(NOTE: The number on each PPT Lecture Slide directly corresponds with the Concepts for Lecture.)*

1 Suggested Sequencing for Physical Exam
- General survey
- Vital signs

2 Head
- Hair, scalp, cranium, face
- Eyes and vision
- Ears and hearing
- Nose and sinuses
- Mouth and oropharynx
- Cranial nerves

3 Neck
- Muscles
- Lymph nodes
- Trachea
- Thyroid gland
- Carotid arteries
- Neck veins

4 Upper Extremities
- Skin and nails
- Muscle strength and tone
- Range of motion

- Brachial and radial pulses
- Biceps and triceps reflexes
- Sensation

**5** Chest and Back
- Skin
- Chest shape and size
- Lungs
- Heart
- Spinal column
- Breasts and axilla

**6** Abdomen
- Skin
- Abdominal sounds
- Specific organs
- Femoral pulses

**7** Genitals
- Testicles
- Vagina
- Urethra

**8** Anus and Rectum

**9** Lower Extremities
- Skin and toenails
- Gait and balance
- Range of motion
- Popliteal, posterior tibial, and pedal pulses
- Tendon and plantar reflexes

---

### SUGGESTIONS FOR CLASSROOM ACTIVITIES

- Show a videotape or DVD of a complete physical examination. Instruct the students to note the sequence of the examination.

### SUGGESTIONS FOR CLINICAL ACTIVITIES

- If possible and appropriate, assign students to perform a complete physical examination using the nursing physical examination form used in the institution. Discuss outcomes.

---

## LEARNING OUTCOME 7

Discuss variations in examination techniques appropriate for clients of different ages.

### CONCEPTS FOR LECTURE

1. When assessing adults it is important to recognize that people of the same age differ markedly.

    Be aware of normal physiologic changes that occur with age. Also be aware of stiffness of muscles and joints from aging changes or history of orthopedic surgery. Expose only areas of the body to be examined, and permit ample time for the client to answer questions and assume the desired positions. Be aware of cultural differences, arrange for an interpreter if the client's language differs from that of the nurse, and ask clients how they wish to be addressed. Adapt assessment techniques to any sensory impairment.

### POWERPOINT LECTURE SLIDES

*(NOTE: The number on each PPT Lecture Slide directly corresponds with the Concepts for Lecture.)*

**1** Variations in Examination Techniques
- Adult
  - Be aware of normal physiologic changes
  - Be aware of stiffness of muscles and joints from aging changes or history of orthopedic surgery
  - Expose only areas to be examined
  - Permit ample time to answer questions and assume desired positions
  - Be aware of cultural differences

## CONCEPTS FOR LECTURE *continued*

If clients are elderly or frail it is wise to plan several assessment times in order not to overtire them.

The sequence of the assessment differs with children. When assessing children, proceed from the least invasive or uncomfortable to the more invasive. Examination of the head and neck, heart and lungs, and range of motion can be done early in the process, while the ears, mouth, abdomen, and genitals should be left for the end of the exam.

Variations in examination techniques for clients of different ages are given at the end of each skill in this chapter:

## POWERPOINT LECTURE SLIDES *continued*

- ○ Arrange for an interpreter if needed
- ○ Ask clients how wish to be addressed
- ○ Adapt techniques to any sensory impairment
- Elderly
  - ○ Plan several assessment times in order not to overtire
- Children
  - ○ Proceed from the least invasive or uncomfortable to the more invasive
  - ○ Examination of the head and neck, heart and lungs, and range of motion can be done early
  - ○ Ears, mouth, abdomen, and genitals should be left for the end

## SUGGESTIONS FOR CLASSROOM ACTIVITIES

- Show a videotape or DVD of physical examinations performed on children and elderly adults. Compare and contrast.

## SUGGESTIONS FOR CLINICAL ACTIVITIES

- Assign students to observe in clinics where clients of various ages are seen (e.g., well-child clinics, clinics in Veterans Administration facilities). Have the students report on observations of variation in techniques that were used to accommodate the needs of the clients in these settings.

# CHAPTER 31
## ASEPSIS

## RESOURCE LIBRARY

### 💿 PRENTICE HALL NURSING MEDIALINK DVD-ROM

Audio Glossary
NCLEX® Review
Skill Checklists:
   *Donning a Sterile Gown and Gloves*
      *(Open Method)*
   *Donning and Removing Personal Protective*
      *Equipment*
   *Donning and Removing Sterile Gloves*
      *(Open Method)*
   *Establishing and Maintaining a Sterile*
      *Field Handwashing*
Videos and Animations: *Handwashing and Gloving*

### 📖 IMAGE LIBRARY

**Figure 31.1** The chain of infection.
**Figure 31.2** Biohazard alert.
**Skill 31.1** Hand hygiene.
**Skill 31.2** Donning and Removing Personal Protective
Equipment (Gloves, Gown, Mask, Eyewear).

### 🌐 COMPANION WEBSITE

Additional NCLEX® Review
Case Study: *Client with Mycoplasma Pneumonia*
Care Plan Activity: *Client on Radiation Therapy and*
   *Medication*
Application Activity: *Infection Control Today*
Links to Resources

**Skill 31.3** Establishing and Maintaining a Sterile Field
**Skill 31.4** Donning and Removing Sterile Gloves
   (Open Method)
**Skill 31.5** Donning a Sterile Gown and Gloves
   (Closed Method)

## LEARNING OUTCOME 1

Explain the concepts of medical and surgical asepsis.

### CONCEPTS FOR LECTURE

1. Asepsis is the freedom from disease-causing microorganisms. To decrease the possibility of transferring microorganisms from one place to another, aseptic technique is used.

    Medical asepsis includes all practices intended to confine a specific microorganism to a specific area, limiting the number, growth, and transmission of microorganisms. In medical asepsis, objects are referred to as clean, which means the absence of almost all microorganisms, or dirty (soiled, contaminated), which means likely to have microorganisms, some of which may be capable of causing infection.

2. Surgical asepsis, or sterile technique, refers to those practices that keep an area or object free of all microorganisms. It includes practices that destroy all microorganisms and spores (microscopic dormant structures formed by some pathogens that are very hardy and often survive common cleaning techniques). Surgical asepsis is used for all procedures involving sterile areas of the body.

### POWERPOINT LECTURE SLIDES

*(NOTE: The number on each PPT Lecture Slide directly corresponds with the Concepts for Lecture.)*

🎞 1 Medical Asepsis
   • Practices intended to confine a specific
     microorganism to a specific area
   • Limits the number, growth, and transmission of
     microorganisms
   • Objects referred to as clean or dirty (soiled,
     contaminated)

🎞 2 Surgical Asepsis
   • Sterile technique
   • Practices that keep an area or object free of all
     microorganisms
   • Practices that destroy all microorganisms and
     spores
   • Used for all procedures involving sterile areas of
     the body

## SUGGESTIONS FOR CLASSROOM ACTIVITIES

- Provide students with examples of various activities or procedures and have them identify whether these are examples of medical or surgical asepsis.

## SUGGESTIONS FOR CLINICAL ACTIVITIES

- Review the institution's policies and procedures for handling dirty objects.
- Arrange for students to observe a surgical procedure. Have them discuss their observations regarding the principles of surgical asepsis, opening and manipulating sterile supplies, sterilization procedures, and communication among personnel about breaks in technique.

# LEARNING OUTCOME 2

Identify signs of localized and systemic infections.

## CONCEPTS FOR LECTURE

1. Signs of localized infections include localized swelling, localized redness, pain or tenderness with palpation or movement, palpable heat in the infected area, and loss of function of the body part affected, depending on the site and extent of involvement. In addition, open wounds may exude drainage of various colors.

2. Signs of systemic infection include fever, increased pulse and respiratory rate if the fever is high, malaise and loss of energy, anorexia and, in some situations, nausea and vomiting, and enlargement and tenderness of lymph nodes that drain the area of infection.

3. Laboratory data that indicates the presence of an infection include the following: elevated leukocyte (white blood cell or WBC) count; increases in specific types of WBCs revealed in the differential count; elevated erythrocyte sedimentation rate; and urine, blood, sputum, or other drainage culture.

## POWERPOINT LECTURE SLIDES

*(NOTE: The number on each PPT Lecture Slide directly corresponds with the Concepts for Lecture.)*

**1** Signs of Localized Infection
- Localized swelling
- Localized redness
- Pain or tenderness with palpation or movement
- Palpable heat in the infected area
- Loss of function of the body part affected, depending on the site and extent of involvement
- Wound exudate of various colors

**2** Signs of Systemic Infection
- Fever
- Increased pulse and respiratory rate if the fever high
- Malaise and loss of energy
- Anorexia and, in some situations, nausea and vomiting
- Enlargement and tenderness of lymph nodes that drain the area of infection

**3** Laboratory Data
- Elevated WBC count
- Increases in specific WBC types
- Elevated erythrocyte sedimentation rate (ESR)
- Cultures of urine, blood, sputum, or other drainage

## SUGGESTIONS FOR CLASSROOM ACTIVITIES

- Review the types and functions of WBCs. Discuss the relevance of increases or decreases in each type of cell.

## SUGGESTIONS FOR CLINICAL ACTIVITIES

- Have the students provide examples to illustrate signs and symptoms of localized and systemic infections observed in assigned clients and interventions for these clients.

# LEARNING OUTCOME 3

Identify risks for nosocomial infections.

## CONCEPTS FOR LECTURE

1. Nosocomial infections are associated with the delivery of health care services in a health care facility.

   A number of factors contribute to nosocomial infections. Diagnostic or therapeutic procedures may cause iatrogenic infections.

   Another factor contributing to the development of nosocomial infections is the compromised host, that is, a client whose normal defenses have been lowered by surgery or illness.

   Hands of personnel are a common vehicle for the spread of microorganisms. Insufficient hand cleansing is thus an important factor contributing to the spread of nosocomial infections.

## POWERPOINT LECTURE SLIDES

*(NOTE: The number on each PPT Lecture Slide directly corresponds with the Concepts for Lecture.)*

1. Risks for Nosocomial Infections
   - Diagnostic or therapeutic procedures (iatrogenic infections)
   - Compromised host
   - Insufficient hand cleansing

## SUGGESTIONS FOR CLASSROOM ACTIVITIES

- Have the students provide examples of potential therapeutic procedures that may cause iatrogenic infections. Discuss measures to prevent these infections.

## SUGGESTIONS FOR CLINICAL ACTIVITIES

- Have the students use the Assessment Interview: Clients at Risk for Infections for identifying the client at risk for infections to determine whether their assigned client is at risk for infection. Discuss interventions to reduce the risk for infections for these clients.

# LEARNING OUTCOME 4

Identify factors influencing a microorganism's capability to produce an infectious process.

## CONCEPTS FOR LECTURE

1. The extent to which any microorganism is capable of producing an infectious process depends on the number of microorganisms present, the virulence and potency of the microorganisms (pathogenicity), the ability of the microorganisms to enter the body, the susceptibility of the host, and the ability of the microorganisms to live in the host's body.

## POWERPOINT LECTURE SLIDES

*(NOTE: The number on each PPT Lecture Slide directly corresponds with the Concepts for Lecture.)*

1. Factors Influencing Microorganism's Capability to Produce Infection
   - Number of microorganisms present
   - Virulence and potency of the microorganisms (pathogenicity)
   - Ability to enter the body
   - Susceptibility of the host
   - Ability to live in the host's body

## SUGGESTIONS FOR CLASSROOM ACTIVITIES

- Invite a member of the microbiology faculty to discuss pathogenicity of common microorganisms.
- Discuss the growth of antibiotic-resistant organisms and measures to prevent this.

## SUGGESTIONS FOR CLINICAL ACTIVITIES

- Invite the infection control nurse to discuss how MRSA is controlled in the institution.

# LEARNING OUTCOME 5

Identify anatomic and physiologic barriers that defend the body against microorganisms.

## CONCEPTS FOR LECTURE

1. Intact skin and mucous membranes are the body's first line of defense against microorganisms. The dryness of the skin, resident bacteria of the skin, and the normal secretions of the skin also inhibit bacterial growth.

   The moist mucous membranes and cilia of the nasal passages and the alveolar macrophages are also barriers against microorganisms.

   Each body orifice also has protective mechanisms. The oral cavity sheds mucosal epithelium to rid the mouth of colonizers; saliva flow, and buffering action help prevent infection. Saliva also contains microbial inhibitors.

   The eyes are protected by tears. The high acidity of the stomach inhibits microbial growth, the resident flora of the large intestine helps prevent the establishment of disease-producing organisms, and peristalsis also tends to move microbes out of the body.

   The low pH of the vagina inhibits the growth of many disease-producing microorganisms. It is believed that the urine flow through the urethra has a flushing and bacteriostatic action.

## POWERPOINT LECTURE SLIDES

*(NOTE: The number on each PPT Lecture Slide directly corresponds with the Concepts for Lecture.)*

 Anatomic and Physiologic Barriers Defend Against Infection
- Intact skin and mucous membranes
- Moist mucous membranes and cilia of the nasal passages
- Alveolar macrophages
- Shedding of mucosal epithelium of oral cavity
- Saliva
- Tears
- High acidity of the stomach
- Resident flora of the large intestine
- Peristalsis
- Low pH of the vagina
- Urine flow through the urethra

## SUGGESTIONS FOR CLASSROOM ACTIVITIES

- Have students identify factors that may alter normal anatomic and physiologic barriers. Discuss interventions to prevent these alterations.

## SUGGESTIONS FOR CLINICAL ACTIVITIES

- Have students present examples of intact and nonintact anatomic and physiologic barriers present in assigned clients. Discuss nursing interventions to maintain these intact barriers and support the client with nonintact barriers.

# LEARNING OUTCOME 6

Differentiate active from passive immunity.

## CONCEPTS FOR LECTURE

1. In active immunity, the host produces antibodies in response to natural antigens or artificial antigens. The duration of active immunity tends to be long. In natural active immunity, antibodies are formed in the presence of active infection in the body and the duration of this type of immunity is lifelong. In artificial active immunity, antigens are administered to stimulate antibody formation. This type of active immunity lasts for many years, but artificial immunity must be reinforced by booster.
2. In passive (or acquired) immunity, the host receives natural or artificial antibodies produced from another source. The duration of passive immunity tends to be short. In natural passive immunity, the antibodies are

## POWERPOINT LECTURE SLIDES

*(NOTE: The number on each PPT Lecture Slide directly corresponds with the Concepts for Lecture.)*

 Active Immunity
- Antibodies produced in response to antigens
- Natural
  - Antibodies formed in presence of active infection
  - Duration lifelong
- Artificial
  - Antigens administered to stimulate antibody formation (vaccines)
  - Lasts for many years
  - Reinforced by booster

transferred naturally from an immune mother to her baby through the placenta or in colostrum. This type of immunity lasts 6 months to 1 year. Artificial passive immunity occurs when immune serum (antibody) from an animal or another human is injected. This immunity lasts 2 to 3 weeks.

2 Passive Immunity
- Antibodies produced from another source transferred to host
- Natural
  - Antibodies transferred naturally through the placenta or in colostrum
  - Lasts 6 months to 1 year
- Artificial
  - Immune serum (antibody) from an animal or another human injected
  - Lasts 2 to 3 weeks

## SUGGESTIONS FOR CLASSROOM ACTIVITIES

- Review the immunization schedule for adults and children. Identify the types of vaccines.
- Discuss the fears some parents have about immunizing their children.

## SUGGESTIONS FOR CLINICAL ACTIVITIES

- Have the students interview their assigned clients to determine whether they are current with their immunizations.

## LEARNING OUTCOME 7

Identify relevant nursing diagnoses and contributing factors for clients at risk for infection and who have an infection.

### CONCEPTS FOR LECTURE

1. The NANDA nursing diagnostic label for problems associated with the transmission of microorganisms is *Risk for Infection*, the state in which an individual is at increased risk for being invaded by pathogenic microorganisms.

   When using this diagnosis, the nurse should identify risk factors, including inadequate primary defenses such as inadequate anatomic and physiologic barriers, or inadequate secondary defenses such as leukopenia, immunosuppression, decreased hemoglobin, or suppressed inflammatory response.

2. Clients who have or are at risk for an infection are prime candidates for other physical and psychologic problems. Examples of nursing diagnoses or collaborative problems that may arise from the actual presence of an infection include *Potential Complication of Infection: Fever; Imbalanced Nutrition: Less Than Body Requirements; Acute Pain; Impaired Social Interaction or Social Isolation;* and *Anxiety*.

### POWERPOINT LECTURE SLIDES

*(NOTE: The number on each PPT Lecture Slide directly corresponds with the Concepts for Lecture.)*

1 *Risk for Infection*
- NANDA diagnostic label
- State in which an individual is at increased risk for being invaded by pathogenic microorganisms
- Risks Factors
  - Inadequate primary defenses
  - Inadequate secondary defenses

2 Related Diagnoses
- Potential complication of infection: fever
- Imbalanced nutrition: less than body requirement
- Acute pain
- Impaired social interaction or social isolation
- Anxiety

## SUGGESTIONS FOR CLASSROOM ACTIVITIES

- Provide the students with a case study illustrating a client who has the nursing diagnosis of *Risk for Infection* and another of a client who has an infection and defining characteristics of a collaborative problem and related nursing diagnoses. Have the students develop the nursing diagnosis and collaborative problem statement.

## SUGGESTIONS FOR CLINICAL ACTIVITIES

- Have the students identify clients who are at risk for infection and identify the factors that place these clients at risk.

# LEARNING OUTCOME 8

Identify interventions to reduce risks for infections.

## CONCEPTS FOR LECTURE

1. Many nosocomial infections can be prevented using proper hand hygiene techniques, environmental controls, sterile technique when warranted, and identification and management of clients at risk for infections.
    Nurses use critical thinking and agency policy in implementing infection control procedure.

## POWERPOINT LECTURE SLIDES

*(NOTE: The number on each PPT Lecture Slide directly corresponds with the Concepts for Lecture.)*

1 Interventions to Reduce Risk for Infection
- Proper hand hygiene techniques
- Environmental controls
- Sterile technique when warranted
- Identification and management of clients at risk

## SUGGESTIONS FOR CLASSROOM ACTIVITIES

- Have students locate research studies related to interventions to reduce risk of infection. Discuss findings.
- Have the students identify interventions that require sterile technique.

## SUGGESTIONS FOR CLINICAL ACTIVITIES

- Have the students identify environmental controls to reduce risks of infection in the institution.
- Have the students review the policies and procedures for proper hand hygiene in the institution.

# LEARNING OUTCOME 9

Identify measures that break each link in the chain of infection.

## CONCEPTS FOR LECTURE

1. The chain of infection includes the etiologic agent, reservoir, portal of exit from the reservoir, method of transmission, portal of entry to the susceptible host, and a susceptible host link.
2. Interventions that affect the etiologic agent (microorganism) include correctly cleaning, disinfecting, or sterilizing articles before use and educating clients and support persons about appropriate methods to clean, disinfect, and sterilize articles.
3. Interventions to reduce the reservoir (source) include changing dressings and bandages when soiled or wet, assisting clients to carry out appropriate skin and oral hygiene, disposing of damp and soiled linens appropriately, disposing of feces and urine in appropriate receptacles, ensuring that all fluid containers are covered or capped, and emptying suction and drainage bottles at the end of each shift or before they become full or according to agency policy.
4. The portal of exit from the reservoir can be controlled by avoiding talking, coughing, or sneezing over open wounds or sterile fields, and covering the mouth and nose when coughing or sneezing.
5. The method of transmission can be controlled by cleansing hands properly; instructing clients and support persons to cleanse hands before handling food or eating, after eliminating, and after touching infectious material; wearing gloves when handling secretions and excretions; wearing gowns if there is danger of

## POWERPOINT LECTURE SLIDES

*(NOTE: The number on each PPT Lecture Slide directly corresponds with the Concepts for Lecture.)*

1 Chain of Infection
- Etiologic agent
- Reservoir
- Portal of exit from the reservoir
- Method of transmission
- Portal of entry to the susceptible host
- Susceptible host

2 Breaking the Chain of Infection
- Etiologic agent
  - Correctly cleaning, disinfecting or sterilizing articles
  - Educating clients and support persons

3 Reservoir (Source)
- Changing dressings and bandages
- Skin and oral hygiene
- Disposing of damp, soiled linens appropriately
- Disposing of feces and urine appropriately
- Covering or capping all fluid containers
- Emptying suction and drainage bottle before full or according to agency policy

4 Portal of Exit
- Avoiding talking, coughing, or sneezing over open wounds or sterile fields
- Covering the mouth and nose when coughing or sneezing

soiling clothing with body substances; placing discarded soiled materials in moisture-proof refuse bags; holding used bedpans steadily to prevent spillage; disposing of urine and feces in appropriate receptacles; initiating and implementing aseptic precautions for all clients; wearing masks and eye protection when in close contact with clients who have infections transmitted by droplets from the respiratory tract; and wearing masks and eye protection when sprays of body fluid are possible.

6. The portal of entry to the susceptible host can be broken by using sterile technique for invasive procedures, using sterile techniques when exposing open wounds or handling dressings, placing used disposable needles and syringes in puncture-resistant containers for disposal, and providing all clients with their own personal care items.

7. The susceptible host link can be broken by maintaining the integrity of the client's skin and mucous membranes, ensuring that the client receives a balanced diet, and educating the public about the importance of immunizations (see Table 31–7).

**5** Method of Transmission
- Using proper hand cleansing
- Teaching appropriate hand hygiene
- Wearing gloves when necessary
- Wearing gowns when necessary
- Discarding soiled materials appropriately
- Holding used bedpans steadily to prevent spillage
- Disposing of urine and feces appropriately
- Implementing aseptic precautions for all clients
- Wearing masks and eye protection when necessary

**6** Portal of Entry
- Using sterile technique when necessary
- Using puncture-resistant containers for disposal of sharps
- Providing all clients with own personal care items

**7** Susceptible Host
- Maintaining the integrity of the client's skin and mucous membranes
- Ensuring that the client receives a balanced diet
- Educating the public about the importance of immunizations

---

### SUGGESTIONS FOR CLASSROOM ACTIVITIES

- Divide the students into groups. Assign each group a link in the chain of infection. Ask each group to identify additional interventions to break the assigned link. Share with the class.

### SUGGESTIONS FOR CLINICAL ACTIVITIES

- Have the students observe health care personnel on the clinical unit. Ask the students to identify instances of proper medical and surgical asepsis.

---

## LEARNING OUTCOME 10

Compare and contrast category-specific, disease-specific, universal, body substance, standard, and transmission-based isolation precaution systems.

### CONCEPTS FOR LECTURE

1. Isolation refers to measures designed to prevent the spread of infections or potentially infectious microorganisms to health personnel, clients, and visitors. Several sets of guidelines have been used in hospitals and other health care settings.

    Category-specific isolation precautions use seven categories: strict, contact, respiratory, and tuberculosis isolation, and enteric, drainage/secretions, and blood/body fluid precautions.

2. Disease-specific isolation precautions provide precautions for specific diseases. They may delineate use of private rooms with special ventilation, having the client share a room with other clients infected with the same organism, and gowning to prevent gross soilage of clothes for specific infectious diseases.

### POWERPOINT LECTURE SLIDES

*(NOTE: The number on each PPT Lecture Slide directly corresponds with the Concepts for Lecture.)*

**1** Category-specific Isolation Precautions
- Strict isolation
- Contact isolation
- Respiratory isolation
- Tuberculosis isolation
- Enteric precautions
- Drainage/secretions precautions
- Blood/body fluid precautions

**2** Disease-specific Isolation Precautions
- Delineate practices for control of specific diseases such as the following: use of private rooms with special ventilation

3. Universal precautions (UP) are techniques to be used with all clients to decrease the risk of transmitting unidentified pathogens. These obstruct the spread of bloodborne pathogens, namely hepatitis B and C viruses and HIV. The CDC did not recommend that universal precautions replace disease-specific or category-specific precautions, but that they be used in conjunction with them.

4. The body substance isolation (BSI) system employs generic infection control precautions for all clients except those with the few diseases transmitted through the air. The BSI system is based on three premises: (a) all people have an increased risk for infection from microorganisms placed on their mucous membranes and nonintact skin; (b) all people are likely to have potentially infectious microorganisms in all of their moist body sites and substances; and (c) an unknown portion of clients and health care workers will always be colonized or infected with potentially infectious microorganisms in their blood and other moist body sites and substances. The term *body substances* includes blood, some body fluids, urine, feces, wound drainage, oral secretions, and any other body product or tissue.

5. Standard precautions are used in the care of all hospitalized persons regardless of their diagnosis or possible infection status. They apply to blood; all body fluids, secretions, and excretions except sweat (whether or not blood is present or visible); nonintact skin; and mucous membranes. They combine the major features of UP and BSI (see Box 31–1)

6. Transmission-based precautions are used in addition to standard precautions for clients with known or suspected infections that are spread in one of three ways: by airborne transmission, by droplet transmission, or by contact. The three types of transmission-based precautions may be used alone or in combination but always in addition to standard precautions.

- cohorting clients infected with the same organism
- gowning to prevent gross soilage of clothes

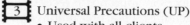 3 Universal Precautions (UP)
- Used with all clients
- Decrease the risk of transmitting unidentified pathogens
- Obstruct the spread of bloodborne pathogens (hepatitis B and C viruses and HIV)
- Used in conjunction with disease-specific or category-specific precautions

4 Body Substance Isolation (BSI)
- Employs generic infection control precautions for all clients
- Body substances include:
  - Blood
  - Urine
  - Feces
  - Wound drainage
  - Oral secretions
  - Any other body product or tissue

5 Standard Precautions
- Used in the care of all hospitalized persons
- Apply to
  - Blood
  - All body fluids, secretions, and excretions except sweat (whether or not blood is present or visible)
  - Nonintact skin and mucous membranes
- Combine the major features of UP and BSI

6 Transmission-based Precautions
- Used in addition to standard precautions
- For known or suspected infections that are spread in one of three ways:
  - Airborne
  - Droplet
  - Contact
- May be used alone or in combination but always in addition to standard precautions

## SUGGESTIONS FOR CLASSROOM ACTIVITIES

- Divide the students into groups. Assign each group a type of isolation or precaution category. Ask each group to select the personal protective equipment necessary to perform vital signs, to provide wound care for a large sacral decubitus, and to administer oral medications for a client diagnosed with hepatitis B, a client diagnosed with pulmonary tuberculosis, and an immunosuppressed client.

## SUGGESTIONS FOR CLINICAL ACTIVITIES

- Invite the infection control nurse to discuss the development of isolation categories and precautions and the role of the infection control nurse in institutions.

# LEARNING OUTCOME 11

Correctly implement aseptic practices, including hand hygiene; donning and removing a facemask, gown, and disposable gloves; managing equipment used for isolation clients; and maintaining a sterile field.

## CONCEPTS FOR LECTURE

1. Skill 31.1: Hand Hygiene, Skill 31.2: Donning and Removing Personal Protective Equipment (Gloves, Gown, Mask, Eyewear), and Skill 31.3: Establishing and Maintaining a Sterile Field present the correct implementation of aseptic practices. (Refer students to the Skill Checklists supplied on the Student CD-ROM.)

   Hand hygiene is important in every setting. It is considered one of the most effective infection control measurement. It is important that both the nurses' and the clients' hands be cleansed at the following times to prevent the spread of microorganisms: before eating, after using the bedpan or toilet, and after the hands have come in contact with any body substances. In addition, health care workers should cleanse their hands before and after giving care of any kind.

   WHO recommends hand washing under a stream of water for at least 20 seconds using plain granule soap, soap-filled sheets, or liquid soap when hands are visibly soiled, after using the restroom, after removing gloves, before handling invasive devices, and after contact with medical equipment or furniture; however, soap and water are inadequate to sufficiently remove pathogens.

   The CDC recommends use of alcohol-based antiseptic hand rubs for use before and after direct client contact. The CDC recommends antimicrobial hand cleansing agents in the following situations: when there are known multiple resistant bacteria; before invasive procedures; in special care units, such as nurseries and ICUs; and before caring for severely immunocompromised clients. Antimicrobial soaps are usually provided in high-risk areas and are frequently supplied in dispensers at the sink.

2. All health care providers must apply clean or sterile gloves, gowns, masks, and protective eyewear according to the risks of exposure to potentially infective materials.

3. The nurse should follow the principles of surgical asepsis when setting up a sterile field: all objects used in a sterile field must be sterile; sterile objects become unsterile when touched by unsterile objects; sterile items that are out of vision or below the waist or table level are considered unsterile; sterile objects can become unsterile by prolonged exposure to airborne microorganisms; fluids flow in the direction of gravity; moisture that passes through a sterile object draws microorganisms from unsterile surfaces above or below to the sterile surface by capillary action; the edges of a sterile field are considered unsterile; the skin cannot be sterilized and is unsterile; and consciousness, alertness, and honesty are essential qualities in maintaining surgical asepsis.

## POWERPOINT LECTURE SLIDES

*(NOTE: The number on each PPT Lecture Slide directly corresponds with the Concepts for Lecture.)*

**1** Hand Hygiene
- Skill 31.1 Hand Hygiene

**2** Protective Equipment
- Skill 31.2 Donning and Removing Personal Protective Equipment (Gloves, Gown, Mask, Eyewear)

**3** Sterile Field
- Skill 31.3 Establishing and Maintaining a Sterile Field

**4** Managing Equipment Used for Isolation Clients
- Many supplied for single use only
- Disposed of after use
- Agencies have specific policies and procedures for handling soiled reusable equipment
- Nurses need to become familiar with these practices

4. Many pieces of equipment are supplied for single use only and are disposed of after use. Some items are reusable. Agencies have specific policies and procedures for handling soiled equipment in order to prevent inadvertent exposure of health care workers to articles contaminated with body substances and to prevent contamination of the environment. Nurses need to become familiar with these practices in the employing agencies.

---

## SUGGESTIONS FOR CLASSROOM ACTIVITIES

- Have the students practice hand hygiene, donning and removing personal protective equipment, and sterile gloving.
- Show a videotape or DVD of these procedures.

## SUGGESTIONS FOR CLINICAL ACTIVITIES

- Review the policies and procedures of the agency for handling equipment for isolation clients.
- Assign students to care for clients who have isolation precautions in place. Discuss with the group how laboratory data relate to the infection, how equipment enters and leaves the room, how nursing procedures are carried out, and how the client is reacting to the isolation.

---

## LEARNING OUTCOME 12

Describe the steps to take in the event of a bloodborne pathogen exposure.

## CONCEPTS FOR LECTURE

1. Report the incident immediately to appropriate personnel within the agency and complete an injury report.
2. Seek appropriate evaluation and follow-up, including identification and documentation of the source individual when feasible and legal; testing of the source for hepatitis B, hepatitis C, and HIV when feasible and consent is given; making results of the test available to the source individual's health care provider; testing of the blood-exposed nurse (with consent) for hepatitis B, hepatitis C, and HIV antibodies; postexposure prophylaxis if medically indicated; and medical and psychologic counseling regarding personal risk of infection or risk of infecting others.
3. For a puncture/laceration, encourage bleeding, wash/clean the area with soap and water, and initiate first aid and seek treatment if indicated. For a mucous membrane exposure (eyes, nose, mouth), flush with saline or water for 5 to 10 minutes.
4. The postexposure protocol (PEP) for HIV includes starting treatment as soon as possible, preferably within hours after exposure. For "high-risk" exposure (high blood volume and source with a high HIV titer), three-drug treatment is recommended; for "increased risk" exposure (high blood volume or source with high HIV titer), three-drug treatment is recommended; for "low-risk" exposure (neither high blood volume nor

## LECTURE SLIDES

*(NOTE: The number on each PPT Lecture Slide directly corresponds with the Concepts for Lecture.)*

[1] Bloodborne Pathogen Exposure
- Report the incident immediately
- Complete injury report

[2] Seek Appropriate Evaluation and Follow-up Including:
- Identification and documentation of the source individual when feasible and legal
- Testing of the source for hepatitis B, C and HIV when feasible and consent is given
- Making results of the test available to the source individual's health care provider
- Testing of blood exposed nurse (with consent) for hepatitis B, C, and HIV antibodies
- Postexposure prophylaxis if medically indicated
- Medical and psychologic counseling

[3] Puncture/laceration
- Encourage bleeding
- Wash/clean the area with soap and water
- Initiate first aid and seek treatment if indicated
- Mucous membrane exposure (eyes, nose, mouth)
- Flush with saline or water flush for 5 to 10 minutes

source with a high HIV titer), two-drug treatment is considered. Drug prophylaxis continues for 4 weeks. Drug regimens vary and new drugs and regimens are continuously being developed. HIV antibody tests should be done shortly after exposure (baseline), and 6 weeks, 3 months, and 6 months afterward.

5. PEP for hepatitis B includes anti-HBs testing 1 to 2 months after the last vaccine dose, and HBIG and/or hepatitis B vaccine within 1 to 7 days following exposure for nonimmune workers.

6. PEP for hepatitis C includes anti-HCV and ALT at baseline and 4 to 6 months after exposure.

**4** Postexposure Protocol (PEP) for HIV
- Start treatment as soon as possible
- For "high-risk" exposure, three drug treatment is recommended
- For "increased risk" exposure, three-drug treatment is recommended
- For "low risk" exposure, two-drug treatment is considered
- Drug prophylaxis continues for 4 weeks
- Drug regimens vary and new drugs and regimens continuously being developed
- HIV antibody tests should be done:
  - Shortly after exposure (baseline)
  - 6 weeks, 3 months, and 6 months afterward

**5** Postexposure Protocol (PEP) for Hepatitis B
- Anti-HBs testing 1 to 2 months after last vaccine dose
- HBIG and/or hepatitis B vaccine within 1 to 7 days following exposure for nonimmune workers

**6** Postexposure Protocol (PEP) for Hepatitis C
- Anti-HCV and ALT at baseline and 4 to 6 months after exposure

| SUGGESTIONS FOR CLASSROOM ACTIVITIES | SUGGESTIONS FOR CLINICAL ACTIVITIES |
| --- | --- |
| • Discuss the legal aspects of testing the source individual. | • Review the institution's policies and procedures for exposure to bloodborne pathogens. |

# CHAPTER 32
## SAFETY

## RESOURCE LIBRARY

 **PRENTICE HALL NURSING MEDIALINK DVD-ROM**

Audio Glossary
NCLEX® Review
Skills Checklists:
   *Applying Restraints*
   *Implementing Seizure Precautions*
   *Using a Bed or Chair Exit Safety Monitoring*
    *Device*
Videos and Animation: *Lead Poisoning*

**COMPANION WEBSITE**

Additional NCLEX® Review
Case Study: *Ensuring Client Safety*
Care Plan Activity: *Safety at Home*
Application Activities:
   *Disaster Nursing and the Red Cross*
   *Safety in Nursing Issues*
Links to Resources

📖 **IMAGE LIBRARY**

**Figure 32.1** Nurses need to teach clients about safety and how to prevent accidents such as using smoke detectors, safety covers for electrical outlets, childproof locks on drawers and cabinets, Mr. Yuk stickers on toxic substances, infant car seats, and by placing poison control information near or on the telephone.
**Figure 32.2** Promoting safety (e.g., by placing hot pots on back burners with handles turned inward) is required to keep children from injury.
**Figure 32.3** Performing the Heimlich maneuver.

**Figure 32.4** Three-pronged grounded plug.
**Figure 32.5** Restraint monitoring and intervention flow sheet.
**Figure 32.6** A belt restraint.
**Figure 32.7** A mitt restraint.
**Figure 32.8** A limb restraint.
**Skill 32.1** Using a Bed or Chair Exit Safety Monitoring Device
**Skill 32.2** Implementing Seizure Precautions
**Skill 32.3** Applying Restraints

## LEARNING OUTCOME 1

Discuss factors that affect people's ability to protect themselves from injury.

### CONCEPTS FOR LECTURE

1. The ability of people to protect themselves from injury is affected by such factors as age and development, lifestyle, mobility and health status, sensory-perceptual alterations, cognitive awareness, emotional state, ability to communicate, safety awareness, and environmental factors.

    Through knowledge and accurate assessment of the environment, people learn to protect themselves from many injuries. Only through knowledge and experience do children learn what is potentially harmful. Elders can have difficulty with movement and diminished sensory acuity that may result in injury.

    Lifestyle factors that place people at risk include unsafe work environments, residence in neighborhoods with high crime rates, access to guns and ammunition, insufficient income to buy safety equipment or make necessary repairs, access to illicit drugs, and risk-taking behaviors.

### POWERPOINT LECTURE SLIDES

*(NOTE: The number on each PPT Lecture Slide directly corresponds with the Concepts for Lecture.)*

 1 Factors Affecting Ability to Protect Self from Injury
- Age and development
- Lifestyle
- Mobility and health status
- Sensory-perceptual alterations
- Cognitive awareness
- Emotional state
- Ability to communicate
- Safety awareness
- Environmental factors

Impaired mobility due to paralysis, muscle weakness, poor balance, or poor coordination increases risk for injury as may illness and surgery.

Accurate perception of environmental stimuli is vital to safety. Impaired touch, hearing, taste, smell, and vision increase susceptibility to injury.

Cognitive awareness is the ability to perceive environmental stimuli and body reactions and to respond appropriately through thought and action. Clients with impaired awareness are at increased risk for injury.

Extreme emotional states can alter the ability to perceive environmental hazards. Stressful situations can reduce a person's level of concentration, cause errors in judgment, and decrease awareness of external stimuli.

The ability to communicate is very important. Individuals with a diminished ability to receive and convey information are at risk for injury.

Safety awareness and accurate information are crucial to safety. Lack of knowledge places people at risk for injury.

The nurse may need to assess the environment of the home, workplace, and/or community. Client safety is affected by the health care setting, and bioterrorism has recently become a national safety concern.

---

## SUGGESTIONS FOR CLASSROOM ACTIVITIES

- Invite a representative of the local public health department to discuss bioterrorism preparedness for the community.
- Invite an occupational nurse to discuss occupational safety measures.

## SUGGESTIONS FOR CLINICAL ACTIVITIES

- Have the students assess their clients for factors that might affect their ability to protect themselves. Discuss findings and possible interventions to prevent injury for these clients.

---

# LEARNING OUTCOME 2

Describe methods to assess clients at risk for injury.

## CONCEPTS FOR LECTURE

1. Assessing clients at risk for injuries involves noting pertinent indicators in the nursing history and physical examination, using specifically developed risk assessment tools, and evaluating the client's home environment.

    The nursing history and physical examination include the following data: age and developmental level, general health status, mobility status, presence or absence of physiologic or perceptual deficits, altered thought processes or other impaired cognitive or emotional capabilities, substance abuse, any indications of abuse or neglect, accident and injury history, awareness of hazards, knowledge of safety precautions both at home and at work, and any perceived threats to safety.

## POWERPOINT LECTURE SLIDES

*(NOTE: The number on each PPT Lecture Slide directly corresponds with the Concepts for Lecture.)*

1. Methods to Assess Clients at Risk for Injury
    - Nursing history and physical examination
    - Risk assessment tools
    - Assessment of client's home environment

---

Risk assessment tools are available to determine clients at risk for specific kinds of injury, such as falls, and to determine the general safety of the home and health care setting. In general, these tools direct the nurse to appraise the factors affecting safety as well as summarizing specific data contained in the client's nursing history and physical examination.

Hazards in the home are major causes of falls, fire, poisoning, suffocation, and other injuries, such as those caused by improper use of household equipment, tools, and cooking utensils.

| SUGGESTIONS FOR CLASSROOM ACTIVITIES | SUGGESTIONS FOR CLINICAL ACTIVITIES |
| --- | --- |
| • Obtain examples of various risk assessment tools used in different health care agencies to share with the class. | • Review the risk assessment tools used in the clinical agency. Have the students assess their clients using these tools. |

# LEARNING OUTCOME 3

Discuss the National Patient Safety Goals (NPSGs).

## CONCEPTS FOR LECTURE

1. As a result of the Institute of Medicine report *To Err Is Human*, the health care industry and national organizations increased their awareness of the need to improve patient safety.

The Joint Commission on Accreditation of Healthcare Organizations (JCAHO) requires its accredited agencies to meet specific National Patient Safety Goals (NPSGs). It is important to remember that the focus of the NPSGs is on system-wide solutions rather than finding out who made the error. This changes the environment from one of fear and scapegoating to analyzing the system to find out why the error was made.

The JCAHO 2006 National Patient Safety Goals are the following: improve the accuracy of patient identification; improve the effectiveness of communication among caregivers; improve the safety of using medications; reduce the risk of health care-associated infections; accurately and completely reconcile medications across the continuum of care; reduce the risk of patient harm resulting from falls; reduce the risk of influenza and pneumococcal disease in institutionalized older adults; reduce the risk of surgical fires; implement applicable National Patient Safety Goals and associated requirements by components and practitioner sites; encourage the active involvement of patients and their families in the patient's care as a patient safety strategy; and prevent health care-associated pressure ulcers (decubitus ulcers).

## POWERPOINT LECTURE SLIDES

*(NOTE: The number on each PPT Lecture Slide directly corresponds with the Concepts for Lecture.)*

**1** National Patient Safety Goals (NPSGs)
- Improve the accuracy of patient identification.
- Improve the effectiveness of communication among caregivers.
- Improve the safety of using medications.
- Reduce the risk of health care–associated infections.
- Accurately and completely reconcile medications across the continuum of care.
- Reduce the risk of patient harm resulting from falls.
- Reduce the risk of influenza and pneumococcal disease in institutionalized older adults.
- Reduce the risk of surgical fires.
- Implement applicable National Patient Safety Goals and associated requirements by components and practitioner sites.
- Encourage the active involvement of patients and their families in the patient's care as a patient safety strategy.
- Prevent health care–associated pressure ulcers (decubitus ulcers).

## LEARNING OUTCOME 4

Identify common potential hazards throughout the life span.

### CONCEPTS FOR LECTURE

1. Hazards to the developing fetus include exposure to maternal smoking, alcohol consumption, addictive drugs, x-rays (first trimester), and certain pesticides.
2. Newborns and infants are at risk for falling, suffocation in cribs, choking from aspirated milk or ingested objects, burns from hot water or other spilled hot liquids, motor vehicle crashes, crib or playpen injuries, electric shock, and poisoning.
3. Hazards to toddlers include physical trauma from falling, banging into objects, or getting cut by sharp objects; motor vehicle crashes; burns; poisoning; drowning; and electric shock.
4. Potential hazards to preschoolers include injury from traffic, playground equipment, and other objects; choking, suffocation, and obstruction of airway or ear canal by foreign objects; poisoning; drowning; fire and burns; and harm from other people or animals.
5. Potentials hazards to adolescents include vehicular (automobile, bicycle) crashes, recreational injuries, firearms, and substance abuse.
6. Older adults are at risk for falling, burns, and pedestrian and motor vehicle crashes.

### POWERPOINT LECTURE SLIDES

*(NOTE: The number on each PPT Lecture Slide directly corresponds with the Concepts for Lecture.)*

1 Common Potential Hazards: Developing Fetus
- Exposure to maternal smoking, alcohol consumption, addictive drugs
- X-rays (first trimester)
- Certain pesticides

2 Common Potential Hazards: Newborns and Infants
- Falling
- Suffocation in cribs
- Choking from aspirated milk or ingested objects
- Burns from hot water or other spilled hot liquids
- Motor vehicle crashes
- Crib or playpen injuries
- Electric shock
- Poisoning

3 Common Potential Hazards: Toddlers
- Physical trauma from falling, banging into objects, or getting cut by sharp objects
- Motor vehicle crashes
- Burns
- Poisoning
- Drowning
- Electric shock

4 Common Potential Hazards: Preschoolers
- Injury from traffic, playground equipment, and other objects
- Choking, suffocation, and obstruction of airway or ear canal by foreign objects
- Poisoning
- Drowning
- Fire and burns
- Harm from other people or animals

5 Common Potential Hazards: Adolescents
- Motor vehicle or bicycle crashes
- Recreational injuries
- Firearms
- Substance abuse

6 Common Potential Hazards: Older Adults
* Falling
* Burns
* Motor vehicle crashes and pedestrian injuries

---

**SUGGESTIONS FOR CLASSROOM ACTIVITIES**

* Have the students design a safety information sheet for parents to provide to their child's caregiver (such as a babysitter).

**SUGGESTIONS FOR CLINICAL ACTIVITIES**

* Have the students assess their clients for potential hazards for the clients' age group.

---

# LEARNING OUTCOME 5

Give examples of nursing diagnoses, outcomes, and interventions for clients at risk for accidental injury.

## CONCEPTS FOR LECTURE

1. NANDA offers a broad diagnostic label related to safety issues: *Risk for Injury*, a state in which the individual is at risk for injury as a result of environmental conditions interacting with the individual's adaptive and defense resources. This broad label consists of subcategories that may be preferred when the nurse wants to describe injury more specifically to direct interventions: *Risk for Poisoning, Risk for Suffocation, Risk for Trauma, Latex Allergy Response, Risk for Latex Allergy Response, Contamination, Risk for Contamination, Risk for Aspiration,* and *Risk for Disuse Syndrome.*

   *Deficient Knowledge (Accident Prevention)* may be another nursing diagnosis.

2. The major goal for clients with safety risks is to prevent injury. To meet this goal, clients often need to change their health behavior and may need to modify their environment.

   Desired outcomes associated with preventing injury depend upon the individual client.

3. Nursing interventions to meet desired outcomes are largely directed toward helping the client and family to accomplish the following: identify environmental hazards in the home and community; demonstrate safety practices appropriate to the home health care agency, community, and workplace; experience a decrease in the frequency or severity of injury; and demonstrate safe child-rearing practices or lifestyle practices.

## POWERPOINT LECTURE SLIDES

*(NOTE: The number on each PPT Lecture Slide directly corresponds with the Concepts for Lecture.)*

 1 Nursing Diagnoses for Clients at Risk for Injury
* Risk for injury
  ○ Risk for poisoning
  ○ Risk for suffocation
  ○ Risk for trauma
  ○ Latex allergy response
  ○ Risk for latex allergy response
  ○ Contamination
  ○ Risk for contamination
  ○ Risk for aspiration
  ○ Risk for disuse syndrome
  ı Deficient knowledge (accident prevention)

2 Major Goal/Desired Outcomes for Clients with Safety Risks
* Prevent injury
* Often need to change health behavior
* Modify their environment
* Desired outcomes depend on individual client

3 Interventions
* Helping the client and family accomplish the following:
  ○ Identify environmental hazards in home and community
  ○ Demonstrate safety practices appropriate to the home health care agency, community, and workplace
  ○ Experience a decrease in the frequency or severity of injury
  ○ Demonstrate safe child-rearing practices or lifestyle practices

## LEARNING OUTCOME 6

Plan strategies to maintain safety in the health care setting, home, and community, including prevention strategies across the life span for thermal injury, falls, seizures, poisoning, suffocation or choking, excessive noise, electric hazards, firearms, radiation, and bioterrorism.

### CONCEPTS FOR LECTURE

1. When planning care to prevent injury, the nurse considers all factors affecting the client's safety, specifies desired outcomes, and selects nursing activities to meet these outcomes.

   Clients should be taught to prevent scalds and burns by making certain that pot handles do not protrude over the edge of a stove; electrical appliances especially those with dangling cords are out of the reach of crawling infants and young children; and that bath water is not excessively hot. In the health care institution, nurses should pay particular attention to assessing clients whose skin sensitivity is impaired, should monitor bath water temperature and take care when using therapeutic applications of heat.

2. To prevent agency fires, nurses must be aware of fire safety regulations and fire prevention practices of the agency in which they work. When a fire occurs, the nurse follows four sequential priorities: protect and evacuate clients who are in immediate danger; report the fire; contain the fire; and extinguish the fire.

3. Preventive strategies for home fires focus on teaching fire safety. Preventive measures include the following: keep emergency numbers near the telephone or stored for speed dialing; be sure smoke alarms are operable and appropriately located; teach clients to change batteries in smoke alarms annually on a special day; have a family "fire drill" plan; keep fire extinguishers available and in working order; and close windows and doors, if possible, cover the mouth and nose with a damp cloth when exiting through a smoke-filled area; and avoid heavy smoke by assuming a bent position with the head as close to the floor as possible.

   Preventive measures for falls are discussed in Outcome #7.

   Outcome #8 list seizures precautions (measures to protect the clients from injury should they have a seizure).

### POWERPOINT LECTURE SLIDES

*(NOTE: The number on each PPT Lecture Slide directly corresponds with the Concepts for Lecture.)*

**1** Preventing Thermal Injuries
- Pot handles should not protrude over the edge of a stove
- Electrical appliances should be out of the reach of crawling infants and young children
- Bath water should not be excessively hot
- Clients whose skin sensitivity is impaired should be monitored
- Care should be taken when using therapeutic applications of heat

**2** Preventing Agency Fires
- Be aware of fire safety regulations and fire prevention practices of the agency
  - If a fire occurs, the nurse should:
    - Protect and evacuate clients who are in immediate danger
    - Report the fire
    - Contain the fire
    - Extinguish the fire

**3** Preventing Home Fires
- Teach fire safety
- Keep emergency numbers near the telephone, or stored for speed dialing
- Be sure smoke alarms are operable and appropriately located
- Teach to change batteries in smoke alarms annually on a special day
- Have a family "fire drill"
- Keep fire extinguishers available and in working order
- If a fire occurs:
  - Close windows and doors, if possible
  - Cover mouth and nose with a damp cloth
  - Avoid heavy smoke by assuming a bent position with the head as close to the floor as possible

4. Measures to prevent poisoning include the following: lock potentially toxic agents in a cupboard or attach special plastic hooks to keep them securely closed; avoid storing toxic liquids or solids in food containers; do not remove container labels or reuse empty containers to store different substances; do not rely on cooking to destroy toxic chemicals in plants; never use anything prepared from nature as a medicine of "tea"; teach children never to eat any part of an unknown plant or mushroom and not to put leaves, stems, barks, seeds, nuts, or berries from any plant into their mouths; place poison warning stickers designed for children on containers of bleach, lye, kerosene, solvent, and other toxic substances; do not refer to medicine as candy or pretend false enjoyment when taking medications; read and follow label directions on all products before using them; keep syrup of ipecac on hand at all times and use only on the advice from the local poison control center or the family primary health care provider; do not keep poisonous plants in the home and avoid planting poisonous plants in the yard; and display the phone number of the poison control center near or on all telephones in the home.

   Prevention of carbon monoxide (CO) poisoning includes learning the steps to prevent CO exposure because all gasoline-powered vehicles, lawn mowers, kerosene stoves, barbecues, and burning wood emit CO. Incomplete or faulty combustion of any fuel, including natural gas used in furnaces, also produces CO. Home CO detectors should be used.

5. Clients should be taught the universal sign of distress, grasping the anterior neck and being unable to speak or cough as well as the Heimlich maneuver, or abdominal thrust, which can dislodge the foreign object and reestablish an airway.

6. It is important for nurses to minimize noise in the hospital setting and to encourage clients to protect their hearing as much as possible. Noise can be minimized in several ways. Acoustic tile on ceilings, walls, and floors as well as drapes and carpeting absorb sound. Background music can mask noise and have a calming effect on some people.

7. To reduce electrical hazards the following actions should be taken: check cords for fraying or other signs of damage before using and do not use if damage is apparent; avoid overloading outlets and fuse boxes with too many appliances; use only grounded plugs and outlets; always pull a plug from the wall outlet by firmly grasping the plug and pulling it straight out; never use electrical appliances near sinks, bathtubs, showers, or other wet areas; keep electric cords and appliances out of the reach of young children; place protective covers over wall outlets to protect young children; have all noninsulated wiring in the home altered to meet safety standards; carefully read instructions before operating electric equipment; always disconnect appliance that had given a tingling sensation or shock

4 Preventing Poisoning
- Lock potentially toxic agents in a cupboard or attach special plastic hooks
- Avoid storing toxic liquids or solids in food containers
- Do not remove container labels or reuse empty containers to store different substances
- Do not rely on cooking to destroy toxic chemicals in plants
- Never use anything prepared from nature as a medicine of "tea"
- Teach children never to eat any part of an unknown plant or mushroom
- Place poison warning stickers designed for children on containers of toxic substances
- Do not refer to medicine as candy or pretend false enjoyment when taking medications
- Read and follow label directions on all products before using them
- Keep syrup of ipecac on hand at all times
- Use only on the advice from the local poison control center or the family primary health care provider
- Do not keep poisonous plants in the home
- Avoid planting poisonous plants in the yard
- Display the phone number of the poison control center near or on all telephones
- Use CO detectors

5 Preventing Choking and Suffocation
- Teach universal distress signal
- Teach Heimlich maneuver

6 Minimizing Excessive Noise
- Minimize noise in the hospital setting
- Encourage clients to protect hearing as much as possible
- Noise can be minimized in several ways:
  - Acoustic tile on ceilings, walls, and floors
  - Drapes and carpeting absorb
  - Background music

7 Reducing Electrical Hazards
- Check cords for fraying or other signs of damage before using and do not use if damage is apparent
- Avoid overloading outlets and fuse boxes with too many appliances
- Use only grounded plugs and outlets
- Always pull a plug from the wall outlet by firmly grasping the plug and pulling it straight out
- Never use electrical appliances near sinks, bathtubs, showers, or other wet areas
- Keep electric cords and appliances out of the reach of young children
- Place protective covers over wall outlets to protect young children

and have an electrician evaluate it for stray current; and keep electric cords coiled or taped to the ground away from areas of traffic to prevent others from damaging the cords or tripping over them.

8. To promote firearm safety, nurses can teach their clients to follow these guidelines: Store all guns in sturdy locked cabinets without glass and make sure the keys are inaccessible to children. Store the bullets in a different location. Tell children never to touch a gun or stay in a friend's house where a gun is accessible. Teach children never to point the barrel of a gun at anyone. Ensure the firearm is unloaded and the action is open when handing it to someone else. Don't handle firearms while affected by alcohol or drugs of any kind, including pharmaceuticals. When cleaning or dry firing a firearm, remove all ammunition to another room and double-check the firearm when you enter the room you will be using to clean the firearm. Have firearms that are regularly used inspected by a qualified gunsmith at least every 2 years.

9. Nurses need to protect themselves from radiation when some clients are receiving radiation therapy. Exposure to radiation can be minimized by limiting time near the source; providing as much distance as possible from the sources; and using shielding devices such as lead aprons when near the source. Nurses need to become familiar with agency protocols related to radiation therapy.

10. No one knows when a bioterrorism attack will occur; thus, it is important that health care personnel and facilities plan and prepare for the unknown. Health care organizations are now expected to address four specific phases of disaster planning—mitigation, preparedness, response, and recovery—as well as to participate annually in at least one community-wide practice drill (See Box 32–3).

- Have all noninsulated wiring in the home altered to meet safety standards
- Carefully read instructions before operating electric equipment
- Always disconnect appliance that had given a tingling sensation or shock and have an electrician evaluate it for stray current
- Keep electric cords coiled or taped to the ground away from areas of traffic to prevent others from damaging the cords or tripping over them.

**8** Firearm Safety
- Store all guns in sturdy locked cabinets without glass
- Make sure the keys are inaccessible to children
- Store the bullets in a different location
- Tell children never to touch a gun or stay in a friend's house where a gun is accessible
- Teach children never to point the barrel of a gun at anyone
- Ensure the firearm in unloaded and the action open when handing to someone else
- Don't handle firearms while affected by alcohol or drugs of any kind, including pharmaceuticals
- When cleaning or dry firing a firearm, remove all ammunition to another room
- Double-check the firearm when entering the room used to clean the firearm
- Have firearms that are regularly used inspected by a qualified gunsmith at least every 2 years

**9** Protecting Against Radiation
- Limit time near the source
- Provide as much distance as possible from the sources
- Use shielding devises such as lead aprons when near the source
- Become familiar with agency protocols related to radiation therapy

**10** Planning for Bioterrorism
- Important health care personnel and facilities plan and prepare for the unknown
- Health care organizations expected to address four specific phases of disaster planning
  - Mitigation
  - Preparedness
  - Response
  - Recovery
- Should participate annually in at least one community-wide practice drill

**SUGGESTIONS FOR CLASSROOM ACTIVITIES**

- Have the students investigate their community to determine the emergency phone numbers.
- Have the students investigate the website for the local health department to determine what information is available for the public on prevention of poisoning, bioterrorism, excessive noise, fire, and other safety issues.

**SUGGESTIONS FOR CLINICAL ACTIVITIES**

- Review the agency's policies and procedures for fire safety, electrical safety, and radiation safety.

---

# LEARNING OUTCOME 7

Explain measures to prevent falls.

## CONCEPTS FOR LECTURE

1. Measures to prevent falls in health care agencies include orienting clients to their surroundings and explaining the call system; carefully assessing the client's ability to ambulate and transfer; providing walking aids and assistance as required; closely supervising the clients at risk for falls, especially at night; encouraging the client to use the call bell to request assistance and ensuring that the bell is within easy reach; placing bedside tables and overbed tables near the bed or chair so that clients do not overreach; always keeping hospital beds in the low position and wheels locked when not providing care so that clients can move in or out of bed easily; encouraging clients to use grab bars mounted in toilet and bathing areas and railings along corridors; making sure nonskid bath mats are available in tubs and showers; encouraging the clients to wear nonskid footwear; keeping the environment tidy, especially keeping light cords from underfoot and furniture out of the way; and using individualized interventions rather than side rails for confused clients.

2. Electronic devices are available to detect that clients are attempting to move or to get out of bed (See Skill 32.1).

3. In the home or community setting, assess potential environmental causes of falls such as inadequate lighting; presence of electrical cords, loose rugs, clutter, and slippery floors; absent or unsteady railings; uneven step height or surfaces; unsteady bases on furniture; lack of armrests on chairs and cabinets that are too high or too low; and inappropriate toilet height, slippery floors, and absence of grab bars in the bathroom.

## POWERPOINT LECTURE SLIDES

*(NOTE: The number on each PPT Lecture Slide directly corresponds with the Concepts for Lecture.)*

1 Measures to Prevent Falls
- Orient clients to surroundings and explain the call system
- Carefully assess the client's ability to ambulate and transfer
- Provide walking aids and assistance as required
- Closely supervise the clients at risk for falls, especially at night
- Encourage the client to use the call bell to request assistance and ensure that the bell is within easy reach
- Place bedside tables and overbed tables near the bed or chair so that clients do not overreach
- Always keep hospital beds in the low position and wheels locked when not providing care so that clients can move in or out of bed easily
- Encourage clients to use grab bars mounted in toilet and bathing areas and railings along corridors
- Make sure nonskid bath mats are available in tubs and showers
- Encourage the clients to wear nonskid footwear
- Keep the environment tidy, especially keeping light cords from underfoot and furniture out of the way
- Use individualized interventions, e.g. electronic devices, rather than side rails for confused client

2 Using a Bed or Chair Exit Safety Monitoring Device
- Skill 32.1

3 Assess Potential Environmental Causes of Falls
- Inadequate lighting
- Presence of electrical cords, loose rugs, clutter, and slippery floors
- Absent or unsteady railings
- Uneven step height or surfaces
- Unsteady base on furniture
- Lack of armrests on chairs
- Cabinets that are too high or too low
- Inappropriate toilet height
- Slippery floors in the bathroom
- Absence of grab bars

### SUGGESTIONS FOR CLASSROOM ACTIVITIES

- Invite several home health nurses to discuss home health safety appraisal.
- Have the students develop possible interventions for potential environmental causes of falls in the home as listed in the textbook.

### SUGGESTIONS FOR CLINICAL ACTIVITIES

- Have the students do a safety check of their clients' rooms. Discuss findings and, if necessary, have students plan interventions to reduce the risk of falls for their clients.

## LEARNING OUTCOME 8

Discuss implementation of seizure precautions.

### CONCEPTS FOR LECTURE

1. Seizure precautions are safety measures taken by the nurse to protect clients from injury should they have a seizure (See Skill 32.2).

   Pad the client's bed by securing blankets and linens around the head, foot, and side rails of the bed.

   Put oral suction equipment in place, and test it to ensure that it is functional.

   Children who have frequent seizures should wear helmets for protection.

   Home safety precautions for a person who has seizures that are not well controlled include restriction of or direct supervision by others for activities such as tub bathing, swimming, cooking, using electrical equipment or machinery, and driving.

### POWERPOINT LECTURE SLIDES

*(NOTE: The number on each PPT Lecture Slide directly corresponds with the Concepts for Lecture.)*

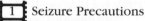 Seizure Precautions
- Pad the bed
- Put oral suction equipment in place and test
- Helmets for children with frequent seizures
- In the home, if seizures are not well-controlled, restrict or directly supervise:
  - Tub bathing
  - Swimming
  - Cooking
  - Using electrical equipment or machinery
  - Driving

### SUGGESTIONS FOR CLASSROOM ACTIVITIES

- Discuss the importance of teaching clients to take anticonvulsant medications as ordered.
- Discuss the state's regulations for obtaining or maintaining a driver's license if a person is diagnosed with a seizure disorder.

### SUGGESTIONS FOR CLINICAL ACTIVITIES

- Review the institution's policies and procedures for seizure precautions.

## LEARNING OUTCOME 9

Describe alternatives to restraints.

### CONCEPTS FOR LECTURE

1. As an alternative to restraints, assign nurses in pairs to act as "buddies" to observe the client when the other leaves the unit.

   Place unstable clients in an area that is constantly or closely supervised.

   Prepare clients before a move to limit relocation shock and resultant confusion.

   Stay with a client using a bedside commode or bathroom if the client is confused, is sedated, has a gait disturbance, or has a high risk score for falling.

   Monitor all the client's medication. If possible, lower or eliminate dosages of sedatives or psychotropics.

   Position beds in the lowest position.

### POWERPOINT LECTURE SLIDES

*(NOTE: The number on each PPT Lecture Slide directly corresponds with the Concepts for Lecture.)*

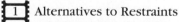 Alternatives to Restraints
- Assign nurses in pairs
- Place unstable clients in an area that is constantly or closely supervised
- Prepare clients before a move to limit relocation shock
- Stay with a confused, sedated, or unstable client using a bedside commode or bathroom
- Monitor all the client's medication and if possible lower or eliminate dosages of sedatives or psychotropics
- Position beds in lowest position

Replace full-length side rails with half-length or three-quarter-length rails to prevent confused clients from climbing over rails or falling from the end of the bed.

Use rocking chairs to help confused clients expend some energy so they will be less inclined to wander.

Wedge pillows or pads against the sides of wheelchairs to keep clients well positioned.

Place a removable lap tray on a wheelchair to provide support and help keep the client in place.

To quiet agitated clients, try a warm beverage, soft lights, a back rub, or a walk.

Use "environmental" restraints such as pieces of furniture or large plants as barriers to keep clients from wandering beyond appropriate areas.

Place a picture or other personal item on the door to the client's room to help the client identify the room.

Try to determine the causes of the client's sundowner syndrome, including poor hearing, poor eyesight, or pain.

Establish ongoing assessments to monitor changes in physical and cognitive functional abilities and risk factors.

- Replace full-length side rails with half- or three-quarter-length rails
- Use rocking chairs to help confused clients expend some energy
- Wedge pillows or pads against the sides of wheelchairs
- Place a removable lap tray on a wheelchair
- Try a warm beverage, soft lights, a back rub or a walk
- Use "environmental restraints"
- Place a picture or other personal item on the door to the client's room
- Try to determine the causes of the client's sundowner syndrome
- Establish ongoing assessment

## SUGGESTIONS FOR CLASSROOM ACTIVITIES

- Have the students identify additional alternatives to restraints.

## SUGGESTIONS FOR CLINICAL ACTIVITIES

- Have the students identify measures they have observed employed by staff of the agency or that they have employed to avoid the use of restraints and the outcomes of these measures.

# LEARNING OUTCOME 10

Discuss the use and legal implications of restraints.

## CONCEPTS FOR LECTURE

1. Because restraints restrict the individual's freedom, their use has legal implications. Nurses need to know their agency's policies and state laws about restraining clients.

   The U.S. Centers for Medicare and Medicaid Services published revised standards for use of restraints in 2001. These standards apply to all health care organizations and specify two standards for applying restraints: the behavior management standard when the client is a danger to self or others, and the acute medical and surgical care standard when temporary immobilization of a client is required to perform a procedure.

2. In the case of the behavior management standard, the nurse may apply restraints but the primary care provider or other licensed independent practitioner must see the client within 1 hour for evaluation. A written restraint order for an adult, following evaluation, is valid for only 4 hours.

## POWERPOINT LECTURE SLIDES

*(NOTE: The number on each PPT Lecture Slide directly corresponds with the Concepts for Lecture.)*

1. Use and Legal Implications of Restraints
   - Restraints restrict the individual's freedom
   - U.S. Centers for Medicare and Medicaid Services standards
     - Behavior management standard
     - Acute medical and surgical care standard

2. Behavior Management Standard
   - Nurse may apply restraints but the physician or other licensed independent practitioner must see the client within 1 hour for evaluation
   - Written restraint order for an adult valid for only 4 hours
   - Must be continual visual and audio monitoring

3. If the client must be restrained and secluded, there must be continual visual and audio monitoring of the client's status.

   The medical and surgical care standard permits up to 12 hours for obtaining the primary care provider written order for the restraints.

   All orders must be renewed daily.

   Standards require that a primary care provider order for restraints state the reason and time period. The use of prn orders for restraints is prohibited.

   Restraints should be used only after every other possible means of ensuring safety have been unsuccessful and documented.

   Nurses must document that the need for the restraint was made clear to both the client and the family.

   Clients have the right to be free from restraints that are nor medically necessary. There must be justification that the use of restraints will protect the client and that less restrictive measures were attempted and found not effective. Restraints cannot be used for staff convenience or client punishment.

 Medical Surgical Care Standard
- Up to 12 hours for obtaining the primary care provider written order
- Orders renewed daily
- Order must state the reason and time period
- PRN order prohibited
- Use only after every possible means of ensuring safety unsucccssful and documented
- Nurses must document need for the restraint made clear both to client and family.
- Can never be used for staff convenience or punishment

---

### Suggestions for Classroom Activities

- Discuss the difference in rules and regulations for the use of restraints in acute care and long-term care institutions.
- Have the students apply various types of restraints to each other using quick release knots. Ask thcm to describe feelings experienced when the restraint was applied.

### Suggestions for Clinical Activities

- Review the agency's policies and procedures for use of restraints. Compare and contrast with information presented in the textbook.

---

# Learning Outcome 11

List desired outcomes to use in evaluating the selected strategies for injury prevention.

### Concepts for Lecture

1. To prevent client injury, the nurse's role is largely educative. Desired outcomes reflect the client's acquisition of knowledge of hazards, behaviors that incorporate safety practices, and skills to perform in the event of certain emergencies. The nurse needs to individualize these for clients.

2. Examples of desired outcomes include describing methods to prevent specific hazards, reporting use of home safety measures, altering the home physical environment to reduce the risk of injury, describing emergency procedures for poisoning and fire, describing age-specific risks or work safety risks or community safety risks, demonstrating correct use of child safety seats, and demonstrating correct administration of cardiopulmonary resuscitation.

### PowerPoint Lecture Slides

*(NOTE: The number on each PPT Lecture Slide directly corresponds with the Concepts for Lecture.)*

 Desired Outcomes to Use in Evaluating the Strategies for Injury Prevention
- Nurse's role largely educative
- Desired outcomes reflect:
  - Acquisition of knowledge of hazards
  - Behaviors that incorporate safety practices
  - Skills to perform in the event of certain emergencies

Examples of desired outcomes include:

- Describe methods to prevent specific hazards
- Report use of home safety measures
- Alter home physical environment to reduce risk of injury
- Describe emergency procedures for poisoning and fire
- Describe age-specific risks or work safety risks or community safety risks
- Demonstrate correct use of child safety seats
- Demonstrate correct administration of cardiopulmonary resuscitation

# CHAPTER 33
## HYGIENE

## RESOURCE LIBRARY

 **PRENTICE HALL NURSING MEDIALINK DVD-ROM**

Audio Glossary
NCLEX® Review
Skills Checklists

**COMPANION WEBSITE**

Additional NCLEX® Review
Case Study: *Providing Basic Hygiene Care*
Care Plan Activity: *Client on Radiation Therapy*
Application Activities:
    *Client with Chickenpox*
    *Caring for Dentures*
Links to Resources

📖 **IMAGE LIBRARY**

**Figure 33.1** Tub/shower seat in the home.

**Figure 33.2** Hand bars on the sides of the bathtub.

**Figure 33.3** A shower chair.

**Figure 33.4** Fingernails are trimmed straight across.

**Figure 33.5** The anatomic parts of a tooth.

**Figure 33.6** Temporary teeth and their times of eruption (stated in months).

**Figure 33.7** Permanent teeth and their times of eruption (stated in years).

**Figure 33.8** Example of a foam swab used to clean the mouth of a dependent client.

**Figure 33.9** An African American's hair styled with braids.

**Figure 33.10** Shaving in the direction of hair growth.

**Figure 33.11** Removing hard contact lenses.

**Figure 33.12** Storing lenses.

**Figure 33.13** Removing a soft lens by pinching it between the pads of the thumb and index finger.

**Figure 33.14** Removing an artificial eye by retracting the lower eyelid and exerting slight pressure below the eyelid.

**Figure 33.15** Holding an artificial eye between the thumb and index finger for insertion.

**Figure 33.16** A, A behind-the-ear hearing aid. B, A behind-the-ear hearing aid attached to glasses.

**Figure 33.17** A, An in-the-ear hearing aid. B, Small hearing aid in ear canal. C, Large hearing aid in ear canal.

**Figure 33.18** Mitering the corner of a bed.

**Skill 33.1** Bathing an Adult or Pediatric Client

**Skill 33.2** Providing Perineal-Genital Care

**Skill 33.3** Providing Foot Care

**Skill 33.4** Brushing and Flossing the Teeth

**Skill 33.5** Providing Special Oral Care for the Unconscious Client

**Skill 33.6** Providing Hair Care for Clients

**Skill 33.7** Shampooing the Hair of a Client Confined to Bed

**Skill 33.8** Removing, Cleaning, and Inserting a Hearing Aid

**Skill 33.9** Changing an Unoccupied Bed

**Skill 33.10** Changing an Occupied Bed

## LEARNING OUTCOME 1

Describe hygienic care that nurses provide to clients.

### CONCEPTS FOR LECTURE

1. Hygiene involves care of the skin, hair, nails, teeth, oral and nasal cavities, eyes, ears, and perineal-genital areas.
2. It is important to know exactly how much assistance a client needs for hygienic care. Clients may require help after urinating or defecating, after vomiting, and whenever they become soiled.

### POWERPOINT LECTURE SLIDES

*(NOTE: The number on each PPT Lecture Slide directly corresponds with the Concepts for Lecture.)*

 Hygienic Care
- Care of the skin
- Hair
- Nails
- Teeth
- Oral and nasal cavities

**POWERPOINT LECTURE SLIDES** *continued*

- Eyes
- Ears
- Perineal-genital area

 Types of Hygienic Care
  - Early morning
  - Morning
  - Hours of sleep (HS) or PM
  - As-needed (prn)

**SUGGESTIONS FOR CLASSROOM ACTIVITIES**

- Have students provide examples of clients who may require help with hygiene care.

**SUGGESTIONS FOR CLINICAL ACTIVITIES**

- Have students discuss the type of assistance their assigned clients require for hygiene care and how they provided this assistance.

# LEARNING OUTCOME 2

Identify factors influencing personal hygiene.

## CONCEPTS FOR LECTURE

1. Factors influencing personal hygiene care include culture, religion, environment, developmental level, health and energy, and personal preference.

   The North American culture places a high value on cleanliness. Many North Americans bathe or shower once or twice a day; whereas people from other cultures bathe only once per week. Some cultures consider privacy essential, and others practice communal bathing. Body odor is offensive in some cultures and accepted as normal in others.

   Some religions practice ceremonial washings.

   For some people, the environment and finances may affect the availability of facilities for bathing and supplies for hygienic care.

   Children learn hygiene in the home. Practices vary according to the individual's age.

   Ill people may not have the motivation or energy to attend to hygiene. Some clients may not have the neuromuscular ability to perform hygienic care.

   Personal preferences also affect hygiene. For example, some people prefer a shower to a tub bath. Some people have preferences regarding the time of bathing.

## POWERPOINT LECTURE SLIDES

*(NOTE: The number on each PPT Lecture Slide directly corresponds with the Concepts for Lecture.)*

 Factors Influencing Personal Hygiene
  - Culture
  - Religion
  - Environment
  - Developmental level
  - Health and energy
  - Personal preference

**SUGGESTIONS FOR CLASSROOM ACTIVITIES**

- Have the students provide other examples of the factors influencing personal hygiene.
- Have students investigate the hygienic practices and preferences of students in the educational setting from difference cultures.

**SUGGESTIONS FOR CLINICAL ACTIVITIES**

- Have the students discuss factors that influence the provision of personal hygiene for their assigned clients.

# LEARNING OUTCOME 3

Identify normal and abnormal assessment findings while providing hygiene care.

## CONCEPTS FOR LECTURE

1. The nurse can use the opportunity of providing hygiene care to physically assess clients as well as assessing psychosocial and learning needs.

    Normal and abnormal skin assessment findings are found in Chapter 30. Common skin problems include abrasion, excessive dryness, ammonia dermatitis, acne, erythema, and hirsutism (see Table 33–3).

2. Normal and abnormal findings on assessment of the feet are listed in Table 33–5. Deviations from normal include excessive dryness, areas of inflammation or swelling, fissures, scaling and cracking of skin, plantar warts, swelling and pitting edema, weak or absent pulses, and cool skin temperature in one or both feet.

3. Normal and abnormal assessment findings of the nails are found in Chapter 30. Abnormal findings include: spoon nails, excessive thickness or clubbing, presence of grooves or furrows, Beau's lines, discolored or detached nails, bluish or purplish tint or pallor of nailbeds, hangnails, paronychia, and delayed capillary refill.

4. Normal and abnormal assessment findings of the mouth are included in Chapter 30. Common problems of the mouth are listed in Table 33–6 and include halitosis, glossitis, gingivitis, periodontal disease, reddened or excoriated mucosa, excessive dryness of the buccal mucosa, cheilosis, dental caries, sordes, stomatitis, and parotitis.

5. Normal and abnormal assessment findings of the hair are included in Chapter 30. Common problems of the hair include dandruff, hair loss, ticks, pediculosis, scabies, and hirsutism.

6. Normal and abnormal assessment findings of the eyes, ears, and nose are included in Chapter 30. Abnormal findings visible during hygiene care include: loss of hair, scaling, and flakiness of the eyebrows; redness, swelling, flaking, crusting, discharge, asymmetrical closing, or ptosis of the eyelids; jaundiced sclera; pale or red conjunctiva; opaque cornea; unequal pupils or pupils that fail to dilate or constrict, and inability to see; asymmetrical, excessively red or tender auricles; lesions, flaky, scaly skin over the auricles; normal voice tones not heard; asymmetrical nose; discharge, localized redness, tenderness or lesions of the nose.

## POWERPOINT LECTURE SLIDES

*(NOTE: The number on each PPT Lecture Slide directly corresponds with the Concepts for Lecture.)*

**1** Abnormal Findings of the Skin Include:
- Abrasion
- Excessive dryness
- Ammonia dermatitis
- Acne
- Erythema
- Hirsutism

**2** Abnormal Findings of the Feet Include:
- Excessive dryness
- Areas of inflammation or swelling
- Fissures
- Scaling and cracking of skin
- Plantar warts
- Swelling and pitting edema
- Weak or absent pulses
- Cool skin temperature in one or both feet

**3** Abnormal Findings of the Nails Include:
- Spoon nails
- Excessive thickness or clubbing
- Presence of grooves or furrows
- Beau's lines
- Discolored or detached nails
- Bluish or purplish tint or pallor of nailbeds
- Hangnails or paronychia
- Delayed capillary refill

**4** Abnormal Findings of the Mouth Include:
- Halitosis
- Glossitis
- Gingivitis
- Periodontal disease
- Reddened or excoriated mucosa
- Excessive dryness of the buccal mucosa
- Cheilosis
- Dental caries
- Sordes
- Stomatitis
- Parotitis

**5** Abnormal Findings of the Hair Include:
- Dandruff
- Hair loss
- Ticks
- Pediculosis
- Scabies
- Hirsutism

**6** Abnormal Findings of the Eyes, Ears, and Nose Include:
- Loss of hair, scaling, and flakiness of the eyebrows
- Redness, swelling, flaking, crusting, discharge, asymmetrical closing, or ptosis of the eyelids

- Jaundiced sclera
- Pale or red conjunctiva
- Opaque cornea
- Unequal pupils or pupils that fail to dilate or constrict
- Inability to see
- Asymmetrical, excessively red or tender auricles
- Lesions, flaky, scaly skin over the auricles
- Normal voice tones not heard
- Asymmetrical nose
- Discharge, localized redness, tenderness or lesions of the nose

## SUGGESTIONS FOR CLASSROOM ACTIVITIES

- Demonstrate how to perform a head-to-toe assessment while providing hygiene care. Use a manikin in the nursing laboratory.

## SUGGESTIONS FOR CLINICAL ACTIVITIES

- Have the students perform assessment of clients as hygiene care is provided. Share assessments in class. Discuss modifications to make this process more efficient and effective.

---

# LEARNING OUTCOME 4

Apply the nursing process to common problems related to hygienic care of the skin, feet, nails, mouth, hair, eyes, ears, and nose.

## CONCEPTS FOR LECTURE

1. Assessment of the client's skin, feet, nails, mouth, hair, eyes, ears, and nose includes a nursing history to determine self-care practices, self-care abilities, and past or current problems. The assessment should also identify clients at risk for developing impairment of these areas.

   Physical assessment of the skin, feet, nails, mouth, hair, eyes, ears, and nose is performed to gather objective data.

2. Nursing diagnoses are derived from the assessment data. *Self-Care Deficit (Bathing/Hygiene, Dressing/Grooming, or Toileting)* diagnoses are used for the client who has problems performing hygiene care. Other common nursing diagnoses include *Deficient Knowledge, Situational Low Self-Esteem, Risk for Impaired Skin Integrity, Impaired Skin Integrity, Risk for Infection, Impaired Oral Mucous Membrane, Disturbed Body Image,* and *Risk for Injury.* The etiology or risk factors are individualized according to client data.

3. In planning care, the nurse and, if appropriate, the client and/or family set goals/desired outcomes for each nursing diagnosis.

   The nurse then identifies interventions to assist the client to achieve the designated outcomes.

## POWERPOINT LECTURE SLIDES

*(NOTE: The number on each PPT Lecture Slide directly corresponds with the Concepts for Lecture.)*

1 Nursing Process Related to Hygienic Care: Assessment
- Nursing history to determine:
  - Self-care practices
  - Self-care abilities
  - Past or current problems
  - Identification of clients at risk for developing impairment
- Physical assessment

2 Nursing Process Related to Hygienic Care: Nursing Diagnoses
- Self-care deficit:
  - Bathing/hygiene
  - Dressing/grooming
  - Toileting
- Deficient knowledge
- Situational low self-esteem
- Risk for impaired skin integrity
- Impaired skin integrity
- Risk for infection
- Impaired oral mucous membrane

General nursing interventions include assisting dependent clients with hygiene activities, educating clients and/or family about appropriate hygienic practices, demonstrating use of assistive equipment and adaptive activities, and assessing and monitoring physical and psychological responses.

The nurse implements the plan as appropriate, evaluates the client's responses as designated in the goals/desired outcomes, and modifies the plan as necessary.

See Identifying Nursing Diagnoses, Outcomes, and Interventions for skin problems, foot problems, oral cavity problems, and hair grooming in the textbook for sample plans.

- Disturbed body image
- Risk for injury
- Etiology or risk factors are individualized

 Nursing Process Related to Hygienic Care: Planning/Intervention/Evaluation
- Nurse and, if appropriate, the client and/or family set goals/desired outcomes
- Nurse identifies interventions to assist the client to achieve the designated outcomes
- General nursing interventions include:
  - Assisting dependent clients with hygiene activities
  - Educating clients and/or family about appropriate hygienic practices
  - Demonstrating use of assistive equipment and adaptive activities
  - Assessing and monitoring physical and psychological responses
- Nurse:
  - Implements the plan
  - Evaluates the clients' responses as designated in the goals/desired outcomes
  - Modifies the plan as necessary

---

## SUGGESTIONS FOR CLASSROOM ACTIVITIES

- Discuss possible risk factors and etiologic factors for the nursing diagnoses related to hygiene as listed in the text.

## SUGGESTIONS FOR CLINICAL ACTIVITIES

- Have the students develop care plans related to hygienic care for assigned clients and present their plans in conference.

---

# LEARNING OUTCOME 5

Identify the purposes of bathing.

## CONCEPTS FOR LECTURE

1. The purposes of bathing are to remove transient microorganisms, body secretions and excretions, and dead skin cells; to stimulate circulation to the skin; to promote a sense of well-being; to produce relaxation and comfort; and to prevent or eliminate unpleasant body odors.

## POWERPOINT LECTURE SLIDES

*(NOTE: The number on each PPT Lecture Slide directly corresponds with the Concepts for Lecture.)*

 Purposes of Bathing
- Remove transient microorganisms, body secretions and excretions, and dead skin cells
- Stimulate circulation
- Promote a sense of well-being
- Produce relaxation and comfort
- Prevent or eliminate unpleasant body odors

---

## SUGGESTIONS FOR CLINICAL ACTIVITIES

- Have the students discuss the purposes of bathing that relate to their clients.

---

# LEARNING OUTCOME 6

Describe various types of baths.

## CONCEPTS FOR LECTURE

1. There are two categories of baths. Cleansing baths are given chiefly for hygiene purposes. Therapeutic baths are given for physical effects, such as to soothe irritated skin or to treat an area (e.g., perineum).
2. Types of cleansing baths include the complete bed bath, self-help bath, partial bath (abbreviated), bag bath, tub bath, sponge bath, and shower.

    When giving a complete bed bath, the nurse washes the entire body of a dependent client in bed.

    For a self-help bath, a client confined to bed is able to bathe self with help from the nurse for washing the back and perhaps the feet.

    In a partial bath (abbreviated), only the parts of the client's body that might cause discomfort or odor, if neglected, are washed: face, hands, axillae, perineal area, and the back.

    A bag bath is a commercially prepared product that contains 10 to 12 presoaked disposable washcloths that contain no-rinse cleanser solution.

    A tub bath is often preferred to a bed bath because it is easier to wash and rinse in a tub. Tubs are also used for therapeutic baths. There are tubs specially designed for dependent clients.

    A sponge bath is suggested for newborns because daily tub baths are not considered necessary.

    A shower may be appropriate for many ambulatory clients who are able to use shower facilities and require only minimal assistance from the nurse.

## POWERPOINT LECTURE SLIDES

*(NOTE: The number on each PPT Lecture Slide directly corresponds with the Concepts for Lecture.)*

**1** Categories of Baths
- Cleansing baths
- Therapeutic baths

**2** Types of Baths
- Complete bed
- Self-help
- Partial (abbreviated)
- Bag
- Tub
- Sponge
- Shower

## SUGGESTIONS FOR CLASSROOM ACTIVITIES

- Obtain a sample of a bag bath and demonstrate this type of bath on a manikin.
- Discuss situations in which a complete bed bath may be more desirable than a bag bath.
- Discuss various types of therapeutic baths.

## SUGGESTIONS FOR CLINICAL ACTIVITIES

- Discuss the types of baths and available equipment for performing baths in the institution.
- Demonstrate how to use shower chairs.

# LEARNING OUTCOME 7

Explain specific ways in which nurses help hospitalized clients with hygiene.

## CONCEPTS FOR LECTURE

1. Early morning care is provided to clients as they awaken. This care consists of providing a urinal or bedpan to the client confined to bed, washing the face and hands, and giving oral care.
2. Morning care is often provided after clients have breakfast, although it may be provided before breakfast. It usually includes elimination needs, a bath or

## POWERPOINT LECTURE SLIDES

*(NOTE: The number on each PPT Lecture Slide directly corresponds with the Concepts for Lecture.)*

**1** Early Morning Care
- Urinal or bedpan
- Washing face and hands
- Oral care

shower, perineal care, back massage, and oral, nail, and hair care. Making the bed is part of morning care.

3. Hour of sleep (HS) or PM care is provided to clients before they retire for the night. It usually involves providing for elimination needs, washing face and hands, giving oral care, and giving a back massage.

4. As-needed (prn) care is provided as required by the client.

**2** Morning Care
- Usually after breakfast
- Elimination
- Bath or shower
- Perineal care
- Back massage
- Oral, nail, and hair care

**3** Hour of Sleep (HS) or PM
- Elimination
- Washing face and hands
- Oral care
- Back massage

**4** As Needed (prn)
- As required by client need

---

## SUGGESTIONS FOR CLASSROOM ACTIVITIES

- Have students provide examples of clients who may require as-needed (prn) hygiene care. Discuss the importance of providing this care in terms of preventing client problems such as reduced skin integrity.

## SUGGESTIONS FOR CLINICAL ACTIVITIES

- Discuss the agency's routine bathing schedule and variations from this schedule.

---

# LEARNING OUTCOME 8

Describe steps for identified hygienic-care procedures.

## CONCEPTS FOR LECTURE

1. Nurses should understand the purposes of hygienic procedures as well as assessment that should be done prior to, during, and after the procedures.

   Planning includes decisions about delegating the performance of the procedure and gathering the equipment needed to complete the procedure.

   Implementation includes preparation of the client and equipment as well as performance of the procedure. This step is individualized according to the client's needs.

   Evaluation is the last step in hygienic-care procedures. It involves assessing the client's response to the procedures, conducting appropriate follow-up, and relating findings to prior assessment data.

   Refer to the textbook and the Skill Checklists on the Student DVD-Rom for the following:

2. Bathing an Adult or Pediatric Client: Skill 33.1
3. Providing Perineal-Genital Care: Skill 33.2
4. Providing Foot Care: Skill 33.3
5. Brushing and Flossing the Teeth: Skill: 33.4
6. Providing Special Oral Care for the Unconscious Client: Skill: 33.5
7. Providing Hair Care for Clients: Skill 33.6
8. Shampooing the Hair of a Client Confined to Bed: Skill 33.7

## POWERPOINT LECTURE SLIDES

*(NOTE: The number on each PPT Lecture Slide directly corresponds with the Concepts for Lecture.)*

**1** Steps for Hygienic-Care Procedures
- Assessing
- Planning
- Implementing
- Evaluating

**2** Bathing an Adult or Pediatric Client
- Skill 33.1

**3** Providing Perineal-Genital Care
- Skill 33.2

**4** Providing Foot Care
- Skill 33.3

**5** Brushing and Flossing the Teeth
- Skill 33.4

**6** Providing Special Oral Care for the Unconscious Client
- Skill 33.5

**7** Providing Hair Care for the Client
- Skill 33.6

**8** Shampooing the Hair of a Client Confined to Bed
- Skill 33.7

## SUGGESTIONS FOR CLASSROOM ACTIVITIES

- Have the students practice hygiene procedures on manikins.

## SUGGESTIONS FOR CLINICAL ACTIVITIES

- Have the students provide hygiene care for their assigned clients.
- Discuss the pros and cons of delegating hygiene care.

# LEARNING OUTCOME 9

Identify steps in removing contact lenses and inserting and removing artificial eyes.

## CONCEPTS FOR LECTURE

1. Hard contact lenses must be positioned directly over the cornea for proper removal. If the lens is displaced, the nurse asks the client to look straight ahead, and gently exerts pressure on the upper and lower lids to move the lens back onto the cornea. Figure 33.11 shows the steps needed to remove a hard lens.

   Removal of soft lenses varies in two ways. First, have the client look forward. Retract the lower lid with one hand. Using the pad of the index finger of the other hand, move the lens down to the inferior part of the sclera. This reduces the risk of damage to the cornea.

   Second, remove the lens by gently pinching the lens between the pads of the thumb and index finger. Figure 33.13 shows a client removing her own contact lens using the method described. The nurse would need to wear gloves.

2. To remove an artificial eye, the nurse puts on clean gloves and retracts the client's lower eyelid down over the infraorbital bone while exerting slight pressure below the eyelid to overcome the suction (See Figure 33.14). An alternative method is to compress a small rubber bulb and apply the tip directly to the eye; as the nurse gradually releases the finger pressure on the bulb, the suction of the bulb counteracts the suction holding the eye in the socket and draws the eye out of the socket.

   The eye is cleaned with warm normal saline and placed in a container filled with water or saline solution. The socket and tissues around the eye are usually cleaned with cotton wipes and normal saline.

   To reinsert the eye, the nurse uses the thumb and index finger of one hand to retract the eyelids, exerting pressure on the supraorbital and infraorbital bones. Holding the eye between the thumb and index finger of the other hand, the nurse slips the eye gently into the socket (See Figure 33.15).

## POWERPOINT LECTURE SLIDES

*(NOTE: The number on each PPT Lecture Slide directly corresponds with the Concepts for Lecture.)*

1. Removing Contact Lenses

2. Inserting and Removing Artificial Eye

## SUGGESTIONS FOR CLASSROOM ACTIVITIES

- If possible, obtain various types of contact lenses for students to view.

## SUGGESTIONS FOR CLINICAL ACTIVITIES

- If the agency has an eye clinic, arrange for students to observe fittings for contact lenses and the education given to clients obtaining contact lenses.

# LEARNING OUTCOME 10

Describe steps for removing, cleaning, and inserting hearing aids.

## CONCEPTS FOR LECTURE

1. Skill 33.8 provides the steps in removing, cleaning, and inserting a hearing aid. (See the textbook and the Skill Checklist provided on the Student DVD-ROM.)

    Remove the hearing aid.

    Turn the hearing aid off and lower the volume. The on/off switch may be labeled "O" (off), "M" (microphone), "T" (telephone), or "TM" (telephone/microphone).

    Remove the earmold by rotating it slightly forward and pulling it outward.

    If the hearing aid is not to be used for several days, remove the battery.

    Store the hearing aid in a safe place and label with the client's name. Avoid exposure to heat and moisture.

2. Clean the earmold.

    Detach the earmold if possible. Disconnect the earmold from the receiver of a body hearing aid or from the hearing aid case of behind-the-ear and eyeglass hearing aids where the tubing meets the hook of the case. Do not remove the earmold if it is glued or secured by a small metal ring.

    If the earmold is detachable, soak it in a mild soapy solution. Rinse and dry it well. Do not use isopropyl alcohol.

    If the earmold is not detachable or is for an in-the-ear aid, wipe the earmold with a damp cloth.

    Check that the earmold opening is patent. Blow any excess moisture through the opening or remove debris (e.g., earwax) with a pipe cleaner or toothpick.

    Reattach the earmold if it was detached from the rest of the hearing aid.

3. Insert the hearing aid.

    Determine from the client if the earmold is for the left or the right ear.

    Check that the battery is inserted in the hearing aid. Turn off the hearing aid, and make sure the volume is turned all the way down.

    Inspect the earmold to identify the ear canal portion. Some earmolds are fitted for only the ear canal and concha; others are fitted for all the contours of the ear. The canal portion, common to all, can be used as a guide for correct insertion.

    Line up the parts of the earmold with the corresponding parts of the client's ear.

    Rotate the earmold slightly forward, and insert the ear canal portion.

    Gently press the earmold into the ear while rotating it backward.

    Check that the earmold fits snugly by asking the client if it feels secure and comfortable.

    Adjust the other components of a behind-the-ear or body hearing aid.

    Turn the hearing aid on, and adjust the volume according to the client's needs.

## POWERPOINT LECTURE SLIDES

*(NOTE: The number on each PPT Lecture Slide directly corresponds with the Concepts for Lecture.)*

**1** Removing a Hearing Aid
- Turn off
- Remove earmold
- Remove battery, prn
- Store in a safe place

**2** Cleaning a Hearing Aid
- Detach earmold, if possible
- Soak detachable mold in mild soapy solution
- Do not use alcohol
- Wipe the nondetachable earmold with damp cloth
- Check patency of earmold opening
- Reattach the earmold

**3** Inserting a Hearing Aid
- Determine appropriate ear for insertion
- Replace battery, if removed
- Line up parts of earmold with client's ear
- Rotate the earmold slightly forward
- Insert the ear canal portion
- Gently press earmold into the ear while rotating it backward
- Check fit with client
- Adjust other components as necessary
- Turn on hearing aid

**SUGGESTIONS FOR CLASSROOM ACTIVITIES**

- If possible, invite a representative from a hearing aid company to bring samples of various hearing aids to class and discuss appropriate care of these devices.

**SUGGESTIONS FOR CLINICAL ACTIVITIES**

- Have the students review the policy and procedure for care of clients' hearing aids while in the institution.

## LEARNING OUTCOME 11

Identify safety and comfort measures underlying bed-making procedures.

### CONCEPTS FOR LECTURE

1. A smooth, wrinkle-free bed foundation minimizes sources of skin irritation. This is achieved by pulling and tucking the sheet under the mattress tightly.

    To provide for client comfort and safety after making a bed: Attach the signal cord so that the client can conveniently reach it; if the bed is currently being used by a client, either fold back the top covers at one side or fanfold them down to the center of the bed; place the bedside table and the overbed table so that they are available to the client; leave the bed in the high position if the client is returning by stretcher, or place in the low position if the client is returning to bed after being up.

    When turning the client to the side while making an occupied bed, raise the side rail nearest the client to protect the client from falling out of bed.

2. To ensure continued safety of the client after making an occupied bed: Raise the side rails; place the bed in the low position before leaving the bedside; attach the signal cord to the bed linen within the client's reach; put items used by the client within easy reach.

### POWERPOINT LECTURE SLIDES

*(NOTE: The number on each PPT Lecture Slide directly corresponds with the Concepts for Lecture.)*

 Bed-Making
- Provide smooth, wrinkle-free bed foundation
- Place the bedside table/overbed table within reach
- Leave the bed in the high position if returning by stretcher
- Leave in the low position if returning to bed after being up
- When turning the client to the side while making an occupied bed, raise the side rail nearest the client

 To Ensure Continued Safety of the Client after Making an Occupied Bed:
- Raise the side rails
- Place the bed in the low position
- Put items used by the client within easy reach
- Attach the signal cord

**SUGGESTIONS FOR CLASSROOM ACTIVITIES**

- Have the students practice making unoccupied and occupied beds in the nursing laboratory.

**SUGGESTIONS FOR CLINICAL ACTIVITIES**

- Discuss the schedule for linen change in the institution and reasons to deviate from this.
- Have the students perform safety checks of the environment after completing the linen change.

# CHAPTER 34
## DIAGNOSTIC TESTING

## RESOURCE LIBRARY

### PRENTICE HALL NURSING MEDIALINK DVD-ROM

Audio Glossary
NCLEX® Review
Skills Checklists
Animations: *MRI*
   *PET*
   *Ultrasounds*

### COMPANION WEBSITE

Additional NCLEX® Review
Case Study: *Checking Lab Results*
Care Plan Activity: *Client Waiting for Diagnosis*
Application Activity: *Diagnostic Tests*
Links to Resources

###  IMAGE LIBRARY

**Figure 34.1** Composition of blood.

**Figure 34.2** Blood glucose monitor, test strips, and lancet injector.

**Figure 34.3** A, Opening the front cover of a Hemoccult slide and applying a thin smear of feces on the slide. B, Opening the flap on the back of the slide and applying two drops of developing fluid over each smear.

**Figure 34.4** Disposable clean-catch specimen equipment.

**Figure 34.5** Obtaining a urine specimen from a retention catheter. A, From a specific area near the end of the catheter; B, from an access port in the tubing.

**Figure 34.6** Obtaining a urine specimen from a retention catheter using a needleless port.

**Figure 34.7** After dipping the reagent strip (dipstick) into fresh urine, wait the stated time period and compare the results to the color chart.

**Figure 34.8** Sputum specimen container.

**Figure 34.9** Depressing the tongue to view the pharynx.

**Figure 34.10** Enhanced color x-ray of the colon during a barium enema exam.

**Figure 34.11** Bronchoscopy.

**Figure 34.12** MRI lab.

**Figure 34.13** PET scan comparing the metabolic activity levels of a normal brain and the brain of an individual with Alzheimer's disease.

**Figure 34.14** A spinal needle with the stylet protruding from the hub.

**Figure 34.15** A diagram of the vertebral column, indicating a site for insertion of the lumbar puncture needle into the subarachnoid space of the spinal canal.

**Figure 34.16** Supporting the client for a lumbar puncture.

**Figure 34.17** A preassembled lumbar puncture set. Note the manometer at the top of the set.

**Figure 34.18** A common site for an abdominal paracentesis.

**Figure 34.19** A trocar and cannula may be used for an abdominal paracentesis.

**Figure 34.20** Two positions commonly used for a thoracentesis.

**Figure 34.21** Needle is inserted into the pleural space on the lower posterior chest to withdraw fluid.

**Figure 34.22** The sternum and the iliac crests are common sites for a bone marrow biopsy.

**Figure 34.23** A cross section of a bone.

**Figure 34.24** A common site for a liver biopsy.

**Figure 34.25** The position to provide pressure on a liver biopsy site.

**Skill 34.1** Obtaining a Capillary Blood Specimen to Measure Blood Glucose

**Skill 34.2** Collecting a Urine Specimen for Culture and Sensitivity by Clean Catch

# LEARNING OUTCOME 1

Describe the nurse's role for each of the phases involved in diagnostic testing.

## CONCEPTS FOR LECTURE

1. Diagnostic testing involves three phases: pretest, intratest, and post-test.
2. The major focus of the pretest phase is client preparation. The nurse educates the client about the test based on client assessment as well as knowledge about the test ordered. In addition, the nurse needs to know what equipment and supplies are needed (see Client Teaching: Preparing for Diagnostic Testing).
3. The intratest phase focuses on specimen collection and performing or assisting with certain diagnostic testing. The nurse provides emotional and physical support while monitoring the client as needed. Correct labeling, storage, and transportation of the specimen is also important.
4. During the post-test period, the focus is on the nursing care of the client, follow-up activities, and observations. The nurse compares the previous and current test results and modifies nursing interventions as needed. Reporting the results to appropriate health team members is also important.

## POWERPOINT LECTURE SLIDES

*(NOTE: The number on each PPT Lecture Slide directly corresponds with the Concepts for Lecture.)*

**1** Three Phases of Diagnostic Testing
- Pretest
- Intratest
- Post-test

**2** Pretest Phase
- Preparing the client
- Knowing about the test ordered
- Gathering equipment and supplies

**3** Intratest Phase
- Collecting the specimen
- Performing or assisting
- Providing emotional and physical support
- Monitoring
- Correct labeling, storage, and transportation of specimen

**4** Post-Test Period
- Nursing care of client
- Performing follow-up activities and observations
- Comparing the previous and current test results
- Modifying nursing interventions as needed
- Reporting the results

## SUGGESTIONS FOR CLASSROOM ACTIVITIES

- Ask the students to bring the laboratory and diagnostic test book required in the curriculum. Divide the students into groups and assign each group a specific diagnostic test. Have the students describe the nurse's role for each phase of the assigned diagnostic test. Share with the class.

## SUGGESTIONS FOR CLINICAL ACTIVITIES

- Have the students review the agency's policies and procedures for the nurse's role in common laboratory or diagnostic procedures.

# LEARNING OUTCOME 2

List common blood tests.

## CONCEPTS FOR LECTURE

1. Common blood tests include the complete blood count (See Table 34-1), serum electrolytes (see Box 34-1), serum osmolality, drug monitoring (peak and trough levels), blood urea nitrogen and creatinine, arterial blood gases, blood chemistry (see Table 34-2), metabolic screening, and capillary blood glucose levels.
2. The complete blood count includes hemoglobin, hematocrit, erythrocyte (RBC) count, leukocyte (WBC) count, RBC indices, and WBC differential.

## POWERPOINT LECTURE SLIDES

*(NOTE: The number on each PPT Lecture Slide directly corresponds with the Concepts for Lecture.)*

**1** Common Blood Tests
- Complete blood count
- Serum electrolytes
- Serum osmolality
- Drug monitoring
- Blood urea nitrogen and creatinine
- Arterial blood gases

Hemoglobin, the main intracellular protein of the RBCs, carries oxygen to and carbon dioxide from the tissues; hematocrit measures the percentage of RBC to total blood volume; the RBC count is the number of RBCs per cubic milliliter of whole blood; RBC indices evaluate the size, weight, and hemoglobin concentration; the WBC count is the number of WBCs per cubic milliliter of whole blood; the WBC differential identifies the type and percentage of each type of WBC.

3. The most commonly ordered serum electrolytes are for sodium, potassium, chloride, and bicarbonate ions. These are ordered to screen for electrolyte and acid-base imbalances.

4. Serum osmolality is the measure of the solute concentration in the blood.

5. Therapeutic drug monitoring is conducted when the client is taking a medication with a narrow therapeutic range. The peak level is the highest concentration of the drug and the trough level is the lowest concentration of the drug.

6. Blood levels of urea and creatinine are used to evaluate renal function. Urea, the end product of protein metabolism, is measured as blood urea nitrogen (BUN); creatinine is produced by muscles.

7. Arterial blood gases are explained in Chapter 50.

8. Blood chemistry includes liver function tests, cardiac markers, lipoprotein profile, serum glucose, hormones, and other substances. These tests provide valuable diagnostic cues.

9. Metabolic screening evaluates newborns for congenital metabolic conditions such as phenylketonuria (PKU) and congenital hypothyroidism.

10. Capillary blood glucose specimen is taken to measure blood glucose.

- Blood chemistry
- Metabolic screening
- Capillary blood glucose levels

**2** Complete Blood Count
- Hemoglobin
- Hematocrit
- RBC count
- RBC indices
- WBC count
- WBC differential

**3** Serum Electrolytes
- Sodium
- Potassium
- Chloride
- Bicarbonate ions

**4** Serum Osmolality
- Measure of solute concentration in the blood

**5** Drug Monitoring
- Therapeutic drug monitoring — client is taking medication with a narrow therapeutic range
- Peak level = highest concentration of drug
- Trough level = lowest concentration of drug

**6** Blood Urea Nitrogen and Creatinine
- Evaluate renal function
- Urea is end product of protein metabolism (measured as BUN)
- Creatinine produced by muscles

**7** Arterial Blood Gases
- Usually taken by specialty nurses, respiratory therapists
- Take specimens of blood from radial, brachial, or femoral arteries

**8** Blood Chemistry
- Liver function tests
- Cardiac markers
- Lipoprotein profile
- Glucose
- Hormones
- Other substances (i.e., cholesterol)

**9** Metabolic Screening
- Phenylketonuria (PKU)
- Hypothyroidism

**10** Capillary Blood Glucose
- Often taken to measure blood glucose
- Clients can perform on themselves

---

### SUGGESTIONS FOR CLASSROOM ACTIVITIES

- Select specific laboratory test results for memorization. Have a laboratory test "spelling bee" type game.

### SUGGESTIONS FOR CLINICAL ACTIVITIES

- Ask the students to relate the blood tests performed for their assigned clients to the clients' diagnosis and treatment plans, medical and nursing.

---

# LEARNING OUTCOME 3

Accurately measure blood glucose from a capillary blood specimen using a blood glucose meter.

## CONCEPTS FOR LECTURE

1. Skill 34.1 describes how to obtain a capillary blood specimen and measure blood glucose using a portable meter. (Refer to the textbook and the Skill Checklists included on the Student DVD-ROM.)

## POWERPOINT LECTURE SLIDE

*(NOTE: The number on each PPT Lecture Slide directly corresponds with the Concepts for Lecture.)*

[1] Capillary Blood Glucose Measurement
  • Skill 34.1

## SUGGESTIONS FOR CLASSROOM ACTIVITIES

• If possible, obtain several glucometers. Have the students read the directions for using these glucometers.
• Have the students go to several drugstores and price various types of glucometers and glucometer supplies. Share findings with the class.

## SUGGESTIONS FOR CLINICAL ACTIVITIES

• Assign the students to perform blood glucose measurement and relate findings to the client's previous values. Discuss necessary follow-up.
• Review the agency's policy and procedures for performing capillary blood glucose monitoring. Discuss protocols for abnormal capillary blood glucose results.

# LEARNING OUTCOME 4

Discuss the nursing responsibilities for specimen collection.

## CONCEPTS FOR LECTURE

1. Nursing responsibilities associated with specimen collection include the following: Explain the purpose of the specimen collection and the procedure for obtaining the specimen; provide client comfort, privacy, and safety; use the correct procedure for obtaining a specimen or ensure that the client or staff follows the correct procedure; note relevant information on the laboratory requisition slip; transport the specimen to the laboratory promptly; report abnormal laboratory findings to the health care provider in a timely manner consistent with the severity of the abnormal results.

## POWERPOINT LECTURE SLIDES

*(NOTE: The number on each PPT Lecture Slide directly corresponds with the Concepts for Lecture.)*

 Nursing Responsibilities for Specimen Collection
  • Explain the purpose of the specimen collection and the procedure
  • Provide client comfort, privacy, and safety
  • Use the correct procedure or ensure that client or staff follows the correct procedure
  • Note relevant information on the laboratory requisition slip
  • Transport the specimen to the laboratory promptly
  • Report abnormal laboratory findings to the health care provider in a timely manner

## SUGGESTIONS FOR CLASSROOM ACTIVITIES

• Ask the students to bring the laboratory and diagnostic test book required in the curriculum. Divide the students into groups and assign each group a specific diagnostic test. Have the students describe the nurse's responsibilities for each assigned diagnostic test. Share with the class.

## SUGGESTIONS FOR CLINICAL ACTIVITIES

• Arrange for the students to have an observational experience in several of the agency's laboratories. Ask the students to record observations as to how the laboratory personnel handle various specimens.
• Discuss the agency's policies and procedures for reporting laboratory results to health providers.
• Review procedures for delivery of specimens to the laboratory.

# LEARNING OUTCOME 5

Explain the rationale for the collection of each type of specimen.

## CONCEPTS FOR LECTURE

1. The stool specimen is used to determine the presence of occult (hidden) blood, to analyze for dietary products and digestive secretions, to detect the presence of ova and parasites, and to detect the presence of bacteria or viruses.
2. Urine specimens are collected by the nurse for a number of tests: clean voided specimens for routine urinalysis, clean-catch or midstream urine specimens for urine culture, and timed urine specimens for a variety of tests that depend on the client's specific health problem.
3. Sputum specimens are usually collected for one or more of the following reasons:
   - For culture and sensitivity to identify a specific microorganism and its drug sensitivities
   - For cytology to identify the origin, structure, function, and pathology of cells
   - For acid-fast bacillus (AFB), which also requires serial collection, often for 3 consecutive days, to identify the presence of tuberculosis (TB)
   - To assess the effectiveness of therapy
4. Throat culture samples are collected from the mucosa of the oropharynx and tonsillar regions using a culture swab. The sample is then cultured and examined for the presence of disease-producing microorganisms.

## POWERPOINT LECTURE SLIDES

*(NOTE: The number on each PPT Lecture Slide directly corresponds with the Concepts for Lecture.)*

**1** Stool Specimens
- Used to determine:
  - The presence of occult (hidden) blood
  - To analyze for dietary products and digestive secretions
  - To detect the presence of ova and parasites
  - To detect the presence of bacteria or viruses

**2** Urine Specimens
- Clean voided specimens for routine urinalysis
- Clean-catch or midstream urine specimens for urine culture
- Timed urine specimens for a variety of tests

**3** Sputum Specimens
- Collected for one or more of the following reasons:
  - To identify a specific microorganism and its drug sensitivities
  - For cytology to identify the origin, structure, function, and pathology of cells
  - For acid-fast bacillus (AFB)
  - To assess the effectiveness of therapy

**4** Throat Specimens
- Collected from the mucosa of the oropharynx and tonsillar regions for the presence of disease producing microorganisms

## SUGGESTIONS FOR CLASSROOM ACTIVITIES

- Divide students into groups and assign each group a type of specimen. Ask students to develop a pamphlet or information sheet for clients describing the purposes for obtaining the specimen.

## SUGGESTIONS FOR CLINICAL ACTIVITIES

- Have students discuss the rationales for the types of specimens that have been obtained from their assigned clients.

# LEARNING OUTCOME 6

Collect and test stool specimens.

## CONCEPTS FOR LECTURE

1. The nurse needs to determine the reason for collecting the stool specimen and the correct method of obtaining and handling.
2. When obtaining a stool specimen, the nurse gives the following instructions to the client: Defecate in a clean bedpan or bedside commode; if possible, do not contaminate the specimen with urine or menstrual

## POWERPOINT LECTURE SLIDES

*(NOTE: The number on each PPT Lecture Slide directly corresponds with the Concepts for Lecture.)*

**1** Collecting and Testing Stool Specimens
- Determine reason for collecting the stool specimen
- Determine correct method of obtaining and handling

discharge; void before the specimen collection; do not place toilet tissue in the bedpan after defecation; and notify the nurse as soon as possible after defecation.

3. When obtaining the stool specimen from the bedpan or bedside commode, the nurse should follow medical aseptic technique meticulously, wear gloves, and take care not to contaminate the outside of the specimen container.

   The amount of stool to be sent depends on the purpose for which the specimen is collected. Usually about 2.5 cm (1 in.) of formed stool or 15 to 30 mL of liquid stool is adequate. For some timed specimens, the entire stool passed must be sent. Visible pus, mucus, or blood should be included in sample specimens.

   The specimen label and the laboratory requisition must have the correct information and be securely attached to the specimen container. The specimen should be sent to the laboratory immediately or refrigerated because fresh specimens provide the most accurate results.

   All relevant information must be documented including date and time of the collections and all nursing assessments (e.g., color, odor, consistency, and amount of feces), presence of abnormal constituents, results of the test for occult blood if obtained, discomfort during or after defecation, status of perianal skin, and any bleeding from the anus after defecation.

4. For a stool culture, the nurse dips a sterile swab into the specimen, preferably where purulent fecal matter is present, and, using sterile technique, places the swab in a sterile test tube.

5. A commonly used test product to measure occult blood is the Hemoccult test. To perform this test, the nurse or client uses a tongue blade to place a small amount of stool on a slide or card and then closes the card. The card is turned over and a few drops of a reagent are placed onto the smear or on the back of the card. The nurse then observes for a color change. A blue color indicates a guaiac positive result (presence of blood). No color change or any other color than blue is a negative finding, indicating the absence of blood in the stool.

   Certain foods, medications, and vitamin C can produce inaccurate test results. False-positive results can occur if the client has recently ingested red meat, raw vegetables or fruits (particularly radishes, turnips, horseradish, and melons), or certain medications that irritate the gastric mucosa and cause bleeding such as aspirin or other nonsteroidal anti-inflammatory drugs, steroids, iron preparations, and anticoagulants. False-negative results can occur if the client has taken more than 250 mg per day of vitamin C from all sources (dietary and supplemental) up to 3 days before the test, even if bleeding is present. (Guidelines for instructing clients to assess their stool for occult blood are listed in Client Teaching.)

**2** Instructions to the Client:
- Defecate in clean bedpan or bedside commode
- If possible, do not contaminate specimen with urine or menstrual discharge
- Do not place toilet tissue in bedpan after defecation
- Notify the nurse

**3** Collecting and Testing Stool Specimens
- Follow medical aseptic technique meticulously
- Know the amount of stool to collect
- Correctly label and complete the laboratory requisition
- Send to the laboratory immediately or refrigerate
- Document all relevant information

**4** Stool Culture
- Dip a sterile swab into the specimen
- Using sterile technique, place the swab in a sterile test tube

**5** Hemoccult Test
- Instruct about foods and medications to be restricted prior to test
- Use tongue blade to place small amount of stool on slide or card
- Close card
- Turn card over
- Add few drops of a reagent onto the smear or on the back of the card
- Observe for a color change

## SUGGESTIONS FOR CLASSROOM ACTIVITIES

- Have the students review the laboratory book required for the curriculum to determine other methods of detecting occult blood in the stool. Compare with the Hemoccult method.

## SUGGESTIONS FOR CLINICAL ACTIVITIES

- If possible, have students perform Hemoccult testing if required on their assigned clients and present the results.
- Discuss the agency's policies and procedures for occult blood testing (e.g., is this a nursing responsibility or is this a procedure delegated to the laboratory?).

# LEARNING OUTCOME 7

Compare and contrast the different types of urine specimens.

## CONCEPTS FOR LECTURE

1. There are several types of urine specimens: clean voided for routine urinalysis, clean-catch or midstream urine specimen for urine culture (see Skill 34.2), and timed urine specimens for a variety of tests. Some urine specimen collection may require collection via straight catheter insertion.
2. A clean voided specimen is usually collected by the client with minimal instructions. Male clients generally are able to void directly into the specimen container, and female clients usually sit or squat over the toilet, holding the container between their legs during voiding. Routine urine examinations are usually done on the first voided specimen in the morning because it tends to have a higher, more uniform concentration and a more acidic pH than specimens later in the day. A urine specimen of 10 mL is generally sufficient.
3. Clean-catch or midstream urine specimens are collected when a urine culture is ordered to identify microorganisms causing urinary tract infection. Clean-catch specimens are collected into a sterile specimen container with a lid. Care is taken to ensure that the specimen is as free as possible from contamination by microorganisms around the urinary meatus. Skill 34.2 explains how to collect a clean-catch urine specimen.
4. Timed urine specimens require collection of all urine produced and voided over a specific period of time, ranging from 1 to 2 hours to 24 hours. Timed specimens are either refrigerated or contain a preservative to prevent bacterial growth or decomposition of urine components.

## POWERPOINT LECTURE SLIDES

*(NOTE: The number on each PPT Lecture Slide directly corresponds with the Concepts for Lecture.)*

**1** Types of Urine Specimens
- Clean voided
- Clean-catch or midstream
- Timed

**2** Clean Voided Urine Specimen
- Routine urinalysis
- Nonsterile specimen
- Usually first-morning urine

**3** Clean-Catch or Midstream Urine Specimen
- Skill 34.2
- Urine culture to identify microorganisms causing urinary tract infection
- Sterile specimen

**4** Timed Urine Specimen
- Collection of all urine produced and voided over a specific time period
- Generally refrigerated or treated to prevent bacterial growth or decomposition of urine components
- Nonsterile specimen

## SUGGESTIONS FOR CLASSROOM ACTIVITIES

- Review the procedures for obtaining each type of specimen.
- Show the equipment used for obtaining each type of specimen.
- Review "dipstick" urine testing.

## SUGGESTIONS FOR CLINICAL ACTIVITIES

- Have the students obtain necessary urine specimens for assigned clients.
- Have the students discuss results of urine testing performed on their assigned clients and relate the results to the clients' diagnosis and plan of care, medical and nursing.

# LEARNING OUTCOME 8

Collect sputum and throat specimens.

## CONCEPTS FOR LECTURE

1. To collect a sputum specimen, the nurse follows these steps: Offer mouth care so that the specimen will not be contaminated with microorganisms from the mouth. Ask the client to breathe deeply and then cough up 1 to 2 tablespoons or 15 to 30 mL of sputum. Wear gloves and personal protective equipment to avoid direct contact with the sputum (if TB is suspected, obtain the specimen in a room equipped with a special airflow system or ultraviolet light, or outdoors, or wear a mask capable of filtering droplet nuclei). Ask the client to expectorate the sputum into the specimen container. Make sure that the sputum does not contact the outside of the container. Following sputum collection, offer mouthwash. Label and transport the specimen to the laboratory. Document the collection of the sputum specimen on the client's chart, including the amount, color, odor, consistency (thick, tenacious, watery), presence of hemoptysis, measures needed to obtain the specimen (postural drainage), and any discomfort experienced by the client.
2. To obtain a throat culture specimen, the nurse puts on clean gloves, then inserts the swab into the oropharynx and runs the swab along the tonsils and areas on the pharynx that are reddened or contain exudates.

## POWERPOINT LECTURE SLIDES

*(NOTE: The number on each PPT Lecture Slide directly corresponds with the Concepts for Lecture.)*

 Collecting Sputum Specimens
- Offer mouth care
- Wear gloves and PPE
- Ask client to do the following:
  - Breathe deeply
  - Cough up 1 to 2 tablespoons or 15 to 30 mL of sputum
  - Expectorate sputum into specimen container
  - Make sure sputum does not contact outside of container
- Offer mouthwash
- Label and send to laboratory
- Document

 Collecting Throat Cultures
- Put on clean gloves
- Insert swab into the oropharynx
- Run swab along tonsils and areas that are reddened or contain exudates
- Place swab in sterile test tube
- Label and send to laboratory
- Document

## SUGGESTIONS FOR CLASSROOM ACTIVITIES

- Demonstrate how to use suction to obtain sputum specimens (e.g., sputum traps).

## SUGGESTIONS FOR CLINICAL ACTIVITIES

- Have the students obtain sputum specimens on assigned clients if appropriate.

# LEARNING OUTCOME 9

Describe visualization procedures that may be used for the client with gastrointestinal, urinary, and cardiopulmonary alterations.

## CONCEPTS FOR LECTURE

1. Visualization procedures include indirect (noninvasive) and direct (invasive) techniques for visualizing body organ and system functions.
2. Direct gastrointestinal visualization techniques include anoscopy, the viewing of the anal canal; proctoscopy, the viewing of the rectum; proctosigmoidoscopy, the viewing of the rectum and sigmoid colon; and colonoscopy, the viewing of the large intestines.
3. Indirect viewing of the gastrointestinal tract is possible with x-rays that can detect strictures, obstructions,

## POWERPOINT LECTURE SLIDES

*(NOTE: The number on each PPT Lecture Slide directly corresponds with the Concepts for Lecture.)*

 Visualization Procedures
- Direct (invasive)
- Indirect (noninvasive)
- Techniques for visualizing body organ and system function

## CONCEPTS FOR LECTURE *continued*

tumors, ulcers, inflammatory disease, or other structural changes such as hiatal hernias. Viewing may be enhanced by introduction of a radiopaque substance such as barium through swallowing or enema. These x-rays usually include fluoroscopic examination.

4. Visualization of the urinary tract includes x-rays of the kidneys/ureters/bladder (KUB), intravenous pyelography (IVP), and retrograde pyelography. For an intravenous pyelogram, contrast medium is injected intravenously. During retrograde pyelography, the contrast medium is instilled directly into the kidney pelvis via the urethra, bladder, and ureters. Renal ultrasonography is a noninvasive test that uses reflected sound waves to visualize the kidneys. During a cystoscopy, the bladder, ureteral orifices, and urethra can be directly visualized using a cystoscope, a lighted instrument inserted through the urethra.

5. A number of visualization procedures can be done to examine the cardiovascular system and respiratory tract. Electrocardiography (ECG) provides a graphic recording of the heart's electrical activity. Stress electrocardiography uses ECG to assess the client's response to an increased cardiac workload during exercise. Angiography is an invasive procedure requiring informed consent of the client. A radiopaque dye is injected into the vessels to be examined; using fluoroscopy and x-rays the flow through the vessels is assessed. An echocardiogram is a noninvasive test that uses ultrasound to visualize structures of the heart and evaluate left ventricular functions. X-ray examination of the chest is done both to diagnose and to assess the progress of a disease.

6. A lung scan, also known as a V/Q (ventilation/perfusion) scan, records the emissions from radioisotopes that indicate how well gas and blood are traveling through the lungs. The perfusion scan (Q scan) is used to assess blood flow through the pulmonary vascular system. A radioisotope is injected intravenously and measured as it circulates through the lung. The ventilation scan (V scan) detects ventilation abnormalities, particularly in clients with emphysema. The client inhales a radioactive gas through a mask and then exhales it into the room air. Laryngoscopy and bronchoscopy are sterile procedures that are conducted with a laryngoscope and bronchoscope. Tissue samples may be taken for biopsy.

## POWERPOINT LECTURE SLIDES *continued*

**2** Gastrointestinal System Visualization
- Direct
  - Anoscopy
  - Proctoscopy
  - Proctosignmoidoscopy
  - Colonscopy

**3** Gastrointestinal System Visualization
- Indirect
  - X-rays
  - May be enhanced by introduction of a radiopaque substance such as barium through swallowing or enema
  - Include fluoroscopic examination

**4** Urinary System Visualization
- X-rays of the kidneys/ureters/bladder (KUB)
- Intravenous pyelography (IVP) and retrograde pyelography
- Renal ultrasonography
- Cystoscopy

**5** Cardiopulmonary System Visualization
- Electrocardiography (ECG)
- Stress electrocardiography
- Angiography
- Echocardiogram

**6** V/Q (Ventilation/Perfusion) Scan
- Lung scan
- Perfusion scan (Q scan)
- Ventilation scan (V scan)
- Laryngoscopy
- Bronchoscopy

---

### SUGGESTIONS FOR CLASSROOM ACTIVITIES

- If possible, obtain videotapes or DVDs of various visualization procedures and show to the class.
- Ask the students to bring the laboratory and diagnostic test book required in the curriculum. Divide the students into groups and assign each group a specific diagnostic test. Have the students describe the nurse's responsibilities for each assigned diagnostic test. Share with the class.

### SUGGESTIONS FOR CLINICAL ACTIVITIES

- Arrange for the students to have an observational experience in various diagnostic centers in the agency (e.g., GI and cardiac lab). Have the students share observations of how the client is prepared and monitored during the procedure.

# LEARNING OUTCOME 10

Compare and contrast CT, MRI, and nuclear imaging studies.

## CONCEPTS FOR LECTURE

1. Computed tomography (CT) is a painless, noninvasive x-ray procedure that has the unique capability of distinguishing minor differences in the density of tissues. CT produces a three-dimensional image of the organ or structure, making it more sensitive than the x-ray machine.

2. Magnetic resonance imaging (MRI) is a noninvasive diagnostic scanning technique in which the client is placed in a magnetic field. Clients with implanted metal devices cannot undergo MRI because of the strong magnetic field. There is no exposure to radiation. If a contrast medium is injected during the procedure, it is not an iodine contrast. MRI provides a better contrast between normal and abnormal tissue than the CT scan. MRIs are commonly used for visualization of the brain, spine, limbs and joints, heart, blood vessels, abdomen, and pelvis.

3. Nuclear imaging studies study the physiology or function of an organ system in contrast to CT, MRI, or x-ray studies which visualize anatomic structures. Nuclear imaging studies use a radiopharmaceutical, a pharmaceutical (targeted to a specific organ) labeled with a radioisotope, which is administered through various routes. Clients retain the radioisotopes a relatively short period of time. A gamma camera converts the emission of the radioisotope and forms a detailed image.

4. Positron emission tomography (PET) is a noninvasive radiologic study that involves the injection or inhalation of a radioisotope. Images are created as the radioisotope is distributed in the body. This allows study of various aspects of organ function and may include evaluation of blood flow and tumor growth.

## POWERPOINT LECTURE SLIDES

*(NOTE: The number on each PPT Lecture Slide directly corresponds with the Concepts for Lecture.)*

**1** Computerized Tomography (CT)
- Painless, noninvasive x-ray procedure
- Distinguishes minor differences in the density of tissues
- Produces a three-dimensional image of organ or structure
- More sensitive than the x-ray machine

**2** Magnetic Resonance Imaging (MRI)
- Noninvasive diagnostic scanning technique
- Magnetic field
- Clients with implanted metal devices cannot undergo MRI
- No exposure to radiation
- Provides a better contrast between normal and abnormal tissue than the CT scan

**3** Nuclear Imaging Studies
- Study physiology and function
- Uses a radiopharmaceutical labeled with a radioisotope
- Administered through various routes
- Retain radioisotope for short period of time
- A gamma camera converts emission to form of detailed image

**4** Positron Emission Tomography (PET)
- Nuclear imaging study
- Involves the injection or inhalation of a radioisotope
- Images created as the radioisotope distributed in the body
- Allows study of various aspects of organ function
- May include evaluation of blood flow and tumor growth

## SUGGESTIONS FOR CLASSROOM ACTIVITIES

- Obtain examples of CT, MRI, and nuclear imaging scans to share with the class.

## SUGGESTIONS FOR CLINICAL ACTIVITIES

- Arrange for the students to have an observational experience in nuclear medicine, CT, and MRI. Have them share observations of how the client is prepared and monitored during the procedure.

# LEARNING OUTCOME 11

Describe the nurse's role in caring for clients undergoing aspiration/biopsy procedures.

## CONCEPTS FOR LECTURE

1. Aspiration is the withdrawal of fluid that has abnormally collected or to obtain a specimen (e.g., cerebral spinal fluid). A biopsy is the removal and examination of tissue.

2. The nurse's role in assisting with lumbar puncture, abdominal paracentesis, thoracentesis, bone marrow biopsy, and liver biopsy is extensive and is required before, during, and after these procedures. The full extent of the nurse's role is presented in Table 34–3: Assisting with Aspiration and Biopsy.

   When caring for the client undergoing a lumbar puncture, the nurse should explain that a local anesthetic will be given, a sensation of pressure will be felt when the spinal needle is inserted, and that the client must lie still for about 15 minutes as the procedure is performed.

3. During the lumbar puncture procedure the nurse assists the client to maintain the position by supporting the client behind the neck and knees; encourages normal breathing and relaxation; observes the client's color, respirations, and pulse; asks the client to report headache or persistent pain at the insertion site; handles specimen with gloves; labels and sends the specimen to laboratory immediately; and places a small sterile dressing over the puncture site.

4. After the lumbar puncture procedure, the nurse assists the client into the dorsal recumbent position with one pillow for 1 to 12 hours; provides analgesics, if ordered, for headache as necessary; offers oral fluids; monitors for swelling or bleeding at the puncture site, changes in neurologic status, numbness, tingling, or pain radiating down the legs; and documents the date and time and person performing the procedure, color, characteristics, amount of CSF withdrawn, number of specimens, CSF pressures, and nursing assessment and interventions.

5. When caring for a client undergoing an abdominal paracentesis, the nurse explains that the client must remain still during the procedure, helps the client assume a sitting position and provides a blanket for warmth.

6. During the abdominal paracentesis procedure the nurse provides verbal support; observes for signs of distress, monitors color, pulse, blood pressure and for signs of hypovolemic shock (pallor, dyspnea, diaphoresis, drop in blood pressure, restlessness or increased anxiety); places a small, sterile dressing over the puncture site; labels and sends specimens to the laboratory.

7. After the abdominal paracentesis procedure the nurse monitors for signs of hypovolemic shock, scrotal edema, vital signs, urine output, drainage from the puncture site every 15 minutes for 2 hours and then

## POWERPOINT LECTURE SLIDES

*(NOTE: The number on each PPT Lecture Slide directly corresponds with the Concepts for Lecture.)*

**1** Aspiration and Biopsy
- Aspiration
  - Withdrawal of fluid that has abnormally collected
  - To obtain specimen
- Biopsy
  - Removal and examination of tissue

**2** Lumbar Puncture: Before the Procedure
- Explain that a local anesthetic will be given
- A sensation of pressure will be felt when the spinal needle is inserted
- Client must lie still for about 15 minutes as the procedure is performed

**3** Lumbar Puncture: During the Procedure
- Support the client behind the neck and knees
- Encourage normal breathing and relaxation
- Observe the client's color, respirations and pulse
- Ask the client to report headache or persistent pain
- Handle specimen with gloves
- Label and send the specimen to laboratory immediately
- Place a small sterile dressing over the puncture site

**4** Lumbar Puncture: After the Procedure
- Assist the client into the dorsal recumbent position with one pillow for 1 to 12 hours
- Provide analgesics, if ordered, for headache as necessary
- Offer oral fluids
- Monitor for the following:
  - Swelling or bleeding at the puncture site
  - Changes in neurologic status
  - Numbness, tingling, pr pain radiating down the legs
- Document the following:
  - Date and time and person performing the procedure
  - Color, characteristics, amount of CSF withdrawn
  - Number of specimens
  - CSF pressures
  - Nursing assessment and interventions

**5** Abdominal Paracentesis: Before the Procedure
- Explain that must remain still during the procedure
- Help assume a sitting position

every four hours as ordered or as the client's condition dictates; measures the abdominal girth at the level of the umbilicus; documents date, time, and name of health care provider performing the procedure, abdominal girth before and after the procedure, color, clarity, amount of fluid drained, nursing assessment and interventions.

8. When caring for a client undergoing a thoracentesis, the nurse explains that some discomfort and pressure may be felt when the needle is inserted but that ease of breathing may increase as fluid is drained; reminds the client to avoid coughing when the needle is inserted; helps position the client.

9. During the thoracentesis procedure the nurse provides verbal support, observes for signs of distress (dyspnea, pallor, and coughing); places a small, sterile dressing over the puncture site; collects the fluid, labels and sends any specimens to the laboratory.

10. After the thoracentesis procedure, the nurse monitors pulse, respirations, skin color; removes no more than 1000 mL within the first 30 minutes; observes for changes in cough, sputum, respiratory depth, breath sounds, and notes complaints of chest pain; positions the client according to agency protocol; and documents date, time, and name of health care provider performing the procedure, amount, color, clarity of the fluid as well as nursing assessment and interventions.

11. When caring for a client undergoing a bone marrow biopsy, the nurse explains that pain may occur when the marrow is aspirated and that a crunching sound may be heard as the needle punctures the cortex of the bone; positions the client appropriately and administers sedation if ordered.

12. During the bone marrow biopsy procedure, the nurse provides verbal support; observes for pallor, diaphoresis, or faintness; applies a small, sterile dressing over the site; and applies direct pressure for 5 to 10 minutes after the procedure; assists in preparing the specimens; labels and sends to the laboratory.

13. After the bone marrow biopsy procedure the nurse assesses for discomfort, bleeding; provides analgesics; and documents the procedure as well as nursing assessment and interventions.

14. When caring for a client undergoing a liver biopsy, the nurse gives preprocedure medications 30 minutes prior to the procedure or as ordered; gives vitamin K as ordered for several days prior to the procedure if ordered; explains that a sedative and local anesthesia will be given and that the client may experience slight discomfort on injection of the anesthetic and feels sensation of pressure as the needle is inserted; reminds the client to remain NPO for two hours prior to the procedure; and assists the client to a supine position with the upper right quadrant of the abdomen exposed.

15. During the liver biopsy procedure the nurse provides verbal support; instructs the client to take several deep inhalations and expirations, and then hold breath after

6. Abdominal Paracentesis: During the Procedure
- Provide verbal support
- Observe for signs of distress
- Monitor for the following
  - Color, pulse, blood pressure
  - Signs of hypovolemic shock
- Place a small, sterile dressing over the puncture site
- Label and send specimens to the laboratory

7. Abdominal Paracentesis: After the Procedure
- Monitor for the following:
  - Signs of hypovolemic shock
  - Scrotal edema
  - Vital signs
  - Urine output
  - Drainage from the puncture site
- Measure the abdominal girth at the level of the umbilicus
- Document the following:
  - Date, time, and name of health care provider performing the procedure
  - Abdominal girth before and after the procedure
  - Color, clarity, amount of fluid drained
  - Nursing assessment and interventions

8. Thoracentesis: Before the Procedure
- Explain some discomfort and pressure may be felt when the needle is inserted
- Ease of breathing may increase as fluid is drained
- Remind to avoid coughing when the needle is inserted
- Help position the client

9. Thoracentesis: During the Procedure
- Provide verbal support
- Observe for signs of distress (dyspnea, pallor, and coughing)
- Collects the fluid
- Place a small, sterile dressing over the puncture site
- Label and send any specimens to the laboratory

10. Thoracentesis: After the Procedure
- Monitor pulse, respirations, skin color
- Remove no more than 1000 mL within the first 30 minutes
- Observe for changes in cough, sputum, respiratory depth, breath sounds
- Note complaints of chest pain
- Position the client according to agency protocol
- Document the following:
  - Date, time, and name of health care provider performing the procedure
  - Amount, color, clarity of the fluid
  - Nursing assessment and interventions

11. Bone Marrow Biopsy: Before the Procedure
- Explain that pain may occur when the marrow is aspirated
- A crunching sound may be heard as the needle punctures the cortex of the bone

the final exhalation as the needle is inserted, biopsy obtained, and needle withdrawn; instructs the client to resume normal respirations; applies pressure to the puncture site; applies a small, sterile dressing to the puncture site; labels and send specimens to the laboratory.

16. After the liver biopsy procedure the nurse assists the client to a right-side lying position with a small pillow or bath blanket under the biopsy site for several hours as ordered; monitors vital signs as ordered or as needed; monitors for abdominal pain; checks the puncture site for bleeding; and documents the procedure and nursing assessment and interventions.

- Position appropriately
- Administer sedation if ordered

**12** Bone Marrow Biopsy: During the Procedure
- Provide verbal support
- Observe for pallor, diaphoresis, or faintness
- Apply a small, sterile dressing over the site
- Apply direct pressure for 5 to 10 minutes after the procedure
- Assist in preparing the specimens
- Label and send to the laboratory

**13** Bone Marrow Biopsy: After the Procedure
- Assess for discomfort, bleeding
- Provide analgesics
- Documents the procedure as well as nursing assessment and interventions

**14** Liver Biopsy: Before the Procedure
- Give vitamin K as ordered for several days prior to the procedure
- Give preprocedure medications
- Explain that a sedative and local anesthesia will be given
- May experience slight discomfort on injection of the anesthetic
- Feel sensation of pressure as the needle is inserted
- Remind the client to remain NPO for two hours prior to the procedure
- Assist to a supine position with the upper right quadrant of the abdomen exposed

**15** Liver Biopsy: During the Procedure
- Provide verbal support
- Instruct the client to take several deep inhalations and expirations
- Then hold breath after the final exhalation as the needle is inserted, biopsy obtained and needle withdrawn
- Instruct the client to resume normal respirations
- Apply pressure to the puncture site
- Apply a small, sterile dressing to the puncture site
- Label and send specimens to the laboratory

**16** Liver Biopsy: After the Procedure
- Assist the client to a right-side lying position
- Place a small pillow or bath blanket under the biopsy site for several hours
- Monitor vital signs as ordered or as needed
- Monitor for abdominal pain
- Check the puncture site for bleeding
- Document the procedure and nursing assessment and interventions

| SUGGESTIONS FOR CLASSROOM ACTIVITIES | SUGGESTIONS FOR CLINICAL ACTIVITIES |
| --- | --- |
| • If possible, obtain equipment used to perform these procedures. Demonstrate the equipment for the students. | • Review the institution's policies for performance of these procedures and the nurse's role. |

## RESOURCE LIBRARY

**PRENTICE HALL NURSING MEDIALINK DVD-ROM**

Audio Glossary
NCLEX® Review
Skills Checklist
Animations:
  *Drug Metabolization*
  *Agonist/Antagonist Mechanism of Action*
  *Injections*
Videos:
  *Medical Drugs*
  *Metered-Dose Inhaler (MDI)*
  *Small Volume Nebulizer (SVN) Treatment*

**COMPANION WEBSITE**

Additional NCLEX® Review
Case Study: *Preparing Medications*
Care Plan Activity: *Client on Insulin*
Application Activity: *Calculating Dosages*
Links to Resources

**IMAGE LIBRARY**

---

# Learning Outcome 1

Define selected terms related to the administration of medications.

## Concepts for Lecture

1. There are many important definitions related to the administration of medications. These are defined throughout the chapter (see Key Terms in the textbook and the audio glossary on the student DVD-ROM and the Companion Website).

2. A *medication* is a substance administered for the diagnosis, treatment, or relief of a symptom or for the prevention of diseases. This term is used interchangeably with the word *drug*; however, the word *drug* also has the connotation of an illegally obtained substance such as heroin.

   A *prescription* is the written directions for the preparation and administration of a drug.

   The generic name of a drug is given before a drug becomes officially approved as a medication.

## PowerPoint Lecture Slides

*(NOTE: The number on each PPT Lecture Slide directly corresponds with the Concepts for Lecture.)*

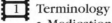 Terminology
- Medication
  - Substance administered for the diagnosis, treatment, or relief of a symptom or for the prevention of diseases
  - Used interchangeably with the word *drug*
  - *Drug* also has the connotation of an illegally obtained substance

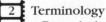 Terminology
- Prescription
  - Written directions for the preparation and administration of a drug
- Generic name of a drug

The official name of a drug is the name under which it is listed in one of the official publications such as the *United States Pharmacopeia.*

3. The chemical name of a drug is the name by which a chemist knows the drug.

The trade or brand name is the name given by the drug manufacturer and is usually short and easy to remember.

Pharmacology is the study of the effect of drugs on living organisms.

Pharmacy is the art of preparing, compounding, and dispensing drugs, and also refers to the place where drugs are prepared.

- ○ Name given before a drug becomes officially approved as a medication
- Official name of a drug
- ○ Name under which it is listed in one of the official publications

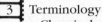 Terminology
- Chemical name of a drug
  - ○ Name by which a chemist knows the drug
- Trade or brand name
  - ○ Name given by the drug manufacturer
  - ○ Usually short and easy to remember
- Pharmacology
  - ○ Study of the effect of drugs on living organisms
- Pharmacy
  - ○ Art of preparing, compounding, and dispensing drugs
  - ○ Also refers to the place where drugs are prepared

## SUGGESTIONS FOR CLASSROOM ACTIVITIES

- Provide examples of the generic, official, chemical, and trade (brand) names of common medications.

## SUGGESTIONS FOR CLINICAL ACTIVITIES

- Identify the name of drugs (generic, official, trade or brand) used in the agency.

# LEARNING OUTCOME 2

Describe legal aspects of administering medications.

## CONCEPTS FOR LECTURE

1. The administration of drugs in both the United States and Canada is controlled by law. Table 35–2 provides a summary of U.S. drug legislation (Food, Drug, and Cosmetic Act of 1938, Durham-Humphrey Amendment of 1952, Kefauver-Harris Amendment of 1962, and the Comprehensive Drug Abuse Prevention and Control Act of 1970).

2. Table 35–3 summarizes Canadian drug legislation (Proprietary or Patent Medicine Act of 1908, Canada Food and Drug Act of 1953, and Canadian Narcotic Control Act of 1961).

3. Nurses need to know how nursing practice acts in their areas define and limit their functions and be able to recognize the limits of their own knowledge and skills. Under the law, nurses are responsible for their own actions regardless of whether there is a written order. Therefore, nurses should question any order that appears unreasonable and refuse to give the medication until the order is clarified.

4. Another aspect of nursing practice governed by law is the use of controlled substances. Controlled substances are kept under lock. Special inventory forms

## POWERPOINT LECTURE SLIDES

*(NOTE: The number on each PPT Lecture Slide directly corresponds with the Concepts for Lecture.)*

1 U.S. Drug Legislation
- Food, Drug, and Cosmetic Act (1938)
- Durham-Humphrey Amendment (1952)
- Kefauver-Harris Amendment (1962)
- Comprehensive Drug Abuse Prevention and Control Act (1970)

2 Canadian Drug Legislation
- Proprietary or Patent Medicine Act (1908)
- Canada Food and Drug Act (1953)
- Canadian Narcotic Control Act (1961)

3 Legal Aspects of Administering Medications
- Nursing practice acts
- Responsibility for actions
- Question any order that appears unreasonable
- Refuse to give the medication until the order is clarified

4 Controlled Substances
- Kept under lock
- Special inventory forms

are used for recording the use of these substances. The information usually required on these forms include the name of the client, date and time of administration, name of the drug, dosage, and signature of the person who prepares and gives the drug. The name of the primary care provider who ordered the drug may also be listed. A verifying signature of another RN may be required by the agency when a drug is administered. Careful inventory control is maintained. When a portion or all of a controlled substance is discarded, the nurse must ask another nurse to witness the discarding. In most agencies, counts of controlled substances are taken at the end of each shift and the count total should tally with the total at the end of the last shift minus the number used.

- Documentation requirements
- Counts of controlled substances
- Procedures for discarding

## SUGGESTIONS FOR CLASSROOM ACTIVITIES

- Discuss nursing actions the nurse should take when a primary care provider ordered medication is inappropriate. Have the students role-play contacting a primary care provider and discussing the medication order.
- Have the students review the state nurse practice act to determine how the act defines and limits nursing practice as it relates to medication administration. In addition, have the students identify what statements are made about administration of medication by LPNs/LVNs

## SUGGESTIONS FOR CLINICAL ACTIVITIES

- Review the agency's policies and procedures for administering controlled substances.

## LEARNING OUTCOME 3

Identify physiologic factors and individual variables affecting medication action.

## CONCEPTS FOR LECTURE

1. Medication action may be affected by developmental factors, gender, culture, ethnicity, genetics, diet, environment, psychologic factors, illness and disease, and time of administration.

   The nurse needs to be aware of developmental factors. Pregnant women must be careful about taking medications, especially in the first trimester, because of the possible adverse effects on the fetus. Infants usually require smaller doses because of their body size and the immaturity of their organs. Older adults have different responses to medications due to physiologic changes that accompany aging and because they may be prescribed multiple drugs and incompatibilities may occur.

   Gender differences in medication action are chiefly related to the distribution of body fat and fluid and hormonal differences. In addition, most research studies on medications have been done on men.

## POWERPOINT LECTURE SLIDES

*(NOTE: The number on each PPT Lecture Slide directly corresponds with the Concepts for Lecture.)*

 1 Factors Affecting Medication Action
- Developmental
- Gender
- Cultural, ethnic, and genetic
- Diet
- Environment
- Psychologic
- Illness and disease
- Time of administration

In addition to gender, a client's response to drugs is also influenced by genetic variations such as size and body composition (pharmacogenetics).

Ethnopharmacology is the study of the effects of ethnicity on response to prescribed medications. Cultural factors and practices (values and beliefs) can also affect a drug's action; for example, an herbal remedy may speed up or slow down the metabolism of certain drugs (see Culturally Competent Care).

The diet may contain nutrients that can interact with medications and increase or decrease action.

It is important to consider the effects of a drug in the context of the client's personality, milieu, and environmental conditions (e.g., temperature, noise).

Psychologic factors, such as a client's expectations about what a drug can do, can affect the response to the medication.

Illness and disease can affect how a client responds to a medication. For example, aspirin can reduce body temperature of a feverish client but has no effect on body temperature of a client without a fever.

Time of administration is important because medications are absorbed more quickly if the stomach is empty; however, some medications irritate the gastrointestinal tract and are given after a meal.

---

### SUGGESTIONS FOR CLASSROOM ACTIVITIES

- Divide the students into groups. Assign a medication to each group. Have the students use the medication book required by the curriculum to illustrate how individual factors could affect the action of the assigned medication and nursing interventions to counter these, if possible.

### SUGGESTIONS FOR CLINICAL ACTIVITIES

- Have the students review the medications prescribed for their assigned clients and apply the individual factors that could affect the action of each medication. Discuss how the nurse might facilitate the desired action of the medication and reduce adverse reactions, if possible.

---

## LEARNING OUTCOME 4

Describe various routes of medication administration.

### CONCEPTS FOR LECTURE

1. Routes of medication administration include oral, sublingual, buccal, parenteral, and topical.

In oral administration the drug is swallowed. It is the most common, least expensive, and most convenient route for most clients.

In sublingual administration a drug is placed under the tongue, where it dissolves.

Buccal means "pertaining to the cheek." In buccal administration a medication is held in the mouth against the mucous membranes of the cheek until the drug dissolves.

The parenteral route is defined as other than the alimentary or respiratory tract. Some common routes

### POWERPOINT LECTURE SLIDES

*(NOTE: The number on each PPT Lecture Slide directly corresponds with the Concepts for Lecture.)*

 Routes of Medication Administration
- Oral
- Sublingual
- Buccal
- Parenteral
  - Subcutaneous
  - Intramuscular
  - Intradermal
  - Intravenous
  - Intra-arterial
  - Intracardiac

for parenteral administration include subcutaneous (hypodermic), into the subcutaneous tissue just below the skin; intramuscular, into the muscle; intradermal, under the epidermis (into the dermis); intravenous, into a vein; intra-arterial, into an artery; intracardiac, into the heart muscle; intraosseous, into the bone; intrathecal or intraspinal, into the spinal canal; epidural, into the epidural space; and intra-articular, into a joint.

2. Topical applications are those applied to a circumscribed surface area of the body. Routes for topical applications include dermatologic, applied to the skin; instillations and irrigations, applied into body cavities or orifices such as the urinary bladder, eyes, ears, nose, rectum, or vagina; ophthalmic, otic, nasal, rectal, and vaginal topical preparations; and inhalations, administered into the respiratory system by a nebulizer or positive pressure breathing apparatus.

Table 35-6 lists some of the routes of administration with advantages and disadvantages of each.

- ○ Intraosseous
- ○ Intrathecal (intraspinal)
- ○ Epidural
- ○ Intra-articular

 Topical
- Dermatological
- Instillations and irrigations
- Inhalation
- Ophthalmic, otic, nasal, rectal, and vaginal

---

### SUGGESTIONS FOR CLASSROOM ACTIVITIES

- Assign the students to look up specific medications to determine the various routes available for administration. Ask the students to suggest when the various routes would be appropriate.

### SUGGESTIONS FOR CLINICAL ACTIVITIES

- Have the students review the medications prescribed for their clients, indicating the various routes for each.

---

## LEARNING OUTCOME 5

Identify essential parts of a medication order.

### CONCEPTS FOR LECTURE

1. Essential parts of a medication order include the full name of the client, date and time the order is written, name of the drug to be administered, dosage of the drug, frequency of administration, route of administration, and signature of the person writing the order (see Box 35-1).

### POWERPOINT LECTURE SLIDES

*(NOTE: The number on each PPT Lecture Slide directly corresponds with the Concepts for Lecture.)*

 Parts of a Medication Order
- Full name of the client
- Date and time the order written
- Name of drug to be administered
- Dosage
- Frequency of administration
- Route of administration
- Signature of person writing the order

---

### SUGGESTIONS FOR CLASSROOM ACTIVITIES

- Provide the students with several medication orders. Ask them to identify the essential parts of the medication order in each.

### SUGGESTIONS FOR CLINICAL ACTIVITIES

- Have the students review the process of ordering medications in the agency, identifying how the essential components of a medication order are included.

---

# LEARNING OUTCOME 6

List examples of various types of medication orders.

## CONCEPTS FOR LECTURE

1.  There are four common medication orders: stat order, single order, standing order, and prn order.
    A stat order indicates that the medication is to be given immediately and only once (e.g., Demerol 100 mg IM stat).
    The single order or one-time order is for medication to be given once at a specified time (e.g., Seconal 100 mg hs before surgery).
    The standing order may or may not have a termination date, may be carried out indefinitely (e.g., multiple vitamins daily) until an order is written to cancel it, or may be carried out for a specified number of days (e.g., Demerol 100 mg IM q4h × 5 days).
    A prn order or as-needed order permits the nurse to give a medication when, in the nurse's judgment, the client requires it (e.g., Amphojel 15 mL prn).

## POWERPOINT LECTURE SLIDES

*(NOTE: The number on each PPT Lecture Slide directly corresponds with the Concepts for Lecture.)*

 1   Types of Medication Orders and Examples
- Stat order
  - Demerol 100 mg IM stat
- Single order
  - Seconal 100 mg hs before surgery
- Standing order
  - Multivitamin 1 capsule po daily
  - Demerol 100 mg IM q 4 h x 5 days
- prn order
  - Amphojel 15 mL prn

## SUGGESTIONS FOR CLASSROOM ACTIVITIES

- Provide the students with a list of various types of medication orders. Have the students identify the type of order for each.

## SUGGESTIONS FOR CLINICAL ACTIVITIES

- Discuss the policies and procedures of the agency for verbal orders.
- Discuss the policies and procedures of the agency for medication orders when a client is transferred from one clinical unit to another, when transferred to and from the operating room, and when discharged to home or another facility.

# LEARNING OUTCOME 7

State systems of measurement that are used in the administration of medications.

## CONCEPTS FOR LECTURE

1.  Systems of measurement used in the administration of medications include metric, apothecaries, and household.
    The metric system is strongly suggested for safety reasons because many practitioners are unfamiliar with the apothecary system.

## POWERPOINT LECTURE SLIDES

*(NOTE: The number on each PPT Lecture Slide directly corresponds with the Concepts for Lecture.)*

1   Systems of Measurement
- Metric
- Apothecary
- Household
- Use of metric system strongly suggested for safety reasons

## SUGGESTIONS FOR CLASSROOM ACTIVITIES

- Provide the students with medication calculation problems requiring conversion from one system to another. Review the calculations.

## SUGGESTIONS FOR CLINICAL ACTIVITIES

- Review the policies and procedures of the agency in terms of the measurement system used for medication orders.

# LEARNING OUTCOME 8

List six essential steps to follow when administering medication.

## CONCEPTS FOR LECTURE

1. When administering any drug, regardless of the route of administration, the nurse must identify the client, inform the client, administer the drug, provide adjunctive interventions as indicated, record the drug administered, and evaluate the client's response to the drug.

   JCAHO's National Patient Safety Goals require a nurse to use at least two client identifiers whenever administering medications. Acceptable identifiers may be the person's name, an assigned identification number, a telephone number, a photograph, or another personal identifier.

   If the client is unfamiliar with the medication, the nurse should explain the intended action as well as any side effects or adverse reactions that might occur. It is also very important to listen to the client.

   Before administering the drug, the nurse should read the medication administration record (MAR) carefully and perform three checks with the labeled medication (See Box 35-3). In addition the ten "rights" of medication administration must be observed (See Box 35-4).

   The nurse should provide adjunctive interventions as indicated. Clients may require physical assistance in assuming positions for parenteral medications or may need guidance about measures to enhance drug effectiveness and prevent complications.

   The nurse must record the drug administered, following agency regulations.

   In order to evaluate the client's response to the drug, the nurse should know the kinds of behavior that reflect the action or lack of action of the drug and its untoward effects (both minor and major) for each medication the client is receiving. The nurse may also report the client's response directly to the nurse manager and primary care provider.

## POWERPOINT LECTURE SLIDES

*(NOTE: The number on each PPT Lecture Slide directly corresponds with the Concepts for Lecture.)*

 Six Essential Steps for Administering Medications
- Identify the client
- Inform the client
- Administer the drug
- Provide adjunctive interventions as indicated
- Record the drug administered
- Evaluate the client's response to the drug

---

## SUGGESTIONS FOR CLASSROOM ACTIVITIES

- Invite a quality assurance representative to discuss common medication errors and how they can be prevented.
- Provide the students with various scenarios that may occur when administering medications (e.g., another nurse asks the student to administer medications that the student has not prepared). Have the students provide appropriate responses to these situations.

## SUGGESTIONS FOR CLINICAL ACTIVITIES

- Invite a staff nurse to demonstrate the procedure used for administering medications in the agency, including acceptable patient identifiers, how to perform the three checks, use of the medication administration record (MAR), and documentation of administration of medications.
- Review the policies and procedures of the agency in terms of standardized time for administering medications (e.g., what is considered to be administering the medication on time, what to do if the client is scheduled for a test or therapy at the time a medication is due, what to do if a client refuses a medication).

# LEARNING OUTCOME 9

State the "rights" to accurate medication administration.

## CONCEPTS FOR LECTURE

1. The ten "rights" of medication include the right medication, right dose, right time, right route, right client, right client education, right documentation, right to refuse, right assessment, and right evaluation (See Box 35-4).

## POWERPOINT LECTURE SLIDES

*(NOTE: The number on each PPT Lecture Slide directly corresponds with the Concepts for Lecture.)*

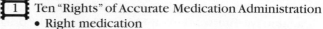 Ten "Rights" of Accurate Medication Administration
- Right medication
- Right dose
- Right time
- Right route
- Right client
- Right client education
- Right documentation
- Right to refuse
- Right assessment
- Right evaluation

## SUGGESTIONS FOR CLASSROOM ACTIVITIES

- Discuss the nursing responsibility when a client refuses to take a prescribed medication.

## SUGGESTIONS FOR CLINICAL ACTIVITIES

- Review the agency's policies and procedures for administering medications.
- Have the students review each of the ten "rights" as they administer medications to assigned clients.

# LEARNING OUTCOME 10

Describe physiologic changes in older adults that alter medication administration and effectiveness.

## CONCEPTS FOR LECTURE

1. Physiologic changes in older adults that alter medication administration and effectiveness include altered memory; decreased visual acuity; decreased renal function, resulting in slower elimination of drugs and higher drug concentration in the bloodstream for longer periods; less complete and slower absorption from the gastrointestinal tract; increased proportion of fat to lean body mass, which facilitates retention of fat-soluble drugs and increases the potential for toxicity; decreased liver function, which hinders biotransformation of drugs; decreased organ sensitivity, which means that the response to the same drug concentration in the vicinity of the target organ is less in older people than in the young; altered quality of organ responsiveness, resulting in adverse effects becoming pronounced before therapeutic effects are achieved; and decreased manual dexterity due to arthritis and/or decreased flexibility (See Box 35-5).

## POWERPOINT LECTURE SLIDES

*(NOTE: The number on each PPT Lecture Slide directly corresponds with the Concepts for Lecture.)*

 Elder Considerations
- Altered memory
- Decreased visual acuity
- Decrease in renal function
- Less complete and slower absorption from the gastrointestinal tract
- Increased proportion of fat to lean body mass
- Decreased liver function
- Decreased organ sensitivity
- Altered quality of organ responsiveness
- Decrease in manual dexterity

## SUGGESTIONS FOR CLASSROOM ACTIVITIES

- Divide the students into groups. Ask each group to develop guidelines for safely administering medications to elders based upon the physiologic changes of aging.

## SUGGESTIONS FOR CLINICAL ACTIVITIES

- Ask the students to review medications ordered for their elderly clients in terms of the physiologic changes of aging.

# LEARNING OUTCOME 11

Outline steps required to administer oral medications safely.

## CONCEPTS FOR LECTURE

1. Refer to the Skill 35.1 in the textbook and the Skill Checklist included on the Student DVD-ROM.

   Prior to administering oral medications, the nurse should assess for allergies to medications (See Table 35–5: Common Mild Allergic Responses); the client's ability to swallow the medication; presence of vomiting or diarrhea; specific drug action, side effects, interactions, and adverse reactions; the client's knowledge of and learning needs about the medication; and determine if assessment data influences administration of the medications.

   In preparation for administering the medication, the nurse should know the reason why the client is receiving the medication, the drug classification, contraindications, usual dosage range, side effects, and nursing considerations for administering and evaluating the intended outcomes for the medication. The nurse should check the MAR, verify the client's ability to take medication orally, and organize the supplies.

## POWERPOINT LECTURE SLIDES

*(NOTE: The number on each PPT Lecture Slide directly corresponds with the Concepts for Lecture.)*

1 Administering Oral Medications
   • Skill 35.1

## SUGGESTIONS FOR CLASSROOM ACTIVITIES

• Obtain practice medications, MARs, and administration equipment. Develop client scenarios, and have the students practice safely administering oral medications for the clients in these scenarios.

## SUGGESTIONS FOR CLINICAL ACTIVITIES

• Assign the students to administer oral medications for their clients following the agency's policies and procedures.
• Require students to have medication cards for each medication administered according to the requirements of the curriculum and to state the reason the client is receiving the medication, actions of the medication, possible side effects and adverse reactions, and related nursing interventions.

# LEARNING OUTCOME 12

Outline steps required for nasogastric and gastrostomy tube medication administration.

## CONCEPTS FOR LECTURE

1. Check with the pharmacist to see if the client's medications come in a liquid form because these are less likely to cause tube obstruction.

   If medications do not come in liquid form, check to see if they may be crushed. (Note that enteric-coated, sustained action, buccal, and sublingual medications should never be crushed.)

   Crush a tablet into a fine powder and dissolve in at least 30 mL of warm water. Cold liquids may cause client discomfort. Use only water for mixing and flushing. Some medications are mixed with other fluids, such as normal saline, in order to maximize dissolution. Nurses are encouraged to consult with a pharmacist.

## POWERPOINT LECTURE SLIDES

*(NOTE: The number on each PPT Lecture Slide directly corresponds with the Concepts for Lecture.)*

 1 Nasogastric/Gastrostomy Tube Medication Administration
   • Check with the pharmacist for a liquid form
   • Check to see if medication may be crushed
   • Crush a tablet into a fine powder and dissolve in at least 30 mL of warm water
   • Open capsules and mix the contents with water only with the pharmacist's advice
   • Do not administer whole or undissolved medications

Read medication labels carefully before opening a capsule. Open capsules and mix the contents with water only with the pharmacist's advice.

Do not administer whole or undissolved medications because they will clog the tube.

Assess tube placement (see Chapter 47 for methods to verify tube placement).

Before giving the medication, aspirate all the stomach contents and measure the residual volume. Check agency policy if residual volume is greater than 100 mL.

2. When administering the medication(s):
   • Remove the plunger from the syringe and connect the syringe to a pinched or kinked tube.
   • Put 15 to 30 mL (5 to 10 mL for children) of water into the syringe barrel to flush the tube before administering the first medication. Raise or lower the barrel of the syringe to adjust the flow as needed. Pinch or clamp the tubing before all the water is instilled to avoid excess air entering the stomach.
   • Pour liquid or dissolved medication into the syringe barrel and allow to flow by gravity into the enteral tube.
   • When giving several medications, administer each one separately and flush with at least 15 to 30 mL (5 mL for children) of tap water between each medication.
   • When finished administering all medications, flush with another 15 to 30 mL (5 to 10 mL for children) of warm water to clear the tube.
3. If the tube is connected to suction, disconnect the suction and keep the tube clamped for 20 to 30 minutes after giving the medication to enhance absorption.

• Assess tube placement
• Aspirate stomach contents and measure the residual volume

 Nasogastric/Gastrostomy Tube Medication Administration
• Remove the plunger from the syringe and connect the syringe to a pinched or kinked tube
• Put 15 to 30 mL (5 to 10 mL for children) of water into the syringe barrel to flush the tube before administering the first medication
• Pour liquid or dissolved medication into the syringe barrel and allow to flow by gravity into the enteral tube
• Administer each medication separately and flush with at least 15 to 30 mL water between each medication
• When you have finished administering all medications, flush with another 15 to 30 mL (5 to 10 mL for children) of warm water to clear the tube

 If the tube is connected to suction, disconnect the suction and keep the tube clamped to enhance absorption

---

## SUGGESTIONS FOR CLASSROOM ACTIVITIES

• Set up the manikins with nasogastric or gastrostomy tubes. Prepare scenarios for the students to practice administering medications through these tubes.

## SUGGESTIONS FOR CLINICAL ACTIVITIES

• Review the agency's policies and procedures for administering medications through nasogastric and gastrostomy tubes, including assessing placement of the tubes and checking for residual volume.
• Discuss the difference in procedure for administering medications through small- and large-bore tubes.

---

# LEARNING OUTCOME 13

Identify equipment required for parenteral medications.

## CONCEPTS FOR LECTURE

1. To administer parenteral medications, nurses use syringes and needles to withdraw medications from ampules and vials.
2. Syringes have three parts: the tip, the barrel, and the plunger. There are several kinds of syringes, differing in size, shape, and material.

## POWERPOINT LECTURE SLIDES

*(NOTE: The number on each PPT Lecture Slide directly corresponds with the Concepts for Lecture.)*

 Parenteral Medications
• Common nursing procedure
• Absorbed more quickly than oral

3. The three most commonly used types are the standard hypodermic syringe, the insulin syringe, and the tuberculin syringe. Injectable medications are frequently supplied in disposable prefilled unit-dose systems available as a prefilled syringe ready for use or prefilled sterile cartridges and needles that require attachment to a reusable holder. Needleless systems are also available.
4. Needles are made of stainless steel, and most are disposable. A needle has three parts: the hub, the cannula or shaft, and the bevel.
5. Needles used for injections have three variable characteristics: the slant or length of the bevel, the length of the shaft, and the gauge.

- Requires careful and accurate administration
- Aseptic technique

**2** Syringes
- Parts
  - Tip
  - Barrel
  - Plunger

**3** Types of Syringes
- Standard hypodermic syringe
- Insulin syringe
- Tuberculin syringe
- Disposable prefilled unit-dose or prefilled cartridges

**4** Needles
- Stainless steel
- Most disposable
- Parts
  - Hub
  - Cannula or shaft
  - Bevel

**5** Characteristics of Needles
- Slant or length of the bevel
- Length of the shaft
- Gauge

## SUGGESTIONS FOR CLASSROOM ACTIVITIES

- Obtain various types of syringes and needles. Make a poster illustrating the components of the syringes and needles.
- Provide the students with various medication orders and indicate how the medications are supplied (e.g., the number of mg/mL). Have the students identify the appropriate syringe to use to draw up the medication.
- Have the students identify the length and gauge of needle to use to administer an intradermal, subcutaneous, and intramuscular injection for an "average" size adult, an adult who is obese, and an elder who is frail.

## SUGGESTIONS FOR CLINICAL ACTIVITIES

- Review the types of equipment used for administering parenteral medications in the agency.

# LEARNING OUTCOME 14

Describe how to prepare selected drugs from ampules and vials.

## CONCEPTS FOR LECTURE

1. An ampule is a glass container usually designed to hold a single dose of a drug. It has a distinctive shape with a constricted neck. Ampules vary in size and most have colored marks around the necks indicating where they are prescored.

## POWERPOINT LECTURE SLIDES

*(NOTE: The number on each PPT Lecture Slide directly corresponds with the Concepts for Lecture.)*

**1** Preparing Medications from Ampules
- Skill 35.2

**2** Preparing Medications from Vials
- Skill 35.3

To access the medications, the ampule must be broken at its constricted neck. A plastic ampule opener may be used to prevent injury from broken glass. Once an ampule has been broken, the fluid is aspirated into a syringe using a filter needle that prevents aspiration of any glass particles.

Skill 35.2 describes the specific steps of how to prepare medications from ampules. (See the Skill Checklist provided on the Student DVD-ROM.

2. A vial is a small glass bottle with a sealed rubber cap that comes in different sizes, from single to multidose vials. To access the medication, the vial must be pierced with a needle. In addition, air must be injected into a vial before the medication can be withdrawn in order to avoid creating a vacuum that makes withdrawal difficult.

Several drugs are dispensed as powders in vials. A liquid (diluent) must be added to a powdered medication before it can be injected (reconstitution).

Rubber particulate has been found in medications withdrawn from vials. As a result, it is strongly recommended that the nurse use a filter needle when withdrawing medications. The filter needle is then replaced with the regular needle for injections.

Skill 35.3 describes the specific steps of how to prepare medications from vials. (See the textbook and the Skill Checklist provided on the Student DVD-ROM.)

3. Sometimes it is desirable to mix medications in one syringe after checking for compatibility. Skill 35.4 presents the steps for this procedure. (See the textbook and the Skill Checklist on the Student DVD-ROM.)

3 Mixing Medications Using One Syringe
• Skill 35.4

---

## SUGGESTIONS FOR CLASSROOM ACTIVITIES

• Using practice vials and ampules, have the students practice withdrawing medications safely.
• Using practice vials and ampules, have the students practice mixing medications in one syringe.
• Using practice insulin vials, have the students withdraw insulin doses requiring the use of either the 100-U or 50-U syringe.

## SUGGESTIONS FOR CLINICAL ACTIVITIES

• When appropriate, have the students prepare parenteral medications for their assigned clients.
• Discuss how parenteral medications are prepared by the pharmacy and sent to the clinical unit in this institution (e.g., already prepared in unit dose syringes, or sent with diluent and instructions on how to prepare).

---

# LEARNING OUTCOME 15

Identify sites used for intradermal, subcutaneous, and intramuscular injections.

## CONCEPTS FOR LECTURE

1. Intradermal injection sites include the inner lower arm, the upper chest, and the back beneath the scapula.
2. Subcutaneous injection sites include the outer aspect of the upper arms and the anterior aspect of the thighs. Other areas that may be used are the abdomen, the

## POWERPOINT LECTURE SLIDES

*(NOTE: The number on each PPT Lecture Slide directly corresponds with the Concepts for Lecture.)*

1 Sites for Intradermal Injections
• Inner lower arm
• Upper chest
• Back beneath the scapula

scapular areas of the upper back, and the ventrogluteal and dorsogluteal areas.

3. Sites used for intramuscular injections include the ventrogluteal, vastus lateralis, dorsogluteal, deltoid, and rectus femoris.

**2** Sites for Subcutaneous Injections
- Outer aspect of the upper arms
- Anterior aspect of the thighs
- Abdomen
- Scapular areas of the upper back
- Ventrogluteal and dorsogluteal areas

**3** Sites for Intramuscular Injections
- Ventrogluteal
- Vastus lateralis
- Dorsogluteal
- Deltoid
- Rectus femoris

---

## SUGGESTIONS FOR CLASSROOM ACTIVITIES

- Have the students identify the bony landmarks for intramuscular injections on a skeleton.
- Have the students identify sites for intradermal, subcutaneous, and intramuscular injections on at least two other students.

## SUGGESTIONS FOR CLINICAL ACTIVITIES

- Review the agency's policies and procedures for sites used for intradermal, subcutaneous, and intramuscular injections.

---

## LEARNING OUTCOME 16

Describe essential steps for safely administering parenteral medications by intradermal, subcutaneous, intramuscular, and intravenous routes.

---

## CONCEPTS FOR LECTURE

1. Refer to Skill 35.5: Administering an Intradermal Injection for Skin Tests. See the Skill Checklist provided on the Student DVD-ROM.

2. Subcutaneous: Refer to Skill 35.6: Administering a Subcutaneous Injection. See the Skill Checklist provided on the Student DVD-ROM.

3. Intramuscular: Refer to Skill 35.7: Administering an Intramuscular Injection. See the Skill Checklist provided on the Student DVD-ROM.

   Perform hand hygiene and observe other appropriate infection control procedures (e.g., clean gloves). Prepare the medication, and provide for client privacy. Prepare the client. Select, locate, and clean the site.

   Remove the needle cover and discard it without contaminating the needle. If using a prefilled unit-dose medication, take caution to avoid dripping medication on the needle prior to injection. If this does occur, wipe the medication off the needle with a sterile gauze. Some sources recommend changing the needle if possible.

   Inject the medication using a Z-track technique.
   - Use the ulnar side of the nondominant hand to pull the skin approximately 2.5 cm (1 inch) to the side.

## POWERPOINT LECTURE SLIDES

*(NOTE: The number on each PPT Lecture Slide directly corresponds with the Concepts for Lecture.)*

**1** Administering Intradermal Injections
- Skill 35.5

**2** Administering Subcutaneous Injections
- Skill 35.6

**3** Administering Intramuscular Injections
- Skill 35.7

**4** Administering Intravenous Injections
- Skill 35.8

Under some circumstances, such as for an emaciated client or an infant, the muscle may be pinched.

- Holding the syringe between the thumb and forefinger (as if holding a pencil), pierce the skin quickly and smoothly at a 90-degree angle, and insert the needle into the muscle.
- Hold the barrel of the syringe steady with the nondominant hand and aspirate by pulling back on the plunger with the dominant hand. Aspirate for 5 to 10 seconds. If blood appears in the syringe, withdraw the needle, discard the syringe, and prepare a new injection. This step determines whether the needle has been inserted into a blood vessel.
- If blood does not appear, inject the medication steadily and slowly (approximately 10 seconds per milliliter) while holding the syringe steady.
- After injection, wait 10 seconds to permit the medication to disperse into the muscle tissue, thus decreasing the client's discomfort.

Withdraw the needle smoothly at the same angle of insertion. Release the skin and apply gentle pressure at the site with a dry sponge. If bleeding occurs, apply pressure with a dry sterile gauze until it stops.

4. Adding medications to intravenous fluid containers: Refer to Skill 35.8: Adding Medications to Intravenous Fluid Containers. See the Skill Checklist provided on the Student DVD-ROM.

Adding medications using IV push: Refer to Skill 35.9: Administering Intravenous Medications Using IV Push. See the Skill Checklist provided on the Student DVD-ROM.

---

## SUGGESTIONS FOR CLASSROOM ACTIVITIES

- Using manikins, injection simulators, or oranges, have the students practice administering intradermal, subcutaneous, and intramuscular injections.
- Set up the manikins or simulator arms for practice administering intravenous medications. Develop various medication orders requiring administering intravenous medication using various methods. Have the students practice administering the medications.
- Show videotaped demonstrations of administering parenteral medications. Compare and contrast with skills in the textbook.

## SUGGESTIONS FOR CLINICAL ACTIVITIES

- Review the policies and procedures for administering various types of parenteral medications, including any restrictions on intravenous medications that nurses may administer.
- Assign students to administer parenteral medications to assigned clients.

# LEARNING OUTCOME 17

Describe essentials steps in safely administering topical medications: dermatologic, ophthalmic, otic, nasal, vaginal, respiratory inhalation, and rectal preparations.

## CONCEPTS FOR LECTURE

1. Topical skin or dermatologic preparations include ointments, pastes, creams, lotions, powders, sprays, and patches. See Table 35–1. Also see Practice Guidelines for applying skin preparations. Before applying a dermatologic preparation, thoroughly clean the area with soap and water and dry it with a patting motion. Skin encrustations harbor microorganisms, and these as well as previously applied applications can prevent the medication from coming in contact with the area to be treated. Nurses should wear gloves when administering skin applications and always use surgical asepsis when an open wound is present. Refer to Skill 35.10: Administering Ophthalmic Instillations. See the Skill Checklist provided on the Student DVD-ROM.

2. Refer to Skill 35.11: Administering Otic Instillations. See the Skill Checklist included on the Student DVD-ROM.
   To treat the ethmoid and sphenoid sinuses, instruct the client to lie back with the head over the edge of the bed or a pillow under the shoulders so that the head is tipped backward.

   To treat the maxillary and frontal sinuses, instruct the client to assume the same back-lying position, with the head turned toward the side to be treated. The client should also be instructed to (a) breathe through the mouth to prevent aspiration of medication into the trachea and bronchi, (b) remain in a back-lying position for at least 1 minute so that the solution will come into contact with all of the nasal surface, and (c) avoid blowing the nose for several minutes.

3. Refer to Skill 35.12: Administering Vaginal Instillations. See the Skill Checklist included on the Student DVD-ROM.

4. Rectal preparations:
   - Assist the client to a left lateral or left Sims' position, with the upper leg flexed.
   Fold back the top bedclothes to expose the buttocks.
   - Put a glove on the hand used to insert the suppository.
   - Unwrap the suppository and lubricate the smooth rounded end, or see the manufacturer's instructions. The rounded end is usually inserted first, and lubricant reduces irritation of the mucosa.
   - Lubricate the gloved index finger.
   - Encourage the client to relax by breathing through the mouth. This usually relaxes the external anal sphincter.
   - Insert the suppository gently into the anal canal, rounded end first (or according to manufacturer's instructions), along the rectal wall using the

## POWERPOINT LECTURE SLIDES

*(NOTE: The number on each PPT Lecture Slide directly corresponds with the Concepts for Lecture.)*

**1** Administering Ophthalmic Medications
- Skill 35.10

**2** Administering Otic Medications
- Skill 35.11

**3** Administering Vaginal Medications
- Skill 35.12

**4** Inserting Rectal Suppositories

**5** Respiratory Inhalation

gloved index finger. For an adult, insert the
suppository beyond the internal sphincter
(i.e., 10 cm [4 in.]).
- Avoid embedding the suppository in feces in order
  for the suppository to be absorbed effectively.
- Press the client's buttocks together for a few
  minutes.
- Ask the client to remain in the left lateral or supine
  position for at least 5 minutes to help retain the
  suppository. The suppository should be retained for
  varying lengths of time according to the
  manufacturer's instructions.
5. Respiratory inhalation:
- Nebulizers deliver most medications administered
  through the inhaled route. A nebulizer is used to
  deliver a fine spray (fog or mist) of medication or
  moisture to a client. There are two kinds of
  nebulization: atomization and aerosolization.
- A metered-dose inhaler (MDI) is a handheld
  nebulizer. It is a pressurized container of
  medication that can be used by the client to
  release the medication through a nosepiece or
  mouthpiece. The nurse should provide the
  following instructions and periodically assess the
  client's techniques for using an inhaler spacer or
  chamber correctly:
    ○ Ensure that the canister is firmly and fully
      inserted into the inhaler.
    ○ Remove the mouthpiece cap. Holding the
      inhaler upright, shake the inhaler vigorously for
      3 to 5 seconds to mix the medication evenly.
    ○ Exhale comfortably (as in a normal full breath).
    ○ Hold the canister upside down.
    ○ Press down once on the MDI canister (which
      releases the dose) and inhale slowly (for 3 to 5
      seconds) and deeply through the mouth.
    ○ Hold your breath for 10 seconds or as long as
      possible. This allows the aerosol to reach
      deeper airways.
    ○ Remove the inhaler from or away from the
      mouth.
    ○ Exhale slowly through pursed lips. Controlled
      exhalation keeps the small airways open
      during exhalation.
    ○ Repeat the inhalation if ordered. Wait 20 to 30
      seconds between inhalations of bronchodilator
      medications so the first inhalation has a chance
      to work and the subsequent dose reaches
      deeper into the lungs.
    ○ Following use of the inhaler, rinse the mouth
      with tap water to remove any remaining
      medication and reduce irritation and risk of
      infection.
    ○ Clean the MDI mouthpiece after each use. Use
      mild soap and water, rinse it, and let it air dry
      before replacing it on the device.

## SUGGESTIONS FOR CLASSROOM ACTIVITIES

- Show a videotape of administration of topical medications. Compare and contrast with the related skills in the textbook.
- Obtain samples of various types of topical medications for the students to view.

## SUGGESTIONS FOR CLINICAL ACTIVITIES

- Review the agency's policies and procedures for administering various topical medications.
- Assign students to administer topical medications for assigned clients.

# CHAPTER 36
# SKIN INTEGRITY AND WOUND CARE

## RESOURCE LIBRARY

### PRENTICE HALL NURSING MEDIALINK DVD-ROM

Audio Glossary
NCLEX® Review
Skills Checklists
Animations:
    *Pressure Ulcers*
    *Feature Integument*
    *Layers of the Skin*
    *Integumentary Repair*

### COMPANION WEBSITE

Additional NCLEX® Review
Case Study: *Clients with Chronic Illnesses*
Care Plan Activity: *Client with Pressure Ulcer*
Application Activity: *Enterostomal Therapist*
Links to Resources

### IMAGE LIBRARY

**Figure 36.1** Four stages of pressure ulcers.
**Figure 36.2** Braden Scale for Predicting Pressure Sore Risk.
**Figure 36.3** Body pressure areas.
**Figure 36.4** Pressure Ulcer Scale for Healing (PUSH) Tool.
**Figure 36.5** Wound/skin documentation sheet.
**Figure 36.6** Heel protector.
**Figure 36.7** Alternating pressure mattress (Ease).
**Figure 36.8** Low-air-loss bed.
**Figure 36.9** Low-air-loss and air-fluidized combo bed (Clinitron/Rite Hite).
**Figure 36.10** The strips of tape should be placed at the ends of the dressing and must be sufficiently long and wide to secure the dressing.
**Figure 36.11** Dressings over moving parts must remain secure in spite of the client's movement.
**Figure 36.12** Montgomery straps, or tie tapes, are used to secure large dressings that require frequent changing.

**Figure 36.13** Vacuum-assisted closure (VAC) system for wounds.
**Figure 36.14** Starting a bandage with two circular turns.
**Figure 36.15** Applying spiral turns.
**Figure 36.16** Applying spiral reverse turns.
**Figure 36.17** Starting a recurrent bandage.
**Figure 36.18** Completing a recurrent bandage.
**Figure 36.19** Applying a figure-eight bandage.
**Figure 36.20** Large arm sling.
**Figure 36.21** A straight abdominal binder.
**Figure 36.22** An aquathermia heating unit.
**Figure 36.23** Commercially prepared disposable hot packs.
**Skill 36.1** Obtaining a Wound Drainage Specimen for Culture.
**Skill 36.2** Irrigating a Wound.

## LEARNING OUTCOME 1

Describe factors affecting skin integrity.

### CONCEPTS FOR LECTURE

1. Genetics and heredity determine many aspects of a person's skin, including color, sensitivity to light, and allergies.
    Age influences skin integrity. The skin of both the very young and the very old is more fragile and susceptible to injury than that of most adults. However, wounds tend to heal more rapidly in infants and children.
    Many chronic illnesses and their treatments affect skin integrity. People with impaired peripheral arterial

### POWERPOINT LECTURE SLIDES

*(NOTE: The number on each PPT Lecture Slide directly corresponds with the Concepts for Lecture.)*

 **1** Factors Affecting Skin Integrity
- Genetics and Heredity
- Age
- Chronic Illnesses and Related Treatments
- Medications
- Poor Nutrition

## CONCEPTS FOR LECTURE *continued*

circulation may have skin on the legs that appears shiny, has lost its hair distribution, and damages easily.

Some medications, corticosteroids for example, cause thinning of the skin and allow it to be much more readily harmed. Many medications increase sensitivity to sunlight and can predispose one to severe sunburn. Some of the most common medications that can cause this damage are certain antibiotics, chemotherapy drugs for cancer, and some psychotherapeutic drugs.

Poor nutrition alone can interfere with the appearance and function of normal skin.

---

### SUGGESTIONS FOR CLASSROOM ACTIVITIES

• Provide additional examples of disease conditions and medications. Ask the students to identify why these conditions or medications may influence skin integrity.

### SUGGESTIONS FOR CLINICAL ACTIVITIES

• Have the students identify factors that may influence the skin integrity of their assigned clients.

---

## LEARNING OUTCOME 2

Identify clients at risk for pressure ulcers.

### CONCEPTS FOR LECTURE

1. Risk factors for pressure ulcers include friction and shearing, immobility, inactivity, inadequate nutrition, fecal and urinary incontinence, decreased mental status, diminished sensation, excessive body heat, advanced age, and chronic conditions.

   Other factors contributing to formation of pressure ulcers are poor lifting and transferring techniques, incorrect positioning, hard support surfaces, and incorrect application of pressure-relieving devices.

2. Several risk assessment tools are available that provide the nurse with systematic means of identifying clients at high risk for pressure ulcer development. The U.S. Public Health Service's Panel for the Prediction and Prevention of Pressure Ulcers in Adults (PPPPUA) (1992a) recommends that the tool include data collection in the areas of immobility, incontinence, nutrition, and level of consciousness.

   The Braden Scale for Predicting Pressure Sore Risk (Figure 36.2) consists of six subscales: sensory perception, moisture, activity, mobility, nutrition, and friction and shear. A total score of 23 points is possible. An adult who scores below 18 points is considered at risk.

   Norton's Pressure Area Risk Assessment Form Scale (Table 36–2) includes the categories of general physical condition, mental state, activity, mobility, incontinence, and medications. The total possible score is 24. Scores of 15 or 16 should be viewed as indicators, not predictors, of risk.

### POWERPOINT LECTURE SLIDES

*(NOTE: The number on each PPT Lecture Slide directly corresponds with the Concepts for Lecture.)*

 Risk Factors for Pressure
  • Friction and shearing
  • Immobility and inactivity
  • Inadequate nutrition
  • Fecal and urinary incontinence
  • Decreased mental status
  • Diminished sensation
  • Excessive body heat
  • Advanced age
  • Chronic mental conditions
  • Poor lifting and transferring techniques
  • Incorrect positioning
  • Hard support surfaces
  • Incorrect application of pressure-relieving devices

 Risk Assessment Tools
  • Braden Scale for Predicting Pressure Sore Risk
  • Norton's Pressure Area Risk Assessment Form Scale

---

## SUGGESTIONS FOR CLASSROOM ACTIVITIES

- Give the students outlines of the human body in supine, prone, and side-lying positions. Have the students mark a potential pressure site on the outlines.
- Divide the students into groups. Assign each group a pressure ulcer risk factor. Have each group develop specific interventions to prevent pressure ulcer formation for their assigned risk factor.

## SUGGESTIONS FOR CLINICAL ACTIVITIES

- Have the students assess their assigned clients using the pressure ulcer risk tool used in the agency.

---

# LEARNING OUTCOME 3

Describe the four stages of pressure ulcer development.

## CONCEPTS FOR LECTURE

1. Stage I: Nonblanchable erythema signals potential ulceration.
2. Stage II: Partial-thickness skin loss (abrasion, blister, or shallow crater) involves the epidermis and possibly the dermis.
3. Stage III: Full-thickness skin loss involves damage or necrosis of subcutaneous tissue that may extend down to, but not through, underlying fascia. The ulcer presents clinically as a deep crater with or without undermining of adjacent tissue.
4. Stage IV: There is full-thickness skin loss with tissue necrosis or damage to muscle, bone, or supporting structures such as tendons or joint capsules. Undermining and sinus tracts may also be present.

## POWERPOINT LECTURE SLIDES

*(NOTE: The number on each PPT Lecture Slide directly corresponds with the Concepts for Lecture.)*

1. Stage I
   - Nonblanchable erythema signals potential ulceration
2. Stage II
   - Partial-thickness skin loss
3. Stage III
   - Full-thickness skin loss
4. Stage IV
   - Full-thickness skin loss

## SUGGESTIONS FOR CLASSROOM ACTIVITIES

- Show slides or pictures of pressure ulcers in various stages. Have the students identify the ulcer stage and write nursing notes describing the ulcer.
- Discuss the method used in the agency to stage pressure ulcers.

## SUGGESTIONS FOR CLINICAL ACTIVITIES

- If there is a client on the clinical unit who has a pressure ulcer, arrange for the students to observe assessment of the ulcer and a dressing change or assign one of the students to provide care for the client and report assessment data and care provided in clinical conference.

---

# LEARNING OUTCOME 4

Differentiate primary and secondary wound healing.

## CONCEPTS FOR LECTURE

1. Primary intention healing occurs when the tissue surfaces have been approximated (closed) and there is minimal to no tissue loss; it is characterized by minimal granulation tissue and scarring. It is also called primary union or first intention healing. An example is a closed surgical incision.
2. A wound that is extensive and involves considerable tissue loss, and in which the edges cannot or should not be approximated, heals by secondary intention

## POWERPOINT LECTURE SLIDES

*(NOTE: The number on each PPT Lecture Slide directly corresponds with the Concepts for Lecture.)*

1. Primary Intention Healing
   - Tissue surfaces approximated
   - Minimal or no tissue loss
   - Formulation of minimal granulation and scarring
2. Secondary Intention Healing
   - Extensive tissue loss

healing. The repair time is longer, the scarring is greater, and the susceptibility to infection is greater. An example is a pressure ulcer.

3. Wounds that are left open for 3 to 5 days to allow edema or infection to resolve or exudate to drain and are then closed with sutures, staples, or adhesive skin closures heal by tertiary intention. This is also called delayed primary intention.

- Edges cannot be closed
- Repair time longer
- Scarring greater
- Susceptibility to infection greater

**3** Tertiary Intention Healing (Delayed Primary Intention)
- Initially left open
- Edema, infection, or exudate resolves
- Then closed

### SUGGESTIONS FOR CLASSROOM ACTIVITIES

- Obtain pictures of wounds that demonstrate primary, secondary, and tertiary healing.

### SUGGESTIONS FOR CLINICAL ACTIVITIES

- Locate clients who have wounds in various stages of healing. Ask permission for the students to assess the wounds. Compare and contrast assessment findings.

# LEARNING OUTCOME 5

Describe the three phases of wound healing.

### CONCEPTS FOR LECTURE

1. The inflammatory phase of wound healing is initiated immediately after injury and lasts 3 to 5 days. Two major processes occur during this phase: hemostasis (the cessation of bleeding) and phagocytosis (engulfing of microorganisms and cellular debris by macrophages).

2. The proliferative phase of wound healing extends from day 3 or 4 to about day 21 postinjury. Fibroblasts (connective tissue cells) begin to synthesize collagen, a protein that adds tensile strength to the wound. Capillaries grow across the wound, increasing the blood supply. Fibroblasts deposit fibrin, and granulation tissue is formed. Granulation tissue is a translucent red color. It is fragile and bleeds easily. When the edges of a wound aren't sutured, the area must be filled in with granulation tissue. When granulation tissue matures, marginal epithelial cells migrate to it, proliferating over this connective tissue base to fill the wound.

3. The maturation phase (or remodeling) of wound healing begins about day 21 and can extend 1 or 2 years after the injury. Fibroblasts continue to synthesize collagen, and the collagen fibers reorganize into a more orderly structure. The wound is remodeled and contracted. The scar becomes stronger but is never as strong as the original tissue.

### POWERPOINT LECTURE SLIDES

*(NOTE: The number on each PPT Lecture Slide directly corresponds with the Concepts for Lecture.)*

**1** Inflammatory Phase of Wound Healing
- Immediately after injury; lasts 3 to 5 days
- Hemostasis
- Phagocytosis

**2** Proliferative Phase of Wound Healing
- From postinjury day 3 or 4 until day 21
- Collagen synthesis
- Granulation tissue formation

**3** Maturation Phase of Wound Healing
- From day 21 until 1 or 2 years postinjury
- Collagen organization
- Remodeling or contraction
- Scar stronger

### SUGGESTIONS FOR CLASSROOM ACTIVITIES

- If possible, locate pictures of wounds in various stages of healing. Describe the associated findings.

### SUGGESTIONS FOR CLINICAL ACTIVITIES

- Have students assess clients who have surgical wounds. Ask students to describe findings.

# LEARNING OUTCOME 6

Identify three major types of wound exudate.

## CONCEPTS FOR LECTURE

1. Exudate is material such as fluid and cells that have escaped from blood vessels during the inflammatory process. It is deposited in tissue or on the tissue surface. There are three major types of exudate: serous, purulent, and sanguineous (hemorrhagic).

2. Serous exudate consists chiefly of serum (the clear portion of the blood) derived from blood and the serous membranes of the body. It looks watery and has few cells. An example of serous exudate is the fluid in a blister.

   Purulent exudate is thicker than serous exudate because of the presence of pus, which consists of leukocytes, liquefied dead tissue debris, and dead and living bacteria. Purulent exudates vary in color. Some acquire tinges of blue, green, or yellow, depending on the causative organisms.

   A sanguineous (hemorrhagic) exudate consists of large amounts of red blood cells, indicating damage to capillaries that is severe enough to allow the escape of red blood cells from the plasma.

   Mixed exudates include serosanguineous (consisting of clear and blood-tinged drainage) and purosanguineous discharge (consisting of pus and blood).

## POWERPOINT LECTURE SLIDES

*(NOTE: The number on each PPT Lecture Slide directly corresponds with the Concepts for Lecture.)*

 Exudate
- Material such as fluid and cells that have escaped from blood vessels during inflammatory process
- Deposited in tissue or on tissue surface
- Three major types
  ○ Serous
  ○ Purulent
  ○ Sanguineous

2 Serous Exudate
- Mostly serum
- Watery, clear of cells
- E.g. Fluid in a blister
- Purulent Exudate
  ○ Thicker
  ○ Presence of pus
  ○ Color varies with organisms
- Sanguineous (hemorrhagic) Exudate
  ○ Large numbers of RBCs
  ○ Indicates severe damage to capillaries
- Mixed
  ○ Serosanguineous
    ⁻ Clear and blood-tinged drainage
  ○ Purosanguineous
    ⁻ Pus and blood

## SUGGESTIONS FOR CLASSROOM ACTIVITIES

- Obtain pictures of various types of wound drainage and have the students identify them.

## SUGGESTIONS FOR CLINICAL ACTIVITIES

- If there are clients on the unit who have wound drainage or wound drainage systems, have the students assess the type of drainage present.

# LEARNING OUTCOME 7

Identify the main complications of and factors that affect wound healing.

## CONCEPTS FOR LECTURE

1. The main complications of wound healing include hemorrhage, infection, and dehiscence and evisceration.

   Hemorrhage is excessive bleeding either internally or externally; infection is the multiplication of colonizing organisms and invasion of tissues; dehiscence is the partial or total rupturing of a wound; and evisceration is the protrusion of internal viscera through an incision.

2. Characteristics of the individual such as age, nutritional status, lifestyle, and medications influence the speed of wound healing.

   Elders, who may have chronic diseases that affect wound healing, heal more slowly (see Box 36–2);

## POWERPOINT LECTURE SLIDES

*(NOTE: The number on each PPT Lecture Slide directly corresponds with the Concepts for Lecture.)*

 Complications of Wound Healing
- Hemorrhage
- Infection
- Dehiscence
- Evisceration

2 Factors Affecting Wound Healing
- Age
- Nutritional status
- Lifestyle
- Medications

individuals who are malnourished or obese heal more slowly and are at risk for infection; those who exercise regularly heal faster and those who smoke heal more slowly; anti-inflammatory medications slow healing and prolonged antibiotic use may lead to development of resistant organisms.

---

## SUGGESTIONS FOR CLASSROOM ACTIVITIES

- Discuss the signs and symptoms of dehiscence and evisceration and the appropriate nursing interventions.

## SUGGESTIONS FOR CLINICAL ACTIVITIES

- Have the students discuss how clients' developmental stage, nutritional status, lifestyle, and medications can affect wound healing.
- Have the students discuss discharge instructions that should be provided for clients who have wounds, in terms of recognizing and reporting signs and symptoms of complications and proper nutrition for wound healing.

---

# LEARNING OUTCOME 8

Identify assessment data pertinent to skin integrity, pressure sites, and wounds.

## CONCEPTS FOR LECTURE

1. During the review of systems as part of the nursing history, information regarding skin diseases, previous bruising, general skin condition, skin lesions, and usual healing of sores is elicited.

2. Inspection and palpation of the skin focuses on determination of skin color distribution, skin turgor, presence of edema, and characteristics of any skin lesions that are present. Particular attention is paid to areas that are most likely to break down such as skin folds under the breasts, moist areas such as the perineum, and areas that receive extensive pressure such as bony prominences.

3. Nurses commonly assess both untreated and treated wounds. Assessing untreated wounds includes assessing the location and extent of tissue damage; measuring the wound length, width, and depth; inspecting the wound for bleeding; inspecting the wound for foreign bodies; assessing associated injuries; and, if the wound is contaminated with foreign material, determining when the client last had a tetanus toxoid injection. (See Practice Guidelines: Assessing Untreated Wounds.)

4. Assessing treated wounds, or sutured wounds, involves observation of appearance, size, drainage, presence of swelling or pain, and status of drains or tubes. In some agencies photographs are taken weekly for a visual record of progress.

5. When a pressure ulcer is present, the nurse notes location of the ulcer related to a bony prominence; size of the ulcer in centimeters including length (head to toe), width (side to side), and depth; presence of undermining or sinus tracts, assessed as face on a clock

## POWERPOINT LECTURE SLIDES

*(NOTE: The number on each PPT Lecture Slide directly corresponds with the Concepts for Lecture.)*

**1** Nursing Management: Assessment
- Nursing history
  - Review of systems
  - Skin diseases
  - Previous bruising
  - General skin condition
  - Skin lesions
  - Usual healing of sores

**2** Nursing Management: Assessment
- Inspection and Palpation
  - Skin color distribution
  - Skin turgor
  - Presence of edema
  - Characteristics of any skin lesions
  - Particular attention paid to areas that are most likely to break down

**3** Nursing Management: Assessment
- Untreated Wounds
  - Location
  - Extent of tissue damage
  - Wound length, width, and depth
  - Bleeding
  - Foreign bodies
  - Associated injuries
  - Last tetanus toxoid injection

**4** Nursing Management: Assessment
- Treated Wounds
  - Appearance
  - Size

with 12 o'clock as the client's head; stage of the ulcer; color of the wound bed and location of necrosis or eschar; condition of the wound margins; integrity of surrounding skin; and clinical signs of infection such as redness, warmth, swelling, pain, odor, and exudate.

6. When assessing common pressure sites, the nurse inspects pressure areas for discoloration and capillary refill or blanch response when gently palpated by the end of a finger or thumb. The nurse also inspects pressure areas for abrasions and excoriations, and palpates the surface temperature of the skin over the pressure area sites for increased temperature and over bony prominences and dependent body areas for the presence of edema, which feels spongy or boggy. (See Practice Guidelines: Assessing Common Pressure Sites.)

7. Laboratory data, such as leukocyte count, hemoglobin level, blood coagulation studies, serum protein analysis (albumin level), and results of wound culture and sensitivities, can often support the nurse's clinical assessment of the wound's progress.

- ○ Drainage
- ○ Presence of swelling
- ○ Pain
- ○ Status of drains or tubes

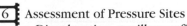 5 Assessment of Pressure Ulcers
- Location
- Size of ulcer in centimeters
  - ○ Length (head to toe)
  - ○ Width (side to side), and depth
- Presence of undermining or sinus tracts
- Stage
- Color of the wound bed
- Location of necrosis or eschar
- Condition of the wound margins
- Integrity of surrounding skin
- Clinical signs of infection

6 Assessment of Pressure Sites
- Discoloration, capillary refill or blanche response
- Abrasions and excoriations
- Surface temperature
- Presence of edema

7 Assessment of Laboratory Data
- Leukocyte count
- Hemoglobin level
- Blood coagulation studies
- Serum protein analysis (especially albumin level)
- Results of wound culture and sensitivities

---

## SUGGESTIONS FOR CLASSROOM ACTIVITIES

- Set up manikins with wounds and dressings. Simulate exudate. Divide the students into groups and have them describe the wound characteristics.

## SUGGESTIONS FOR CLINICAL ACTIVITIES

- Have the students assess their clients' skin integrity. Discuss findings at postconference.

---

## LEARNING OUTCOME 9

Identify nursing diagnoses associated with impaired skin integrity.

### CONCEPTS FOR LECTURE

1. The NANDA nursing diagnoses (2007) that relate to clients who have skin wounds or who are at risk for skin breakdown are *Risk for Impaired Skin Integrity* (at risk for skin being adversely altered), *Impaired Skin Integrity* (altered epidermis and/or dermis), and *Impaired Tissue Integrity* (damage to mucous membranes or corneal, integumentary, or subcutaneous tissue).

   Additional nursing diagnoses that may be appropriate for clients with existing impaired skin or tissue integrity include *Risk for Infection* (if the skin impairment is severe, the client is immunosuppressed, or the wound is caused by trauma) and *Pain* (related to nerve involvement within the tissue impairment or as a consequence of procedures used to treat the wound).

### POWERPOINT LECTURE SLIDES

*(NOTE: The number on each PPT Lecture Slide directly corresponds with the Concepts for Lecture.)*

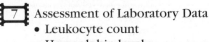 1 NANDA Nursing Diagnoses
- Risk for impaired skin integrity
- Impaired skin integrity
- Impaired tissue integrity
- Risk for infection
- Pain

**SUGGESTIONS FOR CLASSROOM ACTIVITIES**

- Using the nursing diagnoses reference book required by the curriculum, have the students look up the defining characteristics, etiology, or risk factors for the nursing diagnoses related to skin integrity.

**SUGGESTIONS FOR CLINICAL ACTIVITIES**

- Have the students develop nursing diagnoses for an assigned client who has risk factors for or actual impaired skin integrity. Discuss the defining characteristics, etiology, or risk factors that the client demonstrates.

# LEARNING OUTCOME 10

Identify essential aspects of planning care to maintain skin integrity and promote wound healing.

## CONCEPTS FOR LECTURE

1. The major goals for clients at *Risk for Impaired Skin Integrity* (pressure ulcer development) are to maintain skin integrity and to avoid potential associated risks. Clients with *Impaired Skin Integrity* need goals to demonstrate progressive wound healing and regain intact skin within a specified time frame.

2. Increasingly, wound care is provided in the home, and the client and family assume much of the responsibility for assessing and treating existing wounds and for helping to prevent pressure ulcers. Nurses are accountable for teaching the client and family wound preventive and care measures. A critical pathway can also be useful for planning client care at home. (See Home Care Assessment: Wound Care and Prevention of Pressure Ulcer, Client Teaching: Skin Integrity, and Critical Pathway: Wound Management.)

## POWERPOINT LECTURE SLIDES

*(NOTE: The number on each PPT Lecture Slide directly corresponds with the Concepts for Lecture.)*

1. Goals in Planning Client Care
   - Risk for impaired skin integrity
     - Maintain skin integrity
     - Avoid or reduce risks factors
   - Impaired skin integrity
     - Progressive wound healing
     - Regain intact skin

2. Client and Family Education
   - Assess and treat existing wound
   - Prevention of pressure ulcers

## SUGGESTIONS FOR CLASSROOM ACTIVITIES

- Divide the students into groups. Provide each group with a case study of a client who has impaired skin integrity. Ask the students to identify the nursing diagnoses related to skin integrity and write specific goals/desired outcomes for this client. Compare and contrast plans.

## SUGGESTIONS FOR CLINICAL ACTIVITIES

- Have the students develop care plans for their clients who have impaired skin integrity or who are at risk for impaired skin integrity. Review these in clinical conference.

# LEARNING OUTCOME 11

Discuss measures to prevent pressure ulcer formation.

## CONCEPTS FOR LECTURE

1. Measures to prevent pressure ulcers include providing nutrition, maintaining skin hygiene, avoiding skin trauma, and providing supportive devices.

2. Nutrition: Maintain fluid intake of at least 2500 mL per day unless contraindicated, sufficient protein, vitamins C, A, $B_1$, $B_5$, and zinc. Dietary consultation and nutritional supplements should be considered for nutritionally compromised clients. Weight should be monitored

## POWERPOINT LECTURE SLIDES

*(NOTE: The number on each PPT Lecture Slide directly corresponds with the Concepts for Lecture.)*

1. Measures to Prevent Pressure Ulcers

2. Providing Nutrition
   - Fluid intake
   - Protein, vitamins, zinc
   - Dietary consult
   - Weight/laboratory data monitoring

as should lymphocyte count, protein (especially albumin), and hemoglobin levels.

3. Skin Hygiene: Use mild cleansing agents that do not disrupt the skin's "natural barriers," avoid using hot water, exposure to cold and low humidity; apply moisturizing lotions while the skin is moist after bathing; keep skin clean, dry and free of irritation and maceration by urine, feces, sweat, and dry skin completely after a bath. Apply skin protection (dimethicone-based creams or alcohol-free barrier films) if indicated. Avoid massaging over bony prominences since massage may lead to deep tissue trauma.

4. Avoiding skin trauma: Provide a smooth, firm, and wrinkle-free foundation on which to sit or lie; position, transfer, and turn clients correctly. Elevate the head of the bed to no more than 30 degrees if not contraindicated to reduce shearing force. Avoid the use of baby powder and cornstarch which create harmful abrasive grit and are a respiratory hazard. Teach clients to shift weight 10 to 15 degrees every 15 to 30 minutes and exercise or ambulate to stimulate blood circulation. Use a lifting device rather than dragging the skin against a sheet. Reposition clients confined to bed at least every 2 hours using the prone, supine, right and left lateral (side-lying), and right and left Sims position. Avoid positioning the client directly on the trochanter. Establish a written schedule for turning and repositioning.

5. Supportive devices: Keep pressure on the bony prominences below capillary pressure for as much time as possible through a combination of turning, positioning, and use of pressure-relieving surfaces. Use an overlay mattress, a replacement mattress made of foam and gel combinations, or a specialty bed (high-air-loss beds, low-air-loss beds, and beds that provide kinetic therapy) for clients confined to bed (See Table 36–4). Raise the heels completely off the bed using supports such as wedges or pillows. Use pressure-reducing devices to distribute weight over the entire seating surface when the client is sitting.

**3** Maintaining Skin Hygiene
- Mild cleansing agents
- Avoid hot water
- Moisturizing lotions/skin protection
- Reduce irritants

**4** Avoiding Skin Trauma
- Smooth, firm surfaces
- Semi-Fowler's position
- Frequent weight shifts
- Exercise and ambulation
- Lifting devices
- Reposition q 2 hours
- Turning schedule

**5** Providing Supportive Devices
- Mattresses
- Beds
- Wedges, pillows
- Miscellaneous devices

### SUGGESTIONS FOR CLASSROOM ACTIVITIES

- Invite one or more equipment representatives to demonstrate and explain their special support devices for minimizing pressure ulcer formation.
- Have students position manikins or other students in supine, prone, and side-lying positions using appropriate technique to avoid pressure. Have students practice moving the "client" in bed using techniques to avoid friction and shearing.

### SUGGESTIONS FOR CLINICAL ACTIVITIES

- Invite the wound/ostomy/continence nurse from the agency to discuss equipment available in the agency to prevent pressure ulcer formation.

# LEARNING OUTCOME 12

Describe nursing strategies to treat pressure ulcers, promote wound healing, and prevent complications of wound healing.

## CONCEPTS FOR LECTURE

1. To treat pressure ulcers, the nurse should follow agency protocols and the primary care provider's orders, if any. In addition, minimize direct pressure on the ulcer by repositioning the client at least every 2 hours, make a schedule and record position changes on the client's chart, and provide devices to minimize or float pressure areas. Clean the pressure ulcer with every dressing change. The method of cleaning depends on the stage of the ulcer, products available, and agency protocol. Clean and dress the ulcer using surgical asepsis. Never use alcohol or hydrogen peroxide as they are cytotoxic to tissue beds. If the pressure ulcer is infected, obtain a sample of the drainage for culture and sensitivity. Teach the client to move, even if only slightly, to relieve pressure. Provide range-of-motion (ROM) exercise and encourage mobility as the client's condition permits (see Practice Guidelines: Treating Pressure Ulcers).

2. The goals of the RYB color guide to wound care are to protect (cover) red, cleanse yellow, and debride black. Red wounds need to be protected to avoid disturbance to regenerating tissue. The nurse protects the wound by gentle cleansing, covering periwound skin with alcohol-free barrier film, filling dead space with hydrogel or alginate, covering the wound with an appropriate dressing such as transparent film, hydrocolloid dressing, or a clear absorbent acrylic dressing, and changing the dressing as infrequently as possible.

    Yellow wounds are characterized primarily by liquid to semiliquid "slough" that is often accompanied by purulent drainage or previous infection. The nurse cleanses yellow wounds to remove nonviable tissue. Methods used may include applying moist-to-moist normal saline dressings, irrigating the wound, using absorbent dressing materials such as impregnated hydrogel or alginate dressings, and consulting with the primary care provider about the need for a topical antimicrobial to minimize bacterial growth.

    Black wounds are covered by thick necrotic tissue or eschar. They require debridement (removal of dead tissue). Debridement may be achieved in four different ways: sharp, mechanical, chemical, autolytic, and use of fly larvae (maggots). Once eschar is removed, the wound is treated as yellow, then red.

3. To promote wound healing, the client should be assisted to have an oral intake of at least 2,500 mL of fluids a day unless contraindicated. Ensure that the client receives sufficient protein, vitamins C, A, $B_1$, $B_5$, and zinc. Consulting a registered dietitian may be helpful. Nutritional supplements should be considered for nutritionally compromised clients. The client's weight should be monitored, and lymphocyte count, protein (especially albumin), and hemoglobin should be monitored.

## POWERPOINT LECTURE SLIDES

*(NOTE: The number on each PPT Lecture Slide directly corresponds with the Concepts for Lecture.)*

**1** Treating Pressure Ulcers
- Minimize direct pressure
- Schedule and record position changes
- Provide devices to reduce pressure areas
- Clean and dress the ulcer using surgical asepsis
- Never use alcohol or hydrogen peroxide
- Obtain culture and sensitivity, if infected
- Teach the client to move
- Provide range-of-motion (ROM) exercise

**2** RYB Color Guide for Wound Care
- Red (protect)
- Yellow (cleanse)
- Black (debride)

**3** Promoting Wound Healing
- Fluid intake
- Protein, vitamin, and zinc intake
- Dietary consult
- Nutritional supplements
- Monitor weight/laboratory values

**4** Preventing Complications of Wound Healing
- Prevent entry of microorganisms
- Prevent the transmission of pathogens

4. Two major aspects to controlling wound infection include preventing microorganisms from entering the wound, and preventing the transmission of blood-borne pathogens to or from the client to others (see Table 36–3: Guidelines for Preventing Infection and the Transmission of Bloodborne Pathogens).

---

| SUGGESTIONS FOR CLASSROOM ACTIVITIES | SUGGESTIONS FOR CLINICAL ACTIVITIES |
|---|---|
| • Invite a wound/ostomy/continence nurse to discuss current trends in pressure ulcer treatment. | • Review the agency's policies and procedures for care of pressure ulcers. |

---

## LEARNING OUTCOME 13

Identify purposes of commonly used wound dressing materials and binders.

### CONCEPTS FOR LECTURE

1. Table 36–5 lists selected types of wound dressings, purposes, indications, and examples.

   Transparent film is used to provide protection against contamination and friction, to maintain a clean moist surface that facilitates cellular migration, to provide insulation by preventing fluid evaporation, and to facilitate wound assessment.

   Impregnated nonadherent dressings are used to cover, soothe, and protect partial- and full-thickness wounds without exudate.

   Hydrocolloid dressings are used to absorb exudate; to produce a moist environment that facilitates healing but does not cause maceration of surrounding skin; to protect the wound from bacterial contamination, foreign debris, and urine or feces; and to prevent shearing.

   Clear absorbent acrylic dressings maintain a transparent membrane for easy wound bed assessment, provide bacterial and shearing protection, maintain moist wound healing, and can be used with alginates to provide packing to deeper wound beds.

   Hydrogels are used to liquefy necrotic tissue or slough, rehydrate the wound bed, and fill in dead space.

   Polyurethane foams absorb up to heavy amounts of exudate, providing and maintaining moist wound healing.

   Alginates (exudate absorbers) are used to provide a moist wound surface by interacting with exudate to form a gelatinous mass, to absorb exudate, to eliminate dead space or pack wounds, and to support debridement.

2. Bandages and binders serve various purposes, such as supporting a wound, immobilizing a wound, applying pressure, and retaining warmth. When applied correctly, they promote healing, provide comfort, and can prevent injury.

### POWERPOINT LECTURE SLIDES

*(NOTE: The number on each PPT Lecture Slide directly corresponds with the Concepts for Lecture.)*

1. Types of Wound Dressings
   - Transparent film
   - Impregnated nonadherent
   - Hydrocolloids
   - Clear absorbent acrylic
   - Hydrogel
   - Polyurethane foam
   - Alginate

2. Bandages
   - Gauze
     - Retain dressings on wounds
     - Bandage hands and feet
   - Elasticized
     - Provide pressure to an area
     - Improve venous circulation in legs
   - Binders
     - Support large areas of body
     - e.g. Triangular arm sling, straight abdominal binder

Many bandages are made of gauze, which is light and porous and readily molds to the body. Gauze is used to retain dressings on wounds and to bandage the fingers, hands, toes, and feet. It supports dressings and permits air to circulate. It can be impregnated with petroleum jelly or other medications for application to wounds.

Elasticized bandages are applied to provide pressure to an area, to provide support, and to improve venous circulation in the legs.

A binder is a type of bandage designed for a specific body part. Binders are used to support large areas of the body such as the abdomen, arm, or chest. They can be made of inexpensive materials or can be of commercial design, which are easier to use, more expensive, and slightly less modifiable. Examples include the triangular arm sling and straight abdominal binder.

## SUGGESTIONS FOR CLASSROOM ACTIVITIES

• Prepare a display of different types of wound dressings and a description of when each should be used.

## SUGGESTIONS FOR CLINICAL ACTIVITIES

• Review wound dressings used in the agency as well as the agency's policies and procedures related to these.

# LEARNING OUTCOME 14

Identify essential steps of obtaining wound specimens, applying dressings, and irrigating a wound.

## CONCEPTS FOR LECTURE

1. The steps in obtaining wound specimens are listed in Skill 36.1. Essential steps include determining whether the wound is to be cleansed prior to obtaining the specimen, whether the site from which to obtain the specimen has been indicated, whether the specimen to be collected is for an aerobic or anaerobic organism, and whether the client has been complaining of pain at the wound site and will require an analgesic before the culture is obtained. An aerobic or anaerobic culture is then obtained following the steps listed.

2. The essential steps in applying dressings include following the manufacturer's instruction for applying the dressings described in outcome #13 (see Table 36-5). Dressings are placed so that the entire wound is covered. When securing dressings the nurse places tape so that dressings cannot be folded back to expose the wound placing tapes at the ends of the wound and in the middle (See Figure 36.10 A). The tape should extend for several inches on either side of the wound (See Figure 36.10A, B). Tape should be placed in the opposite directions of body action (See Figure 36.11A, B, C) and Montgomery straps (tie tapes) should be used for wounds that require frequent changing (See Figure 36.12)

## POWERPOINT LECTURE SLIDES

*(NOTE: The number on each PPT Lecture Slide directly corresponds with the Concepts for Lecture.)*

1. Obtaining a Wound Specimen
   • Skill 36.1

2. Applying a Dressing
   • Cover entire wound

3. Irrigating a Wound
   • Skill 36.2

3. The steps in irrigating a wound are listed in Skill 36.2. Essential steps include checking for the type of irrigating solution to be used, the frequency of the irrigations, and the temperature of the irrigating solution; positioning the client so that the irrigating solution will flow from the top to the bottom of the wound and into the basin; using a piston syringe to prevent aspiration of drainage and to provide safe pressure (4 to 15 psi). The wound is then irrigated following the steps listed.

---

## SUGGESTIONS FOR CLASSROOM ACTIVITIES

- Prepare manikins with various types of wounds and dressings. Have the students practice changing the dressings.
- Have the students practice irrigating wounds on manikins.
- Have the students practice obtaining wound cultures on manikins.
- Have the students practice bandaging on manikins.

## SUGGESTIONS FOR CLINICAL ACTIVITIES

- Assign the students to assist with dressing changes and suture/staple removal.
- Show types of equipment available to obtain wound cultures in the agency.

---

## LEARNING OUTCOME 15

Identify physiologic responses to and purposes of heat and cold.

### CONCEPTS FOR LECTURE

1. The physiologic effects of heat include causing vasodilation, increasing capillary permeability, increasing cellular metabolism, increasing inflammation, and producing a sedative effect.
2. Indications for heat include (a) muscle spasms (heat relaxes muscles and increases their contraction); (b) inflammation (heat increases blood flow and softens exudate); (c) pain (heat relieves pain possibly by promoting muscle relaxation, increasing circulation, promoting psychologic relaxation and a feeling of comfort, and acting as a counterirritant); (d) contracture (heat reduces contracture and increases joint mobility by allowing greater distention of muscles and connective tissue); and (e) joint stiffness (heat reduces stiffness by decreasing viscosity of synovial fluid and increasing tissue distensibility).
3. The physiologic effects of cold include causing vasoconstriction, decreasing capillary permeability, decreasing cellular metabolism, slowing bacterial growth, decreasing inflammation, and producing a local anesthetic effect (See Table 36-6).
4. Indications for cold include (a) muscle spasms (cold relaxes muscles and decreases muscle contractility); (b) inflammation (vasoconstriction decreases capillary permeability, decreases blood flow, and slows cellular metabolism); (c) pain (cold decreases pain by slowing nerve conduction rate and blocking nerve

### POWERPOINT LECTURE SLIDES

*(NOTE: The number on each PPT Lecture Slide directly corresponds with the Concepts for Lecture.)*

**1** Physiologic Effects of Heat
- Vasodilation
- Increases capillary permeability
- Increases cellular metabolism
- Increases inflammation
- Produces sedative effect

**2** Indications for Heat
- Muscle spasms
- Inflammation
- Pain
- Contracture
- Joint stiffness

**3** Physiologic Effects of Cold
- Vasoconstriction
- Decreases capillary permeability
- Decreases cellular metabolism
- Slows bacterial growth
- Decreases inflammation
- Local anesthetic effect

**4** Indications for Cold
- Muscle spasms
- Inflammation
- Pain
- Traumatic injury

impulses, produces numbness, acts as a counterirri-tant, and increases pain threshold); and (d) traumatic injury (cold decreases bleeding by constricting blood vessels and decreases edema by reducing capillary per-meability). (See Table 36–8.)

| SUGGESTIONS FOR CLASSROOM ACTIVITIES | SUGGESTIONS FOR CLINICAL ACTIVITIES |
|---|---|
| • Discuss contraindications for use of heat or cold. | • Have the students provide examples of indications for the use of heat or cold that they have observed clinically or have used with assigned clients. Ask the students to provide rationale for the selection of heat or cold in terms of the physiologic effect. |

# LEARNING OUTCOME 16

Describe methods of applying dry and moist heat and cold.

## CONCEPTS FOR LECTURE

1. Heat can be applied to the body in both dry and moist forms. Dry heat is applied locally by means of a hot wa-ter bottle, aquathermia pad, disposable heat pack, or electric pad. Moist heat can be provided by compress, hot pack, soak, or sitz bath.

   To use a hot water bag, measure the temperature of the water using a bath thermometer. Fill the bag about two-thirds full, expel the remaining air, and se-cure the top. Dry the bag and hold it upside down to test for leakage. Wrap the bag in a towel or cover and place it on the body site. Remove it after 30 minutes or in accordance with agency protocol.

   To use an aquathermia pad, fill the reservoir of the unit two-thirds full of distilled water. Set the desired temperature (check the manufacturer's instructions; most units are set at 40.5°C for adults). Cover the pad, plug in the unit, and apply the pad to the body part. The treatment is usually continued for 30 minutes. Check orders and agency protocol (See Figure 36.22).

   To use a hot or cold pack, follow the manufac-turer's direction on the package to initiate the heating or cooling process (striking, squeezing, or kneading) (See Figure 36.23).

   When using an electric pad, do not insert sharp objects into the pad, ensure that the body area is dry unless there is a waterproof cover on the pad, use pads with a preset heating switch so the client cannot in-crease the heat, and do not place the pad under the client.

2. Dry cold is generally applied locally by means of a cold pack, ice bag, ice glove, or ice collar. Moist cold can be provided by compress or a cooling sponge bath.

## POWERPOINT LECTURE SLIDES

*(NOTE: The number on each PPT Lecture Slide directly corresponds with the Concepts for Lecture.)*

 Methods for Applying Dry and Moist Heat
- Dry Heat
  - Hot water bottle
  - Aquathermia pad
  - Disposable heat pack
  - Electric pad
- Moist Heat
  - Compress
  - Hot pack
  - Soak
  - Sitz bath

 Methods for Applying Dry and Moist Cold
- Dry Cold
  - Cold pack
  - Ice bag
  - Ice glove
  - Ice collar
- Moist Cold
  - Compress
  - Cooling sponge bath

Ice bags, ice gloves, and ice collars are filled with either ice chips or an alcohol-based solution. Always wrap the container in a towel or cover.

Compresses can be either warm or cold. Moist gauze dressings are heated to the temperature indicated by the order or according to agency protocol. When there is a break in the skin, sterile technique is necessary.

A soak refers to immersing a body part in a solution or wrapping a part in gauze dressings and then saturating the dressing with a solution. Sterile technique is indicated for open wounds. Determine agency protocol regarding the temperature of the solution.

A sitz bath or hip bath is used to soak the pelvic area. The temperature of water should be from 40°C to 43°C. Determine the agency's protocol. The duration of the bath is generally 15 to 20 minutes. Assist the client into the tub, provide a bath blanket for the client's shoulders, and eliminate drafts. Observe the client closely during the bath for signs of faintness, dizziness, weakness, accelerated pulse rate, and pallor. Maintain the water temperature. Following the sitz bath, assist the client out of the tub and help the client to dry.

The temperature for a cooling sponge bath ranges from 18°C to 32°C. Sponge the face, arms, legs, back, and buttocks slowly and gently. Leave each area wet and cover with a damp towel. Place ice bags and cold packs, if used, or a cool cloth on the forehead for comfort and in each axilla and at the groin. Sponge one body part and then another. The sponge bath should take about 30 minutes. Discontinue the bath if the client becomes pale or cyanotic or shivers or if the pulse becomes rapid or irregular. Reassess the vital signs at 15 minutes and after completing the sponge bath.

## SUGGESTIONS FOR CLASSROOM ACTIVITIES

- Have the students form groups and select one method of applying dry or moist heat. Make certain all methods are selected. Ask the students to develop a pamphlet or information sheet for clients that describes purposes, steps in applying, and assessment data to collect before, during, and after application as well as essential safety measures required.

## SUGGESTIONS FOR CLINICAL ACTIVITIES

- Have the students investigate and report on the agency's equipment, policies, and procedures for local application of heat and cold.

# CHAPTER 37
## PERIOPERATIVE NURSING

## RESOURCE LIBRARY

###  PRENTICE HALL NURSING MEDIALINK DVD-ROM

Audio Glossary
NCLEX® Review
Skills Checklist
End of Unit Concept Map Activity
Animation: *Diazepam*
Video: *Role of Scrub Nurse*

### 📖 IMAGE LIBRARY

**Figure 37.1** PACU nurse provides constant assessment and care for clients recovering from anesthesia and surgery.
**Figure 37.2** Nasogastric tubes used for gastric decompression.
**Figure 37.3** Wall suction unit for generating negative pressure for nasogastric suction.
**Figure 37.4** Hemovac closed-wound drainage system.
**Figure 37.5** Two Jackson-Pratt devices compressed to facilitate collection of exudates.
**Figure 37.6** Emptying drainage from Hemovac drainage system.
**Figure 37.7** With one hand, press the top and bottom together.

### 🌐 COMPANION WEBSITE

Additional NCLEX® Review
Case Study: *Clients Having Surgical Procedures*
Care Plan Activity: *Coronary Artery Bypass Procedure*
Application Activities:
 *Developing Operative Care Policies*
 *Preadmission Testing*
Links to Resources

**Figure 37.8** Common sutures.
**Figure 37.9** A surgical incision with retention sutures.
**Figure 37.10** Suture scissors.
**Figure 37.11** Staple remover.
**Figure 37.12** Removing a plain interrupted skin suture.
**Figure 37.13** Mattress interrupted sutures.
**Figure 37.14** Removing surgical clips or staples.
**Skill 37.1** Teaching Moving, Leg Exercises, Deep Breathing, and Coughing
**Skill 37.2** Applying Antiemboli Stockings
**Skill 37.3** Managing Gastrointestinal Suction
**Skill 37.4** Cleaning a Sutured Wound and Applying a Sterile Dressing

## LEARNING OUTCOME 1

Discuss various types of surgery according to degree of urgency, degree of risk, and purpose.

### CONCEPTS FOR LECTURE

1. Surgery is classified by its urgency and necessity to preserve the client's life, body part, or body function. Emergency surgery is performed immediately to preserve function or the life of the client (for example, to control internal hemorrhage). Elective surgery is performed when surgical intervention is the preferred treatment for a condition that is not immediately life threatening, but may ultimately threaten life or well-being, or to improve the client's life (for example, hip replacement surgery).

   Surgery is also classified as major or minor according to the degree of risk to the client. Major surgery involves a high degree of risk. It may be complicated or prolonged, large losses of blood may occur, vital organs may be involved, or postoperative complications may be likely (for example, open heart

### POWERPOINT LECTURE SLIDES

*(NOTE: The number on each PPT Lecture Slide directly corresponds with the Concepts for Lecture.)*

🎞 1 Various types of surgery
 • Degree of urgency
  ○ Emergency
  ○ Elective
 • Degree of risk
  ○ Major
  ○ Minor
 • Purposes of surgical procedures
  ○ Diagnostic
  ○ Palliative
  ○ Ablative
  ○ Constructive
  ○ Transplant

surgery). Minor surgery normally involves little risk, produces few complications, and is often performed on an outpatient basis (for example, breast biopsy).

Surgical procedures have various purposes. A diagnostic procedure confirms or establishes a diagnosis (for example, breast biopsy). A palliative procedure relieves or reduces pain or symptoms of a disease; it does not cure (for example, resection of nerve roots). An ablative procedure removes a diseased body part (for example, removal of gallbladder). A constructive procedure restores function or appearance that has been lost or reduced (for example, breast implant). A transplant replaces malfunctioning structures (for example, kidney replacement). (See Box 37-1.)

## SUGGESTIONS FOR CLASSROOM ACTIVITIES

- Have the students discuss the following statement: Surgery is never "minor" for a client.

## SUGGESTIONS FOR CLINICAL ACTIVITIES

- Have the students classify the type and purpose of surgery for various clients on the surgical unit.

# LEARNING OUTCOME 2

Describe the phases of the perioperative period.

## CONCEPTS FOR LECTURE

1. Surgery is a unique experience of a planned physical alteration encompassing three phases: preoperative, intraoperative, and postoperative.

   The preoperative phase begins when the decision to have surgery is made and ends when the client is transferred to the operating table. The nursing activities associated with this phase include assessing the client, identifying potential or actual health problems, planning specific care based on the individual's needs, and providing preoperative teaching for the client, the family, and significant others.

   The intraoperative phase begins when the client is transferred to the operating table and ends when the client is admitted to the postanesthesia care unit (PAC). The nursing activities related to this phase include a variety of specialized procedures designed to create and maintain a safe therapeutic environment for the client and the health care personnel. The activities include providing for the client's safety, maintaining an aseptic environment, ensuring proper functioning of equipment, and providing the surgical team with the instruments and supplies needed during the operation.

   The postoperative phase begins with the admission of the client to the postanesthesia area and ends when healing is complete. During the postoperative phase, nursing activities include assessing the client's response (physiologic and psychologic) to surgery, performing interventions to facilitate healing and prevent complications, teaching, providing support to the client and support people, and planning for home care.

## POWERPOINT LECTURE SLIDES

*(NOTE: The number on each PPT Lecture Slide directly corresponds with the Concepts for Lecture.)*

1. Phases of the Perioperative Period
   - Preoperative
     - Begins with decision to have surgery
     - Ends when client transferred to operating table
   - Intraoperative
     - Begins when client transferred to operating table
     - Ends when client admitted to PAC
   - Postoperative
     - Begins with admission of client to PAC
     - Ends when healing complete

# LEARNING OUTCOME 3

Identify essential aspects of preoperative assessment.

## CONCEPTS FOR LECTURE

1. Preoperative assessment includes collecting and reviewing physical, psychological, and social client data to determine the client's needs throughout the three preoperative phases.

    Preoperative assessment data include current health status, allergies, medications, previous surgeries, mental status, understanding of the surgical procedure and anesthesia, smoking, alcohol and other mind-altering substances, coping, social resources, and cultural and spiritual considerations (See Box 37–3).

2. A brief but complete physical assessment pays particular attention to systems that could affect the client's response to anesthesia and surgery. It also includes a brief "mini" mental status. Respiratory, cardiovascular, and other systems (gastrointestinal, genitourinary, and musculoskeletal) are examined to provide baseline data.

    The surgeon and/or anesthesiologist orders preoperative diagnostic tests. The nurse's responsibility is to check the orders carefully to see that they are carried out and to ensure that the results are obtained and in the client's record prior to surgery. Table 37–2 lists routine preoperative screening tests. In addition to these tests, diagnostic tests directly relating to the client's disease are performed.

    See Lifespan Considerations: Preoperative Teaching for children and elders.

## POWERPOINT LECTURE SLIDES

*(NOTE: The number on each PPT Lecture Slide directly corresponds with the Concepts for Lecture.)*

**1** Preoperative Assessment
- Current health status
- Allergies
- Medications
- Previous surgeries
- Mental status
- Understanding of the surgical procedure and anesthesia
- Smoking, alcohol and other mind-altering substances
- Coping
- Social resources
- Cultural and spiritual considerations

**2** Physical Assessment
- "Mini" mental status
- Respiratory
- Cardiovascular
- Other systems (gastrointestinal, genitourinary, and musculoskeletal)
- Preoperative laboratory and diagnostic tests

# LEARNING OUTCOME 4

Give examples of pertinent nursing diagnoses for surgical clients.

## CONCEPTS FOR LECTURE

1. Nursing diagnoses that may be appropriate for the preoperative client include *Deficient Knowledge, Anxiety, Disturbed Sleep Pattern, Anticipatory Grieving, and Ineffective Coping.*
2. Nursing diagnoses that may be appropriate for the intraoperative client include *Risk for Aspiration, Ineffective Protection, Impaired Skin Integrity, Risk for Perioperative-Positioning Injury, Risk for Impaired Body Temperature, Ineffective Tissue Perfusion,* and *Risk for Deficient Fluid Volume.*
3. Nursing diagnoses that may be appropriate for the postoperative client include *Acute Pain; Risk for Infection; Risk for Injury; Risk for Deficient Fluid Volume; Ineffective Airway Clearance; Ineffective Breathing Pattern; Self-Care Deficit: Bathing/Hygiene, Dressing/ Grooming, Toileting; Ineffective Health Maintenance; and Disturbed Body Image.*

## POWERPOINT LECTURE SLIDES

*(NOTE: The number on each PPT Lecture Slide directly corresponds with the Concepts for Lecture.)*

**1** NANDA Nursing Diagnoses: Preoperative Phase
- Deficient knowledge
- Anxiety
- Disturbed sleep pattern
- Anticipatory grieving
- Ineffective coping

**2** NANDA Nursing Diagnoses: Intraoperative Phase
- Risk for aspiration
- Ineffective protection
- Impaired skin integrity
- Risk for perioperative-positioning injury
- Risk for impaired body temperature
- Ineffective tissue perfusion
- Risk for deficient fluid volume

**3** NANDA Nursing Diagnoses: Postoperative Phase
- Acute pain
- Risk for infection
- Risk for injury
- Risk for deficient fluid volume
- Ineffective airway clearance
- Ineffective breathing pattern
- Self-care deficit: bathing/hygiene, dressing/grooming, toileting
- Ineffective health maintenance and disturbed body image

## SUGGESTIONS FOR CLASSROOM ACTIVITIES

- Using the nursing diagnosis book required by the school, have the students review the defining characteristics, etiology, or risk factors for each diagnosis.
- Provide the students with several case studies. Ask them to develop nursing diagnoses related to the specific perioperative phase in each case study and to document the defining characteristics, etiology, or risk factors.

## SUGGESTIONS FOR CLINICAL ACTIVITIES

- Have the students review critical pathways or preprinted nursing care plans for clients who are having various types of surgical procedures.
- Have the students develop care plans for their assigned clients who are in the preoperative or postoperative phase. Compare and contrast plans in postconference.

# LEARNING OUTCOME 5

Identify nursing responsibilities in planning perioperative nursing care.

## CONCEPTS FOR LECTURE

1. The overall goal in the preoperative period is to ensure that the client is mentally and physically prepared for surgery. Planning should involve the client, the client's family, and significant others. Examples of nursing activities to achieve these goals include preoperative teaching

## POWERPOINT LECTURE SLIDES

*(NOTE: The number on each PPT Lecture Slide directly corresponds with the Concepts for Lecture.)*

**1** Planning Perioperative Nursing Care: Preoperative Phase
- Overall goal is to ensure client mentally and physically prepared for surgery

(covered in outcome 6), physical preparation (covered in outcome 7), and psychological preparation.

For the perioperative client, discharge planning begins before admission. Early planning to meet the discharge needs of the client is particularly important for outpatient procedures as the client is generally discharged within hours after the procedure is performed.

Discharge planning incorporates an assessment of the client's, family's, and significant others' abilities and resources for care, their financial resources, and the need for referrals and home health services. (See Home Care Considerations: Postoperative Instructions.)

2. The overall goals of care in the intraoperative period are to maintain the client's safety and to maintain homeostasis. Examples of nursing activities to achieve these goals include positioning the client appropriately; performing preoperative skin preparation; assisting in preparing and maintaining the sterile field; opening and dispensing sterile supplies during surgery; providing medications and solutions for the sterile field; monitoring and maintaining a safe, aseptic environment; managing catheters, tubes, drains, and specimens; performing sponge, sharp, and instrument counts; and documenting nursing care provided and the client's response to interventions.

3. Overall goals in postoperative period include promotion of comfort and healing; restoration of the highest possible level of wellness; and prevention of associated risks. Postoperative care planning and discharge planning begin in the preoperative phase when preoperative teaching is implemented. To plan for continuity of care for the surgical client after discharge, the nurse considers the client's needs for assistance with care in the home setting and incorporates an assessment of the client's and family's abilities for self-care, financial resources, and the need for referrals and home health services. (See Home Care Assessment: Surgical Clients.)

- Preoperative teaching
- Physical preparation
- Psychological preparation
- Discharge planning

**2** Planning Perioperative Nursing Care: Intraoperative Phase
- Overall goals:
  - Maintain the client's safety
  - Maintain homeostasis

**3** Planning Perioperative Nursing Care: Postoperative Phase
- Overall goals:
  - Promote comfort and healing
  - Restore highest possible level of wellness
  - Prevent associated risks

---

**SUGGESTIONS FOR CLASSROOM ACTIVITIES**

- Invite a nurse educator from a hospital operating room to discuss current trends in perioperative nursing. Ask the nurse to discuss such issues as the qualifications of each member of the surgical team and beliefs about skin preparation.

**SUGGESTIONS FOR CLINICAL ACTIVITIES**

- Have the students discuss with clients the clients' perspectives on the perioperative experience.
- Arrange for students to spend a day in the operating room. Have them complete a postobservation sheet indicating the roles of each member of the surgical team; client, procedure, and site verification; interventions to prevent complications during surgery; and safety measures.

# LEARNING OUTCOME 6

Describe essential preoperative teaching, including pain control, moving, leg exercises, and coughing and deep-breathing exercises.

## CONCEPTS FOR LECTURE

1. Four dimensions of preoperative teaching have been identified as important to clients: information including what will happen to the client, when it will happen, and what the client will experience, such as expected sensations and discomfort; psychological support to reduce anxiety; roles of the client and support people in preoperative preparation, during the surgical procedure, and during the postoperative period; and skills training such as moving, deep breathing, coughing, splinting incisions with the hands or pillow, and using an incentive spirometer.

2. Preoperative teaching includes instruction about preoperative and postoperative regimens.

Preoperative regimen teaching includes: need for preoperative testing; discuss bowel preparation if necessary, skin preparation, preoperative medications, specific preoperative therapies, visit by anesthetist, need to restrict food and fluids, general timetable of events, need to remove jewelry, makeup and prostheses, preoperative holding area and waiting room; teach deep breathing and coughing exercises, how to turn, move, and splinting of incisions.

Postoperative regimen teaching includes: explain PACU routine and emergency equipment; review type and frequency of assessment; discuss pain management; explain usual activity restrictions and precaution when getting up for the first time postoperatively; describe usual dietary alterations; discuss dressings and drains; and provide an explanation and tour of ICU if client is to be transferred there postoperatively.

For outpatient surgical clients explain the usual preoperative and postoperative regimens; confirm place and time of surgery, when to arrive, where to register and what to wear; explain the need for a responsible adult to drive or to accompany the client home; discuss medications; communicate by telephone the evening before surgery to confirm time of surgery and arrival time; communicate by telephone within 48 hours postoperatively to evaluate surgical outcomes and identify any problems or complications.

Refer to Skill 37.1: Teaching Moving, Leg Exercises, Deep Breathing, and Coughing for actual performance of these skills

3. The purposes for performing each of these skill include the following:

Moving: to promote venous return, mobilize secretions, stimulate gastrointestinal motility, and facilitating early ambulation.

Leg exercises: to promote venous return; prevent thrombophlebitis and thrombus formation.

Deep breathing and coughing: to enhance lung expansion and mobilize secretions; prevent atelectasis and pneumonia.

## POWERPOINT LECTURE SLIDES

*(NOTE: The number on each PPT Lecture Slide directly corresponds with the Concepts for Lecture.)*

**1** Four Dimensions of Preoperative Teaching
- Information - explain what will happen, when, and what the client will experience
- Psychological support to reduce anxiety
- Explain roles of the client and support people in preoperative preparation, during the surgical procedure, and during the postoperative period
- Skills training

**2** Preoperative Instruction
- Preoperative regimen
- Postoperative regimen
- Special instructions for outpatient surgical clients
- Skill 37.1: Teaching Moving, Leg Exercises, Deep Breathing, and Coughing

**3** Purpose of Skills
- Moving
  - Promote venous return
  - Mobilize secretions
  - Stimulate gastrointestinal motility
  - Facilitate early ambulation
- Leg Exercises
  - Promote venous return
  - Prevent thrombophlebitis and thrombus formation
- Deep breathing and coughing
  - Enhance lung expansion
  - Mobilize secretions
  - Prevent atelectasis and pneumonia

## LEARNING OUTCOME 7

Describe essential aspects of preparing a client for surgery, including skin preparation.

### CONCEPTS FOR LECTURE

1. Physical preparation includes the following: nutrition and fluids, elimination, hygiene, medications, rest, care of valuables and prostheses, special orders, vital signs, safety protocols, and surgical skin preparation.

   The nurse should identify and record any signs of malnutrition or fluid imbalance. The nurse should also determine whether the client is to be "NPO after midnight" or is permitted food or fluids as recommended by the American Society for Anesthesiology (ASA) revised guidelines.

   Enemas prior to surgery are no longer routine but may be ordered if bowel surgery is planned. Prior to surgery, straight catheterization or the insertion of an indwelling catheter into the urinary bladder may be ordered. If the client does not have a catheter, the client should empty the bladder prior to receiving preoperative medication.

   The client may be asked to shower, bathe, and shampoo the evening or morning of surgery (or both). The nails should be trimmed and free of polish, and all cosmetics should be removed. Before going to the operating room the client should remove all hair pins and clips, and put on an operating room gown and surgical cap.

   The anesthetist or anesthesiologist may order routinely taken medications be held the day of surgery as well as preoperative medications which are given "on call" or at a scheduled time prior to surgery.

   To promote rest and sleep, a sedative may be ordered the night before surgery. The nurse should do everything possible to help the client sleep.

   All prostheses must be removed before surgery. However, hearing aids are often left in place and the operating room personnel are notified. Valuables should be sent home with the client's family or significant others or be labeled and placed in a locked storage area per agency policy.

   The nurse checks the surgeon's orders for any special orders such as insertion of a nasogastric tube, administration of medications, or application of antiemboli stockings (see Skill 37.2).

   JCAHO has established the Universal Protocol for Preventing Wrong Site, Wrong Procedure, Wrong

### POWERPOINT LECTURE SLIDES

*(NOTE: The number on each PPT Lecture Slide directly corresponds with the Concepts for Lecture.)*

 Preparing a Client for Surgery
- Nutrition and fluids
- Elimination
- Hygiene
- Medications
- Rest and sleep
- Valuables
- Special orders
- Skin preparation
- Safety protocols
- Vital signs
- Antiemboli stockings (Skill 37.2)
- Sequential compression devices

Person Surgery. This involves three steps: The first step is client verification at the time surgery is scheduled, during admission, and repeated whenever the client is transferred to another caregiver. The second step involves marking of the operative site in an unambiguous manner. The third step is called "time-out." The surgical team takes a time-out to conduct a final verification of the correct client, procedure, and site.

In most agencies skin preparation is carried out during the intraoperative phase. The site is cleansed with an antimicrobial to remove soil and decrease resident microbial count to subpathogenic levels.

The nurse assesses and documents vital signs and reports abnormal findings.

Antiembolic stockings or sequential compression devices (SCD) may be applied.

## SUGGESTIONS FOR CLASSROOM ACTIVITIES

- Discuss the importance of reviewing the plan for postoperative analgesia with the client and family prior to surgery.

## SUGGESTIONS FOR CLINICAL ACTIVITIES

- Examine postoperative clients' medication records and have the students discuss the nursing implications of the particular anesthetics and postoperative analgesics used.
- Discuss the nurse's role in witnessing the signature on the surgical consent form.

# LEARNING OUTCOME 8

Compare various types of anesthesia.

## CONCEPTS FOR LECTURE

1. Anesthesia is classified as general, regional, or local.
2. General anesthesia is the loss of all sensation and consciousness. Protective reflexes such as cough and gag reflexes are lost. General anesthetics act by blocking awareness centers in the brain so that amnesia, analgesia, hypnosis, and relaxation occur. They are generally administered by intravenous infusion or by inhalation of gases.
3. Regional anesthesia is the temporary interruption of the transmission of nerve impulses to and from a specific area or region of the body. The client loses sensation in an area of the body but remains conscious. Techniques include the following: topical or surface (applied directly to the skin and mucous membranes, open skin surfaces, wounds, and burns); local or infiltration (injected into a specific area and used for minor surgical procedures); nerve block (injected into and around a nerve or small nerve group that supplies sensation to a small area of the body); intravenous block or Bier block (used most often for procedures involving the arm, wrist, and hand; an occlusion tourniquet is applied to the extremity to prevent infiltration and

## POWERPOINT LECTURE SLIDES

*(NOTE: The number on each PPT Lecture Slide directly corresponds with the Concepts for Lecture.)*

1. Types of Anesthesia
   - General
   - Regional or local

2. General Anesthesia
   - Loss of all sensation and consciousness
   - Loss of protective reflexes
   - Block awareness centers in brain
   - Administered by IV or inhalation

3. Regional or Local Anesthesia
   - Loss of sensation in area of body but client remains conscious
   - Topical or surface
   - Local or infiltration
   - Nerve block
   - Intravenous block or Bier block
   - Spinal
   - Epidural or peridural
   - Conscious sedation

absorption of the injected intravenous agent beyond the involved extremity); spinal or subarachnoid block (agent is injected into the subarachnoid space); epidural or peridural (injected into the epidural space); and conscious sedation (minimal depression of the level of consciousness in which the client retains the ability to maintain a patent airway and respond appropriately to commands).

---

## SUGGESTIONS FOR CLASSROOM ACTIVITIES

- Discuss different types of anesthesia and have the students identify the nursing implications of each.
- Invite a panel of nurse anesthetists to discuss their roles and various types of anesthesia.

## SUGGESTIONS FOR CLINICAL ACTIVITIES

- During the operating room observation, have the students spend time observing the administration of various types of anesthesia.

---

# LEARNING OUTCOME 9

Identify essential nursing assessments and interventions during the immediate postanesthetic phase.

## CONCEPTS FOR LECTURE

1. Essential nursing assessments during the immediate postanesthetic phase include adequacy of airway; oxygen saturation; adequacy of ventilation; cardiovascular status; level of consciousness; presence of protective reflexes; activity; ability to move extremities; skin color; fluid status; condition of operative site; patency of and amount and character of drainage from catheters, tubes, and drains; discomfort; and safety.

2. Interventions include positioning the client on the side, with the face slightly down; elevating the upper arm on a pillow; suctioning as needed until cough and swallowing reflexes return; and helping the client to cough and deep breathe once the oral airway or endotracheal tube is removed. If the client has had spinal anesthesia, keep the client flat for the specified period of time.

## POWERPOINT LECTURE SLIDES

*(NOTE: The number on each PPT Lecture Slide directly corresponds with the Concepts for Lecture.)*

**1** Nursing Care During the Immediate Postanesthetic Phase
- Assessment:
  - Adequacy of airway
  - Oxygen saturation
  - Adequacy of ventilation
  - Cardiovascular status
  - Level of consciousness
  - Presence of protective reflexes
  - Activity, ability to move extremities
  - Skin color
  - Fluid status
  - Condition of operative site
  - Patency of and amount and character of drainage from catheters, tubes, and drains
  - Discomfort
  - Safety

 **2** Nursing Interventions During Immediate Postanesthetic Phase
- Position client on side, with the face slightly down
- Elevate upper arm on a pillow
- Suction as needed until cough and swallowing reflexes return
- Help client to cough and deep breathe
- Keep the client flat for specified period of time if the client had spinal anesthesia

## LEARNING OUTCOME 10

Demonstrate ongoing nursing assessments and interventions for the postoperative client.

### CONCEPTS FOR LECTURE

1. As soon as the client returns to the nursing unit, the nurse conducts an initial assessment. The sequence of assessment varies with the situation.

   The nurse consults the surgeon's postoperative orders for the following: food and fluids, IV fluids and position, medications, laboratory tests, intake and output and activity permitted. In addition, the nurse reviews the PACU record for the following: operation performed, presence and location of drains, anesthetic used, postoperative diagnosis, estimated blood loss, and medications administered in the PACU.

   The nurse assesses level of consciousness, vital signs, skin color and temperature, comfort, fluid balance, dressing and bedclothes, and drains and tubes.

2. Nursing interventions designed to promote client recovery and prevent complications include pain management, appropriate positioning, incentive spirometry, deep breathing and coughing exercises, leg exercises, early ambulation, adequate hydration, diet, promoting urinary and bowel elimination, suction maintenance, and wound care.

   See Lifespan Considerations: Postoperative Care, and Home Care Assessment: Surgical Clients.

### POWERPOINT LECTURE SLIDES

*(NOTE: The number on each PPT Lecture Slide directly corresponds with the Concepts for Lecture.)*

 Nursing Care During Postoperative Phase
- Initial Assessment:
  - Level of consciousness
  - Vital signs
  - Skin color and temperature
  - Comfort
  - Fluid balance
  - Dressing and bedclothes
  - Drains and tubes
- Review surgeon's postoperative orders and PACU record

 Nursing Interventions During Postoperative Phase
- Pain management
- Appropriate positioning
- Incentive spirometry
- Deep breathing and coughing exercises
- Leg exercises
- Early ambulation
- Adequate hydration
- Diet
- Promoting urinary and bowel elimination
- Suction maintenance
- Wound care

# LEARNING OUTCOME 11

Identify potential postoperative complications and describe nursing interventions to prevent them.

## CONCEPTS FOR LECTURE

1. Potential postoperative problems and preventive nursing interventions include: pneumonia (deep breathe, cough; moving in bed, early ambulation); atelectasis (deep, breathe, cough, moving in bed, early ambulation); pulmonary embolism (turning, ambulation, antiembolic stockings, SCD); hypovolemia (early detection of signs, fluid and or blood replacement); hemorrhage (early detection of signs); hypovolemic shock (maintain blood volume through fluid replacement, prevent hemorrhage, early detection of signs); thrombophlebitis (early ambulation, leg exercises, antiembolic stockings, SCD, adequate fluid intake); thrombus (venous-same as thrombophlebitis; arterial maintain prescribed position, early detection of signs); embolus (turn, ambulate, leg exercises, SCD, careful maintenance of IV catheters); urinary retention (monitor I&O, interventions facilitating voiding, catheterization); urinary tract infection (adequate fluids, early ambulation, straight catheterization, good perineal hygiene); nausea and vomiting ( IV fluids until peristalsis returns, then progression of diet, antiemetic drugs if ordered and analgesics); constipation (adequate fluids, high fiber diet, early ambulation); tympanites (early ambulation, avoid using straws, ice chips and water at room temperature); postoperative ileus (no interventions listed); wound infection (keep wound clean and dry, use surgical asepsis when changing dressings); wound dehiscence and evisceration (adequate nutrition, appropriate incisional support and avoidance of strain); and postoperative depression (adequate rest, physical activity, opportunity to express anger and other negative feelings).

## POWERPOINT LECTURE SLIDES

*(NOTE: The number on each PPT Lecture Slide directly corresponds with the Concepts for Lecture.)*

1. Potential Postoperative Complications
   - Respiratory
     - Pneumonia
     - Atelectasis
     - Pulmonary embolism
   - Circulatory
     - Hypovolemia
     - Hemorrhage
     - Hypovolemic shock
     - Thrombophlebitis
     - Thrombus
     - Embolus
   - Urinary
     - Urinary retention
     - Urinary tract infection
   - Gastrointestinal
     - Nausea and vomiting
     - Constipation
     - Tympanites
     - Postoperative ileus
   - Wound
     - Wound infection
     - Wound dehiscence
     - Wound evisceration
   - Psychologic
     - Postoperative depression

## SUGGESTIONS FOR CLASSROOM ACTIVITIES

- Provide the students with case studies of clients who are experiencing postoperative complications. Have the students identify the problem and related nursing responsibilities and interventions. Also ask them to identify interventions to prevent the complications, if possible.

## SUGGESTIONS FOR CLINICAL ACTIVITIES

- Have the students review agency protocols for responding to postoperative complications (e.g., pulmonary embolism, dehiscence, and evisceration).
- Review charts of clients experiencing postoperative complications for risk factors, signs and symptoms, and nursing interventions.

# LEARNING OUTCOME 12

Identify essential aspects of managing gastrointestinal suction.

## CONCEPTS FOR LECTURE

1. Suction can be continuous or intermittent. Intermittent suction is used when single lumen gastric tubes are used to prevent damaging the mucous membrane near the distal port. Continuous suction can be used when

## POWERPOINT LECTURE SLIDES

*(NOTE: The number on each PPT Lecture Slide directly corresponds with the Concepts for Lecture.)*

1. Management of Gastrointestinal Suction
   - Continuous or intermittent

double-lumen tubes are used. Type and amount of suction is ordered by the primary care provider.

Fluid and electrolytes must be replaced intravenously when gastric suction or continuous drainage is ordered.

Nasogastric tubes may be irrigated if lumen becomes clogged. A physician's order may be required.

Refer to Skill 37.3: Managing Gastrointestinal Suction. Major components in managing gastrointestinal suction include initiating suction (position client appropriately, confirm tube is in stomach, set and check suction, establish suction, assess the drainage), maintaining suction (assess client and suction system regularly, relieve blockages if present, prevent reflux into the vent lumen of a Salem sump tube, ensure client comfort, change drainage receptacle according to policy, and irrigate the gastrointestinal tube); irrigating a gastrointestinal tube (prepare client and equipment, irrigate the tube, reestablish suction, and document all relevant information).

- Replace fluid and electrolytes
- May need to irrigate tube if lumen clogged
- Skill 37.3: Managing Gastrointestinal Suction

---

## SUGGESTIONS FOR CLASSROOM ACTIVITIES

- Have the students practice inserting and irrigating various types of nasogastric tubes on manikins.
- Obtain various types of nasogastric tubes for the students to handle.

## SUGGESTIONS FOR CLINICAL ACTIVITIES

- Discuss potential complications that occur postoperatively, including signs and symptoms and nursing interventions.
- Demonstrate the suction apparatus used in the agency.

---

# LEARNING OUTCOME 13

Describe appropriate wound care for a postoperative client.

## CONCEPTS FOR LECTURE

1. Most clients return from surgery with a sutured wound covered by a dressing. Dressings are inspected regularly to ensure that they clean, dry and intact. Excessive drainage may indicate hemorrhage, infection or an open wound.

When dressings are changed, the nurse assesses the wound for appearance, size, drainage, swelling, pain, and status of drains or tubes.

Refer to Skill 37.4: Cleaning a Sutured Wound and Applying a Sterile Dressing. See the Skill Checklist included on the Student DVD-ROM. Major steps include remove binders and tape; remove and dispose of soiled dressings appropriately; set up sterile supplies; use surgical aseptic technique; cleanse wound, if indicated; apply dressings to drain site and incision; and document procedure and assessments.

## POWERPOINT LECTURE SLIDES

*(NOTE: The number on each PPT Lecture Slide directly corresponds with the Concepts for Lecture.)*

1 Wound Care for the Postoperative Client
- Dressings should be clean, dry, and intact
- Assess wound for:
  - Appearance
  - Size
  - Drainage
  - Swelling
  - Pain
  - Drains or tubes
- Skill 37.4: Cleaning a Sutured Wound and Applying a Sterile Dressing

## SUGGESTIONS FOR CLASSROOM ACTIVITIES

- Set up manikins with various types of wounds and dressings. Have the students practice assessing and providing care for the wounds.
- Demonstrate use of various types of wound drainage systems.

## SUGGESTIONS FOR CLINICAL ACTIVITIES

- Have the students perform wound care, including wound assessment. Compare and contrast variations among assessments, findings, and type of wound care required.

# LEARNING OUTCOME 14

Evaluate the effectiveness of perioperative nursing interventions.

## CONCEPTS FOR LECTURE

1. Using the goals established during the pre-, intra-, and postoperative phases, the nurse collects data to evaluate whether the identified goals and desired outcomes have been achieved.

   Examples of client outcomes and related indicators are shown in the Identifying Nursing Diagnoses, Outcomes, and Interventions boxes.

   If the desired outcomes are not achieved, the nurse and client (and support people, if appropriate) need to explore the reasons before modifying the care plan.

   For example, if the outcome "Pain control" is not met, questions to be considered include:
   - What is the client's perception of the problem?
   - Does the client understand how to use patient-controlled analgesia (PCA)?
   - Is the prescribed analgesic dose adequate for the client?
   - Is the client allowing pain to become intense prior to requesting medication or using PCA?
   - Where is the client's pain? Could it be due to a problem unrelated to surgery (e.g., chronic arthritis, anginal pain)?
   - Is there evidence of a complication that could cause increased pain (an infection, abscess, or hematoma)?

## POWERPOINT LECTURE SLIDES

*(NOTE: The number on each PPT Lecture Slide directly corresponds with the Concepts for Lecture.)*

1. Evaluating Perioperative Care
   - Evaluate pre-intra-and postoperative goals according to specific desired outcomes
   - If not achieved, explore the reasons before modifying the care plan

## SUGGESTIONS FOR CLASSROOM ACTIVITIES

- Provide the students with case studies of clients in various perioperative phases with nursing diagnoses already identified. Ask the students to develop appropriate goals/desired outcomes that will be used for evaluation.

## SUGGESTIONS FOR CLINICAL ACTIVITIES

- Have the students develop a complete care plan for a client who is in one of the perioperative phases, including evaluation. Compare and contrast effectiveness of the plan and proposed revision.

# CHAPTER 38
## SENSORY PERCEPTION

## RESOURCE LIBRARY

###  PRENTICE HALL NURSING MEDIALINK DVD-ROM

Audio Glossary
NCLEX® Review
Skills Review
Animations:
   *Components of a Reflex Arc*

###  COMPANION WEBSITE

Additional NCLEX® Review
Case Study: *Clients with Altered Sensory Perception*
Care Plan Activity: *The Confused and Agitated Client*
Application Activity: *Client with Second-Degree Burns*
Links to Resources

### IMAGE LIBRARY

**Figure 38.1** The nerve impulses run along the ascending sensory tracts to reach the reticular activating system (RAS); then certain impulses reach the cerebral cortex where they are perceived.

**Figure 38.2** A client in an ICU may experience sensory overload.

**Figure 38.3** Promoting orientation to time and date is essential for clients who are confused or have a memory loss.

---

## LEARNING OUTCOME 1

Discuss anatomic and physiologic components of the sensory-perception process.

### CONCEPTS FOR LECTURE

1. The sensory process involves two components: sensory reception, the process of receiving stimuli or data, and sensory perception, the conscious organization and translation of the data or stimuli into meaningful information.
2. Four aspects of the sensory process must be present: a stimulus, a receptor, impulse conduction, and perception.

   The stimulus is an agent or act that stimulates a nerve receptor. A receptor is a nerve cell that acts as a receptor by converting the stimulus to a nerve impulse. Impulse conduction is the transmission of the stimulus along the nerve pathways to the spinal cord or directly to the brain. Perception, or awareness of stimuli, takes place in the brain, where specialized brain cells interpret the nature and the quality of the sensory stimuli. The level of consciousness affects the perception of the stimuli.

   For the person to receive and interpret stimuli, the brain must be alert. The reticular activating system (RAS) in the brain stem is thought to mediate the arousal mechanism. There are two components of the RAS: the reticular excitatory area (REA) and the reticular inhibitory area (RIA). The REA is responsible for stimulus arousal and wakefulness.

### POWERPOINT LECTURE SLIDES

*(NOTE: The number on each PPT Lecture Slide directly corresponds with the Concepts for Lecture.)*

 Sensory Process
- Sensory reception
  - Process of receiving stimuli or data
- Sensory perception
  - Conscious organization and translation of data into meaningful information

Sensory Process: Four Aspects Must be Present
- Stimulus
- Receptor
- Impulse conduction
- Perception
  - Arousal mechanism

---

SUGGESTIONS FOR CLASSROOM ACTIVITIES

• Obtain models of eyes, ears, nose, skin, and brain and identify anatomical locations involved in sensory perception.

# LEARNING OUTCOME 2

Describe factors influencing sensory function.

## CONCEPTS FOR LECTURE

1. A number of factors affect the amount and quality of sensory stimulation, including a person's developmental stage, culture, level of stress, medications and illness, and lifestyle.

   Perception of sensation is crucial to the intellectual, social, and physical development of infants and children. Adults have many learned responses to sensory cues. The sudden loss or impairment of any sense has a profound effect on both the child and adult. Normal physiologic changes in older adults put them at higher risk for altered sensory function.

   An individual's culture often determines the amount of stimulation that a person considers usual or normal. The normal amount of stimulation associated with ethnic origin, religious affiliation, and income level also affects the amount of stimulation an individual desires and believes to be meaningful. A sudden change in cultural surroundings may also result in sensory overload or cultural shock.

   During times of increased stress, people may find their senses already overloaded and thus seek to decrease sensory stimulation. On the other hand, clients may seek sensory stimulation during times of low stress.

   Certain medications can alter an individual's awareness of environmental stimuli; some depress awareness of stimuli. Anyone taking several medications concurrently may show alterations in sensory function. Elders are especially at risk and need to be monitored carefully. Some medications, if taken over a long period, become ototoxic. Certain diseases restrict blood flow to the receptor organs and the brain, decreasing awareness and slowing responses. Uncontrolled diabetes mellitus can impair vision and is a leading cause of blindness. Some central nervous system diseases cause varying degrees of paralysis and sensory loss.

   Lifestyle and personality influence the quality and quantity of stimulation to which an individual is accustomed. People's personalities differ in terms of the stimuli with which they are comfortable.

## POWERPOINT LECTURE SLIDES

*(NOTE: The number on each PPT Lecture Slide directly corresponds with the Concepts for Lecture.)*

 Factors Influencing Sensory Function
- Developmental stage
- Culture
- Level of stress
- Medications and illness
- Lifestyle

SUGGESTIONS FOR CLASSROOM ACTIVITIES

• Have the students experience alterations in sensation by being blindfolded, having ears plugged, wearing glasses that simulate visual disturbances, and wearing gloves. Assign the students to perform simple activities and report their feelings related to how the sensory alteration interfered with the activities.

• Have the students review their assigned clients' history and identify factors that might interfere with sensory function.

## LEARNING OUTCOME 3

Identify clinical signs and symptoms of sensory overload and deprivation.

### CONCEPTS FOR LECTURE

1. Clinical manifestations of sensory overload include complaints of fatigue and sleeplessness; irritability, anxiety, and restlessness; periodic or general disorientation; reduced problem-solving ability and task performance; increased muscle tension; and scattered attention and racing thoughts.
2. Clinical manifestations of sensory deprivation include excessive yawning, drowsiness, and sleeping; decreased attention span, difficulty concentrating, and decreased problem solving; impaired memory; periodic disorientation, general confusion, or nocturnal confusion; preoccupation with somatic complaints, such as palpitations; hallucinations or delusions; crying, annoyance over small matters, and depression; and apathy and emotional liability.

### POWERPOINT LECTURE SLIDES

*(NOTE: The number on each PPT Lecture Slide directly corresponds with the Concepts for Lecture.)*

 Clinical Manifestations of Sensory Overload
- Complaints of fatigue, sleeplessness
- Irritability, anxiety, and restlessness
- Periodic or general disorientation
- Reduced problem-solving ability and task performance
- Increased muscle tension
- Scattered attention and racing thoughts

 Clinical Manifestations of Sensory Deprivation
- Excessive yawning, drowsiness, and sleeping
- Decreased attention span, difficulty concentrating, and decreased problem-solving
- Impaired memory; periodic disorientation, general confusion, or nocturnal confusion
- Preoccupation with somatic complaints, such as palpitations
- Hallucinations or delusions
- Crying, annoyance over small matters and depression
- Apathy and emotional liability

### SUGGESTIONS FOR CLASSROOM ACTIVITIES

• Invite a panel of nurses who practice in critical care and in nursing home settings to discuss interventions used to prevent or reduce sensory overload or deprivation in their settings.

### SUGGESTIONS FOR CLINICAL ACTIVITIES

• Arrange for students to have an observational experience in critical care settings and in nursing homes. Have the students note the situations that could create sensory overload or deprivation and interventions employed in these areas to prevent these from occurring.

## LEARNING OUTCOME 4

Describe essential components in assessing a client's sensory-perception function.

### CONCEPTS FOR LECTURE

1. Nursing assessment of sensory-perceptual functioning includes six components: nursing history, mental status examination, physical examination, identification of clients at risk, the client's environment, and the social support network.

### POWERPOINT LECTURE SLIDES

*(NOTE: The number on each PPT Lecture Slide directly corresponds with the Concepts for Lecture.)*

 Assessment of Sensory-Perceptual Function
- Nursing history
- Mental status examination

When conducting the nursing history, the nurse assesses present sensory perceptions, usual functioning, sensory deficits, and potential problems. In some instances, significant others can provide data the client cannot. Assessment Interview: Sensory-Perceptual Functioning lists questions to ask to assess visual, auditory, gustatory, olfactory, tactile, and kinesthetic function.

To evaluate mental status, the nurse assesses level of consciousness, orientation, memory, and attention span. It is important to note that sensory alterations can cause changes in cognitive function.

During the physical examination, the nurse assesses vision and hearing, and the olfactory, gustatory, tactile, and kinesthetic senses. Specific sensory tests include visual acuity (Snellen chart or other reading materials) and visual fields; hearing acuity (response to conversation, whisper, Weber and Rinne); olfactory sense (identification of aromas); gustatory sense (identification of three tastes); and tactile tests (light touch, sharp and dull sensations, two-point discrimination, hot and cold sensation, vibration sense, position sense, and stereognosis).

The nurse identifies clients at risk for sensory disturbances (see Outcome 5).

The nurse assesses the client's environment for quantity, quality, and type of stimuli. For example, the nurse would look for the presence of a radio or other auditory device, television, clock or calendar, reading material, number and compatibility of roommates, and number of visitors. In the client's home, the nurse notes the presence of a video/DVD recorder, pets, bright colors, and adequate lighting. To assess a health care environment for excessive stimuli, the nurse would consider factors such as bright lights, noise, therapeutic measures, and frequency of assessments and procedures.

In evaluating the client's social support network, the nurse assesses whether the client lives alone, who visits and when, and any signs indicating social deprivation, such as withdrawal from contact with others to avoid embarrassment or dependence on others, negative self-image, reports of lack of meaningful communication with others, and absence of opportunities to discuss fears or concerns that facilitate coping mechanisms.

- Physical examination
- Identification of clients at risk
- Environment
- Social support network

## SUGGESTIONS FOR CLASSROOM ACTIVITIES

- Have the students select partners and practice special physical assessments related to sensory function (e.g., Snellen vision screening, visual fields, Weber and Rinne tests).

## SUGGESTIONS FOR CLINICAL ACTIVITIES

- Have the students perform a sensory assessment on assigned clients and report findings in clinical conference.

# LEARNING OUTCOME 5

Discuss factors that place a client at risk for sensory disturbances.

## CONCEPTS FOR LECTURE

1. Clients at risk for sensory deprivation include clients who are confined in a nonstimulating or monotonous environment, have impaired vision or hearing, have mobility restrictions, are unable to process stimuli, have emotional disorders, and have limited social contact.
2. Clients at risk for sensory overload include clients who have pain or discomfort, are acutely ill and have been admitted to an acute care facility, are being closely monitored in an intensive care unit and have invasive tubes, and have decreased cognitive ability.

## POWERPOINT LECTURE SLIDES

*(NOTE: The number on each PPT Lecture Slide directly corresponds with the Concepts for Lecture.)*

**1** Risk Factors for Sensory Deprivation
- Nonstimulating or monotonous environment
- Impaired vision or hearing
- Mobility restrictions
- Inability to process stimuli
- Emotional disorders
- Limited social contact

**2** Risk Factors for Sensory Overload
- Pain or discomfort
- Admission to an acute care facility
- Monitoring in intensive care units
- Invasive tubes
- Decreased cognitive ability

## SUGGESTIONS FOR CLASSROOM ACTIVITIES

- Have the students provide examples of situations where they have been either over- or understimulated and how they responded to these situations.
- Discuss methods the nurse can employ to prevent sensory overload or deprivation.

## SUGGESTIONS FOR CLINICAL ACTIVITIES

- Ask the students to assess the clinical environment, including the clients' rooms, for risk factors for sensory overload or deprivation and provide suggestions to reduce these factors.

# LEARNING OUTCOME 6

Develop nursing diagnoses and outcome criteria for clients with impaired sensory function.

## CONCEPTS FOR LECTURE

1. NANDA includes the following diagnostic label for sensory perception alterations: *Disturbed Sensory Perception (Specify: Visual, Auditory, Kinesthetic, Gustatory, Tactile, Olfactory)*. This diagnostic label is used to describe clients whose perception has been altered by physiologic factors.

    Other diagnostic labels that can relate to sensory perception alterations include *Acute Confusion, Chronic Confusion,* and *Impaired Memory*.
2. Examples of nursing diagnoses for which sensory-perceptual disturbances are the etiology include *Risk for Injury, Impaired Home Maintenance, Risk for Impaired Skin Integrity, Impaired Verbal Communication, Self-Care Deficit: Bathing/Hygiene,* and *Social Isolation*.
3. The overall outcome criteria for clients with sensory-perception alterations are to prevent injury, maintain the function of existing senses, develop an effective communication mechanism, prevent sensory overload or deprivation, reduce social isolation, and perform activities of daily living independently and safely.

## POWERPOINT LECTURE SLIDES

*(NOTE: The number on each PPT Lecture Slide directly corresponds with the Concepts for Lecture.)*

**1** NANDA Nursing Diagnoses
- Disturbed sensory perception (specify: visual, auditory, kinesthetic, gustatory, tactile, olfactory)
- Acute confusion
- Chronic confusion
- Impaired memory

**2** NANDA Nursing Diagnoses
- Examples of nursing diagnoses for which sensory-perceptual disturbances are the etiology
  - Risk for injury
  - Impaired home maintenance
  - Risk for impaired skin integrity
  - Impaired verbal communication
  - Self-care deficit: bathing/hygiene
  - Social isolation

**3** Outcome Criteria
- Prevent injury
- Maintain the function of existing senses

- Develop an effective communication mechanism
- Prevent sensory overload or deprivation
- Reduce social isolation
- Perform activities of daily living independently and safely

---

**SUGGESTIONS FOR CLASSROOM ACTIVITIES**

- Provide the students with a case study and ask them to identify nursing diagnoses related to impaired sensory function.

**SUGGESTIONS FOR CLINICAL ACTIVITIES**

- Have the students identify appropriate nursing diagnoses related to impaired sensory function in assigned clients and discuss the etiology or risk factors for these diagnoses.

---

## LEARNING OUTCOME 7

Discuss nursing interventions to promote and maintain sensory function.

### CONCEPTS FOR LECTURE

1. Nurses can assist clients with sensory alterations by promoting healthy sensory function, by adjusting environmental stimuli, and by helping clients to manage acute sensory deficits.

   Healthy sensory function can be promoted with environmental stimuli that produce appropriate sensory input. Sensory input should be varied and neither too excessive nor too limited. As many senses as possible should be stimulated using various colors, sounds, textures, smells, and body positions. Also clients at risk for sensory alterations should be taught to prevent sensory disturbances by obtaining regular health and vision examinations; seeking medical attention if signs or symptoms suggest visual impairment; obtaining proper immunizations (rubella, measles, and mumps) to prevent hearing loss; learning age-appropriate safety measures and use of dark glasses to protect eyes from UV rays. Nurses must implement safety precautions for clients with sensory deficits.

   Clients function best when the environment is somewhat similar to that of individuals' ordinary lifestyle. Sometimes nurses need to take steps to adjust clients' environment to prevent either sensory overload or sensory deprivation. Measures to prevent sensory overload include: minimize unnecessary light, noise or distraction; control pain; introduce self and call client by name; provide orienting cues; provide a private room; limit visitors; plan care to provide uninterrupted rest or sleep; use a regular schedule for care; speak in low tones and in an unhurried manner; provide new information gradually; describe tests and procedures; decrease noxious odors; take time to discuss client's problems and correct misunderstandings; and assist client with stress-reducing techniques.

### POWERPOINT LECTURE SLIDES

*(NOTE: The number on each PPT Lecture Slide directly corresponds with the Concepts for Lecture.)*

1. Nursing Interventions to Promote/Maintain Sensory Function
   - Promote healthy sensory function
     - Appropriate sensory stimulation
     - Prevention of sensory disturbances
   - Adjust environmental stimuli
     - Prevent sensory overload
     - Prevent sensory deprivation
   - Manage acute sensory deficits
     - Use of sensory aids
     - Use of other senses
     - Effective communication

---

Measures to prevent sensory deprivation include: encourage use of eyeglasses or hearing aids, address by name and touch client if culturally appropriate; communicate frequently and meaningfully with client; provide telephone, TV, radio, clock, and calendar; provide murals, pictures, wall hangings and sculpture; have family and friends bring in flowers and plants; consider a resident pet with regular visits; include different tactile stimuli through objects or physical care measures; encourage social interaction, use of puzzles, or games to stimulate mental function; encourage environmental changes through walks or changes where sitting; encourage self-stimulation such as singing or humming.

When assisting clients who have sensory deficits the nurse needs to encourage use of sensory aids to support residual sensory function, promote use of other senses, communicate effectively, and ensure client safety.

Sensory aids for visual deficits include: eyeglasses with appropriate prescription; adequate lighting, protection against glare; bright, contrasting colors in the environment; magnifying glasses; phone dialer with large numbers; clock and wristwatch with large numbers; color coding of appliances; color or raised rims of dishes; large print reading materials; Braille or recorded books and seeing-eye dog.

Sensory aids for hearing deficits include: hearing aids in good repair; lip reading; sign language; amplified telephone, ringers and doorbells; telecommunication devices for the deaf (TDD); and flashing alarm clocks and smoke detectors.

Promotion of the use of other senses is similar to that provided to prevent sensory deprivation; however, these methods are adapted to the client's specific deficit.

Communicating effectively with a person who has a visual deficit includes: announcing your presence; staying in the person's visual field; speaking in a warm and pleasant tone of voice; explaining what you are about to do prior to doing it; explaining sounds in the environment; and indicating when the conversation has come to an end and you are leaving the room. When communicating with a person who has a hearing deficit the nurse should move into the person's line of vision; decrease background noise; talk at a moderate rate and in a normal tone of voice; address the person directly; avoid talking with something in your mouth or hands covering your mouth; keep tone of voice at same volume throughout the sentence; speak clearly and accurately but not "overarticulating"; us longer phrases; pronounce the names with care and provide a frame of reference for each name; and change the subject slowly.

## SUGGESTIONS FOR CLASSROOM ACTIVITIES

- Using the nursing diagnosis reference book required by the school, ask the students to develop a list of nursing activities to assist clients who have various sensory impairments (e.g., problems with hearing or vision).

# LEARNING OUTCOME 8

Identify strategies to promote and maintain orientation to person, place, time, and situation for the client with acute confusion/delirium.

## CONCEPTS FOR LECTURE

1. The following strategies can be used by the nurse to promote a therapeutic environment for the client with acute confusion/delirium: wear a readable name tag; address the person by name and introduce yourself frequently; identify time and place as indicated; ask the client "Where are you?" and orient the client to place if indicated; place a calendar and clock in the client's room and mark holidays with ribbons, pins, or other means; speak clearly and calmly, allowing time for your words to be processed and for the client to respond; encourage family to visit frequently except if this causes the client to become hyperactive; provide clear, concise explanations of each treatment, procedure, or task; eliminate unnecessary noise; reinforce reality by interpreting unfamiliar sounds, sights, and smells and correct any misconceptions; schedule activities at same time each day and provide same caregiver if possible; provide adequate sleep; keep glasses and hearing aids within reach; ensure adequate pain management; keep familiar items in client's environment and keep the environment uncluttered; and keep the room well lit during waking hours.

## POWERPOINT LECTURE SLIDES

*(NOTE: The number on each PPT Lecture Slide directly corresponds with the Concepts for Lecture.)*

 Orientation Strategies for Client with Acute Confusion/Delirium

• Wear a readable name tag
• Address the person by name
• Introduce yourself frequently
• Identify time and place as indicated
• Ask the client "Where are you?"
• Orient the client to place if indicated
• Place a calendar and clock in the client's room
• Mark holidays with ribbons, pins or other means
• Speak clearly and calmly, allowing time for words to be processed and for a response
• Encourage family to visit frequently
• Provide clear, concise explanations of each treatment, procedure or task
• Eliminate unnecessary noise
• Interpret unfamiliar sounds, sights, smells
• Correct misinterpretations
• Schedule activities at same time each day
• Provide adequate sleep
• Keep glasses and hearing aids within reach
• Ensure adequate pain management
• Keep familiar items in an uncluttered environment
• Keep room well lit during waking hours

Promote structured sensory stimulation for the unconscious client.

## CONCEPTS FOR LECTURE

1. Coma stimulation consists of providing sensory stimulation to promote brain recovery by waking the RAS.

   It is important that the stimulation be delivered in a quiet environment and be done slowly to allow time for a response to occur. Sessions are of a certain time duration (e.g., 30 to 45 minutes) and the number of sessions will vary in a 12-hour day.

   It is also important to provide the client with sleep/rest periods that alternate with the structured sensory stimulation sessions.

   Box 38–7 lists ways to promote sensory stimulation for the unconscious client: auditory (introduce self, orient to time, month, year, location, and what happened and inform client prior to performing care; read to client; play tape recording of familiar voices; converse directly with the client); visual (sit client upright in chair or bed); olfactory (provide aromatic stimulation that may include the client's favorite smells); gustatory (use flavored mouth care products; place different tastes on tongue); tactile (provide during hygiene care); and kinesthetic (provide range-of-motion exercises and position changes).

## POWERPOINT LECTURE SLIDES

*(NOTE: The number on each PPT Lecture Slide directly corresponds with the Concepts for Lecture.)*

 Promoting Structured Sensory Stimulation for Unconscious Client
- Auditory
  - Introduce yourself to the client
  - Orient the client to time, month, year, location
  - Inform client beforehand the care to be provided
  - Read literature to client
  - Play a tape recording of familiar voice
  - Converse directly to client
- Visual
  - Sit client upright in a chair or bed
- Olfactory
  - Provide aromatic stimuli that may include client's favorites
- Gustatory
  - Provide mouth care
  - Place different tastes on tongue
- Tactile
  - Incorporate during bath activities
- Kinesthetic
  - Perform range-of-motion exercises
  - Change client's position

## SUGGESTIONS FOR CLASSROOM ACTIVITIES

- Discuss interventions the students can employ to provide stimulation when caring for clients who are unconscious.
- Invite a nurse who practices in a rehabilitation facility to discuss coma stimulation used in the agency.

## SUGGESTIONS FOR CLINICAL ACTIVITIES

- Have the students observe nurses caring for unconscious clients. Discuss interventions used by these nurses to provide stimulation.
- If possible, assign students to care for clients who are confused or who are unconscious. Have the students develop a care plan for the client, including interventions for stimulation. In postconference, discuss the effectiveness of the plan and any modifications needed.

# CHAPTER 39
## SELF-CONCEPT

## RESOURCE LIBRARY

### 💿 PRENTICE HALL NURSING MEDIALINK DVD-ROM

Audio Glossary
NCLEX® Review

### 🌐 COMPANION WEBSITE

Additional NCLEX® Review
Case Study: *Refusal to Accept a Medical Diagnosis*
Care Plan Activity: *Client Who Lost His Job*
Application Activity: *A Change in Attitude*
Links to Resources

### 📖 IMAGE LIBRARY

**Figure 39.1** Body image is the sum of a person's conscious and unconscious attitudes about his or her body.

**Figure 39.2** A child is often pulled in opposite directions by family and peer expectations.

---

## LEARNING OUTCOME 1

Identify four dimensions of self-concept.

### CONCEPTS FOR LECTURE

1. Four dimensions of self-concept are self-knowledge, self-expectation, social self, and social evaluation.

    Self-knowledge is the knowledge that one has about oneself, including insights into one's abilities, nature, and limitations.

    Self-expectation is what one expects of oneself. It may be a realistic or unrealistic expectation.

    Social self is how a person is perceived by others and society.

    Social evaluation is the appraisal of oneself in relationship to others, events, or situations.

### POWERPOINT LECTURE SLIDES

*(NOTE: The number on each PPT Lecture Slide directly corresponds with the Concepts for Lecture.)*

🎞 1 Four Dimensions of Self-Concept
- Self-knowledge
- Self-expectation
- Social self
- Social evaluation

---

### SUGGESTIONS FOR CLASSROOM ACTIVITIES

- Have the students provide examples of situations in which a positive self-concept assists a nurse to help clients meet their needs.

---

## LEARNING OUTCOME 2

Give Erikson's explanation of the effects of psychosocial tasks on self-concept and self-esteem.

### CONCEPTS FOR LECTURE

1. A person is not born with a self-concept; rather it develops as a result of social interaction with others.

    According to Erikson, throughout life people face developmental tasks associated with eight psychosocial stages. The success with which a person copes with

### POWERPOINT LECTURE SLIDES

*(NOTE: The number on each PPT Lecture Slide directly corresponds with the Concepts for Lecture.)*

🎞 1 Erikson's Explanation of Development of Self Concept and Self Esteem
- Self concept develops through social interaction

these developmental tasks largely determines the development of self-concept. Difficulty in coping results in self-concept problems at the time and, often, later in life.

Table 39–1 lists examples of behaviors indicating successful and unsuccessful resolution of these developmental tasks.

- People face developmental tasks
- Success in coping with these tasks determine self-concept
- Difficulty in coping results in problems with self-concept

## SUGGESTIONS FOR CLASSROOM ACTIVITIES

- Divide the students into eight groups. Assign each group a developmental stage. Have the students develop suggestions for assisting individuals to successful resolution of the developmental tasks.

## SUGGESTIONS FOR CLINICAL ACTIVITIES

- Have the students provide examples of verbal or behavioral data that support the positive or negative resolution of developmental tasks for their assigned clients.

# LEARNING OUTCOME 3

Describe the four components of self-concept.

## CONCEPTS FOR LECTURE

1. Components of self-concept include personal identity, body image, role performance, and self-esteem.
2. Personal identity is the conscious sense of individuality and uniqueness that is constantly evolving throughout life. It includes the individual's identity in terms of name, gender, age, race, ethnic origin or culture, occupation or roles, talents, and other situational characteristics. It also includes beliefs and values, personality, and character. Identity is what distinguishes self from others.
3. Body image is the image of the physical self and is how a person perceives the size, appearance, and functioning of the body and its parts. Body image has cognitive aspects (knowledge of the material body) and affective aspects (sensations of the body, such as pain, pleasure, fatigue, and physical movement). Body image also includes clothing, makeup, hairstyle, jewelry, and other things intimately connected to the person as well as prostheses and devices required for functioning. Body image develops partly from others' attitudes and responses and partly from the individual's exploration of the body.
4. Role performance relates what a person in a particular role does to the behaviors expected of a role. To act appropriately, people need to know who they are in relation to others and what society expects for the positions they hold. Role mastery means that the person's behaviors meet social expectations. Role development involves socialization into a particular role. Role ambiguity occurs when expectations are unclear and people do not know what to do or how to do it and are unable to predict the reactions of others to their behavior. Failure to master a role creates frustration

## POWERPOINT LECTURE SLIDES

*(NOTE: The number on each PPT Lecture Slide directly corresponds with the Concepts for Lecture.)*

**1** Four Components of Self-Concept
- Personal identity
- Body image
- Role performance
- Self-esteem

**2** Personal Identity
- Conscious sense of individuality and uniqueness
- Constantly evolves throughout life
- Includes name, gender, age, race, culture, occupation, talents
- Also includes beliefs, values, personality, character
- Identify distinguishes self from others

**3** Body Image
- Image of physical self
- How a person perceives size, appearance and functioning of body and its parts
- Has cognitive aspects (knowledge of the body)
- Has affective aspects (sensations of body)
- Also includes clothing, hairstyle, make-up, accessories, prostheses
- Develops partly from attitudes and responses of others and partly from self-exploration of body

**4** Role Performance
- Relates what a person in a particular role does to the behaviors expected of a role
- Role mastery means person's behaviors meet social expectations

## CONCEPTS FOR LECTURE *continued*

and feelings of inadequacy, often with the consequent lowered self-esteem. Self-concept is also affected by role strain and role conflicts.

5. Self-esteem is one's judgment of one's own worth, that is, how that person's standards and performances compare to others and to one's ideal self. There are two types of self-esteem: global and specific. Global self-esteem is how much one likes oneself as a whole, and specific self-esteem is how much one approves of a certain part of oneself. Self-esteem is derived from self and others. The foundation for self-esteem is established during early life experiences, usually within the family structure. However, an adult's level of overall self-esteem may change markedly from day to day and moment to moment.

## POWERPOINT LECTURE SLIDES *continued*

- Failure to master a role creates frustration and feelings of inadequacy and lowered self-esteem
- Self-concept also affected by role strain and role conflicts

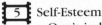 Self-Esteem
- One's judgment of one's own worth
- Two types
  ○ Global—how much one likes oneself as a whole
  ○ Specific—how much one approves of a specific part of oneself
- Derived from self and others
- Foundation established during early life experiences
- Overall self-esteem may change from day to day and moment to moment

---

## SUGGESTIONS FOR CLASSROOM ACTIVITIES

- Divide the students into four groups, each representing one component of self-concept: body image, role performance, personal identity, or self-esteem. Provide a case study and ask each group to describe how the assigned component of self-concept is evidenced in this case.
- Have the students discuss the role of the student nurse as it relates to role performance, role mastery, role development, role ambiguity, role strain, and role conflict.

## SUGGESTIONS FOR CLINICAL ACTIVITIES

- Explore personal identity, body image, role performance, and self-esteem as they relate to the students' assigned clients. Have the students provide examples of clients' verbal comments or behavior related to these concepts.

---

## LEARNING OUTCOME 4

Identify common stressors affecting self-concept and coping strategies.

### CONCEPTS FOR LECTURE

1. Box 39–1 lists stressors affecting self-concept.
2. Identity stressors include change in physical appearance; declining physical, mental, or sensory abilities; inability to achieve goals; relationship concerns; sexuality concerns; and unrealistic ideal self.
3. Body image stressors include loss of body parts; loss of body functions; disfigurement; and unrealistic body ideal.
4. Self esteem stressors include lacking positive feedback from significant others; repeated failures; unrealistic expectations; abusive relationships; loss of financial security.
5. Role stressors include loss of parent, spouse, child, or close friend; change or loss of job or other significant role; divorce, illness, ambiguous or conflicting role expectations; inability to meet role expectations.

### POWERPOINT LECTURE SLIDES

*(NOTE: The number on each PPT Lecture Slide directly corresponds with the Concepts for Lecture.)*

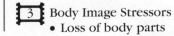 Common Stressors Affecting Self-Concept
- Identity stressors
- Body image stressors
- Self-esteem stressors
- Role stressors

2 Identity Stressors
- Change in physical appearance
- Declining physical, mental, or sensory abilities
- Inability to achieve goals
- Relationship concerns
- Sexuality concerns
- Unrealistic ideal self

3 Body Image Stressors
- Loss of body parts

---

- Loss of body functions
- Disfigurement
- Unrealistic ideal self

4 Self-Esteem Stressors
- Lacking positive feedback from significant others
- Repeated failures
- Unrealistic expectations
- Abusive relationships
- Loss of financial security

5 Role Stressors
- Loss of parent, spouse, child, close friend
- Change or loss of job or other significant role
- Divorce
- Illness
- Ambiguous or conflicting role expectations
- Inability to meet role expectations

## Suggestions for Classroom Activities

- Discuss identity, body image, self-esteem, and role stressors that may occur as a result of illness or disability.

## Suggestions for Clinical Activities

- Have the students provide examples of identity, body image, self-esteem, and role stressors identified in their assigned clients.

# Learning Outcome 5

Describe the essential aspects of assessing role relationships.

## Concepts for Lecture

1. The nurse assesses the client's satisfaction and dissatisfaction associated with role responsibilities and relationships.

   To obtain data related to the client's family relationships and satisfaction or dissatisfaction with work roles and social roles, the nurse might ask some of the following questions (see Assessment Interview: Role Performance): What is home like? How is your relationship with your spouse/partner/significant other (if appropriate)? What are your relationships like with your other relatives? How are important decisions made in your family? What are your responsibilities in the family? Do you like your work? How do you get along at work? What about your work would you like to change if you could? How do you spend your free time? Are you involved in any community groups?

   Questions need to be tailored to individuals and their culture, age, and situations.

## PowerPoint Lecture Slides

*(NOTE: The number on each PPT Lecture Slide directly corresponds with the Concepts for Lecture.)*

1 Assessing Role Relationships
- Assess satisfaction and dissatisfaction with role responsibilities and relationships
- Assessment Interview: role performance
- Tailor questions to individual, culture, age, and situation

**SUGGESTIONS FOR CLASSROOM ACTIVITIES**

- Using the Assessment Interview guides in the textbook, have the students assess each other. Discuss feelings of the "client" during this assessment process.
- Discuss cultural and life span considerations when assessing self-concept.

**SUGGESTIONS FOR CLINICAL ACTIVITIES**

- Have the students perform a self-concept assessment on their assigned clients. Discuss their findings in postconference.

## LEARNING OUTCOME 6

Identify nursing diagnoses related to altered self-concept.

### CONCEPTS FOR LECTURE

1. Three of the NANDA nursing diagnostic labels relating specifically to the domain of Self-Perception and the classes of self-concept, self-esteem, and body image are *Disturbed Body Image, Ineffective Role Performance,* and *Chronic Low Self-Esteem.*
2. Additional nursing diagnoses that may apply to clients with problems of self-concept include *Disturbed Personal Identity, Anxiety, Impaired Adjustment, Ineffective Coping, Anticipatory Grieving, Dysfunctional Grieving, Hopelessness, Powerlessness, Parental Role Conflict, Readiness for Enhanced Self-Concept, Disturbed Sleep Pattern, Social Isolation, Spiritual Distress,* and *Disturbed Thought Processes.*

### POWERPOINT LECTURE SLIDES

*(NOTE: The number on each PPT Lecture Slide directly corresponds with the Concepts for Lecture.)*

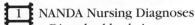 NANDA Nursing Diagnoses
- Disturbed body image
- Ineffective role performance
- Chronic low self-esteem

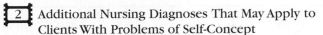 Additional Nursing Diagnoses That May Apply to Clients With Problems of Self-Concept
- Disturbed personal identity
- Impaired adjustment
- Anticipatory grieving
- Hopelessness
- Parental role conflict
- Social isolation
- Disturbed thought processes
- Readiness for enhanced self-concept
- Anxiety
- Ineffective coping
- Dysfunctional grieving
- Powerlessness
- Disturbed sleep pattern
- Spiritual distress

**SUGGESTIONS FOR CLASSROOM ACTIVITIES**

- Using the nursing diagnosis reference book required by the curriculum, have the students review the defining characteristics, etiology, or risk factors for the three specific NANDA diagnoses related to self-perception.

**SUGGESTIONS FOR CLINICAL ACTIVITIES**

- Have the students identify nursing diagnoses related to self-concept, self-esteem, or body image of their assigned clients, providing subjective and objective data to support the diagnoses.

## LEARNING OUTCOME 7

Describe nursing interventions designed to achieve identified outcomes for clients with altered self-concept.

### CONCEPTS FOR LECTURE

1. Nursing interventions to promote a positive self-concept include helping a client to identify areas of strength. For clients who have an altered self-concept, nurses should establish a therapeutic relationship and assist the clients to evaluate themselves and make behavioral changes.

### POWERPOINT LECTURE SLIDES

*(NOTE: The number on each PPT Lecture Slide directly corresponds with the Concepts for Lecture.)*

1 Nursing Interventions for Clients with Altered Self-Concept
- Help client to identify areas of strength

When a client has difficulty identifying personality strengths and assets, the nurse provides the client with a set of guidelines or a framework for identifying personality strengths (see Box 39–2).

2.  Nurses can employ the following specific strategies to reinforce strengths: stress positive thinking; notice and verbally reinforce client strengths; encourage the setting of attainable goals; acknowledge goals that have been attained; and provide honest, positive feedback.

- Assist clients to evaluate themselves and make behavioral changes
- Framework for identifying personality strengths

 2 Specific Strategies to Reinforce Strengths
- Stress positive thinking
- Notice and verbally reinforce client strengths
- Encourage the setting of attainable goals
- Acknowledge goals that been attained
- Provide honest, positive feedback

---

**SUGGESTIONS FOR CLASSROOM ACTIVITIES**

- Using the framework presented in Box 39–2, have the students identify their own strengths.
- Discuss how positive self-talk can be used to prevent negative self-talk.

**SUGGESTIONS FOR CLINICAL ACTIVITIES**

- Have the students list examples of how a nurse can assist clients to reinforce client strengths.

---

## LEARNING OUTCOME 8

Describe ways to enhance client self-esteem.

### CONCEPTS FOR LECTURE

1.  The nurse assisting a client who has an altered self-concept must establish a therapeutic relationship. To do this, the nurse must have self-awareness and effective communication skills.

    The nurse can use the following techniques to help clients analyze the problem and enhance self-esteem:
    - Encourage clients to appraise the situation and express their feelings.
    - Encourage clients to ask questions.
    - Provide accurate information.
    - Become aware of distortions, inappropriate or unrealistic standards, and faulty labels in clients' speech.
    - Explore and encourage clients' positive qualities and strengths.
    - Encourage clients to express positive self-evaluation more than negative self-evaluation.
    - Avoid criticism.
    - Teach clients to substitute negative self-talk with positive self-talk.

### POWERPOINT LECTURE SLIDES

*(NOTE: The number on each PPT Lecture Slide directly corresponds with the Concepts for Lecture.)*

 1 Enhancing Client Self-Esteem
- Encourage clients to appraise situations and express feelings
- Encourage clients to ask questions
- Provide accurate information
- Become aware of distortions, inappropriate or unrealistic standards, and faulty labels in clients' speech
- Explore clients' positive qualities and strengths
- Encourage clients' positive qualities and strengths
- Encourage clients to express positive self-evaluation more than negative self-evaluation
- Avoid criticism
- Teach clients to substitute negative self-talk with positive self-talk

---

**SUGGESTIONS FOR CLASSROOM ACTIVITIES**

- Review life span considerations for enhancing self-esteem in children and elders.

**SUGGESTIONS FOR CLINICAL ACTIVITIES**

- Have the students observe health care personnel's interactions with clients and document how each maintained the clients' self-esteem. Have the students also note any interactions that were not supportive of client self-esteem. Ask them to offer suggestions for how these interactions could be changed into positive interactions.

# CHAPTER 40
## SEXUALITY

## RESOURCE LIBRARY

 **PRENTICE HALL NURSING MEDIALINK DVD-ROM**

Audio Glossary
NCLEX® Review
Animations:
   *Spermatogenesis*
   *Oogenesis and Spermatogenesis*
Videos:
   *Gender Identity*
   *Sexual and Physical Abuse*

**COMPANION WEBSITE**

Additional NCLEX® Review
Case Study: *Client in a Motor Vehicle Crash*
Care Plan Activity: *Client with a Mastectomy*
Application Activities:
   *Society for Human Sexuality*
   *Campus Health Promotion*
Links to Resources

### 📖 IMAGE LIBRARY

**Figure 40.1** Phases of the sexual response cycle.
**Figure 40.2** Rolling the testicle between the thumb and fingers.

**Figure 40.3** Adolescents require age-appropriate teaching about sexuality and sexually transmitted diseases.
**Figure 40.4** Methods of contraception.

---

## LEARNING OUTCOME 1

Describe sexual development and concerns across the life span.

### CONCEPTS FOR LECTURE

1. Birth to 18 months: From birth, infants are assigned the gender of male or female. The infant differentiates self from others gradually. External genitals are sensitive to touch. Male infants have penile erections; females have vaginal lubrication.
2. Toddler (1–3 years): Continues to develop gender identity; able to identify own gender.
3. Preschooler (4–5 years): Becomes increasingly aware of self. Explores own and classmates' body parts; learns correct names for body parts; learns to control feelings and behaviors; focuses love on parent of the opposite sex.
4. School age (6–12 years): Has strong identification with parent of same gender; tends to have friends of same gender; has increasing awareness of self; increased modesty; desire for privacy; continues self-stimulating behavior; learns the roles and concepts of own gender as part of the total self-concept; at about 8 or 9 years becomes concerned about specific sex behavior and often approaches parents with explicit concerns abour sexuality and reproduction.

### POWERPOINT LECTURE SLIDES

*(NOTE: The number on each PPT Lecture Slide directly corresponds with the Concepts for Lecture.)*

**1** Sexual Development : Birth to 18 Months
- From birth, infants assigned gender of male or female
- Infant gradually differentiates self from others
- External genitals are sensitive to touch
- Males have penile erections
- Females have vaginal lubrication

**2** Sexual Development: Toddler (1–3 Years)
- Continues to develop gender identify
- Can identify own gender

**3** Sexual Development: Preschooler (4–5 Years)
- Becomes increasingly aware of self
- Explores own and classmates' body parts
- Learns correct name for body parts
- Learns to control feelings and behaviors
- Focuses love on parent of opposite sex

**4** Sexual Development: School Age (6–12 Years)
- Strong identification with parent of same gender

## CONCEPTS FOR LECTURE *continued*

5. Adolescence (12-18 years): Primary and secondary sexual characteristics develop; menarche usually takes place; develops relationships with interested partners; masturbation is common; may participate in sexual activity; may experiment with homosexual relationships; are at risk for pregnancy and sexually transmitted diseases.

6. Young adulthood (18-49 years): Sexual activity is common; establishes own lifestyle and values; homosexual identity is established by the mid-20s; many couples share financial obligations and household tasks.

7. Middle adulthood (40-65 years): Men and women experience decreased hormone production; menopause occurs in women, usually anywhere between 40-55 years; the climacteric occurs gradually in men; quality rather the number of sexual experiences becomes important; individuals establish independent moral and ethical standards.

8. Late adulthood (65 years and older): Interest in sexual activity often continues; sexual activity may be less frequent; women's vaginal secretions diminish and breasts atrophy; men produce fewer sperm and need more time to achieve an erection and to ejaculate.

## POWERPOINT LECTURE SLIDES *continued*

- Friends of same gender
- Increasing awareness of self
- Increased modesty, desire for privacy
- Continues self-stimulating behavior
- Learns roles and concepts of own gender as part of self-concept
- Age 8 or 9 often have specific concerns about sexuality and reproduction

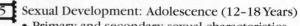 Sexual Development: Adolescence (12-18 Years)
- Primary and secondary sexual characteristics develop
  - Menarche
  - Develops relationships with interested partners
  - Masturbation common
  - May participate in sexual activity
  - May experiment with homosexuality
  - At risk for pregnancy and STDs

6 Sexual Development: Young Adulthood (18-49 Years)
- Sexual activity is common
- Establishes own lifestyle and values
- Homosexual identity established in mid-20s
- Couples may share financial and household responsibilities

7 Sexual Development: Middle Adulthood (40-65 Years)
- Decreased hormone production
- Menopause in women between 40-55 years
- Climacteric occurs gradually in men
- Quality rather than number of occurrences becomes important
- Individuals establish independent moral and ethical standards

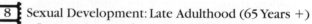 Sexual Development: Late Adulthood (65 Years +)
- Interest in sexual activity continues but may be less frequent
- Women's vaginal secretions diminish, breasts atrophy
- Men produce fewer sperm and need more time to achieve erection and ejaculate

---

## SUGGESTIONS FOR CLASSROOM ACTIVITIES

- Divide the students into groups. Assign each group an age group. Ask each to further develop the nursing interventions and teaching guidelines for the assigned age group based on Table 40-1 in the textbook.

## SUGGESTIONS FOR CLINICAL ACTIVITIES

- Using Table 40-1, have the students review the characteristics, nursing interventions, and teaching guidelines for the age group of their assigned clients.

# LEARNING OUTCOME 2

Define sexual health.

## CONCEPTS FOR LECTURE

1. The World Health Organization (WHO) defined sexual health in 1975 as the integration of the somatic, emotional, intellectual, and social aspects of sexual being, in ways that are positively enriching and that enhance personality, communication, and love. This definition recognizes the biologic, psychologic, and sociocultural dimensions of sexuality.

2. Characteristics of sexual health include: knowledge about sexuality and sexual behavior; ability to express one's full sexual potential, excluding all forms of sexual coercion, exploitation, and abuse; ability to make autonomous decisions about one's sexual life within a context of personal and social ethics; experience of sexual pleasure as a source of physical, psychologic, cognitive, and spiritual well-being; capability to express sexuality through communication, touch, emotional expression, and love; right to make free and responsible reproductive choices; and ability to access sexual health care and treatment for all sexual concerns, problems, and disorders.

## POWERPOINT LECTURE SLIDES

*(NOTE: The number on each PPT Lecture Slide directly corresponds with the Concepts for Lecture.)*

**1** Sexual Health
- World Health Organization (1975) definition:
  - Integration of the somatic, emotional, intellectual, and social aspects of sexual being, in ways that are positively enriching and that enhance personality, communication, and love

**2** Characteristics of Sexual Health:
- Knowledge about sexuality and sexual behavior
- Ability to express one's full sexual potential
- Ability to make autonomous decisions about one's sexual life
- Experience of sexual pleasure as a source of physical, psychologic, cognitive, and spiritual well-being
- Capability to express sexuality through communication, touch, emotional expression, and love
- Right to make reproductive choice
- Ability to access sexual health care

## SUGGESTIONS FOR CLASSROOM ACTIVITIES

- Discuss the components of WHO definition of sexual health.

## SUGGESTIONS FOR CLINICAL ACTIVITIES

- Have students discuss how illness and disease may affect sexual health.

# LEARNING OUTCOME 3

Discuss the varieties of sexuality.

## CONCEPTS FOR LECTURE

1. There are many varieties of sexuality, including sexual orientation, gender identity, and erotic preferences.

2. Sexual orientation is one's attraction to people of the same sex, other sex, or both sexes. It lies along a continuum between exclusively heterosexual attraction and exclusively homosexual attraction.

3. Western culture is deeply committed to the idea that there are only two sexes. Biologically speaking, there are many gradations of gender identity running from female to male; this is known as transgenderism. In some cases gender is clear, in other cases, there is a blending of both genders within the same individual. Intersex is a condition in which there are contradictions among chromosomal gender, gonadal gender, internal organs, and external genital appearance. The gender of such an infant is ambiguous. Transsexuals have a condition called gender dysphoria (strong and

## POWERPOINT LECTURE SLIDES

*(NOTE: The number on each PPT Lecture Slide directly corresponds with the Concepts for Lecture.)*

**1** Varieties of Sexuality
- Sexual orientation
- Gender identity
- Erotic preferences

**2** Sexual Orientation
- Same gender
- Opposite gender
- Both genders

**3** Gender Identity
- Transgenderism
- Intersexuality
- Transsexuality
- Cross-dressers

persistent feelings of discomfort with one's assigned gender) or gender identity disorder. For the transsexual person, sexual anatomy is not consistent with gender identity. Cross-dressers are typically males who cross-dress to express the feminine side of their personality. In most instances they are not interested in permanently altering their bodies through surgical means.

4. Sexual fantasies and single-partner sex are the most common sexual outlets for women and men, single and coupled persons, and heterosexual, gay/lesbian, and bisexual persons. Masturbation is the ongoing love affair that each of us has with ourselves throughout our lifetime. Oral—genital sex is known as cunnilingus and involves kissing, licking, or sucking of the female genitals, including the mons pubis, vulva, clitoris, labia, and vagina. Fellatio is oral stimulation of the penis by licking and sucking. Sixty-nine is simultaneous oral—genital stimulation by two persons. Anal stimulation can be a source of sexual pleasure, and stimulation may be applied with fingers, mouth, or sex toys such as vibrators. Genital intercourse is penile—vaginal intercourse (coitus). The other form of genital intercourse is anal intercourse in which the penis is inserted into the anus and rectum of the partner.

There are many other varieties of sexuality, including several or many partners, nudism, swinging, group sex, fetishism, sexual sadism, and sexual masochism.

**4** Erotic Preferences
- Sexual fantasies
- Masturbation
- Cunnilingus
- Fellatio
- Anal stimulation
- Genital intercourse
- Anal intercourse
- Others

## SUGGESTIONS FOR CLASSROOM ACTIVITIES

- Discuss strategies to deal with clients who have a different sexual orientation than the student.
- Invite representatives from local organizations for gay or lesbian rights to discuss their expectations of health care providers.

## SUGGESTIONS FOR CLINICAL ACTIVITIES

- Review the agency's policies about sexual issues and implications for nursing.

# LEARNING OUTCOME 4

Give examples of how the family, culture, religion, and personal ethics influence one's sexuality.

## CONCEPTS FOR LECTURE

1. Gender identity, body image, sexual self-concepts, and capacity for intimacy are developed within the family. Children observe and model parents. Family messages about sex range from "sex is so shameful it shouldn't be talked about" to "sex is a joyful part of adult relationships."

Sexuality is regulated by the individual's culture. Culture influences the sexual nature of dress, rules about marriage, expectations of role behavior and social responsibilities, and specific sex practices. Cultures differ with regard to which body parts they find to be erotic. Female circumcision and male circumcision are culturally related practices.

## POWERPOINT LECTURE SLIDES

*(NOTE: The number on each PPT Lecture Slide directly corresponds with the Concepts for Lecture.)*

**1** Influences on Sexuality
- Family
- Culture
- Religion
- Personal Expectations and Ethics

Religion influences sexual expression. It provides guidelines for sexual behavior and acceptable circumstances for the behavior, as well as prohibited sexual behavior and the consequences of breaking the sexual rules. Many religious values conflict with the more flexible values of society. These conflicts create marked anxiety and potential sexual dysfunctions in some individuals.

Personal expectations and ethics concerning sexual behavior come from cultural norms. Examples include values regarding masturbation, oral or anal intercourse, and cross-dressing. (Box 40–2 provides a guide for assessing personal values.)

---

## SUGGESTIONS FOR CLASSROOM ACTIVITIES

- Ask the students to provide additional examples of how family, culture, religion, and personal ethics influence one's sexuality.

## SUGGESTIONS FOR CLINICAL ACTIVITIES

- Discuss appropriate responses of a nurse who discovers a client masturbating.

---

# LEARNING OUTCOME 5

Describe physiologic changes in males and females during the sexual response cycle.

## CONCEPTS FOR LECTURE

1. Commonly occurring phases of the human sexual response follow a similar sequence in both females and males regardless of sexual orientation. It does not matter if the motive for being sexually active is true love or passionate lust.
2. Desire phase: Both: response cycle starts in the brain; sexually (erotic) stimuli may be real or symbolic; sight, hearing, smell, touch, and imagination (sexual fantasy) can all evoke sexual arousal.
3. Excitement/plateau:
   - **Both:** Muscle tension increases as excitement increases. Sex flush, usually on chest. Nipple erection.
   - **Male:** Penile erection; glans size increases as excitement increases. Appearance of a few drops of lubricant, which may contain sperm.
   - **Female:** Erection of the clitoris. Vaginal lubrication. Labia may increase 2 to 3 times in size. Breasts enlarge. Inner two-thirds of vagina widens and lengthens; outer third swells and narrows. Uterus elevates.
4. Orgasmic:
   - **Both:** Respirations may increase to 40 breaths per minute. Involuntary spasms of muscle groups throughout the body. Diminished sensory awareness. Involuntary contractions of the anal sphincter. Peak heart rate (110–180 BPM), respiratory rate (40/min or greater), and blood pressure (systolic 30–80 mm Hg and diastolic 20–50 mm Hg above normal).

## POWERPOINT LECTURE SLIDES

*(NOTE: The number on each PPT Lecture Slide directly corresponds with the Concepts for Lecture.)*

**1** Male and Female Sexual Response Cycle
- Desire phase
- Excitement/Plateau
- Orgasmic
- Resolution

**2** Desire Phase
- Men and Women
  - Response cycle starts in brain
  - Sexually erotic stimuli may be real or symbolic

**3** Excitement/Plateau
- Both
  - Muscle tension increases as excitement increases
  - Sex flush, usually on chest
  - Nipple erection
- Male
  - Penile erection
  - Glans size increases as excitement increases
  - Appearance of few drops of lubricant—may contain sperm
- Female
  - Erection of clitoris
  - Vaginal lubrication
  - Labia may increase 2–3 times in size
  - Breasts enlarge
  - Inner two-thirds of vagina widens and lengthens; outer third swells and narrows
  - Uterus elevates

- **Male:** Rhythmic, expulsive contractions of the penis at 0.8-sec intervals. Emission of seminal fluid into the prostatic urethra from contraction of the vas deferens and accessory organs (stage 1 of the expulsive process). Closing of the internal bladder sphincter just before ejaculation to prevent retrograde ejaculation into bladder. Orgasm may occur without ejaculation. Ejaculation of semen through the penile urethra and expulsion from the urethral meatus. The force of ejaculation varies from man to man and at different times but diminishes after the first two to three contractions (stage 2 of the expulsive process).
- **Female:** Approximately 5–12 contractions in the orgasmic platform at 0.8-sec intervals. Contraction of the muscles of the pelvic floor and the uterine muscles. Varied pattern of orgasms, including minor surges and contractions, multiple orgasms, or a simple intense orgasm similar to that of the male.

5. Resolution:
- **Both:** Reversal of vasocongestion in 10–30 min; disappearance of all signs of myotonia within 5 min. Genitals and breasts return to their preexcitement states. Sex flush disappears in reverse order of appearance. Heart rate, respiratory rate, and blood pressure return to normal. Other reactions include sleepiness, relaxation, and emotional outbursts such as crying or laughing.
- **Male:** A refractory period during which the body will not respond to sexual stimulation; varies, depending on age and other factors, from a few moments to hours or days.

 Orgasmic Phase
- Both
  - Respirations may increase to 40 breaths/minute
  - Involuntary spasms of muscle groups throughout body
  - Diminished sensory awareness
  - Involuntary contractions of anal sphincter
  - Peak heart rate 110–180 bpm
  - Blood pressure—systolic 30–80 mm Hg and diastolic 20–50 mm Hg above normal
- Male
  - Rhythmic, expulsive contractions of penis at 0.8-sec intervals
  - Emission of seminal fluid into prostatic urethra from contraction of vas deferens and accessory organs
  - Closing of internal bladder sphincter just before ejaculation
  - May occur without ejaculation
  - Force of ejaculation varies but diminishes after first 2–3 contractions
- Female
  - 5–12 contractions of muscles of pelvic floor and uterine muscles at 0.8-sec intervals
  - Varied patterns of orgasms: minor, multiple, simple intense

 Resolution
- Both
  - Reversal of vasocongestion in 10-30 min
  - Disappearance of all signs of myotonia within 5 min
  - Genitals and breasts return to preexcitement states
  - Sex flush disappears in reverse order of appearance
  - HR, RR, BP return to normal
  - Other reactions include sleepiness, relaxation, emotional outbursts
- Male
  - Refractory period during which body will not respond to sexual stimulation
  - Varies from moments to hours or days

---

### SUGGESTIONS FOR CLASSROOM ACTIVITIES

- Show a DVD or VHS tape presenting the physiologic changes in males and females during the sexual response cycle. Discuss the effects of various diseases on these changes.

# LEARNING OUTCOME 6

Identify the forms of male and female sexual dysfunction.

## CONCEPTS FOR LECTURE

1. Many individuals experience transient problems with their ability to respond to sexual stimulation or to maintain a response. A smaller percentage experience problems that are lifelong in duration.

   Forms of sexual dysfunction may be related to past and current factors and may be classified as sexual desire disorders, sexual arousal disorders, orgasmic disorders, sexual pain disorders, and problems with satisfaction.

2. Past and current problems may be related to sociocultural factors (very restrictive upbringing accompanied by inadequate sex education); psychological factors (negative feelings such as guilt, anxiety, or fear that interfere with the ability to experience pleasure and joy); cognitive factors (internalization of negative expectations and beliefs); relationship problems (conflict and anger with one's partner); or health factors (physical changes brought on by illness, injury, or surgery, or reactions to prescribed medications or street drugs; see Table 40–4).

3. Hypoactive sexual desire disorders refer to a deficiency in or absence of sexual fantasies and persistently low interest or a total lack of interest in sexual activity. Sexual aversion disorders refer to a severe distaste for sexual activity or the thought of sexual activity, which then leads to a phobic avoidance of sex.

4. In female sexual arousal disorder, lack of vaginal lubrication causes discomfort or pain during sexual intercourse. Male erectile disorder or erectile dysfunction (ED) is the inability to have an erection during 25% or more of sexual interactions.

5. In female orgasmic disorder, the sexual response stops before orgasm occurs. Preorgasmic women have never experienced an orgasm. In male orgasmic disorder, the man can maintain an erection for long periods but has extreme difficulty ejaculating (referred to as retarded ejaculation). Rapid ejaculation is absence of voluntary control of ejaculation or ejaculation that is too rapid for mutual satisfaction.

6. Sexual pain disorders include dyspareunia (pain during or immediately after intercourse), vaginismus (involuntary spasm of the outer one-third of the vaginal muscles, making penetration of the vagina painful and sometimes impossible), vulvodynia (constant, unremitting burning that is localized to the vulva with an acute onset), and vestibulitis (severe pain only on touch or attempted vaginal entry).

7. Some people experience sexual desire, arousal, and orgasm and yet feel dissatisfied with their sexual relationships.

## POWERPOINT LECTURE SLIDES

*(NOTE: The number on each PPT Lecture Slide directly corresponds with the Concepts for Lecture.)*

1. Sexual Dysfunction
   - May be related to
     - Past and current factors
     - Sexual desire disorder
     - Sexual arousal disorder
     - Orgasmic disorder
     - Sexual pain disorder
     - Problem with satisfaction

2. Influence of Past and Current Factors
   - Sociocultural
   - Psychological
   - Cognitive
   - Relationship problems
   - Health
   - Medications or street drugs

3. Sexual Desire Disorders
   - Hypoactive sexual desire
   - Sexual aversion disorders

4. Sexual Arousal Disorders
   - Female sexual arousal disorder
   - Male erectile dysfunction or erectile dysfunction (ED)

5. Orgasmic Disorders
   - Female orgasmic disorder
     - Preorgasmic women
   - Male orgasmic disorder
     - Retarded ejaculation
     - Rapid ejaculation

6. Sexual Pain Disorders
   - Dyspareunia
   - Vaginismus
   - Vulvodynia
   - Vestibulitis

7. Problems with Satisfaction
   - Some people experience sexual desire, arousal, and orgasm and yet feel dissatisfied with their sexual relationship

# LEARNING OUTCOME 7

Identify basic sexual questions the nurse should ask during client assessment.

## CONCEPTS FOR LECTURE

1. Information about a client's sexual health status should be an integral part of nursing assessment. The amount and kind of data collected depend on the context of the assessment; that is, the client's reason for seeking health care and how the client's sexuality interacts with other problems.

   It is critical to introduce the topic of sexuality to all clients in order to give them permission to bring up concerns or problems. All nursing histories should at least include a question such as "Have there been any changes in your sexual function that might be related to your illness or medications you take?"

   The Assessment Interview lists basic sexual questions the nurse should ask during client assessment. They include the following:
   • Are you currently sexually active? With men, women, or both? With more than one partner?
   • What are some positive and negative aspects of your sexual functioning?
   • Do you have difficulty with sexual desire? Arousal? Orgasm? Satisfaction?
   • Do you experience any pain with sexual interaction?
   • If there are problems, how have they influenced how you feel about yourself? How have they affected your partner? How have they affected your relationship?
   • Do you expect your sexual functioning to be altered because of your illness?
   • What are your partner's concerns about your future sexual functioning?
   • Do you have any other sexual questions or concerns that I have not addressed?

## POWERPOINT LECTURE SLIDES

*(NOTE: The number on each PPT Lecture Slide directly corresponds with the Concepts for Lecture.)*

1 Client Sexual Assessment
   • Amount and type of data collected depends on reason for seeking health care
   • All clients should be asked "Have there been any changes in your sexual function that might be related to your illness or medications you take?"
   • More specific data may be obtained through the following questions:
   • Are you currently sexually active? With men, women, or both?
   • With more than one partner?
   • Describe positive and negative aspects of your sexual functioning
   • Do you have difficulty with sexual desire: Arousal? Orgasm? Satisfaction?
   • Do you experience any pain with sexual interaction?
   • If there are problems, how have they influenced how you feel about yourself? How have they affected your partner? How have they affected your relationship?
   • Do you expect your sexual functioning to be altered because of your illness?
   • What are your partner's concerns about your future sexual functioning?
   • Do you have any other sexual questions or concerns that I have not addressed?

# LEARNING OUTCOME 8

Formulate nursing diagnoses and interventions for the client experiencing sexual problems.

## CONCEPTS FOR LECTURE

1. The NANDA nursing diagnoses relating specifically to sexuality include *Ineffective Sexuality Pattern* and *Sexual Dysfunction*.
2. Sexual problems can also be the etiology of other diagnoses, including *Deficient Knowledge, Pain, Anxiety, Fear,* and *Disturbed Body Image*.
3. Nursing interventions to promote sexual health and function focus largely on the nurse's teaching role. In addition to teaching, the nurse can do the following to help clients maintain a healthy sexual self-concept: provide privacy during intimate body care, involve the client's partner in physical care, give attention to the client's appearance and dress, and give clients privacy to meet their sexual needs alone or with a partner within physically safe limits.

## POWERPOINT LECTURE SLIDES

*(NOTE: The number on each PPT Lecture Slide directly corresponds with the Concepts for Lecture.)*

**1** NANDA Nursing Diagnoses
- The NANDA nursing diagnoses relating specifically to sexuality
  - Ineffective sexuality pattern
  - Sexual dysfunction

**2** NANDA Nursing Diagnoses
- Sexual problems may be the etiology of other diagnoses
  - Deficient knowledge
  - Pain
  - Anxiety
  - Fear
  - Disturbed body image

**3** Interventions
- Education
- Provide privacy during intimate body care
- Involve the client's partner in physical care
- Give attention to the client's appearance and dress
- Give clients privacy to meet their sexual needs alone or with a partner within physically safe limits

---

## SUGGESTIONS FOR CLASSROOM ACTIVITIES

- Have the students review the defining characteristics and etiology for the related NANDA nursing diagnoses in the nursing diagnosis textbook required by the program.

## SUGGESTIONS FOR CLINICAL ACTIVITIES

- Have the students discuss nursing interventions that they have used to assist a client in promoting a healthy sexual self-concept.
- Have the students review nursing care plan books for suggestions to assist a client with sexuality issues.

---

# LEARNING OUTCOME 9

Recognize health promotion teaching related to reproductive structures.

## CONCEPTS FOR LECTURE

1. Providing education for sexual health is an important component of nursing implementation. Many sexual health problems exist because of sexual ignorance. Many others can be prevented with effective health teaching.

    Nurses can assist clients to understand their anatomy and how the body functions. Details about physiologic changes in sexual function that occur during major developmental crises (puberty, pregnancy, menopause, and male climacteric) should be provided. Parents often need assistance to learn ways to answer questions and what information should be provided for their children starting in the preschool years. Sexual myths and misconceptions should be corrected (See Table 40–2).

## POWERPOINT LECTURE SLIDES

*(NOTE: The number on each PPT Lecture Slide directly corresponds with the Concepts for Lecture.)*

**1** Health Promotion Teaching
- Sex education
- Teaching self examinations
  - Breast Self-examination (BSE)
  - Testicular self-examination (TSE)
- Responsible sexual behavior
  - Prevention of sexually transmitted disease
  - Prevention of unwanted pregnancies
  - Avoidance of sexual harassment and abuse

The nurse should teach the reason and way to perform monthly breast and testicular examinations. Monthly breast self-examination (BSE) is described in Client Teaching: Breast Self-Examination. Monthly testicular self-examination is described in Client Teaching: Testicular Self-Examination.

Responsible sexual behavior involves prevention of sexually transmitted disease (Client Teaching: Preventing Transmission of STIs and HIV), prevention of unwanted pregnancies (See Box 40-3: Methods of Contraception), and avoidance of sexual harassment and abuse.

## SUGGESTIONS FOR CLASSROOM ACTIVITIES

- Divide the students into groups and assign each group a topic (e.g., menopause, BSE). Have each group develop a teaching plan for the assigned topic.
- Invite a nurse from the local STD clinic to discuss client teaching provided in this setting.

## SUGGESTIONS FOR CLINICAL ACTIVITIES

- Arrange for the students to attend an STD clinic. Discuss observations about the education provided for clients in this setting.

# CHAPTER 41
## SPIRITUALITY

## RESOURCE LIBRARY

###  PRENTICE HALL NURSING MEDIA LINK DVD-ROM

Audio Glossary
NCLEX® Review
Video: *Emotional, Social, and Spiritual Needs*

###  COMPANION WEBSITE

Additional NCLEX® Review
Case Study: *Supporting a Client's Spiritual Practices*
Care Plan Activity: *Care of a Paralyzed Client*
Application Activities:
   *Researching Atheism*
   *Spirituality, Health, and Holistic Nursing*
Links to Resources

###  IMAGE LIBRARY

**Figure 41.1** Spirit titer.
**Figure 41.2** Hospital chaplains minister to clients and their families.

**Figure 41.3** Clients may bring objects to the hospital to use in prayer or other religious rituals.
**Figure 41.4** Hindu women dressed in saris.

---

## LEARNING OUTCOME 1

Define the concepts of spirituality and religion as they relate to nursing and health care.

### CONCEPTS FOR LECTURE

1. Spirituality refers to that part of being human that seeks meaningfulness through intra-, inter-, and transpersonal connection (Reed, 1992). It generally involves a belief in a relationship with some higher power, creative force, divine being, or infinite source of energy. Spirituality includes the following aspects (Martsolf & Mickley, 1998): meaning, value, transcendence, connecting, and becoming. Words or concepts reflective of spirituality, such as faith, courage, cheer, and hope, may be used in ordinary speech when discussing spirituality.

2. Religion is an organized system of beliefs and practices. It offers a way of spiritual expression that provides guidance for believers in responding to life's questions and challenges. Organized religions offer a sense of community bound by common beliefs; the collective study of scripture; the performance of ritual; the use of disciplines and practices, commandments, and sacraments; and ways of taking care of the person's spirit.

### POWERPOINT LECTURE SLIDES

*(NOTE: The number on each PPT Lecture Slide directly corresponds with the Concepts for Lecture.)*

**1** Concepts of Spirituality
- Refers to that part of being human that seeks meaningfulness through intra-, inter-, and transpersonal connection
- Generally involves a belief in a relationship with some higher power, creative force, divine being, or infinite source of energy
- Includes the following aspects:
  - Meaning
  - Value
  - Transcendence
  - Connecting
  - Becoming
- Words such as faith, courage, cheer, and hope, may be used in ordinary speech when discussing spirituality

**2** Concepts of Religion
- An organized system of beliefs and practices
- Offers a way of spiritual expression that provides guidance for believers in responding to life's questions and challenges
- Organized religions offer a sense of community bound by common beliefs
- Collective study of scripture

---

- Performance of ritual
- Use of disciplines and practices, commandments, and sacraments
- Ways of taking care of the person's spirit

---

### SUGGESTIONS FOR CLASSROOM ACTIVITIES

- Have the students provide definitions for the following words: faith, courage, cheer, and hope.

---

## LEARNING OUTCOME 2

Identify characteristics of spiritual health.

### CONCEPTS FOR LECTURE

1. Spiritual health or spiritual well-being is manifested by a feeling of being generally alive, purposeful, and fulfilled. As defined by the Nursing Outcomes Classification project, it is the "connectedness with self, others, higher power, all life, nature and the universe that transcends and empowers the self." Box 41-2 lists indicators of spiritual health: uncompromised faith, hope, meaning and purpose of life, achievement of spiritual world, feelings of peacefulness, ability to love, ability to forgive, ability to pray, ability to worship, spiritual experiences, participation in spiritual rites and passages, participation in meditation, participation in spiritual reading, interaction with spiritual leaders, expression through song/music, expression through art, expression through writing, connectedness with inner self, connectedness with others, and interaction with others to share thoughts, feelings, and beliefs.

### POWERPOINT LECTURE SLIDES

*(NOTE: The number on each PPT Lecture Slide directly corresponds with the Concepts for Lecture.)*

1 Characteristics of Spiritual Health
- Faith
- Hope
- Meaning and purpose of life
- Achievement of spiritual world
- Feelings of peacefulness
- Ability to love, to forgive, to pray, to worship
- Spiritual experiences
- Participation in spiritual rites and passages, in meditation, in spiritual reading
- Interaction with spiritual leaders, with other to share thoughts, feelings, and beliefs
- Expression through song/music, art, writing
- Connectedness with inner-self, with others

---

### SUGGESTIONS FOR CLASSROOM ACTIVITIES

- Using the indicators of spiritual health in Box 41-2 of the textbook, have the students provide examples of each of these indicators.

### SUGGESTIONS FOR CLINICAL ACTIVITIES

- Ask the students to provide examples from assigned clients indicative of spiritual health.

---

## LEARNING OUTCOME 3

Identify factors associated with spiritual distress and manifestations of it.

### CONCEPTS FOR LECTURE

1. Spiritual distress refers to a challenge to the spiritual well-being or to the belief system that provides strength, hope, and meaning to life.
2. Some factors that may be associated with or contribute to a person's spiritual distress include physiologic problems, treatment-related concerns, and situational concerns.
3. NANDA offers the following as defining characteristics of spiritual distress: expresses lack of hope, meaning and purpose in life, forgiveness of self; expresses being

### POWERPOINT LECTURE SLIDES

*(NOTE: The number on each PPT Lecture Slide directly corresponds with the Concepts for Lecture.)*

1 Spiritual Distress
- Refers to a challenge to spiritual well-being or belief system that provides strength, hope, and meaning to life

2 Factors Associated with Spiritual Distress
- Physiologic problems
- Treatment-related concerns
- Situational concerns

---

abandoned by or having anger toward God; refuses interaction with friends and family; makes sudden changes in spiritual practices; requests to see a religious leader; and has no interest in nature or reading spiritual literature. No list could be complete, however, considering the complexity and variability of people and their spiritual dimensions.

**3** NANDA Defining Characteristics of Spiritual Distress:
- Expresses lack of hope, meaning and purpose in life, forgiveness of self
- Expresses being abandoned by or having anger toward God
- Refuses interaction with friends, family
- Sudden changes in spiritual practices
- Requests to see a religious leader
- No interest in nature, reading spiritual literature

## SUGGESTIONS FOR CLASSROOM ACTIVITIES

- Invite leaders of various faiths to discuss spiritual distress they have seen in individuals experiencing illness and measures they use to help people through these periods of distress.

## SUGGESTIONS FOR CLINICAL ACTIVITIES

- Invite a member of the agency's chaplain's office to discuss the role of this office in assisting clients and their families to deal with spiritual distress while hospitalized.

---

# LEARNING OUTCOME 4

Describe the spiritual development of the individual across the life span.

## CONCEPTS FOR LECTURE

1. Just as individuals develop physically, cognitively, and morally, they also develop spiritually.

    Neonates and toddlers (0 to 3 years) are acquiring fundamental spiritual qualities of trust, mutuality, courage, hope, and love. Transition to the next stage of faith begins when the child's language and thought begin to allow use of symbolism.

2. The period from age 3 to 7 years is a fantasy-filled, imitative phase when the child can be influenced by examples, moods, and actions. The child relates intuitively to ultimate conditions of existence through stories, images, and the fusion of facts and feelings. Make-believe is experienced as reality (Santa Claus, God as grandfather in the sky).

3. From age 7 to 12 years, and even into adulthood, the child is attempting to sort fantasy from fact by demanding proofs or demonstrations of reality. Stories are important for finding meaning and organizing experience. The child accepts stories and beliefs literally. The child is able to learn the beliefs and practices of the culture and religion.

4. By adolescence, experience of the world is beyond the family unit and spiritual beliefs can aid understanding of the extended environment. Adolescents generally conform to the beliefs of those around them. They begin to examine beliefs objectively, especially in late adolescence.

5. Young adulthood is characterized by development of a self-identity and worldview differentiated from those of others. Young adults form independent commitments, lifestyles, beliefs, and attitudes. The individual

## POWERPOINT LECTURE SLIDES

*(NOTE: The number on each PPT Lecture Slide directly corresponds with the Concepts for Lecture.)*

**1** Spiritual Development: 0–3 Years
- Acquiring qualities of trust, mutuality, courage, hope, love

**2** Spiritual Development: 3–7 Years
- Fantasy-filled, imitative phase
- Stories, images, and fusion of facts and feelings
- Make-believe experienced as reality

**3** Spiritual Development: 7–12 Years, Even Into Adulthood
- Demand proof or demonstrations of reality
- Accepts stories and beliefs literally
- Able to learn beliefs and practices of culture and religion

**4** Spiritual Development: Adolescence
- Spiritual beliefs help understand extended environment
- Generally conform to beliefs of those around them
- Begin to examine beliefs objectively

**5** Spiritual Development: Young Adulthood
- Differentiating beliefs from those of others
- Develop personal meaning for symbols of religion and faith

**6** Spiritual Development: Mid-Adulthood
- Respect for past and one's inner voice
- More awareness of differences because of social background

begins to develop personal meaning for symbols of religion and faith.

6. During mid-adulthood, the individual has newfound appreciation for the past, increased respect for one's inner voice, and more awareness of myths, prejudices, and images that exist because of social background. The adult in this stage attempts to reconcile contradictions in mind and experience and to remain open to others' truths.

7. By mid- to late adulthood, the individual is able to believe in, and live with a sense of participation in, a nonexclusive community. The adult in this stage may work to resolve social, political, economic, or ideological problems in society. The individual is able to embrace life, yet hold it loosely.

- Attempts to reconcile contradictions in mind and experience
- Remain open to others' truths

7 Spiritual Development: Mid- to Late Adulthood
- Believe in, live with, participate in community
- Works to resolve problems in society
- Embraces life, yet holds it loosely

## SUGGESTIONS FOR CLASSROOM ACTIVITIES

- Have the students interview adults of different age groups, asking each to discuss the meaning of spirituality and religion and the importance of each in their lives. Compare and contrast findings.

## SUGGESTIONS FOR CLINICAL ACTIVITIES

- Have students present examples of spiritual development observed in their clients.

## LEARNING OUTCOME 5

Describe the influence of spiritual and religious beliefs about diet, dress, prayer and meditation, and birth and death on health care.

### CONCEPTS FOR LECTURE

1. Clients frequently identify religious practices such as prayer as important strategies for coping with illness.

   Many religions have proscriptions regarding diet. There may be rules about which foods and beverages are allowed and which are prohibited. Some solemn religious observances are marked by fasting. Most religions lift the fasting requirements for seriously ill believers for whom fasting may be a detriment to health. Some religions may exempt nursing mothers or menstruating women from fasting requirements. It is important that health care providers prescribe diet plans with an awareness of the client's dietary and fasting beliefs.

2. Many religions have laws or traditions that dictate dress. Some religions require that women dress in a conservative manner. Hospital gowns may make women wishing to comply with religious dress codes uneasy and uncomfortable. Clients may be especially disconcerted when undergoing diagnostic tests or treatments, such as mammography, that require body parts to be bared.

3. Prayer is a spiritual practice; for many, it is also a religious practice. Some religions require daily prayers or dictate specific times for prayer and worship. People who are ill may want to continue or increase their

### POWERPOINT LECTURE SLIDES

*(NOTE: The number on each PPT Lecture Slide directly corresponds with the Concepts for Lecture.)*

1 Influence of Spiritual and Religious Beliefs on Diet
- Proscriptions about foods and beverages permitted
- Fasting
- Provide diet plans specific to religious beliefs

2 Influence of Spiritual and Religious Beliefs on Dress
- Conservative female dress
- Recognize desire to comply even when hospitalized

3 Influence of Spiritual and Religious Beliefs on Prayer and Meditation
- Daily prayers or worship
- Provide uninterrupted quiet time

4 Influence of Spiritual and Religious Beliefs on Birth
- Rituals and ceremonies
- Assist families in fulfilling these obligations

prayer practices. They may need uninterrupted quiet time during which they have their prayer books, rosaries, malas, or other icons available to them. Meditation is the act of focusing one's thoughts or engaging in self-reflection or contemplation. Some people believe that, through deep meditation, they can influence or control physical and psychologic functioning and the course of illness.

4. For all religions the birth of a child is an important event giving cause for celebration. Many religions have specific rituals or ceremonies that consecrate the new child to God. When nurses are aware of the religious needs of families and their infants, they can assist families in fulfilling their religious obligations. This is especially important when the newborn infant is seriously ill or in danger of dying because some people believe that if religious obligations are not fulfilled the infant will not be accepted into the community of the faithful after death.

5. Spiritual and religious beliefs play a significant role in the believer's approach to death. Some religions have special rituals surrounding dying and death that must be observed by the faithful. During a terminal illness the client and family should be queried about observances or rituals that follow death. Religious symbols or objects should be treated with respect and kept with the body. The nurse can support the family of the deceased by providing an environment conducive to the performance of their traditional death rituals.

**5** Influence of Spiritual and Religious Beliefs on Death
- Observances and rituals
- Provide environment conducive to performance of rituals

---

### SUGGESTIONS FOR CLASSROOM ACTIVITIES

- Invite a panel of religious leaders from various faiths to describe the religious practices relating to birth, illness, and death practiced by members of their faith.

### SUGGESTIONS FOR CLINICAL ACTIVITIES

- Discuss the agency's policies relating to addressing spiritual needs of its clients.

---

## LEARNING OUTCOME 6

Assess the spiritual needs of clients and plan nursing care to assist clients with spiritual needs.

### CONCEPTS FOR LECTURE

1. Data about a client's spiritual beliefs are obtained from the client's general history (religious preference or orientation); through a nursing history; and by clinical observation of the client's behavior, verbalizations, mood, and so on.

2. All clients can be asked a general question or two such as "What spiritual beliefs or practices are important to you now while you live with illness?" or "How would you like your health care team to support you spiritually?" Only those who manifest some type of unhealthful spiritual need or are at risk for spiritual distress need be subjected to a more thorough spiritual assessment (see Assessment Interview: Spirituality).

### POWERPOINT LECTURE SLIDES

*(NOTE: The number on each PPT Lecture Slide directly corresponds with the Concepts for Lecture.)*

**1** Assessment of Spiritual Needs
- Data gathered from the following:
  - General history
  - Nursing history
  - Clinical observation

**2** Assessment of Spiritual Needs
- FICA:
  - F (faith or beliefs)
  - I (implications or influence)
  - C (community)
  - A (address)

Remembering an acronym such as FICA can also help the nurse ask appropriate questions: F (faith or beliefs, e.g., "What spiritual beliefs are most important to you?"), I (implications or influence, e.g., "How is your faith affecting the way you cope now?"), C (community, e.g., "Is there a group or like-minded believers with which you regularly meet?"), and A (address, e.g., "How would you like your health care team to support your spirituality?").

3. During clinical assessment, cues to spiritual and religious preferences, strengths, concerns, or distress may be revealed by one or more of the following: environment (e.g., religious item in room), behavior (e.g., prayer before meals), verbalizations (e.g., mention a higher being in conversation), affect and attitude (e.g., affect, mood), and interpersonal relationships (e.g., visits from religious advisors).

4. In the planning phase, the nurse identifies interventions to help the client achieve the overall goal of maintaining or restoring spiritual well-being so that spiritual strength, serenity, and satisfaction are realized.

5. Planning in relation to spiritual needs should be designed to do one or more of the following: help the client fulfill religious obligations; help the client draw on and use inner resources more effectively to meet the present situation; help the client maintain or establish a dynamic, personal relationship with a supreme being in the face of unpleasant circumstances; help the client find meaning in existence and the present situation; promote a sense of hope; and provide spiritual resources otherwise unavailable.

3 Clinical Assessment
- May find cues to spiritual and religious preferences
  - Environment (religious item in room)
  - Behavior (prayer before meals)
  - Verbalizations (mention of a higher being in conversation)
  - Affect and attitude (mood)
  - Interpersonal relationships (visit from religious advisor)

4 Planning
- Overall goal:
  - Maintaining or restoring spiritual well-being so that spiritual strength, serenity, and satisfaction are realized

5 Planning
- Planning should be designed to do one or more of the following:
  - Help the client fulfill religious obligations
  - Help the client draw on and use inner resources more effectively
  - Help the client maintain or establish a dynamic, personal relationship with a supreme being in the face of unpleasant circumstances
  - Help the client find meaning in existence and the present situation
  - Promote a sense of hope
  - Provide spiritual resources otherwise unavailable

---

## SUGGESTIONS FOR CLASSROOM ACTIVITIES

- Have the students role-play the assessment of spiritual needs using either the Assessment Interview in the textbook or the acronym FICA.

## SUGGESTIONS FOR CLINICAL ACTIVITIES

- Discuss how the clinical agency promotes or interferes with clients' spiritual expressions.
- Describe how the agency assesses spiritual needs of the client.

---

# LEARNING OUTCOME 7

Describe nursing interventions to support clients' spiritual beliefs and religious practices.

## CONCEPTS FOR LECTURE

1. Numerous nursing actions are available to help clients meet their spiritual needs. Although nursing therapeutics that enhance spiritual health are diverse, some of the most common and most desired include providing presence, supporting religious practices, assisting clients with prayer, and referring clients for spiritual counseling.

Presencing is being present, being there, or just being with a client. The distinguishing features of presencing include giving of self in the present moment, being

## POWERPOINT LECTURE SLIDES

*(NOTE: The number on each PPT Lecture Slide directly corresponds with the Concepts for Lecture.)*

1 Nursing Interventions
- Providing presence
- Supporting religious practices
- Assisting clients with prayer
- Referring clients for spiritual counseling

available with all of the self, listening with full aware-ness of the privilege of doing so, and being there in a way that is meaningful to another person.

Nurses need to consider specific religious prac-tices that will affect nursing care. Practice Guidelines: Supporting Religious Practices lists ways to support clients. These guidelines include: create a trusting re-lationship; ask how the nurse can assist in meeting spiritual needs; do not discuss personal spiritual be-liefs unless the client requests; inform the client of spiritual support available; allow time and privacy for spiritual practices; respect and ensure the safety to the client's religious articles; facilitate visits by clergy or spiritual advisor; prepare the environment for these visits; consult dietitian so that dietary needs can be met; become acquainted with religions, spiritual prac-tices, and culture in area of practice; remember the dif-ference between facilitating and supporting and practicing the religion; ask another nurse to assist if a particular religious practice makes the nurse uncom-fortable; and remember that all spiritual interventions must be done within agency guidelines.

Clients may choose to participate in private prayer or want group prayer with family, friends, or clergy. The nurse's major responsibility is to ensure a quiet envi-ronment and privacy. Clients may ask the nurse to pray with them. Prayer should only be done when there is mutual agreement between the clients and those pray-ing with them. Nurses who are unaccustomed to pray-ing aloud or in public may find it helpful to have a formal prayer or a scriptural passage readily available.

Referrals for spiritual counseling can be made for hospitalized clients and their families through the hos-pital chaplain's office if one is available. Nurses in home care can identify spiritual resources by checking directories of community agencies, telephone directo-ries, or religious directories. Referral may be necessary in times of spiritual distress.

## SUGGESTIONS FOR CLASSROOM ACTIVITIES

- Have the students discuss how they would respond if a client asked them to pray with the client.

## SUGGESTIONS FOR CLINICAL ACTIVITIES

- Have each student identify one way to assist the assigned client to meet spiritual needs, if the client so desires.
- Invite one or more nurses to discuss examples of clients who have had unique needs related to spiri-tual beliefs and how they were able to facilitate these needs.
- Have the students discuss items they would like to have available to assist clients to meet spiritual needs (e.g., a small book with inspirational verse, various types of music, or nature sounds).

# LEARNING OUTCOME 8

Identify desired outcomes for evaluating the client's spiritual health.

## CONCEPTS FOR LECTURE

1. Using the measurable outcomes developed during the planning stage, the nurse collects data needed to judge whether client goals and outcomes have been achieved. Please see the general goals and outcomes listed in Outcome # 6.

## POWERPOINT LECTURE SLIDES

*(NOTE: The number on each PPT Lecture Slide directly corresponds with the Concepts for Lecture.)*

 Evaluation
- Use measurable outcomes developed during the planning stage
- Collect data needed to judge whether client goals and outcomes have been achieved

## SUGGESTIONS FOR CLASSROOM ACTIVITIES

- Have the students look up the NOC labels for outcomes related to spiritual needs.

## SUGGESTIONS FOR CLINICAL ACTIVITIES

- Have the students discuss a client who had a spiritual need, the related nursing diagnoses, and the goals/desired outcomes.

# CHAPTER 42
## STRESS AND COPING

## RESOURCE LIBRARY

 **PRENTICE HALL NURSING MEDIALINK DVD-ROM**

Audio Glossary
NCLEX® Review
Animation: *Reuptake Inhibitor*

 **COMPANION WEBSITE**

Additional NCLEX® Review
Case Study: *Becoming Parents*
Care Plan Activity: *Client Going Through a Divorce*
Application Activities:
    *Resources for Stress Management*
    *School Nursing Care of Teenagers*
Links to Resources

 **IMAGE LIBRARY**

**Figure 42.1** Some disorders that can be caused or aggravated by stress.

**Figure 42.2** The three stages of adaptation to stress: The alarm reaction, the stage of resistance, and the stage of exhaustion.

---

## LEARNING OUTCOME 1

Differentiate the concepts of stress as a stimulus, as a response, and as a transaction.

### CONCEPTS FOR LECTURE

1. Three main models of stress are stimulus-based, response-based, and transaction-based.
2. In stimulus-based stress models, stress is defined as a stimulus, a life event, or a set of circumstances that arouses physiologic and/or psychologic reactions that may increase the individual's vulnerability to illness. In this view both positive and negative events are considered stressful.
3. Stress may also be considered as a response. This definition was developed and described by Selye (1956, 1976) as the nonspecific response of the body to any kind of demand made upon it.
4. Transaction-based theories are based on the work of Lazarus (1966) who stated that the stimulus and response theories do not consider individual differences. The Lazarus transactional stress theory encompasses a set of cognitive, affective, and adaptive (coping) responses that arise out of person-environment transactions. The person and the environment are inseparable; each affects and is affected by the other. Stress refers to any event in which the environmental demands, internal demands, or both tax or exceed the adaptive resources of an individual, social system, or tissue system.

### POWERPOINT LECTURE SLIDES

*(NOTE: The number on each PPT Lecture Slide directly corresponds with the Concepts for Lecture.)*

**1** Concepts of Stress
- Stimulus-based models
- Response-based models (Selye)
- Transaction-based models (Lazarus)

**2** Stimulus-Based Models
- Stress defined as a stimulus, a life event, or set of circumstances that arouses physiologic/psychologic reaction
- This stress may increase vulnerability to illness
- Both positive and negative events considered stressful

**3** Response-Based Models
- Stress may be considered a response
- Selye (1956, 1976) defined as nonspecific response of body to any kind of demand made upon it

**4** Transaction-based Models
- Based on work of Lazarus (1966)
- Set of cognitive, affective, and adaptive (coping) responses that arise out of person-environment transactions

- Person and environment are inseparable—each affects and is affected by the other
- Stress refers to any event in which environmental demands, internal demands, or both tax adaptive resources of individual, social system, or tissue system

## SUGGESTIONS FOR CLASSROOM ACTIVITIES

- Have the students provide examples that illustrate stress as a stimulus, response, or transaction.

## SUGGESTIONS FOR CLINICAL ACTIVITIES

- Have the students provide examples of stress observed in their assigned clients and identify whether these examples represent stress as a stimulus, response, or transaction.

# LEARNING OUTCOME 2

Describe the three stages of Selye's general adaptation syndrome.

## CONCEPTS FOR LECTURE

1. Selye's stress response is characterized by a chain or pattern of physiologic events called the general adaptation syndrome (GAS). The three stages of Selye's general adaptation syndrome are alarm reaction (which is divided into two parts: the shock phase and the countershock phase), stage of resistance, and stage of exhaustion.

   The initial reaction of the body is the alarm reaction, which alerts the body's defenses. This stage is divided into two parts; the shock phase and the countershock phase. During the shock phase, the stressor may be perceived consciously or unconsciously by the person. Stressors stimulate the sympathetic nervous system (SNS), which stimulates the hypothalamus. The hypothalamus releases the corticotrophin releasing hormone (CRH) causing the anterior pituitary to release the adrenocorticotropin hormone (ACTH) which stimulates the adrenal medulla to release epinephrine and norepinephrine.

   Epinephrine causes increased myocardial contractility, bronchial dilation, increased blood clotting, increased cellular metabolism, and increased fat mobilization. Norepinephrine causes decreased blood to the kidneys and increased secretion of renin, a hormone that produces angiotensin, which increases blood pressure by constricting arterioles. The net effect is that the person is ready for "fight or flight." This primary response is short-lived, lasting from 1 minute to 24 hours.

   The second part of the alarm reaction is the countershock phase, in which the changes produced in the body during the shock phase are reversed. Thus the person is best mobilized to react during the shock phase of the alarm reaction. The stage of resistance is when the body's adaptation takes place. In other words, the body attempts to cope with the stressor and to limit the stressor to the smallest area of the body that can deal with it.

## POWERPOINT LECTURE SLIDES

*(NOTE: The number on each PPT Lecture Slide directly corresponds with the Concepts for Lecture.)*

 Seyle's General Adaptation Syndrome
- Alarm reaction divided into two parts:
  - Shock phase
  - Countershock phase
- Resistance
- Exhaustion

During the third stage, the stage of exhaustion, the adaptation that the body made during the second stage cannot be maintained. If adaptation has not overcome the stressor, the stress effect may spread to the entire body. At the end of this stage, the body may either rest and return to normal, or death may be the ultimate consequence. The end of this stage depends largely on the adaptive energy resources of the individual, the severity of the stressor, and the external adaptive resources that are provided.

## SUGGESTIONS FOR CLASSROOM ACTIVITIES

- Provide the students with clinical examples demonstrating one of Selye's three stages and have the students identify the appropriate stage.

## SUGGESTIONS FOR CLINICAL ACTIVITIES

- Have the students provide examples of Selye's stages of stress as observed in their assigned clients.

# LEARNING OUTCOME 3

Identify physiologic, psychologic, and cognitive indicators of stress.

## CONCEPTS FOR LECTURE

1. Indicators of stress may be physiologic, psychologic, or cognitive.
2. Physiologic indicators of stress are listed in Clinical Manifestations: Stress. Pupils dilate, sweat production increases, heart rate and cardiac output increase, skin is pallid, sodium and water are retained, rate and depth of respiration increase, urinary output decreases, the mouth may be dry, peristalsis of the intestines decreases; for serious threats, mental alertness improves, and blood sugar increases.
3. Psychologic manifestations of stress include anxiety, fear, anger, depression, and unconscious ego defense mechanisms.
4. Cognitive indicators of stress are thinking responses that include problem solving (thinking through threatening situations using specific steps to arrive at a solution), structuring (arranging or manipulating of a situation so that threatening events do not occur), self-control or self-discipline (assuming a manner and facial expression that convey a sense of being in control or in charge), suppression (consciously or willfully putting thoughts or feelings out of mind), and fantasy or daydreaming (likened to make-believe; unfulfilled wishes or desires are imagined as fulfilled or a threatening situation is reworked or replayed so it ends differently from reality).

## POWERPOINT LECTURE SLIDES

*(NOTE: The number on each PPT Lecture Slide directly corresponds with the Concepts for Lecture.)*

1. Indicators for Stress
   - May be
     - Physiologic
     - Psychologic
     - Cognitive

2. Physiologic Indicators of Stress
   - Pupils dilate
   - Sweat production increases
   - Heart rate and cardiac output increase
   - Skin is pallid
   - Sodium and water retained
   - Rate and depth of respiration increase
   - Urinary output decreases
   - Mouth may be dry
   - Peristalsis of the intestines decrease
   - Mental alertness improves (serious threats)
   - Blood sugar increases

3. Psychologic Indicators of Stress
   - Anxiety
   - Fear
   - Anger
   - Depression
   - Unconscious ego defense mechanisms

4. Cognitive Indicators of Stress
   - Problem-solving
   - Structuring

- Self-control or self-discipline
- Suppression
- Fantasy

| SUGGESTIONS FOR CLASSROOM ACTIVITIES | SUGGESTIONS FOR CLINICAL ACTIVITIES |
|---|---|
| • Discuss the difference between anxiety and fear. | • Have the students review the charts of individuals who have had surgery and identify physiologic indicators of change (e.g., alterations in electrolytes, blood glucose, fluid volume). If there are no indicators, discuss why. |

# LEARNING OUTCOME 4

Differentiate four levels of anxiety.

## CONCEPTS FOR LECTURE

1. The four levels of anxiety are mild, moderate, severe, and panic. Table 42–2 lists the indicators of the levels of anxiety.
2. Indicators of mild anxiety include increased questioning, mild restlessness, sleeplessness, feelings of increased arousal and alertness, and the use of learning to adapt.
3. Indicators of moderate anxiety include voice tremors and pitch changes; tremors, facial twitches, and shakiness; increased muscle tension; narrowed focus of attention; ability to focus but selectively inattentive; slightly impaired learning; slightly increased respiratory and heart rate; and mild gastric symptoms.
4. Indicators of severe anxiety include communication that is difficult to understand, increased motor activity, inability to relax, fearful facial expression, inability to focus or concentrate, easily distracted, severely impaired learning, tachycardia, hyperventilation, headache, dizziness, and nausea.
5. Indicators of panic include communication that may not be understandable, increased motor activity, agitation, unpredictable responses, trembling, poor motor coordination, perception distorted or exaggerated, inability to learn or function, dyspnea, palpitations, choking, chest pain or pressure, feeling of impending doom, paresthesia, and sweating.

## PowerPoint Lecture Slides

*(NOTE: The number on each PPT Lecture Slide directly corresponds with the Concepts for Lecture.)*

**1** Four Levels of Anxiety
- Mild
- Moderate
- Severe
- Panic

**2** Indicators of Mild Anxiety
- Increased questioning
- Mild restlessness
- Sleeplessness
- Feelings of increased arousal and alertness
- Use of learning to adapt

**3** Indicators of Moderate Anxiety
- Voice tremors and pitch changes
- Tremors
- Facial twitches
- Shakiness
- Increased muscle tension
- Narrowed focus of attention
- Ability to focus but selectively inattentive
- Slightly impaired learning
- Slight increased RR and HR
- Mild gastric symptoms

**4** Indicators of Severe Anxiety
- Communication that is difficult to understand
- Increased motor activity
- Inability to relax
- Fearful facial expression
- Inability to focus or concentrate
- Easily distracted
- Severely impaired learning
- Tachycardia, hyperventilation
- Headache, dizziness, nausea

5 Indicators of Panic
- Communication that may not be understandable
- Increased motor activity
- Agitation
- Unpredictable responses
- Trembling
- Poor motor coordination
- Perception distorted or exaggerated
- Inability to learn or function
- Dyspnea, palpitations, choking
- Chest pain or pressure, feeling of impending doom
- Paresthesia, sweating

## SUGGESTIONS FOR CLASSROOM ACTIVITIES

- Have the students relate the indicators of anxiety they have experienced in various situations: giving a speech, performing a skill for the first time, or taking a test. Ask the students to identify the level of anxiety represented and whether the level of anxiety helped or hindered their performance.

## SUGGESTIONS FOR CLINICAL ACTIVITIES

- Have the students identify indicators of anxiety they have observed in their assigned clients. Discuss the situations in which this occurred and possible interventions to assist the clients to reduce the level of anxiety.

## LEARNING OUTCOME 5

Identify behaviors related to specific ego defense mechanisms.

### CONCEPTS FOR LECTURE

1. Table 42–3 lists defense mechanisms, behavioral examples, and the use or purpose of each.

    Defense mechanisms listed include compensation, denial, displacement, identification, intellectualization, introjection, minimization, projection, rationalization, reaction formation, regression, repression, sublimation, substitution, and undoing.

### POWERPOINT LECTURE SLIDES

*(NOTE: The number on each PPT Lecture Slide directly corresponds with the Concepts for Lecture.)*

 Defense Mechanisms
- Compensation
- Denial
- Displacement
- Identification
- Intellectualization
- Introjection
- Minimization
- Projection
- Rationalization
- Reaction formation
- Regression
- Repression
- Sublimation
- Substitution
- Undoing

## LEARNING OUTCOME 6

Discuss types of coping and coping strategies.

### CONCEPTS FOR LECTURE

1. Coping may be described as dealing with change, either successfully or unsuccessfully. A coping strategy (coping mechanism) is a natural or learned way of responding to a changing environment or specific problem or situation.

2. Two types of coping strategies have been described: problem-focused and emotion-focused coping. Problem-focused coping refers to efforts to improve a situation by making changes or taking some action. Emotion-focused coping includes thoughts and actions that relieve emotional distress. It does not improve the situation, but the person often feels better. Both types of strategies usually occur together.

3. Coping strategies are also viewed as long term or short term. Long-term coping strategies can be constructive and realistic. Examples include talking with others, trying to find out more about the situation, changing lifestyle patterns, or using problem solving in decision making instead of anger or other nonconstructive responses.

    Short-term coping strategies can reduce stress to a tolerable limit temporarily but are ineffective ways to permanently deal with reality and may even be destructive or detrimental. Examples include use of alcohol or drugs, daydreaming and fantasizing, relying on the belief that everything will work out, and giving in to others to avoid anger.

    Coping can be adaptive or maladaptive. Adaptive coping helps the person to deal effectively with stressful events and minimizes distress associated with them. Maladaptive coping can result in unnecessary distress for the person and others associated with the person or stressful event. In nursing literature, effective coping results in adaptation and ineffective coping results in maladaptation.

### POWERPOINT LECTURE SLIDES

*(NOTE: The number on each PPT Lecture Slide directly corresponds with the Concepts for Lecture.)*

 Coping
- Dealing with change (either successfully or unsuccessfully)
- Coping strategy is natural or learned way of responding to changing environment or specific problem or situation

 Types of Coping
- Problem-focused
  ○ Efforts to improve situation by making changes or taking action
- Emotion-focused coping
  ○ Thoughts and actions that relieve emotional distress
  ○ Doesn't improve situation but person feels better
- Both types usually occur together

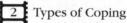 Coping Strategies
- Long term
  ○ Can be constructive and realistic
- Short term
  ○ Reduce stress temporarily but ineffective to deal with reality
  ○ May be destructive or detrimental
- Adaptive
  ○ Helps person deal effectively with stress and minimize distress
  ○ Result of effective coping
- Maladaptive
  ○ Results in unnecessary distress for person and others associated with person or event
  ○ Results from ineffective coping

# LEARNING OUTCOME 7

Identify essential aspects of assessing a client's stress and coping patterns.

## CONCEPTS FOR LECTURE

1. Nursing assessment of a client's stress and coping patterns includes a nursing history and physical examination for indicators of stress or stress-related health problems.

   When obtaining the history, the nurse poses questions about client-perceived stressors or stressful incidents, manifestations of stress, and past and present coping strategies.

2. Questions to elicit data about the client's stress and coping patterns are shown in the accompanying Assessment Interview: Ask the client to rate specific stressors such as home, work, or school on a scale of 1 to 10 where 1 is "very minor" and 10 is "extreme," ask how long has the client been dealing with specific stressors; ask how the client usually handles stressful situations and how well the client's usual coping strategies work.

3. During the physical examination, the nurse observes for verbal, motor, cognitive, or other physical manifestations of stress. However, the clinical signs and symptoms may not occur when cognitive coping is effective.

   In addition, the nurse should be aware of expected developmental transitions. When these tasks are carried over or not resolved, stress increases as the person becomes older. See Table 42-1: Selected Stressors Associated with Developmental Stages.

## POWERPOINT LECTURE SLIDES

*(NOTE: The number on each PPT Lecture Slide directly corresponds with the Concepts for Lecture.)*

1 Assessing Stress and Coping Patterns
   - Nursing history
     - Client-perceived stressors or stressful incidents
     - Manifestations of stress
     - Past and present coping strategies
     - Developmental transitions

2 Assessment Interview
   - Scale to rate specific stressors
   - Duration of stressful situation
   - Usual strategy for handling stressful situations
   - Effectiveness of these strategies

3 Physical Examination
   - Verbal
   - Motor
   - Cognitive
   - Other physical manifestations of stress

---

## SUGGESTIONS FOR CLASSROOM ACTIVITIES

- Using the Assessment Interview in the textbook, have each student perform the assessment on another student. Have the students discuss insights gained from this assessment.

## SUGGESTIONS FOR CLINICAL ACTIVITIES

- Have the students perform a stress and coping assessment on their assigned client, if appropriate. Compare and contrast findings.

---

# LEARNING OUTCOME 8

Identify nursing diagnoses related to stress.

## CONCEPTS FOR LECTURE

1. NANDA diagnostic labels related to stress, adaptation, and coping include *Anxiety, Caregiver Role Strain, Compromised Family Coping, Decisional Conflict (Specify), Defensive Coping, Disabled Family Coping, Fear, Impaired Adjustment, Ineffective Coping, Ineffective Denial, Post-Trauma Syndrome*, and *Relocation Stress Syndrome*.

## POWERPOINT LECTURE SLIDES

*(NOTE: The number on each PPT Lecture Slide directly corresponds with the Concepts for Lecture.)*

1 Nursing Diagnoses Related to Stress
   - Anxiety
   - Caregiver role strain
   - Compromised family coping
   - Decisional conflict (specify)
   - Defensive coping
   - Disabled family coping
   - Fear
   - Impaired adjustment

- Ineffective coping
- Ineffective denial
- Post-trauma syndrome
- Relocation stress syndrome

---

### SUGGESTIONS FOR CLASSROOM ACTIVITIES

- Have the students investigate the definition, defining characteristics, and etiology for each of the NANDA diagnostic labels related to stress, adaptation, and coping.

### SUGGESTIONS FOR CLINICAL ACTIVITIES

- Using the data obtained from assessment of stress and coping performed for their assigned clients, have the students identify appropriate diagnoses validating with defining characteristics and etiology.

---

## LEARNING OUTCOME 9

Describe interventions to help clients minimize and manage stress.

### CONCEPTS FOR LECTURE

1. Some methods to help reduce stress will be effective for one person; other methods will be appropriate for a different person. Several health promotion strategies are often appropriate as interventions for clients with stress-related nursing diagnoses: physical exercise, optimal nutrition, adequate rest and sleep, and time management.
2. Exercise promotes both physical and emotional health. Thirty minutes of daily exercise is recommended by the United States Department of Agriculture.
3. Optimal nutrition is essential for health and increases the body's resistance to stress. Clients should avoid excesses of caffeine, salt, sugar, and fat and deficiencies in vitamins and minerals.
4. Sleep restores the body's energy level. To get adequate rest and sleep, clients may need help to attain comfort and to learn techniques that promote peace of mind and relaxation (see "Using Relaxation Techniques" in the textbook).
5. Time management must address both what is important to the client and what can realistically be achieved. Clients may need to reexamine the "should do," "ought to do," and "must do" situations in their lives and develop realistic self-expectations.
6. Other methods to minimize stress and anxiety include (See Box 42–1); listen attentively; try to understand the client's perspective; provide an atmosphere of warmth and trust; convey a sense of caring and empathy; determine if it is appropriate to include the client in the plan of care; stay with the client to promote a feeling of safety and security; control the environment to minimize additional stressors; implement suicide precautions if necessary; help the client to determine situations that precipitate anxiety; verbalize feelings; identify personal strengths; recognize usual positive and negative coping mechanisms; identify new coping strategies and appropriate support systems.

### POWERPOINT LECTURE SLIDES

*(NOTE: The number on each PPT Lecture Slide directly corresponds with the Concepts for Lecture.)*

**1** Interventions to Minimize and Manage Stress
  - Physical exercise
  - Optimal nutrition
  - Adequate rest and sleep
  - Time management

**2** Physical Exercise
  - Promotes physical and emotional health
  - 30 minutes per day recommended

**3** Optimal Nutrition
  - Essential for health
  - Increases body's resistance to stress
  - Avoid excesses of caffeine, salt, sugar, and fat and deficiencies in vitamins and minerals

**4** Sleep
  - Restores body's energy level
  - May need to use relaxation techniques

**5** Time Management
  - Must address what is important to client and be achievable
  - Clients may need to reexamine the "should do," "ought to do," and "must do"

**6** Other Methods to Reduce Client's Stress
  - Listen attentively, try to understand client's perspective
  - Provide atmosphere of warmth and trust
  - Convey sense of caring and empathy
  - Include client in plan of care
  - Promote feeling of safety and security
  - Minimize additional stressors
  - Help client with recognition of stressors and coping mechanisms

## Suggestions for Classroom Activities

- Invite a psychiatric nurse to discuss suicide prevention and suicide precautions.
- Divide the students into groups and have each group identify a technique to reduce stress and anxiety. Have each group investigate this method and demonstrate it for the class.

## Suggestions for Clinical Activities

- Using the interventions listed in Box 42-1, have the students describe how they can assist a client in reducing stress or anxiety.
- Discuss medications that may be prescribed for short-term use to assist clients to sleep. The discussion should include appropriate use, action, half-life, adverse reactions or side effects, and associated nursing interventions.

# CHAPTER 43
## LOSS, GRIEVING, AND DEATH

## RESOURCE LIBRARY

 **PRENTICE HALL NURSING MEDIALINK DVD-ROM**

Audio Glossary
NCLEX® Review
End of Unit Concept Map Activity
Video: *Terminally Ill Clients*

 **COMPANION WEBSITE**

Additional NCLEX® Review
Case Study: *Helping a Family Accept a Terminal Illness*
Care Plan Activity: *Client with an Arm Amputation*
Application Activities:
    *Dealing with a Pet Loss*
    *Care of a Grieving Parent*
Links to Resources

 **IMAGE LIBRARY**

**Figure 43.1** Children experience the same emotions of grief as adults.

---

## LEARNING OUTCOME 1

Describe types and sources of losses.

### CONCEPTS FOR LECTURE

1. There are two general types of loss: actual and perceived. An actual loss can be recognized by others. A perceived loss is experienced by one person but cannot be verified by others. Psychological losses are often perceived losses in that they are not directly verifiable.

    Both losses can be anticipatory. Anticipatory loss is experienced before the loss actually occurs.

    Loss can be viewed as situational or developmental. Examples of situational losses include the loss of one's job, the death of a child, or the loss of functional ability because of acute illness or injury. Developmental losses occur in the process of normal development, such as the departure of children from the home, or retirement from a career.

2. There are many sources of loss: (a) loss of an aspect of oneself—a body part, a physiologic function, or a psychologic attribute; (b) loss of an object external to oneself; (c) separation from an accustomed environment; and (d) loss of a loved one or valued person.

### POWERPOINT LECTURE SLIDES

*(NOTE: The number on each PPT Lecture Slide directly corresponds with the Concepts for Lecture.)*

 Types of Loss
- Actual
  - Recognized by others
- Perceived
  - Experienced by one person but cannot be verified by others
- Anticipatory
  - Experienced before loss occurs
  - Can be actual or perceived
- Situational
  - i.e., Loss of job, death of child
  - Developmental
  - i.e., Departure of children from home

 Sources of Loss
- Loss of an aspect of oneself
- Loss of an object external to oneself
- Separation from an accustomed environment
- Loss of a loved one or valued person

---

### SUGGESTIONS FOR CLASSROOM ACTIVITIES

- Have the students provide additional examples of actual, perceived, anticipatory, situational, and developmental losses.

### SUGGESTIONS FOR CLINICAL ACTIVITIES

- Have the students identify potential or actual sources of loss for assigned clients.

© 2008 Pearson Education, Inc.

Discuss selected frameworks for identifying stages of grieving.

### CONCEPTS FOR LECTURE

1. Many authors have described stages or phases of grieving. Kübler-Ross (1969) described five stages: denial, anger, bargaining, depression, and acceptance. Table 43–1 lists these stages, behavioral responses, and nursing implications.
2. Engel (1964) identified six stages of grieving: shock and disbelief, developing awareness, restitution, resolving the loss, idealization, and outcome. Table 43–2 lists the stages and behavioral responses.
3. Sanders (1998) described five phases of bereavement: shock, awareness, conservation/withdrawal, healing, and renewal. Table 43–3 lists descriptions and behavioral responses of these phases.
4. Martocchio (1985) described five clusters of grief—shock and disbelief; yearning and protest; anguish, disorganization and despair; identification in bereavement; and reorganization and restitution—and maintained that there is no single correct way, nor a correct timetable, by which a person progresses through the grief process.
5. Rando (1991, 1993, 2000) has described three categories of responses: avoidance, confrontation, and accommodation. Avoidance is similar to Kübler-Ross's phases of denial, anger, and bargaining and Engel's phase of shock and disbelief. Confrontation is the most upsetting phase for the grieving person facing the loss. Accommodation is the phase in which the person begins to resume more usual activities, feels better, and places the loss in perspective.

### POWERPOINT LECTURE SLIDES

*(NOTE: The number on each PPT Lecture Slide directly corresponds with the Concepts for Lecture.)*

**1** Kübler-Ross (1969) Stages of Grieving
- Denial
- Anger
- Bargaining
- Depression
- Acceptance

**2** Engel (1964) Stages of Grieving
- Shock and disbelief
- Developing awareness
- Restitution
- Resolving the loss
- Idealization
- Outcome

**3** Sanders (1998) Phases of Bereavement
- Shock
- Awareness of loss
- Conservation/withdrawal
- Healing: the turning point
- Renewal

**4** Martocchio (1985) Clusters of Grief
- Shock and disbelief
- Yearning and protest
- Anguish, disorganization, and despair
- Identification in bereavement
- Reorganization and restitution

**5** Rando (1991, 1993, 2000) Categories of Response
- Avoidance
- Confrontation
- Accommodation

### SUGGESTIONS FOR CLASSROOM ACTIVITIES

- Compare and contrast the various stages of grieving as identified by the researchers listed in the textbook.

### SUGGESTIONS FOR CLINICAL ACTIVITIES

- Invite a nurse from the hospice or oncology unit to discuss how clients and families demonstrate movement through the stages of grief and how nurses can facilitate this movement.

## LEARNING OUTCOME 3

Identify clinical symptoms of grief.

### CONCEPTS FOR LECTURE

1. Physiologically, the body responds to a current or anticipated loss with a stress reaction. The nurse can assess the clinical signs of this response (see Chapter 42).

### POWERPOINT LECTURE SLIDES

*(NOTE: The number on each PPT Lecture Slide directly corresponds with the Concepts for Lecture.)*

**1** Clinical Symptoms of Grief
- Signs and symptoms of a stress reaction
- Manifestations considered to be normal:

Manifestations of grief that would be considered normal include verbalization of the loss, crying, sleep disturbance, loss of appetite, and difficulty concentrating. Complicated grieving may be characterized by extended time of denial, depression, severe physiologic symptoms, or suicidal thoughts.

- ○ Verbalization of the loss
- ○ Crying
- ○ Sleep disturbance
- ○ Loss of appetite
- ○ Difficulty concentrating
- Complicated grieving
  - ○ Extended time of denial
  - ○ Depression
  - ○ Severe physiologic symptoms
  - ○ Suicidal thoughts

## SUGGESTIONS FOR CLASSROOM ACTIVITIES

- Show a videotape demonstrating the signs and symptoms of grief and interventions to help.

## SUGGESTIONS FOR CLINICAL ACTIVITIES

- Have a nurse from the emergency department describe how individuals react to unexpected loss and how individuals are helped to express and deal with grief in this unit.

# LEARNING OUTCOME 4

Discuss factors affecting a grief response.

## CONCEPTS FOR LECTURE

1. A number of factors affect a person's responses to a loss or death: age, significance of the loss, culture, spiritual beliefs, gender, socioeconomic status, support systems, and the cause of loss or death.

   Age affects a person's understanding of and reaction to loss. With familiarity, people usually increase their understanding and acceptance of life, loss, and death.

   Significance of the loss depends on the perception of the individual experiencing the loss. A number of factors affect the significance: importance of the lost person, object, or function; degree of change required because of the loss; and the person's beliefs and values.

   Culture influences an individual's reaction to the loss. How grief is expressed is often determined by the customs of the culture.

   Spiritual beliefs greatly influence both a person's reaction to loss and subsequent behavior. Most religious groups have practices related to dying, and these are often important to the client and support people.

   Gender roles affect reactions at times of loss. Men are frequently expected to "be strong" and show very little emotion during grief, whereas it is acceptable for women to show grief by crying. Gender role also affects the significance of body image changes to clients.

   Socioeconomic status often affects the support system available at the time of a loss. A pension plan or insurance can offer a widowed or disabled person a choice of ways to deal with a loss. A person who is confronted with both severe loss and economic hardship may not be able to cope with either.

## POWERPOINT LECTURE SLIDES

*(NOTE: The number on each PPT Lecture Slide directly corresponds with the Concepts for Lecture.)*

1 Factors Affecting Grief Response
- Age
- Significance of the loss
- Culture
- Spiritual beliefs
- Gender
- Socioeconomic status
- Support systems
- Cause of death

The people closest to the grieving individual are often the first to recognize and provide emotional, physical, and functional assistance; however, some individuals feel uncomfortable or inexperienced in dealing with losses and may withdraw from the grieving person. In addition, support may be available when the loss first occurs, but as the support people return to usual activities, the ongoing need for support may be unmet. Also, the grieving person may be unable or unready to accept support.

Individual and societal views on the cause of a loss or death may significantly influence the grief response. Some diseases are considered "clean" and engender compassion, whereas others may be viewed as repulsive and less unfortunate. A loss or death that is beyond the control of those involved may be more acceptable than one that is preventable, such as a drunk driving accident. Injuries or deaths occurring during respected activities such as "in the line of duty" are considered honorable, whereas those occurring during illicit activities may be considered the individual's just rewards.

---

## SUGGESTIONS FOR CLASSROOM ACTIVITIES

- Have each student interview a person from a different culture to determine what the cultural group considers to be acceptable losses, how the culture responds to these losses, and rituals or rites used to assist individuals experiencing loss. Share with the class.
- Have the students discuss acceptable and unacceptable gender behaviors related to loss in their family.

## SUGGESTIONS FOR CLINICAL ACTIVITIES

- Have the students interview staff nurses, asking each to discuss factors affecting the grief responses they have observed in practice. Discuss findings in conference.

---

# LEARNING OUTCOME 5

Identify measures that facilitate the grieving process.

## CONCEPTS FOR LECTURE

1. Explore and respect the client's and family's ethnic, cultural, religious, and personal values in their expressions of grief.

    Teach the client or family what to expect in the grief process.

    Encourage the client to express and share grief with support people.

    Teach family members to encourage the client's expression of grief, not to push the client to move on or enforce their own expectations of appropriate reactions.

    Encourage the client to resume activities on a schedule that promotes physical and psychologic health.

## POWERPOINT LECTURE SLIDES

*(NOTE: The number on each PPT Lecture Slide directly corresponds with the Concepts for Lecture.)*

 Measures that Facilitate the Grieving Process
- Explore and respect ethnic, cultural, religious, and personal values
- Teach what to expect in the grief process
- Encourage the client to express and share grief with support people
- Teach family members to encourage the client's expression of grief
- Encourage the client to resume activities on a schedule that promotes physical and psychologic health

---

# LEARNING OUTCOME 6

List clinical signs of impending and actual death.

## CONCEPTS FOR LECTURE

1. Manifestations of impending death include loss of muscle tone (relaxation of the facial muscles, difficulty speaking, difficulty swallowing, gradual loss of the gag reflex, decreased activity of the gastrointestinal tract, possible urinary and rectal incontinence, diminished body movement); slowing of the circulation (diminished sensation, mottling and cyanosis of the extremities, cold skin, slower and weaker pulse, decreased blood pressure); changes in respiration (rapid, shallow, irregular or abnormally slow respirations, noisy breathing, mouth breathing, dry oral mucous membranes); and sensory impairment (blurred vision, impaired sense of taste and smell).

2. The traditional clinical signs of death were cessation of the apical pulse, respirations, and blood pressure, also referred to as heart-lung death. However, since the advent of artificial means to maintain respirations and blood circulation, identifying death is more difficult.

3. In 1968, the World Medical Assembly adopted the following guidelines for physicians as indications of death: total lack of response to external stimuli; no muscular movement, especially during breathing; no reflexes; and a flat encephalogram (brain waves). In instances of artificial support, absence of brain waves for at least 24 hours is an indication of death.

4. Another definition of death is cerebral death or higher brain death which occurs when the higher brain center, the cerebral cortex, is irreversibly destroyed. In this case, there is "a clinical syndrome characterized by the permanent loss of cerebral and brain stem function, manifested by absence of responsiveness to external stimuli, absence of cephalic reflexes, and apnea. An isoelectric electroencephalogram for at least 30 minutes in the absence of hypothermia and poisoning by central nervous system depressants supports the diagnosis" (Stedman's Medical Dictionary, 2005).

## POWERPOINT LECTURE SLIDES

*(NOTE: The number on each PPT Lecture Slide directly corresponds with the Concepts for Lecture.)*

**1** Manifestations of Impending Death
- Loss of muscle tone
- Slowing of the circulation
- Changes in respiration
- Sensory impairment

**2** Traditional Clinical Signs of Death
- Cessation of
  - Apical pulse
  - Respirations
  - Blood pressure

**3** World Medical Assembly Guidelines for Death
- Total lack of response to external stimuli
- No muscular movement, especially during breathing
- No reflexes
- Flat encephalogram (brain waves)
- In instances of artificial support, absence of brain waves for at least 24 hours

**4** Cerebral Death/Higher Brain Death
- Occurs when the cerebral cortex is irreversibly destroyed
- Permanent loss of cerebral and brain stem function, manifested by absence of responsiveness to external stimuli, absence of cephalic reflexes, and apnea
- Isoelectric electroencephalogram for at least 30 minutes in the absence of hypothermia and poisoning by central nervous system depressants

# LEARNING OUTCOME 7

Describe helping clients die with dignity.

## CONCEPTS FOR LECTURE

1. Nurses need to ensure that the client is treated with dignity, that is, with honor and respect. Helping clients die with dignity involves maintaining their humanity, consistent with their values, beliefs, and culture.

    By introducing options available to the client and significant others, nurses can restore and support feelings of control that dying clients often feel they have lost. Some choices that clients can make are the location of care, times of appointments with health professionals, activity schedule, use of health resources, and times of visits from relatives and friends.

2. Clients want to be able to manage the events preceding death so they can die peacefully. Nurses can help clients to determine their own physical, psychologic, and social priorities. Part of the nurse's challenge is to support the client's will and hope. (See Box 43–1: The Dying Person's Bill of Rights.)

3. It is natural for people to be uncomfortable discussing death. Some strategies to be taken to make this discussion easier include: the nurse should identify personal feelings about death and how these may influence interaction with clients; focus on the client's needs; talk to the client and family about how the client usually copes with stress; establish communication relationship that shows concerns for and commitment to the client; determine what the client knows about the illness and prognosis; respond with honesty and directness to the client's questions about death; and make time to be available to the client to provide support and listen and respond.

## POWERPOINT LECTURE SLIDES

*(NOTE: The number on each PPT Lecture Slide directly corresponds with the Concepts for Lecture.)*

**1** Helping Clients Die with Dignity
- Introduce options available to restore and support feelings of control:
  - Location of care
  - Times of appointments with health professionals
  - Activity schedule
  - Use of health resources
  - Times of visits from relatives and friends

**2** Assists Clients to Manage the Events Preceding Death So They Can Die Peacefully
- Can help clients to determine their own physical, psychologic, and social priorities
- Support the client's will and hope

**3** Strategies to Facilitate Discussions About Death
- Identify personal feelings about death
- Focus on client's needs
- Determine client's usual ways of coping
- Establish communication relationship
- Determine what the client knows about the illness and prognosis
- Respond with honesty and directness
- Make time to be available to provide support, listen, and respond

## SUGGESTIONS FOR CLASSROOM ACTIVITIES

- Discuss the Dying Person's Bill of Rights and nursing implications.

## SUGGESTIONS FOR CLINICAL ACTIVITIES

- Discuss how the agency implements regulations related to advance directives.
- Have the students discuss whether the nursing care for a client is altered depending upon "code" status.
- Arrange for students to have a practice experience in an inpatient or outpatient hospice organization.

# LEARNING OUTCOME 8

Describe the role of the nurse in working with families or caregivers of dying clients.

## CONCEPTS FOR LECTURE

1. The most important aspects of providing support to the family members of a dying client involve using therapeutic communication to facilitate their expression of feelings. The nurse can provide an empathetic and caring presence. The nurse also serves as teacher, explaining what is happening and what the family can

## POWERPOINT LECTURE SLIDES

*(NOTE: The number on each PPT Lecture Slide directly corresponds with the Concepts for Lecture.)*

**1** Assisting Families or Caregivers of Dying Clients
- Use therapeutic communication
- Provide an empathetic and caring presence
- Explain what is happening and what to expect

expect. The nurse must have a calm and patient demeanor.

Family members should be encouraged to participate in the physical care of the dying person as much as they wish to and are able. The nurse can suggest they assist with bathing, speak or read to the client, and hold hands. The nurse must not, however, have specific expectations for family members' participation. Those who feel unable to care for or be with the dying person also require support. They should be shown an appropriate waiting area if they wish to remain nearby.

Sometimes, it seems as if the client is "holding on" possibly out of concern for the family not being ready. It may be therapeutic for the family to verbally give permission to the client that they are prepared for the client to "let go," to die when ready.

2. After the client dies, the family should be encouraged to view the body because this has been shown to facilitate the grieving process. They may wish to clip a lock of hair as a remembrance. Children should be included in the events surrounding the death if they wish to.

- Have a calm and patient demeanor
- Encourage participation in the physical care as they are able:
  ○ Assist with bathing
  ○ Speak or read to the client
  ○ Hold hands
- Support those who feel unable to care for or be with the dying
  ○ Show an appropriate waiting area
- May be therapeutic for the family to verbally give permission to the client to "let go" when ready

 After Client Dies
- Encourage the family to view the body
- May wish to clip a lock of hair as a remembrance
- Children should be included in the events if they wish

---

### SUGGESTIONS FOR CLASSROOM ACTIVITIES

- Discuss how nurses can provide support by teaching and assisting family members to participate in care for the dying client. Provide examples.

### SUGGESTIONS FOR CLINICAL ACTIVITIES

- Tour the agency's chapel to identify resources available in this area.
- If possible, arrange for the students to have an experience with a home hospice nurse to observe services and interventions provided for families of dying clients.

---

# LEARNING OUTCOME 9

Describe nursing measures for care of the body after death.

### CONCEPTS FOR LECTURE

1. Nursing personnel may be responsible for care of the body after death. Postmortem care should be carried out according to the policy of the hospital or agency.

   Because care of the body may be influenced by religious law, the nurse should check the client's religion and make every attempt to comply.

   If the deceased's family or friends wish to view the body, it is important to make the environment as clean and as pleasant as possible and make the body appear natural and comfortable. All equipment, soiled linen, and supplies should be removed from the bedside. Some agencies require that all tubes remain in place. In other agencies, tubes may be cut to within 2.5 cm (2 inches) of the skin and taped in place. In others, all tubes are removed.

### POWERPOINT LECTURE SLIDES

*(NOTE: The number on each PPT Lecture Slide directly corresponds with the Concepts for Lecture.)*

 Care of the Body After Death
- Follow policy of the hospital or agency
- Check the client's religious rituals and make every attempt to comply
- If family or friends wish to view the body:
  ○ Make the environment as clean and as pleasant as possible
  ○ Make the body appear natural and comfortable
  ○ All equipment, soiled linen, and supplies should be removed
  ○ Follow agency policy when caring for tubes

2. Normally, the body is placed in a supine position with the arms either at the sides, palm down, or across the abdomen. One pillow is placed under the head and shoulders to prevent blood from discoloring the face by settling in it. The eyelids are closed and held in place for a few seconds so they remain closed. Dentures are usually inserted to help give the face a natural appearance; the mouth is then closed.

3. Soiled areas of the body are washed, absorbent pads are placed under the buttocks to take up any feces and urine released because of relaxation of the sphincter muscles, a clean gown is placed on the client, and the hair is brushed and combed. All jewelry is removed, except a wedding band in some instances, which is taped to the finger. The top bed linens are adjusted to cover the client to the shoulders, and soft lighting and chairs are provided for the family.

4. After the body has been viewed by the family, the deceased's wrist identification tag is left on and additional identification tags are applied. The body is wrapped in a shroud and identification is then applied to the outside of the shroud. The body is taken to the morgue if arrangements have not been made to have a mortician pick it up from the client's room. Nurses have a duty to handle the deceased with dignity and to label the corpse appropriately.

**2** Care of the Body After Death
- Place the body in a supine position
- Place arms either at the sides, palm down, or across the abdomen
- Place one pillow under the head and shoulders
- Close the eyelids for a few seconds
- Insert dentures
- Close the mouth

**3** Care of the Body After Death
- Wash soiled areas of the body
- Place absorbent pads under the buttocks
- Place a clean gown on the client
- Brush and comb the hair
- Remove all jewelry except a wedding band which is taped to the finger
- Adjust the top bed linen to cover the client to the shoulders
- Provide soft lighting and chairs for the family

**4** After Body Viewed by Family:
- Leave wrist identification bracelet on
- Apply additional identification tags
- Wrap the body in a shroud
- Apply identification to the outside of the shroud
- Take the body to the morgue
- Or arrange to have a mortician pick up the body from the client's room
- Handle the deceased with dignity

## SUGGESTIONS FOR CLASSROOM ACTIVITIES

- Obtain a postmortem pack and have the students practice postmortem care on a manikin.
- Invite nurses who work with dying clients and their families to discuss how they deal with death of these clients. Ask the nurses to discuss how they care for themselves to prevent "burnout."

## SUGGESTIONS FOR CLINICAL ACTIVITIES

- If possible, have the students participate in postmortem care and visit the hospital morgue to observe an autopsy. Discuss the experience, including feelings and emotions of the students.
- Review the agency's policies and procedures for postmortem care.

# CHAPTER 44
## ACTIVITY AND EXERCISE

## RESOURCE LIBRARY

### 💿 PRENTICE HALL NURSING MEDIALINK DVD-ROM

Audio Glossary
NCLEX® Review
Skills Checklists
Animations:
  *Classification of Joints*
  *Movement of Joints*
  *Muscle Contraction*

### 🌐 COMPANION WEBSITE

Additional NCLEX® Review
Case Study: *Client with Mobility Problems*
Care Plan Activity: *Activity and Exercise*
Application Activity: *Exercise for Seniors*
Links to Resources

### 📖 IMAGE LIBRARY

**Figure 44.1** The center of gravity and the line of gravity influence standing alignment.

**Figures 44.2–44.30** Selected joint movements and examples of corresponding activity of daily living (ADL).

**Figure 44.31** Example of an isometric exercise for the knees and legs.

**Figure 44.32** Woman in a yoga stretch.

**Figure 44.33** Men and women practicing t'ai chi outdoors in Leshan, China.

**Figure 44.34** Mandala in the floor of Chartres Cathedral, France.

**Figure 44.35** Plantar flexion contracture (foot drop).

**Figure 44.36** Leg veins.

**Figure 44.37** Pooling of secretions in the lungs of an immobile person.

**Figure 44.38** Pooling of urine in the kidney.

**Figure 44.39** Pooling of urine in the urinary bladder.

**Figure 44.40** A standing person with A, good trunk alignment; B, poor trunk alignment. The arrows indicate the direction in which the pelvis is tilted.

**Figure 44.41** The stance and swing phases of a normal gait.

**Figure 44.42** A, Balance is maintained when the line of gravity falls close to the base of support. B, Balance is precarious when the line of gravity falls at the edge of the base of support. C, Balance cannot be maintained when the line of gravity falls outside the base of support.

**Figure 44.43** EZ Lift is an electric client lift that functions to lift clients from bed, chair, toilet, and floor.

**Figure 44.44** The Slipp® Patient Mover is a client-moving device that reduces the nurse's exposure to back injuries and maximizes client comfort.

**Figure 44.45** Using the arm as a lever.

**Figure 44.46** Lifting heavy objects from the floor to waist level.

**Figure 44.47** Low Fowler's (semi-Fowler's) position (supported).

**Figure 44.48** Orthopneic position.

**Figure 44.49** Dorsal recumbent position (supported).

**Figure 44.50** Prone position (supported).

**Figure 44.51** Lateral position (supported).

**Figure 44.52** Sims' position (supported).

**Figure 44.53** A one-piece seat hydraulic lift.

**Figure 44.54** Supporting a limb above and below the joint for passive exercise.

**Figure 44.55** Holding limbs for support during passive exercise.

**Figure 44.56** Tensing the quadriceps femoris muscles before ambulation.

**Figure 44.57** A quad cane.

**Figure 44.58** Steps involved in using a cane to provide maximum support.

**Figure 44.59** Steps involved in using a cane when less than maximum support is required.

**Figure 44.60** A, standard walker. B, Two-wheeled walker.

**Figure 44.61** Types of crutches.

**Figure 44.62** The standing position for measuring the correct length for crutches.

**Figure 44.63** The tripod position.

**Figure 44.64** The four-point alternate crutch gait.

**Figure 44.65** The three-point crutch gait.

## LEARNING OUTCOME 1

Describe four basic elements of normal movement.

### CONCEPTS FOR LECTURE

1. Body movement requires coordinated muscle activity and neurologic integration. It involves four basic elements: body alignment (posture), joint mobility, balance, and coordinated movement.

2. Proper body alignment and posture bring body parts into position in a manner that promotes optimal balance and maximal body function whether the client is standing, sitting, or lying down. A person maintains balance as long as the line of gravity (an imaginary vertical line drawn through the body's center of gravity) passes through the center of gravity (the point at which all the body's mass is centered) and the base of support (the foundation on which the body rests).

3. Range of motion (ROM) of a joint is the maximum movement that is possible for that joint. ROM varies from individual to individual and is determined by genetic makeup, developmental patterns, the presence or absence of disease, and the amount of physical activity in which the person normally engages. (See Table 44–2.)

4. The mechanisms involved in maintaining balance and posture are complex and involve informational inputs from the labyrinth (inner ear), from vision (vestibulo-ocular input), and from stretch receptors of muscles and tendons (vestibulospinal input). Mechanisms of equilibrium respond, frequently without awareness. Proprioception is the term used to describe awareness of posture, movement, and changes in equilibrium and the knowledge of position, weight, and resistance of objects in relation to the body.

5. Balanced, smooth, purposeful movement is the result of proper functioning of the cerebral cortex, cerebellum, and basal ganglia. The cerebral cortex initiates voluntary movement; the cerebellum coordinates motor activity; and the basal ganglia maintain posture.

### POWERPOINT LECTURE SLIDES

*(NOTE: The number on each PPT Lecture Slide directly corresponds with the Concepts for Lecture.)*

**1** Four Basic Elements of Normal Movement
- Body alignment (posture)
- Joint mobility
- Balance
- Coordinated movement

**2** Body Alignment/Posture
- Brings body parts into position that promotes optimal balance and body function
- Person maintains balance as long as line of gravity passes through center of gravity and base of support

**3** Joint Mobility
- ROM is maximum movement possible for joint
- ROM varies and determined by
  - Genetic makeup
  - Developmental patterns
  - Presence or absence of disease
  - Physical activity

**4** Coordinated Movement
- Complex mechanisms
- Proprioception
  - Awareness of posture, movement, changes in equilibrium
  - Knowledge of position, weight, resistance of objects in relation to body

**5** Balance
- Smooth, purposeful movement
- Result of proper functioning of cerebral cortex, cerebellum, basal ganglia
  - Cerebral cortex initiates voluntary movement
  - Cerebellum coordinates motor activity
  - Basal ganglia maintains posture

# LEARNING OUTCOME 2

Differentiate isotonic, isometric, isokinetic, aerobic, and anaerobic exercise.

## CONCEPTS FOR LECTURE

1. Isotonic (dynamic) exercises are those in which the muscle shortens to produce muscle contraction and active movement. Isotonic exercises increase muscle tone, mass, and strength and maintain joint flexibility and circulation. During isotonic exercise, both heart rate and cardiac output quicken to increase blood flow to all parts of the body. Most physical conditioning exercises (e.g., running and walking) are isotonic ADLs and active ROMs.

2. Isometric (static or setting) exercises are those in which there is muscle contraction without moving the joint (muscle length does not change). These exercises involve exerting pressure against a solid object. Isometric exercises produce a mild increase in heart rate and cardiac output but no apparent increase in blood flow to other parts of the body. Isometric exercises are useful for strengthening abdominal, gluteal, and quadriceps muscles used for walking; strengthening muscles immobilized in casts or by traction; and for endurance training.

3. Isokinetic (resistive) exercises involve muscle contraction or tension against resistance. Thus, they can be either isotonic or isometric. During isokinetic exercises, the person moves (isotonic) or tenses (isometric) against resistance. An increase in blood pressure and blood flow to muscles occurs with resistance training. Isokinetic exercises are done for physical conditioning and to build up certain muscle groups.

4. Aerobic exercise is activity during which the amount of oxygen taken in the body is greater than that used to perform the activity. Aerobic exercises improve cardiovascular conditioning and physical fitness.

5. Anaerobic exercise involves activity in which the muscles cannot draw enough oxygen from the bloodstream, and anaerobic pathways are used to provide additional energy for a short time. This type of exercise is used in endurance training for athletes, such as weight lifting and sprinting.

## POWERPOINT LECTURE SLIDES

*(NOTE: The number on each PPT Lecture Slide directly corresponds with the Concepts for Lecture.)*

**1** Isotonic (Dynamic) Exercise
- Muscle shortens to produce muscle contraction and active movement
- Increase muscle tone, mass, and strength
- Maintain joint flexibility and circulation
- Heart rate and cardiac output increase

**2** Isometric (Static or Setting) Exercise
- Muscle contraction without moving the joint (muscle length does not change)
- Involve exerting pressure against a solid object
- Produce a mild increase in heart rate and cardiac output
- No apparent increase in blood flow to other parts of the body

**3** Isokinetic (Resistive) Exercise
- Muscle contraction or tension against resistance
- Can either be isotonic or isometric
- Person moves (isotonic) or tenses (isometric) against resistance
- An increase in blood pressure and blood flow to muscles occurs

**4** Aerobic Exercise
- Amount of oxygen taken in the body is greater than that used to perform the activity
- Improve cardiovascular conditioning and physical fitness

**5** Anaerobic
- Muscles cannot draw enough oxygen from the bloodstream
- Anaerobic pathways are used to provide additional energy for a short time
- Used in endurance training for athletes

## LEARNING OUTCOME 3

Compare the effects of exercise and immobility on body systems.

### CONCEPTS FOR LECTURE

1. The effects of exercise on the musculoskeletal system include maintenance of the size, shape, tone, and strength of muscles (including the heart muscle). Since joints lack a discrete blood supply, it is through activity that joints receive nourishment. Exercise also increases joint flexibility, stability, and ROM. Bone density and strength is maintained through weight bearing. The effects of immobility include disuse osteoporosis, disuse atrophy, contractures, and stiffness and pain in the joints.

2. The effects of adequate moderate-intensity exercise on the cardiovascular system include increases in the heart rate, the strength of the heart muscle contraction, and the blood supply to the heart and muscles through increased cardiac output. Exercise also promotes heart health by mediating the harmful effects of stress. The effects of immobility include diminished cardiac reserve, increased use of the Valsalva maneuver, orthostatic (postural) hypotension, venous vasodilation and stasis, dependent edema, and thrombus formation.

3. The effects of exercise on the respiratory system include an increase in ventilation and oxygen intake during exercise, thereby improving gas exchange. Adequate exercise also prevents pooling of secretions in the bronchi and bronchioles, decreasing the breathing effort and the risk of infection. Exercising the muscles of respiration (deep breathing) throughout activity as well as rest enhances oxygenation improving stamina and circulation of lymph improving immune function. The effects of immobility include decreased respiratory movement, pooling of respiratory secretions, atelectasis, and hypostatic pneumonia.

4. The effects of exercise on the metabolic/endocrine system include elevation of the metabolic rate, thus increasing the production of body heat and waste products and calorie use. Exercise increases use of triglycerides and fatty acids, resulting in a decreased level of triglycerides and cholesterol. Weight loss and exercise stabilize blood sugar and make cells more responsive to insulin. The effects of immobility include decreased metabolic rate, negative nitrogen balance, anorexia, and negative calcium balance.

### POWERPOINT LECTURE SLIDES

*(NOTE: The number on each PPT Lecture Slide directly corresponds with the Concepts for Lecture.)*

1 Effect on the Musculoskeletal System
 • Exercise
  ○ Maintain size, shape, tone, and strength of muscles (including the heart muscle)
  ○ Nourish joints
  ○ Increase joint flexibility, stability, and ROM
  ○ Maintain bone density and strength
 • Immobility
  ○ Disuse osteoporosis
  ○ Disuse atrophy
  ○ Contractures
  ○ Stiffness and pain in the joints

2 Effect on the Cardiovascular System
 • Exercise
  ○ Increases heart rate, strength of contraction, and blood supply to the heart and muscles
  ○ Mediates the harmful effects of stress
 • Immobility
  ○ Diminished cardiac reserve
  ○ Increased use of the Valsalva maneuver
  ○ Orthostatic (postural) hypotension
  ○ Venous vasodilation and stasis
  ○ Dependent edema
  ○ Thrombus formation

3 Effect on the Respiratory System
 • Exercise
  ○ Increase ventilation and oxygen intake improving gas exchange
  ○ Prevents pooling of secretions in the bronchi and bronchioles
 • Immobility
  ○ Decreased respiratory movement
  ○ Pooling of respiratory secretions
  ○ Atelectasis
  ○ Hypostatic pneumonia

4 Effect on the Metabolic/Endocrine System
 • Exercise
  ○ Elevates the metabolic rate, thus increasing the production of body heat and waste products and calorie use

5. The effects of exercise on the gastrointestinal system include improved appetite and increased gastrointestinal tract tone, facilitating peristalsis. The effects of immobility include constipation.

6. The effects of exercise on the urinary system include promotion of blood flow to the kidneys, causing body wastes to be excreted more effectively. In addition, stasis (stagnation) of urine in the bladder is usually prevented. The effects of immobility include urinary stasis, renal calculi, urinary retention, and urinary infection.

7. The effects of exercise on the immune system include more efficient pumping of lymph fluid from tissues into lymph capillaries and vessels throughout the body and increased circulation through lymph nodes where destruction of pathogens and removal of foreign antigens can occur. Although moderate exercise seems to enhance immunity, strenuous exercise may reduce immune function, leaving a window of opportunity for infection during the recovery phase.

8. According to a strong and growing body of evidence, the effects of exercise on the psychoneurologic system include elevating mood and relieving stress and anxiety across the life span. Regular exercise also improves quality of sleep for most individuals. The effects of immobility include a decline in mood-elevating substances. In addition, perception of time intervals deteriorates, problem-solving and decision-making abilities may deteriorate, and loss of control over events can cause anxiety.

9. Current research supports the positive effects of exercise on cognitive functioning, in particular decision-making and problem-solving processes, planning, and paying attention. Physical exertion induces cells in the brain to strengthen and build neuronal connections.

10. There is evidence that a program of Pilates, yoga-style exercise, slow walking a labyrinth (circular mandala) improves spiritual health and alters heart, blood pressure, and respiratory rates.

  The effects of immobility on the integumentary system include reduced skin turgor and skin breakdown.

- ○ Decrease serum triglycerides and cholesterol
- ○ Stabilize blood sugar and make cells more responsive to insulin
- Immobility
  - ○ Decreased metabolic rate
  - ○ Negative nitrogen balance
  - ○ Anorexia
  - ○ Negative calcium balance

**5** Effect on the Gastrointestinal System
- Exercise
  - ○ Improves the appetite
  - ○ Increases gastrointestinal tract tone
  - ○ Facilitates peristalsis
- Immobility
  - ○ Constipation

**6** Effect on the Urinary System
- Exercise
  - ○ Promotes blood flow to the kidneys causing body wastes to be excreted more effectively
  - ○ Prevents stasis (stagnation) of urine in the bladder
- Immobility
  - ○ Urinary stasis
  - ○ Renal calculi
  - ○ Urinary retention
  - ○ Urinary infection

**7** Effect on the Immune System
- Exercise
  - ○ Pumps lymph fluid from tissues into lymph capillaries and vessels throughout the body
  - ○ Increases circulation through lymph nodes where destruction of pathogens and removal of foreign antigens can occur
  - ○ Strenuous exercise may reduce immune function, leaving a window of opportunity for infection during recovery phase

**8** Effect on the Psychoneurologic System
- Exercise
  - ○ Elevates mood and relieving stress and anxiety across the lifespan
  - ○ Improves quality of sleep for most individuals
- Immobility
  - ○ Decline in mood elevating substances
  - ○ Perception of time intervals deteriorates
  - ○ Problem-solving and decision-making abilities may deteriorate
  - ○ Loss of control over events can cause anxiety

**9** Effect on Cognitive Function
- Exercise
  - ○ Positive effects on decision-making and problem-solving processes, planning, and paying attention
  - ○ Induces cells in the brain to strengthen and build neuronal connections

10 Other Effects of Exercise and Immobility
- Evidence that certain types of exercise increase spiritual health
- Immobility causes reduced skin turgor and skin breakdown

---

| SUGGESTIONS FOR CLASSROOM ACTIVITIES | SUGGESTIONS FOR CLINICAL ACTIVITIES |
|---|---|
| • Divide the students into groups and assign each a body system. Have each group develop a pamphlet for adult clients and families, presenting the effect of exercise and the negative effect of immobility on each system. Reproduce and share with the class. | • Have the students assess their clients for the effects of immobility. Share the results in postconference. |

---

# LEARNING OUTCOME 4

Identify factors influencing a person's body alignment and activity.

## CONCEPTS FOR LECTURE

1. A number of factors affect an individual's body alignment, mobility, and daily activity level. These include growth and development, nutrition, personal values and attitudes, certain external factors (such as temperature, humidity, availability of recreational facilities, and safety of the neighborhood), and prescribed limitations (such as casts, braces, traction, and activity restrictions including bed rest).

## POWERPOINT LECTURE SLIDES

*(NOTE: The number on each PPT Lecture Slide directly corresponds with the Concepts for Lecture.)*

1 Factors Affecting Body Alignment, Mobility, and Daily Activity Level
- Growth and development
- Nutrition, personal values, and attitudes
- External factors (such as temperature, humidity, availability of recreational facilities and safety of the neighborhood)
- Prescribed limitations (such as casts, braces, traction, activity restrictions including bed rest)

---

| SUGGESTIONS FOR CLASSROOM ACTIVITIES | SUGGESTIONS FOR CLINICAL ACTIVITIES |
|---|---|
| • Have the students provide examples of how nurses can help individuals adapt to or change factors influencing body alignment and activity.<br>• Show pictures of clients from various age groups and have the students identify body alignment characteristics of each age group. | • Invite a dietitian from the agency to discuss dietary guidelines to support optimal activity and modifications that may need to be made for hospitalized clients. |

---

# LEARNING OUTCOME 5

Assess activity-exercise pattern, alignment, mobility capabilities and limitations, activity tolerance, and potential problems related to immobility.

## CONCEPTS FOR LECTURE

1. Assessment relative to a client's activity and exercise should be routinely addressed. It should include a nursing history and a physical examination of body alignment, gait, appearance and movement of joints, capabilities and limitations for movement, muscle mass and strength, activity tolerance, problems related to immobility, and physical fitness.

## POWERPOINT LECTURE SLIDES

*(NOTE: The number on each PPT Lecture Slide directly corresponds with the Concepts for Lecture.)*

1 Assessment of Activity and Exercise
- Nursing history
- Physical examination of the following:
  ○ Body alignment
  ○ Gait

---

The Assessment Interview: Activity and Exercise lists examples of questions to elicit this information. If the client indicates a recent pattern of change, a more detailed history should include the specific nature of the problem, when it first began and its frequency, its causes if known, how the problem affects daily living, what the client is doing to cope with the problem, and whether these methods have been successful.

Table 44–3: Assessing Problems of Immobility lists assessment activities to identify problems of immobility.

- ○ Appearance and movement of joints
- ○ Capabilities and limitations for movement
- ○ Muscle mass and strength
- ○ Activity tolerance
- ○ Problems related to immobility

---

## SUGGESTIONS FOR CLASSROOM ACTIVITIES

- Have each student use the Assessment Interview to assess another student's activity and exercise patterns.
- Show a videotape of assessment of the musculoskeletal system.
- Demonstrate how to assess body alignment, gait, ROM, muscle mass, strength, and activity tolerance. Have the students practice this assessment.

## SUGGESTIONS FOR CLINICAL ACTIVITIES

- Assign students to assess their assigned clients' activity and exercise. Have them use Table 44–3 in the textbook to assess for problems of immobility.

---

# LEARNING OUTCOME 6

Develop nursing diagnoses and outcomes related to activity, exercise, and mobility problems.

## CONCEPTS FOR LECTURE

1. Mobility problems may be appropriate as the diagnostic label or as the etiology for other nursing diagnoses.

    NANDA includes the following nursing diagnostic labels for activity and exercise problems: *Activity Intolerance, Risk for Activity Intolerance, Impaired Physical Mobility, Sedentary Lifestyle,* and *Risk for Disuse Syndrome.*

2. NANDA diagnoses in which the mobility problem becomes the etiology include *Fear* (of falling), *Ineffective Coping, Low Self-Esteem, Powerlessness, Risk for Falls,* and *Self-Care Deficit.*

3. When problems associated with prolonged immobility arise, many other diagnoses may be necessary. Examples include, but are not limited to, the following: *Ineffective Airway Clearance, Risk for Infection, Risk for Injury, Risk for Disturbed Sleep Pattern,* and *Risk for Situational Low Self-Esteem.*

4. When planning for desired outcomes, NOC labels that pertain to exercise and activity can be helpful. These include the following: activity tolerance; anxiety level and self-control; body image; body positioning; bowel elimination; caregiver physical health; coordinated movement; depression self-control; diabetes self-management; endurance; fall prevention behavior; immobility consequences, both physiological and psycho-cognitive; joint movement; mobility;

## POWERPOINT LECTURE SLIDES

*(NOTE: The number on each PPT Lecture Slide directly corresponds with the Concepts for Lecture.)*

**1** Nursing Diagnoses for Activity and Exercise Problems
- Activity intolerance
- Risk for activity intolerance
- Impaired physical mobility
- Sedentary lifestyle
- Risk for disuse syndrome

**2** NANDA Diagnoses: Mobility Problem Becomes the Etiology
- Fear (of falling)
- Ineffective coping
- Low self-esteem
- Powerlessness
- Risk for falls
- Self-care deficit

**3** Prolonged Immobility
- Ineffective airway clearance
- Risk for infection
- Risk for injury
- Risk for disturbed sleep pattern
- Risk for situational low self-esteem

**4** Examples of Desired Outcomes (NOC labels)
- Activity tolerance
- Body positioning

mood equilibrium; personal well-being; physical fitness; play participation; quality of life; respiratory status; ventilation and gas exchange; role performance; self-care; sleep; stress level; and weight control.

5. The goals established will vary according to the diagnosis and defining characteristics related to each individual. Examples of overall goals for clients with actual or potential problems related to mobility or activity include increased tolerance for physical activity; restored or improved capability to ambulate and/or participate in ADLs; absence of injury from falling or improper use of body mechanics; enhanced physical fitness; absence of any complications associated with immobility; and improved social, emotional, and intellectual well-being.

- Bowel elimination
- Fall prevention behavior
- Immobility consequences both physiological and psycho-cognitive
- Joint movement
- Mobility
- Respiratory status
- Ventilation and gas exchange
- Self-care
- Sleep
- Stress level
- Weight control

**5** Overall Goals for Problems Related to Mobility or Activity
- Increased tolerance for physical activity
- Restored or improved capability to ambulate and/or participate in ADLs
- Absence of injury from falling or improper use of body mechanics
- Enhanced physical fitness
- Absence of any complications associated with immobility
- Improved social, emotional, and intellectual well-being

---

### SUGGESTIONS FOR CLASSROOM ACTIVITIES

- Have the students review the definitions, defining characteristics, etiology, or risk factors for the NANDA diagnoses related to activity and mobility.
- Provide the students with a case study. Ask them to identify nursing diagnoses and the data that support these diagnoses.

### SUGGESTIONS FOR CLINICAL ACTIVITIES

- Have the students develop a care plan for their assigned clients related to exercise and mobility, if appropriate. Share these with the class.

---

## LEARNING OUTCOME 7

Use safe practices when positioning, moving, lifting, and ambulating clients.

### CONCEPTS FOR LECTURE

1. When a nurse assists a person to move, correct body mechanics need to be employed so that the nurse is not injured.

   Correct body alignment for the client must also be maintained so that undue stress is not placed on the musculoskeletal system.

2. Actions and rationales applicable to moving and lifting clients include the following:
   - Before moving a client, assess the degree of exertion permitted, the client's physical abilities (e.g., muscle strength, presence of paralysis) and ability to assist with the move, ability to understand instructions, degree of comfort or discomfort when moving, client's weight, presence of orthostatic

### POWERPOINT LECTURE SLIDES

*(NOTE: The number on each PPT Lecture Slide directly corresponds with the Concepts for Lecture.)*

**1** Safe Practice for Positioning, Moving, Lifting, Ambulating Clients
- Correct body mechanics required for nurse to prevent injury
- Correct body alignment for the client also so that undue stress is not placed on the musculoskeletal system

**2** General Guidelines for Moving and Lifting:
- Before moving, assess
- If indicated, use pain relief modalities
- Prepare any needed assistive devices

hypotension (particularly important when client will be standing), and your own strength and ability to move the client.

- If indicated, use pain relief modalities or medication prior to moving the client.
- Prepare any needed assistive devices and supportive equipment (e.g., pillows, trochanter roll).
- Plan around encumbrances to movement such as an IV or heavy cast.
- Be alert to the effects of any medications the client takes that may impair alertness, balance, strength, or mobility.
- Obtain required assistance from other persons.
- Explain the procedure to the client and listen to any suggestions the client or support people have.
- Provide privacy.
- Perform hand hygiene.
- Raise the height of the bed to bring the client close to your center of gravity.
- Lock the wheels on the bed, and raise the rail on the side of the bed opposite you to ensure client safety.

3. Refer to the textbook and the Skill Checklists included on the Student DVD-ROM:
   - Skill 44.1: Moving a Client Up in Bed
   - Skill 44.2: Turning a Client to the Lateral or Prone Position in Bed
   - Skill 44.3: Logrolling a Client
   - Skill 44.4: Assisting the Client to Sit on the Side of the Bed (Dangling)

4. General guidelines for transferring client include: plan what to do and how to do it; obtain essential equipment before starting; remove obstacles; explain the transfer to the client and nursing personnel who are assisting; always support or hold the client rather than the equipment; during the transfer explain step-by-step what the client should do; and make a written plan including the client's tolerance. Refer to the textbook and the Skill Checklists on the Student DVD-ROM.
   - Skill 44.5: Transferring Between Bed and Chair
   - Skill 44.6: Transferring Between Bed and Stretcher

5. General guidelines for ambulating the client include: assess the amount of assistance the client will require; assess for signs and symptoms of postural (orthostatic) hypotension and return the client to the supine position if necessary; prepare the client for ambulation; ensure client safety by appropriately assisting the client to ambulate, applying a transfer or walking belt, physically supporting the client, obtaining assistance of other nursing personnel to follow with a wheelchair or to assist with physical support, and teaching the client to correctly use mechanical aids for walking. Refer to the textbook and the Skill Checklists included in the Student DVD-ROM:
   - Skill 44.7: Assisting the Client to Ambulate

- Plan around encumbrances
- Be alert to the effects of any medications
- Obtain required assistance
- Explain the procedure to the client

**3** Skills
- Skill 44.1: Moving a Client Up in Bed
- Skill 44.2: Turning a Client to the Lateral or Prone Position in Bed
- Skill 44.3: Logrolling a Client
- Skill 44.4: Assisting the Client to Sit on the Side of the Bed (Dangling)

**4** General Guidelines for Transferring a Client
- Plan what to do and how to do it
- Obtain essential equipment before starting
- Remove obstacles
- Explain the transfer to the client and nursing personnel who are assisting
- Support or hold the client rather than the equipment
- Explain step-by-step what the client should do
- Make a written plan including the client's tolerance
- Skill 44.5: Transferring Between Bed and Chair
- Skill 44.6: Transferring Between Bed and Stretcher

**5** General Guidelines for Ambulating
- Assess the amount of assistance the client will require
- Assess for signs and symptoms of postural (orthostatic) hypotension and take appropriate action
- Prepare the client for ambulation
- Appropriately assist the client to ambulate
- Apply a transfer or walking belt
- Physically support the client
- Obtain assistance of other nursing personnel to follow with a wheelchair or to assist with physical support
- Teach the client to correctly use mechanical aids for walking
- Skill 44.7: Assisting the Client to Ambulate

## SUGGESTIONS FOR CLASSROOM ACTIVITIES

- Using manikins or fellow students, have the students practice all of the above skills in the nursing laboratory.
- Have the students practice positioning the manikins in the above positions with special emphasis on preventing pressure points and maintaining body alignment.
- Have students practice assisting a falling or fainting client.

## SUGGESTIONS FOR CLINICAL ACTIVITIES

- Arrange for the students to attend physical therapy sessions. Ask the physical therapists to demonstrate proper use of crutches, walkers, and canes.
- Demonstrate the assistive devices available in the institution for relieving pressure and maintaining body alignment (e.g., foot splints, hand splints).

# CHAPTER 45
## SLEEP

## LEARNING OUTCOME 1

Explain the functions and the physiology of sleep.

### CONCEPTS FOR LECTURE

1. Sleep is an altered state of consciousness in which the individual's perception of and reaction to the environment are decreased.

    The cyclic nature of sleep is thought to be controlled by centers located in the lower part of the brain. Neurons within the reticular formation, located in the brain stem, integrate sensory information from the peripheral nervous system and relay the information to the cerebral cortex. The upper part of the reticular formation, called the reticular activating system (RAS), is involved with the sleep–wake cycle. An intact cerebral cortex and reticular formation are necessary for the regulation of sleep and waking states.

2. Neurotransmitters affect the sleep–wake cycle. Serotonin is thought to lessen the response to sensory stimulation and gamma-aminobutyric acid (GABA) to shut off the activity in the neurons of the RAS. Acetylcholine, released in the reticular formation, dopamine, in the midbrain, and noradrenalin, in the pons, are associated with cerebral cortical arousal.

3. Another key factor to sleep is exposure to darkness. Darkness and preparing for sleep causes a decrease in the stimulation of the RAS. The pineal gland begins to actively secrete the hormone melatonin and the person feels less alert. During sleep the growth hormone is secreted and cortisol is inhibited.

4. Sleep is a complex biological rhythm. When a person's biological clock coincides with the sleep–wake cycle, the person is said to be in circadian synchronization—the person is awake when the body temperature is

### POWERPOINT LECTURE SLIDES

*(NOTE: The number on each PPT Lecture Slide directly corresponds with the Concepts for Lecture.)*

**1** Physiology of Sleep
- Sleep is an altered state of consciousness where perception of and reaction to environment are decreased
- Cyclic nature of sleep thought to be controlled by lower part of brain
  - Neurons in reticular formation (brain stem) integrate sensory information from PNS and relay it to cerebral cortex
- Reticular Activating System (RAS) involved with sleep–wake cycle
  - Intact cerebral cortex and reticular formation necessary for sleep–wake regulation

**2** Neurotransmitters
- Affect sleep–wake cycle
- Serotonin
  - Thought to lessen response to sensory stimulation
- Gamma-aminobuytyeric acid (GABA)
  - Thought to shut off activity in neurons of RAS
  - Acetylcholine, dopamine, noradrenalin associated with cerebral cortical arousal

**3** Exposure to Darkness
- Darkness and preparing for sleep cause decrease in stimulation of RAS

highest and asleep when the body temperature is lowest. Circadian rhythm regularly begins to develop by the sixth week of life and by 3 to 6 months most infants have a regular sleep–wake cycle.

5. The effects of sleep are not completely known. Sleep exerts physiologic effects on both the nervous system and other body structures. Sleep in some way restores normal levels of activity and normal balance among parts of the nervous system. Sleep is necessary for protein synthesis. The role of sleep in psychological well-being is best noticed by the deterioration in mental functioning related to sleep loss. With inadequate amounts of sleep, people tend to become emotionally irritable, have poor concentration, and experience difficulty making decisions.

- Pineal gland begins to secrete melatonin and person feels less alert
- During sleep GH secreted and cortisol inhibited

**4** Circadian Rhythm
- Circadian synchronization when biological clock coincides with sleep–wake cycle
  ○ Person awake when body temp highest and asleep when body temp lowest
- Begins to develop by 6 weeks of age
- By 3–6 months of age have regular sleep–wake cycle

**5** Functions of Sleep
- Restores normal levels of activity and normal balance among parts of the nervous system
- Necessary for protein synthesis
- Psychological well-being

---

## SUGGESTIONS FOR CLASSROOM ACTIVITIES

- Review the anatomical structures and neurotransmitters involved in the physiology of sleep.

---

## LEARNING OUTCOME 2

Identify the characteristics of the sleep states: NREM and REM sleep.

### CONCEPTS FOR LECTURE

1. Sleep architecture refers to the basic organization of normal sleep. There are two types of sleep: NREM (non-rapid-eye movement) and REM (rapid-eye movement). During sleep, NREM and REM sleep alternate in cycles.

2. NREM sleep occurs when activity in the RAS is inhibited. It constitutes about 75% to 80% of sleep and consists of four stages.

3. Stage I is the stage of very light sleep and lasts only a few minutes. The person feels drowsy and relaxed, eyes roll from side to side, and the heart and respiratory rates drop slightly. The sleeper can be readily awakened and may deny having been sleeping.

4. Stage II is the stage of light sleep during which the body processes continue to slow down. The eyes are generally still, the heart and respiratory rates decrease slightly, and the body temperature falls. This stage lasts only about 10 to 15 minutes but constitutes 44% to 55% of total sleep. More intense stimuli is required to awaken the person.

5. Stages III and IV are the deepest stages of sleep, differing only in the percentage of delta waves recorded during a 30-second period. During delta sleep or deep sleep, the sleeper's heart and respiratory rates drop 20% to 30% below those exhibited during waking hours. The sleeper is difficult to arouse and is not disturbed by sensory stimuli. Skeletal muscles are very

### POWERPOINT LECTURE SLIDES

*(NOTE: The number on each PPT Lecture Slide directly corresponds with the Concepts for Lecture.)*

**1** Sleep Architecture
- Refers to basic organization of sleep
- Two types that alternate in cycles during sleep
  ○ NREM
  ○ REM

**2** NREM Sleep
- Occurs when activity in RAS inhibited
- Constitutes 75%–80% of sleep
- Consists of four stages

**3** NREM Sleep: Stage I
- Very light sleep and lasts only a few minutes
- Feel drowsy and relaxed
- Eyes roll from side to side
- Heart and respiratory rates drop slightly
- Can be readily awakened and may deny sleeping

**4** NREM Sleep: Stage II
- Light sleep lasts only about 10 to 15 minutes
- Body processes continue to slow down
- Eyes are generally still
- Heart and respiratory rates decrease slightly
- Body temperature falls
- 44% to 55% of total sleep
- Requires more intense stimuli to awaken

relaxed, reflexes are diminished, and snoring is most likely to occur. Even swallowing and saliva production are reduced. These stages are essential for restoring energy and releasing important growth hormones.

6. Physiologic changes that occur in NREM sleep include: arterial blood pressure falls; pulse rate decreases; peripheral blood vessels dilate; cardiac output decreases; skeletal muscles relax; basal metabolism rate decreases 10–30%; growth hormone levels peak; and intracranial pressure decreases. (See Box 45-1.)

7. REM sleep usually occurs every 90 minutes and lasts 5 to 10 minutes. Most dreams take place during REM sleep. The brain is highly active, and brain metabolism may increase as much as 20%. Acetylcholine and dopamine are released. Distinctive eye movements occur, voluntary muscle tone is dramatically decreased, and deep tendon reflexes are absent. The sleeper may be difficult to arouse or may wake spontaneously, gastric secretions increase, and heart and respiratory rates often are irregular. It is thought that the regions of the brain that are used in learning, thinking, and organizing information are stimulated during REM sleep.

5. NREM Sleep: Stages III and IV
   - Deepest stages of sleep (delta sleep or deep sleep)
   - Heart and respiratory rates drop 20% to 30% below waking hours
   - Difficult to arouse
   - Not disturbed by sensory stimuli
   - Skeletal muscles very relaxed
   - Reflexes are diminished
   - Snoring is most likely to occur
   - Swallowing and saliva production reduced
   - Essential for restoring energy and releasing important growth hormones

6. Physiologic Changes in NREM Sleep
   - Arterial blood pressure falls
   - Pulse rate decreases
   - Peripheral blood vessels dilate
   - Cardiac output decreases
   - Skeletal muscles relax
   - Basal metabolism rate decreases 10%–30%
   - Growth hormone levels peak
   - Intracranial pressure decreases

7. Characteristics of REM Sleep
   - Occurs every 90 minute
   - Lasts 5 to 10 minutes
   - Acetylcholine and dopamine increased
   - Most dreams take place
   - Brain is highly active
   - Brain metabolism increases as much as 20%
   - Distinctive eye movements occur
   - Voluntary muscle tone dramatically decreased
   - Deep tendon reflexes absent
   - May be difficult to arouse or may wake spontaneously
   - Gastric secretions increase
   - Heart and respiratory rates often are irregular
   - Regions of brain associated with learning, thinking, organizing information stimulated

---

**SUGGESTIONS FOR CLASSROOM ACTIVITIES**

- Invite practitioners from a sleep clinic to discuss the stages and functions of sleep.

---

# LEARNING OUTCOME 3

Describe variations in sleep patterns throughout the life span.

**CONCEPTS FOR LECTURE**

1. Newborns sleep 16 to 18 hours a day, on an irregular schedule with periods of 1 to 3 hours spent awake. They enter REM sleep immediately and spend nearly 50% of their time in each of NREM and REM sleep states. The sleep cycle is about 50 minutes.

**POWERPOINT LECTURE SLIDES**

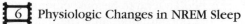

*(NOTE: The number on each PPT Lecture Slide directly corresponds with the Concepts for Lecture.)*

1. Sleep Patterns: Newborns
   - Sleep 16 to 18 hours a day on irregular schedule
   - Periods of 1 to 3 hours spent awake

2.  At first, infants awaken every 3 to 4 hours, eat, and then go back to sleep. Periods of wakefulness gradually increase during the first months. By 6 months, most infants sleep through the night and begin to establish a pattern of daytime naps. At the end of the first year, an infant usually takes two naps per day and should get about 14 to 15 hours of sleep in 24 hours. About half of the infant's sleep time is spent in light sleep.

3.  Toddlers (1 to 3 years of age) require 12 to 14 hours of sleep. Most still need an afternoon nap but the need for midmorning naps gradually decreases. Nighttime fears and nightmares are also common.

4.  The preschool child (3 to 5 years of age) requires 11 to 13 hours of sleep per night, particularly if the child is in preschool. Sleep needs fluctuate in relation to activity and growth spurts. The school-age child (5 to 12 years of age) needs 10 to 11 hours of sleep, but most receive less because of increasing demands.

5.  Adolescents (12 to 18 years of age) require 9 to 10 hours of sleep each night; however, few actually get that much sleep. As children reach adolescence, their circadian rhythms tend to shift. The natural tendency for teenagers is to stay up late at night and wake up later in the morning.

6.  Most healthy adults need 7 to 9 hours of sleep; however, there is individual variation. Some adults may be able to function well with 6 hours of sleep, and others may need 10 hours to function optimally.

7.  A hallmark change with age is a tendency toward earlier bedtime and wake times. Older adults (65 to 75 years) usually awaken 1.3 hours earlier and go to bed approximately 1 hour earlier than younger adults (20 to 30 years). They may show an increase in disturbed sleep that can create a negative impact on their quality of life, mood, and alertness. Although the ability to sleep becomes more difficult, the need to sleep does not decrease with age.

*   Enter REM sleep immediately
*   50% NREM and 50% REM
*   Sleep cycle ~ 50 minutes

**2** Sleep Patterns: Infants
*   Infants awaken every 3 to 4 hours, eat, and then go back to sleep
*   Periods of wakefulness gradually increase
*   By 6 months, most infants sleep through the night
*   Establish a pattern of daytime naps

**3** Sleep Patterns: Toddlers
*   Twelve to 14 hours are recommended
*   Most still need an afternoon nap
*   Nighttime fears and nightmares are also common

**4** Sleep Patterns: Preschool and School-age
*   Preschool child (3–5 years) requires 11 to 13 hours of sleep
    *   Sleep needs fluctuate in relation to activity and growth spurts
*   School-age child (aged 5 to 12) needs 10–11 hours of sleep
    *   Most receive less

**5** Sleep Patterns: Adolescents
*   Require 9–10 hours of sleep each night
*   Few actually get that much sleep
*   Circadian rhythms tend to shift
    *   Tendency to stay up later and wake later

**6** Sleep Patterns: Adults
*   Most healthy adults need 7–9 hours of sleep
*   Individual variations

**7** Sleep Patterns: Elders
*   Tendency toward earlier bedtime and wake times
*   May show an increase in disturbed sleep
*   Need to sleep does not decrease with age

---

**SUGGESTIONS FOR CLASSROOM ACTIVITIES**

*   Have the students interview parents of young children to determine sleep patterns of their children. Compare findings in class.

**SUGGESTIONS FOR CLINICAL ACTIVITIES**

*   Have the students interview assigned clients to determine their usual sleep patterns and how these patterns have changed due to health alterations or hospitalization. Compare and contrast findings.

---

# LEARNING OUTCOME 4

Identify factors that affect normal sleep.

---

**CONCEPTS FOR LECTURE**

1.  Factors that affect normal sleep include illness, environment, lifestyle, emotional stress, stimulants and alcohol, diet, smoking, motivation, and medications.

**POWERPOINT LECTURE SLIDES**

*(NOTE: The number on each PPT Lecture Slide directly corresponds with the Concepts for Lecture.)*

**1** Factors the Affect Sleep
*   Illness
*   Environment

Illness that causes pain or physical distress can result in sleep problems. People who are ill require more sleep than normal and the normal rhythm of sleep and wakefulness are often disturbed.

Any change in environment can inhibit sleep. In addition, noise, room temperature, size and comfort of the bed, snoring of partner, for example, may alter sleep.

Lifestyle factors such as irregular schedules, time of day when a person exercises, and stress may alter sleep.

Emotional stress is the number one cause of short-term sleeping difficulty due to inability to relax sufficiently. The amount of norepinephrine is increased leading to less deep sleep and REM sleep and more stage changes and awakening.

Stimulants such as caffeine-containing stimulate the CNS and may inhibit sleep. Alcohol disrupts REM sleep but hastens the onset of sleep.

Weight gain is associated with decreased total sleep time as well as broken sleep and earlier awakening. Weight loss is associated with increased total sleep time and less broken sleep. L-tryptopan, found in cheese and milk, may induce sleep.

Nicotine is a stimulant and smokers have more difficulty falling asleep and are easily aroused.

Motivation can increase alertness but not sufficiently to overcome circadian rhythm and also cannot overcome sleepiness associated with insufficient sleep.

Some medications affect quality of sleep. See Boxes 45–2 and 45–3.

- Lifestyle
- Emotional stress
- Stimulants and alcohol
- Diet
- Smoking
- Motivation
- Medications

---

## SUGGESTIONS FOR CLASSROOM ACTIVITIES

- Invite several nurses who work the night shift to discuss how they have adapted their sleep–wake patterns. Also have the nurses discuss the sleep patterns of hospitalized clients.
- Divide the students into groups. Assign each group a factor that influences sleep. Have each group investigate research on this factor and present findings to the class.

## SUGGESTIONS FOR CLINICAL ACTIVITIES

- Have the students interview assigned clients to determine factors that have altered their sleep (e.g., illness, environment, change in lifestyle, medications). Compare and contrast findings.

---

# LEARNING OUTCOME 5

Describe common sleep disorders.

## CONCEPTS FOR LECTURE

1. Common sleep disorders include insomnia, excessive daytime sleepiness (hypersomnia and narcolepsy), sleep apnea, insufficient sleep, and parasomnias.
2. Insomnia is described as difficulty falling asleep or remaining asleep. Manifestations include: difficulty falling asleep, waking up frequently during the night,

## POWERPOINT LECTURE SLIDES

*(NOTE: The number on each PPT Lecture Slide directly corresponds with the Concepts for Lecture.)*

 Common Sleep Disorders
- Insomnia
- Excessive daytime sleepiness
- Parasomnias

difficulty returning to sleep, waking up too early in the morning, unrefreshing sleep, daytime sleepiness, difficulty concentrating, and irritability. Insomnia is the most common sleep complaint in America. It may be acute or chronic. Main risk factors are older age and female gender. Incidence increases with age, but it may be caused by some other medical condition. Women experience sleep loss in connection with hormonal changes (menstruation, pregnancy, and menopause).

3. Excessive daytime sleepiness is a result of hypersomnia, narcolepsy, sleep apnea, and insufficient sleep.

4. Hypersomnia refers to conditions where the affected individual obtains sufficient sleep at night but still cannot stay awake during the day and may be caused by medical or psychological disorders.

5. Narcolepsy is a disorder of excessive daytime sleepiness caused by the lack of the chemical hypocretin in the area of the central nervous system that regulates sleep. Clients have sleep attacks or excessive daytime sleepiness, and their sleep at night usually begins with a sleep-onset REM period.

6. Sleep apnea is characterized by frequent short breathing pauses during the night. More than five apneic episodes or five breathing pauses longer than 10 seconds per hour is considered abnormal. Symptoms include loud snoring, frequent nocturnal awakenings, excessive daytime sleepiness, difficulties falling asleep at night, morning headaches, memory and cognitive problems, and irritability. Although sleep apnea is most often diagnosed in men and postmenopausal women, it may also occur in children. Three common types are obstructive, central, and mixed apnea.

7. A parasomnia is behavior that may interfere with sleep or occur during sleep. The *International Classification of Sleep Disorders* (American Sleep Disorders Association, 2005) subdivides parasomnias into arousal disorders (e.g., sleepwalking, sleep terrors), sleep wake transition disorders (e.g., sleep talking), parasomnias associated with REM sleep (e.g., nightmares), and others (e.g., bruxism). Box 45-4 describes examples of parasomnias.

8. Healthy individuals who obtain less sleep than they need will experience sleepiness and fatigue during the day. They may develop attention and concentration deficits, reduced vigilance, distractibility, reduced motivation, fatigue, malaise, and occasionally diplopia and dry mouth. When clients report obtaining more sleep on weekends or days off, it usually indicates that they are not obtaining sufficient sleep.

**2** Insomnia
- Difficulty falling asleep
- Waking up frequently; waking up too early
- Difficulty returning to sleep
- Daytime sleepiness
- Difficulty concentrating
- Irritability
- Risk factors
  - Older age
  - Female

**3** Excessive Daytime Sleepiness
- Hypersomnia
- Narcolepsy
- Sleep apnea
- Insufficient sleep

**4** Hypersomnia
- Sufficient sleep at night but cannot stay awake during day
- Caused by medical or psychological disorders

**5** Narcolepsy
- Caused by lack of hypocretin in CNS that regulates sleep
- Clients have sleep attacks
- Sleep at night usually begins with sleep-onset REM period

**6** Sleep Apnea
- Frequent short breathing pauses during night
- More than 5 apneic episodes greater than 10 seconds per hour considered abnormal
- Symptoms include snoring, frequent awakenings, difficulty falling asleep, morning headaches, memory and cognitive problems, irritability
- Types include obstructive, central, and mixed apnea

**7** Parasomnia
- Behavior that may interfere with or occur during sleep
- Arousal disorders (e.g., sleepwalking, sleep terrors)
- Sleep-wake transition disorders (e.g., sleep talking)
- Associated with REM sleep (e.g., nightmares)
- Others (e.g., bruxism)

**8** Healthy Individuals Who Don't Sleep
- Experience sleepiness and fatigue during day
- Attention and concentration deficits
- Reduced vigilance
- Distractibility
- Reduced motivation
- Fatigue, malaise, diplopia and dry mouth

# LEARNING OUTCOME 6

Identify the components of a sleep pattern assessment.

## CONCEPTS FOR LECTURE

1. A complete assessment of a client's sleep difficulty includes a sleep history, health history, physical exam, and, if warranted, a sleep diary and diagnostic studies.
2. A sleep history includes the following questions: When does the client usually go to sleep, awake, nap and, if a child, any bedtime rituals; does the client have any problems with sleep; has anyone ever told the client that he/she snores loudly or thrashes around during sleep; is the client able to stay awake at work, when driving or engaging in usual activities; does the client take any prescribed medications, OTC or herbals to help sleep or stay awake; and is there anything else the client would like to report about sleep?
3. During the health history the nurse obtains information about any medical or psychiatric problems that may influence sleep as well as a medication history including prescribed, OTC, and herbal medications consumed.
4. The physical examination rarely yields information related to sleep disorders unless the client has obstructive sleep apnea. Signs of this problem include enlarged and reddened uvula and soft palate, enlarged adenoids and tonsils (children), obesity (adults), neck circumference greater than 17.5 inches in men, and occasionally a deviated septum.
5. A sleep specialist may ask the client to keep a sleep diary including all or some of the following: time factors associated with sleep; activities performed 2 to 3 hours prior to sleep; consumption of caffeinated beverages and alcohol and amount consumed; medications; bedtime rituals; any difficulty remaining awake during the day and time when this occurs; any worries the client believes are influencing sleep; and any factors the client believes have a positive or negative effect on sleep.
6. Diagnostic studies performed by sleep disorder laboratory includes polysomnography. This includes electroencephalography (EEG), electromyogram (EMG), and electro-oculogram (EOG).

## POWERPOINT LECTURE SLIDES

*(NOTE: The number on each PPT Lecture Slide directly corresponds with the Concepts for Lecture.)*

**1** Sleep Pattern Assessment
- Sleep history
- Health history
- Physical exam
- If warranted, a sleep diary and diagnostic studies

**2** Sleep History
- When does client usually go to sleep?
- Bedtime rituals?
- Does client snore?
- Can client stay awake during day?
- Taking any prescribed or OTC medications?

**3** Health History
- Obtain information about medical or psychiatric problems that may influence sleep
- Medication history

**4** Physical Examination
- Rarely yields information unless client has obstructive sleep apnea
  - Enlarged and reddened uvula and soft palate
  - Enlarged adenoids and tonsils (children)
  - Obesity (adults)
  - Neck circumference greater than 17.5 inches (men)
  - Occasionally a deviated septum

**5** Sleep Diary
- Client may be asked to keep track of
  - Time factors associated with sleep
  - Activities performed 2–3 hours prior to sleep
  - Consumption of caffeine, alcohol
  - Medications
  - Bedtime rituals
  - Difficulty remaining awake during day
  - Any worries or factors client feels may be contributing

**6** Diagnostic Studies
- Polysomnography
  - EEG
  - EMG
  - EOG

## SUGGESTIONS FOR CLASSROOM ACTIVITIES

- Have the students practice performing a sleep history on each other.
- Have the students keep a sleep diary and share findings with the class.

## SUGGESTIONS FOR CLINICAL ACTIVITIES

- Have the students perform a sleep assessment on their assigned clients. Discuss findings in postconference.

# LEARNING OUTCOME 7

Develop nursing diagnoses, outcomes, and nursing interventions related to sleep problems.

## CONCEPTS FOR LECTURE

1. *Disturbed Sleep Pattern* is the NANDA diagnosis given to clients with sleep problems. It is usually made more specific with descriptions such as "difficulty falling asleep" or "difficulty staying asleep." Various etiologies may be involved and must be specified for the individual.
2. Sleep pattern disturbances may also be stated as the etiology of another diagnosis, in which case the nursing interventions are directed toward the sleep disturbance itself. Examples include *Risk for Injury, Ineffective Coping, Fatigue, Risk for Impaired Gas Exchange, Deficient Knowledge, Anxiety,* and *Activity Intolerance.*
3. The major goal for clients with sleep disturbances is to maintain (or develop) a sleeping pattern that provides sufficient energy for daily activities. Other goals may relate to enhancing the client's feeling of well-being or improving the quality and quantity of the client's sleep.
4. The nurse plans specific nursing interventions to reach the goal based on the etiology of each nursing diagnosis. These interventions may include reducing environmental distractions, promoting bedtime rituals, providing comfort measures, scheduling nursing care to provide for uninterrupted sleep periods, and teaching stress reduction, relaxation techniques, or good sleep hygiene.

## POWERPOINT LECTURE SLIDES

*(NOTE: The number on each PPT Lecture Slide directly corresponds with the Concepts for Lecture.)*

1. NANDA Nursing Diagnoses
   - Disturbed sleep pattern
     - With specific descriptions such as "difficulty falling asleep" or "difficulty staying asleep"
     - Various etiologies may be involved and specified

2. Sleep Pattern Disturbances as Etiology of Other Diagnoses:
   - Risk for injury
   - Ineffective coping
   - Fatigue
   - Risk for impaired gas exchange
   - Deficient knowledge
   - Anxiety
   - Activity intolerance

3. Outcomes for Clients With Sleep Disturbances
   - Maintain (or develop) a sleeping pattern that provides sufficient energy for daily activities
   - Enhance feeling of well-being
   - Improve the quality and quantity of the client's sleep

4. General Nursing Interventions for Sleep Disturbances
   - Reducing environmental distractions
   - Promoting bedtime rituals
   - Providing comfort measures
   - Scheduling nursing care to promote uninterrupted sleep
   - Teaching stress reduction, relaxation techniques, or good sleep hygiene

## SUGGESTIONS FOR CLASSROOM ACTIVITIES

- Have the students review the defining characteristics of the *Disturbed Sleep Pattern* diagnosis.
- Provide the students with a case study in which disturbed sleep is the etiology of another nursing diagnosis. Ask the students to identify the appropriate nursing diagnosis, develop goals and desired outcomes, and select appropriate nursing interventions.

## SUGGESTIONS FOR CLINICAL ACTIVITIES

- If appropriate, have the students develop a care plan related to sleep patterns for their assigned clients.

Describe interventions that promote normal sleep.

## CONCEPTS FOR LECTURE

1. Sleep hygiene is a term referring to interventions used to promote sleep. These involve health teaching about sleep habits, support of bedtime rituals, the provision of a restful environment, specific measures to promote comfort and relaxation, and appropriate use of hypnotic medications.

2. Clients need to learn the importance of sleep in maintaining active and productive lifestyles, the conditions that promote sleep and those that interfere with sleep, safe use of sleep medications, effects of other prescribed medications on sleep, and effects of their disease states on sleep. (See Client Teaching: Promoting Sleep.)

3. Bedtime rituals are routines that are conducive to comfort and relaxation. Altering or eliminating such routines can affect a client's sleep. Common bedtime activities of adults include listening to music, reading, taking a soothing bath, and praying. Children need to be socialized into a presleep routine. Sleep is also usually preceded by hygienic routines. In institutional settings, nurses can provide similar bedtime rituals.

4. Creating a restful environment is important. All people need a sleeping environment with minimal noise, a comfortable room temperature, appropriate ventilation, and appropriate lighting. Children or those in a strange environment may prefer a low light source. Distractions such as environmental noises and staff communication noise are particularly troublesome for hospitalized patients.

5. The environment must also be safe. Patients may feel more secure with side rails. Beds should be placed in low positions, night-lights should be turned on, and call bells should be placed within reach of the patient.

   A concerned, caring attitude, along with the following interventions, can significantly promote client comfort and sleep:
   - Provide loose-fitting nightwear.
   - Assist clients with hygienic routines.
   - Make sure the bed linen is smooth, clean, and dry.
   - Assist or encourage the client to void before bedtime.
   - Offer to provide a back massage before sleep.
   - Position dependent clients appropriately to aid muscle relaxation, and provide supportive devices to protect pressure areas.
   - Schedule medications, especially diuretics, to prevent nocturnal awakenings.
   - For clients who have pain, administer analgesics 30 minutes before sleep.
   - Listen to the client's concerns and deal with problems as they arise.

     People of any age, but especially elders, are unable to sleep well if they feel cold. The bed should be

## POWERPOINT LECTURE SLIDES

*(NOTE: The number on each PPT Lecture Slide directly corresponds with the Concepts for Lecture.)*

**1** Sleep Hygiene
- Interventions used to promote sleep
  ○ Client education
  ○ Supporting bedtime rituals
  ○ Creating a restful environment
  ○ Promoting comfort and relaxation
  ○ Sleep medications, if appropriate

**2** Client Education
- The importance of sleep
- Conditions that promote sleep
- Conditions that interfere with sleep
- Safe use of sleep medications
- Effects of prescribed medications on sleep
- Effects of disease states on sleep

**3** Bedtime Rituals
- Altering or eliminating routines can affect sleep
- Adults
  ○ Listening to music
  ○ Reading
  ○ Soothing bath
  ○ Praying
- Children
  ○ Need to be socialized into presleep routine
  ○ Usually preceded by hygienic ritual

**4** Creating a Restful Environment
- Minimal noise
- Comfortable room temperature
- Appropriate ventilation
- Appropriate lighting

**5** Promoting Comfort and Relaxation
- Ensure a safe environment
- Concerned, caring attitude
- Relaxation techniques

**6** Medications
- Sedative-hypnotics (induce sleep)
- Anti-anxiety or tranquilizers (decrease anxiety/tension)
- Be aware of actions, effects, and risks of specific medications

warmed with prewarmed bath blankets, and 100% flannel sheets or thermal blankets should be provided. Clients should wear their own clothing, such as flannel nightgowns or pajamas, socks, leg warmers, long underwear, sleeping cap (if scalp hair is sparse), or sweater, or use extra blankets.

Relaxation techniques can be encouraged as part of the nightly routine. Deep breathing followed by slow, rhythmic contraction and relaxation of muscles, imagery, meditation, and yoga can be taught.

6. Medications that enhance sleep are often prescribed on a prn basis. They include sedative-hypnotics, which induce sleep, and anti-anxiety drugs or tranquilizers, which decrease anxiety and tension. Both nurses and clients need to be aware of the actions, effects, and risks of the specific medications prescribed. (Table 45–1 presents some of the common medications used for enhancing sleep and the half-life of these medications.)

## SUGGESTIONS FOR CLASSROOM ACTIVITIES

- Invite a certified massage therapist to assist students to practice effleurage on each other.
- Have the students select a relaxation technique to investigate and present to the class.
- Have the students interview people of various ages to discover bedtime rituals. Discuss findings.

## SUGGESTIONS FOR CLINICAL ACTIVITIES

- Have the students review charts to determine hypnotic medications prescribed. Ask the students to review these medications in a drug reference book and identify how the medications induce sleep, how they affect REM and NREM sleep, half-life, any adverse reactions, and any contraindications for use.
- Discuss nursing interventions to assist clients to sleep while hospitalized.
- Invite staff nurses to discuss interventions the institution has introduced to assist clients to sleep.

# CHAPTER 46
## PAIN MANAGEMENT

## RESOURCE LIBRARY

 **PRENTICE HALL NURSING MEDIALINK DVD-ROM**

NCLEX® Review
Skill Checklist
Video: *Pain Management*
Animations:
  *Morphine*
  *Naproxen*

 **COMPANION WEBSITE**

Additional NCLEX® Review
Case Study: *Client with Stomach Cancer*
Care Plan Activity: *Treating Chronic Back Pain*
Application Activities:
  *The Mayday Pain Project*
  *Resources for Arthritis*
Links to Resources

 **IMAGE LIBRARY**

**Figure 46.1** Common sites of referred pain from various body organs.
**Figure 46.2** Substance P assists the transmission of impulses across the synapse from the primary afferent neuron to a second-order neuron in the spinothalamic tract.
**Figure 46.3** Physiology of pain perception.
**Figure 46.4** A schematic illustration of the gate control theory.
**Figure 46.5** Proprioceptive reflex to a pain stimulus.
**Figure 46.6** An 11-point pain intensity scale with word modifiers.
**Figure 46.8** Pain management flow sheet.

**Figure 46.9** The WHO three-step analgesic ladder.
**Figure 46.10** Subcutaneous infusion needle placement.
**Figure 46.11** Placement of intraspinal catheter in the epidural space.
**Figure 46.12** PCA line introduced into the injection port of a primary line.
**Figure 46.13** The older child is able to regulate a PCA pump.
**Figure 46.14** A transcutaneous electric nerve stimulator.
**Skill 46.1** Providing a Back Massage

## LEARNING OUTCOME 1

Discriminate between physiological and neuropathic pain categories.

### CONCEPTS FOR LECTURE

1. Physiological pain is experienced when an intact, properly functioning nervous system signals that tissues are damaged, requiring attention and proper care. This type of pain may be transient (for example, pain from a cut or broken bone) if the cause of the pain is eliminated, or it may be persistent if it is not possible to eliminate the cause of the pain (for example, pain from loss of the protective cartilage in the joints as in osteoarthritis). Subcategories of physiological pain include somatic (originates in the skin, muscles, bone, or connective tissue) and visceral (results from activation of pain receptors in organs and/or hollow viscera).
2. Neuropathic pain is experienced by people who have damaged or malfunctioning nerves. The nerves may be abnormal due to illness, injury, or undetermined reasons. Peripheral neuropathic pain (e.g., phantom limb,

### POWERPOINT LECTURE SLIDES

*(NOTE: The number on each PPT Lecture Slide directly corresponds with the Concepts for Lecture.)*

**1** Physiologic Pain
  • Experienced when an intact, properly functioning nervous system signals that tissues are damaged, requiring attention and proper care
  • Transient
  • Persistent
  • Subcategories
    ○ Somatic
    ○ Visceral

**2** Neuropathic Pain
  • Experienced by people who have damaged or malfunctioning nerves
  • Types

carpal tunnel) follows damage and/or sensitization of peripheral nerves. Central neuropathic pain (e.g., spinal cord injury pain) results from malfunctioning nerves in the central nervous system. Sympathetically maintained pain occurs occasionally when abnormal connections between pain fibers and the sympathetic nervous system perpetuate problems with both the pain and sympathetically controlled functions. Neuropathic pain is typically chronic and tends to be difficult to treat. It may result from a failure to treat pain effectively during the postoperative period.

- ○ Peripheral
- ○ Central
- ○ Sympathetically maintained

---

### SUGGESTIONS FOR CLASSROOM ACTIVITIES

- Provide additional examples of the various types of pain.
- Discuss referred pain.

### SUGGESTIONS FOR CLINICAL ACTIVITIES

- Explore the various types of pain experienced by assigned clients, if appropriate. Compare and contrast.

---

## LEARNING OUTCOME 2

Describe the four processes involved in nociception and how pain interventions can work during each process.

### CONCEPTS FOR LECTURE

1. The physiologic processes related to pain perception are described as nociception. Four physiologic processes are involved: transduction, transmission, perception, and modulation.

   During the transduction phase, noxious stimuli trigger the release of biochemical mediators (e.g., prostaglandins, bradykinin, serotonin, histamine, substance P) that sensitize nociceptors. Noxious or painful stimulation also causes movement of ions across cell membranes, which excite nociceptors. Pain medications can work during this phase by blocking the production of prostaglandin (e.g., ibuprofen or aspirin), by decreasing the movement of ions across the cell membrane (e.g., local anesthetic), or by use of a topical analgesic (e.g., capsaicin) which depletes the accumulation of substance P and blocks transduction.

   Transmission of pain includes three segments. During the first segment, the pain impulse travels from the peripheral nerve fibers to the spinal cord. Substance P serves as a neurotransmitter. Two types of nociceptor fibers cause this type of transmission in the spinal cord: unmyelinated C fibers (transmit dull, aching pain) and thin A-delta fibers (transmit sharp, localized pain). In the dorsal horn, the pain signal is modified by modulating factors (e.g., excitatory amino acids or endorphins) before the amplified or dampened signal travels via spinothalamic tracts. The second segment is transmission from the spinal cord and ascension via the spinothalamic tracts to the brain stem and thalamus. The third segment involves transmission of signals between the thalamus and the sensory cortex

### POWERPOINT LECTURE SLIDES

*(NOTE: The number on each PPT Lecture Slide directly corresponds with the Concepts for Lecture.)*

 Four Processes Involved in Nociception
- Transduction
- Transmission
- Modulation
- Perception

when pain perception occurs. Opioids block the release of neurotransmitters, particularly substance P, which stops the pain at the spinal level. Capsaicin may also deplete substance P and inhibit the transmission of pain signals.

Modulation occurs when neurons in the thalamus and brain stem send signals back down to the dorsal horn of the spinal cord. These descending fibers release substances such as endogenous opioids, serotonin, and norepinephrine that can inhibit (dampen) the ascending noxious (painful) impulses in the dorsal horn. In contrast, excitatory amino acids, e.g., glutamate, *N*-methyl-D-aspartate (NMDA), and the upregulation of excitatory glial cells can facilitate (amplify) these pain fibers. The effects of the excitatory amino acids and glial cells tend to persist, while the effects of the inhibitory neurotransmitters tend to be short-lived as they are reabsorbed into the neurons. Tricyclic antidepressants block the reuptake of norepinephrine and serotonin. NMDA antagonists (e.g., ketamine, dextromethorphan) may be used to help diminish the signals of pain.

Perception, the final process, is when the client becomes conscious of the pain. Pain perception is the sum of complex activities in the central nervous system that may shape the character and intensity of pain perceived and ascribe meaning to the pain. The psychosocial context of the situation and the meaning of the pain based on past experiences and future hopes/dreams help to shape the behavioral responses that follow.

## SUGGESTIONS FOR CLASSROOM ACTIVITIES

- Review the physiology of pain transmission using Figure 46.3 in the textbook.
- Provide the students with other interventions for pain, and have them relate the interventions to the four processes involved in nociception.

## SUGGESTIONS FOR CLINICAL ACTIVITIES

- Have the students explore the care plans for various clients on the clinical unit to determine the pain interventions used, if any. Ask the students to relate these interventions to the four processes involved in nociception.

## LEARNING OUTCOME 3

Describe how the physical, mental, spiritual, and social aspects of pain contribute to concepts such as pain tolerance, suffering, and pain behavior.

### CONCEPTS FOR LECTURE

1. Numerous factors can affect a person's perception of and reaction to pain. These include the person's ethnic and cultural values, developmental level, support people, previous pain experiences, and the meaning of the current pain.

   Ethnic background and cultural heritage have long been recognized as factors that influence both a person's reaction to pain and the expression of that

### POWERPOINT LECTURE SLIDES

*(NOTE: The number on each PPT Lecture Slide directly corresponds with the Concepts for Lecture.)*

 1 Factors Affecting Perception of Pain
- Ethnic and cultural values
- Age and developmental level
- Environmental factors
- Support people
- Previous pain experiences

pain. Behavior related to pain is part of the socialization process. Although there appears to be little variation in pain threshold, cultural background can affect the level of pain that an individual is willing to tolerate. Additionally, there are significant variations in the expressions of pain.

The age and developmental stage of a client is an important variable that will influence both the reaction to and the expression of pain. Age variations and related nursing interventions are presented in Table 46–3.

A strange environment can compound pain. In addition, the lonely person who is without a support network may perceive pain as severe, whereas the person who has supportive people around may perceive less pain. Some people prefer to withdraw when they are in pain, whereas others prefer the distraction of people and activity around them. Expectations of significant others can affect a person's perceptions of and responses to pain. The presence of support people often changes a client's reaction to pain.

Past pain experiences alter a client's sensitivity to pain. People who have personally experienced pain or who have been exposed to the suffering of someone close are often more threatened by anticipated pain than people without a pain experience. In addition, the success or lack of success of pain relief measures influences a person's expectations for relief and future response to interventions.

Some clients may accept pain more readily than others, depending on the circumstances and the client's interpretation of its significance. A client who associates the pain with a positive outcome may withstand pain amazingly well. By contrast, clients with unrelenting chronic pain may suffer more intensely. Chronic pain affects the body, mind, spirit, and social relationships in an undesirable way. Mood often becomes impaired when pain persists as the sadness of being unable to do important or enjoyable activities is combined with self-doubts and learned helplessness to produce depression. Anxiety and worry about coping with the pain experience may escalate to panic.

Spiritually, pain may be viewed in a variety of ways. It may be perceived as a punishment for wrongdoing, a betrayal by the higher power, a test of fortitude, or a threat to the essence of who the person is. As such, pain may be a source of spiritual distress, or be a source of strength and enlightenment.

Socially, pain often strains valued relationships, in part because of the impaired ability to fulfill role expectations.

- Meaning of the current pain
  - Spiritual
  - Social

<table>
<tr><td>

**SUGGESTIONS FOR CLASSROOM ACTIVITIES**

- Invite a panel of clients who are experiencing or have experienced pain to discuss factors that they believe influenced their pain experience and how nurses helped or could have helped them deal with their pain.
- Have the students discuss situations when they have experienced pain and the factors that influenced pain perception and response.

</td><td>

**SUGGESTIONS FOR CLINICAL ACTIVITIES**

- Invite staff nurses to discuss factors they have observed that influence pain perceptions and responses in clients.

</td></tr>
</table>

## LEARNING OUTCOME 4

Describe the gate control theory and its application to nursing care.

### CONCEPTS FOR LECTURE

1. According to Melzack and Wall's gate control theory (1965), small-diameter (A-delta or C) peripheral nerve fibers carry signals of noxious stimuli to the dorsal horn, where these signals are modified when they are exposed to the substantia gelatinosa that may be imbalanced in an excitatory or inhibitory direction.

   Ion channels on the pre- and postsynaptic membranes serve as gates that, when open, permit positively charged ions to rush into the second order neurons, sparking an electrical impulse and sending signals of pain to the thalamus.

   Peripherally, large-diameter (A-delta) nerve fibers, which typically send messages of touch, warm, or cold temperatures, have an inhibitory effect on the substantia gelatinosa, and may activate the descending mechanism that can lessen the intensity of pain perceived or inhibit the transmission of those pain impulses—that is, close the (ion) gates.

   Higher centers of the brain, especially those associated with affect and motivation, are capable of modifying the substantia gelatinosa and influence the opening or closing of the gates.

2. Clinically, nurses can use this model to stop nociceptor firing (treat the underlying cause), apply topical therapies (e.g., heat, ice, electrical stimulation, or massage), and address the client's mood (e.g., reduce fear, anxiety, and anger) and goals (e.g., client education, anticipatory guidance).

### POWERPOINT LECTURE SLIDES

*(NOTE: The number on each PPT Lecture Slide directly corresponds with the Concepts for Lecture.)*

 Gate Control Theory
- Small diameter (A-delta or C) peripheral nerve fibers carry signals of noxious stimuli to the dorsal horn
- Signals are modified when they are exposed to the substantia gelatinosa
- Ion channels on the pre- and postsynaptic membranes serve as gates
- When open, permit positively charged ions to rush into the second order neurons, sparking an electrical impulse and sending signals of pain to the thalamus
- Large diameter (A-delta) fibers have an inhibitory effect on the substantia gelatinosa
- May activate descending mechanism that can lessen or inhibit transmission of pain (close the gate)

 Clinical Application of Gate Control Theory
- Stop nociceptor firing by treating the cause of pain
- Apply topical therapies
- Address client's mood
- Address client's goals

<table>
<tr><td>

**SUGGESTIONS FOR CLASSROOM ACTIVITIES**

- Provide the students with examples of interventions to reduce pain and ask them to use the gate control model to explain the rationale for each intervention.

</td><td>

**SUGGESTIONS FOR CLINICAL ACTIVITIES**

- Arrange for a nurse from a pain control clinic to discuss pain control treatments used in the clinic. Ask the students to apply the gate control model to explain the rationale for each intervention.

</td></tr>
</table>

# LEARNING OUTCOME 5

Identify subjective and objective data to collect and analyze when assessing pain.

## CONCEPTS FOR LECTURE

1. Many health facilities are making pain assessment the fifth vital sign. Pain should be assessed every time vital signs are evaluated with a simple question such as "Are you experiencing any discomfort right now?"

    A comprehensive assessment of the pain experience (physiologic, psychologic, behavioral, emotional, and sociocultural) provides the necessary foundation for optimal pain control.

    Pain assessments consist of two major components: a pain history to obtain facts from the client, and direct observation of behaviors, physical signs of tissue damage, and secondary physiologic responses of the client.

    A mnemonic for assessing pain is COLDERR: Character (describe the sensation), Onset (when it started, how it has changed), Location (where it hurts), Duration (constant or intermittent), Exacerbation (factors that make it worse), Relief (factors that make it better), and Radiation (pattern of shooting, spreading, location away from its origin). Additional data that should be obtained in a comprehensive pain history include intensity, precipitating factors, associated symptoms, effect on ADLs, past pain experiences, meaning of the pain to the person, coping resources, and affective responses.

2. There are wide variations in nonverbal responses to pain, including facial expression, vocalizations like moaning and groaning or crying and screaming, immobilization of the body or body part, purposeless body movements, behavioral changes such as confusion and restlessness, and rhythmic body movements or rubbing.

3. Physiologic responses vary with the origin and duration of pain. Increased blood pressure, pulse rate, respiratory rate, pallor, diaphoresis, and pupil dilation may occur early due to sympathetic nervous system stimulation. These responses may be absent in people with chronic pain because the autonomic nervous system adapts.

    A daily pain diary may help clients who experience chronic pain to identify pain patterns and factors that exacerbate or mediate the pain experience. This record can include time of onset of pain, activity or situation, physical pain characteristics (quality) and intensity (0–10), emotions experienced and intensity 0–10), and use of analgesics or other relief measures.

## POWERPOINT LECTURE SLIDES

*(NOTE: The number on each PPT Lecture Slide directly corresponds with the Concepts for Lecture.)*

 Pain Assessment: Subjective Data
- Comprehensive pain history includes COLDERR:
  - Character (description of the sensation or quality)
  - Onset (when it started; how it has changed)
  - Location (where it hurts)
  - Duration (constant or intermittent)
  - Exacerbation (what makes it worse)
  - Relief (what makes it better)
  - Radiation (pattern of shooting, spreading, location away from its origin)
- Additional data to obtain
  - Intensity associated with symptoms
  - Effect on ADLs
  - Past pain experiences
  - Meaning of the pain to the person
  - Coping resources
  - Affective response

 Pain Assessment: Objective Data
- Nonverbal responses to pain (highly variable)
  - Facial expression
  - Vocalizations like moaning and groaning or crying and screaming
  - Immobilization of the body or body part
  - Purposeless body movements
  - Behavioral changes such as confusion and restlessness
  - Rhythmic body movements or rubbing

 Early Physiologic Responses
  - Increases blood pressure, pulse rate, respiratory rate, pallor, diaphoresis, and pupil dilation
  - May be absent in people with chronic pain
- Pain diary

---

## SUGGESTIONS FOR CLASSROOM ACTIVITIES

- Have the students practice completing a pain assessment on a partner.

## SUGGESTIONS FOR CLINICAL ACTIVITIES

- Discuss the pain assessment tool used in the institution. Have the students assess their clients' pain using the tool, if appropriate. Discuss findings in postconference.

---

# LEARNING OUTCOME 6

Identify examples of nursing diagnoses for clients with pain.

## CONCEPTS FOR LECTURE

1. NANDA includes the following diagnostic labels for clients experiencing pain or discomfort: *Acute Pain* and *Chronic Pain*. The nurse should specify the location. Related factors, when known, can include both physiologic and psychologic factors.
2. Because the presence of pain can affect so many facets of a person's functioning, pain may be the etiology of other nursing diagnoses. Examples include *Ineffective Airway Clearance, Hopelessness, Anxiety, Ineffective Coping, Ineffective Health Maintenance, Self-Care Deficit (Specify), Deficient Knowledge (Pain Control Measures),* and *Disturbed Sleep Pattern.*

## POWERPOINT LECTURE SLIDES

*(NOTE: The number on each PPT Lecture Slide directly corresponds with the Concepts for Lecture.)*

**1** NANDA Nursing Diagnoses for Clients with Pain
- Acute pain and chronic pain
- Specify the location
- Related factors, when known, can include physiologic and psychologic factors

**2** Pain as Etiology of Other Nursing Diagnoses
- Ineffective airway clearance
- Hopelessness
- Anxiety
- Ineffective coping
- Ineffective health maintenance
- Self-care deficit (specify)
- Deficient knowledge (pain control measures)
- Disturbed sleep patterns

## SUGGESTIONS FOR CLASSROOM ACTIVITIES

- Have the students determine the difference in the defining characteristics for *Acute Pain* and *Chronic Pain*.
- Provide the students with a case study of a client with chronic pain. Have them identify appropriate nursing diagnoses for this client.

## SUGGESTIONS FOR CLINICAL ACTIVITIES

- If appropriate, have the students identify nursing diagnoses related to pain for assigned clients, indicating the defining characteristics and etiology.

# LEARNING OUTCOME 7

Individualize a pain treatment plan based on clinical and personal goals, while setting objective outcome criteria by which to evaluate a client's response to interventions for pain.

## CONCEPTS FOR LECTURE

1. The established goals for the client will vary according to the diagnosis and its defining characteristics.

   When planning, nurses need to choose pain relief measures appropriate for the client, based on assessment data and input from the client or support persons.
2. Practice Guidelines: Individualize Care for the Client with Pain lists the following guidelines: establish a trusting relationship; consider the client's ability and willingness to participate actively in pain relief measures; use a variety of pain relief measures; provide measures to relieve pain before it becomes severe; use pain-relieving measures that the client believes are effective; align the pain relief measures with the client's report of the severity of pain; if a pain relief measure is ineffective, encourage the client to try it again before abandoning it; maintain an unbiased attitude about what may relieve the pain; keep trying; prevent harm

## POWERPOINT LECTURE SLIDES

*(NOTE: The number on each PPT Lecture Slide directly corresponds with the Concepts for Lecture.)*

**1** Treatment Plan
- Goals vary according the diagnosis and its defining characteristics
- Select pain relief measures appropriate for the client, based on assessment data and input from the client or support persons

**2** Practice Guidelines
- Establish a trusting relationship
- Consider client's ability and willingness to participate
- Use a variety of pain relief measures
- Provide pain relief measures before pain is severe
- Use pain relief measures the client believes are effective

## CONCEPTS FOR LECTURE *continued*

to the client; and educate the client and caregivers about pain.

3. Nursing interventions may include a variety of pharmacologic and nonpharmacologic interventions.

Developing a plan that incorporates a wide range of strategies is usually most effective. The plan should be documented in the client's record and for in-home care. A copy needs to be made available to the client, support person, and caregivers. Involvement of the client and support persons is essential in pain management.

## POWERPOINT LECTURE SLIDES *continued*

- Align pain relief measures with report of pain severity
- Encourage client to try ineffective measures again before abandoning
- Maintain an unbiased attitude about what may relieve pain
- Keep trying
- Prevent harm to the client
- Educate the client and caregiver about pain

 Pain Treatment Plan
- Include a variety of pharmacologic and nonpharmacologic interventions
- Plan with wide range of strategies usually most effective
- Document the plan in client record and for home care
- Involve the client and support persons

---

### SUGGESTIONS FOR CLASSROOM ACTIVITIES

- Provide the students with a case study of a client experiencing pain. Have the students develop a plan of care for the client.

### SUGGESTIONS FOR CLINICAL ACTIVITIES

- Have the students develop a care plan for a client who is experiencing pain.

---

## LEARNING OUTCOME 8

Compare and contrast barriers to effective pain management affecting nurses and clients.

### CONCEPTS FOR LECTURE

1. Misconceptions and biases can affect pain management. These may involve attitudes of the nurse or the client as well as knowledge deficits.

Clients and families may lack knowledge of the adverse effects of pain and may have misinformation regarding the use of analgesics. Some misconceptions related to the use of nonopioid pain medications include: regular daily use of NSAIDs is much safer than taking opioids; a nonopioid should not be given at the same time as an opioid; administering antacids with NSAIDs is an effective method of reducing gastric distress; nonopioids are not useful for severe pain; and gastric distress is indicative of NSAID-induced gastric ulceration (See Table 46–6).

Common misconceptions about pain include: clients experience pain only when they have had major surgery; the nurse or other health care professional is the authority about a client's pain; administering analgesics regularly for pain will lead to addiction; the amount of tissue damage is related to the amount of pain; and visible physiologic or behavior accompany pain and can be used to verify pain (See Table 46–6)

2. Clients may not report pain because of the following: unwillingness to trouble staff who they believe are

### POWERPOINT LECTURE SLIDES

*(NOTE: The number on each PPT Lecture Slide directly corresponds with the Concepts for Lecture.)*

1 Barriers to Effective Pain Management
- Lack of knowledge of the adverse effects of pain
- Misinformation regarding the use of analgesics
- Misconceptions about pain

2 May Not Report Pain
- Fear of becoming addicted

busy; don't want to be labeled as "complainer" or "bad"; fear of receiving an injection; belief that unrelieved pain is expected (as part of recovery); belief that others will think they are weak; difficulty or inability to communicate discomfort; concern about risks associated with opioid drugs; concerns about unwanted side effects; concern that use of drugs will render drug ineffective later in life; fear that reporting pain will lead to further tests and expenses; belief that nothing can be done to control pain; and the belief that enduring pain may lead to spiritual enlightenment (See Box 46-2).

Another barrier to effective pain management is the fear of becoming addicted, especially when long-term opioid use is prescribed. This fear is often held by both nurses and clients. It is important that all individuals know the difference among the terms tolerance, dependence, and addiction (see Box 46-4).

---

## SUGGESTIONS FOR CLASSROOM ACTIVITIES

- Have the students design a questionnaire about misconceptions regarding pain and administer the questionnaire to college students. Discuss findings.

## SUGGESTIONS FOR CLINICAL ACTIVITIES

- Invite several nurses who work in hospice settings to discuss common misconceptions and biases they have identified in clients, families, and staff and how they help correct these misconceptions and biases.

---

# LEARNING OUTCOME 9

Differentiate tolerance, dependence, and addiction.

## CONCEPTS FOR LECTURE

1. Addiction is a primary, chronic, neurobiologic disease, with genetic, psychosocial, and environmental factors influencing its development and manifestations. It is characterized by behaviors that include one or more of the following: impaired control over drug use, compulsive use, craving, and continued use despite harm.
2. Physical dependence is a state of adaptation that is manifested by a drug class specific withdrawal syndrome that can be produced by abrupt cessation, rapid dose reduction, decreasing blood level of the drug, and/or administration of an antagonist.
3. Tolerance is a state of adaptation in which exposure to a drug induces changes that result in a diminution of one or more of the drug's effects over time. (See Box 46-4.)

## POWERPOINT LECTURE SLIDES

*(NOTE: The number on each PPT Lecture Slide directly corresponds with the Concepts for Lecture.)*

1. Addiction
   - Primary, chronic, neurobiologic disease
   - Genetic, psychosocial, and environmental are influential factors
   - Behaviors can include: impaired control over drug use, compulsive use, craving, and continued use despite harm

2. Dependence
   - State of adaptation
   - Manifested by withdrawal syndrome
   - Produced by abrupt cessation, rapid dose reduction, decreasing blood level of the drug, and/or administration of an antagonist

3. Tolerance
   - State of adaptation
   - Exposure to a drug induces changes
   - Results in a diminution of one or more of the drug's effects over time

## LEARNING OUTCOME 10

Describe pharmacologic interventions for pain.

### CONCEPTS FOR LECTURE

1. Pharmacologic pain management involves the use of opioids (narcotics), nonopioids/nonsteroidal anti-inflammatory drugs (NSAIDs), and coanalgesic drugs (see Box 46–5).
2. There are three primary types of opioids:
   - **Full agonists:** These pure opioid drugs bind tightly to mu receptor sites, producing maximum pain inhibition, an agonist effect. A full agonist analgesic includes morphine (e.g., Kadian, MS Contin), oxycodone (e.g., Percocet, OxyContin), and hydromorphone (e.g., Dilaudid, Palladone). There is no ceiling on the level of analgesia; their dosage can be steadily increased to relieve pain.
   - **Mixed agonists-antagonists:** Agonist-antagonist analgesic drugs can act like opioids and relieve pain (agonist effect) when given to a client who has not taken any pure opioids. However, they can block or inactivate other opioid analgesics when given to a client who has been taking pure opioids (antagonist effect). If a client has been taking a pure opioid agonist daily for several weeks, the administration of a mixed agonist-antagonist may result in an immediate and severe withdrawal reaction. These drugs include dezocine (Dalgan), pentazocine hydrochloride (Talwin), butorphanol tartrate (Stadol), and nalbuphine hydrochloride (Nubain). These drugs also have a ceiling effect and a limit to dosing.
   - **Partial agonists:** Partial agonists have a ceiling effect in contrast to a full agonist. These drugs such as buprenorphine (Buprenex) block the mu receptors or are neutral at that receptor but bind at a kappa receptor site. This drug has good analgesic potency and is emerging as an alternative to methadone for opioid maintenance/narcotic treatment programs.
3. Nonopioids include acetaminophen and NSAIDs such as ibuprofen or aspirin. NSAIDs have anti-inflammatory, analgesic, and antipyretic effects, whereas acetaminophen has only analgesic and antipyretic effects. The anti-inflammatory action relieves pain by interfering with the cyclooxygenase (COX) chemical cascade

### POWERPOINT LECTURE SLIDES

*(NOTE: The number on each PPT Lecture Slide directly corresponds with the Concepts for Lecture.)*

1. Pharmacologic Interventions for Pain
   - Opioids (narcotics)
   - Nonopioids/NSAIDs
   - Coanalgesic drugs

2. Opioids (Narcotics)
   - Full agonists
     - No ceiling on analgesia; dosage can be steadily increased to relieve pain
     - e.g., morphine, oxycodone, hydromorphone
   - Mixed agonist-antagonists
     - Act like opioids and relieve pain
     - Can block or inactivate other opioid analgesics
     - e.g., dezocine, petazocine hydrochloride, butorphanol tartrate, nalbuphine hydrochloride
   - Partial agonist
     - Have a ceiling effect
     - e.g., buprenorphine

3. Nonopioids/NSAIDS
   - e.g., acetaminophen, ibuprofen, aspirin
   - Vary little in analgesic potency but do vary in anti-inflammatory effects, metabolism, excretions, and side effects
   - Have a ceiling effect
   - Narrow therapeutic index

4. Coanalgesic Drugs
   - Antidepressants
   - Anticonvulsants
   - Local anesthetics
   - Others

that is activated by damaged tissue. The COX chemical reactions produce prostaglandins and other inflammatory chemicals that cause a firing of nociceptive fibers. These drugs vary very little in analgesic potency, but do vary in anti-inflammatory effect, metabolism, excretions, and side effects. They have a ceiling effect and narrow therapeutic index. Acetaminophen has a different mechanism of action and side effect profile. Dosing recommendations must be carefully followed.

4. A coanalgesic agent (formerly known as an adjuvant) is a medication that is not classified as a pain medication but has properties that may reduce pain alone or in combination with other analgesics, relieve other discomforts, potentiate the effect of pain medications, or reduce the pain medication's side effects. Examples of coanalgesics that relieve pain are antidepressants (support the function of pain modulating system), anticonvulsants (stabilize nerve membranes, reducing excitability and spontaneous firing), and local anesthetics (block the transmission of pain signals). These drugs appear to be particularly beneficial for managing neuropathic pain.

## SUGGESTIONS FOR CLASSROOM ACTIVITIES

- Invite a nurse practitioner who practices in a hospice setting to discuss common medications used for pain and the process used in pain management.

## SUGGESTIONS FOR CLINICAL ACTIVITIES

- Assign students to review medication administration records and identify common medications used for treatment of pain. Ask the students to relate the medication to the type of pain the client is experiencing.

## LEARNING OUTCOME 11

Describe the World Health Organization's ladder step approach developed for cancer pain control.

## CONCEPTS FOR LECTURE

1. For clients with mild pain (1–3 on a 0–10 scale), step 1 of the analgesic ladder, nonopioid analgesics (with or without a coanalgesic) is the appropriate starting point.

   If the client has mild pain that persists or increases despite full doses of step 1 medications, or if the pain is moderate (4–6 on a 0–10 scale), then a step 2 regimen is appropriate. A weak opioid (e.g., codeine, tramadol, pentazocine) or a combination of opioid and nonopioid medicine (oxycodone with acetaminophen, hydrocodone with ibuprofen) is provided with or without coanalgesic medications.

   If the client has moderate pain that persists or increases despite using full doses of step 2 medications, or if the pain is severe (7–10 on a 0–10 scale), then a step 3 regimen is medically indicated. At the third step, strong opioids (e.g., morphine, hydromorphone, fentanyl) are administered and titrated in around-the-clock scheduled doses until the pain is relieved or dose-limiting respiratory depression occurs.

## POWERPOINT LECTURE SLIDES

*(NOTE: The number on each PPT Lecture Slide directly corresponds with the Concepts for Lecture.)*

1. WHO Ladder Step Approach for Cancer Pain Control
   - Step 1
     - For clients with mild pain (1–3 on a 0–10 scale)
     - Use nonopioid analgesics (with or without a coanalgesic)
   - Step 2
     - Client has mild pain that persists or increases
     - Pain is moderate (4–6 on a 0–10 scale)
     - Use a weak opioid (e.g., codeine, tramadol, pentazocine) or a combination of opioid and nonopioid medicine (oxycodone with acetaminophen, hydrocodone with ibuprofen)
     - With or without a coanalgesic
   - Step 3
     - Client has moderate pain that persists or increases

○ Pain is severe (7–10 on a 0–10 scale)
○ Use strong opioids (e.g., morphine, hydromorphone, fentanyl)

---

## SUGGESTIONS FOR CLASSROOM ACTIVITIES

• Invite a nurse practitioner who practices in hospice or oncology units to discuss the application of the WHO approach for treating cancer pain.

---

# LEARNING OUTCOME 12

Give an example of rational polypharmacy described by the American Pain Society.

## CONCEPTS FOR LECTURE

1. The principles of modern analgesic use are built on a foundation established by the World Health Organization (WHO) three-step approach to treating cancer pain. This approach has evolved into what is currently termed "rational polypharmacy."

   This approach demands that health professionals be aware of all ingredients of medications that alleviate pain, and use combinations to reduce the need for high doses of any one medication and to maximize pain control with a minimum of side effects or toxicity.

   These multidrug strategies, combined with multimodal therapy (use of nondrug approaches like heat/relaxation), may permit opioid dose reduction and improve client outcomes.

## POWERPOINT LECTURE SLIDES

*(NOTE: The number on each PPT Lecture Slide directly corresponds with the Concepts for Lecture.)*

1 Rational Polypharmacy
   • Evolved from the World Health Organization three step approach
   • Demands health professionals be aware of all ingredients of medications that alleviate pain
   • Use combinations to reduce the need for high doses of any one medication
   • Maximize pain control with a minimum of side effects or toxicity
   • Combine with multimodal therapy (e.g., nondrug approaches)

---

## SUGGESTIONS FOR CLASSROOM ACTIVITIES

• Invite a pharmacist to discuss rational polypharmacy.

## SUGGESTIONS FOR CLINICAL ACTIVITIES

• Give the students a list of medications typically used for pain management on the clinical unit. Have them look up the medications in a medication manual to determine composition of each medication, maximum doses, any ceiling effects, adverse effects, and antidotes.

---

# LEARNING OUTCOME 13

Identify risks and benefits of various analgesic delivery routes and analgesic delivery technologies.

## CONCEPTS FOR LECTURE

1. Opioids have traditionally been administered by oral, subcutaneous, intramuscular, and intravenous routes. Newer methods of delivering opiates have been developed to circumvent potential obstacles that occur with these traditional routes. Examples include transnasal, transmucosal, and transdermal drug therapy, continuous subcutaneous infusions, and intraspinal infusions.

   Oral administration is the preferred route of delivery because of ease of administration; however, the duration of action of most opiates is approximately

## POWERPOINT LECTURE SLIDES

*(NOTE: The number on each PPT Lecture Slide directly corresponds with the Concepts for Lecture.)*

1 Oral Administration
   • Preferred because of ease of administration
   • Duration of action is often only 4 to 8 hours
   • Must awaken during night for medication
   • Long-acting preparations developed
   • May need rescue dose of immediate-release medication

---

4 hours. People with chronic pain have had to awaken during the night to medicate themselves for pain. Long-acting or sustained-release forms of morphine with a duration of 8 or more hours have been developed. Clients receiving long-acting morphine may also need prn "rescue" doses of immediate-release analgesics. Liquid preparations enables clients who can swallow only small amounts to continue to take the drug orally. As a transmucosal agent, it immediately enters the bloodstream and begins to work.

2. Transnasal agents enter the bloodstream immediately, and onset of action is rapid. These can be used for individuals who are experiencing nausea, vomiting, and gastroparesis.

3. Transdermal therapy delivers a relatively stable plasma drug level and is noninvasive. Transdermal route differs from topical routes in that the effects of transdermal routes are systemic after absorption whereas topical applications work locally at the site applied.

4. Rectal preparations are particularly useful for clients who have dysphagia or nausea and vomiting.

5. Continuous subcutaneous infusion (CSCI) is particularly helpful for clients whose pain is poorly controlled by oral medications, who are experiencing dysphagia or gastrointestinal obstruction, or who have a need for prolonged use of parenteral narcotics. Continuous subcutaneous administration of a long-acting local anesthetic into or near the surgical site is a technique being used to provide post-operative pain control. Clients receiving continuous local anesthetics for post-operative pain control must be assessed for signs of local anesthetic toxicity and neurological deficit.

6. The intramuscular route should be avoided if possible because of variable absorption, unpredictable onset of action and peak effect, as well as the tissue damage that may result, even if properly administered.

7. The intravenous (IV) route provides rapid and effective relief with few side effects. However, just as the onset of pain relief occurs in 5 to 10 minutes, so can adverse effects, like respiratory depression. Caution is needed to prevent the introduction of air or bacteria into the tubing, and to prevent introducing medications that are incompatible with other medications dissolved in the IV solution.

8. The intraspinal route is delivery of opiates into the epidural or intrathecal (subarachnoid) space. The intraspinal route provides superior analgesia with less medication used. The intrathecal route delivers drugs into the cerebrospinal fluid providing quick and efficient binding to the opiate receptor sites in the dorsal horn speeding the onset and peak effect, which prolongs the analgesic's duration of action. Very little drug is absorbed by blood vessels into the systemic circulation. As a result there may be a delayed onset (24 hours after administration) of respiratory depression, as medication that has left the spinal opioid sites travels through the brain to be eliminated.

2 Transmucosa and Transnasal Administration
- Enters the blood immediately
- Onset of action is rapid

3 Transdermal Administration
- Delivers relatively stable plasma drug level
- Noninvasive

4 Rectal Administration
- Useful for clients with dysphagia or nausea and vomiting

5 Continuous Subcutaneous Infusion
- Used for pain poorly controlled by oral medications

6 Intramuscular
- Should be avoided
- Variable absorption
- Unpredictable onset of action and peak effect
- Tissue damage

7 Intravenous
- Provides rapid and effective relief with few side effects

8 Intraspinal
- Provides superior analgesia with less medication
- Types: intrathecal (subarachnoid) and epidural

9 Patient-Controlled Analgesia
- Minimizes peaks of sedation and valleys of pain that occur with prn dosing
- Electronic infusion pump
- Safety mechanisms

In contrast, the epidural space is separated from the spinal cord by the dura mater, which acts as a barrier to drug diffusion. In addition, it is filled with fatty tissues and an extensive venous system. With this diffusion delay, some medications (especially fat-soluble like fentanyl) from the epidural space enter the systemic circulation via the venous plexus. A higher dose of opiate is required to create the desired effect, which can produce side effects of itching, urinary retention, and/or respiratory depression. A local anesthetic may be combined with the opiate to lower the dose of the opioid. This may increase the fall risk for clients who develop muscular weakness in their legs or orthostatic hypotension in response to the local anesthetic.

9. Patient-controlled analgesia (PCA) minimizes the roller-coaster effects of peaks of sedation and valleys of pain that occur with the traditional method of prn dosing. The client administers a predetermined dose of a narcotic by an electronic infusion pump. A more constant level of relief with less medication is achieved. PCA pumps are designed with built-in safety mechanisms to prevent client overdose, abusive use, and narcotic theft. The most significant adverse effects are respiratory depression and hypotension; however, these rarely occur.

## SUGGESTIONS FOR CLASSROOM ACTIVITIES

- Invite a nurse anesthetist to discuss the various methods of providing local analgesia, including advantages, disadvantages, and nursing implications.
- Provide the students with a list of medications used for pain. Ask the students to identify the possible routes of administration, comparing and contrasting the onset and duration of each method of administration.

## SUGGESTIONS FOR CLINICAL ACTIVITIES

- Review the agency's policies and procedures for PCA.
- Demonstrate the equipment used by the agency for PCA.

# LEARNING OUTCOME 14

Describe nonpharmacologic pain control interventions.

## CONCEPTS FOR LECTURE

1. Nonpharmacologic pain management consists of a variety of physical, cognitive-behavioral, and lifestyle pain management strategies that target the body, mind, spirit, and social interactions as well as nonpharmacological invasive therapies..

2. The goals of physical interventions include providing comfort, altering physiologic responses to reduce pain perception, and optimizing functioning. Physical modalities include cutaneous stimulation (massage, application of heat and cold, acupressure, and contralateral stimulation), immobilization/bracing, and transcutaneous electrical nerve stimulation (TENS).

## POWERPOINT LECTURE SLIDES

*(NOTE: The number on each PPT Lecture Slide directly corresponds with the Concepts for Lecture.)*

1. Nonpharmacologic Pain Control Interventions
   - Consists of a variety of pain management strategies
     ○ Physical
     ○ Cognitive-behavioral
     ○ Lifestyle pain management
   - Target body, mind, spirit, and social interactions

2. Physical Modalities
   - Cutaneous stimulation

3. The goals of mind–body (cognitive-behavioral) interventions include providing comfort, altering psychologic responses to reduce pain perception and optimizing function. Selected cognitive-behavioral interventions include distraction, eliciting the relaxation response, repatterning thinking, and facilitating coping with emotions.

4. Lifestyle management approaches include symptom monitoring, stress management, exercise, nutrition, pacing activities, disability management, and other approaches needed by many clients with persistent pain that has drastically changed their life.

5. Spiritual interventions may include rituals that help the individual become part of a community or feel a bond with the universe that is not necessarily religious in nature.

6. Nonpharmacologic invasive techniques include interrupting pain pathways surgically. Because this interruption is permanent, surgery is performed only as a last resort, generally for intractable pain. These techniques include: cordotomy, rhizotomy, neurotomy, sympathectomy, and spinal cord stimulation.

- Immobilization or therapeutic exercises
- Transcutaneous electrical nerve stimulation (TENS)

**3** Cognitive-Behavioral (Mind–Body)
- Providing comfort
- Eliciting relaxation response
- Repatterning thinking
- Facilitating coping with emotions

**4** Lifestyle Management
- Stress management
- Exercise, nutrition
- Pacing activities
- Disability management

**5** Spiritual
- Feel part of a community
- Bond with universe
- Religious activities

**6** Nonpharmacologic Invasive Techniques
- Surgical interventions
  - Cordotomy
  - Rhizotomy
  - Neurotomy
  - Sympathectomy
  - Spinal cord stimulation

---

# LEARNING OUTCOME 15

List three nonpharmacologic interventions directed at each of the following: the body, the mind, the spirit, and social interactions.

## CONCEPTS FOR LECTURE

1. Table 46–8 lists nonpharmacologic interventions for pain control.

   Body interventions include reducing pain triggers, promoting comfort, massage, applying heat or ice, electric stimulation (TENS), positioning and bracing (selective immobilization), acupressure, diet and nutritional supplements, exercise and pacing activities, invasive interventions (e.g., blocks), and sleep hygiene.

2. Mind interventions include relaxation and imagery; self-hypnosis; pain diary and journal writing; distracting attention; repatterning thinking; attitude adjustment; reducing fear, anxiety, stress, sadness, and helplessness; and providing information about pain.

3. Spiritual interventions include prayer, meditation, self-reflection, meaningful rituals, energy work (therapeutic touch, Reiki), and spiritual healing.

4. Social interaction interventions include functional restoration, improved communication, family therapy, problem solving, vocational training, volunteering, and support groups.

## POWERPOINT LECTURE SLIDES

*(NOTE: The number on each PPT Lecture Slide directly corresponds with the Concepts for Lecture.)*

**1** Body Interventions
- Reducing pain triggers
- Massage
- Applying heat or ice
- Electric stimulation (TENS)
- Positioning and bracing (selective immobilization)
- Acupressure
- Diet and nutritional supplements
- Exercise and pacing activities
- Invasive interventions (e.g., blocks)
- Sleep hygiene

**2** Mind Interventions
- Relaxation and imagery
- Self-hypnosis
- Pain diary and journal writing
- Distracting attention
- Repattern thinking

- Attitude adjustment
- Reducing fear, anxiety, stress, sadness, and helplessness
- Providing information about pain

 Spiritual Interventions
- Prayer
- Meditation
- Self-reflection
- Meaningful rituals
- Energy work (therapeutic touch, Reiki)
- Spiritual healing

 Social Interaction
- Functional restoration
- Improved communication
- Family therapy
- Problem-solving
- Vocational training
- Volunteering
- Support groups

| **SUGGESTIONS FOR CLASSROOM ACTIVITIES** | **SUGGESTIONS FOR CLINICAL ACTIVITIES** |
|---|---|
| • Invite a panel of practitioners who have used therapeutic touch, Reiki, acupressure, acupuncture, and hypnosis or other alternative or complementary interventions to discuss or demonstrate these techniques with the class. | • Investigate resources available in the clinical setting to assist clients with nonpharmacologic pain relief measures. |

# CHAPTER 47
## NUTRITION

## RESOURCE LIBRARY

### PRENTICE HALL NURSING MEDIALINK DVD-ROM

Audio Glossary
NCLEX® Review
Skills Checklists
Videos:
    *Anorexia*
    *Bulimia*
    *Eating Disorders*
Animations:
    *Carbohydrates*
    *Lipids*
    *Inserting a Nasogastric Tube*

### COMPANION WEBSITE

Additional NCLEX® Review
Case Study: *Client with PEG Tube*
Care Plan Activity: *Client Experiencing Loss of Appetite*
Application Activity: *Vegetarian Nutrition*
Links to Resources

### IMAGE LIBRARY

**Figure 47.1** The Food Guide Pyramid.
**Figure 47.2** Food guide pyramid for young children.
**Figure 47.3** A modified food guide pyramid for people older than 70 years of age.
**Figure 47.4** The Nutrition Facts Label.
**Figure 47.5** Scored Patient-Generated Subjective Global Assessment (PG-SGA).
**Figure 47.6** Examples of nutritional deficiencies.
**Figure 47.7** Measuring the triceps skinfold.
**Figure 47.8** Measuring the mid-arm circumference.
**Figure 47.9** For a client who is blind, the nurse can use the clock system to describe the location of food on the plate.
**Figure 47.10** Left to right: glass holder, cup with hole for nose, two-handled cup holder.
**Figure 47.11** Dinner plate with guard attached and lipped plate facilitate scooping; wide-handled spoon and knife facilitate grip.

**Figure 47.12** A, Single-lumen Levin tube. B, Double-lumen Salem sump tub with filter on vent port and connector on suction port.
**Figure 47.13** Nasoenteric feeding tubes.
**Figure 47.14** Percutaneous endoscopic gastrostomy (PEG) tube.
**Figure 47.15** Percutaneous endoscopic jejunostomy (PEJ) tube.
**Figure 47.16** Low profile gastrostomy feeding tube.
**Figure 47.17** An enteric feeding pump.
**Skill 47.1** Inserting a Nasogastric Tube
**Skill 47.2** Removing a Nasogastric Tube
**Skill 47.3** Administrering a Tube Feeding
**Skill 47.4** Administering a Gastronomy or Jejunostomy Feeding

## LEARNING OUTCOME 1

Identify essential nutrients and their dietary sources.

### CONCEPTS FOR LECTURE

1. The body's most basic nutrient need is water. The energy-providing nutrients are carbohydrates, fats, and proteins. Micronutrients (vitamins and minerals) are required in small amounts to metabolize the energy-providing nutrients.

### POWERPOINT LECTURE SLIDES

*(NOTE: The number on each PPT Lecture Slide directly corresponds with the Concepts for Lecture.)*

 **1** Essential Nutrients and Sources
    • Water

Carbohydrates are sugars (simple carbohydrates) and starches and fiber (complex carbohydrates).

Sugars may be monosaccharides (one molecule) or disaccharides (double molecules). Glucose is the most common monosaccharide. Most sugars are produced naturally by plants, especially fruits, sugar cane, and sugar beets. However, other sugars are from an animal source such as lactose found in animal milk. Processed or refined sugars have been extracted from natural sources.

Starches are insoluble, nonsweet forms of carbohydrates that exist naturally in plants such as grains, legumes, and potatoes. Cereals, breads, flour, and puddings are processed from starches.

Fiber is derived from plants and is found in the outer layer of grains, bran, and in the skin, seeds, and pulp of many vegetables and fruits. The Nutritional Reference Guide lists sources of fiber-rich foods.

Proteins are composed of amino acids (essential and nonessential). Most animal proteins, including meat, poultry, fish, dairy products, and eggs, are complete proteins (contain all of the essential amino acids plus many nonessential ones). Incomplete proteins lack one or more essential amino acids and are usually derived from vegetables. (Box 47–5 presents combinations of plant proteins that provide complete proteins.)

Fats are lipids that are solid at room temperature and oils are lipids that are liquid at room temperature. Fatty acids are the basic structural units of most lipids. Fatty acids are either saturated (for example, butyric acid found in butter) or unsaturated.

Unsaturated fatty acids may be monounsaturated or polyunsaturated (for example, linoleic acid found in vegetable oil). Lipids are classified as simple (glycerides) or compound (triglycerides which may be saturated or unsaturated). Saturated triglycerides are found in animal products such as butter. Unsaturated triglycerides are found in plant products such as olive oil and corn oil. Cholesterol is a fatlike substance produced by the body and found in foods of animal origin (milk, egg yolk, and organ meat).

Vitamins are either water soluble (vitamin C and the B-complex vitamins) or fat soluble (vitamins A, D, E, K). Vitamin content is highest in fresh foods that are consumed as soon as possible after harvest.

Minerals are found in organic compounds, as inorganic compounds, and as free ions. Macrominerals are those that people require daily in amounts over 100 mg (calcium, phosphorus, sodium, potassium, magnesium, chloride, and sulfur). Microminerals are those that people require daily in amounts less than 100 mg (iron, zinc, manganese, iodine, fluoride, copper, cobalt, chromium, and selenium). The Nutritional Reference Guide lists major food sources of calcium and iron.

- Carbohydrates
- Protein
- Fats
- Micronutrients
  - Vitamins
  - Minerals

## LEARNING OUTCOME 2

Describe normal digestion, absorption, and metabolism of carbohydrates, proteins, and lipids.

### CONCEPTS FOR LECTURE

1. Major enzymes of carbohydrate digestion include ptyalin (salivary amylase), pancreatic amylase, and the disaccharidases: maltase, sucrase, and lactase. The desired end products are monosaccharides. Essentially all monosaccharides (glucose, fructose, and galactose) are absorbed by the small intestines in healthy people. After the body breaks carbohydrates into glucose, some glucose continues to circulate in the blood to maintain blood levels and to provide a readily available source of energy. Insulin is secreted by the pancreas and aids the transport of glucose into cells. Carbohydrates are stored either as glycogen or fat. Almost all body cells are capable of storing glycogen; however, most is stored in the liver or skeletal muscles for conversion back to glucose. Glucose that cannot be stored as glycogen is converted to fat.

2. Digestion of protein foods begins in the mouth, where the enzyme pepsin breaks protein down into smaller units. However, most protein is digested in the small intestine. The pancreas secretes the proteolytic enzymes trypsin, chymotrypsin, and carboxypeptidase. Glands in the intestinal wall secrete aminopeptidase and dipeptidase, which break protein down into smaller molecules and eventually into amino acids. Amino acids are absorbed by active transport through the small intestines into the portal blood circulation. Protein metabolism includes three activities: anabolism (building tissue), catabolism (breaking down tissue), and nitrogen balance (a measure of the degree of protein anabolism and catabolism).

3. Lipid digestion begins in the stomach, but they are mainly digested in the small intestine, primarily by bile, pancreatic lipase, and enteric lipase. End products of lipid digestion are glycerol, fatty acids, and cholesterol. They are immediately reassembled inside the intestinal cells into triglycerides and cholesterol esters, which are not water soluble. The small intestine and the liver must convert these into soluble compounds called lipoproteins. Converting fat into usable energy occurs through lipase that breaks down triglycerides in adipose cells, releasing glycerol and fatty acids into the blood. Only the glycerol molecules in fat can be converted to glucose.

### POWERPOINT LECTURE SLIDES

*(NOTE: The number on each PPT Lecture Slide directly corresponds with the Concepts for Lecture.)*

**1** Digestion, Absorption, and Metabolism: Carbohydrates
- Major enzymes include ptyalin (salivary amylase), pancreatic amylase, and the disaccharidases
- End products are monosaccharides
- Absorbed by the small intestine in healthy people
- Body breaks carbohydrates into glucose
  ○ Maintain blood levels
  ○ Provide a readily available source of energy stored as glycogen or fat

**2** Digestion, Absorption, Metabolism: Protein
- Digestion begins in the mouth with enzyme pepsin
- Most protein digested in the small intestine
- Pancreas secretes the proteolytic enzymes trypsin, chymotrypsin, and carboxypeptidase
- Glands in the intestinal wall secrete aminopeptidase and dipeptidase, which eventually break proteins into amino acids
- Amino acids are absorbed by active transport through the small intestines into the portal blood circulation
- Protein metabolism includes anabolism, catabolism, and nitrogen balance

**3** Digestion, Absorption, Metabolism: Lipids/Fats
- Digestion begins in the stomach, but mainly digested in the small intestine
- Digestion primarily by bile, pancreatic lipase, and enteric lipase
- End products of lipid digestion are glycerol, fatty acids, and cholesterol
- Reassembled inside the intestinal cells into triglycerides and cholesterol esters
- Small intestine and the liver convert these into soluble compounds called lipoprotein
- Converting fat into useable energy occurs through lipase that breaks down triglycerides in adipose cells releasing glycerol and fatty acids into the blood

## LEARNING OUTCOME 3

Explain essential aspects of energy balance.

### CONCEPTS FOR LECTURE

1. Energy balance is the relationship between the energy derived from food and the energy used by the body. The body obtains energy in the form of calories from carbohydrates, protein, fat, and alcohol. The body uses energy for voluntary activities such as walking and talking and for involuntary activities such as breathing and secreting enzymes. A person's energy balance is determined by comparing his or her energy intake with energy output.

   The amount of energy that nutrients or foods supply to the body is their caloric value. The energy liberated from the metabolism of food has been determined to be 4 calories/gram of carbohydrate and protein, 9 calories/gram of fat, and 7 calories/gram of alcohol.

   Metabolism refers to all biochemical and physiologic processes by which the body grows and maintains itself. The basal metabolic rate (BMR) is the rate at which the body metabolizes food to maintain the energy requirements of a person who is awake and at rest. The energy in food maintains the BMR and provides energy for activities such as running and walking.

   Resting energy expenditure (REE) is the amount of energy required to maintain basic body functions— in other words, the calories required to maintain life. The REE of healthy persons is generally about 1 cal/kg of body weight/hr for men and 0.9 cal/kg for women, although there is great variation among individuals. The actual daily expenditure of energy depends on the degree of activity of the individual.

### POWERPOINT LECTURE SLIDES

*(NOTE: The number on each PPT Lecture Slide directly corresponds with the Concepts for Lecture.)*

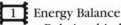 Energy Balance
   • Relationship between the energy derived from food and the energy used by the body
   • Caloric value is the amount of energy that nutrients or foods supply to the body
   • Basal metabolic rate (BMR) is the rate at which the body metabolizes food to maintain the energy requirements of a person who is awake and at rest
   • Resting energy expenditure (REE) is the amount of energy required to maintain basic body functions (calories required to maintain life)

## LEARNING OUTCOME 4

Discuss body weight and body mass standards.

### CONCEPTS FOR LECTURE

1. Maintaining a healthy or ideal body weight requires a balance between the expenditure of energy and the intake of nutrients. Generally, when the energy requirements of an individual equate with the daily caloric intake, the body weight remains stable.

### POWERPOINT LECTURE SLIDES

*(NOTE: The number on each PPT Lecture Slide directly corresponds with the Concepts for Lecture.)*

1 Healthy Body Weight
   • Balance between the expenditure of energy and the intake of nutrients

Ideal body weight (IBW) is the optimal weight recommended for optimal health. IBW can be determined by consulting standardized tables or by calculating the Rule of 5 for women and the Rule of 6 for men (See Box 47-1). Many health professionals consider the body mass index (BMI) to be the more reliable indicator of a person's healthy weight. However, the results must be used with caution in people who have fluid retention, in athletes, or in elders. BMI of < 18.5 is considered to be underweight; 18.5-24.9 normal; 25-29.9 overweight; 30.39.9 obesity; and >40 extreme obesity.

2. Another measure of body mass is percent body fat, which can be measured by underwater weighing and dual-energy x-ray (DEXA). Other indirect but more practical measures include waist circumference (see Box 47-2), skinfold testing, and near-infrared interactance. Bioelectrical impedance analysis (BIA) is used by some modern weight scales and is considered one of the most accurate methods of body fat determination.

Box 47-2 provides the classification of overweight and obesity by BMI, waist circumference, and associated disease risks.

- Ideal body weight (IBW) is the optimal weight recommended for optimal health
- Body mass index (BMI) is considered to be the more reliable indicator by health professionals

 Other Indirect Body Mass Measures
- Percent body fat
- Waist circumference
- Skinfold testing
- Near-infrared interactance
- Bioelectrical impedance analysis (BIA)

## SUGGESTIONS FOR CLASSROOM ACTIVITIES

- Have the students calculate BMI for themselves.
- Have the students practice skinfold testing on a partner.
- Have the students obtain waist circumference on a partner.

## SUGGESTIONS FOR CLINICAL ACTIVITIES

- Have the students obtain BMI of assigned clients and classify BMI according to Box 47-2 in the textbook.

# LEARNING OUTCOME 5

Identify factors influencing nutrition.

## CONCEPTS FOR LECTURE

1. Habits about eating are influenced by developmental considerations, gender, ethnicity and culture, beliefs about food, personal preferences, religious practices, lifestyle, economics, medications and therapy, health, alcohol consumption, advertising, and psychologic factors.

People in rapid periods of growth (infants and adolescents) have increased need for nutrients. Elders need fewer calories and dietary changes related to the risk of coronary heart disease osteoporosis, and hypertension, for example.

Because of body composition differences and the effects of reproductive function, men and women require different amounts of certain nutrients, calories, and fluid.

Ethnicity and culture may influence food preferences.

Food beliefs may be related to the popular media. Food fads may also influence nutrition.

## POWERPOINT LECTURE SLIDES

*(NOTE: The number on each PPT Lecture Slide directly corresponds with the Concepts for Lecture.)*

 Factors Influencing Nutrition
- Developmental considerations
- Gender
- Ethnicity and culture
- Beliefs about food
- Personal preferences
- Religious practices
- Lifestyle
- Economics
- Medications and therapy
- Health
- Alcohol consumption
- Advertising
- Psychologic factors

People develop food preferences based on associations developed with certain foods. Preferences may also be related to familiarity and preferences in tastes, smells, flavors, temperature, color, shapes, size, and texture.

Fasting and avoidance of certain foods may be related to religious practices.

Because of lifestyle people may select convenience foods. There are also individual differences in cooking skills, concerns about health, and necessity to work shifts which can influence nutrition. The amount of muscular activity performed daily will also influence the type and amount of nutrients required.

What, how much, and how often a person eats is related to socioeconomic status. Financial resources will also influence nutrition.

Medications may affect appetite, taste, absorption, excretions. There may also be drug-food interactions. Therapy (chemotherapy and radiation) also influence nutrition.

Dental problems, dysphagia, disease processes, and surgery can influence nutrition.

Alcohol consumption may cause weight gain and excessive use may cause nutritional deficiencies. Some research has shown some health benefits of moderate alcohol consumption.

Advertising attempts to persuade people to purchase certain foods and may target specific age groups.

Some people who are stressed, depressed, or lonely may overeat while others eat less. Certain psychophysiologic diseases (anorexia nervosa and bulimia) will influence nutrition.

## SUGGESTIONS FOR CLASSROOM ACTIVITIES

- Have the students obtain menus from various ethnic restaurants and compare and contrast the essential nutrients found in various foods offered.
- Have the students compare the cost of fresh fruits and vegetables to the cost of canned or frozen fruits and vegetables. Have the students read the food labels on the canned and frozen vegetables for additives.
- Have the students bring in various magazines geared to specific age groups and identify the types of food advertising in each. Compare and contrast.

## SUGGESTIONS FOR CLINICAL ACTIVITIES

- Have the students investigate the factors that influence the eating habits of their assigned clients as identified in the textbook (e.g., ethnicity, lifestyle, health, alcohol consumption). Discuss findings.

## LEARNING OUTCOME 6

Identify developmental nutritional considerations.

### CONCEPTS FOR LECTURE

1. The neonate's fluid and nutritional needs are met by breast milk or formula. The fluid needs of infants are proportionately greater than those of adults because of higher metabolic rate, immature kidneys, and greater

### POWERPOINT LECTURE SLIDES

*(NOTE: The number on each PPT Lecture Slide directly corresponds with the Concepts for Lecture.)*

1 Developmental Nutritional Considerations: Neonate to 1 Year

water losses through the skin and the lungs. The addition of solid food to the diet usually takes place between 4 and 6 months of age. At about 6 months of age, infants require iron supplementation to prevent iron deficiency anemia. Weaning from the breast or bottle to the cup takes place gradually and is usually achieved by 12 to 24 months. It is recommended that infants be breast-fed until 1 year of age (American Academy of Pediatrics, 2005). By the age of 1, most infants can be completely fed on table food, and milk intake is about 20 ounces per day.

2. Toddlers can eat most foods and adjust to three meals each day. By the age of 3 when most of the deciduous teeth have emerged, the toddler is able to bite and chew adult table food. The toddler is less likely to have fluid imbalances than infants. The caloric requirement is 900 to 1,800 Kcal/day. Developing independence may be exhibited through the toddler's refusal of certain foods. Toddlers often display their liking of rituals by eating foods in a certain order, cutting food in a specific way, or accompanying certain foods with a particular drink. The need for adequate iron, calcium, and vitamins C and A, which are common toddler deficiencies, should be addressed.

3. Preschoolers eat adult foods, are very active, and often require snacks between meals. Cheese, fruits, yogurt, raw vegetables, and milk are good choices. Preschoolers are even less susceptible than the toddler to fluid imbalances. The average 5-year-old weighing 20 kg (45 lb) requires at least 75 mL of liquid per kilogram of body weight per day or 1,500 mL every 24 hours.

4. The school-age child requires a balanced diet including 2,400 Kcal/day. School-age children eat three meals a day and one or two nutritious snacks. Children need a protein-rich food at breakfast to sustain the prolonged physical and mental effort required at school. The average healthy 8-year-old weighing 30 kg (66 lb) requires about 1,750 mL of fluid per day. The school-age child generally eats lunch at school. Many dietary problems stem from this independence in food choices, and poor eating habits may result in obesity.

5. During adolescence, the need for nutrients and calories increases, particularly during the growth spurt. In particular, the need for protein, calcium, vitamin D, iron, and the B vitamins increases. An adequate diet for an adolescent is 1 quart of milk per day as well as appropriate amounts of meat, vegetables, fruits, breads, and cereals. Adequate calcium intake (1,200 to 1,500 mg/day) may help decrease osteoporosis in later years. Parents can provide healthy snacks such as fruits and cheese and at the same time limit the amount of junk food available in the home. Common problems related to nutrition and self-esteem among adolescents include obesity, anorexia nervosa, and bulimia.

6. The nutritional habits established during young adulthood often lay the foundation for the patterns maintained throughout a person's life. Young adult females need to maintain adequate iron intake, ingesting 18 mg

- Fluid and nutritional needs are met by breast milk or formula
- Addition of solid food to the diet between 4 and 6 months of age
- By the age of 1, most infants can be completely fed on table food, and milk intake is about 20 ounces per day

2 Developmental Nutritional Considerations: Toddler
- Can eat most foods and adjust to three meals each day
- By the age of 3 is able to bite and chew adult table food
- Caloric requirement is 900 to 1,800 Kcal/day
- Iron, calcium, and vitamins C and A are common deficiencies

3 Developmental Nutritional Considerations: Preschooler
- Eat adult foods
- Very active and often require snacks between meals
- Cheese, fruits, yogurt, raw vegetables, and milk are good choices

4 Developmental Nutritional Considerations: School-aged
- Require a balanced diet including 2,400 Kcal/day
- Eat three meals a day and one or two nutritious snacks
- Need a protein-rich food at breakfast to sustain effort required at school

5 Developmental Nutritional Considerations: Adolescent
- Increased need for nutrient and calories during growth spurts
- Adequate calcium intake (1,200 to 1,500 mg/day)
- Healthy snacks and limits on junk foods
- Anorexia nervosa and bulimia may occur

6 Developmental Nutritional Considerations: Adults
- Continue to eat a healthy diet, with special attention to protein, calcium, and limiting cholesterol and caloric intake
- Two or three liters of fluid should be included in the daily diet
- Postmenopausal women need to ingest sufficient calcium and vitamin D to reduce osteoporosis
- Antioxidants such as vitamin A, C, and E may be helpful in reducing the risks of heart disease

7 Developmental Nutritional Considerations: Elders
- Require the same basic nutrition as the younger adult
- Fewer calories are needed because of the lower metabolic rate and the decrease in physical activity
- Some may need more carbohydrates for fiber and bulk

of iron daily. Calcium is needed in young adulthood to maintain bones and help decrease the chances of developing osteoporosis in later life. The person must also have adequate vitamin D, which is necessary for the calcium to enter the bloodstream. Obesity may occur as the active teen becomes the sedentary adult but does not decrease caloric intake. Low-fat and/or low-cholesterol diets play a significant role in both the prevention and treatment of cardiovascular disease.

The middle-aged adult should continue to eat a healthy diet, following the recommended portions of the food groups, with special attention to protein, calcium, and limiting cholesterol and caloric intake. Two or three liters of fluid should be included in the daily diet. Postmenopausal women need to ingest sufficient calcium and vitamin D to reduce osteoporosis, and antioxidants such as vitamins A, C, and E may be helpful in reducing the risks of heart disease in women. Iron supplements are no longer needed. Decreased metabolic activity and decreased physical activity mean a decrease in caloric needs. During late middle age, gastric juice secretion and free acid gradually decline.

7. Elders require the same basic nutrition as the younger adult. However, fewer calories are needed by elders because of the lower metabolic rate and the decrease in physical activity. Some may need more carbohydrates for fiber and bulk, but most nutrient requirements remain relatively unchanged. Physical changes such as tooth loss and impaired sense of taste and smell may affect eating habits. Decreased saliva and gastric juice secretion may also affect a person's nutrition. Psychosocial factors may also contribute to nutritional problems. Some elders may live alone and do not want to cook for themselves or eat alone. They may adopt poor dietary habits. Lack of transportation, poor access to stores, and inability to prepare the food also affect nutritional status. Loss of spouse, anxiety, depression, dependence on others, and lowered income all affect eating habits (see Table 47–2).

- Physical changes as tooth loss and impaired sense of taste and smell may affect eating habits
- Decreased saliva and gastric juice secretion may also affect nutrition
- Psychosocial factors may also contribute to nutritional problems

---

**SUGGESTIONS FOR CLASSROOM ACTIVITIES**

- Divide the students into groups. Assign an age group to each group. Ask the students to develop a pamphlet addressing nutritional requirements, nutritional issues (e.g., food jags), and suggestions for addressing these for the assigned age group.

**SUGGESTIONS FOR CLINICAL ACTIVITIES**

- Ask a dietician from the agency to discuss how the institution addresses the nutritional needs of the age group served by the institution.

---

## LEARNING OUTCOME 7

Evaluate a diet using a food guide pyramid.

### CONCEPTS FOR LECTURE

1. The Food Guide Pyramid is a graphic aid that was developed by the USDA as a guide in making daily food choices. In 2005, the USDA issued a new pyramid in a food guidance system on the Internet to allow people to customize their pyramid based on a variety of characteristics. On the new pyramid, the food groups—grains, vegetables, fruits, milk, oils, and meat and beans—are drawn from the base of the pyramid to the apex (See Figure 47.1).
2. The pyramid has been modified for young children (See Figure 47.2).
3. The pyramid has been modified for elders (See Figure 47.3) and the pyramid has been translated into other languages.

### POWERPOINT LECTURE SLIDES

*(NOTE: The number on each PPT Lecture Slide directly corresponds with the Concepts for Lecture.)*

1 Food Guide Pyramid

2 Food Guide Pyramid for Young Children

3 Food Guide Pyramid for People Older than 70 Years

### SUGGESTIONS FOR CLASSROOM ACTIVITIES

- Have the students use the *www.mypyramid.gov* site to develop a meal plan for themselves and track their intake for one week. Discuss results.

### SUGGESTIONS FOR CLINICAL ACTIVITIES

- Have the students ask their assigned clients to save their menus for one day. Have the students evaluate the foods eaten by the clients for that day using the *www.mypyramid.gov* site. Discuss the results.

## LEARNING OUTCOME 8

Discuss essential components and purposes of nutritional assessment and nutritional screening.

### CONCEPTS FOR LECTURE

1. A nutritional screen is an assessment performed to identify clients at risk for malnutrition or those who are malnourished. Clients who are found to be at moderate or high risk are followed with a comprehensive assessment by a dietician (see Box 47-6). Medicare standards for nursing homes require that any resident whose percent of meals eaten falls below 75% receive a full nutritional assessment by a nurse.
2. Nurses carry out nutritional screens through routine nursing histories and physical examinations. Custom-designed screening tools for specific populations and specific disorders are available and can be incorporated into the nursing history. Other data include but are not limited to age; gender; activity level; difficulty eating; condition of the mouth, teeth, and presence of dentures; changes in appetite and weight; physical disabilities that affect purchasing, preparing, and eating food; cultural and religious beliefs that affect food choices; living arrangements; general health status and medical conditions; and medication history.

  The physical examination focuses on rapidly proliferating tissues such as skin, hair, nails, eyes, and

### POWERPOINT LECTURE SLIDES

*(NOTE: The number on each PPT Lecture Slide directly corresponds with the Concepts for Lecture.)*

1 Nutritional Screening and Assessment
  - Purposes
    ○ Assessment performed to identify risk for malnutrition or those who are malnourished
    ○ Clients found to be at moderate or high risk are followed with a comprehensive assessment by a dietician
    ○ Nursing home residents whose percent of meals eaten falls below 75% receive a full nutritional assessment by a nurse

2 Nutritional Screening and Assessment
  - Nursing history
  - Physical examination
  - Calculating percentage of weight loss
  - Dietary history
  - Anthropometric measurements
  - Laboratory data
  - Measuring skinfold
  - Measuring mid-arm circumference

mucosa, but also includes a systematic review comparable to any routine physical examination. See Clinical Manifestations and Figure 47.6 for signs associated with malnutrition. These signs must be viewed as suggestive because the signs are nonspecific.

Additional assessment data can be provided by calculating percentage of weight loss and obtaining a dietary history, anthropometric measurements, and laboratory data. (Table 47–3 lists components of a screening and an in-depth nutritional assessment.)

---

## SUGGESTIONS FOR CLASSROOM ACTIVITIES

- Have the students select a partner and perform a 24-hour food recall.
- Have the students practice performing a physical examination (skin, hair, nails, eyes, and mucosa) on a partner to assess for signs associated with malnutrition.

## SUGGESTIONS FOR CLINICAL ACTIVITIES

- Have the students perform a nutritional screening assessment and physical examination on their assigned clients. Discuss findings.
- Invite a dietitian from the agency to discuss the components of an in-depth nutritional assessment.

---

# LEARNING OUTCOME 9

Identify risk factors for and clinical signs of malnutrition.

## CONCEPTS FOR LECTURE

1. Box 47–6 presents a summary of risk factors for nutritional problems. These include factors identified in the diet history (chewing and swallowing difficulties; inadequate food budget, food intake, preparation and storage facilities; intravenous fluids; living and eating alone; no intake for longer than 7 days; physical disabilities; and restricted or fad diets); those identified in the medical history (adolescent pregnancy or closely spaced pregnancies; alcohol/substance abuse; catabolic or hypermetabolic conditions; chronic illnesses; dental problems; neurologic or cognitive impairments; oral and gastrointestinal surgeries; and unintentional weight loss or gain); and those identified in the medication history (antacid, antidepressants, antihypertensives, anti-inflammatory, antineoplastic, aspirin, digitalis, diuretics, laxatives and potassium chloride medication use).

2. Clinical signs of malnutrition are listed in Clinical Manifestations: Malnutrition. These include changes in appearance and vitality; over or underweight; dry, flaky, pale or pigmented skin; presence of petechiae, bruises and lack of subcutaneous fat and edema; brittle, pale, ridges or spoon-shaped nails; dry, dull, sparse, brittle hair with loss of color; pale or red conjunctiva, dryness, soft or dull cornea and night blindness; swollen, red lips cracked at side of the mouth or vertical fissures; swollen, beefy, red or magenta, smooth tongue or an increased or decreased size of the tongue; spongy, swollen or inflamed and bleeding gums; underdeveloped, flaccid, wasted or soft muscles; anorexia, indigestion,

## POWERPOINT LECTURE SLIDES

*(NOTE: The number on each PPT Lecture Slide directly corresponds with the Concepts for Lecture.)*

 Malnutrition Risk Factors
- Diet history
  - Chewing and swallowing difficulties
  - Inadequate food budget, food intake, preparation, and storage facilities
  - Intravenous fluids
  - Living and eating alone
  - No intake for longer than 7 days
  - Physical disabilities; and restricted or fad diets
- Medical history
  - Adolescent pregnancy or closely spaced pregnancies
  - Alcohol/substance abuse
  - Catabolic or hypermetabolic conditions
  - Chronic illnesses
  - Dental problems
  - Neurologic or cognitive impairments
  - Oral and gastrointestinal surgeries
  - Unintentional weight loss or gain
- Medication history
  - Antacid
  - Antidepressants
  - Antihypertensives
  - Anti-inflammatory
  - Antineoplastic
  - Aspirin
  - Digitalis

diarrhea, constipation; enlarged liver and protruding abdomen; decreased reflexes, sensory loss, burning and tingling of hands and feet, mental confusion or irritability.

- ○ Diuretics
- ○ Laxatives
- ○ Potassium chloride

 Malnutrition Clinical Signs
- Changes in appearance and vitality
- Over or underweight
- Dry, flaky, pale or pigmented skin
- Presence of petechiae, bruises
- Lack of subcutaneous fat and edema
- Brittle, pale, ridges or spoon-shaped nails
- Dry, dull, sparse, brittle hair with loss of color
- Pale or red conjunctiva
- Eye dryness
- Soft or dull cornea
- Night blindness
- Swollen, red lips cracked at side of the mouth or with vertical fissures
- Swollen, beefy, red or magenta, smooth tongue or an increased or decreased size of the tongue
- Spongy, swollen or inflamed and bleeding gums
- Underdeveloped, flaccid, wasted or soft muscles
- Anorexia, indigestion, diarrhea, constipation
- Enlarged liver and protruding abdomen
- Decreased reflexes, sensory loss
- Burning and tingling of hands and feet
- Mental confusion or irritability

---

**SUGGESTIONS FOR CLASSROOM ACTIVITIES**

- Discuss the most common risks for malnutrition in the local community.

**SUGGESTIONS FOR CLINICAL ACTIVITIES**

- Examine laboratory test results to identify clients who may have problems with their nutritional status.
- Ask the students to review the history and physical examination of their assigned clients for risk factors for malnutrition.

---

# LEARNING OUTCOME 10

Describe nursing interventions to promote optimal nutrition.

## CONCEPTS FOR LECTURE

1. Nursing interventions to promote optimal nutrition for hospitalized clients are often provided in collaboration with the primary care provider who writes the diet orders and the dietician who informs clients about special diets. The nurse reinforces this interaction and, in addition, creates an atmosphere that encourages eating, provides assistance with eating, monitors the client's appetite and food intake, administers enteral and parenteral feedings, and consults with the primary care provider and dietician about nutritional problems that arise.

## POWERPOINT LECTURE SLIDES

*(NOTE: The number on each PPT Lecture Slide directly corresponds with the Concepts for Lecture.)*

 Nursing Interventions for Optimal Nutrition
- Hospitalized client
  - ○ Provided in collaboration with the primary care provider and the dietician
  - ○ Reinforce information presented by dietician
  - ○ Create an atmosphere that encourages eating
  - ○ Provide and assist with eating
  - ○ Monitor the client's appetite and food intake
  - ○ Administer enteral and parenteral feedings

2. In the community setting, the nurse's role is largely educational. In the home setting, nurses initiate nutritional screens, refer clients at risk to appropriate resources, instruct clients about enteral and parenteral feedings, and offer nutritional counseling as needed.

   Nutrition counseling involves more than simply providing information. The nurse must help clients integrate diet changes into their lifestyle and provide strategies to motivate them to change their eating habits.

○ Consult with primary care provider and dietician about nutritional problems

 Community Setting
- Education
- Home setting
  ○ Refer clients at risk to appropriate resources
  ○ Instruct clients about enteral and parenteral feedings
  ○ Offer nutritional counseling as needed
  ○ Assist clients with special diets
  ○ Stimulate the appetite
  ○ Assist clients with meals
  ○ Refer to special community nutritional services
  ○ Provide enteral and parenteral nutrition

---

## SUGGESTIONS FOR CLASSROOM ACTIVITIES

- Have the students plan a presentation for the educational institution on optimal nutrition.

## SUGGESTIONS FOR CLINICAL ACTIVITIES

- Discuss how the nurse can promote an environment for clients that encourages optimal nutrition.
- Have the students investigate the resources used by the agency to educate clients on optimal nutrition.

---

# LEARNING OUTCOME 11

Discuss nursing interventions to treat clients with nutritional problems.

## CONCEPTS FOR LECTURE

1. Nursing interventions include assisting clients with special diets, stimulating the appetite, assisting clients with meals, referring to special community nutritional services, and providing enteral and parenteral nutrition.

   Assisting clients and support persons with special diets is a function shared by the dietician or nutritionist and the nurse. The dietician informs the client and support persons about the specific foods allowed and not allowed and assists the client with meal planning. The nurse reinforces this instruction, assists the client to make changes, and evaluates the response.

   Stimulating a person's appetite requires the nurse to determine the reason for the lack of appetite and then deal with the problems. Some general interventions for improving the client's appetite are summarized in Box 47–10.

   Guidelines for providing meals to clients are summarized in Box 47–11. When feeding a client, ask in which order the client would like to eat the food. Allow ample time for the client to chew and swallow the food. Provide fluids as requested. If the client is unable to communicate, offer fluids after every three or four mouthfuls of solid food. Make the time pleasant, choosing topics of conversation that are of interest to clients who want to talk.

## POWERPOINT LECTURE SLIDES

*(NOTE: The number on each PPT Lecture Slide directly corresponds with the Concepts for Lecture.)*

 Nursing Intervention for Nutritional Problems
- Assisting with special diets
- Stimulating the appetite
- Referring to community nutritional services
- Providing enteral and parenteral nutrition

Special community nutritional services may include Meals on Wheels or similar organizations, grocery delivery services, and the USDA food stamp programs.

Enteral nutrition is an alternative feeding method to ensure adequate nutrition. Enteral feedings are administered through nasogastric and small-bore feeding tubes or through gastrostomy or jejunostomy tubes.

Parenteral nutrition (PN), also referred to as total parenteral nutrition (TPN) or intravenous hyperalimentation (IVH), is provided when the gastrointestinal tract is nonfunctional because of an interruption in its continuity or because its absorption capacity is impaired. PN is administered intravenously such as through a central venous catheter into the superior vena cava.

---

## SUGGESTIONS FOR CLASSROOM ACTIVITIES

- Provide or ask students to bring a "meal" to the classroom. Have the students feed each other. Discuss feelings and insights experienced.

## SUGGESTIONS FOR CLINICAL ACTIVITIES

- Arrange for several students to observe the preparation of TPN by the pharmacy, and ask these students to share their observations with the clinical group.
- Invite a social worker from the agency to discuss community nutritional resources, including availability, qualifications for use, and type of services provided.

---

# LEARNING OUTCOME 12

Perform the skills of inserting enteral tubes, administering feedings and medications through enteral tubes, and removing enteral tubes.

## CONCEPTS FOR LECTURE

1. Skill 47.1 Inserting a Nasogastric Tube lists the steps in this procedure. Essential steps include: assess the nares to determine obstructions to airflow; select the nostril with greatest airflow; prepare the tube by ensuring that the stylus or guidewire is secured; determine how far to insert the tube by measuring from the tip of the client's nose, to the ear lobe, to the tip of the xiphoid process and mark with adhesive tape; glove and lubricate the tube with water-soluble lubricant; explain how the client can help during the procedure; ask the client to hyperextend his head and insert along the floor of the nasal passage through the nasopharynx; withdraw if resistance is met; once the tube is in the oropharynx, ask the client to tilt the head forward and swallow as the tube is passed to the predetermined mark; ascertain correct placement by aspirating stomach contents and testing the pH or for presence of bilirubin, confirm placement by x-ray or insert 10–30 mL of air while listening with a stethoscope over the stomach for whooshing sound (should not be the primary way to assess placement); secure the tube to the client's nose and gown; attach to suction if ordered; document relevant information; establish a plan for providing daily tube care including inspection of

## POWERPOINT LECTURE SLIDES

*(NOTE: The number on each PPT Lecture Slide directly corresponds with the Concepts for Lecture.)*

1 Skill 47.1 Inserting a Nasogastric Tube

2 Skill 47.2 Removing a Nasogastric Tube

3 Skill 47.3 Administering a Tube Feeding

---

the nares, cleaning the nares and around the tube, changing the adhesive tape securing the tube, prn, and providing frequent mouth care.

2. Skill 47.2 Removing a Nasogastric Tube lists the steps in this procedure. Essential steps include: detach the tube from suction, the client's nose, and gown; remove the tube, glove, instill 50 mL of air, pinch the tube and instruct the client to take a deep breath and hold until the tube is removed; smoothly withdraw the tube, check the tube for intactness and appropriately discard; provide the client with tissues to blow nose; provide mouth care, and document.

3. Skill 47.3 Administering a Tube Feeding lists the steps in this procedure. Essential steps include: correctly positioning the client prior to feeding; assess tube placement; assess residual feeding volume and hold if greater than 100 mL or greater than $\frac{1}{2}$ volume of last feeding according to agency policy; reinstill residual according to agency policy; check residual volume for continuous feedings at least every 4 to 6 hours; administer feeding; if using an open system, hang container approximately 12 inches above point of tube entry; clamp tubing, add feeding, run feeding through tubing, attach to the feeding tube and adjust rate according to order; if using syringe feeding remove the plunger from the syringe and attach the syringe to the feeding tube, pinch the tube and add the feeding; permit the feeding to run in by gravity raising or lowering the syringe to adjust rate to client comfort; if using a closed or prefilled system, attach the administration set, squeeze the drip chamber and run feeding through the tubing, attach to the feeding tube and adjust the rate; at the end of the feeding flush the feeding tube, clamp the tube, and ask the client to remain in upright position (or at least with head elevated 30 degrees) or in a slightly elevated right lateral position for at least 30 minutes; document relevant information and care properly for the equipment. Tube feedings may also be administered using an enteral feeding pump. Directions for use of the pump provided by the manufacturer should be followed.

---

## SUGGESTIONS FOR CLASSROOM ACTIVITIES

- Show videotapes (DVDs) of the skills of inserting and removing nasogastric tubes and administering enteral feedings.
- Show various types of nasogastric, gastrostomy, and jejunostomy tubes.
- Have the students practice performing insertion of nasogastric tubes and administering feeding on manikins.

## SUGGESTIONS FOR CLINICAL ACTIVITIES

- Review the agency's policies and procedures for administering enteral feedings.
- If possible, arrange for students to observe insertion of gastrostomy and jejunostomy tubes.
- Demonstrate the use of the feeding pumps used in the institution.
- Whenever possible, assign students to insert nasogastric tubes, provide care for clients who have enteral tubes, and administer enteral feedings.

# LEARNING OUTCOME 13

Plan, implement, and evaluate nursing care associated with nursing diagnoses related to nutritional problems.

## CONCEPTS FOR LECTURE

1. NANDA includes the following diagnostic labels for nutritional problems: *Imbalanced Nutrition: More Than Body Requirements, Imbalanced Nutrition: Less Than Body Requirements, Readiness for Enhanced Nutrition,* and *Risk for Imbalanced Nutrition: More Than Body Requirements.* Many other NANDA diagnoses may apply because nutritional problems often affect other areas of human functioning. Examples include *Activity Intolerance, Constipation, Low Self-Esteem,* and *Risk for Infection.*

2. Major outcomes for clients with or at risk for nutritional problems include the following: maintain or restore optimal nutritional status, promote healthy nutritional practices, prevent complications associated with malnutrition, decrease weight, and regain specified weight.

3. Specific interventions and associated nursing interventions are selected to meet the individual needs of the client.

   The outcomes established in the planning phase are evaluated according to specific outcomes, also established in that phase. If outcomes are not achieved, the nurse should explore the reasons.

## POWERPOINT LECTURE SLIDES

*(NOTE: The number on each PPT Lecture Slide directly corresponds with the Concepts for Lecture.)*

**1** Nursing Diagnoses Related to Nutritional Problems
- Imbalanced nutrition: more than body requirements
- Imbalanced nutrition: less than body requirements
- Readiness for enhanced nutrition
- Risk for imbalanced nutrition: more than body requirements
- Examples of nursing diagnoses related to nutritional problems as etiology
  - Activity intolerance
  - Constipation
  - Low self-esteem
  - Risk for infection

**2** Desired Outcomes for Clients with Nutritional Problems
- Maintain or restore optimal nutritional status
- Promote healthy nutritional practices
- Prevent complications associated with malnutrition
- Decrease weight
- Regain specified weight

**3** Planning and Evaluation
- Intervention selected to meet goals
- Evaluation based upon criteria set in outcomes

## SUGGESTIONS FOR CLASSROOM ACTIVITIES

- Have the students review the defining characteristics, etiology, and risk factors for the NANDA diagnoses related to nutrition.
- Have the students review care plans for nutrition in various care plan references.

## SUGGESTIONS FOR CLINICAL ACTIVITIES

- Have the students develop a care plan for assigned clients related to nutrition and share these care plans with the clinical group.
- Share standard care plans, computer-generated care plans, or clinical pathways that include nutritional support used by the institution.

# CHAPTER 48
## URINARY ELIMINATION

## RESOURCE LIBRARY

###  PRENTICE HALL NURSING MEDIALINK DVD-ROM

Audio Glossary
NCLEX® Review
Skills Checklists
Animations:
    *Kidney*
    *Female Catheterization*

###  COMPANION WEBSITE

Additional NCLEX® Review
Case Study: *Intermittent Self-Catheterization*
Care Plan Activity: *Client with Urinary Retention Catheter*
Application Activity: *Urinary Incontinence*
Links to Resources

###  IMAGE LIBRARY

**Figure 48.1** Anatomic structures of the urinary tract.
**Figure 48.2** The nephrons of the kidney are composed of six parts: the glomerulus, Bowman's capsule, proximal convoluted tubule, loop of Henle, distal convoluted tubule, and collecting duct.
**Figure 48.3** The male urogenital system.
**Figure 48.4** The female urogenital system.
**Figure 48.5** A urine "hat"—a urine collection device for the toilet.
**Figure 48.6** Urine being measured from a urine collection bag.
**Figure 48.7** Red-rubber or plastic Robinson straight catheters.
**Figure 48.8** A coudé catheter.
**Figure 48.9** An indwelling/retention (Foley) catheter with the balloon inflated.

**Figure 48.10** A three-way Foley catheter often used for continuous bladder irrigation.
**Figure 48.11** Positioning the collecting bag and tubing when sitting in a chair.
**Figure 48.12** A suprapubic catheter in place.
**Figure 48.13** A nephrostomy.
**Figure 48.14** An incontinent urinary diversion (ileal conduit).
**Figure 48.15** The Kock pouch—a continent urinary diversion.
**Figure 48.16** A neobladder.
**Skill 48.1** Applying an External Catheter
**Skill 48.2** Performing Urethral Urinary Catheterization
**Skill 48.3** Performing Bladder Irrigation

## LEARNING OUTCOME 1

Describe the process of urination, from urine formation through micturition.

### CONCEPTS FOR LECTURE

1. Urinary elimination depends on effective functioning of the upper urinary tract (kidneys and ureters) and the lower urinary tract (urinary bladder, urethra, and pelvic floor) as well as normal functioning of the cardiovascular and nervous systems.
2. Urine is formed in the nephron, the functional unit of the kidney. Each nephron has a glomerulus, a tuft of capillaries surrounded by Bowman's capsule. Fluids and solutes readily move across the endothelium of the capillaries into the capsule. From Bowman's capsule the filtrate moves into the tubule of the nephron. In the proximal convoluted tubule, most of the water

### POWERPOINT LECTURE SLIDES

*(NOTE: The number on each PPT Lecture Slide directly corresponds with the Concepts for Lecture.)*

**1** Process of Urination
- Depends on effective functioning of
  - Upper urinary tract (kidneys, ureters)
  - Lower urinary tract (bladder, urethra, pelvic floor)
  - Cardiovascular system
  - Nervous system

**2** Urine Formation
- Nephron
  - Functional unit of the kidney
  - Urine is formed here

and electrolytes are reabsorbed. Solutes such as glucose are reabsorbed in the loop of Henle, and other substances are secreted into the filtrate. In the distal convoluted tubule, additional water and sodium are reabsorbed under the control of hormones such as the antidiuretic hormone (ADH) and aldosterone. Once urine is formed it moves into the calyces of the renal pelvis and from there into the ureters and then into the bladder.

3. The normal process of urination is stimulated when sufficient urine collects in the bladder, stimulating special stretch receptors in the bladder wall. Stretch receptors transmit impulses to the spinal cord voiding reflex center located at the level of the second to fourth sacral vertebrae, causing the internal sphincter to relax and stimulating the urge to void. If the time and place are appropriate, the conscious portion of the brain relaxes the external urethral sphincter muscle and urine is eliminated through the urethra.

- Glomerulus
  - Tuft of capillaries surrounded by Bowman's capsule
  - Fluids and solutes move across endothelium of the capillaries into the capsule
- Bowman's capsule
  - Filtrate moves from here into the tubule of the nephron
- Proximal convoluted tubule
  - Most of water and electrolytes are reabsorbed
- Loop of Henle
  - Solutes such as glucose reabsorbed here
  - Other substances secreted
- Distal convoluted tubule
  - Additional water and sodium reabsorbed here under control of hormones (ADH and aldosterone)
- Formed urine then moves to
  - Calyces of the renal pelvis
  - Ureters
  - Bladder

 Process of Micturition
- Urine collects in the bladder
- Pressure stimulates special stretch receptors in the bladder wall
- Stretch receptors transmit impulses to the spinal cord voiding reflex center
- Internal sphincter relaxes stimulating the urge to void
- If appropriate, the conscious portion of the brain relaxes the external urethral sphincter muscle
- Urine eliminated through the urethra

---

## SUGGESTIONS FOR CLASSROOM ACTIVITIES

- Ask the students to review their anatomy and physiology textbooks and notes on urinary elimination.

---

## LEARNING OUTCOME 2

Identify factors that influence urinary elimination.

### CONCEPTS FOR LECTURE

1. Numerous factors affect the volume and characteristics of the urine produced and the manner in which it is secreted such as developmental factors, psychosocial factors, fluid and food intake, medications, muscle tone, pathologic conditions, and surgical and diagnostic procedures.

    The fetal kidneys begin to excrete urine between the 11th and 12th weeks of development; the ability to concentrate urine is minimal in infants leading to light yellow urine; kidney function matures between the first and second year; urine is concentrated and

### POWERPOINT LECTURE SLIDES

*(NOTE: The number on each PPT Lecture Slide directly corresponds with the Concepts for Lecture.)*

 Factors Influencing Urinary Elimination
- Developmental factors
- Psychosocial factors
- Fluid and food intake
- Medications
- Muscle tone
- Pathologic conditions
- Surgical and diagnostic procedures

urine becomes amber color; between 18 and 24 months the child is able to recognize bladder fullness and hold beyond the urge to void; between 2 $\frac{1}{2}$ and 3 years the child can perceive bladder fullness, hold, and communicate need to urinate; between 4 and 5 years the child develops full urinary control with daytime control occurring prior to nighttime control; kidneys continue to grow in relation to body growth; kidneys reach maximum size between 35–40 years; after 50 years the kidneys decrease in size and function; most shrinkage occurs in the cortex as nephrons are lost; approximately 30% of nephrons are lost by age 80; renal blood flow decreases because of vascular changes and decreased cardiac output; bladder tone diminishes leading to increased frequency and nocturia; decreased bladder tone and contractility may lead to residual urine and an increased risk of bladder infection; and urinary incontinence may occur due to mobility problems or neurological impairments (See Table 48-1). In addition an enlarged prostate gland in men and hormonal changes in older women may also affection urinary elimination.

Some psychosocial factors influencing urinary elimination include privacy, normal position, sufficient time, occasional sound of running water, change in accustomed conditions, voluntary suppression due to perceived time pressure.

Some fluid and food factors affecting urinary output include as fluid intake increases, urine output also increase. Certain fluids (alcohol and caffeinated fluids) increase urine output and fluids and foods with high sodium content cause fluid retention and other foods such as beets can change the color of the urine.

Medications that affect the autonomic nervous system can interfere with normal urinary processes; diuretics increase urine output, and some medictions change the color of urine. Box 48-1 lists additional medications that may cause urinary retention.

Retention catheters that have been in place for a long period of time may create poor bladder tone and poor tone of the pelvic muscles contribute to changes in the ability to store urine and empty the bladder.

Some pathological conditions affect the formation and excretion of urine including diseases of the kidneys, heart and circulatory system; conditions causing abnormal fluid loss (vomiting and fever); obstruction of the flow of urine; and hypertrophy of the prostate gland.

Some surgical and diagnostic procedures may affect passage of urine and urine production itself, e.g., urethral tissues may swell after cystoscopy; surgery on any part of the urinary system may cause bleeding; and spinal anesthesia may cause decreased awareness of the need to void and the ability to void until recovery from the anesthesia.

## LEARNING OUTCOME 3

Identify common causes of selected urinary problems.

### CONCEPTS FOR LECTURE

1. Polyuria refers to the production of abnormally large amounts of urine. It is associated with ingestion of fluids containing caffeine or alcohol, prescribed diuretics, presence of thirst, dehydration, weight loss, and a history of diabetes mellitus, diabetes insipidus, or kidney disease.

   Oliguria (low urine output) and anuria (no urine production) are associated with a decrease in fluid intake; signs of dehydration; presence of hypotension, shock, or heart failure; history of kidney disease; signs of renal failure such as elevated blood urea nitrogen (BUN) and serum creatinine; edema; and hypertension.

   Frequency (voiding at frequent intervals) and nocturia (voiding two or more times a night) are associated with pregnancy, increase in fluid intake, and urinary tract infection.

   Urgency, the sudden strong desire to void, is associated with presence of psychologic stress and urinary tract infections.

   Dysuria, voiding that is either painful or difficult, is associated with urinary tract inflammation, infection, or injury. It is also associated with hesitancy, hematuria, pyuria, and frequency.

   Enuresis, involuntary urination in children beyond the age when voluntary bladder control is normally acquired, is associated with family history of enuresis, difficult access to toilet facilities, and home stresses.

   Incontinence, involuntary urination, is associated with bladder inflammation or disease; difficulties in independent toileting; leakage when coughing, laughing, or sneezing; and cognitive impairment.

   Retention, bladder overdistention due to inability to empty the bladder, is associated with distended bladder on palpation and percussion; signs and symptoms such as pubic discomfort, restlessness, frequency, and small urine volume; recent anesthesia; recent perineal surgery; presence of perineal swelling; medications

### POWERPOINT LECTURE SLIDES

*(NOTE: The number on each PPT Lecture Slide directly corresponds with the Concepts for Lecture.)*

 Selected Urinary Problems
- Polyuria
- Oliguria, anuria
- Frequency or nocturia
- Urgency
- Dysuria
- Enuresis
- Incontience
- Retention
- Neurogenic bladder

prescribed; and lack of privacy or other factors inhibiting micturition (See Table 48–3).

A neurogenic bladder is flaccid and distended or spastic with frequent involuntary urination. It is associated with impairment of neurologic function.

---

## SUGGESTIONS FOR CLASSROOM ACTIVITIES

- Review common pathologic conditions contributing to urinary problems and related nursing interventions.
- Discuss incontinence (types and causes) and have the students investigate interventions to assist clients to cope with this problem.

## SUGGESTIONS FOR CLINICAL ACTIVITIES

- Demonstrate the use of the bladder scanner.
- Review the agency's policies and procedures for identifying and treating urinary retention.

---

# LEARNING OUTCOME 4

Describe nursing assessment of urinary function, including subjective and objective data.

## CONCEPTS FOR LECTURE

1. A complete assessment of a client's urinary function includes the following: nursing history, physical assessment of the genitourinary system, hydration status, examination of the urine, and relating the data obtained from the results of any diagnostic tests and procedures.
2. The nursing history should include the client's normal voiding patterns and frequency, appearance of the urine and any recent changes, any past or current problems with urination, the presence of an ostomy, and factors influencing the elimination patterns. Examples of the interview questions are shown in the Assessment Interview.
3. The physical assessment usually involves percussion of the kidneys to detect areas of tenderness; palpation and percussion of the bladder are also performed. If the client's history or current problems indicate a need for it, the urethral meatus of both male and female clients is inspected for swelling, discharge, and inflammation. It is also important to assess the skin for color, texture, and tissue turgor as well as the presence of edema. If incontinence, dribbling, or dysuria is noted in the history, the skin of the perineum should be inspected for irritation.
4. For information on the assessment of urine, see Outcome 5.

    To measure urinary output and residual urine, the nurse assesses the amount of urine eliminated per hour (approximately 60 mL) or per day (about 1,500 mL). Residual urine is normally 50 to 100 mL and can be measured by catheterization after the client voids or by bladder scanner.
5. The blood levels of urea and creatinine are routinely used to evaluate renal function. Urea is the end product

## POWERPOINT LECTURE SLIDES

*(NOTE: The number on each PPT Lecture Slide directly corresponds with the Concepts for Lecture.)*

**1** Nursing Assessment of urinary Function
- Nursing history
- Physical assessment of genitourinary system
- Hydration status
- Examination of urine
- Data from any diagnostic tests and procedures

**2** Nursing History
- Normal voiding patterns
- Appearance of urine
- Recent changes
- Past or current problems

**3** Physical Assessment
- Percussion of kidneys and bladder to detect tenderness
- Inspect utrethral meatus for swelling, discharge, inflammation
- Skin color, texture, turgor, signs of irritation
- Edema

**4** Assessing Urine
- Measuring urinary output
- Measuring residual urine

**5** Diagnostic Tests
- Blood urea nitrogen
- Creatinine

of protein metabolism and is measured as blood urea nitrogen (BUN). Creatinine is produced in relatively constant quantities by the muscles. The creatinine clearance test uses 24-hour urine and serum creatinine levels to determine the glomerular filtration rate, a sensitive indicator of renal function.

---

### SUGGESTIONS FOR CLASSROOM ACTIVITIES

- Review the common laboratory tests performed to diagnose urinary alterations and related nursing responsibilities.

### SUGGESTIONS FOR CLINICAL ACTIVITIES

- Review forms and measurement guides used for intake and output recording in the agency.
- Review laboratory results that reflect alterations in urinary function.

---

## LEARNING OUTCOME 5

Identify normal and abnormal characteristics and constituents of urine.

### CONCEPTS FOR LECTURE

1. Normal urine consists of 96% water and 4% solutes. Organic solutes include urea, ammonia, creatinine, and uric acid. Inorganic solutes include sodium, chloride, potassium sulfate, magnesium, and phosphorus. Variations in color can occur.
2. Normal characteristics of urine include: volume of 1,200–1,500 mL/day for adults; straw colored and transparent; faint aromatic odor, absence of microorganisms, glucose, ketones, or blood, pH of 4.5 to 8, and specific gravity between 1.010 to 1.025.

    Abnormal characteristics of urine include: volume of less than 1,200 mL/day or large volume over the amount of fluid intake; dark amber, dark orange, red, dark brown color; viscid, thick urine; presence of mucous plugs; presence of microorganisms, glucose, ketones, and blood; pH greater than 8 or less than 4.5; and specific gravity greater than 1.025 and less than 1.010.

### POWERPOINT LECTURE SLIDES

*(NOTE: The number on each PPT Lecture Slide directly corresponds with the Concepts for Lecture.)*

 Characteristics of Urine
- Normal urine
  - 96% water and 4% solutes
  - Organic solutes include urea, ammonia, creatinine, and uric acid
  - Inorganic solutes include sodium, chloride, potassium sulfate, magnesium, and phosphorus

 Characateristics of Normal and Abnormal Urine
- Volume
- Color, clarity
- Odor
- Sterility
- pH
- Specific gravity
- Glucose
- Ketone bodies
- Blood

---

### SUGGESTIONS FOR CLASSROOM ACTIVITIES

- Discuss the appropriate performance of "dipstick" urine testing.
- Discuss the significance of each of the organic solutes found in normal and abnormal urine.

### SUGGESTIONS FOR CLINICAL ACTIVITIES

- Arrange for the students to observe urinary testing in the agency's laboratory.
- Ask the students to review the urinalysis results of several clients with different types of diagnoses. Compare and contrast findings.

# LEARNING OUTCOME 6

Develop nursing diagnoses, desired outcomes, and interventions related to urinary elimination.

## CONCEPTS FOR LECTURE

1. NANDA includes one general diagnostic label for urinary elimination problems: *Impaired Urinary Elimination.* NANDA also includes several labels that are more specific: *Functional Urinary Incontinence, Reflex Urinary Incontinence, Stress Urinary Incontinence, Total Urinary Incontinence, Urge Urinary Incontinence,* and *Urinary Retention.* Box 48–2 lists definitions of each of the NANDA diagnoses related to incontinence.

2. Problems of urinary elimination also may become the etiology for other problems experienced by the client. Examples include *Risk for Infection, Low Self-Esteem, Risk for Impaired Skin Integrity, Self-Care Deficit: Toileting, Risk for Deficient Fluid Volume* or *Excess Fluid Volume, Disturbed Body Image, Deficient Knowledge, Risk for Caregiver Role Strain,* and *Risk for Social Isolation.*

3. The desired outcomes established will vary according to the diagnosis and defining characteristics. Examples of overall general goals may include the following: maintain or restore a normal voiding pattern; regain normal urine output; prevent associated risks such as infection, skin breakdown, fluid and electrolyte imbalance, and lowered self-esteem; perform toilet activities independently with or without assistive devices; and contain urine with the appropriate device, catheter, ostomy appliance, or absorbent product.

4. Appropriate preventive and corrective nursing interventions that relate to these must be specified. Specific nursing activities associated with each of these interventions can be selected to meet the client's individual needs.

   General nursing interventions include promoting fluid intake, maintaining normal voiding patterns, assisting with toileting, preventing urinary tract infections, managing urinary incontinence, providing continence (bladder) training, teaching pelvic muscle exercises, maintaining skin integrity, applying external urinary drainage devices, managing urinary retention, performing urinary catheterizations, performing bladder irrigations, and providing care for clients with indwelling urinary catheters and urinary diversion.

## POWERPOINT LECTURE SLIDES

*(NOTE: The number on each PPT Lecture Slide directly corresponds with the Concepts for Lecture.)*

**1** NANDA Nursing Diagnoses
- Impaired urinary elimination
- Functional urinary incontinence
- Reflex urinary incontinence
- Stress urinary incontinence
- Total urinary incontinence
- Urge urinary incontinence
- Urinary retention

**2** Related Nursing Diagnoses
- Risk for infection
- Low self-esteem
- Risk for impaired skin integrity
- Self-care deficit
- Risk for deficient fluid volume or excess fluid volume
- Disturbed body image
- Deficient knowledge
- Risk for caregiver role strain
- Risk for social isolation

**3** Desired Outcomes
- Maintain or restore a normal voiding pattern
- Regain normal urine output
- Prevent associated risks such as infection, skin breakdown, fluid and electrolyte imbalance, and lowered self-esteem
- Perform toilet activities independently with or without assistive devices
- Contain urine with the appropriate device, catheter, ostomy appliance, or absorbent product

**4** General Nursing Interventions
- Promoting fluid intake
- Maintaining normal voiding patterns
- Assisting with toileting
- Preventing urinary tract infections
- Managing urinary incontinence
- Managing urinary retention
- Continence (bladder) training
- Teaching pelvic muscle exercises
- Maintaining skin integrity
- Applying external urinary drainage devices
- Performing urinary catheterizations
- Performing bladder irrigations
- Providing care for clients with indwelling urinary catheters and urinary diversions

## SUGGESTIONS FOR CLASSROOM ACTIVITIES

- Compare and contrast NANDA diagnoses related to urinary incontinence based on definition, defining characteristics, and etiology.
- Discuss interventions the nurse may use to assist clients to perform toilet activities.

## SUGGESTIONS FOR CLINICAL ACTIVITIES

- Discuss the current research on care of the client who has an indwelling catheter. Compare to the agency's procedure for providing care for the client with an indwelling catheter.
- Have the students review care plans for clients who have nursing diagnoses related to urinary incontinence. Ask the students to compare and contrast interventions. Have them develop a care plan for assigned clients with urinary incontinence, if appropriate.

## LEARNING OUTCOME 7

Delineate ways to prevent urinary infection.

## CONCEPTS FOR LECTURE

1. Gastrointestinal bacteria can colonize the perineal area and move into the urethra, especially when there is urethral trauma, irritation, or manipulation. Women are at particular risk.

   The following guidelines are useful to prevent urinary infection:

   - Drink eight 8-ounce glasses of water per day.
   - Practice frequent voiding (every 2 to 4 hours).
   - Avoid use of harsh soaps, bubble bath, powder, or sprays in the perineal area.
   - Avoid tight-fitting pants or other clothing that creates irritation to the urethra and prevents ventilation of the perineal area.
   - Wear cotton rather than nylon underclothes.
   - Girls and women should always wipe the perineal area from front to back following urination or defecation.
   - If recurrent urinary infections are a problem, take showers rather than baths.

## POWERPOINT LECTURE SLIDES

*(NOTE: The number on each PPT Lecture Slide directly corresponds with the Concepts for Lecture.)*

 Preventing Urinary Tract Infections
- Drink eight-ounce glasses of water per day
- Practice frequent voiding (every 2 to 4 hours)
- Avoid use of harsh soaps, bubble bath, powder, or sprays in the perineal area
- Avoid tight-fitting pants or other clothing
- Wear cotton rather than nylon underclothes
- Always wipe the perineal area from front to back following urination or defecation (girls and women)
- Take showers rather than baths if recurrent urinary infections are a problem

## SUGGESTIONS FOR CLASSROOM ACTIVITIES

- Have the students review current evidence-based practice related to prevention of urinary tract infections and develop an information sheet for clients based on their findings.

## SUGGESTIONS FOR CLINICAL ACTIVITIES

- Invite a staff nurse to discuss practices used to prevent urinary tract infections for clients on the clinical unit.

## LEARNING OUTCOME 8

Explain the care of clients with retention catheters or urinary diversions.

### CONCEPTS FOR LECTURE

1. Nursing care of the client with an indwelling catheter and continuous drainage is largely directed toward preventing infection of the urinary tract and encouraging urinary flow through the drainage system. This includes encouraging large amounts of fluid intake, accurately recording the fluid intake and output, changing the retention catheter and tubing, maintaining the patency of the drainage system, preventing contamination of the drainage system, and teaching these measures to the client.

    Fluids are important. The client should drink up to 3,000 mL/day if permitted to flush the bladder, decrease likelihood of urinary stasis, infection, and decrease risk of sediment obstructing the tubing.

    Dietary measures are also important. Acidifying the urine may reduce the risk of urinary tract infection and calculus formation. Foods such as eggs, cheese, meat and poultry, whole grains, cranberries, plums, prunes, and tomatoes tend to increase the acidity of the urine. Conversely, most fruits, vegetables, legumes, milk, and milk products result in alkaline urine.

    For perineal care, no special cleaning other than routine hygiene is necessary for clients with retention catheters.

    Routine changing of the catheter and tubing is not recommended. Collection of sediment in the catheter or tubing or impaired urine drainage are indicators for changing the catheter and drainage system.

    Guidelines to prevent catheter-associated urinary tract infections are given in Practice Guidelines and include: an established infection control program; catheterize clients only when absolutely necessary; maintain a sterile closed-drainage system; do not discontinue unless absolutely necessary; remove the catheter as soon as possible; follow good hand hygiene; perform routine perineal care; and prevent contamination by feces in the incontinent client.

2. Ongoing assessment of clients with retention catheters is a high priority. To maintain patency of the drainage system and prevent contamination of the drainage system, the nurse should ensure that there are no obstructions in the drainage tubing and that the drainage tubing is not clogged with mucus or blood. Check that there is no tension on the catheter or tubing, ensure that gravity drainage is maintained, make sure there are no loops in the tubing below its entry to the drainage receptacle and that the drainage receptacle is below the level of the client's bladder, and ensure that the drainage system is well sealed or closed. Observe the flow of urine every 2 or 3 hours, and note color, odor, and any abnormal constituents. If sediment is present, check the catheter more frequently to ascertain whether it is plugged (See Box 48-4).

### POWERPOINT LECTURE SLIDES

*(NOTE: The number on each PPT Lecture Slide directly corresponds with the Concepts for Lecture.)*

**1** Nursing Care of Client with an Indwelling or Retention Catheter
- Goal: Prevent infection and maintain urinary flow through drainage system
- Interventions to prevent infection include:
  ○ Encourage fluid intake
  ○ Intake of foods that create acidic urine
  ○ Perineal care
  ○ Change catheter and drainage system only when necessary
  ○ Catheterize only when necessary
  ○ Maintain sterile closed-drainage system
  ○ Remove catheter as soon as possible
  ○ Follow good hand hygiene
  ○ Prevent fecal contamination

**2** Interventions to Maintain Urinary Flow Through Drainage System
- Ensure that there are no obstructions in the drainage tubing
- Ensure that drainage tubing is not clogged with mucus or blood
- Ensure that there is no tension on the catheter or tubing
- Ensure that gravity drainage is maintained
- Make sure there are no loops in the tubing below its entry to the drainage receptacle
- Keep the drainage receptacle below the level of the client's bladder
- Ensure that the drainage system is well sealed or closed
- Observe the flow of urine every 2 or 3 hours
- Note color, odor, and any abnormal constituents
- If sediment is present, check the catheter more frequently to ascertain whether it is plugged

**3** Nursing Care of Client With a Urinary Diversion
- Assess intake and output
- Note any changes in urine color, odor, or clarity (mucous shreds are commonly seen in the urine of clients with an ileal diversion)
- Frequently assess the condition of the stoma and surrounding skin
- Consult with the wound ostomy continence nurse (WOCN)

3. When caring for clients with a urinary diversion, the nurse must accurately assess intake and output; note any changes in urine color, odor, or clarity (mucous shreds are commonly seen in the urine of clients with an ileal diversion); and frequently assess the condition of the stoma and surrounding skin. The nurse should consult with the wound ostomy continence nurse (WOCN) to identify strategies for management of the stoma and peristomal problems and the most appropriate appliance for the client's needs.

## SUGGESTIONS FOR CLASSROOM ACTIVITIES

- Review the Centers for Disease Control (CDC) recommendations for care of clients with retention catheters.
- Invite an ostomy nurse to discuss care of the client who has a urinary ostomy.
- Show videotaped performance of insertion of a straight and indwelling catheter and ostomy care.
- Show various types of catheters and ostomy equipment.
- Have the students practice insertion of straight and retention catheters on manikins.

## SUGGESTIONS FOR CLINICAL ACTIVITIES

- Invite a dietician to discuss appropriate foods for clients who have alterations in urinary function.
- Review the agency's policies and procedures for maintaining the integrity of a retention catheter.
- Discuss methods of assisting a client to maintain appropriate fluid intake.
- Review the agency's procedures for catheterization, and assign students to perform catheterizations when possible.

# CHAPTER 49
## FECAL ELIMINATION

## RESOURCE LIBRARY

 **PRENTICE HALL NURSING MEDIALINK DVD-ROM**

Audio Glossary
NCLEX® Review
Skills Checklists
Animations:
   *Performing an Enema*

**COMPANION WEBSITE**

Additional NCLEX® Review
Case Study: *Client After Abdominal Surgery*
Care Plan Activity: *Client Who Had a Stroke*
Application Activity:
   *The United Ostomy Association*
   *Wound Ostomy Nurse*
Links to Resources

### IMAGE LIBRARY

**Figure 49.1** The large intestine.
**Figure 49.2** Internal and external hemorrhoids.
**Figure 49.3** The rectum, anal canal, and anal sphincters.
**Figure 49.4** The locations of bowel diversion ostomies.
**Figure 49.5** End colostomy: the diseased portion of bowel is removed and a rectal pouch remains.
**Figure 49.6** Loop colostomy.
**Figure 49.7** Divided colostomy with two separated stomas.
**Figure 49.8** Double-barreled colostomy.
**Figure 49.9** A commode with overlying seat.
**Figure 49.10** Top, The high-back or regular bedpan; Bottom, the slipper or fracture pan.
**Figure 49.11** Placing a slipper pan under the buttocks.

**Figure 49.12** Placing a regular bedpan against the client's buttocks.
**Figure 49.13** A drainable fecal collector pouch.
**Figure 49.14** Inflatable artificial sphincter.
**Figure 49.15** Adjustable ostomy belt.
**Figure 49.16** A, A one-piece ostomy appliance or pouching system, and B, a two-piece ostomy appliance or pouching system.
**Figure 49.17** A, A closed pouch, and B, a drainable pouch.
**Figure 49.18** Applying a pouch clamp.
**Skill 49.1** Administering an Enema
**Skill 49.2** Changing a Bowel Diversion Ostomy Appliance

## LEARNING OUTCOME 1

Understand the physiology of defecation.

### CONCEPTS FOR LECTURE

1. Defecation is the expulsion of feces from the anus and rectum. When peristaltic waves move the feces into the sigmoid colon and the rectum, the sensory nerves in the rectum are stimulated and the individual becomes aware of the need to defecate.

   When the internal anal sphincter relaxes, feces move into the anal canal. If appropriate, the external anal sphincter is relaxed voluntarily. Expulsion of the feces is assisted by contraction of the abdominal muscles and the diaphragm, which increases abdominal pressure, and by contraction of the muscles of the pelvic floor, which moves the feces through the anal canal.

### POWERPOINT LECTURE SLIDES

*(NOTE: The number on each PPT Lecture Slide directly corresponds with the Concepts for Lecture.)*

 Physiology of Defecation
   • Peristaltic waves move the feces into the sigmoid colon and the rectum
   • Sensory nerves in the rectum are stimulated
   • Individual becomes aware of the need to defecate
   • Feces move into the anal canal when the internal and external sphincter relax
   • External anal sphincter is relaxed voluntarily if timing is appropriate

Normal defecation is facilitated by thigh flexion, which increases the pressure within the abdomen, and a sitting position, which increases the downward pressure on the rectum.

- Expulsion of the feces assisted by contraction of the abdominal muscles and the diaphragm
- Moves the feces through the anal canal and expelled through the anus
- Facilitated by thigh flexion and a sitting position

## SUGGESTIONS FOR CLASSROOM ACTIVITIES

- Review the related anatomy of the structures involved in defecation.

## LEARNING OUTCOME 2

Identify factors that influence fecal elimination and patterns of defecation.

### CONCEPTS FOR LECTURE

1. Factors that affect defecation include developmental stage, diet, fluid, activity, psychologic factors, defecation habits, medications, diagnostic procedures, anesthesia, surgery, pathologic conditions, and pain.

   Newborns, infants, children, and elders are groups within which members have similarities in elimination patterns, e.g. newborns pass meconium within 24 hours of birth; control of defecation usually starts at 2 ⅔ to 3 years of age; and constipation is the most common bowel management problem in the elderly.

   Sufficient bulk (cellulose, fiber) is necessary to provide fecal volume. Therapeutic diet may affect fecal elimination as may individual difficulties in digesting certain foods, the effects of certain foods (e.g., spicy, gas-forming).

   Health elimination requires 2,000–3,000 mL per day of fluid.

   Activity stimulates peristalsis facilitating the movement of chyme. Weak abdominal muscles from lack of exercise, immobility, or neurologically impaired can lead to alterations in fecal elimination.

   Some people who are anxious or angry may experience increased peristalsis and those with depression may experience decreased peristalsis.

   Regular defecation patterns provide fecal elimination. When normal defecation reflexes are ignored, water is continued to be reabsorbed leading to hard feces that is difficult to expel.

   Some medications have side effects that interfere with normal elimination. Some directly affect elimination (laxatives). Some medications appear in the feces.

   For accuracy of certain diagnostic procedures, food and fluids may be restricted and enemas may need to be administered which interfere with normal patterns.

   General anesthesia can block the parasympathetic nervous system stimulation to the colon and

### POWERPOINT LECTURE SLIDES

*(NOTE: The number on each PPT Lecture Slide directly corresponds with the Concepts for Lecture.)*

 Factors that Influence Fecal Elimination
- Developmental stage
- Diet
- Fluid
- Activity
- Psychologic factors
- Defecation habits
- Medications
- Diagnostic procedures
- Anesthesia
- Surgery
- Pathologic conditions
- Pain

handling of the bowel during surgery can cause temporary cessation of peristalsis.

Spinal cord and head injuries may decreased sensory stimulation and impaired mobility may decrease the ability to respond to urge to defecate.

Painful elimination may cause the client to suppress the urge to defecate. One of the side effects of narcotic analgesics given for pain is constipation.

---

### SUGGESTIONS FOR CLASSROOM ACTIVITIES

- Discuss additional pathologic conditions that may influence fecal elimination.
- Discuss the signs and symptoms of colorectal cancer.

### SUGGESTIONS FOR CLINICAL ACTIVITIES

- Have students discuss factors that have altered fecal elimination patterns of assigned clients.

---

## LEARNING OUTCOME 3

Distinguish normal from abnormal characteristics and constituents of feces.

### CONCEPTS FOR LECTURE

1. Normal feces are made of about 75% water and 25% solid materials.

    Some normal characteristics of fecal matter include: feces in adults that are brown in color and yellow in infants; formed, soft, semisolid, and moist consistency; cylindrical shape with about 2.5 cm (1 in) diameter; amount varies with diet about 100 to 400 g/day; aromatic odor that is affected by ingested food and individual bacterial flora; constituents include small amount of undigested roughage, sloughed dead bacterial and epithelial cells, fat, protein, dried elements of digestive juices.

    Some abnormal characteristics of fecal matter include; clay, white, black, tarry, red, pale, orange or green color; hard, dry, diarrhea consistency; narrow, pencil-shaped, string-like consistency; pungent odor; pus, mucus, parasites, blood, large quantities of fat or foreign objects within the feces.

### POWERPOINT LECTURE SLIDES

*(NOTE: The number on each PPT Lecture Slide directly corresponds with the Concepts for Lecture.)*

 Characteristics of Normal and Abnormal Feces
- Color
- Consistency
- Shape
- Amount
- Odor
- Constituents

---

### SUGGESTIONS FOR CLASSROOM ACTIVITIES

- Have students review various fecal tests, e.g., fecal cultures, testing for occult blood, in the laboratory/diagnostic manual used in the curriculum.

### SUGGESTIONS FOR CLINICAL ACTIVITIES

- Have students discuss variation in fecal characteristics observed in assigned clients with various disease conditions.

---

# LEARNING OUTCOME 4

Identify common causes and effects of selected fecal elimination problems.

## CONCEPTS FOR LECTURE

1. Four common problems related to fecal elimination are constipation, diarrhea, bowel incontinence, and flatulence.

2. Defining characteristics for constipation include decreased frequency of defecation; hard, dry, formed stools; straining at stool; painful defecation; reports of rectal fullness or pressure or incomplete bowel evacuation; abdominal pain, cramps, or distention; anorexia or nausea; and headache (See Box 49-1). Many causes and factors contribute to constipation, including insufficient fiber and fluid intake, insufficient activity or immobility, irregular defecation habits, change in daily routine, lack of privacy, chronic use of laxatives or enemas, irritable bowel syndrome (IBS), pelvic floor dysfunction or muscle damage, poor motility or slow transit, neurological conditions, stroke or paralysis, emotional disturbances such as depression or mental confusion, and medications such as opioids, iron supplements, antihistamines, antacids, and antidepressants.

3. Fecal impaction is a mass or collection of hardened feces in the folds of the rectum. Fecal impaction can be recognized by the passage of liquid fecal seepage (diarrhea) and no normal stool. The liquid portion of the feces seeps out around the impacted mass. Other symptoms include frequent but nonproductive desire to defecate, rectal pain, a generalized feeling of illness, anorexia, distended abdomen, nausea, and vomiting. Causes of fecal impaction are usually poor defecation habits and constipation. The barium used in radiologic examinations of the upper and lower gastrointestinal tracts can be a causative factor.

4. Diarrhea refers to the passage of liquid feces and an increased frequency of defecation. Often spasmodic cramps occur, and bowel sounds are increased. Irritation of the anal region extending to the perineum and buttocks generally results with persistent diarrhea. Fatigue, weakness, malaise, and emaciation are the results of prolonged diarrhea. Major causes of diarrhea include psychologic stress; medications (antibiotics, iron, cathartics); allergy to foods, fluid, and drugs; intolerance of food or fluids; and diseases of the colon (malabsorption syndrome, Crohn's disease).

5. Bowel incontinence, also called fecal incontinence, refers to the loss of voluntary ability to control fecal and gaseous discharges through the anal sphincter. Incontinence may occur at specific times or it may occur irregularly. Partial incontinence is the inability to control flatus or to prevent minor soiling. Major incontinence is the inability to control feces of normal consistency. Fecal incontinence is generally associated with impaired functioning of the anal sphincter or its nerve supply, such as in some neuromuscular diseases,

## POWERPOINT LECTURE SLIDES

*(NOTE: The number on each PPT Lecture Slide directly corresponds with the Concepts for Lecture.)*

**1** Selected Fecal Elimination Problems
- Constipation
- Diarrhea
- Bowel incontinence
- Flatulence

**2** Constipation
- Decreased frequency of defecation
- Hard, dry, formed stools
- Straining at stool
- Painful defecation
- Causes include insufficient fiber and fluid intake, insufficient activity, irregular habits, and others

**3** Fecal Impaction
- Mass or collection of hardened feces in folds of rectum
- Passage of liquid fecal seepage and no normal stool
- Causes leave usually poor defecation habits and constipation

**4** Diarrhea
- Passage of liquid feces and increased frequency of defecation
- Spasmodic cramps, increased bowel sounds
- Fatigue, weakness, malaise, emaciation
- Major causes: stress, medications, allergies, intolerance of food or fluids, disease of colon

**5** Bowel Incontinence
- Loss of voluntary ability to control fecal and gaseous discharges
- Generally associated with impaired functioning of anal sphincter or nerve supply and with some neuromuscular diseases, spinal trauma, tumors

**6** Flatulence
- Excessive flatus in intestines
- Leads to stretching and inflation of intestines
- Can occur from variety of causes: foods, abdominal surgery, narcotics

spinal cord trauma, and tumors of the external anal sphincter muscle.

6. Flatulence is the presence of excessive flatus in the intestines and leads to stretching and inflation of the intestines. Flatulence can occur in the colon from a variety of causes, such as foods, abdominal surgery, or narcotics.

---

## SUGGESTIONS FOR CLASSROOM ACTIVITIES

- Review common medications including over-the-counter medications, used in treatment of constipation and diarrhea. Stress the appropriate use and misuse of these medications and associated client education related to use of these medications.

## SUGGESTIONS FOR CLINICAL ACTIVITIES

- Have students discuss examples of clients who have had constipation, diarrhea, fecal incontinence, or flatus including contributing factors, signs and symptoms exhibited, treatment, and nursing intervention.

---

# LEARNING OUTCOME 5

Describe methods used to assess the intestinal tract.

---

## CONCEPTS FOR LECTURE

1. Assessment of fecal elimination includes taking a nursing history; performing a physical examination of the abdomen, rectum, and anus; and inspecting the feces. The nurse should also review any data obtained from relevant diagnostic tests.

2. A nursing history helps the nurse ascertain the client's normal pattern, a description of usual feces, and any recent changes. The nurse collects information about any past or current problems with elimination, the presence of an ostomy, and factors influencing the elimination pattern. Examples of questions to elicit this information are shown in the Assessment Interview.

3. Physical examination of the abdomen, rectum, and anus is discussed in Chapter 30. Auscultation precedes palpation because palpation can alter peristalsis.

   Inspecting the feces includes observing the client's stool for color, consistency, shape, amount, odor, and the presence of abnormal constituents (See Table 49–1).

   Diagnostic studies include direct visualization techniques, indirect visualization, and laboratory tests for abnormal constituents.

## POWERPOINT LECTURE SLIDES

*(NOTE: The number on each PPT Lecture Slide directly corresponds with the Concepts for Lecture.)*

1 Assessment of Fecal Elimination
- Nursing history
- Physical examination
- Review of data from any diagnostic tests

2 Nursing History
- Ascertains the client's normal pattern
- Description of usual feces
- Recent changes
- Past problems with elimination
- Presence of an ostomy
- Factors influencing the elimination pattern

3 Physical Examination
- Examination of the abdomen, rectum, and anus
- Auscultation precedes palpation because palpation alters peristalsis
- Inspection of the feces for color, consistency, shape, amount, odor, abnormal constituents
- Review any data obtained from relevant diagnostic tests

---

## SUGGESTIONS FOR CLASSROOM ACTIVITIES

- Have students practice obtaining a nursing history related to fecal elimination using the Assessment Interview: Fecal Elimination in the textbook on another student.
- Divide students into groups and assign each a diagnostic test related to fecal elimination. Have the groups report on client preparation and nursing responsibilities related to the study.

## SUGGESTIONS FOR CLINICAL ACTIVITIES

- If possible, assign students to observe the performance of diagnostic studies such as barium enema, colonoscopy, etc. and share observations with the group.
- Have students gather appropriate assessment data concerning fecal elimination on their assigned clients and report findings with the group.

---

# LEARNING OUTCOME 6

Identify examples of nursing diagnoses, outcomes, and interventions for clients with elimination problems.

## CONCEPTS FOR LECTURE

1. NANDA includes the following diagnostic labels for fecal elimination problems: *Bowel Incontinence, Constipation, Risk for Constipation, Perceived Constipation,* and *Diarrhea*.

2. Fecal elimination problems may affect many other areas of human functioning and as a consequence may be the etiology of other NANDA diagnoses. Examples include *Risk for Deficient Fluid Volume, Risk for Impaired Skin Integrity, Low Self-Esteem, Disturbed Body Image, Deficient Knowledge (Bowel Training, Ostomy Management),* and *Anxiety*.

3. The major goals for clients with fecal elimination problems are to maintain or restore a normal bowel elimination pattern, maintain or regain normal stool consistency, and prevent associated risks such as fluid and electrolyte imbalance, skin breakdown, abdominal distention, and pain.

4. Appropriate preventive and corrective nursing interventions that relate to these must be identified. Specific nursing activities associated with each of these interventions can be selected to meet the client's individual needs.

   General nursing interventions include promoting regular defecation, teaching about medications, decreasing flatulence, administering enemas, digital removal of a fecal impaction (if agency policy permits), instituting bowel training programs, applying a fecal incontinence pouch, and ostomy management.

## POWERPOINT LECTURE SLIDES

*(NOTE: The number on each PPT Lecture Slide directly corresponds with the Concepts for Lecture.)*

**1** NANDA Nursing Diagnoses
- Bowel incontinence
- Constipation
- Risk for constipation
- Perceived constipation
- Diarrhea

**2** Related Nursing Diagnoses
- Risk for deficient fluid volume
- Risk for impaired skin integrity
- Low self-esteem
- Disturbed body image
- Deficient knowledge (bowel training, ostomy management)
- Anxiety

**3** General Goals
- Maintain or restore normal bowel elimination pattern
- Maintain or regain normal stool consistency
- Prevent associated risks such as fluid and electrolyte imbalance, skin breakdown, abdominal distention and pain

**4** General Nursing Interventions
- Promoting regular defecations
- Teaching about medications
- Decreasing flatulence
- Administering enemas
- Digital removal of a fecal impaction (if agency policy permits)
- Instituting bowel training programs
- Applying a fecal incontinence pouch
- Ostomy management

---

## SUGGESTIONS FOR CLASSROOM ACTIVITIES

- Have students review the definitions, defining characteristics, etiology, and risk factors for the NANDA diagnoses related to problems with fecal elimination.
- Have students practice assisting a client onto a bedpan using manikins.

## SUGGESTIONS FOR CLINICAL ACTIVITIES

- Have students develop care plans for clients who have fecal elimination problems.
- When possible, have students perform enema administration.

## CONCEPTS FOR LECTURE

1. The nurse can help clients achieve regular defecation by attending to provision of privacy, timing, nutrition and fluids, exercise, and positioning.

   Privacy during defecation is extremely important to many people. The nurse should provide as much privacy as possible for such clients but may need to stay with those who are too weak to be left alone.

   A client should be encouraged to defecate when the urge is recognized. To establish regular bowel elimination, the client and nurse can discuss when mass peristalsis normally occurs and provide time for defecation. Other activities should not interfere with defecation time.

   The diet a client needs for regular normal elimination varies, depending on the kind of feces the client currently has, the frequency of defecation, and the types of foods that the client finds assist with normal defecation. Clients who have constipation should be encouraged to increase fluid intake, hot liquids, fruit juices, and fiber in the diet. Clients with diarrhea should be encouraged to continue oral intake and bland food, eat smaller meals, avoid excessively hot or cold fluids and any foods known to increase diarrhea. Clients with flatulence should be encouraged to limit carbonated beverages, drinking straws, and gas-forming foods.

   Regular exercise helps clients develop a regular defecation pattern. Weak abdominal and pelvic muscles may be strengthened with isometric exercises.

   Although the squatting position best facilitates defecation, on a toilet seat the best position for most people seems to be leaning forward.

   For clients who have difficulty sitting down and getting up from the toilet, an elevated toilet seat can be attached to a regular toilet. A bedside commode can be used for an adult client who can get out of bed but is unable to walk to the bathroom. Appropriate positioning of the client on the bedpan should be used.

## POWERPOINT LECTURE SLIDES

*(NOTE: The number on each PPT Lecture Slide directly corresponds with the Concepts for Lecture.)*

 1 Measures to Maintain Normal Fecal Elimination Patterns
- Privacy
- Timing
- Nutrition and fluids
- Exercise
- Positioning

## SUGGESTIONS FOR CLASSROOM ACTIVITIES

- Divide students into groups and ask each to develop a teaching aid to develop a teaching guide to assist an adult to maintain normal fecal elimination patterns.

## SUGGESTIONS FOR CLINICAL ACTIVITIES

- Have students discuss methods to provide privacy for clients to help maintain normal fecal elimination patterns.
- Show equipment available in the agency to assist client with fecal elimination needs.

# LEARNING OUTCOME 8

Describe the purpose and action of commonly used enema solutions.

## CONCEPTS FOR LECTURE

1. Table 49–4 lists commonly used enema solutions and actions.

   Hypertonic solutions draw water into the colon. A commonly used hypertonic enema is the commercially prepared Fleet phosphate enema. Hypotonic solutions (tap water) distend the colon, stimulate peristalsis, and soften feces. Isotonic solutions (physiologic saline) distend the colon, stimulate peristalsis, and soften feces. Soapsuds (pure soap such as castile) enemas irritate the mucosa and distend the colon. Oil lubricates the feces and the colonic mucosa.

2. There are four types of enemas: cleansing, carminative, retention, and return-flow enemas.

   Cleansing enemas are given to prevent escape of feces during surgery, to prepare the intestine for certain diagnostic tests, and to remove feces in instances of constipation or impaction. Hypertonic, hypotonic, and isotonic solutions may be used.

   Carminative and return-flow enemas are given primarily to expel flatus.

   Retention enemas introduce oil or medication into the rectum and sigmoid colon.

   Return-flow enema is used occasionally to expel flatus.

## POWERPOINT LECTURE SLIDES

*(NOTE: The number on each PPT Lecture Slide directly corresponds with the Concepts for Lecture.)*

 Enemas
- Common enema solutions and actions
  - Hypertonic (Fleet phosphate)—draws water into the colon
  - Hypotonic (tap water)—distends the colon, stimulates peristalsis, softens feces
  - Isotonic (physiologic saline)—distends the colon, stimulates peristalsis, softens feces
  - Soapsuds (pure soap such as castile)—irritates mucosa and distends the colon
  - Oil—lubricates the feces and the colonic mucosa

2 Types of Enemas
- Cleansing
  - Prevents escape of feces during surgery
  - Prepare the intestines for certain diagnostic tests
  - Removes feces in instances of constipation or impaction
- Carminative and return-flow—used primarily to expel flatus
- Retention—introduces oil or medication into the rectum and sigmoid colon

## SUGGESTIONS FOR CLASSROOM ACTIVITIES

- Show videotape or DVD of administration of enemas and insertion of rectal tubes and have students practice these on manikins.
- Review the safety measures associated with enema administration, e.g., temperature of solutions.
- Review the procedure for removing a fecal impaction.
- Review the procedure for application of a fecal incontinence pouch.

## SUGGESTIONS FOR CLINICAL ACTIVITIES

- Review the procedures used for administering enemas in the agency.
- Assign students to administer enemas whenever possible.
- Review agency policy and procedure for removing a fecal impaction.

# LEARNING OUTCOME 9

Describe essentials of fecal stoma care for clients with an ostomy.

## CONCEPTS FOR LECTURE

1. Care of the stoma is important for all clients who have ostomies. The fecal material from a colostomy or ileostomy is irritating to the peristomal skin. This is particularly true of the stool from an ileostomy, which contains digestive enzymes.

## POWERPOINT LECTURE SLIDES

*(NOTE: The number on each PPT Lecture Slide directly corresponds with the Concepts for Lecture.)*

 Stoma Care for Clients with an Ostomy
- Normal stoma should appear red (like mucosal lining of the inner cheek) and may bleed slightly when touched

The stoma should appear red, similar in color to the mucosal lining of the inner cheek, and slightly moist. Slight bleeding may occur when the stoma is touched and this is normal. It is important to assess the peristomal skin for irritation each time the appliance is changed. Any irritation or skin breakdown needs to be treated immediately.

The skin is kept clean by washing off any excretion and drying thoroughly.

An ostomy appliance should protect the skin, collect stool, and control odor.

- Assess the peristomal skin for irritation each time the appliance is changed
- Treat any irritation or skin breakdown immediately
- Keep skin clean by washing off any excretion and drying thoroughly
- Protect skin, collect stool, and control odor with an ostomy appliance

## SUGGESTIONS FOR CLASSROOM ACTIVITIES

- Show videotape or DVD on the care of ostomies.
- Show equipment used in care of the stoma.

## SUGGESTIONS FOR CLINICAL ACTIVITIES

- Invite the enterostomal nurse to discuss the types of ostomies, care of ostomies, and assisting clients in adjusting to ostomies.

# CHAPTER 50
## OXYGENATION

## RESOURCE LIBRARY

### 💿 PRENTICE HALL NURSING MEDIALINK DVD-ROM

Audio Glossary
NCLEX® Review
Skills Checklists
Animations:
>  *Gas Exchange in the Lung*
>  *Carbon Dioxide Transport*
>  *Oxygen Transport*
>  *Pulmonary Diseases*

Videos:
>  *Incentive Spirometer*
>  *Humidifier*
>  *Nasal Cannula*
>  *Face Mask*
>  *Nonrebreather Mask*

### 🌐 COMPANION WEBSITE

Additional NCLEX® Review
Case Study: *Coping with Emphysema*
Care Plan Activity: *Deep Breathing and Coughing*
Application Activities:
>  *Learning About Lung Disease*
>  *Tracheostomy Nursing Care*

Links to Resources

### 📖 IMAGE LIBRARY

**Figure 50.1** A, Organs of the respiratory tract. B, Respiratory bronchioles, alveolar ducts, and alveoli.

**Figure 50.2** Gas exchange occurs between the air on the alveolar side and the blood on the capillary side.

**Figure 50.3** The relationship of lung volumes and capacities.

**Figure 50.4** A client using the overbed table to assist with breathing.

**Figure 50.5** A, Flow-oriented SMI; B, volume-oriented SMI.

**Figure 50.6** Percussing the upper posterior chest.

**Figure 50.7** Vibrating the upper posterior chest.

**Figure 50.8** An oxygen humidifier attached to a wall outlet oxygen flow meter.

**Figure 50.9** Insert flow meter into the wall unit.

**Figure 50.10** This flow meter is set to deliver 2 L/minute.

**Figure 50.11** A nasal cannula.

**Figure 50.12** A simple face mask.

**Figure 50.13** A partial rebreather mask.

**Figure 50.14** A nonrebreather mask.

**Figure 50.15** A Venturi mask.

**Figure 50.16** An oxygen face tent.

**Figure 50.17** Pediatric oxygen tent.

**Figure 50.18** An "E" cylinder oxygen tank on a wheeled stand.

**Figure 50.19** A portable liquid oxygen supply.

**Figure 50.20** An oropharyngeal airway in place.

**Figure 50.21** A nasopharyngeal airway in place.

**Figure 50.22** An endotracheal tube (ET).

**Figure 50.23** A tracheostomy tube in place.

**Figure 50.24** Components of a tracheostomy tube.

**Figure 50.25** A tracheostomy tube with a low-pressure cuff.

**Figure 50.26** A tracheostomy tube with a foam cuff.

**Figure 50.27** A tracheostomy mist collar.

**Figure 50.28** Types of suction catheters: A, open tipped; B, whistle tipped.

**Figure 50.29** Oral (Yankauer) suction tube.

**Figure 50.30** A wall suction unit.

**Figure 50.31** A closed airway suction (in-line) system.

**Figure 50.32** A disposable chest drainage system.

**Figure 50.33** Heimlich chest drain valve.

**Figure 50.34** The Pneumostat is an example of a device often used for clients with a pneumothorax.

**Skill 50.1** Administering Oxygen by Cannula, Face Mask, or Face Tent

**Skill 50.2** Oropharygneal, Nasopharygneal, and Nasotracheal Suctioning

**Skill 50.3** Suctioning a Tracheostomy or Endotracheal Tube

**Skill 50.4** Providing Tracheostomy Care

# LEARNING OUTCOME 1

Outline the structure and function of the respiratory system.

## CONCEPTS FOR LECTURE

1. The function of the respiratory system is gas exchange. Oxygen from inspired air diffuses from alveoli in the lungs into the blood in the pulmonary capillaries. Carbon dioxide produced during cell metabolism diffuses from the blood into the alveoli and is exhaled.

2. The respiratory system is divided structurally into the upper respiratory system and the lower respiratory system. The mouth, nose, pharynx, and larynx compose the upper respiratory system. The lower respiratory system includes the trachea and lungs, with the bronchi, bronchioles, alveoli, pulmonary capillary network, and pleural membranes. Inspired air is warmed, humidified, and filtered by the nose. Inspired air passes from the nose to the pharynx (composed of the nasopharynx and oropharynx), which is supplied with lymphoid tissue that traps and destroys pathogens entering with the air.

   The larynx has a role in providing speech, maintaining airway patency, and protecting the lower airways from swallowed food by closing the epiglottis to route food to the esophagus.

   The trachea and bronchi are lined with mucosal epithelium that produce a thin layer of mucus (the mucous blanket) that traps pathogens and microscopic particulate. Foreign particles are swept upward to the larynx and throat by cilia.

   No gas exchange occurs until the air enters the respiratory bronchioles and alveoli. Alveoli have very thin walls, composed of a single layer of cells covered by a network of pulmonary capillaries (the respiratory membrane) where gas exchange occurs.

   The outer surface of the lungs is covered by a thin, double layer of tissue known as the pleura. Between the layers is a potential space that contains a small amount of pleural fluid which prevents friction during movement of breathing.

## POWERPOINT LECTURE SLIDES

*(NOTE: The number on each PPT Lecture Slide directly corresponds with the Concepts for Lecture.)*

**1** Function of the Respiratory System
- The function of the respiratory system is gas exchange
- Oxygen from inspired air diffuses from alveoli in the lung into the blood in the pulmonary capillaries
- Carbon dioxide produced during cell metabolism diffuses from the blood into the alveoli and is exhaled

**2** Structures of the Respiratory System
- Upper respiratory tract
  - Mouth
  - Nose
  - Pharynx
  - Larynx
- Lower respiratory tract
  - Trachea
  - Bronchi
  - Bronchioles
  - Alveoli
  - Pulmonary capillary network
  - Pleural membranes

---

## SUGGESTIONS FOR CLASSROOM ACTIVITIES

- Ask the students to review the chapter on the respiratory system in their anatomy and physiology textbook.

## SUGGESTIONS FOR CLINICAL ACTIVITIES

- Arrange for the students to observe diagnostic testing of the respiratory tract in order to see the anatomical structures.

# LEARNING OUTCOME 2

Describe the processes of breathing (ventilation) and gas exchange (respiration).

## CONCEPTS FOR LECTURE

1. Ventilation of the lungs is accomplished through the act of breathing: inspiration (inhalation) when air flows into the lungs and expiration (exhalation) as air moves out of the lungs.
2. The intrapulmonary pressure (pressure within the lungs) always equalizes with atmospheric pressure. Inspiration occurs when the diaphragm and intercostal muscles contract, increasing the size of the thoracic cavity. The volume of the lungs increases, decreasing intrapulmonary pressure. Air then rushes into the lungs to equalize this pressure with atmospheric pressure.
3. Conversely, when the diaphragm and intercostal muscles relax, the volume of the lungs decreases, intrapulmonary pressure rises, and air is expelled.
4. After the alveoli are ventilated, the second phase of the respiratory process—the diffusion of oxygen from the alveoli and into the pulmonary blood vessels—begins. Pressure differences in the gases on each side of the respiratory membrane affect diffusion. The partial pressure (the pressure exerted by each individual gas in a mixture of gases according to its concentration in the mixture) of oxygen ($PO_2$) in the alveoli is about 100 mm Hg, whereas the $PO_2$ in the venous blood of the pulmonary arteries is about 60 mm Hg. These pressures rapidly equalize, however, so that the arterial oxygen pressure also reaches about 100 mm Hg. By contrast, carbon dioxide in the venous blood entering the pulmonary capillaries has a partial pressure of about 45 mm Hg, whereas that in the alveoli has a partial pressure of about 40 mm Hg. Therefore, carbon dioxide diffuses from the blood into the alveoli, where it can be eliminated with expired air.

## POWERPOINT LECTURE SLIDES

*(NOTE: The number on each PPT Lecture Slide directly corresponds with the Concepts for Lecture.)*

**1** Process of Breathing
- Inspiration—air flows into lungs
- Expiration—air flows out of lungs

**2** Inspiration
- Diaphragm and intercostals contact
- Thoracic cavity size increases
- Volume of lungs increases
- Intrapulmonary pressure decreases
- Air rushes into the lungs to equalize pressure

**3** Exhalation
- Diaphragm and intercostals relax
- Volume of the lungs decreases
- Intrapulmonary pressure rises
- Air is expelled

**4** Gas Exchange
- Occurs after the alveoli are ventilated
- Pressure differences in the gases on each side of the respiratory membranes affect diffusion
- Diffusion of oxygen from the alveoli into the pulmonary blood vessels
- Diffusion of carbon dioxide from the pulmonary blood vessels into the alveoli

## SUGGESTIONS FOR CLASSROOM ACTIVITIES

- Review the lung volume and capacities.

## SUGGESTIONS FOR CLINICAL ACTIVITIES

- Arrange for the students to observe pulmonary function testing.

# LEARNING OUTCOME 3

Explain the role and function of the respiratory system in transporting oxygen and carbon dioxide to and from body tissues.

## CONCEPTS FOR LECTURE

1. The third part of the respiratory process involves the transport of respiratory gases. Oxygen is transported from the lungs to the tissues, and carbon dioxide must be transported from the tissues to the lungs.

   Normally, most of the oxygen (97%) combines loosely with hemoglobin in the red blood cells and is carried to the tissues as oxyhemoglobin. The remaining

## POWERPOINT LECTURE SLIDES

*(NOTE: The number on each PPT Lecture Slide directly corresponds with the Concepts for Lecture.)*

**1** Oxygen Transport
- Transported from the lungs to the tissues
- 97% of oxygen combines with hemoglobin in red blood cells and carried to tissues as oxyhemoglobin

oxygen is dissolved and transported in the fluid of the plasma and cells.

2. Carbon dioxide, continually produced in the processes of cell metabolism, is transported from the cells to the lungs in three ways. The majority (about 65%) is carried inside the red blood cells as bicarbonate ($HCO_3$) and is an important component of the bicarbonate buffer system. A moderate amount of carbon dioxide (30%) combines with hemoglobin as carbhemoglobin for transport. Smaller amounts (5%) are transported in solution in the plasma and as carbonic acid (the compound formed when carbon dioxide combines with water).

- Remaining oxygen is dissolved and transported in plasma and cells

 Carbon Dioxide Transport
- Must be transported from the tissues to the lungs
- Continually produced in the process of cell metabolism
- 65% is carried inside the red blood cells as bicarbonate
- 30% combines with hemoglobin as carbhemoglobin
- 5% transported in solution in plasma and as carbonic acid

---

## SUGGESTIONS FOR CLINICAL ACTIVITIES

- Review arterial blood gases.

---

# LEARNING OUTCOME 4

Identify factors influencing respiratory function.

## CONCEPTS FOR LECTURE

1. Factors that influence respiratory function affect the cardiovascular system as well. These factors are age, environment, lifestyle, health status, medications, and stress.

    Profound changes occur in the respiratory system at birth when the fluid-filled lungs drain, $PCO_2$ rises, and the neonate, take the first breath. Changes of aging affect the respiratory system and may become especially important if the system is compromised by infection, stress, surgery, anesthesia, or other procedures.

    Altitude, heat, cold, and air pollution affect oxygenation.

    Physical exercise or activity increases the rate and depth of respirations and hence the supply of oxygen in the body. Certain occupations may predispose the individual to lung disease.

    Diseases of the respiratory system adversely affect oxygenation of the blood.

    A variety of medications can decrease the rate and depth of respirations (benzodiazepines, sedative-hypnotics, and antianxiety and narcotics such as morphine).

    Some people hyperventilate in response to stress. During stress the sympathetic nervous system is stimulated and epinephrine is released. Epinephrine dilates bronchioles increasing blood flow and oxygen to active muscles.

## POWERPOINT LECTURE SLIDES

*(NOTE: The number on each PPT Lecture Slide directly corresponds with the Concepts for Lecture.)*

 Factors that Influence Respiratory Function
- Age
- Environment
- Lifestyle
- Health status
- Medications
- Stress

## SUGGESTIONS FOR CLASSROOM ACTIVITIES

- Divide the students into groups. Assign each a factor that may influence respiratory function. Have each group develop a pamphlet describing these factors and interventions to prevent alterations.

## SUGGESTIONS FOR CLINICAL ACTIVITIES

- Ask the students to review the chart of assigned clients to determine factors that may influence respiratory function as listed in the textbook. Discuss findings in postconference.

---

# LEARNING OUTCOME 5

Identify common manifestations of impaired respiratory function.

## CONCEPTS FOR LECTURE

1. Three major alterations in respiration are hypoxia, altered breathing patterns, and an obstructed or partially obstructed airway.
2. Hypoxia is a condition of insufficient oxygen anywhere in the body, from the inspired gas to the tissue. Common manifestations of hypoxia include rapid pulse; rapid, shallow respirations and dyspnea; increased restlessness or light-headedness; flaring of the nares; substernal or intercostal retractions; and cyanosis.
3. Breathing patterns refer to the rate, volume, rhythm, and relative ease or effort of respiration. Tachypnea (rapid rate), bradypnea (abnormally slow rate), and apnea (cessation of breathing) are alterations in rate. Kussmaul's breathing is a type of hyperventilation (increased movement of air into and out of the lungs) by which the body attempts to compensate by blowing off the carbon dioxide that accompanies metabolic acidosis. Abnormal respiratory rhythms create an irregular breathing pattern. Cheyne-Stokes respirations (marked waxing and waning of respirations from very deep to very shallow and temporary apnea) and Biot's respirations (shallow breaths interrupted by apnea) are irregular breathing patterns seen in disease states. Orthopnea is the inability to breathe except in an upright or standing position. Dyspnea is difficult or uncomfortable breathing. The dyspneic person often appears anxious and may experience shortness of breath (SOB). Often the nostrils are flared, the skin may be dusky, and the heart rate is increased.
4. Obstructed airway (completely or partially) can occur anywhere along the upper or lower respiratory passageways. Partial obstruction is indicated by a low-pitched snoring sound during inhalation. Air passing through accumulated secretions may cause gurgly or bubbly respiratory sounds. Complete obstruction is indicated by extreme inspiratory effort that produces no chest movement and an inability to cough or speak. The client may also exhibit marked sternal and intercostal retractions. Stridor, a harsh, high-pitched sound, may be heard on inspiration. The client may have altered arterial blood gases, restlessness, dyspnea, and adventitious breath sounds.

## POWERPOINT LECTURE SLIDES

*(NOTE: The number on each PPT Lecture Slide directly corresponds with the Concepts for Lecture.)*

 Common Manifestations of Impaired Respiratory Function
- Hypoxia
- Altered breathing patterns
- Obstructed or partially obstructed airway

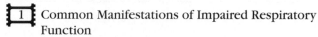 Hypoxia
- Condition of insufficient oxygen anywhere in the body
- Rapid pulse
- Rapid, shallow respirations and dyspnea
- Increased restlessness or light-headedness
- Flaring of the nares
- Substernal or intercostal retractions
- Cyanosis

3 Altered Breathing Patterns
- Alterations in respiratory rate:
  ○ Tachpnea (rapid rate)
  ○ Bradypnea (abnormally slow rate)
  ○ Apnea (cessation of breathing) alteration in volume and rhythm
  ○ Kussmaul's breathing
  ○ Cheyne-Stokes respirations
  ○ Biot's respirations
- Alterations in ease of breathing
  ○ Orthopnea
  ○ Dyspnea

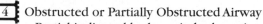 Obstructed or Partially Obstructed Airway
- Partial indicated by low-pitched snoring during inhalation
- Complete indicated by extreme inspiratory effort with no chest movement

## LEARNING OUTCOME 6

Describe nursing measures to promote respiratory function and oxygenation.

### CONCEPTS FOR LECTURE

1. Examples of nursing interventions to facilitate pulmonary ventilation may include ensuring a patent airway, positioning, encouraging deep breathing and coughing, ensuring adequate hydration, and giving medications.

   The semi-Fowler's or high Fowler's position allows maximum chest expansion in clients who are confined to bed. The nurse should encourage clients to turn from side to side frequently so that alternate sides of the chest are permitted maximum expansion. Leaning over the overbed table with a pillow for support may help dyspneic or orthopneic clients by pressing the lower chest against the table to help exhaling and preventing abdominal organs are not pressing on the diaphragm.

   Deep breathing and coughing assist the client to remove secretions from the airways. Breathing exercises such as abdominal (diaphragmatic) and pursed-lip breathing are frequently indicated for clients with restricted chest expansion. Forceful coughing often is less effective than using controlled or huff coughing techniques (see Client Teaching).

   Hydration maintains the moisture of the respiratory mucous membranes. Thin secretions are moved more readily by ciliary action. Fluid intake should be as great as the client can tolerate. Humidifiers are devices that add water vapor to inspired air. Nebulizers are used to deliver humidity and medications. They may be used with oxygen delivery systems to provide moistened air directly to the client to prevent mucous membranes from drying and becoming irritated and to loosen secretions for easier expectoration.

### POWERPOINT LECTURE SLIDES

*(NOTE: The number on each PPT Lecture Slide directly corresponds with the Concepts for Lecture.)*

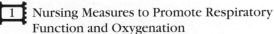 Nursing Measures to Promote Respiratory Function and Oxygenation
- Ensuring a patent airway
- Positioning
- Encouraging deep breathing and coughing
- Ensuring adequate hydration
  - Fluid intake
  - Humidifiers
  - Nebulizers

## LEARNING OUTCOME 7

Explain the use of therapeutic measures such as medications, inhalation therapy, oxygen therapy, artificial airways, airway suctioning, and chest tubes to promote respiratory function.

### CONCEPTS FOR LECTURE

1. Medications such as bronchodilators, anti-inflammatory drugs, expectorants, and cough suppressants may be used to treat respiratory problems.
   - Bronchodilators reduce bronchospasm, opening tight or congested airways and facilitating ventilation.
   - Anti-inflammatory drugs work by decreasing edema and inflammation in the airways and allowing a better air exchange.
   - Leukotriene modifiers suppress the effects of leukotrienes, which cause bronchoconstriction, mucous production, and edema of the respiratory tract.
   - Expectorants help "break up" mucus, making it more liquid and easier to expectorate.
   - Cough suppressants may be used when frequent or prolonged coughing interrupts sleep.

   Incentive spirometers measure the flow of air inhaled through a mouthpiece. They are used to improve pulmonary ventilation, counteract the effects of anesthesia or hypoventilation, loosen respiratory secretions, facilitate respiratory gaseous exchange, and expand collapsed alveoli. Percussion, vibration, and postural drainage are dependent nursing functions performed according to a primary care provider's order. Percussion over congested lung areas can mechanically dislodge tenacious secretions from the bronchial walls. Vibration is used after percussion to increase the turbulence of the exhaled air and thus loosen thick secretions. Postural drainage is the drainage by gravity of secretions from various lung segments.

   Oxygen therapy is used for clients who have difficulty ventilating all areas of their lungs, those whose gas exchange is impaired, or people with heart failure to prevent hypoxia. Oxygen therapy is prescribed by the primary care provider. Safety precautions are essential during oxygen therapy (see Box 50–2). A number of systems are available to deliver oxygen to the client. The choice will depend upon the client's oxygen needs, comfort, and developmental considerations. Nasal cannula, face mask (simple, partial rebreather, nonrebreather, and Venturi), and face tent may be used.

   Artificial airways are inserted to maintain a patent air passage for clients whose airways have become or may become obstructed. Four of the more common types of airways are oropharyngeal, nasopharyngeal, endotracheal, and tracheostomy. Oropharyngeal and nasopharyngeal airways are used to keep the upper air passages open when they may become obstructed by secretions or the tongue. Endotracheal tubes are most commonly inserted for clients who have had general anesthetics or for those in emergency situations where

### POWERPOINT LECTURE SLIDES

*(NOTE: The number on each PPT Lecture Slide directly corresponds with the Concepts for Lecture.)*

 Therapeutic Measures to Promote Respiratory Function
- Medications
- Incentive spirometry
- Chest PT
- Postural drainage
- Oxygen therapy
- Artificial airways
- Airway suctioning
- Chest tubes

mechanical ventilation is required. A tracheostomy is an opening into the trachea through the neck; it is used for clients who need long-term airway support.

Suctioning is aspirating secretions through a catheter connected to a suction machine or wall suction outlet for clients who have difficulty handling their secretions or who have an airway in place.

Chest tube and drainage systems are used when the pleural membrane is disrupted by lung disease, surgery, or trauma. The negative pressure between the pleural layers may be lost, and the lung then collapses. Air (pneumothorax) or blood may accumulate in the pleural space (hemothorax), placing pressure on the lung tissue and interfering with lung expansion. Chest tubes may be inserted into the pleural cavity to restore negative pressure and drain collected fluid, blood, or air. When chest tubes are inserted, they must be connected to a sealed drainage system or a one-way valve that allows air and fluid to be removed from the pleural space but prevents air from entering from the outside. A Heimlich valve (a one-way flutter valve that allows air to escape but prevents air from reentering) may be used for ambulatory clients. The Pneumostat (also has a one-way valve and a small, built-in collection chamber) may be used for a pneumothorax, which usually has a small amount of fluid.

---

## SUGGESTIONS FOR CLASSROOM ACTIVITIES

- Show videotaped demonstrations of administration of respiratory medications, suctioning, and obtaining respiratory specimens.
- Compile a poster showing various types of oxygen equipment, suction catheters, and artificial airways for the students to review.
- Have the students practice suctioning techniques on manikins.
- Use a drinking straw and a glass of water to illustrate the principles of chest tube function.
- Invite a respiratory therapist to demonstrate percussion, vibration, and postural drainage on a student.

## SUGGESTIONS FOR CLINICAL ACTIVITIES

- Invite a respiratory nurse clinical specialist or respiratory therapist to demonstrate proper use of oxygen equipment.
- Arrange for the students to spend time with a respiratory therapist, observing the collection of specimens, assessment of respiratory status, implementation of therapeutic measures, and client teaching.
- Have the students visit an intensive care unit and observe the use of artificial airways, chest tubes, and suctioning techniques. Ask the students to share observations in postconference.

---

# LEARNING OUTCOME 8

State outcome criteria for evaluating client responses to measures that promote adequate oxygenation.

## CONCEPTS FOR LECTURE

1. Overall goals/outcomes for a client with oxygenation problems are to maintain a patent airway; improve comfort and ease of breathing; maintain or improve pulmonary ventilation and oxygenation; improve the ability to participate in physical activities; and prevent risks associated with oxygenation problems such as skin and tissue breakdown, syncope,

## POWERPOINT LECTURE SLIDES

*(NOTE: The number on each PPT Lecture Slide directly corresponds with the Concepts for Lecture.)*

☐1☐ Desired Outcomes for Client With Oxygenation Problem
- Maintain a patent airway
- Improve comfort and ease of breathing

---

acid–base imbalances, and feelings of hopelessness and social isolation.

2. Using the goals and desired outcomes identified in the planning stage, the nurse collects data to evaluate the effectiveness of interventions. If outcomes are not achieved, the nurse, client, and support person (if appropriate) need to explore the reasons before modifying the care plan.

- Maintain or improve pulmonary ventilation and oxygenation
- Improve ability to participate in physical activities
- Prevent risks associated with oxygenation problems

 Evaluation

- Collect data to evaluate the effectiveness of interventions
- If outcomes not achieved, explore the reasons before modifying the care plan

## SUGGESTIONS FOR CLINICAL ACTIVITIES

- Have students develop care plans for clients with respiratory problems.

# CHAPTER 51
## CIRCULATION

## RESOURCE LIBRARY

### 💿 PRENTICE HALL NURSING MEDIALINK DVD-ROM

Audio Glossary
NCLEX® Review
Skill Checklist
Animations:
   *Heart*
   *Blood Flow Atria*
   *Blood Pressure*
   *Hemodynamics*
   *Congenital Heart Defects*
   *Dysrhythmias*
   *Ventricular Contraction*
Videos:
   *Coronary Artery Disease*
   *Dysrhythmia*
   *Heart Attack*

### 🌐 COMPANION WEBSITE

Additional NCLEX® Review
Case Study: *Client with Diabetes*
Care Plan Activity: *Client Experiencing Pain from Walking*
Application Activity: *Health Promotion for a Healthy Heart*
Links to Resources

### 📖 IMAGE LIBRARY

**Figure 51.1** The layers of the heart: the epicardium, the myocardium, and the endocardium.
**Figure 51.2** Heart valves in closed position viewed from the top.
**Figure 51.3** Blood flow through the heart.
**Figure 51.4** The coronary arteries supply the heart muscle with oxygenated blood.
**Figure 51.5** The electrical system of the heart.

**Figure 51.6** The heart and blood vessels.
**Figure 51.7** Vein with competent valve and vein with incompetent valve that allows blood to pool in the veins.
**Figure 51.8** A client with cardiac monitoring.
**Figure 51.9** The sequential venous compression device enhances venous return.
**Skill 51.1** Sequential Compression Devices

## LEARNING OUTCOME 1

Outline the structure and function of the cardiovascular system.

### CONCEPTS FOR LECTURE

1. The cardiovascular system is made up of the heart, blood vessels, and blood.
2. The heart is a hollow organ covered by the pericardium (double layer fibroserous membrane). The three layers of the heart are the epicardium, myocardium, and endocardium. There are four hollow chambers—right and left atria and right and left ventricles—separated by the interventricular septum. The atria and ventricles are separated by the atrioventricular (AV) valves, the tricuspid on the right and bicuspid (mitral) on the left. The ventricles are separated from the great vessels (pulmonary arteries and aorta) by the

### POWERPOINT LECTURE SLIDES

*(NOTE: The number on each PPT Lecture Slide directly corresponds with the Concepts for Lecture.)*

**1** Structures of the Cardiovascular System
- Heart
- Blood vessels
- Blood

**2** The Heart

**3** Blood Vessels
- Arteries
  - Arterioles
  - Capillaries

semilunar valves, pulmonic on the right and aortic on the left (See Figure 51.2). The valves serve to direct the flow of blood, allowing it to move from atria to ventricles and ventricles to the great vessels, but preventing backflow. Deoxygenated blood from the superior and inferior vena cava flows into the right atria, through the tricuspid valve into the right ventricle, through the pulmonic valve into the pulmonary arteries to the lungs for exchange of gases. Oxygenated blood from the lungs flows into the pulmonary veins and into the left atria, through the bicuspid (mitral) valve into the left ventricle and through the aortic valve to the aorta and then to the tissues of the body (See Figure 51.3).

The heart receives nourishment from the coronary arteries (See Figure 51.4). Electrical stimulation to cause contraction of the chambers of the heart is supplied by the cardiac conduction system: the sinoatrial (SA) node, the atrioventricular (AV) node, the bundle of His, the right and left bundle branches, and the Purkinje fibers (See Figure 51.5).

The function of the heart is to pump deoxygenated blood through the pulmonary arteries into the lungs for gas exchange and freshly oxygenated blood through the aorta into the systemic circulation.

3. A closed system of blood vessels transports blood to the tissues and returns it to the heart. The blood flows from the aorta into arteries, arterioles, and into the capillaries. From the capillaries the blood flows into venules and then veins returning to the heart through the venae cavae. With the exception of capillaries, blood vessel walls have three distinct layers, or tunics: the tunica intima (smooth endothelium), the tunica media (elastic fibers and smooth muscle cells innervated by the autonomic nervous system), and the tunica adventitia (connective tissue). Capillaries contain only one thin layer of tunica intima.

The function of the arterial system is to transport oxygenated blood to the tissues, and the venous system returns deoxygenated blood from the tissues to the heart.

4. The blood consists of formed elements (blood cells) suspended in fluid (plasma).

The primary functions of the blood are (a) transporting oxygen, nutrients, and hormones to cells, and metabolic wastes from the tissues for elimination; (b) regulating body temperature, pH, and fluid volume; and (c) preventing infection and blood loss.

- Venous system
  - Venules
  - Veins

 Blood
- Blood cells
- Plasma
- Functions

---

## SUGGESTIONS FOR CLASSROOM ACTIVITIES

- Ask the students to review the chapter on the cardiovascular system in their anatomy and physiology textbook.
- Review the RBC indices and other related laboratory tests.

## SUGGESTIONS FOR CLINICAL ACTIVITIES

- If possible, arrange for the students to observe laboratory testing of blood.
- If possible, arrange for the students to observe cardiovascular diagnostic testing to see the heart and blood vessels in a living person.

# LEARNING OUTCOME 2

Identify factors influencing cardiovascular function.

## CONCEPTS FOR LECTURE

1. Factors influencing cardiovascular function include cardiac output (the amount of blood ejected from the heart each minute), stroke volume (amount of blood ejected from the heart with each beat), heart rate (number of beats per minute), contractility (inotropic state of the myocardium, strength of contraction), preload (left ventricular end diastolic volume, stretch of the myocardium), and afterload (resistance against which the heart muscle must pump).

    Also refer to Outcome 3.

## POWERPOINT LECTURE SLIDES

*(NOTE: The number on each PPT Lecture Slide directly corresponds with the Concepts for Lecture.)*

 Factors Influencing Cardiovascular Function
- Cardiac output—amount of blood ejected from the heart each minute
- Stroke volume—amount of blood ejected from the heart with each beat
- Heart rate—number of beats per minute
- Contractility—inotropic state of the myocardium, strength of contraction
- Preload—left ventricular end diastolic volume, stretch of the myocardium
- Afterload—resistance against which the heart muscle must pump

## SUGGESTIONS FOR CLASSROOM ACTIVITIES

- Provide the students with examples of how changes in stroke volume and rate can affect cardiac output.

## SUGGESTIONS FOR CLINICAL ACTIVITIES

- If possible, arrange for the students to observe in the cardiac catheterization laboratory.

# LEARNING OUTCOME 3

Identify major risk factors for the development of coronary heart disease.

## CONCEPTS FOR LECTURE

1. Box 51-1 lists the risk factors for coronary heart disease, separating these into nonmodifiable, modifiable, and other risk factors.

    Nonmodifiable risk factors include heredity, age, and gender (women's risk increases with menopause).

    Modifiable risk factors include elevated serum lipid levels, hypertension, cigarette smoking, diabetes, obesity, and sedentary lifestyle.

    Other risk factors include heat and cold, previous health status, stress and coping, dietary factors, alcohol intake, and elevated homocysteine level.

## POWERPOINT LECTURE SLIDES

*(NOTE: The number on each PPT Lecture Slide directly corresponds with the Concepts for Lecture.)*

 Risk Factors for Coronary Heart Disease
- Nonmodifiable risks
  - Heredity
  - Age
  - Gender
- Modifiable risk factors
  - Elevated serum lipid levels
  - Hypertension
  - Cigarette smoking
  - Diabetes
  - Obesity
  - Sedentary lifestyle
- Other risk factors
  - Heat and cold
  - Previous health status
  - Stress and coping
  - Dietary factors
  - Alcohol intake
  - Elevated homocysteine level

## SUGGESTIONS FOR CLASSROOM ACTIVITIES

- Ask the students to interview a classmate to determine risk factors for coronary heart disease.
- Have the students review the Framingham Heart Study and related website. Discuss the importance of this study.
- Ask the students to review evidence-based interventions for prevention of coronary heart disease.

## SUGGESTIONS FOR CLINICAL ACTIVITIES

- Ask the students to review the charts of assigned clients and interview these clients to determine risk factors for coronary heart disease. Discuss findings in postconference.
- Share literature and programs available in the institution for teaching clients about coronary heart disease and prevention.

# LEARNING OUTCOME 4

Discuss the manifestations of cardiovascular disorders.

## CONCEPTS FOR LECTURE

1. Cardiovascular function can be altered by conditions that affect the following:
   - The function of the heart as a pump
   - Blood flow to organs and peripheral tissues
   - The composition of the blood and its ability to transport oxygen and carbon dioxide
2. Three major alterations in cardiovascular function are decreased cardiac output, impaired tissue perfusion, and disorders that affect the composition or amount of blood available for transport of gases.
3. Conditions that may decrease cardiac output include myocardial infarction (heart attack), heart failure, irregular heart rhythms (dysrhythmias), and structural heart conditions (congenital or acquired).
4. Conditions that may affect tissue perfusion include atherosclerosis particularly of the coronary arteries (angina pectoris), of the vessels supplying the brain (transient ischemic attacks or a stroke), and peripheral arteries (peripheral vascular disease), vessel inflammation, arterial spasms, blood clots (thrombus), incompetent valves of the veins, and pulmonary emboli.
5. Conditions that affect the composition of the blood are various types of anemia.
6. Conditions that affect volume of blood include hemorrhage, dehydration, fluid retention, and kidney failure.

## POWERPOINT LECTURE SLIDES

*(NOTE: The number on each PPT Lecture Slide directly corresponds with the Concepts for Lecture.)*

**1** Cardiovascular Function Can Be Altered by Conditions that Affect
- The function of the heart as a pump (cardiac output)
- Blood flow to organs and peripheral tissues
- The composition of the blood and its ability to transport oxygen and carbon dioxide

**2** Alterations in Cardiovascular Function
- Decreased cardiac output
- Impaired tissue perfusion
- Disorders that affect composition or amount of blood available for transport of gases

**3** Conditions That Affect Cardiac Output
- Myocardial infarction (heart attack)
- Heart failure
- Irregular heart rhythms (dysrhythmias)
- Structural heart conditions (congenital or acquired)

**4** Conditions That May Affect Tissue Perfusion
- Atherosclerosis of the following:
  - Coronary arteries (angina pectoris)
  - Brain (transient ischemic attacks or a stroke)
  - Peripheral arteries (peripheral vascular disease)
- Vessel inflammation
- Arterial spasms
- Blood clots (thrombus)
- Incompetent valves of the veins
- Pulmonary emboli

**5** Conditions That Affect the Composition of the Blood
- Anemias

**6** Conditions That Affect Blood Volume
- Hemorrhage
- Dehydration
- Fluid retention
- Kidney failure

## LEARNING OUTCOME 5

Identify common responses to alterations in cardiovascular status.

### CONCEPTS FOR LECTURE

1. Decreased cardiac output may occur when vessels that supply the heart muscle become occluded by atherosclerosis or a blood clot shutting off the blood supply to a portion of the heart. Tissues in the affected area become necrotic and die, a condition known as myocardial infarction (MI) or heart attack.
2. Heart failure may develop if the heart isn't able to keep up with the body's need for oxygen and nutrients to the tissues. Heart failure usually occurs because of myocardial infarction, but it may also result from chronic overwork of the heart, such as in clients with uncontrolled hypertension or extensive arteriosclerosis. In left-sided heart failure, the vessels of the pulmonary system become congested or engorged with blood. This may cause fluid to escape into the alveoli and interfere with gas exchange, a condition known as pulmonary edema.
3. Atherosclerosis is the most common cause of impaired blood flow to organs and tissues. Vessels narrow and become constricted, and distal tissues receive less oxygen and nutrients. Ischemia is a lack of blood supply due to obstructed circulation. Coronary arteries, vessels supplying blood to the brain, and arteries in the peripheral tissues are most often affected. Obstruction in the coronary arteries causes myocardial ischemia, leading to angina pectoris. Obstruction in vessels supplying the brain results in transient ischemic attack (TIA) or stroke. Obstruction in peripheral arteries leads to peripheral vascular disease.
4. Incompetent venous valves may allow blood to pool in veins, causing edema and decreasing venous return to the heart. Veins may also become inflamed, reducing blood flow and increasing the risk of thrombus formation. Thrombi may break loose, becoming emboli, occluding blood supply to the capillary side of the alveolar-capillary membrane. No gas exchange occurs there because of impaired blood flow. This condition is known as an acute pulmonary embolism.
5. Because most oxygen is transported to the tissues in combination with hemoglobin, the problems of inadequate red blood cells (RBCs), low hemoglobin levels, or abnormal hemoglobin structure can affect tissue oxygenation. Anemia (low hemoglobin level) may be caused by loss of RBCs due to acute or chronic bleeding,

### POWERPOINT LECTURE SLIDES

*(NOTE: The number on each PPT Lecture Slide directly corresponds with the Concepts for Lecture.)*

**1** Decreased Cardiac Output
- Occurs when vessels supplying heart muscle become occluded
- Tissues in affected area die (MI)

**2** Heart Failure
- Can develop if heart not able to keep up with body's need for oxygen and nutrients
- Usually occurs because of MI
- May result from chronic overwork of heart
- Left-sided heart failure can result in pulmonary edema

**3** Atherosclerosis
- Most common cause of impaired blood flow to organs and tissues
- Vessels narrow and become constricted
- Distal tissues receive less oxygen and nutrients
- Coronary arteries most affected
- Obstruction of coronary arteries leads to myocardial ischemia leads to angina pectoris
- Obstruction in vessels supplying brain results in TIA or stroke

**4** Incompetent Venous Valves
- May allow blood to pool in veins
  ○ Edema
  ○ Decreased venous return to heart
- Veins become inflamed
  ○ Reduce blood flow
  ○ Increased risk of thrombus formation
- Thrombi may break loose
  ○ Emboli
  ○ Occlude blood supply A/C membrane
  ○ Acute pulmonary embolism

**5** Problems with Oxygen Transport
- Inadequate RBCs
- Low hemoglobin
- Abnormal hemoglobin

dietary deficiencies of iron or folic acid, inadequately formed hemoglobin or RBCs (sickle-cell disease), and some disorders that cause RBCs to break down excessively.

## SUGGESTIONS FOR CLASSROOM ACTIVITIES

- Demonstrate and have the students practice apical-radial pulse assessment using two people.
- Demonstrate the assessment of the peripheral vascular system and have students practice this assessment on another student.

## SUGGESTIONS FOR CLINICAL ACTIVITIES

- Identify clients on the clinical unit who have abnormal heart sounds. Obtain permission from these clients to have students listen to their heart sounds.
- If possible, assign students to observe venous ultrasound procedures.
- Have students present the signs and symptoms exhibited by assigned clients who have cardiovascular diseases.

# LEARNING OUTCOME 6

List signs of alterations in cardiovascular function.

## CONCEPTS FOR LECTURE

1. Signs and symptoms of a myocardial infarction include chest pain (substernal and/or radiating to the left arm or jaw), nausea, shortness of breath, and diaphoresis.
2. Signs of heart failure may include pulmonary congestion; adventitious breath sounds; shortness of breath; increased heart rate; increased respiratory rate; peripheral vasoconstriction; cold, pale extremities; and distended neck veins. Box 51–2 gives examples of conditions that may precipitate heart failure.
3. Signs of impaired peripheral arterial circulation may include decreased peripheral pulses, pale skin color, cool extremities, and decreased hair distribution.
4. Signs and symptoms of acute pulmonary embolism include sudden onset of shortness of breath and pleuritic chest pain.
5. Signs and symptoms of anemia include chronic fatigue, pallor, shortness of breath, and hypotension.

## POWERPOINT LECTURE SLIDES

*(NOTE: The number on each PPT Lecture Slide directly corresponds with the Concepts for Lecture.)*

**1** Myocardial Infarction
- Chest pain
- Substernal and/or radiating to the left arm jaw
- Nausea
- Shortness of breath
- Diaphoresis

**2** Heart Failure
- Pulmonary congestion
- Adventitious breath sounds
- Shortness of breath
- Increased heart rate
- Increased respiratory rate
- Peripheral vasoconstriction
- Cold, pale extremities
- Distended neck veins

**3** Impaired Peripheral Arterial Circulation
- Decreased peripheral pulses
- Pale skin color
- Cool extremities
- Decreased hair distribution

**4** Acute Pulmonary Embolism
- Sudden onset of shortness of breath
- Pleuritic chest pain

**5** Anemia
- Chronic fatigue
- Pallor
- Shortness of breath
- Hypotension

# LEARNING OUTCOME 7

Identify and describe nursing measures to promote circulation.

## CONCEPTS FOR LECTURE

1. There are many nursing interventions that can help clients maintain cardiac and vascular function.

    To maintain vascular function, the nurse may elevate the client's legs to promote venous return to the heart unless the client has cardiac dysfunction because this will increase preload and may stress the dysfunctional heart. Avoid placing pillows under the knees or providing more than 15 degrees of knee flexion to improve blood flow to the lower extremities and reduce venous stagnation. Encourage leg exercises (such as flexion and extension of the feet, active contraction and relaxation of calf muscles) for a client on bed rest, and promote ambulation as soon as possible. Encourage or provide frequent position changes.

2. To maintain cardiac function, the nurse can position the client in high Fowler's position to decrease preload and reduce pulmonary congestion. Monitor intake and output. Fluid restriction is not usually required unless the client has severe heart failure.

3. The nurse administers prescribed medication to promote cardiovascular function. An important role of the nurse is to help the client understand the purposes, effects, and side effects of the medications. In addition, the nurse is responsible for assessing the effects of medications and also for potential complications. Examples include assessing intake and output and potassium levels, if appropriate, for clients receiving diuretics; assessing blood pressure, heart rate, peripheral pulses, and lung sounds as indicators of cardiac output for clients receiving positive inotropic medications; and monitoring blood pressure (including postural blood pressure) when antihypertensive medications are administered.

4. Preventing venous stasis is an important nursing intervention to reduce the risk of complications following surgery, trauma, or major medical problems. Interventions to prevent venous stasis include positioning and leg exercises (Chapter 50), applying antiembolic stockings (Chapter 37), and use of sequential compression devices (SCDs). Skill 51.1 provides steps in

## POWERPOINT LECTURE SLIDES

*(NOTE: The number on each PPT Lecture Slide directly corresponds with the Concepts for Lecture.)*

1. To Maintain Vascular Function
   - Elevate the client's legs
   - Avoid placing pillows under the knees or providing more than 15° knee flexion
   - Encourage leg exercises for a client on bed rest
   - Promote ambulation as soon as possible
   - Encourage or provide frequent position changes

2. To Maintain Cardiac Function
   - Position the client in high Fowler's position
   - Monitor intake and output
   - Fluid restriction

3. Administering Prescribed Medication
   - Help the client understand the purposes, effects, and side effects of the medications
   - Assess effects of medications and potential complications
   - Assess intake and output and potassium levels, if appropriate, for clients receiving diuretics
   - Assess blood pressure, heart rate, peripheral pulses, and lung sounds for clients receiving positive inotropic medications
   - Monitor blood pressure (including postural blood pressure) for client receiving antihypertensive medications

4. Preventing Venous Stasis
   - Positioning and leg exercises
   - Applying antiembolic stockings
   - Applying sequential compression devices (SCDs)

applying SCDs, which inflate and deflate plastic sleeves wrapped around the legs to promote venous return. The ankle area inflates first, followed by the calf region, and then the thigh region, assisting the leg muscles in moving the blood toward the heart.

## SUGGESTIONS FOR CLASSROOM ACTIVITIES

- Have the students demonstrate proper positioning to promote circulation on a manikin.
- Ask a student to role-play teaching leg exercises to another person.
- Provide the students with a list of medications prescribed for cardiovascular conditions. Ask them to identify assessment that should be done prior to giving each medication and assessment to be performed to evaluate effectiveness of the medication.

## SUGGESTIONS FOR CLINICAL ACTIVITIES

- Demonstrate proper measurement and application of antiembolic stockings.
- Demonstrate use of the SCD equipment and related agency policies and procedures.

# LEARNING OUTCOME 8

Describe the critical nature of cardiopulmonary resuscitation.

## CONCEPTS FOR LECTURE

1. Cardiopulmonary resuscitation (CPR) is a combination of oral resuscitation and external cardiac massage that is intended to reestablish cardiac function and circulation of blood.

   A cardiac arrest is the cessation of cardiac function; the heart stops beating. When it occurs, the heart no longer pumps blood to any of the organs of the body. Breathing then stops and the person becomes unconscious and limp. Within 20 to 40 seconds of a cardiac arrest the victim is clinically dead. After 4 to 6 minutes the lack of oxygen supply to the brain causes permanent and extensive damage.

   It is vital that all nurses be trained to perform CPR so resuscitation measures can be initiated immediately.

## POWERPOINT LECTURE SLIDES

*(NOTE: The number on each PPT Lecture Slide directly corresponds with the Concepts for Lecture.)*

 Importance of Cardiopulmonary Resuscitation
- Within 20 to 40 seconds of a cardiac arrest the victim is clinically dead
- After 4 to 6 minutes the lack of oxygen supply to the brain causes permanent and extensive damage
- Must initiate CPR immediately

## SUGGESTIONS FOR CLASSROOM ACTIVITIES

- Ensure that all students are currently certified in CPR for health care providers, or provide certification for all students.
- Invite an instructor in CPR to demonstrate the use of an automated external defibrillator (AED).

## SUGGESTIONS FOR CLINICAL ACTIVITIES

- Show the students the location of CPR equipment.
- Review the emergency notification system used in the institution.
- Review the functions of members of the responding team.
- Review the functions of student nurses in case of a cardiac or respiratory arrest on the unit.

# CHAPTER 52

## FLUID, ELECTROLYTE, AND ACID–BASE BALANCE

## RESOURCE LIBRARY

###  PRENTICE HALL NURSING MEDIALINK DVD-ROM

Audio Glossary
NCLEX® Review
Skills Checklists
Animations:
  *Membrane Transport*
  *Filtration Pressure*
  *Fluid Balance*
  *Acid–Base Balance*
  *Furosemide Drug*
  *Applying a Central Venous Line*

### COMPANION WEBSITE

Additional NCLEX® Review
Case Study: *Client with Suspected Electrolyte Imbalance*
Care Plan Activity: *Client with Heart Failure*
Application Activities:
  *Determining Body Fluid Problems*
  *Arterial Blood Gases and Acid–Base Balance*
Links to Resources

### 📖 IMAGE LIBRARY

**Figure 52.1** Total body fluid represents 40 L in an adult male weighing 70 kg (154 lb).

**Figure 52.2** Electrolyte composition (cations and anions) of body fluid compartments.

**Figure 52.3** Osmosis: Water molecules move from the less concentrated area to the more concentrated area in an attempt to equalize the concentration of solutions on two sides of a membrane.

**Figure 52.4** Diffusion: The movement of molecules through a semipermeable membrane from an area of higher concentration to an area of lower concentration.

**Figure 52.5** Schematic of filtration pressure changes within a capillary bed.

**Figure 52.6** An example of active transport.

**Figure 52.7** Factors stimulating water intake through the thirst mechanism.

**Figure 52.8** Antidiuretic hormone (ADH) regulates water excretion from the kidneys.

**Figure 52.9** Body fluids are normally slightly alkaline, between a pH of 7.35 and 7.45.

**Figure 52.10** Carbonic acid–bicarbonate ratio and pH.

**Figure 52.11** Evaluation of edema.

**Figure 52.12** The extracellular sodium level affects cell size.

**Figure 52.13** A, Positive Chvostek's sign. B, Positive Trousseau's sign.

**Figure 52.14** A sample 24-hour fluid intake and output record.

**Figure 52.15** A, Format for a diagram of serum electrolyte results. B, Example that may be seen in a primary care provider's documentation notes.

**Figure 52.16** Commonly used venipuncture sites of the A, arm; B, hand.

**Figure 52.17** Central venous lines with A, subclavian vein insertion, and B, left jugular insertion.

**Figure 52.18** An implantable venous access device.

**Figure 52.19** An implantable venous access device (right) and a Huber needle with extension tubing.

**Figure 52.20** A plastic intravenous fluid container.

**Figure 52.21** A standard IV administration set.

**Figure 52.22** Cannulae used to connect the tubing of additive sets to primary infusions.

**Figure 52.23** Schematic of an over-the-needle catheter.

**Figure 52.24** Schematic of a butterfly needle with adapter.

**Figure 52.25** Infusion set spikes and drip chambers: nonvented macrodrip, vented macrodrip, nonvented microdrip.

**Figure 52.26** Timing label on an intravenous container.

**Figure 52.27** The Dial-A-Flo in-line device.

**Figure 52.28** An intravenous infusion pump.

**Figure 52.29** Programmable infusion pumps.

**Figure 52.30** Schematic of a Y-set for blood administration.

**Skill 52.1** Starting an Intravenous Infusion

**Skill 52.2** Monitoring an Intravenous Infusion

**Skill 52.3** Changing an Intravenous Container, Tubing, and Dressing

**Skill 52.4** Discontinuing an Intravenous Infusion

**Skill 52.5** Changing an Intravenous Catheter to an Intermittent Infusion Lock

**Skill 52.6** Initiating, Maintaining, and Terminating a Blood Transfusion Using a Y-Set

# LEARNING OUTCOME 1

Discuss the function, distribution, movement, and regulation of fluids and electrolytes in the body.

## CONCEPTS FOR LECTURE

1. A delicate balance of fluids, electrolytes, and acids and bases is maintained in the body. This balance depends on multiple physiologic processes that regulate fluid intake and output and the movement of water and substances dissolved in it between body compartments.

2. Water is vital to health and normal cellular function. It serves as a medium for metabolic reactions within the cells; a transporter for nutrients, waste products, and other substances; a lubricant; an insulator; a shock absorber; and one means of regulating and maintaining body temperature.

    The body's fluid is divided into two major compartments: intracellular and extracellular. Intracellular fluid (ICF) is found within the cells, and extracellular fluid (ECF) is found outside the cells. The two main compartments of the ECF are intravascular fluid (plasma) and interstitial fluid (surrounds the cells). Other compartments of ECF include lymph and transcellular fluids such as cerebrospinal, pericardial, pancreatic, pleural, intraocular, biliary, peritoneal, and synovial fluids. Intracellular fluid is vital to normal cell functioning. It contains solutes such as oxygen, electrolytes, and glucose, and it provides a medium in which metabolic processes of the cell take place. Extracellular fluid is the transport system that carries nutrients to and waste products from the cells.

3. Fluids and electrolytes move among the body compartments by osmosis, diffusion, filtration, and active transport. The volume and composition of body fluids is regulated through several homeostatic mechanisms: the kidneys, the endocrine system, the cardiovascular system, the lungs, and the gastrointestinal system. The antidiuretic hormone (ADH), also called arginine vasopressin (AVP), the renin-angiotensin-aldosterone system, and the atrial natriuretic factor are also involved in maintaining fluid balance.

4. Normally fluid intake balances fluid loss. The thirst mechanism is the primary regulator of fluid intake. There are four routes of fluid loss: urine, insensible loss through the skin as perspiration and through the lungs as water vapor in the expired air, noticeable loss through the skin, and loss through the intestines in feces. (See Table 52-2.)

    ECF and ICF contain ions (charged particles). Anions are negative ions and cations are positive ions called electrolytes. The number of cations and anions in should be equal. The principal electrolytes in the ECF are sodium, chloride, and bicarbonate. Other electrolytes such as potassium, calcium, and magnesium but in much smaller quantities. Plasma and interstitial fluids (major components of ECF) contain essentially the same electrolytes and solutes with the exception

## POWERPOINT LECTURE SLIDES

*(NOTE: The number on each PPT Lecture Slide directly corresponds with the Concepts for Lecture.)*

1 Distribution of Body Fluids

2 Composition of Body Fluids

3 Movement of Body Fluids
- Osmosis
- Diffusion
- Filtration
- Active transport

4 Regulating Body Fluids
- Fluid intake
  - Thirst
- Fluid output
  - Urine
  - Insensible loss
  - Feces
- Maintaining homeostasis
  - Kidneys
  - Antidiuretic hormone
  - Renin-angiotensin-aldosterone system
  - Atrial natriuretic system

5 Regulating Electrolytes
- Sodium
- Potassium
- Calcium
- Magnesium
- Chloride
- Phosphate
- Bicarbonate

of proteins, which are plentiful in the plasma. The primary electrolytes in the ICF are potassium, magnesium, phosphate, and sulfate. As in ECF, other electrolytes are present within the cells, but in smaller concentrations.

5. Table 52–3 lists the regulation and function of sodium, potassium, calcium, magnesium, chloride, phosphate, and bicarbonate.

---

## SUGGESTIONS FOR CLASSROOM ACTIVITIES

- Using the example of a tea bag and a glass of hot water, have the students explain diffusion, osmosis, and filtration and how this relates to the movement of body fluids and electrolytes.
- Divide the students into groups. Assign each group an electrolyte. Have the students develop a pamphlet about the function of the electrolyte, foods that are high and low in the electrolyte, and problems associated with either high or low values of the electrolyte.

## SUGGESTIONS FOR CLINICAL ACTIVITIES

- Arrange for the students to observe measurements of electrolytes in the laboratory.
- Have the students review the electrolyte values of their assigned clients. Discuss results relating to the clients' medical diagnoses, medications, or other treatments.

---

# LEARNING OUTCOME 2

Describe the regulation of acid–base balance in the body, including the roles of the lungs, the kidneys, and buffers.

## CONCEPTS FOR LECTURE

1. An important part of regulating the chemical balance or homeostasis of body fluids is regulating their acidity or alkalinity, which is measured as pH. The pH reflects the hydrogen concentration of the solution. The higher the hydrogen ion concentration, the lower the pH (more acidic) and vice versa. Body fluids are maintained within a narrow range that is slightly alkaline (arterial blood is between 7.35 and 7.45). Several body systems, including buffers, the respiratory system, and the renal system, are actively involved in maintaining the narrow pH range necessary for optimal function. The lungs and kidneys help maintain a normal pH by either excreting or retaining acids and bases.

2. Buffers prevent excessive changes in the pH by removing or releasing hydrogen ions. The major buffer system in ECF is the bicarbonate ($HCO_3^-$) and carbonic acid ($H_2CO_3$) system. The amounts of bicarbonate and carbonic acid in the body vary. However, as long as a ratio of 20 parts of bicarbonate to 1 part of carbonic acid is maintained, pH remains within normal limits. In addition, plasma proteins, hemoglobin, and phosphates function as buffers.

3. The lungs help regulate acid–base balance by eliminating or retaining carbon dioxide, a potential acid. Combined with water, carbon dioxide forms carbonic acid. This chemical reaction is reversible. Working together with the bicarbonate–carbonic acid buffer

## POWERPOINT LECTURE SLIDES

*(NOTE: The number on each PPT Lecture Slide directly corresponds with the Concepts for Lecture.)*

**1** Regulation Acid–Base Balance
- Low pH = acidic
- High pH = alkalinic
- Body fluids maintained between pH of 7.35 and 7.45 by
  - Buffers
  - Respiratory system
  - Renal system

**2** Buffers
- Prevent excessive changes in the pH
- Major buffer in ECF is $HCO_3$ and $H_2CO_3$
  - 20 parts $HCO_3$ to 1 part $H_2CO_3$
- Other buffers include plasma proteins, hemoglobin, phosphates

**3** Lungs
- Regulate acid–base balance by eliminating or retaining carbon dioxide
- Does this by altering rate and depth of respirations
  - Faster rate/more depth = get rid of more $CO_2$ = pH rises
  - Slower rate = retain $CO_2$ = pH lowers

system, the lungs regulate acid–base balance and pH by altering the rate and depth of respirations. Carbon dioxide is a powerful stimulator of the respiratory center. When blood levels of carbonic acid and carbon dioxide rise, the respiratory center is stimulated and the rate and depth of respiration increase. Carbon dioxide is exhaled and carbonic acid levels fall. By contrast when bicarbonate levels are excessive, the rate and depth of respirations are reduced, causing carbon dioxide to be retained, carbonic acid to rise, and excess bicarbonate to be neutralized. The respiratory system response to changes in pH is rapid, occurring within minutes.

4. The kidneys are the ultimate long-term regulator of acid–base balance. They are slower to respond to changes, requiring hours to days to correct imbalances, but their response is more permanent and selective than that of the other systems. Kidneys maintain acid–base balance by selectively excreting or conserving bicarbonate and hydrogen ions. When excess hydrogen ion is present and the pH falls (acidosis), the kidneys reabsorb and regenerate bicarbonate and excrete hydrogen ions. In the case of alkalosis and a high pH, excess bicarbonate is excreted and a hydrogen ion is retained. The relationship of the respiratory and renal regulation of acid–base balance is further explained in Box 52-2.

**4** Kidneys
- Regulate by selectively excreting or conserving bicarbonate and hydrogen ions
- Slower to respond to change

---

### SUGGESTIONS FOR CLASSROOM ACTIVITIES

- Invite a critical care clinical specialist to review acid–base balance and the importance of assessing and interpreting these values in the setting where the nurse practices.
- Invite a faculty member of the chemistry department to present a visual demonstration of buffers, acids, and bases, relating this to the biochemistry of the human body.

### SUGGESTIONS FOR CLINICAL ACTIVITIES

- Invite a nurse from a critical care unit to discuss the procedure for obtaining arterial blood gases (ABGs), and discuss the responses of clients exhibiting alterations in ABGs and related nursing interventions.
- Review laboratory values for acid–base balance.

---

## LEARNING OUTCOME 3

Identify factors affecting normal body fluid, electrolyte, and acid–base balance.

### CONCEPTS FOR LECTURE

1. Factors affecting normal body fluid, electrolyte, and acid–base balance include age, gender and body size, environmental temperature, and lifestyle.

   Age—infants and growing children have much greater fluid turnover than adults because of their higher metabolic rates, increase fluid loss, immature kidneys (infants), rapid respiratory rate (infants), and greater body surface area (infants). In elderly people normal aging process and the likelihood of the presence of chronic diseases may affect fluid balance.

### POWERPOINT LECTURE SLIDES

*(NOTE: The number on each PPT Lecture Slide directly corresponds with the Concepts for Lecture.)*

 **1** Factors Affecting Body Fluid, Electrolyte, and Acid–Base Balance
- Age
- Gender
- Body size
- Environmental temperature
- Lifestyle

Thirst is blunted; nephrons are less able to conserve water in response to ADH; the increased level of atrial nutriuretic hormone may contribute to impaired ability to conserve water in older people.

Gender and body size—fat cells contain little water and lean tissue has an increased water content. People with a greater percentage of body fat have less body fluid. Women have proportionally greater body fat than men and have less body water than men.

Environmental temperature—individuals with illness and participation in strenuous exercise are at risk for fluid and electrolyte imbalances when the environmental temperature in high the loss of water and salt in sweat.

Lifestyle—diet (intake of fluid and electrolytes), exercise (calcium balance), and stress (increases cellular metabolism, blood glucose concentration, and catecholamine levels) affect fluid and electrolyte and acid–base balance. Heavy alcohol consumption decreases calcium, magnesium, and phosphate levels and increases the risk of acidosis from breakdown of fat.

## SUGGESTIONS FOR CLASSROOM ACTIVITIES

- Provide examples of the factors affecting normal body fluid, electrolyte, and acid–base balance and have the students identify the effect each may have.

## SUGGESTIONS FOR CLINICAL ACTIVITIES

- Ask the students to review the chart and care plan of assigned clients to determine factors that might influence normal body fluid, electrolyte, and acid–base balance. Share findings with the clinical group in postconference.

# LEARNING OUTCOME 4

Discuss the risk factors for and the causes and effects of fluid, electrolyte, and acid-base imbalances.

## CONCEPTS FOR LECTURE

1. Common risk factors for fluid, electrolyte, and acid–base imbalances are listed in Box 52-3 and include: chronic diseases (e.g., lung disease, heart failure, Cushing's or Addison's diseases, diabetes mellitus, and cancer), acute conditions (e.g., acute gastroenteritis, burns, crushing injuries, surgery, or fever), medications (e.g., diuretics, corticosteroids, and NSAIDs), treatments (e.g., chemotherapy, intravenous therapy or total peripheral nutrition, nasogastric suction, enteral feedings, mechanical ventilation) and other factors (such as the very young and the very old, inability to access food and fluids independently).

2. Fluid imbalances are of two basic types: isotonic and osmolar. Isotonic imbalances occur when water and electrolytes are lost or gained in equal proportions so that the osmolality of body fluids remains constant. Osmolar imbalances involve the loss of only water so that the osmolality of the serum is altered. Thus there are four categories of fluid imbalances: an isotonic loss

## POWERPOINT LECTURE SLIDES

*(NOTE: The number on each PPT Lecture Slide directly corresponds with the Concepts for Lecture.)*

1 Factors for Fluid, Electrolyte, and Acid–Base Imbalances
  - Chronic diseases
  - Acute conditions
  - Medications
  - Treatments
  - Extremes of age
  - Inability to access food and fluids

2 Fluid Imbalances
  - Isotonic loss of water and electrolytes (fluid volume deficit)
  - Isotonic gain of water and electrolytes (fluid volume excess)
  - Hyperosmolar loss of only water (dehydration)
  - Hypo-osmolar gain of only water (overhydration)

of water and electrolytes (fluid volume deficit), an isotonic gain of water and electrolytes (fluid volume excess), a hyperosmolar loss of only water (dehydration), and a hypo-osmolar gain of only water (overhydration).

Table 52–4 lists risk factors, clinical manifestations, and nursing interventions for isotonic fluid volume deficit. Table 52–5 lists risk factors, clinical manifestations, and nursing interventions for isotonic fluid volume excess. The risk for dehydration increases with older age due to decreased thirst sensation. Also at risk for dehydration are clients who are hyperventilating or have prolonged fever or are in diabetic ketoacidosis and those receiving enteral feedings with insufficient water. Common manifestations of dehydration include weight loss, decreased skin turgor and capillary refill, dry mucous membranes, weak, rapid pulse, decreased blood pressure and orthostatic hypotension, increased specific gravity of the urine, hematocrit and blood urea nitrogen. Overhydration may occur if only water is replaced or from the syndrome of inappropriate antidiuretic hormone (SIADH), which can result from some malignant tumors, AIDS, head injury, or administration of certain drugs such as barbiturates or anesthetics. Common manifestations of overhydration include weight gain, full bounding pulse, tachycardia, elevated blood pressure, distended neck and peripheral veins, adventitious lung sounds, shortness of breath, and confusion.

3. Table 52–6 lists electrolyte imbalances (hypo- and hypernatremia, hypo- and hyperkalemia, hypo- and hypercalcemia, hypo- and hypermagnesemia) and associated risk factors, clinical manifestations, and nursing interventions.

4. Table 52–7 lists acid–base imbalances (respiratory acidosis and alkalosis, and metabolic acidosis and alkalosis) and associated risk factors, clinical manifestations, and nursing interventions.

**3** Electrolyte Imbalances
- Hyponatremia
- Hypernatremia
- Hypokalemia
- Hyperkalemia
- Hypocalcemia
- Hypercalcemia
- Hypomagnesemia
- Hypermagnesemia
- Hypochloremia
- Hyperchloremia
- Hypophosphatemia
- Hyperphosphatemia

**4** Acid–Base Imbalances
- Respiratory acidosis
- Respiratory alkalosis
- Metabolic acidosis
- Metabolic alkalosis

---

## SUGGESTIONS FOR CLASSROOM ACTIVITIES

- Divide the students into groups. Assign each group a fluid or acid-base imbalance. Ask the students to develop a teaching sheet for clients and families describing the problem, causes, signs and symptoms, and treatment in a way that clients will understand.
- Divide the students into groups. Assign each group an electrolyte. Have the students develop a pamphlet about the function of the electrolyte, foods that are high and low in the electrolyte, and problems associated with either high or low values of the electrolyte.

## SUGGESTIONS FOR CLINICAL ACTIVITIES

- Invite a nurse from the renal dialysis unit to discuss fluid and electrolyte problems commonly seen in clients needing dialysis and how these are demonstrated in the clients.
- Review intake and output records of various clients. Analyze the results.

# LEARNING OUTCOME 5

Collect assessment data related to the client's fluid, electrolyte, and acid–base balances.

## CONCEPTS FOR LECTURE

1. Components of the assessment include the nursing history, physical assessment of the client, clinical measurement, and review of laboratory test results.

   The nursing history includes current and past medical history, medications, and functional, developmental, and socioeconomic factors. Common risk factors for fluid and electrolyte imbalances are listed in Box 52-3 (Outcome 4). The nurse also needs to elicit data about the client's food and fluid intake, fluid output, and the presence of signs or symptoms suggestive of altered fluid and electrolyte balance. The Assessment Interview provides examples of questions to elicit information regarding fluid, electrolyte, and acid–base balance.

   Table 52-8 lists the focused physical assessment of fluid, electrolyte, or acid–base imbalances, including assessment of the skin, mucous membranes, eyes, fontanels (infants), cardiovascular system, respiratory system, neurologic and muscular status. Figure 52.11 presents an illustration on assessing edema.

   Clinical measurement includes daily weights, vital signs, and fluid intake and output.

   Table 52-9 lists arterial blood gas values in common acid–base disorders (respiratory acidosis and alkalosis and metabolic acidosis and alkalosis). Box 52-5 lists normal electrolyte values for adults (sodium, potassium, chloride, calcium, magnesium, phosphate, and serum osmolality). Box 52-6 lists normal values of arterial blood gases (ABGs), and Box 52-7 presents a method for interpreting ABGs. Figure 52.15AB presents a method to diagram serum electrolytes.

   Other laboratory tests to review include complete blood count, osmolality (serum and urine), urine pH, urine specific gravity, urine sodium, and chloride excretion.

## POWERPOINT LECTURE SLIDES

*(NOTE: The number on each PPT Lecture Slide directly corresponds with the Concepts for Lecture.)*

 Collecting Assessment Data
- Nursing history
- Physical assessment
- Clinical measurement
- Review of laboratory test results
- Evaluation of edema

## SUGGESTIONS FOR CLASSROOM ACTIVITIES

- Invite respiratory or critical care nurses to discuss interpretation of blood gases and assessment criteria related to them.
- Have the students use the Assessment Interview to practice obtaining information about fluid, electrolyte, and acid–base balance on each other.
- Have the students practice the focused physical assessment in Table 52-8 in the textbook on each other.

## SUGGESTIONS FOR CLINICAL ACTIVITIES

- Assign students to collect assessment data related to the client's fluid, electrolyte, and acid–base balances using either the tools presented in the text or the assessment form used by the clinical agency. Discuss findings as they are related to the client's medical diagnosis.
- Have the students perform specific gravity measurements using the equipment provided by the agency.

# LEARNING OUTCOME 6

Identify examples of nursing diagnoses, outcomes, and interventions for clients with altered fluid, electrolyte, or acid–base balance.

## CONCEPTS FOR LECTURE

1. NANDA diagnostic labels that relate to fluid and acid–base imbalances include *Deficient Fluid Volume, Excess Fluid Volume, Risk for Imbalanced Fluid Volume, Risk for Deficient Fluid Volume,* and *Impaired Gas Exchange.*

2. Fluid, electrolyte, and acid–base imbalances affect many other body areas and as a consequence may be the etiology of other nursing diagnoses such as *Impaired Oral Mucous Membrane, Impaired Skin Integrity, Decreased Cardiac Output, Ineffective Tissue Perfusion, Activity Intolerance, Risk for Injury,* and *Acute Confusion.*

3. When planning care the nurse identifies nursing interventions that will assist the client to achieve the following broad goals: maintain or restore normal fluid balance, maintain or restore normal balance of electrolytes in the intracellular and extracellular compartments, maintain or restore pulmonary ventilation and oxygenation, and prevent associated risks (tissue breakdown, decreased cardiac output, confusion, other neurologic signs). Obviously, goals will vary according to the diagnosis and defining characteristics.

    Nursing activities include monitoring fluid intake and output, cardiovascular and respiratory status, and results of laboratory tests; assessing the client's weight, location and extent of edema if present, skin turgor and skin status, specific gravity of urine, level of consciousness, and mental status; fluid intake modifications; dietary changes; parenteral fluid, electrolyte, and blood replacement; and other appropriate measures such as administering prescribed medications and oxygen, providing skin care and oral hygiene, positioning the client appropriately, and scheduling rest periods.

4. Specific nursing interventions are found in Tables 52-6 and 52-7.

## POWERPOINT LECTURE SLIDES

*(NOTE: The number on each PPT Lecture Slide directly corresponds with the Concepts for Lecture.)*

**1** Nursing Diagnoses Related to Fluid and Acid–Base Imbalances
- Deficient fluid volume
- Excess fluid volume
- Risk for imbalanced fluid volume
- Risk for deficient fluid volume
- Impaired gas exchange

**2** Fluid and Acid–Base Imbalances as Etiology
- Impaired oral mucous membrane
- Impaired skin integrity
- Decreased cardiac output
- Ineffective tissue perfusion
- Activity intolerance
- Risk for injury
- Acute confusion

**3** Desired Outcomes
- Maintain or restore normal fluid balance
- Maintain or restore normal balance of electrolytes in the intracellular and extracellular compartments
- Maintain or restore pulmonary ventilation and oxygenation
- Prevent associated risks (tissue breakdown, decreased cardiac output, confusion, other neurologic signs)

**4** Nursing Interventions
- Monitoring
  - Fluid intake and output
  - Cardiovascular and respiratory status
  - Results of laboratory tests
- Assessing
  - Client's weight
  - Location and extent of edema, if present
  - Skin turgor and skin status
  - Specific gravity of urine
  - Level of consciousness, and mental status
- Fluid intake modifications
- Dietary changes
- Parenteral fluid, electrolyte, and blood replacement
- Other appropriate measures such as
  - Administering prescribed medications and oxygen
  - Providing skin care and oral hygiene
  - Positioning the client appropriately
  - Scheduling rest periods

# LEARNING OUTCOME 7

Teach clients measures to maintain fluid and electrolyte balance.

## CONCEPTS FOR LECTURE

1. Client Teaching: Wellness Care and Promoting Fluid and Electrolyte Balance includes measures to teach clients such as: consume 6–8 glasses of water daily; avoid foods with excess amounts of salt, sugar, and caffeine; eat a well-balanced diet; limit alcohol intake; increase fluid intake before, during, and after strenuous exercise and replace lost electrolytes for excess perspiration with commercially prepared electrolyte solutions; maintain normal body weight; learn about, monitor and manage side effects of medications that affect fluid and electrolytes; recognize possible risk factors for fluid and electrolyte imbalances; and seek prompt professional health care for notable signs of fluid imbalances.

2. Client Teaching: Home Care and Fluid, Electrolyte, and Acid–Base Balance includes additional teaching topics. Topics include monitoring of fluid intake and output; maintaining food and fluid intake; safety; referrals, measures specific to the client's problem, and community and other sources of help.

3. Practice Guidelines: Facilitating Fluid Intake includes reasons for required intake and amount needed; establish a 24-hour plan for ingesting fluids; set short-term goals; identify fluids the client likes and obtain if permitted; help clients to select foods that tend to become liquid at room temperature; supply cups, glasses, and straws for clients confined to bed; serve fluids at the proper temperature; encourage participation in recording intake; and be alert to cultural implications.

4. Practice Guidelines: Helping Clients Restrict Fluid Intake includes reason and the amount of the restriction; help client establish a schedule for ingestion of fluids; identify preferences and obtain if permitted; set short term goals; place fluids in small containers; offer ice chips and mouth care; teach client to avoid ingesting chewy, salty, or sweet foods or fluids; and encourage participation in recording intake.

## POWERPOINT LECTURE SLIDES

*(NOTE: The number on each PPT Lecture Slide directly corresponds with the Concepts for Lecture.)*

1. Wellness Care and Promoting Fluid and Electrolyte Balance
   - Consume 6–8 glasses of water daily
   - Avoid foods with excess amounts of salt, sugar, and caffeine, eat a well-balanced diet
   - Limit alcohol intake
   - Increase fluid intake before, during, and after strenuous exercise
   - Replace lost electrolytes for excess perspiration with commercially prepared electrolyte solutions
   - Maintain normal body weight
   - Learn about, monitor and manage side effects of medications that affect fluid and electrolytes
   - Recognize possible risk factors for fluid and electrolyte imbalances
   - Seek prompt professional health care for notable signs of fluid imbalances

2. Teaching Client to Maintain Fluid and Electrolyte Balance
   - Promoting fluid and electrolyte balance
   - Monitoring fluid intake and output
   - Maintaining food and fluid intake
   - Safety
   - Medications
   - Measures specific to client's problems
   - Referrals
   - Community agencies and other sources of help
   - Facilitating fluid intake

3. Practice Guidelines: Facilitating Fluid Intake
   - Explain reason for required intake and amount needed
   - Establish a 24-hour plan for ingesting fluids
   - Set short-term goals
   - Identify fluids the client likes and obtain if permitted
   - Help clients to select foods that tend to become liquid at room temperature

- Supply cups, glasses, and straws for clients confined to bed
- Serve fluids at the proper temperature
- Encourage participation in recording intake
- Be alert to cultural implications

**4** Practice Guidelines: Helping Clients Restrict Fluid Intake
- Explain reason and the amount of the restriction
- Help client establish a schedule for ingestion of fluids
- Identify preferences and obtain if permitted
- Set short-term goals; place fluids in small containers
- Offer ice chips and mouth care
- Teach client to avoid ingesting chewy, salty, or sweet foods or fluids
- Encourage participation in recording intake

---

### SUGGESTIONS FOR CLASSROOM ACTIVITIES

- Have the students review the Client Teaching and Practice Guidelines features in the textbook. Ask them to suggest additions to these guidelines.

### SUGGESTIONS FOR CLINICAL ACTIVITIES

- If appropriate, have the students use the Client Teaching and Practice Guidelines features to teach clients about promoting fluid, electrolyte, and acid–base balance.

---

## LEARNING OUTCOME 8

Implement measures to correct imbalances of fluids and electrolytes or acids and bases such as enteral or parenteral replacements and blood transfusions.

### CONCEPTS FOR LECTURE

1. Fluids and electrolytes can be provided orally if the client is not vomiting, has not experienced an excessive fluid loss, and has an intact gastrointestinal tract and gag and swallow reflexes. Increased fluids are often prescribed for clients with actual or potential fluid volume deficits. Restricted fluids may be necessary for clients who have fluid retention. These may vary from "nothing by mouth" to a precise amount ordered by a primary care provider.

    Specific fluid and electrolyte imbalances may require simple dietary changes (e.g., increase intake of foods high in potassium, avoid foods high in sodium, or increase intake of foods rich in calcium).

2. Some clients can benefit from oral supplements of electrolytes, particularly when a medication is prescribed that affects electrolyte balance, when dietary intake is inadequate for a specific electrolyte, or when fluid and electrolyte losses are excessive. Clients taking potassium supplements are instructed to take the medication with juice to mask the unpleasant taste and reduce the possibility for gastric distress, to take

### POWERPOINT LECTURE SLIDES

*(NOTE: The number on each PPT Lecture Slide directly corresponds with the Concepts for Lecture.)*

 Correcting Fluids and Electrolyte Imbalances
- Oral replacement in following situations:
  - If the client is not vomiting
  - Has not experienced an excessive fluid loss
  - Has an intact gastrointestinal tract and gag and swallow reflexes
- Restricted fluids may be necessary for fluid retention
  - Vary from "nothing by mouth" to a precise amount ordered
- Dietary changes

 Oral supplements
- Potassium
- Calcium
- Multivitamins
- Sports drink

the medication as prescribed, to see a primary care provider on a regular basis, to never increase the amount taken without an order to do so, and to consult with a primary care provider before using a salt substitute since many contain potassium. People who ingest insufficient milk and milk products or on long-term corticosteroid therapy may benefit from calcium supplements. When taking calcium supplements, the client should consume at least 2,500 mL per day of fluids to reduce the risk of kidney stones. People who have poor dietary habits, who are malnourished, or who have difficulty accessing or eating fresh fruits and vegetables may benefit from a daily multiple vitamin with minerals. People who engage in strenuous activity in a warm environment need to be encouraged to replace water and electrolytes lost through excessive perspiration by consuming a sports drink. Liquid nutritional supplements may be given to clients who are malnourished or have poor eating habits. Some supplements are very high in protein and high in potassium so labels should be carefully read.

3. Parenteral fluid and electrolyte replacement interventions are described in Skill 52.1: Starting an Intravenous Infusion; Skill 52.2: Monitoring an Intravenous Infusion; Skill 52.3: Changing an Intravenous Container, Tubing, and Dressing; Skill 52.4: Discontinuing an Intravenous Infusion; Skill 52.5: Changing an Intravenous Catheter to an Intermittent Infusion Lock; and Skill 52.6: Initiating, Maintaining, and Terminating a Blood Transfusion Using a Y-Set.

   Practice Guidelines Include: Vein Selection, General Tips for Easier IV Starts, and Caring for Clients with a Venous Access Device.

3 Parenteral Fluid and Electrolyte Replacement Interventions
- Skill 52.1: Starting an Intravenous Infusion
- Skill 52.2: Monitoring an Intravenous Infusion
- Skill 52.3: Changing an Intravenous Container, Tubing, and Dressing
- Skill 52.4: Discontinuing an Intravenous Infusion
- Skill 52.5: Changing an Intravenous Catheter to an Intermittent Infusion Lock
- Skill 52.6: Initiating, Maintaining, and Terminating a Blood Transfusion Using a Y-Set

## SUGGESTIONS FOR CLASSROOM ACTIVITIES

- Invite nurses who serve on an IV team to discuss assessment criteria related to clients receiving intravenous therapy, including nursing interventions for infiltrated intravenous lines.
- Make a poster with various intravenous catheters, including central lines, and types of fluids and dressing materials for the students to review.
- Show videotaped demonstrations for starting, hanging, changing, maintaining, and discontinuing intravenous infusions, and have students perform these skills on manikins.
- Discuss blood products, uses of each, and assessments that must be done prior to, during, and after administration of these products. Include discussion of common transfusion reactions.
- Review the composition of common intravenous solutions and the rationale for their use.

## SUGGESTIONS FOR CLINICAL ACTIVITIES

- If possible, arrange for each student to spend time with the IV team observing assessment, procedures for insertion of devices, and care provided for clients who have intravenous lines.
- Examine the agency policies and procedures for intravenous infusions, including time frames for container, tubing, needle (catheter), and dressing changes. Compare to protocols for TPN.
- Demonstrate the use of the intravenous pumps used in the institution.
- Assign students to care for clients requiring IV infusions.
- Review the agency's policies and procedures related to administration of blood products.
- Invite a member of the blood bank to discuss donation, storage, testing, and types of blood products.

# LEARNING OUTCOME 9

Evaluate the effect of nursing and collaborative interventions on the client's fluid, electrolyte, or acid-base balance.

## CONCEPTS FOR LECTURE

1. The nurse collects data to evaluate the effectiveness of goals, desired outcomes, and nursing and collaborative interventions as identified in the plan of care. If desired outcomes are not achieved, the nurse, client, and support person (if appropriate) need to explore the reasons before modifying the care plan.

## POWERPOINT LECTURE SLIDES

*(NOTE: The number on each PPT Lecture Slide directly corresponds with the Concepts for Lecture.)*

 Evaluation
- Collect data as identified in the plan of care
- If desired outcomes are not achieved, explore the reasons before modifying the care plan

## SUGGESTIONS FOR CLASSROOM ACTIVITIES

- Have the students review the nursing diagnosis reference book used by the agency for suggested goals/outcomes/ interventions for NANDA diagnoses related to fluid, electrolyte, and acid-base balance. Have the students identify evaluation data required to determine the effectiveness of each of these.

## SUGGESTIONS FOR CLINICAL ACTIVITIES

- Have the students evaluate the effectiveness of the interventions used to assist their clients to maintain or restore fluid, electrolyte, or acid-base balance, if possible.

# TEST BANK QUESTIONS

The following questions are similar to those that may appear on the NCLEX-RN® exam. Some questions may have one or more correct responses. During this review you should select the best response(s).

## CHAPTER 1

**1.1** Organize these events in chronological order, beginning with the earliest (1) and ending with the most recent (5):

_____ The Order of Deaconesses opens a small hospital in Kaiserswerth, Germany.

_____ The Knights of St. Lazarus dedicate themselves to the care of people with leprosy, syphilis, and chronic skin conditions.

_____ Harriet Tubman provides care to slaves fleeing on the Underground Railroad.

_____ The Cadet Nurse Corps is established.

_____ Florence Nightingale administers to soldiers during the Crimean War.

Answer:

___2___ The Order of Deaconesses opens a small hospital in Kaiserswerth, Germany.

___1___ The Knights of St. Lazarus dedicate themselves to the care of people with leprosy, syphilis, and chronic skin conditions.

___4___ Harriet Tubman provides care to slaves fleeing on the Underground Railroad.

___5___ The Cadet Nurse Corps is established.

___3___ Florence Nightingale administers to soldiers during the Crimean War.

Rationale: Religion played a significant role in the development of nursing. The Crusades saw the formation of several orders of knights who provided care to the sick and injured, including the Knights of St. Lazarus. In 1836, Theodore Fliedner reinstituted the Order of Deaconesses and opened a small hospital and training school in Kaiserswerth, Germany, where Florence Nightingale received her training. During the Crimean War (1854–1856), Ms. Nightingale administered to the soldiers following a request by Sir Sidney Herbert of the British War Department. During the American Civil War (1861–1865), Harriet Tubman (among other nurses) administered to the care of slaves and injured soldiers. World War II casualties created an acute shortage of care, and the Cadet Nurse Corps was established in response to the shortage of nurses.

Assessment

Safe, effective care environment—resource management

Application

Learning Outcome 1.1

**1.2** In alignment with the contributions of Florence Nightingale, the Vietnam Women's Memorial was established to honor which of the following?

1. The memory of Ms. Nightingale
2. Those who brought a human touch to the suffering and dying
3. The image of the angel of mercy
4. Surgical advancements and the use of anesthetic agents

Answer: 2

Rationale: The Vietnam Women's Memorial was established to "honor the women who served and also for the families who lost loved ones during the war . . . to let them know about the women who provided comfort, care, and a human touch for those who were suffering and dying" (Vietnam Women's Memorial Foundation, n.d.). Florence Nightingale brought respectability to the nursing profession, and her contributions allowed nurses to be viewed as noble, compassionate, moral, religious, dedicated, and self-sacrificing. The image of the guardian angel or angel of mercy arose in the latter part of the 19th century, largely from Ms. Nightingale's work. The monument "The Spirit of Nursing" stands in Arlington National Cemetery, honoring nurses who served in World War I—a time of progress in health care, particularly in the field of surgery.

Assessment

Safe, effective care environment

Application

Learning Outcome 1.1

**1.3** Public health and health promotion roles for nurses are components of nursing envisioned by which of the following nurse leaders?

1. Clara Barton
2. Lillian Wald
3. Mary Brewster
4. Florence Nightingale

Answer: 4

Rationale: Florence Nightingale's vision of nursing included public health and health promotion roles for nurses, but it was only partly addressed in the early days of nursing. Her focus tended to be on developing the profession within the hospitals. Clara Barton is noted for establishing the American Red Cross. She persuaded Congress to ratify the Treaty of Geneva in 1882 so that the Red Cross could perform humanitarian efforts in times of peace. Lillian Wald is considered the founder of public health nursing. She and Mary Brewster were the first to offer trained nursing services to the poor in the New York slums and developed the Visiting Nurse Service, along with the Henry Street Settlement.

| | Implementation<br>Safe, effective care environment<br>Analysis<br>Learning Outcome 1.1 |
|---|---|
| **1.4** Which of the following nurse leaders campaigned for the legislation that allows nurses, rather than physicians, to control the nursing profession?<br>　1.　Mary Breckinridge<br>　2.　Lavinia Dock<br>　3.　Margaret Higgins Sanger<br>　4.　Virginia Henderson | Answer: 2<br>Rationale: Lavinia Dock was a feminist, writer, and activist. She participated in protest movements for women's rights that resulted in passage of the 19th Amendment, which allowed women the right to vote. In addition, Dock campaigned for legislation to allow nurses, rather than physicians, to control their profession. Mary Breckinridge established the Frontier Nursing Service. Margaret Higgins Sanger is considered the founder of Planned Parenthood. Virginia Henderson was one of the first modern nurses to define nursing (1966).<br>Assessment<br>Safe, effective care environment<br>Application<br>Learning Outcome 1.1 |
| **1.5** Which of the following themes are common in the definitions of nursing? (Select all that apply.)<br>＿＿＿＿＿ Adaptive<br>＿＿＿＿＿ Client centered<br>＿＿＿＿＿ Goal directed according to the needs of the client<br>＿＿＿＿＿ Diagnosis and treatment of disease<br>＿＿＿＿＿ An art<br>＿＿＿＿＿ A science | Answer:<br>＿＿x＿＿ Adaptive<br>＿＿x＿＿ Client centered<br>＿＿＿＿ Goal directed according to the needs of the client<br>＿＿＿＿ Diagnosis and treatment of disease<br>＿＿x＿＿ An art<br>＿＿x＿＿ A science<br>Rationale: Adaptive; client centered; art; science; holistic; caring; concerned with health promotion, health maintenance, and health restoration; and a helping profession are themes that are common to many definitions formulated about nursing. In 1973, the American Nurses Association (ANA) described nursing practice as goal oriented and adaptable to the needs of the individual, the family, and the community (not just the client).<br>In 1980, the ANA's definition was changed to "Nursing is the diagnosis and treatment of the *human responses* to actual or potential health problems." Diagnosis and treatment of disease is a definition of the medical model.<br>Implementation<br>Safe, effective care environment<br>Application<br>Learning Outcome 1.2 |
| **1.6** The term *patient* usually implies that the person is:<br>　1.　Seeking assistance because of illness.<br>　2.　Proactive in his or her health care needs.<br>　3.　A collaborator in his or her care.<br>　4.　Using a service or commodity. | Answer: 1<br>Rationale: The word *patient* comes from a Latin word meaning "to suffer" or "to bear." Usually, people become patients when they seek assistance because of illness or for surgery. Some nurses believe that the word patient implies passive acceptance of the decisions and care of health professionals, which would be opposite of being proactive in one's health care needs. The term *client* presents the recipient of health care as a collaborator in that care, along with the people who are providing service. A consumer is an individual, a group of people, or a community that uses a service or commodity.<br>Implementation<br>Safe, effective care environment<br>Application<br>Learning Outcome 1.2 |
| **1.7** A nurse has decided to focus on educating the community about health promotion and wellness. Which of the following would be an example of this?<br>　1.　Initiating prenatal and infant care<br>　2.　Holding classes on prevention of sexually transmitted disease | Answer: 4<br>Rationale: Wellness is a process that engages in activities and behaviors that enhance quality of life and maximize personal potential. This involves individual and community activities to enhance healthy lifestyles such as improving nutrition and physical fitness, preventing drug and alcohol misuse, restricting smoking, and preventing accidents in the home and workplace. The goal of illness prevention is to maintain optimal health by preventing |

| | |
|---|---|
| 3. Implementing an exercise class for clients who have had a stroke<br>4. Teaching a class about home accident prevention | disease—which would include immunization, prenatal and infant care, and prevention of sexually transmitted disease. Teaching clients about recovery activities, such as exercises that accelerate recovery after a stroke, would focus on health restoration.<br>Implementation<br>Health promotion and maintenance<br>Application<br>Learning Outcome 1.3 |
| **1.8** Nursing students offer free occult blood screening at a community health fair. This activity would be an example of which area of nursing practice?<br>1. Promoting health and wellness<br>2. Illness prevention<br>3. Restoring health<br>4. Rehabilitation | Answer: 3<br>Rationale: Restoring health focuses on the ill client, and it extends from early detection (such as checking for occult blood in feces) through helping the client during the recovery period. Health promotion and wellness activities enhance the quality of life and maximize personal potential. Rehabilitation is an activity of health restoration.<br>Implementation<br>Health promotion and maintenance<br>Application<br>Learning Outcome 1.3 |
| **1.9** A new graduate has starting working in a state other than the one in which the nursing education program was located. Which of the following should this nurse consult in order to understand the implications of this change of venue?<br>1. American Nurses Association (ANA)<br>2. National League for Nursing (NLN)<br>3. National Council of State Boards of Nursing (NCSBN)<br>4. Nurse State Practice Act | Answer: 4<br>Rationale: Nurse practice acts regulate the practice of nursing in the United States and Canada. Each state and each province has its own act. Nurses are responsible for knowing their state's nurse practice act as it governs their practice. The ANA is the professional organization of nursing, the NLN is responsible for accrediting schools of nursing, and the NCSBN handles licensure of professional nurses.<br>Implementation<br>Safe, effective care environment<br>Application<br>Learning Outcome 1.4 |
| **1.10** A seasoned nurse who acts as a mentor for a new graduate is practicing which of the standards of professional performance?<br>1. Collaboration<br>2. Leadership<br>3. Collegiality<br>4. Evaluation | Answer: 3<br>Rationale: Collegiality describes interaction with and contributions to the professional development of peers and colleagues, which is what a mentoring relationship would involve. Collaboration involves working with the client, the family, and others in the conduct of nursing practice. Leadership provides direction in a professional practice setting, and evaluation involves a comparison between one's own nursing practice and professional practice standards.<br>Implementation<br>Safe, effective environment of care<br>Application<br>Learning Outcome 1.4 |
| **1.11** A nurse is careful to cover the client during a bath. This action describes which of the following nursing roles?<br>1. Caregiver<br>2. Communicator<br>3. Teacher<br>4. Client advocate | Answer: 1<br>Rationale: The caregiver role includes those activities that assist the client physically and psychologically while preserving the client's dignity. As a communicator, the nurse identifies client problems, then communicates these verbally or in writing to other members of the health team. As a teacher, the nurse helps clients learn about their health and the health care procedures they need to perform to maintain or restore their health. A client advocate acts to protect clients and represents their needs and wishes to other health professionals.<br>Implementation<br>Safe, effective care environment<br>Application<br>Learning Outcome 1.5 |

| | |
|---|---|
| **1.12** A client wishes to discontinue treatment for his cancer. Acting as the client advocate, the nurse makes this statement to the client's physician:<br>1. "The client is making his own decision."<br>2. "The client would benefit from additional information about treatment options."<br>3. "The family must be involved in this decision."<br>4. "Let's educate the family about the consequences of this decision." | Answer: 1<br>Rationale: A client advocate acts to protect the client and may represent the client's needs and wishes to other health professionals, such as relaying the client's wishes for information to the physician. Providing additional information to the client about treatment options and bringing the family into the decision-making process would be examples of the nurse acting as teacher or counselor.<br>Implementation<br>Psychosocial integrity<br>Application<br>Learning Outcome 1.5 |
| **1.13** The nurse has assumed the responsibilities of case manager. Which of the following would these include?<br>1. Managing an acute hospital stay<br>2. Delegating activities to other nurses<br>3. Evaluating performance of ancillary workers<br>4. Identifying areas of client concern or problems | Answer: 1<br>Rationale: The case manager oversees the care of a specific caseload or may act as the primary nurse to provide some level of direct care to the client and family. Responsibilities may vary from managing acute hospitalizations to managing high-cost clients or case types. Delegating activities to other nurses and evaluating performance of ancillary workers are responsibilities of the nurse manager. Identifying areas of researchable problems would fall to the research consumer.<br>Evaluation<br>Safe, effective care environment<br>Application<br>Learning Outcome 1.5 |
| **1.14** Throughout the course of the nursing program, professionalism is exemplified by the faculty. The student nurse practices professionalism by which of the following?<br>1. Acquiring characteristics considered to be professional<br>2. Maintaining specific character and spirit<br>3. Learning about the influences of Florence Nightingale<br>4. Promising to uphold the standards of the profession | Answer: 2<br>Rationale: Professionalism refers to professional character, spirit, or methods. It is a set of attributes and a way of life that implies responsibility and commitment. Florence Nightingale influenced nursing professionalism a great deal, but simply learning about her influence does not constitute professionalism because it refers to a way of life. Professionalization is the process of becoming professional, which is acquiring characteristics considered to be professional and upholding the standards of a profession.<br>Implementation<br>Safe, effective care environment<br>Analysis<br>Learning Outcome 1.7 |
| **1.15** The nurse is caring for several acutely ill clients during the shift. Which of the following is an example of the nurse practicing the professional criteria of autonomy?<br>1. Delivering medications and prescribed treatments in a timely manner<br>2. Deciding to prioritize care according to client needs<br>3. Communicating with peers when help is needed<br>4. Complaining to the supervisor about high acuity level and staff-to-client ratio | Answer: 2<br>Rationale: Autonomy in nursing means independence at work, responsibility, and accountability for one's actions. Making decisions about which client requires care according to needs is an example of autonomy. Carrying out physician orders would be an example of nursing care, but not independence. Communication is important in any profession as well as making concerns known to supervisors, but these are not examples of controlling activity—a hallmark of autonomy.<br>Evaluation<br>Safe, effective care environment<br>Application<br>Learning Outcome 1.7 |

**1.16** A student nurse has set up study groups, complete with objectives and goals for each session. This student is practicing which attribute of organization?

1. Governance
2. Socialization
3. Service orientation
4. Specialized education

Answer: 2

Rationale: Socialization involves learning to behave, feel, and see the world in a manner similar to other persons occupying the same role. The goal is to instill in others the norms, values, attitudes, and behaviors deemed essential. One of the most powerful mechanisms of professional socialization is interacting with fellow students and becoming bound together by feelings of mutual cooperation, support, and solidarity. Governance is the establishment and maintenance of social, political, and economic arrangements by which practitioners control their practice, working conditions, and professional affairs. Service orientation differentiates nursing from an occupation pursued primarily for profit. Specialized education is an important aspect of professional status and is focused on the course of study and curriculum particular to the profession.

Evaluation
Safe, effective care environment
Application
Learning Outcome 1.7

---

**1.17** Explaining the present economic challenges to students in the community health course, the nurse educator would emphasize the importance of nurses being familiar with which of the following?

1. Emphasis shift from inpatient to outpatient care
2. Consumer representatives on governing boards of nursing associations and regulatory agencies
3. Diagnostic-related groups (DRGs)
4. Advances in science and technology

Answer: 1

Rationale: Economics is one of the social forces currently influencing the profession of nursing. As a result of the shift from inpatient to outpatient care, more nurses are being employed in community-based health settings. Other forces include consumer demands, family structure, and science and technology. DRGs are a classification system that categorically establishes pretreatment billing based on diagnosis. Though this is an aspect of economic factors affecting nursing, it is not the underlying cause of more personnel being employed in community-based settings.

Evaluation
Safe, effective care environment
Application
Learning Outcome 1.7

---

**1.18** The community health nurse is working primarily with teenage mothers and their children. The nurse recognizes that these clients have increased vulnerability, mainly due to which of the following?

1. Distance separation from their nuclear families
2. Increased poverty
3. Raising children without the support of family
4. Normal difficulties of adolescence

Answer: 4

Rationale: Teenage mothers have the normal needs of teenagers as well as those of new mothers, with motherhood compounding the difficulties of adolescence. Though many teenage mothers are raising children alone, without the support of the baby's father or perhaps their own family, and many live in poverty, *all* are vulnerable because of their age.

Assessment
Psychosocial integrity
Evaluation
Learning Outcome 1.9

---

**1.19** The client questions information gathered from a website. Which of the following is the best response by the nurse to these questions?

1. "Information from the Internet isn't accurate."
2. "We'll have to check this information with your physician."
3. "Bring your information to the clinic so we can go through it together."
4. "Don't trust anything you haven't received from our office."

Answer: 3

Rationale: Nurses may need to interpret Internet sources of information to clients and their families. Though not all Internet-based information is accurate, some may be high quality and valid. Nurses need to become information brokers so they, not just the physician, can help clients access and evaluate information to determine its usefulness.

Evaluation
Safe, effective care environment
Analysis
Learning Outcome 1.9

---

| | |
|---|---|
| **1.20** The nurse practitioner is working with the staff nurse to change the plan of care for a client. This is an example of which of the ANA standards of practice?<br>   1. Assessment<br>   2. Outcomes identification<br>   3. Planning<br>   4. Implementation | Answer: 4<br>Rationale: Consultation—as in advanced practice nurses and staff nurses working together—is a way for those involved with the client's care to influence the plan, enhance the abilities of others, and effect change. Consultation is part of Standard 5: Implementation. Assessment deals with data collection. Outcomes identification sets identified goals for a plan specific to the client or situation. Planning prescribes strategies and alternatives to attain expected outcomes.<br>Implementation<br>Safe, effective care environment<br>Application<br>Learning Outcome 1.9 |
| **1.21** The advanced practice nurse refers the client to physical therapy for further rehabilitation. This is an example of which of the ANA standards of practice?<br>   1. Assessment<br>   2. Diagnosis<br>   3. Planning<br>   4. Implementation | Answer: 4<br>Rationale: Standard 5: Implementation includes prescriptive authority and treatment, which would include a referral for further treatment and therapy in accordance with state and federal laws and regulations. Assessment is data collection. Diagnosis analyzes the assessment data. Planning prescribes strategies and alternatives to reach the expected goals.<br>Implementation<br>Safe, effective care environment<br>Application<br>Learning Outcome 1.4 |
| **1.22** The client recovered to a greater level than what was previously expected. The staff nurse responsible for the client's care is following which of the ANA standards of practice?<br>   1. Diagnosis<br>   2. Planning<br>   3. Implementation<br>   4. Evaluation | Answer: 4<br>Rationale: Evaluation, Standard 6, evaluates the progress toward attainment of outcomes. Since the progress was recovery in this case, and at a greater level than expectations, the nurse would be evaluating the plan of care. Diagnosis analyzes the assessment data to determine problems. Planning involves prescribing strategies and alternatives to attain expected outcomes. Implementation consists of coordinating care, teaching, consultation, prescriptive authority, and treatment/evaluation.<br>Evaluation<br>Safe, effective care environment<br>Analysis<br>Learning Outcome 1.4 |
| **1.23** A practicing RN decides that attending an upcoming workshop about new pharmacological treatments would benefit his or her practice. This RN is modeling which of the standards of professional performance?<br>   1. Quality of practice<br>   2. Education<br>   3. Professional practice evaluation<br>   4. Research | Answer: 3<br>Rationale: Standards of professional performance describe a competent level of behavior in the professional role. Professional practice evaluation, Standard 9, is behavior that evaluates one's own nursing practice in relation to professional practice standards and guidelines, relevant statutes, rules, and regulations. Deciding to enhance one's current knowledge base, in relationship to one's own practice, would describe this standard. Quality of practice is a systematic approach to enhance the quality and effectiveness of nursing practice. Education is knowledge attainment and competency that reflects current nursing practice. Research integrates research findings into practice.<br>Implementation<br>Safe, effective care environment<br>Application<br>Learning Outcome 1.7 |
| **1.24** A nurse is working closely with a client regarding a chemotherapy regimen, providing consultation, education, and direction for the client and the client's family. This nurse would most likely be certified as which of the following?<br>   1. Nurse practitioner<br>   2. Clinical nurse specialist | Answer: 2<br>Rationale: A clinical nurse specialist has an advanced degree or expertise and is considered to be an expert in a specialized area of practice (oncology in this case). The nurse provides direct client care, educates others, consults, conducts research, and manages care. A nurse practitioner has an advanced education, is a graduate of a nurse practitioner program, and usually deals with nonemergency acute or chronic illness and provides primary ambulatory care. The nurse educator is responsible for classroom and often clinical teaching. A nurse |

| | |
|---|---|
| 3. Nurse educator<br>4. Nurse entrepreneur | entrepreneur usually has an advanced degree, manages a health-related business, and may be involved in education, consultation, or research.<br>Implementation<br>Safe, effective care environment<br>Application<br>Learning Outcome 1.6 |
| **1.25** A nursing program utilizes nurse preceptors in some of its clinical experiences. These nurses are considered proficient in their clinical area. According to Benner's stages of nursing expertise, these nurses would belong to which stage?<br>  1. Stage II<br>  2. Stage III<br>  3. Stage IV<br>  4. Stage V | Answer: 3<br>Rationale: Stage IV is a proficiency stage. The person has 3 to 5 years of experience and has a holistic understanding of the client, which improves decision making and focuses on long-term goals. Stage II is advanced beginner. The person demonstrates marginally acceptable performance. Stage III is competent. The nurse has 2 or 3 years of experience and demonstrates organizational/planning abilities. Stage V is considered expert. Performance is fluid, flexible, and highly proficient. The expert nurse no longer requires rules, guidelines, or maxims to connect an understanding of the situation to appropriate action. This person has highly intuitive and analytic abilities in new situations.<br>Assessment<br>Safe, effective care environment<br>Analysis<br>Learning Outcome 1.8 |

## CHAPTER 2

| | |
|---|---|
| **2.1** A high school graduate is considering entering a nursing program that offers a baccalaureate degree. Which of the following is the entity that accredits baccalaureate programs (or higher)?<br>  1. NLN (National League for Nursing)<br>  2. CCNE (Commission on Collegiate Nursing Education)<br>  3. NCLEX (National Council Licensure Examination)<br>  4. NCSBN (National Council of State Boards of Nursing) | Answer: 2<br>Rationale: The CCNE accredits baccalaureate and graduate degree nursing programs. The NLN accredits nursing programs at all levels, including LVN and LPN. Both of these offer voluntary accreditation. The NCLEX is the licensure examination administered by each state, and the NCSBN is the council to which all state boards of nursing belong.<br>Assessment<br>Safe, effective care environment<br>Application<br>Learning Outcome 2.1 |
| **2.2** If the RN has several LPNs on the shift to supervise, which of the following responsibilities will fall to the RN?<br>  1. Evaluating the care provided to the client<br>  2. Administering scheduled injectable medications<br>  3. Performing complex dressing changes<br>  4. Supervising unlicensed client care providers (such as a nurse's aide) | Answer: 1<br>Rationale: The RN has the knowledge and skill to make more sophisticated nursing judgments and is responsible for assessing the client's condition, planning care, and evaluating the effect of the care provided. LPNs practice under the supervision of an RN in a hospital, nursing home, rehabilitation center, or home health agency, and usually provide basic, direct technical care to clients.<br>Implementation<br>Safe, effective care environment<br>Application<br>Learning Outcome 2.1 |
| **2.3** Several nurse educators are working together to promote articulation agreements between prospective nursing programs in their state. Funding for this type of program was made possible by which of the following?<br>  1. Pew Health Professions Commission<br>  2. Goldmark report | Answer: 4<br>Rationale: The Robert Wood Foundation funded 20 nationwide Colleagues in Caring (CIC) projects to facilitate a collaborative approach to nursing workforce development whose focus is providing seamless articulation between educational levels. The Pew Health Professions Commission developed a set of competencies needed by all health professional groups for successful practice in the 21st century. The Goldmark report and the Brown report were studies that supported the development of 2-year programs in the United States. |

| | |
|---|---|
| 3. Brown report<br>4. Colleagues in Caring | Implementation<br>Safe, effective care environment<br>Application<br>Learning Outcome 2.1 |
| **2.4** A nurse faculty member is speaking to prospective students to the BSN program at their educational institution. Which of the following is a major incentive for students to select a BSN program over an ADN program?<br><br>   1. Ability to work in critical care areas<br>   2. Easier transition to graduate school<br>   3. Better opportunity for career advancement<br>   4. Liberal arts education | Answer: 3<br>Rationale: The nurse who holds a baccalaureate degree enjoys greater autonomy, responsibility, participation in institutional decision making, and career advancement. A liberal arts education is also a positive point, though not as major an incentive. RNs, regardless of their education level, can work in critical care areas. There are some programs offering RN to MSN completion studies at this point in time.<br>Evaluation<br>Safe, effective care environment<br>Application<br>Learning Outcome 2.1 |
| **2.5** The ANA's proposal for entry level for professional practice initiated debate among nurses. Which of the following would be most at risk if the ANA proposal were implemented?<br><br>   1. An RN with an associate degree who has a head nurse position<br>   2. An RN with a BSN who is a staff nurse<br>   3. An RN with a diploma who works overtime<br>   4. An RN with an associate degree who is currently in school | Answer: 1<br>Rationale: According to the ANA's proposal, only the baccalaureate graduate would be licensed under the legal title registered nurse. The graduate with an associate degree or diploma would be considered a technical nurse. If the ANA proposal is implemented, nurses who are currently licensed and educated in associate degree or diploma programs would have to be considered under a grandfather clause, provided that their performance meets established standards. If an institution required a minimum of a baccalaureate degree for the position of head nurse, an RN who is currently employed as a head nurse but who does not hold the baccalaureate degree would have no guarantee of retaining that position.<br>Implementation<br>Safe, effective care environment<br>Application<br>Learning Outcome 2.2 |
| **2.6** Although Florence Nightingale demonstrated the importance of research in nursing care as early as 1854, the research approach did not take hold in nursing until the beginning of the 20th century. Put these events in chronological order, starting with the earliest (1) and proceeding to the most recent (4):<br><br>_____ The National Center for Nursing Research was created.<br>_____ The National Institute for Nursing Research was created.<br>_____ The journal *Nursing Research* was established.<br>_____ End-of-life/palliative care research was conducted. | Answer:<br>\_\_\_\_2\_\_\_\_ The National Center for Nursing Research was created.<br>\_\_\_\_3\_\_\_\_ The National Institute for Nursing Research was created.<br>\_\_\_\_1\_\_\_\_ The journal *Nursing Research* was established.<br>\_\_\_\_4\_\_\_\_ End-of-life/palliative care research was conducted.<br>Rationale: The journal *Nursing Research* was established in 1952. The National Center for Nursing Research was created in 1985 at the National Institutes of Health (NIH). In 1993, it was promoted to the National Institute for Nursing Research (NINR). End-of-life/palliative care was identified at NINR as an area of research for 2000–2004.<br>Assessment<br>Safe, effective care environment<br>Application |
| **2.7** Some nursing students have been given an assignment to develop a research question from a quantitative approach. Which of the following would be an example of a quantitative research question in the clinical area?<br><br>   1. How do siblings react to a new baby of a second marriage after divorce of their parents? | Answer: 2<br>Rationale: Quantitative research is often viewed as "hard" science. It progresses through systematic, logical steps to collect information under controlled conditions. The information is analyzed using statistical procedures. Qualitative research most often explores the subjective experiences of human beings, which would be exemplified in options 1, 3, and 4.<br>Evaluation |

| | |
|---|---|
| 2. What dressing selections work best for a wound dehiscence?<br><br>3. What support do terminal cancer clients find least beneficial in hospice care?<br><br>4. Does expression of client spirituality affect recovery time? | Safe, effective care environment<br>Analysis<br>Learning Outcome 2.5 |
| **2.8** A client has agreed to participate in a research study. Which of the following would constitute risk of harm to this client?<br><br>1. Withholding information about the study<br><br>2. Suggesting that participation would greatly benefit the client's financial situation<br><br>3. Giving the client false information about his or her participation<br><br>4. Providing the client's name as a participant in the study | Answer: 4<br>Rationale: Risk of harm to a research subject is exposure to the possibility of injury, which could involve physical or psychological injury such as loss of confidentiality or loss of privacy. Withholding information or giving false information would be violations of full disclosure. Participants should feel free from coercion or undue influence to participate in a study or this would be a violation against the right of self-determination.<br>Assessment<br>Psychosocial integrity<br>Application<br>Learning Outcome 2.6 |
| **2.9** A nursing instructor is researching the implementation of assigning study guides for homework points and the effect this has on the students' test grades. The instructor reports group data for published research. This is an example of which of the rights in research?<br><br>1. Right of full disclosure<br><br>2. Right of confidentiality<br><br>3. Right of self-determination<br><br>4. Risk of harm | Answer: 2<br>Rationale: Confidentiality means that any information a participant relates will not be made public and investigators must inform research participants about the measures to provide for these rights. Such measures may include the use of code numbers or reporting only group or aggregate data in published research. Right of full disclosure is the act of making clear the client's role in a research situation. Right of self-determination means that participants should feel free from undue influence. Risk of harm is exposure to the possibility of injury going beyond everyday situations.<br>Implementation<br>Safe, effective care environment<br>Application<br>Learning Outcome 2.6 |
| **2.10** A nurse researcher is exploring and formulating research problems. Which of the following criteria should the nurse researcher consider in this process? (Select all that apply.)<br>_____ Significance<br>_____ Confidentiality<br>_____ Researchability<br>_____ Design<br>_____ Feasibility<br>_____ Interest to the researcher | Answer:<br>____x____ Significance<br>_____ Confidentiality<br>____x____ Researchability<br>_____ Design<br>____x____ Feasibility<br>____x____ Interest to the researcher<br>Rationale: Polit and Beck suggest that several criteria be used when formulating a research problem: significance (the potential to contribute to nursing science by enhancing client care); researchability (the problem can be subjected to scientific investigation); and feasibility (the availability of time as well as material and human resources, space, money, etc.). Since researchers spend much time and energy while conducting a research project, it would also be important that they have genuine interest in the project. Confidentiality is one of the rights of the participant in research, and design focuses on how the research is done.<br>Assessment<br>Safe, effective care environment<br>Application<br>Learning Outcome 2.7 |

| | |
|---|---|
| **2.11** The nurse researcher is considering whether the findings of a project may present uncertain results in the clinical area. The criteria this researcher is reflecting on would be which of the following?<br>1. Significance<br>2. Researchability<br>3. Confidentiality<br>4. Variables | Answer: 2<br>Rationale: Researchability means that the problem can be subjected to scientific investigation. If a significant problem produces ambiguity or uncertainty in clinical situations, it may not be appropriate to research. Significance deals with whether the research problem has the potential to contribute to nursing science by enhancing nursing care. Confidentiality is one of the research participant's rights. Quantitative research problems address relationships between independent and dependent variables.<br>Implementation<br>Safe, effective care environment<br>Application<br>Learning Outcome 2.7 |
| **2.12** A nurse researcher is considering the use of various nonpharmacological distraction techniques that have shown success for behavior control in troubled adolescents. The criteria this researcher is considering is which of the following?<br>1. Significance<br>2. Researchability<br>3. Feasibility<br>4. Interest | Answer: 1<br>Rationale: The research problem has significance if it has the potential to contribute to nursing science by enhancing client care, testing or generating a theory, or resolving a day-to-day clinical problem. If the adolescents are showing improved behavior, then these techniques have significance in enhancing client care. Researchability means that the problem can be subjected to scientific investigation, without ambiguity or uncertainty. Feasibility pertains to the time and material as well as human resources needed to investigate a problem or question. Interest can be a factor for successful completion, depending on the attitude of the researcher.<br>Assessment<br>Psychosocial integrity<br>Application<br>Learning Outcome 2.7 |
| **2.13** A nurse educator has asked the question, "Do students who form study groups fare better on the NCLEX® exam when compared to their peers who study independently?" An example of a dependent variable would be which of the following?<br>1. Number of students in a study group<br>2. NCLEX® scores of both groups<br>3. Students' college GPAs<br>4. Time between graduation and sitting for the NCLEX® | Answer: 2<br>Rationale: The dependent variable is the behavior, characteristic, or outcome that the researcher wishes to explain or predict. The independent variable is the presumed cause of or influence on the dependent variable. In this situation, the prediction is the success on NCLEX®. All the other options would be examples of independent variables, or those things that cause or have an influence on the dependent variable.<br>Assessment<br>Safe, effective care environment<br>Analysis<br>Learning Outcome 2.7 |
| **2.14** A nurse has defined the current research problem. What is the next step in the process?<br>1. Formulate a hypothesis<br>2. Define variables<br>3. Review the literature<br>4. Select a design | Answer: 3<br>Rationale: Before progressing with the research design, the researcher determines what is known and not known about the problem. A thorough review of the literature provides the foundation on which to build new knowledge. Next, a hypothesis is formulated, variables are defined, and the research design is selected.<br>Implementation<br>Safe, effective care environment<br>Application<br>Learning Outcome 2.7 |
| **2.15** A nurse researcher is testing the effects of a new dressing preparation on certain participants, while continuing to use older but more familiar products on others. This is an example of which type of research design?<br>1. Quasi-experimental<br>2. Experimental | Answer: 2<br>Rationale: Experimental design is one in which the investigator manipulates the independent variable by administering an experimental treatment to some participants while withholding it from others. This would be the situation if some of the participants were exposed to new products while others were not. Quasi-experimental design is when the investigator manipulates the independent variable but without either randomization or control. In a nonexperimental design, the investigator does no manipulation of the |

| | |
|---|---|
| 3. Nonexperimental<br>4. Pilot study | independent variable. A pilot study is a test study before the actual one begins and is not a type of research design.<br>Implementation<br>Health promotion and maintenance<br>Application<br>Learning Outcome 2.7 |
| **2.16** A researcher is conducting a study involving only the single-parent families of a school system. The sample in this situation is which of the following?<br>1. The school system<br>2. Children<br>3. Parents<br>4. Single-parent families | Answer: 4<br>Rationale: The sample is the segment of the population from which the data will actually be collected—in this case, single-parent families. The school system, parents, and children would be more representative of the population, which includes all possible members of the group who meet the criteria for the study.<br>Assessment<br>Health promotion and maintenance<br>Application |
| **2.17** A nurse researcher is using an instrument that provides similar results each time it's implemented. This is an example of which of the following?<br>1. Validity<br>2. Reliability<br>3. Consistency<br>4. Variability | Answer: 2<br>Rationale: Reliability is the degree of consistency with which an instrument measures a concept or variable. If it is reliable, repeated measurement of the same variable should yield similar or nearly similar results. Validity is the degree to which an instrument measures what it is supposed to measure. Consistency is a component of reliability. Variability does not describe instrument measurement, but variances in data.<br>Implementation<br>Health promotion and maintenance<br>Application<br>Learning Outcome 2.7 |
| **2.18** The student nurse is examining the dispersion of data in a research study. Measurements would include which of the following?<br>1. Mean, median, and mode<br>2. Range, variance, and standard deviation<br>3. Mean, range, and standard deviation<br>4. Measures of central tendency | Answer: 2<br>Rationale: Measures of variability indicate the degree of dispersion or spread of the data. They include the range, variance, and standard deviation. Measures of central tendency describe the center of distribution of the data, denoting where most of the subjects lie. They include the mean, median, and mode.<br>Evaluation<br>Safe, effective care environment<br>Analysis |
| **2.19** After the data have been analyzed, the nurse realizes that the probability has a value of less than .05. This means that the findings are which of the following?<br>1. Statistically significant<br>2. Statistically insignificant<br>3. Chance occurrences<br>4. Generalized | Answer: 1<br>Rationale: If findings in a research study are statistically significant—which means they did not occur by chance—the probability value is less than .05, the acceptable level of significance. Values greater than .05 are considered to be statistically insignificant and there is a greater probability that the results were due to chance occurrences. In other words, options 2 and 3 mean the same thing. It is not known what the generalized findings would be.<br>Evaluation<br>Safe, effective care environment<br>Analysis |
| **2.20** The student nurse is doing a literature review on evidence-based practice (EBP). Which of the following demonstrates the student's understanding of EBP?<br>1. Presenting a paper about EBP<br>2. Repositioning a client at risk for skin breakdown every 2 hours<br>3. Explaining EBP to fellow students | Answer: 2<br>Rationale: In evidence-based practice, the nurse integrates research findings with clinical experience, the client's preferences, and available resources in planning and implementing care. Evidence-based practice would support frequent repositioning to prevent skin breakdown in an at-risk client, demonstrating that this student is able to incorporate research into practice. Presenting papers or explaining what EBP is to someone else does not *demonstrate* the ability to put into practice that which is learned. |

| | |
|---|---|
| 4. Trying to find other problems to implement EBP | Implementation<br>Health promotion and maintenance<br>Application<br>Learning Outcome 2.4 |
| **2.21** A group of nurses is researching how care providers of Stage I/II Alzheimer's clients use prior coping skills in dealing with their current situation. Which qualitative research tradition does this exemplify?<br>1. Grounded theory<br>2. Ethnography<br>3. Phenomenology<br>4. Substantive dimension | Answer: 3<br>Rationale: Phenomenology is research that investigates people's life experiences and how they interpret those experiences. Using prior coping skills (life experiences) and applying them to current situations in order to interpret the process of Alzheimer's disease is an example of phenomenology. Grounded theory is research to understand social structures and social processes. Ethnography is research that provides a framework to focus on the culture of a group of people. Substantive dimension is not a research tradition, rather a way to critique research reports.<br>Assessment<br>Psychosocial integrity<br>Application<br>Learning Outcome 2.5 |
| **2.22** In evaluating a research question regarding the safety of pharmacological interventions used to stop preterm labor, the nurse looks specifically at the various medications used and what effect, if any, they had on the baby. The nurse is critiquing the research based on which dimension?<br>1. Methodologic<br>2. Interpretive<br>3. Substantive and theoretical<br>4. Presentation and stylistic | Answer: 3<br>Rationale: For substantive and theoretical dimensions, the nurse needs to evaluate the significance of the research problem (preterm labor is a critical concern in obstetric nursing) and the congruence between the research question and the methods used to address it (in this case, using accepted means to treat preterm labor). Methodologic dimensions pertain to the appropriateness of the research design, of which we have no information for this situation. To critique interpretive dimensions, the nurse needs to ascertain the accuracy of the discussion, conclusions, and implications of the study results (no information is given regarding the results in this situation).<br>The manner in which the research plan and results are communicated refers to the presentation and stylistic dimensions. Again, we have no examples of this dimension for this scenario to critique.<br>Evaluation<br>Safe, effective care environment<br>Analysis |
| **2.23** A nurse practitioner feels it is important to participate in nursing research. Which activity is most appropriate for this nurse's level of education and position?<br>1. Helping to identify clinical problems in direct client care<br>2. Using research findings to develop policies and procedures<br>3. Critically analyzing and interpreting research for application to practice<br>4. Participating in data collection | Answer: 3<br>Rationale: The nurse practitioner, having a graduate level education as well as prior nursing experience, would most likely be analyzing and interpreting research for application. All nurses, including new graduates, could help to identify clinical problems in direct client care or participate in data collection. Nurse managers would most likely use research findings to develop policies and procedures and may not necessarily have an advanced degree.<br>Implementation<br>Health promotion and maintenance<br>Application<br>Learning Outcome 2.4 |
| **2.24** A significant research study was conducted on surgical clients in Pennsylvania hospitals. Findings concluded that:<br>1. Years of nursing experience increased client survival.<br>2. Hospital size did not affect client survival.<br>3. Nurses with BSN or higher degrees were associated with lower mortality. | Answer: 3<br>Rationale: This research study has generated much debate over the relationship of higher educational level of nursing staff and client mortality rate. For every 10% increase in proportion of higher-degree nurses, there was a 5% reduction in mortality. Years of nursing experience did not correlate with client survival, but nurse staffing and certified surgeons were also statistically significant in reducing mortality. Hospital data included the size, but this was not an outcome of the findings. |

| | |
|---|---|
| 4. Nurse-to-client ratios did not have a bearing on significant reduction in client mortality. | Evaluation<br>Safe, effective care environment<br>Analysis |

# CHAPTER 3

| | |
|---|---|
| **3.1** Nursing students have been assigned to develop their own theory of nursing. Which of the following would they include in their theory, often referred to as the metaparadigm for nursing?<br>1. Society, medicine, nursing, and biology<br>2. Patient, facility, health, and nursing<br>3. Organization, discipline, nursing, and client<br>4. Client, environment, health, and nursing | Answer: 4<br>Rationale: Four major concepts—person (or client), environment, health, and nursing—can be superimposed on almost any theoretical work in nursing. They are collectively referred to as a metaparadigm for nursing. All other options listed do not include the "pattern" associated with these four concepts.<br>Assessment<br>Health promotion and maintenance<br>Application<br>Learning Outcome 3.3 |
| **3.2** Nursing students have been studying the "stability model" of nurse theorists. This view can be described as which of the following? (Select all that apply.)<br>_____ Dominant<br>_____ Stress/adaptation framework<br>_____ Martha Rogers's theory<br>_____ Caring/complexity framework<br>_____ Callista Roy's theory<br>_____ Systems framework | Answer:<br>____x____ Dominant<br>____x____ Stress/adaptation framework<br>_____ Martha Rogers's theory<br>_____ Caring/complexity framework<br>____x____ Callista Roy's theory<br>____x____ Systems framework<br>Rationale: The dominant view of nursing theories is considered the "stability model" (Hood & Leddy, 2003). These theories use systems or stress/adaptation as frameworks. The theories of Callista Roy, Betty Neuman, and Imogene King would fit in the stability model. The emerging view is considered the "growth model" with theories using caring or complexity as frameworks. This model includes the theories of Dorothea Orem, Jean Watson, Hildegard Peplau, Martha Rogers, and Rosemarie Parse.<br>Assessment<br>Health promotion and maintenance<br>Application<br>Learning Outcome 3.4 |
| **3.3** Nursing students are researching how cultural practices affect the dying process of terminal cancer clients. For their research, they most likely will explore which of the following?<br>1. Critical theory<br>2. Midlevel theories<br>3. Grand theories<br>4. Stability models | Answer: 1<br>Rationale: Critical theory research used in nursing helps explain how structures such as race, gender, sexual orientation, and economic class affect patient experiences and health outcomes. In this scenario (the influences of culture on the dying process), research on critical theory would help educate how these structures affect the human experience of death. Midlevel theories focus on exploring concepts such as pain, self-esteem, and learning. Grand theories are only occasionally used in nursing research. The stability model describes the dominant view of nursing theories.<br>Implementation<br>Health promotion and maintenance<br>Application<br>Learning Outcome 3.4 |
| **3.4** A nurse is caring for a client with a severe head trauma. Each shift, the nurse pays attention to the lighting, atmosphere, and surroundings the client is exposed to. The nurse is functioning according to the assumptions of which nursing theorist? | Answer: 3<br>Rationale: Florence Nightingale defined nursing more than 100 years ago as "the act of utilizing the environment of the patient to assist him in his recovery." Attending to the client's surroundings, including the lighting and atmosphere, is being attentive to the client's environment. Deficiencies in environmental factors (especially air, water, drainage, cleanliness, and light) have produced lack of health or illness. Dorothea Orem's theory focused on |

| | |
|---|---|
| 1. Dorothea Orem<br>2. Martha Rogers<br>3. Florence Nightingale<br>4. Jean Watson | self-care, Rogers's theory is the science of unitary human beings, and Jean Watson defined nursing in relationship to caring.<br>Implementation<br>Psychosocial integrity<br>Application |
| **3.5** Nursing staff members from an acute psychiatric unit have been asked to establish a nurse theorist they can easily identify within their practice. Understanding the importance of developing a therapeutic relationship between themselves and their clients, especially in this unit, which theorist would they most likely be drawn to?<br>1. Florence Nightingale<br>2. Hildegard Peplau<br>3. Jean Watson<br>4. Dorothea Orem | Answer: 2<br>Rationale: Hildegard Peplau, a psychiatric nurse, introduced a theory in which a therapeutic relationship between the nurse and client is central. Florence Nightingale's theory focused around environmental controls. Jean Watson's theory has caring as its central theme. Dorothea Orem's theory focused on self-care deficit.<br>Implementation<br>Psychosocial integrity<br>Application |
| **3.6** During a hospital stay, the client has taken control of her recovery and rehabilitation and is utilizing available resources for her needs. This describes which level of Peplau's model?<br>1. Orientation<br>2. Identification<br>3. Exploitation<br>4. Resolution | Answer: 3<br>Rationale: The nurse–client relationship is described in four phases, according to Peplau's interpersonal relations model. The exploitation phase occurs when the client derives full value from what the nurse offers through the relationship, using available services based on self-interest and needs. Power shifts from the nurse to the client. Orientation is the first phase, when the client seeks help and the nurse provides the client with understanding and assistance. Identification is the second phase, where the client assumes dependence, interdependence, or independence in relation to the nurse. The last phase is resolution, where old needs and goals are put aside and new ones adopted.<br>Assessment<br>Psychosocial integrity<br>Application |
| **3.7** Which of the following nurse theorists focused her theory on 14 fundamental needs of individuals?<br>1. Dorothea Orem<br>2. Florence Nightingale<br>3. Martha Rogers<br>4. Virginia Henderson | Answer: 4<br>Rationale: Henderson conceptualized the nurse's role as assisting sick or healthy individuals to gain independence in meeting 14 fundamental needs, from breathing normally to discovering the curiosity that leads to normal development and health. Dorothea Orem's theory focused on self-care deficit. Florence Nightingale's theory centered around the client's environment, and Martha Rogers related her theory to multiple scientific disciplines.<br>Assessment<br>Physiologic integrity<br>Knowledge |
| **3.8** A nurse has implemented the use of noncontact therapeutic touch. Which theorist applied the concept surrounding this intervention?<br>1. Florence Nightingale<br>2. Martha Rogers<br>3. Virginia Henderson<br>4. Rosemarie Parse | Answer: 2<br>Rationale: Rogers states that humans are dynamic energy fields. Nurses applying Rogers's theory seek to promote interaction between the two energy fields. The use of noncontact therapeutic touch is based on the concept of human energy fields. Nightingale's theory centered on the client's environment. Henderson conceptualized the nurse's role as assisting individuals to gain independence in meeting 14 fundamental needs. Rosemarie Parse's theory revolves around *human becoming*.<br>Assessment<br>Physiologic integrity<br>Knowledge |

**3.9** The nurse is teaching health and wellness principles to junior high students. According to Orem's theory, which category of self-care requisite are these students experiencing?

1. Universal
2. Developmental
3. Health deviation
4. Deficit

Answer: 2

Rationale: Developmental requisites result from maturation or are associated with conditions or events, such as adjusting to a change in body image (adolescent maturation, in this case) or to the loss of a spouse. Universal requisites are common to all people and include nutrition, hydration, elimination, and rest. Health deviation requisites result from illness, injury, or disease or its treatment. They include actions such as seeking health care assistance, carrying out prescribed therapies, and learning to live with the effects of illness or treatment. Self-care deficit is not a self-care requisite, but it results when self-care agency is not adequate to meet the known self-care demand.

Implementation

Health promotion and maintenance

Application

---

**3.10** According to Orem's self-care deficit theory, people are assisted through which of the following methods of helping? (Select all that apply.)

_____ Balancing rest
_____ Teaching
_____ Supporting
_____ Guiding
_____ Preventing hazards to life

Answer:

_____ Balancing rest
___x___ Teaching
___x___ Supporting
___x___ Guiding
_____ Preventing hazards to life

Rationale: Orem's self-care deficit theory explains not only when nursing is needed, but also how people can be assisted through five methods of helping: acting or doing for, guiding, teaching, supporting, and providing an environment that promotes the individual's abilities to meet current and future demands. Balancing rest and preventing hazards to life are part of the universal requisites of Orem's self-care needs.

Assessment

Health promotion and maintenance

Application

---

**3.11** Nursing students are working with clients on a secured Alzheimer's unit. Most of the clients are Stage II/III Alzheimer's disease. Which of the following types of nursing systems, according to Orem's theory, would be appropriate for this unit?

1. Supportive
2. Educative
3. Partly compensatory
4. Wholly compensatory

Answer: 4

Rationale: Wholly compensatory systems are required for individuals who are unable to control and monitor their environment and process information. This would describe clients with Stage II/III Alzheimer's—those who need constant supervision and at some point in the near future, total care with all ADLs. Supportive-educative systems (developmental) are designed for persons who need to learn to perform self-care measures and need assistance to do so. This would not be attainable for this group of clients. Partly compensatory systems are designed for individuals who are unable to perform some, but not all, self-care activities. Because the clients are in the end stage of the disease, their ability to care for themselves is greatly diminished. Some would not be able to care for themselves at all.

Assessment

Safe, effective care environment

Application

---

**3.12** A nurse educator incorporates stress, power, authority, and personal space along with other concepts and considers these concepts essential knowledge for use by nurses. The educator is applying principles from which theorist into the curriculum?

1. Dorothea Orem
2. Imogene King
3. Jean Watson
4. Hildegard Peplau

Answer: 2

Rationale: Imogene King's theory of goal attainment is based on 15 concepts from nursing literature she selected as essential knowledge for use by nurses. These include self, role, perception, communication, interaction, transaction, growth and development, stress, time, personal space, organization, status, power, authority, and decision making. Orem's theory focuses on self-care/self-care deficit. Jean Watson's theory centers on caring interaction, and Hildegard Peplau's theory centers on the use of a therapeutic relationship between the nurse and client.

Implementation

Health promotion and maintenance

Analysis

---

| | |
|---|---|
| **3.13** Nursing students must apply Neuman's systems model in the clinical area. Which of the following would represent an intrapersonal stressor to a client?<br>  1. Inadequate health insurance coverage<br>  2. Family members who quarrel frequently about the client's care<br>  3. Adverse reaction to medication<br>  4. Expectations regarding rehab | Answer: 3<br>Rationale: Neuman categorizes stressors as intrapersonal—those that occur within the individual (like a drug reaction); interpersonal—those that occur between individuals (family members who quarrel or expectations regarding rehabilitation); and extrapersonal—those that occur outside the person (financial/insurance concerns).<br>Assessment<br>Psychosocial integrity<br>Application |
| **3.14** A client is being seen in the clinic for the final follow-up appointment after an extensive course of rehabilitation. According to Neuman's model, which level of intervention does this describe?<br>  1. Primary prevention<br>  2. Secondary prevention<br>  3. Resistant prevention<br>  4. Tertiary prevention | Answer: 4<br>Rationale: According to Neuman's model, nursing interventions focus on retaining or maintaining system stability and are carried out on three preventive levels: primary, secondary, and tertiary. Tertiary prevention focuses on readaptation and stability and protects reconstitution or return to wellness following treatment. A final follow-up appointment following extensive rehabilitation would be an example of tertiary prevention. Primary prevention focuses on protecting the normal line of defense and strengthening the flexible line of defense. Secondary prevention focuses on strengthening internal lines of resistance, reducing the reaction, and increasing resistance factors.<br>Implementation<br>Health promotion and maintenance<br>Application |
| **3.15** A student is caring for a client who contracted an infection following surgery. The client is afebrile during the student's shift, but still receiving IV antibiotics. This is an example of which level of prevention, according to Neuman's model?<br>  1. Primary<br>  2. Secondary<br>  3. Tertiary<br>  4. Critical | Answer: 2<br>Rationale: Secondary prevention focuses on strengthening internal lines of resistance (fighting the infection with IV antibiotics), reducing the reaction, and increasing resistance factors. The fact that the client is now afebrile shows that the treatment is working to improve the client's condition. Primary prevention focuses on protecting the normal line of defense and strengthening the flexible line of defense. Tertiary prevention focuses on readaptation and stability and protects reconstitution or return to wellness following treatment. Critical prevention is not part of Neuman's model.<br>Assessment<br>Physiologic integrity<br>Application |
| **3.16** Nursing students who help to set up an immunization clinic are initiating which level of prevention, according to Neuman's model?<br>  1. Educational<br>  2. Primary<br>  3. Secondary<br>  4. Tertiary | Answer: 2<br>Rationale: Primary prevention focuses on protecting the normal line of defense. Providing immunizations would be doing just that—protecting the body's normal response to disease by helping it to build antibodies. Secondary prevention focuses on strengthening internal lines of resistance, and tertiary prevention focuses on readaptation and stability. Educational is not one of Neuman's levels of prevention.<br>Implementation<br>Health promotion and maintenance<br>Application |
| **3.17** A nursing student would like to explore the meaning of spirituality among clients and their response to spiritually centered interventions in nursing practice. The work of which theorist would be most beneficial for this student?<br>  1. Roy<br>  2. Neuman | Answer: 1<br>Rationale: Sr. Callista Roy's work focuses on the increasing complexity of person and environment and the relationship between and among persons, the universe, and what can be considered a supreme being or God. She uses characteristics of "creation spirituality" in her work and philosophy. Neuman developed her model based on the individual's relationship to stress. Nightingale's theory focuses on environmental manipulation, and Peplau's centers on the therapeutic relationship between nurse and client. |

| | 3. Nightingale<br>4. Peplau | Assessment<br>Psychosocial integrity<br>Application |
|---|---|

| | |
|---|---|
| **3.18** The client is working to include his spouse in the treatment and recovery process of his illness. Which of Roy's modes does this exemplify?<br>   1. Physiologic<br>   2. Self-concept<br>   3. Role function<br>   4. Interdependence | Answer: 4<br>Rationale: The goal of Roy's model is to enhance life processes through adaptation in four adapative modes. The interdependence mode involves one's relations with significant others and support systems that provide help, affection, and attention. Involving a spouse with the treatment and recovery process would be an example of this mode. The physiologic mode involves the body's basic physiologic needs and ways of adapting with regard to function of the body's systems. The self-concept mode includes the physical self and the personal self. The role function mode is determined by the need for social integration and refers to the performance of duties based on given positions within society.<br>Implementation<br>Health promotion and maintenance<br>Application |
| **3.19** The client is experiencing metabolic acidosis, a condition that involves the body's pH level, carbon dioxide, and bicarbonate balance. According to Roy's model, which mode is this client responding to?<br>   1. Physiologic<br>   2. Self-concept<br>   3. Role function<br>   4. Interdependence | Answer: 1<br>Rationale: The physiologic mode involves the body's basic physiologic needs and ways of adapting with regard to fluid and electrolytes, activity and rest, circulation and oxygen, nutrition and elimination, protection, the senses, and neurologic and endocrine function. The pH level as well as levels of the carbon dioxide and bicarbonate ion would be physiologic mechanisms at work in the body. The self-concept mode includes the physical self and the personal self. The role function mode is determined by the need for social integration and refers to the performance of duties based on given positions within society. The interdependence mode involves one's relations with significant others and support systems that provide help, affection, and attention.<br>Assessment<br>Physiologic integrity<br>Analysis |
| **3.20** A nurse has agreed to delay a client's treatment until the matriarch of the family can be present. Understanding that this is an important consideration for this client's cultural practices, the nurse is implementing which of Leininger's intervention modes? Culture care:<br>   1. Preservation and maintenance<br>   2. Accommodation, negotiation<br>   3. Restructuring<br>   4. Repatterning | Answer: 2<br>Rationale: The three modes, according to Leininger, that nurses intervene in client care are culture care: preservation and maintenance; accommodation, negotiation, or both; and restructuring and repatterning. By allowing flexibility in scheduling client treatment in order to allow for the client's family member to be present—which in this case is an important aspect of their cultural practices—the nurse accommodates the client's needs.<br>Implementation<br>Psychosocial integrity<br>Application |
| **3.21** The nurse implements being authentically present to clients by supporting them in their beliefs and helping to instill a hopefulness in their recovery. The nurse has taken on the processes of which of the following theorists?<br>   1. Florence Nightingale<br>   2. Hildegard Peplau<br>   3. Jean Watson<br>   4. Rosemarie Parse | Answer: 3<br>Rationale: Jean Watson believes the practice of caring is central to nursing and has developed nursing interventions referred to as clinical caritas processes. Of these, "being authentically present, and enabling and sustaining the deep belief system and subjective life world of self and one-being cared for" is an example. Nightingale's theory involved environmental manipulation. Peplau focused on the therapeutic relationship between nurse and client. Parse developed the theory of human becoming.<br>Implementation<br>Psychosocial integrity<br>Application |

| | |
|---|---|
| **3.22** A nurse has been working with a difficult client and at one point, elects to put aside the nurse's own beliefs and is able to experience a sense of true empathy for the client's situation. This is an example of which assumption, according to Parse's human becoming theory?<br>  1. Meaning<br>  2. Rhythmicity<br>  3. Intersubjectivity<br>  4. Cotranscendence | Answer: 4<br>Rationale: In her theory, Rosemarie Parse proposed three assumptions which focus on meaning, rhythmicity, and cotranscendence. Contranscendence is the process of reaching out beyond the self, which would be what the nurse in this scenario has implemented. Meaning arises from a person's interrelationship with the world. Rhythmicity is the movement toward greater diversity. Intersubjectivity is not one of Parse's three assumptions.<br>Implementation<br>Psychosocial integrity<br>Application |
| **3.23** When a client who had a stroke gives up all hope of any amount of recovery, the nurse solicits a visit from a former stroke client who has physical limitations but has since gone back to work and through adaptation, can function independently at home. This nurse has fulfilled which role, according to Parse?<br>  1. Mobilizing transcendence<br>  2. Synchronizing rhythm<br>  3. Illuminating meaning<br>  4. True presence | Answer: 3<br>Rationale: According to Parse's theory, illuminating meaning refers to uncovering what was and what will be. In this situation, the stroke is what was, and the client who is now independent is what could be for the nurse's current client. Synchronizing rhythm involves leading through discussion to recognize harmony. Mobilizing transcendence is dreaming of possibilities and planning to reach them. Nurses must provide a "true presence" to their clients, but this is not a role in Parse's theory; it is a behavior.<br>Implementation<br>Psychosocial integrity<br>Application |
| **3.24** The pediatric nurse implements Watson's assumption regarding a caring environment by which of the following?<br>  1. Providing all needs and cares to the nurse's clients<br>  2. Ensuring that a zone of professionalism is present between the nurse and client<br>  3. Allowing the clients to have choices, as appropriate, in their care<br>  4. Selecting games and activities that are age appropriate for the clients | Answer: 3<br>Rationale: A caring environment, according to Watson's assumptions of caring, offers the development of potential while allowing the person to choose the best action for the self at a given point in time. The nurse may not need to provide *all* needs and cares to the clients. Being conscientious of a "zone" of professionalism (i.e., keeping distant) would not be a characteristic of caring according to Watson. Taking choices away from clients by making selections for them is also not a good example of true caring, as defined by Watson.<br>Evaluation<br>Psychosocial integrity<br>Analysis |
| **3.25** Grounding nursing research among theories from other disciplines is argued to be undesirable by some scholars. The reason for this is which of the following? (Select all that apply.)<br>_____ It detracts from developing nursing as a separate discipline.<br>_____ It makes nursing less relevant.<br>_____ It helps bring a broader perspective and insight to nursing.<br>_____ Other disciplines are not unique to the human condition. | Answer:<br>\_\_\_\_\_x\_\_\_ It detracts from developing nursing as a separate discipline.<br>\_\_\_\_\_x\_\_\_ It makes nursing less relevant.<br>_____ It helps bring a broader perspective and insight to nursing.<br>_____ Other disciplines are not unique to the human condition.<br>Rationale: Some nursing scholars think that grounding research in theories from other disciplines detracts from the development of nursing as a separate discipline and makes nursing research less relevant. Other scholars believe that bringing insights and perspectives from other disciplines helps to broaden values of the profession.<br>Assessment<br>Safe, effective care environment<br>Analysis<br>Learning Outcome 3.5 |

**4.1** A client was given the wrong dose of medication and died. The case is being tried in court and similar cases are used by the court in comparison to arrive at a decision. What doctrine is being applied here?
1. Common law
2. Public law
3. Administrative law
4. *Stare decisis*

Answer: 4
Rationale: *Stare decisis*, "to stand by things decided," is a doctrine courts adhere to when arriving at a ruling in a particular case. The courts apply the same rules and principles applied in previous, similar cases. Common law, public law, and administrative law are all types of laws, enacted by different entities.
Implementation
Safe, effective care environment
Application
Learning Outcome 4.1

---

**4.2** The student nurse is studying the various applications of law to understand the regulations surrounding nursing practice in the state. What is the type of law that implements and enforces the nurse practice act of any given state?
1. Statutory law
2. Administrative law
3. Common law
4. Public law

Answer: 2
Rationale: Administrative agencies are given authority to create rules and regulations to enforce statutory law when the state legislature passes a statute. State boards of nursing write rules and regulations to implement and enforce a nurse practice act, which was created through statutory law but is enforced by administrative law. Common law refers to laws evolved from court decisions. Public law refers to the body of law that deals with relationships between individuals and the government and governmental agencies.
Assessment
Safe, effective care environment
Application
Learning Outcome 4.1

---

**4.3** The admitting nurse explains the process of signing forms to allow for the client's insurance company to be billed for services. If the insurance fails to pay for services, the client is responsible for payment. This is an example of which of the following?
1. Contract law
2. Tort law
3. Statutory law
4. Administrative law

Answer: 1
Rationale: Contract law involves the enforcement of agreements among private individuals or the payment of compensation for failure to fulfill the agreements. Signing a form prior to receipt of health care services makes the client responsible for cost, regardless of insurance payment. Tort law defines and enforces duties and rights among private individuals that are not based on contractual agreements. Statutory laws are laws enacted by any legislative body. Administrative laws give administrative agencies the authority to create rules and regulations to enforce statutory laws.
Implementation
Safe, effective care environment
Application
Learning Outcome 4.1

---

**4.4** A nurse forgets to put the call light within the client's reach and then leaves the room. The client reaches for it and falls out of bed. The nurse could be charged with which of the following?
1. Assault
2. Battery
3. Negligence
4. Malpractice

Answer: 3
Rationale: Negligence is an example of a tort law. Negligence occurs when something is accidental and harm results, as in this case. Another example of negligence would be if surgical instruments or bandages are accidentally left in a client during surgery. Assault is the threat to touch another person unjustifiably. Battery is the willful touching of a person that may cause harm. Malpractice is professional negligence.
Evaluation
Safe, effective care environment
Analysis
Learning Outcome 4.11

---

**4.5** Before a case goes to court, the nurse and the attorney will make an effort to understand and obtain all the facts surrounding a situation—for example, other staff who were working with the client, anyone who might have had access to the client's information,

Answer: 3
Rationale: Discovery is an effort by both parties to obtain all the facts of the situation. It occurs before the trial. Burden of proof falls to the plaintiff and is the duty to prove wrongdoing. Complaint is a document filed by a person (plaintiff) who claims that his or her legal rights have been infringed on by one or more persons (defendants). Civil action is a legal action that deals with the relationships among individuals in society.

---

| | |
|---|---|
| and the client's mental status and condition. This is referred to as which of the following?<br>  1. Burden of proof<br>  2. Complaint<br>  3. Discovery<br>  4. Civil action | Implementation<br>Safe, effective care environment<br>Application |
| **4.6** Before the nurse can apply for relicensure, the state board of nursing requires 30 hours of continuing education in nursing in-service or education. This practice exemplifies which of the following?<br>  1. Licensure<br>  2. Competency<br>  3. Credentialing<br>  4. Certification | Answer: 3<br>Rationale: Credentialing is the process of determining and maintaining competence in nursing practice. It is one way to maintain the professional standards of practice and accountability for the members' educational preparation. Licensure is the process of granting a legal permit to practice or engage in a profession, such as nursing. Credentialing is part of licensure. Competency is a level of acceptable performance, and credentialing ensures this in licensure. Certification is also part of credentialing. It validates that an individual has met minimum standards of nursing competency in a specialty area.<br>Implementation<br>Safe, effective care environment<br>Application<br>Learning Outcome 4.2 |
| **4.7** A high school graduate wants to attend a nursing school that is highly regarded for its program. Which of the following entities must accredit or approve nursing programs?<br>  1. State board of nursing<br>  2. NLNAC<br>  3. CCNE<br>  4. ANA | Answer: 1<br>Rationale: *All* states require that schools of nursing are approved/accredited by the state board of nursing. *Some* states require that programs be both state approved and accredited by a national accrediting agency such as NLNAC or CCNE. Voluntary accreditation is a means of informing the public and prospective students that the nursing program has met certain criteria. The ANA (American Nurses Association) is nursing's professional organization.<br>Assessment<br>Safe, effective care environment<br>Application<br>Learning Outcome 4.2 |
| **4.8** The nurse carries out a medication order, incorrectly written by the physician and subsequently filled by the pharmacist. Who, in this situation, is liable for the action?<br>  1. Physician<br>  2. Pharmacist<br>  3. Hospital<br>  4. Nurse | Answer: 4<br>Rationale: The responsibility for the nursing activity—in this case, giving the medication—belongs to the nurse. Liability is legal responsibility for one's action. Even though the physician wrote the order incorrectly and the pharmacist filled it, it was the nurse who carried it out, making that person ultimately responsible for the action.<br>Evaluation<br>Safe, effective care environment<br>Application<br>Learning Outcome 4.7 |
| **4.9** A nurse was responsible for a client's injury after failing to implement proper safety precautions in the client's care. The client's family is now pursuing damages from the hospital as well as the nurse. The doctrine that holds the hospital responsible as well as the nurse is which of the following?<br>  1. Contractual relationship<br>  2. Stare decisis<br>  3. Respondeat superior<br>  4. Res ipsa loquitur | Answer: 3<br>Rationale: "Let the master answer," or respondeat superior, means that the master (in this case the hospital/employer) assumes responsibility for the conduct of the servant (the nurse) and can be held responsible for the nurse's failure to act in a competent way. A contractual relationship is not a doctrine; it is what the nurse and hospital, for example, enter when the hospital hires the nurse as an employee. "To stand by things decided," or stare decisis, is the same thing as following precedent, or applying the same rules to a situation as were applied in similar situations. "The thing speaks for itself," or res ipsa loquitur, is a doctrine in cases where harm occurs but cannot be traced to a specific health care provider or standard. The harm does not normally occur unless there has been a negligent act.<br>Evaluation<br>Safe, effective care environment<br>Analysis<br>Learning Outcome 4.2 |

**4.10** A client is to undergo an invasive procedure by a physician. The client is questioning some of the terminology in the consent form. Which of the following is the best response by the nurse?

1. "Just sign the form, and I'll make sure your physician talks to you before he begins the procedure."
2. "I'll explain whatever you don't understand."
3. "You should have asked your physician when he was in here."
4. "I'll call your physician back in the room to answer your questions."

Answer: 4

Rationale: Obtaining informed consent for specific medical treatment is the responsibility of the person who is going to perform the procedure, in this case the physician. Informed consent suggests that the client has been given complete information, including benefits, risks, and alternatives if the treatment is not given. An element of informed consent is that the client must be given enough information to be the ultimate decision maker. If not, it is the physician's responsibility to make sure the client's understanding is clear. It is important that the person obtaining the consent (the physician in this case) answer the client's questions. If the client has questions, he should not sign the form, and it is not the nurse's responsibility to answer the questions. Telling the client what he "should have" done is demeaning and not an appropriate therapeutic response.
Implementation
Safe, effective care environment
Analysis
Learning Outcome 4.4

---

**4.11** The client presents her hand when the nurse makes this statement: "I need to start an IV so you can get your antibiotics." This is an example of which of the following?

1. Informed consent
2. Express consent
3. Implied consent
4. Compliance

Answer: 3

Rationale: Implied consent exists when the individual's nonverbal behavior indicates agreement. In this case, presenting the hand for IV initiation would be a nonverbal behavior indicating agreement with the treatment. Informed consent is an agreement by a client to accept a course of treatment or a procedure after being provided complete information, including the benefits and risks of treatment. In this case, the nurse did not give benefits/risks of the IV antibiotic. Express consent may be either an oral or written agreement. In this case, there were neither spoken words nor a written consent form for the IV initiation. Compliance occurs when clients agree to follow the recommended treatment, usually by their own actions as in taking prescribed medications or following a prescribed diet.
Assessment
Physiologic integrity
Analysis
Learning Outcome 4.4

---

**4.12** An adult client who cannot read needs surgery and is competent to make his own decisions. The best action of the nurse is to:

1. Tell the client in the nurse's own words what the surgical procedure involves.
2. Read the consent form to the client and have the client state understanding.
3. Make sure the physician explains the procedure to the client.
4. Have a family member who can read sign the consent form.

Answer: 2

Rationale: If a client cannot read, the consent form must be read to the client and the client must state understanding before the form is signed. Telling the client in words other than what is on the consent form is not appropriate as some meaning and information may be lost in the transfer. The physician should explain the procedure to the client, regardless of the client's literacy. Since the client is a competent adult, he must be the one giving consent. Illiteracy does not make one incompetent.
Implementation
Psychosocial integrity
Application
Learning Outcome 4.2

---

**4.13** An elderly adult fell at home and fractured a hip, which requires surgical repair. After admittance to the emergency department, the client was given sedation for pain before a surgical permit was signed. What is the best action necessary to obtain consent?

1. The physician should have the client's wife sign the consent form.

Answer: 1

Rationale: A client who is confused, disoriented, or sedated is not considered functionally competent and a legal guardian or representative can provide or refuse consent for the client. In this case, since the client was given medication that sedated him, the wife would be appropriate for giving consent for the surgical procedure. Waiting until the effects of the medication wear off would not be in the best interest of the client. Thorough explanation may or may not matter in this case since the client is considered functionally incompetent. Besides, it is the physician's responsibility to obtain informed consent. Implied consent may be used in a medical emergency, but in this case, option 1 would be most appropriate.

---

| | |
|---|---|
| 2. The physician should wait until the effects of the medication wear off and have the client sign.<br>3. Since the client has been medicated, the nurse should thoroughly explain the consent form to the client.<br>4. This would be considered an emergency situation and consent would be implied. | Implementation<br>Safe, effective care environment<br>Analysis<br>Learning Outcome 4.4 |
| **4.14** A client is brought to the emergency department after being involved in a motor vehicle crash. Although the client is conscious, her condition is critical and will require emergency surgery. The client does not speak English. What is the best action of the staff?<br>1. Read the consent form and have the client sign it anyway.<br>2. Explain as best they can using pictures and gestures.<br>3. Have the hospital interpreter explain the procedure.<br>4. Proceed with surgery as implied consent would be the case in this situation. | Answer: 3<br>Rationale: If the client does not speak the same language as the health professional who is providing the information, an interpreter must be present. Reading the consent form to someone who doesn't understand the words is pointless. If there is not an interpreter available and the situation is emergent, trying as best they can to explain the procedure with pictures and gestures would be the next best in this situation. Implied consent indicates that the person understands what will be done. Having an interpreter present the information is the best course of action.<br>Implementation<br>Safe, effective care environment<br>Application<br>Learning Outcome 4.4 |
| **4.15** The nurse has delegated the task of obtaining vital signs on a new admission to a UAP (unlicensed assistive personnel). The task is completed, but the vitals were not recorded accurately. Who is responsible for this action?<br>1. The UAP<br>2. The nurse<br>3. Both the UAP and the nurse<br>4. The nurse manager on the unit | Answer: 2<br>Rationale: While taking vital signs was an appropriate task to delegate to the UAP, the responsibility of the action—in this case, the inaction since the vitals were recorded inaccurately—remains with the nurse.<br>Evaluation<br>Safe, effective care environment<br>Analysis<br>Learning Outcome 4.7 |
| **4.16** A nurse is caring for a client in the emergency department who was brought in by her adult child for vague, flu-like symptoms. While helping the client to change into a gown, the nurse notices numerous bruises on the client's back and arms. When questioned, the client is distracted and ambiguous with her answers. The nurse should:<br>1. Report the situation to law enforcement.<br>2. Report the situation to social services.<br>3. Question the adult child who brought the client to the ED.<br>4. File a written report in the client's chart. | Answer: 2<br>Rationale: Nurses are considered mandated reporters. As a result, they must report any situation when an injury is present and appears to be the result of abuse, neglect, or exploitation. The situation described may or may not be one of abuse or neglect, but the nurse is required to report it to the proper authorities. In this case, social services should be notified. Law enforcement would be notified if the results of social services' investigation warrant it. Questioning the client's adult child is appropriate, but the incident needs to be reported. Documentation in the chart is also extremely important, but this would be part of the nurse's notes, not a separate written report.<br>Implementation<br>Psychosocial integrity<br>Application<br>Learning Outcome 4.7 |

**4.17** A nurse who has been a longtime employee of a hospital, providing bedside care to clients, was seriously injured and is paralyzed from the shoulders down, with limited use of the upper arms. Through rehabilitation, the nurse is able to mobilize with a wheelchair and has no cognitive or psychological deficits. The nurse wants to return to the same position held prior to the injury. Under the guidelines of the ADA, the hospital:

1. Is required to accommodate the nurse.
2. Must find another job for the nurse.
3. Could claim undue hardship to accommodate this nurse.
4. Will have to terminate the nurse's employment.

Answer: 3
Rationale: According to the ADA, it is the employer's responsibility to provide *reasonable* accommodations that would allow the person with a disability to perform the job satisfactorily. With limited use of upper arms, this nurse would not be able to perform the tasks required of a nurse working at the bedside. However, the hospital *could* help find another position that utilizes the nurse's experience and desire to continue in the field of nursing, but this would have to be a collaborate effort with the nurse. Terminating employment may or may not occur, but not until all other options have been explored.
Evaluation
Safe, effective care environment
Analysis
Learning Outcome 4.5

**4.18** A nurse on the unit notices that a co-worker exhibits a pattern of behavior suggestive of drug abuse. The nurse should:

1. Report the situation to the unit charge nurse.
2. Send an anonymous letter to the director of nursing.
3. Let other co-workers know about the situation.
4. Report the situation, then let management take care of it.

Answer: 1
Rationale: As a mandatory reporter, the nurse is required to report situations where co-workers are suspected of impairment, which includes alcohol/drug abuse as well as mental illness. The nurse should report the matter starting at the lowest possible level in the agency hierarchy. In this case, the charge nurse would be appropriate. The nurse should also take responsibility for the report by being open about it, not making an anonymous report to the higher level of management. The nurse should also obtain support from at least one other trustworthy person before filing the report. This doesn't mean telling the whole unit, which could be detrimental to both the nurse reporting the incident and the co-worker. After the report is made, the nurse should see the problem through, not assume that management will take care of the situation.
Implementation
Safe, effective care environment
Application
Learning Outcome 4.6

**4.19** A nurse's co-worker makes a practice of telling offensive jokes or stories with a sexual undertone during the shift. The best action of the nurse is to:

1. Ignore the co-worker and walk away.
2. Report the incident to the nurse manager.
3. Tell the co-worker to stop the activity because the conduct is offensive.
4. Ask to be scheduled opposite this co-worker.

Answer: 3
Rationale: Nurses must develop skills of assertiveness to deter sexual harassment in the workplace. Telling the co-worker to stop and why, is the first step in putting an end to the situation. Ignoring the situation or asking to be scheduled opposite this person is not addressing the situation in an assertive manner. Reporting the incident to the nurse manager would be a second step if the behavior doesn't stop after the nurse's approach.
Implementation
Safe, effective care environment
Application

**4.20** A nurse who is opposed to abortion works in a hospital where they are done. According to the Supreme Court's conscience clause, the nurse:

1. Cannot interfere with a woman's constitutional right.
2. Should not be working in this particular hospital.

Answer: 4
Rationale: In *Roe v. Wade* and *Doe v. Bolton*, the Supreme Court upheld that a woman's right to privacy includes control over her own body to the extent that she can abort her fetus. Although the nurse cannot interfere with this, the conscience clause states that nurses, as well as other health care personnel, have a right to refuse to participate in abortions and hospitals have the right to deny admission to abortion clients. Counseling a woman prior to an abortion would

| | |
|---|---|
| 3. Can counsel women before they have an abortion.<br>4. Has the right to refuse to participate in abortions. | not be an appropriate action since the nurse has chosen to work in a hospital where these procedures are done.<br>Evaluation<br>Psychosocial integrity<br>Analysis<br>Learning Outcome 4.7 |
| **4.21** A nurse is being sued for malpractice. Which of the following specific elements must be present for the nurse to lose the case? (Select all that apply.)<br>_____ Negligence<br>_____ Damages<br>_____ Injury<br>_____ Malpractice<br>_____ Causation<br>_____ Foreseeability<br>_____ Breach of duty<br>_____ Duty | Answer:<br>_____ Negligence<br>___x___ Damages<br>___x___ Injury<br>_____ Malpractice<br>___x___ Causation<br>___x___ Foreseeability<br>___x___ Breach of duty<br>___x___ Duty<br>Rationale: Six elements (those selected) must be present for a case of nursing malpractice to be proven. Negligence is misconduct or practice that falls below acceptable or expected standards. Malpractice is "professional negligence"—negligence that occurs while the person performs as a professional.<br>Assessment<br>Safe, effective care environment<br>Application<br>Learning Outcome 4.10 |
| **4.22** A client woke in the middle of the night, confused and unaware of the surroundings. Although the call light was within reach, the client got out of bed unassisted, tripped on the bedside chair, and fell. Which of the following elements of malpractice is missing in this case?<br>1. Foreseeability<br>2. Damages<br>3. Injury<br>4. Duty | Answer: 1<br>Rationale: Foreseeability is the link between the nurse's act and the injury suffered. The call light was within reach, but the client did not use it and got out of bed unassisted. Nighttime confusion occurs with some clients but unless the nurse had knowledge or awareness that this would happen, there was no link between the nurse's action and the client's fall. Duty is present in this case since the call light was within reach. Damages and injury may well be present, but these probably are not due to any action or inaction on the nurse's part.<br>Evaluation<br>Safe, effective care environment<br>Analysis<br>Learning Outcome 4.10 |
| **4.23** A client is scheduled to have surgery, has signed the consent form, but refuses to have a Foley catheter placed, saying "That's not part of the surgery." The nurse should:<br>1. Explain that this is part of the surgical prep and continue with the procedure.<br>2. Explain that the client has already signed the consent, and place the catheter.<br>3. Respect the client's wishes and document accordingly.<br>4. Call the physician. | Answer: 3<br>Rationale: Consent is required before procedures are performed. Depending on the invasiveness of the procedure, a written consent may be required. The client signed a consent form for surgery, and the refusal for placement of a catheter should be respected. The nurse should document the incident and not continue with the procedure. Battery exists when there is not consent, even if the client was not asked. In this case, the client has the right to refuse other treatment surrounding pre- and postop care.<br>Implementation<br>Safe, effective care environment<br>Application<br>Learning Outcome 4.4 |
| **4.24** The nurse makes this entry in a client's medical record: "The client is a drug addict and is always asking for more medication than what is necessary." In this situation, the nurse may be charged with which of the following? | Answer: 3<br>Rationale: Libel is defamation of character by means of print, writing, or pictures. Putting a statement such as this in the client's medical record is, first, making a diagnosis which the nurse is not qualified to do and, second, making an assumption about the client's need for medication which is a personal attitude about how the client responds. Defamation is communication that is false or made with a careless disregard for the truth and that results in injury to the reputation of a person. Slander is defamation by the spoken word. |

| | |
|---|---|
| 1. Defamation<br>2. Slander<br>3. Libel<br>4. Incompetence | Libel is part of defamation, but in this case is a more accurate description of the incident.<br>Evaluation<br>Psychosocial integrity<br>Analysis<br>Learning Outcome 4.1 |
| **4.25** Nurses are protected by laws such as Good Samaritan acts. Which of the following situations would apply as part of these acts? (Select all that apply.)<br>_____ A nurse gives CPR to a client brought to the emergency department; later the client is found to have a "Do Not Resuscitate" order.<br>_____ A nurse gives first aid to a child injured in a sporting event.<br>_____ A nursing student tries to insert an airway in an unconscious client.<br>_____ A nurse leaves the scene of an emergency to call for help.<br>_____ A nurse helps deliver the baby of a neighbor during a snowstorm. | Answer:<br>_____x_____ A nurse gives CPR to a client brought to the emergency department; later the client is found to have a "Do Not Resuscitate" order.<br>_____x_____ A nurse gives first aid to a child injured in a sporting event.<br>_____ A nursing student tries to insert an airway in an unconscious client.<br>_____ A nurse leaves the scene of an emergency to call for help.<br>_____x_____ A nurse helps deliver the baby of a neighbor during a snowstorm.<br>Rationale: The Good Samaritan acts are laws designed to protect health care providers against claims of malpractice in cases of emergency, unless it can be shown that there was a gross departure from the normal standard of care. Giving CPR would be considered a level of care provided by any other reasonable person under similar circumstances. The fact that the client had a DNR order was not apparent at the time of care rendered by the nurse. A nursing student trying to insert an airway is not appropriate, since it would be above the level of care a student is able to do. A nurse should not leave the scene of an emergency until another qualified person takes over. The nurse should have someone else call or go for additional help.<br>Evaluation<br>Safe, effective care environment<br>Analysis<br>Learning Outcome 4.5 |

## CHAPTER 5

| | |
|---|---|
| **5.1** A student is attending a school with a high first-time pass rate on the NCLEX®. A belief that the nursing student has about faculty in the program could be expressed as which of the following? Faculty:<br>1. Expect high academic standards from their students.<br>2. Are concerned with job placement of their graduates.<br>3. Are more concerned with licensure than anything else.<br>4. Work hard to make sure students are successful. | Answer: 3<br>Rationale: Beliefs are interpretations or conclusions that people accept as true. They are based more on faith than fact and may or may not be true. Stating that faculty are more concerned with licensure would be a belief that the student has. It may or may not be true and it may be something that the student believes only for a short time—for example, until the student has had experiences with more of the faculty than just a few. Beliefs may last only briefly. The rest of the options would express attitudes. Attitudes are mental positions or feelings that continue over time. These options describe how the student *feels* about the faculty.<br>Assessment<br>Safe, effective care environment (ethical practice)<br>Application<br>Learning Outcome 5.1 |
| **5.2** A nurse manager has a staff nurse who observes certain religious holidays. The manager tries to make sure that these observances can be met if possible. The manager is practicing which of the following values?<br>1. Human dignity<br>2. Social justice<br>3. Autonomy<br>4. Altruism | Answer: 4<br>Rationale: Altruism is a concern for the welfare and well-being of others. A professional behavior of this value is demonstrating the understanding of cultures, beliefs, and perspectives of others. Human dignity is respect for the inherent worth and uniqueness of individuals and populations. Providing culturally competent and sensitive care is an example of this professional behavior. Social justice is upholding moral, legal, and humanistic principles. Autonomy is the right to self-determination, and professional practice reflects autonomy when the nurse respects patients' rights to make decisions about their health care.<br>Implementation<br>Psychosocial integrity<br>Analysis<br>Learning Outcome 5.2 |

**5.3** Parents of a terminally ill child have decided to remove their child from life support, a decision that has met with much negative support. The nurse practices the value of autonomy through which of the following?

1. Showing respect for the family
2. Respecting the parents' decision
3. Referring the parents to social services
4. Asking to be assigned to a different client

Answer: 2
Rationale: Autonomy is the right to self-determination, and professional practice reflects autonomy when the nurse respects patients' rights to make decisions about their health care. A nurse can show respect for the family without respecting the decision of the parents. Referring the parents to another entity points to feelings of unease about the parents' choice. Asking to be assigned to another client does not honor the right of patients and families to make decisions about health care.
Evaluation
Psychosocial integrity
Analysis
Learning Outcome 5.2

**5.4** A nurse is working with a local agency to provide care to the inadequately insured by helping to staff an after-hours clinic. This nurse is demonstrating which of the following professional values?

1. Human dignity
2. Altruism
3. Social justice
4. Integrity

Answer: 3
Rationale: Social justice is upholding moral, legal, and humanistic principles. This value is demonstrated in professional practice when the nurse works to ensure equal treatment under the law and equal access to quality health care. Human dignity is respect for the worth and uniqueness of individuals and populations. Altruism is concern for the welfare and well-being of others. Integrity is acting in accordance with an appropriate code of ethics and accepted standards of practice.
Implementation
Health maintenance and promotion
Analysis
Learning Outcome 5.3

**5.5** A nurse mistakenly gave a client who was NPO a morning breakfast tray. After realizing the mistake, the nurse notified the physician as well as the client; explained the consequences of this mistake, which included a delay in the client's scheduled procedure; and documented the situation in the client's medical record. This nurse demonstrates which of the following?

1. Altruism
2. Integrity
3. Social justice
4. Human dignity

Answer: 2
Rationale: Integrity is acting in accordance with an appropriate code of ethics and accepted standards of practice. Integrity is reflected in professional practice when the nurse is honest and provides the care based on an ethical framework that is accepted within the profession. Behavior that demonstrates integrity includes providing honest information to patients and documentation that is accurate and honest. By taking the responsibility for the mistake, the nurse is honest with the physician as well as the client and provides accurate documentation of the action. Altruism is a concern for the welfare and well-being of others. Social justice is upholding moral, legal, and humanistic principles. Human dignity is respect for the worth and uniqueness of individuals and populations.
Implementation
Safe, effective care environment
Analysis
Learning Outcome 5.3

**5.6** A pregnant client says her main concern is that her baby will be born healthy, even though she admits to drinking alcohol on a regular basis. This client is struggling with which of the following?

1. Values transmission
2. Values clarification
3. Morals
4. Ethics

Answer: 2
Rationale: Behavior that indicates unclear values includes ignoring a health professional's advice, such as using alcohol during pregnancy. Values transmission means that values are learned through observation and experience and are influenced by sociocultural environment and traditions. Morals refer to personal standards of what is right and wrong. Ethics refers to the practices or beliefs of a certain group.
Assessment
Psychosocial integrity
Analysis
Learning Outcome 5.3

**5.7** A client who has been blinded as result of an injury informs the rehabilitation staff that she plans to return to her counseling practice and will continue to work on a full-time basis. This client is demonstrating which aspect of values clarification?

Answer: 3
Rationale: The "acting" component of values clarification is a behavioral action in which chosen beliefs are affirmed to others, incorporated into one's behavior, and repeated consistently in one's life. Stating the intention to return to prior employment on a full-time basis would be an affirmation of the client's plan. Choosing is a cognitive action. Beliefs are chosen freely without outside pressure, from among alternatives, and after reflecting

1. Choosing
2. Prizing
3. Acting
4. Clarifying

and considering consequences. Prizing is an affective action where chosen beliefs are prized and cherished. Clarifying values is the process in which choosing, prizing, and acting are accomplished.
Implementation
Psychosocial integrity
Analysis
Learning Outcome 5.3

---

**5.8** A client has been complaining of pain, even though the nurse has given the client the maximum amount of medication as ordered by the physician. Which of the following demonstrates the nurse's respect for the client's autonomy?
1. Telling the client that he will have to "tough it out"
2. Calling the physician for further orders
3. Telling co-workers that this client has no pain tolerance
4. Believing the client is drug seeking

Answer: 2
Rationale: Honoring the principle of autonomy means that the nurse respects the client's right to make decisions, treating others with consideration and not as impersonal sources of knowledge or training. Believing the client continues to have pain would be an example of treating with consideration. For whatever reason, this particular client is not responding to the medication ordered by the physician and other medications or treatment should be initiated. The other three options do not exemplify the nurse's respect for or consideration of the client's situation.
Evaluation
Safe, effective care environment
Analysis
Learning Outcome 5.3

---

**5.9** A client has chosen to discontinue hemodialysis. His family is not supportive of his decision. The nurse who uses the theory of principles-based reasoning would make which of the following statements?
1. "This client is of sound mind and is capable of making his own decisions regarding health care. It really is his decision to make."
2. "I need to try and help the family understand the client's decision so they can work through this situation together."
3. "This client's health is so deteriorated that the treatment is not saving his life. It is prolonging the ultimate outcome, which is his death."
4. "The client understands his decision and the advanced stage of his disease. If he quits treatment, he will die."

Answer: 1
Rationale: Principles-based theories stress individual rights, like autonomy. The client has the ability to make the decision and it is his right to autonomy to do that. Caring theories, or relationship theories, stress courage, generosity, commitment, and the need to nurture and maintain relationships. Caring theories promote the common good or the welfare of the group. Trying to help the family understand the client's decision is an example of a caring-based theory in practice. Consequence-based theories look at the outcomes of an action in judging whether that action is right or wrong. Consequence theories are exemplified by the nurse looking at the outcomes of the client's decision.
Implementation
Safe, effective care environment
Application
Learning Outcome 5.3

---

**5.10** The administration of a hospital, along with nursing services, is planning to incorporate a struggling private clinic into the infrastructure of the hospital. Although relocating the clinic may cause transportation difficulty for some clients, keeping the clinic running will allow current employees as well as clients the continued benefit of the service. This is a specific example of which theory?
1. Teleological theory
2. Deontological theory

Answer: 3
Rationale: Utilitarianism views a good act as one that brings the most good and the least harm for the greatest number of people. Continuing to provide a service, even though it has to be relocated, is better than discontinuing something that clients continue to use and employees depend on. Teleological theories look at the outcomes of an action and judge it to be right or wrong. Utilitarianism is one form of consequentialist theory, and this scenario is more specific to this theory. Deontological theories, which are also principles based, emphasize individual rights, duties, and obligations. In this situation, a number of people are involved with the clinic, not just one person. Caring theories stress courage, generosity, commitment, and the need to nurture and maintain relationships.
Implementation

---

| | 3. Utilitarianism | Safe, effective care environment |
| | 4. Caring theory | Application |
| | | Learning Outcome 5.3 |

**5.11** A nurse is having difficulty with the decision for aggressive cancer therapy in an elderly client, wondering if the therapy will actually be more harmful than the disease and knowing that the client will be subjected to harmful chemicals. This nurse is struggling with which of the following principles?
1. Autonomy
2. Justice
3. Beneficence
4. Nonmaleficence

Answer: 4
Rationale: Nonmaleficence is duty to "do no harm." Doing intentional harm is never acceptable in nursing. Placing a client at risk of harm is what is depicted in this scenario, and it occurs as a known consequence of a nursing intervention or some other type of treatment. It is unknown how much therapy will be of benefit to the client or whether it will actually do more harm. Autonomy refers to the right to make one's own decisions. Justice is often referred to as fairness. Beneficence means "doing good." In this case the benefits are not known, making the harm more real. Aggressive cancer therapy is difficult to endure, and given the age of the client, this case is more suggestive of nonmaleficence than beneficence.
Evaluation
Safe, effective care environment
Analysis
Learning Outcome 5.3

**5.12** A toddler who has just been admitted to the pediatric unit is crying and scared. No treatment has been initiated at this point. The nurse needs to start an IV and the parent asks, "Will this be painful to my child?" In practicing veracity, the nurse responds:
1. "I won't lie to you. It may be easier for you if you step out until we get the line in."
2. "We'll take every care not to hurt your child."
3. "It shouldn't be too bad and I'll be quick."
4. "We do this all the time, so don't worry."

Answer: 1
Rationale: Veracity refers to telling the truth. Even though telling the truth may frighten the parent, starting an IV on a frightened, scared, ill child is a difficult task. Because of the developmental stage, any explanation given by the nurse won't be understood. Being honest to the parent will help the nurse gain trust and will outweigh any benefits that may be gained by downplaying the situation. Saying that the nurse will not hurt the child is simply not true. A needle going into a vein is not a comfortable procedure. The nurse really doesn't know how bad it will be, and telling the parent not to worry is pointless.
Implementation
Safe, effective care environment
Analysis
Learning Outcome 5.3

**5.13** A student nurse accidentally left the call light outside the reach of an elderly client. Luckily another nurse found the situation and was able to rectify the matter before something happened. The student responded, "I know better. I should've double-checked where the light was before I left the room." This student is demonstrating which of the following?
1. Justice
2. Fidelity
3. Responsibility
4. Accountability

Answer: 4
Rationale: Accountability means "answering to oneself and others for one's own actions." By admitting that he or she knew better and should have double-checked the situation, the student shows accountability. Responsibility refers to the liability associated with the performance of duties of a particular role. The student had the responsibility to provide safe care to the client (i.e., make sure the call light was within reach) but did not follow through with it. Justice is being fair. Fidelity means to be faithful to agreements and promises.
Evaluation
Safe, effective care environment
Analysis
Learning Outcome 5.3

**5.14** The ANA (American Nurses Association) and the CNA (Canadian Nurses Association) have both adopted a code of ethics. Which of the following describes characteristics of a code of ethics? (Select all that apply.)
_____ Formal statement
_____ Same standards as legal standards
_____ Shared by group members

Answer:
____x____ Formal statement
_____ Same standards as legal standards
____x____ Shared by group members
_____ Reflects legal judgments
____x____ Serves as a standard for professional actions
Rationale: A code of ethics is a formal statement of a group's ideals and values. It is a set of ethical principles that (a) is shared by members of the group, (b) reflects their moral (not legal) judgments over time, and (c) serves as a standard for their professional actions. Codes of ethics usually have *higher* requirements

| | |
|---|---|
| _____ Reflects legal judgments<br>_____ Serves as a standard for<br>professional actions | than legal standards, and they are never lower than the legal standards of the profession.<br>Implementation<br>Safe, effective care environment<br>Application<br>Learning Outcome 5.4 |
| **5.15** Which of the following fundamental responsibilities of nurses are included in the preamble of the International Council of Nurses Code of Ethics? (Select all that apply.)<br>_____ Promote health<br>_____ Restore health<br>_____ Inform the public about minimum standards of nursing conduct<br>_____ Provide self-regulation in the profession<br>_____ Prevent illness<br>_____ Alleviate suffering | Answer:<br>_____x_____ Promote health<br>_____x_____ Restore health<br>_____ Inform the public about minimum standards of nursing conduct<br>_____ Provide self-regulation in the profession<br>_____x_____ Prevent illness<br>_____x_____ Alleviate suffering<br>Rationale: These are the four fundamental responsibilities of nurses, according to the International Council of Nurses Code of Ethics. Informing the public and providing self-regulation are purposes of nursing codes of ethics.<br>Assessment<br>Safe, effective care environment<br>Application<br>Learning Outcome 5.4 |
| **5.16** A 20-year-old client with Down syndrome is able to live in an assisted environment and work part-time for a local bookstore. The parent of this client is adamant about not initiating a course of treatment whose side effects are unknown with Down syndrome clients. According to the nursing code of ethics, the nurse's first loyalty is to which of the following?<br>1. The client<br>2. The parent<br>3. The physician<br>4. The nurse | Answer: 1<br>Rationale: The nurse's first loyalty is to the client. Conflicts among obligations to families, physicians, employing institutions, and clients may arise because of the nurse's unique position. It is not always easy to determine which action best serves the client's needs.<br>Implementation<br>Safe, effective care environment<br>Application<br>Learning Outcome 5.4 |
| **5.17** A hospice nurse has been working closely with a client who, on several occasions, has asked about guidance and support in ending her life. The nurse, in making an ethical and moral decision, should recognize that:<br>1. Passive euthanasia is an easy decision to arrive at.<br>2. Legal issues are not the same as moral or ethical ones.<br>3. Active euthanasia is supported in the Code for Nurses.<br>4. Assisted suicide is illegal in all states. | Answer: 2<br>Rationale: Determining whether an action is legal is only one aspect of deciding whether it is ethical. Legality and morality are not one and the same. The nurse must know and follow the legal statutes of the profession and boundaries within the state before making any decision. Passive euthanasia involves the withdrawal of extraordinary means of life support and is never an easy decision. Active euthanasia and assisted suicide are in violation of the Code for Nurses, according to the position statement by the ANA (1995). Some states and countries have laws permitting assisted suicide for clients who are severely ill, are near death, and wish to commit suicide.<br>Implementation<br>Safe, effective care environment<br>Application<br>Learning Outcome 5.4 |
| **5.18** A client with terminal cancer is dying. For the past several days, the client has refused food and fluids, and pushes the caregiver's hands away when attempts are made to feed the client or offer any kind of fluid. The family is considering placing a gastrostomy tube because they feel the client is "starving to death." The nurse should: | Answer: 3<br>Rationale: A nurse is morally obligated to withhold food and fluids if it is determined to be more harmful to administer them than to withhold them. The nurse must also honor competent patients' refusal of food and fluids. This position is supported by the ANA's Code of Ethics for Nurses, through the nurse's role as a client advocate and through the moral principle of autonomy. Clients, not their families, should make decisions about their own health care and treatment. The physician may or may not be involved, but not to disregard the client's refusal. An ethics committee is usually |

| | |
|---|---|
| 1. Honor the family's wishes and have them sign a consent form.<br>2. Talk to the physician so he or she can move forward with the family's wishes.<br>3. Honor the client's refusal and help the family come to terms with the situation.<br>4. Take the case to the hospital's ethics committee. | considered when there is a ethical dilemma and more input is needed to make a decision. In this case, the client has made a decision and it should be honored.<br>Implementation<br>Psychosocial integrity<br>Application<br>Learning Outcome 5.4 |
| **5.19** A client comes to the clinic and is found to have an STD (sexually transmitted disease). The client states to the nurse, "Promise you won't tell anyone about my condition." The nurse, according to the Health Insurance Portability and Accountability Act (HIPAA) of 1996, must do which of the following?<br>1. Honor the client's wishes<br>2. Not disclose any information to anyone<br>3. Respect the client's privacy and confidentiality<br>4. Communicate only necessary information | Answer: 4<br>Rationale: HIPAA includes standards that protect the confidentiality, integrity, and availability of data as well as standards that define appropriate disclosures of identifiable health information and patient rights protection. Nurses are entrusted with sensitive information which, at times, must be revealed to other health care personnel in order to provide appropriate health care. In this case, the nurse may be required to report information to the state health department. Clients must be able to trust that their information is secure and will only be shared with appropriate entities. Nurses should not make promises to keep necessary information private.<br>Implementation<br>Safe, effective care environment<br>Application<br>Learning Outcome 5.4 |
| **5.20** A home health client has been prescribed nutritional supplements three times a day. The formula is expensive and the client tells the home health nurse that she is taking them three times a day, but diluting them so she can use only one can, not three, per day. As a client advocate, the nurse should:<br>1. Help the client look for available community resources that may be of assistance.<br>2. Tell the client that she needs to take the prescribed amount.<br>3. Report the situation to the physician.<br>4. Weigh the client on a weekly basis to monitor weight gain or loss. | Answer: 1<br>Rationale: Resource allocation and financial considerations are major issues in home health care. When clients are in their own home, they operate from their own values and client autonomy must be respected. Community resources may be of benefit for this client to be able to afford the proper supplement at the correct dose or to provide assistance in other financial areas so the client has the treatment needs met. The client probably knows she should take the prescribed amount, and telling the physician will not help to solve the situation. Weighing the client merely assesses the need, which has already been established, and is something that's probably being done anyway.<br>Implementation<br>Safe, effective care environment<br>Application<br>Learning Outcome 5.7 |

## CHAPTER 6

| | |
|---|---|
| **6.1** *Healthy People 2010* has two primary goals. Which of the following is in alignment with one of the goals?<br>1. Providing free screening to schoolchildren<br>2. Opening a wellness clinic<br>3. Creating new pharmacological treatments<br>4. Developing better insurance controls | Answer: 2<br>Rationale: Two primary goals of *Healthy People 2010* are to (1) increase quality and years of healthy life; and (2) eliminate health disparities. Opening a wellness clinic focuses on bettering health, which would be in line with goal 1. Free screening to schoolchildren is already being done in most states as well as creating new pharmacological treatments—neither of which are new ideas. Developing insurance control was a goal of health care reform during the Clinton administration.<br>Assessment<br>Safe, effective care environment<br>Application<br>Learning Outcome 6.1 |

| | |
|---|---|
| **6.2** A group of nurses are working to open a clinic that focuses on health promotion. Which of the following is an example of a health promotion activity?<br>   1. Teaching biofeedback techniques for stress reduction<br>   2. Providing immunization clinics<br>   3. Evaluating regional industrial centers for environmental pollution<br>   4. Teaching smoking cessation classes to adolescents | Answer: 1<br>Rationale: Health promotion programs address nutrition, weight control, exercise, and stress reduction. Health promotion activities emphasize the role of clients in maintaining their own health and provide encouragement in maintaining the highest level of wellness they can achieve. Providing immunization clinics, evaluating industrial centers for pollution, and teaching smoking cessation classes are examples of illness prevention, not health promotion.<br>Assessment<br>Safe, effective care environment<br>Application<br>Learning Outcome 6.1 |
| **6.3** A client is in the end stages of cancer. By which type of service would this client best be served?<br>   1. Rehabilitation<br>   2. Health restoration<br>   3. Acute care<br>   4. Palliative care | Answer: 4<br>Rationale: Palliative care is service that provides comfort and treatment of symptoms. This type of care is for clients who cannot be returned to health. It may be conducted in many settings, including the home. Rehabilitation is a process of restoring ill or injured people to optimum and functional levels of wellness, emphasizing the importance of assisting clients to function adequately in the physical, mental, social, economic, and vocational areas of their lives. Health restoration is service that helps bring ill or injured clients back to their former state of health. Acute care is the typical service provided in a hospital.<br>Assessment<br>Safe, effective care environment<br>Application<br>Learning Outcome 6.1 |
| **6.4** Several nurses are looking for an agency to sponsor a program that would meet the needs of a community group lacking in health promotion education. The nurses should seek help from which of the following?<br>   1. State health department<br>   2. Local health department<br>   3. Local hospital<br>   4. Federal government | Answer: 2<br>Rationale: The local health department has the responsibility for developing programs to meet the health needs of the people, providing the necessary staff and facilities to carry out those programs, evaluating their effectiveness, and monitoring changing needs. State health organizations are responsible for assisting the local health departments. The U.S. Department of Health and Human Services is an agency at the federal level whose functions include conducting research and providing training in the health field, providing assistance to communities in planning and developing health facilities, and assisting states and local communities through financing and provision of trained personnel. Local hospitals provide the majority of acute care services in a community.<br>Implementation<br>Safe, effective care environment<br>Application<br>Learning Outcome 6.2 |
| **6.5** A nurse has begun working in a hospital that provides services in all specialty areas (medical, surgical, pediatrics, obstetrics). This hospital is classified as which of the following?<br>   1. General hospital<br>   2. Specialty hospital<br>   3. Long-term care hospital<br>   4. Short-term hospital | Answer: 1<br>Rationale: Hospitals are classified by the services they provide as well as by their ownership. General hospitals admit clients requiring a variety of services such as medical, surgical, obstetric, pediatric, and psychiatric services. Some hospitals offer only specialty services such as psychiatric or pediatric. Hospitals can also be classified as acute care or chronic care. Acute care hospitals provide assistance to clients whose illness and need for hospitalization are relatively short term, such as several days. Long-term care hospitals provide services for longer periods—sometimes years or for the remainder of the client's life.<br>Assessment<br>Safe, effective care environment<br>Application<br>Learning Outcome 6.2 |

**6.6** A client is being discharged following an extensive illness. The client continues to require IV antibiotics, is not able to complete ADLs (activities of daily living) without assistance, and has no family available to assist in the recovery phase. The nurse should make a recommendation for this client to:

1. Stay in the hospital until the client is fully capable of self-care.
2. Remain in the hospital until the antibiotic course is completed.
3. Be discharged to an extended care facility.
4. Go to a nursing home.

Answer: 3

Rationale: Extended care facilities provide care for clients who require rehabilitation and custodial care after discharge from an acute care hospital. Since this client still receives antibiotic therapy and requires some custodial care, this type of facility can provide the best care until the client is ready for discharge home. An acute care hospital stay is no longer required, and extended care facilities could provide skilled care with less cost. The client may require a nursing home or long-term care facility at some point, but it is too early in the recovery to make this decision.

Implementation

Safe, effective care environment

Application

Learning Outcome 6.2

---

**6.7** An elderly client has no family in the same community, lives alone in a small house, and is having greater difficulty with mobility due to advanced osteoarthritis. Cognitively, this client is alert, is able to manage her own business matters, and does her own cooking, but does not enjoy "cooking for one." The home health nurse who visits has noticed that the client is losing weight and does not have as much energy or interest in activities as on previous visits. The nurse should recommend that the client:

1. See a psychiatrist since the client appears depressed.
2. Check out joint replacement options for the osteoarthritis.
3. Start thinking about long-term care.
4. Consider moving to an assisted living facility.

Answer: 4

Rationale: Assisted living facilities offer meals, laundry services, nursing care, transportation, and social activities to residents who are able to live relatively independently. They are intended to meet the needs of people who are unable to remain at home but do not require hospital or nursing home care. The client in this scenario has some physical limitations, but could benefit from socialization and interaction with peers as well as have staff available who provide limited care and health promotion activities. Diagnosing depression is outside the scope of nursing practice, and other interventions can be implemented before this action should be considered. Joint replacement may or may not be an option, but it would not be the nurse's responsibility to recommend this. This client does not require long-term care at this point.

Implementation

Safe, effective care environment

Application

Learning Outcome 6.2

---

**6.8** The spouse of a client diagnosed with Stage I/II Alzheimer's disease must continue to work full-time. The spouse tells the occupational health nurse that the client has started to wander outside the house, forgets to turn off the stove after preparing food, and tries to drive the car if the client finds the keys. The nurse should recommend which of the following?

1. Long-term care placement for the client
2. That the spouse consider early retirement
3. Placing the client in an adult day-care environment
4. Considering increasing the client's medications to slow the progress of the disease

Answer: 3

Rationale: Day-care centers provide care and nutrition for adults who cannot be left at home alone but do not need to be in an institution. These centers often provide care involving socializing, exercise programs, and stimulation. Some provide counseling and physical therapy. Nurses who are employed in day-care centers may provide medications, treatment, and counseling. Placing a client from an independent home situation to long-term care would be more detrimental than a gradual progression of care. Telling the spouse to consider early retirement is neither therapeutic nor realistic. Increasing medications is a decision that needs to be made by the client's primary caregiver, not the nurse.

Implementation

Safe, effective care environment

Application

Learning Outcome 6.2

**6.9** A client has just been referred to hospice care, and the spouse asks the hospice nurse why the client needs the change in services. The best response by the nurse is:

1. "So we can see if there's any way to improve your spouse's life."
2. "There is no need for acute care any longer."
3. "It's best for your spouse to be cared for at home."
4. "Hospice care is cheaper than acute care."

Answer: 1

Rationale: The central concept of the hospice movement is not saving life but improving or maintaining the quality of life until death. Hospice care provides a variety of services given to the terminally ill, their families, and support persons. The place of care varies, but includes home, hospital, or skilled nursing facilities. Acute care may be warranted as the client's condition changes. Hospice care may well be cheaper, but this is not the main reason for referral to hospice services.

Implementation

Safe, effective care environment

Analysis

Learning Outcome 6.2

---

**6.10** A client has been recovering after an injury that left him partially paralyzed. The client is a young adult and intent on living independently, as before the injury. The best referral for this client would be to which of the following?

1. Paramedical technologist
2. Physical therapist
3. Occupational therapist
4. Case manager

Answer: 3

Rationale: An occupational therapist assists clients with impaired function to gain the skills necessary for activities of daily living. The therapist teaches skills that are therapeutic but at the same time provide fulfillment.

Helping a client with paralysis learn to use equipment or different methods of doing daily tasks will enable him to be as independent as possible. The term *paramedical technologist* includes laboratory technologists, radiological technologists, and nuclear medicine technologists. This title is given to those professionals having some connection with medicine. A physical therapist helps clients regain physical strength and mobility. In this case, the client would probably also see a physical therapist, but not for the focus on independent living. A case manager's role is to ensure that clients receive fiscally sound, appropriate care in the best setting. Again, this client may well have a case manager to coordinate all the necessary care, but the question focuses on the return to independent living.

Implementation

Safe, effective care environment

Analysis

Learning Outcome 6.3

---

**6.11** Which of the following factors have an effect on health care delivery? (Select all that apply.)

_____ Increased use of complementary and alternative medicine
_____ More knowledgeable consumers
_____ Increase in the number of elderly
_____ Decrease in chronic disease
_____ Technological advances
_____ Economics

Answer:

_____ Increased use of complementary and alternative medicine
___X___ More knowledgeable consumers
___X___ Increase in the number of elderly
_____ Decrease in chronic disease
___X___ Technological advances
___X___ Economics

Rationale: Today's health care consumers have greater knowledge about their health than in previous years and are increasingly influencing health care delivery. By the year 2020, it is estimated that the number of U.S. adults over the age of 65 will be more than 53 million. People over age 85 are projected to be the fastest growing population in the United States. Chronic illness is prevalent in this group. Technology related to health care is rapidly increasing and includes improved diagnostic procedures and equipment that permits early recognition of diseases. Computers, bedside charting, and the ability to store and retrieve large volumes of information in databases are common in health care organizations. Inflation increases all costs, and paying for health care services is becoming a greater problem. Though there is an increase in complementary and alternative medicine use, this does not affect how health care is delivered.

Assessment

Safe, effective care environment

Application

Learning Outcome 6.4

**6.12** Nurses are directly involved in cost containing or cost control measures. Which of the following reasons are related to cost increases? (Select all that apply.)

_____ Rising numbers of uninsured
_____ Total population is decreasing
_____ Inflation
_____ Use of prescription drugs is leveling off

Answer:

____x____ Rising numbers of uninsured
_____ Total population is decreasing
____x____ Inflation
_____ Use of prescription drugs is leveling off

Rationale: The total population is growing, especially in the older adult segment who tend to have greater health care needs compared to younger persons. The cost of prescription drugs is increasing and represents 19% of total health care expenditures in the United States. The uninsured numbers are on the rise—17% of persons under age 65. Inflation increases all costs.
Assessment
Safe, effective care environment
Application
Learning Outcome 6.5

**6.13** A nurse is interviewing a client at a clinic near a shelter for the homeless. Understanding the increased risk poor physical environment creates for this client, the nurse will focus on which of the following during the intake phase of the interview?

1. Lack of social support
2. Recent history of chills and body aches
3. Improper nutrition
4. Few personal resources

Answer: 2
Rationale: Poor physical environment results in increased susceptibility to infections. The client's recent history of chills and body aches should alert the nurse that this client may have an infection. All other options are factors that contribute to health problems in general.
Assessment
Physiological integrity
Analysis
Learning Outcome 6.4

**6.14** A nurse is working in a clinic whose emphasis is on cost control, customer satisfaction, health promotion, and preventive services. This represents which type of system?

1. Managed care
2. Case management
3. Differentiated practice
4. Patient-focused care

Answer: 1
Rationale: Managed care describes a health care system whose goals are to provide cost-effective, quality care that focuses on decreased costs and improved outcomes for groups of clients. Case management describes a range of models for integrating health care services for individuals or groups. Differentiated practice is a system in which the best possible use of nursing personnel is based on their educational preparation and resultant skill sets. Patient-focused care is a delivery model that brings all services and care providers to the client.
Assessment
Safe, effective care environment
Application
Learning Outcome 6.5

**6.15** The manager of a small clinic has cross-trained the nurses to not only provide basic nursing care, but also perform ECG testing, phlebotomy, and some respiratory therapy interventions. This clinic is an example of which delivery model?

1. Managed care
2. Case management
3. Patient-focused care
4. Critical pathways

Answer: 3
Rationale: Patient-focused care is a delivery model that brings all services and care providers to the client. Activities provided by auxiliary personnel (physical therapy, respiratory therapy, ECG testing, and phlebotomy) are moved close to the client, thereby decreasing the number of personnel involved and the number of steps to get the work done. Managed care focuses on cost-effective, quality care which results in decreased costs and improved outcomes. Case management is a way to integrate health care services for individuals or groups and involves multidisciplinary teams that assume collaborative responsibility for planning, assessing needs, and coordinating, implementing, and evaluating care. Critical pathways are used to track the client's progress in case management.
Assessment
Safe, effective care environment
Application
Learning Outcome 6.5

**6.16** A new graduate nurse is looking for employment and is hoping to find a facility that utilizes nursing personnel based on their educational preparation and skill set. Which of the following systems implements this practice?
1. Patient-focused care
2. Shared governance
3. Differentiated practice
4. Managed care

Answer: 3
Rationale: Differentiated practice is a system in which the best possible use of nursing personnel is based on their educational preparation and resultant skill sets. This model consists of specific job descriptions for nurses according to their education or training. Patient-focused care is a delivery model that brings all services and care providers to the client. Shared governance is an organizational model in which nursing staff are cooperative with administrative personnel in making, implementing, and evaluating client care policies. Managed care focuses on cost containment, consumer satisfaction, health promotion, and preventive services.
Assessment
Safe, effective care environment
Application
Learning Outcome 6.5

**6.17** A nurse has just moved from a facility that utilized differentiated practice. Which of the following delivery systems would most resemble this system?
1. Case method
2. Shared governance
3. Functional method
4. Team nursing

Answer: 4
Rationale: Team nursing is the delivery of individualized nursing care to clients by a team led by a professional nurse. The nursing team consists of registered nurses, licensed practical nurses, and unlicensed assistive personnel. The registered nurse retains responsibility and authority for client care but delegates appropriate tasks to the other team members. This enables nurses to progress and assume roles and responsibilities appropriate for their level of experience, capability, and education—much like the differentiated practice system. Case method is a client-centered model where one nurse is assigned to and responsible for the comprehensive care of a group of clients during a shift. In this method a client has consistent contact with one nurse during a shift, but may have different nurses on other shifts. Shared governance is an organizational model in which nursing staff are cooperative with administrative personnel in making, implementing, and evaluating client care policies. The functional nursing method focuses on the jobs to be completed. It is a task-oriented approach in which personnel with less preparation than the professional nurse perform less complex care requirements.
Assessment
Safe, effective care environment
Application
Learning Outcome 6.5

**6.18** A seasoned RN is especially competent in knowledge of the computerized charting system in a facility and is able to assume the team leader role on a regular basis. These two characteristics are the basis of which system?
1. Primary nursing
2. Team nursing
3. Differentiated practice
4. Case method

Answer: 1
Rationale: Primary nursing is a system in which one nurse is responsible for total care of a number of clients, 24 hours a day, 7 days a week. It is a method of providing comprehensive, individualized, and consistent care. Primary nursing uses the nurse's technical knowledge and management skills in assessing and prioritizing each client's needs, implementing the plan of care, and evaluating its effectiveness. Team nursing is the delivery of individualized nursing care to clients by a team led by a professional nurse and consisting of RNs, LPNs, and UAPs. Differentiated practice is a system in which the best possible use of nursing personnel is based on their education preparation and resultant skill sets. Case method is also referred to as total care, in which one nurse is assigned to and is responsible for the comprehensive care of a group of clients during an 8- or 12-hour shift.
Assessment
Safe, effective care environment
Application
Learning Outcome 6.5

| | |
|---|---|
| **6.19** A client who is at least 65 years of age is asking the nurse how he will afford his hospitalization, which has now been extended, involving extremely expensive drugs. The best response by the nurse is:<br>    1. "Don't worry. I'm sure everything will work out OK."<br>    2. "You need to focus on recovering, not worrying about finances."<br>    3. "Much of your care will be covered by Medicare."<br>    4. "I'll have someone from the business office come and talk to you about your bill." | Answer: 3<br>Rationale: The Medicare amendment to the Social Security Act provided a national and state health insurance program for older adults. By the mid-1970s, virtually everyone over 65 years of age was protected by hospital insurance under Part A. In 1988, Congress expanded Medicare to include extremely expensive hospital care, "catastrophic care," and expensive drugs. Ignoring the client's concerns by telling him not to worry is not therapeutic communication and does little, if anything, to confront the client's concerns. Giving the concern to the business office is merely "passing the buck." Nurses should have some knowledge about the payment sources of their clients, especially those who have automatic coverage with Medicare because of their age.<br>Implementation<br>Psychosocial integrity<br>Application<br>Learning Outcome 6.5 |
| **6.20** A clinic in a rural area depends primarily on the services of a nurse practitioner. The legislation that allows this opportunity is which of the following?<br>    1. Medicare<br>    2. Medicaid<br>    3. Rural Health Clinics Act<br>    4. National Health Planning and Resources Development Act | Answer: 3<br>Rationale: In 1978, the Rural Health Clinics Act provided for the development of health care in medically underserved rural areas. This act opened the door for nurse practitioners to provide primary care. Medicare and Medicaid are amendments to the Social Security Act. Medicare provides insurance coverage for people over age 65, and Medicaid provides service to people who require financial assistance for health care. The National Health Planning and Resources Development Act established health systems agencies throughout the United States for the development of health care in medically underserved rural areas.<br>Assessment<br>Safe, effective care environment<br>Application<br>Learning Outcome 6.5 |
| **6.21** Principles recommended by the Institute of Medicine to address the problem of insurance coverage include which of the following? (Select all that apply.)<br>  _____ Health coverage should be for everyone.<br>  _____ Families and individuals should have coverage they can afford.<br>  _____ Coverage should be provided by private companies.<br>  _____ Health coverage should be ongoing and uninterrupted.<br>  _____ Hospitals should be financed through taxation. | Answer:<br>\_\_\_\_x\_\_\_\_ Health coverage should be for everyone.<br>\_\_\_\_x\_\_\_\_ Families and individuals should have coverage they can afford.<br>_____ Coverage should be provided by private companies.<br>\_\_\_\_x\_\_\_\_ Health coverage should be ongoing and uninterrupted.<br>_____ Hospitals should be financed through taxation.<br>Rationale: Between 2001 and 2004, the Institute of Medicine issued six research reports identifying the scope of the problem of the underinsured in America. They recommended five principles for addressing this problem: health coverage should be for everyone, health coverage should be ongoing/uninterruptible, individuals and families need to have coverage they can afford, a national approach must be cost-effective and able to be maintained by society, and the care provided under this coverage must ensure care that is "effective, safe, timely, patient centered, and equitable."<br>The Canada Health Act in 1984 provided financing for hospitals through taxation.<br>Assessment<br>Safe, effective care environment<br>Application<br>Learning Outcome 6.5 |
| **6.22** A client has just been enrolled (through her employer) in an HMO. The client's previous experience with health care coverage through her employer was with a PPO. The client asks the occupational health nurse to explain the difference. The best response by the nurse is which of the following? | Answer: 3<br>Rationale: HMO plans emphasize wellness, and members choose a primary care provider who evaluates their health status and coordinates their care. Clients are limited in their ability to select health care providers and services, but available services are at minimal and predetermined cost to the client. PPOs consist of a group of physicians that provides an insurance company or employer with health services at a discounted rate. One advantage of the PPO is that it provides clients with a choice of health care providers and services. Telling the client not to |

1. "You'll have good health care benefits, so don't worry."
2. "Both the HMO and PPO are covered by your employer so it's really not your concern."
3. "Your PPO offered you a choice in your health care provider as well as services. Now, you will choose a primary care provider who will evaluate your health and will coordinate all of your care."
4. "You really should be happy about the HMO. You'll pay little, if any, out-of-pocket expense."

worry does not address the client's question, which is to explain the difference. Even though telling the client that she will have little out-of-pocket expense may be truthful, it doesn't answer the question.
Implementation
Safe, effective care environment
Application
Learning Outcome 6.5

# CHAPTER 7

**7.1** The ANA recommended several changes for health care reform. How many of them have been implemented since 1991? _____

Answer: Few
Rationale: The ANA published Nursing's Agenda for Health Care Reform in 1991, which highlighted several recommendations for health care reform. Although the agenda called for "immediate" changes, the majority of the recommendations have still not been implemented over 15 years later.
Assessment
Safe, effective care environment
Application
Learning Outcome 7.1

**7.2** Primary health care is incorporated into five major principles. Which of the following apply?
_____ Focus on individual participation
_____ Appropriate technology
_____ Focus on disease management
_____ Equitable distribution
_____ Multisectoral approach

Answer:
_____ Focus on individual participation
____x_____ Appropriate technology
_____ Focus on disease management
____x_____ Equitable distribution
____x_____ Multisectoral approach
Rationale: Primary health care is defined as essential health care based on practical, scientifically sound, and socially acceptable methods and technology made universally accessible to individuals and families in the community. Primary health care incorporates five principles: equitable distribution, appropriate technology, focus on health promotion and disease prevention, community participation, and a multisectoral approach.
Assessment
Safe, effective care environment
Application
Learning Outcome 7.1

**7.3** A nurse educator is explaining primary health care (PHC) and the extension of its boundaries beyond traditional health care services. Issues related to PHC include which of the following?
1. Distribution and participation
2. Environment, agriculture, and housing
3. Consumerism and governmental subsidies
4. Low life expectancies and high mortality rates among children

Answer: 2
Rationale: PHC involves issues of the environment, agriculture, and housing. It also involves other social, economic, and political issues such as poverty, transportation, unemployment, and economic development to sustain the population. Distribution and participation are two of the five principles incorporated in PHC. Consumerism and governmental subsidies are not part of the PHC makeup. Low life expectancies and high mortality rates among children are two concerns about health care that led to the global health strategy of primary health care.
Assessment
Safe, effective care environment
Application
Learning Outcome 7.5

| | |
|---|---|
| **7.4** After a community was hit by a tornado, the nurses of the local Red Cross Chapter helped to make sure people had adequate food and clothing. Which function of community were these nurses focused on restoring?<br>1. Social control<br>2. Social interparticipation<br>3. Mutual support<br>4. Distribution of goods and services | Answer: 4<br>Rationale: Production, distribution, and consumption of goods and services are the means by which the community provides for the economic needs of its members. It includes supplying food and clothing as well as providing water, electricity, police and fire protection, and the disposal of refuse.<br>Implementation<br>Physiological integrity<br>Application<br>Learning Outcome 7.2 |
| **7.5** A nurse is helping to set up an elder social group at a local senior center where residents can come to play cards or participate in structured activities three times a week. This nurse is working in which function of community?<br>1. Socialization<br>2. Social control<br>3. Social interparticipation<br>4. Mutual support | Answer: 3<br>Rationale: Social interparticipation refers to community activities that are designed to meet people's needs for companionship. Socialization refers to the process of transmitting values, knowledge, culture, and skills to others. Social control refers to the way in which order is maintained in a community. Mutual support refers to the community's ability to provide resources at a time of illness or disaster.<br>Implementation<br>Psychosocial integrity<br>Application<br>Learning Outcome 7.2 |
| **7.6** When explaining the difference between community and population, the nurse educator uses which of the following as an example for population?<br>1. Commuters on the subway<br>2. A grade school class<br>3. Graduating nursing students<br>4. A group of employees at a local plant | Answer: 1<br>Rationale: A population is composed of people who share some common characteristic, but who do not necessarily interact with each other—as people on a subway might behave. They are all riding, but not really interacting. The other options are examples of community—people or a social system in which the members interact formally or informally and form networks that operate for the benefit of all people in the community. A grade school class or nurse graduates would fall into this category as would employees at a local plant—people who share some part of their lives in such a way that all benefit.<br>Assessment<br>Safe, effective care environment<br>Application<br>Learning Outcome 7.8 |
| **7.7** When completing a community assessment, the community health nurse will take several aspects into account. What is the first stage of this assessment?<br>1. Learn about the people in the community.<br>2. Understand the major illnesses present in the community.<br>3. Identify the boundaries of the community.<br>4. Make sure resources are available in the community. | Answer: 1<br>Rationale: The first stage in assessment is to learn about the people in the community. When completing a community assessment, the nurse needs to focus on a much larger "client"—which is the whole community. Identifying boundaries is part of a community assessment, not the first stage. Other aspects to consider are types of dwellings, education present, safety and transportation services, politics and government, health and social services, communication, economics, and recreation.<br>Assessment<br>Safe, effective care environment<br>Application<br>Learning Outcome 7.2 |
| **7.8** A nurse is completing a community assessment and must understand where the main health facilities are located and how many residents in the community are welfare recipients. The best source for this information would be which of the following?<br>1. Police department<br>2. City health planning board | Answer: 3<br>Rationale: The county health department would be able to supply information about location of health facilities, occupational health programs, numbers of health professionals, numbers of welfare recipients, and so on. The police department has statistics regarding incidence of crime, vandalism, and drug addiction. The city health planning board has information about health needs and practices. The state census data describe population composition and characteristics.<br>Assessment |

| | |
|---|---|
| 3. County health department<br>4. State census data | Safe, effective care environment<br>Application<br>Learning Outcome 7.2 |
| **7.9** Several student nurses are compiling information about their community and want to understand more about services to maintain and promote health. What entity would be most helpful to them?<br>    1. Chamber of commerce<br>    2. Public and university libraries<br>    3. Recreational directors<br>    4. Teachers and school nurses | Answer: 4<br>Rationale: Teachers and school nurses provide information about the incidence of children's health problems and information on facilities and services to maintain and promote health. The chamber of commerce can supply statistics about employment, major industries, and primary occupations. Public and university libraries contain district social and cultural research reports. Recreational directors provide information about programs and participation levels.<br>Assessment<br>Safe, effective care environment<br>Application<br>Learning Outcome 7.2 |
| **7.10** Nursing students are required to attend at least two community activities related to health and wellness. What resource would best help them identify the type and time of these activities?<br>    1. Online computer services<br>    2. Recreational directors<br>    3. Local newspapers<br>    4. Telephone book | Answer: 3<br>Rationale: Local newspapers contain information—including date and time—about community activities related to health and wellness, such as health lectures or health fairs. Online computer services may provide access to public documents related to community health. Recreational directors have information about programs provided and participation levels. The telephone book would include the location of social, recreational, and health organizations, as well as committees and facilities.<br>Assessment<br>Safe, effective care environment<br>Application |
| **7.11** Several nurses at the county health department are involved in planning community health. In order to create a plan that will be acceptable to members of the community, who else should be involved in this venture?<br>    1. As many people from the community as possible<br>    2. Physicians and other nurses<br>    3. Members of the chamber of commerce and governing board of the community<br>    4. Just the nurses at the county health department | Answer: 1<br>Rationale: A broadly based planning group is most likely to create a plan that is acceptable to members of the community. People who are involved in planning become educated about problems, resources, and interrelationships within the system. Responsibility for planning at the community level is usually broadly based and needs to include as many of the community partners as possible.<br>Implementation<br>Safe, effective care environment<br>Application<br>Learning Outcome 7.7 |
| **7.12** After implementing health promotion activities and plans to prioritize health problems, the community must evaluate the effectiveness of the interventions. Which groups would be involved in this process?<br>    1. Health care providers at the community level<br>    2. Hospital and clinic personnel who administered health care needs<br>    3. Health care providers, consumers, community leaders, and politicians<br>    4. Those consumers who were directly affected by the services provided | Answer: 3<br>Rationale: Because community health is usually a collaborative process between health providers, community leaders, politicians, and consumers, all may be involved in the evaluation process. Often, the community health nurse is the agent of evaluation, collecting and assessing data that determine the effectiveness of implemented programs.<br>Evaluation<br>Safe, effective care environment<br>Application<br>Learning Outcome 7.7 |

**7.13** A large community clinic provides health education, illness prevention, acute care, screening, and rehabilitation and health promotion services for the chronically ill. In assessing the type of approach this represents, the community health nurse would identify this as which of the following?

1. Community-based setting
2. Integrated health care system
3. Wellness center
4. Community outreach center

Answer: 2

Rationale: An integrated health care system makes all levels of care available in an integrated form, including primary care (education and illness prevention), secondary care (acute care and screening), and tertiary care (rehabilitation and services for the chronically ill). Community-based settings are provided in county and state health departments and may include day-care centers, senior centers, storefront clinics, homeless shelters, and the like. A wellness center provides services such as health promotion, maintenance education, counseling, and screening. Community outreach centers are small, freestanding clinics providing services similar to those traditionally provided by large public health clinics, but focused on a narrower population.
Assessment
Safe, effective care environment
Application

---

**7.14** A parish health nurse is working with a particular congregation in setting up a support program for shut-ins within the congregation who are not able to come to regular prayer services. In this capacity, the nurse is working in which of the following roles?

1. Counselor
2. Educator
3. Referral source
4. Facilitator

Answer: 4

Rationale: A facilitator recruits and coordinates volunteers within the congregation and develops support groups. A counselor discusses health issues and problems with individuals and makes home, hospital, and nursing home visits as needed. An educator works to support individuals through health education activities that promote an understanding of the relationship between values, attitudes, lifestyle, faith, and well-being. A referral source is a liaison to other congregations and community resources.
Implementation
Psychosocial integrity
Application
Learning Outcome 7.4

---

**7.15** A parish nurse is helping a group of new parents within the congregation find appropriate health care providers within the community who specialize in infant/child and family health care needs. This nurse is functioning in which of the following roles?

1. Health educator
2. Referral source
3. Facilitator
4. Integrator

Answer: 2

Rationale: A referral source acts as a liaison to other congregational and community resources. Helping new parents find appropriate sources for health care would be an example of a referral source. A health educator supports individuals through health education activities that promote understanding of the relationship between values, attitudes, lifestyle, faith, and well-being. A facilitator recruits and coordinates volunteers within the congregation and develops support groups. An integrator brings the entities of faith and health together.
Assessment
Safe, effective care environment
Application
Learning Outcome 7.4

---

**7.16** A public health nurse is working with a group of home health nurses in an isolated, mountainous region where access to smaller communities and individuals is quite difficult, especially in the winter and early spring—seasons when health needs of these individuals are quite high. The public health nurse has set up video conferencing and video clinics for these home health nurses regarding various client teaching and health promotion activities. This is an example of which of the following?

1. Community-based nursing
2. Parish nursing
3. Telenursing
4. Collaborative health care

Answer: 3

Rationale: Telehealth projects use communication and information technology to provide health information and health care services to people in rural, remote, or underserviced areas. Video conferences and video clinics enable health care workers to provide distant consultation to assess and treat ambulatory clients who have a variety of health care needs. Telenursing enables nurses to provide client teaching and health promotion to distant clients. Community-based nursing is nursing care directed toward specific individuals, on a much broader scale than what is described in this scenario. Parish nursing focuses on integrating aspects of faith and members of a particular congregation and health care or nursing needs. Collaborative health care describes a process of teamwork in providing comprehensive health care.
Evaluation
Safe, effective care environment
Analysis
Learning Outcome 7.4

**7.17** Several nurses are working in concert with other health care providers for a group of individuals within the community who have complications of diabetes mellitus and require extensive dressing changes and comprehensive education. The nurses and providers are working within the context of which of the following?

1. Collaboration
2. Case management
3. Health promotion
4. Health education

Answer: 1

Rationale: Collaboration means a collegial working relationship with other health care providers to supply patient care. Collaborative practice requires the discussion of diagnoses and management in the delivery of care. Case management involves one person overseeing the needs and requirements of a particular individual's health. Health promotion activities include disease prevention and healthy lifestyle interventions. Health education would be included in this particular situation but collaboration is a more inclusive definition of what is occurring with these individuals and the care they require.

Assessment
Physiological integrity
Analysis
Learning Outcome 7.9

**7.18** A nurse is working in collaboration with a group of health care providers in a community clinic setting. They have defined a problem and now are focusing on objectives and considering various viewpoints presented by the group. Which of the competencies of collaboration does this describe?

1. Mutual respect
2. Trust
3. Communication
4. Decision making

Answer: 4

Rationale: Decision making involves shared responsibility for the outcome. The team must follow specific steps of the decision-making process, beginning with a clear definition of the problem. Team decision making must be directed at the objectives of the effort and requires full consideration and respect for various and diverse viewpoints. Mutual respect occurs when two or more people show or feel honor or esteem toward one another. Trust occurs when a person is confident in the actions of another person. Both imply mutual process and outcome and may be expressed verbally or nonverbally. Communication is necessary in effective collaboration. It occurs only if the involved parties are committed to understanding each other's professional roles and appreciating each other as individuals.

Assessment
Safe, effective care environment
Application
Learning Outcome 7.7

**7.19** A nurse case manager must be vigilant in protecting the client's health information. Because the nursing office is in a cluster of offices that share a fax machine, which action by the nurse ensures that HIPAA requirements are met?

1. Have the client sign a consent for information to be released.
2. Have sending agencies call ahead before any information is sent.
3. Do not utilize the fax machine; depend on the mail system.
4. Take relevant information over the phone.

Answer: 2

Rationale: Case manager nurses need to maintain vigilance to protect the privacy of client health care information when sending and receiving messages. In this case, having the sending agency call prior to faxing information would alert the nurse to collect the information from the fax machine at the time it is received, securing that information so others do not have access to it. Signing a consent form for information to be released is necessary to share information, but this would not ensure the privacy aspect of HIPAA—only the disclosure aspect. Sending information through the mail takes time and does not ensure the privacy of the information. Phone conversations and information taken during the conversation must be protected and taken in a secured way to ensure HIPAA privacy aspects have not been breached.

Implementation
Psychosocial integrity
Application
Learning Outcome 7.9

**7.20** The nurse is helping in discharge planning of a client who needs extensive rehabilitation and is on a complicated medication schedule. The nurse would want to include which of the following persons in this client's plan?

1. Client's spouse
2. Physician
3. Pharmacist
4. Social worker

Answer: 1

Rationale: Effective discharge planning necessitates health team conferences and family conferences and gives the client, family, and health care professionals the opportunity to plan care and set goals. Involving the client's spouse would be important in this situation because of the complexity of the client's situation. The physician, pharmacist, and social worker may also be included, but by their own decision—not necessarily by the nurse's invitation.

Implementation
Physiologic integrity
Application
Learning Outcome 7.9

**7.21** A client is getting ready to go home from an intermediate care facility following surgery and a lengthy recovery period. Which item will the home health nurse focus on in order to determine effectiveness of the discharge teaching plan?
1. Activity restrictions
2. Follow-up appointment dates
3. Return demonstration of dressing change
4. Signs of complications

Answer: 3
Rationale: Clients need teaching before discharge that includes information about medications, dietary and activity restrictions, signs of complications that need to be reported to the physician, follow-up appointments, and where supplies can be obtained. Clients, and perhaps caregivers, also need to demonstrate safe performance of any necessary treatments. Clients need help to understand their situation, to make health care decisions, and to learn new health behaviors. All the options would be important for the client to retain, but to determine whether the task of changing the dressing was learned, the client would have to demonstrate the skill back to the nurse.
Evaluation
Physiologic integrity
Analysis
Learning Outcome 7.9

# CHAPTER 8

**8.1** Home care nursing is a fast growing sector of the health care system. Which of the following factors have contributed to the growth of home health care? (Select all that apply.)
_____ The need for custodial care
_____ Third-party payers who support cost control measures
_____ The increase in the older adult population
_____ The decreasing need for acute care

Answer:
_____ The need for custodial care
____x____ Third-party payers who support cost control measures
____x____ The increase in the older adult population
_____ The decreasing need for acute care
Rationale: Factors that have contributed to the growth of home care services include the increase in the older population, who are frequent recipients of home care; third-party payers who favor home care to control costs; consumers who prefer to receive care in the home rather than in an institution; and the ability of agencies and institutions to successfully deliver high-technology services in the home. A common misconception about home health nursing is that it is custodial in its scope of practice. Acute care has not decreased, but the length of stay in acute care has.
Assessment
Safe, effective care environment
Application
Learning Outcome 8.1

**8.2** A nursing student wants to understand the difference in care delivery between home health nursing and community nursing. Unlike the community nurse, the focus for the home health nurse is which of the following?
1. Individuals, families, and groups
2. The individual and his or her family
3. The terminally ill client and his or her family
4. The client in a home setting

Answer: 2
Rationale: The focus of home health care nursing is individuals and their families. Community health nursing focuses on individuals, families, and aggregate groups. Hospice nursing supports the care of the dying client and the client's family. A home setting identifies the location of home health nursing, but not the focus.
Assessment
Psychosocial integrity
Application
Learning Outcome 8.2

**8.3** Home health nurses experience a variety of challenges in caring for their clients. Unlike the acute care setting, entry into the home is _____.

Answer: granted, not assumed
Rationale: The home is the family's territory, and issues in delivering care differ from those in the hospital. Entry into a client's hospital room is assumed, or the client would not be hospitalized. Entry into a client's home is an invited, trusting process which does not occur as quickly as it might in the acute care facility.
Implementation
Psychosocial integrity
Application
Learning Outcome 8.2

| | |
|---|---|
| **8.4** A home health client is having difficulty with the medication regimen that is prescribed by the physician. The nurse helps with this situation by consulting the pharmacist for ideas on how to improve the situation. This is an example of which of the following?<br><br>1. Hands-on care<br>2. Direct care<br>3. Advocacy<br>4. Indirect care | Answer: 4<br>Rationale: Indirect care is provided by the home health nurse to the client each time the nurse consults with other health care providers about ways to improve nursing care for the client. This consultation may manifest itself in care conferences with multiple disciplines where the role of the home health nurse is client advocate. However, in this situation, the client's rights or decisions about care is not the problem. The client needs help with certain medications. Hands-on care includes physical assessments, dressing changes, managing IV sites for therapies, and so on. Direct care is the same as hands-on care.<br>Assessment<br>Physiologic integrity<br>Application<br>Learning Outcome 8.4 |
| **8.5** A client is currently seeing a physician who recommends that the client now see a physical therapist. The therapist sees the need to call in a nurse for a wound that is not healing, and the nurse contacts a social worker to help the client with sorting through mounting medical bills. The client will be referred to a home health care provider. Who, in this situation, must write the order to meet the legal reimbursement requirement?<br><br>1. Physician<br>2. Nurse<br>3. Social worker<br>4. Physical therapist | Answer: 1<br>Rationale: A client may be referred to home health care by providers, nurses, social workers, and therapists, but home care cannot begin without a physician's order and a physician-approved treatment plan. This is a legal reimbursement requirement.<br>Implementation<br>Safe, effective care environment<br>Application<br>Learning Outcome 8.3 |
| **8.6** The client is being seen for the first time by the home health nurse. The nurse determines that the client will need speech therapy, physical therapy, and custodial care several times a week. When can the client's care begin?<br><br>1. As soon as the nurse completes the initial assessment<br>2. The care has already begun<br>3. When the physician signs the plan of care the nurse develops<br>4. Within 48 hours of the nurse's visit | Answer: 3<br>Rationale: At the initial visit, the nurse develops a plan of care that identifies the client's needs. This plan must by reviewed, approved, authorized, and signed by the attending physician before the home health agency providers can continue with services.<br>Implementation<br>Safe, effective care environment<br>Application<br>Learning Outcome 8.5 |
| **8.7** A home health client has a complicated case involving occupational therapy, respiratory therapy, a dietitian, the nurse, and a nurse's aide who provides assistance with bathing, housekeeping, and grocery shopping. Who is responsible for coordinating the client's care?<br><br>1. Physician<br>2. Nurse<br>3. Social worker<br>4. Home health agency | Answer: 2<br>Rationale: Because clients often require the services of several professionals, case coordination is essential and generally rests with the registered nurse.<br>Implementation<br>Physiologic integrity<br>Application<br>Learning Outcome 8.4 |

**8.8** The home health agency in a community is operated by the state health department and financed by taxes. This is an example of which type of agency?

1. Institution based
2. Private
3. Not-for-profit
4. Official

Answer: 4

Rationale: Official or public agencies are operated by state or local governments and financed primarily by tax funds. Institution-based agencies operate under a parent organization such as a hospital and are funded by the same sources as the parent. Private, proprietary agencies are for-profit organizations and are governed by either individual owners or national corporations. Not-for-profit or voluntary agencies are supported by donations, endowments, charities such as the United Way, and third-party reimbursement.

Assessment

Safe, effective care environment

Application

Learning Outcome 8.3

---

**8.9** A client's insurance company has coverage for DME. Which of the following client needs would be covered under this clause?

1. Dressings and bandages
2. Medications
3. A hospital bed
4. Visits by the home health nurse

Answer: 3

Rationale: Durable medical equipment (DME) ranges from hospital beds to bedside commodes to ventilators and apnea monitors. In other words, equipment that will not be "used up" is considered DME. Supplies that the client uses and cannot be reused is not considered DME. Visits by the home health nurse are not equipment.

Assessment

Physiologic integrity

Application

Learning Outcome 8.3

---

**8.10** Clients are entitled to home health care reimbursement if they meet certain criteria. The nurse would like to admit a client to home health care, but is worried about insurance reimbursement because the client:

1. Lives with a spouse.
2. Needs skilled care.
3. Needs intermittent care.
4. Drives a car for trips to the barber.

Answer: 4

Rationale: Clients must meet certain criteria, including homebound status, except for occasional outings. Barber trips are included as "occasional outings," but the client is not the driver. Living with a spouse and needing intermittent and skilled care are criteria that allow for reimbursement by insurance companies.

Assessment

Physiologic integrity

Application

Learning Outcome 8.3

---

**8.11** A client who has been the recipient of home health care has made the decision to discontinue hemodialysis. The client understands all the consequences of this decision and is not supported by his family. The nurse is meeting with the family to help them understand the significance of the client's decision and to help them support the client during this difficult time. In this situation, the nurse is acting in which of the following roles?

1. Caregiver
2. Advocate
3. Educator
4. Counselor

Answer: 2

Rationale: As a client advocate, the nurse explores and supports the client's choices in health care. Advocacy includes having discussions about the client's rights, advance medical directives, living wills, and durable power of attorney for health care. At times, the client's views may vary from those of other family members. In the event of conflict, the nurse ensures that the client's rights and desires are upheld. The home health nurse's major role as caregiver is to assess and diagnose the client's actual and potential health problems. The educator role focuses on teaching illness care, prevention of problems, and promotion of optimal wellness or well-being. Counselor is not a role for the home health nurse.

Implementation

Psychosocial integrity

Application

Learning Outcome 8.4

---

**8.12** A home health client has terminal cancer and has signed a DNR (do not resuscitate) order. The client has a respiratory arrest during one of the home health nurse's visits. The client's spouse is second-guessing the client's wishes and tells the nurse to call 911. The nurse should:

Answer: 4

Rationale: In the event of conflict between the client's desires and the family's wishes, the nurse, being the client's primary advocate, ensures that the client's rights and desires are upheld. This is a difficult situation, but the nurse is bound to the client's desires.

---

| | |
|---|---|
| 1. Ignore the spouse.<br>2. Call 911.<br>3. Start CPR.<br>4. Remind the spouse of the client's desires. | Implementation<br>Psychosocial integrity<br>Application<br>Learning Outcome 8.4 |
| **8.13** A home health nurse explains the procedures for preventing infection in a client's central venous access device and has the client's spouse watch while the nurse hooks the client to the medication infusion. The nurse is acting in which of the following roles?<br>1. Caregiver<br>2. Advocate<br>3. Educator<br>4. Coordinator | Answer: 3<br>Rationale: Education can be the most essential aspect of home care practice, the goal of which is to help clients learn to manage as independently as possible. Involving the spouse in care and educating the spouse along with the client promotes wellness and helps prevent problems. The role of caregiver involves assessing and diagnosing actual or potential health problems, planning care, and evaluating the client's outcomes. The advocate role ensures that the rights and desires of the client are upheld. The home health nurse coordinates the activities of all other home health team members involved in the client's treatment plan.<br>Evaluation<br>Physiologic integrity<br>Evaluation<br>Learning Outcome 8.4 |
| **8.14** The home health nurse is assessing the client's environment for safety concerns and finds that most of the rooms in the house have only one outlet with various cords entering the outlet. The nurse notes this concern to the client and the client's spouse. They inform the nurse that "this is the way we've lived for years." The nurse should:<br>1. Provide telephone numbers for local electricians.<br>2. Continue to persuade the client to have the home rewired.<br>3. Not bring the subject up again.<br>4. Document the findings and the client and spouse's response to the concern. | Answer: 4<br>Rationale: Home health nurses cannot expect to change a family's living space and lifestyle. However, they can express concern when a situation suggests the possibility for injury. Nurses must document information they provide and the family's response to instruction as well as make ongoing assessments about the family's use of safety precautions.<br>Implementation<br>Health promotion and maintenance<br>Application<br>Learning Outcome 8.6 |
| **8.15** A home health client lives alone in a small apartment and has only one phone, which is a land line. What safety recommendation might the visiting home health nurse make for this particular client?<br>1. Suggest that the client move to a nursing home or assisted living dwelling.<br>2. Recommend that the client be enrolled in an emergency response system.<br>3. Enroll the client in a program that places all the client's vital medical information in one place for emergency personnel.<br>4. Have the client post a list of emergency numbers (fire, police, ambulance) near the phone. | Answer: 2<br>Rationale: An emergency response system provides a small device with a help button that attaches to the client's wrist or is worn around the neck. The client can send a signal to a home base which would indicate if the client is in trouble (i.e., has fallen or become ill) and can't get to the phone. This system is particularly useful for clients who live alone. Making suggestions for the client to relocate may be a possibility, but this might be premature to suggest at this point. Having all of the client's medical information in one place is a helpful idea, as is having emergency numbers in a visible spot, but would not help as much as an alert system if the client falls while alone.<br>Implementation<br>Health promotion and maintenance<br>Application<br>Learning Outcome 8.6 |

| | |
|---|---|
| **8.16** The home health nurse has scheduled a visit to a client who lives in a neighborhood that is known to be unsafe because of gang activity. Before going to the client's home, the nurse should:<br>  1. Call for an escort.<br>  2. Call the client to let them know the nurse is on the way.<br>  3. Ask if the client could meet the nurse at the agency.<br>  4. Take a second nurse along on the visit. | Answer: 1<br>Rationale: Some less desirable living locations pose safety concerns for the nurse. Many home health agencies have contracts with security firms to escort nurses needing to see clients in potentially unsafe neighborhoods. If there is no such firm for escort, the police can also provide security for the nurse. Calling ahead to the client's home is routine practice, regardless of where the client lives. Having the client meet the nurse at the agency is inappropriate, especially if the client meets the criteria for home care. Taking a second nurse along may be a good idea, but it is not as safe as having security or police escort.<br>Implementation<br>Physiologic integrity<br>Application<br>Learning Outcome 8.6 |
| **8.17** A home health nurse has a weekly visit to a client living in less than desirable cleanliness. The client has a central venous access device and requires weekly infusion therapy. What is the best way for the nurse to protect the client against infection?<br>  1. Have the client wash her hands before the infusion begins.<br>  2. Practice strict aseptic technique during the infusion process.<br>  3. Help the client clean the room before starting the infusion.<br>  4. Suggest that the client have a housekeeper come on the morning of the infusion. | Answer: 2<br>Rationale: Infection control can present a challenge to the home health nurse, especially if the home care facilities are not conducive to basic aseptic requirements. The most important ways to prevent infection are making sure the site is clean, accessing the port following sterile procedure, and following Standard Precautions while accessing the line. The nurse's major role in infection control is health teaching. Even if the client's environment is not clean, that doesn't necessarily mean the client is unclean. Teaching about health practices that prevent infection is important, but the nurse cannot expect to change the client's lifestyle.<br>Implementation<br>Health promotion and maintenance<br>Application<br>Learning Outcome 8.6 |
| **8.18** A home health client has multiple sclerosis. In the last 6 months, his condition has deteriorated significantly. The home health nurse is concerned about the spouse experiencing caregiver role strain. Which of the following, if present, would the nurse expect to see or hear if this could be the situation? (Select all that apply.)<br>_____ The home appears more unkempt and cluttered.<br>_____ The spouse expresses feelings of anger.<br>_____ The spouse reports decreased energy.<br>_____ The spouse reports that she is learning how to manage finances. | Answer:<br>\_\_\_\_x\_\_\_\_ The home appears more unkempt and cluttered.<br>\_\_\_\_x\_\_\_\_ The spouse expresses feelings of anger.<br>\_\_\_\_x\_\_\_\_ The spouse reports decreased energy.<br>_____ The spouse reports that she is learning how to manage finances.<br>Rationale: Caregiver role strain occurs when caregivers experience physical, emotional, social, and financial burdens that can seriously jeopardize their own health and well-being. Signs of caregiver overload or strain include those identified in the answer as well as difficulty performing routine tasks for the client; concerns that the caregiver's responsibilities interfere with other roles as parent, spouse, worker, and friend; anxiety about meeting future needs of the client; and feelings of depression. Learning how to manage finances is a positive statement and would not indicate strain.<br>Assessment<br>Psychosocial integrity<br>Application<br>Learning Outcome 8.7 |
| **8.19** After completing the initial assessment, the nurse is able to identify the client's teaching needs as well as the support system in the home environment. The main reason that education is a common intervention in the home care setting is related to:<br>  1. Lack of knowledge related to health conditions and self-care.<br>  2. The fact that there is little time to complete education in the acute care setting. | Answer: 1<br>Rationale: One of the most common health issues that nurses address with clients in home care settings is lack of knowledge related to health conditions and self-care. Client education is considered a skill reimbursed by Medicare. Not all home care clients come from acute care, and education is still implemented in this setting. Not all home clients are willing or ready to learn, even though they are in their own home environment.<br>Evaluation<br>Health promotion and maintenance<br>Application<br>Learning Outcome 8.5 |

3. The fact that teaching someone who is willing to learn is easier in the home.
4. The need for reimbursement for education by Medicare.

---

**8.20** An elderly client is being discharged home after a short illness and stay in acute care. The physician has written an order for home health follow-up. In order to better understand the need for any assistive devices, when should the home health nurse make an assessment?
1. At the initial home visit, in order to see the client in the home environment
2. While the client is still in the hospital
3. After the client has been home a few days and can help the nurse decide what is needed
4. When the spouse is available to assist

Answer: 2
Rationale: Assessment for the elderly client being discharged to home health should be initiated while the client is in the hospital to determine the need for assistive devices or environmental changes before the client returns home. Once the client is at home, the need for the devices will be immediate and the client may have to wait unnecessarily for the required items. Waiting a few days or until the spouse is able to help is a delay that is not beneficial for the client who requires these items upon arriving home.
Assessment
Health promotion and maintenance
Application
Learning Outcome 8.5

---

**8.21** Once the client has been receiving home care for a period of time, the nurse is able to evaluate the effectiveness of the education and interventions provided. The responsibility for assurance that the client is receiving prescribed therapy at the appropriate times belongs to which of the following?
1. Client
2. Nurse
3. Physician
4. Client's spouse

Answer: 2
Rationale: Even though the client and family may become independent in self-care skills, the home health nurse still has the ultimate responsibility to ensure that the client is receiving the prescribed therapy at the appropriate timed intervals. On subsequent home visits, the nurse observes the same parameters assessed on the initial visit.
Implementation
Safe, effective care environment
Application
Learning Outcome 8.4

---

# CHAPTER 9

**9.1** A nursing student is doing clinicals at a hospital implementing a new computer system. Trying to generalize the information is key, since the student nurse plans to move after graduation. This is due to the fact that:
1. Each hospital will have its own system.
2. Facilities never use the same computer system.
3. Computer standards change routinely.
4. Students are not expected to know all the details of a computer system.

Answer: 3
Rationale: All nurses must have a basic level of computer literacy in order to perform their jobs. Although facilities may utilize the same computer program, it will be customized to each individual facility. Students are expected to know the basic terminology and function of hospital or facility computer systems, but the science of computers changes so quickly that keeping an open mind about change is extremely important.
Implementation
Safe, effective care environment
Application
Learning Outcome 9.2

---

**9.2** A nurse manager is responsible for scheduling the staff of all units in a critical care hospital. Which of the following programs would work best for computer scheduling?

Answer: 4
Rationale: Spreadsheets are programs that can manipulate numbers. Data are arranged in columns and rows. Spreadsheets are used for budgets and are useful for working with staffing, scheduling, invoicing, research, and other analyses. A database is used to manage detailed information.

---

| | |
|---|---|
| 1. Database<br>2. Word processing<br>3. Graphics program<br>4. Spreadsheet | Word processing is one of the most commonly used computer applications. Documents are checked for spelling and grammar, and individualized to include pictures, charts, and designs. Graphics programs have become popular with their ability to create charts, tables, and pictures.<br>Assessment<br>Safe, effective care environment<br>Application<br>Learning Outcome 9.2 |
| **9.3** A client asks the nurse about her medications and tells the nurse she has been investigating on the Internet. The nurse's best response to this is:<br>1. "I'm glad you're interested in your therapy."<br>2. "Information on the Internet cannot be trusted. You should check with your pharmacist."<br>3. "Your physician is the one you should be asking these kinds of questions."<br>4. "Let's look at some of the sites you've been visiting." | Answer: 4<br>Rationale: Thousands of health-related sites exist on the Internet, new ones occurring daily. There are no controls to ensure that information provided on these sites is accurate. Therefore, the nurse should help the client find reliable and accurate information. Clients are involved consumers. Wanting more information about their medications, disease processes, and treatment options is taking a proactive approach to their care. It is appropriate to ask questions and seek information at a variety of sources. However, nurses must assist clients in making sure the information they gather is credible and accurate.<br>Implementation<br>Health promotion and maintenance<br>Application<br>Learning Outcome 9.3 |
| **9.4** Nursing students are participating in an online delivery course in their nursing program. For their next assignment, they are to evaluate nursing research articles for credibility and reliability. One of the best databases to search for these articles would be which of the following?<br>1. CINAHL<br>2. Google<br>3. ERIC<br>4. PsychINFO | Answer: 1<br>Rationale: The Cumulative Index to Nursing and Allied Health Literature (CINAHL) focuses on nursing and allied health articles, including research. In this database, the user can search systematically for articles that are related to nursing research, peer reviewed, published, and so on. Google search engine gives a variety of sites, both health-related and non-health-related, but there are no restrictions for accuracy with this database. Educational Resources Information Center (ERIC) would include all areas of academia, not just nursing. PsychINFO includes only psychological abstracts.<br>Assessment<br>Health promotion and maintenance<br>Application<br>Learning Outcome 9.3 |
| **9.5** A small nursing program has limited access to clinical sites, especially those that might contain specialty areas (cardiac intensive care, neonatal intensive care, trauma/neuro intensive care, etc.). Which of the following might be an alternative option for nurse educators to allow their students "hands-on" simulated clinical experience in these areas?<br>1. A field trip to a larger city<br>2. Videos<br>3. CAI<br>4. Workbook with written study guides | Answer: 3<br>Rationale: Computer-assisted instruction (CAI) helps students as well as nurses learn and demonstrate learning. Programs cover topics from drug dosage calculations to ethical decision making, drill and practice, simulation, and testing. CAI simulations can provide a virtual experience for the student through a computer program. Taking field trips is a great idea, but may not be economically feasible. Videos also provide instruction, but not simulation. Written study guides allow for learning, but not "hands-on" experience.<br>Implementation<br>Safe, effective care environment<br>Application<br>Learning Outcome 9.3 |
| **9.6** A nursing student is able to continue studies while visiting abroad. This student's nursing program has implemented which of the following to make this possible?<br>1. Classroom technology<br>2. Distance learning | Answer: 2<br>Rationale: Distance learning is a model to deliver information and class sessions via audio or video transmission. The use of computers is required to offer this type of delivery in education. Classroom technology is just one piece of distance learning. Computer-assisted instruction (CAI) is a method to allow for practice and simulation via CD-ROM. Nursing informatics is the science of using computer |

| | |
|---|---|
| 3. CAI<br>4. Informatics | information systems in the practice of nursing, not necessarily the education of nursing.<br>Implementation<br>Safe, effective care environment<br>Application<br>Learning Outcome 9.3 |
| **9.7** A nurse educator has taught the same courses for the past 5 years and each year implements a few minor changes. Over this time, the educator has stored the grade data, including homework and assignment scores, in order to track trends following the implemented changes. This educator is utilizing which of the following?<br>1. Informatics<br>2. Student record management<br>3. Data warehousing<br>4. MIS | Answer: 3<br>Rationale: Data warehousing is the accumulation of large amounts of data that are stored over time and can be examined for output in different types of reports (charts and tables). Informatics is the use of computer technology in nursing practice. Student and course record management are programs that help maintain results of students' grades or attendance using spreadsheets. MIS (management information system) is designed to facilitate the organization and application of data used to manage an organization or department.<br>Implementation<br>Safe, effective care environment<br>Application<br>Learning Outcome 9.3 |
| **9.8** Electronic client data that can be retrieved by caregivers, administrators, and accreditors have the ability to improve health care by which of the following? (Select all that apply.)<br>_____ Ability to monitor quality<br>_____ Access warehoused data (stored data)<br>_____ Possess greater security of client records<br>_____ Constant availability of client health information<br>_____ Ability for clients to share in knowledge and activities influencing their health | Answer:<br>\_\_\_\_x\_\_\_\_ Ability to monitor quality<br>\_\_\_\_x\_\_\_\_ Access warehoused data (stored data)<br>_____ Possess greater security of client records<br>\_\_\_\_x\_\_\_\_ Constant availability of client health information<br>\_\_\_\_x\_\_\_\_ Ability for clients to share in knowledge and activities influencing their health<br>Rationale: Security concerns are the major drawback for computerizing health care and storing client records. However, the Computer-Based Patient Record Institute identified these four ways that CPR (computer-based patient records) could improve health care.<br>Assessment<br>Safe, effective care environment<br>Application<br>Learning Outcome 9.4 |
| **9.9** A client in a health care facility asks the nurse about the facility's computerized system for keeping client information, especially confidentiality issues. Which is the best response by the nurse?<br>1. "Don't worry, your information is always safe."<br>2. "Information in our system requires a password to retrieve."<br>3. "Our system was designed with a lot of input from nursing staff."<br>4. "I can see why you're worried, with all the computer hackers out there these days." | Answer: 2<br>Rationale: Maintaining privacy and security of data is a significant issue. One way that computers can protect data is by the use of passwords—only those persons who have a legitimate need to access the data receive the password. Information in a computer data system may not always be safe, and it would be inappropriate for the nurse to say this. Nurses need to be involved with the design, implementation, and evaluation of client-based patient records (CPRs) to maximize their use and effectiveness, but this does not ensure security. Reminding the client that there is indeed cause for privacy concerns is not as therapeutic as explaining that the system requires a password.<br>Implementation<br>Psychosocial integrity<br>Analysis<br>Learning Outcome 9.4 |
| **9.10** Standard classification of terms used in health care, particularly nursing data, along with definitions would greatly benefit computer-based patient records. Which of the following are among those systems used in the United States? (Select all that apply.)<br>_____ HIPAA<br>_____ NIC | Answer:<br>_____ HIPAA<br>\_\_\_\_x\_\_\_\_ NIC<br>\_\_\_\_x\_\_\_\_ NANDA<br>\_\_\_\_x\_\_\_\_ The Omaha system<br>\_\_\_\_x\_\_\_\_ HHCC<br>\_\_\_\_x\_\_\_\_ NOC<br>_____ ANA<br>_____ ICN |

| | |
|---|---|
| _____ NANDA<br>_____ The Omaha system<br>_____ HHCC<br>_____ NOC<br>_____ ANA<br>_____ ICN | Rationale: HIPAA is a piece of legislation that increased privacy access to health records. The ANA has a position statement on privacy, confidentiality of medical records, and the nurse's role, but it is not one of the classification systems used in the United States. The ICN has proposed an International Classification for Nursing Practice, but it may take years to determine which standards will allow optimal access to and manipulation of computerized records.<br>Assessment<br>Safe, effective care environment<br>Application<br>Learning Outcome 9.4 |

# CHAPTER 10

| | |
|---|---|
| **10.1** Nurses must use critical thinking in their day-to-day practice, especially in circumstances surrounding client care and wise use of resources. In which of the following situations would critical thinking be most beneficial?<br>1. Administering IV push meds to critically ill clients<br>2. Educating a home health client about treatment options<br>3. Teaching new parents car seat safety<br>4. Assisting an orthopedic client with the proper use of crutches | Answer: 2<br>Rationale: Nurses who utilize good critical-thinking skills are able to think and act in areas where there are neither clear answers nor standard procedures. Treatment options, especially for the home health client, can be extensive. There are many points to consider (good and bad), and choosing between treatment options can cause conflict among family members. The nurse in this case must use creativity, analysis based on science, and problem-solving skills—all of which contribute to critical-thinking skills. Administering IV meds (even to critically ill clients), teaching correct use of crutches, and teaching new parents about car seat safety do not require as much reasoning. There are standard procedures to follow and, most of the time, clear answers about the rationale.<br>Implementation<br>Health promotion and maintenance<br>Analysis<br>Learning Outcome 10.2 |
| **10.2** A rehab client has orders for active range of motion exercises to her shoulder following a stroke. The client doesn't like to do these because they are uncomfortable and she can't understand "what good they will do anyway." Which of the following statements by the nurse demonstrates the critical-thinking component of creativity?<br>1. "You'll only get worse if you don't do these exercises."<br>2. "As soon as you get these into your routine, you'll feel better."<br>3. "Your physician wouldn't have ordered these if they weren't important."<br>4. "Here's a marker. See how many circles you can make on this board in 10 minutes." | Answer: 4<br>Rationale: Making the exercise routine into something more—like a game, or drawing a picture, or even "decorating the walls," for example—would raise a challenge to the client, take the focus off the *why,* and still achieve the end result. Explaining the rationale for doing or not doing the exercises is not using creativity. It is merely explaining the reason.<br>Implementation<br>Physiologic integrity<br>Analysis<br>Learning Outcome 10.4 |
| **10.3** A student nurse who claims to be very *un*creative doesn't understand why it is necessary to learn and develop new ideas in the clinical area. The best response by the nurse educator is:<br>1. "Creativity allows unique solutions to unique problems."<br>2. "Not all your answers are going to be from your textbook."<br>3. "Creativity makes nursing more fun." | Answer: 1<br>Rationale: Creativity is thinking that results in the development of new ideas and products and is the ability to develop and implement new and better solutions. When nurses incorporate creativity into their thinking, they are able to find unique solutions to unique problems. Creativity does make the nurse look beyond the answers found in the text, but it also brings originality and individuality to nursing. The other options listed are not really explaining the best reason creativity is a major component to critical thinking.<br>Implementation<br>Health promotion and maintenance |

| | |
|---|---|
| 4. "You'll get bored if you don't learn to be creative." | Analysis<br>Learning Outcome 10.1 |
| **10.4** A nurse educator assigned students an activity to implement Socratic questioning in their daily lives. Which of the following is a question about reason using this technique?<br>　1. "What makes you think cramming for a test is an ineffective way to study?"<br>　2. "What other ways of studying could you implement?"<br>　3. "If you didn't study for your test, what is the probability you will fail?"<br>　4. "If you study all the unit outcomes, what effect will that have?" | Answer: 1<br>Rationale: Socratic questioning is a technique one can use to look beneath the surface, recognize and examine assumptions, search for inconsistencies, examine multiple points of view, and differentiate what one knows from what one merely believes. Questions about evidence and reason focus on just that (e.g., what evidence is there, how do you know, what would change your mind). Asking about ways to study would be a question about the problem (studying). Asking about the effects of studying is questioning about implications and consequences.<br>Evaluation<br>Health promotion and maintenance<br>Analysis<br>Learning Outcome 10.1 |
| **10.5** A client comes into the emergency department (ED) with a productive cough, audible coarse crackles, elevated temperature of 102.3°F, chills, and body aches. The nurse identifies the problem as respiratory compromise. The nurse is using which of the following?<br>　1. Deductive reasoning<br>　2. Inductive reasoning<br>　3. Socratic questioning<br>　4. Critical analysis | Answer: 1<br>Rationale: Deductive reasoning is reasoning from the general to the specific. The nurse starts with a framework and makes descriptive interpretations of the client's condition in relation to the framework. Productive cough, crackles, fever, and chills all point to problems with respiratory status. Inductive reasoning would be making a generalization from a set of facts or observation. In this case, the nurse using inductive reasoning could presume that the client has bronchitis or a bacterial respiratory infection. Socratic questioning is a technique of critical analysis, looking beneath the surface and asking questions to come to a conclusion about the situation.<br>Evaluation<br>Physiologic integrity<br>Analysis<br>Learning Outcome 10.1 |
| **10.6** A nurse is taking a health history from a client who states that he has been to numerous physicians and has had a lot of laboratory tests (all of which were abnormal) and exploratory surgery, but no one is able to explain the etiology of his problem. The client also states that he has a PhD in epidemiology and he has a rare form of a neurological disorder. The nurse who utilizes critical thinking will make this statement:<br>　1. "Why don't you just tell your physician what you think you have?"<br>　2. "Did you bring your prior tests and results with you, so we don't repeat anything?"<br>　3. "If you know what you have, what do you want from us?"<br>　4. "Describe what tests you've had and explain the symptoms of this disorder." | Answer: 4<br>Rationale: In critical thinking, the nurse also differentiates statements of fact, inference, judgment, and opinion. The nurse will have to ascertain the accuracy of information and evaluate the credibility of the information sources. "Why" questions make clients very defensive. Asking a "yes/no" question offers little other information. Asking the client what he wants does not help to find out more information about the client's situation or prior history.<br>Implementation<br>Physiologic integrity<br>Application<br>Learning Outcome 10.4 |

| | |
|---|---|
| **10.7** Critical-thinking nurses must develop which of the following specific attitudes or traits? (Select all that apply.)<br><br>_____ Independence<br>_____ Egocentricity<br>_____ Intellectual humility<br>_____ Fair-mindedness<br>_____ Acceptance of rituals<br>_____ Perseverance<br>_____ Confidence | Answer:<br><br>\_\_\_\_x\_\_\_\_ Independence<br>_____ Egocentricity<br>\_\_\_\_x\_\_\_\_ Intellectual humility<br>\_\_\_\_x\_\_\_\_ Fair-mindedness<br>_____ Acceptance of rituals<br>\_\_\_\_x\_\_\_\_ Perseverance<br>\_\_\_\_x\_\_\_\_ Confidence<br>Rationale: Attitudes that foster critical thinking include independence, fair-mindedness, *insight into* egocentricity (which is open to the possibility that biases or social pressures and customs may affect one's thinking), intellectual humility, intellectual courage to *challenge* (not accept) the status quo and rituals, integrity, perseverance, confidence, and curiosity.<br>Assessment<br>Psychosocial integrity<br>Application<br>Learning Outcome 10.1 |
| **10.8** A nurse educator has always believed that lectures with focused outlines are the best way to present theory content in class. A colleague who teaches the same group of students, but a different subject, utilizes group work and in-class activities to teach difficult content and finds that students perform as well, or better, on their tests. The first educator in this situation is starting to rethink her position. This is an example of which of the following?<br><br>1. Integrity<br>2. Perseverance<br>3. Fair-mindedness<br>4. Humility | Answer: 1<br>Rationale: Intellectual integrity requires that individuals apply the same rigorous standards of proof to their own knowledge and beliefs as they apply to the knowledge and beliefs of others. Trying new teaching techniques in the hope that students might respond positively shows that the first educator is willing to question her own practices, just as she would question those of another. Perseverance is determination that enables critical thinkers to clarify concepts and sort out related issues, in spite of difficulties and frustrations. Fair-mindedness is assessing all viewpoints with the same standards and not basing judgments on personal or group bias or prejudice. Intellectual humility means having an awareness of the limits of one's own knowledge. Critical thinkers are willing to admit what they do not know, seek new information, and rethink their conclusions in light of new knowledge.<br>Implementation<br>Safe, effective care environment<br>Application<br>Learning Outcome 10.1 |
| **10.9** A nurse who just moved from an urban area to a sparsely populated rural area understands that certain customs and practices the nurse is familiar with may be quite foreign to the people in the new area. This nurse is practicing which of the attitudes of critical thinking?<br><br>1. Fair-mindedness<br>2. Insight into egocentricity<br>3. Intellectual humility<br>4. Intellectual courage to challenge the status quo and rituals | Answer: 2<br>Rationale: Critical thinkers are open to the possibility that their personal biases or social pressures and customs could unduly affect their thinking. They actively try to examine their own biases and bring them to awareness each time they make a decision. Understanding that how things were done and what practices were common may be completely different in the new surroundings is an example of the nurse implementing this attitude. Fair-mindedness means assessing all viewpoints with the same standards and not basing judgments on personal or group bias or prejudice. Intellectual humility means having an awareness of the limits of one's own knowledge. Intellectual courage to challenge the status quo and rituals is taking a fair examination of one's own ideas or views, especially those to which one may have a strongly negative reaction.<br>Evaluation<br>Safe, effective care environment<br>Analysis<br>Learning Outcome 10.1 |
| **10.10** A new graduate nurse learns a quicker way to set up and initiate an IV. This graduate nurse still follows safe practice, but implements changes that help with time management. This nurse is practicing which of the attitudes of critical thinking? | Answer: 1<br>Rationale: Nurses who can think for themselves and consider different methods of performing technical skills—not just the way they may have been taught in school—develop an attitude of independence. Courage to challenge the status quo comes from recognizing that sometimes beliefs are false or misleading. Integrity requires that individuals apply the same rigorous standards of proof to their own knowledge and beliefs. Critical thinkers |

1. Independence
2. Intellectual courage to challenge the status quo or rituals
3. Integrity
4. Confidence

believe that well-reasoned thinking will lead to trustworthy conclusions. They cultivate an attitude of confidence in the reasoning process and examine emotion-laden arguments using the standards for evaluating thought.
Evaluation
Safe, effective care environment
Analysis
Learning Outcome 10.1

---

**10.11** A nurse continues to question the practice of administering rectal suppositories to residents in a long-term care facility at bedtime, rather than earlier in the day. When told that this is the best time for staff and that's the routine that has been practiced for a long time, the nurse continues to research whether there would be a better time, especially in the best interest of the residents. This nurse is practicing which of the critical-thinking attitudes?
1. Confidence
2. Perseverance
3. Curiosity
4. Integrity

Answer: 3
Rationale: The internal conversation going on within the mind of a critical thinker is filled with questions. The curious nurse may value tradition but is not afraid to examine traditions to be sure they are still valid, as in this case. This nurse is asking valid questions. Confidence comes from cultivating reasoning and examining arguments. In this case, the nurse did not reason anything out, but is still asking questions. Perseverance happens from determination in clarifying concepts and sorting out related issues, in spite of difficulties and frustrations. This nurse is still asking questions, not making any changes in spite of difficulties or frustrations. Integrity requires that individuals apply the same rigorous standards of proof to their own knowledge and beliefs as they apply to the knowledge and beliefs of others.
Implementation
Physiologic integrity
Application
Learning Outcome 10.1

---

**10.12** A nurse is learning how to operate a new ventilator that the hospital is considering to purchase. Many of the functions available on the old model are also available on the new, and the setup is quite similar between the two machines. In this case, the nurse is utilizing a _____ order of critical-thinking skill.

Answer: lower
Rationale: Psychomotor skills in nursing often involve minimal thinking, such as operating a familiar piece of equipment or, in this case, a newer model of a familiar piece of equipment. Higher order skills of critical thinking are put into play as soon as a new idea is encountered or a less-than-routine decision must be made.
Implementation
Safe, effective care environment
Application
Learning Outcome 10.1

---

**10.13** A seasoned nurse works in a busy ICU unit. When a particularly complex client is admitted, the nurse uses past experiences and knowledge gained from those situations to help care for this client. The nurse is fully aware that in the future, an even more complex case may be in the workload. This nurse is practicing which of the attributes of critical thinking?
1. Reflection
2. Context
3. Dialogue
4. Time

Answer: 4
Rationale: The attribute of time emphasizes the value of using past learning in current situations that then guide future actions. Reflection involves being able to determine what data are relevant and to make connections between that data and the decisions reached. Context is an essential consideration in nursing since care must always be individualized, taking knowledge and applying it to real people.
Implementation
Safe, effective care environment
Analysis
Learning Outcome 10.1

---

**10.14** A nurse is taking an admission history from a client who is easily distracted and offers much information about his health and social history. Although careful to document what the client relates, the nurse sorts out the relevant data to determine the best nursing care for this client. This nurse is practicing which attribute of critical thinking?

Answer: 1
Rationale: Reflection involves being able to determine what data are relevant and to make connections between that data and the decisions reached. Context is an essential consideration in nursing since care must always be individualized, taking knowledge and applying it to real people. Dialogue, which need not involve other persons, refers to the process of serving as both teacher and student in learning from situations. Time emphasizes the value of using past learning in current situations that then guide future actions.

---

| | |
|---|---|
| 1. Reflection<br>2. Context<br>3. Dialogue<br>4. Time | Implementation<br>Safe, effective care environment<br>Analysis<br>Learning Outcome 10.1 |

**10.15** A client has just been admitted, is complaining of shortness of breath, has no pallor, no cyanosis, and no accessory muscle use with respirations. The client's respiratory rate is 16 breaths per minute. The nurse is performing the assessment and continues to ask herself how the client's report and the physical findings conflict. This nurse is using which universal standard of critical thinking?

1. Clarity
2. Accuracy
3. Logicalness
4. Significance

Answer: 3
Rationale: Logicalness would ask if the report follows from the evidence. In this case, it does not. However, the nurse is still questioning which shows she is engaged in critically thinking through the situation. Clarity provides examples. Accuracy is asking if something is true. Significance is prioritizing the facts.
Assessment
Physiologic integrity
Application
Learning Outcome 10.3

**10.16** A nurse enters the room of a critically ill child and has a sense that "something" isn't right. After performing an initial physical assessment and finding that the child is stable, the nurse continues to perform a check of all the lines and equipment in the room and finds that the last IV solution hung by the previous nurse was not the correct solution. This nurse was utilizing which method of problem solving?

1. Trial and error
2. Intuition
3. Judgment
4. Scientific method

Answer: 2
Rationale: Intuition is the understanding or learning of things without the conscious use of reasoning. It is also known as sixth sense, hunch, instinct, feeling, or suspicion. Clinical experience allows the nurse to recognize cues and patterns and begin to reach correct conclusions using intuition. Finding no cause for concern in the physical assessment of the client, the nurse is not satisfied and continues to assess the client's surroundings, finding the error. Trial and error is solving problems through a number of approaches until a solution is found. Judgment is not part of problem solving. The scientific method requires that the nurse evaluate potential solutions to a given problem in an organized, formal, and systematic approach.
Implementation
Safe, effective care environment
Analysis
Learning Outcome 10.3

**10.17** A client has had a nonhealing wound for a period of time. The home health nurse decides to implement a variety of wound care products to see if any of them work. Each day, the nurse switches to a different brand or product. In this situation, the nurse is utilizing which method of problem solving?

1. Intuition
2. Scientific method
3. Research process
4. Trial and error

Answer: 4
Rationale: Trial and error is solving problems by utilizing a number of approaches. Trial-and-error methods can be dangerous in nursing because the client might suffer harm if an approach is inappropriate. In this case, the client may not suffer harm, but there will be no way to know if one product used is effective since the nurse is changing them on a daily basis. Intuition is the learning of things without conscious use of reasoning—also known as the sixth sense, hunch, or instinct. Scientific method and research process are both formalized, systematic, and logical approaches to solving problems.
Implementation
Physiologic integrity
Analysis
Learning Outcome 10.3

**10.18** A nurse is caring for a client who has unstable cardiac dysrhythmias. The client has orders for medications, one of which is by oral route, the other by IV delivery. The nurse realizes that the IV route would be fastest, but is also concerned about the side effects that this drug may produce and the fact that the client has never taken the drug, so

Answer: 2
Rationale: In this step, the decision maker (nurse) identifies possible ways to meet the criteria. Alternatives considered are which route to give a certain medication: IV versus oral. The nurse is utilizing his experience, taking what he knows about cardiac problems and pharmacology, and will make a selection based on that information. Identifying the purpose, in this case, would be determining that the client needs intervention to control the dysrhythmia. Projecting is when the nurse applies creative thinking and skepticism to determine what might go wrong as a result of a decision and develops plans to

any adverse effect is unknown. The nurse is implementing which step of the decision-making process?
1. Identify the purpose
2. Seek alternatives
3. Project
4. Implement

prevent, minimize, or overcome any problems. Implementation is taking the plan into action.
Assessment
Physiologic integrity
Application
Learning Outcome 10.3

---

**10.19** A nurse is checking over the past charting of the previous shift, paying special attention to how a particular client responded to nursing interventions throughout the day. The nurse is caring for this client and wants to see what has been effective, as well as what didn't work. This nurse is utilizing which of the steps of the decision-making process?
1. Set the criteria
2. Examine alternatives
3. Implement
4. Evaluate the outcome

Answer: 4
Rationale: In evaluating, the nurse determines the effectiveness of the plan and whether the initial purpose was achieved. In this situation, the nurse wants to determine what worked on the previous shift and what didn't. This will help with deciding on interventions for the client during the shift. Setting criteria is based on three questions: What is the desired outcome? What needs to be preserved? What needs to be avoided? Examining alternatives ensures that there is an objective rationale in relation to the established criteria for choosing one strategy over another. In this case, the nurse is evaluating the previous nurse's alternatives, not choosing new ones. Implementation is putting a plan into action.
Evaluation
Safe, effective care environment
Analysis
Learning Outcome 10.3

---

**10.20** A nurse is being questioned by the parents of a client whose physician ordered a battery of invasive tests. They are wondering why their child should have to go through all the pain and discomfort of these studies. The nurse is not familiar with the situation and has just come on duty for the evening shift. A limited report was given by the previous shift. The nurse understands that the child is stable at this time and has no pain, but the nurse has not been able to review the chart or do an initial assessment at this point. The best response by the nurse is:
1. "I'm not sure I can answer your question just now."
2. "It's a good idea to listen to what your physician wants."
3. "Your child's doctor is the best there is. I don't see why you wouldn't follow his advice."
4. "Maybe you should get another opinion if you're not comfortable with your doctor."

Answer: 1
Rationale: Suspending judgment means tolerating ambiguity for a time. If an issue is complex it may not be resolved quickly and judgment should be postponed. In this case, the nurse just doesn't have enough information to give a good answer to the parents. For a while, the nurse will need to say, "I don't know" and be comfortable with that answer. Telling the parents to agree with the physician before the nurse knows all the facts might be premature, even if he is the best physician in the area. It would also be premature to tell the parents to get another opinion. Nurses should not give advice or counsel, merely information.
Evaluation
Safe, effective care environment
Analysis
Learning Outcome 10.4

---

**10.21** A client comes into the clinic with complaints of "extreme" low back pain after helping to move a heavy object. The client is pale and diaphoretic and walks bent at the waist. Before taking vital signs, the nurse projects that the blood pressure as well as heart rate will be elevated. This is an example of which of the following?
1. Fact
2. Inference
3. Judgment
4. Opinion

Answer: 2
Rationale: Inferences are conclusions drawn from facts, going beyond facts to make a statement about something that is not currently known. In this case, acute, severe pain will most likely cause the blood pressure as well as pulse rate to be elevated as the body's response to the painful experience. Fact can be verified through investigation. In this case, fact would be the elevated pulse and blood pressure readings. Judgment is evaluating facts and information that reflect values or other criteria; it is a type of opinion. Because the nurse understands the pathophysiology of pain, thinking about changes in vital signs is more than a judgment—it is an inference. Opinions are beliefs formed over time and include judgments that may fit facts or be in error.

---

Assessment
Physiologic integrity
Application
Learning Outcome 10.1

**10.22** A nurse is completing a plan of care for a client. The statement "client will be able to walk 10 feet, twice a day without shortness of breath" is which part of the nursing process (in comparison to the decision-making process)?
1. Assess
2. Diagnose
3. Plan
4. Evaluate

Answer: 3
Rationale: The planning portion of the nursing process involves setting criteria (walking 10 feet twice a day), weighting the criteria, and seeking/examining alternatives when compared to the decision-making process. Assessment is the same as identifying the purpose. Diagnosing is putting a label on the problem. Evaluating is reviewing the outcome.
Implementation
Physiologic integrity
Application
Learning Outcome 10.3

**10.23** A nurse is caring for a client of a different culture. The nurse is not familiar with the customs of this particular client and becomes disturbed when the client's spouse makes all the decisions about care and treatments. The nurse's reaction is an example of which of the following?
1. Inference
2. Judgment
3. Opinion
4. Evaluation

Answer: 3
Rationale: Opinions are beliefs formed over time and include judgments that may fit facts or be in error. In this case, the nurse may not understand that culturally, this may be very appropriate and fitting for this client. If this is the case, the nurse should not become disturbed by the spouse's attention. Inferences are conclusions drawn from the facts, going beyond facts to make a statement about something not currently known. Judgment is an evaluation of facts or information that reflects values or other criteria; it is a type of opinion. Evaluation is considering the results or outcome.
Assessment
Safe, effective care environment
Application
Learning Outcome 10.1

**10.24** Before beginning a particularly stressful shift in a critical care nursery, a nurse is in the practice of reviewing his attitudes and feelings about death and dying, dignity of people, and the parental role in understanding and questioning cares and treatments. This nurse is cultivating which of the following?
1. Critical-thinking attitudes
2. Dissonance
3. Ambiguity
4. Self-assessment

Answer: 4
Rationale: Nurses are in and around situations that require attitudes of curiosity, fair-mindedness, humility, courage, and perseverance. They need attitudes that foster critical thinking. A rigorous personal assessment may help determine what attitudes a nurse already possesses and which need to be cultivated. Identifying weak or vulnerable attitudes and reflecting on situations where decisions were made and then later regretted helps to assess the nurse's own biases and perceptions.
Assessment
Safe, effective care environment
Application
Learning Outcome 10.2

**10.25** A nurse educator senses that a student has been struggling with clinical skills learned in lab. In the clinical area, this student is usually lagging behind and seems to be involved when the other students have opportunities to perform some of the tasks. The educator pairs the student with a particularly outgoing staff nurse who has a number of unique clients with a variety of treatments and cares. The educator is utilizing which type of problem solving?
1. Trial and error
2. Intuition
3. Research process
4. Experience

Answer: 2
Rationale: Intuition is the understanding or learning of things without the conscious use of reasoning. It is also known as the sixth sense, hunch, instinct, feeling, or suspicion. In this case, the educator has a sense that the student is struggling, though there are no real facts to support it. Experience is part of intuition, but by itself, not a particular way to problem solve. Trial and error uses a number of approaches until a solution is found, which is not the case here. Trial-and-error methods in nursing care can be dangerous because the client might suffer harm if an approach is inappropriate. The research process is a systematic, analytical, and logical way to problem solve.
Implementation
Safe, effective care environment
Analysis
Learning Outcome 10.3

**11.1** When learning how to implement the nursing process into a plan of care for a client, the student nurse realizes that part of the purpose of the nursing process is to:

1. Deliver care to a client in an organized way.
2. Implement a plan that is close to the medical model.
3. Identify client needs and deliver care to meet those needs.
4. Make sure that standardized care is available to clients.

Answer: 3
Rationale: The purpose of the nursing process is to identify a client's health status and actual or potential health care problems or needs, to establish plans to meet the identified needs, and to deliver specific nursing interventions to meet those needs. Delivery or organized care is not part of the nursing process, though each phase is interrelated. The nursing process is not part of the medical model as nurses treat the client's *response* to the disease or problem. The nursing process is individualized for each client's care plan. It is not about standardizing care.
Implementation
Health promotion and maintenance
Application
Learning Outcome 11.2

---

**11.2** The nurse is performing a dressing change for a client and notices that there is a new area of skin breakdown near the site of the dressing. On closer examination, it appears to be caused from the tape used to secure the dressing. This would be an example of which phase of the nursing process?

1. Assessment
2. Diagnosis
3. Implementation
4. Evaluation

Answer: 1
Rationale: Assessment is the collection, organization, validation, and documentation of data. Assessment is carried throughout the nursing process, as in this case. Even though performing the dressing change is implementation, noticing the new skin breakdown is assessment. Diagnosis is identifying the client's response to the problem. Implementation is what the nurse does to help the client reach a goal, and then the goal is evaluated.
Assessment
Physiologic integrity
Application
Learning Outcome 11.1

---

**11.3** A nurse is performing an initial assessment on a new admission. Which of the following is part of the database? (Select all that apply.)

_____ Reports from physical therapy the client received as an outpatient
_____ Documentation of the nurse's physical assessment
_____ Physician's orders
_____ A list of current medications
_____ Information about the client's cultural preferences
_____ Discharge instructions

Answer:

___x___ Reports from physical therapy the client received as an outpatient
___x___ Documentation of the nurse's physical assessment
_____ Physician's orders
___x___ A list of current medications
___x___ Information about the client's cultural preferences
_____ Discharge instructions

Rationale: The database is all the information about a client. It includes the nursing health history, physical assessment, the physician's history and physical examination, results of laboratory and diagnostic tests, and material contributed by other health personnel. It would not include the physician's orders for this admission, nor would it include discharge instructions.
Assessment
Safe, effective care environment
Application
Learning Outcome 11.4

---

**11.4** The nurse is taking information for the client's database. The client is not very talkative; is pale, diaphoretic, and restless in the bed; and tells the nurse to just "leave me alone." Which of the following is subjective data?

1. Restlessness
2. "Leave me alone"
3. Not talkative
4. Pale and diaphoretic

Answer: 2
Rationale: Subjective data can be described or verified only by that person and are apparent only to the person affected. Subjective data include the client's sensations, feelings, beliefs, attitudes, and perceptions of personal health status and life situations. Restlessness, not being talkative, and paleness with diaphoresis are what the nurse is observing.
Assessment
Physiologic integrity
Application
Learning Outcome 11.5

---

| | |
|---|---|
| **11.5** The nurse is collecting information from a client's family. The client is confused and not able to contribute to the conversation. The spouse states, "This is not his normal behavior." The nurse documents this as which of the following?<br>　1. Inference<br>　2. Subjective data<br>　3. Objective data<br>　4. Secondary subjective data | Answer: 3<br>Rationale: Information supplied by family members, significant others, or other health professionals is considered subjective if it is not based on fact. Since this information is factual, in that the spouse is able to provide the nurse with information about the client's routine behavior and patterns, that is objective data. Inference is making a judgment.<br>Assessment<br>Psychosocial integrity<br>Application<br>Learning Outcome 11.5 |
| **11.6** A nurse is providing a back rub to a client just after administering a pain medication, with the hope that these two actions will help decrease the client's pain. Which phase of the nursing process is this nurse implementing?<br>　1. Assessment<br>　2. Diagnosis<br>　3. Implementation<br>　4. Evaluation | Answer: 3<br>Rationale: Implementation is that part of the nursing process in which the nurse applies knowledge to perform interventions. Assessment is gathering data. Diagnosis is identifying patterns and making inferences. Evaluation is making criterion-based evaluations.<br>Implementation<br>Physiologic integrity<br>Application<br>Learning Outcome 11.1 |
| **11.7** A nurse has just been informed that a new admission is coming to the unit. According to the 2005 JCAHO requirements, how long does the nurse have to complete a physical assessment and have a documented history and physical on the chart?<br>　1. 1 hour<br>　2. 12 hours<br>　3. 48 hours<br>　4. 24 hours | Answer: 4<br>Rationale: The Joint Commission on Accreditation of Healthcare Organizations (JCAHO) requires that each client have an initial assessment consisting of a history and physical performed and documented within 24 hours of admission as an inpatient.<br>Assessment<br>Safe, effective care environment<br>Application<br>Learning Outcome 11.4 |
| **11.8** An infant has been admitted to the pediatric unit. The parents are quite worried and upset, and the grandmother is also present. In this situation, what would be the best source of data?<br>　1. Medical record from the child's birth<br>　2. Grandmother, since the parents are upset<br>　3. Parents<br>　4. Admitting physician | Answer: 3<br>Rationale: The best source of data is usually the client, unless the client is too ill, young, or confused to communicate clearly. Even though the parents are upset, they would be able to provide the nurse with the most accurate, current information regarding the baby (diet, schedule, symptoms, etc.). The grandmother can support the parents during this time and may be able to offer some helpful information. The baby's birth record and admitting physician will also be able to provide necessary information, but not to the extent as the parents.<br>Assessment<br>Safe, effective care environment<br>Application<br>Learning Outcome 11.5 |
| **11.9** A client was admitted just prior to the shift change. The admitting nurse reported most of the information to oncoming staff, but did not have all of the client's past records. The second nurse is completing the assessment and database and continues to question the client about much of the same information as the previous nurse. The client says, "Why don't you people talk to each other and quit asking the same things over and over?" The best response of the nurse is: | Answer: 2<br>Rationale: Repeated questioning can be stressful and annoying, especially for hospitalized clients, and cause concern about the lack of communication among health professionals. The nurse should review previous records that contain data about the client's occupation, religion, and marital status, as well as take time to review all the information the previous nurse collected. Validating the client's feelings is always a good idea and helps to build rapport between the nurse and client. Before asking more questions, the nurse should review what is already at hand. Telling the client "we're only doing our jobs" is belittling to the client and doesn't offer any therapeutic response.<br>Implementation |

| | |
|---|---|
| 1. "In order to make sure all of your information is complete, I need to ask these questions."<br>2. "You're right. Let me know if there's anything you need right now."<br>3. "I'll be done shortly, just give me a few more minutes."<br>4. "You shouldn't be upset. We're only doing our jobs." | Psychosocial integrity<br>Analysis<br>Learning Outcome 11.4 |
| **11.10** The nurse makes this entry in the client's chart: "Client avoids eye contact and gives only vague, nonspecific answers to direct questioning by the professional staff. However, is quite animated (laughs aloud, smiles, uses hand gestures) in conversation with spouse." This is an example of which method of data collection?<br>1. Examining<br>2. Interviewing<br>3. Listening<br>4. Observing | Answer: 4<br>Rationale: Observation is a conscious, deliberate skill that is developed through effort and with an organized approach. Observation occurs whenever the nurse is in contact with the client or support persons. Examining is the major method used in the physical health assessment. Interviewing is used mainly while taking the nursing health history. Listening is part of observing.<br>Assessment<br>Safe, effective care environment<br>Application<br>Learning Outcome 11.6 |
| **11.11** A nurse has worked in the trauma critical care area for several years. Which of the following noises may become indiscriminate for this particular nurse?<br>1. A client with audible breathing<br>2. Moaning of a client in pain<br>3. Whirring of ventilators<br>4. Co-workers discussing their clients' conditions | Answer: 3<br>Rationale: Nurses often need to focus on specific data in order not to be overwhelmed by a multitude of data. Observing involves discriminating data in a meaningful manner (i.e., noticing things that may indicate cause for concern or action on the nurse's part). Listening to a client's breathing helps the nurse become attentive to changes in breathing patterns. A client's moans of pain should never become easy to listen to. Listening to co-workers discuss other clients on the unit is helpful in case the nurse has to attend to any one of them. The noises of machines and other equipment noises—except alarms—would be easy to ignore as these are the usual, normal sounds of the unit.<br>Evaluation<br>Safe, effective care environment<br>Analysis<br>Learning Outcome 11.6 |
| **11.12** A client has been using the call light routinely throughout the evening. Upon entering the room, the nurse observes the following details. Organize them according to priority sequencing (1 is first priority; 6 is least priority).<br>_____ Family is at bedside.<br>_____ The IV pump is running on battery.<br>_____ ECG monitor shows tachycardia.<br>_____ Client is pale and restless.<br>_____ O₂ tubing is not attached to wall regulator.<br>_____ Bedding is damp and soiled. | Answer:<br>\_\_\_6\_\_\_ Family is at bedside.<br>\_\_\_4\_\_\_ The IV pump is running on battery.<br>\_\_\_2\_\_\_ ECG monitor shows tachycardia.<br>\_\_\_1\_\_\_ Client is pale and restless.<br>\_\_\_3\_\_\_ O₂ tubing is not attached to wall regulator.<br>\_\_\_5\_\_\_ Bedding is damp and soiled.<br>Rationale: Nurses develop a sequence for observing events, usually focused on the client first. The color and disposition of the client is observed as soon as the nurse enters the room. Taking view of the monitors would be next. Threats to client safety would be third. Checking equipment functioning would be next, and taking stock of the client's immediate environment would follow.<br>Assessment<br>Safe, effective care environment<br>Application<br>Learning Outcome 11.6 |

| | |
|---|---|
| **11.13** During an initial interview, the client makes this statement: "I don't understand why I have to have surgery, I'm really not that sick or in pain right now." The nurse's best response is:<br>  1. "It's OK to be worried. Surgery is a big step."<br>  2. "What kind of questions do you have about your surgery?"<br>  3. "I think these are things you should be asking your doctor."<br>  4. "Have you had surgery before?" | Answer: 2<br>Rationale: The nurse should use a combination of directive and nondirective approaches during the interview to determine areas of concern for the client. Simply noting the concern, without dealing with it, can leave the impression that the nurse does not care about the client's concerns or dismisses them as unimportant. Passing the questions off for the doctor would do the same. A closed question (Have you had surgery before?) does not allow the client to offer much information, besides yes/no or one-word answers.<br>Assessment<br>Psychosocial integrity<br>Application<br>Learning Outcome 11.7 |
| **11.14** The nurse is taking a health history from a client who has complications from chronic asthma. Which of the following is an example of an open-ended question?<br>  1. "How would you describe your sleep pattern?"<br>  2. "Can you describe your coughing pattern?"<br>  3. "Is there anything that makes your breathing worse?"<br>  4. "What medications are you on?" | Answer: 1<br>Rationale: Open-ended questions invite clients to discover and explore, elaborate, clarify, or illustrate their thoughts or feelings. They specify only the broad topic to be discussed. Open-ended questions invite long answers—longer than one or two words. Closed questions can be answered with short, factual, and specific information.<br>Assessment<br>Health promotion and maintenance<br>Application<br>Learning Outcome 11.8 |
| **11.15** Wanting to know more about the client's pain experience, the nurse continues to explore different questioning techniques. Which of the following is the best example of an open-ended question for this situation?<br>  1. "Is your pain worse at night?"<br>  2. "What brought you to the clinic?"<br>  3. "How has the pain impacted your life?"<br>  4. "You're feeling down about having pain, aren't you?" | Answer: 3<br>Rationale: An open-ended question would be beneficial to explore more about the client's experience and should be asked with a "how" or "what." Closed questions can be answered with one or two words. A neutral question is a question that the client can answer without direction or pressure from the nurse. A neutral question is open-ended and is used in nondirective interviews, which is what would be used if the nurse didn't understand the reason for the client's visit. A leading question is usually closed and directs the client's answer (the nurse stating how the client is feeling, for example).<br>Assessment<br>Health promotion and maintenance<br>Application<br>Learning Outcome 11.8 |
| **11.16** A client is coming in to the clinic for the first time. In order for the nurse to allow the client the most comfort during the interview, the nurse should:<br>  1. Sit next to the client, a few feet apart.<br>  2. Sit behind a desk.<br>  3. Stand at the side of the client's chair.<br>  4. Stand at the counter to take notes during the interview. | Answer: 1<br>Rationale: A seating arrangement in which the client and nurse are seated in chairs, a few feet apart, at right angles to each other and with no table between creates a less formal atmosphere, with the nurse and client feeling on equal terms. This would allow for more comfort and relaxation during the interview phase. Sitting behind a desk creates a formal arrangement that suggests a business meeting between a superior and subordinate. Standing and looking down at a client who is in a chair risks intimidating the client.<br>Implementation<br>Psychosocial integrity<br>Application<br>Learning Outcome 11.9 |
| **11.17** A client comes into the emergency department with a non-life-threatening wound to the hand that will require stitches. The department is quite busy with other clients, their families, | Answer: 3<br>Rationale: The interview setting should be in a well-lighted, well-ventilated room that is relatively free of noise, movements, and distractions in order to encourage communication. The interview should also take place in an area where others cannot overhear or see the client if possible. In this situation, at least pulling a |

and other people in the waiting room. The best way for the nurse to conduct an interview with this client is to:
1. Have the client wait until the department quiets down, since the wound is not too serious.
2. Tell the client to wait in the waiting room and fill out the paperwork.
3. Draw curtains around the client and nurse to provide as much privacy as possible.
4. Make sure the client's back is to the rest of the room so as not to be heard by passersby.

privacy curtain will help keep the client from view of others in the department. Merely making sure the client's back is to the rest of the room is not as acceptable. Having the client wait may cause an unnecessary delay in treatment.
Implementation
Safe, effective care environment
Application
Learning Outcome 11.9

---

**11.18** A client has been admitted for acute dehydration, secondary to nausea and diarrhea. When is the best time for the nurse to conduct this client's interview?
1. As soon as the client gets to the floor
2. After the client has settled in and been oriented to the room
3. When the family is available to help
4. After the client has been medicated

Answer: 2
Rationale: Interviews should be planned when the client is physically comfortable and free of pain, and when interruptions by the family are minimal. After the client has been oriented to where the bathroom and nurse call light are, the nurse should start the interview process. In this situation, the nurse may have to pace the interview according to the client's comfort level. The nurse will also have to select focused questions and get information in a quick manner since the client is acutely ill. Medication may affect the client's ability to think clearly, so again, getting as much information quickly is key here.
Assessment
Physiologic integrity
Application
Learning Outcome 11.9

---

**11.19** A nurse has been assigned a new client who cannot speak English. In order that the client receives accurate information, the nurse should:
1. Have a member of the housekeeping staff who speaks the same language translate.
2. Use the translation services supplied by the hospital.
3. Make sure a family member who does speak English is available.
4. Conduct the interview using hand gestures.

Answer: 2
Rationale: Live translation is preferred since the client can then ask questions for clarification. Many large facilities are establishing their own translator services for the languages commonly spoken in their geographical regions. Nurses must be cautious when asking family members, client visitors, or agency nonprofessional staff to assist with translation. Issues of confidentiality or gender mismatch can interfere with effective communication.
Implementation
Safe, effective care environment
Application
Learning Outcome 11.9

---

**11.20** A nursing student is meeting an assigned client for the first time. In order to begin the establishment of rapport, the best statement by the student is:
1. "Hello, I'm your nursing student and I'll be helping to take care of you today."
2. "You're lucky, you have students and nurses taking care of you today."
3. "Good morning, is there anything you need right now?"
4. "Hi. If you need anything, either your nurse or I will get it for you."

Answer: 1
Rationale: Establishing rapport is a process of creating goodwill and trust and usually begins with a greeting and self-introduction, accompanied by nonverbal gestures such as a smile, a handshake, and a friendly manner. Telling a hospitalized client he or she is lucky is probably not the best therapeutic comment. Making introductions, especially offering the use of name, is especially good in establishing rapport.
Implementation
Psychosocial integrity
Application
Learning Outcome 11.6

**11.21** The nurse has just completed an admission interview with a new client. Which response by the nurse is an example of a remark used during the closing phase of the interview?
1. "I'm going to set up your physical assessment now. Do you have any questions?"
2. "Tell me more about how you feel."
3. "Could you give examples of what types of other treatments you've had?"
4. "Is there anything you're worried about?"

Answer: 1
Rationale: Closing the interview is important for maintaining the rapport and trust between the client and nurse as well as to facilitate future interactions. The closing should contain an offer for questions, conclusions, plans for the next meeting, and a summary to verify accuracy. The other options are what would be part of the body of the interview—questions designed to gather the most information about the situation.
Implementation
Safe, effective care environment
Application
Learning Outcome 11.6

**11.22** During an assessment interview, the nurse understands that the client has decided not to take the physician's advice about an elective surgical procedure. The client shares that this is "just not part of what I have in mind for my life's goals." This would fall into which of Gordon's functional health patterns?
1. Cognitive/perceptual pattern
2. Coping/stress-tolerance pattern
3. Health-perception/health-management pattern
4. Value/belief pattern

Answer: 4
Rationale: The value/belief pattern describes the patterns of values, beliefs (including spiritual), and goals that guide the client's choices or decisions. The client in this situation has decided against a surgical procedure because it doesn't coincide with the client's beliefs and goals. Cognitive perceptual patterns describe sensory-perceptual and cognitive patterns. Coping/stress-tolerance patterns describe the client's general coping pattern and the effectiveness of the patterns in terms of stress tolerance. Health-perception/health-management pattern describes the client's perceived pattern of health and well-being and how health is managed.
Assessment
Health promotion and maintenance
Analysis
Learning Outcome 11.10

**11.23** A client comes to the emergency department with injuries to her upper shoulders and back area. When questioned about how the injuries occurred, the client becomes less talkative and states that she "fell." The client has a history of frequent ED visits, always with believable excuses about how her injuries occurred. The nurse begins to suspect that this client is a victim of abuse. This is an example of the nurse making which of the following?
1. Observation of cues
2. Validation
3. Inference
4. Judgment

Answer: 3
Rationale: Inferences are the nurse's interpretations of conclusions made based on the cues, which in this case would be the frequent visits to the emergency department and the client's injuries. Data must be based on cues, and the nurse must be careful not to jump to conclusions. Validation is the act of "double-checking" or verifying data to confirm that they are accurate and factual. Judgment is not part of validation.
Evaluation
Health promotion and maintenance
Analysis
Learning Outcome 11.4

**11.24** A nursing student is learning how to implement the nursing process in the clinical area. The purpose of the diagnosis phase includes which of the following? (Select all that apply.)
_____ Develop a list of problems.
_____ Identify client strengths.
_____ Develop a plan.
_____ Specify goals and outcomes.
_____ Identify problems that can be prevented.

Answer:
____x____ Develop a list of problems.
____x____ Identify client strengths.
_____ Develop a plan.
_____ Specify goals and outcomes.
____x____ Identify problems that can be prevented.
Rationale: Diagnosing is analyzing and synthesizing data in order to identify client strengths and health problems that can be prevented or resolved by collaborative and independent nursing interventions as well as developing a list of nursing and collaborative problems. Developing a plan and specifying goals and outcomes is part of the planning phase.

Nursing diagnosis
Health promotion and maintenance
Application
Learning Outcome 11.1

| | |
|---|---|
| **11.25** The nurse makes the decision to look at alternatives for wound care with a client who has a stasis ulcer that has been treated over the past 2 weeks. The nurse was hopeful to see some improvement by this time. This represents which phase of the nursing process?<br>   1. Diagnosis<br>   2. Implementation<br>   3. Evaluation<br>   4. Assessment | Answer: 3<br>Rationale: Evaluation is measuring the degree to which goals/outcomes have been achieved and identifying factors that positively or negatively influence goal achievement. Activities of evaluation include judging whether goals/outcomes have been achieved and making decisions about problem status. The client's wound is not healing and the nurse decides to modify the nursing interventions. Diagnosis is problem identification. Implementation is carrying out (or delegating) the planned nursing interventions. Wound care would be the implementation of this particular case. Assessment is collecting and organizing data.<br>Evaluation<br>Physiologic integrity<br>Analysis<br>Learning Outcome 11.1 |
| **11.26** A nurse is working in the operating room with a client just prior to the procedure. While setting up for the procedure, the nurse notices that the client has become unresponsive and respirations have become shallow. What type of assessment would be necessary in this situation?<br>   1. Initial assessment<br>   2. Problem-focused assessment<br>   3. Emergency assessment<br>   4. Time-lapsed assessment | Answer: 3<br>Rationale: An emergency assessment is performed during any physiologic or psychologic crisis of the client to identify life-threatening problems. Initial assessment is performed within a specific time after admission to a health care agency. Problem-focused assessment is an ongoing process integrated with nursing care. Time-lapsed assessment occurs several months after the initial assessment to compare the client's current status to baseline data previously obtained.<br>Assessment<br>Physiologic integrity<br>Application |
| **11.27** A nurse has delegated to a nurse's aide to obtain vital signs for a newly admitted client. The aide reports the following: temperature = 99.3(F), respirations = 26, pulse = 98 bpm, and blood pressure = 200/146. To validate the data, the best action by the nurse is:<br>   1. Retake the vital signs.<br>   2. Call the physician.<br>   3. Continue with the physical assessment as soon as possible.<br>   4. Report the findings to the charge nurse. | Answer: 1<br>Rationale: Guidelines for validating assessment data that are out of normal range include repeating the measurements, using another piece of equipment as needed to confirm abnormalities, or asking someone else to collect the same data. In this situation, the nurse needs to be sure that the vital signs are accurate. Calling the physician and reporting the findings to the charge nurse before they have been validated would be premature. The physical assessment should be done as soon as possible anyway, but not until after the vital signs have been validated.<br>Assessment<br>Physiologic integrity<br>Application<br>Learning Outcome 11.4 |

# CHAPTER 12

| | |
|---|---|
| **12.1** A nursing student is learning the application of the nursing process to client care. When questioned by the student about the reason for implementing a nursing diagnosis, the nursing professor responds: The nursing diagnosis statement:<br>   1. "Describes client problems that nurses are licensed to treat."<br>   2. "Helps other health care professionals understand the plan of care." | Answer: 1<br>Rationale: The domain of nursing diagnoses includes only those health states that nurses are educated and licensed to treat. A nursing diagnosis is a judgment made only after data collection. Nursing diagnoses describe a continuum of health states: deviations from health, presence of risk factors, and areas of enhanced personal growth. The nursing diagnosis statement is specific to nursing and nurses and does not include the medical diagnosis. The nursing diagnosis, like the plan of care, is specific to each individual client and the client's situation.<br>Nursing diagnosis<br>Safe, effective care environment<br>Application<br>Learning Outcome 12.3 |

| | |
|---|---|
| 3. "Includes the disease the client has during the treatment of care."<br>4. "Helps standardize care for all clients." | |
| **12.2** A client comes to the clinic seeking information and education regarding healthy lifestyles and eating habits. The most appropriate diagnosis for this client is which of the following?<br>1. Risk nursing diagnosis<br>2. Syndrome diagnosis<br>3. Wellness diagnosis<br>4. Actual diagnosis | Answer: 3<br>Rationale: A wellness diagnosis describes the human response to levels of wellness in an individual. This client is seeking information about behavior changes and improvement to assist him in making choices and changes to enhance his life. A risk diagnosis is a clinical judgment that a problem does not exist, but the presence of risk factors indicates that a problem is likely to develop unless nurses intervene. A syndrome diagnosis is associated with a cluster of other diagnoses. An actual diagnosis is a client problem that is present at the time of the nursing assessment.<br>Nursing diagnosis<br>Health promotion and maintenance<br>Application<br>Learning Outcome 12.1 |
| **12.3** A client who has been in a wheelchair for several years is currently experiencing problems with skin breakdown and urinary retention. Aside from this, the client is having bouts of depression. When formulating a nursing diagnosis, an appropriate selection would be which of the following?<br>1. Syndrome diagnosis<br>2. Risk nursing diagnosis<br>3. Actual diagnosis<br>4. Wellness diagnosis | Answer: 1<br>Rationale: A syndrome diagnosis is a diagnosis that is associated with a cluster of other diagnoses (in this situation, *Urinary elimination alteration*, *Impaired skin integrity*, and *Powerlessness*). Currently, there are <u>six</u> syndrome diagnoses on the NANDA International list. A risk nursing diagnosis is a clinical judgment that a problem does not exist, but the presence of risk factors indicates that a problem is likely to develop unless the nurse intervenes. An actual diagnosis is a client problem that is present at the time of the nursing assessment. A wellness diagnosis describes human responses to levels of wellness in an individual, family, or community that has a readiness for enhancement.<br>Nursing diagnosis<br>Physiological integrity<br>Application<br>Learning Outcome 12.1 |
| **12.4** Which of the following is true of the NANDA label? (Select all that apply.)<br>_____ Must contain three components<br>_____ Describes the health problem for which nursing therapy is given<br>_____ Helps define medical diagnoses for nursing<br>_____ Promotes a taxonomy of nursing | Answer:<br>____x____ Must contain three components<br>____x____ Describes the health problem for which nursing therapy is given<br>_____ Helps define medical diagnoses for nursing<br>____x____ Promotes a taxonomy of nursing<br>Rationale: The purpose of NANDA is to define, refine, and promote a taxonomy of nursing diagnostic terminology of general use to professional nurses. This label describes the health problem or response by the client for which nursing therapy is given. It contains three components: the problem and its definition, the etiology, and the defining characteristics. The nursing diagnosis is not equated nor defined by medical diagnoses.<br>Nursing diagnosis<br>Safe, effective care environment<br>Application<br>Learning Outcome 12.2 |
| **12.5** The nurse has formulated a nursing diagnosis of *Impaired skin integrity* related to poor hygienic practice, secondary to current living conditions. Which of the following data would support this diagnosis? (Select all that apply.)<br>_____ Skin is dry, cracked<br>_____ One large with several smaller open, ulcerated areas on right leg | Answer:<br>____x____ Skin is dry, cracked<br>____x____ One large with several smaller open, ulcerated areas on right leg<br>_____ Client does not drive<br>_____ Client states that does not use alcohol or drugs<br>____x____ Clothes are soiled<br>____x____ Client has obvious body odor<br>Rationale: Data that support this problem are clustered around the condition of the client's skin, clothes, and general appearance. The facts that the client does not drive and does not use alcohol or drugs do not play a part in this client's skin condition. |

| | |
|---|---|
| _____ Client does not drive<br>_____ Client states that does not use<br>alcohol or drugs<br>_____ Clothes are soiled<br>_____ Client has obvious body odor | Assessment<br>Physiologic integrity<br>Application<br>Learning Outcome 12.7 |
| **12.6** An experienced nurse has just walked into the room of a client to whom the nurse has been assigned for the shift. Which of the following might be a significant cue?<br>1. The client's eyes are closed.<br>2. The client's skin is pale and mottled.<br>3. The client's spouse is asleep in the chair next to the bed.<br>4. The TV is on and the volume is turned up. | Answer: 2<br>Rationale: Nurses draw on knowledge and experience to compare client data to standards and norms and to identify significant and relevant cues. A cue is considered significant if it points to changes in the client's health status or pattern, varies from norms of the client population, or indicates a developmental delay. Pale, mottled skin could indicate coldness, a problem with circulation, or even death. Since the client's eyes are closed and the spouse is asleep, the experienced nurse may immediately consider that there is something very wrong with this picture.<br>Assessment<br>Physiologic integrity<br>Application<br>Learning Outcome 12.4 |
| **12.7** A nursing diagnosis of _Enhanced readiness for spiritual well-being_ has been formulated for a particular family. Which of the following data clusters would support this diagnosis?<br>1. The family visits different congregations, the parents have been reflecting on their own spiritual upbringings, and the children are questioning rituals of their friends and friends' families.<br>2. The children attend Sunday school classes, the parents take turns driving and doing errands during this time, and the parents have little interaction with congregational activities.<br>3. The grandparents go to weekly services and have formal interaction with clergy.<br>4. The children have attended private school, and the parents are involved minimally in school activities. | Answer: 1<br>Rationale: A wellness diagnosis describes human responses to levels of wellness in an individual family or community that has a readiness for enhancement or improvement. The data cluster that describes the questioning, searching, and reflecting would support an attitude of readiness. The other options merely show activities but no real interest in improvement.<br>Assessment<br>Psychosocial integrity<br>Application<br>Learning Outcome 12.6 |
| **12.8** The student nurse understands that clustering data comes with experience and recognizing cues. The best way for this student to recognize patterns or cues in the data is to:<br>1. Depend on knowledge gained from peers' experiences.<br>2. Work with seasoned and experienced nurses and learn from them.<br>3. Take assessment notes and utilize information from textbooks for comparison.<br>4. Know that this will take time, and experience is the best teacher. | Answer: 3<br>Rationale: The novice nurse must take careful assessment notes, search data for abnormal cues, and use textbook resources for comparing the client's cues with the defining characteristics and etiologic factors of the accepted nursing diagnoses. Learning from peers and seasoned nurses is helpful, but does not take the place of didactic information in textbooks. Experience teaches much information, but it never takes the place of concrete, scientific theory from a textbook.<br>Implementation<br>Safe, effective care environment<br>Application<br>Learning Outcome 12.4 |

**12.9** The nurse has formulated a diagnosis of *Activity intolerance* related to decreased airway capacity for a client with chronic asthma. In looking at the client's coping skills, the nurse realizes that the client has a vast knowledge about the disease and what exacerbates symptoms in particular situations. The nurse will utilize this information because:

1. Strengths can be an aid to mobilizing health and the healing process.
2. The client will be more active in the plan.
3. It will be easier for the nurse to educate the client about other interventions.
4. The nurse won't have to spend time going over the pathology of the client's disease.

Answer: 1
Rationale: Establishing strengths, resources, and ability to cope help the client develop a more well-rounded self-concept and self-image. Strengths can be an aid to mobilizing health and regenerative processes. Yes, the client may be more active in the plan, but the selected option is more inclusive and gives the real reason *why* the client will be more active. Looking at what will be easier for the nurse is not the reason strengths are included in the client's plan.
Implementation
Health promotion and maintenance
Application
Learning Outcome 12.6

---

**12.10** A client has been having pain without any clear pathology for cause. The x-rays are normal, the client did not have an injury or fall, and there has been no recent trauma. The most appropriately written nursing diagnosis for this client would be which of the following?

1. *Pain* due to unknown factors
2. *Pain* related to unknown etiology
3. *Pain* caused by psychosomatic condition
4. *Pain* manifested by client's report

Answer: 2
Rationale: The second part of the nursing diagnosis statement is the *etiology (E)*—the factors contributing to or probable causes—and should be joined to the first part, the *problem (P)*, by the words *related to* rather than *due to*. The phrase *related to* implies a relationship between the problem and the cause. In this situation, the cause is unknown, but the problem is evident. Making an assumption that the cause is psychosomatic is not within the nurse's scope of practice. The third part of the nursing diagnosis statement is the *manifested by (S)* portion, which includes the signs and symptoms.
Nursing diagnosis
Physiologic integrity
Application
Learning Outcome 12.7

---

**12.11** A client is diagnosed with pneumonia and has been hospitalized for several days. A priority nursing diagnosis for this client is which of the following?

1. *Altered oral mucous membranes*, related to dry mouth
2. *Activity intolerance*, related to oxygen supply imbalance
3. *Knowledge deficit*, related to medication regimen
4. *Ineffective airway clearance*, related to increased secretions

Answer: 4
Rationale: Prioritizing care must begin with the basic needs, in this case, the airway. All other options are appropriate but do not match the need for a clear airway. The nurse must attend to this first, before acting on other needs of the client.
Nursing diagnosis
Physiological integrity
Application
Learning Outcome 12.7

---

**12.12** A client just had a baby following a long labor and difficult delivery. Which of the following nursing diagnoses is formulated correctly?

1. *Constipation*, due to tissue trauma, manifested by no bowel movement for 2 days
2. *Risk for infection*, because of new incision, related to episiotomy

Answer: 3
Rationale: The *problem* statement is listed first (NANDA label), followed by the *etiology*—factors that contribute to or are the cause of the client's response. The two parts are joined by the words *related to*, implying a relationship between the two. Adding a second part to the etiology statement makes it more descriptive and useful. *Due to* and *because of* are not appropriate wording of the NANDA statement.
Nursing diagnosis
Physiologic integrity

---

| | |
|---|---|
| 3. *Ineffective breast-feeding*, related to lack of motivation, secondary to exhaustion<br>4. *Altered urinary elimination*, secondary to childbirth | Application<br>Learning Outcome 12.7 |
| **12.13** A client has a long, extensive history of psychiatric problems, beginning in childhood. The client has been in and out of institutions his whole life and is now being placed in a long-term, structured mental health hospital. When formulating nursing diagnoses for this client, the nurse looks at the etiologic factors involved in the client's situation. Which of the following would be the most correctly formulated diagnosis for this client?<br>  1. *Chronic low self-esteem*, related to factors too numerous to mention<br>  2. *Risk for self-harm*, related to many psychiatric problems<br>  3. *Impaired social interaction*, due to long history of institutionalization<br>  4. *Alteration in thought processes*, related to complex factors | Answer: 4<br>Rationale: The phrase *complex factors* may be used when there are too many etiologic factors or when they are too complex to state in a brief phrase. The actual cause of this client's altered thought process may be due to psychiatric diagnoses, medication tolerances and noncompliance, history of institutionalization, and life history of mental disease. This is a variation of the basic two-part statement, but acceptable to use.<br>Nursing diagnosis<br>Psychosocial integrity<br>Application<br>Learning Outcome 12.7 |
| **12.14** The nurse is reviewing the client's care plan and checking the quality of the nursing diagnosis statements. Criteria to use for guidelines in formulating nursing diagnoses include which of the following? (Select all that apply.)<br>_____ Nonjudgmental statements<br>_____ Stated in terms of a need<br>_____ Must be legally advisable<br>_____ Cause/effect are correctly stated<br>_____ Use medical terminology to describe the cause<br>_____ Word the diagnosis specifically and precisely | Answer:<br>\_\_\_\_x\_\_\_\_ Nonjudgmental statements<br>_____ Stated in terms of a need<br>\_\_\_\_x\_\_\_ Must be legally advisable<br>\_\_\_\_x\_\_\_ Cause/effect are correctly stated<br>_____ Use medical terminology to describe the cause<br>\_\_\_\_x\_\_\_ Word the diagnosis specifically and precisely<br>Rationale: A nursing diagnosis statement must be stated in terms of a problem, not a need. Nursing terminology rather than medical terminology is used to describe the client's response and the probable cause of the client's response. Other guidelines include making sure that both elements of the statement do not say the same thing.<br>Assessment<br>Safe, effective care environment<br>Application<br>Learning Outcome 12.6 |
| **12.15** A nurse is reviewing the problem list he has compiled with a client and the client's family. The nurse is also relating the various diagnoses he has formulated to this client, then asking for input from the client and family. The nurse is utilizing which of the following to minimize diagnostic error?<br>  1. Understanding what is normal vs. what is not normal<br>  2. Verifying<br>  3. Consulting resources<br>  4. Basing diagnoses on patterns | Answer: 2<br>Rationale: The nurse, while taking the information and collecting data, begins to hypothesize possible explanations of the data and then realizes all diagnoses are only tentative until they are verified. The client and family should be included in the beginning and also at the end of the diagnostic process to verify the nurse's diagnoses. Nurses must apply knowledge from various areas to recognize cues and patterns to understand what is normal and not normal. This comes from principles of chemistry, anatomy, and pharmacology—not the client or the family. Both novices and experienced nurses should consult appropriate resources whenever in doubt about a diagnosis. Professional literature, colleagues, and other professionals are all appropriate resources. Diagnoses should be based on patterns and behavior over time, not an isolated incident. |

| | |
|---|---|
| | Implementation<br>Safe, effective care environment<br>Application<br>Learning Outcome 12.7 |
| **12.16** The nurse, after formulating several diagnoses for a client, does not understand the reason for some of the discrepancies in the client's lab values and diagnostic tests, when comparing to norms and standards. Which of the following is the best action of the nurse?<br>  1. Verify the information with the client.<br>  2. Compare all findings to the national norms and standards.<br>  3. Consult other professionals and colleagues.<br>  4. Improve critical-thinking skills so answers come more easily. | Answer: 3<br>Rationale: Both novices and experienced nurses should consult appropriate resources whenever in doubt about a diagnosis. Professional literature, nursing colleagues, and other professionals are all appropriate resources. Verifying the information with the client would be inappropriate since the information does not come from subjective data, rather from testing and lab values. The nurse already has compared the findings to the norms and standards. Critical-thinking skills help the nurse be aware of and avoid errors. This comes with experience and is a learned and practiced process.<br>Implementation<br>Safe, effective care environment<br>Application<br>Learning Outcome 12.7 |
| **12.17** The student nurse is learning the Taxonomy II nursing diagnoses system. This system is coded according to which of the following axes? (Select all that apply.)<br>_____ Gordon's health pattern groupings<br>_____ Age<br>_____ Time<br>_____ Health status<br>_____ Gender<br>_____ Unit of care | Answer:<br>_____ Gordon's health pattern groupings<br>\_\_\_x\_\_\_ Age<br>\_\_\_x\_\_\_ Time<br>\_\_\_x\_\_\_ Health status<br>_____ Gender<br>\_\_\_x\_\_\_ Unit of care<br>Rationale: The Taxonomy II system codes diagnoses according to seven axes: diagnostic concept, time, unit of care, age, health status, descriptor, and topology. Diagnoses are listed alphabetically by concept, not by first word.<br>Assessment<br>Health promotion and maintenance<br>Application<br>Learning Outcome 12.7 |
| **12.18** The nurse has completed the initial assessment of a client and has analyzed and clustered the data. The nurse's next step in the diagnostic process is to:<br>  1. Formulate a diagnosis.<br>  2. Verify the data.<br>  3. Research collaborative and nursing-related interventions.<br>  4. Identify the client's problem, health risks, and strengths. | Answer: 4<br>Rationale: The three phases of the diagnostic process are data analysis; identification of the client's health problems, health risks, and strengths; and formulation of diagnostic statements. Verifying the data should be done at the end of the assessment/interview phase. Researching collaborative and nursing-related interventions comes after setting goals or outcomes and is not part of the diagnostic process, rather part of the implementation phase.<br>Assessment<br>Health promotion and maintenance<br>Application<br>Learning Outcome 12.4 |
| **12.19** Nursing diagnoses are different from medical diagnoses and collaborative problems in _____, _____, and _____. | Answer:<br>Orientation, duration, and nursing focus<br>Nursing diagnosis<br>Safe, effective care environment<br>Knowledge<br>Learning Outcome 12.3 |
| **12.20** The nurse has formulated the following diagnosis: *Activity intolerance*, related to weakness and debilitation, manifested by reports of fatigue after any physical activity. What is the defining characteristic of this label? | Answer: 3<br>Rationale: The defining characteristics are those reports given by the client—or the signs and symptoms. Activity intolerance is the NANDA label and identifies the problem. Weakness and debilitation are the etiology (underlying cause). Physical activity is what brings on the reports of fatigue (defining characteristic) and a part of the manifestation, but not by itself.<br>Nursing diagnosis |

| | |
|---|---|
| 1. Activity intolerance<br>2. Weakness and debilitation<br>3. Reports of fatigue<br>4. Physical activity | Physiologic integrity<br>Application<br>Learning Outcome 12.6 |
| **12.21** A client who has just been diagnosed with pancreatic cancer is quite upset and verbal. The nurse has formulated the following diagnosis: *Anxiety*, related to unfamiliarity of disease process, manifested by restlessness and tachycardia. The etiology of this diagnosis is which of the following?<br>    1. Unfamiliarity of disease process<br>    2. Anxiety<br>    3. Restlessness<br>    4. Tachycardia | Answer: 1<br>Rationale: The etiology is the underlying cause and a contributing factor of the client's response. In this case, the uncertainty of the diagnosis, fear of the unknown, and response to the diagnosis cause the client to become anxious and upset. Anxiety is the NANDA label—the problem identified. Restlessness and tachycardia are the defining characteristics which the client exhibits.<br>Nursing diagnosis<br>Psychosocial integrity<br>Application<br>Learning Outcome 12.7 |
| **12.22** A client has been admitted to the cardiac intensive care unit following an acute myocardial infarction. The nurse formulates the following nursing diagnosis: *Acute pain*, related to tissue damage, secondary to infarction, manifested by pallor, client report, and shallow, rapid breathing. Which of the following would be an example of a collaborative intervention?<br>    1. Provide a calm, quiet atmosphere in the client's room.<br>    2. Administer pain medication.<br>    3. Educate the client and family regarding treatment and therapies.<br>    4. Monitor for changes in the client's condition. | Answer: 2<br>Rationale: Collaboration occurs between the nurse, physician, and other health care professionals to treat the client's problem. In this case, the physician prescribes medications, and the nurse administers them—a primarily dependent action that requires physician orders. The other options are nurse mediated, which the nurse can implement independently.<br>Implementation<br>Physiologic integrity<br>Application<br>Learning Outcome 12.3 |
| **12.23** A 2-year-old has been admitted to the pediatric unit with a 2-day history of vomiting and diarrhea. Which of the following would be a cue the nurse identifies as being outside the normal standard?<br>    1. The child's weight is 25 lb.<br>    2. The child cries when parents leave the room.<br>    3. The child is not able to stand alone.<br>    4. The child is able to hold finger foods. | Answer: 3<br>Rationale: A developmental delay that should cue the nurse to a probable problem would be that this 2-year-old is not able to stand by himself. Most children are walking between 12 months and 18 months. The other data are considered normal behavior for a 2-year-old.<br>Assessment<br>Physiologic integrity<br>Application<br>Learning Outcome 12.6 |

# CHAPTER 13

| | |
|---|---|
| **13.1** The client is admitted to a comprehensive rehabilitation center for continuing care following a motor vehicle crash. The admitting nurse will develop the initial plan of care. Of the following, who might be involved with the ongoing planning of this client's care? | Answer: 3<br>Rationale: Planning is basically the nurse's responsibility but input from the client and support persons is essential if a plan is to be effective. In this case, therapies from other disciplines (occupational, physical, speech, etc.) would be involved since the client is in a comprehensive rehabilitation center. The client's support people and caregivers are also going to be involved in the plan of care, but not exclusively.<br>Implementation |

| | |
|---|---|
| 1. The admitting nurse is still responsible<br>2. All nurses who work with the client<br>3. Everybody involved in this client's care<br>4. The client and the client's support system | Health promotion and maintenance<br>Application<br>Learning Outcome 13.1 |
| **13.2** A client is admitted for complications following a routine diagnostic procedure of the colon. The type of care plan that will most likely be implemented for this client is which of the following?<br>　1. Informal nursing care plan<br>　2. Formal nursing care plan<br>　3. Standardized care plan<br>　4. Individualized care plan | Answer: 4<br>Rationale: An individualized care plan is tailored to meet the unique needs of a specific client—needs that are not addressed by the standardized care plan. In this situation, the client had complications following a relatively routine procedure—something that is unplanned and a rare occurrence and must fit with the needs of the client. An informal nursing care plan is a strategy for action that exists in the nurse's mind. A formal nursing care plan is a written or computerized guide that organizes information about the client's care. A standardized care plan is a formal plan that specifies the nursing care for groups of clients with common needs.<br>Implementation<br>Physiologic integrity<br>Application<br>Learning Outcome 13.2 |
| **13.3** A client is admitted for a scheduled, elective hip replacement after having pain and limited mobility for several years. The client's plan of care would most likely be taken from which of the following?<br>　1. Informal nursing care plan<br>　2. Formal nursing care plan<br>　3. Standardized care plan<br>　4. Individualized care plan | Answer: 3<br>Rationale: A standardized care plan is a formal plan that specifies the nursing care for groups of clients with common needs. For example, all clients undergoing hip replacement surgery would have basic, similar needs or problems such as pain, skin integrity disruption, risk for infection, decreased mobility, or risk for fall or injury. An informal nursing care plan is a strategy for action that exists in the nurse's mind. A formal nursing care plan is a written or computerized guide that organizes information about the client's care. An individualized care plan is tailored to meet the unique needs of a specific client—needs not addressed by the standardized plan.<br>Implementation<br>Physiologic integrity<br>Application<br>Learning Outcome 13.2 |
| **13.4** A nurse is just starting a job at a new hospital. As part of the orientation process, the nurse must review the hospital's policies and procedures for nursing care. Standards of care, standardized care plans, protocols, policies, and procedures are developed and accepted by the nursing staff for which of the following reasons? (Select all that apply.)<br>＿＿＿ Make sure all clients have the same types of care<br>＿＿＿ Ensure that minimally accepted standards are met<br>＿＿＿ Promote efficient use of the nurse's time<br>＿＿＿ Eliminate care disparities among clients | Answer:<br>＿＿＿ Make sure all clients have the same types of care<br>＿x＿ Ensure that minimally accepted standards are met<br>＿x＿ Promote efficient use of the nurse's time<br>＿＿＿ Eliminate care disparities among clients<br>Rationale: Ensuring that all clients receive the same type of care is not appropriate as care must be individualized to meet the client's needs. Standardized approaches to care planning are common in many health care agencies.<br>Implementation<br>Safe, effective care environment<br>Knowledge<br>Learning Outcome 13.3 |

**13.5** A nurse is working in the neonatal intensive care unit. A newly admitted, premature baby is having difficulty maintaining body temperature. The nurse implements several actions to prevent further complications. The nurse finds these actions in what type of document?
1. Standardized care plan
2. Protocol
3. Standards of care
4. Policy and procedure manual

Answer: 2
Rationale: Protocols are preprinted to indicate the actions commonly required for a particular group of clients (in this case, premature infants). Protocols may include both physicians' orders and nursing interventions. Standardized care plans are preprinted guides for the nursing care of a client who has a need that arises frequently in the agency—or all nursing diagnoses associated with a particular medical condition. In this situation, the nurse is not working from the written care plan, since the baby has just been admitted. Standards of care describe nursing actions for clients with similar medical conditions rather than individuals, and they describe achievable rather than ideal nursing care. Policies and procedures are developed to govern the handling of frequently occurring situations.
Implementation
Physiologic integrity
Application
Learning Outcome 13.2

---

**13.6** A nurse is caring for a client in a trauma ICU in the middle of the night. The client is having difficulty maintaining blood pressure, and the nurse administers a routinely used medication for this problem. This is an example of the nurse implementing which of the following?
1. A STAT order
2. A one-time order
3. A prn order
4. A standing order

Answer: 4
Rationale: Standing orders are a written document about policies, rules, regulations, or orders regarding client care. Standing orders give the nurses authority to carry out specific actions under certain circumstances, often when a physician is not immediately available. A STAT order is one that must be carried out immediately. A one-time order is for an action to be done only once; prn is *pro re nata*—Latin for "as needed."
Implementation
Physiologic integrity
Application
Learning Outcome 13.2

---

**13.7** A nurse manager is implementing computerized care plans for the units of the hospital. Which of the following guidelines must be followed when writing care plans? (Select all that apply.)
_____ Plans must be dated and signed.
_____ Categories must have headings.
_____ Plans must be specific.
_____ Plans must include preventive and health maintenance.
_____ Standardized or approved medical or English symbols may be used.
_____ Plans must include interventions for ongoing assessment.
_____ Plans are standardized and generalized for all clients.

Answer:
____x____ Plans must be dated and signed.
____x____ Categories must have headings.
____x____ Plans must be specific.
____x____ Plans must include preventive and health maintenance.
____x____ Standardized or approved medical or English symbols may be used.
____x____ Plans must include interventions for ongoing assessment.
_____ Plans are standardized and generalized for all clients.
Rationale: Other guidelines include reference to procedure books or other sources of information rather than including all the steps on a written plan. Tailor the plan to the unique characteristics of the client by ensuring that the client's choices are included. Include collaborative and coordination activities in the plan, and include discharge and home care needs in the plan.
Assessment
Safe, effective care environment
Application
Learning Outcome 13.4

---

**13.8** A child is admitted to the hospital for complications from diabetes. Which of the following nursing diagnoses will the nurse focus on as priority?
1. *Fear*, related to unfamiliar surroundings
2. *Ineffective management of therapeutic regimen*, related to complexity
3. *Altered nutrition, less than body requirements*, related to inability to maintain glucose level

Answer: 3
Rationale: Prioritizing is the process of establishing sequencing for addressing nursing interventions. The nurse in this case must decide which diagnosis requires attention first. Physiologic needs are basic to life and receive higher priority than the need for security and education. Identifying a potential problem, but one that is not present, would take the lowest priority.
Nursing diagnosis
Physiologic integrity
Application
Learning Outcome 13.5

---

| | |
|---|---|
| 4. *Risk for infection, related to circulatory changes*, secondary to high blood glucose levels | |
| **13.9** A nurse is seeing a home health client who requires extensive treatment for chronic airway disease. According to the care plan, the client is to receive chest physiotherapy twice daily. The client lives alone in a rural area, does not drive, and is 40 miles away from a hospital. When setting priorities, the home health nurse will:<br><br>1. Make sure that he or she is able to get to the client's home.<br>2. Assist the client in finding an alternative plan for the therapy.<br>3. Tell the client that this therapy will be impossible to receive.<br>4. Make arrangements to have the client moved to a long-term care facility. | Answer: 2<br>Rationale: The nurse must consider a variety of factors when assigning priorities, including resources available to the nurse and client. Factors in this case include the distance between the client's home and the hospital and the fact that therapy is ordered on a twice daily basis. Driving 80 miles two times a day may not be feasible, but perhaps there are other alternatives that could be considered (e.g., a neighbor who might be willing to drive the client, or someone in the area who may be able to assist with the therapy). Telling the client that the therapy is impossible or making arrangements for the client to move is premature at this point in time.<br>Implementation<br>Physiologic integrity<br>Application<br>Learning Outcome 13.5 |
| **13.10** When implementing a care plan, the nurse involves a client who is ready for discharge in the planning. One of the goals is that the client will have improved mobility. Which of the following might be an appropriate desired outcome statement for this goal?<br><br>1. Client will ambulate without a walker by 6 weeks.<br>2. Client will ambulate freely in house.<br>3. Client will not fall.<br>4. Client will have freer movement in daily activities. | Answer: 1<br>Rationale: Desired outcomes are the more specific, observable criteria used to evaluate whether the goals have been met. Ambulating without a walker by a certain date is specific as well as measurable. "Ambulate freely" does not give a time frame, therefore it is not as specific. Goals stated as "will not fall" or "have freer movement in daily activities" are too vague, have no time limit, and do not give the nurse a good set of criteria to evaluate the goal.<br>Planning<br>Physiologic integrity<br>Application<br>Learning Outcome 13.9 |
| **13.11** A nursing diagnosis of *Fluid volume deficit,* related to active fluid loss, secondary to diarrhea has been formulated for a client. An appropriately written goal statement for this diagnosis would be which of the following?<br><br>1. Client will drink more fluids by tomorrow.<br>2. Client will have good skin turgor.<br>3. Client will have moist mucous membranes.<br>4. Client will have intake of at least 1000 mL within 24 hours. | Answer: 4<br>Rationale: The goal statement must be specific with observable outcomes in order for the nurse to evaluate client progress. Modifiers like "more" and "good" could be more specific, and all options must have a time frame for evaluating the desired performance.<br>Planning<br>Physiologic integrity<br>Analysis<br>Learning Outcome 13.9 |
| **13.12** A nurse moves to a new city and begins work in a hospital that utilizes the NOC classification taxonomy. The nurse understands that this system can be compared to which of the following?<br><br>1. Nursing diagnosis statement<br>2. Planning portion of the care plan<br>3. Goal statement of the traditional care plan<br>4. Implementation phase of the care plan | Answer: 3<br>Rationale: The Nursing Outcomes Classification (NOC) describes client outcomes that respond to nursing interventions. The nursing diagnosis statement must follow the NANDA format. Goal setting is part of the planning, but the NOC outcome is narrower in use than general planning. Implementation is compared to the Nursing Interventions Classification (NIC) taxonomy.<br>Planning<br>Safe, effective care environment<br>Application<br>Learning Outcome 13.7 |

**13.13** A nurse is helping a client with planning following a surgery in which the client had a permanent colostomy placed. Which of the following would be considered a short-term goal for this client? Client will:

1. Be able to state signs and symptoms of skin breakdown.
2. Have a formed bowel movement every 2 days.
3. Identify food sources that are problematic for the situation.
4. Maintain a positive self-esteem.

Answer: 1
Rationale: Initially, a client with a new colostomy must be aware of the signs and symptoms of skin breakdown and have a good knowledge base about basic skin care regimen. This should be accomplished before the client leaves the hospital in order to prevent problems at home. Normal bowel elimination patterns may not be present for some time, depending on the client's diet and activity level. This would be a long-term goal. Knowledge about what particular foods may cause problems for this client would be information the client gathers as time goes on. What perhaps was not a problem prior to the surgery may now cause gas, bloating, diarrhea, or constipation. Overcoming body image changes for this client may take some time and this would be considered a long-term goal.
Planning
Physiologic integrity
Application
Learning Outcome 13.8

---

**13.14** A client has been seeing a nurse practitioner for counseling following a rape. A long-term goal for this client would be which of the following?

1. Client will devise a list of phone numbers for support people.
2. Client will be able to share feelings of fear with counselor.
3. Client will return to level of purpose and functioning as before the rape.
4. Client will state signs and symptoms of physical trauma.

Answer: 3
Rationale: Clients who have been raped may require extensive counseling and therapy work to deal with the assault. Some may never regain their prior level of functioning as before the attack, and for most, it will require some time to do this. Short-term goals are the other options listed—those that the client can implement in the first few days following the rape in order to feel safe and share feelings of fear and anger. The physical injuries following a rape may be minor, but the client should know to watch for any unusual symptoms (i.e., discharge, bruising, or bleeding).
Planning
Psychosocial integrity
Application
Learning Outcome 13.8

---

**13.15** A client with beginning stages of Alzheimer's disease is being admitted to an assisted living facility. The nurse is helping the client and family with the adjustment process and planning long- and short-term goals for the client as well as the family. An appropriate, realistic short-term goal for this client would be which of the following?

1. Client will not wander out of facility.
2. Client will maintain a normal weight.
3. Client will be able to verbalize feelings of anger, fear, and trust, when appropriate.
4. Client will be oriented to the surroundings.

Answer: 4
Rationale: This type of client should be oriented to his new surroundings within a few days. The client should know which room is his, where the meals are served, where the bathroom is, and so on. All other options listed would be either unrealistic (no wandering, and verbalizing feelings are probably not within the realm of possibilities) or long-term goals (maintaining a normal weight would be an ongoing, long-term goal).
Planning
Psychosocial integrity
Application
Learning Outcome 13.8

---

**13.16** A client with Parkinson's disease is working to improve fine motor skills, especially for completing activities of daily living. Which of the following would be considered a collaborative intervention?

1. Provide assistance as needed with dressing and grooming.
2. Provide assistive devices and educate client to use grab bar and large handled utensils.

Answer: 2
Rationale: Collaborative interventions are actions the nurse carries out with other health team members, such as physical therapists, social workers, dietitians, and physicians. Collaborative nursing activities reflect the overlapping responsibilities of, and collegial relationships between, health personnel. Providing assistive devices and educating on their proper use would fall into the discipline of physical/occupational therapy, although the nurse will have to assist with reinforcing the teaching and information. Providing assistance and attending to the client's space would be independent interventions. Administering medications would be a dependent intervention.

| | |
|---|---|
| 3. Make sure lighting and space are adequate for client.<br>4. Administer medications to improve muscle tone. | Implementation<br>Health promotion and maintenance<br>Application<br>Learning Outcome 13.10 |
| **13.17** A client is on a regular surgical unit following a knee repair. When caring for the client, the nurse performs independent as well as dependent interventions. Which of the following is an example of a dependent intervention?<br>1. Repositioning the client every 2 hours<br>2. Assisting the client with transfers to the bathroom<br>3. Providing ongoing physical assessment, especially of the incisional sites<br>4. Administering medications for pain | Answer: 4<br>Rationale: Dependent interventions are those activities carried out under the physician's orders or supervision or according to specified routines. The nurse is responsible for assessing the need for and administering medications, but the physician prescribes them. All other options listed are examples of independent interventions—those activities that the nurse is licensed to initiate on the basis of knowledge and skills.<br>Implementation<br>Physiologic integrity<br>Application<br>Learning Outcome 13.10 |
| **13.18** A nurse is devising a care plan for a client with complex health issues and current acute health problems. Nursing interventions must meet which of the following criteria? (Select all that apply.)<br>_____ Congruent with the client's values, beliefs, and culture<br>_____ Within established standards of care<br>_____ Based on scientific and medical knowledge<br>_____ Achievable with the resources available | Answer:<br>____x____ Congruent with the client's values, beliefs, and culture<br>____x____ Within established standards of care<br>_____ Based on scientific and medical knowledge<br>____x____ Achievable with the resources available<br>Rationale: The plan must be based on *nursing* knowledge and experience or knowledge from relevant sciences (based on rationale). Other criteria for interventions are that they must be safe and appropriate for the client's age, health, and condition, and they must be collaborative with other therapies.<br>Implementation<br>Safe, effective care environment<br>Application<br>Learning Outcome 13.10 |
| **13.19** One of the interventions for a client with a nursing diagnosis of *Impaired swallowing* is to position the client upright in a chair (60 to 90 degrees) during feeding times. The modifier in this intervention is which of the following?<br>1. 60 to 90 degrees during feeding times<br>2. Position in chair<br>3. Upright in a chair<br>4. Impaired swallowing | Answer: 1<br>Rationale: Conditions or modifiers may be added to the verb to explain the circumstances under which the behavior is to be performed. They explain what, where, when, or how. In this case, defining "upright" as 60 to 90 degrees and "during feeding times" gives when this should be done. The words "positioning" and "upright" are not descriptive enough for modifiers. Impaired swallowing is the NANDA label.<br>Implementation<br>Safe, effective care environment<br>Application<br>Learning Outcome 13.10 |
| **13.20** A nurse is working with a client who has a diagnosis of *Impaired skin integrity,* related to immobility, secondary to neurologic dysfunction. Of the following listed, which would be considered an observation intervention?<br>1. Turn and reposition client every 2 hours.<br>2. Cushion bony prominences with soft foam while in bed. | Answer: 3<br>Rationale: Observations include assessments made to determine whether a complication is developing as well as observations of the client's responses to nursing and other therapies. Assessment for skin breakdown would fall under this category. Prevention interventions prescribe the care needed to avoid complications or reduce risk factors. Turning and repositioning as well as cushioning bony prominences would help prevent any further skin breakdown. Application of lotion or other treatments to areas of skin impairment would be considered a treatment intervention. |

| | |
|---|---|
| 3. Provide ongoing assessment for skin breakdown every shift.<br>4. Apply lotion to dry skin twice daily. | Implementation<br>Physiologic integrity<br>Application<br>Learning Outcome 13.10 |
| **13.21** A student nurse is working on a care plan for an assigned client. One of the interventions the student nurse would like to include in the plan is to assist the client with ambulation. Which of the following is the best way to state this plan?<br>1. Assist client with ambulation.<br>2. Ambulate with client, using a gait belt, twice daily for 15 minutes.<br>3. Make sure client understands the rationale for using the gait belt.<br>4. Client will ambulate in hallway twice daily. | Answer: 2<br>Rationale: A written intervention should include a verb, conditions, and modifiers, plus a time element. Identifying what to do (ambulate), how to do it (with a gait belt), and how long (twice daily for 15 minutes) is the most precise statement. "Client will ambulate in the hallway" is a goal statement, not an intervention.<br>Implementation<br>Safe, effective care environment<br>Application<br>Learning Outcome 13.10 |
| **13.22** A hospital is implementing the use of NIC (Nursing Interventions Classification) taxonomy. This taxonomy will:<br>1. Help the nurse with documentation of the care plan.<br>2. Still require that the nurse use sound judgment and knowledge of the client.<br>3. Match nursing diagnoses to exact interventions.<br>4. Help the nurse choose activities that are individualized to the client. | Answer: 2<br>Rationale: The NIC taxonomy, like NOC, is similar to NANDA diagnoses—broadly stated interventions that are standardized in language and generalized in nature. Each nursing diagnosis contains suggestions for several interventions under the NIC taxonomy, and nurses must select the appropriate interventions based on their judgment and knowledge of the client. The NIC taxonomy may or may not help with documentation. Although it would utilize standard language for all nurses and offer suggestions of interventions for each diagnosis, finding the most appropriate interventions still requires individualization for each client. This taxonomy is general and standardized and must be tailored to fit the needs, outcomes, and goals of the individual client.<br>Implementation<br>Safe, effective care environment<br>Application<br>Learning Outcome 13.11 |
| **13.23** A client has been in the hospital for several days following a CVA (cerebrovascular accident). One of the diagnoses formulated for this client is *Risk for aspiration,* related to neuromuscular dysfunction. Of the following interventions, which includes a rationale?<br>1. Have suction equipment available at all times.<br>2. Clear secretions from oral/nasal passageways as needed.<br>3. Keep client in low-Fowler's position to prevent reflux.<br>4. Provide frequent assessment for presence of obstructive material in mouth and throat. | Answer: 3<br>Rationale: A rationale is the scientific principle given as the reason for selecting a particular nursing intervention. It helps explain "why" an intervention would be implemented. Keeping the client in a position with the head elevated 30 to 45 degrees helps prevent the risk of reflux (food/liquids returning up through the esophagus after having been swallowed). None of the other options state "why" they are being performed.<br>Implementation<br>Physiologic integrity<br>Application<br>Learning Outcome 13.10 |
| **13.24** A client has just given birth to a premature infant via emergency C-section. Which of the following nursing diagnoses would receive the lowest priority for the new mother?<br>1. *Acute pain,* related to surgical procedure | Answer: 4<br>Rationale: A problem identified as potential (at risk for development) receives the lowest priority since it is currently not present. It is a potential for this client and therefore must be assessed and monitored as a possible complication. The other options are active problems and would receive a higher priority for care.<br>Nursing diagnosis |

| | |
|---|---|
| 2. *Impaired skin integrity*, related to new incision<br>3. *Anxiety*, related to unpredictability of newborn's health<br>4. *Risk for infection*, related to surgical incision | Physiologic integrity<br>Analysis<br>Learning Outcome 13.5 |

## CHAPTER 14

| | |
|---|---|
| **14.1** The home health nurse must devise a way to administer IV antibiotics to a client who insists on being outside during the infusion. Using creativity and critical thinking, the nurse is able to meet the client's requests. This is an example of which of the following?<br>  1. Technical skill<br>  2. Interpersonal skill<br>  3. Creativity<br>  4. Cognitive skill | Answer: 4<br>Rationale: Cognitive skills include problem solving, decision making, critical thinking, and creativity. Finding a unique way to provide the treatment while keeping the client's wishes in mind is an example of the nurse using cognitive abilities. Technical skills are "hands-on" skills such as manipulating equipment, giving injections, bandaging, moving, lifting, and repositioning clients. Though this task in the scenario involves some technical skill, the more apparent one is that of a cognitive level. Interpersonal skills are all of the activities, verbal and nonverbal, people use when interacting directly with one another. Creativity is part of cognitive skill.<br>Implementation<br>Physiologic integrity<br>Application<br>Learning Outcome 14.2 |
| **14.2** The student nurse must accurately perform a sterile dressing change before completing a unit of the course. This student is being evaluated on which of the following?<br>  1. Technical skill<br>  2. Cognitive skill<br>  3. Interpersonal skill<br>  4. Academic skill | Answer: 1<br>Rationale: Technical skills are "hands-on" skills such as manipulating equipment, giving injections, bandaging, moving, lifting, and repositioning clients. These skills can also be called tasks, procedures, or psychomotor skills. Cognitive skills are intellectual skills that involve problem solving, decision making, critical thinking, and creativity. Interpersonal skills are necessary for all nursing activities: caring, comforting, advocating, referring, counseling, and supporting, to name a few. Academic skills would fall under the category of cognitive skills.<br>Implementation<br>Physiologic integrity<br>Application<br>Learning Outcome 14.2 |
| **14.3** A nurse works in an acute psychiatric setting and sees clients as they are admitted for inpatient psychiatric care. Many of the clients exhibit paranoid behavior. The most important skill this nurse can utilize for these clients is which of the following?<br>  1. Cognitive skill<br>  2. Interpersonal skill<br>  3. Technical skill<br>  4. Therapeutic skill | Answer: 2<br>Rationale: Interpersonal skills are all of the activities, verbal and nonverbal, people use when interacting directly with one another. The effectiveness of a nursing action often depends largely on the nurse's ability to communicate with others. Interpersonal skills are necessary for all nursing activities including comforting, counseling, and supporting—all of which are extremely important in the acute psychiatric setting. Cognitive skills are intellectual skills and include problem solving, decision making, critical thinking, and creativity. Technical skills are "hands-on" skills such as manipulating equipment, giving injections, bandaging, and repositioning clients.<br>Implementation<br>Psychosocial integrity<br>Application<br>Learning Outcome 14.2 |
| **14.4** During the process of implementing cares and treatments for a client, the nurse realizes there are several entities included in this phase. Select all that apply: | Answer:<br>_____ Evaluating the outcome of the interventions<br>\_\_\_\_x\_\_\_\_ Reassessing the client<br>_____ Documenting the history and physical<br>\_\_\_\_x\_\_\_\_ Supervising delegated care<br>\_\_\_\_x\_\_\_\_ Implementing the nursing interventions |

| | |
|---|---|
| _____ Evaluating the outcome of the interventions<br>_____ Reassessing the client<br>_____ Documenting the history and physical<br>_____ Supervising delegated care<br>_____ Implementing the nursing interventions | Rationale: Other components of the implementation process include determining the nurse's need for assistance, and documenting nursing activities. Documentation of the history and physical is part of the initial assessment. Evaluating the outcome of the interventions is part of the evaluation phase.<br>Implementation<br>Safe, effective care environment<br>Application<br>Learning Outcome 14.3 |
| **14.5** A client is struggling to learn how to care for a new colostomy. The nurse is following the written care plan and has selected to provide written information along with a demonstration on how to accurately measure the stoma for attaching the appliance. Upon entering the room, the client is crying along with the client's spouse. The nurse decides to sit with both of them, offering presence and listening to their fears instead of the planned education. This is an example of which of the following?<br>1. Implementing nursing intervention<br>2. Determining the nurse's need for assistance<br>3. Supervising delegated care<br>4. Reassessing the client | Answer: 4<br>Rationale: Just before implementing an intervention, the nurse must reassess the client to make sure the intervention is still needed or to discover if there are new data that indicate a need to change the priorities of care. In this case, the client and the spouse are not in a good frame of mind to listen to or retain any kind of teaching/learning experience. Instead, the nurse reassesses the situation and implements a more appropriate intervention. In this situation, the nurse does not need assistance, nor is this a situation where the nurse must supervise care that has been delegated.<br>Assessment<br>Psychosocial integrity<br>Application<br>Learning Outcome 14.3 |
| **14.6** The nurse is teaching new parents how to bathe their baby for the first time. An action that allows the parents to feel in control of this situation would be when the nurse:<br>1. Tells the parents everything the nurse is doing and why.<br>2. Lets the parents watch a video after the bath.<br>3. Lets the parents bathe the baby with direction and guidance from the nurse.<br>4. Gives lots of advice and suggestions about different methods. | Answer: 3<br>Rationale: Active participation enhances a client's sense of independence and control. In this situation, the baby and parents will do best with future bathing times if they are allowed to complete the bath themselves. Explaining, watching a video, and giving advice or suggestions are all helpful, but do not provide the clients with a sense of independence and control in the situation.<br>Implementation<br>Health promotion and maintenance<br>Application<br>Learning Outcome 14.4 |
| **14.7** A client is learning how to administer insulin. The nurse makes sure that the client understands how to activate the safety mechanism on the syringe to prevent needlestick injuries. This is an example of which of the guidelines for implementing interventions?<br>1. Adapt activities to the individual client.<br>2. Encourage clients to participate actively in implementing nursing interventions.<br>3. Base nursing interventions on scientific knowledge, research, and standards of care.<br>4. Implement safe care. | Answer: 4<br>Rationale: Showing the client how to avoid injury with needlesticks is part of implementing safe care. Encouraging clients to participate enhances their sense of independence and control. This particular activity, though, is more directed at safe care. Adapting activities would involve learning the client's beliefs, values, age, health status, and environment as factors that can affect the success of a nursing action. The nurse must be aware of scientific rationale, as well as possible side effects or complications of all interventions so that implementing them centers around specific knowledge and care standards.<br>Implementation<br>Safe, effective care environment<br>Application<br>Learning Outcome 14.4 |

**14.8** A new graduate nurse was working with a nurse mentor during the first 3 months of employment. On one of the first days working alone, the nurse is assigned to care for a client with a new tracheostomy and must provide teaching to the client as well as the client's spouse. This nurse is not familiar with the teaching aspect. The best action for the nurse is to:

1. Ask the nurse mentor to assist with the teaching after reviewing the procedure.
2. Read the policy and procedure manual before the teaching session.
3. Do the best the nurse can by remembering what was taught in nursing school.
4. Ask for a different assignment until the nurse feels comfortable with this one.

Answer: 1
Rationale: When implementing some nursing interventions, the nurse may require assistance. In this case, the nurse lacks the knowledge or skills to implement a particular nursing activity (teaching). Reading and reviewing the policy and procedure are important, but should be followed up with asking for assistance. "Doing the best the nurse can" would not be acceptable and neither would asking for a different assignment.
Implementation
Safe, effective care environment
Application
Learning Outcome 14.4

**14.9** A nurse is working in a busy research hospital. One of the clients assigned to the nurse's care is to receive a medication that the nurse is not familiar with and is not listed in the drug reference manual. The best action of the nurse is to:

1. Follow the physician's orders as written and give the medication.
2. Call the pharmacy and do further investigating before administering the medication.
3. Ask the client about this medication.
4. Call the physician and ask what the medication is and what it is for.

Answer: 2
Rationale: The nurse should clearly understand all nursing interventions to be implemented and question any that are not understood. The nurse is responsible for intelligent implementation of medical and surgical plans of care. Following the physician's order is important, but the nurse is still responsible to know and understand the medication, its action, and adverse actions as well as interactions with other medications. The client should be informed about the medications and treatments, but the nurse does not utilize the client for scientific knowledge and professional standards of care. The pharmacist would be the most appropriate reference point for this nurse to begin to research this problem.
Implementation
Safe, effective care environment
Application
Learning Outcome 14.4

**14.10** The nurse understands that respect for the dignity of the client is extremely important in providing nursing care. Which of the following is an example of this aspect?

1. Allowing clients to complete their own hygienic cares when possible
2. Providing all cares to all clients whenever possible
3. Telling the other staff that the client is demanding, so they are able to meet the client's needs
4. Presenting information to the client's family about the client's condition

Answer: 1
Rationale: Respecting the dignity of each client enhances their self-esteem and is an important aspect of implementing interventions. Providing privacy and allowing clients to make their own decisions, or doing their own cares when possible, is a way of respecting dignity and increasing self-esteem. It is not necessary, nor appropriate, to provide *all* cares at all times. Telling peers and other staff members that a client is demanding is the nurse's opinion and should not be part of the reporting process. Information should be presented to other family members only with the consent of the client.
Implementation
Psychosocial integrity
Analysis
Learning Outcome 14.4

**14.11** A nurse has provided routine morning cares to a client, including all the medications and scheduled treatments. The most appropriate action after this is completed is for the nurse to:

1. Move on to the next assignment to increase the nurse's efficiency.
2. Report this to the charge nurse.
3. Document all cares in the progress notes.
4. Get supplies organized for the next client's medications and treatments.

Answer: 3
Rationale: After carrying out the nursing activities, the nurse completes the implementing phase by recording the interventions and client responses in the progress notes. Administering medications should be recorded when completed to prevent errors. At times, documentation may be done at the end of the shift, but in some instances, as in medication administration, it is important to record immediately after implementation. This information must be accurate and up to date for other nurses and health care professionals. Reporting to the charge nurse would be done at the end of the shift, unless the client's condition is not stable.
Implementation
Safe, effective care environment
Application
Learning Outcome 14.4

---

**14.12** After implementing interventions and reassessing the client's response, the nurse completes the process by evaluating. Evaluation includes which of the following? (Select all that apply.)
_____ Purposeful activity
_____ Nursing accountability
_____ Continuous
_____ Judgments
_____ Opinions

Answer:
____x____ Purposeful activity
____x____ Nursing accountability
____x____ Continuous
____x____ Judgments
_____ Opinions
Rationale: Evaluating is a planned, ongoing, purposeful activity in which clients and health care professionals determine the client's progress toward achievement of goals/outcomes and the effectiveness of the nursing care plan. Evaluation is continuous and done while or immediately after implementing a nursing order. Through evaluating, nurses demonstrate responsibility and accountability for their actions. To evaluate is to judge or appraise. Through evaluation, the nurse is able to establish whether nursing interventions should be terminated, continued, or changed. Evaluation does not rest on opinion.
Evaluation
Safe, effective care environment
Application
Learning Outcome 14.6

---

**14.13** A nursing student does not understand the difference between evaluation and assessment—both are ongoing, and both are areas of data collection. In order to differentiate between the two, the student should remember that:

1. Assessment is done at the beginning of the process.
2. Evaluation is completed at the end of the process.
3. They are the same and there is no need to differentiate.
4. The difference is in how the data are used.

Answer: 4
Rationale: Though the two processes overlap, there is a difference between the data collected. Assessment data are collected for the nurse to make a diagnosis and evaluate desired outcomes. Evaluation data are collected for the purpose of comparing them to prescribed goals and judging the effectiveness of the nursing care. Though assessment is the first phase of the nursing process and evaluation is the final, assessment is carried out during all phases.
Evaluation
Health promotion and maintenance
Application
Learning Outcome 14.5

---

**14.14** A client had an outcome goal stated as follows: Client will have a decrease in pain level (down to a 3) within 45 minutes of receiving oral analgesic. Which statement by the client will the nurse use to evaluate this goal?

1. "I'm getting really sleepy from that medication. I think I'll take a nap."
2. "My pain is a 4."
3. "I still have some pain."
4. "Will the pain ever go away?"

Answer: 2
Rationale: The nurse collects data so that conclusions can be drawn about whether goals have been met. If the goal is clearly stated, precise, and measurable, it will be easy to evaluate. If the goal was a pain level of 3, the client should be able to give a numerical rating to the pain in order for the nurse to evaluate it. All other options do not address the pain level.
Evaluation
Physiologic integrity
Analysis
Learning Outcome 14.6

**14.15** The goal statement for a client's care plan read as follows: Client will be able to state two positive aspects of rehab therapy by the end of the week. Which of the following is an appropriately written evaluation statement?

1. Goal not met, client able to state one positive aspect by the end of the week.
2. Goal met, client able to state one positive aspect by the end of the week.
3. Goal met, client able to state two positive aspects of therapy by week's end.
4. Goal incomplete, client not able to positively state anything about rehab.

Answer: 3
Rationale: An evaluation statement consists of two parts: a conclusion and supporting data. The conclusion is a statement that the goal/desired outcome was met, partially met, or not met. The supporting data are the list of the client responses that support the conclusion. In this situation, the goal was met if the client was able to state two positive aspects of rehab by the end of the week and the evaluation statement should reveal that. If the client can only state one or it takes longer than a week, then the goal could be partially met. Using the word "incomplete" is not appropriate for the evaluation statement.
Evaluation
Health promotion and maintenance
Analysis
Learning Outcome 14.6

**14.16** The written goal statement in a client's care plan is: Client will have clear lung sounds bilaterally within 3 days. One of the interventions to meet this goal is that the nurse will teach the client to cough and deep breathe and have the client do this several times every 2 hours. At the end of the third day, the client's lungs are indeed clear. In order to relate the intervention to the outcome, the nurse should:

1. Ask how many times per day the client practiced the coughing and deep breathing exercises.
2. Tell the client that the lungs are clear.
3. Document the assessment findings to show the effectiveness of the intervention.
4. Write this evaluation statement: Goal met, lung sounds clear by third day.

Answer: 1
Rationale: Part of the evaluating process is determining whether the nursing activities had any relation to the outcomes. Did the lungs clear because the client actually did the coughing and deep breathing? In order to know for sure, the nurse must collect more data and not assume that this particular nursing intervention had any relation to the outcome. Documenting does not show effectiveness of the intervention, and neither does writing an evaluation statement. The nurse needs to ask if the client even did any coughing or deep breathing.
Evaluation
Health promotion and maintenance
Analysis
Learning Outcome 14.6

**14.17** A nursing diagnosis of *Risk for Deficient Fluid Volume* related to excessive fluid loss, secondary to diarrhea and vomiting was implemented for a home health client who began with these symptoms 5 days ago. A goal was that the client's symptoms would be eliminated within 48 hours. The client is being seen after a week, and has had no diarrhea or vomiting for the past 5 days. The nurse should:

1. Keep the problem on the care plan, in case the symptoms return.
2. Document that the problem has been resolved and discontinue the care for the problem.

Answer: 2
Rationale: In this case, the risk factors no longer exist because the causative factors have stopped. The nurse should document that the goal has been met and discontinue the care for the problem. If the problem returns, it can be implemented again and addressed at that time.
Evaluation
Health promotion and maintenance
Analysis
Learning Outcome 14.7

3. Assume that whatever the cause was, the symptoms may return, but document that the goal was met.
4. Document that the potential problem is being prevented since the symptoms have stopped.

| | |
|---|---|
| **14.18** A client with terminal cancer has this nursing diagnosis: *Pain* related to neuromuscular involvement of disease process. The goal statement is as follows: Client will be free of pain within 48 hours. As an intervention, the nurse will administer narcotic analgesics and titrate to an appropriate level. What is the flaw in this plan?<br>1. The goal statement is written inaccurately.<br>2. The interventions are dependent of nursing.<br>3. The goal is unrealistic.<br>4. The interventions are not clear enough. | Answer: 3<br>Rationale: When a care plan needs to be modified, discontinued, or changed in some manner, several decisions need to be made. If the nursing diagnosis is accurate, as it is in this case, the nurse should check to see if the goals are attainable and realistic—the flaw in this plan. A client with terminal cancer is not going to be pain-free, regardless of the amount of medication delivered. To think otherwise is inappropriate. The goal statement is written accurately. Dependent interventions would be appropriate, and in this case they are clear.<br>Evaluation<br>Physiologic integrity<br>Application<br>Learning Outcome 14.7 |
| **14.19** A teenage client has been having problems with peer support, school performance, and parental expectations, all of which have led to an eating disorder. After gathering this assessment data, the nurse formulates the diagnosis *Activity Intolerance* related to weakness. After evaluating this information, the nurse should realize which of the following?<br>1. The data collected would support the diagnosis.<br>2. The diagnosis is directly related to the data presented.<br>3. The nursing diagnosis is not relevant to the data.<br>4. The data are not sufficient enough to support this diagnosis. | Answer: 4<br>Rationale: An incomplete database influences all steps of the nursing process and care plan. The nurse must complete the assessment before formulating a diagnosis about weakness and fatigue. Perhaps this diagnosis is appropriate for this client, but there are not enough data presented to know that for sure. Once data are complete, the diagnosis and information need to be relevant to each other.<br>Evaluation<br>Health promotion and maintenance<br>Analysis<br>Learning Outcome 14.5 |
| **14.20** A client has neurologic deficits that are causing tremors, unsteadiness, and weakness. An appropriate diagnosis of *Risk for Falls* related to unsteady gait, secondary to neurologic dysfunction has been formulated. A goal for this client is not to sustain any injuries for the next month. The client however, has fallen several times. In this situation, the nurse should do which of the following?<br>1. Review the data and make sure that the diagnosis is relevant.<br>2. Investigate whether the best nursing interventions were selected.<br>3. Modify the whole nursing plan.<br>4. Discard the nursing plan and start over from the assessment phase. | Answer: 2<br>Rationale: Even if all sections of the care plan appear to be satisfactory, the manner in which the plan was implemented may have interfered with goal achievement. The nurse needs to check and see if the interventions were appropriate for the client. If the interventions selected did not help the client achieve the goal, then rearranging or implementing new ones may be necessary. The data presented are relevant for the diagnosis selected in this case, and it is not necessary to modify the whole plan. It would also not be necessary to discard the whole plan and start over. Modifications may be the key to a successful outcome for the client.<br>Evaluation<br>Safe, effective care environment<br>Analysis<br>Learning Outcome 14.7 |

**14.21** A nurse manager has been charged with implementing a quality assurance program at the hospital. Quality assurance requires evaluation of several components of care. Select those that apply:

_____ Methods
_____ Structure
_____ Finances
_____ Process
_____ Outcome

Answer:

_____ Methods
___x___ Structure
_____ Finances
___x___ Process
___x___ Outcome

Rationale: Quality assurance is an ongoing, systematic process designed to evaluate and promote excellence in the health care provided to clients. It requires evaluation of three components of care: structure, process, and outcome. Each type of evaluation requires different criteria and methods, and each has a different focus.
Evaluation
Safe, effective care environment
Application
Learning Outcome 14.8

---

**14.22** A nursing unit has been short staffed for the past month with a heavy client load and high acuity. The nurses on this unit have been working extra as well as double shifts and often do not have time to make sure that properly working equipment is cleaned, returned, and stored in the appropriate areas. This unit should be evaluated at which level?
1. Management
2. Structure
3. Process
4. Outcome

Answer: 2
Rationale: Structure evaluation focuses on the setting in which care is given. Structural standards describe desirable environmental and organizational characteristics that influence care, such as equipment and staffing. Process evaluation focuses on how the care was given. Outcome evaluation focuses on demonstrable changes in the client's health status as a result of nursing care. Management is not one of the three components of quality assurance evaluation.
Evaluation
Safe, effective care environment
Application
Learning Outcome 14.10

---

**14.23** A nursing unit has had a large number of negative client responses about various aspects of their care in the previous quarter. The quality assurance officer is evaluating this unit, paying particular attention to which of the components of care?
1. Competency
2. Structure
3. Process
4. Outcome

Answer: 3
Rationale: Process evaluation focuses on how the care was given. Is the care relevant to the clients' needs? Is it appropriate, complete, and timely? Process standards focus on the manner in which the nurse uses the nursing process. Competency is not one of the components of quality assurance evaluation. Structure evaluation focuses on the setting in which the care is given. Outcome evaluation focuses on demonstrable changes in the client's health status as a result of nursing care.
Evaluation
Safe, effective care environment
Application
Learning Outcome 14.10

---

**14.24** A nursing unit's records of client care have been reviewed for accuracy in documentation. This type of review is which of the following?
1. Nursing audit
2. Peer review
3. Individual audit
4. Concurrent audit

Answer: 1
Rationale: An audit is an examination or review of records. A nursing audit is a type of peer review that focuses on evaluating nursing care through the review of records. The success of these audits depends on accurate documentation. Peer review is a type of evaluation where nurses functioning in the same capacity perform the audit. Peer review is based on preestablished standards or criteria. An individual audit focuses on the performance of an individual nurse. Concurrent audits are reviews of a client's health care and occur while the client is still receiving the care.
Evaluation
Safe, effective care environment
Application
Learning Outcome 14.8

**14.25** A nurse has taken a position with an insurance company to review clients' records and the care they received while they were inpatient status. Part of the job description requires the nurse to make sure the client (and insurance company) were billed for services and treatment/therapies rendered and that there were no errors in billing. This type of audit is which of the following?
1. Concurrent
2. Peer review
3. Nursing audit
4. Retrospective

Answer: 4
Rationale: A retrospective audit is the evaluation of a client's record after discharge from an agency. The word *retrospective* means "relating to the past." If the nurse is reviewing records after the client has been discharged, the information being examined is in the past. Concurrent audit is the evaluation of a client's health care while the client is still receiving the care from an agency. A nursing audit is a type of peer review, in which the audit focuses on evaluating nursing care through the review of records.
Evaluation
Safe, effective care environment
Application
Learning Outcome 14.8

**14.26** A nurse is working on a medical unit and assigns a nurse's aide to take vital signs for several clients. The aide completes this task and documents them accordingly. One of the clients had a blood pressure reading of 180/110, and it wasn't until the end of the shift that the nurse realized this value. The physician was notified and orders were received for treatment, but not until much later in the shift. Which of the two responsibilities of delegation did the nurse fail to carry out? _____

Answer: adequate supervision
Rationale: The nurse has two responsibilities in delegating and assigning duties: (1) appropriate delegation of duties (that is, giving people duties within their scope of practice) and (2) adequate supervision of personnel to whom work is delegated or assigned. In this situation, the nurse gave an unlicensed person a duty that was appropriate. The aide completed the duty and documented the findings. The nurse is still responsible for analyzing data, planning care, and evaluating outcomes. In this case, the nurse failed to follow up (supervise) after the duty was performed and analyze the findings.
Implementation
Safe, effective care environment
Analysis
Learning Outcome 14.4

# CHAPTER 15

**15.1** A client who has been hospitalized for a period of time is now being transferred to a rehabilitation center for more long-term care. As he is preparing to be discharged, the client asks the nurse if he can take his chart with them, since it's his record. The nurse responds correctly by saying:
1. "You'll have to ask your doctor for permission to do that."
2. "Actually, the original record is the property of the hospital, but you are welcome to copies of your records."
3. "We'll make sure that all of your records are sent ahead to the rehab hospital, so you don't really have to worry about those details."
4. "There's a new law that protects your records, so you're not going to be able to have access to them."

Answer: 2
Rationale: Although the client's record is protected legally as private, access to the record is restricted to health professionals involved in the client's care. The institution or agency is the rightful owner of the client's record, but the client has the right to access all information contained within his own record and to have a copy of the original record. The hospital has the right to charge a fee for the copying costs. The Health Insurance Portability and Accountability Act (HIPAA) is a law enacted to protect health information and maintain confidentiality of client records.
Implementation
Safe, effective care environment
Application
Learning Outcome 15.1

**15.2** After classroom discussion regarding confidentiality policies and laws protecting client records, a student asks why it's OK for them to review and have access to client records in the clinical area. The nurse educator responds correctly by stating that:

1. "Confidentiality and privacy laws don't apply to students."
2. "Most students review so many records and charts that they could not possibly remember details from any one of them."
3. "Records are used in educational settings and for learning purposes, but the student is bound to hold all information in strict confidence."
4. "As long as the clinical instructor is in the area, accessing client records is part of the education process."

Answer: 3

Rationale: For purposes of education and research, most agencies allow students and graduate health professionals access to client records. The student or graduate is bound by a strict ethical code and legal responsibility to hold all information in confidence. It is the responsibility of the student or health professional to protect the client's privacy by not using a name or any statements in the notations that would identify the client.

Implementation
Safe, effective care environment
Application
Learning Outcome 15.1

---

**15.3** A nurse is employed as an MIS (medical information system) trainer at a hospital where a new computerized record system is being installed. According to the Security Rule of HIPAA, which of the following should be implemented to help ensure the security of client records? (Select all that apply.)

_____ Install a firewall to protect the server from unauthorized access.

_____ Give each unit the same password to protect the unit's information.

_____ Log off a terminal after using it.

_____ Make sure the monitor is turned away from view when unattended.

_____ Shred all computer-generated worksheets.

Answer:

___x___ Install a firewall to protect the server from unauthorized access.
_____ Give each unit the same password to protect the unit's information.
___x___ Log off a terminal after using it.
_____ Make sure the monitor is turned away from view when unattended.
___x___ Shred all computer-generated worksheets.

Rationale: The Security Rule of HIPAA became mandatory in 2005 and governs the security of electronic protected health information. Guidelines for confidentiality and security of computerized records also include assignment of a personal password to enter and log off computer files. The password should not be shared with anyone, including other team members. Client information should not be displayed if the terminal is unattended. Never leave a monitor unattended after logging on. Understand the facility's policy for correcting entry errors, and follow agency procedures for documenting sensitive material.

Implementation
Safe, effective care environment
Application
Learning Outcome 15.1

---

**15.4** A nurse manager is conducting a survey of personnel to see what the general feeling is before implementing computerized charting in an acute care hospital. Which of the following would the nurse select as positive aspects of implementing this type of system? (Select all that apply.)

_____ The system is relatively inexpensive to maintain.
_____ Bedside terminals eliminate worksheets and note taking.
_____ The system links to various sources of client information.
_____ The system better protects client privacy.

Answer:

_____ The system is relatively inexpensive to maintain.
___x___ Bedside terminals eliminate worksheets and note taking.
___x___ The system links to various sources of client information.
_____ The system better protects client privacy.
___x___ Information is legible.
___x___ Results, requests, and client information can be sent and received quickly.

Rationale: Other positive aspects of computer documentation include the following: computer records can facilitate a focus on client outcomes; bedside terminals can synthesize information from monitoring equipment; more efficient use is made of nurses' time; monitors are linked to improve accuracy of documentation; and computer documentation incorporates and reinforces standards of care.

Negative aspects of computer documentation include the following: the system is expensive; privacy may be infringed if security measures are not used;

---

| | |
|---|---|
| _____ Information is legible.<br>_____ Results, requests, and client information can be sent and received quickly. | breakdowns make information temporarily unavailable; and extended training periods may be required for updates.<br>Assessment<br>Safe, effective care environment<br>Application<br>Learning Outcome 15.3 |
| **15.5** A hospital is not able to be reimbursed for care a particular client received while in the emergency department. The client came in with chest pain, which was later diagnosed as gastric reflux. A problem in documentation that may have caused the lack of reimbursement would be which of the following?<br>　1.　The client's record contained an incorrect DRG.<br>　2.　The client was charged for an ECG.<br>　3.　A code cart opened and the client was charged for medications the client did not use.<br>　4.　The physician made a diagnostic mistake. | Answer: 1<br>Rationale: Documentation helps a facility receive reimbursement from the federal government. The client's clinical record must contain the correct diagnosis-related group (DRG) codes and reveal that the appropriate care has been given. Codable diagnoses, such as DRGs, are supported by accurate, thorough recording by nurses.<br>Implementation<br>Safe, effective care environment<br>Application<br>Learning Outcome 15.2 |
| **15.6** A student nurse is reviewing an assigned client's chart. When trying to locate recent lab results, the student notices that each department has a separate section in the chart. This type of documentation system is called which of the following?<br>　1.　Source-oriented record<br>　2.　Problem-oriented record<br>　3.　Case management<br>　4.　Focus charting | Answer: 1<br>Rationale: The traditional client record is a source-oriented record in which each person or department makes notations in a separate section or sections of the client's chart. In the problem-oriented medical record, the data are arranged according to the problems the client has rather than the source of the information. Case management uses a multidisciplinary approach to documenting client care, called critical pathways. Focus charting is intended to make the client and client concerns the focus of care, utilizing a three-column format.<br>Implementation<br>Safe, effective care environment<br>Application<br>Learning Outcome 15.3 |
| **15.7** A nurse makes an entry in a client's chart that includes documentation about the routine care, assessment findings, and client problems. This documentation is arranged in a chronological order, from the time the nurse started the shift until the nurse entered the documentation in the client's record. This is an example of which of the following?<br>　1.　Problem-oriented recording<br>　2.　Source-oriented recording<br>　3.　Narrative charting<br>　4.　Plan of care | Answer: 3<br>Rationale: Narrative charting is a traditional part of the source-oriented record. It consists of written notes that include routine care, normal findings, and client problems. There is no right or wrong order to the information, although chronological order is frequently used. Problem-oriented recording is arranging the data according to the problem the client has. Source-oriented recording is arranged in separate sections for each department that contributes to the client's care. Plan of care is part of the problem-oriented medical record.<br>Implementation<br>Safe, effective care environment<br>Application<br>Learning Outcome 15.3 |
| **15.8** A nurse is reviewing a client's chart in a facility that utilizes problem-oriented recording. In looking for the most recent physician orders, the nurse should look in which section? | Answer: 3<br>Rationale: The initial list of orders or plan of care is made with reference to the client's active problems in this type of charting. Physicians write physician orders or the medical care plan. Nurses write nursing orders or the nursing care plan. The database consists of all known information |

1. Database
2. Problem list
3. Plan of care
4. Progress notes

about the client upon admission. The problem list includes those identified problems, listed in the order in which they are identified. Progress notes are chart entries made by all health professionals involved in the client's care.

Assessment
Safe, effective care environment
Application
Learning Outcome 15.3

---

**15.9** A client has specific cultural needs in regard to the plan of care. This information would be found in which of the following?
1. Database
2. Problem list
3. Plan of care
4. Progress notes

Answer: 2
Rationale: The problem list is derived from the database and is usually kept at the front of the chart. The problem list serves as an index to the numbered entries in the progress notes. All caregivers contribute to the problem list, which includes the client's physiologic, psychologic, social, cultural, spiritual, developmental, and environmental needs. The database includes information about the client when admitted to the facility. The plan of care is made with reference to the active problems. Progress notes are chart entries made by all health professionals involved in a client's care.

Assessment
Psychosocial integrity
Application
Learning Outcome 15.4

---

**15.10** The client states: "I really don't want anyone to visit me who has not been OK'd with me first." If utilizing SOAP format, this statement would be documented under which category?
1. Subjective data
2. Objective data
3. Assessment
4. Planning

Answer: 1
Rationale: Subjective data consist of information obtained from what the client says. When possible, the nurse quotes the client's words; otherwise, they are summarized. Objective data consist of information that is measured or observed. Assessment is the interpretation or conclusion drawn about the subjective and objective data. This is the area where the problems are documented initially. Then the client's condition and level of progress are subsequently described. Planning is the care designed to resolve the problem.

Assessment
Safe, effective care environment
Application
Learning Outcome 15.3

---

**15.11** The nurse administered analgesic medications to an assigned client via central line. This information should be documented in which section if using PIE charting?
1. Plan
2. Intervention
3. Evaluation
4. Progress notes

Answer: 2
Rationale: The interventions employed to manage the problem are labeled "I" and numbered according to the problem. The problem statement is labeled "P" and referred to by number. The "E" is evaluation of the effectiveness of the intervention and is also labeled and numbered according to the problem. Progress notes are not part of the identified labels of PIE charting.

Implementation
Physiologic integrity
Application
Learning Outcome 15.3

---

**15.12** The client, after receiving emergency treatment for an acute asthma attack, had diminished wheezing in both lungs. When utilizing focus charting, this information would be included in the _____ section.

Answer: response
Rationale: Focus charting is intended to make the client and client concerns and strengths the focus of care. The progress notes are organized into data (D), action (A), and response (R). The response category reflects the evaluation phase of the nursing process and describes the client's response to any nursing and medical care. The data section reflects the assessment phase of the nursing process and consists of observations of client status and behaviors, including data from flow sheets. The action category reflects planning and implementation and includes immediate and future nursing action.

Evaluation
Physiologic integrity
Application
Learning Outcome 15.3

---

| | |
|---|---|
| **15.13** At the end of the shift, the nurse is reviewing client documentation for the shift. Among the documentation entries the nurse checks, special attention is paid to the flow sheets and abnormal assessment findings for each client. This type of charting is an example of which of the following?<br>1. Computerized documentation<br>2. Focus charting<br>3. SOAP charting<br>4. Charting by exception | Answer: 4<br>Rationale: Charting by exception (CBE) is a documentation system in which only abnormal or significant findings or exceptions to norms are recorded. Flow sheets, standards of nursing care, and bedside access to chart forms are all incorporated into CBE. Computerized documentation is a way to manage the volume of information required in a client's chart, and different systems may include a variety of setups and programs. Focus charting is organized into data, action, and response sections, referred to as DAR. SOAP charting is a way to organize data and information in the client's record: S − subjective data; O = objective data; A = assessment; P = plan.<br>Evaluation<br>Safe, effective care environment<br>Application<br>Learning Outcome 15.3 |
| **15.14** A nurse works in a hospital that utilizes a charting by exception documentation system. When providing care and performing assessments, the nurse may not address all of the sections on a client's flow sheet, especially if the client did not require this particular care. In order for the nurse to identify that these areas were addressed, but no care was needed, the best action is to:<br>1. Leave them blank.<br>2. Leave them blank, but then add an extensive explanation in the progress notes section of the chart.<br>3. Write N/A on the flow sheet in the areas that are not applicable to that client.<br>4. Make sure this information gets passed along in the shift report. | Answer: 3<br>Rationale: Many nurses are uncomfortable with the CBE system and believe that if something was not charted, it was not done. A suggestion to address this would be to write N/A on the flow sheets where the items are not applicable to the client, and not leave the spaces blank. This would avoid the possible assumption that the assessment or intervention was not done by the nurse. It is never a good idea to leave blanks in any charting area. Passing information along in the report is a good way to ensure continuity of care for clients, but this would only be an oral report, not written documentation.<br>Implementation<br>Safe, effective care environment<br>Analysis<br>Learning Outcome 15.3 |
| **15.15** A client did not meet the goal of walking unassisted, without assistive devices, by discharge from rehabilitation. The case manager using a critical pathway would identify this as which of the following?<br>1. An unattainable goal<br>2. A variance<br>3. An incorrectly written care plan<br>4. An error in judgment on the case manager's part | Answer: 2<br>Rationale: Critical pathways are a multidisciplinary approach to planning and documenting client care. Flow sheets, as well as some types of charting by exception, are utilized in critical pathways. When a goal is not reached, it is called a variance. Variances are deviations to what is planned in the critical pathway—unexpected occurrences that affect the planned care or the client's response to care. In this case, the client may need more time or different interventions to reach the goal. The goal and problem may be appropriate, but the interventions may need to be adjusted.<br>Planning<br>Safe, effective care environment<br>Analysis<br>Learning Outcome 15.4 |
| **15.16** A cardiac specialty hospital has several written plans in place for clients who are admitted, according to specific medical diagnoses and nursing interventions. Typical nursing diagnoses as well as standard nursing interventions are included in these plans. This hospital is utilizing which of the following?<br>1. Standardized care plans<br>2. Traditional care plans | Answer: 1<br>Rationale: Standardized care plans were developed to save documentation time. These plans may be based on an institution's standards of practice, thereby helping to provide a high quality of nursing care. Standardized care plans are usually individualized to address each client's specific needs. Traditional care plans are written for each client, are specific, and are individualized for that client. Critical pathways are used in case management, involving a multidisciplinary approach to planning and documenting client care. The Kardex is a concise method of organizing and recording data about a client—making information quickly accessible for all health professionals.<br>Implementation |

| | |
|---|---|
| 3. Critical pathways<br>4. Kardex | Safe, effective care environment<br>Application<br>Learning Outcome 15.4 |
| **15.17** A nursing student has been assigned to a specific client for one of the clinical experiences on a surgical unit. Before the clinical experience begins, the student must be aware of the client's pertinent history, daily treatments, diagnostic procedures, allergies, problems, and other information in order to provide the most appropriate care during the shift. In order to help the student save time in researching all of this information, what should be the first place to start the review?<br>1. The client's medical record<br>2. The MAR (medication administration record)<br>3. The written care plan<br>4. The Kardex | Answer: 4<br>Rationale: The Kardex is a concise method of organizing and recording data about a client, making information quickly accessible to all health professionals. The system is on either an index-type file or a computer-generated form. Information is usually organized into sections: client history/information, list of medications, IV fluids, daily treatments and procedures, diagnostic procedures, allergies, how the client's physical needs are met (type of diet, bathing needs, etc.), and a problem list with stated goals. The medical record contains this same type of information and the Kardex is included in the record at discharge, but the complete chart is lengthy and would take the student more time to review. The MAR includes only those medications that are prescribed or scheduled to be administered during the client's stay. It would not include other information like diagnostic tests, daily cares, and so on. The written care plan may be included in the Kardex, or at least a portion of the care plan, but it would not be as inclusive as the Kardex.<br>Assessment<br>Safe, effective care environment<br>Application<br>Learning Outcome 15.4 |
| **15.18** The nurse is doing teaching regarding medication administration for a client who is being discharged. Which of the following instructions should be rewritten for this client?<br>1. Lasix, 20 mg, po bid<br>2. Lasix, 20 mg, po twice daily<br>3. Lasix, 20 mg by mouth, twice a day<br>4. Lasix, 20 mg by mouth 8 AM and 2 PM | Answer: 1<br>Rationale: If the discharge plan is given directly to the client and family, it is imperative that instructions be written in terms that can be readily understood. For example, medications, treatments, and activities should be written in layman's terms, and use of medical abbreviations should be avoided. Twice a day should be written out, not abbreviated as bid.<br>Implementation<br>Physiologic integrity<br>Application<br>Learning Outcome 15.5 |
| **15.19** A client in long-term care is scheduled for a review of the assessment and care screening process. This assessment will be documented in which of the following?<br>1. MDS<br>2. OBRA<br>3. CBE<br>4. Kardex | Answer: 1<br>Rationale: The Minimum Data Set (MDS) for assessment and care screening must be performed within 4 days of a client's admission to a long-term care facility and reviewed every 3 months. Laws influencing the kind and frequency of documentation required are the Health Care Financing Administration and the Omnibus Budget Reconciliation Act (OBRA) of 1987. It is under the OBRA law that the MDS is identified. CBE stands for charting by exception. The Kardex is a system of organizing client information so it can be accessed quickly. It is usually used in the acute care area.<br>Implementation<br>Safe, effective care environment<br>Application<br>Learning Outcome 15.5 |
| **15.20** The nurse responds to a client's call light. When entering the room, the nurse sees that the client is lying on the floor, with the bed linens around the legs. The most correctly written chart entry is:<br>1. Client fell out of bed, but did push the call button for assistance.<br>2. Client became tangled in the bed linens, then called for assistance after falling out of bed. | Answer: 3<br>Rationale: Accurate notations consist of facts or observations rather than opinions or interpretations. The client was found on the floor, and the call light was activated. Those are the only things known until the nurse learns further information from questioning the client. It should never be assumed that the client fell out of bed, became tangled in bedding, or anything else.<br>Assessment<br>Safe, effective care environment<br>Analysis<br>Learning Outcome 15.6 |

| | |
|---|---|
| 3. Recorder responded to client's call light, upon entering the room, found client on floor. <br> 4. Client found on floor, appeared to have fallen out of bed as a result of getting tangled in bed linens. | |
| **15.21** The client is brought to the emergency department by the police. There are numerous large areas of bruising around the client's throat and upper arms, the client's lip is cut, and the client's clothes are ripped. The documentation that is most correctly written for this situation is: <br> 1. Client brought to the ED, victim of some type of abuse, in the custody of the police. <br> 2. Client had areas of bruising on throat and upper arms—as if someone had choked the client—clothing ripped. <br> 3. Client brought to ED by police. Bruising to throat and upper arms, measuring _____ to _____ cm. Clothes ripped. <br> 4. Police brought client to the ED after getting beat up. Clothes ripped, bruising to throat and upper arms. Lip cut. | Answer: 3 <br> Rationale: Notations on records must be accurate and correct. Accurate notations consist of facts or observations rather than opinions or interpretations. Data should be specific. In this case the bruises would be measured and measurements recorded, or pictures could be taken according to some departments' policies. Assuming that the client is a victim of abuse, or that the client had been beaten or choked is opinion and interpretation, not fact and observation. <br> Implementation <br> Safe, effective care environment <br> Application <br> Learning Outcome 15.6 |
| **15.22** After completing the clinical and documenting in the progress notes, the nursing student discovered he had written in the wrong chart. The correct action is to: <br> 1. Use white-out over the mistake. <br> 2. Take a wide permanent marker and blacken out all the documentation. <br> 3. Put an "X" through the entire page, identify it as an "error," initial, and move on to the correct chart. <br> 4. Draw a single line through the documentation, write "mistaken entry" next to the original entry, and initial it. | Answer: 4 <br> Rationale: When a mistake is recorded, a line should be drawn through it and the words "mistaken entry" written above or next to the original entry then initial or signature—whichever is agency policy. The original entry must remain visible. Erasure, blotting out, or correction fluid should not be used. <br> Implementation <br> Safe, effective care environment <br> Application <br> Learning Outcome 15.6 |

## CHAPTER 16

| | |
|---|---|
| **16.1** When working within the total care context of the individual, the nurse considers which of the following? <br> 1. The individualism of the client <br> 2. Principles that are applicable to the client at this moment <br> 3. Principles that are general to all clients of the same age and condition <br> 4. The person's self-identity | Answer: 3 <br> Rationale: In the total care context, the nurse considers all the principles and areas that apply when taking care of any client of that age and condition. In the individualized care context, the nurse becomes acquainted with the client as an individual, referring to the total care principles and using those principles that apply to this person at this time. The person's self-identity is part of the individual health dimension of any one client. <br> Assessment |

Health promotion and maintenance
Application
Learning Outcome 16.1

| | |
|---|---|
| **16.2** A nurse is practicing the concept of holism to the client. Which of the following is the best example of this?<br>1. The nurse considers how the loss of a client's job will affect the regulation of the client's diabetes.<br>2. The nurse makes sure to do complete teaching regarding pharmacological interventions.<br>3. The nurse is careful to follow physician treatments on schedule.<br>4. The nurse is able to prioritize the needs of the client assigned according to Maslow's hierarchy. | Answer: 1<br>Rationale: The concept of holism emphasizes that nurses must keep the whole person in mind and strive to understand how one area of concern relates to the whole person. In this situation, the stress from a job loss will affect the person's chronic condition. The nurse must also consider the relationship of the individual to the external environment and to others. The rest of the options are only focused on the physiology of the person's condition, not the rest of the situation.<br>Implementation<br>Health promotion and maintenance<br>Application<br>Learning Outcome 16.1 |
| **16.3** Main characteristics of homeostatic mechanisms include which of the following? (Select all that apply.)<br>_____ They are self-regulating.<br>_____ They are compensatory.<br>_____ They are regulated by negative feedback systems.<br>_____ They may require several feedback mechanisms to correct only one physiologic imbalance.<br>_____ They are relatively stable and constant. | Answer:<br>\_\_\_\_\_x\_\_\_\_\_ They are self-regulating.<br>\_\_\_\_\_x\_\_\_\_\_ They are compensatory.<br>\_\_\_\_\_x\_\_\_\_\_ They are regulated by negative feedback systems.<br>\_\_\_\_\_x\_\_\_\_\_ They may require several feedback mechanisms to correct only one physiologic imbalance.<br>_____ They are relatively stable and constant.<br>Rationale: Homeostatic mechanisms have the four main characteristics identified. The *definition* of homeostasis is that the internal environment of the body is relatively stable and constant.<br>Assessment<br>Health promotion and maintenance<br>Application<br>Learning Outcome 16.2 |
| **16.4** Psychologic homeostasis is maintained by a variety of mechanisms. Which of the following clients is the most likely candidate to obtain psychologic homeostasis?<br>1. A child who is used to getting ready for school alone<br>2. A teenager whose circle of friends includes single parents of the same age<br>3. An elderly person who has just moved to a long-term care facility<br>4. A young adult who is in a long-term relationship | Answer: 4<br>Rationale: Psychologic homeostasis is acquired or learned through the experience of living and interacting with others. Individuals can develop psychologic homeostasis if they are in a stable physical environment where they feel safe and secure (a child who is alone while getting ready for school may not feel safe and secure). Individuals also need a stable psychologic environment from infancy onward so that feelings of love and trust develop, a social environment that includes adults who are healthy role models, and a life experience that provides satisfaction. Having friends of the same age who are parents may eliminate healthy adult role models for the teenager. Moving into a long-term care facility can be a huge adjustment for some people, which may affect feelings of safety and security. A young adult who has a relationship that lasts is the one option that would fit most of these mechanisms.<br>Assessment<br>Health promotion and maintenance<br>Application<br>Learning Outcome 16.2 |
| **16.5** A client is having difficulty with feelings of self-loathing and disgust after being attacked and raped. According to Maslow's human needs theory, which level is the client struggling with? | Answer: 4<br>Rationale: Self-esteem and esteem from others includes feelings of independence, competence, self-respect, recognition, respect, and appreciation. Self-hatred and disgust is opposite of what one would expect in the self-esteem level of Maslow's model. Physiological needs include air, food, water, rest, and sleep. Safety and security needs are those things, both psychological and physiological, that help the person feel safe. Love and belonging needs include |

| | |
|---|---|
| 1. Physiological<br>2. Safety and security<br>3. Love and belonging<br>4. Self-esteem | giving and receiving affection, attaining a place in a group, and maintaining the feeling of belonging.<br>Assessment<br>Psychosocial integrity<br>Application<br>Learning Outcome 16.4 |
| **16.6** A client is hospitalized with numerous acute health problems. According to Maslow's basic needs model, which nursing diagnosis would take the highest priority?<br>　1. *Risk for Injury* related to unsteady gait<br>　2. *Altered Nutrition, Less than Body Requirements* related to inability to absorb nutrients<br>　3. *Self-Care Deficit* related to weakness and debilitation<br>　4. *Powerlessness* related to chronic disease state | Answer: 2<br>Rationale: In needs theories, human needs are ranked on an ascending scale according to how essential the needs are for survival. Physiologic needs are those such as air, food, water, shelter, rest, sleep, activity, and temperature maintenance, which are all crucial for survival. Nutritional deficits would fall into this level and take priority over the others listed. *Self-Care Deficit* would fall in the fourth level—self-esteem needs. *Powerlessness* is part of the need to develop one's maximum potential. It falls into the fifth and highest level of self-actualization. A potential problem is one that is likely unless interventions are provided. Since the situation does not exist at this time, *Risk for Injury* would be the lower priority need.<br>Nursing Diagnosis<br>Physiological integrity<br>Application<br>Learning Outcome 16.4 |
| **16.7** Which of the following clients is exhibiting a level of Kalish's adaptation of Maslow's hierarchy? The client who:<br>　1. Has a homosexual encounter for the first time.<br>　2. Has a need to participate in school sports and be "on the team."<br>　3. Strives to become the CEO of a company.<br>　4. Is sleep deprived because of musculoskeletal discomfort. | Answer: 1<br>Rationale: Richard Kalish added a sixth level to Maslow's five levels and referred to it as stimulation needs. This level includes sexual activity, exploration, manipulation, and novelty. A client who "wants to be on the team" is exhibiting characteristics of love and belonging needs. Striving to be in charge of a company is part of self-actualization, and sleep is one of the basic physiological needs.<br>Assessment<br>Psychosocial integrity<br>Application<br>Learning Outcome 16.4 |
| **16.8** A nurse is delivering a workshop regarding health promotion to a group of elderly clients. In describing *Healthy People 2010,* which of the goals will the nurse emphasize for this group?<br>　1. Eliminating health disparities<br>　2. Believing that individual health is closely related to community health<br>　3. Increasing quality and years of life<br>　4. Developing partnerships between individual and community health | Answer: 3<br>Rationale: *Healthy People 2010* has two main goals. The first is to increase quality and years of healthy life, which applies to the clients who will be the focus of this workshop. The second goal is to eliminate health disparities, which reflects the diversity of the population.<br>　　The foundation for this document is the belief that individual health is closely linked to community health and the reverse. In order to bring this about, partnerships are important to improve the health of individuals and communities.<br>Implementation<br>Health promotion and maintenance<br>Application<br>Learning Outcome 16.5 |
| **16.9** A client comes to the clinic seeking information regarding smoking cessation classes and ways to improve respiratory function. This client is modeling which behavior?<br>　1. Health promotion<br>　2. Health protection<br>　3. Tertiary prevention<br>　4. Primary prevention | Answer: 2<br>Rationale: Health protection or illness prevention is "behavior motivated by a desire to actively avoid illness, detect it early, or maintain functioning within the constraints of illness." Expressing a desire to quit smoking would be modeling this behavior. The information we are given does not tell us if the client has pathology or not, but the client certainly has been exposed to a health hazard. Health promotion is behavior motivated by the desire to increase well-being and actualize human health potential. Primary prevention measures focus on health promotion, and tertiary prevention measures focus on restoration and rehabilitation—they are not behaviors. |

| | Implementation<br>Health promotion and maintenance<br>Application<br>Learning Outcome 16.6 |
|---|---|
| **16.10** A community health nurse wants to provide health promotion classes through the local hospital. Which of the following topics might be included in this endeavor?<br>_____ Time management<br>_____ Healthy eating habits<br>_____ Exercise after stroke<br>_____ Bicycle safety for children | Answer:<br>_____x_____ Time management<br>_____x_____ Healthy eating habits<br>_____ Exercise after stroke<br>_____x_____ Bicycle safety for children<br>Rationale: Health promotion activities include those items that increase well-being and overall health. Teaching about exercise following a stroke focuses on rehabilitation, not health promotion.<br>Assessment<br>Health promotion and maintenance<br>Application<br>Learning Outcome 16.7 |
| **16.11** A client has joined a fitness club and is working with the nurse to design a program for weight reduction and increased muscle tone. The client has tried exercise in the past with success, but has not been participating in a program for some time. In order to assess the potential for success with this client, the nurse should evaluate which of the behavior-specific cognitions?<br>1. Interpersonal influences<br>2. Perceived benefits of action<br>3. Situational influences<br>4. Perceived self-efficacy | Answer: 2<br>Rationale: Behavior-specific cognitions and affect are considered to be of major motivational significance for acquiring and maintaining health-promoting behaviors. Perceived benefits of action affect the person's plan to participate in health-promoting behaviors and may facilitate continued practice. If this client has prior positive experience with the behavior or observations of others engaged in the behavior, he or she may be motivated to success. Interpersonal influences are a person's perceptions concerning the behaviors, beliefs, or attitudes of others—including family, peers, and health professionals who can influence their success. Situational influences are direct and indirect influences on health-promoting behaviors and include perceptions of options, demand characteristics, and the aesthetic features of the environment. Perceived self-efficacy refers to the conviction that a person can successfully carry out the behavior necessary to achieve a desired outcome.<br>Assessment<br>Health promotion and maintenance<br>Application<br>Learning Outcome 16.8 |
| **16.12** A client has been working hard in rehab following a traumatic brain injury. She has a weak support system in that her family lives a far distance away, she has no children, and her co-workers are not involved. Which of the following behavior-specific cognitions will the nurse focus on to assist this client with success in the rehab course?<br>1. Situational influences<br>2. Perceived benefits of action<br>3. Perceived barriers to action<br>4. Interpersonal influences | Answer: 4<br>Rationale: Interpersonal influences are a person's perceptions concerning the behaviors, beliefs, or attitudes of others. Family, peers, and health professionals are sources of interpersonal influences that can affect a person's health-promoting behaviors. Since this particular client does not have a close support system, the nurse will look to other possibilities (i.e., the other health professionals involved in the client's care such as other nurses, therapists, and physicians). Situational influences are direct and indirect influences on health-promoting behaviors and include perceptions of available options, demand characteristics, and the aesthetic features of the environment.<br><br>    Perceived benefits of action affect the person's plan to participate in health-promoting behaviors and may facilitate continued practice. Perceived barriers to action may be real or imagined and may affect health-promoting behaviors by decreasing the individual's commitment to a plan of action.<br>Assessment<br>Health promotion and maintenance<br>Application<br>Learning Outcome 16.8 |

**16.13** A client is learning how to manage his asthma. In providing teaching, the nurse stresses the importance of using the peak flow meter every morning to help determine changes in respiratory status. The nurse is stressing which of the following behaviors of health promotion?

1. Competing preferences
2. Competing demands
3. Situational influences
4. Interpersonal influences

Answer: 1

Rationale: Competing preferences are behaviors over which an individual has a high level of control and depend on the individual's ability to be self-regulating. In this case, the individual must make a choice to use his peak flow meter every day. It's really his choice—either he uses it or he doesn't. Competing demands are behaviors over which an individual has a low level of control; something unexpected competes with a planned activity. Situational influences are direct and indirect influences on health-promoting behaviors and include perceptions of available options, demand characteristics, and the aesthetic features of the environment. Interpersonal influences are a person's perceptions concerning the behaviors, beliefs, or attitudes of others.
Implementation
Health promotion and maintenance
Application
Learning Outcome 16.8

---

**16.14** Health behavior change is cyclic and involves progress through several stages. Arrange the following stages in the correct order:

_____ Preparation stage
_____ Contemplation stage
_____ Maintenance stage
_____ Precontemplation stage
_____ Termination stage
_____ Action stage

Answer:

___3___ Preparation stage
___2___ Contemplation stage
___5___ Maintenance stage
___1___ Precontemplation stage
___6___ Termination stage
___4___ Action stage

Rationale: In the stage model proposed by Prochaska, Norcross, and DiClemente, there are five stages people progress through before a change in behavior occurs. By the time the person reaches the final stage, he or she is successfully maintaining the change in behavior. If the person does not succeed in the change of behavior, relapse happens.
Assessment
Health promotion and maintenance
Application
Learning Outcome 16.9

---

**16.15** Several nursing students have been discussing the benefits of joining a study group. They realize the importance of applying nursing knowledge to the clinical area and figure that together they may be more effective in retaining this information than if they continued in their individual settings. Which stage of behavior change are they exemplifying?

1. Termination stage
2. Preparation stage
3. Contemplation stage
4. Action stage

Answer: 3

Rationale: During the contemplation stage, the person acknowledges the problem, considers changing a specific behavior, actively gathers information, and verbalizes plans to change the behavior in the near future. Discussing benefits of a study group would fall into this stage. They haven't started a group nor have they made any preparation toward it; they have merely been talking about it. The termination stage is the ultimate goal where the individual has complete confidence that the problem is no longer a temptation or threat. The preparation stage occurs when the person undertakes cognitive and behavioral activities that prepare the person for change. The action stage occurs when the person actively implements behavioral and cognitive strategies to interrupt previous behavior patterns and adopt new ones.
Implementation
Health promotion and maintenance
Application
Learning Outcome 16.9

---

**16.16** A client with diabetes wants to have better control over her blood sugar levels. She has set a goal that she will have laboratory values that reflect this, and she has been monitoring her blood sugar twice a day for the past month. Along with regular checks, she has kept all appointments with her nutritionist. This client is modeling which of the following?

Answer: 4

Rationale: The action stage occurs when the person actively implements behavioral and cognitive strategies to interrupt previous behavior patterns and adopt new ones. This stage requires the greatest commitment of time and energy and is where the person is actually *doing* something to change the behavior. The termination stage occurs when the individual has complete confidence that the problem is no longer a temptation or a threat. The maintenance stage is where the person integrates adopted behavior patterns into his or her lifestyle. This stage lasts until the person no longer has temptation to return to previous unhealthy behaviors. In the contemplation stage, the person acknowledges

| | |
|---|---|
| 1. Termination stage<br>2. Maintenance stage<br>3. Contemplation stage<br>4. Action stage | having a problem, seriously considers changing a specific behavior, actively gathers information, and verbalizes plans to change the behavior in the near future.<br>Implementation<br>Health promotion and maintenance<br>Application<br>Learning Outcome 16.9 |
| **16.17** The health nurse of a busy university campus is implementing a health promotion activity by placing posters about proper hand washing in all of the public restrooms on campus. This is an example of which type of health promotion program?<br>   1. Environmental control<br>   2. Information dissemination<br>   3. Health risk appraisal and wellness assessment<br>   4. Lifestyle and behavior change | Answer: 2<br>Rationale: Information dissemination is the most basic type of health promotion program. This method makes use of a variety of media to offer information to the public about the risk of a particular lifestyle choice and personal behavior as well as the benefits of changing that behavior. Environmental control programs have been developed as a result of the continuing increase of contaminants of human origin that have been introduced into the environment. Health risk appraisal and wellness assessment programs are used to describe risk factors to people and motivate them to reduce specific risks and develop positive health habits. Lifestyle and behavior change programs require participation of the individual and are geared toward enhancing the quality of life and extending life span.<br>Implementation<br>Health promotion and maintenance<br>Application<br>Learning Outcome 16.7 |
| **16.18** The nurse is preparing information packets for incoming college students regarding sexually transmitted disease, drug and alcohol abuse, and the use of stimulants among this age group. In this situation, the nurse has assumed which of the following roles?<br>   1. Facilitator<br>   2. Advocate<br>   3. Teacher<br>   4. Coordinator of services | Answer: 3<br>Rationale: The teaching role focuses on self-care strategies such as enhancing fitness, improving nutrition, managing stress, and enhancing relationships. A facilitator is involved in the assessment, implementation, and evaluation of health goals. The advocate helps implement changes that promote a healthy environment. A coordinator helps to guide and reinforce the client's development in effective problem solving and decision making as well as reinforces personal and family health-promoting behaviors.<br>Implementation<br>Health promotion and maintenance<br>Application<br>Learning Outcome 16.10 |
| **16.19** The client is making a list of past experiences that have brought joy, peace, and hope into the client's life. This is part of which of the following?<br>   1. Lifestyle assessment<br>   2. Social support systems review<br>   3. Health beliefs review<br>   4. Spiritual health assessment | Answer: 4<br>Rationale: Spiritual health is the ability to develop one's spiritual nature to its fullest potential, including the discovery of how to experience love, joy, peace, and fulfillment. An assessment of spiritual well-being is a part of evaluating the person's overall health. Lifestyle assessment focuses on personal lifestyle and habits of the client as they affect health. Physical activity, nutritional practices, and stress management would be included in a lifestyle assessment. A social support systems review takes into account the social context in which a person lives and works and is important in health promotion. This includes individuals, groups, and interpersonal relationships that provide comfort, assistance, encouragement, and information. A health beliefs review is a clarification of those beliefs that determine how a person maintains control of his or her own health status.<br>Assessment<br>Health promotion and maintenance<br>Application<br>Learning Outcome 16.11 |
| **16.20** A client has received a high score on the Life-Change Index. This component would be part of which of the following?<br>   1. Life stress review | Answer: 1<br>Rationale: The Life-Change Index is a tool that assigns numerical values to life events and is a way to identify clients in stress. Studies have shown that high levels of stress are associated with an increased possibility of illness in an individual. A social support systems review takes into account |

2. Social support systems review
3. Lifestyle assessment
4. Health beliefs review

the social context in which a person lives and works. A lifestyle assessment focuses on the personal lifestyle habits of the client as they affect health. A health beliefs review provides information about how much clients believe they can influence or control health through personal behaviors.
Assessment
Psychosocial integrity
Application
Learning Outcome 16.11

---

**16.21** The client is a high school student who is also a single parent. She is attending parenting classes while studying full time and living in an apartment with her child. The student also meets twice a week with a teen peer group and participates in a nutrition program through the county. Which of the following is the most appropriate diagnosis for this client?
1. *Risk for Situational Low Self-Esteem*
2. *High Risk for Caregiver Role Strain*
3. *Readiness for Enhanced Coping*
4. *Readiness for Enhanced Nutrition*

Answer: 3
Rationale: Wellness diagnoses describe the human responses to levels of wellness in an individual. In this situation, even though the client is young and single, she is making every effort to be well in her situation. Attending parenting classes, meeting with peers, and learning about nutrition all point to a person who has a positive outlook but requires teaching. The information given in the scenario does not indicate that the client is experiencing problems of self-esteem or role strain. The client is doing much more than just learning about nutrition. She is learning how to cope and be well in her life and the life of her child.
Nursing diagnosis
Psychosocial integrity
Application
Learning Outcome 16.12

---

**16.22** A nurse educator takes students into the school system and provides developmental testing for kindergarten through third grade. The nurse educator and students are providing care at which level of prevention?
1. Primary
2. Secondary
3. Tertiary
4. Community

Answer: 2
Rationale: Secondary prevention emphasizes early detection of disease and health maintenance for individuals experiencing health problems. This would include providing assessment of the growth and development of children. Primary prevention is true health promotion and precedes disease or dysfunction. Tertiary prevention begins after an illness, when a defect or disability is fixed, stabilized, or determined to be irreversible. Community health is a broad category that includes many facets. It is not a level of prevention.
Implementation
Health promotion and maintenance
Application
Learning Outcome 16.12

---

**16.23** A client has had a severe brain injury and has been in a rehab hospital for several months. Recently, the client developed pneumonia and is currently on IV antibiotic therapy for this. Which level of prevention addresses the pneumonia?
1. Primary
2. Secondary
3. Tertiary
4. Acute

Answer: 2
Rationale: Secondary prevention emphasizes early detection of disease, prompt intervention, and health maintenance for individuals experiencing health problems. Because the pneumonia is a current health problem, interventions focused on that would be considered secondary prevention. All cares related to rehabilitation following the brain injury would be tertiary prevention. Tertiary prevention focuses on rehabilitating individuals to an optimum level of functioning. Primary prevention is true health promotion and provides specific interventions against disease. Acute care is a part of health care, but not one of the levels of prevention.
Implementation
Physiologic integrity
Analysis
Learning Outcome 16.12

---

**16.24** A nurse in charge of an assisted living complex that includes independent living apartments understands the unique needs of individuals of this age group. In planning health promotion strategies, the nurse takes which of the following factors into consideration?

1. Rest and exercise
2. Adjusting to physiologic changes and limitations
3. High obesity percentages
4. Safety promotion and injury prevention

Answer: 2

Rationale: In the elderly population, health promotion and illness prevention are important, but the focus is often on learning to adapt to and live with increasing changes and limitations. Maximizing strengths continues to be of prime importance in maintaining optimal function and quality of life. Rest and exercise are life span considerations of children as are high obesity percentages. Safety promotion and injury prevention are life span considerations for adolescents.

Implementation

Health promotion and maintenance

Application

Learning Outcome 16.12

---

**16.25** A nurse is working with various cultures while implementing health promotion activities for the community center. Bringing the minister of the church into the planning stage of these activities would be sensitive to which of the following cultural groups?

1. Latino American
2. Asian American
3. Native American
4. African American

Answer: 4

Rationale: In the African American community, the family and church have been major providers of social support. Latino Americans and Asian Americans view the family as being a major social support system. The Native American people live in social networks that foster mutual assistance and support.

Implementation

Psychosocial integrity

Application

Learning Outcome 16.12

---

# CHAPTER 17

**17.1** When working with clients and defining the term *health,* the nurse uses examples from a variety of sources such as Nightingale, the World Health Organization, the President's Commission on Health, and the ANA. Broadly, health is which of the following? (Select all that apply.)

_____ A process
_____ A state of well-being
_____ Purely the absence of disease
_____ A dynamic state of being
_____ Affected solely by physiological factors
_____ The ability to maintain normal roles

Answer:

____x____ A process
____x____ A state of well-being
_____ Purely the absence of disease
____x____ A dynamic state of being
_____ Affected solely by physiological factors
____x____ The ability to maintain normal roles

Rationale: Broad definitions of the term *health* have been developed by various entities, including those mentioned above. It is not merely the absence of disease. It involves the whole person as well as the environment.

Assessment

Safe, effective care environment

Application

Learning Outcome 17.1

---

**17.2** A client is attending classes on building positive relationships with significant others as well as learning skills to be open-minded and respectful to those whose opinions are different. This client is focusing on which component of wellness?

1. Physical
2. Social
3. Emotional
4. Environment

Answer: 2

Rationale: The social component of wellness focuses on the ability to interact successfully with people and within the environment of which each person is a part, to develop and maintain intimacy with significant others, and to develop respect and tolerance for those with different opinions and beliefs. The physical component of wellness is the ability to carry out daily tasks, achieve fitness of all body systems, and practice positive lifestyle habits. The emotional component deals with the ability to manage stress and express emotions appropriately. The environmental component focuses on the health measures that improve the standard of living and quality of life in the community.

Assessment

Psychosocial integrity

Application

Learning Outcome 17.2

| | |
|---|---|
| **17.3** The nurse is assisting a client and his family after the client had a stroke and is no longer able to return to his previous employment. The nurse has made a referral to vocational rehabilitation for assistance in retraining the client in a different occupation. Which component of wellness is the nurse assisting in for this client?<br>    1.  Intellectual<br>    2.  Environmental<br>    3.  Occupational<br>    4.  Emotional | Answer: 3<br>Rationale: Occupational components deal with a balance between work and leisure time. A person's beliefs about education, employment, and home influence personal satisfaction and relationships with others. Assisting a client in retraining to find gainful employment and to attain satisfaction in his work is part of the occupational component of wellness. The intellectual component focuses on learning and using information effectively for personal, family, and career development. It also involves striving for continued growth and learning to deal with new challenges effectively. Because the client requires retraining, he must learn anew those aspects of a job that allow for growth, which would better fit under the occupational component of wellness. Environmental components focus on standards of living and quality of life in the community and include basic human needs such as water, air, and food. Emotional components of wellness involve the ability to manage stress and express emotions appropriately.<br>Implementation<br>Health promotion and maintenance<br>Application<br>Learning Outcome 17.2 |
| **17.4** A nurse educator is explaining the concept of health and parallels this with interruption of body systems and symptoms of disease or injury. This educator is interpreting health according to which model?<br>    1.  Health-illness continua<br>    2.  Eudemonistic<br>    3.  Adaptive<br>    4.  Clinical | Answer: 4<br>Rationale: The narrowest interpretation of health occurs in the clinical model, where people are viewed as physiologic systems with related functions and health is defined by the absence of signs and symptoms of disease or injury. The health-illness continua is often used to measure a person's perceived level of wellness in which health and illness are at opposite ends of a health continuum. The eudemonistic model incorporates a comprehensive view of health, where health is seen as a condition of actualization or realization of a person's potential. In the adaptive model, health is seen as a creative process and disease is seen as a failure in adaptation or maladaptation.<br>Implementation<br>Health promotion and maintenance<br>Application<br>Learning Outcome 17.3 |
| **17.5** A nurse is working in a rehabilitation center with a client who had a serious injury. Part of the client's care plan includes working on coping with her current limitations since the injury. This nurse is working within which of the following models of health?<br>    1.  Role performance<br>    2.  Adaptive<br>    3.  Eudemonistic<br>    4.  Clinical | Answer: 2<br>Rationale: In the adaptive model, health is a creative process; disease is a failure in adaptation or maladaptation. The aim of treatment is to restore the ability of the person to adapt and cope, as in a rehabilitation setting. The role performance model defines health in terms of the individual's ability to fulfill societal roles or to perform work. According to this model, people who fulfill their roles are healthy, even though they may have an illness. The eudemonistic model incorporates a comprehensive view of health, which is seen as a condition of actualization or realization of a person's potential. The clinical model is a narrow interpretation of health, which is defined by the absence of disease.<br>Implementation<br>Health promotion and maintenance<br>Application<br>Learning Outcome 17.3 |
| **17.6** A nurse is conducting a community assessment to determine which diseases are prevalent and most likely to occur. The nurse is basing the assessment on which model of health?<br>    1.  Role performance<br>    2.  Eudemonistic<br>    3.  Ecological<br>    4.  Adaptive | Answer: 3<br>Rationale: The ecological model—also called the agent-host-environment model of health and illness—is used primarily in predicting illness rather than promoting wellness. Identification of risk factors results from interactions between agent, host, and environment, and is helpful in promoting and maintaining health. The role performance model defines health according to how individuals are able to fulfill their roles or perform their work. The eudemonistic model incorporates a comprehensive view of health, which is seen as a condition of actualization or realization of a person's potential. The adaptive model defines health as a creative process and |

| | disease as a maladaptation. The aim of treatment is restoration of the person's ability to cope.<br>Implementation<br>Health promotion and maintenance<br>Application<br>Learning Outcome 17.3 |
|---|---|
| **17.7** A nurse is assessing a client who practices yoga for relaxation, is following a nutritionally sound diet, and has supportive, sound relationships with her spouse and children. According to Dunn's high-level wellness grid, this client would exemplify which of the following?<br>1. Emergent high-level wellness in a favorable environment<br>2. Emergent high-level wellness in an unfavorable environment<br>3. Protected health in a favorable environment<br>4. High-level wellness in a favorable environment | Answer: 4<br>Rationale: Dunn describes a health grid in which a health axis and an environmental axis intersect. The intersection of the two axes forms four quadrants of health and wellness. High-level wellness in a favorable environment involves biopsychosocial, spiritual, and economic resources that support healthy lifestyles. Emergent high-level wellness and protected health are not part of Dunn's four quadrants of health and wellness. Emergent high-level wellness in an unfavorable environment would be exemplified by a client who has the knowledge to implement healthy lifestyles, but does not implement them because of family responsibilities, job demands, or other factors.<br>Assessment<br>Health promotion and maintenance<br>Analysis<br>Learning Outcome 17.3 |
| **17.8** A nurse has volunteered to go on a health mission to rural Haiti, where the majority of the people do not have access to health care and live in poverty. According to Dunn's high-level wellness grid, the nurse will be working with clients in which quadrant?<br>1. Emergent high-level wellness in an unfavorable environment<br>2. Protected poor health in a favorable environment<br>3. Poor health in an unfavorable environment<br>4. Protected poor health in an unfavorable environment | Answer: 3<br>Rationale: According to Dunn's grid, the health axis extends from peak wellness to death, and the environmental axis extends from very favorable to very unfavorable. A health mission to an environment such as rural Haiti would involve clients who are not being treated for problems because of poor access and who also live in poor environmental conditions such as poverty and below standard sanitation. Emergent high-level wellness in an unfavorable environment would include clients who have the knowledge to implement healthy lifestyle practices, but cannot implement them because of other factors or demands. Protected poor health in a favorable environment is where clients have an illness but their needs are met by the health care system. These clients have adequate access to appropriate medications, diet, and health care instruction. Protected poor health in an unfavorable environment is not one of Dunn's quadrants.<br>Assessment<br>Health promotion and maintenance<br>Application<br>Learning Outcome 17.3 |
| **17.9** A nurse educator is reviewing internal variables that affect people's health status. Among them are which of the following? (Select all that apply.)<br>1. Genetic makeup<br>2. Age<br>3. Developmental level<br>4. Environment<br>5. Spiritual and religious beliefs | Answer: 1,2,3,5<br>Rationale: Internal variables that affect people's health include biologic, psychologic, and cognitive dimensions. Biologic dimensions include genetic makeup, gender, age, and developmental level. Psychologic dimensions include the mind–body interactions. Cognitive dimensions include lifestyle choices and spiritual and religious beliefs. Environment is an example of an external variable that affects a person's health.<br>Assessment<br>Health promotion and maintenance<br>Application<br>Learning Outcome 17.4 |
| **17.10** An occupational health nurse is surveying employees. Which of the following employees would be predisposed to develop an illness? | Answer: 1<br>Rationale: Some industrial workers may be exposed to carcinogenic agents. People who hold management positions are in stressful occupational roles that predispose them to stress-related diseases. Working as a custodian or longer shifts would not pose the same type of stress as the management position. |

| | |
|---|---|
| 1. An employee who is in a middle-management position and takes stress from administration as well as the employees<br>2. An employee who works in the janitorial department<br>3. An employee who works 12-hour days, 3 days a week<br>4. An employee who works 4 days on and 3 days off | Assessment<br>Health promotion and maintenance<br>Application<br>Learning Outcome 17.4 |
| **17.11** A community health nurse is testing the theory of locus of control (LOC). Which of the following clients demonstrates the internal control concept of this theory?<br>1. A client who takes an active role in all health decisions<br>2. A client who allows the primary care provider to make all the decisions<br>3. A client who does not make any decisions without his or her spouse's input<br>4. A client who relies on information from the local hospital for his or her health needs | Answer: 1<br>Rationale: Locus of control (LOC) is a concept from social learning theory. People who exercise internal control are more likely than others to take the initiative on their own health care and to be more knowledgeable about their health. They are also more likely to adhere to prescribed health care regimens such as taking medication, making and keeping appointments with physicians, maintaining diets, and giving up smoking. People who believe their health is largely controlled by outside forces (chance or others) are referred to as externals.<br>Assessment<br>Health promotion and maintenance<br>Application<br>Learning Outcome 17.4 |
| **17.12** The nurse case manager is concerned about a particular client being discharged from the hospital. Which of the following factors, if present for this client, would alert the nurse to possible problems with treatment adherence?<br>1. The prescribed therapy is costly and of unknown duration.<br>2. The therapy will require no lifestyle changes of the client.<br>3. The client has not had difficulty understanding the regimen.<br>4. The client's culture is supportive of Western medicine. | Answer: 1<br>Rationale: Adherence to a particular therapy can be compromised if the therapy is expensive or if the complexity, side effects, and duration of the proposed therapy are large. Other factors influencing adherence include client motivation to become well; degree of lifestyle change necessary; perceived severity of the health care problem; value placed on reducing the threat of illness; difficulty in understanding and performing basic behaviors; degree of inconvenience of the illness itself or of the regimen; beliefs that the prescribed therapy or regimen will or will not help; complexity, side effects, and duration of the proposed therapy; specific cultural heritage that may make adherence difficult; and degree of satisfaction with the quality and type of relationship with the health care providers.<br>Assessment<br>Health promotion and maintenance<br>Application<br>Learning Outcome 17.5 |

# CHAPTER 18

| | |
|---|---|
| **18.1** A community health nurse is learning about the REACH initiative and has decided to implement community education on the following topics that relate to this approach. Select those that apply:<br>1. Child and adult immunizations<br>2. Cardiovascular disease<br>3. Chronic lower respiratory disease<br>4. Stroke<br>5. Infant mortality | Answer: 1, 2, 5<br>Rationale: REACH: Racial and Ethnic Approaches to Community Health is an initiative of the Centers for Disease Control and Prevention. Six core health areas that are the focus of this initiative include infant mortality, deficits in breast and cervical cancer screening and management, cardiovascular diseases, diabetes, HIV infections/AIDS, and child and adult immunizations. This initiative was congruent with the identification of the leading causes of death in the United States, which include chronic lower respiratory disease and stroke, along with heart disease, cancer, unintentional injuries, and diabetes.<br>Assessment<br>Health promotion and maintenance<br>Application<br>Learning Outcome 18.1 |

**18.2** A new graduate nurse is working in a busy emergency department of a hospital, situated in a culturally diverse area of the city. In striving to be culturally sensitive, the nurse will:

1. Try to learn about the attitudes toward health care and traditions of the different cultures in that area.
2. Understand and attend to the total context of the client's situation, using knowledge, attitudes, and skills.
3. Possess the underlying background knowledge that will provide these clients with the best possible health care.
4. Strive to be culturally sensitive, culturally appropriate, and culturally competent.

Answer: 1
Rationale: Cultural sensitivity implies that nurses possess some basic knowledge of and constructive attitudes toward the health traditions observed among the diverse cultural groups found in the setting in which they are practicing. The definition of cultural *appropriateness* is to understand and attend to the total context of the client's situation, using knowledge, attitudes, and skills. Cultural *competence* is possessing the underlying background knowledge that will provide clients with the best possible health care. The definition of professional nursing care is to strive for cultural sensitivity, cultural appropriateness, and cultural competence.
Implementation
Psychosocial integrity
Application
Learning Outcome 18.2

---

**18.3** A nurse educator uses Madeleine Leininger's model and describes a formal area of study and practice focused on comparative human-care differences and similarities of the beliefs, values, and patterned lifeways of cultures to provide culturally congruent, meaningful, and beneficial health care to people. This is a definition of _____ .

Answer: Transcultural nursing
Rationale: Madeleine Leininger promulgated this term and defined it as above. She also created the theory of culture care diversity and universality based upon various research projects.
Implementation
Psychosocial integrity
Application
Learning Outcome 18.2

---

**18.4** A client is the child of an African American father and Asian American mother. The client has been exposed to cultural foods, traditions, and customs from both parents throughout life. This client exemplifies which of the following?

1. Diversity
2. Subculture
3. Biculture
4. Cultural sensitivity

Answer: 3
Rationale: Biculture is used to describe a person who has dual patterns of identification and crosses two cultures, lifestyles, and sets of values. Diversity refers to the fact or state of being different. A subculture is usually composed of people who have a distinct identity yet are related to a larger cultural group. Nurses demonstrate cultural sensitivity when they possess some basic knowledge of and constructive attitudes toward the health traditions observed among the diverse cultural groups found in a setting in which they are practicing.
Assessment
Psychosocial integrity
Application
Learning Outcome 18.2

---

**18.5** A nurse is working with a home health client whose spouse was not born in the United States. During the home visit, the nurse realizes that the client has acquired the identity of her spouse's culture and has adopted some of the health practices of that culture. The nurse understands this process as which of the following?

1. Acculturation
2. Assimilation
3. Diversity
4. Heritage consistency

Answer: 2
Rationale: Assimilation is the process by which an individual develops a new cultural identity. It encompasses various aspects such as behavior, marital, identification, and civic. The underlying assumption is that the person from a given cultural group loses his or her original cultural identity to acquire the new one. Acculturation occurs when people adapt to or borrow traits from another culture. Acculturation can also be defined as the changes of one's cultural patterns to those of the host society. Diversity is the fact or state of being different. Heritage consistency relates to the observance of beliefs and practices of a person's traditional cultural system.
Assessment
Psychosocial integrity
Application
Learning Outcome 18.2

**18.6** The nurse is working with clients from different cultural backgrounds than the nurse's own. Which of the following situations would illustrate prejudice on the nurse's part?

1. Making an assumption that all members of each culture are alike
2. Understanding that all culture members will have the same beliefs
3. Bringing previous negative information and experiences into this situation
4. Taking general knowledge from literature and applying it to the situation

Answer: 3
Rationale: Prejudice is a negative belief or preference that is generalized about a group, which leads to "prejudgment." Prejudice occurs when the person making the judgment generalizes an experience of one individual from a culture to all members of that group. The other options describe stereotypical behavior, which is assuming that all members of a culture or ethnic group are alike.
Evaluation
Psychosocial integrity
Analysis
Learning Outcome 18.2

---

**18.7** A new graduate nurse is moving from a small rural college town to a metropolitan area to begin work in a county hospital. The nurse has had limited prior experience with the various cultural groups that are served by the hospital. This nurse is at risk for which of the following?

1. Prejudice
2. Stereotyping
3. Discrimination
4. Culture shock

Answer: 4
Rationale: Culture shock is a disorder that occurs in response to transition from one cultural setting to another. A person's former behaviors are ineffective in such a setting, and basic cues for social behavior are absent. Since the question is an "at risk" scenario, this may not occur, but there is potential for the problem to exist. Prejudice is a negative belief or preference that is generalized about a group and leads to "prejudging." Stereotyping is assuming that all members of a culture or ethnic group are alike. Discrimination occurs when a person acts on prejudice and denies another person one or more of the fundamental rights.
Assessment
Psychosocial integrity
Application
Learning Outcome 18.2

---

**18.8** A client has requested that she have a special item present in her room and explains that it gives her a feeling of comfort and a sense of organization. This client is focusing on which component of heritage consistency?

1. Culture
2. Religion
3. Ethnicity
4. Socialization

Answer: 2
Rationale: Religion is one of the four overlapping components of heritage consistency. It may be defined by a system of beliefs, practices, and ethical values about divine or superhuman power and is closely related to ethnicity. Religion gives a person a frame of reference and a perspective with which to organize information. Culture is a learned behavior and depends on underlying societal traits including knowledge, beliefs, art, law, morals, and customs. Ethnicity describes the traits and common religious customs and language of a group within the social system. Socialization is the process of being raised within a culture and acquiring the characteristics of that group.
Assessment
Psychosocial integrity
Application
Learning Outcome 18.2

---

**18.9** Before a client goes to surgery, he requests to have his spiritual leader present and pray over him. According to the HEALTH traditions model, which traditional methods is the client invoking?

1. Maintaining HEALTH
2. Protecting HEALTH
3. Restoring HEALTH
4. Changing HEALTH

Answer: 3
Rationale: Traditional methods of restoring HEALTH—physical, mental, and spiritual—include the use of herbal remedies, exorcism, and health rituals. This situation describes a healing ritual. Methods of maintaining HEALTH include following a proper diet, wearing proper clothing, concentrating and using the mind, and practicing one's religion. Traditional methods of protecting HEALTH include wearing protective objects such as amulets, avoiding people who may cause trouble, and placing religious objects in the home. Changing HEALTH is not one of the traditional methods in the HEALTH traditions model.
Assessment
Health promotion and maintenance
Application
Learning Outcome 18.3

---

**18.10** A client makes the following statement: "I must be paying for all the wrongs I did in my life, to have such a diagnosis as this." The nurse understands that this client views health from which of the following beliefs?
1. Magico-religious belief
2. Holistic health belief
3. Biomedical health belief
4. Folk medicine

Answer: 1
Rationale: In the magico-religious health belief view, health and illness are controlled by supernatural forces. The client may believe that illness is the result of "being bad" or opposing God's will. The holistic health belief holds that the forces of nature must be maintained in balance or harmony. Human life is one aspect of nature that must be in harmony with the rest of nature. Biomedical health belief, also scientific belief, is based on the belief that life and life processes are controlled by physical and biochemical processes that can be manipulated by humans. Folk medicine is defined as those beliefs and practices related to illness prevention and healing that derive from cultural traditions rather than from modern medicine's scientific base.
Assessment
Psychosocial integrity
Application
Learning Outcome 18.3

**18.11** A Chinese client is hospitalized with a fever of unknown origin and follows a very traditional, cultural view of illness. Which of the following foods will the client prefer?
1. Hot tea
2. Soup and coffee
3. Spicy meat
4. Cold liquids

Answer: 4
Rationale: The concept of yin and yang in the Chinese culture is an example of a holistic health belief. A Chinese client who has a yang illness, or a "hot" illness, may prefer a yin or "cold" treatment. In this case, the fever would be considered a "hot" illness and the client may prefer the opposite or yin treatment. All of the other options would be similar to the illness the client is experiencing.
Implementation
Health promotion and maintenance
Application
Learning Outcome 18.3

**18.12** A community health nurse works with a variety of cultures providing health care services that include preventive care, acute treatment, and education. Of the following clients, which is most likely to use folk medicine?
1. The client who speaks little English and does not have a job
2. A family who has numerous relatives in a Spanish-American sector of the city
3. A female client whose culture is one of male dominance
4. A Chinese client who has a small, family run business in the area

Answer: 1
Rationale: Folk medicine is defined as beliefs and practices that relate illness prevention and healing derived from cultural traditions rather than modern medicine's scientific base. People who have limited access to scientific health care may turn to folk medicine or folk healing. Because folk healing is more culturally based, it may be more comfortable and less frightening for the client who is not fluent in the English language and has limited access to scientific health care. Folk medicine is thought to be more humanistic than biomedical health care. Even though any of the clients mentioned above could utilize folk medicine, it is more likely to be used by the first one described.
Assessment
Health promotion and maintenance
Application
Learning Outcome 18.4

**18.13** A female client is being discharged after a lengthy hospitalization. The family is from a male-dominated culture. Before discharge instructions are given, the nurse should:
1. Make sure instructions are understood by the client.
2. Arrange for teaching when the spouse is available.
3. Make sure that the physician gives the instructions.
4. Ask the client when the best time for teaching would be.

Answer: 2
Rationale: The nurse needs to identify who has the "authority" to make decisions in a client's family. If the decision maker is someone other than the client, as in this situation, the nurse needs to include that person in health care discussions. In this situation, we do not know if the nurse is male or female, so the best answer given with the information that is known is to arrange for teaching when the spouse is available. Regardless of who is present during the teaching, it's always necessary to make sure that the instructions are understood, but difficult to do that before instructions are given. In some cultures, men dominate and clients may be more receptive to instruction from a male nurse or physician, but not knowing the gender of the nurse, this may or may not be a suitable situation.
Implementation
Health promotion and maintenance
Application
Learning Outcome 18.5

**18.14** A client from a different culture than the nurse's has had numerous visitors during his stay. In fact, there are visitors in the room at all times. In order to address this in a culturally sensitive manner, the nurse should:
1. Tell the client that he has to limit visitors.
2. Evaluate the benefits of family participation in the client's care.
3. Question the family as to how they see their interaction with the client.
4. Have the physician limit the number of visitors the client can have.

Answer: 2

Rationale: Cultural family values may dictate the extent of the family's involvement in the hospitalized client's care. In some cultures, the entire community may want to visit and participate in the client's care. The nurse should evaluate the positive benefits of family participation in the client's care and modify visiting policies as appropriate. Telling the client he has to limit visitors or having the physician do this may be in conflict with cultural values and not be helpful to the client at all. It would be more appropriate to question the client, not the family, about the positive benefits of the family interactions. Obviously the family is supportive of their presence.
Implementation
Health promotion and maintenance
Application
Learning Outcome 18.5

**18.15** A client from a culture different from the nurse's has just been admitted to a unit. The unit is busy and the nurse has limited time to complete the nursing admission assessment. The best way for the nurse to show cultural sensitivity is to:
1. Break the assessment into shorter intervals and discuss general topics first.
2. Thoroughly explain the reason for asking many questions before beginning the assessment.
3. Pick a time when the family is present and can help with the admission assessment questions.
4. Wait until there is adequate time to complete the assessment.

Answer: 1

Rationale: Clients may be offended when the nurse immediately asks personal questions. In some cultures, courtesies should be established before business or personal topics are discussed. Discussing general topics can convey that the nurse is interested and has time for the client. This enables the nurse to develop a rapport with the client before progressing to discussion that is more personal. Even if the explanation is given, clients from some cultures may still find questions of a personal nature offensive so early in the nurse–client association. Waiting to complete the assessment is not a good idea as there is certain, initial information that needs to be collected from the client.
Implementation
Safe, effective care environment
Application
Learning Outcome 18.5

**18.16** A client is brought to the emergency department, does not speak English, and needs to have an emergency surgical procedure. The hospital has an interpreter available to explain the procedure and help with the consent form. When the interpreter arrives, the staff should make sure that:
1. The interpreter uses words the client is familiar with for the best understanding.
2. They ask the interpreter to translate as closely as possible the same words used by the professional staff.
3. The staff addresses the questions to the interpreter, so nothing is missed.
4. The client's family is included in the process and exchange of information.

Answer: 2

Rationale: An interpreter is an individual who mediates spoken or signed communication between people using different languages without adding, omitting, or distorting meaning or editorializing. The objective of the professional interpreter is for the complete transfer of the thought behind the utterance in one language into an utterance in a second language (California Healthcare Interpreters Association, 2002). Asking the client's family, especially a child or spouse, to act as an interpreter should be avoided. The questions should be addressed to the client, not the interpreter.
Implementation
Safe, effective care environment
Application
Learning Outcome 18.5

**18.17** A nurse is taking an admission history from a client of a different cultural group than the nurse's own. During the interview, the client averts her eyes and refrains from answering questions for long periods of time. The nurse should:

1. Come back at a different time, when the client is feeling more communicative.
2. Have another nurse finish the interview, since there is something uncomfortable the client senses.
3. Understand that this may be completely appropriate and take cues accordingly.
4. Leave the room and come back after having learned more about this particular culture.

Answer: 3
Rationale: Nonverbal communication includes silence, touch, eye movement, facial expressions, and body posture. Some cultures are quite comfortable with long periods of silence. Many people value silence and view it as essential to understanding a person's needs or use silence to preserve privacy. Before assigning meaning to nonverbal behavior, the nurse must consider the possibility that the behavior may have a different meaning for the client and family.
Implementation
Psychosocial integrity
Application
Learning Outcome 18.5

---

**18.18** The school nurse is doing school screening on children, and checking for head lice is part of the screening process. Before checking the head of an Asian child, the nurse should first:

1. Ask permission.
2. Make sure the child understands the reason for the contact.
3. Put gloves on.
4. Ask the child to wait until last, to avoid embarrassing the child.

Answer: 1
Rationale: In some Asian cultures, only certain elders are permitted to touch the head of others, and children are never patted on the head. Nurses should, therefore, touch a client's head only with permission. The nurse can explain the reason after permission is granted. Nurses should always wear gloves for this type of screening process. Asking the child to wait until last to avoid embarrassment is not appropriate.
Implementation
Psychosocial integrity
Application
Learning Outcome 18.5

---

**18.19** The nurse must complete a focused, physical assessment on a client after coming to the unit from another floor. Before performing the cardiac assessment, the nurse should:

1. Explain the procedure, then wait for permission to continue.
2. Tell the client what the nurse is doing during the assessment.
3. Ask the client to stay quiet since the nurse will be listening to the heart.
4. Take the baseline vital signs, then determine if cardiac auscultation is necessary.

Answer: 1
Rationale: Cardiac assessment requires that the nurse move into the client's intimate space. Before beginning this, the nurse should explain the procedure and then await permission to continue. Telling while doing or asking the client to stay quiet is not explaining the procedure and may make the client more uncomfortable, which will affect the outcome of the assessment. Taking baseline vitals is important but does not take the place of auscultating the cardiac system for irregularities or adventitious heart sounds.
Implementation
Safe, effective care environment
Application
Learning Outcome 18.5

---

**18.20** Time can take on different meanings in different cultural settings. When a nurse is teaching a client about a dressing change that should be done twice a day and the client is from a culture that is "present oriented," the nurse should instruct the client to perform the dressing change at which of the following times?

1. At times that the client selects
2. After breakfast and before going to bed

Answer: 2
Rationale: For clients who are "present oriented," it is important to avoid fixed schedules. The nurse can offer a time range for activities and treatments, such as in the morning or after breakfast, and in the evening or before going to bed. This would fit better with the client who isn't focused on times of the day, such as 10 AM and 4 PM, but at least would get the notion of twice daily into the client's schedule.
Implementation
Health promotion and maintenance
Application
Learning Outcome 18.5

| | |
|---|---|
| 3. At 10 AM and 4 PM<br>4. Whenever the client chooses, as long as it gets done twice daily | |
| **18.21** A client on a medical unit is a Jew who observes kosher customs. Which of the following food items would be appropriate to serve this client, assuming all have been properly inspected and prepared?<br>1. Hamburger, fruit, and milk<br>2. Fish, vegetables, and hot tea<br>3. Ham, baked potato, and fresh fruit<br>4. Cream soup, sausage, and toast | Answer: 2<br>Rationale: Orthodox Judaism and Islam prohibit the ingestion of pork or pork products (ham and sausage). Orthodox Jews observe kosher customs, eating certain foods only if they have been inspected by a rabbi and prepared according to dietary laws. The eating of milk products (milk and cream soup) and meat products (hamburger) at the same meal is prohibited.<br>Implementation<br>Psychosocial integrity<br>Application<br>Learning Outcome 18.5 |
| **18.22** A community health nurse is exploring the concept of heritage consistency among clients the nurse works with. Which of the following examples are indicative of heritage consistency? (Select all that apply.)<br>1. A client frequently visits the "old neighborhood" in the United States.<br>2. A client was raised by a single parent.<br>3. The client's childhood development occurred in an immigrant neighborhood.<br>4. The client participates in religious festivals and cultural events. | Answer: 1, 3, 4<br>Rationale: Other examples of heritage consistency include the following: extended family members encourage participation in traditional religious and cultural activities; the individual's family home is within the ethnic community of which he or she is a member; the individual was raised in an extended family setting; the individual maintains regular contact with the extended family; the individual's name has not been Americanized; the individual was educated in a parochial school; the individual engages in social activities primarily with others of the same religious or ethnic background; the individual has knowledge of the culture and language of origin; and the individual expresses pride in his or her heritage.<br>Assessment<br>Psychosocial integrity<br>Application<br>Learning Outcome 18.7 |
| **18.23** The nurse is working in a clinic setting and is meeting a new client for the first time. In order to convey cultural sensitivity, the nurse should introduce herself in the following way:<br>1. "I'm Jane, and I'll be your nurse today."<br>2. "I'm Dr. Smith's nurse, Jane."<br>3. "I'm Jane Brown, and I'm a nurse here at the clinic."<br>4. "I'm glad to meet you. You can call me Jane." | Answer: 3<br>Rationale: Ways for nurses to be culturally sensitive and to convey sensitivity to clients include introducing themselves by full name, then explaining their role. This helps establish a relationship and provides an opportunity for clients, others, and nurses to learn the pronunciation of one another's names and their roles.<br>Implementation<br>Safe, effective care environment<br>Application<br>Learning Outcome 18.8 |
| **18.24** A home health client participates in cultural health practices that the nurse feels may be detrimental to his health. In order to remain attentive to cultural sensitivity and provide appropriate cultural nursing care, the nurse should:<br>1. Explain the right and wrong of the client's treatment and try to persuade him to follow the scientific perspective.<br>2. Have the client's physician explain the care to the client in a firm but gentle manner. | Answer: 4<br>Rationale: Negotiation acknowledges that the nurse–client relationship is reciprocal and that different views exist of health, illness, and treatment. During the negotiation process, the client's views are explored and acknowledged, then relevant scientific information is provided. If the client's views can lead to harmful behavior or outcomes, then an attempt is made to shift the client's perspectives to the scientific view. "Right" and "wrong" terms should be avoided in culturally sensitive areas and where differing views are present. The nurse, not the physician, is the caregiver in this situation, so it is the nurse's responsibility to teach and see that the plan of care is carried out. If the client's practice is indeed harmful to his health, the nurse must try to negotiate to a better end.<br>Implementation<br>Safe, effective care environment<br>Application<br>Learning Outcome 18.8 |

3.  Validate the client's practices and understand that for this client, it may be beneficial to continue with his preferences.
4.  Try to negotiate with the client by exploring his views and then provide relevant scientific information.

---

**18.25** The nurse is evaluating the following goal: Client will select low-fat foods from a list by the end of the month. The client, who is from a different culture, has not been able to achieve this goal. The nurse should:
1.  Consider whether the client's belief system has been an influencing factor.
2.  Extend the time frame and give the client a longer period to achieve the goal.
3.  Make sure that the client understands the importance of the goal.
4.  Select a different goal.

Answer: 1
Rationale: If the outcomes are not achieved for a client from a different culture, the nurse should be especially careful to consider whether the client's belief system has been adequately included as an influencing factor. Extending the time frame, selecting a different goal, or checking how the client understands the importance of the goal may not be as helpful as looking at the cultural practices—including dietary ones—of the client.
Evaluation
Health promotion and maintenance
Application
Learning Outcome 18.8

# CHAPTER 19

**19.1** A nurse is helping a hospice client who has had difficulty with making end-of-life decisions. The nurse has encouraged the client to focus on her self-worth, her accomplishments, and having a positive self-esteem in order to process through some of these decisions. The nurse is helping the client to achieve balance in which of the following components?
1.  Environmental
2.  Physical
3.  Mental
4.  Spiritual

Answer: 3
Rationale: Mental aspects include feelings of self-worth, a positive identity, a sense of accomplishment, and the ability to appreciate and create. In terms of optimal wellness, balance consists of mental, physical, emotional, spiritual, and environmental components. Each component needs to be balanced, and a sense of equality among the components is needed. Environmental aspects include physical, biologic, economic, social, and political conditions. Physical aspects include optimal functioning of all body systems. Spiritual aspects involve moral values, a meaningful purpose in life, and a feeling of connectedness to others and a divine source.
Implementation
Psychosocial integrity
Application
Learning Outcome 19.1

---

**19.2** A home health nurse is working with a client who has had to quit his job after a serious injury and whose future employability is uncertain. The client states that his life has no meaning or purpose anymore and he feels so lonely, as if everyone has abandoned him. Which of the following is an appropriate nursing diagnosis for this client?
1.  *Body Image Disturbance*
2.  *Health-Seeking Behavior*
3.  *Altered Family Processes*
4.  *Spiritual Distress*

Answer: 4
Rationale: Spirituality is that which gives people meaning and purpose in their lives. It involves finding significant meaning in the entirety of life, including illness and death. The NANDA label *Spiritual Distress* is defined as disruption of the life principle that pervades one's biological and psychosocial nature. The feelings the client expresses have little to do with his body image or family processes, and he is not expressing the desire to increase his level of well-being.
Nursing diagnosis
Psychosocial integrity
Application
Learning Outcome 19.1

---

| | |
|---|---|
| **19.3** The nurse is working with a client who, during her interview, expresses feelings of groundedness. The nurse interprets this to mean that the client:<br>1. Is full of energy.<br>2. Feels connected to her reality.<br>3. Is focused on her center of energy.<br>4. Feels "down in the dumps." | Answer: 2<br>Rationale: Grounding relates to one's connection with reality. Being grounded suggests stability, security, independence, having a solid foundation, and living in the present. Energy is viewed as the force that integrates the body, mind, and spirit. Centering refers to the process of bringing oneself to the center or middle.<br>Evaluation<br>Psychosocial integrity<br>Application<br>Learning Outcome 19.1 |
| **19.4** A nurse has been working overtime shifts on a regular basis for the past month. Having a difficult time saying "no" when the supervisor asks, the nurse begins to feel overwhelmed and irritable. As a method to promote self-healing, this nurse should:<br>1. Clarify values and beliefs.<br>2. Set realistic goals.<br>3. Learn to manage stress.<br>4. Challenge the belief that others always come first. | Answer: 4<br>Rationale: Overwork and overinvolvement leave little time for fulfillment of personal needs. Nurses need to learn to ask for what they need and avoid feelings of selfishness when not responding to someone else's needs. Identification of things that are important, meaningful, and valuable is part of clarifying values and beliefs. Identifying long-term goals, then short-term goals that help in meeting the long-term ones, is a realistic way to accomplish both. Stress management requires acknowledgement of the mind–body connection and monitoring of stress signals.<br>Implementation<br>Psychosocial integrity<br>Application<br>Learning Outcome 19.3 |
| **19.5** During an interview assessment, the client states a belief in nutritional lifestyle counseling and the belief that the body's vital energy circulates through the body, which can be manipulated through specific anatomical points. This client most likely practices which of the following?<br>1. Traditional Chinese medicine<br>2. Native American healing<br>3. Ayurveda<br>4. Curanderismo | Answer: 1<br>Rationale: Traditional Chinese medicine (TCM) is based on the premise that the body's vital energy or qi circulates through pathways and meridians and can be accessed and manipulated through specific anatomical points along the surface of the body. Practitioners use a variety of ancient methods including acupuncture, acupressure, herbal medicine, massage, heat therapy, qigong, t'ai chi, and nutritional counseling. Native American healing is very connected to spirituality, and health is viewed as a balance or harmony of body and mind. Ayurveda emphasizes the interdependence of the health of the individual and the quality of societal life. Curanderismo is a cultural healing tradition found in Latin American cultures and utilizes Western biomedical beliefs, treatment, and practices.<br>Assessment<br>Psychosocial integrity<br>Application<br>Learning Outcome 19.1 |
| **19.6** The client asks whether herbal medicines are a "good idea." The nurse's best response is:<br>1. "Things found in nature are always healthy."<br>2. "If your doctor didn't prescribe it, don't take it."<br>3. "Are there specific ones you're wondering about?"<br>4. "Everything is good in moderation." | Answer: 3<br>Rationale: Not all plant life is beneficial. Nurses must be open to exploring and discussing their clients' uses of and questions regarding herbal medicine. There are cautions and contraindications with some herbal preparations and OTC as well as prescription drugs. The most important role the nurse plays in regard to herbal medicine is to find out what the client is taking, at what dosage, and have a full list of the client's prescription medications as well as anything taken that is OTC.<br>Assessment<br>Physiologic integrity<br>Application<br>Learning Outcome 19.4 |
| **19.7** A client comes to the family planning clinic for follow-up and is currently taking an oral contraceptive. During the interview assessment, the client states she has been using some "natural medicines." Which of the | Answer: 4<br>Rationale: Milk thistle reduces the effectiveness of oral contraceptives. Valerian may increase sedative effects of antianxiety medication. Echinacea may reduce effectiveness of immunosuppressants. Garlic may cause a need for an increased dose of antihypertensives. |

| | |
|---|---|
| following would alert the nurse to a possible interaction with oral contraceptives?<br>  1. Valerian<br>  2. Echinacea<br>  3. Garlic<br>  4. Milk thistle | Assessment<br>Physiologic integrity<br>Application<br>Learning Outcome 19.4 |
| **19.8** A client who has a long-standing history of depression has been on a prescribed antidepressant for several months. During his follow-up clinic visit, he states that he has also been trying St. John's wort, because he heard it was helpful in treating depression. Which vital signs should the nurse be attentive to, for possible adverse effects?<br>  1. Temperature<br>  2. Respiratory rate<br>  3. Oxygen saturation<br>  4. Pulse rate | Answer: 4<br>Rationale: St. John's wort may potentiate antidepressant medications, causing severe agitation, nausea, confusion, and possible cardiac problems. It would not affect the respiratory system.<br>Assessment<br>Physiologic integrity<br>Application<br>Learning Outcome 19.4 |
| **19.9** A client diagnosed with glaucoma has been using a prescribed medication for this condition. During a clinic appointment, the client complains of vision problems. When taking a medication history, which of the following herbal preparations should the nurse identify as being problematic for this client?<br>  1. Ginseng<br>  2. Echinacea<br>  3. Valerian<br>  4. St. John's wort | Answer: 1<br>Rationale: Ginseng may interact with caffeine and cause irritability and may also decrease the effectiveness of glaucoma medication. Echinacea may reduce the effectiveness of immunosuppressants. Valerian may increase the sedative effects of antianxiety medication. St. John's wort may potentiate antidepressant medications, causing severe agitation, nausea, confusion, and possible cardiac problems.<br>Assessment<br>Physiologic integrity<br>Application<br>Learning Outcome 19.4 |
| **19.10** A client diagnosed with hypertension has had well-controlled follow-up of her blood pressure for the past 6 months. At today's clinic appointment, the client's blood pressure is 198/102. The client insists she has been taking her prescribed antihypertensive medication, but also added an "herbal" tablet because she heard it was supposed to be good for her. Of the following, which is most likely interfering with the client's antihypertensive?<br>  1. Valerian<br>  2. Milk thistle<br>  3. Ginseng<br>  4. Garlic | Answer: 4<br>Rationale: Garlic may cause a need for an increased dose of antihypertensives. Valerian may increase the sedative effects of antianxiety medication. Milk thistle reduces the effectiveness of oral contraceptives. Ginseng may decrease the effectiveness of glaucoma medications.<br>Assessment<br>Physiologic integrity<br>Application<br>Learning Outcome 19.4 |
| **19.11** The nurse attended a workshop on the use of essential oils and their effects on body functions such as sleep, eating habits, and the immune system. The nurse works in a multispecialty clinic where a variety of clients are seen on a daily basis. The nurse should be attentive to clients with which chronic disease if they are using essential oils? | Answer: 3<br>Rationale: Some oils can trigger bronchial spasms, so persons with asthma should consult their primary health care provider before using oils. Different oils can calm, stimulate, improve sleep, change eating habits, or boost the immune system.<br>Implementation<br>Physiologic integrity<br>Application<br>Learning Outcome 19.4 |

1. Hypertension
2. Cardiac problems
3. Asthma
4. Cancer

| | |
|---|---|
| **19.12** A client with degenerative joint disease comes to the clinic and states that he has been reading a lot about essential oils that are helpful for body aches, for pain relief, and as anti-inflammatories. The nurse may offer the client information about the use of which oil?<br>　1. Chamomile<br>　2. Eucalyptus<br>　3. Lavender<br>　4. Tea tree | Answer: 2<br>Rationale: Eucalyptus feels cool to the skin and warm to muscles; decreases fever; relieves pain; and acts as an anti-inflammatory, antiseptic, antiviral, and expectorant to the respiratory system in a steam inhalation. It can also boost the immune system. Chamomile oil soothes muscle aches, sprains, and swollen joints and is helpful as a GI antispasmodic. Lavender oil is calming and is used as a sedative for insomnia. It may be massaged around the temples for headache, inhaled to speed recovery from colds or flu, and massaged into the chest to decrease congestion. It can also be used to heal burns. Tea tree oil is good for athlete's foot as an antifungal. It can be used to soothe insect bites, stings, cuts, and wounds. It can be bathed in for yeast infection, and drops on a handkerchief can be used for coughs or congestion.<br>Implementation<br>Physiologic integrity<br>Application<br>Learning Outcome 19.4 |
| **19.13** Systems of healing with emphasis on client responsibility, client education, disease prevention, or natural substances that stimulate a person's self-healing capacity are components of which of the following? (Select all that apply.)<br>　1. Naturopathic medicine<br>　2. Homeopathic medicine<br>　3. Aromatherapy<br>　4. Chiropractic | Answer: 1, 2<br>Rationale: Homeopathy is a self-healing system that utilizes remedies to stimulate a person's self-healing capacity. Naturopathic medicine is a way of life with emphasis on client responsibility, client education, health maintenance, and disease prevention. Aromatherapy is the use of essential oils of plants in which the odor or fragrance, when applied to the body, results in physiologic or psychologic benefit. Chiropractic is a type of manual healing method.<br>Assessment<br>Physiologic integrity<br>Application<br>Learning Outcome 19.1 |
| **19.14** Goals of chiropractic intervention include which of the following? (Select all that apply.)<br>　1. Improvement of blood and lymph flow through the body<br>　2. Stimulation of specific points to help with pain relief, cure certain illnesses, and promote wellness<br>　3. Reduce or eliminate pain<br>　4. Correct spinal dysfunction<br>　5. Preventive maintenance | Answer: 3, 4, 5<br>Rationale: By correcting spinal dysfunction, biomechanical balance is restored to the body to reestablish shock absorption, leverage, and range of motion. Muscles and ligaments are strengthened by spinal rehabilitative exercises to increase resistance to further injury. Preventive maintenance of chiropractic medicine ensures that the problem does not recur. Massage therapy improves blood flow and lymph fluid through the body. Acupressure and acupuncture are techniques of applying pressure or stimulation to specific points on the body in order to relieve pain, cure certain illnesses, and promote wellness.<br>Assessment<br>Physiologic integrity<br>Knowledge<br>Learning Outcome 19.6 |
| **19.15** A client who resides in a long-term care facility has no family or visitors. Her only social contacts are with the staff. The client is confined to bed and is not able to communicate verbally. As part of the client's care plan, the nurses provide massage therapy three times a week. Which of the following is the main benefit of this intervention for this client?<br>　1. Stretch and loosen the muscles | Answer: 3<br>Rationale: Massage would be an appropriate intervention to address all of the options listed. However, the question is the main benefit for this client. Since she has no family, no visitors, and her only contacts are with the staff, this client will benefit at the emotional level as massage satisfies the need for caring and nurturing touch. It also increases feelings of well-being, decreases mild depression, enhances self-image, reduces levels of anxiety, and increases awareness of mind–body connection.<br>Implementation<br>Psychosocial integrity |

| | |
|---|---|
| 2. Speed the removal of metabolic waste products<br>3. Help satisfy the need for caring and nurturing touch<br>4. Relieve pain | Application<br>Learning Outcome 19.6 |
| **19.16** A client visits a clinic that integrates Western medicine with complementary therapies. Which of the following therapies might the client utilize and believe to keep the flow of qi at a therapeutic level?<br>1. Acupressure and reflexology<br>2. Therapeutic touch and Reiki<br>3. Aromatherapy and naturopathic remedies<br>4. Chiropractic and massage therapy | Answer: 1<br>Rationale: Reflexology, acupuncture, and acupressure are treatments rooted in the traditional Eastern philosophy that qi, or life energy, flows through the body along pathways known as meridians. When the flow of energy becomes blocked or congested, people experience discomfort or pain on a physical level. They may feel frustrated or irritable on an emotional level and may experience a sense of vulnerability or lack of purpose in life on a spiritual level. Therapeutic touch and Reiki use the hands to alter the biofield or energy field. Aromatherapy and naturopathic remedies utilize essential oils and plants for health benefits. Chiropractic and massage therapy are examples of manual healing methods.<br>Assessment<br>Physiologic integrity<br>Application<br>Learning Outcome 19.7 |
| **19.17** A client is experiencing feelings of spiritual anguish, has been depressed, and has numerous somatic complaints that make the client feel like "everything is out of order." Which of the following is the most appropriate NANDA nursing diagnosis for this person?<br>1. *Energy-field disturbance*<br>2. *Powerlessness*<br>3. *Hopelessness*<br>4. *Anxiety* | Answer: 1<br>Rationale: Energy-field disturbance, defined as a state in which a disruption of the flow of energy surrounding a person's being results in a disharmony of the body, mind, or spirit, is listed as a nursing diagnosis by NANDA. *Powerlessness* is defined as a perception that one's own action will not significantly affect an outcome. *Hopelessness* is a subjective state in which an individual sees no alternatives or personal choices available and is unable to mobilize energy on his or her own behalf. *Anxiety* is defined as a vague, uneasy feeling, the source of which is often nonspecific or unknown to the individual.<br>Nursing diagnosis<br>Psychosocial integrity<br>Application<br>Learning Outcome 19.7 |
| **19.18** A client undergoing chemotherapy becomes very anxious and stressed just before the every-other-day treatments. Which of the following would be an appropriate therapy for this person to learn?<br>1. Meditation<br>2. Aromatherapy<br>3. Homeopathy<br>4. Yoga | Answer: 1<br>Rationale: Meditation is a general term for a wide range of practices that involve relaxing the body and easing the mind. Meditation is a process that anyone can use to calm themselves, cope with stress, and for those with spiritual inclinations, feel as one with God or the universe. Aromatherapy is the use of essential oils that, when absorbed into the body, produce physiologic or psychologic benefit. Homeopathy is a self-healing system in which doses of natural compounds stimulate a person's self-healing capacity. Yoga includes ethical models for behavior and mental and physical exercises aimed at producing spiritual enlightenment.<br>Implementation<br>Psychosocial integrity<br>Application<br>Learning Outcome 19.7 |
| **19.19** A client has been undergoing therapy as a victim of severe emotional abuse. The goal of the client's therapy is to gain self-control of the situation, improve self-esteem, and become self-sufficient. Of the following, which application is most likely used in the client's therapy sessions?<br>1. Yoga<br>2. Meditation | Answer: 3<br>Rationale: Hypnotherapy is an advanced form of relaxation and can be used to help people gain self-control, improve self-esteem, and become more autonomous. Hypnosis is routinely used with a variety of conditions, usually in conjunction with other forms of medical, surgical, psychiatric, or psychological treatment. Yoga includes ethical models for behavior and mental and physical exercises aimed at producing spiritual enlightenment. Meditation is a general term for a wide range of practices that involve relaxing the body and easing the mind. Guided imagery is a state of focused attention, |

| | |
|---|---|
| 3. Hypnotherapy<br>4. Guided imagery | much like hypnosis, that encourages changes in attitudes, behavior, and physiologic reactions.<br>Implementation<br>Psychosocial integrity<br>Application<br>Learning Outcome 19.7 |
| **19.20** A client has been diagnosed with post-traumatic stress syndrome and has difficulty sleeping because of recurrent nightmares. In working with this client to overcome the problem, the nurse may implement which of the following as part of therapy?<br>1. Guided imagery<br>2. Hypnotherapy<br>3. Yoga<br>4. Meditation | Answer: 1<br>Rationale: Guided imagery is a state of focused attention that encourages changes in attitudes, behavior, and physiologic reactions. Guided imagery can help people learn how to stop troublesome thoughts and focus on images that promote relaxation and decrease the negative impact of stressors. Hypnotherapy is an advanced form of relaxation and can be used to help people gain self-control, improve self-esteem, and become more autonomous. Hypnosis is routinely used with a variety of conditions, usually in conjunction with other forms of medical, surgical, psychiatric, or psychological treatment. Yoga includes ethical models for behavior and mental and physical exercises aimed at producing spiritual enlightenment. Meditation is a general term for a wide range of practices that relax the body and help ease the mind.<br>Implementation<br>Psychosocial integrity<br>Application<br>Learning Outcome 19.7 |
| **19.21** A nurse who works in a busy neonatal intensive care unit has been having difficulty with concentration after a long day's work. The nurse states to a co-worker that "it's hard to get my mind to relax after spending 12 hours focusing on alarms, machines, and sick, tiny babies, not to mention their worried parents." Which of the following might be an appropriate therapy for this nurse to utilize?<br>1. Guided imagery<br>2. Hypnotherapy<br>3. Qigong<br>4. Aromatherapy | Answer: 3<br>Rationale: Qigong is a Chinese discipline consisting of breathing and mental exercises combined with body movements. The softness of movements develops energy without nervousness. The slowness of movements quiets the mind and develops one's powers of awareness and concentration. Guided imagery is a state of focused attention that encourages changes in attitudes, behavior, and physiologic reactions. Hypnotherapy is an advanced form of relaxation and can be used to help people gain self-control, improve self-esteem, and become more autonomous. Aromatherapy is the use of essential oils that, when absorbed into the body, produce physiologic or psychologic well-being.<br>Implementation<br>Psychosocial integrity<br>Application<br>Learning Outcome 19.7 |
| **19.22** A nurse working on an Alzheimer's unit notes that just before the supper hour, many of the residents become more anxious and confused—exhibiting typical "sundowner's syndrome"—making the evening meal an unpleasant ordeal. As a method to try to decrease their turmoil during this time, the nurse introduces which therapy into the daily routine?<br>1. Biofeedback<br>2. Music therapy<br>3. Pilates<br>4. Spiritual therapy | Answer: 2<br>Rationale: Quiet, soothing music without words is often used to induce relaxation. Music therapy can be used in a variety of settings, without much added cost and little extra work on the part of staff. In this particular setting, the music may help to soothe the residents and promote a sense of balance or harmony on the unit. If it doesn't work, there is not much energy expended on the staff's behalf. Biofeedback is a relaxation technique that uses electronic equipment to amplify the electrochemical energy produced by body responses. Pilates is a method of physical movement and exercises designed to stretch, strengthen, and balance the body. Spiritual therapy includes prayer and faith practices to promote healing.<br>Implementation<br>Psychosocial integrity<br>Application |
| **19.23** A client comes to the clinic with a chief complaint of feeling "dirty" and asks the nurse how colonics would work to improve the client's overall well-being. Which response is the most appropriate? | Answer: 2<br>Rationale: Colonics is the procedure for washing the inner wall of the colon by filling it with water or herbal solutions and then draining it. Colon cleansing is a controversial method of detoxification, and there tends to be no middle group in the beliefs about the usefulness of colonics. Contraindications include people in a weakened state and those having ulcerative colitis, |

| | |
|---|---|
| 1. "Colonics is a dangerous and not useful technique that no one should try."<br>2. "There is much controversy about colonics. What do you know about it?"<br>3. "This is a good way to get rid of toxins in your system."<br>4. "You'd better ask your doctor about this." | diverticulitis, Crohn's disease, severe hemorrhoids, or tumors of the large intestine or rectum.<br>Implementation<br>Physiologic integrity<br>Application<br>Learning Outcome 19.9 |
| **19.24** A client was in a motor vehicle crash where he sustained injury (but no paralysis) to his spinal cord. The client has difficulty with balance and holding his posture. The nurse working with the client asks if he is familiar with therapy that might help improve these symptoms. The nurse is referring to which of the following?<br>1. Hippotherapy<br>2. Hypnotherapy<br>3. Chelation therapy<br>4. Detoxification | Answer: 1<br>Rationale: Therapeutic horseback riding, or hippotherapy, is the use of the rhythmic movement of the horse to increase sensory processing and improve posture, balance, and mobility in people with movement dysfunctions. Hypnotherapy is an advanced form of relaxation and can be used to help people gain self-control, improve self-esteem, and become more autonomous. Chelation therapy is the introduction of chemicals into the bloodstream that bind with heavy metals in the body. Detoxification is based on the belief that physical impurities and toxins must be cleared from the body to achieve better health.<br>Implementation<br>Physiologic integrity<br>Application<br>Learning Outcome 19.10 |
| **19.25** A client living in a long-term care center has been withdrawn and subdued, and does not eat in the dining room because of embarrassment about her physical decline. The nurse has been researching the use of complementary therapies for this client. Which of the following may provide opportunities for unconditional love, achievement of trust, responsibility, and empathy toward others?<br>1. Chelation therapy<br>2. Animal-assisted therapy<br>3. Meditation<br>4. Pilates | Answer: 2<br>Rationale: Animal-assisted therapy is defined as the use of specifically selected animals as a treatment modality in health and human service settings. The contributions include opportunities for affection, achievement of trust, responsibility, and empathy toward others. Pets in long-term care facilities become so perceptive that they actually gravitate to the rooms of people who are most isolated or depressed. Chelation therapy is the introduction of chemicals into the bloodstream that bind with heavy metals in the body. Meditation is a wide range of practices that relax the body and heal the mind. Pilates is a method of physical movement and exercise designed to stretch, strengthen, and balance the body.<br>Implementation<br>Psychosocial integrity<br>Application<br>Learning Outcome 19.10 |

# CHAPTER 20

| | |
|---|---|
| **20.1** A nurse is plotting the height and weight of children during a school assessment clinic. Monitoring these patterns is assessing which aspect of the child's health?<br>1. Development<br>2. Health<br>3. Growth<br>4. Bone size | Answer: 3<br>Rationale: Growth refers to the physical change and increase in size. Indicators include height, weight, bone size, and dentition. Development is an increase in the complexity of function and skill progression. It is the capacity and skill of a person to adapt to the environment. Health is a dynamic process with varying definitions, all of which point to well-being. Bone size is one of the indicators of growth.<br>Assessment<br>Health promotion and maintenance<br>Application<br>Learning Outcome 20.1 |
| **20.2** A parent brings a 16-month-old child to the clinic for a well-child checkup. During the assessment, the nurse finds that the child cannot stand next to furniture and does not try to pull himself up from a sitting position. | Answer: 2<br>Rationale: Development is an increase in the complexity of function and skill progression. It is the behavioral aspect of growth—the person's ability to walk, talk, and run. Growth is the physical change and increase in size. Height is one of the indicators of growth. Behavior is a component of the developmental stage. |

| | |
|---|---|
| The child is lagging in which of the following processes? <br> 1. Growth <br> 2. Development <br> 3. Height <br> 4. Behavior | Assessment <br> Health promotion and maintenance <br> Application <br> Learning Outcome 20.2 |
| **20.3** A child is starting school and is being screened for certain developmental milestones. How the child interacts with other children is most influenced by which of the following factors? <br> 1. Temperament <br> 2. Physical characteristics <br> 3. Environment <br> 4. Culture | Answer: 1 <br> Rationale: Temperament is the way individuals respond to their external and internal environment and sets the stage for the interactive dynamics of growth and development. Physical characteristics include eye color and potential height and do not affect how children interact, for the most part. Environment includes family, religion, climate, culture, school, community, and nutrition and would not play as big of a role in how the child responds to peers as temperament does. Culture is part of environmental factors. <br> Assessment <br> Health promotion and maintenance <br> Application <br> Learning Outcome 20.4 |
| **20.4** A parent brings a child to the clinic with concerns about the child's inability to sit alone. The nurse explains that development is based on in-born timetables and the child will be able to meet this milestone at a specific time. The nurse is basing this information on which theory of growth and development? <br> 1. Havighurst's theory <br> 2. Task theory <br> 3. Psychosocial theory <br> 4. Maturational theory | Answer: 4 <br> Rationale: The maturational theory (Arnold Gesell) postulates that child development is a maturational process based on an in-born timetable. Although children benefit from experience, they will achieve maturational milestones such as rolling over, sitting, and walking at specific times. Havighurst, in his developmental task theory, described growth and development occurring during six stages, each associated with 6 to 10 tasks to be learned. Psychosocial theory is focused on the development of personality, not physical development. <br> Assessment <br> Health promotion and maintenance <br> Application <br> Learning Outcome 20.5 |
| **20.5** A toddler shows fear and begins to cry when her parent leaves her at day care. According to Havighurst, which developmental task would this child be exhibiting? <br> 1. Building wholesome attitudes toward oneself <br> 2. Learning to get along with age-mates <br> 3. Learning to relate emotionally <br> 4. Achieving personal independence | Answer: 3 <br> Rationale: A toddler would be in the infancy and early childhood age period, of which *learning to relate emotionally to parents, siblings, and other people* is a developmental task. All other tasks listed are part of the middle childhood age period and would not be appropriate for this child. <br> Assessment <br> Health promotion and maintenance <br> Application <br> Learning Outcome 20.8 |
| **20.6** Which of the following developmental tasks are part of Havighurst's early adulthood age period? (Select all that apply.) <br> 1. Taking on civic responsibility <br> 2. Developing adult leisure-time activities <br> 3. Getting started in an occupation <br> 4. Relating oneself to one's spouse as a person <br> 5. Managing a home | Answer: 1, 3, 5 <br> Rationale: Other tasks of this age group include selecting a mate, learning to live with a partner, starting a family, rearing children, and finding a congenial social group. Developing adult leisure-time activities and relating oneself to one's spouse as a person are part of the middle age period. <br> Implementation <br> Health promotion and maintenance <br> Application <br> Learning Outcome 20.8 |
| **20.7** A parent questions the nurse about her 5-year-old who has begun to masturbate and question the parents about sexual differences among the | Answer: 4 <br> Rationale: In the phallic stage, as described by Freud, which occurs from age 4 to 6 years, the child's genitals are the center of pleasure. Masturbation offers pleasure, and questions about sexual topics with parents is normal. |

child's peer mates. The nurse, familiar with Freud's stages of development, responds by saying:

1. "All children are curious, but make sure the child knows that this behavior might be offensive to others."
2. "You should probably consult a child psychologist if you're this concerned."
3. "Let's make sure to ask your physician at the next appointment."
4. "This behavior is a normal part of your child's development."

Assuring the parent that this is a normal part of development is the best response.
Implementation
Health promotion and maintenance
Application
Learning Outcome 20.6

---

**20.8** A young adult has never lived away from his parents. He has difficulty making decisions and feels unable to make decisions on his own. According to Freud's theory of development, this person would be fixated at which stage of development?

1. Phallic
2. Latency
3. Genital
4. Anal

Answer: 3
Rationale: Freud's genital stage is characterized by energy that is directed toward full sexual maturity and function and development of skills needed to cope with the environment. It occurs during puberty and extends beyond. Implications of this stage include separation from parents, achievement of independence, and decision making. Fixation occurs at any stage and is the immobilization or the inability of the personality to proceed to the next stage because of anxiety. The phallic stage is from 4 to 6 years of age. The latency stage is 6 years to puberty. The anal stage is from $1\frac{1}{2}$ to 3 years.
Assessment
Health promotion and maintenance
Application
Learning Outcome 20.6

---

**20.9** A client is being seen in the mental health clinic for antisocial behavior. According to Erikson's stages of development, this client is dealing with which task of development?

1. Initiative versus guilt
2. Industry versus inferiority
3. Intimacy versus isolation
4. Identity versus role confusion

Answer: 4
Rationale: According to Erik Erikson, the adolescent stage is from 12 to 20 years and the central task is identity versus role confusion. Positive resolution indicates sense of self with plans to actualize one's abilities. Negative resolution indicates feelings of confusion, indecisiveness, and possible antisocial behavior. Initiative versus guilt is the late childhood stage and occurs from age 3 to 5 years. Industry versus inferiority occurs from 6 to 12 years, during the school-age stage. Intimacy versus isolation is the task during young adulthood and occurs from 18 to 25 years.
Assessment
Health promotion and maintenance
Application
Learning Outcome 20.7

---

**20.10** A client who has a terminal diagnosis has been using her time to help family members deal with her impending death. Among her activities, she collected pictures for a scrapbook and wrote a journal of favorite memories for family members to read after the client dies. According to Peck, this client is working through which of the following developmental tasks?

1. Body transcendence versus body preoccupation
2. Ego transcendence versus ego preoccupation
3. Ego differentiation versus work-role preoccupation
4. Integrity versus despair

Answer: 2
Rationale: Ego transcendence is the acceptance without fear of one's death as inevitable. This acceptance includes being actively involved in one's own future beyond death. Peck proposes that there are three developmental tasks during old age, in contrast to Erikson's one—integrity versus despair. Body transcendence versus body preoccupation calls for the individual to adjust to decreasing physical capacities and at the same time maintain feelings of well-being. Ego differentiation versus work-role preoccupation maintains that an adult's identity and feelings of worth are highly dependent on that person's work role. On retirement, people may experience feelings of worthlessness unless they derive their sense of identity from a number of roles so that one such role can replace the work role or occupation as a source of self-esteem.
Assessment
Health promotion and maintenance
Application
Learning Outcome 20.9

---

**20.11** A college-age client is seeing the nurse at the student health office. His statements indicate that he is struggling with feelings of independence, then feelings of dependence on his family again. The nurse recognizes this as which stage of development, according to Roger Gould?
1. Stage 2
2. Stage 3
3. Stage 4
4. Stage 5

Answer: 1
Rationale: Roger Gould studied adult development and described seven stages. Stage 2 (ages 18–22) is where individuals have established autonomy, feel it is in jeopardy, and feel they could be pulled back into their families. Stage 3 (ages 22–28) is when individuals feel established as adults and autonomous from their families. They see themselves as well defined, but still feel the need to prove themselves to their parents. Stage 4 (ages 29–34) is when marriage and careers are well established. Individuals question what life is all about and wish to be accepted as they are, no longer finding it necessary to prove themselves. Stage 5 (ages 35–43) is a period of self-reflection. Individuals question values and life itself. They see time as finite, with little time left to shape the lives of adolescent children.
Assessment
Health promotion and maintenance
Application
Learning Outcome 20.9

**20.12** A parent brings his child into the clinic for a well-child screening. He makes a statement to the nurse that the child is learning new words faster than he can write them in the baby book. According to Piaget, this child is in which of the following phases?
1. Intuitive thought phase
2. Preconceptual phase
3. Concrete operations phase
4. Formal operations phase

Answer: 2
Rationale: Ages 2 to 4 years, according to Piaget, is the preconceptual phase where the child uses an egocentric approach to accommodate the demands of an environment. Language development is rapid and the child associates words with objects. The intuitive thought phase is from age 4 to 7 years and is where egocentric thinking diminishes. The child thinks of one idea at a time and includes others in the environment. The concrete operations phase, ages 7 to 11, is where the child solves concrete problems. The child also begins to understand relationships such as size, right, and left, and is cognizant of viewpoints. During the formal operations phase (ages 11 to 15) the child uses rational thinking, and reasoning is deductive and futuristic.
Assessment
Health promotion and maintenance
Application
Learning Outcome 20.10

**20.13** A 20-month-old child is a client on the pediatric unit of a hospital. The nurse notices that this child is lagging in stage 6 of Piaget's phases of cognitive development. Which activity would indicate that this child is struggling at this stage?
1. The child wants the same toy to sleep with during naptime and bedtime.
2. The child merely watches as the other children pretend-play.
3. The child cries when the parents leave the unit.
4. The child does not cooperate with some of the treatments.

Answer: 2
Rationale: In this stage of development, inventions of new means, children interpret the environment by mental image. They use make-believe and pretend-play. A child who is unable to do this would not be demonstrating the behavior that is significant at this stage. Ritual is important for the child of the tertiary circular reaction, age 12 to 18 months. Crying when parents leave the unit and not cooperating with certain medical treatments is normal behavior for children of various ages, especially when hospitalized, and would not indicate lags in development.
Assessment
Health promotion and maintenance
Application
Learning Outcome 20.10

**20.14** A nurse who is exploring the behavior of children and how they interpret right from wrong or bad from good would best be served by studying which of the following theorists?
1. Vygotsky
2. Skinner
3. Kohlberg
4. Piaget

Answer: 3
Rationale: Lawrence Kohlberg's theory specifically addresses the moral development of children and adults. Vygotsky explored the concept of cognitive development within a social, historical, and cultural context, arguing that adults guide children to learn and that development depends on the use of language, play, and extensive social interaction. Skinner's research led to the term "operant conditioning" and most of his work was with laboratory animals. Piaget developed the cognitive theory of development.
Assessment
Health promotion and maintenance
Application
Learning Outcome 20.11

| | |
|---|---|
| **20.15** A nurse educator believes that teaching students without caring about them is an exercise in futility. This educator also believes that in meeting the students' needs, educators must also work to take care of themselves and care for their own needs. This educator's ideals represent which of Gilligan's stages?<br><br>   1. Stage 1<br>   2. Stage 2<br>   3. Stage 3<br>   4. Stage 4 | Answer: 3<br>Rationale: Gilligan's stage 3—caring for self and others—is the last stage of development where a person sees the need for a balance between caring for others and caring for the self. Stage 1 is caring for oneself. Stage 2 is caring for others. Gilligan does not describe more than 3 stages in her theory.<br>Implementation<br>Psychosocial integrity<br>Application<br>Learning Outcome 20.11 |
| **20.16** A nurse educator is working with students and assisting them in addressing their clients' spiritual needs. The educator understands that most traditional, second-year college students are aware of their own spiritual development or working to develop their own system of spirituality. Fowler describes this stage as which of the following?<br><br>   1. Mythic-lyrical<br>   2. Intuitive-projective<br>   3. Universalizing<br>   4. Individuating-reflexive | Answer: 4<br>Rationale: Fowler describes this as a stage in which the person is constructing his or her own explicit system with a high degree of self consciousness. Mythical-lyrical describes the person between ages 7 and 12, in a private world of fantasy and wonder. Symbols refer to something specific; and dramatic stories and myths are used to communicate spiritual meanings. The intuitive-projective stage, ages 4 to 6 years, is a combination of images and beliefs given by trusted others, mixed with the child's own experience and imagination. Universalizing, which may never be reached by an individual, is a stage of becoming incarnate of the principles of love and justice.<br>Assessment<br>Psychosocial integrity<br>Application<br>Learning Outcome 20.12 |
| **20.17** A client with an acute, serious illness has been hospitalized. Entering the room, the nurse observes the client praying. The client states to the nurse: "I don't know how people manage to get through difficult times without their faith. It's where I get my strength." The nurse correctly associates this belief with which theorist?<br><br>   1. Fowler<br>   2. Westerhoff<br>   3. Gilligan<br>   4. Kohlberg | Answer: 2<br>Rationale: Westerhoff describes faith as a way of being and behaving that evolves from an experienced faith guided by parents and others during a person's infancy and childhood to an owned faith that is internalized in adulthood. For the client who is ill, faith provides strength and trust. Fowler's theory describes the development of faith as a force that gives meaning to a person's life. Gilligan and Kohlberg are not spiritual theorists.<br>Assessment<br>Psychosocial integrity<br>Application<br>Learning Outcome 20.12 |
| **20.18** Westerhoff's spiritual theory describes four stages of development. Put these in order of when they occur in the life cycle:<br><br>_____ Owned faith<br>_____ Affiliative faith<br>_____ Experienced faith<br>_____ Searching faith | Answer:<br><br>\_\_\_\_4\_\_\_\_\_ Owned faith<br>\_\_\_\_\_2\_\_\_\_\_ Affiliative faith<br>\_\_\_\_\_1\_\_\_\_\_ Experienced faith<br>\_\_\_\_\_3\_\_\_\_\_ Searching faith<br>Rationale: Experienced faith occurs from infancy to early adolescence. Affiliative faith occurs in late adolescence. Searching faith occurs in young adulthood. Owning faith occurs in middle adulthood through old age.<br>Assessment<br>Psychosocial integrity<br>Application<br>Learning Outcome 20.12 |
| **20.19** A nurse is working with a school-age client who is learning how to use a peak flow meter to monitor his asthma. The child has been frustrated at first, but now is able to give the reason | Answer: 1<br>Rationale: School-age children (6–12 years) are in the preadolescent period where the peer group begins to increasingly influence behavior. The nurse must allow time and energy for the school-age child to pursue hobbies and school activities and should recognize and support the child's achievement. Play and |

to use the meter on a daily basis. Remembering the growth and development characteristics of the adolescent, which of the following is an appropriate response by the nurse?

1. "You should feel very proud for understanding and using your meter."
2. "Think of using the meter as one of your daily chores."
3. "Maybe you could make a game out of the daily use of your meter."
4. "It's too bad if you don't want to use the meter, it's just something you'll have to do."

social activity are more important in the preschool-age child as new experiences and social roles are tried during play.
Implementation
Health promotion and maintenance
Application
Learning Outcome 20.2

---

**20.20** A nurse is working with the residents of an assisted living complex. When planning care for the old-old stage, the nurse realizes that it will be important to:

1. Provide as much care to the residents as possible.
2. Allow as much independence for the residents as possible.
3. Make sure to provide safety measures as needed.
4. Maintain peer interactions and social groups.

Answer: 2
Rationale: The old-old stage, age 85 and older, is characterized by increasing physical problems. The nursing implication for this age group is to assist with self-care as required, but maintain as much independence as possible. Providing as much care as possible does not meet the independence need required in this age group. Safety measures should be applied in the middle-old age group, age 75 to 84 years. Peer interactions become important in the young-old stage, age 65 to 74 years.
Implementation
Health promotion and maintenance
Application
Learning Outcome 20.2

---

**20.21** A community health nurse is planning adult health education classes. According to Erikson's stages of development, the nurse must address which task with this age group?

1. Identity versus inferiority
2. Identity versus role confusion
3. Intimacy versus isolation
4. Generativity versus stagnation

Answer: 4
Rationale: Adulthood, age 25 to 65 years, is characterized by the central task of generativity versus stagnation. Positive resolution is indicated by creativity, productivity, and concern for others. Negative resolution is characterized by self-indulgence, self-concern, and lack of interests and communication.

Identity versus inferiority is the central task of the school-age child. Identity versus role confusion is the central task of the adolescent. Intimacy versus isolation is the central task of the young adult.
Assessment
Health promotion and maintenance
Application
Learning Outcome 20.7

---

**20.22** A parent brings her baby in for a well-child checkup. Which of the following would the nurse identify as an indicator of positive resolution of the central task of this age? The child:

1. Does not cry when the parent allows the nurse to hold the child.
2. Shows mistrust when strangers approach.
3. Becomes willful when disciplined.
4. Does not play with other children.

Answer: 1
Rationale: In the infancy years (birth to 18 months), the child's central task is to form trust or mistrust with people. Positive resolution would indicate a safe feeling when the parents leave the child with someone they are familiar with and can trust. Negative resolution would indicate mistrust, withdrawal, and estrangement. Willfulness and defiance are negative indicators of the early childhood stage. Playing with other children is also part of the self-esteem and self-expression of the early childhood years.
Assessment
Health promotion and maintenance
Application
Learning Outcome 20.7

---

**20.23** A parent tells the nurse that his child is quite creative and learning how to pretend with "almost anything in the house." According to Piaget, this child is descriptive of which stage/phase?

1. Tertiary circular reaction: stage 5
2. Inventions of new means: stage 6
3. Preconceptual phase
4. Concrete operations phase

Answer: 2

Rationale: Stage 6, inventions of new means, is from 18 to 24 months. The significant behavior is identified by interpretation of the environment by mental image. Make-believe and pretend-play are in use during this stage. Stage 5, 12 to 18 months, is characterized by discovery of new goals and ways to attain goals. Rituals are important in this stage. The preconceptual phase, 2 to 4 years, is when the child uses an egocentric approach to accommodate the demands of an environment. The concrete operations phase, 7 to 11 years, is where the child is able to solve concrete problems and begins to understand relationships such as size, right, and left, and is cognizant of viewpoints.

Assessment
Health promotion and maintenance
Application
Learning Outcome 20.10

# CHAPTER 21

**21.1** A client comes to the women's clinic, stating she has had a positive home pregnancy test. The client states that her last menstrual cycle was 2 months ago. According to this time frame, the client would be in which of the following?

1. Fetal phase
2. Second trimester
3. Third trimester
4. Embryonic phase

Answer: 4

Rationale: Traditionally, pregnancy has been divided into three periods called trimesters, each of which lasts 3 months. The embryonic phase is the period during which the fertilized ovum develops into an organism with most of the features of the human. This period is considered to encompass the first 8 weeks of pregnancy. The fetal phase of development is characterized by a period of rapid growth in the size of the fetus and corresponds to the second trimester of pregnancy. The third trimester is the last 3 months of the pregnancy period.

Assessment
Health promotion and maintenance
Application

**21.2** A baby was born prematurely during the sixth month of pregnancy. The new parents question the nurse about the hair all over their baby. The nurse's best response is:

1. "All babies are hairy. It is more noticeable on preemies."
2. "Fine downy hair helps keep the baby insulated in utero."
3. "You should be more concerned with the baby's respiratory function."
4. "Don't worry about how the baby looks. All preemies look funny."

Answer: 2

Rationale: Lanugo, a fine downy hair, covers the body of the baby and usually disappears by the time gestation is full term. Since this baby was born early, the lanugo is more noticeable and will disappear as the baby nears full term.

Implementation
Health promotion and maintenance
Application

**21.3** The nurse is working with a client who hopes to become pregnant within the next year. The client asks about nutritional needs before and during pregnancy. The nurse responds by telling the client she should increase her intake of which of the following food groups?

1. Meats, fish, and poultry
2. A mix of vegetables and fiber
3. Oranges and green leafy vegetables
4. Foods containing low fat and high protein

Answer: 3

Rationale: Folic acid is important to prevent neural tube defects in the fetus. The neural tube defect occurs in the first few weeks of fetal development. Folic-rich foods include green leafy vegetables, oranges, and dried beans. Clients should also be encouraged to take a vitamin supplement that contains folic acid. Protein sources, fiber, and low-fat foods are important for overall health but do not increase intake of folic acid.

Implementation
Physiologic integrity
Application

| | |
|---|---|
| **21.4** A client has just experienced a spontaneous abortion. Which of the following factors would indicate that the client was at risk for this to occur?<br>1. Taking a medication that was a known teratogen<br>2. Smoking<br>3. Having low levels of folic acid<br>4. Genetic history | Answer: 2<br>Rationale: Smoking has been associated with preterm labor, spontaneous abortion, low-birth-weight infants, sudden infant death syndrome, and learning disorders. Teratogens are medications known to adversely affect normal cellular development in the embryo or fetus. Folic acid is necessary for normal neural tube development. Genetic history does not affect the risk for spontaneous abortion.<br>Assessment<br>Physiologic integrity<br>Application |
| **21.5** A nursing student is studying the fetal development and growth process and asks the instructor why the first 3 months after birth are referred to as the "fourth trimester," since this term is used during the pregnancy period. The educator replies:<br>1. "Since it's part of the baby's first year, it is combined with the pregnancy period."<br>2. "The baby's major task is adjustment and he or she is very vulnerable during the first 3 months following delivery."<br>3. "The baby's birth weight is changing so rapidly that this time period is considered growth as during pregnancy."<br>4. "It is in correlation with their developmental stage, as described by Freud." | Answer: 2<br>Rationale: A newborn's basic task is adjustment to the environment as an individual. This makes them very vulnerable to the outside world. This stage is referred to, by some, as the fourth trimester. It is a time of rapid growth and development, but that's not the underlying reason for this term. Freud's developmental stage for this age group is the oral stage, since many of the infant's activities and pleasures are mouth centered.<br>Implementation<br>Health promotion and maintenance<br>Application<br>Learning Outcome 21.1 |
| **21.6** A 1-year-old is brought into the clinic for a well check. Her birth weight was 8 lb. If she is following normal growth and development patterns, what should her weight be at this point in her life?<br>1. 32 lb<br>2. 16 lb<br>3. 20 lb<br>4. 24 lb | Answer: 4<br>Rationale: Normal growth patterns dictate that infants usually reach three times their birth weight by 12 months, and twice their birth weight at 6 months. They typically gain weight at a rate of 5 to 7 ounces weekly for 6 months.<br>Implementation<br>Health promotion and maintenance<br>Application<br>Learning Outcome 21.2 |
| **21.7** New parents are discovering their baby and all his features the day after the baby is born. They ask the nurse why the baby's head seems lopsided and not round, as they thought it should be. The nurse's best response is:<br>1. "I don't think it looks unusual."<br>2. "Your baby's head had to shape itself to the birth canal. It will look round in a few days."<br>3. "You're right. We'll make sure your doctor checks this out."<br>4. "Babies' heads always look funny. Once his hair grows out, you'll hardly notice it." | Answer: 2<br>Rationale: Molding of the head is made possible by the fontanels and occurs during vaginal deliveries as the head comes through the birth canal. Within a week, the newborn's head usually regains its symmetry. It is normal with vaginal deliveries. Babies born via cesarean section do not experience molding. Molding is not permanent—a fact that makes parents feel more reassured.<br>Implementation<br>Physiologic integrity<br>Application<br>Learning Outcome 21.2 |

**21.8** The parents of a newborn ask the nurse about the things their baby can see. The nurse responds correctly by saying:

1. "Babies aren't able to see until they are around 4 months old."
2. "Babies won't track moving objects until about 5 months."
3. "Newborns blink in response to bright lights and sound and will follow large objects."
4. "Newborns aren't able to focus, so everything looks blurry to them."

Answer: 3
Rationale: Newborns can follow large, moving objects and blink in response to bright lights and sound. Their pupils respond slowly, and the eyes cannot focus on close objects. We don't know what they "see" or how it looks to them. At 4 months, the infant recognizes a parent's smile, though social smiles may appear at 2 months. At 5 months, the infant reaches for objects, but starts tracking them much sooner.
Implementation
Health promotion and maintenance
Application
Learning Outcome 21.2

---

**21.9** The parents of a newborn male ask the nurse about pain during circumcision. The nurse correctly responds with which of the following?

1. "Newborns can't feel pain, so don't worry about it."
2. "We'll make sure to bring your baby to you right after the procedure, so you can comfort him."
3. "I'll have the pediatrician speak to you about it."
4. "Newborns' pain experience is real. We'll use some medication to help your baby feel more comfortable."

Answer: 4
Rationale: Young babies react diffusely to pain and cannot isolate the discomfort. The pain of circumcision is not isolated in the genital region, but may be felt more diffusely, throughout the body. Newborns certainly do feel pain and it is important to comfort the child, but option 2 does not answer the parents' question. Nurses who care for newborns should be able to explain expected reactions to the parents.
Implementation
Physiologic integrity
Application
Learning Outcome 21.2

---

**21.10** An expectant parent asks the nurse about health problems of newborns. The nurse will provide information on which of the following? (Select all that apply.)

1. Infant colic
2. Respiratory tract infections
3. Failure to thrive
4. Injuries
5. SIDS

Answer: 1, 3, 5
Rationale: Health problems of newborns include infant colic, failure to thrive, and SIDS. Respiratory tract infections are more common for toddlers and in the school-age child. Injuries are more problematic as the child grows, especially in the school-age child.
Implementation
Physiologic integrity
Application
Learning Outcome 21.8

---

**21.11** New parents are concerned about the things their baby is and is not doing at age 8 months. The nurse might suggest screening the baby with which of the following?

1. DDST-II
2. Growth and development charts from the CDC
3. Assessment tools utilized by the state education department
4. Apgar scoring system

Answer: 1
Rationale: The Denver Developmental Screening Test (DDST-II) can be used to assess the infant's behavior and can be used from birth to 6 years. It is intended to estimate the abilities of a child compared to those of an average group of children of the same age. The CDC utilizes growth charts for physical assessment, but these do not address developmental issues. The school system assessment tools would be focused on the school-age child. The Apgar scoring system is used to provide information about the baby's physiologic adaptation within minutes after birth.
Assessment
Health promotion and integrity
Application
Learning Outcome 21.8

---

**21.12** The parents of a toddler are concerned that their child is so messy during eating, so they just feed him. The nurse's best response to this is:

Answer: 3
Rationale: Fine muscle coordination and gross motor skills improve during toddlerhood. At 2 years, the toddler should be able to hold a spoon and put it into the mouth correctly, albeit with some messes while he is learning. Assuring the parents that this will improve may help them with their patience during the messy times. Simply doing the skill for the child will allow no room for practice

---

1. "That's probably best. I'm sure it makes your meal time more pleasant."
2. "At least you're sharing meals as a family. That's the most important."
3. "Motor skills keep improving with age. Try not to get frustrated with the mess."
4. "Your child will never learn if you don't let him experience."

and error. However, the nurse must be careful in how this is worded, so as not to sound "scolding" to the parents.
Implementation
Health promotion and maintenance
Application
Learning Outcome 21.2

---

**21.13** A 4-year-old was hospitalized for several days with an acute illness. Though the child had control of bowel and bladder prior to hospitalization, now she has been wetting the bed at night and is having incontinent accidents during the day. The nurse addresses the parents' concerns with the following statement:

1. "Maybe your child should be seen by a specialist, just to make sure there are no physical problems."
2. "It is normal for some children to go through a stage of regression after separation from their family or after an acute illness. Try not to be too discouraged."
3. "You'll have to be very strict with discipline, so your child knows this behavior is not acceptable."
4. "I'd be upset too. It must be hard to go back to using diapers."

Answer: 2
Rationale: Regression is reverting to an earlier development stage (bed-wetting, using baby talk, etc.) as part of the child's experiences with separation anxiety. Nurses can assist parents by helping them understand that this behavior is normal and will pass as the child reestablishes herself as part of the family and works through her own frustration with the situation. Regressive behavior is not based on physiology and, unless it lasts, would not have to be further investigated. Strict discipline may not be the best solution over understanding and caring.
Implementation
Health promotion and maintenance
Application
Learning Outcome 21.1

---

**21.14** A kindergarten class is being screened by a group of nursing students who are working in a community health course. Few of the children have 20/20 vision. Most have 20/30, and some have 20/40. What observation would the nursing students make to their instructor?

1. "These children have normal vision abilities."
2. "We should check into the health of these children. Maybe their diet is lacking in essential vitamins since they all have poor eyesight."
3. "These kids will all be wearing glasses when we come back next year."
4. "We should use a different eye chart. Maybe the kids would understand it better."

Answer: 1
Rationale: Preschool children are generally farsighted and not able to focus on near objects. By the end of the preschool years, visual ability has improved. Normal vision for the 5-year-old is 20/30. The Snellen E chart should be used to assess the preschooler's vision. Unless there are other concerns, these findings should be considered normal and further investigation would be unnecessary.
Evaluation
Health promotion and maintenance
Analysis
Learning Outcome 21.2

**21.15** During an auditory screening of third graders, the school nurse identifies a hearing deficit for one of the students. When the parents ask the nurse about the findings, the nurse should respond:

1. "Hearing acuity is not fully developed in your child. Let's recheck next year."
2. "I'd like to recheck at the clinic. Then we may have to have your child seen by an auditory specialist."
3. "It was too noisy when we were testing, so I wouldn't be concerned if I were you."
4. "Your child will probably need a hearing aid."

Answer: 2

Rationale: Auditory perception is fully developed in school-age children, who are able to identify fine differences in voices, both in sound and pitch. Rechecking the results with a possible referral would be appropriate at this level. Auditory testing should be done in a quiet environment or none of the testing is accurate. The child's hearing test could be affected by a number of physiological variables (recent respiratory illness or excess cerumen in the ears), and telling the parents their child needs a hearing aid is both premature and not within the nurse's realm of practice.

Evaluation

Physiologic integrity

Application

Learning Outcome 21.2

---

**21.16** A school nurse is working with teachers in helping them address the developmental needs of grade school students, according to Erikson's theory of industry versus inferiority. The nurse suggests which of the following activities?

1. Providing time for running and playing sports, such as basketball, to increase gross motor skills
2. Allowing "pretend" time during their classes, like dress-up or role-playing
3. Presenting diversity in culture and practices as part of classroom study
4. Helping them develop skills needed in the adult world, like allowance budgeting

Answer: 4

Rationale: School-age children are motivated by activities that provide a sense of worth. They concentrate on mastering skills that will help them function in the adult world. Gross motor skills should be the focus of the preschool child, as well as make-believe and pretend opportunities. Understanding diversity, role preference, and performance is the task of the adolescent.

Implementation

Health promotion and maintenance

Application

Learning Outcome 21.3

---

**21.17** According to Kohlberg's moral developmental theory, school-age children progress through several stages of their development. Put the following stages in order, from 1 to 4.

_____ Punishment and obedience
_____ Law-and-order orientation
_____ Instrumental-relativist orientation
_____ "Good boy–nice girl" stage

Answer:

___1___ Punishment and obedience
___4___ Law-and-order orientation
___2___ Instrumental-relativist orientation
___3___ "Good boy–nice girl" stage

Rationale: Kohlberg's stage 1 of the preconventional level is punishment and obedience. Stage 2 is instrumental-relativist orientation. The conventional level has two stages. Stage 3 is the "good boy–nice girl" stage, and stage 4 is the law-and-order orientation.

Implementation

Health promotion and maintenance

Application

Learning Outcome 21.5

---

**21.18** A school health nurse is working on education programs for high school students. As part of the plan, the nurse wants to address health concerns of this age group, but focus on other topics besides the dangers of unprotected sex, or drug and alcohol abuse. Which class topic would be appropriate to present?

Answer: 1

Rationale: The 2003 Youth Risk Behavior Surveillance reported that most deaths in the age group from 10 to 24 years were caused by motor vehicle crashes, unintentional injuries (falls, drowning, poisoning), homicides, and suicides. Risky behaviors contributed to these statistics, but since suicide is one of the four major causes of death in this age group and depression or depressed behavior often leads to this end, it would be good if students understood what to look for in their peers. Injury prevention should be the focus in the school-age child. Cancer and heart disease are not prevalent problems among high school age students. Normal physiological

| | |
|---|---|
| 1. Warning signs of depression for peers to identify among their classmates<br>2. Injury prevention<br>3. Early signs of cancer and heart disease<br>4. Normal physiological changes of this age group | changes would not address health problems of this age group, just give general information.<br>Implementation<br>Health promotion and maintenance<br>Application<br>Learning Outcome 21.8 |
| **21.19** The school nurse is teaching a group of parents and their teenage sons a class about puberty and sexual growth. A parent asks the nurse about fertility in teenage males, specifically: "Does fertility coincide with ejaculation?" The nurse should reply:<br>  1. "Yes, if your son is ejaculating, he also possesses fertility."<br>  2. "Sexual maturity does not occur until age 18, so don't worry about anything until then."<br>  3. "Fertility follows several months after the first ejaculation."<br>  4. "You'll have to ask your physician about this since it is a sensitive subject." | Answer: 3<br>Rationale: The milestone of male puberty is considered to be the first ejaculation, which commonly occurs at about 14 years of age. Fertility follows several months later, with sexual maturity achieved by age 18. Ejaculation does not mean the same thing as fertility, which does occur before sexual maturity. The nurse, in presenting topics of a sensitive nature, should be able to answer questions regarding the topic, not referring the audience to a physician's opinion.<br>Implementation<br>Health promotion and maintenance<br>Application<br>Learning Outcome 21.2 |
| **21.20** A school nurse is counseling adolescents about risks for STDs. Using recent statistics, the nurse presents information that the number of new cases of STDs in this age group, each year, will be approximately:<br>  1. 1 million<br>  2. 2 million<br>  3. 3 million<br>  4. 4 million | Answer: 4<br>Rationale: According to statistics from the U.S. Department of Health and Human Services (2000), almost 4 million of the new cases of sexually transmitted diseases (STDs) each year occur in adolescents. One million teenagers become pregnant each year.<br>Implementation<br>Health promotion and maintenance<br>Application<br>Learning Outcome 21.7 |
| **21.21** A teenage girl spends most of her free time with friends or at school. Sharing their concerns about this behavior with the school nurse, the parents are worried about their child seeming to draw away from them. The nurse's best reply is:<br>  1. "You should really keep better track of your child. It's hard to tell what kinds of trouble they may be getting into."<br>  2. "Independence is really important for this age group. Try to be extra attentive when your child does spend time at home."<br>  3. "Use stricter guidelines for curfew and punishment if curfew is broken."<br>  4. "Is it possible that your child might be taking drugs?" | Answer: 2<br>Rationale: Many adolescents gradually draw away from the family and gain independence. This sometimes creates conflict within the family. The young person may appear hostile or depressed. It is not uncommon for adolescents to prefer to be with their peers, rather than their families. Parents should try not to increase controls as this may cause more rebellion in the child. Speaking with the child openly about concerns, the parents should be encouraged to provide a safe, secure home environment with enough freedom that the adolescent can appreciate.<br>Implementation<br>Health promotion and maintenance<br>Application<br>Learning Outcome 21.7 |

**21.22** An adolescent comes to the school nurse's office seeking advice about his friends and feeling pressure to participate in activities he isn't comfortable with (i.e., drinking parties and sexual explorations). The nurse should:

1. Tell the adolescent to stay away from "friends like that."
2. Be open to the concerns and provide accurate information about any questions.
3. Make a judgment about the adolescent's parents and encourage psychosocial counseling.
4. Give the adolescent pamphlets on sexually transmitted diseases.

Answer: 2
Rationale: The nurse must present an open, accepting attitude to the adolescent's questions while encouraging the adolescent to find relationships that promote discussion of feelings, concerns, and fears. Giving directions (option 1) or suggesting counseling may turn the student from seeking help. Just giving written information on a particular topic will not address the complete situation the student comes seeking assistance with.
Implementation
Psychosocial integrity
Application
Learning Outcome 21.7

**21.23** A nurse is teaching a class to new parents on how to handle some of the behaviors that could be demonstrated by toddlers. One of the parents asks what to do when their child throws a temper tantrum. The nurse should reply:

1. "Try to be more attentive to the behaviors that lead into a tantrum. Then you can avoid them."
2. "Put the child in a room alone and ignore the tantrum."
3. "Make sure the child is safe, then walk away."
4. "Hold the child tightly until he stops crying."

Answer: 3
Rationale: Making sure of safety, then walking away is part of fostering the toddler's psychosocial development. Sometimes, even with all the best intentions, toddlers throw tantrums. Parents should not be made to feel like it was something they did wrong or could have prevented. Placing the child away from supervision (in a room alone) could increase the risk of injury. Holding the child tight will only add to the child's frustration and make things worse.
Implementation
Psychosocial integrity
Application
Learning Outcome 21.7

**21.24** A school nurse is implementing a program to promote psychosocial development among adolescent teens at a high school. Which of the following activities should be included? (Select all that apply.)

1. Career planning
2. Establishing peer groups
3. Playing musical instruments
4. Developing a mentor program with teachers and parents

Answer: 1, 4
Rationale: Establishing peer groups would be part of psychosocial development of the school-age child. Learning to play a musical instrument would be motor development for the school-age child. Other psychosocial activities for the adolescent include activities to promote self-esteem, lifestyle choices that fit their identity, and determining belief and value systems.
Implementation
Psychosocial integrity
Application
Learning Outcome 21.8

**21.25** A baby was born with flaccid muscle tone, regular respirations with crying, heart rate of 85, and blue extremities. What would the Apgar score be?

1. 6
2. 7
3. 5
4. 8

Answer: 1
Rationale: Flaccid muscle tone = 0. Regular respirations = 2. Crying = 2. Heart rate of 85 = 1. Blue extremities = 1. Total = 6.
Assessment
Physiologic integrity
Application
Learning Outcome 21.7

**22.1** The nurse is working with a group of adults, ages 30 to 40, assisting them with preemployment physicals at a local industrial plant. This age group is representative of which of the following?
1. Baby Boomers
2. Generation X
3. Generation Y
4. Millennials

Answer: 2
Rationale: The Baby Boomers were born in the years 1945 to 1964. Generation X includes individuals born in years 1965 to 1978. Generation Y is the same as the Millennials, born between the years 1979 and 2000.
Assessment
Health promotion and maintenance
Application
Learning Outcome 22.1

**22.2** When working with young adults, the community health nurse realizes that the psychosocial developmental tasks include which of the following? (Select all that apply.)
1. Selecting a mate
2. Rearing children
3. Achieving civic responsibility
4. Finding a congenial social group
5. Developing adult leisure-time activities

Answer: 1, 2, 4
Rationale: Other tasks include learning to live with a partner, starting a family, managing a home, getting started in an occupation, and taking on civic responsibility. Achieving civic responsibility and developing adult leisure-time activities are tasks of the middle-aged adult.
Assessment
Health promotion and maintenance
Application
Learning Outcome 22.3

**22.3** A colleague is telling the community health nurse that their adult child has just moved back in with them. They are finding this situation somewhat difficult to adjust to. The nurse offers support and listens, while understanding that which of the following contribute to this particular trend? (Select all that apply.)
1. Maladaptive behavior
2. High unemployment rate
3. High housing costs
4. High incidence of chronic disease

Answer: 1, 2, 3
Rationale: These young adults, known as "Boomerang Kids," have moved back into their parents' homes after an initial period of independent living. Another factor that has contributed to this trend is high divorce rates. Chronic disease is not in high incidence among this age group.
Assessment
Psychosocial integrity
Application
Learning Outcome 22.3

**22.4** A nurse works with young adults, all assigned to the same shift in a manufacturing plant. There have been several episodes of discussion regarding working schedules over the holidays. They will be able to balance the emotional as well as logical side of the discussion based on which of the following?
1. Formal operational stage
2. Postformal thought process
3. Kohlberg's theory of moral development
4. Fowler's spiritual development theory

Answer: 2
Rationale: Postformal thought, sometimes called the problem finding stage, is characterized by creative thought, realistic thinking, problem forming, and solving. Postformal thinkers are able to comprehend and balance arguments created by both logic and emotion. Piaget's theory ended at the adolescent's formal operational stage. Young adults enter the postconventional level of Kohlberg's moral theory. This would not be considered a spiritual dilemma, so Fowler's theory would not be utilized.
Implementation
Psychosocial integrity
Application
Learning Outcome 22.3

**22.5** A nurse is working in a community health office that is often frequented by young adults. In assessing for potential problems, the nurse realizes that a leading cause of death in this age group is suicide. Which of the following factors may indicate a problem in this area? (Select all that apply.)

Answer: 1, 2, 3, 5
Rationale: Other factors indicating problems include a variety of physical complaints, digestive disorders, increase in isolation, problems with close relationships, and financial failure. Brain tumors are not an indicator for suicide.
Assessment
Psychosocial integrity
Application
Learning Outcome 22.7

1. Decreased interest in work
2. Weight loss
3. Depression
4. Brain dysfunction, including tumors
5. Sleep disturbances

| | |
|---|---|
| **22.6** An occupational health nurse is providing a hypertension screening at a local manufacturing plant. Among the employees, which group presents with the greatest risk for this problem?<br>   1. Male and female employees, equally<br>   2. African American males<br>   3. Asian American females<br>   4. White females | Answer: 2<br>Rationale: Hypertension is a major problem for young African American adults, particularly men. The causes for this are unknown. The other groups mentioned are not at higher risk than any other of this age group.<br>Assessment<br>Physiologic integrity<br>Application<br>Learning Outcome 22.7 |
| **22.7** A nurse is working in a community of mostly blue-collar workers and is planning an educational session for wellness, targeting the young adult group. In order to address one of the health problems of this group, the nurse plans to:<br>   1. Become more aware of marketing efforts by tobacco companies.<br>   2. Tell this group that smoking is unacceptable.<br>   3. Make sure the group is aware of the increased risk of liver disease and cancer of the esophagus.<br>   4. Counsel the group regarding addiction. | Answer: 1<br>Rationale: Smoking is a type of drug abuse prevalent in this age group, which can lead to lung cancer and cardiovascular disease (not esophageal cancer and liver disease). The nurse's role regarding smoking is to serve as a role model by not smoking, provide educational information regarding the dangers of smoking (not just "tell" or "counsel" about it), help make smoking socially unacceptable, suggest resources such as hypnosis, and assist with lifestyle training and behavior modification to clients who desire to stop smoking.<br>Implementation<br>Health promotion and maintenance<br>Application<br>Learning Outcome 22.9 |
| **22.8** During an educational session regarding physical changes of the middle-aged adult, a question is asked regarding weight loss. The nurse's best response is:<br>   1. "Weight loss is no different during this time than any other time of your life."<br>   2. "Metabolism slows during middle age, which may result in weight gain."<br>   3. "As long as you exercise appropriately, weight loss will be ensured."<br>   4. "Weight loss is always a good idea, regardless of your age." | Answer: 2<br>Rationale: The nurse should educate clients regarding physical changes occurring in their bodies. Statements that generalize weight loss with all other age groups are neither accurate nor helpful to the person asking the question. Age does make a difference in how the body responds to diet and exercise, and it is important for nurses to be well informed and educated regarding age-related changes.<br>Implementation<br>Health promotion and maintenance<br>Application<br>Learning Outcome 22.2 |
| **22.9** A client comes to the clinic with a history of pain in his testicle. During the interview assessment, which of the following should be of concern to the nurse?<br>   1. The client works as an auto-detailer.<br>   2. He smokes ½ pack of cigarettes per week. | Answer: 3<br>Rationale: Testicular cancer is the most common neoplasm in men between the ages of 20 and 34. Monthly testicular self-examination, a means of early identification of malignancy, used to be recommended for all men. More recent recommendations from the American Cancer Society (ACS) are that men should have a testicular exam as part of a yearly physical exam. Auto-detailing and smoking would put the client at risk for respiratory problems.<br>Assessment |

| | |
|---|---|
| 3. He has not had a yearly exam for 5 years.<br>4. He does not perform testicular self-exam. | Physiologic integrity<br>Application<br>Learning Outcome 22.7 |
| **22.10** A young female client comes into the emergency department with vague physical symptoms and does not make eye contact with the nurse during the interview. In order to understand exactly what might be going on, the nurse should ask which of the following questions?<br>1. "Can you tell me what's been going on in your life lately?"<br>2. "What kind of problems are you having?"<br>3. "Is someone hurting you?"<br>4. "Can you explain what your family life is like?" | Answer: 3<br>Rationale: A nurse who works with women should explicitly ask if the young adult is frightened or hurt by someone she knows. It is essential that nurses make assessment for domestic violence part of their routine. Generalized questions about family life, life problems, or events in the person's life only allow for the topic of domestic abuse to be skirted and perhaps avoided altogether. The nurse needs to address it pointedly and directly.<br>Assessment<br>Psychosocial integrity<br>Application<br>Learning Outcome 22.7 |
| **22.11** The nurse is providing education regarding early detection of breast cancer to a group of women between the ages of 30 and 40. According to recommendations from the American Cancer Society, the nurse explains that it is important for these women to:<br>1. Do monthly breast self-exams.<br>2. Have a yearly mammogram.<br>3. See a physician if there is a strong family history of breast cancer.<br>4. Have an annual breast exam performed by a health care provider. | Answer: 4<br>Rationale: Breast self-exam is no longer recommended for all women. The American Cancer Society recommends that young women who choose to do breast self-exam have their technique validated by a health care practitioner at a yearly physical exam. The earlier a lump is discovered, the greater the effectiveness of treatment. Yearly mammography for all women over the age of 40 is encouraged as it decreases the mortality from breast cancer.<br>Implementation<br>Health promotion and maintenance<br>Application<br>Learning Outcome 22.7 |
| **22.12** A community health nurse is doing a screening for cervical cancer at a women's health fair. Which of the following clients would have the highest risk factor for cervical cancer?<br>1. The client who had a difficult vaginal delivery 2 years ago<br>2. The client who has a history of genital herpes<br>3. The client who was married at age 27<br>4. The client who has a sister with breast cancer | Answer: 2<br>Rationale: High risk factors for cervical cancer include sexual activity at an early age, multiple sexual partners, and a history of syphilis, herpes genitalis, or *Trichomonas vaginitis*. Risk factors not included are options 1, 3, and 4. A first-degree relative with breast cancer would be a high-risk factor if the nurse was screening for breast cancer.<br>Assessment<br>Health promotion and maintenance<br>Application<br>Learning Outcome 22.7 |
| **22.13** A 30-year-old client who plans to do some traveling within the United States asks the nurse about appropriate immunizations. The nurse should recommend that the client:<br>1. Have a tetanus booster if the client has not had one within the last 5 years.<br>2. Have the hepatitis B immunization series. | Answer: 3<br>Rationale: Recommended immunizations for this age group include tetanus-diphtheria booster every 10 years and meningococcal vaccine if not given in early adolescence. The hepatitis B series would not be recommended for travel within the United States.<br>Implementation<br>Health promotion and maintenance<br>Application<br>Learning Outcome 22.8 |

| | |
|---|---|
| 3. Receive a meningococcal vaccine if the client did not receive one as a teen.<br>4. Not worry about immunizations as they are not recommended for this age group. | |
| **22.14** A nurse is working with a group of middle-aged adults and has decided to set up an educational session regarding the psychosocial development of this age group. According to Erikson's theory, what activity would best meet the needs of this stage?<br>1. Providing opportunity to mentor school-age children<br>2. Giving the group handouts regarding peer socialization<br>3. Helping the members of this group find appropriate civic responsibility<br>4. Assisting the group members to look at their life accomplishments | Answer: 1<br>Rationale: Erikson viewed the developmental choice of the middle-aged adult as generativity versus stagnation. Generativity is defined as concern for establishing and guiding the next generation. This could be accomplished through a mentor program with school-age children. Peer socialization and finding civic responsibility are tasks of the young adult and adolescent. Taking inventory of past accomplishments is the task of the older adult.<br>Implementation<br>Health promotion and maintenance<br>Application<br>Learning Outcome 22.3 |
| **22.15** The nurse is assisting in a community health project for middle-aged adults and wants to research which members of the community have been successful in the tasks identified by Erikson. Which indicators would the nurse look for in middle-aged adults?<br>1. Ability to have satisfaction in their volunteer activities<br>2. Ability to find an acceptable social group<br>3. Satisfaction with rearing children<br>4. Ability to manage a home | Answer: 1<br>Rationale: Erikson identifies this stage as generativity versus stagnation. Generative middle-aged persons are able to feel a sense of comfort in their lifestyle and receive gratification from charitable endeavors. The other options identify tasks associated with the young adult stage.<br>Assessment<br>Physiologic integrity<br>Application<br>Learning Outcome 22.3 |
| **22.16** The nurse is providing assistance at a community health fair that targets the middle-aged client. Which of the following statements is true for this age group?<br>1. The middle-aged person has decreased physical and cognitive abilities as a result of the normal aging process.<br>2. Adults make the transition into this stage easily and without problems.<br>3. Physical capabilities and functions decrease with age, but mental and social capacities tend to increase in the latter part of life.<br>4. Cognitive and intellectual abilities are somewhat decreased due to slower reaction time, loss of memory, and changes in perception and problem solving. | Answer: 3<br>Rationale: Physical capabilities and functions do decrease with age, but the mental and social capacities actually increase in the latter part of life. Transition into middle life can be as critical as during adolescence. Some refer to the "midlife crisis" and call the decade between 35 and 45 years the "deadline decade." Cognitive and intellectual abilities change very little during this time.<br>Assessment<br>Health promotion and maintenance<br>Application<br>Learning Outcome 22.8 |

**22.17** A client has been coming to the same clinic for a long time. The nurse can identify movement into Kohlberg's postconventional level when the client, after being asked about work, makes this statement:

1. "Oh, the work isn't so bad anymore. I'm getting close to retirement."
2. "Work is fine, but my family and friends are so much more important to me."
3. "I've done a good job for the company. I'm proud of my years there."
4. "I don't like to talk about work when I'm not there."

Answer: 2
Rationale: According to Kohlberg, the extensive experience of personal moral choice and responsibility is required to move into the postconventional level. Movement from a law-and-order orientation to a social contract orientation requires that the individual move to a stage in which rights of others take precedence—as in the statement that work is OK, but family and friends are more important. Statements about work not being so bad or not wanting to talk about it show a complacency about work—it's coming to an end because the person is nearing retirement. Stating that the person has pride about work and the time spent doing it would be an example of Erikson's stage of integrity versus despair.
Assessment
Psychosocial integrity
Evaluation
Learning Outcome 22.5

**22.18** The nurse is performing a community assessment. Which of the listed assessment data from this community would follow the national norms regarding disease for the middle-aged adult?

1. Cancer is the leading cause of death in the age group from 25 to 64 years.
2. Coronary heart disease is the leading cause of death.
3. Leading causes of death include suicide and motor vehicle crashes.
4. Injuries and chronic disease are the leading causes of death in this age group.

Answer: 4
Rationale: Motor vehicle crashes as well as occupational injuries along with chronic disease such as cancer and cardiovascular disease *combined* make up the leading causes of death in the middle-aged adult group. Coronary heart disease is the leading cause of death among all age groups in the United States. Cancer is the second leading cause of death among people between the ages of 25 and 64 years.
Assessment
Physiologic integrity
Application
Learning Outcome 22.7

**22.19** A middle-aged client is struggling with life changes, including menopause. The best response by the nurse to this client is:

1. "Don't worry, menopause can't last forever."
2. "There are some very good antidepressants you can take."
3. "What did your mother do to get through menopause?"
4. "There is a menopause support group that meets every 2 weeks."

Answer: 4
Rationale: Clients experiencing developmental stressors like menopause, the climacteric, aging, impending retirement, or any other situational stressors may experience anxiety and depression. These clients may benefit from support groups or individual therapy to help them cope with specific crises. Telling a client who is struggling not to worry is not therapeutic and does not address the problem. Advice about medications is not within nurses' scope of practice, since they do not prescribe. Comparing this client's situation to her mother's is neither relevant nor therapeutic. Her mother's age group was going through experiences in a different time and culture.
Implementation
Health promotion and maintenance
Application
Learning Outcome 22.7

**22.20** A group of middle-aged clients is coming to the community health center inquiring about health problems inherent in their age group. If the nurse wants to focus on a nutritional aspect in order to address the physiological changes of this age group, the nurse should:

1. Provide information, including a website, regarding diet plans.

Answer: 1
Rationale: Decreased metabolic activity and decreased physical activity mean a decrease in caloric needs. This particular age group must be educated regarding nutrition, exercise, and the relationship to chronic diseases such as diabetes mellitus and heart problems. Recent changes in the U.S. Department of Agriculture's Food Pyramid encourage nutrient intake based on physical activity, age, and gender. Clients may be directed to the food pyramid website at www.My Pyramid.gov to design a customized, healthy diet plan for themselves. It is the nurse's responsibility to

| | |
|---|---|
| 2. Give all clients a handout on diets recommended by the ADA.<br>3. Tell the clients to check with their physician before dieting.<br>4. Have them write to the U.S. Department of Agriculture. | provide information, education, and sources for clients seeking improvement in their nutritional lives.<br>Implementation<br>Health promotion and maintenance<br>Application<br>Learning Outcome 22.9 |

# CHAPTER 23

| | |
|---|---|
| **23.1** A nurse is working with a group of clients in a community center, all over the age of 85. This group is referred to as which of the following?<br>  1. Young-old<br>  2. Middle-old<br>  3. Old-old<br>  4. Elite-old | Answer: 3<br>Rationale: Ages 65 to 74 years are referred to as the young-old. Ages 75 to 84 are the middle-old. Ages 85 to 100 are the old-old, and individuals over 100 are considered the elite-old.<br>Assessment<br>Health promotion and maintenance<br>Knowledge<br>Learning Outcome 23.1 |
| **23.2** When working with the older adult age group, the nurse realizes that physiological and psychosocial changes will be evident. Those in this age group who will have at least one chronic disease condition will constitute what portion of the group?<br>  1. 50% of the group<br>  2. 80% of the group<br>  3. 100% of the group<br>  4. 90% of the group | Answer: 2<br>Rationale: According to the CDC (Centers for Disease Control and Prevention, 2004), 80% of older adults have one chronic health condition and 50% have two.<br>Assessment<br>Physiologic integrity<br>Knowledge<br>Learning Outcome 23.2 |
| **23.3** A nurse is presenting a health education program to a group of older adults at a senior citizens center. Considering the physiological changes of this age group, how should the temperature of the room be set?<br>  1. It should be set at a temperature that is comfortable for the nurse.<br>  2. It should be set cooler than what is comfortable for the nurse.<br>  3. It should be set warmer than the nurse's preference.<br>  4. Temperature of the room is not one of the nurse's concerns. | Answer: 3<br>Rationale: Because elderly persons have a loss of subcutaneous fat, their tolerance of cold is decreased and they typically enjoy warmer temperatures. If the environment is not comfortable to the audience, they will be distracted and not be able to focus or concentrate on the presentation and any information the nurse shares.<br>Implementation<br>Physiologic integrity<br>Application<br>Learning Outcome 23.8 |
| **23.4** The nurse is reviewing the chart of an elderly client before the client comes into the clinic. In this review, the nurse reads that the client has sarcopenia. What will the nurse expect to find the client complaining of?<br>  1. Weight loss and nausea<br>  2. Hair loss and thin skin<br>  3. Bleeding and bruising tendencies<br>  4. Lack of strength and tiring easily | Answer: 4<br>Rationale: Sarcopenia is defined as a steady decrease in muscle fibers, a normal physiological change of aging. The age-related mechanism appears to be related to denervation of the muscle and causes elders to often complain about their lack of strength and how quickly they tire. Alopecia is loss of hair. Thrombocytopenia may cause bleeding and bruising.<br>Implementation<br>Physiologic integrity<br>Application<br>Learning Outcome 23.8 |
| **23.5** An elderly client comes to the clinic for follow-up after a long hospitalization. When the client asks about increasing strength and endurance, the nurse should respond with which of the following? | Answer: 1<br>Rationale: There is evidence that an older adult's muscles can be strengthened through exercise and training, with concomitant improvements in functional status. It would be inappropriate for the nurse to assume that there is no room for improvement or that the client is a |

| | |
|---|---|
| 1. "Your muscles can be strengthened which might help you function better." <br> 2. "It won't matter if you exercise. At your age, there's little room for improvement." <br> 3. "Once muscle mass is decreased, there's nothing that can be done for strength improvement." <br> 4. "Maybe you should think about going to a nursing home. At least the people there will be able to help with your needs." | suitable candidate for long-term care. Physical changes associated with the aging process are normal, but not something that can't be improved upon. <br> Implementation <br> Physiologic integrity <br> Application <br> Learning Outcome 23.8 |
| **23.6** A group of elderly women come to the community center for exercise classes taught by the community health nurse. This activity will help with which of the following? <br> 1. Reverse the effects of aging and cure pain. <br> 2. Slow bone density loss and decrease muscle atrophy. <br> 3. Eliminate the risk for osteoporosis. <br> 4. Prevent pathologic fractures. | Answer: 2 <br> Rationale: Programs of physical activity and proper nutrition will slow bone density loss and decrease muscle atrophy and stiffness that occurs with aging. Exercise and proper nutrition will NOT reverse the effects of aging, nor will they eliminate the risk for osteoporosis. Weight-bearing exercise and calcium supplements taken earlier in life may reduce the risk for osteoporosis. Pathologic fractures occur spontaneously, without a fall or trauma to the bone. Many are a result of low bone density or tumor. <br> Implementation <br> Physiologic integrity <br> Application <br> Learning Outcome 23.8 |
| **23.7** A nurse is teaching a wellness class for older adults. In order to address the sensory loss that accompanies the aging process, the nurse should recommend that these clients: <br> 1. Use hearing aids and glasses. <br> 2. Wear shaded glasses indoors to reduce glare. <br> 3. Switch to brighter lighting in their home. <br> 4. Exercise more and eat higher amounts of calcium. | Answer: 3 <br> Rationale: Changes in vision associated with aging include loss of visual acuity, less power of adaptation to darkness and dim light, decrease in accommodation to near and far objects, loss of peripheral vision, and difficulty in discriminating similar colors. Having brighter lighting in their home may help with some of these vision changes. Wearing darker glasses will not increase the brightness of the home. Not all elderly people need glasses or hearing aids. Exercise and nutrition do not address sensory problems. <br> Implementation <br> Physiologic integrity <br> Application <br> Learning Outcome 23.8 |
| **23.8** A school nurse is bringing a group of students to a nursing home for a social exchange project. Before the students arrive, the nurse reminds them to do which of the following when speaking to the residents? <br> 1. Speak as loud as they can. <br> 2. Speak into the residents' ears. <br> 3. Write out what they want to say on a piece of paper. <br> 4. Speak distinctly, while facing the residents. | Answer: 4 <br> Rationale: Hearing loss in the elderly is greater in the higher frequencies than the lower. Older adults with hearing loss usually hear speakers with low, distinct voices best and it is always appropriate to speak while facing a target. The first three options assume that all residents have significant hearing loss, which is ageism. <br> Implementation <br> Health promotion and maintenance <br> Application <br> Learning Outcome 23.8 |
| **23.9** A nurse is preparing an education program on safety concerns for elderly adults living in their own homes. To address the sensory changes in this age group, the nurse will recommend that this group have which of the following? <br> 1. Carbon monoxide detectors that are checked on a scheduled basis | Answer: 1 <br> Rationale: Decreased or absent sense of smell adds to the safety issues of this age group. Because of this, and if the elderly person's home has natural gas appliances or furnace, a carbon monoxide detector would alert the person of any gas leaks or problems present. Emergency numbers by the phone is a good idea, but does not address sensory changes. Telephones that utilize a blinking light are used for people who are significantly hearing impaired. It is not necessary for someone to do cooking for this age group, |

| | |
|---|---|
| 2. A list of emergency numbers near the phone<br>3. Telephones that use a blinking light instead of a ringer<br>4. Someone to do their cooking for them | though they may be inclined to use more salt due to decreased sense of smell and taste.<br>Implementation<br>Health promotion and maintenance<br>Application<br>Learning Outcome 23.8 |
| **23.10** An elderly client comes to the clinic after checking his blood pressure several times in the local discount store. The nurse checks the blood pressure and finds that it is 146/80. The nurse's best response to this client is:<br>1. "Having blood pressure a little high is normal at your age. Yours is fine."<br>2. "I'll recheck this in a while, but your systolic pressure is too high."<br>3. "We'll wait and see what the doctor says, but I doubt he will be concerned."<br>4. "You should be on high blood pressure medicine." | Answer: 2<br>Rationale: Isolated systolic hypertension was considered to be "normal" in older adults and was frequently not treated. Now, evidence indicates that a systolic pressure of greater than 140 mm Hg is as problematic in older adults as in younger ones and should be treated. It would be up to the physician or primary care provider whether or not to treat. The nurse does not make this decision.<br>Evaluation<br>Physiologic integrity<br>Application<br>Learning Outcome 23.8 |
| **23.11** The elderly client comes in complaining of gastrointestinal problems, including frequent constipation and indigestion. The client has not had any recent weight loss. What should the nurse realize about these symptoms?<br>1. They indicate a concern and could be caused by cancer.<br>2. They indicate the need for an upper and lower GI x-ray series.<br>3. They could be related to normal changes in muscle tone and activity.<br>4. They are probably indicative of a gastric ulcer or colitis. | Answer: 3<br>Rationale: With the normal aging process, there is a decrease in muscle tone, digestive juices, and intestinal activity. These together may lead to indigestion and constipation in the older adult. It would be premature, as well as outside the scope of nursing practice, for the nurse to consider any other pathology or to tell the client that there is a need for invasive testing.<br>Assessment<br>Physiologic integrity<br>Application<br>Learning Outcome 23.8 |
| **23.12** A client comes to the clinic and complains of not being able to hold her urine, stating: "I feel so terrible. This shouldn't happen at my age." The nurse's best response is:<br>1. "You shouldn't feel badly. Lots of people have this trouble."<br>2. "You'll probably have to start wearing incontinent briefs. Then you won't be worried about accidents."<br>3. "Getting old isn't much fun, is it?"<br>4. "There could be a number of causes for this. I need to ask you some more questions about it." | Answer: 4<br>Rationale: Elders may be susceptible to urinary incontinence (UI) because of changes in the kidney and bladder. UI is *never* normal and the nurse must promptly investigate the cause, onset, and any other symptoms. Incontinent briefs are useful products for people who have UI, but the cause for all cases must be investigated. The client already feels badly—the nurse only makes this feeling worse by adding guilt on top of it.<br>Implementation<br>Physiologic integrity<br>Application<br>Learning Outcome 23.8 |
| **23.13** An elderly male client comes to the clinic and states to the nurse that he hasn't been interested in sexual intercourse lately. He states: "I guess this | Answer: 4<br>Rationale: The major age-related change in sexual response is timing. It takes longer to become sexually aroused, longer to complete intercourse, and longer before sexual arousal can occur again. Libido may decrease but not disappear. If an older man reports a loss in sexual interest, the nurse should be as concerned |

is part of getting old, too." What should the nurse understand about decreased sexual interest in elderly clients?

1. It does decrease and gradually disappears.
2. It should not be taken as seriously as if the client were a younger person.
3. It is caused by decreased hormone activity and there is little that can be done about it.
4. It decreases but does not disappear.

as when a younger man reports a loss in sexual activity. Decrease in hormone secretion and activity is a normal aging process, but there may be treatment measures that can help if this is the case.
Implementation
Physiologic integrity
Application
Learning Outcome 23.8

---

**23.14** The nurse is working with a group of elderly adults at a community health center. In planning any health program, the nurse will implement Erikson's theory of task development. The nurse realizes that in this stage, the successful completion of the task allows the person to:

1. Have a feeling of satisfaction from past accomplishments.
2. Make connections with the younger generation.
3. Wish they had their life to live over again.
4. Live out their last years in physical health.

Answer: 1
Rationale: Erikson's task of this developmental stage is integrity versus despair. People who develop integrity accept their life with a sense of wholeness and satisfaction with their past accomplishments. People who despair often believe they made poor choices during life and wish they could live life over. Physical health is not part of psychosocial development. Making connections with the younger generation is part of the task of the middle adult age group.
Evaluation
Psychosocial integrity
Application
Learning Outcome 23.10

---

**23.15** When contemplating Erikson's developmental theory, the nurse assesses several elderly clients. Which of the following will have the least difficulty being successful with this task?

1. A client who felt success through her children's accomplishments.
2. A client who held his job and work status as the defining feature of his life.
3. A client who maintained a balance between work and home.
4. A client who planned to really enjoy life once she retired.

Answer: 3
Rationale: People who learned early in life to live well-balanced and fulfilling lives are generally more successful in retirement. People who attempt suddenly to refocus and enrich their lives at retirement usually have difficulty. The woman who has been concerned only with the accomplishments of her children or the man who has been concerned only with the paycheck and his job status can be left with a feeling of emptiness when children leave or the job no longer exists.
Evaluation
Psychosocial integrity
Analysis
Learning Outcome 23.10

---

**23.16** A nurse is helping a potential home health client acquire the supplies that will be needed once the client is discharged from acute care. When considering these supplies, the nurse should remember that:

1. Medicare will cover supplies, but only with a physician's written order.
2. Between insurance supplements and Medicare, the elderly client shouldn't have any difficulty with coverage.

Answer: 3
Rationale: Financial needs of this age group vary considerably, and problems with income are related to low retirement benefits, lack of pension plans, and increasing length of retirement years. Nurses should be aware of the costs of health care and use supplies that are as economical as possible. Assuming that all supplies are covered by Medicare and/or supplemental insurance is erroneous. The nurse should assist the client to apply for whatever assistance programs are available.
Implementation
Health promotion and maintenance
Application
Learning Outcome 23.9

---

| | |
|---|---|
| 3. Most clients in this age group live on a fixed income, and supplies used should be as economical as possible.<br>4. Clients have to be responsible for their own supplies. | |
| **23.17** A group of elderly clients are interested in living options available in the community when they may need some assistance with their daily needs. Which of the following would the nurse suggest as possibilities to meet these needs? (Select all that apply.)<br>1. Adult foster care<br>2. Group homes<br>3. Retirement villages<br>4. Long-term care facilities<br>5. Adult day-care centers | Answer: 1, 2, 5<br>Rationale: Retirement villages provide social support, but do not provide assistance with medication and ADLs. Long-term care facilities provide all care when elderly persons are no longer able to care for themselves; they are not considered "assistance" living. Other options include assisted living centers.<br>Assessment<br>Health promotion and maintenance<br>Application<br>Learning Outcome 23.6 |
| **23.18** An elderly client who has had a stroke is ready for hospital discharge. How should the nurse case manager support this client's independence?<br>1. Allow the client to be actively involved in all decisions made.<br>2. Make arrangements based on what the nurse feels is in the best interest of the client.<br>3. Work closely with the social worker and physician to make the decisions necessary for the client.<br>4. Set up a meeting with the family members so decisions can be made. | Answer: 1<br>Rationale: Nurses need to acknowledge the older client's ability to think, reason, and make decisions. Most elders are willing to listen to suggestions and advice, but they do not want to be ordered around. It would be quite appropriate to include the physician or primary care provider, social worker, as well as the family in the decision-making process, but always and foremost, to include the client.<br>Implementation<br>Health promotion and maintenance<br>Application<br>Learning Outcome 23.12 |
| **23.19** A group of nursing students are doing their first clinical rotation in a long-term care facility. The nurse educator, in meeting the needs of this particular client group, reminds students to:<br>1. Do all cares for the clients, since they're unable to do them independently.<br>2. Always remember that the client's self-respect must be maintained in all interactions of the students.<br>3. Make sure the clients' cares are done in a timely manner, and sometimes that means doing things for the client.<br>4. Treat this group of clients with a different level of respect than younger clients. | Answer: 2<br>Rationale: Older people appreciate the same thoughtfulness, consideration, and acceptance of their abilities as younger people do. The aging client may be slower and less meticulous in many activities, and many young people err in thinking they are helpful to older people when they take over for them and do the job much faster and more efficiently. There is much diversity among older clients, and nurses should be wary of stereotyping this group.<br>Implementation<br>Psychosocial integrity<br>Application<br>Learning Outcome 23.3 |
| **23.20** A nurse is working with clients in an assisted living facility. In the past month, there have been several deaths— some partners of the residents, and some single members of the facility. In | Answer: 2<br>Rationale: Independence established prior to the loss of a mate makes adjustment easier. A person who had meaningful relationships and friendships or economic security, ongoing interests in the community or private hobbies, and a peaceful philosophy of life copes more easily with bereavement. Not |

helping the remaining residents deal with these deaths, the nurse understands that adjustment may be easier for which of the following residents who just lost their partner? (Select all that apply.)

1. A resident who spent most of her days attending to her partner who is now deceased
2. A resident who had a wide circle of friends, besides her spouse
3. A resident who was not inclined to participate in any activities offered at the facility
4. A resident who started to become more dependent on the nursing staff at the facility

participating in functions offered or becoming more dependent on the staff may indicate feelings of inadequacy or insecurity after a death has occurred.
Assessment
Psychosocial integrity
Application
Learning Outcome 23.11

---

**23.21** A nurse who works in a long-term care facility has noticed that one of the residents has been forgetting names of staff members and has not been doing some of the cares that this resident was able to do just in the week prior. The nurse should:

1. Remember that memory loss is a normal, age-related change.
2. Investigate for possible physiologic problems.
3. Instruct the staff to be extra attentive as this person needs more assistance.
4. Inform the resident's family that the resident probably has some form of dementia.

Answer: 2
Rationale: Cognitive impairment that interferes with normal life is not considered part of normal aging. A decline in intellectual abilities that interferes with social or occupational functions should always be regarded as abnormal. Family members, and certainly nurses, should be advised to seek prompt medical evaluation.
Implementation
Psychosocial integrity
Application
Learning Outcome 23.12

---

**23.22** A client has been diagnosed with dementia. The family wants to know how to plan for the future. The best response by the nurse is:

1. "Your family member's symptoms will get worse, but there are medications to stop the progress."
2. "You should plan right now on which long-term care facility you will want to utilize when the time comes."
3. "Dementia is a progressive deterioration. It's important for you to clearly understand what to look for in symptoms."
4. "Dementia can be treated once the cause is known."

Answer: 3
Rationale: Dementia is a progressive loss of cognitive function. The most common type is Alzheimer's disease. The cause is unknown. The most prominent symptoms are cognitive dysfunctions, including decline in memory, learning, attention, judgment, orientation, and language skills. Family members must be educated on the course of dementia and be encouraged to learn as much about coping skills as possible. There are no cures, but some medications may help to slow the progression.
Implementation
Psychosocial integrity
Application
Learning Outcome 23.15

---

**23.23** A client has had Alzheimer's dementia for a period of time and continues to live at home with his spouse. Which of the following is the nurse's responsibility?

1. Make sure the client is getting appropriate medication.

Answer: 2
Rationale: The nurse's responsibility is to provide supportive nursing care, accurate information, and referral assistance, if necessary, to the caregiver. Caregivers may experience physical and emotional exhaustion while they render continuous care. It is important for the nurse to do an *ongoing* assessment of both the client and the caregiver as the client's condition deteriorates.

---

| | |
|---|---|
| 2. Provide support for the spouse.<br>3. Assess the client early to ensure proper care.<br>4. Find a suitable long-term care facility for the client. | Implementation<br>Psychosocial integrity<br>Application<br>Learning Outcome 23.15 |
| **23.24** The elderly client is at risk to develop dementia as well as delirium. Which of the following statements is correct?<br>1. Delirium is easily distinguished from dementia.<br>2. Dementia is reversible and treatable.<br>3. Delirium is an acute and reversible syndrome.<br>4. Dementia is the only condition that is characterized by changes in memory, judgment, language, mathematic calculation, abstract reasoning, and problem-solving ability. | Answer: 3<br>Rationale: Both dementia and delirium have many of the same characteristics although delirium is an acute, reversible syndrome. Once the underlying pathology is treated, the delirium disappears. Causes of delirium include infection, medication interactions, and dehydration. Dementia is progressive and may be slowed with some medications.<br>Assessment<br>Physiologic integrity<br>Application<br>Learning Outcome 23.15 |
| **23.25** A hospitalized elderly client is recovering from an acute illness. As the client nears the end of his hospitalization, he questions the nurse about medications and care after discharge. The nurse should:<br>1. Tell the physician the client needs to go to a nursing home.<br>2. Assess the client's independence and ability to function in his own home before discharge.<br>3. Tell the client not to worry about going home.<br>4. Invite the client's family to come to the hospital so the nurse can explain the client's care to them. | Answer: 2<br>Rationale: Older adults often perceive that being in the hospital could change their ability to be autonomous and independent. As a result, the nurse needs to assess the older adult's stage or perception of need for control and autonomy during his hospitalization and his fears and hopes about being discharged from the hospital setting. Telling the physician the client needs long-term care is inappropriate at this point. So is inviting the family to come so the nurse can explain the client's care to them. The client is a capable adult and should be included in all decision-making situations. Telling the client not to worry is not therapeutic and does not address his concerns.<br>Implementation<br>Health promotion and maintenance<br>Application<br>Learning Outcome 23.15 |
| **23.26** The community health nurse is providing information to elderly clients in the community regarding health tests and screening. Which of the following would be recommended for these clients? (Select those that apply.)<br>1. Annual hearing screen<br>2. Annual total cholesterol and HDL protein measurement<br>3. Annual vision screen<br>4. Annual flu vaccine<br>5. Annual pneumococcal vaccine after age 65 | Answer: 1, 3, 4<br>Rationale: Total cholesterol and HDL protein measurement every 3 to 5 years until age 75 is recommended. Pneumococcal vaccine is recommended at age 65, then every 10 years thereafter. Other recommendations include a daily aspirin, 81 mg, if in a high-risk group; diabetes mellitus screen every 3 years, if in a high-risk group; smoking cessation; mammography screen every 1 to 2 years for women; clinical breast exam yearly for women; Pap smear annually if there is a history of abnormal smears or previous hysterectomy for malignancy; annual digital rectal exam; annual PSA for men; annual fecal occult blood test; depression screen, periodically; family violence screen, periodically; annual height and weight measurements; STD testing, if in a high-risk group; annual flu vaccine, if over 65 or in a high-risk group; Td vaccine every 10 years.<br>Implementation<br>Health promotion and maintenance<br>Application<br>Learning Outcome 23.16 |
| **23.27** During care activities, the 80-year-old client talks about "the good old days" and often repeats the same stories. What action should the nurse plan? | Answer: 2<br>Rationale: This type of conversation is a necessary part of successful aging, and the nurse should support the reminiscence. There is no need for a psychological consult. It is not necessary to redirect the client to |

1. Request a psychological consult
   for the client.
2. Support this as reminiscence
   therapy.
3. Redirect the client to other
   topics of conversation.
4. Vary caregivers assigned to the
   client.

other topics of conversation, and elders generally respond better to familiar caregivers.
Planning
Psychosocial integrity
Application
Learning Outcome 23.12

# CHAPTER 24

**24.1** A client is asked during an admission interview to describe her family. She proceeds to list parents, siblings, grandparents, aunts, uncles, and cousins. This client is describing which type of family?
1. Nuclear
2. Extended
3. Traditional
4. Blended

Answer: 2
Rationale: The extended family includes parents and offspring (nuclear) along with relatives such as grandparents, aunts, and uncles. A traditional family is viewed as one in which both parents reside in the home with their children—the mother assuming the nurturing role and the father providing the necessary economic resources. A blended family consists of existing family units joined together to form new families, also known as stepfamilies or reconstituted families.
Assessment
Health promotion and maintenance
Application
Learning Outcome 24.2

**24.2** A nurse is working with a particular cultural group in which it is not uncommon for grandparents to live with their married children and to assist with child rearing and discipline issues. This is an example of which of the following?
1. Two-career family
2. Blended family
3. Intragenerational family
4. Traditional family

Answer: 3
Rationale: In some cultures and as people live longer, more than two generations may live together in an intragenerational setting, as described. A two-career family is one where both partners are employed. A blended family occurs when existing family units join together to form new families. A traditional family is viewed as an autonomous unit in which both parents reside in the home.
Assessment
Health promotion and maintenance
Application
Learning Outcome 24.2

**24.3** Two nursing students, both single parents, have decided to move into a larger house. Part of their rationale includes providing support for studying and sharing responsibilities of parenting. This is an example of which of the following?
1. Cohabiting family
2. Blended family
3. Foster family
4. Intragenerational family

Answer: 1
Rationale: Cohabiting (or communal) families consist of unrelated individuals or families that live under one roof. Reasons for cohabiting may be a need for companionship, a desire to achieve a sense of family, sharing expenses, and household management. A blended family occurs when existing family units join together to form new families, also known as stepfamilies or reconstituted families. Foster family situations occur when children can no longer live with their birth parents and require placement with a family that has agreed to include them temporarily. Intragenerational families occur when more than two generations live together.
Assessment
Health promotion and maintenance
Application
Learning Outcome 24.2

**24.4** Which of the following is the purpose of a family assessment? (Select all that apply.)
1. Determine the level of family functioning.
2. Identify family strengths and weaknesses.
3. Provide legal guidelines for consent to health care.
4. Clarify family interaction patterns.

Answer: 1, 2, 4
Rationale: One other purpose is to describe the health status of the family and its individual members. Legal guidelines regarding health care issues such as insurance coverage and the right to consent for health care are important when working with same-sex couples.
Assessment
Health promotion and maintenance
Application
Learning Outcome 24.4

**24.5** A nurse is conducting a family assessment as part of the process for services provided through the community. Of the following, which would provide the best information in identifying existing or potential health problems?

1. Ecomap
2. Genogram
3. Cultural assessment
4. Family communication patterns

Answer: 2

Rationale: The health history is one of the most effective ways of identifying existing or potential health problems. A genogram will help the nurse to visualize how all family members are genetically related to each other and how patterns of chronic conditions are present within the family unit. An ecomap provides a visualization of how the family unit interacts with the external community—for example, schools, religious commitments, occupational duties, and recreational pursuits. A cultural assessment will provide information about health beliefs and health practices of a particular family. Family communication patterns determine the family's ability to function as a cooperative, growth-producing unit.

Assessment
Health promotion and maintenance
Application
Learning Outcome 24.4

---

**24.6** A family struggles with clear communication, and members of the family often seek the help of other systems for personal validation and gratification. What would be an appropriate nursing diagnosis for this family?

1. *Altered Family Processes* related to communication patterns
2. *Impaired Verbal Communication* related to inability to communicate
3. *Ineffective Family Coping* evidenced by assistance from outside sources
4. *Knowledge Deficiency* (communication patterns) related to dysfunctional patterns of communication

Answer: 1

Rationale: This describes a state in which a family with previous normal functioning experiences a dysfunction. The communication patterns have affected how the family works as a unit. *Impaired Verbal Communication* means that the members are not able to communicate because of complications with speaking or saying the words, which is not the case in this situation. *Ineffective Family Coping* must be related to an etiology, so this option is not worded correctly. *Knowledge Deficiency* is not correct as the family does recognize the problem since members of the family seek assistance from outside sources, as given in the scenario.

Nursing diagnosis
Health promotion and maintenance
Application
Learning Outcome 24.6

---

**24.7** A nurse is conducting a family assessment and is focusing, for the moment, on the family members' communication patterns. Which of the following indicate that there are existing or potential problems with family communication?

1. All members are participating in the discussion equally, some quite vocally.
2. The verbal communication is congruent with the nonverbal messages.
3. A few of the members just sit and listen.
4. Disagreements are not addressed among members, rather ignored by the person who does the most talking.

Answer: 4

Rationale: This option describes an authoritarian setting where other members may be cautious in expressing their feelings because of power struggles, hostility, or anger. Nurses should pay special attention to who does the talking for the family, which members are silent, how disagreements are handled, and how well the members listen to one another and encourage the participation of others. Nonverbal communication is important because it gives valuable clues about what people are feeling. Even though some members are more vocal, at least all are participating in the discussion. Verbal communication should be congruent with nonverbal cues. Listening is an art, and not all members of a family need to speak in the same setting.

Assessment
Health promotion and maintenance
Application
Learning Outcome 24.4

---

**24.8** A nurse is conducting a family assessment and asks the following question: "How, as a family, do you deal with disappointments or stressful changes that occur and affect the members of your family?" The nurse is trying to identify _____ .

Answer: coping mechanisms or family coping mechanisms

Rationale: Family coping mechanisms are behaviors that families use to deal with stress or changes imposed from either within or without. The coping mechanisms families and individuals develop reflect their individual resourcefulness. The assessment of coping mechanisms is a way to determine how families relate to stress.

Assessment

---

Health promotion and maintenance
Application
Learning Outcome 24.4

| | |
|---|---|
| **24.9** A nurse has identified a coping problem in a family that recently lost their house and all of their belongings in a fire. The nurse will next assess the family's external support systems. These would include which of the following? (Select all that apply.)<br>　1. Friends<br>　2. Religious affiliations<br>　3. Individual members of the family<br>　4. Health care professionals | Answer: 1, 2, 4<br>Rationale: *External* support also includes extended family members and social services. Individual family members, along with knowledge, skills, and effective communication patterns, provide internal support.<br>Assessment<br>Health promotion and maintenance<br>Application<br>Learning Outcome 24.4 |
| **24.10** A nurse has been working with a family at the community health office and is alert to signs of family violence. Which of the following would the nurse be *most* concerned about, in this regard?<br>　1. The baby always seems to have a cold.<br>　2. One of the children never speaks and seems "on guard" when in the presence of a parent.<br>　3. The family's clothes are relatively clean, but the children usually have some kind of dirt stain on their shirt or pants.<br>　4. The family does not have a regular physician. | Answer: 2<br>Rationale: Family violence includes abuse between intimate partners, child abuse, and elder abuse, and may include physical, mental, and verbal abuse as well as neglect. Early symptoms are evident in burns, cuts, fractures, and even death. Later manifestations often seen are depression, alcohol and substance abuse, and suicide attempts. Not having a regular physician would be a concern for health promotion and maintenance, but not for abuse. The baby may have an untreated condition, but chronic cold symptoms are not evidence of abuse. Dirty clothes or clothes not meeting the nurse's standards are not signs of abuse—maybe for this family, appearance is not a high priority. A child who doesn't speak and is watchful when parents are near would be a significant indicator of a possible abuse situation. The nurse, however, must be careful in assessing for this and would possibly want to speak to the child on a one-to-one basis for further assessment information.<br>Assessment<br>Psychosocial integrity<br>Application<br>Learning Outcome 24.5 |
| **24.11** The nurse is performing a family risk assessment. Which of the following factors would indicate that this family is at risk of developing health problems?<br>　1. The family is an elderly couple who are active in their retirement community.<br>　2. The family is a teenage mother and child. The mother is enrolled in parenting classes at the high school.<br>　3. The family belongs to the local synagogue and has family members still living in Germany.<br>　4. The family depends on two incomes with a limit on their health insurance spending. | Answer: 3<br>Rationale: Tay-Sachs is a neurodegenerative disease that occurs primarily in descendants of Eastern European Jews. Simply because of this family's race, they are at risk for developing this health problem. The elderly couple is active and so is not at as high of risk simply because of age—neither is the teenage mother, even though maturity is one of the factors the nurse will assess in this situation. Although poverty is a major problem that affects the family, the fact that there is health insurance is a positive sociologic factor.<br>Assessment<br>Health promotion and maintenance<br>Application<br>Learning Outcome 24.5 |
| **24.12** During a previous family assessment, the nurse realized that the mother did most of the talking and was quick to make decisions, which appeared to be acceptable to the father. When one of their children is hospitalized, the nurse will:<br>　1. Make sure that both parents are involved in all decision making. | Answer: 3<br>Rationale: The nurse uses information gained from the assessment to help diagnose, plan, and implement care. Understanding that the mother assumes the authority role in this particular family, the nurse may find it easier to address things with both present but not be surprised if this pattern continues during the child's hospitalization. However, the nurse should not assume that in a crisis situation or during stress that family processes will be the same and will want to make sure that the father is present during the process. |

| | |
|---|---|
| 2. Allow the mother to make the decisions.<br>3. Include both parents in the decision making, but not be surprised if the mother retains control.<br>4. Make sure that the physician understands the family dynamics so parental consent comes from the mother. | Implementation<br>Health promotion and maintenance<br>Application<br>Learning Outcome 24.6 |
| **24.13** A family member is hospitalized with an illness. Which of the following factors will the nurse assess to determine the impact this illness will have on the family? (Select all that apply.)<br>1. Nature of the illness<br>2. Duration of the illness<br>3. Cause of the illness<br>4. Financial impact of the illness<br>5. Effect of the illness on future family functioning | Answer: 1, 2, 4, 5<br>Rationale: Other factors include residual effects of the illness, meaning of the illness to the family, and its significance to family systems. The cause of the illness is not a factor that determines the impact on the family.<br>Assessment<br>Health promotion and maintenance<br>Application<br>Learning Outcome 24.6 |
| **24.14** A father of a family was killed in a motor vehicle crash. Which of the following would the nurse consider a "normal" reaction to this event?<br>1. Family disorganization may occur.<br>2. Family members become detached from extended family.<br>3. The family feels that their place in the community has been eliminated.<br>4. The family withdraws into seclusion during the grief process. | Answer: 1<br>Rationale: The death of a family member often has a profound effect on the whole family—especially if the deceased, as in this situation, was the head of the family. Family disorganization would be common, but as the family begins to recover, a new sense of normalcy develops and the family reintegrates its roles and functions. Families need support from extended family members, their community, and spiritual advisers. The other options are not considered "normal" patterns of family grieving, and the nurse should be alert for problems that may develop if these are present.<br>Assessment<br>Health promotion and maintenance<br>Analysis<br>Learning Outcome 24.6 |

# CHAPTER 25

| | |
|---|---|
| **25.1** The student nurse is following a preceptor on the assigned clinical shift. Which of the following behaviors of the nurse would the student interpret as caring?<br>1. Making sure that all medications and treatments are done on time<br>2. Using aseptic technique when performing a dressing change<br>3. Advising the physician that the client wants to speak to him or her prior to a procedure<br>4. Explaining an invasive procedure to the client, then asking if it is all right to begin the procedure | Answer: 4<br>Rationale: Caring practice involves connection, mutual recognition, and involvement. It is more than just performing skills adequately or even efficiently. It's a sense that the nurse has made a difference to someone else. Caring means that people, relationships, and things matter. Explaining a procedure, then seeking permission to begin lets the client know that the nurse respects the client as an individual. All other options are examples of appropriate and professional nursing care, but do not address a caring aspect.<br>Evaluation<br>Psychosocial integrity<br>Application<br>Learning Outcome 25.4 |

| | |
|---|---|
| **25.2** According to Mayeroff's philosophy of caring, which of the following ingredients are necessary for this process? (Select all that apply.)<br>  1.  Honesty<br>  2.  Trust<br>  3.  Humility<br>  4.  Professionalism<br>  5.  Courtesy | Answer: 1, 2, 3<br>Rationale: Professionalism and courtesy are not ingredients described by Mayeroff. Other listed major ingredients are knowing, alternating rhythms, hope, and courage.<br>Assessment<br>Psychosocial integrity<br>Knowledge<br>Learning Outcome 25.2 |
| **25.3** A nurse is emulating the characteristics of caring, as described by Mayeroff. Which of the following is an example of *knowing,* in relationship to caring?<br>  1.  Seeing that a client is withdrawn and sullen, and spending extra time when providing cares or treatments<br>  2.  Understanding the reason a client's lab values are elevated<br>  3.  Seeing the connection between the pathophysiology of the cardiac condition and treatment and giving the rationale for certain medications when the client asks<br>  4.  Getting an extra blanket when the client says he is cold | Answer: 1<br>Rationale: *Knowing* means understanding the other's needs and how to respond to those needs. Sensing that a client is withdrawn and sullen, the nurse knows that spending extra time can sometimes allow the client to feel comfortable in talking about what might be bothering him. Understanding the reason for elevated lab values and the connection between the pathophysiology and treatment of a condition are examples of knowing in the didactic sense. Getting an extra blanket is responding to client needs after being told what those needs are, not sensing or understanding them.<br>Evaluation<br>Psychosocial integrity<br>Analysis<br>Learning Outcome 25.2 |
| **25.4** A nurse manager has been dealing with staffing problems and high patient acuity on the unit. The director of nursing has been sensitive to other issues in the past, so the nurse manager decides to approach her with these new concerns. This is an example of which aspect of caring, as proposed by Mayeroff?<br>  1.  Knowing<br>  2.  Trust<br>  3.  Humility<br>  4.  Courage | Answer: 4<br>Rationale: Courage is the sense of going into the unknown, informed by insight from past experiences. Since the manager had prior experience that was positive from the director of nursing, the manager will use this information to address a problem that has not been introduced before. *Knowing* means understanding the other's needs and how to respond to these needs. Trust involves letting go, to allow the other to grow in his own way and own time. Humility means acknowledging that there is always more to learn, and that learning may come from any source.<br>Evaluation<br>Psychosocial integrity<br>Analysis<br>Learning Outcome 25.2 |
| **25.5** A new nurse has just started work on an oncology unit. One of the clients has decided to discontinue treatment, even though he understands that his life will be shortened extensively if he does. The nurse is having difficulty with this situation and decides to approach a seasoned nurse for insight and a way to help support this particular client. The nurse is exemplifying which of the following?<br>  1.  Hope<br>  2.  Humility<br>  3.  Honesty<br>  4.  Patience | Answer: 3<br>Rationale: Honesty includes awareness and openness to one's own feelings and genuineness in caring for the other. In this situation, the nurse has her own feelings about what the client should do, but truly wants to provide good care so she seeks out the assistance from someone who may be able to enlighten her. Hope is belief in the possibilities of the other's growth. Humility means acknowledging that there is always more to learn, and that learning may come from any source. Patience enables the other to grow in his own way and time.<br>Implementation<br>Psychosocial integrity<br>Application<br>Learning Outcome 25.2 |

**25.6** A nurse is researching the concept of caring as it relates to specific situations in the clinical area. More specifically, the nurse is interested in caring as it relates to cultural differences. Of the following theorists, which would be of the most help to this nurse researcher?
1. Florence Nightingale
2. Jean Watson
3. Dorothea Orem
4. Madeline Leininger

Answer: 4
Rationale: Leininger's theory of culture care diversity and universality is based on the assumption that nurses must understand different cultures in order to function effectively. Nightingale's theory focuses on the environment. Watson's theory focuses on caring in itself. Orem's theory is about self-care and deficit.
Assessment
Safe, effective care environment
Application
Learning Outcome 25.2

---

**25.7** According to Leininger's theory of cultural congruent care, which of the following characterize the way that care should be provided? (Select all that apply.)
1. Care should be influenced by the organizational structure.
2. The client's familiar lifeways are preserved.
3. Accommodations should be satisfying to clients.
4. Nursing care must be repatterned to help the client move toward wellness.

Answer: 2, 3, 4
Rationale: Along with these three specifics, Leininger defines care as assisting, supporting, or enabling one another or a group with evident or anticipated needs to improve life. Care influenced by organizational structure is in line with Ray's theory of bureaucratic caring.
Assessment
Health promotion and maintenance
Knowledge
Learning Outcome 25.2

---

**25.8** A nurse is evaluating how care is delivered at various hospitals. In the process, the nurse is able to identify a facility where caring in the emergency department is perceived differently than caring in the rehabilitation unit. This type of example reflects whose theory of caring?
1. Leininger
2. Ray
3. Roach
4. Boykin and Schoenhofer

Answer: 2
Rationale: Ray's theory of bureaucratic caring suggests that caring in nursing is contextual and is influenced by the organizational structure. Each unit had its own specific meaning of caring and how it was influenced. Leininger's theory is focused on cultural congruency. Roach focuses on the philosophical concept of caring and proposes that caring is the human mode of being. Boykin and Schoenhofer's theory suggests that caring is a lifelong process, lived moment to moment by the nurse and constantly unfolding.
Assessment
Psychosocial integrity
Application
Learning Outcome 25.2

---

**25.9** A nurse is working in a busy intensive care unit. A client is admitted with extensive medical problems and requires a ventilator. Because the nurse already has two other clients assigned to his care, he requests that the nurse manager change assignments so that appropriate attention can be given to this new admission. According to Roach's six C's of caring, which one is the nurse emulating?
1. Compassion
2. Confidence
3. Commitment
4. Conscience

Answer: 4
Rationale: Conscience deals with morals, ethics, and an informed sense of right and wrong as well as an awareness of personal responsibility. This nurse understands the situation of taking on a critically ill client when he is already busy enough and makes an appropriate request for a change in assignment. Compassion is about being aware of one's relationship to others; sharing joys, sorrows, pain, and accomplishments; and participating in the experience of another. Confidence is the quality that fosters trust. It means the nurse has comfort with himself, his clients, and his family. Commitment is a convergence between one's desires and obligations and the deliberate choice to act in accordance with them.
Assessment
Safe, effective care environment
Analysis
Learning Outcome 25.2

---

**25.10** A nurse has been working a 12-hour shift in a labor and delivery unit. A client was admitted early in the shift and is now ready to deliver. The client had a difficult labor experience, was worried and anxious throughout,

Answer: 1
Rationale: Compassion is being aware of one's relationship to others; sharing their joys, sorrows, pain, and accomplishments; and participating in the experience of another. The nurse exemplifies this by staying until the delivery is over and the birth is accomplished. Competence is having the knowledge, skills, energy, experience, and motivation to respond adequately to others, within the

and had physiological problems with blood pressure as well as pain management. The nurse decides to stay until the delivery is over, after having it approved by her manager. This nurse is exhibiting which of the following?

1. Compassion
2. Competence
3. Confidence
4. Conscience

demands of the professional responsibilities. Confidence is the quality that fosters trusting relationships. It is comfort with self, patient, and family. Conscience is focused on morals, ethics, and an informed sense of right and wrong. Awareness of personal responsibility is part of conscience.

Evaluation
Psychosocial integrity
Analysis
Learning Outcome 25.2

---

**25.11** A nurse educator is teaching students about the philosophy of caring in nursing and states that nurses can only be truly caring if they are true to themselves first. This action then emphasizes the importance of nurses knowing themselves, which brings about a process that allows the nurse to be with another person. The educator is teaching the concept of caring according to whose theory?

1. Roach
2. Ray
3. Boykin and Schoenhofer
4. Watson

Answer: 3
Rationale: Boykin and Schoenhofer emphasize the importance of the nurse knowing oneself as caring. Through knowing oneself as a caring person, the nurse can be authentic to self, freeing oneself to truly be with others. Roach's theory focuses on caring as a philosophical concept and proposes that caring is the human mode of being, or the "most common, authentic criterion of humanness." Ray's theory of caring focuses on caring in organizations and is influenced by the organizational structure. Watson views caring as the essence and the moral ideal of nursing.

Assessment
Psychosocial integrity
Analysis
Learning Outcome 25.2

---

**25.12** A labor and delivery nurse wants to conduct research focused on the response of new parents toward their babies. The approach the nurse would like to use suggests that caring is a nurturing process. Which of the following theorists is best in line with this research?

1. Swanson
2. Watson
3. Roach
4. Benner

Answer: 1
Rationale: Swanson defines caring as a nurturing way of relating to a valued "other" toward whom one feels a personal sense of commitment and responsibility. Watson views caring as the essence and moral ideal of nursing. Roach identifies caring as a philosophical concept and proposes that caring is the human mode of being. Benner describes caring as the essence of excellence in nursing.

Implementation
Psychosocial integrity
Application
Learning Outcome 25.2

---

**25.13** A nurse is working with students on a medical unit. A client with respiratory acidosis is being monitored closely, and the nurse is able to describe to the students the pathophysiology surrounding this client's condition as well as specific assessment findings. This nurse is demonstrating which type of knowledge?

1. Aesthetic
2. Empirical
3. Personal
4. Creative

Answer: 2
Rationale: Empirical knowing ranges from factual, observable phenomena to theoretical analysis. Empirical knowledge is systematic and helps to describe, explain, and predict phenomena. Aesthetic knowledge is the art of nursing and is expressed by nurses in their creativity and style in meeting the needs of clients. Personal knowledge is concerned with the knowing, encountering, and actualizing of the concrete, individual self. Creativity is part of aesthetic knowledge.

Assessment
Physiologic integrity
Application
Learning Outcome 25.3

---

**25.14** During a midterm evaluation, the nurse educator tells the students they need to work on improving their aesthetic knowledge. A good way for the students to accomplish this is to:

1. Study harder.
2. Take better notes.

Answer: 4
Rationale: Aesthetic knowing is the art of nursing and is expressed by the individual nurse through his or her creativity and style in meeting the needs of clients. Understanding how other nurses meet the needs of their clients and seeing a variety of methods to provide the same care will help improve this type of knowledge for the students. The other options are ways to improve empirical knowing.

---

| | |
|---|---|
| 3. Read about the same topic from a variety of sources.<br>4. Spend time in the clinical area with seasoned nurses. | Implementation<br>Safe, effective care environment<br>Application<br>Learning Outcome 25.3 |
| **25.15** A nurse has been asked to be a member of a hospital's internal review board and evaluate research studies. Which of the following does this nurse most likely possess?<br>1. Sound empirical knowledge<br>2. Sound personal knowledge<br>3. Sound aesthetic knowledge<br>4. Sound ethical knowledge | Answer: 4<br>Rationale: Ethical knowing focuses on matters of obligation or what ought to be done and goes beyond simply following the ethical codes of the discipline. Internal review boards review research projects and determine whether they meet sound, ethical standards. The more sensitive and knowledgeable the nurse is to these issues, the more "ethical" the nurse will be. Empirical knowledge is systematically organized into laws and theories for the purpose of describing, explaining, and predicting phenomena. Personal knowledge promotes wholeness and integrity in the personal encounter. Aesthetic knowledge is the art of nursing and is expressed by the individual nurse through his or her creativity and style in meeting the needs of clients.<br>Assessment<br>Psychosocial integrity<br>Application<br>Learning Outcome 25.3 |
| **25.16** A student asks the nursing instructor which of the different types of knowledge are important in the clinical area. The best response by the nurse is:<br>1. "Empirical knowledge. You have to know the physiology of the problem before you decide which interventions to use."<br>2. "A good nurse will have a mix of all four types."<br>3. "Ethical knowledge. Nurses must be able to identify principles and norms, handle conflicts, and be sensitive to sensitive issues."<br>4. "Aesthetic knowledge. A nurse must appreciate the special qualities of each client and the individual situation." | Answer: 2<br>Rationale: The nurse who practices effectively is able to integrate all types of knowledge to understand situations more holistically. All options are true, but a nurse must possess all four types of knowledge.<br>Implementation<br>Safe, effective care environment<br>Analysis<br>Learning Outcome 25.2 |
| **25.17** A nurse is working in an acute psychiatric unit. The nurse makes this statement to a co-worker after reviewing a newly admitted client's medical record: "Another client with bipolar disorder. We better be ready for a busy night." This nurse is exemplifying which process of Swanson's theory of caring?<br>1. Knowing<br>2. Being with<br>3. Doing for<br>4. Enabling | Answer: 1<br>Rationale: Knowing, according to Swanson, is striving to understand an event as it has meaning in the life of the other. A subdimension of this process is avoiding assumptions. The nurse in this situation made an assumption about clients with bipolar disorder. Being with is being emotionally present to another person. Doing for is providing for others as they would do for themselves if it were at all possible. Enabling is facilitating the other's passage through life transitions and unfamiliar events.<br>Assessment<br>Psychosocial integrity<br>Analysis<br>Learning Outcome 25.2 |
| **25.18** A nurse is working in the school system with a group of students who are struggling with the death of a classmate. The nurse encourages the students to talk about their friend, bring pictures, and share memories with each other. The nurse also invites the deceased's | Answer: 4<br>Rationale: Enabling is facilitating the other's passage through life transitions and unfamiliar events. Being supportive of the students and encouraging them to share and talk about their friend is allowing them to move through the grief process. Enabling also includes supporting, assisting, guiding, and validating. Knowing is striving to understand an event as it has meaning in the life of the other. If this were the case in this situation, the nurse would be asking the |

family to come to the school and visit with their child's classmates. This nurse is working in which of Swanson's processes?

1. Knowing
2. Being with
3. Doing for
4. Enabling

students to explain what they are going through, or what it feels like to lose a friend. Being with is being emotionally present to the other. Doing for is providing for others as they would do for themselves if it were at all possible.
Implementation
Psychosocial integrity
Analysis
Learning Outcome 25.2

---

**25.19** Compassion is often associated with caring. Of the following, which situation is the *best* example of compassionate nursing care?

1. The nurse has expert technical skills and has the most experience with critical care.
2. The nurse routinely gives back rubs to clients before they go to sleep.
3. The nurse has written procedures and policies in language that is both professional and realistic.
4. The nurse takes time to understand the spiritual needs of clients.

Answer: 4
Rationale: Attention to spiritual needs is part of compassionate care, particularly in the face of death and bereavement. Technical skills, experience, and writing abilities focus on competency of the nurse. Giving routine back rubs focuses on comfort. All of these are important aspects of nursing care.
Evaluation
Psychosocial integrity
Application
Learning Outcome 25.4

---

**25.20** A nurse educator teaches students about caring nursing practice. Which of the following situations shows that the nurse is able to implement the *whole* idea of caring?

1. The nurse is able to carve out time for a favorite hobby, at least once a week.
2. The nurse is a volunteer at church and school events.
3. The nurse makes lists every morning so the day stays organized and planned.
4. The nurse takes care of his elderly parents as well as providing care to his immediate family.

Answer: 1
Rationale: It is imperative that nurses attend to their own needs, because caring for self is central to caring for others. As nurses take on multiple commitments to family, work, school, and community, they risk exhaustion, burnout, and stress. None of the other options depict the nurse caring for self, only for other people or trying to stay on top of the many tasks involved in a daily routine.
Evaluation
Psychosocial Integrity
Analysis
Learning Outcome 25.5

---

**25.21** A nurse understands that certain activities are required for a healthy lifestyle. Which of the following is the best example of this?

1. Exercising every day, at least for an hour and a half
2. Buying only fat-free foods and allowing absolutely no deviation from this
3. Balancing good nutrition and exercise in moderation
4. Exercising more on days when feeling "guilty" about a snack

Answer: 3
Rationale: Nutrition and exercise are necessary for a healthy lifestyle, but key words to remember are *balance* and *moderation*. Completely avoiding a certain nutrient or keeping the nutritional aspects of one's life so strict that there can be no variance is difficult and indicates more of a compulsive nature than a healthy one.
Evaluation
Safe, effective care environment
Application
Learning Outcome 25.5

---

**25.22** A nurse practitioner emphasizes the importance of the staff engaging in activities that help restore peace and balance between the mind and body. Which of the following might be an appropriate therapy for this?
1. Bike riding
2. Cake decorating
3. Reading
4. Storytelling

Answer: 4
Rationale: Mind–body therapies include imagery, meditation, storytelling, music therapy, and yoga—all of which are complementary therapies that bring balance to thoughts and emotions. Practice of one or more mind–body therapies is an effective self-care strategy to help restore peace and balance. The other three options are not considered mind–body therapies.
Assessment
Psychosocial integrity
Application
Learning Outcome 25.5

**25.23** A nursing student was involved in a very difficult situation with a client, the client's family, and a physician. The student felt like she was caught in the middle and wasn't sure how to respond to some of the questions that were being asked about care, treatment, and scheduling. Instead of getting her instructor, the student fielded these questions as best she could. In order to help the student work through this situation, the nursing instructor might advise the student to try which of the following?
1. Meditation
2. Guided imagery
3. Reflection
4. Music therapy

Answer: 3
Rationale: Reflection is thinking from a critical point of view, analyzing why one acted in a certain way and assessing the results of one's actions. Reflection must be personal and meaningful. In this example, it will help the student understand how the situation could have been handled better. Meditation is quieting the mind and focusing it on the present. It helps the individual release fears, worries, and doubts. Guided imagery is a mind–body intervention that uses the power of imagination as a therapeutic tool. Music therapy includes listening, singing, rhythm, and body movement. It is often used to induce relaxation.
Implementation
Psychosocial integrity
Application
Learning Outcome 25.6

**25.24** A nurse is providing bathing assistance to a young client who was seriously injured and is unable to care entirely for herself. Which of the following actions would be an example of Swanson's *doing for* process, in her theory of caring?
1. Allowing the client to wash her perineal area
2. Drying the client completely
3. Seeing the client is uncomfortable with the whole bathing process
4. Touching the client's shoulder when she starts to cry

Answer: 1
Rationale: *Doing for* is providing for the client as she would do for herself if it were possible. Subdimensions of this process include preserving dignity. Drying the client completely, if she is able to do some herself, would not be part of *doing for.* Sensing that the client is uncomfortable fits in the subdimension of *knowing* (sensing cues). Touching the client's shoulder is comforting, a subdimension of *being with*.
Assessment
Psychosocial integrity
Application
Learning Outcome 25.2

# CHAPTER 26

**26.1** A nurse explains to a client that he will need to have a bowel prep before going to his esophagogastroscopy. The nurse should focus on improving which of the following?
1. Pace
2. Intonation
3. Simplicity
4. Clarity

Answer: 3
Rationale: Simplicity includes the use of commonly understood words, brevity, and completeness. A "bowel prep" may be completely meaningless to a client, but telling him that he needs to drink a gallon of laxative-like medication gets the point across better. Esophagogastroscopy is a complicated word. Using words like "small camera looking down your throat into your stomach" will make much more sense to the client. Pace and intonation help indicate interest, anxiety, boredom, or fear—all of which modify the feeling and impact of the message. Clarity and brevity imply that the message is direct and simple—saying precisely what is meant and using the fewest words necessary.
Implementation
Psychosocial integrity
Application
Learning Outcome 26.1

**26.2** The nurse is changing a client's dressing and notes that the wound is obviously infected. The drainage is purulent and has a foul odor. When asked how the wound looks, the nurse says "it looks fine" even though his face tells a different story. This nurse needs to work on which aspect of communication?
1. Adaptability
2. Credibility
3. Timing and relevance
4. Clarity and brevity

Answer: 1
Rationale: Adaptability is adjusting tone of speech and facial expression to match the spoken message. Clearly, if the nurse's face doesn't match his words, the client will identify a problem with the situation. Credibility means worthiness of belief, trustworthiness, and reliability. Timing and relevance affect how the message is taken or heard. Clarity and brevity is preciseness and use of few words.
Assessment
Psychosocial integrity
Application
Learning Outcome 26.1

---

**26.3** A nurse is working on a telemetry unit when one of the clients has a cardiac arrest. The client's spouse is in the room when the code team arrives. Which statement by the nurse is the best, in this situation?
1. "I know you're worried about your loved one. I'm sure this is a difficult situation for you. Do you have any questions right now?"
2. "Your spouse's heart stopped. All these people are here to help get it started."
3. "Your spouse's physician will be here shortly and explain all of the medication and treatment that your spouse is receiving right now."
4. "Is there someone you would like to call? I'm sure this is a scary situation and you may feel more comfortable if someone were with you during this time."

Answer: 2
Rationale: Clarity and brevity provide a message that is simple and clear. In this situation, taking time to explain and/or address all of the spouse's needs and concerns is inappropriate. Not only will the client be unable to process extra information, but the nurse doesn't have time to give long, drawn out explanations about the situation. Dealing with the spouse's fears and concerns right now is not the priority need—the client's emergency situation is.
Evaluation
Safe, effective care environment
Analysis
Learning Outcome 26.1

---

**26.4** The nurse enters a client's room and finds that the phone is lying in the client's lap, tissues are wadded up on the bed, and the client's eyes are red and watery. The best response by the nurse is:
1. "Can I hang that phone up for you?"
2. "Well, it's a beautiful day outside. Let's open the blinds."
3. "Has your doctor been in to talk to you yet?"
4. "You look upset. Is there anything you'd like to talk about?"

Answer: 4
Rationale: Nonverbal communication, or body language, often tells the nurse more about what a person is feeling than what is actually said. The interpretation of such observations requires validation with the client. The other options do not address the nonverbal cues. The client's appearance, the phone off the hook, and the tissues lead the nurse to at least consider that perhaps the client had an upsetting phone call. This should be addressed by the nurse.
Evaluation
Psychosocial integrity
Analysis
Learning Outcome 26.1

---

**26.5** A client has been sullen and withdrawn since receiving the news of her cancer diagnosis. As the nurse enters the room, the client asks for assistance with a shower. Which comment by the nurse is the most appropriate?
1. "If you look better, you might feel better."

Answer: 3
Rationale: How a person dresses or looks may be an indicator of how the person feels. A change in grooming habits may signal that the client is feeling better, but the nurse must be careful in this situation that the focus is not on the client's spouse—but on the client. Telling the client that she might feel better if she looks better and washes away the "gloom and doom" indicates that the client's looks are objectionable.
Evaluation

| | |
|---|---|
| 2. "Taking a shower might wash away some of that gloom and doom."<br>3. "This is a positive sign. I'll be right back with your supplies."<br>4. "Your spouse will be glad to see that you're feeling better." | Psychosocial integrity<br>Analysis<br>Learning Outcome 26.1 |
| **26.6** A nurse is working in a pediatric clinic and has to explain a nebulizer treatment to a child. Which of the following would be the most appropriate?<br>1. Give the child's parent a full explanation, but make sure the child hears what is said.<br>2. Let the child handle the equipment first, then demonstrate on the child's doll.<br>3. Start the treatment, but make sure that the parent is there to comfort the child if she becomes afraid.<br>4. Make sure that the physician is available for questions. | Answer: 2<br>Rationale: The knowledge of the client's developmental stage will allow the nurse to modify the message accordingly. The use of dolls and games with simple language may help explain a procedure to a child. The nurse should not talk over or around the child, just because of her age, but include her in conversation and communication. Before any treatment or therapy, explanation should be given. Otherwise the child will be frightened and the treatment will not be effective. Nurses should always be prepared to give explanation and teaching to their clients.<br>Implementation<br>Safe, effective care environment<br>Application<br>Learning Outcome 26.2 |
| **26.7** A nurse is giving a demonstration of new equipment to the rest of the nursing unit. Which level of proxemics would be appropriate for this situation?<br>1. Intimate<br>2. Personal<br>3. Social<br>4. Public | Answer: 3<br>Rationale: Social distance is characterized by a clear, visual perception of the whole person and generally 4 to 12 feet in distance. Social distance is important in accomplishing the business of the day. It is expedient in communicating with several people at the same time or within a short time, which would be the case in this situation. Intimate distance is touching or up to $1\frac{1}{2}$ feet. This would be appropriate when cuddling a baby, touching a sightless client, repositioning a client, observing an incision, and restraining a toddler for an injection. Personal distance is $1\frac{1}{2}$ to 4 feet and is less overwhelming than intimate distance. Much communication between nurses and clients occurs at this distance, such as sitting with a client, giving medications, or establishing an IV. Public distance is 12 to 15 feet and requires loud, clear vocalizations. It is used most often with a group of people or in the community.<br>Implementation<br>Psychosocial integrity<br>Application<br>Learning Outcome 26.2 |
| **26.8** A nurse must perform a catheterization on a male client. Which of the zones of proximity would be most appropriate?<br>1. Personal distance<br>2. Intimate distance<br>3. Social distance<br>4. Public distance | Answer: 2<br>Rationale: Intimate distance is characterized by body contact and used frequently by nurses when they are required to perform a procedure. Distance in this category is touching to $1\frac{1}{2}$ feet. Personal distance is $1\frac{1}{2}$ to 4 feet and is less overwhelming than intimate distance. Much communication between nurses and clients occurs at this distance, such as sitting with a client, giving medications, or establishing an IV infusion. Social distance is characterized by clear, visual perception of the whole person and is important in accomplishing the business of the day. Public distance requires loud, clear vocalizations and is used for groups of people or in the community for presentations.<br>Evaluation<br>Safe, effective care environment<br>Application<br>Learning Outcome 26.2 |

| | |
|---|---|
| **26.9** A nurse enters a client's room and asks about his level of pain. The client, grimacing, says "It's fine." Which of the factors of communication is the client struggling with?<br><br>1. Territoriality<br>2. Environment<br>3. Congruence<br>4. Attitude | Answer: 3<br>Rationale: In congruent communication, the verbal and nonverbal aspects of the message match. Saying his pain level is "fine," but then showing with facial grimacing that it is not, would be in conflict. Territoriality is a concept of the space and things that an individual considers as belonging to the self. The environment involved in communication must be comfortable. Otherwise it may distract and impair communication. Attitudes can convey beliefs, thoughts, and feelings about people and events—not what is described in this scenario.<br>Assessment<br>Psychosocial integrity<br>Application<br>Learning Outcome 26.2 |
| **26.10** A nurse is working with an elderly male client on a medical unit. Which statement by the nurse is an example of elderspeak?<br><br>1. "It's time for us to go to physical therapy."<br>2. "I think it would be better if you were planning to go to a nursing home after discharge."<br>3. "Your children must really love their dad."<br>4. "Your wife must be having trouble adjusting to your illness." | Answer: 1<br>Rationale: Elderspeak is a speech style, similar to baby talk, that gives a message of dependence and incompetence to older adults. Characteristics of elderspeak include inappropriate terms of endearment, inappropriate plural pronoun use (it's time for *us* to go to physical therapy), tag questions, and slow, loud speech. Telling the client that he needs to go to a nursing home is just insensitive. Noting that the children love their father or making comments about the wife's adjustments to the illness are not examples of elderspeak, merely the nurse making observations to the client.<br>Evaluation<br>Psychosocial integrity<br>Application<br>Learning Outcome 26.2 |
| **26.11** A client has just lost her second baby to preterm complications. The best therapeutic response by the nurse is:<br><br>1. "Don't be so sad. You can always try again."<br>2. "Didn't your doctor advise you about genetic counseling?"<br>3. "I know how you feel. I have children of my own."<br>4. "I am so sad for you. I'll stay with you for a while if you need to talk." | Answer: 4<br>Rationale: Therapeutic communication promotes understanding and is client directed. Nurses need to respond to the feelings expressed by the client. The nurse has no way of knowing how this client feels, and saying so is just insensitive. Asking about genetic counseling implies that the client could have done something to possibly prevent this situation. The client's feelings must be validated, not dismissed ("Don't be so sad, you can always try again"). Sometimes clients need time to deal with their feelings and the best thing the nurse can provide is presence and listening.<br>Evaluation<br>Psychosocial integrity<br>Application<br>Learning Outcome 26.2 |
| **26.12** The nurse is conducting an admission interview. Which of the following indicates that the nurse is attentively listening to the client's explanations?<br><br>1. "Can you explain what your symptoms are like?"<br>2. "When was the last time you saw a doctor for this?"<br>3. "Uh-huh," while nodding the head<br>4. "I'm sorry, say that again?" | Answer: 3<br>Rationale: A nurse can convey attentiveness in listening to clients in various ways. Common responses are nodding the head, uttering "uh-huh" or "mmm," repeating the words the client has used, or saying "I see what you mean." The other options listed are examples of open-ended questions or simply examples of clarifying techniques.<br>Evaluation<br>Safe, effective care environment<br>Application<br>Learning Outcome 26.2 |
| **26.13** During the introductory phase of the helping relationship there are specific stages. Which of the following apply?<br><br>1. Opening the relationship | Answer: 1, 2, 3<br>Rationale: The introductory phase, also referred to as the orientation phase or prehelping phase, sets the tone for the rest of the relationship. Other important tasks of the introductory phase include getting to know each other and developing a degree of trust. Planning before the interview is part of the preinteraction phase. |

| | |
|---|---|
| 2. Clarifying the problem<br>3. Structuring and formulating the contract<br>4. Planning before the interview | Assessment<br>Psychosocial integrity<br>Application<br>Learning Outcome 26.3 |
| **26.14** During an interaction between a nurse and client, the nurse conveys respect and an attitude that shows the nurse takes the client's opinions seriously. This would happen during which stage of the working phase?<br>   1. Exploring and understanding thoughts and feelings<br>   2. Facilitating and taking action<br>   3. Confrontation<br>   4. Concreteness | Answer: 1<br>Rationale: The working phase has two major stages: exploring and understanding thoughts and feelings and facilitating and taking action. Confrontation and concreteness are some of the skills required for the first phase. Other skills necessary include empathetic listening and responding, respect, and genuineness.<br>Implementation<br>Psychosocial integrity<br>Application<br>Learning Outcome 26.3 |
| **26.15** Several nurses have been asked to put together a proposal to help implement a method for self-scheduling. They are given the task of developing a rotation schedule that provides adequate staffing of all shifts. This is an example of which type of group?<br>   1. Self-help group<br>   2. Task group<br>   3. Teaching group<br>   4. Therapy group | Answer: 2<br>Rationale: The task group is one of the most common types of work-related groups to which nurses belong. The focus of such groups is the completion of a specific task (self-scheduling method). A self-help group is a small, voluntary organization composed of individuals who share a similar health, social, or daily living problem. A teaching group has as its major purpose to impart information to the participants. A therapy group works toward self-understanding, more satisfactory ways of relating or handling stress, and changing patterns of behavior toward health.<br>Assessment<br>Safe, effective care environment<br>Application<br>Learning Outcome 26.5 |
| **26.16** A client is nonverbal and the nurse is implementing strategies to promote communication. Which of the following would be appropriate for the client in this situation?<br>   1. Using a picture board to facilitate communication<br>   2. Facing the client when speaking<br>   3. Employing an interpreter<br>   4. Making sure that the language spoken is the client's dominant language | Answer: 1<br>Rationale: The client is nonverbal, so speaking en face or using an interpreter or even using the client's dominant language do not address the client's ability to communicate. Only the picture board, of the options listed, would be of assistance.<br>Implementation<br>Psychosocial integrity<br>Application<br>Learning Outcome 26.6 |
| **26.17** A nurse needs to evaluate the effectiveness of a teaching session with a client. Which of the following would provide the best feedback?<br>   1. Client communication<br>   2. Process recording<br>   3. Therapeutic communication<br>   4. Verbal communication | Answer: 2<br>Rationale: A process recording is a word-for-word account of a conversation. It includes all verbal and nonverbal interactions of both the client and nurse. It would be appropriate to use for evaluating the effectiveness of a teaching session. Client communication, therapeutic communication, and verbal communication are simply types of communication—all of which are helpful in client interactions but do not provide a vehicle for evaluation.<br>Evaluation<br>Psychosocial integrity<br>Knowledge<br>Learning Outcome 26.6 |
| **26.18** Communication among health professionals is a vital component of health care to clients. It can affect the quality of care provided and staff satisfaction. It even plays a role in | Answer: 1, 2, 3<br>Rationale: In the report *Silence Kills*, these areas were found to be difficult for many health care workers to discuss with their colleagues. Also included in this list are mistakes, lack of support, and disrespect. When these topics were not discussed among co-workers, poorer health outcomes were seen for clients. |

medical errors and client safety. Of the following, which are categories of conversation that are especially difficult, are very important for staff to perform well, and yet are often left in silence?
1. Broken rules
2. Micromanagement
3. Incompetence
4. Intimidating behaviors

When co-workers were confident in their communication abilities and did discuss their concerns, better client outcomes were observed along with more satisfaction and commitment to stay in health by the workers themselves.
Assessment
Safe, effective care environment
Application
Learning Outcome 26.7

---

**26.19** Assertive communication is an appropriate approach for nurses to use in the clinical area. It decreases the risk for miscommunication with colleagues, clients, and their families. Which of the following would be an example of this type of communication technique when a nurse is addressing a physician?
1. "You need to check the laboratory results of the client in room 423."
2. "You should visit with the client's family about the upcoming procedure."
3. "We need to be more aware of the situation among the client and the client's family."
4. "I am concerned that the client does not have adequate pain management."

Answer: 4
Rationale: An important characteristic of assertive communication includes the use of "I" statements versus "you" statements. "You" statements place blame and put the listener in a defensive position. "I" statements encourage discussion.
Evaluation
Safe, effective care environment
Analysis
Learning Outcome 26.8

---

**26.20** In order to gain the necessary information about a client's situation, the nurse must be able to ask open-ended questions. Which of the following is an example of this type of communication?
1. "What brings you to the hospital?"
2. "Are you having pain?"
3. "Does your pain feel better or worse today?"
4. "Is there anything I can do for you?"

Answer: 1
Rationale: An open-ended question is one that cannot be answered with a simple yes/no or a one-word response. Often they begin with the words *What, Describe for me, Explain,* or *Tell me about....* All other options listed can be answered with one word or a yes/no response.
Evaluation
Safe, effective care environment
Analysis
Learning Outcome 26.8

---

# CHAPTER 27

**27.1** The nurse has completed client teaching regarding medication administration. Which of the following statements by the client best illustrates compliance?
1. "I'm glad to know about my medications. It makes taking them a lot easier."
2. "I already knew most of what you told me."
3. "I think you should have waited until I was ready to go home. Maybe I'd remember better."
4. "If I take my medications as prescribed, I'll feel better."

Answer: 1
Rationale: Compliance is best illustrated when the person recognizes and accepts the need to learn, then follows through with appropriate behaviors that reflect learning. Learning about the medications helps the client understand why they're prescribed and improves the possibility for following the prescribed regimen. Statements of prior knowledge do not necessarily lead to compliance and neither does merely following the advice of the health care prescriber.
Evaluation
Health promotion and maintenance
Analysis
Learning Outcome 27.2

---

**27.2** A nurse is planning a community health education project that deals with organ donation, and the target audience is a group of adults. When following andragogic concepts, the nurse should make sure that the teaching includes which of the following?

1. Past statistics about organ donors
2. Written pamphlets
3. Directions about how to become an organ donor
4. Information on how this group can influence their children

Answer: 3

Rationale: An adult is more oriented to learning when the material is useful immediately, not sometime in the future. For this audience, giving clear directions on how to become an organ donor would be more helpful than past information and future activities like influencing their children. Written information may or may not be helpful, depending on what types of learners are included in the group.

Implementation

Health promotion and maintenance

Application

Learning Outcome 27.3

---

**27.3** A nurse educator is working with a group of students and demonstrates how to administer an intramuscular injection. The nurse is using which theoretical construct of learning?

1. Thorndike's behaviorism
2. Skinner's positive reinforcement
3. Pavlov's conditioning response
4. Bandura's imitation

Answer: 4

Rationale: Bandura claims that most learning comes from observation and instruction. Imitation is the process by which individuals copy or reproduce what they have observed. Edward Thorndike originally advanced the theory of behaviorism and maintained that learning should be based on the learner's behavior. Skinner and Pavlov focused their work on conditioning behavioral responses to a stimulus that causes the response or behavior.

Implementation

Health promotion and maintenance

Application

Learning Outcome 27.4

---

**27.4** According to Lewin's theory of cognitivism, learning is a complex activity that involves what four types of changes? (Select all that apply.)

_____ Cognitive structure
_____ Perception
_____ Motivation
_____ Sense of belonging to the group
_____ Emotions
_____ Voluntary muscle control

Answer:

_____x_____ Cognitive structure
_____ Perception
_____x_____ Motivation
_____x_____ Sense of belonging to the group
_____ Emotions
_____x_____ Voluntary muscle control

Rationale: Perception and emotions are not part of the four different types of changes that occur in Lewin's theory of learning.

Implementation

Health promotion and maintenance

Application

Learning Outcome 27.4

---

**27.5** A nursing student must present a teaching project to the class, using each of Bloom's domains. The student has several activities included in the project. Which of the following activities is an example of the affective domain?

1. Each member of the class must identify two attitudinal changes that have occurred in their lives since beginning their nursing education.
2. All members must list the technical skills they've learned.
3. Members must demonstrate a favorite nursing skill at the end of the class period.
4. Members must read a paragraph about a new clinical trial, summarize the information, and present it to the rest of the class.

Answer: 1

Rationale: The affective domain of Bloom's theory of learning is also known as the "feeling" domain. It includes emotional responses to tasks such as feelings, emotions, interests, attitudes, and appreciations. Listing technical skills and reading or summarizing information is part of the "thinking" domain, which includes knowing, comprehending, application, analysis, synthesis, and evaluation. The psychomotor domain is the "skill" domain and includes hands-on motor skills such as demonstration.

Implementation

Health promotion and maintenance

Application

Learning Outcome 27.5

| | |
|---|---|
| **27.6** A client is practicing using an incentive spirometer after surgery. The nurse has explained the use, demonstrated how it works, and also given rationale for the client to continue to use this device. By mastering the use of this device, the client will demonstrate learning in which of Bloom's domains?<br>1. Cognitive<br>2. Psychomotor<br>3. Affective<br>4. Imitation | Answer: 2<br>Rationale: The psychomotor domain is the "skill" domain and includes motor skills, such as being able to use an incentive spirometer. Cognitive abilities include the "thinking" process that begins with knowing, comprehending, and applying knowledge. The affective domain involves the attitudes or emotional responses and includes feelings, emotions, interests, and appreciations. Imitation is not one of Bloom's domains of learning.<br>Evaluation<br>Health promotion and maintenance<br>Analysis<br>Learning Outcome 27.5 |
| **27.7** Nurses working in an outpatient clinic setting are developing teaching strategies for clients with complex treatment requirements. Utilizing the behaviorist theory of learning, these nurses will do which of the following? (Select all that apply.)<br>_____ Convey sympathy in the nurse–client relationship.<br>_____ Praise the learner for correct behavior.<br>_____ Provide role models of desired behavior.<br>_____ Encourage the learners to establish goals.<br>_____ Provide sufficient practice time.<br>_____ Provide opportunities for learning to use trial-and-error techniques. | Answer:<br>_____ Convey sympathy in the nurse–client relationship.<br>___x___ Praise the learner for correct behavior.<br>___x___ Provide role models of desired behavior.<br>_____ Encourage the learners to establish goals.<br>___x___ Provide sufficient practice time.<br>___x___ Provide opportunities for learning to use trial-and-error techniques.<br>Rationale: Another trait of behaviorist theory is to select teaching strategies that avoid distracting information and that evoke the desired response. Conveying sympathy and encouragement for the learner's established goals are attributes of the humanistic behavior theory.<br>Implementation<br>Health promotion and maintenance<br>Application<br>Learning Outcome 27.4 |
| **27.8** A nurse is presenting teaching sessions to a group of residents in a home for long-term physical rehabilitation. Which of the clients described exhibits the highest motivation?<br>1. An individual who has been struggling with following nursing directives regarding discharge goals<br>2. The client who has just moved in and is already waiting for discharge<br>3. A client who is excited to learn about his new prosthesis<br>4. A client who has been there the longest and is a great "coach" for newcomers | Answer: 3<br>Rationale: Motivation is the desire to learn and influences how quickly and to what extent a person learns. It is generally greatest when a person recognizes a need and believes the need will be met through learning. The client who is excited to learn about his prosthesis understands that learning about it will help take his recovery to a high level. Motivation must be experienced by the client, not by someone else (as in being a "coach" for newcomers). Clients who struggle with rules or following prescribed courses of treatment are not motivated to learn the best reason for their particular plan of action. They may be "bucking" the system. The client who is already waiting to go home may be motivated for that, but not to the extent of being ready to learn how to achieve this end.<br>Assessment<br>Health promotion and maintenance<br>Application<br>Learning Outcome 27.6 |
| **27.9** A nurse is working in a neonatal intensive care unit, teaching parents how to care for their tiny babies while they are still in the hospital. Which of the following statements by a parent reflects a readiness to learn?<br>1. "I'm so afraid I'll hurt my baby with all these tubes." | Answer: 2<br>Rationale: Readiness to learn is the demonstration of behaviors or cues that reflect a learner's motivation, desire, and ability to learn at a specific time. The client who wants the spouse involved is demonstrating motivation and willingness, but also wants support from the spouse as well. Statements about fear of the situation need to be addressed so the fear will not inhibit the learning process. Wanting to wait until discharge |

| | |
|---|---|
| 2. "I want to make sure my spouse is here, in case I don't hear everything that's said."<br>3. "If my baby is just a little bigger, I'll be able to handle him."<br>4. "You'll give us written instructions before we go home, correct?" | or at least until the baby is older reflects uncertainty and possibly fear and should be addressed before learning can occur.<br>Evaluation<br>Health promotion and maintenance<br>Application<br>Learning Outcome 27.6 |
| **27.10** The nurse is working with a client who has been diagnosed with diabetes and must learn how to self-administer insulin. Which statement regarding feedback will be most beneficial to the client?<br>1. "You know, there are children who can learn to do this."<br>2. "Maybe it would be better if we taught your spouse to help you with this?"<br>3. "Next time, dart the needle in your skin, instead of pushing it in."<br>4. "If you don't learn this, you can't be discharged." | Answer: 3<br>Rationale: Feedback should be meaningful to the learner and should support the desired behavior through praise, positively worded corrections, and suggestions of alternative methods. Ridicule or sarcasm can lead to withdrawal from learning as in reminding an adult client that a child can perform the task or not being discharged until the skill is learned. Statements about having somebody else learn the technique may also cause the learner to avoid the teaching moment and to avoid learning the technique altogether.<br>Evaluation<br>Health promotion and maintenance<br>Application<br>Learning Outcome 27.6 |
| **27.11** A home health client is having difficulty keeping his medication schedule organized. He makes this statement to the nurse at their next visit: "There are so many pills and the names are all confusing to me. I don't even understand what they're for." The nurse should:<br>1. Help the client remember color and size in relationship to dosing time.<br>2. Write out the generic and trade name of all the pills for the client.<br>3. Fill a pill bar and tell the client not to worry, just take the pills according to that system.<br>4. Have the physician talk to the client about his medications. | Answer: 1<br>Rationale: Learning is facilitated by material that is logically organized and proceeds from the simple to the complex. This helps the learner comprehend new information, apply it to previous learning, and form new understandings. Naming the pills by color and size and dosing time helps the client move from that level to learning what each medication is for and why he is taking it—simple to complex. Learning generic and trade names is memorization and may not make sense for this client. Filling a pill box or bar is not helping the client learn about his meds, it merely puts them into an order without information. Nurses must rely on their own creativity and resourcefulness—not depend on physician input.<br>Implementation<br>Safe, effective care environment<br>Application<br>Learning Outcome 27.6 |
| **27.12** A nurse educator is working with a group of students who are in their first clinical rotation. They have had a particularly busy clinical day. All have felt rushed to complete medication administration as well as personal cares for their assigned clients. Charting has been completed and they are ready to leave the clinical area for the day.<br>A client on the unit needs medication delivered by a Z-track injection, and the staff nurse asks the instructor if one of the students would like to perform this. The instructor, understanding the important concepts surrounding timing | Answer: 2<br>Rationale: People retain information and psychomotor skills best when the time between learning and active use is short. An optimal environment is one that has reduced distraction and physical and psychological comfort. After a busy day in the clinical area, students may not be ready for the learning experience, even though it would be a good opportunity for them. Taking time to explain the procedure first might put the learning moment in the wrong time and environment, and the students may not retain the information as best they could. Allowing them to observe the staff nurse, then coming back when they are more refreshed would allow a better learning experience for the students. It is up to the instructor to decide when "teachable" moments occur in the clinical area, but the instructor works closely with staff members to find appropriate experiences. Simply declining the opportunity doesn't make for good rapport with the staff nurses. Allowing a student to simply volunteer puts the instructor's license at risk, especially if it is a skill the student has not learned or practiced. |

and environment in a learning experience, makes this comment to the staff nurse:

1. "It will take me a moment to explain the procedure to the students since we've not practiced this, but I'll find somebody to administer it."
2. "Would it be OK if the students observed today? Then, we'll do it next time we're here."
3. "We're leaving now, but thanks for asking."
4. "I'll check with the students and see if one of them would like to volunteer."

Evaluation
Safe, effective care environment
Analysis
Learning Outcome 27.6

---

**27.13** A client has an incision with a complex dressing change. The client is scheduled to be discharged home and the wound will require continued dressings at home. Which statement by the client indicates a need to postpone teaching?

1. "It's going to take time for me to understand this whole thing."
2. "Let's make sure my spouse is around before you start explaining."
3. "I wish my doctor would have explained this more in depth."
4. "I'm feeling nauseous, but go ahead and start anyway."

Answer: 4
Rationale: Learning can be inhibited by physiologic events such as illness, pain, or sensory deficits. The client must be able to concentrate and apply adequate energy to the learning or the learning itself will be impaired. If the client is experiencing nausea, the nurse should first try to reduce this symptom before beginning the teaching session. The other statements show interest as well as realism in attitude toward learning. The nurse should be attentive to cues that may enhance the learning experience, such as amount of time spent on the process, having the spouse available to learn along with the client, and giving thorough explanations about the rationale for the treatment.
Evaluation
Health promotion and maintenance
Analysis
Learning Outcome 27.6

---

**27.14** A nurse is working with a family of a child who is hospitalized with asthma. The family members speak little English, and the child is being sent home on nebulizer treatments as well as an inhaler. In addition to enlisting an interpreter to help with the language barrier, the nurse should:

1. Provide written instructions before discharge.
2. Address any healing beliefs the family has.
3. Make sure the child comes back for the follow-up appointment.
4. Make sure the parents can set up the treatments for their child.

Answer: 2
Rationale: The client who does not understand will learn little, and providing an interpreter to assist with communication is extremely important in this situation. However, if the prescribed treatment conflicts with the client/family's cultural healing beliefs, the client may not be compliant with the recommended treatments. To be effective, nurses must deal directly with any conflicts and differing values held by the client. It is also important to provide written material and assess the psychomotor skills of the child's parents, but the first priority is ascertaining any belief conflicts that may interfere with the treatment.
Assessment
Safe, effective care environment
Application
Learning Outcome 27.6

---

**27.15** A home health client requires vitamin B$_{12}$ injections every 2 weeks and insists on self-administration. The client is legally blind. The best way to assist this client is for the nurse to:

1. Teach the spouse to draw up the medication, then the client can give the injection.
2. Make sure that the injection is scheduled during a visit, so the nurse can supervise.

Answer: 3
Rationale: Clients who have visual impairment may need assistance of a support person or creative care in order to remain compliant with their treatment. Since the client insists on self-administration, prefilling syringes (and keeping them away from light and heat) would be a plausible solution. The client is concerned with independence, and allowing the client to maintain that would be quite important. Teaching a spouse or using sneaky tactics, such as scheduling injections and visits to coincide or making sure the client is at the clinic when the dose is due, are demeaning and do not support the client's wishes for independence.

---

| | |
|---|---|
| 3. Prefill syringes with the correct dose, so the client can use them for self-administration.<br>4. Schedule the client's clinic appointments in accordance with the dosing schedule, then give the injection when the client is at the clinic. | Implementation<br>Psychosocial integrity<br>Application<br>Learning Outcome 27.6 |
| **27.16** When making an assessment of the client's learning needs, the nurse will focus on which of the following elements? (Select all that apply.)<br>_____ Nurse's own knowledge<br>_____ Client's age<br>_____ Client's understanding of health problem<br>_____ Sensory acuity<br>_____ Learning style<br>_____ Client's support systems | Answer:<br>_____ Nurse's own knowledge<br>____x_____ Client's age<br>____x_____ Client's understanding of health problem<br>_____ Sensory acuity<br>____x_____ Learning style<br>____x_____ Client's support systems<br>Rationale: Other elements include the client's health beliefs and practices, cultural factors, and economic factors. The nurse's own knowledge of common learning needs is a source of information, but not part of the nurse's assessment of the client's learning needs. Sensory acuity is part of the psychomotor ability that the nurse must be aware of when planning a teaching session, but not part of assessment of the client's learning needs.<br>Assessment<br>Health promotion and maintenance<br>Application<br>Learning Outcome 27.6 |
| **27.17** A client has been diagnosed with diabetes mellitus and must learn how to do his own finger stick blood sugar analysis as part of his treatment. The client has been sullen and uncommunicative since receiving the diagnosis. How can the nurse best increase the client's motivation to learn?<br>1. Demonstrating the finger stick on the nurse<br>2. Offering to do the procedure for the client each time it is scheduled<br>3. Teaching the client's support system how to perform the procedure<br>4. Encouraging the client's participation each time the procedure is performed | Answer: 4<br>Rationale: Nurses can increase a client's motivation in several ways, including encouragement of self-direction and independence. Demonstrating the procedure on the nurse may or may not help the client become interested in the learning process, and offering to do the procedure only allows the client's current state of mind to continue. Giving the responsibility to someone else does not encourage the client to learn it.<br>Implementation<br>Health promotion and maintenance<br>Application<br>Learning Outcome 27.6 |
| **27.18** The nurse is working with a group of elderly clients through a community senior citizens center. Utilizing an understanding of health literacy, the nurse will make sure that:<br>1. Information given to this group is written at a third-grade level.<br>2. Teaching includes a variety of approaches.<br>3. Information includes pictures.<br>4. There is ample time for teaching. | Answer: 4<br>Rationale: When working with the elderly population, the nurse must realize that increased time for teaching is necessary because processing of information is slower. Health literacy is the ability to understand, read, and act on health information. Health literacy skills are often limited among certain groups, including older adults, people with limited education, poor or minority populations, and people with limited English proficiency. The average reading ability of many American adults is at the fifth-grade level. Information provided to this group should be large print, on buff-colored paper, and presented at the fifth- to sixth-grade reading level. A variety of approaches should be included regardless of the audience, as people learn by different methods.<br>Implementation |

Safe, effective care environment
Application
Learning Outcome 27.6

**27.19** A client is being discharged from the hospital after a myocardial infarction and has several new medications that have been added to her therapy. She also has been prescribed to follow a low-fat diet. The client states: "I'm never going to understand what to do, when to do it, and why I should be doing all these things." The nurse formulates which of the following diagnoses for this client and her situation?

1. *Health-Seeking Behavior* related to desire to prevent heart problems
2. *Deficient Knowledge* (diet and medication regimen) related to inexperience
3. *Noncompliance* related to situational factors
4. *Risk for Myocardial Infarction* related to deficient knowledge

Answer: 2
Rationale: The NANDA label *Deficient Knowledge* is used when the client is seeking health information or when the nurse has identified a learning need, as in this case. The area of deficiency (diet and medication regimen) should always be included in the diagnosis. *Health-Seeking Behavior* is a diagnostic label used when the client is seeking health information, which is not the case here. *Noncompliance* is used when the client or caregiver fails to follow a plan, which is too early to tell in this case. *Risk for Myocardial Infarction* is not a NANDA label. If a risk exists, the label could be *Risk for Noncompliance* related to deficient knowledge.
Nursing diagnosis
Health promotion and maintenance
Application
Learning Outcome 27.9

**27.20** The nursing diagnosis *Health-Seeking Behavior* (nutrition and diet) related to desire to improve nutritional intake has been formulated for a client who has decided to change his eating habits to be more nutritionally sound. An appropriate outcome for this client would be which of the following?

1. Client will understand the importance of eating healthy.
2. Client will be able to lose weight.
3. Client will list foods that are nutritionally sound, low fat, and high fiber.
4. Client will appreciate the value of using the food guide pyramid.

Answer: 3
Rationale: Learning outcomes, like client outcomes, must be specific and observable so they can be measured. Words like "understand" or "appreciate" are not measurable and are not observable. "Be able to lose weight" is not specific enough, and with the information given, it is not known if that is really what the client wants to attain.
Planning
Health promotion and maintenance
Application
Learning Outcome 27.9

**27.21** A home health nurse is working with a client who has pulmonary fibrosis. Of the following teaching priorities, which will take the highest priority?

1. Client will be able to set up and administer a nebulizer treatment by the end of the day.
2. Client will have increased activity level by the end of the week.
3. Client will be able to do ADLs (activities of daily living) without shortness of breath in 3 days.
4. Client will have a positive attitude about the diagnosis by the end of the month.

Answer: 1
Rationale: Learning outcomes state the client behavior and are ranked according to priority. Nurses can use theoretical frameworks such as Maslow's hierarchy of needs to establish priorities. In this case, the physiological need of learning how to administer medication takes priority over activity and attitudinal needs.
Planning
Health promotion and maintenance
Application
Learning Outcome 27.9

| | |
|---|---|
| **27.22** A school nurse is putting together a program for adolescents about positive lifestyle choices. The nurse should keep in mind that content presented to this age group must be which of the following? (Select all that apply.)<br>  1. Based on learning outcomes<br>  2. Current<br>  3. Adjusted to the adolescent client<br>  4. Based on sources available within the school system | Answer: 1, 2, 3<br>Rationale: Nurses can select among many sources of information, including books, nursing journals, and other nurses and physicians. Whatever sources the nurse chooses, content should be accurate; current; based on learning outcomes; adjusted to the learner's age, culture, and ability; consistent with information the nurse is teaching; and selected with consideration of how much time and what resources are available for teaching.<br>Implementation<br>Health promotion and maintenance<br>Application<br>Learning Outcome 27.9 |
| **27.23** The nurse is going to be working with a client who has a permanent colostomy and is ready to go home within the next several days. When organizing the teaching/learning experience, the nurse should:<br>  1. Start from the beginning and proceed through all material.<br>  2. Break up sessions into shortened time periods.<br>  3. Discover what the learner knows before proceeding with further teaching.<br>  4. Make sure the client's spouse is present before the teaching session begins. | Answer: 3<br>Rationale: Nurses should save time in constructing their own teaching sessions and should follow basic guidelines when sequencing the learning experience. The nurse should find out what the learner knows, and then proceed to the unknown. This gives the learner confidence. This information can be elicited either by asking questions or by having the client take a pretest or fill out a form. Going over information already taught and learned isn't practicing good time management for the nurse or the client. Unless the client has attention problems or may be elderly, breaking up the sessions may not be necessary. Having the spouse present is always a good idea, but may not be possible all the time.<br>Implementation<br>Physiologic integrity<br>Application<br>Learning Outcome 27.11 |
| **27.24** A client needs discharge teaching regarding the use of a walker before going home. The client's room is small and adjacent to a soda machine and small lounge area. In planning a teaching session, the best thing the nurse can do is:<br>  1. Wait until just prior to discharge, then do the teaching in the hospital lobby.<br>  2. Close the door to the client's room and make sure there is no clutter on the floor before the teaching session begins.<br>  3. Take the client to a larger area (treatment room, for example) for teaching, then evaluate on the way back to the client's room.<br>  4. Make sure a physical therapist is available to do the teaching and can see the client before discharge. | Answer: 3<br>Rationale: Noise or interruptions can interfere with concentration, whereas a comfortable environment can promote learning. If possible, the client should be out of bed for learning activities. Going to a larger area and then evaluating the learning by watching the client ambulate back to the room would be the best way to implement teaching in this particular situation. The hospital lobby does not provide privacy and can be noisy. There also would be little time to reinforce any teaching needs that might be necessary. Not all hospitals have a physical therapist available to help implement teaching for clients.<br>Implementation<br>Health promotion and maintenance<br>Application<br>Learning Outcome 27.11 |
| **27.25** A community health nurse runs a clinic that provides health screening to mainly Mexican American and Native American clients. The nurse wants to have a class on smoking cessation for interested adults of this group. In order to adjust to their time orientation, the nurse should: | Answer: 2<br>Rationale: Cultures with a predominant orientation to the present include the Mexican American, Navajo Native American, Appalachian, Eskimo, and Filipino American cultures. Schedules have to be very flexible in present-oriented societies. Time constraints are not significant for cultures who are oriented to the present, so advertising about specific classes may not be effective. The nurse must be quite flexible, treat the culture's beliefs with respect, and not expect that cultural practices will change to reflect the nurse's needs. |

| | |
|---|---|
| 1. Make sure that the classes are held at specific times.<br>2. Begin classes when a group of clients are gathered.<br>3. Mail letters ahead of time to make sure clients are informed about the upcoming class.<br>4. Make posters and place them in areas of the community frequented by these groups. | Implementation<br>Health promotion and maintenance<br>Application<br>Learning Outcome 27.12 |
| **27.26** At the completion of a teaching session, the nurse must evaluate the effectiveness. In a situation where the client was learning a bandaging technique, the most effective evaluation is which of the following?<br>1. Shared by the nurse and client<br>2. A return demonstration by the client<br>3. When the nurse is satisfied that the client can complete the technique<br>4. If the wound heals | Answer: 1<br>Rationale: Both the client and the nurse should evaluate the learning experience. The client can tell the nurse what was helpful and provide a demonstration that shows mastery of the skill. The nurse needs to evaluate whether the client has an understanding of the rationale behind the technique, understands infection control standards, and so on. Using only the return demonstration or focusing on the nurse's satisfaction with the client's performance is one-sided. The evaluation is of the bandaging technique, and it may or may not be covering a wound.<br>Evaluation<br>Health promotion and maintenance<br>Analysis<br>Learning Outcome 27.13 |
| **27.27** The nurse has completed a teaching session for a client with a tracheostomy. Documentation of the session should include which of the following? (Select all that apply.)<br>1. Diagnosed learning needs<br>2. Supplies required<br>3. Client outcomes<br>4 Need for additional teaching<br>5. Topics taught | Answer: 1, 3, 4, 5<br>Rationale: The parts of the teaching process that should be documented in the client's chart include diagnosed learning needs, learning outcomes, topics taught, client outcomes, need for additional teaching, and resources provided.<br>Implementation<br>Health promotion and maintenance<br>Application<br>Learning Outcome 27.14 |

# CHAPTER 28

| | |
|---|---|
| **28.1** According to the National Council of State Boards of Nursing, which of the following are among the "rights" of delegation? (Select all that apply.)<br>1. Supervision<br>2. Evaluation<br>3. Client<br>4. Time<br>5. Task | Answer: 1, 2, 5<br>Rationale: According to the NCSBN, the nurse delegates the right task under the right circumstances to the right person with the right direction and communication and the right supervision and evaluation. The right client and the right time are part of the rights of medication administration.<br>Assessment<br>Safe, effective care environment<br>Knowledge<br>Learning Outcome 28.10 |
| **28.2** An unlicensed assistive person (UAP) is working on a rehabilitation unit. Which of the following tasks would be appropriate for this person to delegate?<br>1. Taking and recording vital signs<br>2. Assisting with bathing<br>3. Making a bed<br>4. An unlicensed assistive person may not delegate tasks. | Answer: 4<br>Rationale: The unlicensed person may not delegate tasks to another person. Delegation is part of the registered nurse's role. Tasks such as taking and recording vital signs, and making a bed are appropriate tasks for the RN to delegate to the UAP.<br>Implementation<br>Safe, effective care environment<br>Application<br>Learning Outcome 28.9 |

| | |
|---|---|
| **28.3** An RN delegates the task of taking a newly admitted client's vital signs to a nurse's aide. The client's blood pressure was 182/98, but did not get reported to the physician for several hours. Who is responsible for the lapse in time between discovery and action?<br>   1. Nurse manager<br>   2. Aide<br>   3. Client<br>   4. RN | Answer: 4<br>Rationale: The RN is ultimately responsible for the action, reporting it, and following through on any action. Part of delegation is supervision and evaluation—ultimate responsibilities that belong to the RN.<br>Evaluation<br>Safe, effective care environment<br>Application<br>Learning Outcome 28.9 |
| **28.4** A nurse has worked on the same unit for a number of years. He is highly respected by his peers and physicians and is able to influence his co-workers to achieve group goals. This is an example of a/an _____ leader. | Answer: informal<br>Rationale: An informal leader is not officially appointed to direct the activities of others, but because of seniority, age, or special abilities, is selected by the group as its leader and plays an important role in influencing colleagues, co-workers, or other group members to achieve the group's goals.<br>Assessment<br>Safe, effective care environment<br>Knowledge<br>Learning Outcome 28.4 |
| **28.5** A nurse manager has the reputation of being an autocratic leader. Which of the following statements by this manager would support that reputation?<br>   1. "I'd like to hear from you (addressing the staff) what your ideas are for promoting better morale in this unit."<br>   2. "I'm putting a suggestion box in the break room if anyone has ideas that would be helpful to the unit."<br>   3. "The new work schedule is posted for the next 6 weeks."<br>   4. "I put the new procedure manual out. Please add your comments to the blank sheet of paper attached to the front." | Answer: 3<br>Rationale: An autocratic leader makes decisions for the group. This style is likened to a dictator in that the autocratic leader gives orders and directions to the group, determines policies, and solves problems without input from the group. Creativity, autonomy, and self-motivation are group attributes that are not met with this type of leadership style. The other options would be more reflective of a democratic style leader.<br>Assessment<br>Safe, effective care environment<br>Application<br>Learning Outcome 28.3 |
| **28.6** During a particularly heated staff meeting regarding staff assignments, the nurse manager makes this comment: "When you all can come to a decision, let me know and we'll move on from there." This leader is best identified as which of the following?<br>   1. Democratic leader<br>   2. Permissive leader<br>   3. Bureaucratic leader<br>   4. Situational leader | Answer: 2<br>Rationale: The permissive leader recognizes the group's need for autonomy and self-regulation by assuming a "hands-off" approach. Allowing the group to come to their own decision, then accepting that would be the case in this situation. The democratic leader encourages group discussion and decision making, provides constructive criticism, offers information, makes suggestions, and asks questions. The bureaucratic leader relies on the organization's rules, policies, and procedures to direct the group's work efforts. A situational leader is one who adapts his or her leadership style to the situation.<br>Assessment<br>Safe, effective care environment<br>Application<br>Learning Outcome 28.3 |

**28.7** A nurse manager allows the staff to make their own schedules and do their own client assignments on their shifts. However, during a code situation, the nurse manager will make decisions for the staff—instructing which nurse to assume which responsibility in the code situation. This manager is exemplifying which style of leadership?
  1. Permissive
  2. Democratic
  3. Situational
  4. Bureaucratic

Answer: 3
Rationale: According to contingency theorists, effective leaders adapt their leadership style to the situation. Unlike the singular style of authoritarian, democratic, and permissive leaders, the situational leader adapts his or her leadership to the readiness and willingness of the group to perform the assigned task. Permissive leaders assume a "hands-off" approach. The democratic leader encourages group discussion and decision making. A bureaucratic leader relies on the organization's rules, policies, and procedures to direct the group's work efforts.
Assessment
Safe, effective care environment
Application
Learning Outcome 28.4

**28.8** A group of community health nurses work together in the same office. They are each responsible for their own caseloads and scheduling of appointments. Their major leadership directives come from the state health office, several hundred miles away. This group of nurses is functioning under what type of leadership?
  1. Charismatic
  2. Shared
  3. Transformational
  4. Transactional

Answer: 2
Rationale: Shared leadership recognizes that a professional workforce is made up of many leaders. No one person is considered to have knowledge or ability beyond that of other members of the work group, as in this situation. A charismatic leader is characterized by an emotional relationship between the leader and group members. A transactional leader has a relationship with followers based on an exchange for some resource valued by the followers. A transformational leader fosters creativity, risk taking, commitment, and collaboration by empowering the group to share in the organization's vision.
Assessment
Safe, effective care environment
Application
Learning Outcome 28.3

**28.9** A charge nurse has just started working on a rehabilitation unit. This nurse's responsibilities include the day-to-day management and coordination of therapies for the clients, client assignments, and scheduling. This is an example of which level of management?
  1. Top-level
  2. Middle-level
  3. First-level
  4. Upper-level

Answer: 3
Rationale: First-level managers are responsible for managing the work of nonmanagerial personnel and the day-to-day activities of a specific work group (rehabilitation unit in this case). Middle-level managers supervise a number of first-level managers and are responsible for the activities in the departments they supervise. Upper-level (same as top-level) managers are organizational executives who are primarily responsible for establishing goals and developing strategic plans.
Assessment
Safe, effective care environment
Application
Learning Outcome 28.5

**28.10** Risk management is part of the planning function of management. Put the following steps of risk management in order from the first step (1) to the last (5):
_____ Analyzing, classifying, and prioritizing risks
_____ Evaluating and modifying risk reduction programs
_____ Anticipating and seeking sources of risk
_____ Developing a plan to avoid and manage risk
_____ Gathering data that indicate success at avoiding or minimizing risk

Answer:
____2____ Analyzing, classifying, and prioritizing risks
____5____ Evaluating and modifying risk reduction programs
____1____ Anticipating and seeking sources of risk
____3____ Developing a plan to avoid and manage risk
____4____ Gathering data that indicate success at avoiding or minimizing risk
Rationale: Risk management is having a system in place to reduce danger to clients and staff. Central to the process of risk management is communication among all involved persons.
Planning
Safe, effective care environment
Application
Learning Outcome 28.6

| | |
|---|---|
| **28.11** A nurse manager is working on new job descriptions for all nursing units of the hospital. This is an example of which function of management?<br>1. Planning<br>2. Organizing<br>3. Directing<br>4. Coordinating | Answer: 2<br>Rationale: Organizing is an ongoing process of management that involves determining responsibilities, communicating expectations (which job descriptions would fall under), and establishing the chain of command for authority and communication. Planning involves assessing a situation, establishing goals and objectives that identify priorities, delineating who is responsible, determining deadlines, and describing how the intended outcome is to be achieved and evaluated. Directing is the process of getting the organization's work accomplished. Coordinating is the process of ensuring that plans are carried out and evaluating outcomes.<br>Implementation<br>Safe, effective care environment<br>Application<br>Learning Outcome 28.6 |
| **28.12** A hospital was named in a lawsuit after a client had to undergo a second surgical procedure because an arthroscopy was performed on the wrong knee during surgery. The hospital settled out of court with the client for damages. This is an example of which principle of management?<br>1. Authority<br>2. Responsibility<br>3. Coordination<br>4. Accountability | Answer: 4<br>Rationale: Principles of management include authority, accountability, and responsibility. Accountability is the ability and willingness to assume responsibility for one's actions and to accept the consequences of one's behavior. The hospital had a responsibility to the client for quality care and service. That was not the case; therefore, the hospital was willing to accept the consequences of the injury experienced by the client. Authority is defined as the right to direct the work of others. Coordination is a function of management, not one of the principles.<br>Evaluation<br>Safe, effective care environment<br>Analysis<br>Learning Outcome 28.5 |
| **28.13** A nurse manager has had to handle a particularly difficult physician who is demanding as well as demeaning. Through this situation, the nurse manager has learned that assertiveness, accuracy, and honesty are attributes of which skill necessary for managers?<br>1. Critical thinking<br>2. Communication<br>3. Networking<br>4. Responsibility | Answer: 2<br>Rationale: Good communication skills are essential to managers and include assertiveness, clear expression of ideas, accuracy, and honesty. Critical thinking is a creative process that includes problem solving and decision making. Networking is a process whereby professional links are established through which people can share ideas, knowledge, and information; offer support and direction to each other; and facilitate accomplishment of professional goals. Responsibility is one of the principles of management, not a management skill.<br>Assessment<br>Safe, effective care environment<br>Application<br>Learning Outcome 28.8 |
| **28.14** A nursing student would like to do an observation on one of the inpatient units at a hospital. In assisting the student to meet this desire, the educator would look for which of the following?<br>1. Mentor<br>2. Manager<br>3. Team leader<br>4. Preceptor | Answer: 4<br>Rationale: The preceptor is a person of experience who assists a "new" nurse in improving clinical skills and nursing judgment. A mentor acts in a more nurturing role, perhaps for a longer period of time, and provides support, guidance, assistance, advice, and inspiration to a younger nurse. Manager and team leader are different management roles.<br>Implementation<br>Safe, effective care environment<br>Application<br>Learning Outcome 28.8 |
| **28.15** A hospital is implementing a computerized charting system, and all nursing staff are required to be oriented to the system by a specific deadline. This is an example of which type of change?<br>1. Overt change<br>2. Covert change | Answer: 1<br>Rationale: An overt change is one that is planned and that people are aware of. Implementing a new computer system is certainly a planned, purposeful event. Covert change is hidden or occurs without the individual's awareness—it may be gradual, subtle, and unplanned. An unplanned change is an alteration imposed by external events or persons and occurs when unexpected events force a reaction. |

| 3. Unplanned change<br>4. Drift | Drift is a type of unplanned change in which change occurs without effort on anyone's part.<br>Assessment<br>Safe, effective care environment<br>Application<br>Learning Outcome 28.4 |
|---|---|
| **28.16** Through the process of implementing a computerized charting system, nursing staff have demonstrated various attitudes. During a particularly busy month with high client census and acuity, the nursing staff was aware of the need for changing the current system of record keeping and charting to make it more efficient. This is an example of which stage of change?<br>1. Refreezing<br>2. Unfreezing<br>3. Moving<br>4. Drift | Answer: 2<br>Rationale: Three stages are involved in change: unfreezing, moving, and refreezing. During the unfreezing stage, the need for change is recognized, driving and restraining forces are identified, alternative solutions are generated, and participants are motivated to change. During the second stage, moving, participants agree that the status quo is undesirable and the actual change is planned in detail and implemented. In the final stage, refreezing, the change is integrated and stabilized. Drift is a type of unplanned change in which change occurs without effort on anyone's part.<br>Implementation<br>Safe, effective care environment<br>Application<br>Learning Outcome 28.4 |

# CHAPTER 29

| **29.1** The following vital signs were taken and given to the RN by the UAP: 97.2-68-18-130/70. The client from whom these vital signs were obtained is a 75-year-old male. Which of the following rationales would explain this client's low temperature?<br>1. Anxiety level of the client has increased.<br>2. Hormones have fluctuated in this client.<br>3. Muscle activity has increased during the client's therapy session.<br>4. Loss of subcutaneous fat is noted. | Answer: 4<br>Rationale: This client is 75 years old, and research shows that older people are at risk for hypothermia. When one ages, subcutaneous fat is lost. If a client is anxious or stressed, this response stimulates the sympathetic nervous system. This in turn increases the production of epinephrine and norepinephrine, which increases metabolic and heat production, causing the temperature to rise. Women experience more hormonal fluctuations than men, and this is usually true with the secretion of progesterone at the time of ovulation. Since this client is a male, this is not a factor. Exercise, which represents hard work or strenuous activity, increases body temperature. That is not the case with this client. No reference has been made to a therapy session, and the temperature is decreased.<br>Evaluation<br>Safe, effective care environment<br>Analysis<br>Learning Outcome 29.1 |
|---|---|
| **29.2** Which of the following nursing interventions would assure the RN of an accurate temperature reading for a client?<br>1. Assess that the equipment used is working properly.<br>2. Place the client in a position that is most comfortable for the health care provider.<br>3. Take the temperature with a chemical disposable thermometer when the client is perspiring.<br>4. Wait at least 10 minutes before taking the temperature after a client has been smoking. | Answer: 1<br>Rationale: If the equipment is not working properly, no accuracy will be obtained in the readings. The type of equipment or method that is chosen will dictate client position, not the position of the health care provider. In order to use a chemical disposable thermometer, the client's skin must be dry for the thermometer to adhere to the skin. The recommended time to wait to assess an oral temperature is 30 minutes after one smokes, not 10 minutes.<br>Implementation<br>Physiological integrity<br>Application<br>Learning Outcome 29.1 |

| | |
|---|---|
| **29.3** Which of the following sites would be the most appropriate choice to use to measure a client's temperature who has a history of heart disease and has just eaten a bowl of vegetable soup?<br>   1. Axilla<br>   2. Oral<br>   3. Popliteal<br>   4. Rectal | Answer: 2<br>Rationale: Body temperature is frequently measured orally even if the client has eaten or drank something cold or hot. One only needs to wait 30 minutes, and then this site can be used. Rectal would be contraindicated in this client given the history of heart disease; the nurse would not want to risk stimulating the vagus nerve. Axilla is the preferred site for newborns, not adults. The popliteal site would not be used given the history of heart disease. There could be circulatory issues that might affect accurate reading since this site is much farther away from the heart.<br>Assessment<br>Physiological integrity<br>Analysis<br>Learning Outcome 29.5 |
| **29.4** Which of the following is an appropriate nursing intervention for lowering a client's elevated temperature?<br>   1. Bathe the client with ice water.<br>   2. Give the client an antipyretic.<br>   3. Increase fluid intake.<br>   4. Lower room temperature. | Answer: 3<br>Rationale: Elevated body temperature contributes to dehydration, which leads to body tissues drying out and malfunctioning. Rehydrating the client's tissues will allow the temperature to return to normal. Giving a client an antipyretic requires a doctor's order. Bathing the client in ice water and setting the air conditioner to a lower temperature would lower the client's temperature too fast, possibly causing hypothermia.<br>Implementation<br>Safe, effective care environment<br>Analysis<br>Learning Outcome 29.4 |
| **29.5** A client has returned to the nursing unit from having a cardiac catheterization. The RN is assessing the client's right pedal pulse (dorsalis pedis) and assesses no pulse present. On further investigation, the extremity is found to be warm and pink, and nail beds blanch well with 2 to 3 seconds capillary refill. How would the RN explain these findings?<br>   1. A change in the client's health status has occurred.<br>   2. The client has thrown a blood clot in that extremity.<br>   3. The RN's watch has stopped working.<br>   4. Too much pressure was applied over the pulse site. | Answer: 4<br>Rationale: Too firm of pressure on a pulse site will obliterate that pulse since assessing the dorsalis pedis pulse requires one to apply some pressure over the dorsalis pedis artery, making contact with the bones in the foot. The information provided gives no indication that any health change has occurred. A complication of a cardiac catheterization is a blood clot, but the assessment data given (warm, pink, etc.) are not symptoms of a blood clot. There are no data given in regard to equipment malfunction like a watch.<br>Assessment<br>Safe, effective care environment<br>Analysis<br>Learning Outcome 29.6 |
| **29.6** The RN assesses a client who is recovering from femoral popliteal bypass surgery and discovers that it is difficult to assess the dorsalis pedis pulses. Which of the following nursing interventions would be most appropriate for the nurse to use?<br>   1. Ask another nurse to assess the pulses.<br>   2. Document the findings.<br>   3. Obtain a Doppler ultrasound stethoscope.<br>   4. Wait and just try again later. | Answer: 3<br>Rationale: Obtaining a Doppler ultrasound stethoscope is the appropriate action to take. The Doppler will ensure accuracy by helping to exclude environmental sounds. If one nurse is having difficulty with the pulse and accuracy, getting another nurse is not going to be the best choice. Just documenting the findings does not address the problem of getting an accurate pulse reading. Waiting until later may be harmful to the client, creating an unsafe environment.<br>Assessment<br>Safe, effective care environment<br>Application<br>Learning Outcome 29.6 |

**29.7** When assessing a client's peripheral pulse, the health care provider is also assessing which of the following?
1. Depth
2. Rhythm
3. Sound
4. Stress

Answer: 2
Rationale: When assessing peripheral pulses, one of the characteristics being assessed is rhythm along with rate, volume, and equality. Heart sounds are assessed with the apical pulse. Depth is a term used when assessing edema. Stress will affect the rate of both pulse and respiration, but it is not a characteristic of pulse assessment.
Assessment
Physiological integrity
Application
Learning Outcome 29.6

**29.8** On the diagram below, place an X over the point of maximal impulse (PMI) where the stethoscope is placed to assess the apical pulse.

Answer:
X should be placed over the dot indicated by the term mitral.
Assessment
Physiological Integrity
Knowledge
Learning Outcome 29.7

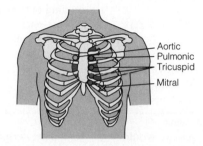

**29.9** An apical-radial pulse is determined by the RN to be the procedure to use on a client with cardiovascular disorders. Which of the following rationales did the RN use to make this decision?
1. A forceful radial pulse is much too difficult to count correctly.
2. Both arteriole and venous sounds were heard simultaneously.
3. The pulse was bounding and easily obliterated.
4. The thrust of blood from the heart is too feeble for the wave to be felt at the peripheral pulse site.

Answer: 4
Rationale: Knowing there is a history of cardiovascular disorders would alert the RN to the importance of the utmost accuracy for the client's pulse assessment. The apical-radial pulse is used to assess this type of client due to the feebleness of the wave of blood flow felt at the peripheral sites. A forceful radial pulse would be ideal for assessing a client's peripheral pulse, and a bounding pulse is *not* easily obliterated. Arteriole and venous sounds would be detected when using the Doppler, but there is no indication for Doppler use given this situation.
Planning
Physiological integrity
Analysis
Learning Outcome 29.7

**29.10** A client in a motor vehicle crash has arrived at the trauma unit in respiratory distress and unconscious. Knowing that chemoreceptors respond to changes in the concentrations of oxygen, carbon dioxide, and hydrogen, which of the following circumstances would account for this client's decrease in respiratory rate?
1. Exercise
2. Increased intracranial pressure
3. Increased environmental temperature
4. Stress

Answer: 2
Rationale: Factors that decrease respirations are decreased environmental temperature, certain medications, and increased intracranial pressure. Exercise, stress, and increased environmental temperature increase respiration rates.
Evaluation
Physiological integrity
Analysis
Learning Outcome 29.9

| | |
|---|---|
| **29.11** Which of the following positions does the RN assist the client in to *best* assess respiratory status?<br>   1. Prone<br>   2. Semi-Fowler's<br>   3. Side-lying<br>   4. Supine | Answer: 2<br>Rationale: Persons in a semi-Fowler's position will better aid themselves and the nurse to assess their respiratory status. Other positions such as prone, side-lying, and supine increase the volume of blood inside the thoracic cavity and compress the chest, compromising the client's respirations.<br>Intervention<br>Safe, effective care environment<br>Application<br>Learning Outcome 29.9 |
| **29.12** A client is being treated for congestive heart failure. Which of the following physical findings would lead the RN to believe the client's condition has *not* improved?<br>   1. Temperature of 98.6°F (37°C)<br>   2. Moderate amount of clear thin mucus<br>   3. Pulse oximetry reading of 96%<br>   4. Wheezing of breath sounds in all lobes | Answer: 4<br>Rationale: Wheezing heard when assessing breath sounds is indicative of abnormal breath sounds, which are characteristic in congestive heart failure. A temperature reading of 98.6°F, moderate clear mucus, and a pulse oximetry reading of 96% are all normal findings and not an indication of heart failure.<br>Evaluation<br>Physiological integrity<br>Analysis<br>Learning Outcome 29.1 |
| **29.13** Which of the following determinants of blood pressure would explain a client's blood pressure reading of 120/100?<br>   1. Blood viscosity<br>   2. Blood volume<br>   3. Pumping action of the heart<br>   4. Peripheral vascular resistance | Answer: 4<br>Rationale: Peripheral vascular resistance especially affects diastolic blood pressure readings. A reading of 120/100 would be indicative of peripheral vascular resistance. A diastolic reading of 100 is too high when a normal reading is 80. Determinants of blood pressure such as blood volume, blood viscosity, and pumping action of the heart mainly affect the systolic reading portion of the blood pressure.<br>Evaluation<br>Physiological integrity<br>Analysis<br>Learning Outcome 29.10 |
| **29.14** Which of the following sounds will be heard during phase 2 of Korotkoff's sounds?<br>   1. A murmur or swishing sound<br>   2. Disappearance of sound<br>   3. Faint, clear tapping sound<br>   4. Increased intensity of sound | Answer: 4<br>Rationale: Phase 1 of Korotkoff's sounds starts with a faint, clear tapping sound. Phase 2 produces a murmur sound. Phase 3 is marked by an increased intensity of sound. Phase 4 produces a muffled sound. Phase 5, the final phase, is where the sound disappears.<br>Evaluation<br>Physiological integrity<br>Application<br>Learning Outcome 29.11 |
| **29.15** Which of the following arteries is most commonly used to obtain a blood pressure reading?<br>   1. Brachial<br>   2. Femoral<br>   3. Radial<br>   4. Ulnar | Answer: 1<br>Rationale: The brachial is the most common artery used to assess a blood pressure reading because it is the most accessible. The radial and ulnar could be used but they are not as accurate. The femoral is not as accessible as the brachial.<br>Assessment<br>Physiological integrity<br>Application<br>Learning Outcome 29.12 |
| **29.16** In the palpatory method of blood pressure determination, instead of listening for the blood flow sounds, light to moderate pressure is used over the artery as the pressure in the cuff is released. When is the pressure read from the sphygmomanometer? | Answer: 3<br>Rationale: The first pulsation that is felt after the cuff is slowly deflated is the blood pressure reading that is recorded if the palpatory method is used to assess a client's blood pressure. Assessing the pulse before the cuff is applied is not the pressure. When inflating the cuff, no pressure is felt. If the second pulsation is recorded, that would be an inaccurate reading. |

| | |
|---|---|
| 1. When the cuff is applied<br>2. When the cuff is being deflated<br>3. When the first pulsation is felt<br>4. When the second pulsation is felt | Implementation<br>Physiological integrity<br>Application<br>Learning Outcome 29.12 |
| **29.17** Which condition would lead the RN to choose the dorsalis pedis pulse as the site for further assessing the client's status?<br>  1. Altered level of consciousness<br>  2. Decreased urine output<br>  3. Irregular radial pulse<br>  4. Toes cool to touch | Answer: 4<br>Rationale: The dorsalis pedis pulse site is in the foot, so this is the ideal site to assess the pulse for toes that are cool to touch. Decreased urine output, irregular radial pulse, and altered level of consciousness would best be assessed at the source of the origin, which is the apical pulse.<br>Assessment<br>Physiological integrity<br>Analysis<br>Learning Outcome 29.5 |
| **29.18** Which of the following factors can affect oxygen saturation readings?<br>  1. Activity<br>  2. Environmental conditions<br>  3. Nutrition<br>  4. Skin color | Answer: 1<br>Rationale: Factors affecting oxygen saturation readings are hemoglobin, circulation, and activity. If there is shivering or excessive movement of the sensor site, this will interfere with an accurate reading. Environmental conditions, nutrition, and skin color are not factors.<br>Implementation<br>Physiological integrity<br>Application<br>Learning Outcome 29.13 |
| **29.19** As the RN is suctioning a client, the pulse oximetry reading drops to 83%. What would be the next action taken by the RN?<br>  1. Allow the client to take some extra deep breaths.<br>  2. Continue to suction but only intermittently.<br>  3. Keep the catheter in place and wait a few minutes.<br>  4. Stop suctioning and give supplemental oxygen. | Answer: 4<br>Rationale: Not only does suctioning remove secretions, but it also removes the client's air. By stopping suctioning, the RN stops removing both. This allows the client to recoup from the procedure, and giving oxygen will also increase the saturation ability back to a normal range. Continuing to suction continuously or intermittently will only decrease the saturation levels more. Allowing the client to take a few deep breaths will help but not quickly enough to compensate for the hypoxia experienced. Leaving the catheter in place obstructs air flow, thus compromising an already poor situation.<br>Implementation<br>Physiological integrity<br>Application<br>Learning Outcome 29.13 |
| **29.20** The RN needs vital signs taken on the four clients that have been assigned. Which of the four clients should be taken by the RN and not the UAP?<br>  1. Cardiac catheterization client returning to the nursing unit<br>  2. COPD client on 2 Lpm oxygen via nasal cannula<br>  3. Pneumonia client nearing discharge<br>  4. Postop client of 2 days from gallbladder surgery | Answer: 1<br>Rationale: The cardiac catheterization client will need a thorough assessment since she is just returning to the nursing unit. Invasive procedures, such as a catheterization, will need to be closely assessed. More than likely a Doppler will be needed to ensure the pedal pulse is present and stable in the extremity used during the procedure. Unlicensed personnel are not usually delegated Doppler ultrasound device use. The COPD client is a chronic condition client, and her vital signs would be considered routine. The client with pneumonia nearing discharge and the client who is 2 days postop from gallbladder surgery would be considered medically stable and are also considered to be routine. Therefore, these clients are within the UAP's capability.<br>Assessment<br>Safe, effective care environment<br>Analysis<br>Learning Outcome 29.14 |

| | |
|---|---|
| **29.21** In which phase of Korotkoff's sounds would the nurse hear crisper sounds, increasing in intensity? _____ | Answer: Phase 3<br>Evaluation<br>Physiological Integrity<br>Application<br>Learning Outcome 29.11 |

## CHAPTER 30

| | |
|---|---|
| **30.1** The nurse is preparing to perform a health assessment of the abdomen. Which of the following is the correct order to perform the assessment?<br>  1. Auscultate, percuss, palpate, inspect<br>  2. Inspect, auscultate, palpate, percuss<br>  3. Inspect, auscultate, percuss, palpate<br>  4. Palpate, percuss, auscultate, inspect | Answer: 3<br>Rationale: Palpation should always be performed last when performing an abdominal health assessment. Auscultation is done before palpation and percussion because palpation and percussion cause movement or stimulation of the bowel, which can increase bowel motility and thus heighten bowel sounds, creating false results.<br>Assessment<br>Physiological integrity<br>Application<br>Learning Outcome 30.2 |
| **30.2** The nurse is performing a health assessment and notes a yellow tinge to the sclera of the eye. The nurse would document this as which of the following?<br>  1. Cyanosis<br>  2. Jaundice<br>  3. Pallor<br>  4. Erythema | Answer: 2<br>Rationale: Jaundice is a yellow tinge that is abnormal and is often noticed in the sclera of the eye.<br>Assessment<br>Physiological integrity<br>Analysis<br>Learning Outcome 30.3 |
| **30.3** While performing an assessment of the integument system, the nurse notes the client's eyeballs are protruding and the upper eyelids are elevated. What term would the nurse use to document this finding?<br>  1. Erythema<br>  2. Cyanosis<br>  3. Exophthalmos<br>  4. Normocephalic | Answer: 3<br>Rationale: Hyperthyroidism can cause exophthalmos, a protrusion of the eyeballs with elevation of the upper eyelids, resulting in a startled or staring expression.<br>Assessment<br>Physiological integrity<br>Analysis<br>Learning Outcome 30.3 |
| **30.4** The nurse is preparing for morning rounds. Which of the following may not be delegated to the nursing assistant?<br>  1. Vital signs<br>  2. Fill water pitchers<br>  3. Skull and face assessment<br>  4. Ambulate surgical clients | Answer: 3<br>Rationale: Assessment of the skull and face may not be delegated to unlicensed assistive personnel.<br>Assessment<br>Physiological integrity<br>Comprehension |
| **30.5** The nurse is preparing to perform an eye assessment. Which of the following equipment will the nurse need to gather? (Select all that apply.)<br>  1. Penlight<br>  2. Snellen's chart<br>  3. Sterile gloves<br>  4. Gauze square<br>  5. Millimeter ruler | Answer: 1, 2, 4, 5<br>When performing an eye examination, the nurse needs the following: cotton-tip applicator, gauze square, clean gloves, millimeter ruler, penlight, Snellen's or E chart, and opaque card.<br>Assessment<br>Physiological integrity<br>Comprehension<br>Learning Outcome 30.5 |

| | |
|---|---|
| **30.6** The nurse is performing a lung assessment on a client with suspected pneumonia. Which of the following assessments should the nurse report to the physician immediately?<br>1. Chest symmetrical<br>2. Breath sounds equal bilaterally<br>3. Asymmetric chest expansion<br>4. Bilateral symmetric vocal fremitus | Answer: 3<br>Rationale: Chest expansion should be symmetrical.<br>Assessment<br>Physiological integrity<br>Analysis<br>Learning Outcome 30.4 |
| **30.7** The nurse is preparing to conduct an assessment of the heart. Which of the following areas would the nurse place the stethoscope for auscultation? (Select all that apply.)<br>1. Aortic<br>2. Pulmonic<br>3. Tricuspid<br>4. Abdomen<br>5. Mitral | Answer: 1, 2, 3, 5<br>Rationale: All options except 4 are areas the nurse would place the stethoscope when auscultating heart sounds.<br>Assessment<br>Physiological integrity<br>Analysis<br>Learning Outcome 30.5 |
| **30.8** While performing a health assessment, in which position should the nurse place the client for inspection of the jugular veins?<br>1. 90-degree angle<br>2. 30- to 45-degree angle<br>3. 15-degree angle<br>4. 60-degree angle | Answer: 2<br>Rationale: The nurse should place the client in the semi-Fowler's postion (30- to 45-degree angle) while inspecting the jugular veins for distention.<br>Assessment<br>Physiological integrity<br>Application<br>Learning Outcome 30.5 |
| **30.9** The nurse is assessing peripheral pulses on a client with suspected peripheral vascular disease. Which of the following should the nurse report to the physician immediately?<br>1. Pulses equal bilaterally<br>2. Full pulsations<br>3. Thready pulses<br>4. Pulses present bilaterally | Answer: 3<br>Rationale: Thready, weak, or decreased pulses are abnormal and should be reported to the physician.<br>Assessment<br>Physiological Integrity<br>Analysis<br>Learning Outcome 30.3 |
| **30.10** The nurse is assessing a female's breasts. The nurse finds both breasts rounded, slightly unequal in size, skin smooth and intact, and nipples without discharge. What is the nurse's next action?<br>1. Notify the charge nurse.<br>2. Notify the physician.<br>3. Document the findings in the nurse's notes as normal.<br>4. Document the findings in the nurse's notes as abnormal. | Answer: 3<br>Rationale: The findings are all normal, so the nurse would document the assessment in the nurse's notes as normal.<br>Assessment<br>Physiological integrity<br>Analysis<br>Learning Outcome 30.3 |
| **30.11** The nurse is preparing a client for an abdominal examination. Which of the following should be performed before the examination?<br>1. Ask client to urinate.<br>2. Ask client to drink 8 ounces of water.<br>3. Assess vital signs.<br>4. Assess heart rate. | Answer: 1<br>Rationale: The nurse should ask the client to urinate since an empty bladder makes the assessment more comfortable.<br>Implementation<br>Physiological integrity<br>Application<br>Learning Outcome 30.5 |

| | |
|---|---|
| **30.12** The nurse is performing a musculoskeletal assessment on a client admitted with a possible stroke. When testing for muscle grip strength, the nurse should ask the client to:<br>1. Grasp the nurse's index and middle fingers while the nurse tries to pull the fingers out.<br>2. Hold an arm up and resist while the nurse tries to push it down.<br>3. Flex each arm and then try to extend it against the nurse's attempt to keep the arm in flexion.<br>4. Shrug the shoulders against the resistance of the nurse's hands. | Answer: 1<br>Rationale: Although all options are included in testing muscle strength, only option 1 is testing muscle grip strength.<br>Implementation<br>Physiological integrity<br>Application<br>Learning Outcome 30.5 |
| **30.13** Assessment of mental status reveals the client's general cerebral function. These include which of the following?<br>1. Cognitive and affective functions<br>2. Cognitive and effective functions<br>3. Affective and memory functions<br>4. Affective and knowledge functions | Answer: 1<br>Rationale: Cognitive (intellectual) and affective (emotional) functions are assessed.<br>Assessment<br>Physiological integrity<br>Comprehension<br>Learning Outcome 30.4 |
| **30.14** The nurse is caring for a client following a cerebrovascular accident (stroke). The client is able to comprehend what is being said to him; however, he is unable to respond by speech or writing. What is this form of aphasia called?<br>1. Auditory aphasia<br>2. Acoustic aphasia<br>3. Sensory aphasia<br>4. Expressive aphasia | Answer: 4<br>Rationale: Motor or expressive aphasia involves loss of the power to express oneself by writing, making signs, or speaking. Clients may find that even though they can recall words, they have lost the ability to combine speech sounds into words.<br>Implementation<br>Physiological integrity<br>Analysis<br>Learning Outcome 30.3 |
| **30.15** The Glasgow Coma Scale is used for assessing level of consciousness. It tests in which of the following areas? (Select all that apply.)<br>1. Eye response<br>2. Motor response<br>3. Verbal response<br>4. Orientation<br>5. Musculoskeletal response | Answer: 1, 2, 3<br>Rationale: The Glasgow Coma Scale was originally developed to predict recovery from a head injury; however, it is used by many professionals to assess locus of control (LOC). It tests in three major areas: eye response, motor response, and verbal response.<br>Assessment<br>Physiological integrity<br>Knowledge<br>Learning Outcome 30.5 |
| **30.16** The nurse is preparing to assess a client's reflexes. Which of the following equipment should the nurse gather before entering the room?<br>1. Sterile gloves<br>2. Clean gloves<br>3. Percussion hammer<br>4. Penlight | Answer: 3<br>Rationale: A percussion hammer is used to test reflexes.<br>Assessment<br>Physiological integrity<br>Comprehension<br>Learning Outcome 30.5 |

| | |
|---|---|
| **30.17** The nurse is assisting the physician who is preparing to test a sexually active female client for cervical cancer. The nurse would expect the physician to perform which of the following?<br>    1. Pap test<br>    2. Breast exam<br>    3. Rectal exam<br>    4. Abdominal exam | Answer: 1<br>Rationale: For sexually active adolescent and adult women, a Papanicolaou test (Pap test) is used to detect cancer of the cervix.<br>Implementation<br>Physiological integrity<br>Analysis<br>Learning Outcome 30.5 |
| **30.18** The nurse is preparing the morning assignments. Which of the following assessments could the nurse delegate to the nursing assistant?<br>    1. Neurological assessment<br>    2. Musculoskeletal assessment<br>    3. Vital signs assessment<br>    4. Female genital assessment | Answer: 3<br>Rationale: Of the four options, the nursing assistant can only assess vital signs.<br>Implementation<br>Physiological integrity<br>Application |
| **30.19** The nurse is caring for a client with abdominal pain. Which of the following assessments should the nurse perform to assess this complaint? (Select all that apply.)<br>    1. Inspect the abdomen.<br>    2. Auscultate the abdomen.<br>    3. Palpate the abdomen.<br>    4. Assess vital signs.<br>    5. Assess peripheral pulses. | Answer: 1, 2, 3, 4<br>Rationale: Although peripheral pulses may be palpated, it is not specific to a client with abdominal pain.<br>Assessment<br>Physiological integrity<br>Analysis<br>Learning Outcome 30.5 |
| **30.20** The nurse is preparing to administer a cardiotonic drug to a client. Which of the following assessments should the nurse perform before administering the medication?<br>    1. Respiratory rate<br>    2. Apical pulse<br>    3. Popliteal pulse<br>    4. Capillary blanch test | Answer: 2<br>Rationale: The apical pulse should be assessed before administering any cardiotonic medication.<br>Assessment<br>Physiological integrity<br>Application<br>Learning Outcome 30.5 |

# CHAPTER 31

| | |
|---|---|
| **31.1** Which of the following techniques best exhibits surgical asepsis?<br>    1. Disinfecting an item before adding it to a sterile field<br>    2. Allowing sterile gloved hands to fall below the waist<br>    3. Suctioning the oral cavity of an unconscious client<br>    4. Touching only the inside surface of the first glove while pulling it onto the hand | Answer: 4<br>Rationale: Touching only the inside surface of the first glove while pulling it onto the hand is the correct technique when applying sterile gloves. This prevents contamination of the outside of the glove, which must remain sterile. Disinfecting an item is an example of medical asepsis, not sterile. If sterile gloved hands fall below the waist, they are considered to be unsterile. Suctioning the oral cavity of a client is considered contaminating.<br>Implementation<br>Safe, effective care environment<br>Application<br>Learning Outcome 31.1 |
| **31.2** Which of the following techniques would be an example of medical asepsis?<br>    1. Administering parenteral medications<br>    2. Changing a dressing | Answer: 4<br>Rationale: Using personal protective equipment is a technique used in demonstrating medical asepsis. Administering parenteral medications, changing a dressing, and performing a urinary catheterization are all techniques that require surgical asepsis.<br>Implementation |

| | |
|---|---|
| 3. Performing a urinary catheterization<br>4. Using personal protective equipment | Safe, effective care environment<br>Application<br>Learning Outcome 31.1 |
| **31.3** Which of the following clients would be most at risk for a nosocomial infection?<br>　1. A client in the emergency department with abdominal pain<br>　2. A 19-year-old woman in her first trimester of pregnancy<br>　3. A 72-year-old male client with COPD<br>　4. An 86-year-old female client on steroid therapy | Answer: 4<br>Rationale: The client most at risk for a nosocomial infection is the client who is 86 years old and on steroid therapy. The very old and very young are most susceptible to infections. The 86-year-old client is also on steroid therapy, which compromises the immune system. A client in the emergency department with abdominal pain has just arrived in the facility, and not enough time has elapsed for this client to be considered to have a nosocomial infection. If this client has an infection, it would be community acquired. The 19-year-old female who is pregnant is at a low risk. The 72-year-old male with COPD is at a higher risk for infection than the 19-year-old due to his age and chronic respiratory condition, but the 86-year-old is older and has a weakened immune system because of taking steroids.<br>Evaluation<br>Physiological integrity<br>Analysis<br>Learning Outcome 31.2 |
| **31.4** Which of the following instructions is the most important to give a client who is about to be discharged and has a surgical wound?<br>　1. Adjust your diet so it contains more fruits and vegetables.<br>　2. Apply lubricating lotion to the edges of the wound.<br>　3. Notify your physician if you notice edema, heat, or tenderness at the wound site.<br>　4. Thoroughly irrigate the wound with hydrogen peroxide. | Answer: 3<br>Rationale: A client being discharged with an open surgical wound has to be instructed on the detection of infection since the skin is the first line of defense. Signs such as edema, heat, and tenderness would indicate a local infection. Increasing fruits and vegetables would increase vitamin C, which helps with wound healing, but more protein would be the best choice. Applying lubricating lotion to the edges of a wound would impede the healing process. Irrigating with hydrogen peroxide would break down good granulating tissue, so this also would not increase healing.<br>Implementation<br>Physiological integrity<br>Analysis<br>Learning Outcome 31.3 |
| **31.5** Which of the following groups of symptoms is most commonly found in a client who has systemic infection?<br>　1. Edema, rubor, heat, and pain<br>　2. Fever, malaise, anorexia, nausea, and vomiting<br>　3. Palpitations, irritability, and heat intolerance<br>　4. Tingling, numbness, and cramping of the extremities | Answer: 2<br>Rationale: Fever, malaise, anorexia, nausea, and vomiting are symptoms of a systemic infection. Edema, rubor, heat, and pain are symptoms of a local infection. Palpitations, irritability, and heat intolerance are symptoms of a thyroid condition. Tingling, numbness, and cramping of the extremities would indicate symptoms of hypocalcemia.<br>Assessment<br>Physiological integrity<br>Application<br>Learning Outcome 31.6 |
| **31.6** An 80-year-old client with gallbladder disease has had a cholecystectomy. Which of the following factors would influence this client's susceptibility to produce an infection?<br>　1. Active bowel sounds<br>　2. Dry skin<br>　3. Intact mucous membranes<br>　4. Susceptibility of the client | Answer: 4<br>Rationale: How susceptible the client is for an infection is one of the factors that influences microorganism growth. This client is 80 years old and has a surgical incision, so the first line of defense, the skin, is not intact. Active bowel sounds, dry skin, and intact mucous membranes are factors that help defend the body against infection.<br>Implementation<br>Physiological integrity<br>Application<br>Learning Outcome 31.5 |

| | |
|---|---|
| **31.7** Which of the following physiological barriers helps defend the body against microorganisms?<br>  1. Heavy smoking<br>  2. Moisturizing the skin<br>  3. Breakdown of skin<br>  4. Voiding quantity sufficient | Answer: 4<br>Rationale: Voiding quantity sufficient is a barrier that helps the body defend itself against microorganisms. The act of voiding flushes those organisms that might try to enter the body through the urinary meatus. Heavy smoking does not defend the body from microorganisms; it destroys the cilia in the nose that helps to filter organisms. Moisturizing the skin and breakdown of the skin can both allow microorganisms to enter the body.<br>Evaluation<br>Physiological integrity<br>Analysis<br>Learning Outcome 31.3 |
| **31.8** Which of the following circumstances would render a client with active immunity?<br>  1. Becoming ill with tetanus and receiving tetanus toxoid<br>  2. Having chickenpox<br>  3. Receiving a rabies shot after being bitten by a rabid dog<br>  4. Receiving an injection of gamma globulin | Answer: 2<br>Rationale: When the client has the disease, the body stimulates the process of acquired active immunity. Receiving injections for rabies, tetanus, and gamma globulin are examples of artificially acquired passive immunity.<br>Implementation<br>Physiological integrity<br>Application<br>Learning Outcome 31.4 |
| **31.9** Which of the following interventions is appropriate for a client who has been bitten by a rabid raccoon?<br>  1. A tetanus toxoid injection<br>  2. An immunization for rabies<br>  3. An injection of immunoglobulin<br>  4. Mother's breast milk with antibodies in it | Answer: 2<br>Rationale: Receiving an immunization for rabies is an example of artificially acquired passive immunity. Receiving tetanus and immunoglobulin are also examples but not specifically for rabies. Mother's breast milk is another example of passive immunity, but not for rabies.<br>Implementation<br>Physiological integrity<br>Application<br>Learning Outcome 31.4 |
| **31.10** Which of the following nursing interventions would be appropriate in reducing the risk of infections?<br>  1. Assess vital signs only once daily.<br>  2. Raise the temperature in the client's room.<br>  3. Wash hands.<br>  4. Wear a mask for all client care. | Answer: 3<br>Rationale: Washing hands is always the first and best way to stop the spread of microorganisms, which cause infections. Assessing vital signs is important but should be taken more frequently than once daily. Wearing a mask for all clients is not practical and is unnecessary unless a microorganism is airborne and the client is in isolation. Raising the temperature in a client's room would contribute to the growth of microorganisms.<br>Implementation<br>Safe, effective care environment<br>Application<br>Learning Outcome 31.8 |
| **31.11** Which of the following nursing measures is appropriate in breaking a link in the chain of infection?<br>  1. Cover one's mouth and nose when sneezing.<br>  2. Place contaminated linens in a paper bag.<br>  3. Use personal protective equipment (PPE) sparingly.<br>  4. Wear gloves at all times. | Answer: 1<br>Rationale: Covering one's mouth and nose when sneezing prevents airborne droplets from escaping into the air for others to contract in the chain of infection. Placing linens in a paper bag would allow germs to come out through the bag, and the linen would act as a fomite thus allowing the chain to continue. PPE, according to OSHA standards, has to be used whenever the situation dictates, not just to save money. Gloves have to be worn but are to be changed between clients and hands washed.<br>Implementation<br>Safe, effective care environment<br>Application<br>Learning Outcome 31.9 |

**31.12** Which of the following techniques is standard care for promoting proper hand washing technique in a client with hepatitis A?
1. Allow the water to splatter forcibly when it is cut on.
2. Clean the faucet after use.
3. Hold the hands upward under the faucet.
4. Use approximately a teaspoon of soap.

Answer: 4
Rationale: One should use a teaspoon of soap when performing proper hand washing technique. When the water is cut on, it should be adjusted so it does not splatter even if the flow is not very forceful. Cleaning the faucet after use would defeat the whole purpose of washing one's hands. If the sink needs cleaning, clean it before washing one's hands. Holding the hands upward under the faucet is incorrect. They should be held downward so the soap, germs, and water are washed downward from the hands and down the sink.
Implementation
Safe, effective care environment
Application
Learning Outcome 31.11

**31.13** Which of the following interventions demonstrates the appropriate technique for removing a mask?
1. Bend the strip at the top of the mask.
2. Loop the ties over the ears.
3. Tie the strings in a bow.
4. Touch the mask by the strings only.

Answer: 4
Rationale: Touching the mask by the strings for both putting on and taking off is the appropriate intervention because the mask is considered contaminated. Bending the strip at the top of the mask, looping the ties over the ears, and tying the strings in a bow under the chin are all interventions used when applying a mask.
Implementation
Safe, effective care environment
Application
Learning Outcome 31.11

**31.14** Which of the following nursing interventions should be performed first when removing gloves?
1. Drop the gloves into the appropriate waste receptacle.
2. Ease the fingers into the gloves.
3. Grasp the outside of the nondominant glove.
4. Hook the bare thumb inside the other glove.

Answer: 3
Rationale: In order to remove gloves after use, one must grasp the outside of the nondominant glove. Hooking the bare thumb inside the other glove, and dropping the gloves into the appropriate waste receptacle will come after the gloves are removed. Easing the fingers into the glove is an intervention used when applying gloves.
Planning
Safe, effective care environment
Application
Learning Outcome 31.11

**31.15** Which of the following actions by the RN would render a sterile field unsterile?
1. Grasping the edge of the outermost flap and opening it away from oneself
2. Keeping objects on the field 1 inch from the edge
3. Keeping the sterile field in eyesight
4. Transferring a sterile object to a sterile field with a gloved hand

Answer: 4
Rationale: Transferring a sterile object onto a sterile field with a gloved hand would render the field unsterile only if the gloves are sterile. Grasping the edge of the outermost flap and opening it away from oneself, keeping objects on the field 1 inch from the edge, and keeping the sterile field in eyesight are all actions that will maintain sterility of a field.
Planning
Safe, effective care environment
Application
Learning Outcome 31.11

**31.16** Which of the following items most likely would be included in the room of a client who is on contact isolation?
1. Cabinet stocked with gloves and gowns
2. Cards and records
3. Paper towels, sink, and blood pressure cuff
4. Sign on the door

Answer: 3
Rationale: Paper towels and a sink for hand washing should be in the client's room so they can be used before the staff leaves the room. A blood pressure cuff is needed to stay in the client's room to prevent cross contamination. A cabinet stocked with gloves and gowns would be on the outside of the room. Cards and records should never be taken into an isolation room. The sign explaining the kind of isolation should be on the outside of the door to alert the staff of what is needed to enter.
Assessment
Health promotion and maintenance
Application
Learning Outcome 31.10

**31.17** The RN has just stuck herself with a syringe while dropping it into a sharps container that was too full in a client's room. Which of the following steps should be taken next, for a puncture?

1. Complete an injury report.
2. Encourage bleeding.
3. Initiate first aid.
4. Wash/clean the area with soap and water.

Answer: 2
Rationale: Encouraging bleeding, initiating first aid, completing an injury report, and washing and cleaning the area with soap and water are all steps to be taken with a puncture wound. But encouraging bleeding is the first step.
Implementation
Health promotion and maintenance
Application
Learning Outcome 31.12

**31.18** Which of the following nursing interventions demonstrates the correct technique to remove a grossly soiled gown when leaving isolation?

1. Grasp the sleeve of the dominant arm, and remove it with a gloved hand.
2. Release the neck ties of the gown and allow the gown to fall forward.
3. Untie the strings at the neck first.
4. Untie the strings at the waist first.

Answer: 4
Rationale: To leave an isolation room where a gown has been worn, one must untie the gown at the waist first, not at the neck. Gloves are removed next. They are not left on while taking the gown off as stated in option 1. After the neck ties are untied, the gown is allowed to fall forward.
Implementation
Safe, effective care environment
Application
Learning Outcome 31.11

**31.19** The RN is conducting a staff in-service on Standard Precautions. Which of the following statements is correct and should be included in the presentation?

1. Cut the needle off a syringe after using it to give a client an injection.
2. Dispose of blood-contaminated materials in a biohazard container.
3. Gloves should not be worn for client care unless body fluids are seen.
4. Wear a mask when in direct contact with all clients.

Answer: 2
Rationale: Disposal of blood-contaminated materials in a biohazard container is a Standard Precaution. Needles should never be cut, bent, or altered in any way as this would place the health care provider at risk to be stuck. Gloves should be worn when providing client care whether body secretions are seen or not. Masks need not be worn when giving routine direct client care unless the client's condition so warrants.
Planning
Health promotion and maintenance
Analysis
Learning Outcome 31.10

**31.20** The unit has been notified that a client with tuberculosis is on the way up. Which of the following actions demonstrated by the staff shows measures of preventing the transmission of this disease?

1. Have the client wear a mask when coming from admission.
2. Stock the supply cart at the beginning of each shift.
3. Wash the hands only after leaving the room.
4. Wear a mask when exiting the room.

Answer: 1
Rationale: When a client has an airborne disease and must go elsewhere in the hospital, the client must wear a mask. Supplies to prevent transmission of disease should be stocked at the end of the shift so that adequate supplies will be available for the next health care provider. The mask should be removed just as the staff leaves the client's room, not when coming out of the room. Hands should be washed before and after client care.
Implementation
Safe, effective care environment
Application
Learning Outcome 31.10

| | |
|---|---|
| **31.21** A client is admitted to the medical unit with an infected decubitus ulcer. The most appropriate nursing action would be to place the client on _____ precautions. | Answer: contact<br>Rationale: A client with a wound infection like a decubitus ulcer, according to the CDC, is placed on contact precautions because the infection can be transmitted by direct contact or contact with items in the client's environment.<br>Implementation<br>Safe, effective care environment<br>Application<br>Learning Outcome 31.10 |
| **31.22** Identify three examples of personal protective equipment (PPE).<br>1. _____<br>2. _____<br>3. _____ | Answer: gloves, gowns, shoe covers, masks<br>Implementation<br>Safe, effective, calm environment<br>Knowledge<br>Learning Outcome 31.10 |

# CHAPTER 32

| | |
|---|---|
| **32.1** Which of the following safety hazards would be taken into consideration in planning care for an elderly client?<br>1. Burns<br>2. Drowning<br>3. Poisoning<br>4. Suffocation | Answer: 1<br>Rationale: Falls, burns, and pedestrian and motor vehicle crashes are safety hazards in older adults. Drowning and poisoning are seen in the toddler age client, and suffocation is a hazard in newborns and infants.<br>Planning<br>Safe, effective care environment<br>Application<br>Learning Outcome 32.4 |
| **32.2** Which of the following are methods of assessing clients at risk for injury? (Select all that apply.)<br>1. Cognitive awareness<br>2. Mobility and health status<br>3. Nursing history<br>4. Physical examination | Answer: 3, 4<br>Rationale: A nursing history and a physical examination are methods to assess a client at risk for injury. Cognitive awareness, mobility, and health status are factors affecting safety.<br>Assessment<br>Physical integrity<br>Analysis<br>Learning Outcome 32.2 |
| **32.3** Which of the following would the nurse identify as a safety hazard in the infant?<br>1. Alcohol consumption<br>2. Drowning<br>3. Pedestrian accidents<br>4. Suffocation in the crib | Answer: 4<br>Rationale: Suffocation in the crib is a safety hazard for both newborns and infants. Drowning is seen in toddlers and preschoolers. Exposure to alcohol consumption is a safety hazard to the fetus, and pedestrian accidents are seen in the older adult.<br>Assessment<br>Physiological integrity<br>Analysis<br>Learning Outcome 32.4 |
| **32.4** Which of the following safety hazards affects a developing fetus?<br>1. Banging into objects<br>2. Bicycle rides<br>3. Recreational activities<br>4. X-rays | Answer: 4<br>Rationale: Exposure to x-rays in the first trimester could cause harm to the developing fetus. Bicycle rides and recreational activities would be good for the developing fetus; the mother should stay as active as possible during the pregnancy. Physical activity promotes good health. Banging into objects is what a toddler would be likely to do, not an expectant mother.<br>Assessment<br>Physiological integrity<br>Analysis<br>Learning Outcome 32.4 |

**32.5** How do the JCAHO 2006 National Patient Safety Goals improve the effectiveness of communication among caregivers?

1. Annually review a list of look-alike/sound-alike drugs used in the organization.
2. Conduct a verification process to confirm the correct procedure.
3. Standardize a list of abbreviations that are not to be used throughout the organization.
4. Use the client's room number as an identifier.

Answer: 3
Rationale: Standardizing a list of abbreviations, acronyms, and symbols that are not to be used throughout the organization is one of the ways the National Patient Safety Goals improve the effectiveness of communication among caregivers. Using the client's room number as an identifier is a passive technique that would improve the accuracy of client identification. Conducting a verification process to confirm that the correct procedure for the correct client is to be performed is another way to improve the accuracy of client identification. Annually reviewing a list of look-alike/sound-alike drugs is used to improve the safety of use of medication in an organization—not to improve effective communication.
Assessment
Safe, effective care environment
Analysis
Learning Outcome 32.3

---

**32.6** Which of the following nursing diagnoses would the nurse expect to find on the care plan of a client prone to falls?

1. *Deficient Knowledge*
2. *Risk for Injury*
3. *Risk for Disuse Syndrome*
4. *Risk for Suffocation*

Answer: 2
Rationale: *Risk for Injury* is a state in which the individual is at risk as a result of environmental conditions like a fall. *Deficient Knowledge* deals with injury prevention. A client who is already prone to falls may not have the cognitive ability for a knowledge deficient. *Risk for Disuse Syndrome* is a deterioration of body system as the result of prescribed or unavoidable musculoskeletal inactivity. *Risk for Suffocation* is inadequate air available for inhalation.
Planning
Safe, effective care environment
Application
Learning Outcome 32.5

---

**32.7** The nurse's major goal for a client who is at risk for injury is to:

1. Assess the client's mental status.
2. Keep the client dependent on the staff for all care.
3. Make all choices for the client.
4. Remain free from injury.

Answer: 4
Rationale: The nurse's major goal for a client who is at risk for injury is for the client to remain injury-free. The nurse will need to assess the client's mental status to help accomplish this goal. Keeping the client dependent on the staff for care and making all choices for the client does not encourage independence, which would contribute to the client's overall self-esteem.
Planning
Safe, effective care environment
Application
Learning Outcome 32.5

---

**32.8** Which of the following interventions is used to prevent falls in a health care agency?

1. Display the phone number to the nurses' station.
2. Keep electrical cords under the bed.
3. Keep the environment tidy.
4. Read label directions.

Answer: 3
Rationale: Keeping the environment tidy and free of clutter will go a long way in preventing falls. The call system to the nurses' station is direct for help. A number has to be displayed or dialed. Electrical cords should only be used if necessary, and the maintenance department can help if any of them present a hazard. Reading label directions will prevent the wrong use of substances given to the client, but would not directly prevent falls.
Intervention
Safe, effective care environment
Application
Learning Outcome 32.7

---

**32.9** Which of the following interventions would help prevent falls in the elderly client?

1. Check vision every 5 years.
2. Exercise regularly.
3. Place socks on feet.
4. Turn the light on after getting out of bed.

Answer: 2
Rationale: The client needs to exercise regularly to maintain strength, flexibility, mobility, and balance, which prevents falls. Vision can be a cause of falls, but it should be checked at least once a year; every 5 years is not often enough. Elderly clients should have something on their feet when walking, but not socks that will allow them to fall. A nonskid-type sock or shoe will help prevent falls. The client should be able to turn the light on before getting out of bed as inadequate lighting is another cause for falls.

| | Implementation |
| --- | --- |
| | Safe, effective care environment |
| | Application |
| | Learning Outcome 32.6 |

| | |
| --- | --- |
| **32.10** The mother of a 2-year-old expresses concern to the nurse that her child continually climbs out of the crib at home. The nurse advises the mother that she should:<br>  1.  Omit the afternoon nap.<br>  2.  Place a crib net over the top of the crib.<br>  3.  Remove all objects from around the crib.<br>  4.  Restrain the child if he gets up more than once. | Answer: 2<br>Rationale: A crib net will prevent an active child from climbing out of the crib but will allow him freedom to move about in the crib. Just removing objects off the floor from around the crib would not prevent a child from climbing out of a crib. Restraining the child would be dangerous and contribute even more to his determination of getting out of the crib. A child of 2 years should still be taking a nap, and that poses a dangerous situation, naptime or bedtime, if the child is still crawling out of the crib.<br>Implementation<br>Safe, effective care environment<br>Application<br>Learning Outcome 32.6 |
| **32.11** Which of the following nursing interventions is appropriate when a client has a seizure?<br>  1.  Insert a tongue blade into the client's mouth.<br>  2.  Loosen any clothing around the neck and chest.<br>  3.  Restrain the client.<br>  4.  Turn the client to the supine position if possible. | Answer: 2<br>Rationale: Loosening any clothing around the neck and chest prevents constriction that might occur during the seizure that could compromise the airway. Research has found that more injury can occur to the client if the caregiver tries to place anything in the mouth during the seizure. A client should never be restrained during a seizure. The nurse should stay with the client and call for assistance, if needed. If possible, the client should be turned onto the lateral position, not supine, to allow for any secretions to drain out of the mouth.<br>Implementation<br>Safe, effective care environment<br>Application<br>Learning Outcome 32.8 |
| **32.12** Which of the following charges could the nurse be brought up on if the nurse were to restrain a client against his or her will?<br>  1.  Assault and battery<br>  2.  Defamation of character<br>  3.  Negligence<br>  4.  Slander | Answer: 1<br>Rationale: Assault and battery is the charge that could be brought against a nurse who restrains a client against his will. Defamation of character is a spoken or written statement made maliciously and intentionally that may injure the client's reputation. Negligence is the failure of commission of an act or the omission of an act that a reasonably prudent person would have done in a similar situation that leads to harming another person. Slander is malicious or untrue spoken words about another person that are brought to the attention of others.<br>Assessment<br>Physiological integrity<br>Application<br>Learning Outcome 32.10 |
| **32.13** When applying restraints on a client, the nurse would secure a doctor's order and:<br>  1.  Assess the restraints every 10 minutes.<br>  2.  Pad bony prominences.<br>  3.  Secure the restraint to the side rail.<br>  4.  Tie the restraint with a square knot. | Answer: 2<br>Rationale: Padding bony prominences will prevent possible skin breakdown. The limb with a restraint should be assessed frequently, but every 10 minutes is not necessary. At least every 32 minutes is appropriate. When a restraint is secured in place, a clove-hitch knot should be used, not a square knot. The clove-hitch knot will not tighten when pulled. Restraints are never tied to a side rail. The ends should be secured to the part of the bed that moves to elevate the head.<br>Intervention<br>Physiological integrity<br>Application<br>Learning Outcome 32.10 |

**32.14** Identify the restraint shown below and explain what is wrong with the application.

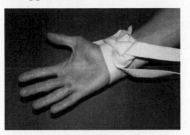

Answer: Wrist restraint
Rationale: Padding should have been placed under this restraint when it was applied.
Intervention
Physiological integrity
Application
Learning Outcome 32.10

---

**32.15** An 86-year-old client with Alzheimer's disease continually tries to get out of bed at night. Which alternative safety measure would the staff choose to use with this client?
  1. Explain all procedures and treatments.
  2. Place a bed safety monitoring device on the bed.
  3. Orient the client to her surroundings.
  4. Use relaxation techniques.

Answer: 2
Rationale: Alzheimer's disease causes impaired intellectual functioning, so a safety device that is weight sensitive would alert the nurse when the client is trying to get out of bed. Explaining procedures, orienting to surroundings, and using relaxation techniques would not be appropriate alternatives to use with this client.
Planning
Safe, effective care environment
Analysis
Learning Outcome 32.9

---

**32.16** There is a very confused client on the unit and she is wandering. Which of the following alternatives to using a restraint would be chosen to use with this client?
  1. Assign this client to the farthest room from the nurses' station.
  2. Place a rocking chair in her room.
  3. Pull up all the side rails on the bed.
  4. Wedge pillows against the side rails on the bed.

Answer: 2
Rationale: Placing a rocking chair in the client's room will help her to expend some of her energy so that she will be less inclined to walk and wander. Pulling up all the side rails is a restraint, so that action would not be an alternative. Assigning the client to the farthest room from the nurses' station would be an unsafe move toward the client; closer would be safer than farther. Keeping pillows wedged against the side rails will not keep the client from wandering. She is not in the bed.
Planning
Safe, effective care environment
Analysis
Learning Outcome 32.9

---

**32.17** Which of the following desired outcomes/goals would be appropriate for an elderly client in preventing injury?
  1. The client will demonstrate an understanding of all limitations.
  2. The client will establish a buddy system.
  3. The client will make uninformed choices when addressing health issues.
  4. The client will take his medication as desired.

Answer: 2
Rationale: Establishing a buddy system provides social contact, safeguards against abuse, and offers respite for caregivers. It also provides a way for elders to be checked up on daily. The client may resent limitations if he is imposed and act out in such a way to cause injury. Making uninformed choices about one's health could be unsafe instead of safe to the client. A routine should be established for medication administration with correct dosage to prevent the possibility of overdose toxicity.
Planning
Safe, effective care environment
Analysis
Learning Outcome 32.6

---

**32.18** Which of the following strategies would contribute to maintaining safety in the home?
  1. Always pull a plug at the plug-in from the wall outlet.
  2. Keep plants in the home.
  3. Use overloaded outlets when necessary.
  4. Remove labels from containers and refill for recycling.

Answer: 1
Rationale: Always pull a plug at the plug-in from the wall outlet. Pulling a plug by its cord can damage the cord and plug unit, creating a dangerous situation. Not knowing which plants are poisonous and which are not may pose a serious problem for children in the home. Always avoid overloading outlets at anytime because this a cause of fire. Do not remove container labels or reuse empty containers to store different substances. Laws mandate that the labels of all substances specify an antidote.

---

| | Planning<br>Safe, effective care environment<br>Analysis<br>Learning Outcome 32.6 |
|---|---|
| **32.19** Bioterrorism has become another threat to homeland security. Keeping this threat in mind, which of the following agents is of highest concern?<br>　1. Cancer<br>　2. Flu<br>　3. Tuberculosis<br>　4. Smallpox | Answer: 4<br>Rationale: Smallpox, anthrax, botulism, plague, viral hemorrhagic fevers, and tularemia are the agents that are of highest concern with bioterrorism.<br>Assessment<br>Safe, effective care environment<br>Analysis<br>Learning Outcome 32.6 |
| **32.20** While eating in a restaurant, a nurse notices that a customer at the next table begins to clutch his throat while eating a steak. Which of the following responses would the nurse perform first?<br>　1. Ask the customer if he is choking.<br>　2. Attempt to give five back blows.<br>　3. Perform the Heimlich maneuver.<br>　4. Start chest compressions. | Answer: 1<br>Rationale: The first step is to ask if the person is choking. If he indicates he is, the next step would be to perform the Heimlich maneuver. Five back blows are reserved for an infant who is choking. Chest compressions would be given if the person was unconscious; this client is not. He is clutching his throat.<br>Implementation<br>Physiological integrity<br>Application<br>Learning Outcome 32.5 |
| **32.21** Which of the following steps helps to promote a safe environment for the client?<br>　1. Keep clutter to a minimum in the client's room.<br>　2. Have the client wear terry cloth slippers.<br>　3. Provide adequate lighting.<br>　4. Turn off alarms to reduce noise. | Answer: 3<br>Rationale: Providing adequate lighting will help prevent the client from falling. The environment should be clutter-free because any clutter can cause the client to fall. Wearing terry cloth slippers would allow the client to fall. The client should have rubber skid-resistant soles. Noise should be kept to a minimum, but turning off alarms would endanger a client.<br>Planning<br>Health promotion and maintenance<br>Application<br>Learning Outcome 32.7 |

# CHAPTER 33

| | |
|---|---|
| **33.1** Which of the following purposes would the RN explain to the client is the reason for her daily bath?<br>　1. To assess skin integrity<br>　2. To develop a nurse–client relationship<br>　3. To moisturize the skin<br>　4. To stimulate circulation | Answer: 4<br>Rationale: The three major reasons for a bath are to remove waste products like perspiration, stimulate circulation, and refresh the client. Giving a bath to a client will allow the nurse to assess the skin, develop a nurse–client relationship, and moisturize the skin, but these are not the most important purposes.<br>Implementation<br>Physiological integrity<br>Application<br>Learning Outcome 33.5 |
| **33.2** Which nursing intervention should take priority when giving a bath to a surgical client on his first postop day?<br>　1. Apply lotion to the extremities.<br>　2. Change the water when it becomes cold.<br>　3. Raise side rails when gathering supplies.<br>　4. Remove the soiled dressing during the bath. | Answer: 3<br>Rationale: Raising the side rails would take priority when planning care. This is a safety issue, and safety is second on Maslow's hierarchy of needs. The client is only 1 day postop and may still be sedated, posing a risk for a potential fall. Changing the water needs to be done before it becomes cold, but raising the side rail first in order to get the water takes priority. Applying lotion to the skin and a dressing change would be performed before or after, not during, the bath and only with a doctor's order.<br>Implementation<br>Physiological integrity<br>Application<br>Learning Outcome 33.8 |

**33.3** A client has had a hemorrhoidectomy and has been ordered a sitz bath BID. Which of the following interventions is appropriate in assisting the client with his bath?

1. Flatten the reservoir bag on a hard surface and press on it to expel air.
2. Have the client use the clamp on the tubing to regulate the flow of water.
3. Leave the client sitting on the basin for 45 minutes.
4. Place the sitz bath on the commode seat, and fill the reservoir with warm water at 110°F to 115°F.

Answer: 2
Rationale: Having the client use the clamp on the tubing to regulate the flow of water is a correct intervention. Flattening the reservoir is performed when an ice bag or hot water bottle is filled. The time for a sitz bath usually ranges from 15 to 20 minutes, not 45 minutes. The water in the reservoir should be about 105°F, not 110°F to 115°F, which would be too hot.
Implementation
Physiological integrity
Application
Learning Outcome 33.8

---

**33.4** Which of the following assessment findings would be normal with the client's hair when giving her a shampoo?

1. Dry, dark, thin
2. Smooth, taut, shiny
3. Smooth texture and not oily or dry
4. Tender, warm scalp

Answer: 3
Rationale: The hair should be smooth in texture and neither oily nor dry. Skin is assessed as being smooth, taut, or shiny, not hair. The hair should not be dry or thin. This could be a sign of alopecia. Darkness would depend on hair color through the gene pool. A tender, warm scalp could indicate a problem, so this would not be normal.
Assessment
Physiological integrity
Application
Learning Outcome 33.3

---

**33.5** Which of the following expected outcomes is correct for a client with the nursing diagnosis *Self-Care Deficit* related to cognitive impairment?

1. The client will be able to name the staff that works on the day shift.
2. The client will eliminate safety hazards in her environment.
3. The client, with supervision, will brush her teeth.
4. The nurse will stress the importance of adequate fluid intake.

Answer: 3
Rationale: A client with cognitive impairment would be able to brush her teeth but only with supervision. She would not voluntarily brush her teeth without prompting from the staff. Cognitive impairment limits the client's ability to understand and comprehend; therefore, stressing adequate fluid intake, naming the staff, and eliminating safety hazards are not within her realm of understanding.
Planning
Health promotion and maintenance
Application
Learning Outcome 33.2

---

**33.6** Which of the following situations could pose a threat to a client's personal hygiene?

1. A client has a newly formed ileostomy.
2. A client performs meticulous foot care.
3. A German client refuses to bathe everyday.
4. The room temperature is set at 72°F.

Answer: 1
Rationale: Some of the factors that influence one's personal hygiene are social practices, body image, knowledge of physical condition, and cultural variables. A client who has had an ileostomy has had a body image change which can greatly influence whether he will care for it or rely on others. This can pose a threat if the client chooses not to care for it. Performing meticulous foot care, bathing every other day, and room temperature of 72°F do not pose a threat to one's hygiene.
Evaluation
Physiological integrity
Analysis
Learning Outcome 33.2

---

| | |
|---|---|
| **33.7** Hygienic care that nurses provide to clients includes _____ care.<br>1. Clothes<br>2. Family<br>3. Hair<br>4. Nutritional | Answer: 3<br>Rationale: Hygiene care consists of skin, hair, hands, feet, eyes, nose, mouth, back, and perineum. The client's clothes, family, and nutrition do not come under hygiene care.<br>Implementation<br>Physiological integrity<br>Application<br>Learning Outcome 33.1 |
| **33.8** Which of the following steps is correct in removing a client's soft contact lens?<br>1. Gently pinch the lens and lift it out.<br>2. Have the client look up.<br>3. Pull the lower eyelid upward.<br>4. Use the pad of the ring finger. | Answer: 1<br>Rationale: Gently pinching the lens and lifting it out is one of the correct steps for removing a client's soft contact lens. The nurse should have the client look straight ahead, not up. The upper eyelid is pulled down gently. The nurse would use the pad of the index finger, not the ring finger.<br>Planning<br>Physiological integrity<br>Application<br>Learning Outcome 33.9 |
| **33.9** The RN has been assigned to a client who is newly diagnosed with diabetes. What should the nurse include in the plan for foot care for this client?<br>1. Cut toenails around and file.<br>2. Dry toes thoroughly.<br>3. Wash feet with water at a temperature of 90°F to 98.6°F.<br>4. Inspect feet thoroughly once a week. | Answer: 2<br>Rationale: Toes should be dried thoroughly after being washed to impede fungal growth and prevent maceration. Toenails should be cut straight across, and nurses do not cut diabetic clients' toenails. Only a podiatrist should handle this task. The water to wash the feet should be 100°F to 110°F. Feet should be inspected each day, not once a week, for early detection of any problems.<br>Planning<br>Health promotion and maintenance<br>Application<br>Learning Outcome 33.4 |
| **33.10** Which of the following nursing interventions should be applied to a client with a nursing diagnosis of *Risk for Skin Integrity Impairment* related to immobility?<br>1. Encourage client to eat at least 40% of meals.<br>2. Keep linens dry and wrinkle-free.<br>3. Restrict fluid intake.<br>4. Turn client every 3 hours. | Answer: 2<br>Rationale: Keeping linens dry and wrinkle-free will prevent pressure areas. For nutritional support to promote healthy tissue, clients should consume more than 40% of their meals. Fluids should not be restricted unless some other physical condition dictates. The skin should be kept hydrated. To relieve pressure, the client should be turned every 2 hours, not every 3.<br>Intervention<br>Physiological integrity<br>Application<br>Learning Outcome 33.7 |
| **33.11** Which of the following should the health care provider report to the RN when caring for a client's ears?<br>1. Excessive earwax<br>2. Loud talking<br>3. Presence of a hearing aid<br>4. Presence of any drainage | Answer: 4<br>Rationale: The health care provider should report any drainage from the ears to the RN. Loud talking could be an indication the client is hard of hearing, which is not an immediate threat. The presence of a hearing aid should already be noted on the client's admission assessment. Excess earwax is not an immediate problem.<br>Assessment<br>Physiological integrity<br>Analysis<br>Learning Outcome 33.4 |
| **33.12** Which of the following steps is essential when removing a client's hearing aid?<br>1. Assist the client with removal when necessary.<br>2. Instruct the client to remove the aid in the sunroom. | Answer: 1<br>Rationale: The small size of hearing aids may make it difficult for older adults to manipulate, so they may need assistance in the aid's removal. Clients are instructed not to remove their aids in common rooms like a sunroom. The removal of the aid is necessary before bathing or when getting a hairstyle so it is not damaged. The aid should always be stored in the client's bedside table—not sent home with the family—so it is available for later use. |

| | |
|---|---|
| 3. Leave the aid in place when bathing.<br>4. Send the aid home with the family. | Implementation<br>Physiological integrity<br>Application<br>Learning Outcome 33.10 |
| **33.13** Which of the following steps should be taken when cleaning a hearing aid?<br>    1. Clean with a dry, soft cloth.<br>    2. Leave the battery in place when not in use.<br>    3. Store the aid in the bathroom cabinet.<br>    4. Use alcohol to remove any earwax. | Answer: 1<br>Rationale: It is recommended by the manufacturers to clean the aid with a dry, soft cloth to prevent any damage to the aid. The aid should be turned off and the battery removed to preserve the life of the battery. The aid should be stored in a safe place where it will not get damaged. It should not be stored in the bathroom cabinet. Alcohol is not recommended to be used on an aid because it could damage the aid.<br>Implementation<br>Physiological integrity<br>Application<br>Learning Outcome 33.10 |
| **33.14** Which one of the *safety* measures is to be followed when applying bed-making procedures?<br>    1. Begin at the head and move toward the foot, loosening bottom linens.<br>    2. Miter corners at the head of the bed.<br>    3. Place the soiled sheet in a laundry bag.<br>    4. Prepare the client. | Answer: 3<br>Rationale: Placing the soiled sheet in the laundry bag reduces the spread of microorganisms, which is a safety measure for both the nurse and client. Beginning at the head and moving toward the foot, loosening the bottom linens, provides maximum work space. Mitering the corners at the head of the bed prevents linens from becoming easily loosened. Preparing the client readies the client for the procedure.<br>Implementation<br>Physiological integrity<br>Application<br>Learning Outcome 33.10 |
| **33.15** Which of the following instructions is given to a client in regard to a hearing aid?<br>    1. Do not buy extra batteries.<br>    2. Marking the aid is not necessary when living in a long term facility.<br>    3. Do not use hair spray when wearing a hearing aid.<br>    4. Use a hair dryer while wearing a hearing aid. | Answer: 3<br>Rationale: Hair spray can clog a hearing aid, and clients are encouraged not to use it when the aid is in use. Extra batteries are needed to keep on hand because a battery only lasts 1½ to 2 weeks. A hair dryer should not be used around the aid as heat can damage the aid. Marking the aid is necessary for a client living in a long term facility because of the potentially high number of hearing aids.<br>Implementation<br>Physiological integrity<br>Application<br>Learning Outcome 33.10 |
| **33.16** Which of the following steps will provide comfort for the client during occupied bed change of linens?<br>    1. Allow for a toe pleat.<br>    2. Place a bath blanket over the client.<br>    3. Slide the mattress to the head of the bed.<br>    4. Raise the side rail. | Answer: 1<br>Rationale: Allowing for a toe pleat provides for client comfort. Placing the bath blanket over the client prevents unnecessary exposure. Sliding the mattress to the head of the bed makes it easier to tuck in the linens. Raising the side rail maintains client safety.<br>Implementation<br>Physiological integrity<br>Application<br>Learning Outcome 33.11 |
| **33.17** The nurse is expected to shave a client when he is unable. Which of the following steps is a correct procedure for shaving a client?<br>    1. Assist the client to a prone position.<br>    2. Pull the skin taut with the dominant hand. | Answer: 3<br>Rationale: Rinsing the razor after each stroke keeps the cutting edge clean. The skin should be pulled taut with the nondominant hand—not the dominant—because this provides uniform shaving. Assist the client to a sitting position—not a prone position—because this is a more natural position. Short strokes should be used—not long strokes—because this provides for a closer shave without irritation.<br>Intervention |

| | |
|---|---|
| 3. Rinse the razor after each stroke.<br>4. Use long strokes. | Physiological integrity<br>Application<br>Learning Outcome 33.8 |
| **33.18** Which of the following interventions promotes safe handling of a client's dentures?<br>1. Clean biting surfaces.<br>2. Fill emesis basin half full of tepid water.<br>3. Replace the upper dentures first.<br>4. Rinse dentures thoroughly with hot water. | Answer: 2<br>Rationale: Filling the emesis basin half full of tepid water acts as a cushion for the dentures if accidentally dropped. Cleansing biting surfaces prevents bacteria, odor, and stain formation. Replacing the upper dentures first promotes comfort. Dentures should be rinsed thoroughly with tepid water, not hot water, because extreme temperatures will harm dentures.<br>Implementation<br>Physiological integrity<br>Application<br>Learning Outcome 33.8 |
| **33.19** Which of the following activities would be included in taking care of a client's artificial eye?<br>1. Apply lubricant.<br>2. Clean regularly.<br>3. Drape the client.<br>4. Firmly pat dry. | Answer: 2<br>Rationale: The eye and orbit should be cleaned regularly to remove any exudates that may be present. A lubricant is not necessary as it could cause damage to the prosthesis. Draping the client is not necessary, but providing privacy by pulling the curtain or shutting the door to the room may make the client more comfortable. The area should be gently dried once cleaned, but firmly patting dry may cause damage.<br>Planning<br>Physiological integrity<br>Application<br>Learning Outcome 33.9 |
| **33.20** Which of the following techniques is used to remove a client's artificial eye?<br>1. Compress the upper eyelid in, and pop out the eye from the supraorbital bone.<br>2. Grasp the upper eyelid, and turn it inside out.<br>3. Retract the lower eyelid down over the infraorbital bone while exerting slight pressure below the eyelid.<br>4. Use the thumb and index finger to grasp hold of the eye. | Answer: 3<br>Rationale: Retracting the lower eyelid down over the infraorbital bone while exerting slight pressure below the eyelid is the correct technique for removing an artificial eye. Compressing the upper eyelid will not allow the eye to come out. The nurse's fingers cannot get a grasp of the eye with the thumb and the index finger; the suction needs to be released first. Turning the upper eyelid inside out will not release the suction.<br>Implementation<br>Physiological integrity<br>Application<br>Learning Outcome 33.9 |
| **33.21** The temperature of a client's bath water should be _____. | Answer: 110°F to 115°F<br>Implementation<br>Physiological integrity<br>Knowledge<br>Learning Outcome 33.8 |

## CHAPTER 34

| | |
|---|---|
| **34.1** Which of the following roles would the nurse perform in the intratest phase?<br>1. Assess the data.<br>2. Collect the specimen.<br>3. Observe the client.<br>4. Prepare the client. | Answer: 2<br>Rationale: Collecting the specimen comes during the intratest phase. Assessing the data and preparing the client occur in the pretest phase, and observing the client occurs in the post-test phase as follow-up after the testing.<br>Intervention<br>Health promotion and maintenance<br>Application<br>Learning Outcome 34.1 |

| | |
|---|---|
| **34.2** Which of the following blood tests is indicative of heart failure?<br>1. BNP<br>2. CBC<br>3. LDH<br>4. PKU | Answer: 1<br>Rationale: The specific blood test to detect and guide treatment for heart failure is the BNP test. B-type natriuretic peptide is secreted primarily by the left ventricle in response to increased ventricular volume and pressure. A CBC is a complete blood count and measures hemoglobin, hematocrit, erythrocyte count, leukocyte count, red blood cell indices, and a differential white cell count. LDH is a blood chemistry determining the enzyme lactic dehydrogenase, which is a cardiac marker for a heart attack. PKU is a screening test for newborns for congenital metabolic conditions.<br>Assessment<br>Health promotion and maintenance<br>Analysis<br>Learning Outcome 34.2 |
| **34.3** Which of the following diagnostic studies can determine how well blood glucose levels have been controlled?<br>1. Blood chemistry<br>2. Capillary blood glucose<br>3. Hemoglobin $A_{1c}$<br>4. Serum electrolytes | Answer: 3<br>Rationale: The glycosylated hemoglobin or hemoglobin $A_{1c}$ (HbA$_{1c}$) is a measurement of blood glucose that is bound to hemoglobin. Hemoglobin $A_{1c}$ is a reflection of how well blood glucose levels have been controlled. A blood chemistry is a number of tests performed on blood serum. It can include LDH, CK, AST, ALT, serum glucose, thyroid hormones, and others such as cholesterol and triglycerides. Capillary blood glucose measures blood glucose when frequent tests are required. It gives immediate results of the present. Serum electrolytes are sodium, potassium, chloride, and bicarbonate ions.<br>Assessment<br>Health promotion and maintenance<br>Analysis<br>Learning Outcome 34.2 |
| **34.4** Which returned demonstration by the client indicates an accurate understanding of performing a blood glucose monitoring test?<br>1. The client punctures the fingertip.<br>2. The client puts on gloves.<br>3. The client smears the blood on the reagent strip.<br>4. The client washes her hands. | Answer: 4<br>Rationale: One of the first steps the client would perform is hand washing for infection control. If the client is performing the test on herself, then applying gloves is not necessary. Once the appropriate site is selected for puncture, the side of the finger is used where there are fewer nerve endings. Then once the specimen is obtained, one holds the reagent strip under the puncture site until enough blood covers the indicator square. It is not smeared on the pad, which would cause an inaccurate reading.<br>Evaluation<br>Physiological integrity<br>Application<br>Learning Outcome 34.3 |
| **34.5** A client asks the nurse, "Why do I have to monitor my blood glucose levels?" An appropriate response from the nurse would be:<br>1. "Because your doctor ordered it."<br>2. "If I were you, I would monitor the blood glucose when I didn't feel good."<br>3. "Monitoring your blood glucose better enables you to manage your diabetes."<br>4. "You can eat anything you want." | Answer: 3<br>Rationale: Blood glucose monitoring improves diabetes management. By testing one's blood, one can change the insulin regimen to maintain a normal glycemic range. Clients need an explanation for why they have to do something. "Because your doctor ordered it" is not a good enough reason. The nurse should never tell a client what he or she would do; that is only an opinion. Eating anything the client wants would give rise to too many episodes of hyperglycemia and make the diabetes harder to control.<br>Implementation<br>Health promotion and maintenance<br>Application<br>Learning Outcome 34.3 |

**34.6** Which of the following nursing responsibilities is associated with specimen collection?
1. Always accompany the client to collect a specimen.
2. Handle the specimen discreetly.
3. Sterile technique should be used with all specimen collection.
4. Use day-old specimens.

Answer: 2
Rationale: The nurse should provide the client as much privacy as possible and handle the specimen discreetly to avoid embarrassing the client. With proper instruction, many clients are able to collect their own specimens, so the nurse does not have to always accompany the client. Specimens should be transported promptly to the lab. Fresh specimens provide the most accurate results. Aseptic technique is used to collect specimens to prevent contamination.
Implementation
Physiological integrity
Application
Learning Outcome 34.4

**34.7** A doctor's order for a 24-hour stool specimen collection indicates to the nurse that the physician needs to:
1. Analyze the stool for dietary products and digestive secretions.
2. Detect the presence of bacteria or viruses.
3. Detect the presence of ova and parasites.
4. Determine the presence of occult blood.

Answer: 1
Rationale: The nurse needs to collect and send the total quantity of stool expelled at one time instead of a small sample so that the specimen can be analyzed for dietary products and digestive secretions. To detect bacteria, viruses, ova, parasites, or blood requires only a small amount of stool.
Intervention
Health promotion and maintenance
Analysis
Learning Outcome 34.5

**34.8** A client is being treated for tuberculosis, and the doctor writes an order to collect a sputum specimen. What is the rationale behind this order?
1. For acid-fast bacillus
2. To assess the effectiveness of therapy
3. To identify origin, structure, function, and pathology of cells
4. To identify the specific organism

Answer: 2
Rationale: Knowing the client has tuberculosis, the organism has already been identified. TB does not require cytology for identification; therefore, there is no need for identifying origin, structure, and function. It is already known that TB is acid-fast, so the reason for this doctor's order is to assess if the therapy ordered is effective for this client.
Intervention
Physiological integrity
Analysis
Learning Outcome 34.5

**34.9** Which urinary test is advised for type 1 diabetes? _____

Answer: Ketones
Intervention
Health promotion
Knowledge
Learning Outcome 34.7

**34.10** Which of the following steps should the nurse perform when obtaining a sputum specimen?
1. Collect at least 5 mL of sputum.
2. Offer mouth care.
3. Take shallow breaths.
4. Wear a mask.

Answer: 2
Rationale: Offer mouth care so that the specimen will not be contaminated with microorganisms from the mouth. At least 1 to 2 tablespoons or 15 to 30 mL should be collected (5 mL or 1 teaspoon is not enough). The client should be instructed to breathe deeply and then cough, not take shallow breaths as this would not raise the sputum. A mask needs to be worn only if TB is suspected.
Implementation
Physiological integrity
Application
Learning Outcome 34.8

**34.11** Which instruction should the nurse give to the client when a stool specimen is to be collected?
1. Defecate in the toilet.
2. Follow sterile technique.
3. Send at least 60 mL of specimen.
4. Void before the specimen is collected.

Answer: 4
Rationale: To avoid contaminating the specimen, the client should void before the specimen is collected. The client should defecate in a clean bedpan or bedside commode, not the toilet. Aseptic technique should be followed, not sterile, because the bowel contains microorganisms. The usual amount needed for a specimen is 15 to 30 mL, not 60 mL.

| | Implementation<br>Health promotion and maintenance<br>Application<br>Learning Outcome 34.6 |
| --- | --- |
| **34.12** Which of the following instructions should be given to the client for obtaining a clean voided urine specimen?<br>　1. Collect at least 5 mL of urine.<br>　2. Collect the first voided specimen in the morning.<br>　3. Keep the specimen on ice.<br>　4. Void in a sterile cup. | Answer: 2<br>Rationale: Routine urine examination is usually performed on the first voided specimen in the morning because it tends to have a higher, more uniform concentration and a more acidic pH than specimens later in the day. At least 10 mL of urine is generally sufficient for a routine urinalysis. A timed urine specimen should be refrigerated or kept on ice to prevent bacterial growth or decomposition of urine components. A clean voided urine specimen does not need to be placed in a sterile container, but a clean-catch or midstream specimen does.<br>Implementation<br>Health promotion and maintenance<br>Application<br>Learning Outcome 34.7 |
| **34.13** Which of the following methods is correct for collecting a sputum specimen? Have the client:<br>　1. Apply sterile gloves.<br>　2. Clear the throat.<br>　3. Cough to bring up secretions.<br>　4. Rinse the mouth with mouthwash prior to the collection. | Answer: 3<br>Rationale: Clients need to cough to bring sputum up from the lungs, bronchi, and trachea into the mouth in order to expectorate the specimen into a collecting container. Clearing the throat will not help produce the sputum; one has to cough. The client does not need to put on sterile gloves. The only thing that has to remain sterile is the inside of the collecting container. The client is allowed to use mouthwash after the collection but not before because the antiseptic could alter the results.<br>Implementation<br>Physiological integrity<br>Application<br>Learning Outcome 34.8 |
| **34.14** When instructing a client on the procedure of how a throat culture will be collected, which of the following statements by the client would indicate the need for further instruction?<br>　1. "I need to hyperextend my neck."<br>　2. "I need to say 'ah.'"<br>　3. "I will need to sit up."<br>　4. "The nurse will use a light." | Answer: 1<br>Rationale: The client should extend the tongue when a throat culture is to be taken, not hyperextend the neck. Saying "ah," using a light to see the throat, and sitting up are all proper steps to take when collecting a throat specimen.<br>Evaluation<br>Physiological integrity<br>Analysis<br>Learning Outcome 34.8 |
| **34.15** Which of the following should be the nursing care priority for the client who is to have a barium enema?<br>　1. Assess bowel sounds.<br>　2. Assess for allergies.<br>　3. Cleanse the bowel.<br>　4. Keep the client NPO. | Answer: 3<br>Rationale: For visualization of the colon, the bowel has to be cleansed; otherwise the test cannot be performed. Therefore, that is the first priority the nurse must keep in mind. Keeping the client NPO, assessing for allergies, and assessing bowel sounds are important, but if the bowel is not free of feces, the barium enema will not be accurate.<br>Planning<br>Physiological integrity<br>Application<br>Learning Outcome 34.9 |
| **34.16** A client is to have an echocardiogram. Which statement by the client about this test indicates he does not need further teaching?<br>　1. "I'm told this test causes no discomfort."<br>　2. "I will have to walk on a treadmill." | Answer: 1<br>Rationale: An echocardiogram causes no discomfort, although conductive gel is used and it may be cold. One does not need to be NPO, take his pulse, or walk on a treadmill for this test. The echocardiogram is a noninvasive procedure.<br>Evaluation<br>Physiological integrity<br>Analysis<br>Learning Outcome 34.9 |

| | |
|---|---|
| 3. "I will need to remain NPO."<br>4. "I will need to take my pulse prior to the test." | |
| **34.17** Which of the following replies from the client indicates that no further teaching is required regarding the cystoscopy?<br>  1. "During the procedure the physician will take x-rays."<br>  2. "I will be awake for this procedure."<br>  3. "The doctor will be able to see my kidneys."<br>  4. "The scope is a lighted instrument inserted through the urethra." | Answer: 4<br>Rationale: The cystoscope is a lighted instrument inserted through the urethra. Clients are either put to sleep or consciously sedated during this procedure; they are not awake. Only the bladder, ureteral orifices, and urethra are directly visualized. Since it is direct visualization, x-rays are not needed nor taken.<br>Evaluation<br>Physiological integrity<br>Analysis<br>Learning Outcome 34.9 |
| **34.18** Which of the following precautions should the nurse take when a client is to undergo an MRI (magnetic resonance imaging) test and the client has tattooed eyeliner?<br>Have the client:<br>  1. Apply earplugs.<br>  2. Lie very still.<br>  3. Report any burning sensation.<br>  4. Wear goggles. | Answer: 4<br>Rationale: The Society of Permanent Cosmetic Professionals states that the concentration of zinc oxide is low and diagnostic imaging problems are remote. Any potential problems can be avoided by wearing goggles to cover permanent cosmetics around the eyes. Earplugs are offered to reduce the noise. One does have to lie still, but the damage could still occur to the eyes if they are not covered. Covering the eyes would prevent a complication of burning. Burning would not be something to take lightly.<br>Implementation<br>Physiological integrity<br>Application<br>Learning Outcome 34.10 |
| **34.19** For a lumbar puncture, the nurse should place the client in which of the following positions?<br>  1. Lateral with head bent toward the chest and knees flexed onto the abdomen<br>  2. Lying prone, with the knees drawn up toward the abdomen<br>  3. Sitting bent over from the waist with legs extended<br>  4. Supine with knees pulled toward the chest | Answer: 1<br>Rationale: Lying in the lateral position with the head bent toward the chest and knees flexed onto the abdomen is the correct position for a lumbar puncture. In this position the back is arched, increasing the spaces between the vertebrae so that the spinal needle can be readily inserted. Supine with knees pulled toward the chest does not expose the vertebrae to be punctured. Sitting would not arch the back enough to increase the space between the vertebrae for puncture. Lying prone with knees down toward the abdomen would position the client too high for the physician and could lead to increased intracranial pressure.<br>Implementation<br>Health promotion and maintenance<br>Application<br>Learning Outcome 34.11 |
| **34.20** Which of the following actions best describes how the fluid is removed from the abdominal cavity if ascites develops in the cirrhosis client?<br>  1. Insert a catheter in the bladder.<br>  2. Perform a liver biopsy.<br>  3. Perform an abdominal paracentesis.<br>  4. Perform a thoracentesis. | Answer: 3<br>Rationale: An abdominal paracentesis is performed to remove ascites, which relieves pressure on the abdominal organs. A thoracentesis is performed to remove excess fluid or air to ease breathing. Inserting a catheter into the bladder will only relieve urine, not the accumulation of fluid in the abdomen. A liver biopsy is performed to obtain a sample of the liver, not to remove fluid.<br>Evaluation<br>Physiological integrity<br>Analysis |

**34.21** Place an "X" over the preferred site of a bone marrow biopsy.

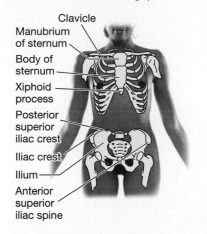

Clavicle
Manubrium of sternum
Body of sternum
Xiphoid process
Posterior superior iliac crest
Iliac crest
Ilium
Anterior superior iliac spine

Answer: Posterior superior iliac crest
Evalution
Physiological integrity
Analysis
Learning Outcome 34.11

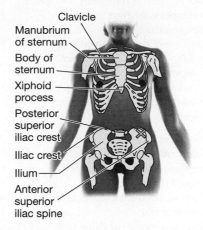

Clavicle
Manubrium of sternum
Body of sternum
Xiphoid process
Posterior superior iliac crest
Iliac crest
Ilium
Anterior superior iliac spine

# CHAPTER 35

**35.1** The nurse is preparing to administer a medication that the agency designates as "high alert." What action should the nurse take?
1. Ask another registered nurse to verify the medication.
2. Call the pharmacist to check the efficacy of the medication.
3. Decline to administer the medication unless there is a physician present.
4. Request that the nursing supervisor administer the medication.

Answer: 1
Rationale: Most health care agencies maintain a list of high-alert medications, including controlled substances, which require the verification of two registered nurses. While the pharmacy is a valuable resource for nurses, the "high-alert" designation does not require pharmacy intervention. High-alert medications do not require the presence of a physician or nursing supervisor for administration.
Implementation
Physiological integrity
Application
Learning Outcome 35.2

**35.2** Hospital regulations now require that the nurse write out the name of the drug morphine sulfate instead of using the abbreviation MS. What is the best rationale for this requirement?
1. The hospital has placed MS on its list of do not use abbreviations.
2. JCAHO requires that the abbreviation MS not be used.
3. Using the abbreviation MS puts the client at risk of medication error.
4. Computerized charting systems will not accept the abbreviation MS.

Answer: 3
Rationale: The best answer is that using the abbreviation MS puts the client at risk of medication error. Although the hospital has probably placed MS on its list of do not use abbreviations, JCAHO does require that the abbreviation not be used, and some computerized charting systems are set up not to accept the abbreviation, those considerations are secondary to the safety of the client.
Planning
Safe, effective care environment
Analysis
Learning Outcome 35.5

**35.3** The hospitalized client has an order for Tylenol 325 mg 2 tablets every 4 hours prn temperature over 101°F. The client complains of a headache. Can the nurse legally administer Tylenol to treat the headache?
1. Yes, since Tylenol is used both for fever and headache.

Answer: 2
Rationale: In the hospital setting, the nurse can only administer medications that are prescribed for the client and can only administer those medications according to the specifics of the prescription. In this case, the medication was ordered for temperature elevation, not pain, so the nurse cannot legally administer the Tylenol to treat the client's headache. The fact that this is an over-the-counter medication and is used both for fever and headache is not pertinent to the nurse's decision. The nurse should never document false information in regard to medication administration.

| | |
|---|---|
| 2. No, not unless the client also has a temperature over 101°F.<br>3. Yes, but the nurse should document the reason why the medication was administered as a temperature elevation.<br>4. Yes, since the medication is available over the counter, an order is not required. | Planning<br>Physiological integrity<br>Analysis<br>Learning Outcome 35.2 |
| **35.4** The nurse identifies that the ordered dose for a medication is twice the amount generally administered. What action should the nurse take?<br>1. Administer the medication as it was ordered.<br>2. Check to see if previous shift nurses gave the medication.<br>3. Collaborate with the prescriber about the order.<br>4. Administer only the standard dose of the medication. | Answer: 3<br>Rationale: When the nurse has doubts about the correctness of a medication or medication dose for a specific client, collaboration with the prescriber is necessary. The nurse is legally and ethically responsible for all actions taken, including medication administration. The fact that previous nurses gave the medication as ordered does not make it the correct action. The nurse cannot change the amount of medication to give without collaborating with the prescriber. Administering the dose as ordered may harm the client.<br>Implementation<br>Physiological integrity<br>Analysis<br>Learning Outcome 35.5 |
| **35.5** The client has required 2 sublingual nitroglycerine tablets that are gr 1/150 per tablet. How many mg of nitroglycerine did the client receive? | Answer: 48 mg<br>Rationale: The client received gr 2/150 of NTG. There are 60 mg in 1 grain. To convert, use ratio-proportion.<br>1 gr/60 mg = 2/150 gr/ x mg<br>x = 120/150<br>x = 48 mg<br>Implementation<br>Physiological integrity<br>Application<br>Learning Outcome 35.9 |
| **35.6** The nurse is preparing to administer a medication to a 6-year-old. What is the nurse's priority action?<br>1. Administer the exact dosage as ordered.<br>2. Give the dosage supplied by the pharmacy.<br>3. Verify that the dosage is within the safe range for this child.<br>4. Administer no more than one-half of the safe adult dosage. | Answer: 3<br>Rationale: The priority action is to verify that the dosage is within the safe range for this child. This verification can be done by figuring the dose per kilogram of body weight or by use of a nomogram. This dose should be compared to the standard dose listed in a reputable drug reference book. This dose may be more or less than one-half the adult dosage. While prescribers and pharmacists are also responsible to figure the correct dose, the nurse who administers the dose is the last possible person to prevent a medication error. The nurse has the final responsibility to ensure that the dose ordered and dose supplied are correct for the client.<br>Implementation<br>Physiological integrity<br>Application<br>Learning Outcome 35.9 |
| **35.7** During the process of administering medications, the nurse checks the name band for the client's name. What should be this nurse's next action?<br>1. Administer the medication as ordered.<br>2. Initial the MAR that the medication will be given. | Answer: 3<br>Rationale: The Joint Commission's National Client Safety Goals require a two-step check of client identification prior to the administration of medications. This nurse should employ a second method to verify the client's identification. After that verification, the nurse should educate the client regarding the medication, administer the medication as ordered, and only then should the nurse initial that the medication was given.<br>Implementation |

| | |
|---|---|
| 3. Double-check the client's identification using a second method.<br>4. Educate the client regarding the medication to be given. | Physiological integrity<br>Analysis<br>Learning Outcome 35.8 |
| **35.8** The nurse is planning to administer a bitter-tasting oral medication to a 4-year-old. What strategy should this nurse plan?<br>1. Give the medication in orange juice or milk to mask the taste.<br>2. Tell the child that the medication tastes good.<br>3. Ask the parents how they give medications at home.<br>4. Get another nurse to assist by holding the client down. | Answer: 3<br>Rationale: Parents are a very good source of ideas for caring for their child, and their input should be sought when performing tasks such as medication administration. Medication should not be placed in essential foods such as orange juice or milk as the child may develop an aversion to the food related to the taste of the medication. Being untruthful about any interventions may cause the client to lose trust in the nurse. Having a second nurse hold the client down to administer the medication is an unnecessary use of force and will frighten the child.<br>Planning<br>Physiological integrity<br>Application<br>Learning Outcome 35.11 |
| **35.9** The nurse is caring for a team of four clients who are seriously ill. One of the clients has just received a new cardiac medication. How should the nurse instruct the unlicensed assistive personnel (UAP) who is also caring for this client?<br>1. Have the UAP assess for any unexpected effects from the medication.<br>2. Tell the UAP to teach the client's family what to expect from the medication.<br>3. Have the UAP look the medication up in a drug reference book to read about drug actions and possible side effects.<br>4. Give the UAP specific instructions regarding what drug actions or side effects to report to the nurse. | Answer: 4<br>Rationale: The nurse should give the UAP specific instructions about what drug actions or side effects should be reported to the nurse. The UAP does not have the skills or legal responsibility to assess the client, but can collect data to report to the nurse. It is also the nurse's responsibility to teach the client or family about the medications. The nurse should not expect that the UAP can determine from the drug reference book what drug actions and possible side effects are pertinent to this client.<br>Planning<br>Safe, effective care environment<br>Application<br>Learning Outcome 35.2 |
| **35.10** The nurse is to administer four oral medications to the client via a nasogastric tube. One of the medications is a tablet that has been crushed, one is a capsule that has been opened and the powder removed, and two are supplied in liquid form. How should the nurse administer these medications?<br>1. Flush the tube, mix the crushed tablet and the capsule powder into the two liquids for administration, and follow by flushing the tube.<br>2. Mix the crushed tablet and capsule powder in warm water and administer. Flush the tube and administer the mixed liquids.<br>3. Flush the tube with the mixed liquids first, then administer the crushed tablet and capsule powder mixed in cold water. | Answer: 4<br>Rationale: When giving medication via a nasogastric or gastric tube, the nurse should individually prepare and administer the medications, flushing the tube before and after each administration. Mixing medications together may result in a chemical reaction that occludes the tube. Failure to flush the tube adequately is the leading cause of tube occlusion.<br>Implementation<br>Physiological integrity<br>Application<br>Learning Outcome 35.12 |

| | |
|---|---|
| 4. Mix the crushed tablet and capsule powder individually in warm water. Administer each medication separately, flushing the tube before and after each administration. | |
| **35.11** At which point of preparing medication from an ampule does the nurse anticipate using a filter needle?<br>  1. Filter needles are not used for this preparation.<br>  2. When drawing the medication from the ampule.<br>  3. When administering the medication to the client.<br>  4. Both for drawing up the medication and for administering the medication. | Answer: 2<br>Rationale: The nurse uses a filter needle to draw medication up from an ampule to remove any possible shards of glass from the liquid. The filter needle is then changed to a regular needle prior to administering the liquid to the client. If the filter needle was used to inject the client, the trapped shards of glass would be injected into the muscle.<br>Planning<br>Physiological integrity<br>Application<br>Learning Outcome 35.14 |
| **35.12** The nurse has discontinued suction to a nasogastric tube to administer medication. For how long should the nurse plan to leave this suction discontinued? | Answer: 20 to 30 minutes<br>Rationale: It will take approximately 20 to 30 minutes for most medications to be absorbed or to move out of the stomach. If the nurse restarts the suction prior to that time, the medication may be removed from the stomach with the suctioned contents. The client may not receive the intended dose or effects from the medication.<br>Planning<br>Physiological integrity<br>Application<br>Learning Outcome 35.12 |
| **35.13** The client is to receive an intramuscular injection of a medication that is supplied in a 2-mL cartridge and a second medication that is supplied in a vial. The total amount to be administered of these medications exceeds the volume of the cartridge by 0.5 mL. How should the nurse proceed?<br>  1. Administer the cartridge medication in one injection and the vial medication in a separate injection.<br>  2. Call the pharmacy for advice on administering these medications.<br>  3. Draw both of the medications up into a syringe for administration.<br>  4. Add as much of the vial medication to the cartridge as possible prior to injection, giving the balance in a separate injection. | Answer: 3<br>Rationale: When the total amount of medication to administer exceeds the volume of the cartridge, the medication is drawn up into a syringe and is administered. Giving two separate injections, no matter how the medication is divided, should be avoided if possible. There is no need for the nurse to consult the pharmacy for this standard technique.<br>Implementation<br>Physiological integrity<br>Application<br>Learning Outcome 35.16 |
| **35.14** During administration of an intradermal injection, the nurse notices that the outline of the needle bevel is visible under the client's skin. How should the nurse proceed?<br>  1. Recognize that this is an expected finding in a properly administered intradermal injection. | Answer: 1<br>Rationale: Intradermal injections are given at a very shallow angle so that the medication is delivered into the area between the dermal layers. When properly given, the outline of the needle bevel will be visible prior to injection of the fluid. There is no need to withdraw the needle and start again. Inserting the needle further into the skin and at a deeper angle would result in delivery of the fluid into the subcutaneous tissues. The needle is inserted with the bevel up.<br>Evaluation |

| | |
|---|---|
| 2. Withdraw the needle, prepare a new injection, and start again.<br>3. Insert the needle further into the skin at a deeper angle.<br>4. Turn the needle so that the bevel is down and inject the medication slowly, looking for development of a bleb. | Physiological integrity<br>Analysis<br>Learning Outcome 35.16 |
| **35.15** The nurse has just injected insulin subcutaneously into the client's abdomen. What action should the nurse take at this point?<br>1. Massage the site to encourage absorption.<br>2. Leave the needle embedded in the client's skin for 5 seconds after administration.<br>3. Remove the needle rapidly by pulling it quickly from the skin.<br>4. Cover the injection site with a pressure dressing for at least 15 minutes or until the bleb disappears. | Answer: 2<br>Rationale: The American Diabetes Association recommends leaving the needle embedded in the client's skin for 5 seconds after injection of medication, particularly insulin. This allows for complete delivery of the dose. Massage is contraindicated for most medications because it alters the delivery rate from the tissues. The needle should be removed slowly and smoothly to minimize pain for the client. Bleeding rarely occurs after subcutaneous injection, but short application of manual pressure (1–3 minutes) should cause bleeding to stop. There is no need for a pressure dressing for 15 minutes. Subcutaneous injections do not result in bleb formation.<br>Implementation<br>Physiological integrity<br>Application<br>Learning Outcome 35.16 |
| **35.16** The nurse who is to administer 2.5 mL of intramuscular pain medication to an adult client notes that the previous injection was administered in the right ventrogluteal site. In which site should the nurse plan to administer this injection?<br>1. The same site<br>2. The deltoid<br>3. The left ventrogluteal<br>4. The rectus femoris | Answer: 3<br>Rationale: Of the options given, the best choice is the left ventrogluteal. This is a site that will accept 2.5 mL of medication, and using the opposite site from the last injection will allow the first site time for recovery. The deltoid site will not accept 2.5 mL of medication. The rectus femoris site is generally used only for self-injection of medication and is a painful site for medication administration.<br>Planning<br>Physiological integrity<br>Analysis<br>Learning Outcome 35.16 |
| **35.17** While administering an intramuscular injection, the nurse notes blood return in the syringe barrel after aspirating. What action should the nurse take?<br>1. Pull the needle out 1/4 inch and inject the medication.<br>2. Inject the medication as planned.<br>3. Notify the physician immediately.<br>4. Discard the medication and start over. | Answer: 4<br>Rationale: Blood return in the syringe barrel after aspiration indicates a strong probability that the needle tip is in a blood vessel. Injection of medication would then be intravenous, not intramuscular. The nurse should discard the medication and start over with new medication and a new syringe. Simply pulling out the needle 1/4 inch does not guarantee that the needle point is not in a vessel, and the presence of blood in the syringe prevents checking the new site. A second consideration is that injection of blood into the muscle is painful. There is no need to notify the physician of this event.<br>Implementation<br>Physiological integrity<br>Application<br>Learning Outcome 35.16 |
| **35.18** The nurse is adding medication to an existing intravenous setup. Which nursing action is indicated?<br>1. Close the infusion clamp.<br>2. Ensure that the IV bag is full prior to adding medication.<br>3. Do not remove the IV bag from the standard.<br>4. Briskly shake the IV bag after injecting the medication. | Answer: 1<br>Rationale: The nurse must close the infusion clamp prior to adding medication to an existing IV bag. Closing the clamp prevents the medication from inadvertently going directly down the tubing and into the client. Medication is frequently added to IV bags that are less than completely full. The nurse must make a determination if the bag contains enough fluid to dilute the medication to the desired strength. The bag can be taken from the IV standard for mixing. The bag should receive a gentle rotation, not brisk shaking, to mix the medication and the fluid. |

| | |
|---|---|
| **35.19** Upon aspirating a saline lock prior to administering intravenous medication, the nurse notes that there is no blood return. What nursing action should be taken?<br><br>1. Discontinue this infiltrated lock and restart another site for medication administration.<br>2. Slowly infuse 1 mL of saline into the lock, assessing for infiltration.<br>3. Reinsert the needle into the lock and aspirate using more pressure.<br>4. Pull the intravenous catheter out $1/8$ inch and attempt aspiration. | Answer: 2<br>Rationale: While the presence of blood upon aspiration confirms that the catheter is in a vein, the absence of blood does not rule out correct placement. If no blood returns, the nurse should slowly infuse 1 mL of saline into the lock while assessing the site for infiltration. If there is no infiltration present, the nurse should administer the medication. Simple lack of blood upon aspiration does not indicate infiltration, so there is no need to discontinue the site. Often the reason for absence of blood return is that the vessel has collapsed around the catheter from the pressure of aspiration. Increasing the pressure will not increase the likelihood of blood return. Pulling the intravenous catheter out 1/8 inch will not increase the likelihood of blood return and may make the site more unstable.<br>Implementation<br>Physiological integrity<br>Analysis<br>Learning Outcome 35.16 |
| **35.20** While preparing to administer an eye ointment, the nurse inadvertently squeezes the tube, discarding the first bead of medication. What action should the nurse take at this point?<br><br>1. Administer the eye ointment as ordered, as the first bead of ointment should be discarded anyway.<br>2. Notify the pharmacy and request a new, unopened tube of ointment.<br>3. Have a second licensed nurse witness the waste and sign the chart.<br>4. Continue to squeeze the tube until a clear line of ointment has been discarded from the tip. | Answer: 1<br>Rationale: The nurse should administer the eye ointment as ordered as the first bead of ointment is considered contaminated and should always be discarded. There is no need to notify the pharmacy for a new tube of ointment or to have the wastage witnessed by another nurse. It is necessary to discard only the first bead of ointment, not an entire line.<br>Implementation<br>Physiological integrity<br>Application<br>Learning Outcome 35.17 |
| **35.21** The nurse is preparing to administer eardrops to a 6-year-old. What nursing action is correct?<br><br>1. Pull the earlobe down and back to straighten the ear canal.<br>2. Insert the tip of the applicator into the ear canal.<br>3. Put the eardrops in the refrigerator for 10 minutes prior to administration.<br>4. Press gently on the tragus of the ear a few times after administration. | Answer: 4<br>Rationale: The nurse should press gently but firmly on the tragus of the ear after eardrops are administered in order to direct the drops into the ear canal. After age 3, the pinna of the ear should be pulled up and back to straighten the ear canal. The tip of the eardrop applicator should not be placed into the ear canal, but should be held just above the canal so that the drops can fall onto the side of the canal. Eardrops should be warmed prior to administration, not cooled.<br>Implementation<br>Physiological integrity<br>Application<br>Learning Outcome 35.17 |
| **35.22** While preparing to administer a transdermal estrogen patch, the nurse finds the previously applied patch in the client's bed linens. How can the nurse avoid this situation with the patch now being applied? | Answer: 4<br>Rationale: In order to affix the patch firmly to the client's skin, press firmly over the patch with the palm of the hand for about 10 seconds after application. Placement of a heating pad is contraindicated as the heat could increase circulation and the rate of absorption. Avoid touching the adhesive edges of the patch prior to placing it on the skin. If hair is a problem in keeping |

| | |
|---|---|
| 1. Shave the area where the patch is being applied.<br>2. Place a heating pad over the area where the patch is applied for 10 minutes after application.<br>3. Run a finger around the adhesive edges of the new patch before placing it on the client's skin.<br>4. Press firmly over the patch with the palm of the hand for about 10 seconds after applying it to the skin. | the patch on, choose a less hairy site for application or clip (do not shave) the hair.<br>Implementation<br>Physiological integrity<br>Application<br>Learning Outcome 35.17 |
| **35.23** The nurse is preparing a small amount of medication for oral administration. Which nursing action is essential?<br>1. Draw up the medication in a syringe with a large-gauge needle.<br>2. Measure the medication at the top of the meniscus.<br>3. Label the syringe with the medication name, amount, and route.<br>4. Dilute the medication with water before measuring. | Answer: 3<br>Rationale: When measuring medication in a syringe, a label must be attached indicating the name of the medication, the amount, and the route. This labeling is essential to prevent the medication from being given via the wrong route. If a regular syringe is used to draw up the medication, the needle should be discarded. A syringe with a needle might also indicate that the medication is to be given parenterally and cause a medication route error. If medications are measured in a cup, the correct measurement is at the bottom of the meniscus. Medication might be diluted after measuring, but dilution before measurement will make it impossible to measure accurately.<br>Implementation<br>Physiological integrity<br>Application<br>Learning Outcome 35.11 |
| **35.24** The diabetic client asks the clinic nurse about the advisability of reusing insulin syringes. Assessment reveals that the client has poor personal hygiene and difficulty with fine motor skills. The nurse also knows the client has financial difficulties. What instruction should the nurse give this client?<br>1. "The American Diabetes Association advises that syringes are single use only."<br>2. "In order to save money, I advise you to reuse syringes up to three times or until the needle feels dull."<br>3. "Only people who practice good personal hygiene can reuse syringes."<br>4. "All clients are different, but I advise you to use a new syringe each injection." | Answer: 4<br>Rationale: While the ADA does indicate that syringes can be reused, that suggestion is not made to people who have poor personal hygiene, acute concurrent illness, open wounds on the hands, or decreased resistance to infection. In this case, the nurse has assessed that this client has poor hygiene and has difficulty with fine motor skills. This may make it difficult for the client to manipulate the syringe and keep it clean. This client does not meet the criteria for suggesting the reuse of syringes. The nurse should not directly confront the client with the statement about personal hygiene as that would damage the nurse–client relationship. The best answer is to suggest that this client use a new syringe for each injection.<br>Implementation<br>Physiological integrity<br>Analysis<br>Learning Outcome 35.13 |
| **35.25** The client who regularly uses a metered-dose inhaler four times a day tells the nurse that it is difficult to tell when the canister is empty. What instruction should the nurse give this client?<br>1. Place the canister in a bowl of water. If the canister floats, it is not empty. | Answer: 2<br>Rationale: The best way to track the number of puffs left in a canister is to start with the new canister, dividing the number of puffs listed on the label by the number of puffs taken each day. The old method of floating the canister in water is not accurate as there may be propellant left in the canister after the medication is all dispensed. Being able to smell the medication is not an indication of the amount left in the canister. Waiting until there is lack of maximum effect from the medication may put the client at risk for respirator illness exacerbation. |

| | |
|---|---|
| 2. When you get a new canister, divide the number of puffs that is listed on the label by four. That will tell you how many days the canister will last. | Implementation<br>Physiological integrity<br>Application<br>Learning Outcome 35.17 |
| 3. You can tell that the canister is empty when you can no longer smell the medication when you activate the plunger. | |
| 4. When you feel like you are no longer getting maximum effect from the medication, your canister is empty. | |

| | |
|---|---|
| **35.26** The nurse is providing discharge teaching for a client who is being dismissed with prescriptions for a bronchodilator inhaler and a corticosteroid inhaler. What information should the nurse provide regarding the dosage schedule for these two medications?<br><br>  1. Always use the corticosteroid inhaler first.<br>  2. Use the bronchodilator first.<br>  3. It makes no difference which inhaler is used first.<br>  4. Use the inhalers on alternate days, not on the same day. | Answer: 2<br>Rationale: These two types of inhalers are frequently prescribed to be used together. The bronchodilator should be used first in order to open the airways so the corticosteroid medication can move deeply into the lungs.<br>Implementation<br>Physiological integrity<br>Application<br>Learning Outcome 35.17 |

| | |
|---|---|
| **35.27** The nurse is planning to administer medications to a new client. What is the nurse's greatest priority in administering these medications?<br><br>  1. Be certain the medications are given within 15 minutes of the time they are scheduled.<br>  2. Before giving the medications, know what the intended effects are for this client.<br>  3. Assess the client's knowledge of the action of the medications.<br>  4. Document the administration accurately so the reimbursement is correct. | Answer: 2<br>Rationale: The nurse should be certain that all of these options occur. However, the greatest priority is to understand the intended effects of the medication for this client. The nurse should never do anything to or for a client without knowing the intended effect.<br>Planning<br>Physiological integrity<br>Analysis<br>Learning Outcome 35.8 |

# CHAPTER 36

| | |
|---|---|
| **36.1** The continuous quality improvement team is monitoring the nursing care of clean-contaminated wounds. Which operative wound would be excluded from this study?<br><br>  1. Gastric resection<br>  2. Uncomplicated abdominal hysterectomy<br>  3. Breast biopsy<br>  4. Lung resection | Answer: 3<br>Rationale: Clean-contaminated wounds are surgical wounds in which the respiratory, alimentary, genital, or urinary tract has been entered. These wounds show no evidence of infection. Of the wounds listed, the only one not meeting the criteria is the breast biopsy.<br>Assessment<br>Safe, effective care environment<br>Application |

**36.2** The surgical report of a newly transferred client indicates that there was a great deal of intestinal spillage into the abdominal cavity during the client's bowel resection. For which category of wound should the receiving nurse plan care?
1. Clean-contaminated
2. Contaminated
3. Dirty
4. Infected

Answer: 2
Rationale: A surgical wound in which there is a large amount of spillage from the gastrointestinal tract is considered a contaminated wound. Clean-contaminated wounds are surgical wounds in which the respiratory, alimentary, genital, or urinary tract has been entered, but minimal to no spillage has occurred. A dirty or infected wound is one that contains dead tissue or that has evidence of a clinical infection, such as purulent drainage.
Planning
Physiologic integrity
Application

**36.3** Emergency medical services contacts the emergency department with the report that they are transporting a client who was the victim of a motor vehicle crash. The paramedics report that the client is stable, but has multiple contusions. How should the nurse prepare for this client?
1. Obtain ice packs to apply to the wounds.
2. Request gauze to pack the wounds.
3. Organize suture material to close the wounds.
4. Notify the surgical staff that a surgical client will soon be arriving.

Answer: 1
Rationale: Contusions are closed wounds in which the skin is ecchymotic or bruised due to damage of blood vessels. These wounds are treated with ice pack application for the first 24 hours. Since these wounds are closed, there is no need for packing, suturing, or surgery.
Planning
Physiologic integrity
Analysis

**36.4** After completing a scheduled every-2-hour turn by turning the client to the left side, the nurse notices a reddened area over the coccyx. The area blanches when the nurse compresses it with thumb pressure. One hour later, the nurse reassesses the area and finds the redness has disappeared. How should the nurse document this area?
1. Reactive hyperemia
2. Stage I pressure ulcer
3. Stage II pressure ulcer
4. Stage III pressure ulcer

Answer: 1
Rationale: If the reddened area blanches with thumb pressure and disappears in one-half to three-quarters of the time pressure was on the area, the condition is reactive hyperemia and no damage to the skin and tissues has occurred. Stage I pressure ulcers are reddened areas that do not blanch with thumb pressure and that do not clear in the allotted amount of time. Stage II pressure ulcers show partial-thickness skin loss and have the appearance of abrasions, blisters, or shallow craters. Stage III pressure ulcers demonstrate full-thickness skin loss involving damage or necrosis of subcutaneous tissue that may extend down to, but not through, underlying fascia.
Evaluation
Physiologic integrity
Application
Learning Outcome 36.3

**36.5** The nurse assesses an open area over a client's greater trochanter that is approximately 10 cm in diameter. The tissue around the area is edematous and feels boggy. The edges of the wound cup in toward the center. Which additional finding would indicate to the nurse that this is a stage IV pressure ulcer?
1. There is undermining of adjacent tissues.
2. The crater extends into the subcutaneous tissue.
3. The joint capsule of the hip is visible.
4. The ulcer has thick dark eschar over the top.

Answer: 3
Rationale: The difference between a stage III and a stage IV pressure ulcer is the depth to which the ulcer extends. Stage III ulcers extend down to, but not through, the underlying fascia. Stage IV ulcers demonstrate damage to muscle, bone, tendons, or the joint capsule. Both stages can include undermining of adjacent tissues. If there is eschar present, the ulcer cannot be staged. Staging can occur only when the bottom of the ulcer can be seen and evaluated.
Assessment
Physiologic integrity
Analysis
Learning Outcome 36.3

| | |
|---|---|
| **36.6** The UAP reports a small skin tear on the client's forearm that occurred during a routine turn. After assessing the wound the nurse should:<br>1. Obtain a transparent dressing for the UAP to place on the wound.<br>2. Request a consult with the wound care nurse.<br>3. Cleanse the wound and apply a dressing.<br>4. Tell the UAP to reevaluate the wound in 20 minutes. | Answer: 3<br>Rationale: The nurse should go to the room, assess the wound, cleanse the wound, and apply a dressing. The UAP is not educationally prepared to evaluate or dress the wound. At this point a consult with the wound care nurse is not required.<br>Implementation<br>Physiologic integrity<br>Analysis<br>Learning Outcome 36.12 |
| **36.7** The newly hired nurse learns that the facility uses the Braden Scale for Predicting Pressure Sore Risk to assess all new admissions. Before using this scale the nurse:<br>1. Should receive specific training.<br>2. Must be certified.<br>3. Is required to ask the client's permission.<br>4. Has to obtain special assessment equipment. | Answer: 1<br>Rationale: The nurse should receive specific training in the use of the Braden scale in order for assessment to be accurate. There is no need for certification. Simple in-house training by an experienced, competent nurse is sufficient. There is no specific permission required from the client. There is no special assessment equipment required.<br>Assessment<br>Health promotion and maintenance<br>Application<br>Learning Outcome 36.8 |
| **36.8** A client has had Braden scores of 18 and 19 and Norton scores of 15 and 17 over the last 2 months. Is trending of these scores significant?<br>1. No, trending can only be accurate if the same scale is used.<br>2. Yes, there is a definite trend of low risk for pressure ulcer development.<br>3. Somewhat, but trending would be more accurate if the same scale was used.<br>4. No, the scores indicate opposite risks for pressure ulcer development. | Answer: 3<br>Rationale: All of these scores indicate risk for development of a pressure ulcer, so some trending is possible, but it would be more accurate if the same scale was always used.<br>Assessment<br>Health promotion and maintenance<br>Analysis<br>Learning Outcome 36.8 |
| **36.9** The emergency department physician has closed a laceration with tissue adhesive. The nurse provides the client with instruction regarding which type of wound healing?<br>1. Primary intention<br>2. Open approximation<br>3. Secondary healing<br>4. Delayed closure | Answer: 1<br>Rationale: The nurse should instruct the client regarding primary intention wound healing. The edges of these wounds are approximated and held together with sutures, bandages, or tissue adhesive. Scarring is minimal with these wounds. Secondary healing involves wounds that cannot be approximated and that must "heal in." These wounds are at higher risk for infection, take longer to heal, and are more prone to scarring.<br>Implementation<br>Physiologic integrity<br>Application<br>Learning Outcome 36.4 |
| **36.10** The client is routinely taking steroid medications to control lung disease. In the discharge teaching plan the nurse includes information on practicing good infection control because steroids cause which of the following? | Answer: 2<br>Rationale: Steroids suppress the inflammatory process, which is a normal part of the healing process. While lung disease may affect oxygenation, the steroid drug regimen would not be implicated in decreased oxygen delivery to tissues. Steroids generally increase blood glucose. Blood vessels are not constricted by steroids.<br>Planning<br>Physiologic integrity |

| | |
|---|---|
| 1. Decreased oxygen supply to tissues<br>2. Suppression of the inflammatory process necessary for healing<br>3. Decrease in the amount of nutrients such as glucose in the blood<br>4. Blood vessel constriction which impairs waste product removal | Analysis<br>Learning Outcome 36.1 |
| **36.11** On the fourth postoperative day, the client has a sudden coughing episode and tells the nurse that "something popped" in the abdominal incision. Upon inspection, the nurse finds that evisceration has occurred. What nursing action should be taken first?<br>  1. Notify the client's surgeon.<br>  2. Cover the area with a large saline-soaked dressing.<br>  3. Position the client in bed with knees bent.<br>  4. Pack the wound with nonadherent gauze. | Answer: 2<br>Rationale: Evisceration occurs when an abdominal wound opens and there is protrusion of the internal viscera through the incision. The nurse's first action should be to cover the area with a large saline-soaked dressing to keep the viscera moist. While notifying the surgeon and positioning the client are important, covering the wound is the priority. Nothing should be packed into this wound.<br>Implementation<br>Physiologic integrity<br>Application<br>Learning Outcome 36.10 |
| **36.12** The night nurse is assuming care of a cardiac client who wears antiembolic stockings. How should this nurse manage assessment of the skin on this client's legs?<br>  1. Defer the assessment since the stockings are in place.<br>  2. Remove the stockings for this assessment.<br>  3. Review the morning assessment, but don't repeat it unless a problem occurs.<br>  4. Assess the skin when the client removes the stockings at bedtime. | Answer: 2<br>Rationale: The stockings should be removed to do this assessment. The nurse is responsible for assessing the skin under the stockings and should not assume that the morning nurse's assessment is still accurate 12 hours later. The stockings are worn day and night, so the client will not remove them for sleep.<br>Assessment<br>Physiologic integrity<br>Application<br>Learning Outcome 36.8 |
| **36.13** Multiple severely injured clients have arrived in the emergency department. On rapid assessment, the nurse notes that a leg wound dressing has a 4 cm × 6 cm blood spot that has soaked through the bandage. The client is otherwise stable. What action should the nurse take?<br>  1. Place a tourniquet above the wound.<br>  2. Remove the dressing and place direct pressure on the wound.<br>  3. Add additional dressing to the wound without removing the original.<br>  4. Remove the dressing and replace it with a new sterile dressing. | Answer: 3<br>Rationale: In this scenario, where there are multiple clients in need of care and since this client is stable, the correct nursing action is to add additional dressing to the wound without removing the original. A tourniquet should not be applied because of the risk of interrupting arterial flow to the tissues. Removing the dressing and applying direct pressure or replacing the dressing with a new sterile dressing would take too much time at this point.<br>Implementation<br>Physiologic integrity<br>Analysis<br>Learning Outcome 36.13 |

**36.14** The nurse is collecting a specimen from an infected wound. From which portion of the wound should the specimen be collected?
1. Clean areas of granulation tissue
2. Exudate in the bottom of the wound
3. A pus-coated area on the side of the wound
4. Intact skin at the edge of the wound

Answer: 1
Rationale: Microorganisms that are most likely to be responsible for wound infections live in viable tissue such as granulation tissue. Exudate and pus contain a variety of components and are unlikely to give good indication of what is causing the infection. The skin at the edge of the wound contains skin organisms that may or may not be present in the wound itself.
Implementation
Physiologic integrity
Application
Learning Outcome 36.14

**36.15** The client has a documented stage III pressure ulcer on the right hip. What NANDA nursing diagnosis problem statement is most appropriate for use with this client?
1. *Altered Tissue Perfusion*
2. *Impaired Skin Integrity*
3. *Impaired Tissue Integrity*
4. *Risk for Injury*

Answer: 3
Rationale: Since a stage III pressure ulcer involves tissues, not just skin, this client has criteria for using the NANDA nursing diagnosis problem statement *Impaired Tissue Integrity*. *Impaired Skin Integrity* deals with the epidermal and dermal layers only and does not extend into the tissue. This client has already suffered injury, so this is not a *Risk for* situation. While it is true that pressure ulcers result from *Altered Tissue Perfusion*, the diagnosis problem statement *Impaired Tissue Integrity* is more specific.
Diagnosis
Safe, effective care environment
Analysis
Learning Outcome 36.9

**36.16** The nurse is selecting dressings for a clean abdominal incision that will be allowed to heal by secondary intention. What principles should the nurse use in choosing this dressing?
1. Materials used in dressing this wound should keep the wound bed moist.
2. The dressing should allow good air circulation through the wound.
3. Dressings should be simple as they will be changed at least every 4 hours.
4. Absorbent material to wick exudates away and support drying should be used.

Answer: 1
Rationale: Wounds that are expected to heal by secondary intention heal by "granulating in." In order to support the growth of granulation tissue, the wound bed should be kept moist and oxygen should be kept out of the wound. Air is drying to tissues and contains oxygen, so air circulation through the dressing is not desirable. The dressings will not be changed that often. Since the goal is to keep the wound bed moist, dressings should not wick exudates away.
Planning
Physiologic integrity
Analysis
Learning Outcome 36.13

**36.17** The adult client is incontinent and wears incontinence briefs when using the wheelchair. An irritated rash has developed in the perianal area. What care should the nurse provide?
1. Wash the area with soap and hot water at every brief change.
2. Apply a petroleum-based cream to the area after cleaning.
3. Wipe the skin with an alcohol-free barrier film agent after cleaning.
4. Keep the client in bed on absorbent pads until the area clears.

Answer: 3
Rationale: The care should include wiping the skin with an alcohol-free barrier film agent after cleaning. Petroleum-based creams are now thought to offer poor overall skin protection and to interfere with incontinence brief absorption. Cleansing should be done with a mild cleansing agent and warm water. Keeping the client in bed to treat this area is not necessary and may lead to problems with immobility.
Application
Implementation
Physiologic integrity
Learning Outcome 36.2

| | |
|---|---|
| **36.18** The nurse is writing the plan of care for a client who is confined to bed. Which intervention should be included to help reduce the effects of shearing forces on the client's skin?<br>   1. Keep the head of the client's bed at 30 degrees.<br>   2. Coat the client's back and buttocks with baby powder after bathing.<br>   3. Use a turn sheet lifted by two staff members to move the client in bed.<br>   4. Dust the linens with cornstarch each morning to allow for easier movement. | Answer: 3<br>Rationale: The nurse should plan to use a turn sheet lifted by two staff members to move the client up in bed. The head of the client's bed should be kept at less than 30 degrees elevation as much as possible. Baby powder and cornstarch should not be used as both agents cause abrasive grit damage to tissues.<br>Planning<br>Safe, effective care environment<br>Application<br>Learning Outcome 36.11 |
| **36.19** The nurse is using an elastic bandage to secure a dressing on an extremity. The bandage should be wrapped in the _____ to _____ direction. | Answer: distal to proximal<br>Rationale: Wrapping the elastic bandage from distal to proximal supports venous return. Wrapping in the other direction can "trap" blood in the distal portion of the extremity.<br>Implementation<br>Physiologic integrity<br>Application<br>Learning Outcome 36.13 |
| **36.20** Upon assessing a pressure ulcer, the nurse notes the presence of red, yellow, and black tissue. Using the RYB color code, which wound care should the nurse plan?<br>   1. Red<br>   2. Yellow<br>   3. Black<br>   4. A combination of all three | Answer: 3<br>Rationale: When using the RYB color code to guide wound care for a wound that contains more than one of the colors, the nurse plans care for the most serious color, in this case black.<br>Planning<br>Physiologic integrity<br>Application<br>Learning Outcome 36.10 |
| **36.21** The nurse has established an expected outcome that the client will demonstrate healing of a stage II pressure ulcer over the coccyx. Which finding, discovered by the nurse during evaluation, might be implicated in the failure to achieve this outcome?<br>   1. The rubber doughnut pressure relief device was not delivered by central supply.<br>   2. The client's serum albumin increased over the last month.<br>   3. Nurses did not document disinfection of the wound with alcohol with each dressing change.<br>   4. Unlicensed assistive personnel (UAP) followed a right side-back-left side-back turning schedule. | Answer: 4<br>Rationale: Since this expected outcome was not met, the nurse looks for problems in the provision of care or changes in the client's condition. Of the options listed, the only one that would result in poor healing is the right side-back-left side-back turning schedule. This schedule places the client on the back for 50% of the time. The schedule should be right side-back-left side-right side. A rubber doughnut should not be used, so the fact that it was not delivered did not cause failure to meet the outcome. An increase in serum albumin is a good finding and would increase wound healing, not decrease wound healing. The use of alcohol interrupts healing, so it is good that nurses did not document its use.<br>Evaluation<br>Physiologic integrity<br>Analysis<br>Learning Outcome 36.12 |

| | |
|---|---|
| **36.22** The nurse is gathering equipment to perform the irrigation of an abdominal wound that is being allowed to heal by secondary intention. A _____ to _____ size syringe should be obtained. | Answer: 30 to 60 mL<br>Planning<br>Physiologic integrity<br>Application<br>Learning Outcome 36.14 |
| **36.23** The nurse has applied an aquathermia pad to a client's back. After 15 minutes of treatment, the client says that the pack no longer is warm and asks the nurse to increase the temperature. How should the nurse evaluate this request?<br>1. Since this client's thermal tolerance is higher than normal, increasing the temperature is necessary.<br>2. This client may be experiencing a rebound effect from the application of moist heat.<br>3. Adaptation of the thermal receptors often results in the decreased sensation of warmth.<br>4. The aquathermia pad should be replaced with a standard hot pack. | Answer: 3<br>Rationale: After about 15 minutes of heat application, the thermal receptors adapt to the temperature increase and the sensation of warmth is diminished. Clients often request that the temperature be increased because they do not feel the same amount of heat. This can lead to burns. There is no evidence that this client has increased thermal tolerance or that the rebound effect is occurring. It is not necessary to replace the aquathermia pad with a hot pack.<br>Evaluation<br>Physiologic integrity<br>Analysis<br>Learning Outcome 36.15 |
| **36.24** The nurse chooses to apply Montgomery ties to secure the dressing over a client's open abdominal wound that is being irrigated and packed every 8 hours. What nursing diagnosis does this intervention specifically support? | Answer: *Risk for Impaired Skin Integrity*<br>Rationale: Montgomery ties are specifically used to prevent skin injury from multiple dressing tape removal. This client is also at risk for other problems like infection, but the Montgomery ties are used specifically to protect the skin.<br>Diagnosis<br>Physiologic integrity<br>Analysis<br>Learning Outcome 36.14 |

# CHAPTER 37

| | |
|---|---|
| **37.1** The operative period that begins when the decision to have surgery is made and ends when the client is transferred to the operating table is which of the following?<br>1. Preoperative phase<br>2. Intraoperative phase<br>3. Postoperative phase<br>4. Perioperative phase | Answer: 1<br>Rationale: Option 2 begins when the client is transferred to the operating table and ends when the client is admitted to the PACU. Option 3 begins with the admission of the client to the postanesthesia area and ends when healing is complete.<br>Assessment<br>Physiological integrity<br>Comprehension<br>Learning Outcome 37.3 |
| **37.2** The nurse is caring for an 80-year-old client preparing for surgery. The nurse knows this client is at increased risk because:<br>1. The physiological deficits of aging increase the surgical risk for older adults.<br>2. The older adult has increased kidney function.<br>3. The older adult has an increase in sensory function.<br>4. The older adult will turn, cough, and deep breathe more effectively. | Answer: 1<br>Rationale: The older adult has more physiological deficits, such as decreased kidney function and decreased thirst, and is at greater risk for fluid and electrolyte imbalances.<br>Assessment<br>Physiological integrity<br>Comprehension<br>Learning Outcome 37.1 |

| | |
|---|---|
| **37.3** The nurse is preparing to complete a physical assessment before surgery. Which of the following should the nurse obtain? (Select all that apply.)<br>   1. Mini mental status<br>   2. Assessment of hearing<br>   3. Assessment of the respiratory system<br>   4. Gastrointestinal assessment<br>   5. Maintain NPO status | Answer: 1, 2, 3, 4<br>Rationale: Option 5 is a nursing intervention. It is not included in the physical assessment.<br>Assessment<br>Physiological integrity<br>Application<br>Learning Outcome 37.3 |
| **37.4** The nurse is preparing to conduct preoperative teaching. Which of the following should be included?<br>   1. Information related to what will happen to the client<br>   2. Referral of the client to the physician for any misconceptions the client may have<br>   3. The role of the nurse during surgery<br>   4. How to perform ADLs following surgery | Answer: 1<br>Rationale: The nurse should provide information including what will happen to the client, when, and what the client will experience. The nurse should clarify any misconceptions the client may have. The nurse should also explain the roles of the client and support people in preoperative preparation, the surgical procedure, and during the postoperative phase.<br>Implementation<br>Health promotion and maintenance<br>Application<br>Learning Outcome 37.6 |
| **37.5** The nurse is preparing a care plan for a client about to undergo surgery. Which of the following nursing diagnoses would take priority during the intraoperative phase of surgery?<br>   1. *Ineffective Protection*<br>   2. *Risk for Aspiration*<br>   3. *Impaired Skin Integrity*<br>   4. *Risk for Falls* | Answer: 2<br>Rationale: Although options 1 and 3 are appropriate for this client, the nurse should remember the ABCs when prioritizing. Option 4 is not appropriate for the intraoperative phase.<br>Diagnosis<br>Physiological integrity<br>Analysis<br>Learning Outcome 37.4 |
| **37.6** The nurse is preparing the skin of a client for surgery. The nurse knows the purpose of the surgical skin preparation is to:<br>   1. Sterilize the skin.<br>   2. Assess the surgical site before surgery.<br>   3. Reduce the risk of postoperative wound infection.<br>   4. Clean any moles the client may have. | Answer: 3<br>Rationale: The purpose of a surgical skin preparation is to reduce the risk of postoperative wound infection.<br>Implementation<br>Physiological integrity<br>Application<br>Learning Outcome 37.7 |
| **37.7** The client is preparing for an upper GI endoscopy. Which of the following types of anesthesia would the nurse anticipate the client to receive?<br>   1. Local anesthesia<br>   2. Spinal anesthesia<br>   3. Epidural anesthesia<br>   4. Conscious sedation | Answer: 4<br>Rationale: Conscious sedation is often used for procedures such as endoscopies and incision and drainage of abscesses.<br>Assessment<br>Physiological integrity<br>Analysis<br>Learning Outcome 37.8 |
| **37.8** The nurse is caring for a client in the recovery area. Which of the following positions should the unconscious client be assuming while in the immediate postanesthesia phase?<br>   1. Supine<br>   2. Prone<br>   3. Side-lying<br>   4. Supine with a pillow under the head | Answer: 3<br>Rationale: The unconscious client should be positioned on the side, with the face slightly down.<br>Implementation<br>Physiological integrity<br>Application<br>Learning Outcome 37.9 |

**37.9** The nurse is admitting a client to the medical-surgical unit following a cholecystectomy. Which intervention should the nurse perform first?
1. Level of consciousness
2. Dressing
3. Drains
4. Skin color

Answer: 1
Rationale: The nurse should assess the client's level of consciousness first.
Implementation
Physiological integrity
Application
Learning Outcome 37.9

**37.10** The nurse is caring for a client on the postoperative unit. Which of the following nursing diagnoses is the priority for this client?
1. *Self-Care Deficit*
2. *Disturbed Body Image*
3. *Ineffective Airway Clearance*
4. *Risk for Falls*

Answer: 3
Rationale: When prioritizing, the nurse should remember the ABCs. Airway should always be the priority.
Diagnosis
Physiological integrity
Application
Learning Outcome 37.4

**37.11** The nurse is assisting the client with turning, coughing, and deep breathing exercises. The client asks why this is important. How should the nurse reply?
1. "These exercises help prevent pneumonia."
2. "The doctor ordered the exercises."
3. "All surgical clients must do these exercises."
4. "These exercises prevent thrombophlebitis."

Answer: 1
Rationale: By increasing lung expansion and preventing accumulation of secretions, deep breathing helps prevent pneumonia and atelectasis.
Implementation
Physiological integrity
Analysis
Learning Outcome 37.6

**37.12** The nurse is assessing an abdominal wound in the postoperative period. Which of the following signs would alert the nurse to an infection?
1. Absence of bleeding
2. Edges warm to the touch
3. Edges well approximated
4. Sutures in place

Answer: 2
Rationale: If the wound becomes warm, red, and edematous, the nurse should suspect an infection and notify the physician.
Evaluation
Physiological integrity
Analysis
Learning Outcome 37.10

**37.13** The nurse is preparing a 23-year-old female client for surgery. The nurse would anticipate which of the following diagnostic tests to be ordered?
1. Pregnancy test
2. ECG
3. EKG
4. BUN and creatinine

Answer: 1
Rationale: A pregnancy test is done on all female clients of childbearing age.
Assessment
Physiological integrity
Analysis

**37.14** The nurse knows the surgical client is at risk for thrombophlebitis. Which of the following nursing interventions would the nurse implement to decrease the risk of this occurring?
1. Administer an anticoagulant
2. Cough every 2 hours
3. Intake and output every 2 hours
4. Early ambulation

Answer: 4
Rationale: Early ambulation, leg exercises, antiemboli stockings, SCDs, and adequate fluid intake are all interventions to reduce the risk for thrombophlebitis.
Implementation
Physiological integrity
Application
Learning Outcome 37.11

| | |
|---|---|
| **37.15** The nurse is preparing a client for a cholecystectomy. The purpose of this surgery is which of the following?<br>  1. Diagnostic<br>  2. Palliative<br>  3. Ablative<br>  4. Constructive | Answer: 3<br>Rationale: When the purpose of surgery is ablative, the diseased body part is removed.<br>Assessment<br>Physiological integrity<br>Analysis<br>Learning Outcome 37.1 |
| **37.16** The nurse is obtaining preoperative assessment data. Which of the following should be included? (Select all that apply.)<br>  1. Current health status<br>  2. Allergies<br>  3. Current medications<br>  4. Mental status<br>  5. Previous surgeries | Answer: 1, 2, 3, 4, 5<br>Rationale: All options should be obtained when completing a preoperative assessment.<br>Assessment<br>Health promotion and maintenance<br>Analysis<br>Learning Outcome 37.3 |
| **37.17** The nurse is caring for a client in the immediate postoperative period (PACU). Which of the following interventions would the nurse implement to reduce the risk of thrombophlebitis?<br>  1. Leg exercises<br>  2. Cough every 2 hours<br>  3. Ambulate every 2 hours<br>  4. Oxygen by mask | Answer: 1<br>Rationale: Leg exercises may be implemented in the PACU to help prevent thrombophlebitis. Options 2 and 4 are not implemented for thrombophlebitis. Option 3 may be implemented in the postoperative unit, but not in the immediate postoperative period.<br>Implementation<br>Physiological integrity<br>Application<br>Learning Outcome 37.9 |
| **37.18** The nurse is preparing to apply antiemboli stockings to a postoperative client. Which of the following should be done first, before applying the stockings?<br>  1. Measure the calf.<br>  2. Assess for circulatory problems.<br>  3. Assess the client's blood pressure.<br>  4. Clean the stockings. | Answer: 2<br>Rationale: Before applying antiemboli stockings, determine any potential or present circulatory problems.<br>Implementation<br>Physiological integrity<br>Application<br>Learning Outcome 37.11 |
| **37.19** The nurse has just inserted a nasogastric tube for gastric suction. Which of the following is the most reliable test for confirming tube placement?<br>  1. Place the stethoscope over the stomach and listen while inserting water into the tube for a swishing sound.<br>  2. Place the stethoscope over the stomach and listen while inserting air into the tube for a swishing sound.<br>  3. Aspirate stomach contents and check the acidity using a pH test strip.<br>  4. Connect the tube to suction and observe the contents. | Answer: 3<br>Rationale: Although option 2 is an option for confirming placement, option 3 is more reliable.<br>Evaluation<br>Physiological integrity<br>Application<br>Learning Outcome 37.12 |

**37.20** The nurse is preparing a 6-year-old child for a tonsillectomy. Which of the following strategies would the nurse use for teaching this client?
  1. Pamphlets
  2. Play
  3. Books
  4. Videotapes

Answer: 2
Rationale: Play is an effective teaching tool with children.
Implementation
Health promotion and maintenance
Application
Learning Outcome 37.6

# CHAPTER 38

**38.1** During review of admission data, the nurse learns that the new client has impairment of kinesthetic sensation. Which nursing intervention should be planned for this client?
  1. Use the clock face as a format for describing the position of food on meal trays.
  2. Provide all teaching materials in very large font.
  3. Ensure that the client has assistance when ambulating.
  4. Use only nonirritating soaps for bathing.

Answer: 3
Rationale: Kinesthetic sensation refers to the awareness of the position and movement of body parts. The client with impairment of this sensation may be prone to injury by falling and should be assisted when ambulating. There is nothing wrong with the client's eyesight or skin.
Planning
Physiologic integrity
Analysis
Learning Outcome 38.7

**38.2** The client has a long history of congestive heart failure and has been treated with large amounts of intravenous furosemide (Lasix). Based upon this history, for which sensory impairment would the nurse monitor this client?
  1. Loss of ability to taste
  2. Hearing loss
  3. Vision loss
  4. Loss of ability to smell

Answer: 2
Rationale: Furosemide (Lasix) can be ototoxic if taken over long periods of time. The nurse would monitor for hearing loss.
Assessment
Physiologic integrity
Application
Learning Outcome 38.2

**38.3** The middle-aged client reports having diabetes mellitus since childhood. Today's blood glucose reading is 180. Because of this history, the nurse would monitor this client for which sensory disturbance?
  1. Loss of ability to taste
  2. Hearing loss
  3. Vision loss
  4. Loss of ability to smell

Answer: 3
Rationale: Uncontrolled diabetes mellitus is a leading cause of blindness in the United States.
Assessment
Physiologic integrity
Application
Learning Outcome 38.2

**38.4** Which recent change, reported by a client's family, would indicate that the client's hearing ability is decreasing? (Select all that apply.)
  1. Inability to follow directions
  2. Mood swings
  3. Decreased appetite
  4. Complaints of dizziness
  5. Answering questions incorrectly

Answer: 1, 2, 4, 5
Rationale: The client who has difficulty hearing may have an inability to follow directions (because the directions were not heard), mood swings (because of the stress of not hearing well), and complaints of dizziness (associated with inner ear disturbances), or may answer questions incorrectly (because the question was not heard or was misinterpreted). Decrease in appetite is not generally associated with hearing loss.
Assessment
Physiologic integrity
Application
Learning Outcome 38.3

| | |
|---|---|
| **38.5** The nurse suspects that the client has a hearing disorder; however, the client denies not being able to hear. What initial assessment technique should the nurse employ?<br><br>1. Schedule a Weber and Rinne test.<br>2. Observe the client's interaction with family.<br>3. Use an otoscope to visualize the inner ear.<br>4. Confront the client with the nurse's suspicion. | Answer: 2<br>Rationale: The most telling of these options would be to observe the client's interactions with family. The nurse should assess for frequent requests to repeat, inattention to conversation, turning one ear to the conversation, and lip-reading. The Weber and Rinne test and use of an otoscope may be a part of assessment, but will not yield as much information as this simple observation. The client has already denied a hearing problem, so confronting the client with the nurse's suspicion will probably only serve to alienate the client from the nurse.<br>Assessment<br>Physiologic integrity<br>Application<br>Learning Outcome 38.4 |
| **38.6** The client has had a cerebral vascular accident (CVA) and now cannot speak. It is unclear from assessment if the client understands spoken words. What NANDA nursing diagnosis problem statement would be used for this client? | Answer: *Disturbed Sensory Perception: Auditory*<br>Rationale: This nursing diagnosis is used when the client exhibits a diminished, exaggerated, distorted, or impaired response to incoming stimuli.<br>Diagnosis<br>Physiologic integrity<br>Analysis<br>Learning Outcome 38.6 |
| **38.7** A hospitalized elderly man suddenly does not recognize his daughter and complains that his wife has not visited him, even though she has been dead for 5 years. The client was clear of mind and thought prior to hospitalization. What NANDA nursing diagnosis problem statement would be used for this client? | Answer: *Acute Confusion*<br>Rationale: The definition of acute confusion is: "the abrupt onset of a cluster of global, transient changes and disturbances in attention, cognition, psychomotor activity, level of consciousness, and/or sleep/wake cycle" (NANDA International, 2005-2006, p. 38).<br>Diagnosis<br>Physiologic integrity<br>Analysis<br>Learning Outcome 38.6 |
| **38.8** The nurse is providing education for the parents of a 7-month-old child who has just been diagnosed with a hearing loss. What guidance should the nurse provide?<br><br>1. Expect that your child will be enrolled in a special hearing intervention program immediately.<br>2. Keep your child in a quiet environment until additional testing is done.<br>3. Interventions to support hearing are not useful until the child is at least 9 months old.<br>4. Hearing loss is not serious until 1 year of age. | Answer: 1<br>Rationale: The Centers for Disease Control and Prevention recommend that children with hearing loss be enrolled in an intervention program by 6 months of age. The child should be stimulated with color, smells, body positions, and textures to develop compensatory mechanisms for the hearing loss. Hearing loss is serious from birth.<br>Implementation<br>Physiologic integrity<br>Application<br>Learning Outcome 38.7 |
| **38.9** The odor from a hospitalized client's draining wound permeates the room and is very overwhelming and distracting to the client and the staff. What intervention would be most helpful?<br><br>1. Spray the room routinely with a floral room spray.<br>2. Instill a vinegar solution into the wound.<br>3. Keep the wound dressing dry and clean.<br>4. Burn a candle in the room. | Answer: 3<br>Rationale: The best way to keep odors controlled is to keep the wound dressing dry and clean. Spraying the room with a floral spray will add to the sensory overload. Burning a candle will also add to the sensory overload, and burning candles are not safe in the hospital environment. Vinegar is not instilled into wounds.<br>Implementation<br>Physiologic integrity<br>Application<br>Learning Outcome 38.2 |

**38.10** The nurse is assisting a visually impaired client with ambulation. How should the nurse proceed with this intervention?

1. Walk slightly behind the client.
2. Walk 1 foot in front of the client.
3. Walk on the right side of the client.
4. Walk on the left side of the client.

Answer: 2
Rationale: The nurse should walk about 1 foot in front of the client, offering the client an arm. The side the nurse walks on will depend upon the preference of the client.
Implementation
Physiologic integrity
Application
Learning Outcome 38.7

**38.11** An older client has become very confused since being hospitalized earlier in the week. Prior to this illness, the client exhibited clear thought processing and was able to maintain an independent lifestyle. How would the nurse document this mental state?

1. As reversible confusion
2. As sundown syndrome
3. As delirium
4. As dementia

Answer: 3
Rationale: Delirium is acute confusion caused by illness, medication, or a change in environment and is the appropriate documentation for this client. Dementia is chronic confusion with symptoms that are gradual in onset and are irreversible. The other options do not reflect proper documentation of this client's situation.
Assessment
Physiologic integrity
Analysis
Learning Outcome 38.4

**38.12** A client who has had a traumatic brain injury is physiologically stable but remains in a coma. Caregivers are participating in a coma stimulation program with this client. Which action is correct for this situation?

1. Provide visual and tactile stimulation concurrently with auditory background.
2. Limit stimulation to a 5- to 10-minute session.
3. Provide continuous auditory stimulation through music tapes.
4. Ensure the client has sleep/rest periods alternating with sensory stimulation.

Answer: 4
Rationale: These coma stimulation programs are a means of providing sensory stimulation to promote brain recovery. Stimulation should be delivered in a quiet environment, should be limited to 30- to 45-minute sessions, and should be done episodically throughout the day, not continuously. Periods of sleep/rest should be alternated with the sensory stimuli.
Planning
Physiologic integrity
Application
Learning Outcome 38.9

**38.13** The nurse is assessing a client who was just brought to the emergency department. The client can be aroused only with extreme or repeated stimuli. How should the nurse describe this client in a report to the ED physician?

1. Somnolent
2. Disoriented
3. Comatose
4. Semicomatose

Answer: 4
Rationale: Since this client can be aroused with extreme stimuli or repeated stimuli, the correct description is semicomatose. The comatose client is not arousable. The somnolent client is very drowsy, but will respond to stimuli. A disoriented client is alert, but not oriented to time, place, or person.
Assessment
Physiologic integrity
Application
Learning Outcome 38.4

**38.14** The nurse is planning care for a client who is experiencing dementia. What essential concept should the nurse consider for this planning?

1. Background noise like music will keep this client calm.
2. Activities should be scheduled at the same time each day.
3. Pain mediation will increase dementia.
4. It is important to talk with the client throughout procedures.

Answer: 2
Rationale: The client with dementia benefits from a routine schedule of activities. The client typically is better oriented when it is quiet. Pain should be controlled. Procedures should be explained in direct, clearly understandable terms, but the nurse should avoid "chatter."
Planning
Psychosocial integrity
Application
Learning Outcome 38.6

**38.15** The client who has the medical diagnosis of Alzheimer's disease is confused and has difficulty interpreting environmental stimuli. Which nursing diagnosis problem statement most accurately describes this client's situation?

    1. *Acute Confusion*
    2. *Altered Role Performance*
    3. *Disturbed Sensory Perception*
    4. *Disturbed Thought Processes*

Answer: 4
Rationale: Since this client has dementia, which interferes with the ability to interpret stimuli, the correct diagnosis problem statement is *Disturbed Thought Processes. Disturbed Sensory Perception* is more useful with the client who has difficulty related to sensory input (perception). Clients with Alzheimer's disease are more likely to exhibit chronic confusion. There is no evidence to support *Altered Role Performance*.
Diagnosis
Physiologic integrity
Analysis
Learning Outcome 38.6

---

**38.16** Which assessment findings would the nurse interpret as being possible signs of sensory overload in a hospitalized client? (Select all that apply.)

    1. Sleeplessness
    2. Anxiety
    3. Apathy
    4. Racing thoughts
    5. Somatic complaints

Answer: 1, 2, 4
Rationale: Sleeplessness, anxiety, and racing thoughts are often indicators of sensory overload. Apathy and somatic complaints are more associated with sensory deprivation.
Assessment
Physiologic integrity
Application
Learning Outcome 38.4

---

**38.17** The client is being treated in an intensive care unit for a complicated myocardial infarction. The client's family lives 150 miles away and is unable to visit. Is this client at greater risk for sensory overload or sensory deprivation?

Answer: Sensory overload
Rationale: Even though the client is separated from family, the risk for sensory overload is greater. This risk is associated with care in the intensive care unit and the seriousness of illness (complicated myocardial infarction).
Planning
Psychosocial integrity
Analysis
Learning Outcome 38.5

---

**38.18** The nurse is caring for a client who has difficulty hearing conversation. What intervention should the nurse implement?

    1. Use short phrases.
    2. Overarticulate words.
    3. Vary the volume of voice through sentences.
    4. Face the client during conversation.

Answer: 4
Rationale: The best intervention is to face the client during conversation so that the client can employ any lip-reading skills. The nurse should use longer phrases that more completely explain concepts. Overarticulation of words makes them difficult to lip-read. The volume of voice should be consistent.
Implementation
Physiologic integrity
Application
Learning Outcome 38.7

---

**38.19** The client who had a traumatic brain injury last week is now persistently unconscious and is being cared for in the intensive care unit. The family asks when attempts to stimulate the client will begin. What is the nurse's best answer?

    1. "There is little hope of improvement from persistently unconscious states."
    2. "Attempts begin while the client is still in the ICU."
    3. "Stimulation will not begin until transfer to a rehabilitation unit."
    4. "The stimulation process will begin when the client is physiologically stable."

Answer: 2
Rationale: Current research indicates that stimulation efforts should begin immediately. The nurse should not discourage hope in this family.
Implementation
Physiologic integrity
Application
Learning Outcome 38.9

---

**38.20** Which health care professionals have the greatest control over the level of sensory input in the hospital?
1. Physicians
2. Administrators
3. Nurses
4. Planners

Answer: 3
Rationale: Nurses have the greatest amount of control over the level of sensory input in the hospital. Nurses can decrease sensory overload by controlling lights, noise, odors, and pain. Nurses can also increase sensory input by stimulating the client as appropriate. Administrators, planners, and physicians are not at the bedside as much as nurses.
Implementation
Physiologic integrity
Application
Learning Outcome 38.7

# CHAPTER 39

**39.1** Which statement, made by the client, would indicate a "me-centered" self-concept?
1. "I couldn't stand to disappoint my parents."
2. "My sister is so much smarter than I am."
3. "My future is based on the decisions I make today."
4. "The world has always been against people like me."

Answer: 3
Rationale: Individuals with a positive self-concept are me-centered and value how they perceive themselves over the opinions of others and have learned to depend on themselves. This is reflected in the statement, "My future is based on the decisions I make today." Other-centered persons have a high need for the approval of others and evaluate themselves in regard to others' opinions. They also compare themselves with others and often believe the world is against them. This outward focus results in a poorer self-concept.
Assessment
Psychosocial integrity
Analysis
Learning Outcome 39.1

**39.2** The charge nurse has instituted a series of classes on self-concept development for staff nurses. Why is it important that the classes include information to improve the nurses' self-concept as well as information to use with clients?
1. The nurse's self-concept is more important than the client's.
2. Poor self-concept is the number-one reason for nursing burnout.
3. Nurses with positive self-concept are better able to help clients.
4. Nurses with poor self-concept are more likely to make errors.

Answer: 3
Rationale: Nurses who have positive self-concept are better prepared to assist clients with their own understanding of needs, desires, feelings, and conflicts. The nurse's self-concept is not more important than the client's, but it is of equal importance in the nurse–client relationship. There is no evidence that nurses with poor self-concept burn out earlier or make more errors than nurses with good self-concept.
Planning
Psychosocial integrity
Application
Learning Outcome 39.1

**39.3** The newly graduated nurse is working with a mentor who has been a nurse for 25 years. The mentor tells the new graduate, "I learn something new about nursing every day." What does this indicate about the mentor's self-awareness?
1. This nurse is not very self-aware.
2. The mentor's self-awareness is behind normal development.
3. Since this mentor has been a nurse for so long, self-awareness is no longer an important issue.
4. Since self-awareness is never complete, this nurse is demonstrating desirable behavior.

Answer: 4
Rationale: Self-awareness takes time and energy and is never completed. Although this mentor has been a nurse for 25 years, there is still room for growth and development of self-awareness. This nurse is demonstrating desirable behavior in that there is still intellectual humility and a desire to learn.
Assessment
Psychosocial integrity
Application
Learning Outcome 39.1

| | |
|---|---|
| **39.4** A nursing student is at the midpoint of a clinical rotation in which the student has had problems getting along with the clinical instructor. The student has just received an evaluation that indicates difficulties with time management and prioritization in the care of clients. How should the student react to this input?<br>   1. Take the feedback seriously and use it to guide personal growth.<br>   2. Blame the student–faculty relationship as the basis of the evaluation.<br>   3. Dismiss the evaluation as invalid.<br>   4. Consider the feedback carefully but not change practice patterns. | Answer: 1<br>Rationale: The student should take the feedback seriously and use it to guide personal growth. Issues with time management and prioritization are common with students and should be addressed. Considering the feedback but not using it to change personal practice, dismissing the feedback, or blaming the student–faculty relationship for the poor review reflects projection of the student's beliefs onto the situation. The student should introspectively look at the situation and use it for growth.<br>Planning<br>Psychosocial integrity<br>Analysis<br>Learning Outcome 39.3 |
| **39.5** Place the following four developmental tasks in order according to Erikson's stages of psychosocial development.<br>a. Expressing one's own opinion<br>b. Guiding others<br>c. Asserting independence<br>d. Working well with others<br>   1. a, d, c, b<br>   2. a, b, c, d<br>   3. c, a, d, b<br>   4. d, c, a, b | Answer: 1<br>Rationale: Expressing one's own opinion is a behavior in the infancy: trust vs. mistrust stage. Working well with others is a behavior in the early school years: industry vs. inferiority stage. Asserting independence is a behavior in the adolescence: identity vs. role confusion stage. Guiding others is a behavior in the middle-aged adults: generativity vs. stagnation stage.<br>Assessment<br>Psychosocial integrity<br>Analysis<br>Learning Outcome 39.2 |
| **39.6** The nurse is developing a tool to document self-concept development among chronically ill children. Included in this tool should be areas to document development in personal identity, body image, role performance/relationships, and _____. | Answer: self-esteem<br>Rationale: When assessing the development of self-concept, the nurse focuses on personal identity, body image, role performance/relationships, and self-esteem. A tool to document this assessment should include all four areas.<br>Assessment<br>Psychosocial integrity<br>Application<br>Learning Outcome 39.3 |
| **39.7** The adolescent male client who weighs 100 pounds tells the nurse that he is considering taking "some herbal stuff" to increase his muscle mass and make him stronger. The nurse should interpret this statement as an indication that this client has which of the following?<br>   1. A strong need for admiration<br>   2. Serious problems with logical thinking<br>   3. Incongruence between reality and ideal self<br>   4. The need for referral to a psychologist | Answer: 3<br>Rationale: The nurse can determine that there is incongruence between reality and this client's ideal self. Any further inferences from these data would not be based on the facts presented in this scenario. While all three other options may be true, further assessment is required.<br>Assessment<br>Psychosocial integrity<br>Analysis<br>Learning Outcome 39.5 |

| **39.8** During assessment, the client frequently refers to her Native American heritage. The nurse assesses that this heritage is a strong part of which of the following?<br>   1. Client's personal identity<br>   2. Client's body image<br>   3. Client's role-performance<br>   4. Client's self-esteem | Answer: 1<br>Rationale: Self-concept consists of personal identity, body image, role-performance, and self-esteem. Personal identity consists of name, sex, age, race, ethnic origin or culture, occupation or roles, talents, and other situational characteristics. Body image is perception of size, appearance, and functioning of the body. Role-performance relates to how a person fulfills his or her own expectations of role. Self-esteem is a judgment of one's own worth.<br>Diagnosis<br>Psychosocial integrity<br>Application<br>Learning Outcome 39.3 |
| --- | --- |
| **39.9** A client who has recently lost the 75 pounds recommended by his physician continues to dress in loose, baggy clothing and frequently refers to himself as "fat." The nurse interprets this finding as most likely indicating which of the following?<br>   1. Role confusion<br>   2. Body image disturbance<br>   3. Fear of success<br>   4. Lack of education | Answer: 2<br>Rationale: The most likely interpretation of this finding is that the client continues to see himself as fat, which is a body image disturbance. Role confusion would be indicated if the client did not have a clear indication of what role he was supposed to fulfill in his life or how to fulfill his chosen role. Fear of success and lack of education are possibilities, but the nurse would need more data to come to this conclusion.<br>Diagnosis<br>Psychosocial integrity<br>Analysis<br>Learning Outcome 39.4 |
| **39.10** A rare malignancy will require the amputation of an adolescent client's leg. The client refuses the surgery, stating: "I would rather die than have my leg amputated." The nurse plans future interventions based upon which of the following?<br>   1. The knowledge that adolescents are very concerned about body image<br>   2. Concern about need for education regarding the danger of delaying surgery<br>   3. The fact that the parents will have the ultimate decision about surgery<br>   4. Ability of the adolescent to understand medical terminology | Answer: 1<br>Rationale: Adolescents are very concerned about body image and will make decisions based upon peer or media opinion even if it puts their health at risk. The nurse's further interventions should be planned with this thought in mind. While there may be a problem with the client understanding medical terminology, a need for further education, and the fact that the parents will make the ultimate decision, the issues regarding the adolescent's focus on body image should be taken into consideration with every new intervention.<br>Planning<br>Psychosocial integrity<br>Analysis<br>Learning Outcome 39.4 |
| **39.11** Which statement, made by a new mother, would indicate to the nurse that there is potential for lowered self-esteem due to role ambiguity?<br>   1. "I don't know if I know how to be a mom."<br>   2. "My husband will be a stay-at-home dad while I work."<br>   3. "I'm so disappointed that this baby is not a girl."<br>   4. "I haven't even finished the baby's room." | Answer: 1<br>Rationale: Role ambiguity occurs when expectations are unclear or a person does not know how to fulfill the role. In this case, the clearest indication of role ambiguity is "I don't know if I know how to be a mom." Disappointment that the baby is not a girl or not having the room finished may indicate other problems, but they are not specific to role ambiguity. Even though the husband staying at home while the mother works may not be the expected role assignment, there is no ambiguity in the arrangement.<br>Diagnosis<br>Psychosocial integrity<br>Application<br>Learning Outcome 39.4 |

| | |
|---|---|
| **39.12** The nurse's functional self-esteem is very low after a week of taking care of several clients who have unexpectedly died. What fact about self-esteem should this nurse remember?<br><br>1. Even during bad times, functional self-esteem will not regress to a level lower than basic self-esteem.<br>2. It is important to focus on errors that contributed to client death.<br>3. Functional self-esteem develops early in life and shouldn't change related to situational problems.<br>4. It is normal for self-esteem to fluctuate related to daily events and problems. | Answer: 4<br>Rationale: It is normal for the adult's functional self-esteem to fluctuate related to daily events and problems. Functional self-esteem can exceed basic self-esteem or can regress to a level lower than basic self-esteem. While reflection on actions is important to prevent further errors, the nurse should not focus on the bad things that have happened.<br>Assessment<br>Psychosocial integrity<br>Analysis<br>Learning Outcome 39.4 |
| **39.13** Which nursing intervention would be helpful when caring for a client who has negative self-esteem?<br><br>1. Find a way to praise the client during each encounter.<br>2. Design a series of "small successes" for the client.<br>3. Correct the client when negativity arises.<br>4. Tell the client how much easier life would be with positive self-esteem. | Answer: 2<br>Rationale: Clients who have negative self-esteem may have a history of failures and disappointments. Designing a series of "small successes" for the client will help foster a more positive attitude. Correcting the client when negativity arises puts the client in a childlike role and will not encourage positive self-esteem. The client likely already knows how much better life would be with positive self-esteem, so reiterating that fact would not be helpful.<br>Implementation<br>Psychosocial integrity<br>Application<br>Learning Outcome 39.8 |
| **39.14** The nurse is conducting a thorough psychosocial assessment of a client who presents with complaints of fatigue, tearfulness, and relationship difficulties. What action by the nurse would support accurate assessment?<br><br>1. Take detailed notes to record client responses.<br>2. Ask as many questions as possible to explore all areas of concern.<br>3. Start the interview by asking a series of yes/no questions.<br>4. Investigate the client's culture prior to the interview. | Answer: 4<br>Rationale: The nurse should consider how the client's behaviors are influenced by culture. In order to understand what is being said or seen, the nurse should investigate the client's culture prior to the interview. Take minimal notes and ask only as many questions as necessary to avoid creating concern that confidential material is being recorded. Questions asked should be open-ended, not yes/no.<br>Implementation<br>Psychosocial integrity<br>Application<br>Learning Outcome 39.7 |
| **39.15** Which statement should the nurse make first when assessing the client's self-concept?<br><br>1. Describe yourself as a person.<br>2. Tell me about your family.<br>3. Describe what you do when you have free time.<br>4. Tell me about the work you do. | Answer: 1<br>Rationale: The first information the nurse gathers when assessing self-concept should focus on the client's personal identity ("Describe yourself as a person"). "Tell me about your family" assesses role performance. "What do you do when you have free time" and "what kind of work do you do" assess work and social roles.<br>Assessment<br>Psychosocial integrity<br>Application<br>Learning Outcome 39.5 |

| | |
|---|---|
| **39.16** During the assessment interview, the client is quiet and answers questions only minimally. What action should the nurse take in regard to this apparent unwillingness to share information?<br><br>1. Document that the client is not cooperative.<br>2. Consider any cultural implications of these actions.<br>3. Assume that the client has something to hide.<br>4. Ask another nurse to sit in on the next interview attempt. | Answer: 2<br>Rationale: The nurse should always consider that there could be a cultural implication to behavior. Documenting that the client is not cooperative or that there is something to hide labels the client for all other health care provider interactions. Asking a second nurse to sit in on the next interview may make the client feel more intimidated.<br>Implementation<br>Psychosocial integrity<br>Application<br>Learning Outcome 39.5 |
| **39.17** Which common characteristic of persons with low self-esteem can make it difficult for the nurse to effectively intervene?<br><br>1. They have low motivation to improve.<br>2. They focus on their problems.<br>3. They express disinterest in working on improvement.<br>4. They are seldom satisfied with their personal situation. | Answer: 2<br>Rationale: Clients with low self-esteem often have difficulty identifying strengths and focus more on their limitations and problems. There is no evidence to support that they are dissatisfied with their current lives, are not motivated to improve, or are disinterested in working on improvement once their focus can be shifted from the negative to a more positive outlook.<br>Assessment<br>Psychosocial integrity<br>Analysis<br>Learning Outcome 39.5 |
| **39.18** The nurse is assisting a client in setting goals as a strategy to reinforce strengths. What intervention should the nurse employ?<br><br>1. Encourage the client to set attainable goals, even if small.<br>2. Help the client choose a significant goal, even if it is time consuming.<br>3. Devise a set of goals from which the client can pick.<br>4. Advise the client to avoid goals that will require too much effort. | Answer: 1<br>Rationale: When attempting to reinforce client strengths, it is important to help the client set attainable goals, even if the goals are small at first. If the goal is too long range, the client may lose sight of the goal before it is attained. However, the goal should not be so effortless that it is not important to the client. Devising goals should be a team effort between the client, significant others, and the nurse.<br>Planning<br>Psychosocial integrity<br>Application<br>Learning Outcome 39.7 |
| **39.19** The nurse and client had set the following expected outcome: "At the next clinic visit, the client will report participation in three activities to increase self-esteem." At today's visit, the client is unable to meet the stated outcome. What should be the nurse's next action?<br><br>1. Explore the possible reasons for not meeting the outcome.<br>2. Reevaluate the accuracy of the outcome statement.<br>3. Collaborate with the client to write a new expected outcome.<br>4. Identify new interventions to help the client achieve the outcome. | Answer: 1<br>Rationale: The nurse's first action should be to explore possible reasons the outcome was not met. Depending upon the results of that investigation, the nurse may need to work with the client to revise or write a new expected outcome or to identify new interventions to move the client toward the expected outcome. Without first identifying why the outcome was not met, there is no direction to further planning or revision.<br>Evaluation<br>Psychosocial integrity<br>Application<br>Learning Outcome 39.7 |

**39.20** The client's wife complains to the nurse that it seems as if her husband is not making much progress in developing a more positive self-esteem. What statement by the nurse would be appropriate?

1. "Most clients make quicker progress than your husband has made."
2. "Self-esteem work takes time and is not easily evaluated."
3. "What have you done to help your husband with this work?"
4. "Do you think that your husband is really trying?"

Answer: 2

Rationale: This wife is expressing concern about her husband's progress, so it would be appropriate to let her know that self-esteem work takes time and that improvement is sometimes not easy to evaluate. It is not appropriate to reinforce her feelings by comparing her husband to other clients. It is not appropriate to make her feel that she is being blamed for the slowness by asking what she has done to help her husband. It is not appropriate to instill doubt in her mind by asking if she thinks her husband is really trying.

Implementation
Psychosocial integrity
Application
Learning Outcome 39.7

---

**39.21** The nurse is teaching a new parents class about self-esteem development in infants. Which information should be included?

1. If the baby awakens at night, let him cry for a few minutes before responding.
2. Keep the baby on a 3-hour feeding schedule, even if it means awakening him.
3. Respond to the baby's needs promptly and consistently.
4. Use firm, loving discipline with the baby from the beginning.

Answer: 3

Rationale: In order to develop self-esteem in their baby, parents should be taught to respond to the baby's needs promptly and consistently. The baby should not be allowed to cry for extended periods of time at this age. A 3-hour feeding schedule might work for some babies, but it should not be presented as the goal to a group of new parents because every baby is different. Babies do not need or respond to discipline.

Planning
Psychosocial integrity
Analysis
Learning Outcome 39.8

---

**39.22** Parents confide to the nurse that they are concerned about their preschooler because she demands to pick out her own clothes in the morning. The parents are concerned that their day-care workers may think they are negligent parents because their daughter often wears unmatched clothing. What should be the nurse's response to this concern?

1. "Don't worry, day-care workers are accustomed to that sort of thing."
2. "Your daughter is normal, and is just practicing skills she will need later in life."
3. "I am glad you brought that to our attention. I will make a note for her pediatrician."
4. "You should have better control of your daughter now if you have any hope of controlling her at sixteen."

Answer: 2

Rationale: The nurse should accept that the parents are concerned and then tell them that this is normal behavior at this age. Preschoolers often begin to exert independence and to "practice" picking out clothing, cooking with play toys, and parenting dolls. Even though day-care workers are accustomed to this stage, the option given discounts the parents' worry and does not give them any information that their daughter is normal. Since this is a normal behavior, there are no issues about controlling their daughter as she gets older. The only reason to notify the pediatrician would be to report this normal behavior.

Implementation
Psychosocial integrity
Application
Learning Outcome 39.8

---

**39.23** The parents of an adolescent report that their child has recently gotten into trouble at school for cheating on an examination and has been barred from participating in a school trip as a consequence of that action. They ask for the nurse's

Answer: 4

Rationale: One of the most important tasks of adolescence and a prime way to develop self-esteem is to take responsibility and to live with the consequences of actions. The nurse does need to respond to these parents, even though the nurse may not have enough information to form an opinion about the situation. Since the nurse does not have all the information, it would be a mistake to agree that the punishment is excessive or that it should be more extensive.

professional opinion about the suitability of the punishment. Which answer best supports self-esteem development in this adolescent?

1. "I think the punishment may be excessive. Have you talked with the school officials about the incident?"
2. "Since my expertise is in health, I really can't respond to your question."
3. "Honesty and respect for authorities is important. I am surprised that the punishment is not more extensive."
4. "Living with the consequences of your actions is a way to help the adolescent develop good self-esteem."

Implementation
Psychosocial integrity
Analysis
Learning Outcome 39.8

---

**39.24** The nurse working in a long-term care facility notices that one of the residents has had a recent decline in self-esteem. What intervention would be appropriate for this resident?

1. Ask the resident for advice in setting up an activity in the dayroom.
2. Keep the resident too busy to dwell in the past.
3. Don't allow the resident to talk about minor concerns.
4. Meet with the social worker to plan all of the client's care.

Answer: 1
Rationale: Asking the client for advice in setting up an activity in the dayroom validates the client's usefulness and worth. Reminiscence therapy is a standard therapy used with older clients. The nurse and staff should listen carefully to client concerns. Clients should be encouraged to be a part of the planning of their care.
Implementation
Psychosocial integrity
Application
Learning Outcome 39.7

---

# CHAPTER 40

**40.1** During discussion of family, the client speaks about an adult son who is a practicing homosexual. The client expresses concern about this son, stating: "I am so worried about him and I know he is going to hell." What is the most important fact for the nurse to consider in formulating a response to this client's concern?

1. Normal sexuality is described as whatever behaviors give pleasure and satisfaction to those adults involved.
2. Since alternative lifestyles are now so well accepted in society, this parent should not feel so much concern.
3. What constitutes normal sexual expression varies among cultures and religions.
4. Sexual development is genetically determined and not affected by environment.

Answer: 3
Rationale: This nurse should remember that culture and religion have a big impact upon what a person believes to be normal sexual behavior. Even though many consider whatever activity gives pleasure and satisfaction to the involved adults to be normal, some cultures and religions do not hold that belief. While alternative lifestyles are well accepted in some cultures, apparently that is not true in this parent's belief patterns. Sexual development has both genetic and environmental components.
Planning
Psychosocial integrity
Analysis
Learning Outcome 40.3

**40.2** The parent of a 20-month-old is very concerned because the baby touches the genital area during diaper changes. How should the nurse respond to this concern?

1. At 20 months this touching is not a sexual experience.
2. Masturbation to orgasm is common and normal at this age.
3. Genital stimulation should not be occurring until the age of 2½ or 3.
4. Babies are sexual beings, but this activity should be discouraged.

Answer: 1
Rationale: At 20 months, exploration and touching of the genital area is no different than exploration and touching of fingers and toes. This touching is not considered a sexual experience. Masturbation to orgasm can occur as early as age 3, although males do not ejaculate until after puberty. At around age 2½ or 3 the child begins to differentiate between genital differences and to identify as a male or female. There is no need to discourage genital exploration at 20 months.
Implementation
Health promotion and maintenance
Application
Learning Outcome 40.1

**40.3** The nurse is teaching a class on body development to a group of middle school girls. One of the girls asks about using tampons for sanitary protection during menstruation. What advice should the nurse include?

1. Tampons should not be used until the menstrual cycle is well established, usually 2 to 3 years after the first period occurs.
2. Super absorbent tampons should be used at night to protect from overflow accidents.
3. Tampons should be alternated with sanitary pads to help decrease infection.
4. Tampons should be changed at least every 8 hours.

Answer: 3
Rationale: The nurse should teach these girls to alternate tampons with sanitary pads to decrease infection. There is no evidence of need to delay tampon use. Sanitary pads, not tampons, should be used at night. Tampons should be changed more frequently than every 8 hours to prevent infection and odor.
Implementation
Health promotion and maintenance
Application
Learning Outcome 40.1

**40.4** The nurse is developing strategies for the relief of menstrual cramping to teach a group of young women. What should be the focus of these strategies?

1. Increase of blood flow to the uterine muscle
2. Avoidance of uterine contraction
3. Minimization of menstrual flow
4. Decrease in estrogen production

Answer: 1
Rationale: Menstrual cramping is a result of the muscle ischemia that occurs when the client experiences powerful uterine contractions. Increase of blood flow to the uterine muscle through rest, some exercises, application of heat to the abdomen, and presence of milder uterine contractions (such as those associated with orgasm) can decrease pain and cramping. There is no connection between the actual amount of flow and pain. Estrogen production should follow normal patterns and should not be altered.
Planning
Health promotion and maintenance
Analysis
Learning Outcome 40.1

**40.5** During a routine physical, an 11-year-old tells the nurse that many students in school are "doing it." How should the nurse respond to this statement?

1. Tell the client to talk with parents about sexual matters.
2. Ask what "doing it" means to this client.
3. State that sexual activity is not appropriate at age 11.
4. Stay silent and wait for the client to continue the discussion.

Answer: 2
Rationale: The nurse should ask what "doing it" means to this 11-year-old client. It is important that the nurse and the client are talking about the same thing before additional information is shared. An 11-year-old may feel uneasy about discussing sexual matters with parents, so this statement to the nurse may be the only opportunity to discuss concerns. This is not the time to tell the client about what is or is not appropriate, it is the time to make the client feel comfortable talking with the nurse. Staying silent may make the client feel as if the nurse is disapproving and would adversely affect the client's comfort level.
Implementation
Health promotion and maintenance
Application
Learning Outcome 40.1

**40.6** The 30-year-old single mother of a second-grade child has to make a decision regarding the teacher her child will have in third grade and asks the nurse for advice. All other variables being equal, which choice is best?

1. A woman with 35 years of teaching experience
2. A man who is 40 years old
3. A newly graduated 22-year-old man
4. A 30-year-old woman

Answer: 2
Rationale: If all other variables are equal, the best choice is the 40-year-old male as this child needs role modeling from both females (the mother) and males (this teacher).
Implementation
Health promotion and maintenance
Application
Learning Outcome 40.1

**40.7** Which statement, made by a postmenopausal woman, would the nurse evaluate as indicating the need for further assessment?

1. "For some reason, I have more sexual desire than ever."
2. "I use water-soluble lubricant to treat my vaginal dryness."
3. "I am so glad that I don't need to worry about sex anymore."
4. "Sex certainly takes longer than it used to, but I'm getting used to that."

Answer: 3
Rationale: The nurse would further assess the client who made the statement, "I am so glad that I don't need to worry about sex anymore." This statement is unclear. Does it mean that the client is glad not to have to engage in sex anymore or does it mean that she will not have to worry about getting pregnant anymore? The other statements reflect normal changes associated with aging and healthy responses to those changes.
Evaluation
Health promotion and maintenance
Application
Learning Outcome 40.1

**40.8** A research article the nurse is reading discusses the prevalence of androgyny in persons 20 to 30 years old. The nurse understands which of the following about androgynous persons?

1. They do not limit behaviors to one gender over the other.
2. They are attracted to people of the same gender.
3. They often repress their sexual feelings.
4. They hold rigid stereotyped gender role expectations.

Answer: 1
Rationale: Androgyny means flexibility in gender roles. The nurse applies this information to identify that androgynous persons do not limit behaviors to one gender over the other, so they do not hold rigid gender role expectations. Androgyny has nothing to do with gender attraction or repression of sexual feelings.
Assessment
Health promotion and maintenance
Application
Learning Outcome 40.3

**40.9** The client experienced female circumcision as a puberty ritual while living in Africa as a child. What condition should the nurse monitor the client for as an adult?

1. Early menopause
2. Increased menstrual flow
3. Chronic urinary tract infection
4. Tendency for postpartum hemorrhage

Answer: 3
Rationale: Female circumcision increases the possibility that the client will have chronic urinary tract infection. There is no indication that early menopause, increased menstrual flow, or tendency for postpartum hemorrhage is a result of female circumcision.
Planning
Physiologic integrity
Application
Learning Outcome 40.4

**40.10** The 45-year-old client reports that she has no interest in sex and that she and her husband have not had intercourse in 16 years. How does the nurse interpret these assessment data?

1. This couple is experiencing from sexual dysfunction.
2. The woman's lack of sexual desire has resulted in impotence in her husband.

Answer: 3
Rationale: If both members of a couple have the same lack of desire and they are comfortable, there is likely no problem with the couple's sexuality. There is no evidence that the wife's lack of desire has resulted in sexual impotence in her husband, but further assessment might be in order. This situation is unnatural in the predominant North American culture, but if both members of the couple are comfortable with the relationship, no dysfunction is present.
Diagnosis
Health promotion and maintenance
Analysis
Learning Outcome 40.4

3.  If both partners share the same lack of desire, there is often not a problem.
4.  This situation is so unnatural, that some dysfunction is present.

---

**40.11** A client is concerned because he was unable to achieve an erection during his last sexual encounter with his wife. He tells the nurse that he has worried about becoming impotent since he had a sexually transmitted infection as a young adult. What is the nurse's best response to this client's concerns?

1.  Sexually transmitted infections may result in sexual problems in adults.
2.  Erectile dysfunction is the correct term for the inability to achieve or sustain an erection.
3.  An occasional incident like this is normal and common and there is no reason to be concerned.
4.  The medical diagnosis of erectile dysfunction is not made until the man has erection difficulties in 25% or more of his interactions.

Answer: 3
Rationale: This client is concerned about his masculinity and sexual abilities. The correct answer at this point is to tell him that it is common and normal for men to experience occasional erectile difficulties. The other options are also true, but they do not serve to alleviate the client's concerns. If the client continues to have difficulties achieving or sustaining an erection, further investigation should take place. Simply correcting the client's use of medical terminology does not address his concerns.
Implementation
Health promotion and maintenance
Analysis
Learning Outcome 40.6

---

**40.12** The nurse is preparing for a pelvic physical examination of a woman who has been medically diagnosed with vaginismus. What equipment should the nurse obtain for this examination?

1.  Culture tubes to assess expected vaginal infection
2.  Extra cleaning supplies to remove thick external secretions
3.  Smaller than normal vaginal speculums
4.  Equipment for preexamination douche

Answer: 3
Rationale: Clients with vaginismus experience involuntary spasm of the outer one-third of the vaginal muscles. This spasm makes internal examination, tampon use, and intercourse difficult. Use of smaller than normal vaginal speculums may make examination easier. There is no increased risk of vaginal infection or need for douche or extra cleaning.
Planning
Safe, effective care environment
Application
Learning Outcome 40.6

---

**40.13** There is disagreement among the nursing unit staff regarding how much sexual history should be included in adult admission history and physicals. What standard is generally the most applicable?

1.  A complete sexual history must be included in the admission history and physicals.
2.  Sexual information should be pursued only if the client's chief complaint indicates possible sexual dysfunction.
3.  Sexual assessment should be done by the physician and not repeated by the nurse.
4.  The amount of sexual information taken will vary on a case-by-case basis.

Answer: 4
Rationale: The amount of sexual information taken will vary on a case-by-case basis. The nurse can open the conversation by asking open-ended questions. This topic should be addressed only after rapport has been established. While the nurse should be sensitive about repeating questions that have already been asked, the client may be more forthcoming with information with the nurse.
Assessment
Health promotion and maintenance
Application
Learning Outcome 40.7

---

**40.14** The mother of a 5-year-old tells the nurse that her daughter has always been closer to her than to her husband. The mother expresses concern that, over the last 2 months, the little girl wants to spend all of her time with her father instead of with the mother. The nurse recognizes that this behavior:

1. May indicate sexual abuse by the father and should be further investigated.
2. Is a normal expectation of a preschooler developing sexuality.
3. Indicates that the girl is overidentifying with the male gender.
4. Can be a sign of precocious puberty and should be monitored.

Answer: 2
Rationale: A part of the normal sexual development of a preschooler is a time in which the child focuses love on the parent of the other gender. The same-gender parent may feel excluded during this time, but can be assured that the behavior is normal. The nurse would be concerned if this attention to the father is accompanied by any manifestation of sexual abuse, but that is not indicated in this question. There is no indication of precocious puberty or overidentification with the male gender.
Diagnosis
Health promotion and maintenance
Analysis
Learning Outcome 40.1

**40.15** A recently married couple is trying to conceive a child. The husband is a collegiate athlete and his coach forbids sexual activity for 2 days prior to a game. The wife asks the nurse if abstinence before the game is necessary. What is the best response?

1. As long as intercourse is not involved, there is no reason to avoid sexual activity.
2. Some residual physical weakness is common for up to 18 hours after sex.
3. This is a common myth among athletes, but there is no basis in fact.
4. In fact, sexual activity before intense physical exercise increases stamina and endurance.

Answer: 3
Rationale: The idea that sexual activity weakens the person physically is a common misconception among athletes, but there is no evidence to support that idea. There is no evidence that avoiding intercourse is necessary. There is no evidence that sexual activity before intense exercise affects stamina or endurance.
Implementation
Health promotion and maintenance
Application
Learning Outcome 40.5

**40.16** The 15-year-old female tells the nurse that she makes her boyfriend stop intercourse before she has an orgasm so she will not get pregnant. What teaching is necessary for this client?

1. Even though she doesn't get pregnant, she might still get a sexually transmitted infection.
2. Intercourse until orgasm may actually reduce conception because the vaginal contractions help to expel sperm.
3. Conceiving is not related to whether or not the female partner experiences an orgasm.
4. As long as her boyfriend does not ejaculate in her vagina, conception is unlikely.

Answer: 3
Rationale: Conceiving is not related to experiencing orgasm. This client is very likely to conceive and is also at risk for getting any sexually transmitted infection her boyfriend might have. The seminal fluid expelled prior to ejaculation also contains sperm and can result in pregnancy even if the male ejaculates outside the vagina.
Implementation
Health promotion and maintenance
Analysis
Learning Outcome 40.9

**40.17** The high school student tells the school nurse that during biology the class learned that alcohol is associated with erectile dysfunction. The student wonders why so many girls get pregnant during evenings when alcohol is consumed. The nurse plans a response based upon which concept?

1. Alcohol is a central nervous system depressant which affects judgment.
2. Erectile dysfunction only occurs after years of alcohol abuse.
3. Alcohol is a sexual stimulant.
4. Erectile dysfunction occurs only in men older than 50.

Answer: 1
Rationale: Alcohol is implicated in behaviors leading to undesired pregnancy because it is a central nervous system depressant and affects judgment. It is not a sexual stimulant. Situational erectile dysfunction often occurs when the male partner is drunk. Chronic erectile dysfunction is more common in older men, and alcohol abuse is associated with this problem.
Planning
Health promotion and maintenance
Analysis
Learning Outcome 40.5

**40.18** The female client has experienced recurrent candidiasis with intense vaginal itching and excoriation. After treatment the client is reexamined, and the nurse practitioner finds presence of a white, cheesy discharge. What recommendation is necessary?

1. Referral to a surgeon for excision of infected tissue
2. Examination and treatment of sexual partner
3. Treatment with a stronger oral antibiotic
4. Routine douches with a topical antibiotic solution

Answer: 2
Rationale: Candidiasis is a sexually transmitted infection. It may be that this woman's sexual partner is also infected with candidiasis and that the couple is transmitting the infection between them. Examination and treatment of the partner is indicated. There is no need for tissue excision. Candidiasis is a yeast infection. Antibiotic therapy is not indicated and may, in fact, complicate treatment.
Evaluation
Health promotion and maintenance
Analysis
Learning Outcome 40.8

**40.19** The nurse enters the room and finds the adult client masturbating. What action should the nurse take?

1. Tell the client that masturbation is harmful to sexual well-being.
2. Say "excuse me" and leave the room.
3. Request that the client stop so that care can be provided.
4. Ask the client if there are any sexual concerns that should be discussed.

Answer: 2
Rationale: In this situation, the nurse should quickly and politely leave the room. Masturbation is not harmful to sexual well-being and does not indicate sexual concerns that should be discussed. It is inappropriate to ask the client to stop so that care can be provided.
Implementation
Health promotion and maintenance
Application
Learning Outcome 40.5

**40.20** The nurse who is teaching a client breast self-examination describes inspection of the breasts before a mirror. Which findings should the nurse tell the client should be evaluated by a health care provider? (Select all that apply.)

1. Puckering of the skin
2. Flattening of the breast from the side view
3. Free movement of the breast over the chest wall
4. Symmetry of the nipples
5. Change in shape

Answer: 1, 2, 5
Rationale: The client should be taught to observe for change in size or shape, lumps or thickenings, rashes or skin irritations, dimpled or puckered skin, and discharge or change in nipples. The nipples should be symmetrical and the breasts should have free movement over the chest wall.
Assessment
Health promotion and maintenance
Application
Learning Outcome 40.9

| | |
|---|---|
| **40.21** A nurse colleague is outraged that a grandchild's day-care center is planning a class on sexuality for 3- and 4-year-olds. Discussion of this plan should include what concept?<br>   1.  At this age, education regarding sexuality should come from parents.<br>   2.  Children are sexual beings from before birth.<br>   3.  Understanding the body and sexuality are a part of growth and development.<br>   4.  Sexual activity is beginning at earlier and earlier ages. | Answer: 1<br>Rationale: While all of these statements are true, the primary consideration is that early childhood education on sex should come primarily from parents.<br>Planning<br>Health promotion and maintenance<br>Analysis<br>Learning Outcome 40.9 |
| **40.22** What self-examination schedules should the nurse teach a class of young adult men and women? (Select all that apply.)<br>   1.  Monthly breast self-exams for women<br>   2.  Yearly breast self-exams for men<br>   3.  Weekly testicular self-exams for men<br>   4.  Monthly breast self-exams for men<br>   5.  Yearly vulvar self-exams for women | Answer: 1, 4<br>Rationale: Both women and men should examine their breasts on a monthly schedule. Men should additionally examine their testicles monthly. There is no need for a yearly scheduled self-vulvar exam for women, as any abnormalities noticed should be examined by the woman or her health care provider immediately.<br>Implementation<br>Health promotion and maintenance<br>Application<br>Learning Outcome 40.9 |
| **40.23** In discussion with teenagers, the nurse chooses to use the term *sexually transmitted infection* rather than *sexually transmitted disease*. What is the rationale for this choice?<br>   1.  Infection is a much more precise term for the transmission that occurs.<br>   2.  The word disease may elicit guilt, shame, and fear in the client.<br>   3.  Sexually transmitted disease does not receive as much third-party reimbursement as does sexually transmitted infection.<br>   4.  These terms can be used interchangeably and there is no good rationale for using one over the other. | Answer: 2<br>Rationale: The term *sexually transmitted disease* can elicit guilt, shame, and fear in the client. Substituting the term *infection* for disease makes the diagnosis less threatening and makes it sound more treatable. Third-party reimbursement is not a reason for choice of terms in this instance. The preciseness of the term is not an issue.<br>Planning<br>Health promotion and maintenance<br>Analysis<br>Learning Outcome 40.9 |
| **40.24** The nurse uses the PLISSIT format in helping clients who have sexual dysfunction. Which action by the nurse best reflects the P section of this format?<br>   1.  Ask the physician for permission to discuss sexual topics with the client.<br>   2.  Obtain signed informed consent from both the client and the spouse or partner prior to providing them with sexual information. | Answer: 3<br>Rationale: The P section of this format reflects permission giving. This giving of permission refers to acknowledging the client's spoken and unspoken sexual concerns and giving the client permission to be a sexual being. There is no need to ask permission from the physician prior to discussing sexual topics. Obtaining signed informed consent from both the client and spouse or partner is not required. Documentation of precertification for benefits from the client's insurance company would be an issue only if the nurse is acting in the role as a sexual therapist for which insurance would reimburse.<br>Assessment<br>Health promotion and maintenance<br>Analysis<br>Learning Outcome 40.8 |

| | |
|---|---|
| 3. Acknowledge the client's spoken and unspoken sexual concerns when providing care.<br>4. Document precertification for benefits from the client's insurance company regarding sexual teaching. | |
| **40.25** The nurse uses the PLISSIT format in helping clients who have sexual dysfunction. Which action by the nurse best reflects the LI section of this format?<br><br>1. In order to avoid causing anxiety, limit the amount of information given to clients regarding adverse sexual side effects of treatments or medications.<br>2. Give the client accurate but concise information in regard to any sexual questions that might be asked.<br>3. Start information using slang terms to refer to sexual body parts because the client is not likely to know the proper terms.<br>4. Review current research literature associated with the sexual concerns of the client and partner. | Answer: 2<br>Rationale: LI represents limited information. The nurse should give accurate but concise information regarding sexual matters. While the nurse should use terms the client understands, assuming that the client only understands slang terms could cause embarrassment for the client and the nurse. A better strategy is to use correct terms while assessing the client's understanding, changing to more common terms if necessary. Clients deserve information regarding sexual side effects, and the nurse is obligated to provide that information. While reviewing current literature is always a good idea, it does not relate to the LI section of the PLISSIT format.<br>Assessment<br>Health promotion and maintenance<br>Application<br>Learning Outcome 40.8 |
| **40.26** The nurse uses the PLISSIT format in helping clients who have sexual dysfunction. Which action by the nurse best reflects the SS section of this format?<br><br>1. Use the nurse's knowledge about how disease affects sexuality to offer specific suggestions for the client.<br>2. Focus interventions on explaining the somatic sexual difficulties and their treatment.<br>3. Offer the client a list of expected sexual side effects of drugs or treatments.<br>4. Identify any concerns the client has regarding attraction to the same sex. | Answer: 1<br>Rationale: SS represents specific suggestions. The nurse should use specialized knowledge and skill about how sexuality and functioning is affected by disease process or therapy to offer specific suggestions for intervention. While some therapy may have somatic effects, the nurse should not focus solely on those effects. Just giving the client a list of expected sexual side effects is not appropriate at this level of the format. SS does not stand for same sex.<br>Intervention<br>Health promotion and maintenance<br>Application<br>Learning Outcome 40.8 |
| **40.27** The nurse uses the PLISSIT format in helping clients who have sexual dysfunction. Which action by the nurse best reflects the IT section of this format?<br><br>1. Use information technology such as the Internet to obtain guidance suggestions for the client.<br>2. Use the technique of informal therapeutic groups to assist the client and partner. | Answer: 4<br>Rationale: IT represents intensive therapy. At this point in intervention, the nurse recognizes that the client requires therapy with a nurse who has specialized preparation and knowledge of sexual and gender identity disorders. Referral or recommendation for intensive therapy is required. Using information technology or informal therapeutic groups does not reflect this need for more intensive therapy. Evaluation of previous interventions and treatments is not a part of the format.<br>Intervention<br>Health promotion and maintenance<br>Application<br>Learning Outcome 40.8 |

| | |
|---|---|
| 3. Evaluate previous interventions and treatment for success.<br>4. Recommend intensive therapy with a qualified sex therapist. | |
| **40.28** The daughters of an 80-year-old man who is aphasic after a cerebrovascular accident (stroke) express concern that their father is "always exposing and playing with himself and his catheter" while they are in the room. Upon assessment, the nurse finds the client pulling on and rubbing his penis. What is the nurse's priority action?<br>1. Tell the client to keep his hands away from his penis.<br>2. Assess the client's penis for irritation from the catheter.<br>3. Ask the client to keep his linens at waist level when he has visitors.<br>4. Collaborate with the physician regarding medications to control this behavior. | Answer: 2<br>Rationale: The nurse should assess whether this client has irritation of the penis that is causing his actions. Telling the client to keep his hands away from his penis or to keep his linens pulled up is inappropriate and assumes the client is masturbating. Medicating the client to control the behavior is also inappropriate and assumes that the client is doing something wrong. All three incorrect options overlook the possibility of a physical reason such as irritation that the client is trying to communicate.<br>Assessment<br>Physiologic integrity<br>Application<br>Learning Outcome 40.8 |

# CHAPTER 41

| | |
|---|---|
| **41.1** As a part of care planning, the nurse considers the client's spiritual needs. What is the rationale for this concern?<br>1. Nurses are the only health professionals that provide this type of holistic care.<br>2. Meeting the client's spiritual needs can decrease suffering.<br>3. Until spiritual needs are met, physical needs cannot be healed.<br>4. It is important that the nurse's idea of spirituality matches the client's ideas. | Answer: 2<br>Rationale: The nurse is concerned about the client's spiritual health because meeting spiritual needs can decrease suffering. Physical needs can be addressed and healed without considering the spiritual side, but in order to provide holistic care both should be addressed. Nurses do provide holistic care, but so do many other health care professionals. While the nurse must assess and understand the client's spirituality, it is not necessary for the nurse's ideas to match those of the client.<br>Planning<br>Psychosocial integrity<br>Application<br>Learning Outcome 41.1 |
| **41.2** The nurse assesses that a client is experiencing spiritual distress. What should be the nurse's primary intervention?<br>1. Establish a trusting nurse–client relationship.<br>2. Have the client describe the basic problem.<br>3. Ask the client what religion is practiced in the home.<br>4. Identify the client's belief in a Supreme Being. | Answer: 1<br>Rationale: The first step in successfully working with a client with spiritual distress is establishing a trusting nurse–client relationship. Until that relationship is established, it will be difficult to complete the other interventions. The nurse should be careful not to confuse spirituality with religion and should be careful not to assume the tenets of the client's spirituality match those of the nurse.<br>Planning<br>Psychosocial integrity<br>Application<br>Learning Outcome 41.6 |
| **41.3** The nurse has identified that many of the clients in the long-term care facility have spiritual concerns and distress. What is the nurse's first step in becoming a competent provider for these clients? | Answer: 1<br>Rationale: The first step of becoming a competent provider for clients who have spiritual distress is for the nurse to possess a healthy spiritual self-awareness. The next step is to learn more about diverse spiritual beliefs and practices. If the nurse attempts step 2 without at least beginning step 1, confusion will result that may actually damage the nurse's ability to help others. Establishing regular |

| | |
|---|---|
| 1. The nurse must possess a healthy spiritual self-awareness.<br>2. The nurse must learn about diverse spiritual beliefs and practices.<br>3. The nurse should start going to church more often.<br>4. The nurse should establish regular religious services in the facility. | religious services in the facility and going to church more often presuppose that spirituality and religion are one, which is not true.<br>Implementation<br>Psychosocial integrity<br>Analysis |
| **41.4** According to Jourard, spirituality can be measured on a "spirit titer." Which client does the nurse assess to have a high spirit titer?<br>1. A client who has experienced multiple life losses who is depressed<br>2. The client who expresses distress over a newly diagnosed terminal disease<br>3. A client who works to be an inspiration to others despite hardships<br>4. The client whose spirituality is not evident to others | Answer: 3<br>Rationale: Jourard's "spirit titer" is a method to measure spirituality that goes from spiritual distress on the low end of the titer to enhanced spirituality on the high end of the titer. The client who works to inspire others despite personal hardships evidences a high spirit titer. The other clients in this question have low or moderate titers or have titers that cannot be assessed.<br>Assessment<br>Psychosocial integrity<br>Application<br>Learning Outcome 41.3 |
| **41.5** During assessment, the client tells the nurse, "I don't believe that the existence of God has been proven. I don't see the scientific evidence I need to be certain." How does the nurse document this finding?<br>1. The client demonstrates polytheism.<br>2. The client is an atheist.<br>3. The client has beliefs that support monotheism.<br>4. The client is agnostic. | Answer: 4<br>Rationale: Agnostics are persons who doubt the existence of God or a supreme being or believe the existence of God has not been proven. Atheists do not believe in a God. Polytheism is the belief in more than one God; monotheism is the belief in one God.<br>Assessment<br>Psychosocial integrity<br>Application<br>Learning Outcome 41.2 |
| **41.6** The 70-year-old client with terminal lung cancer tells the nurse, "I am dying because I sinned by smoking cigarettes." What is the nurse's best response to this dying client?<br>1. "You are correct, but it is too late to do anything about it now."<br>2. "When you started smoking cigarettes we didn't know about the problems they cause. It is not your fault."<br>3. "Why don't we call the hospital chaplain and you can pray about your sins."<br>4. "Smoking cigarettes isn't a sin. There are many worse habits you could have." | Answer: 2<br>Rationale: This client is in distress and is seeking forgiveness. The nurse should offer this forgiveness and a reason the forgiveness is valid. If the nurse tells the client that it is too late to do anything about the problem, there is a possibility that distress will increase. Suggesting that the hospital chaplain be called for prayer reinforces that smoking cigarettes is a sin. The option about worse habits minimizes the client's concerns and does not offer forgiveness.<br>Implementation<br>Psychosocial integrity<br>Application<br>Learning Outcome 41.6 |

**41.7** During assessment, the client says that it has been "a long time" since she has thought very much about religion. The nurse caring for this client has a strong belief in God and the healing power of prayer. What action should be taken by the nurse?

1. Mention the nurse's belief and offer to pray with the client for forgiveness.
2. Tell the client that the nurse will pray for her often.
3. Ask the client if there are any spiritual needs with which the staff can assist.
4. Refer the client for spiritual counseling.

Answer: 3
Rationale: The nurse must understand that personal spiritual beliefs cannot be brought into the work situation unless the client asks for information and the nurse is comfortable sharing. Offering to pray with or for the client is over the boundary of professional practice unless the client requests such intervention and the nurse is comfortable with the arrangement. At this point, there is no information that indicates the client is in need of referral for counseling. This would occur only if the client demonstrates spiritual distress at the level best handled by a specialist.
Implementation
Psychosocial integrity
Application
Learning Outcome 41.7

**41.8** The client being prepared for an elective outpatient colonoscopy asks to be allowed to wear a religious medal during the procedure. The client states, "I have worn this medal and have not removed it since I was a teenager." What action should be taken by the nurse?

1. Tell the client that the medal must be removed as it is policy to remove all jewelry for these procedures.
2. Tell the client that the medal can be worn.
3. Tell the client that the nurse will explain to the colonoscopy staff about the medal and will request that they allow the client to wear it.
4. Remove the medal and place it on the head of the bed where the client will be able to see it during the procedure.

Answer: 3
Rationale: The nurse should explain the significance of the medal to the colonoscopy staff and request that the client be allowed to wear it during the procedure. The nurse should not, however, tell the client that the medal will be allowed as this decision belongs to those directly involved in the procedure. The fact that there is a policy to remove all jewelry is simply a policy, and an exception might be made and documented in this case. Removing the medal and placing it on the head of the bed is not a good choice. There may be no reason to remove the medal. Placing the medal on the head of the bed might allow it to be lost.
Implementation
Psychosocial integrity
Analysis
Learning Outcome 41.7

**41.9** The emergency department nurse contacts the admissions office to request a bed for a bed-bound client who is a practicing Muslim. Acting as an advocate for the client, what request should the nurse make of the admission clerk?

1. Please try to find a private room.
2. A bed that faces east will be best.
3. Have the bed stripped as the client will provide special sheets.
4. If the only available room is semi-private, the other client should be Muslim.

Answer: 2
Rationale: Since this bed-bound client is a practicing Muslim and this religion has a sacred practice of five daily prayers performed while facing east, the logical bed assignment for this client is one that faces east. There is no restriction that the room must be private or that the other client in a semi-private room must be Muslim. There is no indication that the client will have hospital linens replaced by special sheets.
Planning
Psychosocial integrity
Application
Learning Outcome 41.6

**41.10** A client who is devoutly Jewish is hospitalized during Yom Kippur, a time when many of the Jewish faith fast. The client expresses a desire to follow this religious pattern. How should the nurse respond to this wish?

Answer: 1
Rationale: The nurse should support the client's desires to the extent possible. Since this client is a devout follower of Jewish tradition, it is not up to the nurse to instruct the client regarding Jewish law. The nurse should not attempt to convince the client to ignore the tradition. The physician also cannot ethically make this decision for the client.

| | |
|---|---|
| 1. Support the client's desires to the extent possible.<br>2. Remind the client that most religions excuse persons who are ill from fasting.<br>3. Attempt to convince the client to ignore the tradition due to illness.<br>4. Tell the client that the physician must make this decision. | Implementation<br>Psychosocial integrity<br>Analysis<br>Learning Outcome 41.5 |
| **41.11** The female client belongs to a religious community that requires women to dress conservatively in clothing that covers the arms and the knees. This client expresses concern that her body will be exposed during a scheduled cardiac catheterization. How should the nurse respond to this concern?<br>  1. Tell the client that medical personnel have seen so many people's bodies that they don't even notice any longer.<br>  2. Make a note in the client's chart that she is particularly modest.<br>  3. Explain to the client that in order to perform the study, her body must be exposed.<br>  4. Ask the cath lab charge nurse to come to the client's room to talk with her about the concerns. | Answer: 4<br>Rationale: The best plan is to have the cath lab charge nurse talk to the client about her concerns. The charge nurse can then assure the client that even though a small part of her body must be exposed, her modesty will be protected. While medical personnel are often exposed to unclothed bodies, that information will not make this client more at ease. Just making a note in the chart is not sufficient.<br>Implementation<br>Psychosocial integrity<br>Analysis<br>Learning Outcome 41.5 |
| **41.12** During labor, it becomes apparent that the male infant will survive only a short time after birth. Since this baby's parents are Catholic, what planning should the nurse consider?<br>  1. Arrange to have the baby circumcised immediately after birth.<br>  2. Ask the hospital chaplain to be present in the delivery room.<br>  3. Ask the nursing supervisor to find a Catholic nurse to attend the birth.<br>  4. Consider emergency transport of the mother to a Catholic hospital. | Answer: 2<br>Rationale: In this situation, the best choice is to have the hospital chaplain present in the delivery room. The next best answer would be to have a nurse who is Catholic in attendance at the birth. The concern of this family will be baptism of the infant, not circumcision. Transfer of a laboring woman to another facility is not possible.<br>Planning<br>Psychosocial integrity<br>Application<br>Learning Outcome 41.5 |
| **41.13** The family of a dying client has informed the nurse that their religion requires a ritual bath be given by members of the faith after death. Since the hospital unit is very busy and there is an acute need for every bed, how should the nurse respond to this request?<br>  1. Notify the mortuary of the family's request.<br>  2. Arrange for supplies and privacy for the family. | Answer: 2<br>Rationale: When a client is dying, much of the nursing care shifts from the client to support of the family. The nurse should allow this bath and should provide supplies and privacy for the family to complete the ritual. There is no need to notify the mortuary. The nurse should not put a deadline on the bath or tell the family that they will have to delay the bath until the body is removed.<br>Implementation<br>Psychosocial integrity<br>Analysis<br>Learning Outcome 41.5 |

| | |
|---|---|
| 3. Tell the family that the bath will have to take place after the body is removed from the hospital.<br>4. Allow the family to give the bath, but give them a 1-hour deadline for completion. | |
| **41.14** After asking general assessment questions regarding spirituality, the nurse finds the client content and satisfied. How should the nurse conduct the rest of the assessment?<br>1. Specific questions regarding beliefs should be included.<br>2. The nurse should validate spiritual information with the client's family.<br>3. The assessment can now move on to physical assessment.<br>4. No further specific spiritual assessment is currently necessary. | Answer: 4<br>Rationale: If the client is satisfied and content with current levels of spirituality, there is no further specific spiritual assessment necessary. The spiritual assessment should take place at the end of the assessment, so physical assessment should already have been completed. There is no need to validate spiritual assessment with family unless there is a question of the client's reliability as a historian.<br>Assessment<br>Psychosocial integrity<br>Analysis<br>Learning Outcome 41.6 |
| **41.15** The client tells the nurse, "I don't know what to do. The treatment plan my physician has suggested is against some of my religious beliefs." What nursing diagnosis problem statement should the nurse assign to this client?<br>1. *Ineffective Coping*<br>2. *Decisional Conflict*<br>3. *Impaired Religiosity*<br>4. *Anxiety* | Answer: 2<br>Rationale: For this situation, the best nursing diagnosis problem statement is *Decisional Conflict*. This client will be called upon to make a decision between two highly regarded but conflicting plans. There is no evidence that this client is coping ineffectively. *Impaired Religiosity* is impairment of the ability to exercise religious beliefs, which has not yet occurred in this situation. While there may be some anxiety, that nursing diagnosis is not as specific to this case as is *Decisional Conflict*.<br>Diagnosis<br>Psychosocial integrity<br>Analysis<br>Learning Outcome 41.7 |
| **41.16** The nurse caring for wheelchair-dependent residents of a long-term care environment has developed a care plan that includes taking the clients outside and assisting them in planting and maintaining a garden. What is the best rationale for this plan?<br>1. Accreditation agencies require that the residents have regular outings.<br>2. Keeping in touch with nature is a form of spiritual care.<br>3. Fresh vegetables from the garden are good sources of nutritional fiber.<br>4. Sunshine helps activate vitamin D. | Answer: 2<br>Rationale: While all of these options are true, the best rationale for this care is that keeping in touch with nature is a form of spiritual care for these residents.<br>Planning<br>Psychosocial integrity<br>Analysis<br>Learning Outcome 41.7 |
| **41.17** The nurse has obtained supplies to change a complex abdominal dressing on a postoperative client. When the nurse arrives at the room, the client is praying with family. What action should be taken by the nurse? | Answer: 4<br>Rationale: The nurse should wait in the hall until the prayer is over and the client or family give permission to enter the room. Standing inside the room is a violation of privacy and may also unduly influence the length of the prayer session. While it is perfectly acceptable for the nurse to pray with clients, joining the prayer without invitation is not acceptable. The nurse should not interrupt the prayer to request to perform a task. |

| | |
|---|---|
| 1. Stand quietly just inside the room door until the prayer is completed.<br>2. Come to the bedside and join in with the prayer.<br>3. Politely ask the client to allow the dressing change to proceed.<br>4. Quietly shut the door and wait in the hall until asked to enter. | Implementation<br>Psychosocial integrity<br>Application<br>Learning Outcome 41.7 |
| **41.18** The newly hired nurse notices that co-workers routinely pray with clients and their families. The nurse has never been particularly religious or spiritual and is unaccustomed to praying, but holds no strong feeling against prayer. What is the best strategy for the nurse to plan for such situations?<br>1. Try to ensure assignment to clients who are unlikely to request prayer.<br>2. Arrange to have a co-worker substitute for the nurse in these prayer situations.<br>3. Memorize two or three short, formal prayers to use when prayer is requested.<br>4. Just stand silently at the bedside and let others in the room do the praying. | Answer: 3<br>Rationale: Since this nurse has no objection to praying with clients and families, the best plan is to have two or three short, formal prayers or verses memorized to use when prayer is suggested. It is impossible to be certain that the nurse will not be caring for a patient who will ask for prayer, especially since the practice of prayer is somewhat routine on this unit. Having a co-worker substitute for the nurse will be difficult to operationalize and may not always be an option, so the nurse would need some preparation anyway. The second best option is to stand silently at the bedside while others pray.<br>Planning<br>Psychosocial integrity<br>Analysis<br>Learning Outcome 41.7 |
| **41.19** The nurse has developed a strong rapport with a client whose medical care necessitates transfusion of multiple units of blood. The client has a religious objection to this treatment even though it is necessary to sustain life. What action should be taken by the nurse?<br>1. Use the rapport established to influence the client to accept the blood transfusions.<br>2. Explain the scientific reasons that blood transfusions are necessary and why refusal is dangerous.<br>3. Encourage the client, the physician, and the client's spiritual adviser to discuss this conflict and any possible alternative therapies.<br>4. Suggest to the client that as the illness progresses, the blood will probably be transfused despite religious objections. | Answer: 3<br>Rationale: This is a delicate situation for a nurse who has developed a rapport and relationship with a client. The best response is to support the discussion between client, physician, and spiritual adviser. At that point, the nurse must be prepared to support whatever decision the client makes, even if it is to not permit the transfusions. Just explaining scientific reasons will not generally make a difference in the client's decision. Using the rapport established to influence the decision is unethical, as is suggesting that the blood will be transfused anyway if the disease progresses.<br>Implementation<br>Psychosocial integrity<br>Application<br>Learning Outcome 41.7 |
| **41.20** How can the nurse best support the spiritual development of a hospitalized 5-year-old?<br>1. Ask the child who God is.<br>2. Listen to the child's routine bedtime prayer. | Answer: 2<br>Rationale: The nurse should support the routine spiritual practices encouraged by the family. If the client says routine bedtime prayers, the nurse can support this practice by listening to the prayer. If the child does not routinely pray before meals, the nurse should not introduce this activity. Bringing in a Bible storybook to read to the child assumes that the child holds the same religious beliefs as the |

| | |
|---|---|
| 3. Encourage the child to pray before each meal.<br>4. Bring a Bible storybook in to read to the child at bedtime. | nurse. Asking who God is also assumes that the child's religion recognizes God. At this age, the child is a little young to articulate the identity of God.<br>Implementation<br>Psychosocial integrity<br>Application<br>Learning Outcome 41.7 |
| **41.21** During the morning bath, the client asks if the nurse is religious and believes in God. What guideline would be most helpful to the nurse in formulating a response to this question?<br>1. The nurse's personal life is none of the client's business.<br>2. Religion and politics are two subjects not discussed in polite society.<br>3. Will sharing this information positively contribute to the relationship?<br>4. What is the culture of the facility regarding self-disclosure? | Answer: 3<br>Rationale: Practice guidelines regarding support of religious practices indicate that the nurse should first consider whether such self-disclosure will contribute to a therapeutic nurse–client relationship. Although considering the culture of the unit is important, the nurse can make the clinical decision that what is generally done on the unit does not apply in this situation. While it is true that the nurse's personal life is private, the nurse might decide to self-disclose. Some cultures do believe that religion and politics should not be discussed in polite society, but the client does deserve some answer to the question.<br>Implementation<br>Psychosocial integrity<br>Analysis<br>Learning Outcome 41.7 |
| **41.22** The nurse and client have spent several minutes praying together that the client's upcoming surgery will be successful. What action should the nurse take at this point?<br>1. Gently tell the client that the nurse must take care of other duties.<br>2. Smile and pat the client and silently leave the room.<br>3. Stay with the client until the emotion evoked by the prayer dissipates.<br>4. Ask the client if there is anything else the nurse can do. | Answer: 3<br>Rationale: The nurse should stay with the client a few minutes after the prayer has ended until the strong emotions that can be evoked by joint prayer dissipate. Asking if there is anything else the nurse can do makes the prayer look like just another task in a busy day. Smiling and being gentle are correct, but the nurse should stay with the client for at least a few minutes.<br>Implementation<br>Psychosocial integrity<br>Application<br>Learning Outcome 41.7 |
| **41.23** The client who was diagnosed with diabetes mellitus 1 year ago is hospitalized in diabetic ketoacidosis after a religious fast. The client tells the nurse, "I have fasted during this season every year since I became an adult. I am not going to stop now." The nurse is not knowledgeable about this particular religion. What is the best action for this nurse?<br>1. Tell the client that it is different now because of the diabetes.<br>2. Do some research into the meaning of fasting in this religion.<br>3. Ask family members of the same religion to discuss fasting with the client.<br>4. Request a consult from a diabetes educator. | Answer: 4<br>Rationale: The diabetes educator should be contacted to work with the client on strategies that might allow the fasting to occur in a safe manner. Telling the client that life is different now does not support religious beliefs. Research into the meaning of fasting in this religion would be educative for the nurse, but the client requires more immediate intervention. Asking the family to talk to the client might help, but the diabetes educator would be able to provide more direct and helpful information for the client.<br>Planning<br>Psychosocial integrity<br>Analysis<br>Learning Outcome 41.5 |

**41.24** The client states, "I don't know what all this fuss is about religion. God died years ago." The nurse does believe in God and has a strong inclination to share reasons for that belief with the client. What is the best question for the nurse to consider before responding to the client's remark?

1. "Will I get into trouble if I say anything?"
2. "How much longer will I be caring for this client?"
3. "Am I meeting my needs or the client's?"
4. "How can I best make this client understand?"

Answer: 3
Rationale: The nurse should first determine if it is the nurse's needs or the client's needs that would be met by a response. Only after that determination is made would the nurse move on to the other questions in formulating the response.
Implementation
Psychosocial integrity
Application
Learning Outcome 41.6

**41.25** The client who has been hospitalized for 3 weeks following a severe motor vehicle crash tells the nurse that spirituality and spiritual matters mean a great deal more now than before the incident. What nursing diagnosis would the nurse add to this client's care plan?

Answer: *Readiness for Enhanced Spiritual Well-Being*
Rationale: *Readiness for Enhanced Spiritual Well-Being* is a NANDA-approved wellness diagnosis that reflects the client's ability to "experience and integrate meaning and purpose in life through a person's connectedness with self, others, art, music, literature, nature, or a power greater than oneself" (NANDA, 2003).
Diagnosis
Psychosocial integrity
Analysis

**41.26** A client is concerned because hospitalization will interfere with his ability to participate in the religious rituals that traditionally surround the Christmas season. What nursing diagnosis would the nurse add to this client's care plan?

Answer: *Impaired Religiosity*
Rationale: *Impaired Religiosity* is the nursing diagnosis used when the client is unable to participate in religious practices or rituals or to rely on religious beliefs.
Diagnosis
Psychosocial integrity
Analysis

# CHAPTER 42

**42.1** The nurse elects to use a scale of stressful life events to assess the level of a newly admitted client's stress. How should the nurse explain the use of this scale to the client?

1. "We will consider only the negative life events that have happened to you recently."
2. "You should try to remember any stressful event that has occurred to you in the last 10 years to include in the scale."
3. "This scale will give us a definite stress level number that can be used to compare your stress to others your age."
4. "This scale will give us some idea about your stress related to both positive and negative recent events in your life."

Answer: 4
Rationale: Stress scales are useful to give the client and others an idea of the amount of stress that both positive and negative recent life events have placed on the client. The scales do take into consideration both positive and negative events and focus on events that have taken place recently. The scales are only an idea of stress level because each individual reacts to stressful events differently.
Assessment
Psychosocial integrity
Application
Learning Outcome 42.7

| | |
|---|---|
| **42.2** The client has just received news of the death of a relative. Over the next few hours, what physiologic response would the nurse attribute to the shock phase of the alarm reaction caused by the stress of this event?<br><br>1. Drop in blood pressure from 130/80 to 120/75<br>2. A more bounding pulse<br>3. Slight increase in urine output<br>4. Some decrease in oxygen saturation | Answer: 2<br>Rationale: During this shock phase the sympathetic nervous system is stimulated, resulting in increased myocardial contractility which would be reflected in the client as a bounding pulse. Blood pressure rises in response to angiotensin production. Norepinephrine release decreases blood flow to the kidney, which could make urine output decrease. The bronchial tree dilates, allowing more oxygen intake that would result in increased oxygen saturation.<br>Assessment<br>Psychosocial integrity<br>Analysis<br>Learning Outcome 42.1 |
| **42.3** The nursing student admits to being mildly anxious about an upcoming examination. What is the likely result of this level of anxiety?<br><br>1. The student's perception and learning is enhanced.<br>2. The student's attention is focused solely on studying for the examination.<br>3. The student's only topic of conversation is the examination.<br>4. The student cannot talk about the examination without crying. | Answer: 1<br>Rationale: With mild anxiety, the student's perception and learning will be enhanced. Focusing only on studying for the examination would indicate a moderate anxiety level. Severe anxiety is the level at which the examination would consume all of the student's energy. Panic is the state in which the student might lose control of emotions regarding the examination.<br>Evaluation<br>Psychosocial integrity<br>Application<br>Learning Outcome 42.4 |
| **42.4** While attempting to choose a nursing diagnosis, the nurse must decide whether the client is suffering from anxiety or fear. What key point would help the nurse make this decision?<br><br>1. Anxiety is a milder form of fear.<br>2. Fear results in a physiologic response, while anxiety is psychologic.<br>3. The source of fear is identifiable, but anxiety may be vague.<br>4. Anxiety is generally based in reality, fear is not. | Answer: 3<br>Rationale: The source of fear is identifiable, but anxiety is vague. Fear and anxiety can both be based in reality or may not be based in reality. Both fear and anxiety can have physiologic and psychologic components. Fear and anxiety are different, so anxiety is not just a milder form of fear.<br>Diagnosis<br>Psychosocial integrity<br>Analysis<br>Learning Outcome 42.3 |
| **42.5** The newly licensed nurse feels overwhelmed by the demands of working on a busy acute care unit and maintaining a growing family. What strategy should this nurse employ to lessen this stress?<br><br>1. Spend the lunch hour completing documentation while eating a sandwich.<br>2. Set the alarm earlier in order to get to work early.<br>3. Focus on work instead of on family until more familiar with the environment.<br>4. Differentiate between "have to do" and "nice to do" at work. | Answer: 4<br>Rationale: In order to manage stress the nurse must pay close attention to good nutrition, adequate sleep, and exercise. The nurse must also relax by spending time with family. This nurse should differentiate between what is essential care at work, and what is nice to do but can be eliminated on days when stress is high and resources are limited.<br>Implementation<br>Psychosocial integrity<br>Application<br>Learning Outcome 42.6 |
| **42.6** The nurse is caring for a critically ill child. While the nurse is preparing to administer a treatment to the child, the child's mother becomes distraught and | Answer: 4<br>Rationale: In this situation, the nurse must analyze which of the available options would be best for this mother and child. At this level of emotion, the nurse should remove the mother from the room and comfort her. While the mother's |

begins to cry loudly while stroking the child's face. What is the nurse's best response to this occurrence?

1. Tell the mother that she needs to control herself for the benefit of her child.
2. Distract the mother by having her straighten the linens on the bed.
3. Explain the procedure that will occur with the treatment.
4. Take the mother out of the room and comfort her.

expression of anxiety is understandable, the child should be protected from this strongly upsetting situation. Just telling the mother to control herself discounts the seriousness of her anxiety and may serve to alienate the mother from the nurse. This mother is too upset to distract by smoothing linens. Explaining the procedure may help, but the mother should be removed at least temporarily and be comforted so that she will be able to receive the information.
Implementation
Psychosocial integrity
Analysis
Learning Outcome 42.9

---

**42.7** The nurse is caring for a client who was admitted to the intensive care unit to rule out myocardial infarction. The client is upset because he is restricted to the unit and is not allowed to smoke cigarettes. This morning the client became so angry that he threw his breakfast tray at the nurse. How should the nurse respond to this outburst?

1. Call the charge nurse and refuse to take care of this client until he is under control.
2. Apologize to the client for the unit rules, but tell him the rules must be followed.
3. Tell the client that it is understandable that he is upset, but the no smoking rule is not negotiable.
4. Tell the client that he is acting like a child and that such behavior will not be tolerated.

Answer: 3
Rationale: Telling the client that it is understandable that he is upset serves to show that the nurse accepts his right to be angry, but that the anger is the client's. The nurse should not assume responsibility for the anger by apologizing. Admonishing the client by saying that he is acting like a child is not professional and will most likely serve to destroy any hope of resolving this issue. The nurse cannot refuse to care for the client once the assignment has been accepted, since this may constitute client abandonment.
Implementation
Psychosocial integrity
Application
Learning Outcome 42.3

---

**42.8** During a health clinic assessment, the client describes his life as "in crisis." He reports that he has just been fired from his job, his wife has told him she wants a divorce, and he has been sick with a respiratory illness for 1 month. What statement, made by the nurse, reveals understanding of the care of a client in crisis?

1. "Once you reach the crisis state, you may remain there for several months until you recover."
2. "People generally find it easier to work through a crisis if someone is working with them."
3. "Men often handle crisis better individually, while women do better with a counselor."
4. "Experiencing a crisis is never positive, so we must work to relieve your anxiety as soon as possible."

Answer: 2
Rationale: In general, people are more successful in working through a crisis if they have someone to help them. This need for help is not gender dependent. A crisis results in such a state of disequilibrium that it is generally self-limiting and not a long-term event. Experiencing a crisis may actually offer the family or individual a potential for growth and change.
Implementation
Psychosocial integrity
Application
Learning Outcome 42.3

---

| | |
|---|---|
| **42.9** The nurse manager of a busy emergency department is concerned about burnout in the nursing staff. The manager has overheard nurses complaining about their job, absenteeism has increased, and the nurses look tired and anxious. What action, planned by the nurse manager, would best serve to alleviate this burnout?<br>   1. Ask the physician staff to take over some of the tasks they routinely ask the nurses to do.<br>   2. Make certain that the nurses are well prepared for their responsibilities.<br>   3. Assign each nurse to spend 30 minutes with the hospital psychologist daily.<br>   4. Ask administration to require 30 minutes of exercise at the end of each shift. | Answer: 2<br>Rationale: In this situation, the best alternative is to be certain that the nurses are well prepared for the responsibilities of their jobs, as the frustration of being unprepared leads to burnout. Asking physicians to assume nursing tasks is not appropriate. Neither the nurse manager nor the administration can require counseling or exercise programs, particularly after work hours. Instituting such requirements would likely increase stress, frustration, and burnout.<br>Planning<br>Psychosocial integrity<br>Application<br>Learning Outcome 42.6 |
| **42.10** The nurse identifies that a client has not met the expected outcome established for the nursing diagnosis *Ineffective Individual Coping*. What nursing action is priority?<br>   1. Revise the nursing diagnosis.<br>   2. Reassess the patient, looking for previously unknown stressors.<br>   3. Rewrite the interventions used to address the problem.<br>   4. Explore reasons why the outcome was not achieved. | Answer: 4<br>Rationale: When the expected outcome is not met, the nurse, client, and support persons must explore reasons why before modifying the remaining portions of the care plan.<br>Evaluation<br>Psychosocial integrity<br>Application<br>Learning Outcome 42.8 |
| **42.11** The client who has been experiencing slight anxiety is now communicating in a manner that makes it difficult for the nurse to understand the client's needs. When discussing this client with the physician, the nurse indicates the opinion that the client has progressed to which level of anxiety?<br>   1. Mild<br>   2. Moderate<br>   3. Severe<br>   4. Panic | Answer: 3<br>Rationale: Changes in verbalization can be indicative of increasing anxiety. Mild anxiety causes an increase in questioning. Moderate anxiety results in voice tremors and pitch changes. At severe levels, communication is difficult to understand. Communication may not be understandable at all when the client reaches the panic stage.<br>Assessment<br>Psychosocial integrity<br>Application<br>Learning Outcome 42.4 |
| **42.12** The physician has just told the client that the results of a biopsy performed yesterday reveal no malignancy. During discharge teaching the nurse finds the client to be easily distractible and unable to focus. What is the nurse's best interpretation of this situation?<br>   1. The client did not understand that there is no malignancy.<br>   2. Anxiety can result from both positive and negative stimuli. | Answer: 2<br>Rationale: Anxiety can be the result of both positive and negative stimuli. There is no indication that the client doesn't understand the report or that the client discounts the need for teaching. The amount of information retained may be drastically reduced by this level of anxiety, so the nurse should take extra pains to ascertain if the client understands the teaching.<br>Implementation<br>Psychosocial integrity<br>Analysis<br>Learning Outcome 42.4 |

| | |
|---|---|
| 3. Since there is no malignancy present, the client feels there is no need for teaching.<br>4. These findings reflect mild anxiety, but the client should retain information taught despite this distractibility. | |
| **42.13** A client has been admitted to the hospital with severe chest pain and has been medically diagnosed with myocardial infarction. The client tells the nurse, "I don't think this is my heart. That spaghetti I ate for lunch tasted a little strange. I think I have food poisoning." What defense mechanism is this client exhibiting?<br>1. Compensation<br>2. Denial<br>3. Displacement<br>4. Identification | Answer: 2<br>Rationale: Denial is an attempt to ignore unacceptable realities by refusing to acknowledge them. Compensation is covering up weaknesses by emphasizing a strength or by overachievement. Displacement is transferring emotional reactions from one object or person to another object or person. Identification is an attempt to manage anxiety by imitating the behavior of someone feared or respected.<br>Assessment<br>Psychosocial integrity<br>Analysis<br>Learning Outcome 42.5 |
| **42.14** The victim of domestic abuse tells the nurse, "I know my spouse didn't mean to hurt me. The situation just got out of hand." The nurse recognizes that the client is exhibiting which of the following?<br>1. Intellectualization<br>2. Introjection<br>3. Projection<br>4. Minimization | Answer: 4<br>Rationale: Minimization is not acknowledging the significance of a behavior. Intellectualization is a defense mechanism in which an uncomfortable or painful reality is evaded by using a rational explanation that removes personal significance from the event. Introjection is a form of identification in which the person adopts another person's norms or values, even if those norms or values are contrary to what the person would have previously assumed. Projection is blaming another person or the environment for one's own unacceptable thoughts, shortcomings, or failures.<br>Assessment<br>Psychosocial integrity<br>Analysis<br>Learning Outcome 42.5 |
| **42.15** The client tells the nurse that she does not wish to see her mother-in-law during this hospitalization because she does not like her. When the client's husband and her mother-in-law visit, the client is very cordial and acts happy to see both visitors. The nurse recognizes that this client may be using which defense mechanism?<br>1. Reaction formation<br>2. Rationalization<br>3. Regression<br>4. Reparation | Answer: 1<br>Rationale: Reaction formation is a mechanism that causes people to act exactly opposite to the way they feel. Rationalization is justification of behaviors by faulty logic and by ascribing socially acceptable motives to the behavior. Regression is resorting to an earlier, more comfortable level of functioning that is less demanding. Reparation is not a recognized defense mechanism.<br>Assessment<br>Psychosocial integrity<br>Analysis<br>Learning Outcome 42.5 |
| **42.16** The nurse is caring for a 9-year-old client who was sexually abused by a minister. The child's parents are angry and confused as to why someone who was sexually attracted to children would choose to go into the ministry. The nurse explains that displacement of sexual drives into socially acceptable activities is a defense mechanism known as which of the following? | Answer: 2<br>Rationale: Sublimation is displacement of sexual drives into more socially acceptable activities. Repression is an unconscious mechanism by which threatening thoughts and feelings are kept from becoming conscious. Substitution is a mechanism in which highly valued, unacceptable, or unavailable objects are replaced by less valuable, acceptable, or available objects. Undoing is an action or words designed to cancel out some disapproved thoughts, impulses, or acts or in which the person acts to make reparation for a wrong. |

| | |
|---|---|
| 1. Repression<br>2. Sublimation<br>3. Substitution<br>4. Undoing | Assessment<br>Psychosocial integrity<br>Application<br>Learning Outcome 42.5 |
| **42.17** The assessment of a client undergoing testing for an anxiety disorder reveals an increased heart rate, an increased respiratory rate, a low-normal hematocrit, and a low blood sugar. Which finding is contrary to what could be explained by a normal response to anxiety?<br>    1. The heart rate<br>    2. The respiratory rate<br>    3. The hematocrit<br>    4. The blood sugar | Answer: 4<br>Rationale: The normal response to anxiety is increased heart rate and increased rate and depth of respirations. Sodium and water are also retained, which might reflect in a low-normal hematocrit due to increased blood volume. The blood sugar generally increases because of the release of glucocorticoids and gluconeogenesis.<br>Evaluation<br>Psychosocial integrity<br>Analysis<br>Learning Outcome 42.3 |
| **42.18** What nursing intervention should be planned to minimize the stress and anxiety of hospitalization?<br>    1. Explain all procedures in detail before performing them.<br>    2. Let the client make the majority of decisions about the plan of care.<br>    3. Control the environment of healing.<br>    4. Demonstrate staff competence by using multiple nurses for care. | Answer: 3<br>Rationale: The nurse is in charge of the environment of healing and should take responsibility for limiting noise, dimming lights at night, using minimal numbers of nurses to care for one client, and keeping the area clean and comfortable. Explaining all procedures in detail may overwhelm the client. Using short, clear sentences and explaining only enough to satisfy the client is a better plan. A client who is ill cannot be expected to make the majority of decisions about the plan of care, but should be allowed as much autonomy and choice as can be arranged and tolerated.<br>Planning<br>Psychosocial integrity<br>Application<br>Learning Outcome 42.9 |
| **42.19** The parents of a 16-year-old who has a history of depression are concerned because the physician has prescribed an SSRI antidepressant for their child. What information should the nurse use to formulate a response to these parents' concerns?<br>    1. These medications are addictive and difficult to discontinue when the depressive incident is past.<br>    2. It is difficult for teenagers to manage the dosage regimen for many of these drugs because they must be taken with a full meal.<br>    3. There is an FDA warning regarding antidepressant use in teenagers and the increased risk of suicide.<br>    4. Most of the SSRI antidepressant medications will deliver a marked improvement in depression within 3 to 4 days of the first dose. | Answer: 3<br>Rationale: The major concern regarding use of antidepressants and teenagers is the increased risk for suicide. While the client may come to depend upon the medication relieving depression, the drugs are not addictive. The medications must be taken with sufficient water, but a full meal is not necessary. Most of the SSRI antidepressant medications take at least 1 to 2 weeks to improve symptoms.<br>Planning<br>Psychosocial integrity<br>Application<br>Learning Outcome 42.9 |
| **42.20** A 2-year-old child has experienced multiple hospital admissions to treat a congenital heart disorder. Upon today's admission, the nurse notices that the child is lying | Answer: 3<br>Rationale: Toddlers and preschool children often react to anxiety by either withdrawing or acting out. This child is behaving in a normal manner. There is no evidence of parental abuse, of developmental delay, or of clinical depression.<br>Evaluation |

curled in the bed holding a stuffed animal and will not interact with the parents. How should the nurse interpret this withdrawal?

1. The parents may have been abusing this child.
2. The child is probably developmentally delayed secondary to multiple hospitalizations.
3. The child is reacting as a normal 2-year-old.
4. The child could be suffering from a clinical depression.

Psychosocial integrity
Analysis
Learning Outcome 42.3

---

**42.21** The nurse has been working with the family of a client with cystic fibrosis since the child's diagnosis 6 years ago. Over this time, the client's mother has gained 50 pounds and has recently started taking prescription antidepressants. On the last visit, the mother said, "I just don't know how much longer we can go on." What nursing diagnosis should the nurse consider as an addition to the family's care plan?

Answer: *Caregiver Role Strain*
Rationale: The mother's statement, along with the weight gain and need for antidepressants, supports the diagnosis of *Caregiver Role Strain*.
Diagnosis
Psychosocial integrity
Analysis
Learning Outcome 42.8

---

# CHAPTER 43

**43.1** During a home visit, the elderly male client tells the nurse that his wife died 3 years ago. Which action would the nurse interpret as being a possible indicator that this client is experiencing complicated grief?

1. The client has an album of photographs of his wife open on the living room table.
2. He tells the nurse that his wife was an awful cook and that he has eaten better meals since she died.
3. He indicates that he sends his laundry out to be done because he had never figured out how the washer works.
4. He shows the nurse his wife's craft room that remains just as she left it before she died.

Answer: 4
Rationale: Leaving the deceased wife's craft room and belongings intact for over 3 years is considered outside the normal limits of the grief process. Showing photographs of the deceased and talking about her good and bad points are normal responses to grief. Sending out the laundry to be done is a healthy response to a problem that this client identified.
Assessment
Psychosocial integrity
Application
Learning Outcome 43.2

---

**43.2** The nurse is caring for the family of a terminally ill client. The family members have been tearful and sad since the diagnosis was given. What is the best choice of nursing diagnosis problem statements for this family?

1. *Anticipatory Grieving*
2. *Dysfunctional Grieving*
3. *Hopelessness*
4. *Caregiver Role Strain*

Answer: 1
Rationale: Grieving prior to the actual loss is termed anticipatory grieving. There are no assessment findings in the question that indicate dysfunctional grieving or hopelessness. This reaction is typical of family members, so there is no indication that the family is exhibiting caregiver role strain.
Diagnosis
Psychosocial integrity
Analysis

---

| | |
|---|---|
| **43.3** The nurse is counseling a family in which a member is terminally ill. The family has children of varying ages. What should the nurse teach the family about the reactions of children to death?<br>1. Toddlers perceive death as irreversible and unnatural.<br>2. Preschool children view death as a spiritual release.<br>3. At about age 9, children begin to understand death is inevitable.<br>4. Adolescents tend to have better outcomes than adults after a loss. | Answer: 3<br>Rationale: At about age 9, children's concept of death matures and most understand that death is an inevitable part of life. Toddlers fear abandonment, and preschoolers view death as reversible. Adults generally have better outcomes than adolescents when confronted with death.<br>Implementation<br>Psychosocial integrity<br>Application<br>Learning Outcome 43.4 |
| **43.4** The nurse is assigning support personnel to assist the families of clients who have died in dealing with the stress related to the loss of their family member. Which family would the nurse screen as highest risk for complicated grief? The family of a client who:<br>1. Died after a long battle against cancer.<br>2. Died after developing diabetes-induced renal failure.<br>3. Was killed in the robbery of a bank.<br>4. Died from chronic heart disease. | Answer: 3<br>Rationale: While all families are different and all families can respond to grief differently, research supports a greater potential for complicated grief in families whose loved one died suddenly, violently, or unexpectedly. Of the options given, the client who was murdered best fits all three situations. The clients who died of cancer, renal failure, and heart disease had been ill for some time, so they do not meet the criteria as well as the murdered client.<br>Assessment<br>Psychosocial integrity<br>Analysis<br>Learning Outcome 43.8 |
| **43.5** The nurse critically evaluates various models of grief used for terminally ill clients and their families. What should the nurse recognize when applying these models to individual cases?<br>1. The Kübler-Ross model is primarily used to describe anticipatory grief.<br>2. No clear timetables exist, nor are there clear-cut stages of grief.<br>3. The models serve as clear and definitive predictors of grief behaviors.<br>4. There is strong research proving that these models are not useful for many dying clients. | Answer: 2<br>Rationale: Although the models of grief are useful in guiding nursing care of clients who are experiencing loss, there are no clear-cut stages of grief, nor are there exact timetables. Kübler-Ross describes stages of all grief and grieving. None of the models are clear or definitive predictors of grief behaviors.<br>Assessment<br>Psychosocial integrity<br>Application<br>Learning Outcome 43.2 |
| **43.6** A client who is in the terminal phases of a debilitating muscular disease tells his wife that he believes the health care team has "failed" and "given up" on him and "aren't trying as hard." The nurse caring for this client realizes that:<br>1. This idea of abandonment is unfounded.<br>2. This is a common fear in the terminally ill client.<br>3. When clients become terminal, physician care is no longer necessary.<br>4. Clients who feel this way are in denial of the facts of their care. | Answer: 2<br>Rationale: If the client feels that his terminal state is a reflection of failure of the medical system, this fear of abandonment is common. It may not be totally unfounded because failing to cure a client is frustrating and may reflect in the care provided to the client. While nurses do provide much of the care given to terminal clients, physicians continue to be an integral part of care. There is no indication of denial in this client's statements, but powerlessness or hopelessness may be evident.<br>Assessment<br>Psychosocial integrity<br>Application<br>Learning Outcome 43.2 |

**43.7** Which of the following is a useful nursing intervention in treatment of anxiety associated with receiving a terminal diagnosis?

1. Explore the client's history with other stressful life events and how successful coping was at that time.
2. Teach the family that while talking with the client about death and dying is permissible, they should not allow the client to dwell on death.
3. Supply information about the client's disease process and the expected trajectory of death only on a need to know basis.
4. Encourage early pharmaceutical intervention with antianxiety and sedative medications.

Answer: 1
Rationale: It is most helpful for the nurse to know how the client has dealt with previous stressful life events so that support of positive coping mechanisms can occur. The client who has received a terminal diagnosis needs to discuss the future and the implications of the diagnosis. The need for discussion and the amount of time needed will vary from client to client, so "dwelling" is an inappropriate descriptor. The client must be given facts about the disease process and projected trajectory so that final business and relationships can be addressed. Early use of antianxiety and sedative medications is not appropriate because these medications can adversely affect the client's ability to think clearly about the future.
Implementation
Psychosocial integrity
Application
Learning Outcome 43.5

**43.8** A client who has AIDS tells the nurse, "I don't know why I should even keep trying. This disease is so horrible and so many people die from it. It will get me, too." The nurse recognizes this statement as which of the following?

1. An indication of hopelessness that should be further evaluated for treatment
2. A simple statement of the facts regarding AIDS
3. Common and expected in those facing the end of life
4. Proof that the client is accepting the facts of the illness and impending death

Answer: 1
Rationale: This statement reflects hopelessness. Hopelessness is not an expected feeling at end of life and can and should be treated. Despite the inevitability of death, the goal is for the client to continue to express hope of some nature. This hope might take the form of short-term completion of goals prior to death, for peacefulness at the time of death, or for attainment of the individual's personal belief about the afterlife.
Diagnosis
Psychosocial integrity
Analysis
Learning Outcome 43.5

**43.9** A client with terminal cancer of the lung complains of being short of breath with bilateral crackles and wheezes, despite oxygen at 4 Lpm via nasal cannula and diuretic therapy. What nursing interventions are appropriate for this client? (Select all that apply.)

1. Move the client to a room closer to the nurse's desk for closer observation.
2. Help the client assume a position lying on the right side.
3. Place a fan in the room to move air around the client.
4. Change the client's oxygen therapy to a nonrebreathing mask.
5. Elevate the head of the client's bed to a Fowler's position.
6. Consider use of a prn morphine sulfate order.

Answer: 3, 5, 6
Rationale: Placement of a fan to circulate air, elevating the head of the bed, and use of morphine sulfate may relieve shortness of breath. Moving the client who is short of breath is not advisable. Lateral positions are appropriate for unconscious clients, but this client is conscious. Conscious clients who are short of breath do not tolerate oxygen therapy by mask.
Implementation
Health promotion
Analysis
Learning Outcome 43.6

| | |
|---|---|
| **43.10** The client tells the nurse that she has been having problems sleeping since her boss died unexpectedly 3 weeks ago. She confides that she and the boss had been having a secret extramarital affair for years. The nurse recognizes that the sleeping difficulty is most likely a result of which of the following?<br>1. Abbreviated grieving<br>2. Chronic grief<br>3. Disenfranchised grieving<br>4. External grief | Answer: 3<br>Rationale: Sleep disturbances are common during the grieving period. This client is unable to grieve openly for her lost relationship as extramarital affairs are not socially sanctioned. Abbreviated grieving is grieving that is brief, but genuinely felt. This client's grief is not yet chronic as only 3 weeks have passed. External grieving is not a recognized type of grief response.<br>Diagnosis<br>Psychosocial integrity<br>Application<br>Learning Outcome 43.4 |
| **43.11** The nurse is working with a father and his three children, ages 10, 14, and 17. The mother recently died after a long illness. The children are doing poorly in school, and the father is having a difficult time keeping up with household chores. He has recently taken on a second job to help pay his late wife's hospital bills. Which nursing diagnosis should the nurse consider in planning care for this family? (Select all that apply.)<br>1. *Dysfunctional Grieving*<br>2. *Impaired Family Processes*<br>3. *Impaired Adjustment*<br>4. *Caregiver Role Strain*<br>5. *Hopelessness* | Answer: 1, 2, 3, 4, 5<br>Rationale: There may be numerous nursing diagnoses that should be investigated in planning care for this grieving family. This list may not be all inclusive, as problems with sleep, nutrition, self-concept, and role adjustment are common following a long illness and death of a loved one.<br>Diagnosis<br>Psychosocial integrity<br>Analysis<br>Learning Outcome 43.5 |
| **43.12** During the bath, the client suddenly says, "I am not going to get well. I think I am going to die." What response, given by the nurse, is most appropriate?<br>1. "Let's think of something more cheerful."<br>2. "You are doing so well, don't talk like that."<br>3. "What makes you think you are dying?"<br>4. "Whatever is meant to be will happen." | Answer: 3<br>Rationale: The nurse should ask what it is that makes the client think about dying. This allows the nurse to collect and evaluate data before making a further response. "Let's think of something more cheerful" is changing the subject. "You are doing so well, don't talk like that" is offering false reassurance and devaluing the client's concern. "Whatever is meant to be will happen" is being fatalistic and devaluing the client's concerns.<br>Implementation<br>Psychosocial integrity<br>Analysis<br>Learning Outcome 43.6 |
| **43.13** The client has a documented advance health care directive that indicates that no resuscitative measures should be employed in the event of a respiratory or cardiac arrest. The client begins to exhibit severe dyspnea and air hunger and says, "Please do something, I can't breathe." What action should be taken by the nurse?<br>1. Offer the client comfort measures until death occurs.<br>2. Call the client's physician for direction.<br>3. Initiate resuscitative measures.<br>4. Check the medical record to ascertain the terms of the directive. | Answer: 3<br>Rationale: This client has the right to change decisions about resuscitation, and has asked for help. The nurse should initiate resuscitative measures. Just offering comfort measures until the client dies is ignoring the client's wishes. There is no need to call the physician for direction, as the client has clearly given the nurse direction. The nurse should have already known the terms of the directive and would not have time to seek clarification at this point.<br>Implementation<br>Safe, effective care environment<br>Analysis |

**43.14** Upon admitting a client to the hospital, the nurse receives an advance health care directive to include in the medical record. The directive is witnessed by two of the client's three children. How does the nurse interpret this information?

1. This advance directive may not be legal as children cannot witness advance directives in some states.
2. Having the children's signatures on the advance directive is good because it indicates they agree with the client's wishes.
3. The advance directive cannot be honored unless it is witnessed by all three children.
4. In order to be valid, the advance directive must be witnessed by the client's physician.

Answer: 1
Rationale: The nurse must be certain that the advance directive is a legal document. In some states, relatives, heirs, and physicians cannot witness an advance directive. This is to prevent potential abuse of power.
Planning
Safe, effective care environment
Analysis

---

**43.15** The family of an unconscious, terminally ill client cannot come to a decision about requesting a "do-not-resuscitate" order. Two of the children want the order, but one child and the client's sister do not agree. Several heated arguments have occurred in the hall outside the client's room. Efforts to educate the family and mediate in arguments have not helped. What action should the nurse take?

1. Ban the family from the room until they can be polite to each other in front of the client.
2. Have the chaplain attempt mediation.
3. Notify the institutional ethics committee.
4. Talk with each of the children and the client's sister separately in an attempt to understand the conflict.

Answer: 3
Rationale: The best option is to notify the institutional ethics committee. Banning the family from the room, talking individually, and having the chaplain attempt mediation are unlikely to help and may actually inflame the situation more.
Implementation
Safe, effective care environment
Application
Learning Outcome 43.8

---

**43.16** The nurse is providing postmortem care for a client whose family would like to view the body before it is transported to the morgue. Which of the following interventions are necessary for this preparation? (Select all that apply.)

1. Provide a total bed bath.
2. Place absorbent pads beneath the body.
3. Remove dentures.
4. Dress the client in street clothes.
5. Place a pillow under the head.
6. Tape the eyelids closed.

Answer: 2, 5
Rationale: The nurse should place a pillow under the head and place absorbent pads beneath the body. Soiled areas of the body should be washed, but a total bed bath is not necessary. Dentures should be inserted. The eyelids should be held in place until they stay closed and should not be taped. The client should be dressed in a clean gown.
Implementation
Psychosocial integrity
Application
Learning Outcome 43.9

**43.17** The family of a young adult client who has recently been diagnosed with a rapidly progressing terminal illness tells the nurse, "This cannot be happening. There must be some mistake in the testing." What should be the nurse's first step in assisting this family?

1. Provide structure and continuity to promote feelings of security.
2. Examine the nurse's own feelings to ensure denial is not shared.
3. Offer spiritual support.
4. Allow the family to express sadness.

Answer: 2
Rationale: While all of these techniques are appropriate in dealing with a family in this situation, the nurse must first self-examine feelings to ensure that the nurse's behaviors do not demonstrate denial of the situation.
Implementation
Psychosocial integrity
Analysis
Learning Outcome 43.8

**43.18** A client who has just been diagnosed with a slowly progressive terminal illness asks the nurse about the availability of hospice services. What information should the nurse share with this client?

1. When clients are designated as terminally ill, they are automatically assigned to hospice care.
2. Hospice services are generally reserved for those who have a life expectancy of 6 months or less.
3. Only those clients with private insurance can receive hospice benefits.
4. Provision of hospice services is reserved only for those who refuse other palliative treatments.

Answer: 2
Rationale: Hospice services are generally provided only to those who are expected to live less than 6 months.

Those clients whose conditions improve after going on hospice may be removed from those services. Clients are not automatically assigned to hospice. Medicare does provide hospice benefits, and the client may receive both hospice and other palliative care treatments.
Implementation
Safe, effective care environment
Application
Learning Outcome 43.7

**43.19** What is the most important communication strategy for the nurse to use when working with a child who is dying?

1. Talk to the child at the appropriate level of understanding.
2. Be totally open and honest with the child.
3. Avoid discussing death with the child.
4. Encourage the family to talk with the child about the impending death.

Answer: 1
Rationale: While it is very important to be open and honest with the child and may be appropriate to encourage the family to talk with the child about impending death, the most important strategy is to talk with the child at the appropriate level of understanding. Without recognition of this concept, none of the other options will be effective. The nurse should not avoid discussing death with the child if the child brings up the subject.
Implementation
Psychosocial integrity
Analysis
Learning Outcome 43.5

**43.20** The nurse is caring for a client whose family does not want to tell him that he is dying. What is the nurse's best action according to these wishes?

1. Arrange an encounter with the client and tell him the truth.
2. Change the subject when the client asks about his impending death.
3. Tell the family that the patient has the right to know that he is dying.
4. Talk to the family about the situation and their concerns.

Answer: 4
Rationale: In this situation, the best and first thing the nurse should do is talk with the family about what is happening and what their concerns are. The nurse should investigate religious, cultural, and family traditions regarding telling the client about impending death. The nurse should have this discussion with the family before offering such advice as the client has a right to know. The nurse should not change the subject if the client asks about impending death, but should not encourage such an encounter before discussing the situation with the family.
Planning
Psychosocial integrity
Analysis
Learning Outcome 43.8

**43.21** The nurse who is providing postmortem care for a client sees that the client is wearing a ring. What is the most important action regarding this observation?

1. Remove the ring and give it to the family.
2. Call the presence of the ring to the attention of the funeral director.
3. Tape the ring to the client's finger.
4. Document fully whatever action is taken.

Answer: 4
Rationale: Depending upon the circumstances and what kind of ring it is, the nurse might take any of these actions. The most important action is to document what occurred.
Implementation
Safe, effective care environment
Analysis
Learning Outcome 43.9

## CHAPTER 44

**44.1** The nurse is organizing a wellness project to educate teenagers about keeping their bodies healthy. Which information about diet and exercise should be included?

1. Diet is the most important predictor of health.
2. The most important factors for maintaining health are diet and activity.
3. Increase in exercise is sufficient to manage most people's weight gain.
4. Obese women who remain active have a low mortality rate.

Answer: 2
Rationale: Research shows that diet and activity are the most important factors for maintaining health. People who follow a sedentary lifestyle have an increased chance of becoming overweight as well as developing a number of chronic diseases. Although diet is an important predictor of health, activity level appears to be more predictive of future health. Increase in exercise without change in diet will not be sufficient to manage most weight gain and is considered an unhealthy trend in today's society. While obese women who are active are generally healthier than their sedentary counterparts, they still have a higher mortality rate than women who are lean and active.
Planning
Health promotion and maintenance
Analysis

**44.2** During a prenatal visit, the nurse is instructing a newly pregnant woman in regard to exercise. What advice is best for the nurse to give this client?

1. Pregnant women can exercise if exercise was a part of their life prior to pregnancy.
2. Due to the stress of a growing fetus, exercise should be limited to no more than 10 minutes per day.
3. Healthy pregnant women should exercise at least 30 minutes on most if not all days.
4. The pregnant woman's exercise should actually increase above normal recommended levels to prevent water weight gain.

Answer: 3
Rationale: The current recommendation of the American College of Obstetricians and Gynecologists is for healthy pregnant women to get as much exercise as the general population (30 minutes on most if not all days). This is a change from their previous recommendation that pregnant women can exercise. There is no indication that the pregnant woman needs more exercise than the general population.
Implementation
Health promotion and maintenance
Analysis
Learning Outcome 44.4

**44.3** The nurse is caring for a client medically diagnosed with early osteoporosis. Which intervention is most applicable for this client?

1. Institute an exercise plan that includes weight-bearing activities.
2. Increase the amount of calcium in the client's diet.

Answer: 1
Rationale: Osteoporosis is a demineralization of the bone in which calcium leaves the bone matrix. One causative factor is lack of weight-bearing activity. Weight bearing helps to move calcium back into the bone, thereby strengthening them. A standard intervention for those attempting to prevent or reverse osteoporosis is beginning an exercise plan that includes weight-bearing activities. Additional calcium in the diet after osteoporosis has begun is not thought to be effective. Strict bed rest may well make the osteoporosis worse because there is no weight-bearing activity. Assisted range of motion exercises are not weight bearing and do not help delay or reverse osteoporosis.

| | |
|---|---|
| 3. Protect the client's bones with strict bed rest.<br>4. Provide the client with assisted range of motion exercising twice daily. | Planning<br>Health promotion and maintenance<br>Application<br>Learning Outcome 44.6 |
| **44.4** The newly admitted client has contractures of both lower extremities. What nursing intervention should be included in this client's plan of care?<br>1. Frequent position changes to reverse the contractures<br>2. Exercises to strengthen flexor muscles<br>3. Range of motion exercises to prevent worsening of contractures<br>4. Weight-bearing activities to stimulate joint relaxation | Answer: 3<br>Rationale: Once contractures occur they are irreversible except by surgical intervention. The best nursing intervention is to keep the contractures from getting tighter (or worse) by providing range of motion exercises. Frequent position changes will not reverse contractures, nor will weight-bearing activities. The contracture occurs because the flexor muscles are stronger than the extensor muscles. This imbalance in strength pulls the inactive joint into a flexed position, and a permanent shortening of the muscle occurs.<br>Planning<br>Physiologic integrity<br>Analysis<br>Learning Outcome 44.6 |
| **44.5** The nurse has documented that the client has orthostatic hypotension. Which of the following assessment findings would support this assessment? (Select all that apply.)<br>1. Decrease in blood pressure when moving from supine to standing<br>2. Decrease in heart rate when moving from supine to sitting<br>3. Pale color in the legs when lying in bed<br>4. Complaints of dizziness when first sitting up<br>5. Increased respiratory rate on exertion | Answer: 1, 4<br>Rationale: Orthostatic hypotension occurs when the normal vasoconstriction reflex in the legs is dormant and the client's central blood pressure drops when moving from supine to sitting or to standing. The blood pressure drops, the heart rate increases, and the client may complain of dizziness or may faint upon arising. Paleness of the legs is not significant. Increased respiratory rate on exertion is more related to diminished cardiac reserves, not orthostatic hypotension, as it can occur even when the client is lying flat in bed and moving.<br>Assessment<br>Physiologic integrity<br>Analysis<br>Learning Outcome 44.5 |
| **44.6** The client's chief complaint is, "I just can't get around like I used to. I have to stop halfway up the stairs to the bedroom, and just walking to the bathroom makes me so tired." Which nursing diagnosis is most likely appropriate for this client? *Activity Intolerance:*<br>1. Level 1<br>2. Level 2<br>3. Level 3<br>4. Level 4 | Answer: 3<br>Rationale: The NANDA diagnosis *Activity Intolerance* is further individualized to the client's level of intolerance. Level 1 indicates normal activity with slightly more shortness of breath. Level 2 indicates ability to walk about one level city block without difficulty or to climb one flight of stairs without stopping. Level 3 (this client's level) indicates ability to walk no more than 50 feet on level ground without stopping and inability to climb one flight of stairs without stopping. Level 4 indicates dyspnea and fatigue at rest.<br>Diagnosis<br>Physiologic integrity<br>Analysis<br>Learning Outcome 44.6 |
| **44.7** The nurse is considering using the NANDA nursing diagnosis *Impaired Physical Mobility* in the care plan of a newly admitted client. In order to make this problem statement more individual, the nurse should:<br>1. Include what mobility is impaired.<br>2. Use Level 1, 2, 3, or 4 to describe immobility.<br>3. Describe what happens when the client attempts mobility.<br>4. Add strength assessment data. | Answer: 1<br>Rationale: In order to make this broad nursing diagnosis more specific to the client, the nurse should include what mobility is impaired. For example, if the client cannot transfer from bed to chair, a more specific nursing diagnosis is *Impaired Transfer Mobility*. There are NANDA levels of activity intolerance, but not of immobility. Strength assessment data and describing what happens when the client attempts mobility might be used in the "as manifested by" section of the nursing diagnosis, but not in the problem statement section.<br>Diagnosis<br>Physiologic integrity<br>Analysis<br>Learning Outcome 44.6 |

**44.8** The nurse is working on a hospital committee focused on preventing back injury in nurses. Which recommendation by this committee is most likely to result in a decrease in back injuries if followed?

1. Nurses must wear back belts when lifting clients.
2. All nursing personnel must attend annual body mechanics education.
3. In order to prevent injury, nurses must strive to become physically fit.
4. No solo lifting of clients is permitted in the facility.

Answer: 4
Rationale: Research has shown that the only option that has any influence on frequency of back injury is a policy prohibiting solo lifting. Back belts, body mechanics training, and physical fitness of the nurse do not prevent injury.
Planning
Health promotion and maintenance
Application
Learning Outcome 44.7

**44.9** The nurse must lift a 15-pound box of supplies from a low shelf on the supply cart to a table. The nurse should employ which techniques to best protect the back? (Select all that apply.)

1. Place the feet together to provide a strong base of support.
2. Flex the knees to lower the center of gravity.
3. Face the box, pick it up, and rotate the upper body toward the table.
4. Hold the box as close to the body as possible.
5. Bend over and use a jerking motion to pull the box to waist level.

Answer: 2, 4
Rationale: In order to pick up this box as safely as possible, the nurse should spread the feet to shoulder width, flex the knees to lower the center of gravity, smoothly lift the box, holding it as close to the body as possible, and turn the entire body toward the table. Placing the feet together makes the body more unstable and more likely to fall. After picking up the weight, the body should not be rotated, but should be turned to face the table. Rotating the upper body puts strain on the back. The nurse should squat to pick up the box and should lift smoothly with no jerking motions.
Planning
Health promotion and maintenance
Application
Learning Outcome 44.7

**44.10** How should the nurse position a client who is complaining of dyspnea?

1. High Fowler's position with two pillows behind the head
2. Orthopneic position across the overbed table
3. Prone position with knees flexed and arms extended
4. Sims' position with both legs flexed

Answer: 2
Rationale: The orthopneic position across the overbed table facilitates respiration by allowing maximum chest expansion. High Fowler's position should not be used with more than one pillow or with overly large pillows. The prone position places the client on the abdomen and makes chest expansion difficult. Sims' position is a side-lying position and does not support full chest expansion as much as the orthopneic position.
Implementation
Physiologic integrity
Application
Learning Outcome 44.5

**44.11** While assisting the client with a bath, the nurse encourages full range of motion in all the client's joints. Which activity would best support range of motion in the hand and arm?

1. Give the client a washcloth to wash her face.
2. Move the wash basin farther toward the foot of the bed so the client must reach.
3. Have the client brush her own hair and teeth.
4. Move each of the client's hand and arm joints through passive range of motion.

Answer: 3
Rationale: The best range of motion is the natural movement of the client's joints in normal activity. Brushing the hair and teeth includes more of the joints of the hands and the arms than does washing the face. The wash basin should be close to the client to prevent overreaching and possible falls. Passive range of motion is a second best choice after normal use of the joints.
Implementation
Physiologic integrity
Analysis
Learning Outcome 44.1

**44.12** The bed-bound client complains of pain and burning in the right calf area. What action should be taken by the nurse?

1. Deeply palpate the area for rebound tenderness.
2. Percuss over the area for change in tone.
3. Measure the calf and compare to the opposite calf.
4. Medicate the client for pain and reassess in 30 minutes.

Answer: 3

Rationale: Among other assessment activities, the nurse should measure the calf and compare it to the opposite calf. The client may be developing a deep vein thrombosis or thrombophlebitis. Palpating or percussing the area is contraindicated because injury to the vein may induce a thrombus. If a thrombus is present, these actions might embolize it. Medicating the client and reassessing in 30 minutes might allow a worsening of the client's condition.

Assessment

Physiologic integrity

Application

Learning Outcome 44.5

---

**44.13** The client who is bed-bound complains of abdominal pain. Bowel sounds are present. What action should be taken by the nurse?

1. Percuss for flatness over the liver.
2. Palpate for bladder fullness.
3. Use the prn order to medicate the client with an antacid.
4. Inspect the sacral area for edema.

Answer: 2

Rationale: The nurse should palpate for bladder fullness that could cause this discomfort. Flatness is the normal percussion sound over the liver. Sacral edema may occur with the bed-bound client, but should not be a contributor to abdominal pain. The nurse should not medicate the client until assessment is complete.

Assessment

Physiologic integrity

Application

Learning Outcome 44.5

---

**44.14** The client who is unconscious is developing foot drop. What nursing action is indicated?

1. Place high-topped shoes on the client while in bed.
2. Keep the linens on the end of the bed turned back to expose the feet.
3. Use only the prone and Sims' positions for client positioning.
4. Use a device to elevate the linens off the feet.

Answer: 1

Rationale: High-topped shoes will place the client's feet in the anatomical position of dorsal flexion. While a device to elevate linens and turning the linens back will keep the weight of the linens off the feet, foot drop can occur anyway. The prone and Sims' positions are implicated in the development of foot drop.

Implementation

Physiologic integrity

Application

Learning Outcome 44.5

---

**44.15** The nurse is planning care for a client who has limited bed mobility. What instruction should be given to the assistive personnel who will be caring for this client? (Select all that apply.)

1. Place a turn sheet on the bed.
2. Always use two personnel to move the client.
3. Stand at the head of the bed to pull the client up.
4. Slide the client toward the head of the bed.
5. Encourage the client to assist as possible.

Answer: 1, 2, 5

Rationale: Placing a turn sheet on the bed will help overcome inertia and friction during moving. Using two personnel will allow a "lift and move" rather than pulling or sliding the client over linens. The personnel should stand on either side of the bed and use the turn sheet to move the client. Encouraging the client to assist as much as possible will lighten the workload.

Planning

Safe, effective care environment

Application

Learning Outcome 44.6

---

**44.16** Which nursing action is first when assisting the client to a lateral position for placement of a bedpan?

1. Perform hand hygiene.
2. Move the client to the side of the bed.
3. Place the client's arm over the chest.
4. Raise the opposite side rail.

Answer: 1

Rationale: Even though the intervention being performed is placing the client on a bedpan, the nurse should first perform hand hygiene. This prevents cross-transmission of infection from one client to another. Performing this hygiene in front of the client also increases the client's perception of the quality of care being provided and the nurse's concern about infection control.

Implementation

Safe, effective care environment

Application

---

**44.17** Which client would require logrolling for position changes?
1. A client with documented pneumonia
2. The client who has had abdominal surgery
3. The client who fell from a house, sustaining a fractured tibia
4. A client who has a severe headache from hypertensive crisis

Answer: 3
Rationale: Logrolling technique is used in moving any client who may have sustained a spinal injury. Of these clients, the most concern is for the client who fell from a house. There is no documented reason to logroll the remaining clients.
Implementation
Physiologic integrity
Application

**44.18** The nurse is assisting the client to dangle on the bedside. After raising the head of the bed, in which position should the nurse face?
1. Toward the nearest corner of the head of the bed
2. Toward the side of the bed
3. Toward the far corner of the foot of the bed
4. Directly toward the client

Answer: 3
Rationale: The nurse should face the far corner of the foot of the bed because this is the direction in which movement will occur. Facing in any other direction will require the nurse's trunk to twist when swinging the client's legs over the side of the bed and raising the client's head and shoulders.
Planning
Physiologic integrity
Application

**44.19** What is the priority action of the nurse prior to transferring a client from bed to wheelchair?
1. Place the bed in its lowest position.
2. Place the wheelchair parallel to the bed.
3. Lock the brakes on the bed.
4. Place a transfer belt on the client.

Answer: 3
Rationale: While all of these activities are important safety issues, the most important is to lock the wheels on the bed. If the wheels are not locked and the bed moves out from under the client, none of the other safety actions will likely prevent a fall or near fall.
Implementation
Safe, effective care environment
Analysis

**44.20** The nurse is preparing to transfer a client from the bed to a gurney. The correct position for the bed to be placed is parallel to the gurney and which of the following?
1. Slightly higher
2. Slightly lower
3. At the same height
4. At least 2 inches lower

Answer: 1
Rationale: When transferring a client from bed to gurney, the bed should be parallel to the gurney and slightly higher. It is easier for the client to move down a slant to the new surface than to move up to a higher surface or to an even surface.
Planning
Safe, effective care environment
Application

**44.21** The postoperative client is ambulating for the first time since surgery. The client has been able to tolerate sitting up on the side of the bed and has stood at the bedside without difficulty on two occasions. Which staff member should ambulate this client?
1. The UAP
2. A licensed practical (vocational) nurse
3. A registered nurse
4. It makes no difference

Answer: 3
Rationale: Since this is the first time this client has ambulated, the best choice is for the registered nurse to ambulate the client. The registered nurse must assess and evaluate the client's response to the ambulation. Once the client has successfully ambulated, any nursing staff member can assist. The registered nurse should make assistive personnel aware of potential untoward effects of ambulation and of what to report to the nurse.
Planning
Safe, effective care environment
Analysis

**44.22** The nurse is assisting a newly delivered mother in ambulating to the nursery to see her baby. The client complains of light-headedness and begins to faint. What is the nurse's most important action?
1. Ensure the client's modesty as she falls.

Answer: 2
Rationale: All of these actions are important, but the priority is ensuring the client does not strike her head on anything as she falls. The nurse should ease the client down while supporting her body against the nurse, protecting the head and laying it gently on the floor.

| | |
|---|---|
| 2. Be certain the client does not hit her head on anything.<br>3. Call for immediate assistance.<br>4. Check the vital signs and for excessive vaginal bleeding. | Implementation<br>Safe, effective care environment<br>Analysis |
| **44.23** The nurse is providing range of motion exercising to the client's elbow when the client complains of pain. What action should the nurse take?<br>1. Stop immediately and report the pain to the client's physician.<br>2. Discontinue the treatment and document the results in the medical record.<br>3. Reduce the movement of the joint just until the point of slight resistance.<br>4. Continue to exercise the joint as before to loosen the stiffness. | Answer: 3<br>Rationale: Range of motion exercising should never cause discomfort. In this case, the best action is to reduce the movement of the joint just until the point of slight resistance is felt and evaluate the pain response at that level. If there is no pain, the exercise can be continued. Stopping the treatment is not justified until this evaluation has taken place, but continuing at the same level may cause damage to the joint as well as causing pain to the client.<br>Evaluation<br>Safe, effective care environment<br>Analysis<br>Learning Outcome 44.3 |
| **44.24** The client has a history of postural hypotension. Which activities would the nurse advise this client would be likely to cause postural hypotension? (Select all that apply.)<br>1. Hot baths<br>2. Heavy meals<br>3. Use of a rocking chair<br>4. Valsalva maneuvers<br>5. Bending down to the floor | Answer: 1, 2, 4, 5<br>Rationale: Any activity that causes pooling or shifting of blood may cause postural hypotension. Hot baths can cause venous pooling in the lower extremities. Heavy meals divert blood to the gastrointestinal organs. Valsalva maneuvers slow the heart rate, which lowers blood pressure. Bending to the floor can cause rapid changes in blood pressure upon standing up again. Use of a rocking chair can be good for the client as the rocking action exercises the legs.<br>Implementation<br>Safe, effective care environment<br>Application<br>Learning Outcome 44.6 |
| **44.25** The nurse is teaching a client how to use a cane while rehabilitating from a left leg injury. The nurse should advise this client to place the cane on which side of the body? | Answer: Right<br>Rationale: The cane should be placed on the stronger side of the body, in this case the right side. This provides maximum support and the best body alignment.<br>Implementation<br>Safe, effective care environment<br>Application |
| **44.26** The nurse is evaluating the proper fit of crutches for a client who is to be discharged home. What portion of this client's body should support the weight? | Answer: Arms<br>Rationale: The weight of the body should rest on the arms, not the axilla. Weight on the axilla can cause radial nerve damage. Crutches that are too long will divert weight to the axilla. Crutches that are too short will cause the client to hunch over to walk and will alter the center of gravity, perhaps causing a fall.<br>Evaluation<br>Safe, effective care environment<br>Application |

# CHAPTER 45

| | |
|---|---|
| **45.1** The mother of a newborn calls the pediatric clinic and states, "I am concerned about my baby. When she first goes to sleep, her eyes dart around under her eyelids, she doesn't breathe regularly, and she sometimes twitches." What advice should the nurse give this mother? | Answer: 2<br>Rationale: These are indications of normal REM sleep in the newborn. The mother should be reassured that this is normal. Having the mother wait until the next checkup unnecessarily delays this reassurance. There is no need for an immediate trip to the clinic or to the emergency department.<br>Implementation<br>Physiologic integrity |

| | |
|---|---|
| 1. Please bring your baby in immediately for a checkup.<br>2. These are common behaviors in newborns and are normal.<br>3. You should ask the physician about these symptoms at your next checkup.<br>4. If your baby does this again, take her to the emergency department. | Application<br>Learning Outcome 45.1 |
| **45.2** The parents of a 6-month-old tell the nurse that they are exhausted because their baby wakes up several times every night. What advice should the nurse give these parents?<br>  1. Be certain that the baby is truly awake before picking him up for feeding.<br>  2. Let the baby "cry it out" for a few nights until he can sleep through the night.<br>  3. Continue to respond to the baby anytime he is restless during the night.<br>  4. Bring the baby in for a possible sleep study to check for sleeping disorders. | Answer: 1<br>Rationale: Babies often move and make noises while sleeping that do not indicate wakefulness. The parents should be certain the baby is awake before picking him up to feed, change, or comfort. Letting the baby "cry it out" is not appropriate if he really needs care. Continuing to respond to the baby anytime he is restless during the night is not necessary and may result in parental exhaustion. There is no indication for need of a sleep study for this baby.<br>Implementation<br>Physiologic integrity<br>Application<br>Learning Outcome 45.3 |
| **45.3** The 70-year-old woman tells the nurse, "I can go to sleep without a problem, but then I wake up in a couple of hours and can't go back to sleep." What nursing action would help promote rest and sleep in this client?<br>  1. Have the client develop a bedtime ritual of quiet music and a glass of wine.<br>  2. Encourage the client to avoid taking pain medication prior to sleep.<br>  3. Evaluate if the client perceives sleeplessness to be a serious problem.<br>  4. Have the client perform moderate exercises before bedtime. | Answer: 3<br>Rationale: The first intervention is to determine what the pattern of sleeplessness means to the client. Many older clients will "nap" off and on through the day and night and spend wakeful times engaged in activity, even if the active times are not during traditional active hours. Alcohol and exercise can interfere with sleep. If the client has pain, the nurse should not encourage avoidance of medication.<br>Planning<br>Physiologic integrity<br>Application<br>Learning Outcome 45.7 |
| **45.4** During a corporate health fair, an attendee states that he "just can't stay awake" during the daytime, although he "sleeps just fine at night." What advice should the nurse offer this man?<br>  1. Go to your physician for a physical examination.<br>  2. Go to a mental health professional for evaluation of possible depression.<br>  3. Purchase an over-the-counter sleep aid to deepen nighttime sleep.<br>  4. Drink more caffeinated beverages in the daytime to stay awake. | Answer: 1<br>Rationale: Daytime hypersomnia is often due to medical conditions such as kidney, liver, or metabolic disturbances. It is rarely caused by psychologic issues. An over-the-counter sleep aid is not a good choice as the man already sleeps well at night and sleep aids can sometimes cause future sleep disturbances. Caffeinated beverages may increase daytime wakefulness, but will not help any underlying problem that may be present.<br>Implementation<br>Physiologic integrity<br>Application<br>Learning Outcome 45.5 |

| | |
|---|---|
| **45.5** The nurse is developing a plan of care for a 25-year-old client of the outpatient clinic who has just been diagnosed with narcolepsy. Which intervention should the nurse include in this plan of care?<br><br>1. Encourage the client to take an over-the-counter medication to improve nighttime sleep.<br>2. Be certain the client has his prescription for modafinil (Provigil) filled.<br>3. Have the client purchase sodium oxybate (Xyrem) over the counter to prevent daytime drowsiness.<br>4. Be certain the client obtains antihistamines to control nasal stuffiness. | Answer: 2<br>Rationale: The medication modafinil (Provigil) is prescribed to control the daytime drowsiness associated with narcolepsy. There is no reason to take an over-the-counter sleep aid, as most younger clients generally have good nighttime sleep, but cannot stay awake in the daytime. Over-the-counter sleep medications may result in daytime sleepiness as well. Sodium oxybate (Xyrem) is a prescription medication that has very limited availability. The client should avoid antihistamines as they can cause daytime drowsiness to increase.<br>Planning<br>Physiologic integrity<br>Application<br>Learning Outcome 45.5 |
| **45.6** The client is being treated with a nasal continuous positive airway pressure device (CPAP) for sleep apnea. What finding would the nurse evaluate as indicating that this treatment has been helpful to the client?<br><br>1. The client has lost 7 pounds since treatment began.<br>2. The client sleeps so soundly that he snores.<br>3. The client's diabetes is now under control.<br>4. The client reports a decrease in morning headache. | Answer: 4<br>Rationale: The fact that the client experiences a decrease in morning headache indicates the client is sleeping better. Weight loss is not a direct result of CPAP therapy. Snoring is a sign of apnea, not sound sleeping. Successful treatment for sleep apnea will not help control diabetes.<br>Evaluation<br>Physiologic integrity<br>Analysis<br>Learning Outcome 45.7 |
| **45.7** The nurse is admitting a critically ill client to the intensive care unit. What questions should the nurse ask regarding this client's sleep history?<br><br>1. No questions should be asked.<br>2. When do you usually go to sleep?<br>3. Do you have any problems with sleeping?<br>4. What are your bedtime rituals? | Answer: 1<br>Rationale: When the client is critically ill or being admitted for an outpatient procedure, sleep history can be omitted or deferred.<br>Assessment<br>Physiologic integrity<br>Application<br>Learning Outcome 45.6 |
| **45.8** The nurse is completing the admission assessment on a client who has obstructive sleep apnea. Which findings would be probable in this client? (Select all that apply.)<br><br>1. Reddened uvula<br>2. Large soft palate<br>3. Obesity<br>4. Short neck<br>5. Deviated septum | Answer: 1, 2, 3<br>Rationale: Clients with obstructive sleep apnea are likely to have a reddened and enlarged uvula and soft palate. They may be obese. A large, thick neck (over 17.5 inches) is more likely to be problematic than is a short neck. Deviated septum is an unlikely cause of obstructive apnea.<br>Assessment<br>Physiologic integrity<br>Application<br>Learning Outcome 45.5 |
| **45.9** The client who has sleep apnea reports falling asleep while driving, almost being involved in a crash, and frequent episodes of sleepwalking. What nursing diagnosis should be a priority for this client? | Answer: 4<br>Rationale: Although all of these nursing diagnoses may be correct for this client, the priority is *Risk for Injury* related to somnambulism since it reflects the most dangerous situation for the client.<br>Diagnosis |

| | |
|---|---|
| 1. *Disturbed Sleep Pattern* related to difficulty staying asleep<br>2. *Risk for Impaired Gas Exchange* related to sleep apnea<br>3. *Disturbed Thought Processes* related to chronic insomnia<br>4. *Risk for Injury* related to somnambulism | Physiologic integrity<br>Analysis<br>Learning Outcome 45.7 |
| **45.10** The nurse is working with a client to develop an expected outcome for the nursing diagnosis *Disturbed Sleep Pattern,* difficulty staying asleep related to anxiety secondary to multiple life stressors. Which expected outcome would be most applicable to this client's situation? The client will:<br>1. Sleep at least 8 hours each night.<br>2. List three positive coping mechanisms for anxiety relief.<br>3. Report getting sufficient sleep to provide energy for daily activities.<br>4. Manifest less anxiety after taking prescribed medications. | Answer: 3<br>Rationale: The best outcome statement for this client is to report getting sufficient sleep to provide energy for daily activities. The client may require more than 8 hours of sleep to feel rested and have sufficient energy. Simply listing coping mechanisms for anxiety relief is not as helpful as actually getting sleep. Antianxiety medications are probably not the most important factor for this client.<br>Planning<br>Physiologic integrity<br>Application<br>Learning Outcome 45.7 |
| **45.11** The nurse is planning interventions for a client who has difficulty falling asleep. Which intervention regarding sleep times would be most helpful?<br>1. Maintain a regular bedtime and wake-up time for all days of the week.<br>2. If bedtime is delayed on one night, go to bed that much earlier the next night.<br>3. If daytime drowsiness occurs, go to bed earlier that night.<br>4. Sleep at least 1 hour later on mornings you don't have to go to work. | Answer: 1<br>Rationale: The best intervention is to have the client establish and maintain a regular bedtime and wake-up time for all days of the week. Moving bedtimes and awakening times according to drowsiness, delayed bedtime, or work schedules does not promote a sleep routine.<br>Planning<br>Physiologic integrity<br>Application<br>Learning Outcome 45.7 |
| **45.12** The client reports having difficulty sleeping. Which environmental intervention would the nurse recommend?<br>1. Play soft music through the night.<br>2. Keep a television on in the bedroom.<br>3. Provide white noise with a fan.<br>4. Play a talk radio station. | Answer: 3<br>Rationale: Noise should be kept to a minimum. Extraneous noise can be blocked by white noise from a fan, air conditioner, or white noise machine. Music, talk radio, and television are not recommended as they can be interesting enough to promote wakefulness.<br>Planning<br>Physiologic integrity<br>Application<br>Learning Outcome 45.7 |
| **45.13** The client reports having difficulty sleeping and awakening several times during the night. What intervention should the nurse recommend for the client when unable to sleep?<br>1. Get out of bed, go into another room, and pursue some relaxing activity until drowsy. | Answer: 1<br>Rationale: The bed should be used only for sleep or sexual activity, so it is associated with sleep. The client should get up, go into a different room, and pursue some relaxing activity until drowsiness returns. Lying awake in bed or sitting in the bed while watching television will strengthen the association between wakefulness and bed. Exercise within 2 hours of attempting to sleep may cause wakefulness.<br>Planning<br>Physiologic integrity |

| | |
|---|---|
| 2. Get out of bed, go into another room, and exercise until tired before trying to go back to sleep.<br>3. Sit in bed and watch the bedroom television until drowsy.<br>4. Stay in bed with eyes closed and do some mental arithmetic until sleepy. | Application<br>Learning Outcome 45.7 |
| **45.14** The hospitalized client requests a bedtime snack. Which food should the nurse offer this client?<br>1. Hot chocolate<br>2. Tea and crackers<br>3. Cereal with milk<br>4. Chips and salsa | Answer: 3<br>Rationale: The nurse should offer the client a light carbohydrate (cereal) and milk. Hot chocolate and tea contain caffeine which can cause wakefulness and nocturia. Chips and salsa are so spicy that they may cause gastrointestinal upsets that disturb sleep.<br>Implementation<br>Physiologic integrity<br>Application<br>Learning Outcome 45.8 |
| **45.15** The client has been prescribed zolpidem (Ambien) for the short-term management of insomnia. What information should the nurse include in discharge planning for this client?<br>1. For best results, take the medication just prior to bedtime.<br>2. Take the medication at dinnertime to avoid gastric upset.<br>3. Do not take the medication with any liquid that contains calcium.<br>4. Drink an entire glass of water with the dose to avoid kidney stones. | Answer: 1<br>Rationale: Zolpidem (Ambien) has a rapid onset of action, so for best results and decreased sedation while awake, the client should take the medication just prior to bedtime. The client should not take the medication at dinnertime, which is probably some hours before bedtime. There is no reason to avoid calcium, or special need for extra water with the dose.<br>Implementation<br>Physiologic integrity<br>Application<br>Learning Outcome 45.8 |
| **45.16** The client who has obstructive sleep apnea is being treated with a nasal continuous positive airway pressure (CPAP) device, but has just been prescribed modafinil (Provigil). What client statement should the nurse evaluate as indicating understanding of the discharge instructions regarding these two therapies?<br>1. "I am so glad that I won't have to sleep in this machine anymore."<br>2. "Once I get regulated on the Provigil, I will wean myself off the CPAP."<br>3. "I will continue using my CPAP machine at night."<br>4. "I can turn down the pressure on my CPAP machine in about 1 week." | Answer: 3<br>Rationale: Provigil is a medication that is for the treatment of narcolepsy, not sleep apnea. It will not prevent sleep apnea, so the client must continue to use the CPAP machine as it was used prior to the Provigil.<br>Evaluation<br>Physiologic integrity<br>Application<br>Learning Outcome 45.8 |
| **45.17** The client calls the neurology clinic nurse and questions a newly prescribed medication. The client states, "The pharmacist told me this drug is used for Parkinson's disease." Upon checking the medical record the nurse discovers the client was diagnosed with | Answer: 2<br>Rationale: Medications that are commonly prescribed for the treatment of Parkinson's disease are also prescribed for the treatment of PLMD. There is no need for the client to return to the clinic, nor is there an error. If the nurse calls the pharmacy, it should be to collaborate with the pharmacist regarding the use of this medication.<br>Implementation |

| | |
|---|---|
| periodic limb movements disorder (PLMD) this morning. What action should the nurse take? <br>   1. Have the client bring the medication to the clinic for review. <br>   2. Assure the client that medications used to treat Parkinson's disease are also used to treat PLMD. <br>   3. Tell the client not to take the medication because there is most likely an error. <br>   4. Call the pharmacy and reprimand the pharmacist for dispensing the wrong medication. | Physiologic integrity <br> Application <br> Learning Outcome 45.8 |
| **45.18** The nurse is working on a hospital committee tasked with reducing environmental distractions to sleep within the hospital. Which recommendations by the committee would be helpful? (Select all that apply.) <br>   1. Turn off all overhead lights on the unit and use night-lights and flashlights. <br>   2. Establish a time at which radios and televisions should be turned off or down. <br>   3. Discontinue use of the paging system after 2100. <br>   4. Conduct nursing reports in the hallway. <br>   5. Open curtains between beds in semiprivate rooms. | Answer: 2, 3 <br> Rationale: Establishing a time at which radios and televisions should be turned off or down will reduce the amount of disturbance to clients. Discontinuing use of the paging system at 2100 will also reduce noise. It is not possible to turn off all overhead lights and use only night-lights and flashlights, but those lights that can be eliminated should be. Nursing reports should be conducted in an area away from the client beds. Closing the curtains between beds in semiprivate rooms will also decrease disturbance. <br> Planning <br> Physiologic integrity <br> Application <br> Learning Outcome 45.8 |
| **45.19** The client has complained of stiffness and muscle tension in his back. The nurse suggests a back rub, but the client declines the offer. What action should the nurse take? <br>   1. Encourage the client to accept the back rub, saying how much it will relax the back muscles. <br>   2. Document that the client is noncompliant with the nursing plan of care. <br>   3. Accept the declination but tell the client to call if he changes his mind. <br>   4. Instruct the UAP to rub the client's back while assisting him to change into a clean gown. | Answer: 3 <br> Rationale: Some clients are eager to have a back rub, but others are not comfortable with the close physical contact this intervention requires. Respect the client's decision, but keep the offer open if he changes his mind. The client is not noncompliant, he is simply stating his preference. The UAP should not attempt to rub the client's back without permission. <br> Implementation <br> Physiologic integrity <br> Application <br> Learning Outcome 45.8 |
| **45.20** The 5-year-old has recurrent night terrors. What nursing intervention would the nurse plan to help alleviate this problem? <br>   1. Have the child walk around in the room when night terrors occur. <br>   2. The next morning, ask the child to describe the event. | Answer: 3 <br> Rationale: Night terrors are partial awakenings that are sometimes related to excessive tiredness or a full bladder. Having the child empty the bladder before going to bed might be helpful. Since this is a partial awakening, walking the child around the room will not help and the child will probably not awaken. The child will have no memory of the event the next morning. There is no reason to add an additional pillow behind the child's head. <br> Planning |

| | |
|---|---|
| 3. Have the child empty the bladder prior to going to bed.<br>4. Use an additional pillow behind the child's head at night. | Physiologic integrity<br>Application<br>Learning Outcome 45.3 |

# CHAPTER 46

| | |
|---|---|
| **46.1** The nurse is caring for an 8-month-old infant. Which of the following is the best tool the nurse should use for evaluating pain in this infant?<br>   1. FLACC scale<br>   2. Wong-Baker FACES<br>   3. Visual analog scale<br>   4. Any of the above | Answer: 1<br>Rationale: The FLACC scale has been validated in children from 2 months to 7 years old. Options 2 and 3 are not appropriate for this age child.<br>Assessment<br>Health promotion and maintenance<br>Analysis |
| **46.2** The nurse is preparing to discharge a client home with a prescription for ibuprofen. Which of the following is a well-known side effect of this drug?<br>   1. Gastrointestinal (GI) bleeding<br>   2. Shakiness<br>   3. Tremors<br>   4. Rash | Answer: 1<br>Rationale: Gastrointestinal bleeding is a well-known side effect of any NSAID, including ibuprofen.<br>Evaluation<br>Health promotion and maintenance<br>Knowledge<br>Learning Outcome 46.10 |
| **46.3** Which of the following objective assessment data does the nurse know to obtain before administering any opioid?<br>   1. Pain level as stated by client<br>   2. Any nausea the client may be feeling<br>   3. Respiratory rate<br>   4. Color of skin | Answer: 3<br>Rationale: Opioids may depress the respiratory system, so the nurse should assess the respiratory rate before administering opioids. Options 1 and 2 are both subjective data.<br>Assessment<br>Physiological integrity<br>Analysis<br>Learning Outcome 46.5 |
| **46.4** The duration of action for most opiates is how long?<br>   1. 2 hours<br>   2. 4 hours<br>   3. 6 hours<br>   4. 8 hours | Answer: 2<br>Rationale: The duration of action for most opiates is 4 hours.<br>Assessment<br>Physiological integrity<br>Knowledge<br>Learning Outcome 46.10 |
| **46.5** The nurse is to administer acetaminophen (Tylenol) prn for a headache. The client has been vomiting all day. Which of the following routes should the nurse use to administer the medication?<br>   1. Oral<br>   2. Vaginal<br>   3. Rectal<br>   4. Intravenous | Answer: 3<br>Rationale: The rectal route is often used if the client has nausea or vomiting. The nurse should administer an acetaminophen suppository to the client.<br>Assessment<br>Physiological integrity<br>Analysis<br>Learning Outcome 46.10 |
| **46.6** The nurse is caring for a client who underwent a left below-the-knee amputation. The client calls and asks the nurse for pain medication. The client informs the nurse he has left foot pain. What type of pain is the client describing?<br>   1. Phantom limb pain<br>   2. Acute pain | Answer: 1<br>Rationale: When the amputation involves a limb, it is termed *phantom limb pain*.<br>Assessment<br>Physiological integrity<br>Knowledge<br>Learning Outcome 46.1 |

| | |
|---|---|
| 3. Chronic pain<br>4. Narcotic-induced pain | |
| **46.7** The nurse is providing discharge instructions to a client receiving an opioid. Which of the following measures can be used to decrease the risk of constipation?<br>   1. Take an antihistamine three times per day.<br>   2. Drink 6 to 8 glasses of water per day.<br>   3. Assess respiratory rate before taking medication.<br>   4. Assess heart rate before taking medication. | Answer: 2<br>Rationale: Increasing fluid intake can help prevent constipation. Option 1 will not affect constipation. Options 3 and 4 are not interventions that will prevent constipation.<br>Evaluation<br>Physiological integrity<br>Analysis<br>Learning Outcome 46.10 |
| **46.8** The nurse is caring for a client on a PCA pump with morphine. Which of the following medications should the nurse have readily available?<br>   1. Naloxone hydrochloride (Narcan)<br>   2. Acetaminophen (Tylenol)<br>   3. Diphenhydramine hydrochloride (Benadryl)<br>   4. Normal saline | Answer: 1<br>Rationale: Narcan is an opioid antagonist and should be readily available when a client is receiving an opioid.<br>Implementation<br>Physiological integrity<br>Analysis<br>Learning Outcome 46.13 |
| **46.9** The client is taking meperidine (Demerol) and experiencing pruritus. Which of the following medications would the nurse expect the physician to order?<br>   1. Naloxone hydrochloride (Narcan)<br>   2. Acetaminophen (Tylenol)<br>   3. Diphenhydramine hydrochloride (Benadryl)<br>   4. Normal saline | Answer: 3<br>Rationale: When clients experience pruritus, an antihistamine, such as Benadryl, is ordered.<br>Implementation<br>Physiological integrity<br>Analysis<br>Learning Outcome 46.10 |
| **46.10** The nurse is admitting a client to the emergency department with complaints of severe abdominal pain. What is the nurse's first action?<br>   1. Administer IV pain medication as ordered.<br>   2. Start an IV line of lactated Ringer's.<br>   3. Assess pain using a scale of 1 to 10.<br>   4. Place a Foley catheter to bedside drainage. | Answer: 3<br>Rationale: Assessment should always occur before implementation.<br>Implementation<br>Physiological integrity<br>Analysis<br>Learning Outcome 46.5 |
| **46.11** If a client is having cardiac pain, but relates the pain is in the left shoulder and denies chest pain, this client is experiencing which of the following?<br>   1. Phantom pain<br>   2. Referred pain<br>   3. Visceral pain<br>   4. Chronic pain | Answer: 2<br>Rationale: Referred pain appears to arise in different areas of the body, as may occur with cardiac pain.<br>Assessment<br>Physiological integrity<br>Analysis<br>Learning Outcome 46.1 |

| | |
|---|---|
| **46.12** If a client rates his pain a 7 on a scale of 0 to 10, the intensity of his pain would be documented as which of the following?<br>1. Mild pain<br>2. Moderate pain<br>3. Severe pain<br>4. Physiological pain | Answer: 3<br>Rationale: Severe pain is rated a 7–10 on a scale of 0 to 10.<br>Assessment<br>Physiological integrity<br>Knowledge<br>Learning Outcome 46.1 |
| **46.13** The nurse is caring for a client presenting to the emergency department with a possible sprained ankle. This client is most likely experiencing what type of pain?<br>1. Mild pain<br>2. Severe pain<br>3. Somatic pain<br>4. Visceral pain | Answer: 3<br>Rationale: Somatic pain originates in the skin, muscles, bone, or connective tissue. The sharp sensation of a paper cut or aching of a sprained ankle are common examples of somatic pain.<br>Assessment<br>Physiological integrity<br>Analysis<br>Learning Outcome 46.1 |
| **46.14** The client scheduled to undergo a minor surgery states, "The physician will not give me pain medication after surgery because my surgery is only minor." The best response by the nurse is:<br>1. "You can experience pain after minor surgery, so you can have pain medication."<br>2. "You are correct. The physician will not order any pain medication."<br>3. "You are correct. I will need to teach you nonpharmacologic pain relief measures."<br>4. "You can only have about half the dose since your surgery is minor." | Answer: 1<br>Rationale: Clients can experience intense pain after minor surgery, so pain medication may be ordered.<br>Implementation<br>Physiological integrity<br>Analysis<br>Learning Outcome 46.7 |
| **46.15** The nurse is performing discharge teaching for a client taking an NSAID. The client states he has heard taking an antacid with this medication will help decrease the incidence of upset stomach. The nurse's best response is:<br>1. "Antacids reduce the absorption and therefore the effectiveness of the NSAID."<br>2. "Antacids help to reduce the incidence of gastric bleeding that could occur with the use of NSAIDs."<br>3. "Antacids should never be taken with an NSAID."<br>4. "Antacids help to reduce the incidence of pain." | Answer: 1<br>Rationale: Option 1 is the best answer. It is documented that the use of antacids can reduce the risk of gastric distress, but can also reduce the absorption and the effectiveness of the medication.<br>Evaluation<br>Physiological integrity<br>Analysis<br>Learning Outcome 46.10 |

**46.16** The nurse is admitting a client who gave birth 2 hours ago. The client has an epidural catheter in place. Which of the following should be immediately reported to the physician?
1. Pulse rate: 80
2. Respiratory rate: 8
3. Blood pressure: 120/80
4. Pain rating of 4 on scale of 1–10

Answer: 2
Rationale: A respiratory rate below 8 should be reported immediately. Options 1 and 3 are normal. Option 4 does not require the nurse to notify the physician.
Evaluation
Physiological integrity
Analysis
Learning Outcome 46.13

**46.17** The client is admitted to the emergency department with complaints of abdominal pain. The client denies any nausea or vomiting. When asked, the client states the pain started 2 hours ago and describes the pain as "cramping." The client is most likely experiencing what type of pain?
1. Chronic pain
2. Phantom pain
3. Visceral pain
4. Acute pain

Answer: 4
Rationale: Acute pain is pain that is directly related to tissue injury and resolves when tissue heals.
Assessment
Physiological integrity
Analysis
Learning Outcome 46.1

**46.18** While conducting a pain assessment, the nurse knows to assess which of the following? (Select all that apply.)
1. Duration
2. Location
3. Intensity
4. Etiology
5. Neurology

Answer: 1, 2, 3, 4
Rationale: Pain may be described in terms of location, duration, intensity, and etiology.
Assessment
Physiological integrity
Knowledge
Learning Outcome 46.5

**46.19** The nurse is obtaining a comprehensive pain history on a client admitted with complaints of continuous low back pain. Which of the following should be included in the history? (Select all that apply.)
1. Pain location
2. Intensity
3. Quality
4. Alleviating factors
5. Past pain experiences
6. Effect on ADLs

Answer: 1, 2, 3, 4, 5, 6
Rationale: All options should be obtained in the comprehensive pain history.
Assessment
Physiological integrity
Knowledge
Learning Outcome 46.2

**46.20** The nurse is caring for a client with a continuous local anesthetic. Which of the following interventions will the nurse perform?
1. Assess for pain every 2 to 4 hours while the client is awake.
2. Change dressing every 2 to 4 hours.
3. Check the dressing every shift.
4. Assess for signs of toxicity.
5. Check the site of the catheter.

Answer: 1, 3, 4, 5
Rationale: The dressing is not usually changed in order to avoid dislodging the catheter.
Implementation
Physiological integrity
Analysis
Learning Outcome 46.13

**47.1** The parent of a newborn infant calls the pediatrician's office to report that the baby wakes up every 2 hours and only takes about 2 ounces of formula before going back to sleep. What instruction should the nurse give this parent?

1. Make the baby wait at least 3 hours between feedings.
2. Continue to feed the baby with this "on demand" schedule.
3. When the baby gets sleepy during feeding, use techniques such as moving around and tickling to encourage wakefulness.
4. Offer the baby less formula to prevent waste.

Answer: 2

Rationale: Newborns are often fed following an "on demand" schedule. This might include feedings every 2 hours at first. Making the baby wait longer between feedings, offering less formula, or trying to keep the baby awake to feed may result in feeding difficulties later in childhood.

Implementation

Physiological integrity

Application

Learning Outcome 47.6

---

**47.2** What criteria does the nurse evaluate to determine if an infant's regurgitation, or spitting up, should be further investigated?

1. How often the baby spits up
2. How much the baby spits up at a time
3. If the baby is gaining weight adequately
4. The consistency of the regurgitated matter

Answer: 3

Rationale: As long as the baby is gaining weight adequately, it is not abnormal for regurgitation or spitting up to occur. The consistency of the regurgitated material may be thin (just consumed) or curdled (has been partially digested) and either case is normal. Many babies spit up after every meal and some seem to spit up a great deal. As long as the baby continues to gain weight as expected, the spitting up will generally pass once the child is in an upright posture most of the day.

Evaluation

Physiologic integrity

Application

Learning Outcome 47.13

---

**47.3** The parents of a 7-month-old child have started offering solid foods to their baby. The baby has enjoyed and tolerated rice cereal, applesauce, and other fruits. Which food should the nurse recommend to be introduced next?

1. Strained beef
2. Green beans
3. Squash
4. Strained chicken

Answer: 3

Rationale: As the baby develops, foods are offered in the sequence in which they are generally best tolerated. Most experts recommend introducing cereals, fruits, yellow vegetables (squash), green vegetables (green beans), and then meats.

Implementation

Physiological integrity

Application

Learning Outcome 47.6

---

**47.4** The nurse has advised the client to consume alcohol only in moderation. What guideline should the nurse provide as a "moderate" alcohol intake?

1. Two drinks per week for women, three for men
2. Two drinks per day for women, three for men
3. One drink per day for women, two for men
4. One drink per week for women, two for men

Answer: 3

Rationale: Moderate alcohol consumption is considered one drink per day for women, two drinks per day for men.

Evaluation

Physiologic integrity

Application

Learning Outcome 47.5

---

**47.5** The nurse completes triceps skinfold measurement on a client newly admitted to the long-term care facility. In order to obtain the most meaningful data, how soon should the nurse repeat this measurement?

1. Two days
2. Ten days to two weeks
3. One month
4. One year

Answer: 4

Rationale: Anthropometric measurements such as triceps skinfold measurement provide the most meaningful data when monitored over longer periods of time such as several months to years. The changes in this measurement occur so slowly that remeasuring in 2 days, 10 days, 2 weeks, or 1 month would not provide significant data.

Planning
Physiological integrity
Application
Learning Outcome 47.8

---

**47.6** The client's lab studies reveal a normal serum albumin with a prealbumin of 10. How does the nurse interpret the significance of these readings?

1. The client has had recent protein malnutrition.
2. The client is now relatively well nourished with malnutrition 6 to 8 months ago.
3. The client is at risk for development of malabsorption syndromes.
4. Carbohydrate malnutrition has occurred over the last 6 months.

Answer: 1

Rationale: Prealbumin is the most responsive serum protein to rapid changes in nutritional status. A level below 11 indicates that aggressive nutritional intervention is necessary. Serum albumin is the slowest of the serum proteins to reflect changes, so abnormalities indicate prolonged protein malnutrition. There is no specific link to malabsorption syndromes. These tests are indicators of protein malnutrition, not carbohydrate malnutrition.

Evaluation
Physiological integrity
Analysis
Learning Outcome 47.9

---

**47.7** The client reports following the "food pyramid" to guide nutritional intake. How should the nurse evaluate this information?

1. Since this food pyramid is produced by the U.S. Department of Agriculture, the client is likely consuming necessary levels of all essential nutrients.
2. The food pyramid is most useful when applied to the nutritional intake of children.
3. The food pyramid is not very useful because it does not take fluid intake and combination foods into consideration.
4. Following the appropriate food pyramid is helpful, but there are additional factors to consider in a balanced diet.

Answer: 4

Rationale: Since there are numerous food pyramids, the client should be following the appropriate one, and other factors such as fluid intake and activity level should be considered in planning a balanced diet. Overall, the food pyramid is a good guide, but unless the client eats a variety of foods from each group, some recommended nutrient levels may be missed. Food pyramids are available for different age groups, including children, middle adults, and older adults.

Evaluation
Physiologic integrity
Analysis
Learning Outcome 47.7

---

**47.8** The nurse has instructed an overweight client to follow a 2,000-calorie diet by substituting foods considered low in calories for those higher in calories. How does the client interpret the food label to decide if a food is low in calories?

1. The product label will state "lighter" or "reduced calories."
2. The nutrition facts label will have the letter "L" located in the lower right corner.

Answer: 3

Rationale: In order to qualify as a low-calorie food in a 2,000-calorie diet, the food must have less than 40 calories per serving. The words "lighter" or "reduced calories" only mean that this version of the food is lower in calories than a previous version, but the food can still be very high in calories. There is no special label letter that indicates foods lighter in calories. Foods that are lower in fat also contain fewer calories, but low fat is considered less than 5%.

Evaluation
Physiological integrity
Analysis
Learning Outcome 47.13

---

|  |  |
| --- | --- |
| 3. Nutritional labeling on the product will indicate less than 40 calories per serving. <br> 4. The product will contain no more than 11% fat. |  |
| **47.9** The client reports that her teenager has started a vegan diet. Which addition to meals should the nurse recommend to help ensure that this teenager does not become iron deficient? (Select all that apply.) <br> 1. Tofu <br> 2. Soybean milk <br> 3. Brewer's yeast <br> 4. Orange juice <br> 5. Okra <br> 6. Apples | Answer: 1, 2, 4 <br> Rationale: While all these options are good ones for someone on a vegan diet, the ones that would best prevent iron deficiency are tofu, soybean milk, and orange juice. Tofu and soybean milk are good sources of protein and iron. Orange juice supports iron absorption from foods since it is high in vitamin C. Brewer's yeast is a good source of vitamin $B_{12}$, which is often low in vegan diets. <br> Implementation <br> Physiological integrity <br> Analysis <br> Learning Outcome 47.5 |
| **47.10** Nitrogen balance testing is planned for a newly admitted client. What instruction to the staff caring for this client is essential? <br> 1. Remove the client's oxygen cannula 10 minutes prior to the test. <br> 2. Accurate measurement of food intake is very important. <br> 3. All urine output should be collected for 48 hours. <br> 4. Keep the client NPO beginning at midnight before the test. | Answer: 2 <br> Rationale: Nitrogen balance is determined by comparing the grams of protein taken in to the urinary nitrogen output for 24 hours. Accurate food intake is essential. The presence of an oxygen cannula is not associated with preparation for the test. The client must have protein intake during the testing time. <br> Planning <br> Physiological integrity <br> Application <br> Learning Outcome 47.13 |
| **47.11** The client who has undergone a gastrointestinal surgery is permitted to have a clear liquid diet on the second postoperative day. Which fluid should the nurse order from the diet kitchen for this client? <br> 1. Apricot nectar <br> 2. Cranberry juice <br> 3. Chicken broth <br> 4. Cherry ice pop | Answer: 3 <br> Rationale: Chicken broth is the only liquid listed that is clear and not red. Apricot nectar is thick with pulp. Cranberry juice is red, as is a cherry ice pop. Clients who have undergone gastrointestinal surgery are often not allowed to have red liquids because the color can be confused with blood if the client vomits. <br> Planning <br> Physiological integrity <br> Application <br> Learning Outcome 47.10 |
| **47.12** At 7:15 AM, two unlicensed personnel are assigned the task of feeding breakfast to four incapacitated clients. What instruction should the nurse include in this delegation? <br> 1. Breakfast should be completed by 8:00 AM so that baths may begin. <br> 2. Give fluids before and after each bite of solid foods. <br> 3. Stand to the left of right-handed clients during feeding. <br> 4. Engage the client in conversation during the meal. | Answer: 4 <br> Rationale: Of the options given, the best answer is to engage the client in conversation during the meal. This makes the mealtime pleasant and encourages socialization as well as appetite. It may well take over 45 minutes to feed these clients in an unhurried manner. Fluids should be offered when the client requests fluids, or after three to four bites of food. The personnel should sit while feeding the client to convey a relaxed and unhurried atmosphere. <br> Planning <br> Safe, effective care environment <br> Application <br> Learning Outcome 47.13 |

| | |
|---|---|
| **47.13** Arrange the steps of nasogastric tube insertion in the proper order.<br>1. Ask the client to tilt the head forward.<br>2. Insert the tube with its natural curve toward the client.<br>3. Ask the client to hyperextend the neck.<br>4. Have the client swallow a small amount of liquid.<br>5. Employ a slight twisting motion on the tube. | Answer: 2, 3, 5, 1, 4<br>Rationale: The tube should first be inserted with its natural curve toward the client. At this time, having the client hyperextend the neck will reduce the curvature of the nasopharyngeal junction. A slight twisting motion may help pass the tube into the nasopharynx. At this time, have the client tilt the head forward to facilitate passage of the tube into the posterior pharynx and esophagus. The client should then be asked to swallow to move the epiglottis over the opening of the larynx, directing the tube toward the esophagus.<br>Implementation<br>Physiological integrity<br>Application<br>Learning Outcome 47.12 |
| **47.14** What instruction does the nurse give the client as the nasogastric tube is being removed? | Answer: Hold your breath.<br>Rationale: Holding the breath closes the glottis, thereby reducing the possibility of aspiration as the tube is removed.<br>Implementation<br>Physiological integrity<br>Application<br>Learning Outcome 47.12 |
| **47.15** The nursing staff has routinely checked feeding tube placement by testing the pH of aspirated tube contents. The client has been started on an $H_2$ blocker. Should the nurse expect the pH now to be higher or lower? | Answer: Higher<br>Rationale: The $H_2$ blocker lowers the acidity of the stomach content, making the pH higher.<br>Evaluation<br>Physiological integrity<br>Analysis<br>Learning Outcome 47.11 |
| **47.16** The nurse has delegated administration of tube feeding to a specially trained UAP. What action should be taken by the nurse in regard to this delegation?<br>1. Order the equipment to give the feeding.<br>2. Check the tube for placement.<br>3. Set up the equipment and mix the feeding.<br>4. Regulate the rate of the feeding. | Answer: 2<br>Rationale: The nurse is responsible to assess tube placement and to determine that the tube is patent. The UAP can order equipment, set up equipment, mix the feeding, and regulate the rate of feeding.<br>Implementation<br>Safe, effective care environment<br>Application<br>Learning Outcome 47.13 |
| **47.17** The nurse notices that the client's continuous open system tube-feeding set is almost empty. What action should the nurse take?<br>1. Add tube feeding to the set.<br>2. Discontinue the feeding and hang a closed system bag.<br>3. Wash out the set and add new feeding.<br>4. Flush the set with clear carbonated soda and discontinue. | Answer: 3<br>Rationale: The open set should be taken down, washed well, and rehung with new feeding. Feeding is not added to that which has already been hanging. There is no indication to change the type of feeding to a closed system. Carbonated soda should not be used to irrigate the tube as it can lead to occlusion.<br>Implementation<br>Physiological integrity<br>Application<br>Learning Outcome 47.13 |
| **47.18** As the nasogastric tube is passed into the oropharynx, the client begins to gag and cough. What is the correct nursing action?<br>1. Remove the tube and attempt reinsertion.<br>2. Give the client a few sips of water. | Answer: 2<br>Rationale: Swallowing ice or water may help calm the gag reflex and also facilitate the "swallowing" of the tube. This is a common response to the presence of a tube in the oropharynx, so removal of the tube is not necessary. The nurse should not use pressure to pass the tube. The client's head should be tilted forward at this point. Tilting the head back will open the airway, not the esophagus.<br>Implementation |

| | |
|---|---|
| 3. Use firm pressure to pass the tube through the glottis.<br>4. Have the client tilt the head back to open the passage. | Physiological integrity<br>Application<br>Learning Outcome 47.12 |
| **47.19** The nurse notes that the tube-fed client has shallow breathing and dusky color. The feeding is running at the prescribed rate. What is the nurse's priority action?<br>    1. Place the client in high Fowler's position.<br>    2. Turn off the tube feeding.<br>    3. Assess the client's lung sounds.<br>    4. Assess the client's bowel sounds. | Answer: 2<br>Rationale: These findings indicate possible aspiration of the feeding. The priority action is to discontinue the feeding to eliminate the amount of material going into the client's lungs. This should be done before any further assessment or client position change is attempted. If it is discovered that there is no aspiration, the tube feeding can be restarted.<br>Evaluation<br>Physiological integrity<br>Analysis<br>Learning Outcome 47.13 |
| **47.20** The nurse is calculating the body mass index (BMI) of a client admitted to the long-term care facility. The client is 1.75 meters tall and weighs 65 kilograms. What BMI measurement should the nurse document for this client? | Answer: 21<br>Rationale: BMI is calculated by dividing the weight in kilograms by the height in meters squared.<br>Assessment<br>Physiological integrity<br>Analysis<br>Learning Outcome 47.4 |
| **47.21** The client has a body mass index (BMI) of 18. How does the nurse interpret this finding?<br>    1. The client is malnourished.<br>    2. The client is underweight.<br>    3. The client is normal.<br>    4. The client is overweight. | Answer: 2<br>Rationale: A BMI of 18 falls within the category of being underweight (16–19). Clients who have a BMI less than 16 are considered malnourished. Clients with a BMI of 20–25 are considered normal. A BMI of 26–30 is considered overweight.<br>Diagnosis<br>Physiological integrity<br>Analysis<br>Learning Outcome 47.4 |
| **47.22** On admission, the client weighs 165 lb (75 kg). The client reports that this is a weight loss from 180 lb (82 kg). What is the percent weight loss?<br>    1. 4.5%<br>    2. 6.25%<br>    3. 8.3%<br>    4. 10.0% | Answer: 3<br>Rationale: To calculate the percent weight loss, subtract the current weight (165 lb) from the usual weight (180 lb). Divide the result by the usual weight and multiply that result by 100. In this case, the loss is 8.3%.<br>Assessment<br>Physiological integrity<br>Analysis<br>Learning Outcome 47.4 |
| **47.23** The client is weighed each month while residing in the long-term care facility. This month the client weighs 110 lb (50 kg). The nurse compares this weight to the last 3 months' results and discovers the client has lost 22 lb (10 kg). There has been no attempt to lose this weight. How does the nurse interpret this weight loss?<br>    1. No malnutrition<br>    2. Mild malnutrition<br>    3. Moderate malnutrition<br>    4. Severe malnutrition | Answer: 2<br>Rationale: To calculate the level of nutritional deficit, the nurse first figures the current percentage of usual body weight and then compares that result to nutritional standards. To calculate the percent of usual body weight, divide the current weight by the usual body weight and multiply by 100. In this case, the client is at 91% of usual body weight. Mild malnutrition is 85% to 90%, moderate malnutrition is 75% to 84%, and severe malnutrition is less than 74%. This is particularly important in an unintentional weight loss.<br>Diagnosis<br>Physiological integrity<br>Analysis<br>Learning Outcome 47.4 |

| | |
|---|---|
| **47.24** The client who was started on total parenteral nutrition (TPN) yesterday has the following morning lab results. Which result indicates the greatest urgency for the nurse's collaboration with the physician?<br>　1.　BUN of 60<br>　2.　Prealbumin of 15<br>　3.　Serum glucose of 328<br>　4.　Potassium of 3.5 | Answer: 3<br>Rationale: The most important concern in this set of laboratory data is the increased serum glucose. If the client has malnutrition, the BUN and prealbumin may be abnormal, but 1 day of TPN therapy will not change those values. The potassium reading is normal.<br>Diagnosis<br>Physiological integrity<br>Analysis<br>Learning Outcome 47.13 |
| **47.25** What nursing diagnosis is the most important for the nurse to include in the care plan of a client who has just been started on total parenteral nutrition (TPN) therapy?<br>　1.　*Risk for Infection*<br>　2.　*Imbalanced Nutrition: Less than Body Requirements*<br>　3.　*Activity Intolerance*<br>　4.　*Fluid Volume Deficit* | Answer: 1<br>Rationale: TPN is delivered via a venous catheter and is very high in glucose. There is a very high risk for infection. The client already has imbalanced nutrition, so while that nursing diagnosis would be included, it is not as important as the risk for infection. The TPN therapy is already addressing the imbalanced nutrition. The client may have an activity intolerance, but the risk for infection takes priority as it can cause greater physical harm to the client. The client is now at more risk of fluid volume overload from the additional TPN fluid.<br>Diagnosis<br>Physiological integrity<br>Analysis<br>Learning Outcome 47.13 |

## CHAPTER 48

| | |
|---|---|
| **48.1** Which of the following factors influences urinary elimination?<br>　1.　Age<br>　2.　Body image<br>　3.　Knowledge<br>　4.　Socioeconomic status | Answer: 1<br>Rationale: Development factors such as how old the client is influence urinary elimination. Body image, knowledge, and socioeconomic status are not factors that influence urinary elimination.<br>Planning<br>Physiological integrity<br>Analysis<br>Learning Outcome 48.2 |
| **48.2** Which of the following clients is at risk for difficulty in urinary elimination?<br>　1.　A client who had bladder cancer and now has a newly created ileal conduit<br>　2.　A 25-year-old female client with low self-esteem<br>　3.　An 80-year-old male reporting frequent urination at night<br>　4.　The client with hypertension who takes a diuretic every day for her blood pressure | Answer: 3<br>Rationale: The client who is 80 years old with frequent urination at night is having problems with his prostate. Older male adults experience urinary retention due to prostate enlargement causing an alteration in urinary elimination. The 25-year-old experiencing low self-esteem has a psychological problem and will need therapy to find the root of the problem. The client who had bladder cancer and now has an ileal conduit doesn't have kidney damage, only the bladder removed. Continued urine production through the ileal conduit will need to be observed and assessed frequently by the staff. The client with high blood pressure takes her medication to remove excess fluid from her body, and as long as urine elimination increases, there should be no problems.<br>Assessment<br>Physiological integrity<br>Analysis<br>Learning Outcome 48.3 |
| **48.3** Which of the following is a cause of nocturia?<br>　1.　Decrease in bladder capacity<br>　2.　Decrease in blood supply<br>　3.　Decrease in number of nephrons<br>　4.　Decrease in cardiac output | Answer: 1<br>Rationale: Approximately 70% of older women and 50% of older men have to get up two or more times during the night to empty their bladders due to decreased bladder capacity. A decrease in blood supply causes an increase in urine concentration. A decrease in the number of nephrons decreases the filtration rate. A decrease in cardiac output decreases peripheral circulation, which would decrease urinary output day or night.<br>Assessment |

| | Physiological integrity<br>Analysis<br>Learning Outcome 48.3 |
|---|---|
| **48.4** Which of the following nursing interventions would be implemented for the client in preventing a urinary tract infection?<br>  1. Encourage the use of bubble baths.<br>  2. Have the client increase sugar in the diet.<br>  3. Instruct the client to empty the bladder completely.<br>  4. Wipe from back to front. | Answer: 3<br>Rationale: Completely emptying the bladder prevents stasis of urine, which would contribute to a urinary tract infection. Irritating soaps and bubble baths can contribute to infections and should be avoided. The client should wipe from front to back because wiping from back to front would contaminate the urinary meatus. The client should decrease the use of sugar in the diet because sugar promotes bacterial growth.<br>Implementation<br>Physiological integrity<br>Application<br>Learning Outcome 48.7 |
| **48.5** The RN should incorporate which instructions into the teaching plan for a client with a urinary diversion?<br>  1. Change the appliance every day.<br>  2. Increase fluid intake.<br>  3. Notify the physician if the stoma is deep pink and shiny.<br>  4. Strands of blood may appear in the urine. | Answer: 2<br>Rationale: Increasing the fluid intake helps to flush out sediment and mucus and prevents clogging of the stoma. The appliance should be changed every 5 to 7 days. Every day changing is unnecessary. A deep pink, shiny stoma is normal, and there's no need to notify the physician. Strands of mucus, not blood, may appear in urine because of the mucus-producing cells of the ileum.<br>Planning<br>Physiological integrity<br>Application<br>Learning Outcome 48.8 |
| **48.6** Which of the following nursing interventions is appropriate care for a client with a retention catheter?<br>  1. Don sterile gloves.<br>  2. Gently retract the labia majora away from the urinary meatus.<br>  3. Observe urine in the drainage bag.<br>  4. Retape the catheter to the thigh. | Answer: 4<br>Rationale: Retaping the catheter to the thigh after care is given prevents trauma and pain from tension and pulling. Gloves are to be worn for cleaning but not sterile gloves. When giving catheter care to a female, the labia minora is gently retracted away from the urinary meatus, not the labia majora. The urine in the tubing should be observed, not the urine in the bag. Observing the urine in the tubing promotes accurate assessment of urine.<br>Implementation<br>Health promotion and maintenance<br>Application<br>Learning Outcome 48.8 |
| **48.7** Which of the following nursing diagnoses would be appropriate for a client who has a retention catheter if the drainage bag is found lying on the floor?<br>  1. *Risk for Impaired Skin Integrity* related to catheter placement<br>  2. *Risk for Infection* related to improper handling<br>  3. *Self-Care Deficit* related to presence of a retention catheter<br>  4. *Risk for Incontinence* related to an obstruction | Answer: 2<br>Rationale: The floor is the dirtiest place, so the drainage device should never be placed on the floor. There is a possibility of skin impairment with a catheter, but the emphasis here is on where the drainage bag was found. Even though a client has a catheter in place she still can administer her care; it does not restrict one from providing her own basic hygiene. The client may need some assistance. The placement of a catheter prevents incontinence; it does not add to it. Patency of the catheter ensures flow, not obstruction.<br>Planning<br>Physiological integrity<br>Analysis<br>Learning Outcome 48.6 |
| **48.8** Which of the following desired client outcomes is correct for a client with the nursing diagnosis *Stress Urinary Incontinence* related to sphincter incompetence?<br>  1. The client will empty her bladder every time she voids. | Answer: 3<br>Rationale: Performing four to five squeezes for 5 to 10 seconds is the goal to start with when teaching a client Kegel exercises, which are used for stress and urge incontinence. Emptying the bladder completely every time she voids would not be realistic in the beginning. This will take time. Improved continence takes 3 to 6 months, so 1 month is not a realistic goal. Clients are not instructed to stop the flow of urine when voiding because this could lead to retention. |

| | |
|---|---|
| 2. The client will improve her incontinence within 1 month.<br>3. The client will perform four to five squeezes for 5 to 10 seconds.<br>4. The client will stop the flow of urine when voiding. | Planning<br>Physiological integrity<br>Application<br>Learning Outcome 48.6 |
| **48.9** Which of the following expected outcomes or goals is correct for a client with the nursing diagnosis *Urinary Pattern Alteration* related to an enlarged prostate?<br>1. The client will avoid bladder distention.<br>2. The client will maintain fluid imbalance.<br>3. The client will remain free of skin breakdown.<br>4. The client will voice increased discomfort. | Answer: 1<br>Rationale: Avoiding bladder distention will help eliminate stasis of urine in the bladder which contributes to urinary tract infections, a possible complication of urine flow being obstructed from an enlarged prostate. One would want to maintain fluid balance, not imbalance, with a client with urinary obstruction and enlarged prostate. Keeping up with the client's intake and output would be a better goal. It is important to keep urine off the skin to prevent breakdown, but with an enlarged prostate the problem will be more of the client retaining urine instead of it being on the skin. One would hope if the retention subsides, the client would voice less discomfort, not more.<br>Planning<br>Physiological integrity<br>Application<br>Learning Outcome 48.6 |
| **48.10** The RN is admitting a client to the medical unit for a urinary disorder. Which of the following physical assessment techniques will the nurse use in assessing this client's urinary system?<br>1. Auscultation and inspection<br>2. Inspection and percussion<br>3. Observation and auscultation<br>4. Palpation and observation | Answer: 4<br>Rationale: The hands and sense of touch are used with palpation to gather data along with observation or inspection, which visually allows the nurse to observe all responses and nonverbal behavior. It is also the most frequently used technique and the most convenient. Percussion technique is the least frequently used by nurses, and it would cause discomfort if this client is already uncomfortable with a kidney condition. The nurse should not make matters worse. Auscultation is the technique of listening. The three systems that should be assessed using this technique are cardiovascular, respiratory, and gastrointestinal.<br>Assessment<br>Physiological integrity<br>Application<br>Learning Outcome 48.4 |
| **48.11** A client has been admitted with incontinence. Which of the following findings would the nurse expect to assess in this client?<br>1. Client is wearing cotton undergarments.<br>2. Leakage of urine occurs when client laughs.<br>3. Leakage of urine occurs when talking with the client.<br>4. Skin of the client is clear without discoloration. | Answer: 2<br>Rationale: Incontinence involves a small leakage of urine when a client laughs, coughs, or lifts something heavy, not if a client just carries on a conversation. A client with incontinence would wear some kind of undergarment pad. Cotton undergarments alone would not provide protection for catching the urine. If the client has been experiencing incontinence, the nurse might expect to see the skin inflamed and irritated because urine is very irritating to the skin.<br>Assessment<br>Physiological integrity<br>Analysis<br>Learning Outcome 48.4 |
| **48.12** A client is rushed to the emergency department with what the physicians suspect to be necrosis of the urinary diversion stoma. What evidence presented by the client leads to this conclusion?<br>1. Black with sloughing<br>2. Moist stoma<br>3. Pink and shiny<br>4. Slight bleeding from stoma | Answer: 1<br>Rationale: Black color to the stoma and sloughing are signs of necrosis to the stoma. A healthy stoma should appear pink to red and look moist and shiny. Slight bleeding might occur because the intestinal mucosa is very fragile.<br>Assessment<br>Physiological integrity<br>Analysis<br>Learning Outcome 48.3 |

| | |
|---|---|
| **48.13** The client with a urinary disorder is admitted to the urology unit of the hospital. Results from the urinalysis are as follows: pH 5.2, gross cloudiness, WBC 10–15, glucose negative, specific gravity 1.012, and protein negative. How would the nurse interpret the results?<br>  1. Dehydration<br>  2. Diabetic ketoacidosis<br>  3. Trauma<br>  4. Urinary tract infection | Answer: 4<br>Rationale: The pH, glucose, specific gravity, and protein are all within normal limits. Urine is usually clear to slightly cloudy, and WBC count can be from 0–4. Therefore, the gross cloudiness and WBC count of 10–15 are not normal, indicating a urinary tract infection. Diabetic ketoacidosis would show glucose elevated, trauma would show blood in the urine, and dehydration would indicate elevated specific gravity.<br>Assessment<br>Physiological integrity<br>Analysis<br>Learning Outcome 48.4 |
| **48.14** A routine urinalysis is collected by the client and given to the nurse. Results confirm there are no problems involving the urinary system. Which of the following results gives this conclusion?<br>  1. Blood present and no ketones<br>  2. Dark amber color and output less than 500 cc in 24 hours<br>  3. pH 6 and no glucose present<br>  4. Specific gravity 1.035 and faint aromatic odor | Answer: 3<br>Rationale: Normal pH is 4.5–8, so a pH of 6 and no glucose present are two normal characteristics of urine. There should be no blood present as well as no ketones. The urine should be an amber color, not dark amber. For an adult, normal output range is 1,200–1,500 mL in 24 hours. Specific gravity of 1.035 does not fall within the normal range of 1.010–1.025, but a faint aromatic odor is normal.<br>Intervention<br>Physiological integrity<br>Analysis<br>Learning Outcome 48.4 |
| **48.15** The desire to void is reached when there are _____ cc in the bladder. | Answer: 250 to 450 cc.<br>Assessment<br>Physiological integrity<br>Knowledge<br>Learning Outcome 48.1 |
| **48.16** Which of the following instructions should the nurse include when administering a beta-adrenergic like Inderal (propranolol) to the client?<br>  1. Medication should be discontinued abruptly.<br>  2. Notify your physician if you experience urinary retention.<br>  3. Take a laxative every day.<br>  4. Take the medication on an empty stomach. | Answer: 2<br>Rationale: A beta-adrenergic blocker such as propranolol can cause urinary retention; therefore, it would be of the utmost importance to notify one's physician. Clients should always check with their physician before stopping any medication because there could be some major complications. Constipation has been reported from clients taking propranolol, but a laxative should not be taken every day as one can become dependent. This medicine should be taken with food, not on an empty stomach, in order to enhance absorption.<br>Intervention<br>Physiological integrity<br>Application<br>Learning Outcome 48.6 |
| **48.17** Which of the following instructions by the nurse given to the client would help promote urinary elimination?<br>  1. Don't interrupt your day by going to the bathroom; wait until you're at a good stopping place.<br>  2. Drink 8 to 10 glasses of water daily.<br>  3. Urine color changes are not important.<br>  4. Wash with soap and water every other day. | Answer: 2<br>Rationale: Drinking 8 to 10 glasses of water daily will encourage the need for bladder emptying, keeping the system flushed. The client should respond to the urge to void as soon as possible to avoid urinary retention. The client should report any changes in urine color, which could be indicative of a problem. To maintain asepsis, the client should wash with soap and water every day, not every other day.<br>Intervention<br>Physiological integrity<br>Application<br>Learning Outcome 48.2 |

| | |
|---|---|
| **48.18** Which of the following returned demonstrations by the client demonstrates she understands correct technique for caring for an indwelling catheter?<br><br>1. The client empties the drainage bag once a day.<br>2. The client hangs the drainage bag on the towel rod.<br>3. The client refuses to drink adequate amounts of fluids.<br>4. The client takes a shower each day. | Answer: 4<br>Rationale: The client should take a shower rather than a tub bath because sitting in a tub allows bacteria to easily access the urinary tract. The drainage bag should be emptied regularly, not just once a day but at least three times a day. Adequate amounts of fluids should be consumed to help prevent sediments and infections. Hanging the drainage bag on the towel rod is too high. The drainage bag should be hung below the bladder.<br>Intervention<br>Physiological integrity<br>Application<br>Learning Outcome 48.8 |
| **48.19** Which nursing intervention would be appropriate for an elderly male client who has returned from having a transurethral resection of the prostate (TURP) with a three-way indwelling catheter and now tells the nurse he has to urinate?<br><br>1. Deflate and then reinflate the balloon.<br>2. Irrigate the catheter.<br>3. Reposition the catheter.<br>4. Retape the catheter to the abdomen. | Answer: 2<br>Rationale: Blood clots give the client the sensation to urinate when they obstruct the urine outflow; therefore, irrigation will have to remedy the problem. Deflating and reinflating the balloon is not an option. The surgeon knows how much pressure is needed to control bleeding after surgery. The catheter is usually taped to the client's leg after a TURP and is not to be manipulated. This also controls bleeding after surgery. Repositioning the catheter would not be an option right after surgery.<br>Intervention<br>Physiological integrity<br>Application<br>Learning Outcome 48.8 |
| **48.20** Identify the area in the nephron below where solutes such as glucose are reabsorbed.<br><br>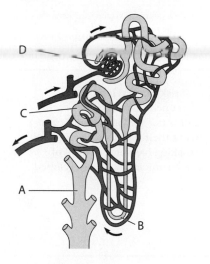 | Answer: b (Loop of Henle)<br>Assessment<br>Physiological integrity<br>Application<br>Learning Outcome 48.1 |
| **48.21** Identify this urinary diversion.<br><br>_____<br><br>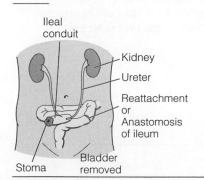 | Answer: Urostomy (ileal conduit)<br>Assessment<br>Physiological integrity<br>Application<br>Learning Outcome 48.1 |

**49.1** A client asks the RN why it is more difficult to use a bedpan for defecating than sitting on the toilet. Which of the following is the best response?

1. The sitting position decreases the contractions of the muscles of the pelvic floor.
2. The sitting position increases the downward pressure on the rectum, making it easier to pass stool.
3. The sitting position increases the pressure within the abdomen.
4. The sitting position inhibits the urge to urinate, allowing one to defecate.

Answer: 2
Rationale: The sitting position increases the downward pressure on the rectum, assisting one to defecate. Thigh flexion increases the pressure within the abdomen. The contractions of the muscles of the pelvic floor are increased, not decreased. The sitting position does not inhibit the urge to urinate.
Implementation
Physiological integrity
Analysis
Learning Outcome 49.1

---

**49.2** The certified nurse assistant informs the RN that one of the clients is passing lots of gas which is very noxious. The assistant asks why the smell is so bad. What should be the nurse's response?

1. The actions of microorganisms within the GI tract are responsible for the odor.
2. The client's emotions are causing the gas formation.
3. The sensory nerves in the rectum are being stimulated.
4. The client has swallowed too much air while eating.

Answer: 1
Rationale: The actions of the microorganisms are responsible for the odor produced and also the color of the feces. Extreme stimulation of the client's emotions would result in large amounts of mucus being secreted. The sensory nerves, when stimulated, give one the desire to defecate not form gas. Eating too fast or talking while eating does cause the formation of gas but does not contribute to the odor.
Implementation
Physiological integrity
Analysis
Learning Outcome 49.2

---

**49.3** Which of the following clients is at greatest risk for developing constipation?

1. An adult who is on bed rest
2. An infant who is breast-fed
3. A school-age child at recess
4. A toddler who is now walking

Answer: 1
Rationale: Adults who are on bed rest are at greatest risk for developing constipation. Infants that are breast-fed pass stools frequently, usually after each feeding, because the intestine is immature and water is not well absorbed. School-age children may delay defecation because of play, but their activity still promotes regular bowel movements. A toddler who is now walking has some control of defecation, and the nervous and muscular systems are sufficiently well developed to permit bowel control.
Assessment
Health promotion and maintenance
Application
Learning Outcome 49.4

---

**49.4** The nurse is taking care of a client who states that he ignores the urge to defecate when he is at work. Which of the following responses by the nurse would explain why this practice should be changed?

1. "If you continue to ignore the urge to defecate, the urge is ultimately lost."
2. "It is best to suppress the urge than suffer embarrassment at work."

Answer: 1
Rationale: When the normal defecation reflexes are inhibited, these conditioned reflexes tend to be progressively weakened. When the urge to defecate is ignored, water continues to be reabsorbed, making the feces hard and difficult to expel. Ignoring the urge repeatedly will eventually cause the urge to be lost.
Implementation
Health promotion and maintenance
Analysis
Learning Outcome 49.1

---

| | |
|---|---|
| 3. "This is a common practice, and it will strengthen the reflex later." <br> 4. "You will get the urge later; don't worry." | |
| **49.5** Which part of the nursing process is the nurse using when obtaining a nursing history of a client's fecal elimination? <br> 1. Assessment <br> 2. Evaluation <br> 3. Implementation <br> 4. Planning | Answer: 1 <br> Rationale: Assessment of fecal elimination includes a nursing history and also a review of any data from the client's records. Performing a physical examination would demonstrate implementation of the nursing process. Interpretation of diagnostic test results would demonstrate evaluation of the nursing process. Setting goals for the client demonstrates the planning step of the nursing process. <br> Assessment <br> Physiological integrity <br> Application <br> Learning Outcome 49.6 |
| **49.6** Which of the following characteristics assessed by the nurse is considered normal for an adult's feces? <br> 1. Black in color <br> 2. Cylindrical in shape <br> 3. Pungent in odor <br> 4. Yellow in color | Answer: 2 <br> Rationale: Cylindrical in contour is a normal characteristic of feces because it takes the shape of the rectum. Yellow is the color of an infant's feces, not an adult's. Black is abnormal. Pungent is abnormal, but aromatic odor is normal. <br> Assessment <br> Physiological integrity <br> Analysis <br> Learning Outcome 49.3 |
| **49.7** The nurse would instruct a client with frequent bouts of diarrhea to: <br> 1. Change her daily routine. <br> 2. Decrease fluid consumption. <br> 3. Increase fiber in the diet. <br> 4. Note the precipitating event. | Answer: 4 <br> Rationale: Psychological stress such as anxiety, medications, food allergies, and certain diseases can cause diarrhea. Noting the event can help identify and stop the cause. Decreasing fluid consumption may cause constipation. If a client has diarrhea and still decreases her fluid intake, this can contribute to dehydration. Changing one's daily routine can cause or contribute to diarrhea. Increasing fiber in the diet when one already has diarrhea would just make matters worse. <br> Implementation <br> Physiological integrity <br> Application <br> Learning Outcome 49.4 |
| **49.8** Which of the following actions by the client would signal to the nurse that client teaching was effective for preventing constipation? <br> 1. The client continues to ask for his pain medication. <br> 2. The client decreases his fluid consumption. <br> 3. The client refuses to eat the bran flakes on his tray. <br> 4. The client walks around the unit several times a day. | Answer: 4 <br> Rationale: Increased activity like walking promotes gastric motility, which increases bowel function. Pain medication contributes to constipation, especially those that are opiates. Decreasing fluid intake further contributes to constipation. Refusing to eat bran flakes would also promote constipation. <br> Evaluation <br> Health promotion and maintenance <br> Analysis <br> Learning Outcome 49.7 |
| **49.9** The nurse is called to the client's room to assess the client's first bowel movement since surgery. Upon investigation, the nurse finds hard, dry, but formed stool. This is characteristic of which of the following? <br> 1. Bowel incontinence <br> 2. Constipation <br> 3. Diarrhea <br> 4. Fecal impaction | Answer: 2 <br> Rationale: Hard, dry, formed stool is characteristic of constipation. Fecal impaction is a mass of hardened feces in the folds of the rectum. Diarrhea is the passage of liquid feces. Bowel incontinence is the loss of voluntary ability to control feces. <br> Assessment <br> Physiological integrity <br> Analysis <br> Learning Outcome 49.4 |

**49.10** Which of the following nursing diagnoses would be most appropriate for a client on bed rest?
1. *Bowel Incontinence*
2. *Constipation*
3. *Diarrhea*
4. *Disturbed Body Image*

Answer: 2
Rationale: Lack of activity, like bed rest, is a major contributor to constipation. Lack of movement slows bowel movements. Lack of sphincter control contributes to bowel incontinence, not bed rest. Diarrhea would come from a GI upset triggered by diseases, medication, or diet. Disturbed body image would affect a client who has undergone a bowel diversion.
Planning
Physiological integrity
Analysis
Learning Outcome 49.6

**49.11** Which of the following goals would be appropriate for a client dealing with a fecal elimination problem like diarrhea?
1. Client will defecate regularly.
2. Client will increase the amount of sugar in the diet.
3. Client will limit fluid intake.
4. Client will regain normal stool consistency.

Answer: 4
Rationale: Since this client is experiencing diarrhea, the goal would be to regain normal stool consistency which would be less water in the stool and more formed consistency. Defecating regularly once the diarrhea has subsided can be a goal, but it is too soon for this goal. The problem needs to be corrected first. Since the client is experiencing diarrhea, which can dehydrate the client and promote electrolyte loss, limiting fluid would not be appropriate. Increasing the amount of sugar in the diet will just add to the diarrhea.
Planning
Health promotion and maintenance
Application
Learning Outcome 49.6

**49.12** Which of the following instructions given to the client will assist him in taking care of his colostomy?
1. Change the drainage pouch daily.
2. Clothing of a special style will be needed now that a pouch is worn.
3. Stick a pin into the drainage pouch to relieve any gas buildup.
4. Secure the faceplate to the drainage pouch so no skin around the stoma is exposed.

Answer: 4
Rationale: The skin around a stoma is very susceptible to irritation and breakdown. To avoid skin irritation, the faceplate to the drainage pouch needs to fit close enough to the stoma so as not to expose any other skin. The drainage pouches are expensive, and they can be used up to a week before being changed. Just daily rinsing and cleaning is necessary. If a pin is stuck into the pouch, a hole will be left and it will cause leakage, which is not recommended. No special clothing has to be worn with a colostomy pouch. The client can wear the same clothes he had prior to his surgery.
Implementation
Health promotion and maintenance
Application
Learning Outcome 49.9

**49.13** Which of the following assessment skills would the RN perform first when examining a client for fecal elimination problems?
1. Auscultation
2. Inspection
3. Palpation
4. Percussion

Answer: 1
Rationale: Auscultation precedes palpation because palpation can alter peristalsis. Examination of the rectum and anus includes inspection and palpation.
Planning
Physiological integrity
Application
Learning Outcome 49.5

**49.14** Which of the following assessment data would indicate compromised gastrointestinal function?
1. Bowel sounds active in all four quadrants
2. Clay color stool
3. Increased appetite
4. Semisolid and moist stool

Answer: 2
Rationale: Clay color stools would be an indication of a problem in the GI tract. Clay color is a sign of the absence of bile pigment (bile obstruction). Bowel sounds active in all four quadrants is indicative of normal bowel activity. If the GI tract were compromised, the client would have a decrease in appetite, not an increase. A semisolid and moist stool indicates normal bowel function.
Assessment
Physiological integrity
Analysis
Learning Outcome 49.5

| | |
|---|---|
| **49.15** Which of the following suggestions by the nurse would be appropriate to maintain a normal fecal elimination pattern?<br>   1. Drink two to four glasses of water daily.<br>   2. Include more spicy foods and sugar in the diet.<br>   3. Include more whole grains in the diet.<br>   4. Use enemas as desired. | Answer: 3<br>Rationale: Eating more whole grains will increase fiber in the diet, which increases bulk and volume. For regular elimination, six to eight glasses of water should be consumed daily. The constant use of enemas and laxatives will promote dependence. Increasing the consumption of spicy foods and sugar will cause diarrhea, which is not a normal fecal pattern.<br>Implementation<br>Health promotion and maintenance<br>Application<br>Learning Outcome 49.7 |
| **49.16** The RN is caring for the stomal area of a client who has a colostomy. Which of the following actions is most appropriate?<br>   1. Apply pressure over the stoma.<br>   2. Clean the stomal area and pat dry.<br>   3. Dilate the stoma.<br>   4. Scrub the stoma. | Answer: 2<br>Rationale: Stomal care includes cleaning the area and patting dry. Applying pressure over the stoma may damage the stoma. Gentle care should be taken with the stoma. Scrubbing would cause the stoma to bleed since the area is very vascular. A physician's order is needed if the stoma is to be dilated. Dilating is not routine.<br>Implementation<br>Physiological integrity<br>Application<br>Learning Outcome 49.9 |
| **49.17** Which of the following is included in client teaching prior to administration of a cleansing enema?<br>   1. Hold the solution for a short time.<br>   2. Lie in the left lateral position.<br>   3. Lie in the right lateral position.<br>   4. Take fast breaths through the nose. | Answer: 2<br>Rationale: The client lies in the left lateral position, not the right, in order to clean the rectum and sigmoid. Once the enema is given, the client should hold the solution as long as possible for the best results. The client should take slow deep breaths through the mouth. This will enable the client to hold the solution being given.<br>Implementation<br>Physiological integrity<br>Application<br>Learning Outcome 49.8 |
| **49.18** Which of the following actions would be expected if a hypertonic solution like saline is used to give an enema?<br>   1. Exerts osmotic pressure and draws fluid from the interstitial space into the colon<br>   2. Exerts a lower osmotic pressure than the surrounding interstitial fluid<br>   3. Exerts the same osmotic pressure as the interstitial fluid surrounding the colon<br>   4. Stimulates peristalsis by increasing the volume in the colon and irritating the colon | Answer: 1<br>Rationale: A hypertonic solution exerts osmotic pressure and draws fluid from the interstitial space into the colon. A hypotonic solution exerts a lower osmotic pressure than the surrounding interstitial fluid. Isotonic solution is the safest enema solution to use. It exerts the same osmotic pressure as the interstitial fluid surrounding the colon. Soapsuds stimulate peristalsis by increasing the volume in the colon and irritating the colon.<br>Planning<br>Physiological integrity<br>Analysis<br>Learning Outcome 49.8 |
| **49.19** Identify the fecal diversion pictured below: _____<br>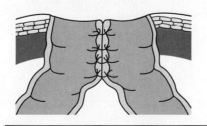 | Answer: Double barrel colostomy<br>Assessment<br>Physiological integrity<br>Application<br>Learning Outcome 49.9 |

**49.20** Indicate with an "X" in the diagram below where the most liquid is in the large intestine.

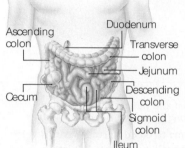

Answer:
Assessment
Physiological integrity
Application
Learning Outcome 49.1

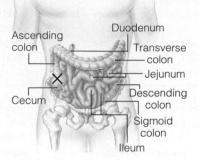

# CHAPTER 50

**50.1** The client has a tracheostomy secondary to head and neck surgery. The nurse monitors the client for complications related to the absence of which important protective mechanism?
1. The ability to cough
2. Filtration and humidification of inspired air
3. The sneeze reflex initiated by irritants in the nasal passages
4. Decrease in oxygen-carrying capacity of the trachea

Answer: 2
Rationale: When the nasal passages are bypassed as they would be in the case of a client with a tracheostomy, the filtration, humidification, and warming of the nasal passages is also bypassed. The client can still cough and sneeze, and there is no decrease in the oxygen-carrying capacity of the trachea.
Planning
Physiological integrity
Analysis
Learning Outcome 50.1

**50.2** Which client would the nurse closely observe for a decreased or absent cough reflex?
1. The client with a nasal fracture
2. The client with impairment of vagus nerve conduction
3. The client with a sinus infection
4. The client with reduction in respiratory membrane conduction

Answer: 2
Rationale: The cough reflex depends upon nerve impulse transmission via the vagus nerve to the medulla. The nurse must monitor clients with vagus nerve impairment (through spinal cord injury, trauma, CNS depression, or other means) for a decreased or absent cough reflex. This decreased or absent reflex places the client at high risk for aspiration or development of pneumonia or other respiratory infections. Nasal fracture and sinus infections do not depress cough reflex. The respiratory membrane is the alveolar/capillary membrane and is not implicated in decreased or absent cough reflex.
Planning
Physiological integrity
Application
Learning Outcome 50.1

**50.3** The client complains of difficulty breathing. Which of the following assessment findings would the nurse commonly associate with that complaint? (Select all that apply.)
1. Use of accessory muscles
2. Increased respiratory depth
3. Increased respiratory rate
4. Decreased respiratory depth
5. Decreased respiratory rate

Answer: 1, 2, 3, 4
Rationale: Rate, depth, and use of accessory muscles often are assessment findings indicating difficulty breathing. The depth of respirations can be deeper (tidal volume greater than 500 mL of air) or more shallow if partial obstruction is present in conditions such as asthma. Rate is generally increased.
Assessment
Physiological integrity
Application
Learning Outcome 50.2

**50.4** The client has been admitted with complaints of shortness of breath of 2 weeks duration and has received the nursing diagnosis *Impaired Gas Exchange*. Which admission laboratory result would support the choice of this diagnosis?

1. Increased hematocrit
2. Decreased BUN
3. Increased blood sugar
4. Increased sedimentation rate

Answer: 1
Rationale: Hematocrit is the percentage of the blood that is erythrocytes, which contain the hemoglobin that carries oxygen. Long-term hypoxia may result in the body's attempt to increase oxygen-carrying capacity by increasing erythrocyte production. BUN is a measure of blood urea nitrogen, not oxygen-carrying capacity. Increases in blood sugar and sedimentation rate are not directly a measure of oxygenation.
Diagnosis
Physiological integrity
Analysis
Learning Outcome 50.5

---

**50.5** The client with chronic obstructive lung disease has oxygen ordered at 1.5 liters per minute via nasal cannula. The client complains of shortness of breath. What action should be taken by the nurse?

1. Increase the oxygen to 3 liters per minute via nasal cannula.
2. Lower the head of the client's bed to semi-Fowler's position.
3. Have the client breathe through pursed lips.
4. Encourage the client to breathe more rapidly.

Answer: 3
Rationale: The client should be taught to breathe out against pursed lips to increase the time it takes to exhale and to help keep airways open. In the client with chronic obstructive lung disease, the drive to breathe is often dependent upon low oxygen concentration. Increasing oxygen delivery by increasing the oxygen from 1.5 Lpm to 3 Lpm may be dangerous to this client. Lowering the head of the bed makes it more difficult to breathe. This client should have the head of the bed elevated to Fowler's position or should be assisted to lean over the overbed table to increase chest excursion. Chronic obstructive lung disease makes it difficult for the client to breathe out, so increasing rate of respirations will not be helpful.
Implementation
Physiological integrity
Application

---

**50.6** The client has just been told that his medical condition is terminal and that he has less than 6 months to live. The client begins to hyperventilate and complains that he is light-headed and that his fingers, toes, and mouth are tingling. What action should be taken by the nurse?

1. Prepare to resuscitate the client.
2. Have the client concentrate on slowing down respirations.
3. Place the client in Trendelenburg's position and ask him to cough forcefully.
4. Administer 25 mg of meperidine (Demerol) according to the prn pain order.

Answer: 2
Rationale: This client is hyperventilating and should be assisted to slow down respirations. Techniques to slow respirations include counting respirations or having the client match respirations with the nurse who then slows down the respiratory rate. There is no indication that this client needs resuscitation nor is there need to place him in Trendelenburg's position for coughing. Demerol may slow breathing, but is not necessary at this time.
Implementation
Physiological integrity
Analysis
Learning Outcome 50.6

---

**50.7** The client is experiencing severe shortness of breath, but is not cyanotic. What lab value would the nurse review in an attempt to understand this phenomenon?

1. Blood sugar
2. Hemoglobin and hematocrit
3. Cardiac enzymes
4. Serum electrolytes

Answer: 2
Rationale: In order to exhibit cyanosis, the client's blood must contain about 5 g or more of unoxygenated hemoglobin per 100 mL of blood and the surface blood capillaries must be dilated. Severe anemia will interfere with the development of cyanosis, so the nurse should review the hemoglobin and hematocrit. Blood sugar, cardiac enzymes, and serum electrolytes are not implicated in this phenomenon.
Assessment
Physiological integrity
Analysis
Learning Outcome 50.5

| | |
|---|---|
| **50.8** The client has a 20-year history of asthma with chronic hypoxia. Which change in the client's fingers would the nurse expect? | Answer: Clubbing<br>Rationale: Clubbing is the increase in the angle between the nail and the base of the nail to more than 180 degrees. The base of the nail becomes swollen and the ends of the fingers increase in size. Clubbing is a classic sign of chronic hypoxia.<br>Assessment<br>Physiological integrity<br>Application<br>Learning Outcome 50.5 |
| **50.9** The client has a medical condition that often results in the development of metabolic acidosis. The nurse should observe this client for the development of which breathing pattern as a result of this condition?<br>   1. Cheyne-Stokes<br>   2. Biot's<br>   3. Cluster<br>   4. Kussmaul's | Answer: 4<br>Rationale: Kussmaul's respirations are a type of hyperventilation that accompanies metabolic acidosis. They represent the body's attempt to compensate for the acidosis by "blowing off" carbon dioxide. Cheyne-Stokes respirations are commonly a result of congestive heart failure, increased intracranial pressure, or drug overdose. Cluster and Biot's respirations are the same and are often the result of central nervous system disorders.<br>Assessment<br>Physiological integrity<br>Application<br>Learning Outcome 50.5 |
| **50.10** Upon assessment, the nurse notes that the client is dyspneic, has bibasilar crackles, and tires easily upon exertion. Which nursing diagnosis is best supported by these assessment details?<br>   1. *Ineffective Breathing Pattern*<br>   2. *Anxiety*<br>   3. *Ineffective Airway Clearance*<br>   4. *Impaired Gas Exchange* | Answer: 3<br>Rationale: The data given for this client best support the nursing diagnosis of *Ineffective Airway Clearance*. The most supportive finding for this diagnosis is bibasilar crackles. There are no data that support *Ineffective Breathing Pattern* or *Impaired Gas Exchange*; however, these diagnoses may be appropriate after additional assessment is performed. There are no data that support *Anxiety* as a diagnosis.<br>Diagnosis<br>Physiologic integrity<br>Analysis<br>Learning Outcome 50.8 |
| **50.11** The client is hypoxic according to arterial blood gas measurement. What nursing diagnosis problem statement is most appropriate for this client? | Answer: *Impaired Gas Exchange*<br>Rationale: The only nursing diagnosis supported by hypoxia as the only finding is *Impaired Gas Exchange*. The client may have other nursing diagnoses such as *Ineffective Breathing Pattern* or *Ineffective Airway Clearance*, but those diagnoses are not supported by the findings in this scenario.<br>Diagnosis<br>Physiological integrity<br>Analysis<br>Learning Outcome 50.8 |
| **50.12** The nurse encourages the client to expectorate sputum rather than swallowing it. What is the rationale for this direction?<br>   1. Sputum contains bacteria that should be expectorated.<br>   2. Swallowing sputum is dangerous to the system.<br>   3. The nurse should view the sputum for quality and quantity.<br>   4. The client is likely to aspirate the sputum while attempting to swallow it. | Answer: 3<br>Rationale: There is no good rationale for having the client expectorate the sputum except for the nurse to view it for quality and quantity. Sputum does contain bacteria, but they are killed by the acid environment of the gastrointestinal tract. There is no danger to swallowing sputum, and the client is no more likely to aspirate sputum than any other fluid.<br>Planning<br>Physiological integrity<br>Application<br>Learning Outcome 50.6 |

| | |
|---|---|
| **50.13** The nurse is planning a time schedule for a client's twice-daily postural drainage. Which time schedule would be best?<br>　1. 0800 and 1100<br>　2. 1200 and 1800<br>　3. 0700 and 2000<br>　4. 0900 and 2100 | Answer: 3<br>Rationale: Postural drainage should be scheduled to avoid hours shortly after meals because the treatment may induce vomiting and can be very tiring for the client. Since this client is getting the treatments only twice each day, the sessions should be separated as far as possible to allow for benefits across a longer time span. Of the options offered, the one that takes into consideration the meal schedule and is most widely distributed is 0700 and 2000.<br>Planning<br>Physiological integrity<br>Application<br>Learning Outcome 50.6 |
| **50.14** The client is receiving oxygen by nonrebreather mask, but the bag is not deflating on inspiration. What action should be taken by the nurse?<br>　1. Turn the client to the left side.<br>　2. Increase the percentage of oxygen being delivered.<br>　3. Check for an airtight seal between the client's face and the mask.<br>　4. Increase the liter flow of oxygen being delivered. | Answer: 4<br>Rationale: If the bag attached to the nonrebreather mask is not deflating on inspiration, the nurse should increase the liter flow of the oxygen being delivered. There is no need to turn the client to either side. The seal between the client's face and the mask should be snug, but will not be airtight. All oxygen is delivered at 100%, so there is no method to increase the percentage of oxygen being delivered.<br>Implementation<br>Physiological integrity<br>Application<br>Learning Outcome 50.7 |
| **50.15** The nurse has placed an oropharyngeal airway in a client. What action should the nurse take at this time?<br>　1. Tape the airway in place.<br>　2. Suction the client.<br>　3. Turn the client's head to the side.<br>　4. Insert a nasal trumpet. | Answer: 3<br>Rationale: The nurse should turn the client's head to the side to allow drainage of oral secretions. The airway should not be taped in place as it would then act as an airway obstruction if dislodged. While suctioning the client is possible with the airway in place, the client should be suctioned only when it is necessary. Insertion of a nasal trumpet or nasopharyngeal airway is not necessary when the oropharyngeal airway is in place.<br>Implementation<br>Physiological integrity<br>Application<br>Learning Outcome 50.7 |
| **50.16** The nurse has received a client immediately after surgery for head and neck cancer. The client has a tracheostomy that was created during the surgery and is being mechanically ventilated. What nursing action should be planned for this client?<br>　1. Deflate the cuff of the tracheostomy tube every 2 hours for 5 minutes.<br>　2. Remove the tracheostomy ties and replace them with an elastic bandage.<br>　3. Remove the tracheostomy inner cannula.<br>　4. Tape the tracheostomy obturator to the head of the bed. | Answer: 4<br>Rationale: The obturator should be taped to the head of the bed so that it will be readily available if the client tracheostomy tube should become dislodged. The cuff should not be deflated if the client is being mechanically ventilated. The tracheostomy ties are only removed when they are soiled and need to be changed. The tracheostomy inner cannula is only removed for cleaning.<br>Planning<br>Physiological integrity<br>Application<br>Learning Outcome 50.7 |

**50.17** The hospital policy and procedure for suctioning requires hyperinflation of the client prior to suctioning. How should the nurse proceed with this requirement?

1. Turn the suction level up to 60 cm prior to inserting the catheter.
2. Increase the oxygen flow to the client by 20% prior to suctioning.
3. Provide 2 to 3 breaths at 1.5 times the tidal volume prior to suction.
4. Instruct the client to cough forcefully from the abdomen prior to suction.

Answer: 3
Rationale: The nurse should provide 2 to 3 breaths at 1.5 times the client's normal tidal volume prior to and after insertion of the suction catheter. Turning up the suction level, increasing the oxygen flow rate, and instructing the client to cough will not hyperinflate the client's lungs.
Implementation
Physiological integrity
Application
Learning Outcome 50.7

**50.18** The nurse who is assessing a client's chest tube insertion site notices a fine crackling sound and feeling upon palpating the area. What action should the nurse take?

1. Discontinue the chest tube suction.
2. Collaborate with the client's physician.
3. Mark the area involved and remove the tube.
4. Reinforce the chest tube dressing.

Answer: 2
Rationale: The nurse should collaborate with the client's physician regarding this finding. Chest tube suction should not be discontinued, nor should the tube be removed. Simply reinforcing the chest tube dressing will not prevent further air loss and does not allow for physician input.
Implementation
Physiological integrity
Application
Learning Outcome 50.7

**50.19** The nurse is preparing to assist with the removal of a chest tube that is a simple insertion without a purse-string suture. What materials should the nurse gather for this procedure?

1. An occlusive dressing
2. A 4 × 4 gauze
3. An adhesive gauze pad dressing
4. A nonadherent gauze dressing

Answer: 1
Rationale: Since this chest tube was put in without a purse-string suture, there is nothing to pull the tissue together once the tube is removed. In order to prevent leakage of air into the chest cavity, an occlusive dressing must be used. None of the other dressings listed are occlusive.
Planning
Physiological integrity
Analysis
Learning Outcome 50.7

**50.20** The nurse has completed discharge teaching for a client who will be going home on oxygen therapy. What statement, made by the client, would indicate that this client needs further instruction?

1. "I will replace my cotton blankets with polyester ones."
2. "My son will not be able to smoke when I am around."
3. "I will have my electrical appliance checked for grounding."
4. "I will buy a fire extinguisher for my bedroom."

Answer: 1
Rationale: Polyester blankets and fabrics tend to produce static electricity, which can cause sparks and can cause oxygen-saturated fabrics to burn more readily. The other statements reflect understanding of the hazards associated with home oxygen therapy.
Evaluation
Physiological integrity
Application
Learning Outcome 50.7

**50.21** The client who has a nasotracheal tube in place has been restless and pulling at the tube. How would the nurse assess if the tube is still in place?
1. Count the client's respirations.
2. Assess the depth of the client's respirations.
3. Auscultate for bilateral breath sounds.
4. Deflate the cuff and listen for minimal leak.

Answer: 3
Rationale: The end of the endotracheal tube should sit just above the bifurcation of the trachea into the two mainstem bronchi. If the tube is in correct position, the nurse should be able to hear equal bilateral breath sounds. Counting the respirations and assessing their depth will not give good information about tube placement. Deflating the cuff and listening for minimal leak is a way to prevent damage to the trachea, not a way to assess placement.
Assessment
Physiological integrity
Application
Learning Outcome 50.7

**50.22** The nurse has just initiated oxygen by nasal cannula for a client with the medical diagnosis of chronic obstructive pulmonary disease. What is the nurse's next action?
1. Fill the humidifier with normal saline.
2. Pad the tubing where it contacts the client's ears.
3. Set the oxygen delivery to 5 liters.
4. Secure the cannula with ties around the client's head.

Answer: 2
Rationale: It is necessary to pad the cannula where it contacts the client's ears as pressure irritation may occur. The humidifier should be filled with water prior to initiating therapy. Since this client has chronic obstructive pulmonary disease, the oxygen should be set at a lower delivery rate (generally no more than 1.5 to 2 Lpm). The cannula does not require ties to secure.
Implementation
Physiological integrity
Analysis
Learning Outcome 50.7

**50.23** The nurse who is performing care for a client with a new tracheostomy determines the ties are very soiled and must be changed. What is the best method for changing these ties?
1. Remove the old ties, clean the area well, and then put on new ties.
2. Attach the new tape and tie with a square knot behind the client's neck.
3. Have an assistant hold the tracheostomy tube in place, remove the soiled ties, and replace the ties.
4. Remove the outer cannula, replace the soiled ties, and reinsert.

Answer: 3
Rationale: Since these ties are very soiled, it is likely that they must be removed before new ties are attached. The safest way to perform this intervention is to have an assistant hold the tracheostomy tube flange in place while the nurse removes the old ties and replaces them. Removing the ties without an assistant could allow the tracheostomy tube to become dislodged. The knot for securing the tracheostomy tube should be tied at the side of the neck to prevent an area of pressure development. The inner cannula is not removed in a new tracheostomy.
Implementation
Physiological integrity
Analysis
Learning Outcome 50.7

**50.24** The nurse is planning the care of a client who has need for frequent suctioning. Which of the following should the nurse delegate to the UAP?
1. Both oral and tracheal suctioning
2. Only oral suctioning
3. Only tracheal suctioning
4. Neither oral nor tracheal suctioning

Answer: 2
Rationale: The suctioning of the oral cavity is a nonsterile procedure and can be delegated to the UAP. Tracheal suctioning is a sterile procedure that requires client assessment and should not be delegated to the UAP.
Planning
Physiological integrity
Analysis
Learning Outcome 50.7

| | |
|---|---|
| **50.25** During tracheal suctioning, the nurse notes that the client's heart rate has increased from 80 to 100 bpm. Based upon this assessment, what action should the nurse take?<br>1. Immediately discontinue suctioning.<br>2. Prepare to resuscitate the client.<br>3. Continue to suction until the airway is clear.<br>4. Complete the suction episode as quickly as possible. | Answer: 4<br>Rationale: An increase in heart rate from 80 to 100 is not an unusual finding during suctioning, but does indicate increased stress on the client. The nurse should complete the suctioning episode as quickly as possible. There is no need to immediately discontinue suctioning or to prepare to resuscitate the client, but the client will likely not tolerate continuing the suction episode until the airway is clear. The nurse should allow the client to rest and reassess whether a second episode of suctioning is indicated.<br>Implementation<br>Physiological integrity<br>Analysis<br>Learning Outcome 50.7 |
| **50.26** The client who is being mechanically ventilated has copious amounts of secretions ranging from thick and tenacious to frothy. In preparing to suction this client the nurse should:<br>1. Hyperventilate the client using settings on the mechanical ventilator.<br>2. Hyperventilate the client using a manual resuscitator.<br>3. Avoid hyperventilation, but instill normal saline into the endotracheal tube.<br>4. Avoid hyperventilation and increase the oxygen to 100% for several breaths. | Answer: 4<br>Rationale: The nurse should avoid hyperventilation and should increase the oxygen to 100% for several breaths prior to initiating suction. Hyperventilating the client will likely serve to force secretions back into the respiratory tract. There is no need to instill normal saline into the tube of a client with copious frothy secretions.<br>Planning<br>Physiological integrity<br>Application<br>Learning Outcome 50.7 |
| **50.27** As a part of preoperative teaching, the nurse is instructing the client on the use of a volume-oriented incentive spirometer. Which instruction should be included in this teaching? (Select all that apply.)<br>1. Blow out into the canister until the enclosed cylinder rises.<br>2. Close your lips tightly around the mouthpiece.<br>3. Inhale sharply to elevate the enclosed cylinder.<br>4. Use a nose clip to occlude nasal passages if necessary.<br>5. Cough after using the device.<br>6. Tilt the device slightly toward yourself while using. | Answer: 2, 4, 5<br>Rationale: The volume-oriented incentive spirometer works best when the client closes the lips around the mouthpiece tightly, inhales slowly and deeply to achieve rise in the enclosed cylinder, and keeps the device level. A nose clip may be used to occlude nasal passages if the client has difficulty breathing only through the nose. The client should also be taught to cough after using the device.<br>Implementation<br>Physiological integrity<br>Application<br>Learning Outcome 50.7 |
| **50.28** The client has been prescribed both a bronchodilator and a steroid medication that is delivered by inhaler. What information is essential to teach this client in regard to these medications?<br>1. The medications cannot be used on the same day.<br>2. The steroid inhaler should be used when immediate effects are necessary. | Answer: 4<br>Rationale: Both of these medications have the possible side effect of increased heart rate. The medications can be used on the same day. It is imperative for the client to understand that the steroid inhaler is not a "rescue" inhaler and should not be used for immediate relief. While the client should be taught to use both inhalers as infrequently as possible, the client should be taught to use the inhaler when necessary. When the inhalers are used together, the bronchodilator is used first, followed by the steroid.<br>Implementation<br>Physiological integrity<br>Analysis<br>Learning Outcome 50.7 |

3. The bronchodilator should be used only when absolutely necessary and only after the steroid inhaler.
4. Both medications have the possible side effect of increased heart rate.

# CHAPTER 51

**51.1** The nurse is planning care for a client who was admitted after having a myocardial infarction. Based upon this history, the nurse's greatest concern is that this client might develop which of the following?
1. Chronic renal failure
2. A gastric ulcer
3. Hypoxemia
4. A cerebral vascular accident

Answer: 3
Rationale: While injury to the heart muscle might affect any or all of the body systems, at this point the nurse is most concerned that the client will develop hypoxemia. The status of the respiratory system is closely linked to and dependent upon the cardiovascular system.
Planning
Physiological integrity
Analysis
Learning Outcome 51.5

**51.2** Cardiac catheterization has shown that the infant has a malformation of the mitral valve. The nurse specifically monitors the client for the development of problems associated with delivery of which of the following?
1. Oxygenated blood to the body
2. Deoxygenated blood to the lung
3. Oxygenated blood to the right atrium
4. Deoxygenated blood to the left ventricle

Answer: 1
Rationale: The mitral valve separates the left ventricle from the left atrium. Problems with this valve will impede flow of oxygenated blood from the left atrium into the left ventricle for delivery to the body. The pulmonic valve separates the right ventricle from the pulmonary artery. Problems with this valve would impede delivery of deoxygenated blood back to the lung. The blood that returns to the right atrium is deoxygenated. The blood delivered to the left ventricle is oxygenated.
Implementation
Physiological integrity
Analysis
Learning Outcome 51.1

**51.3** During assessment, the nurse notes a cardiac murmur that occurs between $S_1$ and $S_2$. The nurse documents this murmur as which of the following?
1. Diastolic
2. Holosystolic
3. Systolic
4. Pansystolic

Answer: 3
Rationale: The period of the cardiac cycle between $S_1$ and $S_2$ is ventricular systole. Any extra heart sounds heard during this period of time would be documented as systolic. The period of time between $S_2$ and the next $S_1$ is diastole.
Assessment
Physiological integrity
Analysis
Learning Outcome 51.1

**51.4** The nurse detects an extra heart sound that occurs "between heartbeats." How would the nurse document the timing of this sound?
1. Diastolic
2. Holosystolic
3. Systolic
4. Pansystolic

Answer: 1
Rationale: The period "between heartbeats" is the time between $S_2$ and the next $S_1$. This period of time is diastole. Systole is the period of time between $S_1$ and $S_2$.
Assessment
Physiological integrity
Analysis
Learning Outcome 51.1

**51.5** The client has experienced a myocardial infarction with damage to the inferior portion of the heart. Due to this history, the nurse monitors the client for the development of rhythm disturbances that are most directly based upon which factor?

Answer: 3
Rationale: Each cardiac cell can generate its own electrical impulse. Myocardial infarction interferes with the flow of blood to these cells, and the resultant ischemia makes the cells more irritable and more likely to generate an impulse. These uncontrolled impulses result in rhythm disturbances. While extreme changes in blood sugar, electrolyte disturbances, and liver damage can result in cardiac disturbances, the most likely cause of rhythm disturbance following myocardial infarction is insult to the cells causing them to be irritable.
Planning

| | |
|---|---|
| 1. The resultant change in blood sugar<br>2. Electrolyte disturbances from tissue damage<br>3. The automaticity of cardiac cells<br>4. Decreased blood flow to the liver | Physiological integrity<br>Application<br>Learning Outcome 51.4 |
| **51.6** The client is admitted to the emergency department with the chief complaint of "My heart is racing." Upon initiated cardiac monitoring, the nurse discovers that the client has a sustained heart rate of 170 beats per minute. The nurse then assesses the client for which of the following?<br>  1. Increased cardiac output<br>  2. Increased preload<br>  3. Decreased afterload<br>  4. Decreased cardiac output | Answer: 4<br>Rationale: Cardiac output equals stroke volume × heart rate. Since this client has a sustained rapid heart rate, the ventricles are most likely not having sufficient time to relax and refill between contractions, so the stroke volume will decrease. At the rate of 170, the compensatory increase in heart rate is no longer helpful in increasing cardiac output. This leads to a decrease in cardiac output. Preload refers to the degree to which muscle fibers in the ventricle are stretched at the end of the relaxation period. Afterload is the reflective of systemic vascular resistance.<br>Assessment<br>Physiological integrity<br>Application<br>Learning Outcome 51.1 |
| **51.7** The client has complaints of being tired, listless, and unable to tolerate activity at usual levels. Which laboratory value would the nurse review first while assessing this complaint?<br>  1. Blood urea nitrogen<br>  2. Hemoglobin and hematocrit<br>  3. Blood sugar<br>  4. Serum potassium | Answer: 2<br>Rationale: While disturbances in all of these laboratory values could be implicated in this client's complaints, the most likely would be a decrease in hemoglobin and hematocrit. Hemoglobin is the oxygen-carrying portion of the blood, and anemia (decrease in hemoglobin and hematocrit) is often associated with client complaint of being tired, listless, and unable to tolerate normal activities.<br>Assessment<br>Physiological integrity<br>Application<br>Learning Outcome 51.2 |
| **51.8** The nurse assessing a 1-day-old infant discovers the heart rate is 140 and irregular. What action should the nurse take?<br>  1. Immediately contact the infant's physician.<br>  2. Prepare to resuscitate the infant.<br>  3. Note this normal finding in the infant's medical record.<br>  4. Stimulate the infant gently. | Answer: 3<br>Rationale: An irregular heart rate of 140 is common and normal in an infant of this age. The finding should be recorded in the medical record. There is no need to contact the physician, prepare to resuscitate the infant, or stimulate the infant.<br>Implementation<br>Physiological integrity<br>Application<br>Learning Outcome 51.4 |
| **51.9** The 50-year-old who is postmenopausal asks the nurse about the use of estrogen replacement therapy to protect the heart. How should the nurse respond?<br>  1. "This therapy is well proven to protect the heart in postmenopausal women."<br>  2. "Estrogen replacement therapy is helpful to reduce the sleep disturbances and hot flashes associated with menopause, but does not protect the heart."<br>  3. "Estrogen replacement therapy has been proven to have no effect on any postmenopausal symptoms and is not protective of the heart." | Answer: 4<br>Rationale: Research on estrogen replacement therapy is ongoing. Currently, it is thought that there may be some benefit in reducing cardiac risk. There is some concern about the risk of administering this therapy and the development of other health problems such as cancers. The choice to use this therapy should be made only after careful consideration of these benefits and risks.<br>Implementation<br>Health promotion/health maintenance<br>Application<br>Learning Outcome 51.3 |

| | |
|---|---|
| 4. "The use of estrogen replacement therapy is complex and requires a thoughtful review of the balance between possible benefits and possible risks." | |
| **51.10** The post-myocardial infarction client asks the nurse about return to exercise. What information should the nurse give this client?<br><br>1. It is better to exercise when it is cold.<br>2. Environmental temperatures have little impact on cardiac function.<br>3. Avoid exercise when the weather is hot or cold.<br>4. Hot temperatures increase peripheral blood vessel contraction. | Answer: 3<br>Rationale: The nurse should advise the client to avoid exercise in hot or cold weather as these extremes of temperature increase the workload on the heart. Cold temperatures increase peripheral blood vessel contraction and therefore peripheral vascular resistance, making it more difficult for the heart to circulate blood. Hot temperatures decrease systemic vascular resistance by dilating peripheral vessels. This decrease makes the heart rate increase, thereby increasing the heart's workload.<br>Implementation<br>Health promotion/health maintenance<br>Application<br>Learning Outcome 51.7 |
| **51.11** What dietary teaching should the nurse provide to the client who has homocysteine elevation?<br><br>1. Reduce salt intake.<br>2. Take a B complex vitamin supplement daily.<br>3. Increase fluid intake to 2,000 mL per day.<br>4. Avoid alcohol intake. | Answer: 2<br>Rationale: Supplementation with a vitamin that provides folate, vitamin $B_6$, vitamin $B_{12}$, and riboflavin can reduce homocysteine levels. While reduction of salt intake may help to prevent hypertension, there is no connection to homocysteine levels. Alcohol in moderation can reduce the risk of heart disease. Increase in fluid intake is not associated with decreased homocysteine levels.<br>Implementation<br>Health promotion/health maintenance<br>Application<br>Learning Outcome 51.2 |
| **51.12** The client has a history of recurrent transient ischemic attack (TIA). Based upon this history the nurse is most concerned about the client's potential to develop which of the following?<br><br>1. Renal failure<br>2. Gangrene<br>3. Myocardial infarction<br>4. Stroke | Answer: 4<br>Rationale: Transient ischemic attacks may result from atherosclerosis of the cerebral vessels. Continued development of this atherosclerosis may result in stroke. Myocardial infarction results from atherosclerosis of the coronary arteries. Gangrene may occur if atherosclerosis reduces blood flow to extremities. Renal failure would result from atherosclerotic changes in the renal artery.<br>Assessment<br>Physiological integrity<br>Application<br>Learning Outcome 51.3 |
| **51.13** The nurse is assessing a newly admitted client for the presence of impaired peripheral arterial circulation. Which finding would be significant to this condition?<br><br>1. Ruddy skin color over legs<br>2. Bounding pedal pulses<br>3. Hot spots on the feet and legs<br>4. Decreased hair on the legs | Answer: 4<br>Rationale: When peripheral arterial blood flow is reduced, the amount of oxygen to support hair growth is decreased and there is a reduction of hair distribution on the legs. The color of the legs is more likely pale, pulses are weak, and feet are cool.<br>Assessment<br>Physiological integrity<br>Application<br>Learning Outcome 51.4 |

| | |
|---|---|
| **51.14** The client is admitted with a possible deep vein thrombosis. Nursing interventions should be designed to prevent which complication?<br>1. Myocardial infarction<br>2. Renal failure<br>3. Pulmonary embolism<br>4. Pneumonia | Answer: 3<br>Rationale: The presence of a deep vein thrombosis is a risk factor for the development of a pulmonary embolism. The nurse should design interventions to help prevent that development. There is less likelihood that the thrombosis would cause an MI, renal failure, or pneumonia.<br>Planning<br>Physiological integrity<br>Application<br>Learning Outcome 51.4 |
| **51.15** The nurse is collecting equipment to assess a newly admitted client's ankle/brachial index (ABI). What equipment should be taken to the client's bedside?<br>1. Blood pressure cuff and a Doppler ultrasound device<br>2. None, as no special equipment is needed<br>3. Stethoscope and penlight<br>4. Reflex hammer and tuning fork | Answer: 1<br>Rationale: The nurse should take a blood pressure cuff and a Doppler ultrasound device to the bedside for this measurement. The ABI is calculated by dividing either the posterior tibial or dorsalis pedis pulse (whichever is higher) by the left or right brachial systolic pressure (whichever is higher). No other equipment is used in this assessment.<br>Assessment<br>Physiological integrity<br>Application<br>Learning Outcome 51.4 |
| **51.16** The nurse has calculated the client's toe brachial pressure index (TBPI) as 0.58. This client is at risk for the development of _____. | Answer: peripheral vascular disease<br>Rationale: A TBPI less than 0.64 indicates risk for development of presence of peripheral vascular disease. This client should have further evaluation and testing.<br>Evaluation<br>Physiological integrity<br>Analysis<br>Learning Outcome 51.6 |
| **51.17** The nurse notes a widely bizarre pattern on the client's cardiac monitor. What is the nurse's priority action?<br>1. Call a code blue.<br>2. Check the client's pulse.<br>3. Immediately defibrillate the client.<br>4. Check the rhythm in a different lead. | Answer: 2<br>Rationale: The nurse should always remember to verify any changes on the cardiac monitor by assessing the client (in this case, checking the pulse). The cardiac monitor reports electrical activity which may not directly reflect the mechanical activity occurring in the heart. The other options may be necessary after the initial pulse check is performed.<br>Assessment<br>Safe, effective care environment<br>Application<br>Learning Outcome 51.7 |
| **51.18** The nurse is reviewing the laboratory results of a client who is being observed for possible myocardial infarction. Which laboratory result would be most important for the nurse to discuss with the physician?<br>1. Increased hemoglobin<br>2. Decreased creatine kinase<br>3. Increased troponin<br>4. High normal potassium | Answer: 3<br>Rationale: Of these options, the most important finding to discuss with the physician is the increase in troponin, which may help diagnose myocardial infarction. Decreased creatine kinase, increased hemoglobin, and high normal potassium levels are important, but do not carry the diagnostic significance of troponin elevation.<br>Implementation<br>Physiological integrity<br>Analysis<br>Learning Outcome 51.3 |

| | |
|---|---|
| **51.19** The client exhibits confusion, decreased capillary refilling time, low oxygen saturation readings, and decreased renal output. What NANDA nursing diagnosis problem statement would the nurse choose for this client?<br>　1. *Ineffective Tissue Perfusion*<br>　2. *Decreased Cardiac Output*<br>　3. *Activity Intolerance*<br>　4. *Risk for Injury* | Answer: 1<br>Rationale: *Ineffective Tissue Perfusion* is the diagnosis assigned when there is a decrease in oxygenation from failure to nourish tissues at the capillary level. Decreased cardiac output occurs when there is inadequate blood pumped by the heart to meet the demands of the body (not supported by this scenario). Activity intolerance occurs when the client does not have the energy for daily activities (not supported by this scenario). Risk for injury occurs when the client has an increased chance of being injured (not supported by this scenario).<br>Diagnosis<br>Physiological integrity<br>Analysis<br>Learning Outcome 51.7 |
| **51.20** The client is on strict bed rest following hip surgery. What nursing intervention would support vascular health?<br>　1. Place pillows under the unaffected knee for support.<br>　2. Position the bed to flex the knees at least 20 degrees.<br>　3. Have the client alternately flex and extend the feet several times a day.<br>　4. Keep the client in a prone position for at least 20 minutes twice a day. | Answer: 3<br>Rationale: Alternating flexion and extension of the feet will help keep clots from forming in the extremities. Active contraction and relaxation of calf muscles is also used for this purpose. Placing pillows under the knees or positioning the bed so that the knees are in more than 15 degrees of flexion supports the development of clotting. The client would not be placed in the prone (on abdomen) position.<br>Implementation<br>Physiological integrity<br>Application<br>Learning Outcome 51.7 |
| **51.21** The nurse is caring for a client who has severe cardiovascular disease. In an attempt to decrease preload and to reduce pulmonary congestion, the nurse places the client in which position? | Answer: High Fowler's<br>Rationale: High Fowler's position decreases preload and reduces pulmonary congestion.<br>Implementation<br>Physiological integrity<br>Application<br>Learning Outcome 51.7 |
| **51.22** Because the client is receiving a diuretic, the nurse closely monitors laboratory levels of which electrolyte? | Answer: Potassium<br>Rationale: Clients who are taking a diuretic lose potassium with the excess urine and often develop hypokalemia.<br>Assessment<br>Physiological integrity<br>Application<br>Learning Outcome 51.2 |
| **51.23** The nurse finds a client pulseless and breathless. The client's skin is pale and cool, but not cyanotic. Because of this finding, the nurse suspects which of the following?<br>　1. Respiratory arrest occurred prior to cardiac arrest.<br>　2. Cardiac arrest occurred prior to respiratory arrest.<br>　3. The client cannot be resuscitated.<br>　4. Arrest was caused by airway obstruction. | Answer: 2<br>Rationale: In the absence of cyanosis, the logical sequence of events would be cardiac arrest followed by respiratory arrest. There is no indication that the arrest was caused by airway obstruction or that the client cannot be resuscitated. Unless the client has do-not-resuscitate orders, a code should be called.<br>Assessment<br>Physiological integrity<br>Analysis<br>Learning Outcome 51.8 |

| | |
|---|---|
| **51.24** The client has a long history of hypertension and has developed heart failure. The nurse would anticipate giving medications to do which of the following?<br>　1. Increase preload.<br>　2. Decrease afterload.<br>　3. Decrease contractility.<br>　4. Decrease cardiac output. | Answer: 2<br>Rationale: The client likely has developed heart failure secondary to the hypertension, which is an increase in afterload. The nurse would anticipate giving medication to decrease afterload. There would be no reason to increase preload, decrease contractility, or decrease cardiac output.<br>Planning<br>Physiological integrity<br>Analysis<br>Learning Outcome 51.4 |
| **51.25** The nurse finds an adult client pulseless and breathless. After calling the code, the nurse begins single rescuer cardiopulmonary resuscitation at what rate?<br>　1. Five compressions to each breath<br>　2. Fifteen compressions to each two breaths<br>　3. Thirty compressions to each two breaths<br>　4. Forty-five compressions to each breath | Answer: 3<br>Rationale: The 2005 guidelines from the American Heart Association recommend a compression to ventilation ratio of 30:2 for single rescuers for all clients except newborns.<br>Implementation<br>Physiological integrity<br>Application<br>Learning Outcome 51.8 |
| **51.26** The client requires defibrillation during resuscitation. What sequence should the nurse use for this defibrillation?<br>　1. Deliver three shocks without CPR between shocks.<br>　2. Deliver two shocks and a precordial thump before beginning CPR.<br>　3. Deliver one shock followed by immediate CPR.<br>　4. Deliver shocks every 3 seconds until conversion occurs. | Answer: 3<br>Rationale: The 2005 guidelines from the American Heart Association recommend delivery of one shock followed by immediate CPR beginning with chest compressions.<br>Implementation<br>Physiological integrity<br>Application<br>Learning Outcome 51.8 |
| **51.27** The nurse is planning morning care for a client who has sequential compression devices in place. How should the nurse instruct the UAP who will be giving the bath?<br>　1. "Come get me when it is time to remove the devices, since that must be done by a nurse."<br>　2. "You may remove the devices, but standards require that only a nurse put them back on the client."<br>　3. "You may leave the devices off until the client's legs air dry."<br>　4. "Put the devices on as quickly as possible after the bath." | Answer: 4<br>Rationale: The nurse should remind the UAP that the devices are being used to support circulation and should be off the client for as short a period of time as possible. The UAP who knows the correct removal and application process may remove and apply these devices.<br>Planning<br>Physiological integrity<br>Application<br>Learning Outcome 51.7 |

**51.28** The nurse is assessing the vital signs of a 5-year-old client. Should the nurse measure this child's blood pressure?

1. Yes, blood pressure is measured for all children over the age of 3 years.
2. No, blood pressure measurements are not required until age 13.
3. Only if the child complains of headache or has an elevated pulse rate.
4. Yes, but the measurement must be taken in the child's thigh.

Answer: 1
Rationale: Blood pressure measurements should be included for all children over the age of 3 years. The blood pressure is measured with a child size cuff and can be taken in any extremity.
Assessment
Physiological integrity
Application
Learning Outcome 51.7

# CHAPTER 52

**52.1** The 154-pound adult client has had vomiting and diarrhea for 4 days secondary to a viral infection. What hourly urine measurement would indicate that efforts to rehydrate this client have not yet been successful and should continue?

1. 35 mL per hour
2. 80 mL per hour
3. 50 mL per hour
4. 30 mL per hour

Answer: 4
Rationale: Normal urine output for adult clients is at least 0.5 mL/kg/hour. This client weighs 70 kg, so adequate urine output would be 35 mL/hour. The only option lower than 35 mL per hour is 30 mL per hour.
Evaluation
Physiological integrity
Analysis
Learning Outcome 52.2

**52.2** Which statement correctly reflects the body's attempt to restore acid–base balance?

1. Respiratory regulation is slow, but very efficient.
2. Primary regulation is through GI system losses.
3. Kidney regulation is powerfully effective.
4. The cardiovascular system is the major buffer.

Answer: 3
Rationale: The major buffering systems are the respiratory system and the renal system. Respiratory regulation is rapid, but temporary. Renal regulation is slower, but powerfully effective.
Assessment
Physiological integrity
Application
Learning Outcome 52.2

**52.3** The nurse is caring for a client who is 3-days postoperative. Which intervention should the nurse implement to decrease the client's possibility of developing hypercalcemia?

1. Measure vital signs every 4 hours.
2. Assist the client to turn, cough, and deep breathe every 2 hours.
3. Assist the client to ambulate around the room at least three times daily.
4. Irrigate the client's nasogastric tube every 2 hours.

Answer: 3
Rationale: Hypercalcemia can occur from immobility. Ambulation of the client helps to prevent leaching of calcium from the bones into the serum. None of the other options are related to the development of hypercalcemia.
Implementation
Physiological integrity
Application
Learning Outcome 52.4

**52.4** The client is admitted to the acute care unit with a phosphorus level of 2.3 mg/dL. Which nursing intervention would support this client's homeostasis?
1. Encourage consumption of milk and yogurt.
2. Enforce strict isolation protocols.
3. Encourage consumption of a high-calorie carbohydrate diet.
4. Strain all urine.

Answer: 1
Rationale: A phosphorus level of 2.3 is low and the client needs additional phosphorus. Provision of phosphorus-rich foods such as milk and yogurt is a good way to provide that additional phosphorus. There is no indication of the need to place this client in strict isolation, to increase the client's carbohydrate calorie intake, or to strain all urine.
Implementation
Physiological integrity
Application
Learning Outcome 52.6

**52.5** The mother of a 1-month-old infant calls the nurse who works in the health clinic. The mother is concerned because the infant has had vomiting and diarrhea for 2 days. What instruction should the nurse give this infant's mother?
1. Bring the infant to the clinic for evaluation.
2. Give the infant at least 2 ounces of juice every 2 hours.
3. Measure the infant's urine output for 24 hours.
4. Provide the infant with 50 mL of glucose water.

Answer: 1
Rationale: Parents and caregivers need to be taught the seriousness of vomiting or diarrhea in infants due to rapid fluid loss that can occur in this age group. They should also be taught the importance of bringing an infant in this situation to health care providers for evaluation. Encouraging fluids for an infant who is actively vomiting will not improve fluid balance status, nor is juice or glucose water the best choice of fluid. Simply monitoring the loss over the next 24 hours would increase the potential for the infant to become dehydrated.
Planning
Physiological integrity
Application
Learning Outcome 52.6

**52.6** The client has just returned to the nursing unit after placement of a subclavian central venous catheter. Because of the dangers associated with this procedure, which assessment finding is the most important in planning care for this client?
1. Presence of bibasilar crackles
2. Tachycardia
3. Decreased pedal pulses
4. Headache

Answer: 2
Rationale: Because insertion of a subclavian central venous catheter may result in hemothorax, pneumothorax, cardiac perforation, thrombosis, or infection, the priority finding for planning care is tachycardia. Bibasilar crackles may develop secondary to fluid overload or to the disease process, but would not be particularly evident just after placement of the subclavian catheter. Decrease in pedal pulses and headache would not likely be associated with the placement of a subclavian catheter.
Planning
Physiological integrity
Analysis
Learning Outcome 52.5

**52.7** The nurse is caring for a client who is receiving intravenous fluids that are not regulated on an electronic controller. In order to calculate the rate of the IV flow in drops per minute, the nurse must know the number of drops per milliliter of fluid the tubing delivers. Where should the nurse look for this information?
1. On the packaging of the tubing
2. In the charting from the nurse who started the infusion
3. In the drug reference book
4. On the roller clamp of the tubing

Answer: 1
Rationale: The drop factor (number of drops per milliliter of fluid) of tubing is located on the packaging. It would not be documented or found in any other place.
Implementation
Physiological integrity
Application
Learning Outcome 52.8

| | |
|---|---|
| **52.8** The physician has ordered 50 mL of an IV solution to infuse over the next 20 minutes. In order to accurately infuse this solution, the electronic controller should be set to deliver how many mL/hr? | Answer: 150 mL/hr<br>Rationale: 50 mL/20 minutes = x mL/60 minutes<br>Planning<br>Physiological integrity<br>Analysis<br>Learning Outcome 52.8 |
| **52.9** The nurse is to administer 75 mL of an antibiotic solution by IV over the next 30 minutes. The tubing has a drop factor of 20. How many drops per minute should the nurse set the controller to deliver? | Answer: 50 drops per minute<br>Rationale: 75 mL/1 hour × 20 drops/30 minutes = 50 drops per minute<br>Planning<br>Physiological integrity<br>Analysis<br>Learning Outcome 52.8 |
| **52.10** The nurse is caring for a client who is receiving IV therapy at a rate of 10 mL/hour. The 500-mL IV bottle was hung at 0900 Monday morning when the IV catheter was initiated. It is now 0900 on Tuesday morning. What nursing action should be taken?<br>  1. Refigure the rate of the IV.<br>  2. Infuse the remaining IV fluid before hanging a new bag.<br>  3. Discard the remaining IV fluid and hang a new bag.<br>  4. Discontinue the IV site and restart an IV in the opposite hand. | Answer: 3<br>Rationale: The remaining IV fluid should be discarded and a new bag hung. IV fluid should be changed every 24 hours, regardless of how much solution remains. This helps to minimize the risk of contamination. There is no need to restart the IV in the opposite hand or to refigure the rate of the IV.<br>Implementation<br>Physiological integrity<br>Application<br>Learning Outcome 52.8 |
| **52.11** A client is brought to the emergency department after passing out in a local department store. The client reports dieting by fasting for the last 4 days. Which acid-base imbalance would the nurse expect to assess in this client?<br>  1. Respiratory acidosis<br>  2. Respiratory alkalosis<br>  3. Metabolic acidosis<br>  4. Metabolic alkalosis | Answer: 3<br>Rationale: A client who is fasting is at risk for development of metabolic acidosis. The body recognizes fasting as starvation and begins to metabolize its own proteins into ketones, which are metabolic acids. Starvation would not result in respiratory acidosis or alkalosis or in metabolic alkalosis.<br>Assessment<br>Physiological integrity<br>Analysis<br>Learning Outcome 52.4 |
| **52.12** A client is admitted to the hospital after vomiting for 3 days. Which arterial blood gas results would the nurse expect to find in this client?<br>  1. pH 7.30; PaCO$_2$ 50; HCO$_3$ 27<br>  2. pH 7.47; PaCO$_2$ 43; HCO$_3$ 28<br>  3. pH 7.43; PaCO$_2$ 50; HCO$_3$ 28<br>  4. pH 7.47; PaCO$_2$ 30; HCO$_3$ 23 | Answer: 2<br>Rationale: The nurse would expect that this client is alkalotic because stomach acids have been lost, so the pH would be above 7.45. This is a metabolic problem, so the PaCO$_2$ is likely normal. The HCO$_3$ will likely be high (above 26). The only option that includes all of these parameters is pH 7.47; PaCO$_2$ 43; HCO$_3$ 28.<br>Assessment<br>Physiological integrity<br>Analysis<br>Learning Outcome 52.4 |

**52.13** The client's arterial blood gas report reveals a pH of 6.58. How does the nurse evaluate this value?
1. There is a slight elevation.
2. This value is incompatible with life.
3. This is a low normal value.
4. This value is extremely elevated.

Answer: 2
Rationale: The body's pH range is normally 7.35 to 7.45. Values lower than 6.8 or higher than 7.8 are generally considered incompatible with life. If the nurse assesses that this client is physiologically more stable than would be expected with this pH, the possibility of a lab error should be considered.
Evaluation
Physiological integrity
Analysis
Learning Outcome 52.9

**52.14** The nurse has admitted a client who was brought to the hospital after a narcotic overdose. What acid–base imbalance does the nurse expect to observe in this client?
1. Respiratory acidosis
2. Respiratory alkalosis
3. Metabolic acidosis
4. Metabolic alkalosis

Answer: 1
Rationale: Since narcotics generally act to decrease or suppress respirations, this client is probably hyperventilating. The expected acid–base imbalance would be respiratory acidosis.
Planning
Physiological integrity
Analysis
Learning Outcome 52.4

**52.15** Ten minutes after the transfusion of a unit of packed red blood cells was initiated, the client complains of a headache. The nurse assesses that the client has slight shortness of breath and feels warm to the touch. What action by the nurse is priority?
1. Notify the client's physician.
2. Discontinue the transfusion.
3. Slow the rate of the transfusion.
4. Prepare to resuscitate the client.

Answer: 2
Rationale: The priority intervention is to discontinue the transfusion. If this client is having a transfusion reaction, it will be better to limit the amount of blood transfused. The nurse would also contact the physician to collaborate on further treatment, but this action should be after the transfusion is discontinued. Slowing the rate of the transfusion allows additional blood to be infused. At this point, there is no need to prepare for resuscitation.
Implementation
Physiological integrity
Analysis
Learning Outcome 52.6

**52.16** The client who has been taking a diuretic has a serum potassium of 3.4. Which food would the nurse encourage this client to choose from the dinner menu?
1. Baked chicken
2. Green beans
3. Cantaloupe
4. Iced tea

Answer: 3
Rationale: A potassium level of 3.4 is low, so the client should be encouraged to consume potassium-rich foods. Of the foods listed, the highest in potassium is cantaloupe.
Planning
Physiological integrity
Analysis
Learning Outcome 52.3

**52.17** The client has orders for the administration of IV fluid at a "keep vein open" rate in preparation for administration of IV antibiotics starting at noon. When the nurse goes to the room to start the IV, the UAP is preparing to bathe the client. What should the nurse do?
1. Instruct the UAP to wait until the IV is started to bathe the client.
2. Let the UAP start the bath on the opposite side of where the nurse will be starting the IV.
3. Tell the UAP to notify the nurse as soon as the bath is completed.
4. Give the UAP permission to skip the client's bath for today.

Answer: 3
Rationale: Since this IV is being initiated to support the administration of IV antibiotic therapy that is not scheduled to start until noon, the nurse should let the UAP give the bath and then start the IV. This will protect the IV site from movement during this bath. There is no reason to skip the bath. Having the UAP bathing one side of the client while the nurse starts the IV on the opposite side would be uncomfortable and stressful for the client and could potentially compromise client modesty. This action would also not protect the IV site from movement while the UAP completes the bath.
Planning
Physiological integrity
Application
Learning Outcome 52.8

| | |
|---|---|
| **52.18** The nurse is preparing to start an IV in the hand of a client who has very small veins. Which actions would be useful in dilating the veins? (Select all that apply.)<br><br>  1.  Position the hand at heart level.<br>  2.  Stroke the vein.<br>  3.  Have the client clench and unclench the fist.<br>  4.  Slap the back of the client's hand.<br>  5.  Massage the vein. | Answer: 2, 3, 5<br>Rationale: Strategies that are helpful in dilating the vein include positioning the hand lower than the heart in a dependent position, stroking and massaging the vein, having the client clench and unclench the fist, and lightly tapping the vein. Slapping the vein is contraindicated and may actually reduce venous filling.<br>Implementation<br>Physiological integrity<br>Application<br>Learning Outcome 52.8 |
| **52.19** The client complains of burning along the vein in which a medicated IV is infusing. Upon assessment, the nurse finds the IV site is slightly reddened, but not warmer than the surrounding skin, and without swelling. What action should be taken by the nurse?<br><br>  1.  Slow the IV infusion and reassess the area in 15 minutes.<br>  2.  Place a cool pack over the IV site and vein.<br>  3.  Discontinue the IV and place a warm pack on the area.<br>  4.  Call the physician for direction. | Answer: 3<br>Rationale: This assessment likely indicates the beginning of phlebitis. The nurse should discontinue the IV and place a warm pack on the area. Simply slowing the IV will not prevent further damage to the vein and will also alter the amount of IV fluid and medication the client is receiving. A cool pack over the IV site will not prevent additional damage to the vein. This assessment and evaluation are within the scope of nursing practice, so at this point, collaboration with the physician is not necessary.<br>Evaluation<br>Physiological integrity<br>Application<br>Learning Outcome 52.8 |
| **52.20** The client who has an IV with an intermittent infusion lock in place wishes to shower. What action should be taken by the nurse?<br><br>  1.  Have the UAP discontinue the lock.<br>  2.  Cover the lock with an occlusive dressing.<br>  3.  Place a piece of cloth tape under the lock, wrapping the top in a U shape.<br>  4.  Tell the client that a bed bath is necessary until the IV is discontinued. | Answer: 2<br>Rationale: The client can shower if the lock is covered with an occlusive dressing. Cloth tape will not protect the lock. Discontinuing the lock is not appropriate unless there is a specific order to do so.<br>Implementation<br>Physiological integrity<br>Application<br>Learning Outcome 52.8 |
| **52.21** The nurse is collecting equipment to administer a unit of packed red blood cells. Which IV fluid should be used to initiate the IV for this transfusion?<br><br>  1.  1,000 mL of lactated Ringer's solution<br>  2.  250 mL of normal saline<br>  3.  500 mL of 5% dextrose and water<br>  4.  100 mL of 5% dextrose and ½ normal saline | Answer: 2<br>Rationale: Blood and blood products should only be administered with normal saline. Other IV fluids may cause damage to the cells being administered.<br>Planning<br>Physiological integrity<br>Application<br>Learning Outcome 52.8 |
| **52.22** The nurse has obtained a unit of packed red blood cells from the laboratory blood bank to administer to a postoperative client. Upon returning to the client's room, the nurse discovers that the client has been taken for an emergency CT scan and is expected to | Answer: 3<br>Rationale: Blood should not be held at room temperature for more than 30 minutes before the transfusion is initiated. The unit refrigerator is not climate controlled for blood storage, so the unit must be returned to the laboratory blood bank until the client has returned from the CT. |

| | |
|---|---|
| be gone from the unit for approximately 45 minutes. What action should the nurse take?<br><br>1. Set up the blood with the IV fluid and y-tubing and place it on the IV standard in the client's room to initiate immediately after the client returns.<br>2. Place the blood in the unit refrigerator until the client returns.<br>3. Return the blood to the laboratory blood bank until the client returns.<br>4. Set up the blood with the IV fluid and y-tubing and place it in the unit medication room to initiate immediately after the client returns. | Implementation<br>Physiological integrity<br>Application<br>Learning Outcome 52.8 |
| **52.23** The nurse has initiated a blood transfusion. Which action is now priority?<br><br>1. Stay with the client and closely observe him for the first 5 to 10 minutes of the transfusion.<br>2. Assign the UAP to sit with the client for 15 minutes.<br>3. Advise the client to notify the nurse if he experiences any chilling, nausea, flushing, or rapid heart rate.<br>4. Return to the room and take a set of vital signs in 15 minutes. | Answer: 1<br>Rationale: The nurse should stay with the client and closely observe him for the first 5 to 10 minutes of the transfusion. The nurse cannot delegate this assessment to the UAP. The client should be advised of reactions to report, but this self-reporting is more indicated after the nurse is no longer in constant attendance.<br>Implementation<br>Physiological integrity<br>Application<br>Learning Outcome 52.8 |
| **52.24** The nurse is providing discharge instructions to a client who has been started on furosemide (Lasix) once daily. What information is essential to include in this information?<br><br>1. Take the medication at bedtime.<br>2. Avoid high-potassium foods.<br>3. Stand up slowly from a sitting position.<br>4. Do not take this medication on the days you take digitalis (Lanoxin). | Answer: 3<br>Rationale: Clients who are taking diuretics must make position changes slowly in order to minimize dizziness from orthostatic hypotension. The medication should be taken in the morning to prevent awakening at night to void. The client should be encouraged to eat potassium-rich foods and will probably be prescribed a potassium supplement. While clients who take digitalis (Lanoxin) and furosemide (Lasix) are at higher risk for the development of digitalis toxicity, the medications are often taken concurrently. The client and health care provider must monitor these clients closely for the development of digitalis toxicity.<br>Implementation<br>Physiological integrity<br>Application<br>Learning Outcome 52.7 |
| **52.25** Which parenteral potassium order is safe for the nurse to implement?<br><br>1. Add 20 mEq of KCL to 1,000 mL of IV fluid<br>2. 10 mEq KCL IV over 1–2 minutes<br>3. Dilute 20 mEq KCL in 3 mL of NS and give IV push<br>4. 10 mEq KCL SQ | Answer: 1<br>Rationale: Parenteral potassium should be well diluted and given IV. It is not given SQ, by IV push, or in limited dilution (such as 20 mEq in 25 mL of fluid). If given in concentrated form, parenteral potassium is lethal to the client.<br>Implementation<br>Physiological integrity<br>Application<br>Learning Outcome 52.6 |

**52.26** The client has been placed on a 1,200 mL oral fluid restriction. How should the nurse plan for this restriction?

1. Allow 600 mL from 7-3, 400 mL from 3-11, and 200 mL from 11-7.
2. Instruct the client that the 1,200 mL of fluid placed in the bedside pitcher must last until tomorrow.
3. Offer the client softer, cold foods such as sherbet and custard.
4. Remove fluids from diet trays and offer them only between meals.

Answer: 1
Rationale: The amount of fluid allowed should be divided between the three major times of the day (7-3, 3-11, 11-7). This helps by taking into consideration meals and medication administration. Sherbet and custard are counted as liquids and should be avoided. The client should be given a choice regarding consumption of fluids at mealtime.
Planning
Physiological integrity
Application
Learning Outcome 52.6

**52.27** The nurse is caring for an 80-year-old client with the medical diagnosis of heart failure. The client has edema, orthopnea, and confusion. Which nursing diagnosis is most appropriate for this client?

1. *Heart Failure* related to edema, as evidenced by confusion
2. *Fluid Volume Deficit* related to loss of fluids as evidenced by edema
3. *Excess Fluid Volume* related to retention of fluids as evidenced by edema and orthopnea
4. *Excess Fluid Volume* related to congestive heart failure as evidenced by edema and confusion

Answer: 3
Rationale: Edema and orthopnea are assessment findings associated with excess fluid volume. Congestive heart failure is a medical diagnosis and cannot be used as the "related to" factor in a nursing diagnosis. This client does not exhibit fluid volume deficit. Heart failure is a medical diagnosis, not a nursing diagnosis.
Diagnosis
Physiological integrity
Analysis
Learning Outcome 52.6

**52.28** The nurse is caring for a client who presented to the emergency department with fever, chills, nausea, and loss of appetite. As a part of the initial assessment, the nurse tests the client for orthostatic hypotension. What action should the nurse take?

1. Assess the client for dependent edema and then raise the legs to the level of the heart and reassess for edema.
2. Measure the client's heart rate and blood pressure in both the sitting and standing position.
3. Measure the client's blood pressure before, during, and after administration of a normal saline fluid challenge.
4. Raise the client's legs above heart level and measure the blood pressure.

Answer: 2
Rationale: The nurse should measure the client's blood pressure and heart rate in the sitting position and then again in the standing position. Assessment of edema is not a part of the assessment of orthostatic hypotension. Normal saline challenges are often administered to clients who are dehydrated, but they are not part of assessment of orthostatic hypotension.
Implementation
Physiological integrity
Application
Learning Outcome 52.5

**52.29** The nurse is caring for a client who is being mechanically ventilated. Arterial blood gas analysis reveals respiratory acidosis. Which change in ventilator settings would the nurse anticipate?

1. Decrease in oxygen delivery
2. Decreased tidal volume of each breath
3. Increased respiratory rate
4. Increase in humidification of inspired air

Answer: 3

Rationale: This client needs to "blow off" more $CO_2$; therefore respiratory rate would be increased. No other option given would serve to decrease $CO_2$ levels.

Planning

Physiological integrity

Application

Learning Outcome 52.9

**52.30** The nurse is caring for an elderly client who has been receiving intravenous fluids at 175 mL/hr. The nurse assesses that the client has crackles, shortness of breath, and distended neck veins. The nurse would recognize these findings as indicating which complication of IV fluid therapy?

1. An allergic reaction to the antibiotics in the fluid
2. Fluid volume excess
3. Pulmonary embolism
4. Speed shock

Answer: 2

Rationale: Fluid volume excess may occur if clients, especially the very young or elderly, receive IV fluid rapidly. The findings given in this scenario do not support the other options.

Evaluation

Physiological integrity

Application

Learning Outcome 52.9